Digest of Education Statistics

1991

Thomas D. Snyder
Project Director
Charlene M. Hoffman
Production Manager
National Center for Education Statistics

U.S. Department of Education
Lamar Alexander
Secretary

Office of Educational Research and Improvement
Diane Ravitch
Assistant Secretary

National Center for Education Statistics
Emerson J. Elliott
Acting Commissioner

National Center for Education Statistics

"The purpose of the Center shall be to collect, and analyze, and disseminate statistics and other data related to education in the United States and in other nations."—Section 406(b) of the General Education Provisions Act, as amended (20 U.S.C. 1221e–1).

November 1991

For sale by the U.S. Government Printing Office
Superintendent of Documents, Mail Stop: SSOP, Washington, DC 20402-9328
ISBN 0–16–035996–1

Foreword

This 1991 edition of the *Digest of Education Statistics* is the 27th in a series initiated in 1962. (The *Digest* has been issued annually except for combined editions for the years 1977–78, 1983–84, and 1985–86.) Its primary purpose is to provide a compilation of statistical information covering the broad field of American education from kindergarten through graduate school. The *Digest* includes a selection of data from many sources, both government and private, and draws especially on the results of surveys and activities carried out by the National Center for Education Statistics (NCES). The publication contains information on a variety of subjects in the field of education statistics, including the number of schools and colleges, teachers, enrollments, and graduates, in addition to educational attainment, finances, Federal funds for education, employment and income of graduates, libraries, and international education. Supplemental information on population trends, attitudes on education, education characteristics of the labor force, government finances, and economic trends provides background for evaluating education data.

The *Digest* is divided into seven chapters: "All Levels of Education," "Elementary and Secondary Education," "Postsecondary Education," "Federal Programs for Education and Related Activities," "Outcomes of Education," "International Education," and "Learning Resources and Technology." To qualify for inclusion, material must be nationwide in scope and of current interest and value. The introduction includes a brief overview of current trends in American education, which supplements the tabular materials in chapters 1 through 7. Information on the structure of the statistical tables is contained in the "Guide to Tabular Presentation." The "Guide to Sources" provides a brief synopsis of the surveys used to generate the tabulations for the *Digest*. Also, a "Definitions" section is included to help readers understand terms.

In addition to updating many of the statistics that have appeared in previous years, this edition contains a substantial amount of new material, including:

- Expenditures for interest on school debt and capital outlay, by State;

- Work-related training;

- Student proficiency in mathematics content areas;

- Student performance on mathematics tests, by State;

- Characteristics of college faculty, by type and control of institution; and

- Faculty salaries, by field of instruction.

In the past, the *Digest of Education Statistics* has proved to be of interest and value to education researchers and administrators, government officials, the media, the business community, and the general public. Recently, we have implemented a program to expand the scope of materials included in the *Digest* to make it even more comprehensive. We welcome comments and suggestions to improve future editions. We trust that the users of this 27th edition will find it even more valuable than its predecessors.

Emerson J. Elliott,
Acting Commissioner
National Center for Education Statistics
November 1991

Acknowledgments

Many people have contributed in one way or another to the development of the *Digest*. Foremost among these contributors is W. Vance Grant, who served as an editor of this series from 1962 to 1986. His developmental work made the publication the widely used and respected report it is today. Thomas D. Snyder was responsible for the overall development and preparation of this *Digest,* which was prepared under the general direction of Jeanne E. Griffith.

Charlene M. Hoffman provided technical assistance in all phases of its preparation and was responsible for Chapter 4, "Federal Programs for Education and Related Activities," and for tables on degrees conferred. Irene Baden compiled tabulations on international education and higher education faculty and finances. John Grymes prepared analyses on elementary and secondary school districts and colleges and universities, computer use, and education outcomes. Debra E. Gerald and William J. Hussar prepared projections of school enrollment and finance statistics. Celestine J. Davis provided statistical assistance.

A number of individuals outside the Center also expended large amounts of time and effort on the *Digest*. James J. Corina, Robert Craig, Chris Graziano, and Frank Schneider of Pinkerton Computer Consultants, Inc., provided computer support. Louise Woerner, Barbara Robinson, Donna Grande, Jeannette Bernardo, Linda Burbank, and Theodore Willis of HCR provided research assistance. In the Public Information Division, Publications Branch, Stephanie Blair, Gerard M. Devlin, and Wilma P. Greene provided editorial assistance, Mamie Brown, typesetting assistance, and Phil Carr designed the cover. Jerry T. Fairbanks and Larry B. Grantham of the U.S. Government Printing Office managed the typesetting, and Evangeline Reese provided typesetting assistance.

This year's edition of the *Digest* has received extensive reviews by individuals within and outside the Department of Education. We wish to thank them for their time and expert advice. In the Office of Educational Research and Improvement (OERI), John Burkett, W. Vance Grant, Mary Frase, and Salvatore Corrallo reviewed the entire manuscript. Elaine El-Khawas (American Council on Education), Lee Greene (National Association of Elementary School Principals) and Rosemary Clark (U.S. Bureau of the Census) also reviewed the entire document. OERI staff who reviewed portions of the manuscript were: Susan Ahmed, Nabeel Alsalam, Patricia Q. Brown, Judy Carpenter, Emmett Fleming, Martin M. Frankel, William Freund, William J. Fowler, Kerry J. Gruber, Edith K. McArthur, Nancy Shantz, and Douglas A. Wright. Agency reviews were conducted by the Office of Under Secretary and the Office of Vocational and Adult Education, U.S. Department of Education.

Contents

Figures

Tables

1. All Levels of Education

Enrollment, Teachers, and Schools

Enrollment Rates

Educational Attainment

2. Elementary and Secondary Education

Enrollment

Schools and School Districts

High School Seniors, Completions, and Dropouts

Educational Achievement

Student Activities and Behavior

3-A. Postsecondary Education: College and University Education

Enrollment

Property

3-B. Postsecondary Education: Vocational and Adult Education

Adult Education

Vocational Education

4. Federal Programs for Education and Related Activities

5. Outcomes of Education

Educational Characteristics of the Workforce

Recent High School and College Graduates

6. International Comparisons of Education

7. Learning Resources and Technology

Libraries

Computers and Technology

Guide to Sources

Appendix Tables

INTRODUCTION

In the fall of 1990, about 60.2 million persons were enrolled in American schools and colleges (table 1). About 3.5 million were employed as elementary and secondary school teachers and as college instructors. Other professional, administrative, and support staff of educational institutions numbered 3.8 million. Thus, more than 67 million Americans were involved, directly or indirectly, in providing or receiving formal education. In a nation with a population of about 250 million, more than 1 out of every 4 persons participated in the educational process.

Elementary/Secondary Enrollment

Enrollment in elementary and secondary schools grew rapidly during the 1950s and 1960s and peaked in 1971 (table 3). This enrollment rise was caused by what is known as the "baby boom," a dramatic increase in births following World War II. From 1971 to 1984, total elementary and secondary school enrollment decreased steadily, reflecting the decline in the school-age population over that period. After these years of decline, enrollment in public elementary and secondary schools showed a small increase in the fall of 1985 (table 3). Enrollment in kindergarten through grade eight rose from 27.0 million in fall 1985 to an estimated 29.7 million in fall 1990. Enrollment in the upper grades declined from 12.4 million to an estimated 11.3 million over the same period. The net result of these two divergent trends was an overall increase in public school enrollment.

Private school enrollment was estimated at 5.2 million in fall 1990. About 4.1 million students were enrolled at the elementary level and 1.1 million at the secondary level. Approximately 11 percent of all elementary and secondary students attend private schools.

Recent increases in elementary enrollment indicate a new trend that will affect elementary and secondary schools for a number of years. Projections of the National Center for Education Statistics (NCES) indicate that public elementary school enrollment will continue to increase, reaching 31.8 million in 1995 and 33.0 million in 2000 (table 3). Between fall 1990 and fall 1995, elementary enrollment is projected to grow by 7 percent, while secondary school enrollment is expected to rise by 12 percent. The growing numbers of young pupils that have been filling the elementary schools will begin to cause increases at

the secondary school level during the early 1990s. Record levels of enrollment are expected by the year 2000.

Postsecondary Education

College enrollment in fall 1990 was estimated at 14.0 million—reflecting a slight increase from the record level of the previous fall. Total college enrollment is expected to rise slightly during the early 1990s, despite decreases in the traditional college-age population (table 2). The number of persons in the 18- to 24-year-old age group peaked in 1981 and then began a decline that is expected to continue throughout most of the next decade (table 14). However, recent trends suggest that total enrollment will remain relatively high because of the increased participation of older women students and a high rate of college attendance for recent high school graduates. Although total enrollment may remain relatively stable, some shifts of students from full-time to part-time status are expected (table 163).

Teachers

About 2.7 million elementary and secondary school teachers were engaged in classroom instruction in the fall of 1990 (table 4). This number has risen in recent years, up about 9 percent since 1984. The number of public school teachers in 1990 was about 2.4 million and the number in private schools was estimated at 0.4 million. About 1.6 million teachers were teaching in elementary schools, while about 1.1 million were employed at the secondary level (table 4).

The number of public school teachers has risen at a faster rate than the number of students in recent years, resulting in a continuing decrease in the pupil/teacher ratio. In the fall of 1990, there were 17.2 pupils per public school teacher compared with 18.7 pupils per teacher 10 years earlier. During the same time period, the pupil/teacher ratio in private schools fell from 17.7 to 14.7. The declining pupil/teacher ratio reflects the trend toward smaller classes and more specialized education programs (table 59).

Teacher salaries, which lost purchasing power to inflation during the 1970s, rose faster than the inflation rate in the 1980s. The rising salaries reflect both an interest by State and local education agencies in boosting teacher salary schedules and an increase in teachers' experience and education levels (table 64). According to data from the National Education Association and NCES projections, the value of teachers' salaries, after adjustment for inflation, rose about 21 percent between 1980–81 and 1990–91. The average salary for teachers in 1990–91 was $33,015, a record-high level (table 72).

Student Performance: Reading

Some improvements have been registered in reading proficiency of elementary and secondary school students. Reading proficiency of 9- and 13-year-olds rose between 1970–71 and 1979–80 (table 102). Reading proficiency of 17-year-olds rose between 1979–80 and 1983–84, but the proficiency of 9-year-olds declined slightly. No significant changes occurred in the overall reading performance of any of the age groups between 1983–84 and 1987–88. Although the reading proficiency of minority children remains below that of other students, blacks have made very large gains. For example, the proportion of black 9-year-olds reading at a basic level or above rose from 22 percent in 1970–71 to 39 percent in 1987–88 (table 106).

Mathematics

Results from assessments of mathematics proficiency also indicate that students have made some improvements in their skill with basic computations. However, performance on more advanced mathematical operations has shown no improvement. The proportion of 9-year-olds who showed beginning skills and understanding rose from 70 percent in 1977–78 to 74 percent in 1985–86, but there was no change in the proportion demonstrating higher levels of performance (table 114).

Similarly, the proportion of 13- and 17-year-olds with an understanding of basic operations rose between 1977–78 and 1985–86, but no change occurred in the proportion with proficiency in moderately complex procedures or multi-step problem solving and algebra. However, notable improvements were made by minority children at all three age groups. The proportion of black 13-year-olds with proficiency in basic operations rose from 30 percent in 1977–78 to 49 percent in 1985–86; for Hispanics the proportion rose from 36 percent to 55 percent (table 115). A 1990 study of eighth graders' mathematics performance found that proficiency varied widely among the 37 States and the District of Columbia which participated in the program (table 116). In general, States with fewer students in large urban areas, smaller proportions of black and Hispanic students, smaller proportions of students watching 6 or more hours of television each day, and fewer numbers from single-parent households scored relatively high.

States in the Northeast and Central region scored higher than States in the Southwest and West.

Science

Small improvements also were registered on science proficiency exams between 1976–77 and 1985–86. The proportion of 9-year-olds who understood simple scientific principles rose from 68 percent in 1976–77 to 71 percent in 1985–86, but no improvement occurred in more advanced levels of achievement. Similarly, the percentage of 13-year-olds demonstrating application of basic scientific information rose from 49 to 53 percent between 1976–77 and 1985–86, but no improvement was registered at the upper levels of achievement. No significant changes occurred in the overall achievement of 17-year-olds between 1976–77 and 1985–86 (table 119).

International Comparisons

Despite some evidence that student achievement has improved, there is still reason for concern. The national assessment measures have not shown a consistent pattern of improvement, especially for upper-level skills. Recent international tests of mathematics and science have highlighted the relatively low level of achievement of U.S. students compared to their peers in other countries (tables 372 to 379). Also, a major U.S. study of writing achievement found that even 11th-grade students had considerable difficulty with persuasive writing assignments (table 109).

Persistence in Education

The number of high school graduates in 1990–91 totaled about 2.5 million. About 2.3 million graduated from public schools and about 0.3 million graduated from private schools. The number of high school graduates has declined from its peak in 1976–77, when 3.2 million persons earned their diplomas. Although the number of graduates has been lower in recent years, the proportion of 17- and 18-year-olds graduating from high school has remained relatively stable for more than two decades, declining slightly in the 1970s and increasing slightly in the 1980s. (Table 95).

The number of postsecondary degrees to be conferred are expected to be at or near an all-time high during the year 1990–91: 470,000 associate degrees; 1,064,000 bachelor's degrees; 327,000 master's degrees; 38,700 doctor's degrees; and 73,800 first-professional degrees (table 228). The number of first-professional degrees is expected to be down slightly from its 1985 peak.

The Bureau of the Census has collected annual statistics on the educational attainment of the population in terms of years of school completed. These data indicate that, between 1980 and 1989, the proportion of the adult population 25 years of age and over with 4 years of high school or more rose from 69 percent to 77 percent, and the proportion of adults with at least 4 years of college increased from 17 percent to 21 percent. In contrast, the proportion of young adults (25- to 29-year-olds) attaining these levels did not change significantly over this time period (table 8).

Expenditures

Expenditures for public and private education, from preprimary through graduate school, are estimated at $365 billion for 1989–90, and projections indicate that they will be about $393 billion in 1990–91 (table 30). The expenditures of elementary and secondary schools are expected to total about $237 billion for 1990–91, while institutions of higher education will spend about $155 billion. The outlays of public schools and colleges are expected to be about $319 billion, while for privately controlled institutions, they are expected to reach $74 billion. Viewed in another context, the total expenditures for education in recent years have amounted to about 7 percent of the gross national product and are expected to remain at that level in 1990–91 (table 29).

The statistical highlights in this section of the report provide a quantitative description of the current American education scene. Clearly, as evidenced by the large number of participants, the number of years that people spend in school, and the vast sums expended by educational institutions, the American people have a high regard for education. Yet, data on student proficiency suggest that improvements in recent years have been limited. Wide variations in mathematics proficiency from State to State and disappointing scores of American students in international tests pose challenges for the future.

NOTE: Readers should be aware of the limitations of statistics. These limitations vary with the exact nature of a particular survey. For example, estimates based on a sample of institutions will differ somewhat from the figures that would have been obtained if a complete census had been taken using the same survey procedures. Although some of the surveys conducted by the National Center for Education Statistics are complete, census-type surveys, all surveys are subject to design, reporting, and processing errors and errors due to nonresponse. More information on survey methodologies can be found in the "Guide to Sources" in the appendix. Price indexes for inflation adjustments can be found in table 36.

CHAPTER 1
All Levels of Education

This chapter provides a broad overview of education in the United States. It brings together material from preprimary, elementary, secondary, and higher education and from the general population to present a composite picture of the American educational system. It contains tables which show the total number of persons enrolled in school, the number of teachers, the number of schools, and total expenditures for education at all levels. This chapter also includes statistics on education-related topics such as education attainment, family characteristics, population, and opinions about schools. Economic indicators and price indexes have been added to assist researchers in preparing comparative analyses.

Figure 1 provides an overview of the structure of education in the United States. It shows the three levels of education (elementary, secondary, and postsecondary) and gives the approximate age of persons at each level. Pupils ordinarily spend from 6 to 8 years in the elementary grades, which may be preceded by 1 or 2 years in nursery school and kindergarten. The elementary school program is followed by a 4- to 6-year program in high school. Pupils normally complete the entire program through grade 12 by age 17 or 18.

High school graduates who decide to continue their education may enter a technical or vocational institution, a 2-year college, or a 4-year college or university. A 2-year college normally offers the first 2 years of a standard 4-year college curriculum and a selection of terminal-vocational programs. Academic courses completed at a 2-year college are transferable for credit at 4-year colleges and universities. A technical or vocational institution offers postsecondary technical training leading to a specific career.

An associate degree requires at least 2 years of college-level work, and a bachelor's degree normally can be earned in 4 years. At least 1 year beyond the bachelor's is necessary for a master's degree, while a doctor's degree usually requires a minimum of 3 or 4 years beyond the bachelor's.

Professional schools differ widely in admission requirements and in program length. Medical students, for example, generally complete a 4-year program of premedical studies at a college or university before they can enter the 4-year program at a medical school. Law programs normally require 3 years of coursework beyond the bachelor's degree level.

Many of the statistics in this chapter are derived from the statistical activities of the National Center for Education Statistics. In addition, substantial contributions have been drawn from the work of other groups, both government and nongovernment, as shown in the source notes of the appropriate tables. Information on survey methodologies is in the "Guide to Sources" in the appendix and in the publications cited in the source notes.

Highlights

- In the fall of 1985, total elementary and secondary school enrollment increased for the first time since 1971. The increase from 1985 to 1990 occurred in the elementary grades, but this pattern is expected to change in the early 1990s. Between fall 1990 and fall 1995, public elementary enrollment is expected to rise 7 percent, while public secondary enrollment is expected to increase by 12 percent. Overall, enrollment is expected to increase by 3.4 million students, or about 8 percent. (Table 3)

- Over the past 10 years, there has been little change in the proportion of students in private schools and colleges. Between 1980 and 1990, the proportion of elementary and secondary school students in private schools has been around 11 to 12 percent. At the same time, the proportion of college students in private institutions has remained at about 22 percent. (Table 3)

- College enrollment rose to a record level of 14.0 million in fall 1990, reflecting a significant increase in public college enrollment. Enrollment is expected to rise during the 1990s because of the high attendance rates of younger age groups and the large number of older students. (Tables 3 and 163)

- The proportion of some age groups attending school has risen over the past decade, but attendance rates for most groups have remained relatively steady. A relatively small change occurred among 3- and 4-year-olds whose attendance rate rose from 37 percent in 1980 to 44 percent in 1990. Also, the proportion of 18- and 19-year-olds attending high school or college rose from 46 to 57 percent between 1980 and 1990. The proportion of 20- to 24-year-olds enrolled in school rose from 22 percent in 1980 to 29 percent in 1990. (Table 6)

- Increases in the amount of education completed by Americans has continued. In 1989, 77 percent of the population 25 years old and over had completed high school and 21 percent had completed 4 or more years of college. This represents an increase from 1980, when 69 percent had completed high school and 17 percent had 4 years of college. (Table 8)

- The gap in high school achievement between white and black young adults has narrowed in recent years. In 1980, 77 percent of black and other minority races 25- to 29-year-olds had completed high school compared to 87 percent for white 25- to 29-year-olds. By 1989, the proportion of young blacks completing high school had risen to 83 percent while the proportion of whites showed no change from the 1980 level. (Table 8)

- About 17 percent of persons over 18 had completed a bachelor's or higher degree in 1987. About 4 percent held a master's degree, 1 percent held a professional degree (e.g., medicine or law), and 0.6 percent held a doctor's degree. (Table 11)

- Between 1970 and 1990, the composition of families shifted substantially. In 1970, 50 percent of families were married-couple families with children under 18, compared to 37 percent in 1990. The proportion of families headed by women (no husband present) who had children under 18 rose from 6 percent to 10 percent. Altogether, more than one out of five children under 18 lived with one parent in 1990. (Tables 17 and 18)

- According to results of a nationwide survey, Americans rated public schools more favorably in the mid-1980s compared to the later 1980s and the early 1980s. In another opinion survey, Americans indicated that the two largest problems facing public schools in 1990 were drugs (38 percent) and discipline (19 percent). (Tables 20 and 21)

- Parents who had not completed high school were less likely than other parents to report having regular talks with their children about school experiences, high school plans, or plans after high school. (Table 22)

- Education expenditures rose to an estimated high of nearly $393 billion in the 1990–91 school year. Elementary and secondary schools spent about 60 percent of this total, and colleges and universities accounted for the remaining 40 percent. An estimated 7.2 percent of the gross national product was spent by elementary and secondary schools and colleges and universities in 1990–91. (Tables 29 and 30)

- The proportion of total State and local government funds spent on education declined between 1979 and 1989, at least partly as a result of the drop in elementary and secondary enrollment and the expansion of other governmental services. Of the 1989 State and local funds spent on education, about 70 percent went to elementary and secondary schools, 26 percent to colleges and universities, and 4 percent to other education programs. (Tables 33 and 35)

Figure 1.—The structure of education in the United States

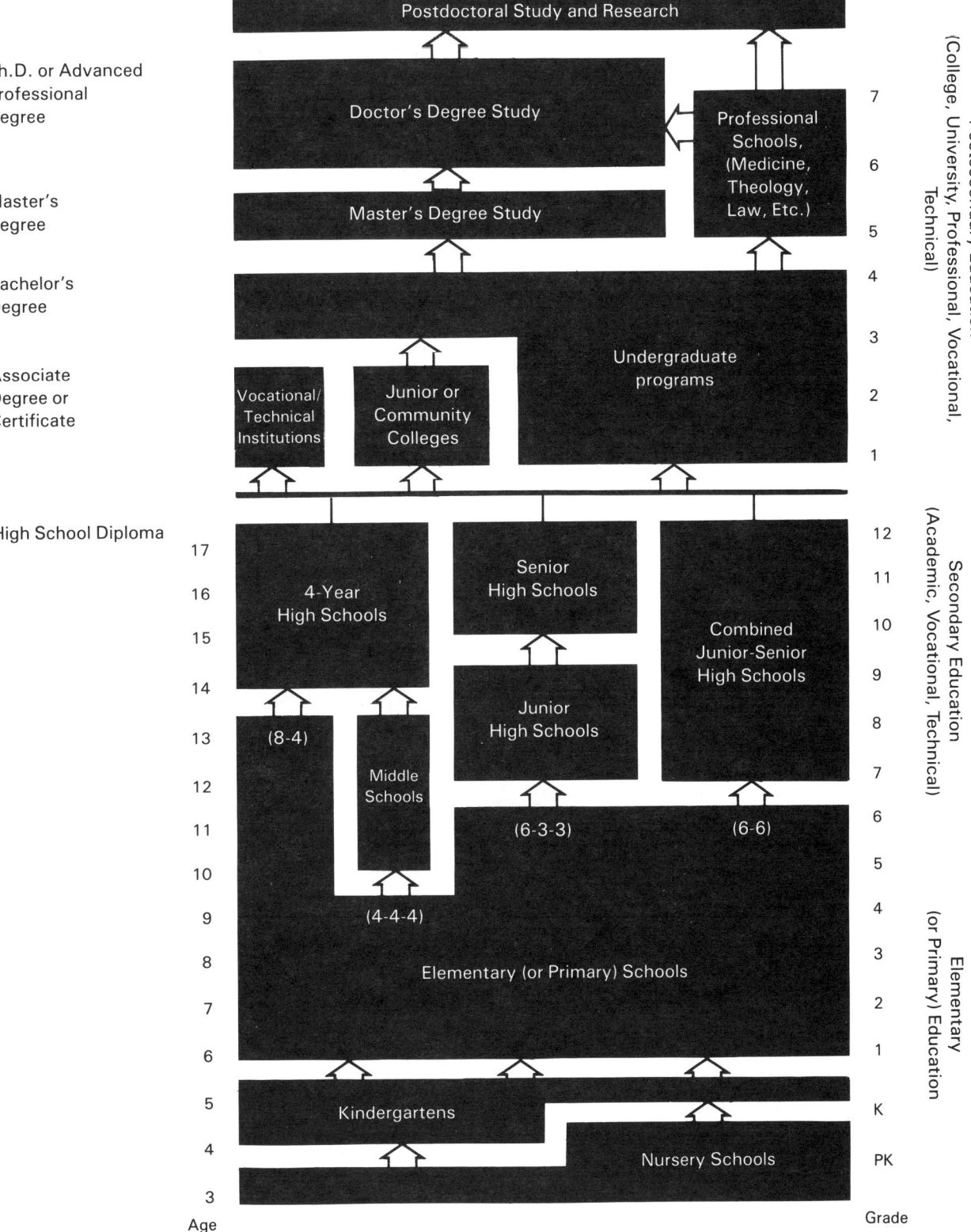

NOTE—Adult education programs, while not separately delineated above, may provide instruction at the elementary, secondary, or higher education level. Chart reflects typical patterns of progression rather than all possible variations.

SOURCE: U.S. Department of Education, National Center for Education Statistics.

**Figure 2.--Enrollment and total expenditures in current and constant dollars,
by level of education: 1960-61 to 1990-91**

Enrollment, in millions

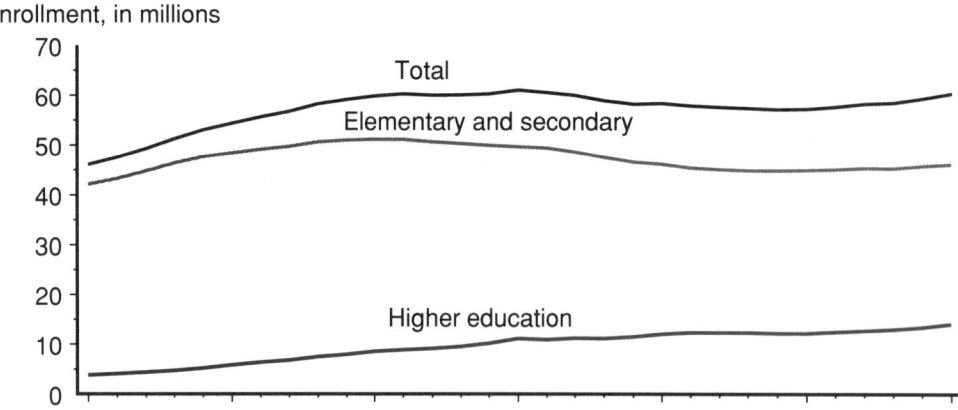

Expenditures, in billions of current dollars

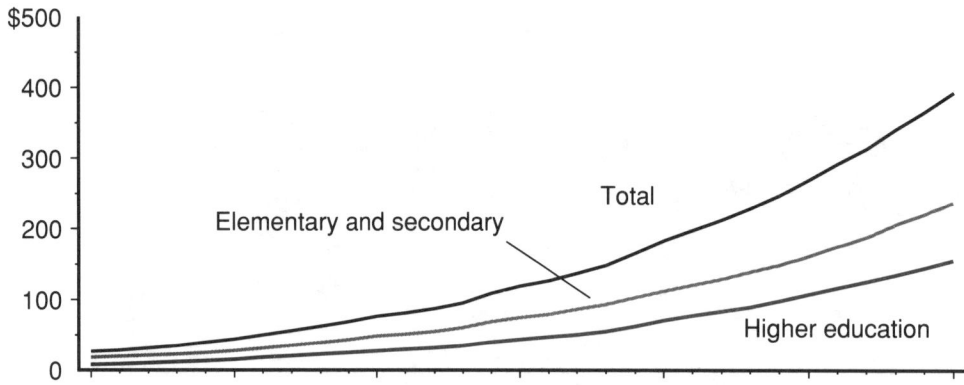

Expenditures, in billions of constant 1990-91 dollars

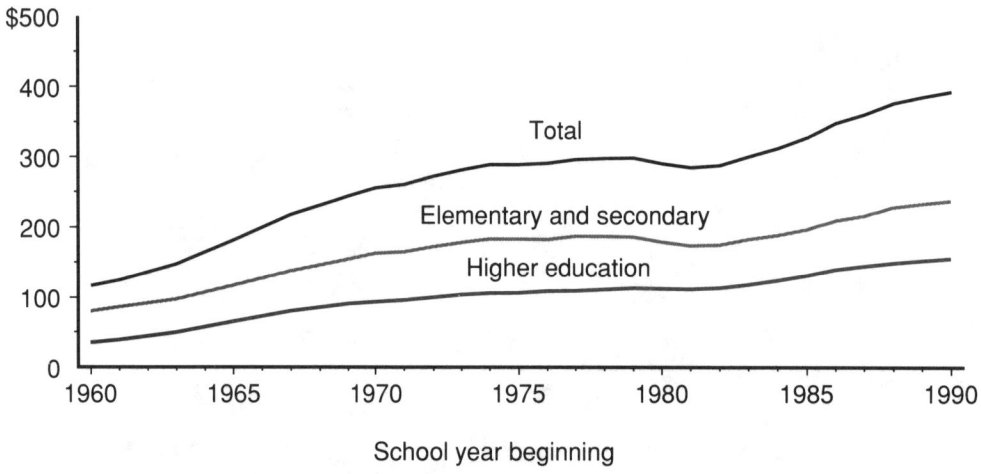

School year beginning

SOURCE: U.S. Department of Education, National Center for Education Statistics, *Statistics of State School Systems; Statistics of Public Elementary and Secondary School Systems; Statistics of Nonpublic Secondary School Systems; Statistics of Nonpublic Elementary and Secondary Schools; Revenues and Expenditures for Public Elementary and Secondary Education; Fall Enrollment in Institutions of Higher Education; Financial Statistics of Institutions of Higher Education;* Common Core of Data surveys; and Integrated Postsecondary Education Data System surveys.

Figure 3.--Years of school completed by persons 25 years old and over: 1940 to1989

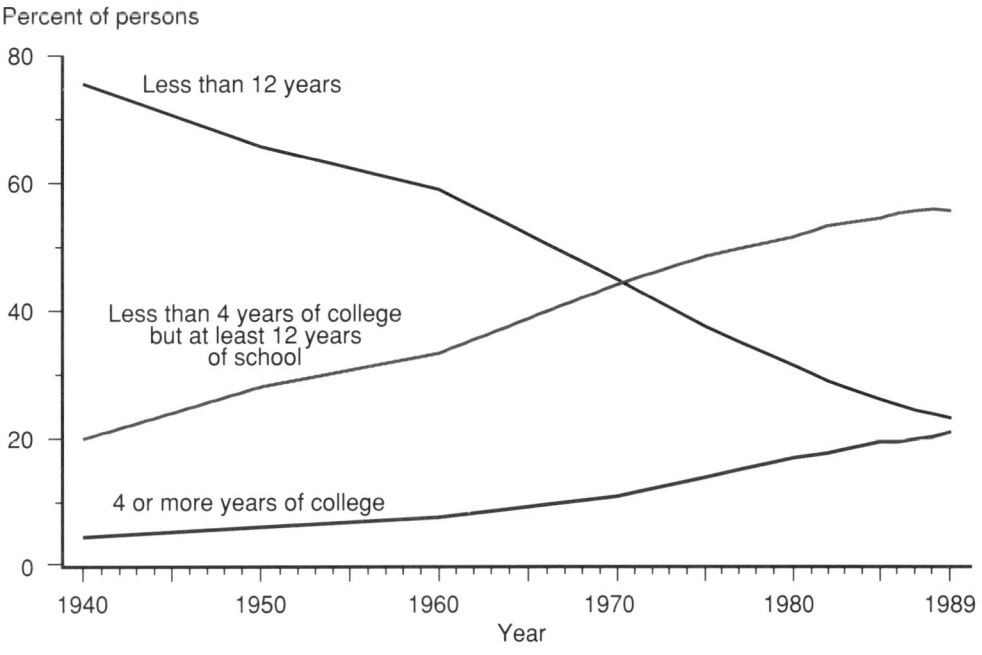

SOURCE: U.S. Department of Commerce, Bureau of the Census, *1960 Census of Population,* Vol. 1, part 1; and *Current Population Reports,* Series P–20, "Educational Attainment in the United States," and U.S. Department of Labor, Bureau of Labor Statistics, Office of Employment and Unemployment Statistics, "Educational Attainment of Workers, March 1989," unpublished.

Figure 4.--Years of school completed by persons 25 to 29 years of age: 1940 to 1989

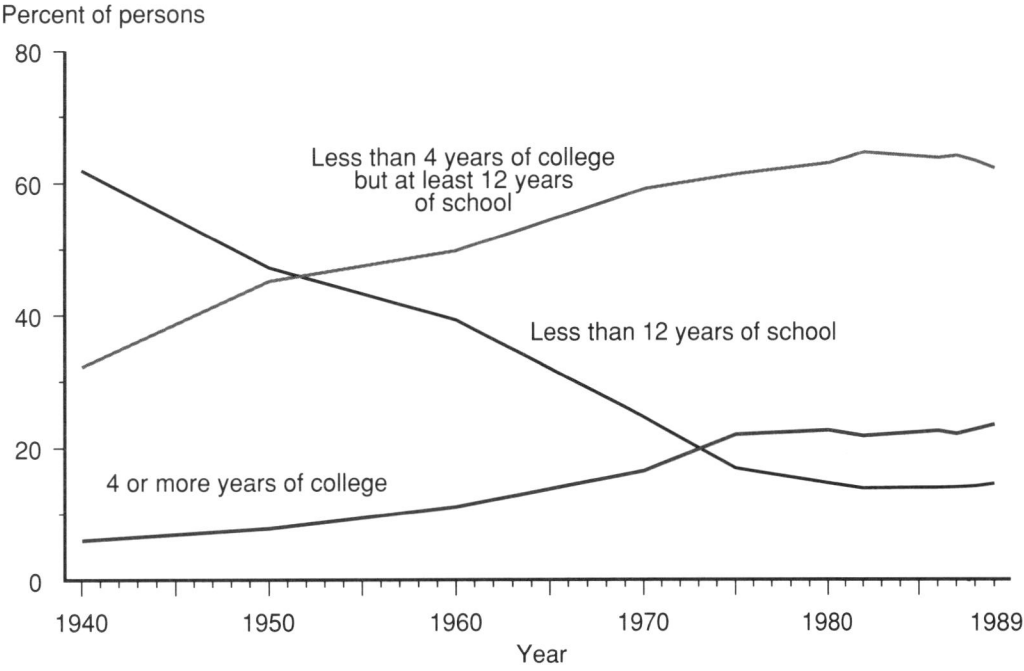

SOURCE: U.S. Department of Commerce, Bureau of the Census, *1960 Census of Population,* Vol. 1, part 1; and *Current Population Reports,* Series P–20, "Educational Attainment in the United States," and U.S. Department of Labor, Bureau of Labor Statistics, Office of Employment and Unemployment Statistics, "Educational Attainment of Workers, March 1989," unpublished.

Figure 5.--Highest degree earned by persons 18 years old and over: 1987

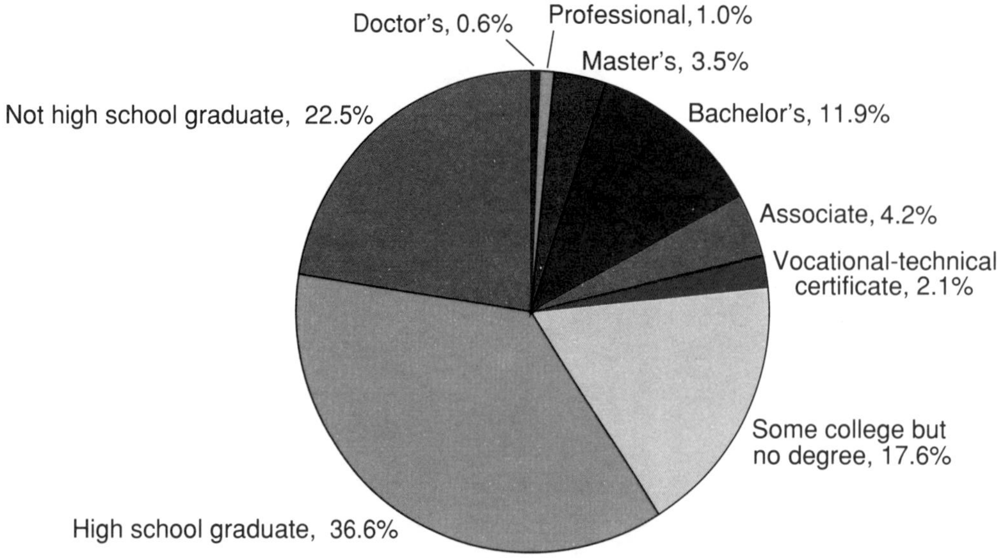

Doctor's, 0.6%
Professional, 1.0%
Master's, 3.5%
Bachelor's, 11.9%
Associate, 4.2%
Vocational-technical certificate, 2.1%
Some college but no degree, 17.6%
High school graduate, 36.6%
Not high school graduate, 22.5%

Total persons age 18 and over = 176 million

SOURCE: U.S. Department of Commerce, Bureau of the Census, *Current Population Reports,* Series P–70, No. 11, Educational Background and Economic Status; Spring 1987.

Figure 6.--Items most frequently cited by the public as a major problem facing the local public schools: 1980 to 1990

Percent citing problem
40
35
30
25
20
15
10
5
Lack of discipline
Use of drugs
Lack of financial support
1980
1981
1982
1983
1984
1985
1986
1987
1988
1989
1990
Year

SOURCE: Phi Delta Kappan, "The 20th Annual Gallup Poll of the Public's Attitudes Toward the Public Schools," September 1990.

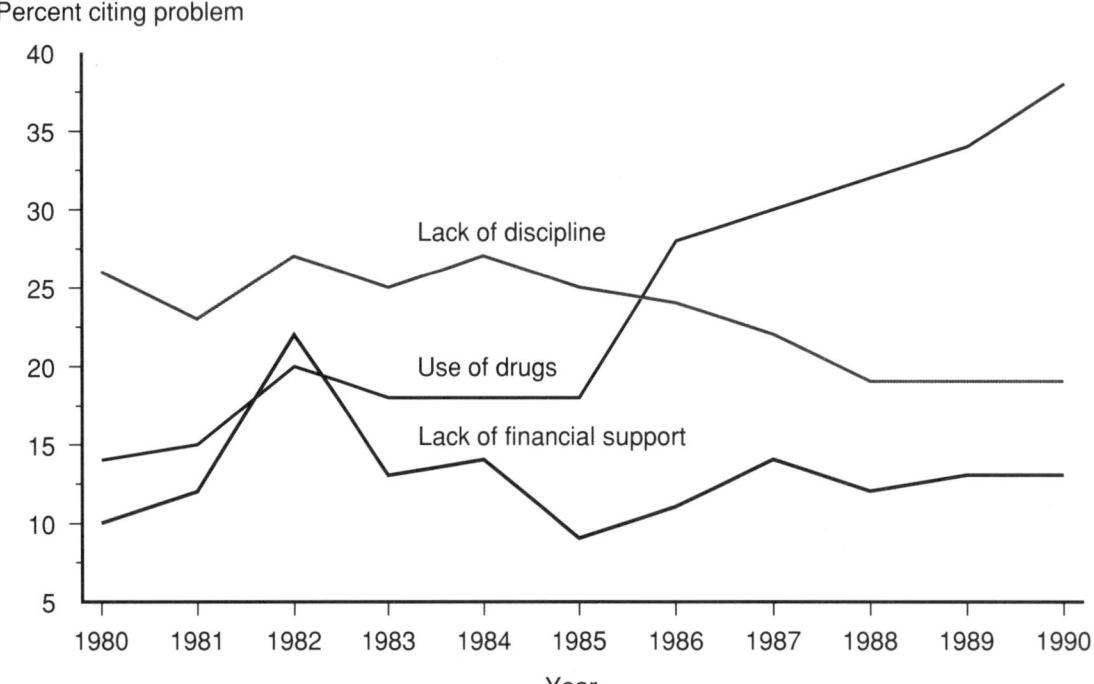

Table 1.—Estimated number of participants in elementary and secondary education and in higher education: Fall 1990

[In millions]

Participants	All levels (elementary, secondary, and higher education)	Elementary and secondary schools			Institutions of higher education
		Total	Public	Private	
1	2	3	4	5	6
Total	**67.5**	**51.2**	**45.5**	**5.7**	**16.3**
Enrollment [1]	60.2	46.2	41.0	5.2	14.0
Teachers and faculty	3.5	2.7	2.4	0.4	[2]0.8
Other professional, administrative, and support staff	3.8	2.3	2.1	0.2	1.6

[1] Includes enrollments in local public school systems and in most private schools (religiously affiliated and nonsectarian). Excludes subcollegiate departments of institutions of higher education, residential schools for exceptional children, and Federal schools. Elementary and secondary includes most kindergarten and some nursery school enrollment. Excludes preprimary enrollment in schools that do not offer first grade or above. Higher education comprises full-time and part-time students enrolled in degree-credit and nondegree-credit programs in universities, other four-year colleges, and two-year colleges.

[2] Includes full-time and part-time faculty with the rank of instructor or above.

NOTE.—The enrollment figures include all students in elementary and secondary schools and colleges and universities. However, the data for teachers and other staff in public and private elementary and secondary schools are reported in terms of full-time equivalents. The staff data for institutions of higher education include all full-time and part-time professional, administrative, and support personnel. Because of rounding, details may not add to totals.

SOURCE: U.S. Department of Education, National Center for Education Statistics, unpublished projections and estimates. (This table was prepared April 1991.)

Table 2.—Enrollment in educational institutions, by level and control of institution: Fall 1980 to fall 2000

[In thousands]

Level of instruction and type of control	Fall 1980	Fall 1983	Fall 1984	Fall 1985	Fall 1986	Fall 1987	Fall 1988	Fall 1989[1]	Estimated fall 1990	Projected fall 1995	Projected fall 2000
1	2	3	4	5	6	7	8	9	10	11	12
All levels	**58,346**	**57,432**	**57,150**	**57,226**	**57,709**	**58,254**	**58,485**	**59,339**	**60,172**	**64,675**	**68,098**
Public	50,376	48,935	48,686	48,901	49,467	49,981	50,350	51,041	51,938	55,835	58,759
Private	7,971	8,497	8,465	8,325	8,242	8,273	8,135	8,298	8,234	8,840	9,339
Elementary and secondary education[2]	46,249	44,967	44,908	44,979	45,205	45,487	45,430	45,881	46,221	50,054	52,406
Public	40,918	39,252	39,208	39,422	39,753	40,008	40,189	40,526	41,026	44,442	46,539
Private	5,331	5,715	[3] 5,700	5,557	[3] 5,452	5,479	5,241	5,355	5,195	5,612	5,867
Grades K-8[4]	31,669	31,294	31,201	31,225	31,537	32,164	32,539	33,320	33,808	36,127	37,548
Public	27,677	26,979	26,901	27,030	27,421	27,932	28,503	29,158	29,742	31,782	33,032
Private	3,992	4,315	[3] 4,300	4,195	[3] 4,116	4,232	4,036	4,162	4,066	4,345	4,516
Grades 9-12	14,581	13,674	13,708	13,754	13,669	13,323	12,892	12,562	12,413	13,927	14,858
Public	13,242	12,274	12,308	12,392	12,333	12,076	11,686	11,369	11,284	12,660	13,507
Private	1,339	1,400	[3] 1,400	1,362	[3] 1,336	1,247	1,206	1,193	1,129	1,267	1,351
Higher education[5]	12,097	12,465	12,242	12,247	12,504	12,767	13,055	13,458	13,951	14,621	15,692
Public	9,457	9,683	9,477	9,479	9,714	9,973	10,161	10,515	10,912	11,393	12,220
Undergraduate[6]	8,442	8,697	8,493	8,477	8,661	8,919	9,103	9,425	9,803	10,065	10,841
First-professional	114	113	114	112	112	110	109	113	115	136	143
Graduate[7]	901	872	870	890	941	945	949	978	994	1,192	1,236
Private	2,640	2,782	2,765	2,768	2,790	2,793	2,894	2,943	3,039	3,228	3,472
Undergraduate[6]	2,033	2,149	2,125	2,120	2,137	2,128	2,213	2,241	2,350	2,384	2,595
First-professional	163	165	165	162	158	158	158	158	161	158	194	205
Graduate[7]	443	468	475	486	494	507	522	541	531	650	672

[1]Preliminary.

[2]Includes enrollments in local public school systems and in most private schools (religiously affiliated and nonsectarian). Excludes subcollegiate departments of institutions of higher education, residential schools for exceptional children, and Federal schools. Excludes preprimary pupils in schools that do not offer first grade or above.

[3]Estimated.

[4]Includes kindergarten and some nursery school pupils.

[5]Includes full-time and part-time students enrolled in degree-credit and nondegree-credit programs in universities and 2-year colleges.

[6]Includes unclassified students below the baccalaureate level.

[7]Includes unclassified postbaccalaureate students.

NOTE.—Higher education enrollment projections based on the middle alternative projections published by the National Center for Education Statistics. Because of rounding, details may not add to totals. Some data have been revised from previously published figures.

SOURCE: U.S. Department of Education, National Center for Education Statistics, Common Core of Data and "Fall Enrollment in Institutions of Higher Education" surveys; Integrated Postsecondary Education Data System (IPEDS), "Fall Enrollment" surveys, and *Projections of Education Statistics to 2002*. (This table was prepared April 1991.)

Table 3.—Enrollment in educational institutions, by level and by control of institution: 1869–70 to fall 2002

[In thousands]

Year	Total enrollment, all levels	Elementary and secondary, total	Public elementary and secondary schools			Private elementary and secondary schools[1]			Higher education[2]		
			Total	Kinder-garten through grade 8	Grades 9 through 12	Total	Kinder-garten through grade 8	Grades 9 through 12	Total	Public	Private
1	2	3	4	5	6	7	8	9	10	11	12
1869-70	—	—	6,872	6,792	80	—	—	—	52	—	—
1879-80	—	—	9,868	9,757	110	—	—	—	116	—	—
1889-90	14,491	14,334	12,723	12,520	203	1,611	1,516	95	157	—	—
1899-1900	17,092	16,855	15,503	14,984	519	1,352	1,241	111	238	—	—
1909-10	19,728	19,372	17,814	16,899	915	1,558	1,441	117	355	—	—
1919-20	23,876	23,278	21,578	19,378	2,200	1,699	1,486	214	598	—	—
1929-30	29,430	28,329	25,678	21,279	4,399	2,651	2,310	341	1,101	—	—
1939-40	29,539	28,045	25,434	18,832	6,601	2,611	2,153	458	1,494	797	698
1949-50	31,151	28,492	25,111	19,387	5,725	3,380	2,708	672	2,659	1,355	1,304
Fall 1959	44,497	40,857	35,182	26,911	8,271	5,675	4,640	1,035	3,640	2,181	1,459
Fall 1964	52,996	47,716	41,416	30,025	11,391	[3]6,300	[3]5,000	1,300	5,280	3,468	1,812
Fall 1965	54,394	48,473	42,173	30,563	11,610	6,300	4,900	1,400	5,921	3,970	1,951
Fall 1966	55,629	49,239	43,039	31,145	11,894	[3]6,200	[3]4,800	[3]1,400	6,390	4,349	2,041
Fall 1967	56,803	49,891	43,891	31,641	12,250	[3]6,000	[3]4,600	[3]1,400	6,912	4,816	2,096
Fall 1968	58,257	50,744	44,944	32,226	12,718	5,800	4,400	1,400	7,513	5,431	2,082
Fall 1969	59,124	51,119	45,619	32,597	13,022	[3]5,500	[3]4,200	[3]1,300	8,005	5,897	2,108
Fall 1970	59,853	51,272	45,909	32,577	13,332	5,363	4,052	1,311	8,581	6,428	2,153
Fall 1971	60,230	51,281	46,081	32,265	13,816	[3]5,200	[3]3,900	[3]1,300	8,949	6,804	2,144
Fall 1972	59,959	50,744	45,744	31,831	13,913	[3]5,000	[3]3,700	[3]1,300	9,215	7,071	2,144
Fall 1973	60,031	50,429	45,429	31,353	14,077	[3]5,000	[3]3,700	[3]1,300	9,602	7,420	2,183
Fall 1974	60,277	50,053	45,053	30,921	14,132	[3]5,000	[3]3,700	[3]1,300	10,224	7,989	2,235
Fall 1975	60,976	49,791	44,791	30,487	14,304	[3]5,000	[3]3,700	[3]1,300	11,185	8,835	2,350
Fall 1976	60,496	49,484	44,317	30,006	14,311	5,167	3,825	1,342	11,012	8,653	2,359
Fall 1977	60,003	48,717	43,577	29,336	14,240	5,140	3,797	1,343	11,286	8,847	2,439
Fall 1978	58,896	47,636	42,550	28,425	14,125	5,086	3,732	1,353	11,260	8,786	2,474
Fall 1979	58,215	46,645	41,645	27,931	13,714	[3]5,000	[3]3,700	[3]1,300	11,570	9,037	2,533
Fall 1980	58,346	46,249	40,918	27,677	13,242	5,331	3,992	1,339	12,097	9,457	2,640
Fall 1981	57,894	45,522	40,022	27,270	12,752	[3]5,500	[3]4,100	[3]1,400	12,372	9,647	2,725
Fall 1982	57,591	45,166	39,566	27,158	12,407	[3]5,600	[3]4,200	[3]1,400	12,426	9,696	2,730
Fall 1983	57,432	44,967	39,252	26,979	12,274	5,715	4,315	1,400	12,465	9,683	2,782
Fall 1984	57,150	44,908	39,208	26,901	12,308	[3]5,700	[3]4,300	[3]1,400	12,242	9,477	2,765
Fall 1985	57,226	44,979	39,422	27,030	12,392	5,557	4,195	1,362	12,247	9,479	2,768
Fall 1986	57,709	45,205	39,753	27,421	12,333	[3]5,452	[3]4,116	[3]1,336	12,504	9,714	2,790
Fall 1987	58,254	45,487	40,008	27,932	12,076	5,479	4,232	1,247	12,767	9,973	2,793
Fall 1988	58,485	45,430	40,189	28,503	11,686	5,241	4,036	1,206	13,055	10,161	2,894
Fall 1989[4]	59,339	45,881	40,526	29,158	11,369	5,355	4,162	1,193	13,458	10,515	2,943
Fall 1990[5]	60,172	46,221	41,026	29,742	11,284	5,195	4,066	1,129	13,951	10,912	3,039
Fall 1991[6]	60,946	46,841	41,575	30,186	11,389	5,267	4,127	1,140	14,105	10,982	3,123
Fall 1992[6]	61,836	47,601	42,250	30,663	11,587	5,351	4,192	1,159	14,235	11,083	3,152
Fall 1993[6]	62,776	48,410	42,971	31,091	11,880	5,439	4,250	1,189	14,366	11,187	3,179
Fall 1994[6]	63,791	49,279	43,749	31,451	12,298	5,530	4,300	1,230	14,512	11,305	3,207
Fall 1995[6]	64,675	50,054	44,442	31,782	12,660	5,612	4,345	1,267	14,621	11,393	3,228
Fall 1996[6]	65,561	50,759	45,074	32,068	13,006	5,685	4,384	1,301	14,802	11,537	3,266
Fall 1997[6]	66,309	51,331	45,585	32,343	13,242	5,746	4,422	1,325	14,978	11,673	3,305
Fall 1998[6]	66,977	51,750	45,955	32,661	13,294	5,795	4,465	1,330	15,227	11,864	3,363
Fall 1999[6]	67,572	52,110	46,276	32,843	13,433	5,834	4,490	1,344	15,462	12,043	3,419
Fall 2000[6]	68,098	52,406	46,539	33,032	13,507	5,867	4,516	1,351	15,692	12,220	3,472
Fall 2001[6]	68,544	52,679	46,782	33,172	13,610	5,897	4,535	1,362	15,865	12,355	3,510
Fall 2002[6]	69,026	52,996	47,068	33,245	13,823	5,928	4,545	1,383	16,030	12,478	3,552

[1] Beginning in fall 1980, data include estimates for an expanded universe of private schools. Therefore, these totals may differ from figures shown in other tables, and direct comparisons with earlier years should be avoided.

[2] Data for 1869-70 through 1949-50 include resident degree-credit students enrolled at any time during the academic year. Beginning in 1959, data include all resident and extension students enrolled at the beginning of the fall term.

[3] Estimated.

[4] Preliminary data.

[5] Based on "Early Estimates" surveys.

[6] Projected.

—Data not available.

NOTE.—Elementary and secondary enrollment includes pupils in local public school systems and in most private schools (religiously affiliated and nonsectarian), but generally excludes pupils in subcollegiate departments of institutions of higher education, residential schools for exceptional children, and Federal schools. Elementary enrollment includes some prekindergarten pupils. Higher education enrollment includes students in colleges, universities, professional schools, teachers colleges, and 2-year colleges. Higher education enrollment projections are based on the middle alternative projections published by the National Center for Education Statistics. Some data have been revised from previously published figures. Because of rounding, details may not add to totals.

SOURCE: U.S. Department of Education, National Center for Education Statistics, *Statistics of State School Systems; Statistics of Public Elementary and Secondary School Systems; Statistics of Nonpublic Elementary and Secondary Schools; Projections of Education Statistics to 2002;* Common Core of Data; "Fall Enrollment in Institutions of Higher Education"; and Integrated Postsecondary Education Data System (IPEDS), "Fall Enrollment" surveys. (This table was prepared April 1991.)

Table 4.—Teachers in elementary and secondary schools, and senior instructional staff in institutions of higher education, by control of institution: Fall 1970 to fall 2002

[In thousands]

Fall	All levels			Elementary and secondary teachers [1]									Higher education senior instructional staff [2]		
				Total			Elementary teachers			Secondary teachers					
	Total	Public	Private	Total	Public	Private	Total	Public	Private	Total	Public	Private	Total	Public	Private
1	2	3	4	5	6	7	8	9	10	11	12	13	14	15	16
1970	2,762	2,369	393	2,288	2,055	233	1,281	1,128	153	1,007	927	80	474	314	160
1975	3,079	2,639	440	2,451	2,196	[3]255	1,352	1,180	[3]172	1,099	1,016	[3]83	628	443	185
1980	3,171	2,679	492	2,485	2,184	301	1,401	1,189	212	1,084	995	89	[3]686	[3]495	[3]191
1981	3,143	2,634	509	2,438	2,125	[3]313	1,380	1,159	[3]221	1,057	965	[3]92	705	509	196
1982	3,156	2,627	529	2,446	2,121	[3]325	1,402	1,171	[3]231	1,044	950	[3]94	[3]710	[3]506	[3]204
1983	3,187	2,638	549	2,463	2,126	337	1,418	1,178	240	1,045	948	97	724	512	212
1984	3,225	2,673	552	2,508	2,168	[3]340	1,448	1,205	[3]243	1,060	963	[3]97	[3]717	[3]505	[3]212
1985	3,265	2,710	555	2,550	2,207	343	1,483	1,237	246	1,067	970	97	[3]715	[3]503	[3]212
1986	3,314	2,754	560	2,592	2,244	[3]348	1,517	1,267	[3]250	1,075	977	[3]98	[3]722	[3]510	[3]212
1987	3,425	2,832	593	2,631	2,279	353	1,554	1,297	257	1,077	982	95	[4]793	[4]553	[4]240
1988	3,409	2,847	562	2,668	2,323	[3]345	1,604	1,353	[3]251	1,064	970	[3]94	[6]741	524	[6]217
1989[5]	3,488	2,890	598	2,734	2,356	[3]377	1,664	1,389	[3]275	1,070	968	[3]102	[6]755	[6]534	[6]221
1990[5]	3,506	2,930	576	2,744	2,391	353	1,632	1,379	253	1,112	1,012	100	[6]762	[6]539	[6]223
1991[6]	3,587	3,004	583	2,826	2,465	360	1,631	1,378	253	1,194	1,087	107	762	539	223
1992[6]	3,546	2,967	579	2,791	2,433	358	1,645	1,389	255	1,146	1,043	103	755	534	221
1993[6]	3,596	3,012	584	2,847	2,482	365	1,674	1,414	260	1,173	1,067	105	749	530	219
1994[6]	3,647	3,057	590	2,902	2,530	372	1,704	1,439	264	1,198	1,090	108	744	527	218
1995[6]	3,701	3,105	596	2,958	2,579	379	1,736	1,467	269	1,222	1,112	110	743	526	217
1996[6]	3,760	3,156	604	3,015	2,628	387	1,770	1,495	275	1,245	1,133	112	745	528	217
1997[6]	3,817	3,205	612	3,066	2,673	393	1,799	1,520	279	1,267	1,153	114	750	532	219
1998[6]	3,865	3,246	619	3,107	2,709	398	1,824	1,541	283	1,283	1,167	115	758	537	221
1999[6]	3,910	3,284	626	3,145	2,742	403	1,846	1,559	286	1,299	1,182	117	765	542	223
2000[6]	3,954	3,321	633	3,181	2,774	408	1,866	1,576	289	1,316	1,198	118	771	547	225
2001[6]	—	—	—	3,217	2,805	412	1,884	1,592	292	1,333	1,213	120	—	—	—
2002[6]	—	—	—	3,254	2,838	417	1,903	1,608	295	1,351	1,230	122	—	—	—

[1] Includes teachers in local public school systems and in most private schools (religiously affiliated and nonsectarian). Excludes subcollegiate departments of institutions of higher education, residential schools for exceptional children, and Federal schools. Teachers are reported in terms of full-time equivalents.

[2] Includes full-time and part-time faculty with the rank of instructor or above in colleges, universities, professional schools, teachers colleges, and 2-year colleges. Excludes teaching assistants.

[3] Estimated on the basis of enrollment.

[4] Based on actual survey data. Methodology is not consistent with figures for other years.

[5] Preliminary data.

[6] Projected.

—Data not available.

NOTE.—Because of rounding, details may not add to totals. Some data have been revised from previously published figures.

SOURCE: U.S. Department of Education, National Center for Education Statistics, Common Core of Data; Projections of Education Statistics, various years; Integrated Postsecondary Education Data System (IPEDS), "Staff" survey; and Equal Employment Opportunity Commission, unpublished data. (This table was prepared April 1991.)

Table 5.—Educational institutions, by level and control of institution: 1976–77 to 1989–90

Level and control of institution	1976–77	1978–79	1980–81	1982–83	1984–85	1986–87	1987–88	1988–89	1989–90
1	2	3	4	5	6	7	8	9	10
All institutions	—	—	**117,707**	—	—	**121,433**	**122,111**	—	—
Elementary and secondary schools	—	—	106,746	—	—	109,071	110,055	—	—
Elementary	74,053	73,062	72,659	—	—	74,104	76,398	—	—
Secondary	26,457	25,259	24,856	—	—	23,844	23,183	—	—
Combined	4,859	4,904	5,202	—	—	6,932	9,475	—	—
Other	—	—	4,029	—	—	4,191	1,000	—	—
Public schools	—	—	85,982	84,740	84,007	83,455	83,248	83,165	83,425
Elementary	61,123	60,312	59,326	58,051	57,231	58,801	59,311	59,296	59,757
Secondary	23,857	22,834	22,619	22,383	22,320	21,406	20,758	20,550	20,359
Combined	1,521	1,670	1,743	1,605	1,596	1,983	2,179	2,235	2,280
Other	—	—	2,294	2,701	2,860	1,265	1,000	1,084	1,029
Private schools	19,910	19,489	20,764	—	—	[1] 25,616	26,807	—	—
Elementary	12,930	12,750	13,333	—	—	[1] 15,303	17,087	—	—
Secondary	2,600	2,425	2,237	—	—	[1] 2,438	2,425	—	—
Combined	3,338	3,234	3,459	—	—	[1] 4,949	7,296	—	—
Other	1,042	1,080	1,735	—	—	[1] 2,926	—	—	—
Postsecondary institutions	—	—	[2] 10,961	—	—	12,362	12,056	11,389	10,606
Public	—	—	[2] 2,393	—	—	2,363	2,250	2,169	2,120
Private nonprofit	—	—	[2] 2,359	—	—	3,432	3,254	3,092	2,942
Proprietary	—	—	[2] 6,209	—	—	6,567	6,552	6,128	5,544
Noncollegiate institutions	—	—	[2] 7,730	—	—	8,956	8,469	7,824	7,071
Public	—	—	[2] 896	—	—	830	659	587	557
Private nonprofit	—	—	[2] 790	—	—	1,797	1,581	1,434	1,286
Proprietary	—	—	[2] 6,044	—	—	6,329	6,229	5,803	5,228
Institutions of higher education [3]	3,046	3,134	3,231	3,280	3,331	3,406	3,587	3,565	3,535
2-year colleges	1,133	1,193	1,274	1,296	1,306	1,336	1,452	1,436	1,408
Public	905	924	945	933	935	960	992	984	968
Private nonprofit	188	188	182	363	186	173	186	180	177
Proprietary	40	81	147	([4])	185	203	274	272	263
4-year colleges	1,913	1,941	1,957	1,984	2,025	2,070	2,135	2,129	2,127
Public	550	550	552	560	566	573	599	598	595
Private nonprofit	1,348	1,376	1,387	1,424	1,430	1,462	1,487	1,478	1,479
Proprietary	15	15	18	([4])	29	35	49	53	53

[1] Data are for 1985–86. Data were collected from a sample survey that differed significantly from earlier surveys. The sample survey was designed to correct an undercount of about 10 percent that was known to have occurred in earlier surveys.

[2] Because of changes in survey procedures, figures are not directly comparable with data for later years.

[3] Includes only those institutions designated as institutions of higher education by the Higher Education General Information Survey system. Includes branch campuses. Beginning in 1980, total includes some schools accredited by the National Association of Trade and Technical Schools.

[4] Included under "private nonprofit."

—Data not available.

NOTE.—Because of changes in survey definitions, figures for "other" schools are not comparable from year to year. Because of rounding, details may not add to totals.

SOURCE: U.S Department of Education, National Center for Education Statistics, Common Core of Data and Private School surveys; Higher Education General Information Survey, "Institutional Characteristics of Colleges and Universities"; and Integrated Postsecondary Education Data System, "Institutional Characteristics." (This table was prepared March 1991.)

Table 6.—Percentage of the population 3 to 34 years old enrolled in school,[1] by age:
April 1940 to October 1990

Year	Total, 3 to 34 years	3 and 4 years	5 and 6 years	7 to 13 years	14 to 17 years	18 and 19 years	20 to 24 years			25 to 29 years	30 to 34 years
							Total	20 and 21 years	22 to 24 years		
1	2	3	4	5	6	7	8	9	10	11	12
1940[2]	—	—	43.0	95.0	79.3	28.9	6.6	—	—	—	—
1945	—	—	60.4	98.1	78.4	20.7	3.9	—	—	—	—
1947	—	—	58.0	98.5	79.3	24.3	10.2	—	—	3.0	—
1948	—	—	56.0	98.1	81.8	26.9	9.7	—	—	2.6	—
1949	—	—	59.3	98.6	81.6	25.3	9.2	—	—	3.8	—
1950	—	—	58.2	98.7	83.4	29.7	9.2	—	—	3.0	0.9
1951	—	—	54.5	99.1	85.2	26.2	8.6	—	—	2.5	—
1952	—	—	54.7	98.8	85.2	28.8	9.7	—	—	2.6	1.2
1953	—	—	55.7	99.4	85.9	31.2	11.1	—	—	2.9	1.7
1954	—	—	77.3	99.4	87.1	32.4	11.2	—	—	4.1	1.5
1955	—	—	78.1	99.2	86.9	31.5	11.1	—	—	4.2	1.6
1956	—	—	77.6	99.3	88.2	35.4	12.8	—	—	5.1	1.9
1957	—	—	78.6	99.5	89.5	34.9	14.0	—	—	—	—
1958	—	—	80.4	99.5	89.2	37.6	13.4	—	—	—	—
1959	—	—	80.0	99.4	90.2	36.8	12.7	—	—	—	—
1960	—	—	80.7	99.5	90.3	38.4	13.1	—	—	4.9	2.4
1961	—	—	81.7	99.3	91.4	38.0	13.7	—	—	—	—
1962	—	—	82.2	99.3	92.0	41.8	15.6	—	—	—	—
1963	—	—	82.7	99.3	92.9	40.9	17.3	—	—	—	—
1964	—	—	83.3	99.0	93.1	41.6	16.8	—	—	5.2	2.6
1965	55.5	10.6	84.9	99.4	93.2	46.3	19.0	27.6	13.2	6.1	3.2
1966	56.1	12.5	85.8	99.3	93.7	47.2	19.9	29.9	13.2	6.5	2.7
1967	56.6	14.2	87.4	99.3	93.7	47.6	22.0	33.3	13.6	6.6	4.0
1968	56.7	15.7	87.6	99.1	94.2	50.4	21.4	31.2	13.8	7.0	3.9
1969	57.0	16.1	88.4	99.2	94.0	50.2	23.0	34.1	15.4	7.9	4.8
1970	56.4	20.5	89.5	99.2	94.1	47.7	21.5	31.9	14.9	7.5	4.2
1971	56.2	21.2	91.6	99.1	94.5	49.2	21.9	32.2	15.4	8.0	4.9
1972	54.9	24.4	91.9	99.2	93.3	46.3	21.6	31.4	14.8	8.6	4.6
1973	53.5	24.2	92.5	99.2	92.9	42.9	20.8	30.1	14.5	8.5	4.5
1974	53.6	28.8	94.2	99.3	92.9	43.1	21.4	30.2	15.1	9.6	5.7
1975	53.7	31.5	94.7	99.3	93.6	46.9	22.4	31.2	16.2	10.1	6.6
1976	53.1	31.3	95.5	99.2	93.7	46.2	23.3	32.0	17.1	10.0	6.0
1977	52.5	32.0	95.8	99.4	93.6	46.2	22.9	31.8	16.5	10.8	6.9
1978	51.2	34.2	95.3	99.1	93.7	45.4	21.8	29.5	16.3	9.4	6.4
1979	50.3	35.1	95.8	99.2	93.6	45.0	21.7	30.2	15.8	9.6	6.4
1980	49.7	36.7	95.7	99.3	93.4	46.4	22.3	31.0	16.3	9.3	6.4
1981	48.9	36.0	94.0	99.2	94.1	49.0	22.5	31.6	16.5	9.0	6.9
1982	48.6	36.4	95.0	99.2	94.4	47.8	23.5	34.0	16.8	9.6	6.3
1983	48.4	37.5	95.4	99.2	95.0	50.4	22.7	32.5	16.6	9.6	6.4
1984	47.9	36.3	94.5	99.2	94.7	50.1	23.7	33.9	17.3	9.1	6.3
1985	48.3	38.9	96.1	99.2	94.9	51.6	24.0	35.3	16.9	9.2	6.1
1986	48.2	38.9	95.3	99.2	94.9	54.6	23.6	33.0	17.9	8.8	6.0
1987	48.6	38.3	95.1	99.5	95.0	55.6	25.5	38.7	17.5	9.0	5.8
1988	48.7	38.2	96.0	99.7	95.1	55.6	26.1	39.1	18.2	8.3	5.9
1989	49.1	39.1	95.2	99.3	95.7	56.0	27.0	38.5	19.9	9.3	5.7
1990	50.2	44.4	96.5	99.6	95.8	57.2	28.6	39.7	21.0	9.7	5.8

[1] Includes enrollment in any type of graded public, parochial, or other private school in regular school systems. Includes nursery schools, kindergartens, elementary schools, colleges, universities, and professional schools. Attendance may be on either a full-time or part-time basis and during the day or night. Enrollments in "special" schools, such as trade schools, business colleges, or correspondence schools, are not included.

[2] Data are as of April 1940. Data for all other years are as of October.

—Data not available.

NOTE.—Data are based upon sample surveys of the civilian noninstitutional population.

SOURCE: U.S. Department of Commerce, Bureau of the Census, *Historical Statistics of the United States, Colonial Times to 1970; Current Population Reports*, Series P–20, various years; and unpublished data. (This table was prepared May 1991.)

Table 7.—Percentage of the population 3 to 34 years old enrolled in school,[1] by race/ethnicity, sex, and age: October 1975 to October 1990

Year and age	Total				Men				Women			
	All races	White, non-Hispanic	Black, non-Hispanic	Hispanic origin	All races	White, non-Hispanic	Black, non-Hispanic	Hispanic origin	All races	White, non-Hispanic	Black, non-Hispanic	Hispanic origin
1	2	3	4	5	6	7	8	9	10	11	12	13
1975												
Total, 3 to 34 years	**53.7**	**53.0**	**57.7**	**54.8**	**56.1**	**55.2**	**60.4**	**58.1**	**51.5**	**50.8**	**55.3**	**51.7**
3 and 4 years	31.5	31.0	34.4	27.3	30.9	31.1	31.4	26.7	32.1	30.9	37.5	27.9
5 and 6 years	94.7	95.1	94.4	92.1	94.4	94.8	94.8	89.7	95.1	95.4	94.0	94.4
7 to 9 years	99.3	99.4	99.3	99.6	99.2	99.2	99.4	99.6	99.5	99.6	99.2	99.5
10 to 13 years	99.3	99.3	99.1	99.2	98.9	99.0	98.9	98.8	99.6	99.6	99.3	99.7
14 and 15 years	98.2	98.5	97.4	95.6	98.4	98.6	97.6	97.4	98.0	98.4	97.2	93.8
16 and 17 years	89.0	89.5	86.8	86.2	90.7	91.2	88.1	88.3	87.2	87.8	85.5	84.0
18 and 19 years	46.9	46.8	46.9	44.0	49.9	49.4	49.6	51.9	44.2	44.2	44.6	37.1
20 and 21 years	31.2	32.1	26.7	27.5	35.3	36.7	28.4	31.3	27.4	27.8	25.3	24.3
22 to 24 years	16.2	16.4	13.9	14.1	20.0	20.8	14.5	15.9	12.6	12.2	13.4	12.5
25 to 29 years	10.1	10.1	9.4	8.3	13.1	13.2	11.6	11.9	7.2	7.2	7.6	5.3
30 to 34 years	6.6	6.6	7.1	5.5	7.7	7.5	8.7	7.2	5.6	5.8	5.9	4.1
1980												
Total, 3 to 34 years	**49.7**	**48.8**	**54.0**	**49.8**	**50.9**	**50.0**	**56.2**	**49.9**	**48.5**	**47.7**	**52.1**	**49.8**
3 and 4 years	36.7	37.4	38.2	28.5	37.8	39.2	36.4	30.1	35.5	35.5	40.0	26.6
5 and 6 years	95.7	95.9	95.5	94.5	95.0	95.4	94.1	94.0	96.4	96.5	97.0	94.9
7 to 9 years	99.1	99.1	99.4	98.4	99.0	99.0	99.5	97.7	99.2	99.2	99.3	99.0
10 to 13 years	99.4	99.4	99.4	99.7	99.4	99.4	99.4	99.4	99.4	99.3	99.3	99.9
14 and 15 years	98.2	98.7	97.9	94.3	98.7	98.9	98.4	96.7	97.7	98.5	97.3	92.1
16 and 17 years	89.0	89.2	90.7	81.8	89.1	89.4	90.7	81.5	88.8	89.0	90.6	82.2
18 and 19 years	46.4	47.0	45.8	37.8	47.0	48.5	42.9	36.9	45.8	45.7	48.3	38.8
20 and 21 years	31.0	33.0	23.3	19.5	32.6	34.8	22.8	21.4	29.5	31.3	23.7	17.6
22 to 24 years	16.3	16.8	13.6	11.7	17.8	18.7	13.4	10.7	14.9	15.0	13.7	12.6
25 to 29 years	9.3	9.4	8.8	6.9	9.8	9.8	10.6	6.8	8.8	9.1	7.5	6.9
30 to 34 years	6.4	6.4	6.9	5.1	5.9	5.6	7.2	6.2	7.0	7.2	6.6	4.1
1985												
Total, 3 to 34 years	**48.3**	**47.8**	**50.8**	**47.7**	**49.2**	**48.7**	**52.6**	**47.5**	**47.4**	**46.9**	**49.2**	**47.9**
3 and 4 years	38.9	40.3	42.8	27.0	36.7	39.1	34.6	26.4	41.2	41.6	50.3	27.7
5 and 6 years	96.1	96.6	95.7	94.5	95.3	95.6	94.5	95.3	97.0	97.6	97.1	93.7
7 to 9 years	99.1	99.4	98.6	98.4	99.0	99.3	98.4	98.9	99.2	99.4	98.9	98.0
10 to 13 years	99.3	99.3	99.5	99.4	99.2	99.2	99.1	99.1	99.4	99.3	99.9	99.7
14 and 15 years	98.1	98.3	98.1	96.1	98.3	98.4	98.5	96.2	97.9	98.1	97.6	96.0
16 and 17 years	91.7	92.5	91.8	84.5	92.4	92.9	92.0	88.9	90.9	92.2	91.6	80.0
18 and 19 years	51.6	53.7	43.5	41.8	52.2	53.4	49.4	38.6	51.0	54.0	37.8	44.7
20 and 21 years	35.3	37.2	27.7	24.0	36.5	38.8	29.9	20.3	34.1	35.7	25.8	27.4
22 to 24 years	16.9	17.5	13.8	11.6	18.8	19.8	13.5	12.6	15.1	15.4	14.0	10.4
25 to 29 years	9.2	9.6	7.4	6.6	9.4	9.7	5.8	8.2	9.1	9.4	8.7	4.9
30 to 34 years	6.1	6.2	5.2	5.7	5.4	5.6	3.9	4.0	6.8	6.9	6.2	7.5
1989												
Total, 3 to 34 years	**49.0**	**48.7**	**51.5**	**45.7**	**49.7**	**49.3**	**52.8**	**45.5**	**48.4**	**48.1**	**50.2**	**45.9**
3 and 4 years	39.1	42.2	39.0	22.3	38.8	42.0	39.9	19.3	39.5	42.4	38.0	25.5
5 and 6 years	95.2	95.7	94.6	93.3	95.1	95.8	92.9	92.8	95.2	95.5	96.3	93.7
7 to 9 years	99.2	99.4	99.0	98.1	99.2	99.6	98.8	97.5	99.2	99.2	99.2	98.7
10 to 13 years	99.4	99.5	99.3	99.1	99.2	99.3	98.8	98.6	99.6	99.6	99.9	99.6
14 and 15 years	98.8	99.1	99.4	96.4	99.2	99.5	99.3	98.0	98.4	98.7	99.5	95.0
16 and 17 years	92.7	93.1	93.8	86.4	93.2	93.0	95.8	88.7	92.2	93.2	91.7	83.7
18 and 19 years	56.0	58.0	49.8	44.6	56.6	58.8	51.5	44.2	55.4	57.2	48.3	45.0
20 and 21 years	38.5	42.8	30.8	18.8	37.3	43.1	23.2	17.1	39.7	42.5	37.4	20.8
22 to 24 years	19.9	21.3	17.1	12.0	20.4	21.7	15.7	12.2	19.5	20.8	18.4	11.9
25 to 29 years	9.3	9.8	6.1	6.6	9.3	9.6	5.0	7.3	9.3	10.0	7.0	5.8
30 to 34 years	5.7	5.8	5.0	3.8	5.0	5.1	3.3	4.1	6.4	6.6	6.4	3.5
1990												
Total, 3 to 34 years	**50.2**	**49.8**	**52.2**	**47.2**	**50.9**	**50.4**	**54.3**	**46.8**	**49.5**	**49.2**	**50.3**	**47.7**
3 and 4 years	44.4	47.2	41.8	30.7	43.9	47.9	38.1	28.0	44.9	46.6	45.5	33.6
5 and 6 years	96.5	96.7	96.5	94.9	96.5	96.8	96.2	95.8	96.4	96.7	96.9	93.9
7 to 9 years	99.7	99.7	99.8	99.5	99.7	99.7	99.9	99.5	99.6	99.7	99.8	99.4
10 to 13 years	99.6	99.7	99.9	99.1	99.6	99.6	99.9	99.0	99.7	99.7	99.8	99.1
14 and 15 years	99.0	99.0	99.4	99.0	99.1	99.2	99.7	99.1	98.9	98.9	99.1	98.8
16 and 17 years	92.5	93.5	91.7	85.4	92.6	93.4	93.0	85.5	92.4	93.7	90.5	85.3
18 and 19 years	57.2	59.1	55.0	44.0	58.2	59.7	60.4	40.7	56.3	58.5	49.8	47.2
20 and 21 years	39.7	43.1	28.3	27.2	40.3	44.2	31.0	21.7	39.2	42.0	25.8	33.1
22 to 24 years	21.0	21.9	19.7	9.9	23.7	23.7	22.3	11.2	19.9	20.3	20.0	8.4
25 to 29 years	9.7	10.4	6.1	6.3	9.2	10.0	4.7	4.6	10.2	10.7	7.3	8.1
30 to 34 years	5.8	6.2	4.5	3.6	4.8	5.0	2.3	4.0	6.9	7.4	6.3	3.1

[1] Includes enrollment in any type of graded public, parochial, or other private school in regular school systems. Includes nursery schools, kindergartens, elementary schools, high schools, colleges, universities, and professional schools. Attendance may be on either a full–time or part–time basis and during the day or night. Enrollments in "special" schools, such as trade schools, business colleges, or correspondence schools, are not included.

NOTE.—Data are based upon sample surveys of the civilian noninstitutional population.

SOURCE: U.S. Department of Commerce, Bureau of the Census, Current Population Survey, and unpublished data. (This table was prepared May 1991.)

Table 8.—Years of school completed by persons age 25 and over and 25 to 29, by race: 1910 to 1989

Race, age, and date	Percent, by years of school completed			Median school years completed	Race, age, and date	Percent, by years of school completed			Median school years completed
	Less than 5 years of elementary school	4 years of high school or more	4 or more years of college			Less than 5 years of elementary school	4 years of high school or more	4 or more years of college	
1	2	3	4	5	1	2	3	4	5
All races					**White [2] (continued)**				
25 and over					25 to 29				
1910 [1]	23.8	13.5	2.7	8.1	1920 [1]	12.9	22.0	4.5	8.5
1920 [1]	22.0	16.4	3.3	8.2	April 1940	3.4	41.2	6.4	10.7
1930 [1]	17.5	19.1	3.9	8.4	April 1950	3.3	56.3	8.2	12.2
April 1940	13.7	24.5	4.6	8.6	April 1960	2.2	63.7	11.8	12.3
April 1950	11.1	34.3	6.2	9.3	March 1970	0.9	77.8	17.3	12.6
April 1960	8.3	41.1	7.7	10.5	March 1975	1.0	84.4	22.8	12.8
March 1970	5.3	55.2	11.0	12.2	March 1980	0.8	86.9	23.7	12.9
March 1975	4.2	62.5	13.9	12.3	March 1982	0.8	86.9	22.7	12.9
March 1980	3.4	68.6	17.0	12.5	March 1985	0.8	86.8	23.2	12.9
March 1982	3.0	71.0	17.7	12.6	March 1986	0.9	86.5	23.5	12.9
March 1985	2.7	73.9	19.4	12.6	March 1987	0.8	86.3	23.0	12.9
March 1986	2.7	74.7	19.4	12.6	March 1988	1.0	86.6	23.5	12.9
March 1987	2.4	75.6	19.9	12.7	March 1989	0.9	86.0	24.4	12.9
March 1988	2.4	76.2	20.3	12.7	**Black and other races [2]**				
March 1989	2.5	76.9	21.1	12.7	25 and over				
25 to 29					April 1940	41.8	7.7	1.3	5.7
April 1940	5.9	38.1	5.9	10.3	April 1950	32.6	13.7	2.2	6.9
April 1950	4.6	52.8	7.7	12.1	April 1960	23.5	21.7	3.5	8.2
April 1960	2.8	60.7	11.0	12.3	March 1970	14.7	36.1	6.1	10.1
March 1970	1.1	75.4	16.4	12.6	March 1975	11.7	46.4	9.2	11.4
March 1975	1.0	83.1	21.9	12.8	March 1980	8.8	54.6	11.1	12.2
March 1980	0.8	85.4	22.5	12.9	March 1982	7.4	58.1	12.4	12.3
March 1982	0.8	86.2	21.7	12.8	March 1985	6.0	63.2	15.4	12.4
March 1985	0.7	86.1	22.2	12.9	March 1986	5.5	65.3	15.2	12.4
March 1986	0.9	86.1	22.4	12.9	March 1987	5.1	66.7	15.7	12.4
March 1987	0.9	86.0	22.0	12.8	March 1988	5.1	66.7	16.4	12.5
March 1988	1.0	85.9	22.7	12.8	March 1989	5.6	67.3	16.9	12.5
March 1989	1.0	85.5	23.4	12.9	25 to 29				
White [2]					1920 [1]	44.6	6.3	1.2	5.4
25 and over					April 1940	27.0	12.3	1.6	7.1
April 1940	10.9	26.1	4.9	8.7	April 1950	16.1	23.6	2.8	8.7
April 1950	8.9	36.4	6.6	9.7	April 1960	7.2	38.6	5.4	10.8
April 1960	6.7	43.2	8.1	10.8	March 1970	2.2	58.4	10.0	12.2
March 1970	4.2	57.4	11.6	12.2	March 1975	0.7	73.8	15.4	12.6
March 1975	3.3	64.5	14.5	12.4	March 1980	1.0	77.0	15.2	12.7
March 1980	2.6	70.5	17.8	12.5	March 1982	0.7	82.2	15.8	12.8
March 1982	2.4	72.8	18.5	12.6	March 1985	0.5	82.4	16.7	12.8
March 1985	2.2	75.5	20.0	12.7	March 1986	0.9	84.3	16.3	12.8
March 1986	2.2	76.2	20.1	12.7	March 1987	1.1	84.1	16.9	12.8
March 1987	2.0	77.0	20.5	12.7	March 1988	1.2	82.0	18.1	12.6
March 1988	2.0	77.7	20.9	12.7	March 1989	1.2	83.1	18.1	12.8
March 1989	2.0	78.4	21.8	12.7					

[1] Estimates based on retrojection, by the Bureau of the Census, of 1940 census data on education by age.

[2] Persons of Hispanic origin are included, as appropriate, in the "white" or in the "black and other races" category.

NOTE.—Data for 1975 and subsequent years are for the noninstitutional population. Some data have been revised from previously published figures.

SOURCE: U.S. Department of Commerce, Bureau of the Census, U.S. Census of Population, 1960, Vol. 1 part 1; Current Population Reports, Series P–20; Series P–19, No. 4; 1960 Census Monograph, "Education of the American Population," by John K. Folger and Charles B. Nam; and unpublished data from the Current Population Survey; and U.S. Department of Labor, Bureau of Labor Statistics, Office of Employment and Unemployment Statistics, "Educational Attainment of Workers, March 1989," unpublished. (This table was prepared March 1991.)

Table 9.—Years of school completed by persons [1] age 18 and over, by age, sex, and race/ethnicity: 1989

[In thousands]

Age, sex, and race	Total population [1]	Elementary level		High school		College		
		Less than 8 years	8 years	1 to 3 years	4 years	1 to 3 years	4 years	5 years or more
1	2	3	4	5	6	7	8	9
Total								
18 and over	179,783	10,741	8,173	22,394	70,340	33,677	20,523	13,934
18 and 19 years old	7,354	128	117	2,671	3,479	960	—	—
20 to 24 years old	18,274	408	340	2,003	7,525	6,104	1,637	255
25 years old and over	154,155	10,206	7,716	17,719	59,336	26,614	18,886	13,679
25 to 29 years old	21,478	539	333	2,242	8,951	4,391	3,575	1,446
30 to 34 years old	21,762	619	307	1,771	8,950	4,681	3,479	1,954
35 to 39 years old	19,369	636	317	1,461	7,171	4,353	3,033	2,396
40 to 49 years old	29,860	1,275	821	2,831	11,593	5,584	4,000	3,757
50 to 59 years old	21,899	1,595	1,156	3,006	8,882	3,090	2,096	2,075
60 to 69 years old	20,783	2,269	1,743	3,331	7,992	2,656	1,549	1,243
70 years old and over	19,005	3,271	3,040	3,077	5,798	1,857	1,154	807
Men								
18 and over	85,799	5,373	3,789	10,590	31,207	16,110	10,536	8,197
18 and 19 years old	3,635	81	63	1,452	1,630	408	—	—
20 to 24 years old	8,939	221	181	1,061	3,680	2,975	679	140
25 years old and over	73,225	5,070	3,545	8,076	25,897	12,725	9,856	8,057
25 to 29 years old	10,650	291	163	1,204	4,314	2,139	1,764	777
30 to 34 years old	10,811	348	147	925	4,345	2,252	1,720	1,073
35 to 39 years old	9,595	343	178	702	3,202	2,174	1,598	1,397
40 to 49 years old	14,548	652	422	1,242	5,069	2,749	2,147	2,268
50 to 59 years old	10,510	813	610	1,294	3,832	1,439	1,169	1,351
60 to 69 years old	9,586	1,190	859	1,488	3,105	1,242	947	757
70 years old and over	7,524	1,436	1,164	1,219	2,030	731	511	433
Women								
18 and over	93,984	5,369	4,383	11,805	39,133	17,568	9,988	5,738
18 and 19 years old	3,719	45	54	1,220	1,849	549	—	—
20 to 24 years old	9,336	188	158	942	3,845	3,128	958	116
25 years old and over	80,930	5,135	4,171	9,643	33,440	13,888	9,030	5,622
25 to 29 years old	10,827	248	170	1,039	4,637	2,253	1,810	669
30 to 34 years old	10,950	271	160	846	4,605	2,428	1,759	881
35 to 39 years old	9,775	294	139	759	3,969	2,179	1,436	999
40 to 49 years old	15,312	624	399	1,588	6,524	2,835	1,852	1,489
50 to 59 years old	11,389	781	545	1,711	5,050	1,651	927	724
60 to 69 years old	11,197	1,080	883	1,842	4,888	1,416	603	486
70 years old and over	11,480	1,836	1,875	1,858	3,768	1,125	643	374
White [2]								
18 and over	154,032	8,042	7,077	18,021	61,031	29,226	18,140	12,497
18 and 19 years old	6,038	101	94	2,096	2,939	808	—	—
20 to 24 years old	15,090	347	281	1,537	6,083	5,184	1,426	234
25 years old and over	132,903	7,593	6,702	14,389	52,010	23,233	16,713	12,263
25 to 29 years old	17,973	476	267	1,779	7,405	3,658	3,139	1,248
30 to 34 years old	18,298	518	247	1,365	7,563	3,875	2,987	1,741
35 to 39 years old	16,437	508	255	1,083	6,057	3,771	2,648	2,115
40 to 49 years old	25,708	994	642	2,194	10,109	4,920	3,468	3,378
50 to 59 years old	18,976	1,120	986	2,385	7,963	2,767	1,908	1,848
60 to 69 years old	18,351	1,586	1,527	2,753	7,399	2,460	1,465	1,162
70 years old and over	17,160	2,389	2,779	2,829	5,514	1,779	1,099	771
Black [2]								
18 and over	19,984	2,089	869	3,854	7,662	3,436	1,347	728
18 and 19 years old	1,072	18	18	487	426	123	—	—
20 to 24 years old	2,517	38	44	407	1,247	635	143	3
25 years old and over	16,395	2,032	807	2,959	5,988	2,679	1,204	725
25 to 29 years old	2,726	28	50	407	1,298	597	272	74
30 to 34 years old	2,662	45	38	369	1,173	666	282	89
35 to 39 years old	2,201	59	40	335	938	446	235	147
40 to 49 years old	3,048	181	138	562	1,178	521	253	216
50 to 59 years old	2,304	394	144	557	759	252	85	114
60 to 69 years old	1,926	579	164	501	447	138	38	56
70 years old and over	1,528	748	234	226	195	56	38	29
Hispanic origin [3]								
18 and over	13,061	3,171	885	2,257	3,879	1,786	696	387
18 and 19 years old	730	67	35	339	245	44	—	—
20 to 24 years old	1,893	261	104	379	727	368	48	6
25 years old and over	10,438	2,843	746	1,539	2,907	1,373	648	382
25 to 29 years old	2,152	350	94	395	731	366	152	65
30 to 34 years old	1,816	380	103	268	530	320	140	75
35 to 39 years old	1,478	344	89	176	465	247	88	70
40 to 49 years old	2,107	598	144	310	583	248	147	77
50 to 59 years old	1,349	465	121	212	304	120	69	56
60 to 69 years old	951	392	113	128	187	62	40	29
70 years old and over	586	313	82	52	105	12	13	10

[1] Civilian noninstitutional population.
[2] Includes persons of Hispanic origin.
[3] Persons of Hispanic origin may be of any race.
—Data not applicable or available.

NOTE.—Data are based on sample surveys of the noninstitutional population. Although cells with fewer than 75,000 people are subject to relatively wide sampling varia-

tion, they are included in the table to permit various types of aggregations. Because of rounding, details may not add to totals.

SOURCE: U.S. Department of Commerce, Bureau of the Census, Current Population Survey, unpublished data. (This table was prepared March 1991.)

Table 10.—Number of persons age 18 and over who hold a bachelor's or higher degree, by field of study, sex, race, and age: Spring 1987

[Numbers in thousands]

Field of study	Total	Sex		Race		Age					
		Men	Women	White	Black	18 to 24 years old	25 to 34 years old	35 to 44 years old	45 to 54 years old	55 to 64 years old	65 years old and over
1	2	3	4	5	6	7	8	9	10	11	12
Total population, 18 and over	176,405	84,106	92,299	151,882	19,290	26,148	42,858	34,352	23,052	21,726	28,268
Number of persons with bachelor's or higher degree	29,910	16,461	13,449	26,832	1,954	1,989	9,815	8,329	4,161	3,073	2,541
Percent of population	17.0	19.6	14.6	17.7	10.1	7.6	22.9	24.2	18.1	14.1	9.0
Agriculture and forestry	658	507	151	628	22	56	256	121	91	76	59
Biology	884	411	473	765	94	94	393	222	76	70	30
Business and management	5,433	3,890	1,543	4,954	358	345	2,044	1,497	771	547	228
Economics	885	662	223	744	73	77	279	251	105	77	95
Education	5,300	1,336	3,964	4,766	389	184	1,265	1,720	808	681	643
Engineering	2,671	2,489	182	2,316	112	279	920	562	383	319	210
English and journalism	1,040	434	606	1,005	16	69	283	335	151	93	109
Home economics	454	14	440	375	60	31	150	104	81	33	54
Law	882	737	145	849	32	13	324	245	52	160	88
Liberal arts and humanities	2,372	1,030	1,342	2,171	79	157	836	620	299	213	248
Mathematics and statistics	560	392	168	456	82	47	140	183	135	12	44
Medicine and dentistry	897	710	187	818	17	42	215	306	140	80	113
Nursing, pharmacy, and health technologies	1,476	210	1,266	1,324	78	48	484	451	219	155	120
Physical and earth sciences	819	539	280	736	43	54	291	187	110	113	66
Police science and law enforcement	223	173	50	185	29	18	96	40	26	15	28
Psychology	839	431	408	731	72	63	228	310	125	53	61
Religion and theology	527	475	52	458	34	17	102	140	110	94	65
Social sciences	2,158	1,084	1,074	1,924	206	205	732	671	257	136	156
Vocational and technical studies	156	131	25	112	44	8	91	23	11	18	5
Other fields	1,677	806	871	1,513	116	183	686	341	214	129	124

Percentage distribution of degree holders, by field

Total	100.0	100.0	100.0	100.0	100.0	100.0	100.0	100.0	100.0	100.0	100.0
Agriculture and forestry	2.2	3.1	1.1	2.3	1.1	2.8	2.6	1.5	2.2	2.5	2.3
Biology	3.0	2.5	3.5	2.9	4.8	4.7	4.0	2.7	1.8	2.3	1.2
Business and management	18.2	23.6	11.5	18.5	18.3	17.3	20.8	18.0	18.5	17.8	9.0
Economics	3.0	4.0	1.7	2.8	3.7	3.9	2.8	3.0	2.5	2.5	3.7
Education	17.7	8.1	29.5	17.8	19.9	9.3	12.9	20.7	19.4	22.2	25.3
Engineering	8.9	15.1	1.4	8.6	5.7	14.0	9.4	6.7	9.2	10.4	8.3
English and journalism	3.5	2.6	4.5	3.7	0.8	3.5	2.9	4.0	3.6	3.0	4.3
Home economics	1.5	0.1	3.3	1.4	3.1	1.6	1.5	1.2	1.9	1.1	2.1
Law	2.9	4.5	1.1	3.2	1.6	0.7	3.3	2.9	1.2	5.2	3.5
Liberal arts and humanities	7.9	6.3	10.0	8.1	4.0	7.9	8.5	7.4	7.2	6.9	9.8
Mathematics and statistics	1.9	2.4	1.2	1.7	4.2	2.4	1.4	2.2	3.2	0.4	1.7
Medicine and dentistry	3.0	4.3	1.4	3.0	0.9	2.1	2.2	3.7	3.4	2.6	4.4
Nursing, pharmacy, and health technologies	4.9	1.3	9.4	4.9	4.0	2.4	4.9	5.4	5.3	5.0	4.7
Physical and earth sciences	2.7	3.3	2.1	2.7	2.2	2.7	3.0	2.2	2.6	3.7	2.6
Police science and law enforcement	0.7	1.1	0.4	0.7	1.5	0.9	1.0	0.5	0.6	0.5	1.1
Psychology	2.8	2.6	3.0	2.7	3.7	3.2	2.3	3.7	3.0	1.7	2.4
Religion and theology	1.8	2.9	0.4	1.7	1.7	0.9	1.0	1.7	2.6	3.1	2.6
Social sciences	7.2	6.6	8.0	7.2	10.5	10.3	7.5	8.1	6.2	4.4	6.1
Vocational and technical studies	0.5	0.8	0.2	0.4	2.3	0.4	0.9	0.3	0.3	0.6	0.2
Other fields	5.6	4.9	6.5	5.6	5.9	9.2	7.0	4.1	5.1	4.2	4.9

NOTE.—Data are based on sample surveys of the civilian noninstitutional population. Because of rounding, details may not add to totals.

SOURCE: U.S. Department of Commerce, Bureau of the Census, *Current Population Reports*, Series P-70, No. 21, "Educational Background and Economic Status: Spring 1987." (This table was prepared March 1991.)

Table 11.—Highest educational level and degree earned by persons age 18 and over, by sex, race, and age: Spring 1987

[Numbers in thousands]

Sex, race, and age	Total	Not high school graduate [1]	High school graduate only	Some college, no degree or certificate	Vocational certificate	Associate degree	Bachelor's degree	Master's degree	Professional degree	Doctor's degree
1	2	3	4	5	6	7	8	9	10	11
Total population, 18 and over	**176,405**	**39,679**	**64,636**	**31,045**	**3,743**	**7,393**	**21,018**	**6,192**	**1,723**	**977**
Men	84,106	19,341	28,494	15,160	1,273	3,376	10,909	3,416	1,344	792
Women	92,299	20,338	36,141	15,884	2,471	4,017	10,109	2,776	379	184
White, total	151,882	31,875	56,240	26,981	3,415	6,538	18,850	5,486	1,605	891
Men	72,862	15,552	24,687	13,404	1,211	3,028	9,982	2,978	1,307	713
Women	79,020	16,323	31,553	13,577	2,205	3,510	8,868	2,508	298	178
Black, total	19,290	6,406	6,911	3,069	245	706	1,445	440	37	33
Men	8,696	3,127	3,176	1,252	41	261	583	221	8	26
Women	10,594	3,279	3,735	1,817	203	445	861	219	29	7
Age										
18 to 24 years old	26,148	4,203	10,596	8,043	389	928	1,912	77	—	—
25 to 34 years old	42,858	5,032	16,202	8,248	987	2,574	7,623	1,575	499	117
35 to 44 years old	34,352	4,921	12,101	5,931	862	2,208	5,359	2,114	509	347
45 to 54 years old	23,052	5,394	9,048	3,208	478	763	2,508	1,211	232	210
55 to 64 years old	21,726	6,668	8,364	2,690	457	473	1,928	656	285	205
65 years old and over	28,268	13,462	8,324	2,924	571	446	1,687	558	198	98

Percentage distribution, by highest degree earned

Sex, race, and age	Total	Not high school graduate [1]	High school graduate only	Some college, no degree or certificate	Vocational certificate	Associate degree	Bachelor's degree	Master's degree	Professional degree	Doctor's degree
Total population, 18 and over	**100.0**	**22.5**	**36.6**	**17.6**	**2.1**	**4.2**	**11.9**	**3.5**	**1.0**	**0.6**
Men	100.0	23.0	33.9	18.0	1.5	4.0	13.0	4.1	1.6	0.9
Women	100.0	22.0	39.2	17.2	2.7	4.4	11.0	3.0	0.4	0.2
White, total	100.0	21.0	37.0	17.8	2.2	4.3	12.4	3.6	1.1	0.6
Men	100.0	21.3	33.9	18.4	1.7	4.2	13.7	4.1	1.8	1.0
Women	100.0	20.7	39.9	17.2	2.8	4.4	11.2	3.2	0.4	0.2
Black, total	100.0	33.2	35.8	15.9	1.3	3.7	7.5	2.3	0.2	0.2
Men	100.0	36.0	36.5	14.4	0.5	3.0	6.7	2.5	0.1	0.3
Women	100.0	31.0	35.3	17.2	1.9	4.2	8.1	2.1	0.3	0.1
Age										
18 to 24 years old	100.0	16.1	40.5	30.8	1.5	3.5	7.3	0.3	(2)	(2)
25 to 34 years old	100.0	11.7	37.8	19.2	2.3	6.0	17.8	3.7	1.2	0.3
35 to 44 years old	100.0	14.3	35.2	17.3	2.5	6.4	15.6	6.2	1.5	1.0
45 to 54 years old	100.0	23.4	39.3	13.9	2.1	3.3	10.9	5.3	1.0	0.9
55 to 64 years old	100.0	30.7	38.5	12.4	2.1	2.2	8.9	3.0	1.3	0.9
65 years old and over	100.0	47.6	29.4	10.3	2.0	1.6	6.0	2.0	0.7	0.3

[1] Some people are still enrolled in high school.
[2] Less than .05 percent.
—Data not available.

NOTE.—Data are based on sample surveys of the civilian noninstitutional population. Because of rounding, details may not add to totals.

SOURCE: U.S. Department of Commerce, Bureau of the Census, Current Population Reports, Series P-70, No. 21, "Educational Background and Economic Status: Spring 1987." (This table was prepared March 1991.)

Table 12.—Years of school completed by persons age 25 and over, by State: April 1980

State	Number of persons 25 years old and over (in thousands)	Percent of population completing at least—			
		High school		College	
		1 to 3 years	4 years	1 to 3 years	4 years or more
1	2	3	4	5	6
United States	132,836	81.7	66.5	31.9	16.2
Alabama	2,217	75.0	56.5	24.7	12.2
Alaska	211	91.0	82.5	43.7	21.1
Arizona	1,559	85.0	72.4	38.0	17.4
Arkansas	1,337	73.2	55.5	22.3	10.8
California	14,044	85.8	73.5	42.0	19.6
Colorado	1,664	89.4	78.6	44.1	23.0
Connecticut	1,900	83.7	70.3	35.9	20.7
Delaware	345	85.2	68.6	32.4	17.5
District of Columbia	399	83.0	67.1	41.5	27.5
Florida	6,250	82.4	66.7	31.6	14.9
Georgia	3,086	76.3	56.4	27.9	14.6
Hawaii	548	83.8	73.8	38.8	20.3
Idaho	514	87.4	73.7	37.2	15.8
Illinois	6,679	81.5	66.5	31.4	16.2
Indiana	3,136	83.4	66.4	24.6	12.5
Iowa	1,700	83.3	71.5	28.6	13.9
Kansas	1,388	85.4	73.3	34.2	17.0
Kentucky	2,087	68.7	53.1	21.8	11.1
Louisiana	2,281	75.1	57.7	26.7	13.9
Maine	662	83.4	68.7	29.4	14.4
Maryland	2,499	83.5	67.4	34.9	20.4
Massachusetts	3,463	85.6	72.2	35.8	20.0
Michigan	5,254	84.9	68.0	30.0	14.3
Minnesota	2,346	83.3	73.1	34.5	17.4
Mississippi	1,368	73.0	54.8	25.6	12.3
Missouri	2,919	78.3	63.5	27.2	13.9
Montana	451	85.7	74.4	36.5	17.5
Nebraska	912	84.9	73.4	32.8	15.5
Nevada	480	90.4	75.5	35.1	14.4
New Hampshire	542	85.3	72.3	35.1	18.2
New Jersey	4,504	82.3	67.4	31.5	18.3
New Mexico	707	82.3	68.9	34.7	17.6
New York	10,721	81.7	66.3	32.2	17.9
North Carolina	3,403	75.4	54.8	27.0	13.2
North Dakota	365	75.2	66.4	35.1	14.8
Ohio	6,292	84.6	67.0	26.5	13.7
Oklahoma	1,770	81.6	66.0	31.2	15.1
Oregon	1,580	88.5	75.6	38.5	17.9
Pennsylvania	7,240	81.6	64.7	24.3	13.6
Rhode Island	575	79.3	61.1	28.3	15.4
South Carolina	1,733	74.3	53.7	26.7	13.4
South Dakota	390	78.0	67.9	31.7	14.0
Tennessee	2,692	72.3	56.2	24.5	12.6
Texas	7,944	79.3	62.6	33.8	16.9
Utah	705	93.0	80.0	44.1	19.9
Vermont	295	83.3	71.0	34.7	19.0
Virginia	3,133	78.4	62.4	34.0	19.1
Washington	2,439	89.7	77.6	40.2	19.0
West Virginia	1,147	72.0	56.0	20.4	10.4
Wisconsin	2,705	82.0	69.6	29.2	14.8
Wyoming	255	90.0	77.9	37.9	17.2

SOURCE: U.S. Department of Commerce, Bureau of the Census, *Statistical Abstract of the United States, 1986.* (This table was prepared September 1986.)

Table 13.—Years of school completed by persons age 25 and over in the 15 largest States and the 15 largest metropolitan areas: March 1987

State	Percent completing—			Metropolitan area [1]	Percent completing—		
	Less than 4 years of high school	4 years of high school or more	4 years of college or more		Less than 4 years of high school	4 years of high school or more	4 years of college or more
1	2	3	4	5	6	7	8
United States [2]	**24.4**	**75.6**	**19.9**				
California	21.1	78.9	23.5	Atlanta, Georgia	20.3	79.7	26.9
Florida	22.9	77.1	19.7	Baltimore, Maryland	27.5	72.5	20.7
Georgia	28.8	71.2	19.1	Boston, Massachusetts	16.0	84.0	33.2
Illinois	23.6	76.4	20.2	Chicago, Illinois	22.8	77.2	24.2
Indiana	24.0	76.0	13.3	Dallas, Texas	18.8	81.2	28.0
Massachusetts	19.6	80.4	26.5	Detroit, Michigan	26.5	73.5	17.8
Michigan	24.5	75.5	16.5	Houston, Texas	20.4	79.6	32.4
Missouri	21.9	78.1	17.9	Los Angeles/Long Beach, California	25.0	75.0	21.4
New Jersey	23.1	76.9	23.3	Minneapolis/St. Paul, Minnesota	12.9	87.1	25.7
New York	25.0	75.0	23.2	Nassau/Suffolk, New York	15.2	84.8	27.3
North Carolina	32.2	67.8	16.6	New York, New York	29.7	70.3	25.0
Ohio	24.4	75.6	15.0	Philadelphia, Pennsylvania	23.2	76.8	20.0
Pennsylvania	24.5	75.5	17.2	Pittsburgh, Pennsylvania	22.9	77.1	14.8
Texas	28.0	72.0	19.8	St. Louis, MO/IL	20.2	79.8	21.7
Virginia	27.7	72.3	23.5	Washington, DC/MD/VA	12.0	88.0	37.5

[1] Standard Metropolitan Statistical Area.
[2] Includes data for all States and the District of Columbia.

SOURCE: U.S. Department of Commerce, Bureau of the Census, *Current Population Reports*, Series P–20, No. 428, "Educational Attainment in the United States: March 1987 and 1986." (This table was prepared October 1988.)

Table 14.—Estimates of resident population, by age group: July 1, 1960 to July 1, 1989

[In thousands]

Year	Total, all ages	Total, 3 to 34 years	3 and 4 years	5 and 6 years	7 to 13 years	14 to 17 years	18 and 19 years	20 and 21 years	22 to 24 years	25 to 29 years	30 to 34 years
1	2	3	4	5	6	7	8	9	10	11	12
1960	179,979	90,722	8,063	7,811	25,155	11,211	4,886	4,443	6,425	10,823	11,905
1961	182,992	92,597	8,207	7,924	25,293	12,046	5,411	4,635	6,587	10,756	11,738
1962	185,771	94,396	8,190	8,108	25,790	12,751	5,617	4,943	6,710	10,740	11,547
1963	188,483	96,275	8,152	8,251	26,326	13,492	5,461	5,467	6,930	10,848	11,348
1964	191,141	98,281	8,206	8,233	27,011	14,264	5,429	5,685	7,258	11,051	11,144
1965	193,526	100,210	8,190	8,190	27,563	14,146	6,450	5,503	7,902	11,226	11,040
1966	195,576	101,993	8,031	8,251	28,032	14,398	7,183	5,417	8,198	11,521	10,962
1967	197,457	103,635	7,888	8,237	28,392	14,727	6,928	6,289	8,278	11,943	10,953
1968	199,399	105,363	7,645	8,074	28,732	15,170	6,988	6,972	8,082	12,624	11,076
1969	201,385	106,931	7,253	7,930	28,907	15,549	7,119	6,787	8,980	13,119	11,287
1970	203,984	108,653	6,962	7,703	28,969	15,921	7,410	6,850	9,728	13,604	11,505
1971	206,827	110,482	6,805	7,344	28,892	16,326	7,644	7,106	10,596	13,927	11,842
1972	209,284	112,287	6,789	7,051	28,628	16,637	7,854	7,447	10,418	15,142	12,321
1973	211,357	113,954	6,938	6,888	28,159	16,864	8,044	7,658	10,615	15,694	13,094
1974	213,342	115,641	7,117	6,864	27,599	17,033	8,196	7,893	10,864	16,428	13,644
1975	215,465	117,006	6,912	7,014	26,904	17,125	8,418	8,089	11,228	17,183	14,131
1976	217,563	118,073	6,437	7,194	26,321	17,117	8,604	8,240	11,554	18,177	14,428
1977	219,760	118,853	6,190	6,978	25,878	17,042	8,613	8,456	11,856	18,180	15,661
1978	222,095	119,414	6,208	6,499	25,593	16,944	8,617	8,628	12,120	18,585	16,218
1979	224,567	120,126	6,252	6,256	25,174	16,610	8,698	8,653	12,443	19,077	16,961
1980	227,255	121,148	6,369	6,293	24,803	16,140	8,713	8,664	12,716	19,697	17,754
1981	229,637	122,057	6,551	6,327	24,428	15,598	8,553	8,723	12,892	20,200	18,786
1982	231,996	121,917	6,689	6,429	24,184	15,041	8,425	8,700	12,887	20,753	18,808
1983	234,284	122,160	6,924	6,606	23,803	14,720	8,204	8,551	12,938	21,202	19,211
1984	236,477	122,426	7,108	6,742	23,495	14,704	7,818	8,424	12,903	21,535	19,696
1985	238,736	122,714	7,212	6,976	23,135	14,865	7,500	8,186	12,814	21,758	20,269
1986	241,107	122,934	7,275	7,160	23,190	14,797	7,322	7,808	12,603	22,005	20,773
1987	243,419	122,937	7,228	7,263	23,560	14,467	7,315	7,491	12,300	21,979	21,333
1988	245,807	123,009	7,282	7,331	24,075	13,982	7,480	7,319	11,865	21,877	21,798
1989	248,239	122,942	7,431	7,283	24,552	13,496	7,643	7,317	11,386	21,699	22,135

NOTE.—Some data have been revised from previously published figures. Because of rounding, details may not add to totals.

SOURCE: U.S. Department of Commerce, Bureau of the Census, *Current Population Reports*, Series P–25, Nos. 519, 917, 1000, 1022, 1045, and 1057. (This table was prepared February 1991.)

Table 15.—Estimates of school-age[1] resident population, by race and sex: July 1, 1960 to July 1, 1989

[In thousands]

Year	Total			White[2]			Black[2]			Other races[2]		
	Total	Male	Female	Total	Male	Female	Total	Male	Female	Total	Male	Female
1	2	3	4	5	6	7	8	9	10	11	12	13
1960	44,176	22,437	21,739	38,366	19,532	18,832	5,366	2,677	2,690	446	228	217
1961	45,263	22,995	22,269	39,220	19,975	19,246	5,575	2,782	2,792	469	238	232
1962	46,648	23,706	22,941	40,352	20,560	19,791	5,802	2,897	2,906	496	251	244
1963	48,070	24,438	23,633	41,524	21,164	20,361	6,025	3,009	3,016	520	264	257
1964	49,509	25,174	24,336	42,692	21,765	20,929	6,272	3,135	3,137	545	275	270
1965	49,900	25,377	24,522	42,891	21,872	21,019	6,440	3,220	3,221	567	285	281
1966	50,681	25,784	24,898	43,469	22,176	21,293	6,619	3,308	3,311	594	300	295
1967	51,357	26,135	25,224	43,969	22,438	21,529	6,768	3,383	3,384	622	314	310
1968	51,974	26,456	25,517	44,422	22,677	21,744	6,903	3,453	3,450	649	325	323
1969	52,386	26,675	25,711	44,697	22,826	21,871	7,016	3,511	3,505	673	338	336
1970	52,593	26,793	25,801	44,783	22,877	21,906	7,108	3,561	3,547	703	355	349
1971	52,562	26,780	25,782	44,644	22,809	21,834	7,182	3,600	3,583	737	371	365
1972	52,316	26,658	25,658	44,336	22,655	21,681	7,211	3,615	3,596	768	388	380
1973	51,910	26,456	25,455	43,898	22,434	21,464	7,213	3,617	3,596	799	405	394
1974	51,498	26,249	25,249	43,454	22,210	21,244	7,213	3,618	3,596	830	420	409
1975	51,044	26,022	25,022	42,950	21,956	20,994	7,199	3,611	3,588	895	456	440
1976	50,633	25,822	24,811	42,477	21,721	20,755	7,208	3,617	3,591	948	483	465
1977	49,897	25,456	24,441	41,737	21,350	20,386	7,167	3,600	3,568	994	506	487
1978	49,038	25,024	24,013	40,883	20,919	19,964	7,116	3,576	3,540	1,039	530	509
1979	48,041	24,524	23,517	39,910	20,427	19,484	7,037	3,538	3,498	1,094	560	536
1980	47,235	24,138	23,098	39,001	19,981	19,021	6,996	3,524	3,473	1,238	633	605
1981	46,352	23,695	22,658	38,118	19,532	18,586	6,924	3,491	3,433	1,309	671	638
1982	45,655	23,347	22,308	37,400	19,169	18,232	6,879	3,473	3,406	1,374	706	669
1983	45,130	23,089	22,041	36,859	18,899	17,960	6,841	3,457	3,385	1,430	733	697
1984	44,942	23,000	21,942	36,597	18,770	17,827	6,848	3,463	3,384	1,498	767	731
1985	44,975	23,026	21,949	36,503	18,727	17,776	6,898	3,492	3,405	1,575	806	769
1986	45,148	23,120	22,028	36,531	18,746	17,786	6,957	3,527	3,430	1,660	848	812
1987	45,291	23,198	22,093	36,530	18,747	17,781	7,023	3,564	3,460	1,740	887	852
1988	45,388	23,253	22,135	36,475	18,722	17,752	7,091	3,601	3,490	1,823	929	894
1989	45,330	23,224	22,106	36,325	18,645	17,680	7,104	3,612	3,494	1,901	968	934

[1] Includes persons 5 to 17 years of age.
[2] Includes persons of Hispanic origin.

NOTE.—Some data have been revised from previously published figures. Because of rounding, details may not add to totals.

SOURCE: U.S. Department of Commerce, Bureau of the Census, *Current Population Reports,* Series P–25, Nos. 519, 917, 1000, 1022, 1045, and 1057. (This table was prepared February 1991.)

Table 16.—Estimated total and school-age populations, by State: [1] 1970 to 1989

[In thousands]

State	1970[2] Total, all ages	1970[2] 5- to 17-year-olds	1980[3] Total, all ages	1980[3] 5- to 17-year-olds	1985[3] Total, all ages	1985[3] 5- to 17-year-olds	1987[3] Total, all ages	1987[3] 5- to 17-year-olds	1988[3] Total, all ages	1988[3] 5- to 17-year-olds	1989[3] Total, all ages	1989[3] 5- to 17-year-olds
1	2	3	4	5	6	7	8	9	10	11	12	13
United States	**203,302**	**52,540**	**226,546**	**47,407**	**238,736**	**44,975**	**243,419**	**45,291**	**245,807**	**45,388**	**248,239**	**45,330**
Alabama	3,444	934	3,894	866	4,021	815	4,084	821	4,102	819	4,118	811
Alaska	303	88	402	92	521	108	524	111	524	110	527	110
Arizona	1,775	486	2,718	578	3,161	604	3,400	643	3,489	653	3,556	671
Arkansas	1,923	498	2,286	496	2,360	472	2,388	475	2,395	476	2,406	476
California	19,971	4,999	23,668	4,681	26,353	4,754	27,653	4,999	28,314	5,113	29,063	5,225
Colorado	2,210	589	2,890	592	3,232	594	3,293	605	3,301	605	3,317	602
Connecticut	3,032	768	3,108	638	3,175	554	3,212	543	3,233	538	3,239	532
Delaware	548	148	594	125	626	116	648	118	660	118	673	119
District of Columbia ...	757	164	638	109	623	90	621	90	617	91	604	91
Florida	6,791	1,609	9,746	1,789	11,367	1,802	12,022	1,892	12,335	1,947	12,671	1,985
Georgia	4,588	1,223	5,463	1,231	5,975	1,224	6,227	1,261	6,342	1,280	6,436	1,286
Hawaii	770	204	965	198	1,050	195	1,082	197	1,098	198	1,112	199
Idaho	713	200	944	213	1,005	223	1,000	223	1,003	223	1,014	225
Illinois	11,110	2,859	11,427	2,401	11,539	2,192	11,584	2,174	11,614	2,144	11,658	2,116
Indiana	5,195	1,386	5,490	1,200	5,500	1,093	5,530	1,080	5,556	1,072	5,593	1,065
Iowa	2,825	743	2,914	604	2,873	545	2,823	526	2,834	523	2,840	519
Kansas	2,249	573	2,364	468	2,448	451	2,475	458	2,495	462	2,513	468
Kentucky	3,221	844	3,661	800	3,724	750	3,723	738	3,727	728	3,727	716
Louisiana	3,645	1,041	4,206	969	4,484	940	4,448	931	4,408	924	4,382	911
Maine	994	260	1,125	243	1,164	221	1,186	219	1,205	220	1,222	220
Maryland	3,924	1,038	4,217	895	4,391	791	4,536	791	4,622	801	4,694	803
Massachusetts	5,689	1,407	5,737	1,153	5,823	978	5,856	947	5,889	932	5,913	924
Michigan	8,882	2,450	9,262	2,067	9,088	1,826	9,205	1,795	9,240	1,776	9,273	1,761
Minnesota	3,806	1,051	4,076	865	4,191	789	4,244	788	4,307	795	4,353	801
Mississippi	2,217	635	2,521	599	2,613	582	2,624	580	2,620	574	2,621	566
Missouri	4,678	1,183	4,917	1,008	5,036	936	5,107	942	5,141	942	5,159	936
Montana	694	197	787	167	825	164	809	160	805	159	806	158
Nebraska	1,485	389	1,570	324	1,605	303	1,594	302	1,602	303	1,611	305
Nevada	489	127	800	160	939	166	1,006	175	1,054	184	1,111	191
New Hampshire	738	189	921	196	998	184	1,056	190	1,085	194	1,107	195
New Jersey	7,171	1,797	7,365	1,528	7,568	1,347	7,674	1,318	7,721	1,302	7,736	1,286
New Mexico	1,017	311	1,303	303	1,450	303	1,496	312	1,507	315	1,528	320
New York	18,241	4,358	17,558	3,552	17,767	3,184	17,835	3,112	17,909	3,081	17,950	3,044
North Carolina	5,084	1,323	5,882	1,254	6,258	1,191	6,409	1,189	6,489	1,187	6,571	1,179
North Dakota	618	175	653	136	685	133	671	132	667	131	660	129
Ohio	10,657	2,820	10,798	2,307	10,774	2,095	10,816	2,064	10,855	2,049	10,907	2,036
Oklahoma	2,559	640	3,025	622	3,302	628	3,259	627	3,242	635	3,224	619
Oregon	2,092	534	2,633	525	2,688	499	2,723	496	2,767	496	2,820	503
Pennsylvania	11,801	2,925	11,864	2,376	11,865	2,097	11,942	2,068	12,001	2,057	12,040	2,039
Rhode Island	950	225	947	186	967	165	986	164	993	164	998	162
South Carolina	2,591	720	3,122	703	3,333	677	3,425	685	3,470	690	3,512	690
South Dakota	666	187	691	147	708	137	709	138	713	140	715	140
Tennessee	3,926	1,002	4,591	972	4,766	922	4,855	923	4,895	921	4,940	915
Texas	11,199	3,002	14,229	3,137	16,382	3,362	16,781	3,486	16,841	3,498	16,991	3,474
Utah	1,059	312	1,461	350	1,644	419	1,680	445	1,690	452	1,707	456
Vermont	445	118	511	109	535	101	547	101	557	101	567	101
Virginia	4,651	1,197	5,347	1,114	5,704	1,030	5,914	1,039	6,015	1,040	6,098	1,039
Washington	3,413	881	4,132	826	4,407	813	4,542	827	4,648	842	4,761	859
West Virginia	1,744	442	1,950	414	1,936	388	1,898	373	1,876	364	1,857	353
Wisconsin	4,418	1,203	4,706	1,011	4,775	917	4,807	913	4,855	916	4,867	899
Wyoming	332	92	470	101	509	106	490	105	479	102	475	100

[1] Includes Armed Forces residing in each State.
[2] As of April 1.
[3] Estimates as of July 1.

NOTE.—Some data have been revised from previously published figures. Because of rounding, details may not add to totals.

SOURCE: U.S. Department of Commerce, Bureau of the Census, *Current Population Reports*, "State Population and Household Estimates: July 1, 1989," Series P-25, No. 1058; and Population Estimates, unpublished data. (This table was prepared February 1991.)

Table 17.—Families, by family status and presence of own children under 18: 1970 to 1990

Family status	1970	1980	1985	1986	1987	1988	1989	1990	Change, 1970 to 1980	Change, 1980 to 1990
1	2	3	4	5	6	7	8	9	10	11
	In thousands								Percent change	
All families	**51,456**	**59,550**	**62,706**	**63,558**	**64,491**	**65,133**	**65,837**	**66,090**	**15.7**	**11.0**
Married-couple family	44,728	49,112	50,350	50,933	51,537	51,809	52,100	52,317	9.8	6.5
No own children under 18	19,196	24,151	26,140	26,304	26,892	27,209	27,365	27,780	25.8	15.0
With own children under 18	25,532	24,961	24,210	24,630	24,645	24,600	24,735	24,537	-2.2	-1.7
One own child under 18	8,163	9,671	9,640	9,868	10,032	9,904	9,829	9,583	18.5	-0.9
Two own children under 18	8,045	9,488	9,456	9,580	9,606	9,576	9,870	9,784	17.9	3.1
Three or more own children under 18	9,325	5,802	5,115	5,182	5,006	5,120	5,035	5,170	-37.8	-10.9
Other family, male householder, no spouse present	1,228	1,733	2,228	2,414	2,510	2,715	2,847	2,884	41.1	66.4
No own children under 18	887	1,117	1,331	1,479	1,554	1,669	1,779	1,731	25.9	55.0
With own children under 18	341	616	896	935	955	1,047	1,068	1,153	80.6	87.2
One own child under 18	179	374	584	600	608	657	619	723	108.9	93.3
Two own children under 18	87	165	213	260	257	296	326	307	89.7	86.1
Three or more own children under 18	75	77	100	75	90	94	121	123	2.7	59.7
Other family, female householder, no spouse present	5,500	8,705	10,129	10,211	10,445	10,608	10,890	10,890	58.3	25.1
No own children under 18	2,642	3,261	4,123	4,106	4,147	4,335	4,371	4,290	23.4	31.6
With own children under 18	2,858	5,445	6,006	6,105	6,297	6,273	6,519	6,599	90.5	21.2
One own child under 18	1,008	2,398	2,885	2,857	3,079	3,017	3,164	3,225	137.9	34.5
Two own children under 18	810	1,817	1,977	2,061	2,072	2,039	2,095	2,173	124.3	19.6
Three or more own children under 18	1,040	1,230	1,144	1,186	1,147	1,217	1,260	1,202	18.3	-2.3
	Percent of all families								Change in percentage points	
All families	**100.0**	**100.0**	**100.0**	**100.0**	**100.0**	**100.0**	**100.0**	**100.0**	—	—
Married-couple family	86.9	82.5	80.3	80.1	79.9	79.5	79.1	79.2	-4.5	-3.3
No own children under 18	37.3	40.6	41.7	41.4	41.7	41.8	41.6	42.0	3.3	1.5
With own children under 18	49.6	41.9	38.6	38.8	38.2	37.8	37.6	37.1	-7.7	-4.8
One own child under 18	15.9	16.2	15.4	15.5	15.6	15.2	14.9	14.5	0.4	1.7
Two own children under 18	15.6	15.9	15.1	15.1	14.9	14.7	15.0	14.8	0.3	1.1
Three or more own children under 18	18.1	9.7	8.2	8.2	7.8	7.9	7.6	7.8	-8.4	-1.9
Other family, male householder, no spouse present	2.4	2.9	3.6	3.8	3.9	4.2	4.3	4.4	0.5	1.5
No own children under 18	1.7	1.9	2.1	2.3	2.4	2.6	2.7	2.6	0.2	0.7
With own children under 18	0.7	1.0	1.4	1.5	1.5	1.6	1.6	1.7	0.4	0.7
One own child under 18	0.3	0.6	0.9	0.9	0.9	1.0	0.9	1.1	0.3	0.5
Two own children under 18	0.2	0.3	0.3	0.4	0.4	0.5	0.5	0.5	0.1	0.2
Three or more own children under 18	0.1	0.1	0.2	0.1	0.1	0.1	0.2	0.2	(¹)	0.1
Other family, female householder, no spouse present	10.7	14.6	16.2	16.1	16.2	16.3	16.5	16.5	3.9	1.9
No own children under 18	5.1	5.5	6.6	6.5	6.4	6.7	6.6	6.5	0.3	1.0
With own children under 18	5.6	9.1	9.6	9.6	9.8	9.6	9.9	10.0	3.6	0.8
One own child under 18	2.0	4.0	4.6	4.5	4.8	4.6	4.8	4.9	2.1	0.9
Two own children under 18	1.6	3.1	3.2	3.2	3.2	3.1	3.2	3.3	1.5	0.2
Three or more own children under 18	2.0	2.1	1.8	1.9	1.8	1.9	1.9	1.8	(¹)	-0.2

¹ Less than .05 percent.

NOTE.—Because of rounding, details may not add to totals.

SOURCE: U.S. Department of Commerce, Bureau of the Census, *Current Population Reports*, Series P-20, Nos. 411, 419, 424, 432, and 447. (This table was prepared February 1991.)

Table 18.—Characteristics of families with own children under 18, by family status and race/ethnicity:[1] 1990

[Numbers in thousands]

Family characteristics	All races				White[2]				Black[2]				Hispanic origin[3]			
	Total	Married-couple families	Other families		Total	Married-couple families	Other families		Total	Married-couple families	Other families		Total	Married-couple families	Other families	
			Male householder, no spouse present	Female householder, no spouse present			Male householder, no spouse present	Female householder, no spouse present			Male householder, no spouse present	Female householder, no spouse present			Male householder, no spouse present	Female householder, no spouse present
	2	3	4	5	6	7	8	9	10	11	12	13	14	15	16	17
Total families	**66,090**	**52,317**	**2,884**	**10,890**	**56,590**	**46,981**	**2,303**	**7,306**	**7,470**	**3,750**	**446**	**3,275**	**4,840**	**3,395**	**329**	**1,116**
Total families with own children under 18	32,289	24,537	1,153	6,599	26,718	21,579	939	4,199	4,378	1,972	173	2,232	3,051	2,188	118	745
Percent of all families	48.9	46.9	40.0	60.6	47.2	45.9	40.8	57.5	58.6	52.6	38.8	68.2	63.0	64.4	35.9	66.8
Families with—																
1 child under 18	13,530	9,583	723	3,225	11,186	8,398	609	2,179	1,894	815	97	982	1,095	748	63	284
2 children under 18	12,263	9,784	307	2,173	10,342	8,700	245	1,397	1,433	680	44	709	1,036	750	40	246
3 children under 18	4,650	3,751	90	809	3,853	3,301	75	477	635	316	13	306	579	419	11	150
4 children under 18	1,279	1,000	24	254	970	854	7	109	256	103	15	139	232	183	3	45
5 children under 18	379	279	7	93	247	217	2	28	107	41	5	61	73	59	—	14
6 or more under 18	188	140	2	46	121	109	2	10	51	16	—	35	35	29	—	6
Total own children under 18	59,013	45,907	1,727	11,378	48,522	40,251	1,356	6,914	8,151	3,722	299	4,131	6,478	4,763	189	1,526
Average number of children per family with children	1.83	1.87	1.50	1.72	1.82	1.87	1.44	1.65	1.86	1.89	1.72	1.85	2.12	2.18	1.61	2.05
Total families with own children under 6	15,186	12,051	436	2,699	12,516	10,616	335	1,565	2,082	953	87	1,042	1,633	1,226	64	343
Percent of all families	23.0	23.0	15.1	24.8	22.1	22.6	14.5	21.4	27.9	25.4	19.5	31.8	33.7	36.1	19.5	30.7
Families with—																
1 child under 6	10,304	8,084	335	1,885	8,508	7,096	261	1,151	1,402	655	65	682	1,096	824	45	227
2 children under 6	4,195	3,464	85	646	3,489	3,076	65	348	546	262	15	269	449	346	16	86
3 children under 6	614	461	16	137	479	409	9	61	104	32	7	66	78	48	3	27
4 or more under 6	73	42	—	31	40	35	—	5	29	4	—	26	11	8	—	3
Total own children under 6	20,216	16,146	544	3,525	16,700	14,289	413	1,999	2,681	1,189	111	1,381	2,339	1,748	88	503
Average number of children per family with children	1.33	1.34	1.25	1.31	1.33	1.35	1.23	1.28	1.29	1.25	1.28	1.33	1.43	1.42	—	1.47
Total families with own children under 3	9,055	7,331	276	1,447	7,493	6,486	211	795	1,194	539	55	600	978	729	42	207
Percent of all families	13.7	14.0	9.6	13.3	13.2	13.8	9.2	10.9	16.0	14.4	12.3	18.3	20.2	21.5	12.8	18.5
Families with—																
1 child under 3	7,895	6,425	250	1,220	6,589	5,686	192	712	981	468	49	464	847	632	39	176
2 or more under 3	1,160	906	26	228	903	800	20	83	213	71	6	136	131	96	4	31
Total own children under 3	10,086	8,155	301	1,629	8,356	7,247	234	876	1,303	557	57	689	1,175	882	48	246
Average number of children per family with children	1.11	1.11	1.09	1.13	1.12	1.12	1.10	1.10	1.09	1.03	—	1.15	1.20	1.21	—	1.19

[1] Race of family is defined as race of head of household.
[2] Includes persons of Hispanic origin.
[3] Persons of Hispanic origin may be of any race.
— Data not available.

NOTE.—Averages and percents are only shown when the base is 75,000 or greater. Even though the standard errors are large, smaller estimated numbers are shown to permit users to combine categories in various ways. Because of rounding, details may not add to totals.

SOURCE: U.S. Department of Commerce, Bureau of the Census, Current Population Reports, Series P-20, No. 447. (This table was prepared February 1991.)

Table 19.—Poverty status of persons, families, and children under 18, by race/ethnicity: 1959 to 1989

Year and race/ethnicity	Number below the poverty level, in thousands						Percent below the poverty level					
	All persons	In all families			In families with female householder, no husband present		All persons	In all families			In families with female householder, no husband present	
		Total	House-holder	Related children under 18	Total	Related children under 18		Total	House-holder	Related children under 18	Total	Related children under 18
1	2	3	4	5	6	7	8	9	10	11	12	13
All races												
1959	39,490	34,562	8,320	17,208	7,014	4,145	22.4	20.8	18.5	26.9	49.4	72.2
1960	39,851	34,925	8,243	17,288	7,247	4,095	22.2	20.7	18.1	26.5	48.9	68.4
1965	33,185	28,358	6,721	14,388	7,524	4,562	17.3	15.8	13.9	20.7	46.0	64.2
1966	28,510	23,809	5,784	12,146	6,861	4,262	14.7	13.1	11.8	17.4	39.8	58.2
1970	25,420	20,330	5,260	10,235	7,503	4,689	12.6	10.9	10.1	14.9	38.1	53.0
1971	25,559	20,405	5,303	10,344	7,797	4,850	12.5	10.8	10.0	15.1	38.7	53.1
1972	24,460	19,577	5,075	10,082	8,114	5,094	11.9	10.3	9.3	14.9	38.2	53.1
1973	22,973	18,299	4,828	9,453	8,178	5,171	11.1	9.7	8.8	14.2	37.5	52.1
1974	23,370	18,817	4,922	9,967	8,462	5,361	11.2	9.9	8.8	15.1	36.5	51.5
1975	25,877	20,789	5,450	10,882	8,846	5,597	12.3	10.9	9.7	16.8	37.5	52.7
1976	24,975	19,632	5,311	10,081	9,029	5,583	11.8	10.3	9.4	15.8	37.3	52.0
1977	24,720	19,505	5,311	10,028	9,205	5,658	11.6	10.2	9.3	16.0	36.2	50.3
1978	24,497	19,062	5,280	9,722	9,269	5,687	11.4	10.0	9.1	15.7	35.6	50.6
1979	26,072	19,964	5,461	9,993	9,400	5,635	11.7	10.2	9.2	16.0	34.9	48.6
1980	29,272	22,601	6,217	11,114	10,120	5,866	13.0	11.5	10.3	17.9	36.7	50.8
1981	31,822	24,850	6,851	12,068	11,051	6,305	14.0	12.5	11.2	19.5	38.7	52.3
1982	34,398	27,349	7,512	13,139	11,701	6,696	15.0	13.6	12.2	21.3	40.6	56.0
1983	35,303	27,933	7,647	13,427	12,072	6,747	15.2	13.9	12.3	21.8	40.2	55.4
1984	33,700	26,458	7,277	12,929	11,831	6,772	14.4	13.1	11.6	21.0	38.4	54.0
1985	33,064	25,729	7,223	12,483	11,600	6,716	14.0	12.6	11.4	20.1	37.6	53.6
1986	32,370	24,754	7,023	12,257	11,944	6,943	13.6	12.0	10.9	19.8	38.3	54.4
1987	32,221	24,725	7,005	12,275	12,148	7,074	13.4	12.0	10.7	19.7	38.1	54.7
1988	31,745	24,048	6,876	11,935	11,972	6,742	13.0	11.6	10.4	19.0	37.2	50.6
1989	31,534	24,066	6,784	12,001	11,668	6,808	12.8	11.5	10.3	19.0	35.9	51.1
White [1]												
1960	28,309	24,262	6,115	11,229	4,296	2,357	17.8	16.2	14.9	20.0	39.0	59.9
1965	22,496	18,508	4,824	8,595	4,092	2,321	13.3	11.7	11.1	14.4	35.4	52.9
1970	17,484	13,323	3,708	6,138	3,761	2,247	9.9	8.1	8.0	10.5	28.4	43.1
1975	17,770	13,799	3,838	6,748	4,577	2,813	9.7	8.3	7.7	12.5	29.4	44.2
1980	19,699	14,587	4,195	6,817	4,940	2,813	10.2	8.6	8.0	13.4	28.0	41.6
1981	21,553	16,127	4,670	7,429	5,600	3,120	11.1	9.5	8.8	14.7	29.8	42.8
1982	23,517	18,015	5,118	8,282	5,686	3,249	12.0	10.6	9.6	16.5	30.9	46.5
1983	23,984	18,377	5,220	8,534	6,017	3,388	12.1	10.7	9.7	17.0	31.2	47.1
1984	22,955	17,299	4,925	8,086	5,866	3,377	11.5	10.1	9.1	16.1	29.7	45.9
1985	22,860	17,125	4,983	7,838	5,990	3,372	11.4	9.9	9.1	15.6	29.8	45.2
1986	22,183	16,393	4,811	7,714	6,171	3,522	11.0	9.4	8.6	15.3	30.6	46.3
1987	21,195	15,593	4,567	7,398	5,989	3,474	10.4	8.9	8.1	14.7	29.6	45.8
1988	20,715	15,001	4,471	7,095	5,950	3,385	10.1	8.6	7.9	14.0	29.2	43.0
1989	20,788	15,179	4,409	7,164	5,723	3,320	10.0	8.6	7.8	14.1	28.1	42.8
Black [1]												
1959	9,927	9,112	1,860	5,022	2,416	1,475	55.1	54.9	48.1	65.5	70.6	81.6
1966	8,867	8,090	1,620	4,774	3,160	2,107	41.8	40.9	35.5	50.6	65.3	76.6
1970	7,548	6,683	1,481	3,922	3,656	2,383	33.5	32.2	29.5	41.5	58.7	67.7
1975	7,545	6,533	1,513	3,884	4,168	2,724	31.3	30.1	27.1	41.4	54.3	66.0
1980	8,579	7,190	1,826	3,906	4,984	2,944	32.5	31.1	28.9	42.1	53.4	64.8
1981	9,173	7,780	1,972	4,170	5,222	3,051	34.2	33.2	30.8	44.9	56.7	67.7
1982	9,697	8,355	2,158	4,388	5,698	3,269	35.6	34.9	33.0	47.3	58.8	70.7
1983	9,882	8,376	2,161	4,273	5,736	3,187	35.7	34.7	32.3	46.2	57.0	68.3
1984	9,490	8,104	2,094	4,320	5,666	3,234	33.8	33.2	30.9	46.2	54.6	66.2
1985	8,926	7,504	1,983	4,057	5,342	3,181	31.3	30.5	28.7	43.1	53.2	66.9
1986	8,983	7,401	1,987	4,037	5,473	3,251	31.1	29.7	28.0	42.7	53.8	67.1
1987	9,520	7,848	2,117	4,234	5,789	3,394	32.4	31.2	29.4	44.4	54.1	68.3
1988	9,356	7,650	2,090	4,148	5,601	3,130	31.3	30.0	28.2	42.8	51.9	61.8
1989	9,305	7,704	2,077	4,257	5,530	3,256	30.7	29.7	27.8	43.2	49.4	62.9
Hispanic origin [2]												
1975	2,991	2,755	627	1,619	1,053	694	26.9	26.3	25.1	33.1	57.2	68.4
1980	3,491	3,143	751	1,718	1,319	809	25.7	25.1	23.2	33.0	54.5	65.0
1981	3,713	3,349	792	1,874	1,465	909	26.5	25.9	24.0	35.4	55.9	67.3
1982	4,301	3,865	916	2,117	1,601	990	29.9	29.2	27.2	38.9	60.1	71.8
1983	4,633	4,113	981	2,251	1,670	1,018	28.0	27.3	25.9	37.7	55.1	70.6
1984	4,806	4,192	991	2,317	1,764	1,093	28.4	27.4	25.2	38.7	56.2	71.0
1985	5,236	4,605	1,074	2,512	1,983	1,247	29.0	28.3	25.5	39.6	55.7	72.4
1986	5,117	4,469	1,085	2,413	1,921	1,194	27.3	26.5	24.7	37.1	52.9	66.7
1987	5,422	4,761	1,168	2,606	2,045	1,241	28.0	27.5	25.5	38.9	55.6	70.1
1988	5,357	4,700	1,141	2,576	2,052	1,208	26.7	26.0	23.7	37.3	55.0	65.5
1989	5,430	4,659	1,133	2,496	1,902	1,163	26.2	25.2	23.4	35.5	50.5	65.0

[1] Includes persons of Hispanic origin.

[2] Persons of Hispanic origin may be of any race.

SOURCE: U.S. Department of Commerce, Bureau of the Census, *Current Population Reports*, Series P–60, No. 168. (This table was prepared February 1991.)

NOTE.—1987 and 1988 figures are revised from previously published data.

Table 20.—Average grade that the public would give the schools in their community and in the Nation at large: 1974 to 1990

Year	All adults		No children in school		Public school parents		Private school parents	
	Nation	Local community	Nation	Local community	Nation	Local community	Nation	Local community
1	2	3	4	5	6	7	8	9
1974	—	2.63	—	2.57	—	2.80	—	2.15
1975	—	2.38	—	2.31	—	2.49	—	1.81
1976	—	2.38	—	2.34	—	2.48	—	2.22
1977	—	2.33	—	2.25	—	2.59	—	2.05
1978	—	2.21	—	2.11	—	2.47	—	1.69
1979	—	2.21	—	2.15	—	2.38	—	1.88
1980	—	2.26	—	—	—	—	—	—
1981	1.94	2.20	—	2.12	—	2.36	—	1.88
1982	2.01	2.24	2.04	2.18	2.01	2.35	2.02	2.20
1983	1.91	2.12	1.92	2.10	1.92	2.31	1.82	1.89
1984	2.09	2.36	2.11	2.30	2.11	2.49	2.04	2.17
1985	2.14	2.39	2.16	2.36	2.20	2.44	1.93	2.00
1986	2.13	2.36	—	2.29	—	2.55	—	2.14
1987	2.18	2.44	2.20	2.38	2.22	2.61	2.03	2.01
1988	2.08	2.35	2.02	2.32	2.13	2.48	2.00	2.13
1989	2.01	2.35	1.99	2.27	2.06	2.56	1.93	2.12
1990	1.99	2.29	1.98	2.27	2.03	2.44	1.85	2.09

—Data not available.

NOTE.—Average based on a scale where A=4, B=3, C=2, D=1, and F=0.

SOURCE: "The Annual Gallup Poll of the Public's Attitudes Toward the Public Schools," *Phi Delta Kappan*, various years. (This table was prepared March 1991.)

Table 21.—Items most frequently cited by the general public as a major problem facing the local public schools: 1970 to 1990

Problems	Percent												
	1970	1975	1980	1981	1982	1983	1984	1985	1986	1987	1988	1989	1990
1	2	3	4	5	6	7	8	9	10	11	12	13	14
Use of drugs	11	9	14	15	20	18	18	18	28	30	32	34	38
Lack of discipline	18	23	26	23	27	25	27	25	24	22	19	19	19
Lack of financial support	17	14	10	12	22	13	14	9	11	14	12	13	13
Getting good teachers	12	11	6	11	10	8	14	10	6	9	11	7	7
Poor curriculum/standards	6	5	11	14	11	14	15	11	8	8	11	8	8
Large schools/overcrowding	—	10	7	5	4	3	4	5	5	8	6	8	7
Moral standards	—	—	—	1	2	4	1	2	5	7	6	3	3
Parents' lack of interest	3	2	6	5	5	6	5	3	4	6	7	6	4
Pupils' lack of interest/truancy	—	3	5	4	5	5	4	5	3	6	5	3	6
Drinking/alcoholism	—	—	2	2	3	3	4	3	5	6	5	4	4
Low teacher pay	—	—	—	—	—	—	4	2	3	5	4	4	6
Integration/busing	17	15	10	11	6	5	6	4	3	4	4	4	5
Teachers' lack of interest	—	—	6	4	7	8	5	4	4	5	3	4	4
Lack of proper facilities	11	3	2	2	2	1	2	1	1	2	1	1	2

—Data not available.

SOURCE: "The Annual Gallup Poll of the Public's Attitudes Toward the Public Schools," *Phi Delta Kappan*, various years. (This table was prepared March 1991.)

Table 22.—Parental involvement in 8th graders' school-related activities, by selected parental characteristics: 1988

Characteristics of parents	Percent of parents[1] who talk with child regularly about			Percent of parents[1] who report family rules about			Percent of parents[1] who report that they			Percent of parents[1] who have contacted school about child's	
	Current school experiences	High school plans	Plans after high school	Number of hours of television watched on school days	Doing home-work	Maintaining certain grade average	Never or seldom help with home-work	Belong to a parent-teacher organization	Attend the parent-teacher organization meeting	Academic performance	Academic program
1	2	3	4	5	6	7	8	9	10	11	12
Total	79.4	47.1	38.3	61.7	92.0	72.7	29.4	31.9	36.2	52.5	34.8
Race/ethnicity											
Asian/Pacific Islander	59.8	41.7	36.5	67.1	89.3	74.7	42.8	29.4	41.2	36.0	29.4
Hispanic	67.1	52.7	44.8	68.7	92.3	79.8	44.7	15.5	43.0	48.3	34.5
Black, non-Hispanic	75.0	57.8	51.4	75.3	95.5	82.3	31.4	30.4	47.8	52.1	34.2
White, non-Hispanic	82.3	45.0	35.4	58.5	91.4	70.1	26.8	34.3	33.3	53.7	35.1
American Indian/Alaskan Native	72.5	44.6	39.9	62.9	95.9	75.7	35.5	16.6	35.0	52.5	42.5
Socioeconomic status[2]											
Lower quartile	66.3	43.0	33.5	64.0	92.2	74.2	41.7	12.2	29.2	38.1	24.2
Middle two quartiles	80.7	46.5	38.4	60.8	93.0	74.9	27.5	29.8	35.2	54.1	34.8
Highest quartile	89.0	52.7	42.9	61.6	89.9	66.9	21.9	54.0	44.4	61.9	44.1
Highest education level of parents											
Two-parent families											
Neither completed high school	60.0	40.7	29.6	64.0	92.6	75.2	47.6	10.6	32.7	32.3	21.2
One did not complete high school	72.9	45.7	34.7	61.6	92.6	74.8	33.7	15.4	28.7	42.8	28.6
Both completed high school	81.9	46.0	37.7	61.3	93.3	75.5	26.6	30.8	35.8	53.6	35.1
One graduated college[3]	87.2	51.8	42.4	61.1	91.5	69.9	21.8	48.6	42.7	60.9	41.1
Both graduated college	89.5	52.3	40.8	63.0	88.1	61.1	20.5	60.7	46.9	61.5	46.4
Single-parent families (female)											
Did not complete high school .	61.0	47.1	34.6	64.3	91.2	73.2	50.3	9.7	25.1	33.9	19.0
Completed high school	77.0	48.1	42.1	62.5	92.7	75.1	33.8	24.6	33.0	53.5	32.7
Graduated college	84.0	51.8	44.8	60.1	87.0	66.3	28.3	46.7	43.9	67.8	45.6
Family composition											
Two-parent family	81.0	47.4	38.0	61.7	92.2	72.6	27.6	34.2	37.3	52.9	35.7
One-parent family	74.2	47.0	40.2	62.1	91.2	73.3	36.2	23.6	32.0	52.0	31.6

[1] The respondent was the parent most knowledgeable about the child's education. The responding parent reported on their own and their spouse's activities.

[2] Socioeconomic status was measured by a composite score on parental education and occupations, and family income.

[3] Includes a small number of cases where one parent was a high school dropout.

NOTE.—Because of rounding, details may not add to totals.

SOURCE: U.S. Department of Education, National Center for Education Statistics, *National Education Longitudinal Study of 1988*, "Base Year Parent Survey." (This table was prepared July 1990.)

Table 23.—Beliefs held by teachers about what activities and programs would help to improve education: 1989

Selected activities and programs	Percent of teachers			
	Help a lot	Help some	Not help much	Not help at all
1	2	3	4	5
Develop non-traditional approaches to education	40	51	6	2
Increase the number of students studying computer literacy and foreign languages ...	36	50	10	3
Restructure classes on the basis of proficiency instead of age	39	42	12	7
Allow parents and students to choose schools	15	38	24	22
Establish magnet or regional schools with specialized curricula	32	52	10	5

SOURCE: Metropolitan Life/Louis Harris Associates, Inc., *The American Teacher, 1989*. (This table was prepared November 1989.)

Table 24.—Rating of school problems by teachers and students: 1988

Selected problems	Percent of teachers who say problem is "very serious" at their school						Percent of students who say they know 10 or more students involved in each problem
	Total	Inner city	Urban	Suburban	Small town	Rural	
1	2	3	4	5	6	7	8
The number of students requiring constant discipline	14	27	19	11	12	10	30
The number of students who lack basic skills (Students' item: can't read)	16	38	16	12	14	13	5
The number of teenage pregnancies [1]	12	28	9	5	13	12	9
The number of students drinking alcohol [2]	33	32	20	24	38	38	47
The number of students using drugs [2]	14	26	11	14	12	15	25
The number of incidents involving violence in school [2]	4	10	4	3	5	—	—
Have threatened or become violent with other students	—	—	—	—	—	—	23
Have threatened or become violent with teachers	—	—	—	—	—	—	5
The number of dropouts [1]	9	30	11	6	6	9	9

[1] Asked of junior high and high school students and teachers only.
[2] Asked of all students and junior high and high school teachers.
—Data not available.

SOURCE: Metropolitan Life/Louis Harris and Associates, Inc., *The American Teacher, 1988.* (This table was prepared May 1989.)

Table 25.—Public's level of confidence in various institutions: 1989

Institution	Percentage of respondents by levels of confidence				
	A great deal	Quite a lot	Some	Very little	Can't say
1	2	3	4	5	6
Private higher education	22.8	35.4	29.1	6.3	6.4
Public higher education	19.3	37.3	32.4	8.1	2.9
Charities providing health or social services	16.0	37.8	37.1	7.2	2.0
Private elementary or secondary education	21.2	31.4	33.8	7.7	5.8
Public elementary or secondary education	20.0	32.2	34.4	11.9	1.6
The military	19.6	31.5	32.0	14.1	2.9
Federated charitable appeals, e.g., United Way	16.5	34.1	32.9	13.5	3.0
Organized religion	23.9	25.5	31.9	16.0	2.8
Community foundations	10.1	27.4	45.7	9.6	7.2
Media, such as newspapers, T.V., T.V., and radio	11.1	26.0	41.8	19.4	1.7
State and local government	9.8	27.0	45.2	16.2	1.8
Federal government	9.5	25.7	45.4	17.5	1.8
Organized labor	11.3	20.0	40.0	24.9	3.8
Organizations that advocate a particular cause	7.6	21.5	47.4	17.3	6.2
Congress	7.3	21.8	43.7	24.4	2.7
Private foundations	6.1	21.1	48.5	16.3	8.1
Big business	7.0	18.8	45.2	25.5	3.5

NOTE.—Institutions are listed in rank order as determined by the combined responses to "a great deal" and "quite a lot" of confidence.

SOURCE: Independent Sector, The Gallup Organization, *Giving and Volunteering in the United States, 1990.* (This table was prepared March 1991.)

Table 26.—Percentage of households contributing to education and other charitable organizations and average annual donation, by type of charity: 1987 and 1989

Type of charity	1987			1989		
	Percentage of total households [1]	Average annual contribution		Percentage of total households [1]	Average annual contribution	
		Per contributing household	Per total households		Per contributing household	Per total households
1	2	3	4	5	6	7
Total	71.1	$790	$562	75.1	$978	$734
Religion [2]	52.5	715	375	53.2	896	477
Health	23.9	130	31	32.4	143	46
Human services	23.9	210	50	23.0	263	60
Youth development	18.5	88	16	21.6	129	28
Education	15.1	293	44	19.1	291	56
Environment	10.8	87	9	13.4	88	12
Arts, culture, and humanities	8.0	260	21	9.6	193	19
Public and societal benefit	6.5	153	10	11.2	120	13
Private and community foundations	4.8	145	7	6.4	116	7
Recreation— adults	(3)	(3)	(3)	6.2	135	8
International, foreign	4.2	281	12	4.2	202	8
Other	1.3	—	10	3.0	195	6

[1] Percents do not total 100 percent because of respondentndents giving to more than one type of charity.

[2] Churches, synagogues, and mosques.

[3] This category was included as part of other categories in 1987.

—Data not available.

SOURCE: Independent Sector, The Gallup Organization, *Giving and Volunteering in the United States, 1988 and 1990*. (This table was prepared February 1991.)

Table 27.—Contributions of all households to religious and other charities, by age and income: 1989

Age and income	Contributions						Average household income
	Average			As a percentage of household income			
	Total	Religious	Other charities	Total	Religious	Other charities	
1	2	3	4	5	6	7	8
Total	$734	$489	$251	2.0	1.3	0.7	$35,972
Age.							
18 to 24 years	261	155	106	0.6	0.4	0.2	36,153
25 to 34 years	625	422	214	1.6	1.1	0.5	36,973
35 to 44 years	825	476	362	2.0	1.2	0.9	40,493
45 to 54 years	863	534	323	1.9	1.2	0.7	43,766
55 to 64 years	1,134	815	327	3.1	2.2	0.9	35,580
65 to 74 years	844	687	150	3.5	2.9	0.6	24,453
75 years and over	534	362	167	2.4	1.7	0.7	21,217
Income.							
Under $10,000	186	124	70	2.5	1.6	0.9	6,709
$10,000 to $19,999	316	219	94	1.9	1.4	0.6	15,065
$20,000 to $29,999	560	358	195	2.1	1.4	0.7	24,911
$30,000 to $39,999	732	508	224	2.0	1.4	0.6	34,770
$40,000 to $49,999	702	496	217	1.5	1.0	0.5	45,000
$50,000 to $74,999	936	580	365	1.5	0.9	0.6	60,870
$75,000 to $99,999	2,575	1,861	811	2.9	2.0	0.9	87,500
$100,000 or more	2,512	1,662	951	2.4	1.5	0.9	100,000

NOTE.—Estimates exclude those respondents who reported "not sure or no answer" to particular questions. Because of rounding, details may not add to totals.

SOURCE: Independent Sector, The Gallup Organization, *Giving and Volunteering in the United States, 1990*. (This table was prepared March 1991.)

Table 28.—Volunteer workers for schools and other organizations, by selected characteristics: Year ending May 1989

Selected characteristics of volunteers	Number of volunteers (in thousands)	Percent distribution by type of organization							
		Total	School or other educational institution	Church or other religious organization	Civic or political organization	Hospital or other health organization	Social or welfare organization	Sports or recreational organization	Other organization
1	2	3	4	5	6	7	8	9	10
Total	38,042	100.0	15.1	37.4	13.2	10.4	9.9	7.8	6.3
Men	16,681	100.0	10.5	35.9	17.2	7.0	10.1	11.8	7.5
Women	21,361	100.0	18.8	38.5	10.1	13.1	9.7	4.6	5.3
Race/ethnicity									
White [1]	34,823	100.0	15.1	36.6	13.5	10.7	9.8	8.0	6.3
Black [1]	2,505	100.0	12.4	50.4	9.6	7.0	10.4	4.6	5.6
Hispanic [2]	1,289	100.0	18.3	42.2	9.6	8.5	8.9	6.9	5.6
Age									
16 to 19 years	1,902	100.0	26.8	34.4	8.9	9.2	7.0	8.2	5.5
20 to 24 years	2,064	100.0	18.5	30.5	12.7	11.9	11.6	8.0	6.8
25 to 34 years	8,680	100.0	18.3	34.9	13.3	9.1	9.3	8.9	6.1
35 to 44 years	10,337	100.0	20.3	33.1	12.6	7.4	8.5	12.1	6.1
45 to 54 years	5,670	100.0	11.8	40.8	15.1	10.1	8.8	7.1	6.3
55 to 64 years	4,455	100.0	6.7	45.7	16.1	12.4	10.9	2.5	5.7
65 years and over	4,934	100.0	4.3	43.3	11.1	17.8	14.5	1.8	7.2
Educational attainment [3]									
Less than 4 years of high school	2,939	100.0	6.6	48.4	10.0	10.0	13.1	4.8	7.0
4 years of high school	11,105	100.0	12.5	41.5	11.2	11.1	8.8	8.2	6.7
1 to 3 years of college	7,572	100.0	14.7	36.8	13.3	10.8	10.1	8.0	6.3
4 years of college or more	12,459	100.0	17.4	32.9	16.4	9.7	10.1	7.8	5.7
Marital status									
Single, never married	6,327	100.0	18.6	29.3	14.0	10.9	12.4	7.6	7.3
Married, spouse present	26,344	100.0	15.2	40.4	13.2	9.0	8.4	8.4	5.4
Married, spouse absent	765	100.0	17.8	29.4	11.6	13.2	12.5	5.0	10.5
Divorced	2,510	100.0	12.6	25.1	15.1	15.0	15.0	8.2	9.0
Widowed	2,096	100.0	5.9	41.2	8.1	20.8	13.9	1.3	8.9

[1] Includes persons of Hispanic origin.

[2] Persons of Hispanic origin may be of any race.

[3] Data relate to persons 25 years old and over.

SOURCE: U.S. Department of Labor, Bureau of Labor Statistics, News release, "Thirty-Eight Million Persons Do Volunteer Work." (This table was prepared April 1990.)

Table 29.—Total expenditures of educational institutions related to the gross national product, by level of institution: 1959–60 to 1990–91

Year	Gross national product (in billions)	School year	Total expenditures for education (amounts in millions)					
			All educational institutions		All elementary and secondary schools		All colleges and universities	
			Amount	As a percent of gross national product	Amount	As a percent of gross national product	Amount	As a percent of gross national product
1	2	3	4	5	6	7	8	9
1959	$495.8	1959–60	$23,860	4.8	$16,713	3.4	$7,147	1.4
1961	533.8	1961–62	28,503	5.3	19,673	3.7	8,830	1.7
1963	606.9	1963–64	34,440	5.7	22,825	3.8	11,615	1.9
1965	705.1	1965–66	43,682	6.2	28,048	4.0	15,634	2.2
1967	816.4	1967–68	55,652	6.8	35,077	4.3	20,575	2.5
1969	963.9	1969–70	68,459	7.1	43,183	4.5	25,276	2.6
1970	1,015.5	1970–71	75,741	7.5	48,200	4.7	27,541	2.7
1971	1,102.7	1971–72	80,672	7.3	50,950	4.6	29,722	2.7
1972	1,212.8	1972–73	86,875	7.2	54,952	4.5	31,923	2.6
1973	1,359.3	1973–74	95,396	7.0	60,370	4.4	35,026	2.6
1974	1,472.8	1974–75	108,664	7.4	68,846	4.7	39,818	2.7
1975	1,598.4	1975–76	118,706	7.4	75,101	4.7	43,605	2.7
1976	1,782.8	1976–77	126,417	7.1	79,194	4.4	47,223	2.6
1977	1,990.5	1977–78	137,042	6.9	86,544	4.3	50,498	2.5
1978	2,249.7	1978–79	148,308	6.6	93,012	4.1	55,296	2.5
1979	2,508.2	1979–80	165,627	6.6	103,162	4.1	62,465	2.5
1980	2,732.0	1980–81	182,849	6.7	112,325	4.1	70,524	2.6
1981	3,052.6	1981–82	197,801	6.5	120,486	3.9	77,315	2.5
1982	3,166.0	1982–83	212,081	6.7	128,725	4.1	83,356	2.6
1983	3,405.7	1983–84	228,597	6.7	139,000	4.1	89,597	2.6
1984	3,772.2	1984–85	247,657	6.6	149,400	4.0	98,257	2.6
1985	4,014.9	1985–86	269,485	6.7	161,800	4.0	107,685	2.7
1986	4,231.6	1986–87	291,823	6.9	175,200	4.1	116,623	2.8
1987	4,515.6	[1] 1987–88	313,000	6.9	187,700	4.2	125,300	2.8
1988	4,873.7	[1] 1988–89	340,600	7.0	206,000	4.2	134,600	2.8
1989	5,200.8	[2] 1989–90	365,400	7.0	220,900	4.2	144,500	2.8
1990	5,463.6	[2] 1990–91	392,600	7.2	237,200	4.3	155,400	2.8

[1] Preliminary.

[2] Estimated.

NOTE.—Total expenditures for public elementary and secondary schools include current expenditures, interest on school debt, and capital outlay. Data for private elementary and secondary schools are estimated. Total expenditures for colleges and universities include current-fund expenditures and additions to plant value. Excludes expenditures of noncollegiate postsecondary institutions. Some data have been revised from previously published figures. Because of rounding, details may not add to totals.

SOURCE: U.S. Department of Education, National Center for Education Statistics, *Statistics of State School Systems; Revenues and Expenditures for Public Elementary and Secondary Education; Financial Statistics of Institutions of Higher Education*, Common Core of Data survey, and "Financial Statistics of Institutions of Higher Education" survey, Integrated Postsecondary Education Data System (IPEDS) "Finance" survey, and unpublished data; Council of Economic Advisers, *Economic Indicators;* and National Education Association, *Estimates of School Statistics*, various years. (This table was prepared April 1991.)

Table 30.—Total expenditures of educational institutions, by level and control of institution: 1899–1900 to 1990–91

[In millions]

School year	Total	Elementary and secondary schools			Colleges and universities		
		Total	Public	Private [1]	Total	Public	Private
1	2	3	4	5	6	7	8
1899–1900	—	—	$215	—	—	—	—
1909–10	—	—	426	—	—	—	—
1919–20	—	—	1,036	—	—	—	—
1929–30	—	—	2,317	—	$632	$292	$341
1939–40	—	—	2,344	—	758	392	367
1949–50	$8,911	$6,249	5,838	$411	2,662	1,430	1,233
1951–52	10,735	7,861	7,344	517	2,874	1,565	1,309
1953–54	13,147	9,733	9,092	641	3,414	1,912	1,502
1955–56	15,907	11,727	10,955	772	4,180	2,348	1,832
1957–58	20,055	14,525	13,569	956	5,530	3,237	2,293
1959–60	23,860	16,713	15,613	1,100	7,147	3,904	3,244
1961–62	28,503	19,673	18,373	1,300	8,830	4,919	3,911
1963–64	34,440	22,825	21,325	1,500	11,615	6,558	5,057
1965–66	43,682	28,048	26,248	1,800	15,634	9,047	6,588
1967–68	55,652	35,077	32,977	2,100	20,575	12,750	7,824
1969–70	68,459	43,183	40,683	2,500	25,276	16,234	9,041
1970–71	75,741	48,200	45,500	2,700	27,541	18,028	9,513
1971–72	80,672	50,950	48,050	2,900	29,722	19,538	10,184
1972–73	86,875	54,952	51,852	3,100	31,923	21,144	10,779
1973–74	95,396	60,370	56,970	3,400	35,026	23,542	11,484
1974–75	108,664	68,846	64,846	4,000	39,818	26,966	12,852
1975–76	118,706	75,101	70,601	4,500	43,605	29,736	13,869
1976–77	126,417	79,194	74,194	5,000	47,223	31,997	15,226
1977–78	137,042	86,544	80,844	5,700	50,498	34,031	16,467
1978–79	148,308	93,012	86,712	6,300	55,296	37,110	18,187
1979–80	165,627	103,162	95,962	7,200	62,465	41,434	21,031
1980–81	182,849	112,325	104,125	8,200	70,524	46,559	23,965
1981–82	197,801	120,486	111,186	9,300	77,315	50,813	26,502
1982–83	212,081	128,725	118,425	10,300	83,356	54,338	29,018
1983–84	228,597	139,000	127,500	11,500	89,597	58,124	31,473
1984–85	247,657	149,400	137,000	12,400	98,257	63,704	34,553
1985–86	269,485	161,800	148,600	13,200	107,685	70,069	37,616
1986–87	291,823	175,200	160,900	14,300	116,623	75,010	41,613
1987–88 [2]	313,000	187,700	172,400	15,300	125,300	80,500	44,800
1988–89 [2]	340,600	206,000	189,800	16,200	134,600	86,100	48,500
1989–90 [1]	365,100	220,600	203,300	17,300	144,500	93,100	51,400
1990–91 [1]	392,200	236,700	218,300	18,500	155,400	100,300	55,100

[1] Estimated.

[2] Preliminary.

—Data not available.

NOTE.—Total expenditures for public elementary and secondary schools include current expenditures, interest on school debt, and capital outlay. Data for private elementary and secondary schools are estimated. Total expenditures for colleges and universities include current-fund expenditures and additions to plant value. Excludes expenditures of noncollegiate postsecondary institutions. Some data have been revised from previously published figures. Because of rounding, details may not add to totals.

SOURCE: U.S. Department of Education, National Center for Education Statistics, *Statistics of State School Systems; Revenues and Expenditures for Public Elementary and Secondary Education; Financial Statistics of Institutions of Higher Education* Common Core of Data survey, "Financial Statistics of Institutions of Higher Education" survey, Integrated Postsecondary Education Data System (IPEDS) "Finance" survey; and National Education Association, *Estimates of School Statistics, various years.* (This table was prepared July 1991.)

Table 31.—Estimated total expenditures of educational institutions, by level, control of institution, and source of funds: 1975–76 to 1987–88

[In billions]

Level and control of institution and source of funds	1975-76 Amount	1975-76 Per-cent	1979-80 Amount	1979-80 Per-cent	1984-85 Amount	1984-85 Per-cent	1985-86 Amount	1985-86 Per-cent	1986-87 Amount	1986-87 Per-cent	1987-88 Amount	1987-88 Per-cent
1	2	3	4	5	6	7	8	9	10	11	12	13
All levels												
Total public and private	$118.7	100.0	$165.6	100.0	$247.7	100.0	$269.5	100.0	$291.8	100.0	$313.0	100.0
Federal	13.4	11.3	18.9	11.4	21.3	8.6	23.5	8.7	25.2	8.6	26.6	8.5
State	45.0	37.9	64.3	38.8	96.1	38.8	105.3	39.1	113.4	38.9	121.1	38.7
Local	34.5	29.0	43.3	26.1	63.3	25.6	67.9	25.2	73.4	25.2	79.2	25.3
All other	25.9	21.8	39.1	23.6	66.9	27.0	72.8	27.0	79.8	27.3	86.1	27.5
Total public	100.3	100.0	137.4	100.0	200.7	100.0	218.7	100.0	235.9	100.0	252.9	100.0
Federal	10.7	10.7	14.8	10.8	15.8	7.9	17.3	7.9	18.1	7.7	19.2	7.6
State	44.7	44.5	63.9	46.5	95.5	47.6	104.6	47.8	112.5	47.7	120.0	47.4
Local	34.4	34.2	43.1	31.4	63.1	31.4	67.7	30.9	73.2	31.0	78.9	31.2
All other	10.6	10.6	15.6	11.3	26.3	13.1	29.1	13.3	32.2	13.6	34.8	13.8
Total private	18.4	100.0	28.2	100.0	47.0	100.0	50.8	100.0	55.9	100.0	60.1	100.0
Federal	2.7	14.5	4.1	14.5	5.5	11.7	6.2	12.2	7.1	12.7	7.4	12.4
State	0.3	1.7	0.4	1.6	0.7	1.4	0.7	1.4	0.9	1.7	1.1	1.9
Local	0.1	0.7	0.2	0.6	0.2	0.5	0.2	0.5	0.3	0.5	0.3	0.5
All other	15.3	83.1	23.5	83.4	40.6	86.4	43.6	85.9	47.6	85.2	51.2	85.3
Elementary and secondary schools												
Total public and private	75.1	100.0	103.2	100.0	149.4	100.0	161.8	100.0	175.2	100.0	187.7	100.0
Federal	6.3	8.4	9.4	9.1	9.1	6.1	9.9	6.1	10.3	5.9	10.9	5.8
State	31.4	41.8	44.7	43.3	66.8	44.7	73.1	45.2	79.7	45.5	85.1	45.3
Local	32.7	43.5	41.6	40.3	60.8	40.7	65.2	40.3	70.4	40.2	75.9	40.4
All other	4.7	6.3	7.5	7.3	12.8	8.6	13.6	8.4	14.8	8.4	15.8	8.4
Total public	70.6	100.0	96.0	100.0	137.0	100.0	148.6	100.0	160.9	100.0	172.4	100.0
Federal	6.3	8.9	9.4	9.8	9.1	6.6	9.9	6.7	10.3	6.4	10.9	6.3
State	31.4	44.5	44.7	46.6	66.8	48.7	73.1	49.2	79.7	49.5	85.1	49.3
Local	32.7	46.3	41.6	43.3	60.8	44.3	65.2	43.8	70.4	43.8	75.9	44.0
All other	0.2	0.3	0.3	0.3	0.4	0.3	0.4	0.3	0.5	0.3	0.5	0.3
Total private [1]	4.5	100.0	7.2	100.0	12.4	100.0	13.2	100.0	14.3	100.0	15.3	100.0
All other	4.5	100.0	7.2	100.0	12.4	100.0	13.2	100.0	14.3	100.0	15.3	100.0
Institutions of higher education												
Total public and private	43.6	100.0	62.5	100.0	98.3	100.0	107.7	100.0	116.6	100.0	125.3	100.0
Federal	7.1	16.3	9.5	15.2	12.2	12.4	13.6	12.6	14.9	12.8	15.7	12.6
State	13.6	31.1	19.6	31.4	29.4	29.9	32.2	29.9	33.7	28.9	36.1	28.8
Local	1.8	4.1	1.7	2.7	2.5	2.6	2.7	2.5	3.0	2.6	3.2	2.6
All other	21.1	48.5	31.6	50.6	54.1	55.1	59.1	54.9	65.0	55.7	70.3	56.1
Total public	29.7	100.0	41.4	100.0	63.7	100.0	70.1	100.0	75.0	100.0	80.5	100.0
Federal	4.4	14.9	5.4	13.1	6.7	10.6	7.4	10.5	7.8	10.4	8.3	10.3
State	13.3	44.6	19.2	46.3	28.7	45.1	31.5	45.0	32.8	43.7	34.9	43.4
Local	1.7	5.6	1.5	3.7	2.3	3.6	2.5	3.6	2.7	3.6	2.9	3.7
All other	10.4	34.9	15.3	36.9	25.9	40.7	28.7	40.9	31.7	42.2	34.3	42.6
Total private	13.9	100.0	21.0	100.0	34.6	100.0	37.6	100.0	41.6	100.0	44.8	100.0
Federal	2.7	19.2	4.1	19.4	5.5	15.9	6.2	16.5	7.1	17.0	7.4	16.6
State	0.3	2.3	0.4	2.1	0.7	1.9	0.7	1.9	0.9	2.2	1.1	2.5
Local	0.1	0.9	0.2	0.8	0.2	0.6	0.2	0.6	0.3	0.7	0.3	0.6
All other	10.8	77.6	16.3	77.7	28.2	81.6	30.4	80.9	33.3	80.1	35.9	80.2

[1] Some private elementary and secondary school revenues come from Federal, State, and local sources. However, comprehensive data are not available to delineate the sources of revenues for private schools.

NOTE.—Estimates of expenditures by source of funds are derived from data collected on revenue sources. Federally supported student aid that goes to higher education institutions through students' tuition payments is shown under "All other" rather than "Federal." Such payments would add substantial amounts and several percentage points to the Federal share. Other Federal programs, not included in this table because they do not support regular educational institutions, would increase the Federal share even further.

Typical examples of these payments would be Federal support for libraries and museums. Additionally, the Federal contribution to education through tax expenditures is not reflected in this table. Because of rounding, details may not add to totals.

SOURCE: U.S. Department of Education, National Center for Education Statistics, Common Core of Data and "Financial Statistics of Institutions of Higher Education" surveys; Integrated Postsecondary Education Data System (IPEDS) "Finance" survey; unpublished data; and National Education Association, Estimates of School Statistics, various years. (This table was prepared April 1991.)

Table 32.—Governmental expenditures, by level of government and function: 1970–71 to 1988–89

In millions

Expenditure, by function	All governments[1]					Federal Government				State and local governments[2]			
	1970–71	1980–81	1986–87	1987–88	1988–89	1970–71	1980–81	1987–88	1988–89	1970–71	1980–81	1987–88	1988–89
1	2	3	4	5	6	7	8	9	10	11	12	13	14
General expenditures[1]	$301,096	$827,877	$1,374,297	$1,461,856	$1,542,571	$150,422	$422,301	$878,523	$910,438	$150,674	$407,449	$704,897	$762,311
Selected Federal programs													
National defense and international relations	80,910	174,564	319,084	329,993	346,338	80,910	174,564	329,993	346,338	—	—	—	—
Postal service	8,683	20,466	32,243	33,892	36,472	8,683	20,466	33,892	36,472	—	—	—	—
Space research and technology	3,334	5,523	7,450	8,866	10,806	3,334	5,523	8,866	10,806	—	—	—	—
Education and libraries	64,042	158,012	244,325	260,736	284,963	4,629	12,408	34,138	39,017	60,174	147,649	246,184	267,681
Social services and income maintenance													
Public welfare	20,446	74,643	106,277	115,125	126,132	2,220	22,395	79,909	87,580	18,226	54,121	89,101	97,879
Hospitals and health	14,835	47,378	72,489	78,789	85,091	3,630	11,277	22,261	23,404	11,205	36,101	61,940	67,757
Social insurance administration	2,031	5,075	6,775	7,166	7,352	1,086	2,799	6,917	7,165	945	2,276	2,853	2,947
Transportation	23,722	46,578	66,237	70,536	74,277	4,062	7,724	21,577	21,931	19,819	39,231	63,861	66,924
Public safety													
Police protection	5,706	16,851	28,720	30,934	32,723	478	1,904	4,954	5,307	5,228	14,947	26,277	27,771
Correction	1,979	7,806	17,561	20,131	22,500	94	413	1,258	1,418	1,885	7,393	18,963	21,197
Environment and housing													
Natural resources	13,740	43,599	92,801	90,119	64,353	10,658	38,896	82,034	55,490	3,082	6,175	10,238	11,092
Housing and community development	4,467	13,894	21,304	25,212	28,230	1,913	6,808	23,405	25,306	2,554	7,086	13,243	14,738
Governmental administration													
Financial administration	3,612	10,944	18,667	20,454	22,125	1,341	3,714	6,865	7,132	2,271	7,230	13,589	14,993
General control[3]	3,567	11,514	25,459	27,656	30,088	540	1,973	3,826	4,158	4,432	12,771	23,830	25,930
Interest on general debt	21,688	97,641	187,971	202,437	220,845	16,599	80,510	158,119	174,288	5,089	17,131	44,318	46,557
Other and unallocable	28,334	93,389	126,936	139,811	150,274	10,245	30,927	60,509	64,626	15,764	55,338	90,500	96,844

Percentage distribution

Expenditure, by function	All governments[1]					Federal Government				State and local governments[2]			
General expenditures[1]	100.0	100.0	100.0	100.0	100.0	100.0	100.0	100.0	100.0	100.0	100.0	100.0	100.0
Selected Federal programs													
National defense and international relations	26.9	21.1	23.2	22.6	22.5	53.8	41.3	37.6	38.0	—	—	—	—
Postal service	2.9	2.5	2.3	2.3	2.4	5.8	4.8	3.9	4.0	—	—	—	—
Space research and technology	1.1	0.7	0.5	0.6	0.7	2.2	1.3	1.0	1.2	—	—	—	—
Education and libraries	21.3	19.1	17.8	17.8	18.5	3.1	2.9	3.9	4.3	39.9	36.2	34.9	35.1
Social services and income maintenance													
Public welfare	6.8	9.0	7.7	7.9	8.2	1.5	5.3	9.1	9.6	12.1	13.3	12.6	12.8
Hospitals and health	4.9	5.7	5.3	5.4	5.5	2.4	2.7	2.5	2.6	7.4	8.9	8.8	8.9
Social insurance administration	0.7	0.6	0.5	0.5	0.5	0.7	0.7	0.8	0.8	0.6	0.6	0.4	0.4
Transportation	7.9	5.6	4.8	4.8	4.8	2.7	1.8	2.5	2.4	13.2	9.6	9.1	8.8
Public safety													
Police protection	1.9	2.0	2.1	2.1	2.1	0.3	0.5	0.6	0.6	3.5	3.7	3.7	3.6
Correction	0.7	0.9	1.3	1.4	1.5	0.1	0.1	0.1	0.2	1.3	1.8	2.7	2.8
Environment and housing													
Natural resources	4.6	5.3	6.8	6.2	4.2	7.1	9.2	9.3	6.1	2.0	1.5	1.5	1.5
Housing and community development	1.5	1.7	1.6	1.7	1.8	1.3	1.6	2.7	2.8	1.7	1.7	1.9	1.9
Governmental administration													
Financial administration	1.2	1.3	1.4	1.4	1.4	0.9	0.9	0.8	0.8	1.5	1.8	1.9	1.9
General control[3]	1.2	1.4	1.9	1.9	2.0	0.4	0.5	0.4	0.5	2.9	3.1	3.4	3.4
Interest on general debt	7.2	11.8	13.7	13.8	14.3	11.0	19.1	18.0	19.1	3.4	4.2	6.3	6.1
Other and unallocable	9.4	11.3	9.2	9.6	9.7	6.8	7.3	6.9	7.1	10.5	13.6	12.8	12.7

—Not applicable.

[1] Excludes duplicative intergovernmental transactions.

[2] General expenditures include expenditures to the Federal Government ($2,106,000 in 1985–86), which are excluded from direct general expenditures.

[3] Includes judicial and legal expenditures and expenditures on general and public buildings and other governmental administration.

SOURCE: U.S. Department of Commerce, Bureau of the Census, *Governmental Finances*, various years, and unpublished data. (This table was prepared February 1991.)

Table 33.—Direct general expenditures of State and local governments for all functions and for education, by level and State: 1988–89

[In millions]

State	Total direct general expenditures [1]	Education expenditures							
		Total	Elementary and secondary education			Higher education			Other education [2]
			Total	Current expenditure	Capital outlay	Total	Current expenditure	Capital outlay	
1	2	3	4	5	6	7	8	9	10
United States ...	$759,380.2	$263,898.2	$185,170.7	$170,586.6	$14,584.1	$67,550.3	$60,699.2	$6,851.1	$11,177.3
Alabama	9,933.6	3,849.3	2,234.4	2,006.4	228.0	1,223.4	1,085.2	138.2	391.4
Alaska	5,187.1	1,196.8	896.1	792.1	104.0	241.2	215.9	25.3	59.5
Arizona	11,422.0	4,089.8	2,747.9	2,235.1	512.8	1,227.7	1,129.4	98.3	114.2
Arkansas	4,924.3	2,041.3	1,362.9	1,206.5	156.4	521.8	500.3	21.5	156.5
California	97,576.1	31,650.4	21,441.6	19,914.9	1,526.7	9,174.2	8,554.4	619.8	1,034.6
Colorado	9,868.9	3,572.5	2,543.1	2,330.5	212.6	949.6	862.4	87.3	79.7
Connecticut	12,391.1	3,794.2	2,922.8	2,713.7	209.0	635.2	600.3	34.9	236.3
Delaware	2,390.2	878.2	511.6	494.5	17.1	298.5	286.3	12.2	68.2
District of Columbia	3,661.3	645.5	550.5	502.4	48.1	94.9	88.3	6.6	—
Florida	35,891.7	11,545.1	8,599.6	7,490.4	1,109.2	2,365.3	2,016.7	348.6	580.2
Georgia	17,919.3	6,261.4	4,669.7	4,132.2	537.5	1,367.9	1,172.9	195.0	223.7
Hawaii	3,707.4	988.2	605.1	527.3	77.7	367.3	324.1	43.2	15.8
Idaho	2,421.9	899.5	589.8	539.9	49.9	274.2	244.4	29.8	35.5
Illinois	31,618.9	10,819.7	7,518.3	6,983.3	535.0	2,720.7	2,414.3	306.5	580.6
Indiana	14,062.6	5,900.3	3,918.2	3,552.5	365.7	1,649.3	1,429.3	220.1	332.8
Iowa	8,307.1	3,283.0	2,034.2	1,919.1	115.1	1,120.6	1,004.6	116.0	128.1
Kansas	6,875.8	2,720.5	1,812.5	1,696.3	116.2	856.5	765.4	91.1	51.6
Kentucky	9,140.4	3,101.1	1,906.5	1,811.1	95.4	931.6	822.2	109.5	263.0
Louisiana	11,852.9	3,703.7	2,565.2	2,406.0	159.1	941.7	879.9	61.8	196.8
Maine	3,683.1	1,315.0	937.2	841.8	95.4	317.6	301.1	16.5	60.1
Maryland	14,769.1	5,003.0	3,496.7	3,228.9	267.8	1,283.3	1,199.5	83.8	223.1
Massachusetts	21,556.9	5,874.6	4,384.5	4,157.2	227.2	1,188.1	1,047.3	140.9	302.0
Michigan	29,773.1	11,343.6	7,670.3	7,209.9	460.4	3,381.0	2,899.6	481.4	292.3
Minnesota	16,138.8	5,441.5	3,756.3	3,414.0	342.3	1,455.7	1,314.6	141.1	229.5
Mississippi	6,324.9	2,381.2	1,521.3	1,393.3	127.9	730.2	669.5	60.7	129.7
Missouri	11,829.9	4,660.7	3,382.1	3,066.8	315.3	1,130.7	1,052.4	78.3	147.9
Montana	2,351.7	865.7	635.4	607.8	27.6	170.5	159.3	11.2	59.8
Nebraska	4,493.4	1,803.0	1,176.1	1,106.5	69.6	559.7	500.2	59.4	67.3
Nevada	3,439.2	988.2	720.9	626.6	94.3	241.7	206.7	35.0	25.6
New Hampshire	3,030.3	1,117.7	849.1	742.3	106.8	225.8	216	9.9	42.8
New Jersey	27,985.0	9,299.1	7,118.8	6,728.3	390.5	1,898.1	1,594.3	303.8	282.1
New Mexico	4,645.4	1,736.8	1,082.7	987.9	94.8	588.7	548.0	40.7	65.4
New York	82,700.4	23,789.0	18,493.8	17,499.0	994.8	4,143.7	3,853.4	290.2	1,151.6
North Carolina	16,532.6	6,854.3	4,410.3	4,012.5	397.8	2,217.9	1,950.3	267.5	226.1
North Dakota	2,128.2	784.8	473.8	431.3	42.4	276.6	257.3	19.3	34.4
Ohio	29,472.2	10,857.4	7,828.6	7,474.7	353.9	2,786.2	2,453.7	332.5	242.5
Oklahoma	8,008.2	3,048.7	2,042.4	1,822.8	219.5	912.3	846.0	66.3	94.0
Oregon	8,886.3	3,418.9	2,392.7	2,313.6	79.2	934.4	827.6	106.8	91.8
Pennsylvania	32,891.2	12,062.9	9,251.6	8,498.2	753.4	1,829.3	1,652.8	176.5	982.0
Rhode Island	3,294.6	1,049.9	688.9	670.1	18.8	252.2	239.4	12.7	108.8
South Carolina	8,646.3	3,431.5	2,276.0	2,051.2	224.8	912.8	847.4	65.5	242.7
South Dakota	1,795.1	627.8	454.3	421.3	32.9	145.9	129.1	16.9	27.6
Tennessee	11,801.2	4,028.6	2,480.4	2,321.6	158.8	1,285.4	1,088.9	196.5	262.8
Texas	43,768.6	17,862.4	12,514.4	11,376.0	1,138.4	4,970.4	4,395.3	575.2	377.5
Utah	4,632.0	1,939.2	1,185.9	1,120.3	65.5	676.3	591.3	85.0	77.1
Vermont	1,815.1	751.6	479.1	448.7	30.3	224.9	206.5	18.4	47.6
Virginia	17,776.5	6,782.8	4,654.6	4,174.5	480.1	1,849.0	1,623.5	225.6	279.2
Washington	14,409.8	5,470.1	3,742.4	3,195.9	546.5	1,590.2	1,417.2	173.0	137.6
West Virginia	4,333.1	1,696.6	1,182.0	1,105.6	76.4	421.9	395.0	26.9	92.7
Wisconsin	15,233.8	5,923.6	3,929.8	3,791.3	138.4	1,785.1	1,636.1	148.9	208.7
Wyoming	2,081.8	747.7	528.4	492.4	36.0	202.4	183.3	19.1	16.9

[1] Includes State and local government expenditures for education services, social services and income maintenance, transportation, public safety, environment and housing, governmental administration, interest on general debt, and other general expenditures.

[2] Includes assistance and subsidies to individuals and private institutions for elementary, secondary, and higher education, as well as miscellaneous education expenditures.

—Not applicable.

NOTE.—Current expenditure data in this table differ from figures appearing in other tables because of slightly varying definitions used in the Governmental Finances and Common Core of Data surveys. Because of rounding, details may not add to totals.

SOURCE: U.S. Department of Commerce, Bureau of the Census, Governments Division, Government Finances: 1988-89. (This table was prepared February 1991.)

Table 34.—Direct general expenditures per capita of State and local governments for all functions and for education, by level and State: 1988–89

State	Total, all direct general expenditures per capita [1]	Education expenditures per capita							
		Total		Elementary and secondary education		Higher education		Other education	
		Amount	As a percent of all functions	Amount	As a percent of all functions	Amount	As a percent of all functions	Amount	As a percent of all functions
1	2	3	4	5	6	7	8	9	10
United States	$3,059.07	$1,063.08	34.8	$745.94	24.4	$272.12	8.9	$45.03	1.5
Alabama	2,412.24	934.74	38.7	542.60	22.5	297.08	12.3	95.06	3.9
Alaska	9,842.64	2,270.99	23.1	1,700.36	17.3	457.72	4.7	112.92	1.1
Arizona	3,212.04	1,150.10	35.8	772.75	24.1	345.25	10.7	32.10	1.0
Arkansas	2,046.69	848.42	41.5	566.46	27.7	216.89	10.6	65.06	3.2
California	3,357.40	1,089.03	32.4	737.76	22.0	315.67	9.4	35.60	1.1
Colorado	2,975.23	1,077.02	36.2	766.69	25.8	286.29	9.6	24.03	0.8
Connecticut	3,825.59	1,171.41	30.6	902.37	23.6	196.10	5.1	72.95	1.9
Delaware	3,551.50	1,304.95	36.7	760.14	21.4	443.53	12.5	101.27	2.9
District of Columbia	6,061.69	1,068.67	17.6	911.50	15.0	157.16	2.6	—	—
Florida	2,832.59	911.14	32.2	678.68	24.0	186.67	6.6	45.79	1.6
Georgia	2,784.23	972.87	34.9	725.56	26.1	212.54	7.6	34.76	1.2
Hawaii	3,334.02	888.64	26.7	544.11	16.3	330.35	9.9	14.18	0.4
Idaho	2,388.43	887.10	37.1	581.68	24.4	270.43	11.3	34.98	1.5
Illinois	2,712.21	928.09	34.2	644.91	23.8	233.38	8.6	49.80	1.8
Indiana	2,514.32	1,054.94	42.0	700.56	27.9	294.89	11.7	59.49	2.4
Iowa	2,925.03	1,155.97	39.5	716.28	24.5	394.59	13.5	45.10	1.5
Kansas	2,736.09	1,082.58	39.6	721.24	26.4	340.83	12.5	20.51	0.7
Kentucky	2,452.47	832.05	33.9	511.52	20.9	249.97	10.2	70.56	2.9
Louisiana	2,704.90	845.21	31.2	585.39	21.6	214.91	7.9	44.91	1.7
Maine	3,013.99	1,076.07	35.7	766.94	25.4	259.94	8.6	49.19	1.6
Maryland	3,146.38	1,065.84	33.9	744.92	23.7	273.39	8.7	47.53	1.5
Massachusetts	3,645.68	993.51	27.3	741.50	20.3	200.94	5.5	51.08	1.4
Michigan	3,210.74	1,223.30	38.1	827.16	25.8	364.61	11.4	31.52	1.0
Minnesota	3,707.52	1,250.05	33.7	862.93	23.3	334.41	9.0	52.71	1.4
Mississippi	2,413.17	908.52	37.6	580.42	24.1	278.61	11.5	49.49	2.1
Missouri	2,293.06	903.41	39.4	655.58	28.6	219.16	9.6	28.67	1.3
Montana	2,917.70	1,074.11	36.8	788.35	27.0	211.59	7.3	74.17	2.5
Nebraska	2,789.19	1,119.21	40.1	730.04	26.2	347.40	12.5	41.77	1.5
Nevada	3,095.57	889.44	28.7	648.83	21.0	217.59	7.0	23.01	0.7
New Hampshire	2,737.41	1,009.70	36.9	767.01	28.0	204.01	7.5	38.68	1.4
New Jersey	3,617.50	1,202.05	33.2	920.22	25.4	245.37	6.8	36.46	1.0
New Mexico	3,040.21	1,136.65	37.4	708.57	23.3	385.29	12.7	42.79	1.4
New York	4,607.26	1,325.29	28.8	1,030.29	22.4	230.84	5.0	64.15	1.4
North Carolina	2,516.00	1,043.11	41.5	671.18	26.7	337.53	13.4	34.40	1.4
North Dakota	3,224.51	1,189.15	36.9	717.84	22.3	419.16	13.0	52.15	1.6
Ohio	2,702.14	995.45	36.8	717.76	26.6	255.46	9.5	22.24	0.8
Oklahoma	2,483.92	945.63	38.1	633.50	25.5	282.97	11.4	29.17	1.2
Oregon	3,151.17	1,212.37	38.5	848.48	26.9	331.34	10.5	32.55	1.0
Pennsylvania	2,731.82	1,001.90	36.7	768.40	28.1	151.94	5.6	81.56	3.0
Rhode Island	3,301.19	1,051.95	31.9	690.32	20.9	252.66	7.7	108.97	3.3
South Carolina	2,461.94	977.08	39.7	648.07	26.3	259.92	10.6	69.10	2.8
South Dakota	2,510.68	878.10	35.0	635.38	25.3	204.08	8.1	38.64	1.5
Tennessee	2,388.92	815.50	34.1	502.11	21.0	260.21	10.9	53.19	2.2
Texas	2,575.98	1,051.28	40.8	736.53	28.6	292.53	11.4	22.22	0.9
Utah	2,713.53	1,136.04	41.9	694.71	25.6	396.18	14.6	45.14	1.7
Vermont	3,201.28	1,325.51	41.4	844.94	26.4	396.66	12.4	83.91	2.6
Virginia	2,915.13	1,112.30	38.2	763.30	26.2	303.22	10.4	45.78	1.6
Washington	3,026.63	1,148.95	38.0	786.04	26.0	334.00	11.0	28.90	1.0
West Virginia	2,333.40	913.63	39.2	636.52	27.3	227.20	9.7	49.91	2.1
Wisconsin	3,130.01	1,217.09	38.9	807.43	25.8	366.77	11.7	42.89	1.4
Wyoming	4,382.68	1,574.11	35.9	1,112.45	25.4	426.07	9.7	35.59	0.8

[1] Includes intergovernmental expenditure to the Federal Government.
—Not applicable.

NOTE.—Per capita amounts are based on population figures as of July 1, 1989, and are computed on the basis of amounts rounded to the nearest thousand. Because of rounding, details may not add to totals.

SOURCE: U.S. Department of Commerce, Bureau of the Census, Governments Division, *Government Finances: 1988-89*. (This table was prepared February 1991.)

Table 35.—Gross national product, State and local expenditures, personal income, disposable personal income, median family income, and population: 1929 to 1990

Year	Gross national product, in billions		State and local expenditures [1] in millions		Personal income, in billions	Disposable personal income, in billions of 1982 dollars	Disposable personal income per capita		Median family income	Total population in thousands	
	Current dollars	Constant 1982 dollars	All general expenditures	Education expenditures			Current dollars	Constant 1982 dollars		Annual averages of quarterly data [2]	As of July 1 [3]
1	2	3	4	5	6	7	8	9	10	11	12
1929	$103.9	$709.6	—	—	$84.3	$498.6	$671	$4,091	—	—	121,878
1933	56.0	498.5	—	—	46.3	370.8	357	2,950	—	—	125,690
1939	91.3	716.6	—	—	72.1	499.5	532	3,812	—	—	131,028
1940	100.4	772.9	$9,229	$2,638	77.6	530.7	568	4,017	—	—	132,122
1941	125.5	909.4	—	—	95.2	604.1	689	4,528	—	—	133,402
1942	159.0	1,080.3	9,190	2,586	122.4	693.0	863	5,138	—	—	134,860
1943	192.7	1,276.2	—	—	150.7	721.4	972	5,276	—	—	136,739
1944	211.4	1,380.6	8,863	2,793	164.5	749.3	1,052	5,414	—	—	138,397
1945	213.4	1,354.8	—	—	170.0	739.5	1,066	5,285	—	—	139,928
1946	212.4	1,096.9	11,028	3,356	177.6	723.3	1,124	5,115	—	—	141,389
1947	235.2	1,066.7	—	—	190.2	694.8	1,171	4,820	$3,031	—	144,126
1948	261.6	1,108.7	17,684	5,379	209.2	733.1	1,283	5,000	3,187	—	146,631
1949	260.4	1,109.0	—	—	206.4	733.2	1,260	4,915	3,107	—	149,188
1950	288.3	1,203.7	22,787	7,177	228.1	791.8	1,368	5,220	3,319	—	151,684
1951	333.4	1,328.2	—	—	256.5	819.0	1,475	5,308	3,709	—	154,287
1952	351.6	1,380.0	26,098	8,318	273.8	844.3	1,528	5,379	3,890	—	156,954
1953	371.6	1,435.3	27,910	9,390	290.5	880.0	1,599	5,515	4,242	—	159,565
1954	372.5	1,416.2	30,701	10,557	293.0	894.0	1,604	5,505	4,167	—	162,391
1955	405.9	1,494.9	33,724	11,907	314.2	944.5	1,687	5,714	4,418	—	165,275
1956	428.2	1,525.6	36,711	13,220	337.2	989.4	1,769	5,881	4,780	—	168,221
1957	451.0	1,551.1	40,375	14,134	356.3	1,012.1	1,833	5,909	4,966	—	171,274
1958	456.8	1,539.2	44,851	15,919	367.1	1,028.8	1,865	5,908	5,087	—	174,882
1959	495.8	1,629.1	48,887	17,283	390.7	1,067.2	1,946	6,027	5,417	177,073	177,830
1960	515.3	1,665.3	51,876	18,719	409.4	1,091.1	1,986	6,036	5,620	180,760	180,671
1961	533.8	1,708.7	56,201	20,574	426.0	1,123.2	2,034	6,113	5,735	183,742	183,691
1962	574.6	1,799.4	60,206	22,216	453.2	1,170.2	2,123	6,271	5,956	186,590	186,538
1963	606.9	1,873.3	63,977	23,729	476.3	1,207.3	2,197	6,378	6,249	189,300	189,242
1964	649.8	1,973.3	69,302	26,286	510.2	1,291.0	2,352	6,727	6,569	191,927	191,889
1965	705.1	2,087.6	74,678	28,563	552.0	1,365.7	2,505	7,027	6,957	194,347	194,303
1966	772.0	2,208.3	82,843	33,287	600.8	1,431.3	2,675	7,280	7,532	196,599	196,560
1967	816.4	2,271.4	93,350	37,919	644.5	1,493.2	2,828	7,513	7,933	198,752	198,712
1968	892.7	2,365.6	102,411	41,158	707.2	1,551.3	3,037	7,728	8,632	200,745	200,706
1969	963.9	2,423.3	116,728	47,238	772.9	1,599.8	3,239	7,891	9,433	202,736	202,677
1970	1,015.5	2,416.2	131,332	52,718	831.8	1,668.1	3,489	8,134	9,867	205,089	205,052
1971	1,102.7	2,484.8	150,674	59,413	894.0	1,728.4	3,740	8,322	10,285	207,692	207,661
1972	1,212.8	2,608.5	168,550	65,814	981.6	1,797.4	4,000	8,562	11,116	209,924	209,896
1973	1,359.3	2,744.1	181,357	69,714	1,101.7	1,916.3	4,481	9,042	12,051	211,939	211,909
1974	1,472.8	2,729.3	198,959	75,833	1,210.1	1,896.6	4,855	8,867	12,902	213,898	213,854
1975	1,598.4	2,695.0	230,721	87,858	1,313.4	1,931.7	5,291	8,944	13,719	215,981	215,973
1976	1,782.8	2,826.7	256,731	97,216	1,451.4	2,001.0	5,744	9,175	14,958	218,086	218,035
1977	1,990.5	2,958.6	274,215	102,780	1,607.5	2,066.6	6,262	9,381	16,009	220,289	220,239
1978	2,249.7	3,115.2	296,983	110,758	1,812.4	2,167.4	6,968	9,735	17,640	222,629	222,585
1979	2,508.2	3,192.4	327,517	119,448	2,034.0	2,212.6	7,682	9,829	19,587	225,106	225,055
1980	2,732.0	3,187.1	369,086	133,211	2,258.5	2,214.3	8,421	9,722	21,023	227,754	227,719
1981	3,052.6	3,248.8	407,449	145,784	2,520.9	2,248.6	9,243	9,769	22,388	230,182	229,945
1982	3,166.0	3,166.0	436,896	154,282	2,670.8	2,261.5	9,724	9,724	23,433	232,549	232,171
1983	3,405.7	3,279.1	466,421	163,876	2,838.6	2,331.9	10,340	9,930	24,674	234,829	234,296
1984	3,772.2	3,501.4	505,008	176,108	3,108.7	2,469.8	11,257	10,419	26,433	237,051	236,343
1985	4,014.9	3,618.7	553,899	192,686	3,325.3	2,542.8	11,861	10,625	27,735	239,322	238,466
1986	4,231.6	3,717.9	605,623	210,819	3,526.2	2,635.3	12,469	10,905	29,458	241,660	240,658
1987	4,515.6	3,845.3	657,134	226,619	3,766.4	2,670.7	13,094	10,946	30,970	243,982	242,820
1988	4,873.7	4,016.9	704,921	242,683	4,070.8	2,800.5	14,123	11,368	[4] 32,191	246,358	245,051
1989	5,200.8	4,117.7	762,311	263,898	4,384.3	2,869.0	14,973	11,531	[4] 34,213	248,810	247,350
1990	5,465.1	4,157.3	—	—	4,645.5	2,893.5	15,695	11,509	—	251,420	249,975

[1] Data for years prior to 1963 include expenditures for government fiscal years ending during that particular calendar year. Data for 1963 and later years are the aggregations of expenditures for government fiscal years which ended on June 30 of the stated year. General expenditures exclude expenditures of publicly owned utilities and liquor stores, and of insurance-trust activities. Intergovernmental payments between State and local governments are excluded. Payments to the Federal Government are included.
[2] Population of the United States including Armed Forces overseas; includes Alaska and Hawaii beginning 1960. Quarterly data are averages for the period.
[3] Population of the United States including Armed Forces overseas; includes Alaska and Hawaii beginning 1958.
[4] Revised methodology.

—Data not available.

NOTE.—GNP data are adjusted by the GNP implicit price deflator. Personal income data are adjusted by the Consumer Price Index. Some data have been revised from previously published figures.

SOURCE: Executive Office of the President, *Economic Report of the President, 1990;* and Council of Economic Advisers, *Economic Indicators, January 1991;* and U.S. Department of Commerce, Bureau of the Census, "Estimates of the Population of the United States to November 1, 1990. (This table was prepared July 1991.)

Table 36.—Gross national product price deflator, Consumer Price Index, education price indexes, and Federal budget composite deflator: 1919 to 1990

Calendar year			School year				Federal fiscal year	
Year	GNP implicit price deflator	Consumer Price Index [1]	Year	Consumer Price Index [2]	Elementary/ Secondary Price Index	Higher Education Price Index	Year	Federal budget composite deflator
1	2	3	4	5	6	7	8	9
1919	—	17.3	1919–20	19.1	—	—	1919	—
1929	14.6	17.1	1929–30	17.1	—	—	1929	—
1934	—	13.4	1934–35	13.6	—	—	1934	—
1939	12.7	13.9	1939–40	14.0	—	—	1939	—
1940	13.0	14.0	1940–41	14.2	—	—	1940	0.1138
1941	13.8	14.7	1941–42	15.6	—	—	1941	0.1213
1942	14.7	16.3	1942–43	16.9	—	—	1942	0.1349
1943	15.1	17.3	1943–44	17.4	—	—	1943	0.1482
1944	15.3	17.6	1944–45	17.8	—	—	1944	0.1431
1945	15.7	18.0	1945–46	18.2	—	—	1945	0.1386
1946	19.4	19.5	1946–47	21.2	—	—	1946	0.1330
1947	22.1	22.3	1947–48	23.3	—	—	1947	0.1621
1948	23.6	24.1	1948–49	24.1	—	—	1948	0.1881
1949	23.5	23.8	1949–50	23.7	—	—	1949	0.1918
1950	23.9	24.1	1950–51	25.1	—	—	1950	0.1930
1951	25.1	26.0	1951–52	26.3	—	—	1951	0.1816
1952	25.5	26.5	1952–53	26.7	—	—	1952	0.1938
1953	25.9	26.7	1953–54	26.9	—	—	1953	0.2071
1954	26.3	26.9	1954–55	26.8	—	—	1954	0.2141
1955	27.2	26.8	1955–56	26.9	—	—	1955	0.2200
1956	28.1	27.2	1956–57	27.7	—	—	1956	0.2307
1957	29.1	28.1	1957–58	28.6	—	—	1957	0.2402
1958	29.7	28.9	1958–59	29.0	—	—	1958	0.2553
1959	30.4	29.1	1959–60	29.4	—	—	1959	0.2655
1960	30.9	29.6	1960–61	29.8	—	25.1	1960	0.2708
1961	31.2	29.9	1961–62	30.1	—	26.1	1961	0.2756
1962	31.9	30.2	1962–63	30.4	—	27.1	1962	0.2784
1963	32.4	30.6	1963–64	30.8	—	28.1	1963	0.2894
1964	32.9	31.0	1964–65	31.2	—	29.3	1964	0.2942
1965	33.8	31.5	1965–66	31.9	—	30.8	1965	0.2996
1966	35.0	32.4	1966–67	32.9	—	32.4	1966	0.3120
1967	35.9	33.4	1967–68	34.0	—	34.3	1967	0.3224
1968	37.7	34.8	1968–69	35.7	—	36.7	1968	0.3390
1969	39.8	36.7	1969–70	37.8	—	39.2	1969	0.3598
1970	42.0	38.8	1970–71	39.7	—	41.6	1970	0.3841
1971	44.4	40.5	1971–72	41.2	—	44.0	1971	0.4126
1972	46.5	41.8	1972–73	42.8	—	46.3	1972	0.4372
1973	49.5	44.4	1973–74	46.6	—	49.6	1973	0.4658
1974	54.0	49.3	1974–75	51.8	51.6	53.8	1974	0.5095
1975	59.3	53.8	1975–76	55.5	56.1	57.4	1975	0.5671
1976	63.1	56.9	1976–77	58.7	59.9	61.1	1976	0.6298
1977	67.3	60.6	1977–78	62.6	64.0	65.2	1977	0.6572
1978	72.2	65.2	1978–79	68.5	69.9	70.2	1978	0.7034
1979	78.6	72.6	1979–80	77.6	76.3	77.2	1979	0.7626
1980	85.7	82.4	1980–81	86.6	85.5	85.5	1980	0.8453
1981	94.0	90.9	1981–82	94.1	93.8	94.0	1981	0.9335
1982	100.0	96.5	1982–83	98.2	100.0	100.0	1982	1.0000
1983	103.9	99.6	1983–84	101.8	105.6	104.7	1983	1.0430
1984	107.7	103.9	1984–85	105.8	112.6	110.5	1984	1.0808
1985	110.9	107.6	1985–86	108.8	119.6	115.6	1985	1.1137
1986	113.8	109.6	1986–87	111.2	125.7	120.4	1986	1.1408
1987	117.4	113.6	1987–88	115.8	132.5	125.7	1987	1.1693
1988	121.3	118.3	1988–89	121.2	139.5	133.1	1988	1.2081
1989	126.3	124.0	1989–90	127.0	—	—	1989	1.2578
1990	131.5	130.7	1990–91	133.9	—	—	1990	1.3100

[1] Index for urban wage earners and clerical workers through 1977; 1978 and later figures are for all urban consumers.

[2] Consumer price index adjusted to a school-year basis (July through June).

—Data not available.

NOTE.—Some data have been revised from previously published figures.

SOURCE: Council of Economic Advisers, Economic Indicators, February 1991; U.S. Department of Education, National Institute of Education, Inflation Measures for Schools and Colleges; U.S. Department of Labor, Bureau of Labor Statistics, Consumer Price Index; Research Associates of Washington, "Higher Education Prices and Price Indexes: 1989 Update" and "School Price Index: 1989 Update;" and U.S. Office of Management and Budget, Budget of the U.S. Government, Fiscal Year 1992. (This table was prepared April 1991.)

CHAPTER 2
Elementary and Secondary Education

This chapter contains a variety of statistics on public and private elementary and secondary education. These data are derived from surveys conducted by the National Center for Education Statistics (NCES) and other public and private organizations.

The Center conducts annual surveys of public schools and periodic surveys of teachers and private schools. The Common Core of Data is an administrative records survey of public elementary and secondary schools and school districts. Each State provides summary data on enrollment, staff, revenues, and expenditures. In addition, listings and selected statistics of school districts and schools are obtained. National and State summary statistics from the Common Core of Data have been published annually in the *Digest* and in a series of reports and bulletins.

The Center has released data from a new Schools and Staffing Survey system, which contains comparative statistics on public and private schools as well as detailed information on teacher and school characteristics. This new survey system will provide more information on the finances of elementary and secondary schools and will allow cross comparisons of teacher and school characteristics. The Center has reported periodically on preprimary education and on offerings and enrollments in high school subjects. The most recent statistics in these areas are summarized in the tables which follow.

This chapter of the *Digest* also makes use of data on student achievement from the National Assessment of Educational Progress; on public school enrollment by race or ethnicity from the Office for Civil Rights, U.S. Department of Education; on the characteristics, subjects taught, and average salaries of public school teachers from the National Education Association and the American Federation of Teachers; on private school enrollment from the National Catholic Educational Association; on mandatory ages of attendance, graduation requirements, and minimum-competency testing for students and teachers from the Education Commission of the States; on the Scholastic Aptitude Test scores of college-bound high school seniors from the College Entrance Examination Board; and on the proportion of high school graduates going to college from the Bureau of Labor Statistics.

Additional information on public school libraries and the use of microcomputers in public and private schools is tabulated in chapter 7. Comparisons of the income and employment of high school graduates and dropouts, and college enrollment of high school graduates are in chapter 3. Tabulations of international data are in chapter 6. Further information on survey methodologies is in the "Guide to Sources" in the appendix and in the publications cited in the table source notes.

Highlights

- In fall 1985, public elementary and secondary school enrollments increased for the first time since 1971. Enrollment has continued to rise, resulting in an increase of 4 percent from 1985 to 1990. (Tables 3 and 39)

- In contrast to the declining elementary and secondary school enrollments during the 1970s and early 1980s, preprimary education enrollment grew substantially. Between 1970 and 1980, preprimary enrollment of 3- to 5-year- olds rose by 19 percent; between 1980 to 1990, it increased an additional 37 percent. An important feature of the increasing participation of young children in preprimary schools is the increasing proportion in full-day programs. In 1990 about 39 percent of the children attended school all day, compared with 32 percent in 1980 and 17 percent in 1970. (Table 45)

- Despite drops in total elementary and secondary school enrollment during the late 1970s and early 1980s, increasing numbers of children were served in programs for the handicapped. In 1976–77, 8 percent of children were served in these programs compared with 11 percent in 1988–89. Most of this increase may be attributed to the proportion of children identified as learning disabled, which rose from less than 2 percent of all children in 1976–77 to 5 percent of all children in 1988–89. (Table 47)

- Schools with religious orientation charged significantly lower tuition than nonsectarian schools. In 1987–88, about 6 percent of Catholic schools and 11 percent of schools with other religious orientations charged more than $2,500 tuition, compared with 58 percent of the nonsectarian private schools. The mean tuition paid by students at Catholic elementary schools was $1,005, compared to $1,619 at other religiously oriented schools, and $3,091 at nonsectarian schools. Mean tuition paid by secondary school students was substantially higher, averaging $2,045 at Catholic schools, $3,592 at other religiously oriented schools, and $6,391 at nonsectarian schools. (Table 56)

- During the 1970s and early 1980s, public school enrollment decreased, while the number of teachers held steady. As a result, the pupil/teacher ratio declined markedly. Between 1970 and 1980, the pupil/teacher ratio for public schools fell from 22.3 to 18.7. After 1980, the number of pupils per teacher continued downward, reaching 17.2 in 1990. (Table 59)

- Of the 307,000 full-time and part-time private school teachers in 1987–88, about 78 percent were women. About 56 percent of the private school teachers were under age 40, and 34 percent had a master's degree or above. In contrast, 71 percent of public school teachers were women, 49 percent were under 40, and more than 47 percent had a master's degree or above. (Table 62)

- In general, public school teachers have higher salaries than private school teachers. In 1987–88, the average base salary for public school teachers was $26,231, compared with $16,562 for private school teachers. (Table 70)

- Teachers have expressed more satisfaction with their jobs in recent years. About 86 percent felt satisfied with their jobs in 1989, compared with 81 percent in 1984 and 1986. (Table 71)

- The average salary for public school teachers has grown rapidly in recent years, reaching $33,015 in 1990–91. After adjustment for inflation, teachers' salaries rose 21 percent between 1980–81 and 1990–91, more than recouping the losses in purchasing power suffered during the 1970s. (Table 72)

- The number of nonteaching staff employed by public schools has grown at a faster rate than the number of pupils and teachers. In 1969–70, there were 13.5 pupils per staff member (total staff) compared with 9.2 pupils per staff member in 1989. During the same period, the proportion of the total staff who were teachers declined from 60 percent to 53 percent. In 1987–88, the number of pupils per staff member at private schools was 10.3, approximately the same as for public schools. (Tables 55 and 77)

- Comparisons of the number of public and private high school graduates with the 17-year-old popula-

tion show that the proportion of young people graduating from high school has not increased over the past 20 years. At its highest point in 1968–69, there were 77.1 graduates for every 100 persons 17 years of age. This ratio declined during the 1970s, falling to a low point of 71.4 in 1979–80. The ratio has risen since then, reaching 75.4 in 1990–91. (Table 95)

- Students at ages 9 and 17 were reading slightly better in 1988 than they were in 1971, but 13-year-olds showed no improvement. Improvements in the achievement of minority students between 1971 and 1988 have reduced the gap between their performance and that of other students. (Tables 102 and 106)

- Results from the 1988 assessment of history proficiency showed that large numbers of students had some command of basic history facts, but their interpretative skills were relatively weak. Among 12th graders, 89 percent knew beginning historical information, but only 5 percent demonstrated an ability to interpret historical information. (Table 112)

- Results from a national assessment of mathematics achievement found that performance on basic skills improved between 1977–78 and 1985–86, but performance on more advanced operations remained the same or deteriorated. Between 1977–78 and 1985–86, the proportion of 13-year-olds who could perform basic operations rose from 65 percent to 73 percent. Similarly, the proportion of 17-year-olds who could perform basic operations rose from 92 percent to 96 percent. (Table 115)

- Student achievement in science rose between 1976–77 and 1985–86 for 9- and 13-year-olds, but showed no significant change for 17-year-olds. Between 1976–77 and 1985–86, the proportion of 9-year-olds who could understand simple scientific principles rose slightly, from 68 to 71 percent. The proportion of 13-year-olds who could apply scientific information rose from 49 percent to 53 percent. (Table 119)

- Between 1979–80 and 1989–90, mathematics SAT scores increased by 10 points, while verbal scores remained relatively stable. However, considerable difference existed among students from different racial/ethnic groups. Between 1979–80 and 1989–90, combined mathematics and verbal scores for white students rose by only 9 points compared with an increase of 47 points for black students and 33 points for Asian American students. (Tables 123 and 125)

- The average number of science and mathematics courses completed by high school graduates increased substantially between 1982 and 1987. The mean number of mathematics courses (Carnegie units) completed in high school rose from 2.5 in 1982 to 3.0 in 1987, and the number of science courses rose from 2.2 to 2.6. As a result of the increased course load, the proportion of students completing the recommendations of the National Commission on Excellence (4 units of English; 3 units of social studies; 3 units of science; 3 units of mathematics; and .5 units of computer science) rose from 2.7 percent in 1982 to 13.6 percent in 1987. (Tables 130 and 132)

- The average number of courses in vocational-technical areas completed by all high school graduates dropped slightly, from 4.0 units in 1982 to 3.6 units in 1987. The average number of vocational units completed by vocational and academic program students remained stable or increased slightly between 1982 and 1987. Thus, the increase in the number of academic credits taken by graduates between 1982 and 1987 did not result in a decrease in the number of vocational-technical credits completed. (Table 131)

- Eighth-grade students at Catholic and other private schools were more likely to say that they "get along well with teachers" than students at public schools. Students at private schools were also more likely to feel that "rules for behavior are strict" than students at public schools. (Table 136)

- The proportion of public and private high school seniors who reported ever using an illicit drug rose from 55 percent in 1975 to 66 percent in 1981. After 1981, the proportion of seniors who had ever used drugs fell, reaching 51 percent in 1989. Also, the proportion of high school seniors who have used cocaine fell from 17 percent in 1985 to 10 percent in 1989. Alcohol remains the most often used drug. The proportion of seniors using alcohol within the previous 30 days declined from 72 percent in 1980 to 60 percent in 1989. (Table 142)

- States are the most important funding source for public elementary and secondary schools. In 1988–89, 48 percent of all revenues came from State sources, 46 percent came from local sources, and 6 percent came from the Federal Government. (Table 152)

- The expenditure per student in public schools has risen significantly in recent years, even after allowing for inflation. In 1990–91, the average current expenditure per student in average daily attendance was $5,266. After adjustment for inflation, this represents an increase of 36 percent since 1980–81. (Table 158)

Figure 7.--Preprimary enrollment of 3- to 5-year-olds, by attendance status: October 1970 to October 1990

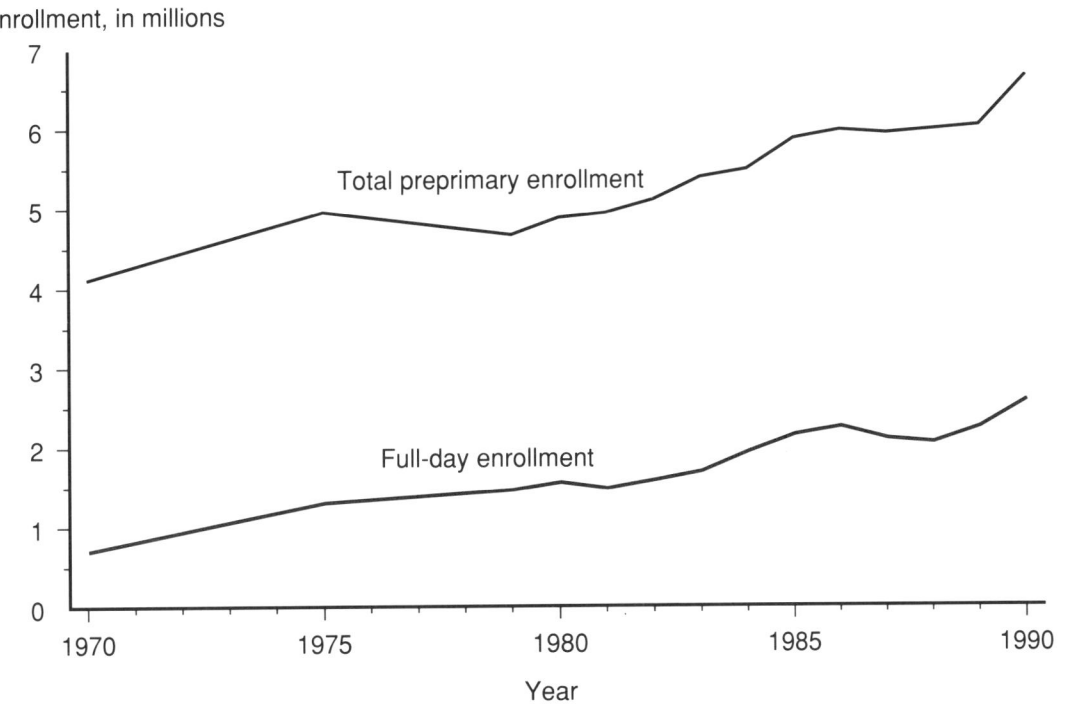

SOURCE: U.S. Department of Education, National Center for Education Statistics, *Preprimary Enrollment,* various years; and U.S. Department of Commerce, Bureau of the Census, Current Population Survey, unpublished data.

Figure 8.--Enrollment, number of teachers, pupil-teacher ratios, and expenditures in public schools: 1960-61 to 1990-91

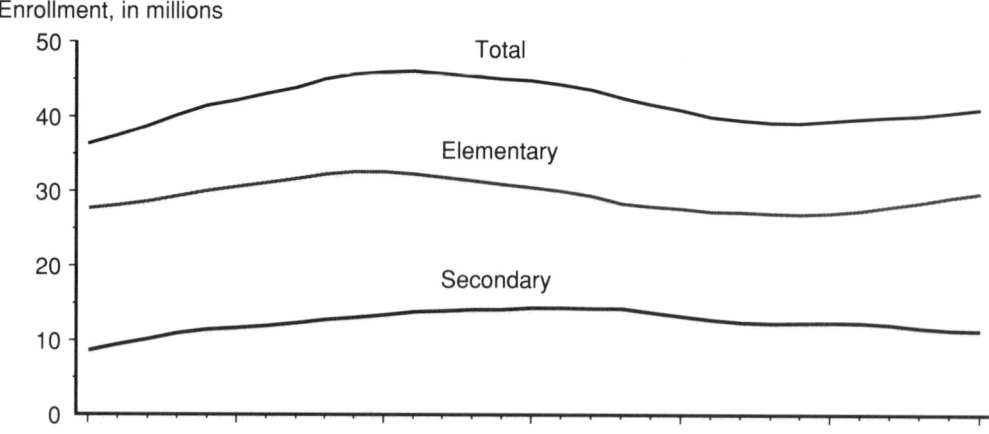

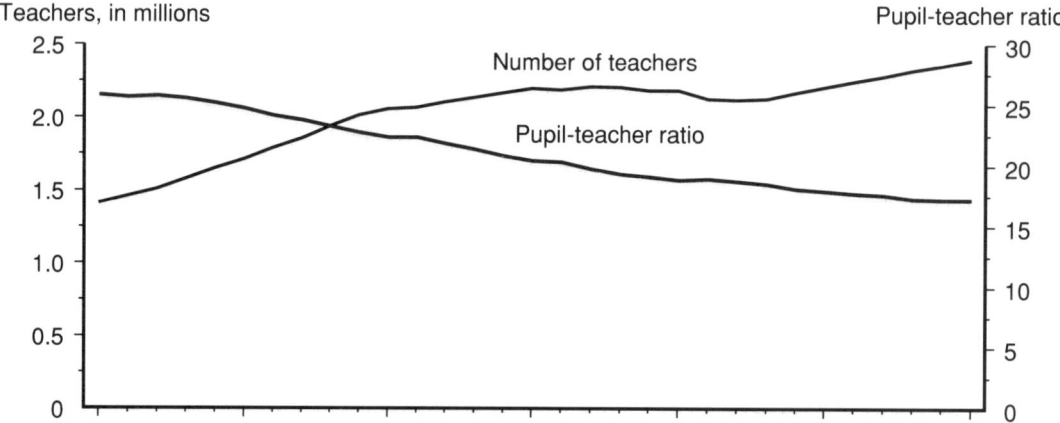

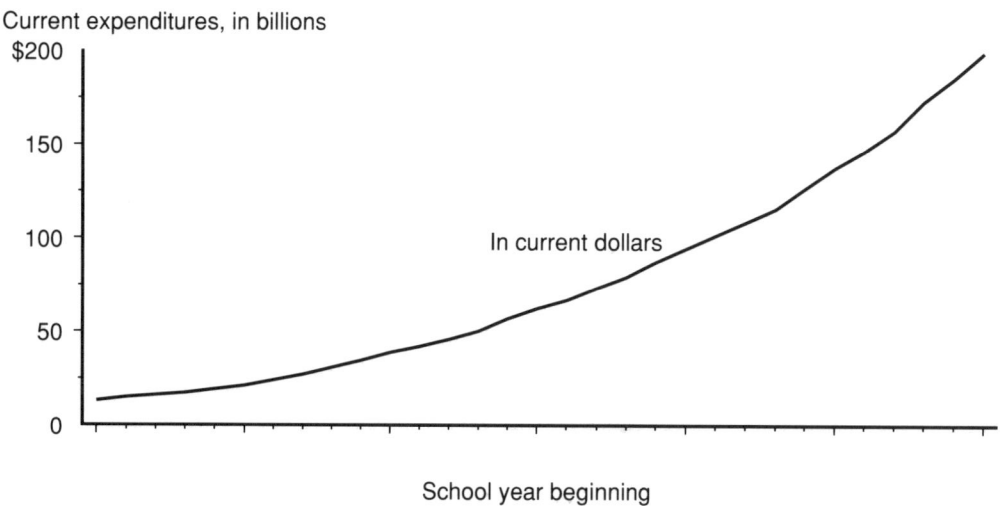

School year beginning

SOURCE: U.S. Department of Education, National Center for Education Statistics, *Statistics of State School Systems; Statistics of Public Elementary and Secondary School Systems; Revenues and Expenditures for Public Elementary and Secondary Education;* and Common Core of Data surveys.

Figure 9.--Percentage change in public elementary and secondary enrollment, by State: Fall 1985 to fall 1990

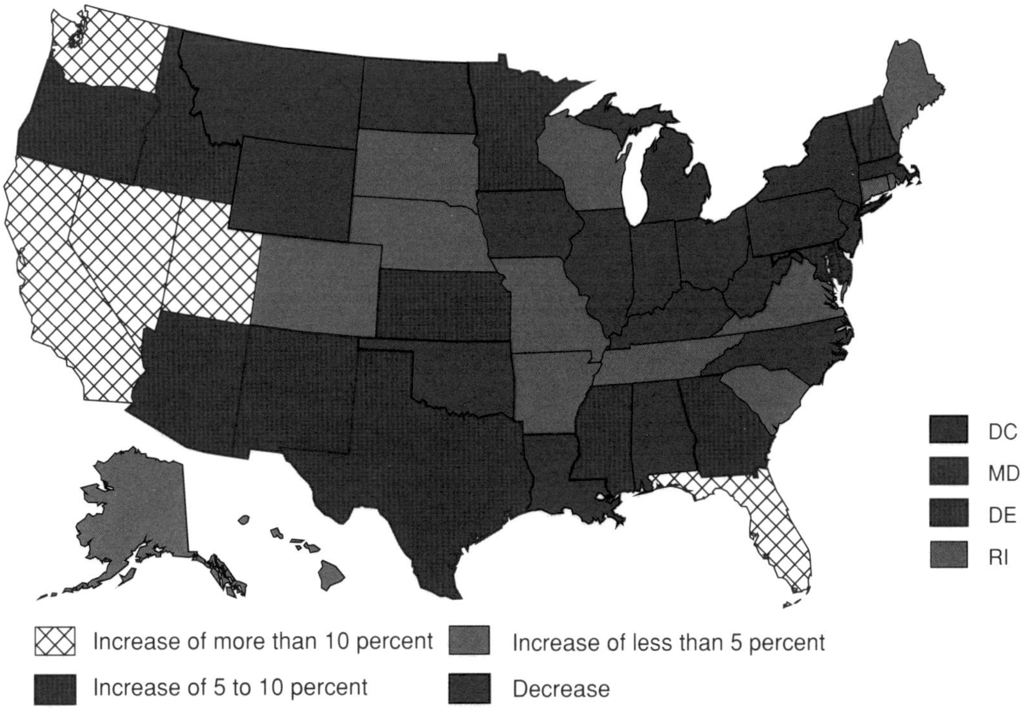

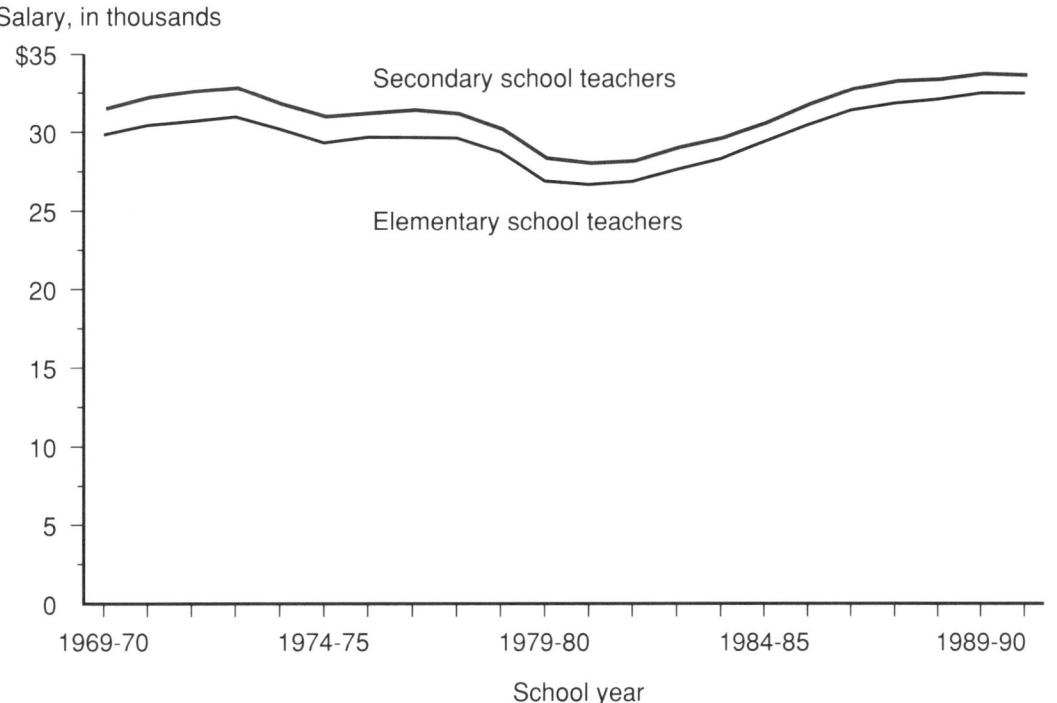

DC
MD
DE
RI
Increase of more than 10 percent
Increase of less than 5 percent
Increase of 5 to 10 percent
Decrease

SOURCE: U.S. Department of Education, National Center for Education Statistics, Common Core of Data surveys.

Figure 10.--Average annual salary for public elementary and secondary school teachers: 1969-70 to 1990-91 [In constant 1990-91 dollars]

Salary, in thousands
$35
30
25
20
15
10
5
0
Secondary school teachers
Elementary school teachers
1969-70
1974-75
1979-80
1984-85
1989-90
School year

SOURCE: National Education Association, *Estimates of School Statistics;* and unpublished data. (Latest edition 1990–91. Copyright © 1991 by the National Education Association. All rights reserved.)

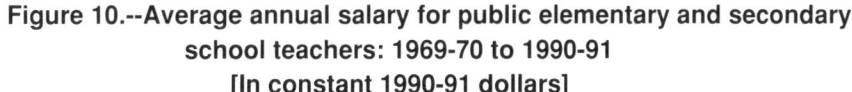

Figure 11.--Sources of revenue for public elementary and secondary schools: 1969-70 to 1988-89

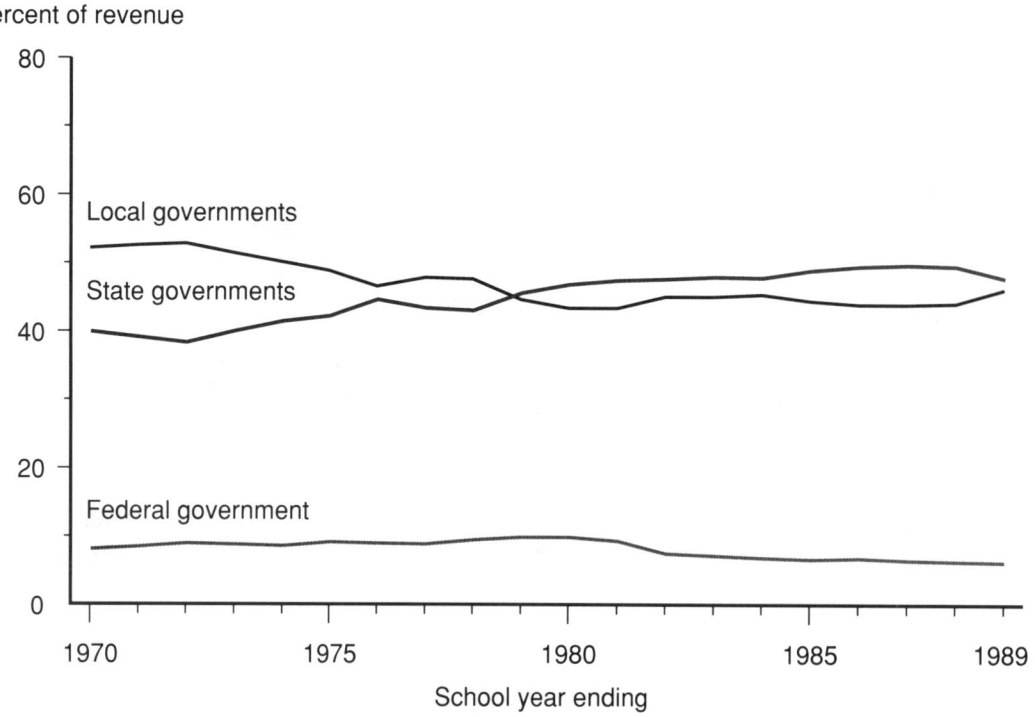

SOURCE: U.S. Department of Education, National Center for Education Statistics, *Statistics of State School Systems; Revenues and Expenditures for Public Elementary and Secondary Education;* and Common Core of Data surveys.

Figure 12.--Current-expenditure per student in average daily attendance in public elementary and secondary schools: 1969-70 to 1989-90

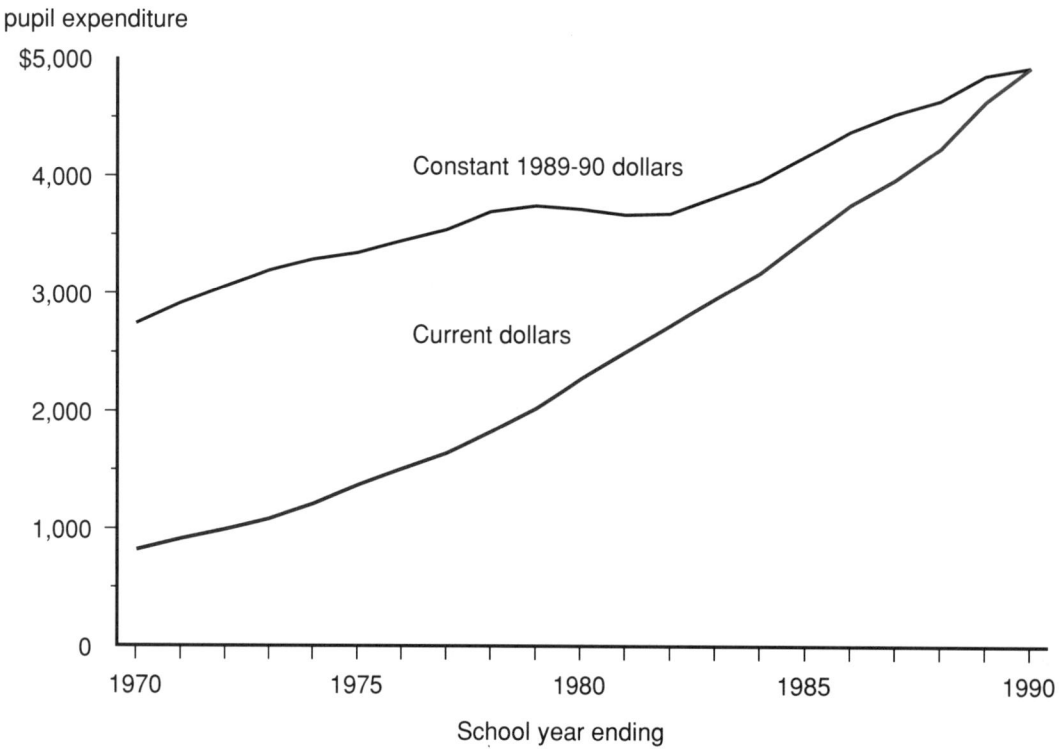

SOURCE: U.S. Department of Education, National Center for Education Statistics, *Statistics of State School Systems; Statistics of Public Elementary and Secondary School Systems; Revenues and Expenditures for Public Elementary and Secondary Education;* and Common Core of Data surveys.

Table 37.—Historical summary of public elementary and secondary school statistics: 1869-70 to 1988-89

Item	1869-70	1879-80	1889-90	1899-1900	1909-10	1919-20	1929-30	1939-40	1949-50	1959-60	1969-70	1979-80	1987-88	1988-89
1	2	3	4	5	6	7	8	9	10	11	12	13	14	15
Population, pupils, and instructional staff														
Total population,[1] in thousands	39,818	50,156	62,948	75,995	90,492	104,512	121,770	130,880	148,665	179,323	201,385	224,567	243,419	245,807
Population aged 5–17 years,[1] in thousands	12,055	15,066	18,543	21,573	24,009	27,556	31,417	30,150	30,168	43,881	52,386	48,041	45,291	45,388
Percent of total population 5–17	30.3	30.0	29.5	28.4	26.5	26.4	25.8	23.0	20.3	24.5	25.8	21.4	18.6	18.5
Total enrollment in elementary and secondary schools,[2] in thousands	6,872	9,867	12,723	15,503	17,814	21,578	25,678	25,434	25,112	36,087	45,619	41,645	40,008	40,189
Kindergarten and grades 1–8, in thousands	6,792	9,757	12,520	14,984	16,899	19,378	21,279	18,833	19,387	27,602	32,597	27,931	27,932	28,503
Grades 9–12, in thousands	[3]80	110	203	519	915	2,200	4,399	6,601	5,725	8,485	13,022	13,714	12,076	11,686
Enrollment as a percent of total population	17.3	19.7	20.2	20.4	19.7	20.6	21.1	19.4	16.9	20.1	22.4	18.5	16.4	16.3
Percent of population aged 5–17 enrolled	57.0	65.5	68.6	71.9	74.2	78.3	81.7	84.4	83.2	82.2	86.9	86.7	88.3	88.5
Percent of total enrollment in high schools (grades 9–12 and postgraduate)	1.2	1.1	1.6	3.3	5.1	10.2	17.1	26.0	22.7	23.5	28.5	32.9	30.2	29.1
High school graduates, in thousands	—	—	22	62	111	231	592	1,143	1,063	1,627	2,589	2,748	2,500	2,401
Average daily attendance, in thousands	4,077	6,144	8,154	10,633	12,827	16,150	21,265	22,042	22,284	32,477	41,934	38,289	37,051	37,282
Total number of days attended by pupils enrolled, in millions	539	801	1,098	1,535	2,011	2,615	3,673	3,858	3,964	5,782	7,501	[4]6,835	—	—
Percent of enrolled pupils attending daily	59.3	62.3	64.1	68.6	72.1	74.8	82.8	86.7	88.7	90.0	90.4	[4]90.1	—	—
Average length of school term, in days	132.2	130.3	134.7	144.3	157.5	161.9	172.7	175.0	177.9	178.0	178.9	[4]178.5	—	—
Average number of days attended per pupil	78.4	81.1	86.3	99.0	113	121.2	143	151.7	157.9	160.2	161.7	[4]160.8	—	—
Total instructional staff, in thousands	—	—	—	—	—	678	880	912	962	1,464	2,253	2,441	—	—
Supervisors, in thousands	—	—	—	—	—	7	7	5	9	14	32	[4]35	—	—
Principals, in thousands	—	—	—	—	—	14	31	32	39	64	91	106	—	—
Teachers, librarians, and other nonsupervisory instructional staff,[5] in thousands	201	287	364	423	523	657	843	875	914	1,387	2,131	2,300	2,398	2,447
Men, in thousands	78	123	126	127	110	93	140	195	195	[4]402	[4]691	[4]782	—	—
Women, in thousands	123	164	238	296	413	585	703	681	719	[4]985	[4]1,440	[4]1,518	—	—
Percent men	38.7	42.8	34.5	29.9	21.1	14.1	16.6	22.2	21.3	[4]29.0	[4]32.4	[4]34.0	—	—
Amounts in millions of current dollars														
Finance														
Total revenue receipts from	—	—	$143	$220	$433	$970	$2,089	$2,261	$5,437	$14,747	$40,267	$96,881	$169,562	$191,210
Federal Government	—	—	—	—	—	2	7	40	156	652	3,220	9,504	10,717	11,872
State governments	—	—	—	—	—	160	354	684	2,166	5,768	16,063	45,349	84,004	91,158
Local sources, including intermediate	—	—	—	—	—	808	1,728	1,536	3,116	8,327	20,985	42,029	74,841	88,180
Percent of revenue receipts from.														
Federal Government	—	—	—	—	—	0.3	0.4	1.8	2.9	4.4	8.0	9.8	6.3	6.2
State governments	—	—	—	—	—	16.5	16.9	30.3	39.8	39.1	39.9	46.8	49.5	47.7
Local sources, including intermediate	—	—	—	—	—	83.2	82.7	68.0	57.3	56.5	52.1	43.4	44.1	46.1
Total expenditures for public schools	$63	$78	$141	$215	$426	$1,036	$2,317	$2,344	$5,838	$15,613	$40,683	$95,962	[4]$172,400	[4]$189,800
Current expenditures	—	—	[6]114	[6]180	[6]356	861	1,844	1,942	4,687	12,329	34,218	86,984	[7]157,098	[7]172,932
Capital outlay	—	—	26	35	70	154	371	258	1,014	2,662	4,659	6,506	—	—
Interest on school debt	—	—	—	—	—	18	93	131	101	490	1,171	1,874	—	—
Other expenditures[8]	—	—	—	—	—	3	10	13	36	133	636	[9]598	—	—
Percent of total expenditures devoted to.														
Current expenditures	—	—	81.3	83.5	83.6	83.1	79.6	82.8	80.3	79.0	[7]84.1	[7]90.6	—	—
Capital outlay	—	—	18.7	16.5	16.4	14.8	16.0	11.0	17.4	17.0	11.5	6.8	—	—
Interest on school debt	—	—	—	—	—	1.8	4.0	5.6	1.7	3.1	2.9	2.0	—	—
Other expenditures[7]	—	—	—	—	—	0.3	0.4	0.6	0.6	0.8	1.6	[8]0.6	—	—
Amounts in current dollars														
Annual salary of instructional staff[10]	$189	$195	$252	$325	$485	$871	$1,420	$1,441	$3,010	$5,174	$8,840	[11]$16,715	[11]$29,235	[11]$30,969
Personal income per member of labor force[1]	—	—	—	—	—	—	$1,634	1,356	3,400	5,413	8,750	19,087	30,973	32,995

Table 37.—Historical summary of public elementary and secondary school statistics: 1869–70 to 1988–89—Continued

Item	1869–70	1879–80	1889–90	1899–1900	1909–10	1919–20	1929–30	1939–40	1949–50	1959–60	1969–70	1979–80	1987–88	1988–89
1	2	3	4	5	6	7	8	9	10	11	12	13	14	15
Total school expenditures per capita of total population	1.59	1.56	2.23	2.83	4.71	9.91	19.03	17.91	39	87	202	427	[4]708	[4]772
National income[1] per capita	—	—	—	—	—	—	667	587	1,520	2,272	3,829	9,117	15,037	16,211
Current expenditure[12] per pupil in ADA[13]	15.55	12.71	[6]13.99	[6]16.67	[6]27.85	53.32	86.70	88.09	209	375	816	2,272	4,240	4,639
Total expenditure[14] per pupil in ADA	—	—	17.23	20.21	33.23	64.16	108.49	105.74	159	472	955	2,506	[4]4,653	[4]5,091
National income per pupil in ADA	—	—	—	—	—	—	3,845	3,502	10,312	12,547	18,656	53,470	98,792	106,886
Current expenditure per day[15] per pupil in ADA	0.12	0.10	[6]0.10	[6]0.12	[6]0.18	0.33	0.50	0.50	1.17	2.11	4.56	12.73	—	—
Total expenditure per day per pupil in ADA	—	—	0.13	0.14	0.21	0.40	0.63	0.60	1.46	2.65	5.34	13.95	—	—

Amounts in constant 1988–89 dollars

Item	1869–70	1879–80	1889–90	1899–1900	1909–10	1919–20	1929–30	1939–40	1949–50	1959–60	1969–70	1979–80	1987–88	1988–89
Annual salary of instructional staff[10]	—	—	—	—	—	$5,539	$10,054	$12,496	$15,403	$21,340	$28,361	[11]$26,094	[11]$30,585	[11]$30,969
Personal income per member of labor force[1]	—	—	—	—	—	—	11,569	11,759	17,399	22,326	28,072	29,797	32,404	32,995
Total school expenditures per capita of total population	—	—	—	—	—	63	135	155	201	359	648	667	[4]741	[4]772
National income[1] per capita	—	—	—	—	—	—	4,723	5,090	7,778	9,371	12,284	14,232	15,731	16,211
Current expenditure[12] per pupil in ADA[13]	—	—	—	—	—	339	614	764	1,069	1,547	2,618	3,546	4,436	4,639
Total expenditure[14] per pupil in ADA	—	—	—	—	—	408	768	917	813	1,947	3,064	3,912	[4]4,868	[4]5,091
National income per pupil in ADA	—	—	—	—	—	—	27,223	30,370	52,769	51,751	59,853	83,471	103,354	106,886
Current expenditure per day[15] per pupil in ADA	—	—	—	—	—	2.10	3.54	4.34	5.99	8.70	14.63	19.87	—	—
Total expenditure per day per pupil in ADA	—	—	—	—	—	2.54	4.46	5.20	7.47	10.93	17.13	21.78	—	—

[1] Data on population and labor force are from the Bureau of the Census, and data on personal income and national income are from the Bureau of Economic Analysis, U.S. Department of Commerce. Population data through 1959–60 are based on total population from the decennial census. Beginning in 1969–70, population data are resident population, excluding armed forces overseas, as of July 1.

[2] Data for 1869–70 through 1959–60 are school year enrollment. Data for later years are fall enrollment.

[3] Data for 1870–71.

[4] Estimated by the National Center for Education Statistics.

[5] Prior to 1919–20, data are for the number of different persons employed rather than number of positions.

[6] Includes interest on school debt.

[7] Because of the modification of the scope of "current expenditures for elementary and secondary schools," data for 1959–60 and later years are not entirely comparable with prior years.

[8] Includes summer schools, community colleges, and adult education. Beginning in 1959-60, also includes community services, formerly classified with "current expenditures for elementary and secondary schools."

[9] Excludes community colleges and adult education.

[10] Average includes supervisors, principals, teachers, and other nonsupervisory instructional staff.

[11] Estimated by the National Education Association.

[12] Excludes current expenditures not allocable to pupil costs.

[13] "A.D.A." means average daily attendance in elementary and secondary schools.

[14] The expenditure figure used here is the sum of current expenditures allocable to pupil costs, capital outlay, and interest on school debt.

[15] Per-day rates derived by dividing annual rates by average length of term.

— Data not reported.

NOTE.—Kindergarten enrollment includes a relatively small number of nursery school pupils. Because of rounding, details may not add to totals. Some data have been revised from previously published figures.

SOURCE: U.S. Department of Education, National Center for Education Statistics, Statistics of State School Systems; Statistics of Public Elementary and Secondary School Systems; Revenues and Expenditures for Public Elementary and Secondary Education, FY 1980; Common Core of Data survey; and Council of Economic Advisers, Economic Indicators. (This table was prepared February 1991.)

Table 38.—Enrollment in public elementary and secondary schools, by grade: Fall 1975 to fall 1989

Grade	Fall 1975	Fall 1976	Fall 1977	Fall 1978	Fall 1979	Fall 1980	Fall 1981	Fall 1982	Fall 1983	Fall 1984	Fall 1985	Fall 1986	Fall 1987	Fall 1988	Fall 1989
1	2	3	4	5	6	7	8	9	10	11	12	13	14	15	16

Numbers in thousands

All grades	44,791	44,317	43,577	42,550	41,645	40,918	40,022	39,566	39,252	39,208	39,422	39,753	40,008	40,189	40,526
Elementary	30,487	30,006	29,336	28,425	27,931	27,677	27,270	27,158	26,979	26,901	27,030	27,421	27,932	28,503	29,158
Kindergarten [1]	2,945	2,919	2,742	2,652	2,675	2,689	2,687	2,845	2,859	3,010	3,192	3,310	3,387	3,433	3,489
lst grade	3,236	3,330	3,295	3,062	2,938	2,894	2,951	2,937	3,080	3,113	3,239	3,358	3,407	3,460	3,485
2nd grade	3,027	3,084	3,199	3,148	2,896	2,800	2,782	2,790	2,781	2,904	2,941	3,054	3,173	3,223	3,289
3rd grade	3,038	2,986	3,060	3,158	3,096	2,908	2,806	2,763	2,772	2,765	2,895	2,933	3,046	3,167	3,235
4th grade	3,112	3,024	2,979	3,046	3,130	3,115	2,918	2,798	2,758	2,772	2,771	2,896	2,938	3,051	3,182
5th grade	3,281	3,115	3,019	2,980	3,055	3,130	3,127	2,912	2,798	2,761	2,776	2,775	2,901	2,945	3,067
6th grade	3,476	3,297	3,111	3,036	2,999	3,038	3,180	3,142	2,928	2,831	2,789	2,806	2,811	2,937	2,987
7th grade	3,619	3,576	3,384	3,228	3,128	3,087	3,183	3,288	3,247	3,036	2,938	2,899	2,910	2,905	3,027
8th grade	3,636	3,581	3,533	3,355	3,168	3,091	3,059	3,123	3,222	3,186	2,982	2,870	2,839	2,853	2,853
Elementary ungraded	567	534	524	760	848	924	576	560	533	524	507	520	520	529	543
Elementary special education	548	561	490	(2)	(2)	(2)	(2)	(2)	(2)	(2)	(2)	(2)	(2)	(2)	(2)
Secondary	14,304	14,310	14,240	14,125	13,714	13,242	12,752	12,407	12,274	12,308	12,392	12,333	12,076	11,686	11,369
9th grade	3,879	3,823	3,779	3,726	3,516	3,380	3,286	3,248	3,330	3,440	3,439	3,256	3,143	3,106	3,124
10th grade	3,723	3,737	3,686	3,610	3,527	3,375	3,218	3,137	3,103	3,145	3,230	3,215	3,020	2,895	2,867
11th grade	3,354	3,373	3,388	3,312	3,241	3,195	3,039	2,917	2,861	2,819	2,866	2,954	2,936	2,749	2,629
12th grade	2,986	3,015	3,026	3,023	2,969	2,925	2,907	2,787	2,678	2,599	2,550	2,601	2,681	2,650	2,473
Postgraduate	23	23	13	(3)	(3)	(3)	(3)	(3)	(3)	(3)	(3)	(3)	(3)	(3)	(3)
Secondary ungraded	63	84	145	454	462	366	302	318	302	304	307	307	296	287	276
Secondary special education	276	254	203	(3)	(3)	(3)	(3)	(3)	(3)	(3)	(3)	(3)	(3)	(3)	(3)

Percent

All grades	100.0	100.0	100.0	100.0	100.0	100.0	100.0	100.0	100.0	100.0	100.0	100.0	100.0	100.0	100.0
Elementary	68.1	67.7	67.3	66.8	67.1	67.6	68.1	68.6	68.7	68.6	68.6	69.0	69.8	70.9	71.9
Kindergarten [1]	6.6	6.6	6.3	6.2	6.4	6.6	6.7	7.2	7.3	7.7	8.1	8.3	8.5	8.5	8.6
lst grade	7.2	7.5	7.6	7.2	7.1	7.1	7.4	7.4	7.8	7.9	8.2	8.4	8.5	8.6	8.6
2nd grade	6.8	7.0	7.3	7.4	7.0	6.8	7.0	7.1	7.1	7.4	7.5	7.7	7.9	8.0	8.1
3rd grade	6.8	6.7	7.0	7.4	7.4	7.1	7.0	7.0	7.1	7.1	7.3	7.4	7.6	7.9	8.0
4th grade	6.9	6.8	6.8	7.2	7.5	7.6	7.3	7.1	7.0	7.1	7.0	7.3	7.3	7.6	7.9
5th grade	7.3	7.0	6.9	7.0	7.3	7.6	7.8	7.4	7.1	7.0	7.0	7.0	7.2	7.3	7.6
6th grade	7.8	7.4	7.1	7.1	7.2	7.4	7.9	7.9	7.5	7.2	7.1	7.1	7.0	7.3	7.4
7th grade	8.1	8.1	7.8	7.6	7.5	7.5	8.0	8.3	8.3	7.7	7.5	7.3	7.3	7.2	7.5
8th grade	8.1	8.1	8.1	7.9	7.6	7.6	7.6	7.9	8.2	8.1	7.6	7.2	7.1	7.1	7.0
Elementary ungraded	1.3	1.2	1.2	1.8	2.0	2.3	1.4	1.4	1.4	1.3	1.3	1.3	1.3	1.3	1.3
Elementary special education	1.2	1.3	1.1	(2)	(2)	(2)	(2)	(2)	(2)	(2)	(2)	(2)	(2)	(2)	(2)
Secondary	31.9	32.3	32.6	33.2	32.9	32.4	31.9	31.4	31.3	31.4	31.4	31.0	30.2	29.1	28.1
9th grade	8.7	8.6	8.7	8.8	8.4	8.3	8.2	8.2	8.5	8.8	8.7	8.2	7.9	7.7	7.7
10th grade	8.3	8.4	8.5	8.5	8.5	8.2	8.0	7.9	7.9	8.0	8.2	8.1	7.5	7.2	7.1
11th grade	7.5	7.6	7.8	7.8	7.8	7.8	7.6	7.4	7.3	7.2	7.3	7.4	7.3	6.8	6.5
12th grade	6.7	6.8	6.9	7.1	7.1	7.1	7.3	7.0	6.8	6.6	6.5	6.5	6.7	6.6	6.1
Postgraduate	0.1	0.1	(4)	(3)	(3)	(3)	(3)	(3)	(3)	(3)	(3)	(3)	(3)	(3)	(3)
Secondary ungraded	0.1	0.2	0.3	1.1	1.1	0.9	0.8	0.8	0.8	0.8	0.8	0.8	0.7	0.7	0.7
Secondary special education	0.6	0.6	0.5	(3)	(3)	(3)	(3)	(3)	(3)	(3)	(3)	(3)	(3)	(3)	(3)

[1] Includes a relatively small number of prekindergarten pupils.
[2] Included in "elementary ungraded."
[3] Included in "secondary ungraded."
[4] Less than 0.05 percent.

NOTE.—Some data have been revised from previously published figures. Because of rounding, details may not add to totals.

SOURCE: U.S. Department of Education, National Center for Education Statistics, *Statistics of Public Elementary and Secondary School Systems;* and Common Core of Data survey. (This table was prepared October 1990.)

Table 39.—Enrollment in public elementary and secondary schools, by level and State: Fall 1980 to fall 1990

State or other area	Fall 1980 Total	Fall 1981 Total	Fall 1982 Total	Fall 1983 Total	Fall 1984 Total	Fall 1985 Total	Fall 1986 Total	Kindergarten through grade 8[2]	Grades 9 to 12
1	2	3	4	5	6	7	8	9	10
United States	40,918,362	40,021,850	39,565,610	39,252,308	39,208,252	39,422,051	39,753,172	27,420,507	12,332,665
Alabama	758,721	743,448	724,037	721,901	712,586	730,460	733,735	518,982	214,753
Alaska[4]	86,514	90,858	89,413	98,206	104,599	107,345	107,848	77,906	29,942
Arizona	513,790	507,199	510,296	506,682	530,062	548,252	534,538	371,419	163,119
Arkansas	447,700	437,121	432,565	432,120	432,668	433,410	437,438	306,851	130,587
California	4,118,022	4,046,156	4,065,486	4,089,017	4,151,110	4,255,554	4,377,989	3,045,684	1,332,305
Colorado	546,033	544,174	545,209	542,196	545,427	550,642	558,415	386,304	172,111
Connecticut[6]	531,459	505,386	486,470	477,585	468,145	462,026	468,847	321,823	147,024
Delaware	99,403	95,072	92,646	91,406	91,767	92,901	94,410	64,807	29,603
District of Columbia	100,049	94,975	91,105	88,843	87,397	87,092	85,612	62,456	23,156
Florida	1,510,225	1,487,721	1,484,734	1,495,543	1,524,107	1,562,283	1,607,320	1,120,938	486,382
Georgia	1,068,737	1,056,117	1,053,689	1,050,859	1,062,315	1,079,594	1,096,425	777,991	318,434
Hawaii	165,068	162,805	162,024	162,241	163,860	164,169	164,640	115,076	49,564
Idaho	203,247	204,524	202,973	206,352	208,080	208,669	208,391	149,613	58,778
Illinois	1,983,463	1,924,084	1,880,289	1,853,316	1,834,355	1,826,478	1,825,185	1,249,340	575,845
Indiana	1,055,589	1,025,172	999,542	984,384	972,659	966,106	966,780	653,613	313,167
Iowa	533,857	516,216	504,983	497,287	491,011	485,332	481,286	323,536	157,750
Kansas	415,291	409,909	407,074	405,222	405,347	410,229	416,091	291,564	124,527
Kentucky	669,798	658,350	651,084	647,414	644,421	643,833	642,778	446,901	195,877
Louisiana	777,560	782,053	784,027	800,193	800,941	788,349	795,188	580,771	214,417
Maine	222,497	216,293	211,986	209,753	207,537	206,101	211,752	143,671	68,081
Maryland	750,665	721,841	699,201	683,491	673,840	671,560	675,747	456,045	219,702
Massachusetts	1,021,885	947,037	908,984	878,844	859,391	844,330	833,918	559,418	274,500
Michigan	1,797,052	1,724,787	1,674,697	1,635,963	1,609,448	1,602,747	1,597,154	1,089,757	507,397
Minnesota	754,318	733,741	715,190	705,236	701,697	705,140	711,134	479,130	232,004
Mississippi	477,059	471,615	468,294	467,744	466,058	471,195	498,639	356,052	142,587
Missouri	844,648	818,705	802,535	795,453	793,793	795,107	800,606	549,348	251,258
Montana	155,193	153,435	152,335	153,646	154,412	153,869	153,327	107,572	45,755
Nebraska	280,430	273,340	269,009	266,998	265,599	265,819	267,139	185,282	81,857
Nevada	149,481	151,339	151,104	150,442	151,633	154,948	161,239	112,164	49,075
New Hampshire	167,232	163,827	160,197	159,030	158,614	160,974	163,717	109,948	53,769
New Jersey	1,246,008	1,199,643	1,172,520	1,147,841	1,129,223	1,116,194	1,107,467	742,324	365,143
New Mexico	271,198	268,091	268,632	269,711	272,478	277,551	281,943	191,037	90,906
New York	2,871,004	2,760,774	2,718,678	2,674,818	2,645,811	2,621,378	2,607,719	1,713,465	894,254
North Carolina	1,129,376	1,108,960	1,096,815	1,089,606	1,088,724	1,086,165	1,085,248	748,451	336,797
North Dakota	116,885	117,708	117,078	117,213	118,711	118,570	118,703	83,930	34,773
Ohio	1,957,381	1,898,501	1,860,245	1,827,300	1,805,440	1,793,965	1,793,508	1,208,110	585,398
Oklahoma	577,807	582,572	593,825	591,389	589,690	592,327	593,183	417,287	175,896
Oregon	464,599	457,165	448,184	447,109	446,884	447,527	449,307	308,527	140,780
Pennsylvania	1,909,292	1,839,015	1,783,969	1,737,952	1,701,880	1,683,221	1,674,161	1,098,115	576,046
Rhode Island	148,956	143,414	139,959	136,412	134,610	133,949	134,690	91,964	42,726
South Carolina	619,223	609,158	608,518	604,553	602,718	606,643	611,629	427,751	183,878
South Dakota	128,507	125,657	123,897	123,060	123,314	124,291	125,458	89,373	36,085
Tennessee	853,569	838,297	828,264	822,057	817,212	813,753	818,073	577,045	241,028
Texas	2,900,073	2,935,547	2,985,659	2,989,796	3,040,305	3,131,705	3,209,515	2,317,454	892,061
Utah	343,618	355,554	370,183	378,208	390,141	403,395	415,994	308,389	107,605
Vermont	95,815	93,183	91,454	90,416	90,089	90,157	92,112	63,392	28,720
Virginia	1,010,371	989,548	975,727	966,110	965,222	968,104	975,135	673,237	301,898
Washington	757,639	750,188	739,215	736,239	741,177	749,706	761,428	521,333	240,095
West Virginia	383,503	377,772	375,115	371,251	362,941	357,923	351,837	243,538	108,299
Wisconsin	830,247	804,262	784,830	774,646	767,542	768,234	767,819	509,584	258,235
Wyoming	98,305	99,541	101,665	99,254	101,261	102,779	100,955	72,239	28,716
Outlying areas									
American Samoa	9,647	9,896	—	10,124	—	—	11,055	8,133	2,922
Guam	26,420	25,084	25,676	26,249	—	26,043	25,676	18,522	7,154
Northern Marianas	—	5,300	—	4,499	4,841	—	—	—	—
Puerto Rico	712,880	721,419	708,794	701,925	692,923	686,914	679,489	503,012	176,477
Trust Territory of the Pacific	—	—	—	39,623	—	—	—	—	—
Virgin Islands	25,201	25,525	25,699	26,126	26,122	25,448	24,435	17,778	6,657

Table 39.—Enrollment in public elementary and secondary schools, by level and State: Fall 1980 to fall 1990—Continued

State or other areas	Fall 1987			Fall 1988			Fall 1989			Estimated fall 1990 [1]
	Total	Kindergarten through grade 8 [2]	Grades 9 to 12	Total	Kindergarten through grade 8 [2]	Grades 9 to 12	Total	Kindergarten through grade 8 [2]	Grades 9 to 12	Total
1	11	12	13	14	15	16	17	18	19	20
United States	40,007,946	27,931,938	12,076,008	40,188,690	28,502,779	11,685,911	40,526,372	29,157,562	11,368,810	41,026,499
Alabama	729,234	521,004	208,230	724,751	521,650	203,101	723,343	525,730	197,613	[3]727,815
Alaska [4]	105,678	76,694	28,984	106,481	78,518	27,963	109,280	81,698	27,582	[5]112,153
Arizona	572,421	412,501	159,920	574,890	417,579	157,311	607,615	451,311	156,304	589,504
Arkansas	437,036	307,248	129,788	436,387	309,268	127,119	434,960	311,060	123,900	[3]434,960
California	4,489,322	3,172,094	1,317,228	4,618,120	3,317,194	1,300,926	4,771,978	3,470,574	1,301,404	4,963,383
Colorado	560,236	391,986	168,250	560,081	399,853	160,228	562,755	407,525	155,230	[3]568,673
Connecticut [6]	465,465	326,250	139,215	460,637	331,697	128,940	461,560	338,378	123,182	[3]468,900
Delaware	95,659	66,714	28,945	96,678	68,886	27,792	97,808	70,699	27,109	[3]99,658
District of Columbia	86,435	62,857	23,578	84,792	62,334	22,458	81,301	60,662	20,639	80,500
Florida	1,664,774	1,171,809	492,965	1,720,930	1,232,007	488,923	1,772,349	1,303,439	468,910	[3]1,861,538
Georgia	1,110,947	795,032	315,915	1,107,994	807,864	300,130	1,126,535	828,426	298,109	[3]1,151,687
Hawaii	166,160	117,514	48,646	167,488	120,385	47,103	169,493	123,496	45,997	[3]171,056
Idaho	212,444	153,356	59,088	214,615	155,505	59,110	214,932	156,602	58,330	[3]220,840
Illinois	1,811,446	1,251,790	559,656	1,794,916	1,259,124	535,792	1,797,355	1,280,021	517,334	1,803,000
Indiana	964,129	658,656	305,473	960,994	667,647	293,347	954,165	671,036	283,129	956,487
Iowa	480,826	328,436	152,390	478,200	333,988	144,212	478,486	338,422	140,064	[3]484,116
Kansas	421,112	298,516	122,596	426,596	306,751	119,845	430,864	313,588	117,276	436,250
Kentucky	642,696	449,033	193,663	637,627	451,805	185,822	630,688	451,858	178,830	[3]630,091
Louisiana	793,093	582,742	210,351	786,683	581,095	205,588	783,025	581,702	201,323	[3]779,161
Maine	211,817	145,499	66,318	212,902	148,904	63,998	213,775	152,267	61,508	[3]215,516
Maryland	683,797	472,909	210,888	688,947	489,115	199,832	698,806	507,007	191,799	[3]715,152
Massachusetts	825,320	565,042	260,278	823,428	577,795	245,633	825,588	590,238	235,350	829,119
Michigan	1,589,287	1,097,004	492,283	1,582,785	1,113,595	469,190	1,576,785	1,127,921	448,864	1,577,000
Minnesota	721,481	496,553	224,928	726,950	511,279	215,671	739,553	528,507	211,046	751,913
Mississippi	505,550	364,129	141,421	503,326	367,593	135,733	502,020	369,513	132,507	[3]500,122
Missouri	802,060	557,073	244,987	806,639	567,860	238,779	807,934	576,243	231,691	810,450
Montana	152,207	108,017	44,190	152,191	109,526	42,665	151,265	109,791	41,474	151,670
Nebraska	268,100	188,166	79,934	269,434	191,302	78,132	270,920	194,227	76,693	[3]274,141
Nevada	168,353	119,077	49,276	176,474	127,414	49,060	186,834	137,455	49,379	196,736
New Hampshire	166,045	114,098	51,947	169,413	119,785	49,628	171,696	124,410	47,286	[3]170,642
New Jersey	1,092,982	747,402	345,580	1,080,871	755,073	325,798	1,076,005	765,810	310,195	1,082,561
New Mexico	287,229	195,413	91,816	292,425	200,129	92,296	296,057	203,157	92,900	[5]299,734
New York	2,594,070	1,735,527	858,543	2,573,715	1,760,596	813,119	2,565,841	1,790,143	775,698	2,563,000
North Carolina	1,085,976	753,595	332,381	1,083,156	761,069	322,087	1,080,744	769,825	310,919	[3]1,082,558
North Dakota	119,004	84,379	34,625	118,809	85,182	33,627	117,816	84,920	32,896	[3]117,134
Ohio	1,793,431	1,219,978	573,453	1,778,544	1,229,384	549,160	1,767,159	1,242,327	524,832	[3]1,770,000
Oklahoma	584,212	410,995	173,217	580,426	413,656	166,770	578,580	420,940	157,640	[3]578,600
Oregon	455,895	317,920	137,975	461,752	328,226	133,526	472,394	340,264	132,130	[3]484,950
Pennsylvania	1,668,542	1,111,171	557,371	1,659,714	1,132,631	527,083	1,655,279	1,150,653	504,626	1,667,630
Rhode Island	134,800	93,623	41,177	133,585	95,285	38,300	135,729	98,412	37,317	[3]137,946
South Carolina	614,921	431,585	183,336	615,774	437,826	177,948	616,177	443,712	172,465	[3]621,776
South Dakota	126,817	91,362	35,455	126,910	92,556	34,354	127,329	93,596	33,733	[3]129,164
Tennessee	823,783	582,432	241,351	821,580	585,972	235,608	819,660	590,121	229,539	822,200
Texas	3,236,787	2,350,856	885,931	3,283,707	2,392,079	891,628	3,328,514	2,443,245	885,269	3,353,270
Utah	423,386	313,953	109,433	431,119	319,423	111,696	437,446	322,889	114,557	[3]444,732
Vermont	92,755	65,012	27,743	93,381	66,761	26,620	94,779	69,103	25,676	[5]96,198
Virginia	979,417	685,172	294,245	982,393	699,064	283,329	985,346	712,297	273,049	[3]998,463
Washington	775,755	540,936	234,819	790,918	563,100	227,818	810,232	585,818	224,414	[3]832,218
West Virginia	344,236	236,926	107,310	335,912	231,819	104,093	327,540	227,251	100,289	[3]323,021
Wisconsin	772,363	521,533	250,830	774,857	535,215	239,642	782,905	549,143	233,762	790,901
Wyoming	98,455	70,369	28,086	97,793	70,415	27,378	97,172	70,130	27,042	[3]98,210
Outlying areas										
American Samoa	11,248	8,313	2,935	11,764	8,911	2,853	12,258	9,309	2,949	[3]12,443
Guam	25,936	18,713	7,223	26,041	18,659	7,382	26,493	19,291	7,202	[3]25,941
Northern Marianas	5,819	4,424	1,395	6,079	4,699	1,380	6,101	4,626	1,475	[5]6,123
Puerto Rico	672,837	498,853	173,984	661,693	491,836	169,857	651,225	486,247	164,978	[3]644,958
Trust Territory of the Pacific	—	—	—	—	—	—	—	—	—	—
Virgin Islands	24,020	17,131	6,889	23,492	17,102	6,390	21,193	15,769	5,424	[3]21,675

[1] Data estimated by State education agencies.
[2] Includes a relatively small number of prekindergarten students.
[3] Actual data.
[4] Beginning in 1983, data include students enrolled in public schools on Federal bases and other special arrangements.
[5] Data estimated by NCES.
[6] Beginning in 1986, data include State vocational/technical schools.

—Data not available.

NOTE.—Some data have been revised from previously published figures.

SOURCE: U.S. Department of Education, National Center for Education Statistics, Common Core of Data survey. (This table was prepared January 1991.)

Table 40.—Enrollment in public elementary and secondary schools, by grade and State: Fall 1989

State or other area	Total, all levels	Prekindergarten through grade 8 and elementary unclassified							
		Total	Prekinder-garten[1]	Kindergarten	Grade 1	Grade 2	Grade 3	Grade 4	Grade 5
1	2	3	4	5	6	7	8	9	10
United States .	40,526,372	29,155,726	264,202	3,224,642	3,484,783	3,289,073	3,234,957	3,182,079	3,066,580
Alabama	723,343	525,730	—	55,478	60,669	57,909	61,085	59,944	57,958
Alaska	109,280	81,698	1,782	9,652	9,893	9,663	9,452	9,010	8,492
Arizona	607,615	451,311	877	49,164	58,644	53,747	51,604	50,508	48,580
Arkansas	434,960	311,060	—	33,543	36,333	34,696	34,540	34,651	33,829
California	4,771,978	3,470,574	—	410,631	423,689	405,057	393,011	379,538	358,578
Colorado	562,755	407,525	3,366	45,412	49,893	48,242	46,839	45,339	43,471
Connecticut	461,560	338,378	4,694	39,264	41,565	37,816	36,545	35,148	34,051
Delaware	97,808	70,699	294	7,814	9,060	8,243	8,242	7,864	7,633
District of Columbia	81,301	60,662	3,645	6,339	7,415	6,754	6,447	5,924	5,691
Florida	1,772,349	1,303,439	14,396	158,907	161,357	151,198	146,938	142,174	137,171
Georgia	1,126,535	828,426	—	95,460	98,413	94,417	97,997	94,825	90,012
Hawaii	169,493	121,660	300	14,147	14,544	14,180	13,661	13,245	12,501
Idaho	214,932	156,602	361	16,259	17,947	17,822	17,498	17,707	17,560
Illinois	1,797,355	1,280,021	29,321	135,793	138,418	135,127	135,780	139,530	133,600
Indiana	954,165	671,036	805	68,409	80,902	75,337	74,526	74,671	72,159
Iowa	478,486	338,422	3,417	38,136	38,181	37,088	37,690	37,298	35,598
Kansas	430,864	313,588	1,398	35,734	37,616	35,331	35,218	34,184	32,405
Kentucky	630,688	451,858	—	46,569	52,447	49,535	49,515	50,256	49,157
Louisiana	783,025	581,702	6,659	64,337	67,802	62,923	62,447	61,886	60,097
Maine	213,775	152,267	1,925	18,798	17,988	16,958	16,523	15,906	15,890
Maryland	698,806	507,007	12,238	54,709	61,668	59,067	56,650	55,009	51,980
Massachusetts	825,588	590,238	6,819	70,464	71,595	66,972	64,588	62,561	60,514
Michigan	1,576,785	1,127,921	10,661	140,356	128,148	121,373	118,338	116,261	113,595
Minnesota	739,553	528,507	7,347	61,916	62,320	61,051	60,403	58,846	56,212
Mississippi	502,020	369,513	379	36,990	43,904	41,772	41,620	41,200	39,365
Missouri	807,934	576,243	—	64,627	68,509	63,596	63,849	64,933	63,099
Montana	151,265	109,791	293	12,183	13,052	12,478	12,334	12,136	11,626
Nebraska	270,920	194,227	1,917	22,834	22,514	22,292	22,379	21,927	20,796
Nevada	186,834	137,455	—	15,408	17,408	16,541	15,997	15,603	14,700
New Hampshire	171,696	124,410	738	7,338	18,800	15,209	14,629	13,826	13,232
New Jersey	1,076,005	765,810	6,531	80,391	88,564	82,757	80,226	79,060	78,222
New Mexico	296,057	203,157	—	23,239	26,005	24,386	23,631	22,829	21,494
New York	2,565,841	1,790,143	28,172	187,957	212,789	198,582	190,267	186,493	180,354
North Carolina	1,080,744	769,825	1,929	86,204	87,934	84,526	83,792	83,168	81,692
North Dakota	117,816	84,920	682	9,510	10,307	9,861	9,711	9,352	9,040
Ohio	1,767,159	1,242,327	3,627	138,256	147,415	141,213	140,862	140,436	136,167
Oklahoma	578,580	420,940	2,940	46,401	56,965	48,615	46,879	45,931	44,052
Oregon	472,394	340,264	1,254	35,715	40,492	39,201	37,717	37,106	37,581
Pennsylvania	1,655,279	1,150,653	2,445	122,594	139,634	128,349	126,009	122,701	119,499
Rhode Island	135,729	98,412	336	10,449	12,997	11,019	10,644	10,418	9,986
South Carolina	616,177	443,712	—	41,490	56,007	51,168	50,880	50,891	49,505
South Dakota	127,329	93,596	214	10,667	10,837	10,779	10,695	10,527	10,028
Tennessee	819,660	590,121	—	61,767	71,367	65,686	64,234	63,539	63,037
Texas	3,328,514	2,443,245	82,711	250,752	298,351	275,020	271,049	268,064	256,649
Utah	437,446	322,889	1,684	33,991	35,486	36,871	36,402	37,301	36,014
Vermont	94,779	69,103	480	8,282	8,999	8,002	7,777	7,429	7,276
Virginia	985,346	712,297	1,569	82,232	81,728	78,398	77,237	75,946	73,618
Washington	810,232	585,818	3,081	65,566	71,750	69,252	67,843	66,144	63,750
West Virginia	327,540	227,251	407	22,455	24,653	24,270	24,445	24,871	23,823
Wisconsin	782,905	549,143	12,508	62,188	63,187	60,588	60,460	59,837	57,355
Wyoming	97,172	70,130	—	7,865	8,622	8,136	7,852	8,126	7,886
Outlying areas									
American Samoa	12,258	9,309	1,509	926	944	911	828	870	797
Guam	26,493	19,291	363	2,279	2,380	2,310	2,176	2,079	2,082
Northern Marianas	6,101	4,626	—	566	565	505	505	511	453
Puerto Rico	651,225	486,247	734	31,975	57,371	54,809	55,539	56,970	56,849
Virgin Islands	21,193	15,769	—	1,580	1,729	1,765	1,696	1,685	1,613

Table 40.—Enrollment in public elementary and secondary schools, by grade and State: Fall 1989—Continued

State or other area	Prekindergarten through grade 8 and elementary unclassified				Grades 9 through 12 and secondary unclassified					
	Grade 6	Grade 7	Grade 8	Elementary unclassified	Total	Grade 9	Grade 10	Grade 11	Grade 12	Secondary unclassified
1	11	12	13	14	15	16	17	18	19	20
United States .	2,987,312	3,027,473	2,853,409	541,216	11,370,646	3,123,694	2,866,939	2,629,325	2,473,144	277,544
Alabama	57,601	60,174	54,912	—	197,613	58,333	49,468	46,330	43,482	—
Alaska	8,143	8,039	7,572	6,526	27,582	7,545	7,109	6,526	6,402	—
Arizona	45,190	45,518	42,172	5,307	156,304	44,106	40,525	35,670	35,618	385
Arkansas	32,814	34,609	33,353	2,692	123,900	32,731	31,965	29,597	28,505	1,102
California	347,629	349,524	330,967	71,950	1,301,404	367,444	349,715	309,689	243,023	31,533
Colorado	41,401	41,056	39,697	2,809	155,230	42,278	38,630	37,391	34,799	2,132
Connecticut	32,948	32,737	31,127	12,483	123,182	33,185	31,306	29,491	29,186	14
Delaware	7,178	7,437	6,934	—	27,109	7,827	7,121	5,847	6,314	—
District of Columbia ...	5,165	5,562	5,119	2,601	20,639	4,852	5,801	4,518	3,778	1,690
Florida	130,179	133,356	127,763	—	468,910	128,151	131,999	112,121	96,639	—
Georgia	87,713	87,085	82,504	—	298,109	93,559	76,412	68,693	59,445	—
Hawaii	11,909	11,429	11,177	6,403	47,833	11,819	10,808	10,748	9,453	3,169
Idaho	17,076	16,962	16,187	1,223	58,330	15,771	15,142	13,589	13,149	679
Illinois	128,048	129,195	122,583	52,626	517,334	132,786	126,084	114,754	110,514	33,196
Indiana	71,963	73,685	70,229	8,350	283,129	76,603	67,895	66,353	65,063	7,215
Iowa	34,654	34,743	33,143	8,474	140,064	35,041	32,489	31,472	33,795	7,267
Kansas	31,526	31,805	30,189	8,182	117,276	30,791	29,065	27,741	26,918	2,761
Kentucky	48,796	49,955	46,242	9,386	178,830	50,010	43,520	41,319	40,186	3,795
Louisiana	58,887	60,387	52,490	23,787	201,323	59,813	49,721	43,291	39,892	8,606
Maine	15,603	15,309	14,917	2,450	61,508	16,282	15,264	14,558	14,552	852
Maryland	51,106	51,443	46,629	6,508	191,799	52,248	46,800	43,185	43,302	6,264
Massachusetts	59,398	59,624	57,364	10,339	235,350	61,890	60,360	57,155	55,945	—
Michigan	111,873	111,085	106,260	49,971	448,864	122,120	109,932	102,068	97,713	17,031
Minnesota	54,249	54,333	51,830	—	211,046	53,878	52,445	50,999	53,724	—
Mississippi	38,330	40,990	36,019	8,944	132,507	37,133	32,917	29,047	27,851	5,559
Missouri	62,268	62,348	58,052	4,962	231,691	64,372	58,526	54,550	52,420	1,823
Montana	11,563	11,464	10,936	1,726	41,474	10,827	10,296	9,806	9,985	560
Nebraska	20,277	20,175	19,116	—	76,693	20,206	19,246	18,142	19,099	—
Nevada	13,811	13,978	13,198	811	49,379	12,999	12,870	12,191	11,297	22
New Hampshire	12,705	12,653	12,058	3,222	47,286	12,838	11,898	11,097	11,131	322
New Jersey	75,446	76,397	72,607	45,609	310,195	78,241	73,767	70,827	70,438	16,922
New Mexico	21,035	20,770	19,768	—	92,900	22,253	20,374	17,684	15,751	16,838
New York	178,863	184,326	171,331	71,009	775,698	203,393	187,596	168,969	148,836	66,904
North Carolina	81,457	83,328	79,280	16,515	310,919	89,470	80,674	72,581	68,194	—
North Dakota	8,883	9,070	8,504	—	32,896	8,524	8,185	8,155	8,032	—
Ohio	131,207	134,903	128,241	—	524,832	145,371	129,228	124,860	125,373	—
Oklahoma	43,374	43,304	40,762	1,717	157,640	40,261	40,670	38,312	37,728	669
Oregon	36,821	36,694	35,253	2,430	132,130	36,213	33,874	31,186	30,018	839
Pennsylvania	118,997	120,714	115,963	33,748	504,626	128,736	120,857	115,499	115,400	24,134
Rhode Island	9,679	9,958	9,388	3,538	37,317	10,123	9,704	8,709	8,346	435
South Carolina	48,787	49,293	45,691	—	172,465	52,848	44,378	38,618	36,621	—
South Dakota	9,633	9,806	9,275	1,135	33,733	8,921	8,313	7,884	8,248	367
Tennessee	61,773	64,114	58,576	16,028	229,539	65,551	59,694	53,443	50,851	—
Texas	250,740	251,852	238,057	—	885,269	270,446	223,419	198,441	192,963	—
Utah	32,787	34,452	32,563	5,338	114,557	30,002	29,213	27,251	24,971	3,120
Vermont	7,086	7,026	6,746	—	25,676	6,357	5,962	5,618	5,719	2,020
Virginia	72,128	73,027	70,040	26,374	273,049	76,727	69,479	63,233	63,501	109
Washington	60,943	60,872	56,617	—	224,414	59,880	56,922	53,772	53,840	—
West Virginia	24,987	27,334	25,292	4,714	100,289	25,953	24,402	23,212	22,831	3,891
Wisconsin	55,420	56,152	51,757	9,691	233,762	59,880	57,923	56,569	56,022	3,368
Wyoming	7,263	7,421	6,959	—	27,042	7,106	6,976	6,564	6,281	115
Outlying areas										
American Samoa	825	841	858	—	2,949	827	738	673	641	70
Guam	1,905	1,861	1,856	—	7,202	2,321	2,006	1,554	1,240	81
Northern Marianas	491	469	427	134	1,475	393	427	355	300	—
Puerto Rico	54,723	57,634	50,732	8,911	164,978	45,952	44,999	37,660	32,700	3,667
Virgin Islands	1,591	2,073	1,463	574	5,424	1,519	1,231	1,226	1,063	385

[1] The U.S. total represents an undercount because prekindergarten enrollment data are not reported by many States.

—Data not reported or not applicable.

SOURCE: U.S. Department of Education, National Center for Education Statistics, Common Core of Data survey. (This table was prepared January 1990.)

Table 41.—Enrollment in public elementary and secondary schools, by grade and State: Fall 1988

State or other area	Total, all levels	Prekindergarten through grade 8 and elementary unclassified							
		Total	Prekinder-garten[1]	Kindergarten	Grade 1	Grade 2	Grade 3	Grade 4	Grade 5
1	2	3	4	5	6	7	8	9	10
United States .	40,188,690	28,501,042	224,750	3,208,374	3,460,049	3,223,428	3,167,036	3,050,506	2,945,065
Alabama	724,751	521,650	—	54,265	61,324	58,390	62,462	57,531	57,035
Alaska	106,481	78,518	1,747	8,637	10,468	9,433	8,905	8,517	8,151
Arizona	574,890	417,579	607	48,132	54,869	48,451	47,970	45,518	43,713
Arkansas	436,387	309,268	—	34,023	36,493	34,935	34,851	33,777	32,648
California	4,618,120	3,317,194	—	403,237	409,608	385,936	370,878	352,076	339,997
Colorado	560,081	399,853	2,396	46,599	49,844	47,005	45,202	43,381	41,272
Connecticut	460,637	331,697	3,884	38,689	40,913	36,728	35,204	34,074	32,902
Delaware	96,678	68,886	293	7,876	9,109	8,199	7,828	7,592	7,072
District of Columbia	84,792	62,334	3,570	6,292	7,614	7,002	6,536	6,242	5,669
Florida	1,720,930	1,232,007	8,317	153,773	152,910	141,231	136,584	132,484	124,848
Georgia	1,107,994	807,864	—	96,054	97,079	94,513	94,992	88,314	85,155
Hawaii	167,488	118,648	261	14,091	14,280	13,796	13,428	12,654	12,075
Idaho	214,615	155,505	—	16,925	18,517	17,637	17,757	17,534	16,996
Illinois	1,794,916	1,259,124	26,945	128,748	139,972	136,281	139,980	133,592	127,458
Indiana	960,994	667,647	814	71,250	81,616	74,717	74,344	71,757	70,788
Iowa	478,200	333,988	3,334	39,067	38,197	37,623	37,112	35,491	34,172
Kansas	426,596	306,751	1,043	36,471	37,173	35,397	34,209	32,345	31,119
Kentucky	637,627	451,805	—	48,112	53,831	50,263	50,576	49,133	48,288
Louisiana	786,683	581,095	1,235	67,051	71,130	64,420	64,873	63,614	61,008
Maine	212,902	148,904	1,761	17,394	18,704	16,609	15,759	15,693	15,389
Maryland	688,947	489,115	10,882	53,667	61,032	56,492	54,629	52,046	49,418
Massachusetts	823,428	577,795	6,017	69,572	70,859	64,884	62,404	60,342	58,819
Michigan	1,582,785	1,113,595	9,549	138,772	128,366	119,621	117,170	113,656	110,733
Minnesota	726,950	511,279	5,827	61,442	62,115	59,960	58,329	55,459	53,457
Mississippi	503,326	367,593	172	37,653	45,268	42,369	41,239	39,849	38,827
Missouri	806,639	567,860	—	65,867	65,599	63,562	64,499	63,098	61,446
Montana	152,191	109,526	268	12,583	13,491	12,550	12,272	11,724	11,621
Nebraska	269,434	191,302	1,509	22,838	23,002	22,465	21,904	20,746	20,077
Nevada	176,474	127,414	—	14,546	16,391	15,395	14,804	13,969	13,242
New Hampshire	169,413	119,785	—	7,364	18,635	14,778	13,749	13,069	12,625
New Jersey	1,080,871	755,073	6,195	79,662	87,426	80,904	79,521	78,262	76,102
New Mexico	292,425	200,129	—	23,587	25,906	24,089	23,180	21,602	21,208
New York	2,573,715	1,760,596	25,005	185,771	211,203	194,350	186,854	183,779	176,457
North Carolina	1,083,156	761,069	1,540	84,798	87,610	82,867	83,087	81,174	79,940
North Dakota	118,809	85,182	633	10,292	10,497	9,963	9,475	9,202	9,020
Ohio	1,778,544	1,229,384	—	138,736	149,861	142,038	140,143	135,733	130,433
Oklahoma	580,426	413,656	2,967	47,326	56,649	46,787	45,532	43,540	42,540
Oregon	461,752	328,226	1,285	32,246	40,413	37,137	36,374	36,978	35,958
Pennsylvania	1,659,714	1,132,631	—	124,878	138,286	126,748	123,106	119,150	115,468
Rhode Island	133,585	95,285	358	9,979	12,733	10,734	10,336	9,813	9,503
South Carolina	615,774	437,826	—	41,433	56,673	50,341	50,365	49,024	47,704
South Dakota	126,910	92,556	376	10,655	11,454	10,795	10,640	10,137	9,496
Tennessee	821,580	585,972	—	62,118	72,103	64,181	63,350	63,206	61,447
Texas	3,283,707	2,392,079	77,548	251,418	295,811	271,568	266,085	255,832	246,934
Utah	431,119	319,423	1,568	35,242	37,350	36,625	37,498	36,190	32,918
Vermont	93,381	66,761	—	8,238	8,562	7,801	7,472	7,214	6,990
Virginia	982,393	699,064	1,610	80,731	81,510	76,780	76,531	73,540	70,604
Washington	790,918	563,100	3,078	65,647	70,615	66,394	64,597	62,240	59,602
West Virginia	335,912	231,819	654	23,567	25,694	24,483	24,873	23,792	25,013
Wisconsin	774,857	535,215	11,502	62,754	62,459	60,142	59,390	56,814	54,375
Wyoming	97,793	70,415	—	8,306	8,825	8,059	8,178	8,007	7,333
Outlying areas									
American Samoa	11,764	8,911	1,354	910	922	823	851	788	804
Guam	26,041	18,659	366	2,203	2,307	2,164	2,056	2,012	1,969
Northern Marianas	6,079	4,699	—	529	535	500	505	457	484
Puerto Rico	661,693	491,836	—	30,788	59,817	56,489	56,489	58,148	57,846
Virgin Islands	23,492	17,102	—	1,760	1,872	1,919	1,821	1,730	1,794

Table 41.—Enrollment in public elementary and secondary schools, by grade and State: Fall 1988—Continued

State or other area	Prekindergarten through grade 8 and elementary unclassified				Grades 9 through 12 and secondary unclassified					
	Grade 6	Grade 7	Grade 8	Elementary unclassified	Total	Grade 9	Grade 10	Grade 11	Grade 12	Secondary unclassified
1	11	12	13	14	15	16	17	18	19	20
United States .	2,936,696	2,905,036	2,853,007	527,095	11,687,648	3,106,280	2,894,602	2,748,750	2,649,674	288,342
Alabama	57,592	57,789	55,262	—	203,101	58,543	51,114	47,873	45,571	—
Alaska	7,826	7,650	7,184	—	27,963	7,468	7,085	6,559	6,851	—
Arizona	42,508	41,345	39,317	5,149	157,311	43,002	39,886	37,050	36,962	411
Arkansas	32,865	33,580	33,461	2,635	127,119	33,009	32,169	30,746	30,074	1,121
California	335,443	330,437	318,856	70,726	1,300,926	356,732	338,871	313,982	257,450	33,891
Colorado	40,698	40,163	39,524	3,769	160,228	41,346	39,464	38,819	37,538	3,061
Connecticut	32,325	31,757	31,713	13,508	128,940	33,688	31,825	31,247	32,164	16
Delaware	6,965	7,095	6,857	—	27,792	7,651	7,062	6,272	6,807	—
District of Columbia ...	5,434	5,930	5,342	2,703	22,458	5,390	5,927	4,951	4,346	1,844
Florida	126,533	127,685	127,642	—	488,923	144,216	130,426	114,622	99,659	—
Georgia	84,951	84,317	82,489	—	300,130	90,716	76,139	67,373	65,902	—
Hawaii	11,938	11,178	10,715	5,969	48,840	11,727	11,147	10,945	10,039	3,245
Idaho	16,688	16,367	15,776	1,308	59,110	15,710	14,692	14,014	13,943	751
Illinois	127,603	124,146	121,810	52,589	535,792	130,732	128,476	121,207	120,267	35,112
Indiana	70,893	70,744	71,967	8,757	293,347	74,505	71,412	69,809	69,641	7,980
Iowa	33,747	32,966	33,186	9,093	144,212	33,373	32,229	34,204	36,157	8,249
Kansas	31,087	30,402	29,543	7,962	119,845	29,962	29,328	28,887	28,783	2,885
Kentucky	48,574	47,516	46,143	9,369	185,822	48,563	46,075	44,841	42,382	3,961
Louisiana	60,410	61,479	54,975	10,900	205,588	60,966	52,871	46,123	41,604	4,024
Maine	15,060	14,923	15,281	2,331	63,998	16,255	15,736	15,462	15,662	883
Maryland	50,235	47,803	46,782	6,129	199,832	52,169	47,541	46,285	47,248	6,589
Massachusetts	58,162	58,134	58,141	10,461	245,633	63,606	61,174	60,265	60,588	—
Michigan	108,896	107,727	109,134	49,971	469,190	123,745	112,605	108,749	107,398	16,693
Minnesota	51,647	51,559	51,484	—	215,671	51,806	52,008	53,522	58,335	—
Mississippi	38,790	38,611	36,129	8,686	135,733	36,909	33,692	30,389	29,129	5,614
Missouri	60,775	59,236	58,880	4,898	238,779	63,567	59,698	57,377	56,218	1,919
Montana	11,452	11,143	10,769	1,653	42,665	10,585	10,267	10,294	10,958	561
Nebraska	19,857	19,243	19,661	—	78,132	19,567	19,029	19,572	19,964	—
Nevada	13,129	12,743	12,310	885	49,060	12,463	12,454	12,199	11,916	28
New Hampshire	12,390	12,144	12,131	2,900	49,628	13,230	11,969	12,219	11,878	332
New Jersey	75,836	74,258	73,684	43,223	325,798	79,268	75,851	75,390	78,033	17,256
New Mexico	20,638	19,980	19,939	—	92,296	21,872	20,136	17,765	16,915	15,608
New York	176,061	180,283	172,302	68,531	813,119	202,098	191,947	187,652	161,593	69,829
North Carolina	81,812	80,085	82,586	15,570	322,087	89,256	83,514	75,722	73,595	—
North Dakota	8,890	8,741	8,469	—	33,627	8,505	8,470	8,219	8,433	—
Ohio	130,444	130,831	131,165	—	549,160	144,343	134,124	133,497	137,196	—
Oklahoma	42,803	41,397	39,041	5,074	166,770	42,824	41,321	40,412	40,073	2,140
Oregon	35,899	35,017	34,398	2,521	133,526	34,447	33,336	32,481	32,320	942
Pennsylvania	115,634	117,340	117,664	34,357	527,083	127,405	124,842	123,717	124,572	26,547
Rhode Island	9,467	9,449	9,375	3,538	38,300	10,228	9,496	9,001	8,954	621
South Carolina	48,577	46,989	46,720	—	177,948	52,835	45,669	40,096	39,348	—
South Dakota	9,486	9,470	9,000	1,047	34,354	8,517	8,251	8,548	8,685	353
Tennessee	61,703	61,699	60,330	15,835	235,608	65,659	60,465	55,784	53,700	—
Texas	246,410	243,086	237,387	—	891,628	264,600	223,162	202,104	201,762	—
Utah	34,446	32,833	29,977	4,776	111,696	28,995	28,023	25,965	25,911	2,802
Vermont	6,937	6,755	6,792	—	26,620	6,350	5,970	5,915	6,199	2,186
Virginia	71,354	69,896	70,402	26,106	283,329	77,510	71,117	66,522	68,064	116
Washington	59,064	56,146	55,717	—	227,818	58,313	56,037	55,547	57,921	—
West Virginia	25,434	26,014	25,547	6,748	104,093	26,038	25,045	24,015	23,488	5,507
Wisconsin	53,887	51,847	52,890	9,155	239,642	59,077	58,555	57,850	60,725	3,435
Wyoming	7,441	7,108	7,158	—	27,378	6,941	6,900	6,691	6,753	93
Outlying areas										
American Samoa	838	836	785	—	2,853	752	679	695	654	73
Guam	1,904	1,880	1,798	—	7,382	2,716	1,849	1,594	1,099	124
Northern Marianas	459	449	421	360	1,380	428	345	326	281	—
Puerto Rico	55,279	57,349	50,127	9,504	169,857	46,330	44,705	39,591	35,307	3,924
Virgin Islands	1,715	2,222	1,653	616	6,390	1,659	1,637	1,446	1,200	448

[1] The U.S. total represents an undercount because prekindergarten enrollment data are not reported by many States.

—Data not reported or not applicable.

NOTE.—Data have been revised from previously published figures.

SOURCE: U.S. Department of Education, National Center for Education Statistics, Common Core of Data survey. (This table was prepared October 1990.)

Table 42.—Membership and attendance in public elementary and secondary schools, by State: 1980–81, 1987–88, and 1988–89

State	1980–81			1987–88			1988–89		
	Estimated average daily membership (ADM)	Average daily attendance (ADA)	ADA as a percent of ADM	Estimated average daily membership (ADM)[1]	Average daily attendance (ADA)	ADA as a percent of ADM	Estimated average daily membership (ADM)[1]	Average daily attendance (ADA)	ADA as a percent of ADM
1	2	3	4	5	6	7	8	9	10
United States .	[1] 40,256,675	37,703,744	93.7	—	37,050,707	—	—	37,281,753	—
Alabama	741,534	701,925	94.7	727,253	689,340	94.8	723,095	684,453	94.7
Alaska	86,604	83,745	96.7	101,144	94,917	93.8	101,442	95,776	94.4
Arizona	491,812	476,149	96.8	566,098	534,812	94.5	609,281	549,219	90.1
Arkansas	441,432	417,080	94.5	431,925	405,196	93.8	431,152	403,106	93.5
California	—	[2] 4,014,917	—	—	[2] 4,531,459	—	—	[2] 4,699,865	—
Colorado	527,721	508,750	96.4	534,783	514,838	96.3	[3] 534,635	[3] 514,232	96.2
Connecticut	534,400	501,085	93.8	467,300	441,150	94.4	465,100	435,227	93.6
Delaware	97,713	89,609	91.7	94,388	87,821	93.0	95,994	88,397	92.1
District of Columbia	98,871	85,773	86.8	85,499	79,801	93.3	84,576	74,398	88.0
Florida	1,510,225	[3] 1,389,487	92.0	1,664,999	1,536,866	92.3	1,719,720	1,587,882	92.3
Georgia	1,046,400	988,612	94.5	1,078,730	1,033,459	95.8	1,105,277	1,039,977	94.1
Hawaii	162,666	151,713	93.3	165,856	155,220	93.6	167,667	156,114	93.1
Idaho	203,250	190,144	93.6	—	199,563	—	—	201,219	—
Illinois	1,876,356	1,765,357	94.1	1,701,834	1,584,745	93.1	1,710,548	1,560,461	91.2
Indiana	994,492	944,424	95.0	933,359	877,942	94.1	920,029	882,175	95.9
Iowa	524,800	501,403	95.5	473,537	450,858	95.2	472,443	449,418	95.1
Kansas	384,870	374,451	97.3	399,666	384,660	96.2	404,895	385,364	95.2
Kentucky	659,950	614,676	93.1	612,105	578,550	94.5	605,932	573,221	94.6
Louisiana	773,000	715,844	92.6	754,300	729,492	96.7	765,713	744,142	97.2
Maine	220,000	207,554	94.3	205,414	197,225	96.0	206,673	194,350	94.0
Maryland	725,818	664,866	91.6	680,095	601,415	88.4	687,371	608,699	88.6
Massachusetts	1,020,382	950,675	93.2	—	749,030	—	—	825,161	756,285	91.7
Michigan	—	1,711,139	—	—	1,473,542	—	—	1,464,766	—
Minnesota	750,073	710,836	94.8	716,120	679,729	94.9	721,340	690,266	95.7
Mississippi	471,100	446,515	94.8	502,554	479,402	95.4	501,160	477,439	95.3
Missouri	831,448	756,536	91.0	—	725,661	—	—	726,451	—
Montana	148,300	141,641	95.5	145,981	139,018	95.2	151,164	138,016	91.3
Nebraska	274,830	263,797	96.0	264,218	252,399	95.5	265,292	253,426	95.5
Nevada	141,825	138,481	97.6	165,218	153,252	92.8	175,500	162,256	92.5
New Hampshire	162,656	150,316	92.4	158,788	152,000	95.7	164,121	152,536	92.9
New Jersey	1,265,089	1,121,272	88.6	1,085,800	1,008,749	92.9	1,071,700	968,176	90.3
New Mexico	271,198	240,496	88.7	272,656	248,231	91.0	276,376	280,921	—
New York	2,808,160	2,475,055	88.1	2,518,000	2,247,588	89.3	2,488,000	2,234,976	89.8
North Carolina	1,123,506	1,055,651	94.0	1,073,763	1,016,742	94.7	1,068,800	1,004,837	94.0
North Dakota	116,416	[2] 111,759	96.0	118,376	109,512	92.5	117,999	109,271	92.6
Ohio	1,948,600	1,801,914	92.5	1,772,217	1,612,592	91.0	1,762,700	1,597,117	90.6
Oklahoma	574,000	542,800	94.6	578,100	547,149	94.6	574,700	542,693	94.4
Oregon	449,925	417,009	92.7	449,300	406,054	90.4	454,800	409,717	90.1
Pennsylvania	1,897,000	1,754,782	92.5	1,634,400	1,539,310	94.2	1,637,100	1,532,806	93.6
Rhode Island	142,457	135,096	94.8	135,365	124,559	92.0	133,500	123,321	92.4
South Carolina	601,708	580,132	96.4	591,500	567,091	95.9	592,706	567,133	95.7
South Dakota	127,068	121,663	95.7	124,893	119,868	96.0	124,976	119,400	95.5
Tennessee	857,373	797,237	93.0	816,678	766,651	93.9	816,507	764,354	93.6
Texas	2,794,671	2,647,288	94.7	—	2,991,242	—	—	3,033,684	—
Utah	340,827	323,048	94.8	419,827	397,214	94.6	422,167	403,294	95.5
Vermont	95,940	90,884	94.7	90,900	87,760	96.5	91,500	88,532	96.8
Virginia	1,000,378	938,794	93.8	971,062	914,354	94.2	974,028	914,445	93.9
Washington	751,287	704,655	93.8	771,297	721,952	93.6	787,398	736,345	93.5
West Virginia	—	351,823	—	—	319,330	—	—	309,691	—
Wisconsin	771,485	743,505	96.4	735,501	698,963	95.0	736,227	700,389	95.1
Wyoming	—	91,381	—	—	97,517	92,434	94.8	—	96,613	91,515	94.7

[1] Total includes estimates for nonreporting States.

[2] Data for California are not strictly comparable with those for other states because California's attendance figures include excused absences.

[3] Data estimated by State education agencies.

—Data not available.

SOURCE: U.S. Department of Education, National Center for Education Statistics, Common Core of Data survey; and National Education Association, *Estimates of School Statistics, 1989-90.* (Copyright © 1990 by the National Education Association. All rights reserved.) (This table was prepared April 1991.)

Table 43.—Average daily attendance in public elementary and secondary schools, by State: 1969-70 to 1988-89

State	1969–70	1975–76	1979–80	1980–81	1984–85	1985–86	1986–87	1987–88	1988–89
1	2	3	4	5	6	7	8	9	10
United States .	41,934,376	41,269,720	38,288,911	37,703,744	36,404,261	36,523,103	36,863,867	37,050,707	37,281,753
Alabama	777,123	716,371	711,432	701,925	684,211	686,716	690,256	689,340	684,453
Alaska	72,489	81,564	79,945	83,745	96,257	98,535	96,004	94,917	95,776
Arizona	391,526	455,692	481,905	476,149	477,520	494,504	518,277	534,812	549,219
Arkansas	414,158	428,720	423,610	417,080	405,077	408,601	409,388	405,196	403,106
California [1]	4,418,423	4,366,617	4,044,736	4,014,917	4,139,461	4,245,090	4,429,792	4,531,459	4,699,865
Colorado	500,388	527,434	513,475	508,750	505,321	507,876	513,587	514,838	514,232
Connecticut	618,881	596,175	507,362	501,085	446,981	452,058	444,285	441,150	435,227
Delaware	120,819	116,553	94,058	89,609	84,407	84,936	86,655	87,821	88,397
District of Columbia	138,600	119,255	91,576	85,773	76,023	76,241	76,822	79,801	74,398
Florida	1,312,693	1,435,570	1,464,461	1,389,487	1,416,104	1,442,921	1,489,146	1,536,866	1,587,882
Georgia	1,019,427	998,898	989,433	988,612	989,713	1,004,799	1,023,127	1,033,459	1,039,977
Hawaii	168,140	162,903	151,563	151,713	150,572	151,174	152,287	155,220	156,114
Idaho	170,920	182,215	189,199	190,144	197,902	198,141	198,449	199,563	201,219
Illinois	2,084,844	1,990,158	1,770,435	1,765,357	1,600,380	1,604,265	1,574,128	1,584,745	1,560,461
Indiana	1,111,043	1,049,889	983,444	944,424	883,592	870,463	873,733	877,942	882,175
Iowa	624,403	574,773	510,081	501,403	461,392	454,341	453,150	450,858	449,418
Kansas	470,296	419,022	382,019	374,451	369,524	371,655	378,073	384,660	385,364
Kentucky	647,970	622,484	619,868	614,676	579,441	577,190	579,226	578,550	573,221
Louisiana	776,555	768,097	727,601	715,844	732,864	732,230	736,474	729,492	744,142
Maine	225,146	227,841	211,400	207,554	198,125	198,358	197,539	197,225	194,350
Maryland	785,989	793,848	686,336	664,866	596,478	592,383	595,618	601,415	608,699
Massachusetts	1,056,207	1,070,996	935,960	950,675	779,869	745,991	727,680	749,030	756,285
Michigan	1,991,235	1,971,774	1,758,427	1,711,139	1,490,452	1,481,068	1,476,471	1,473,542	1,464,766
Minnesota	864,595	827,239	748,606	710,836	669,930	669,385	674,245	679,729	690,266
Mississippi	524,623	479,076	454,401	446,515	435,587	448,117	473,424	479,402	477,439
Missouri	906,132	864,958	777,269	756,536	712,197	714,230	724,710	725,661	726,451
Montana	162,664	156,473	144,608	141,641	139,905	138,829	139,199	139,018	138,016
Nebraska	314,516	296,915	270,524	263,797	250,647	250,975	252,457	252,399	253,426
Nevada	113,421	128,106	134,995	138,481	140,402	143,941	149,136	153,252	162,256
New Hampshire	140,203	159,836	154,187	150,316	144,655	147,561	149,963	152,000	152,536
New Jersey	1,322,124	1,310,042	1,140,111	1,121,272	1,043,047	1,029,797	1,024,611	1,008,749	968,176
New Mexico	259,997	256,764	253,453	240,496	248,758	252,892	243,340	248,231	280,921
New York	3,099,192	3,012,893	2,530,289	2,475,055	2,309,169	2,276,842	2,266,283	2,247,588	2,234,976
North Carolina	1,104,295	1,120,207	1,072,150	1,055,651	1,018,795	1,014,795	1,020,702	1,016,742	1,004,837
North Dakota	141,961	126,277	118,986	111,759	109,427	108,947	109,074	109,512	109,271
Ohio	2,246,282	2,103,243	1,849,283	1,801,914	1,675,530	1,660,718	1,664,709	1,612,592	1,597,117
Oklahoma	560,993	558,528	548,065	542,800	552,835	553,370	550,949	547,149	542,693
Oregon	436,736	425,126	418,593	417,009	401,154	401,476	402,855	406,054	409,717
Pennsylvania	2,169,225	2,064,312	1,808,630	1,754,782	1,571,831	1,560,746	1,554,642	1,539,310	1,532,806
Rhode Island	163,205	158,752	139,195	135,096	122,653	122,109	122,024	124,559	123,321
South Carolina	600,292	591,900	569,612	580,132	559,340	558,716	564,508	567,091	567,133
South Dakota	158,543	141,120	124,934	121,663	117,137	118,269	118,902	119,868	119,400
Tennessee	836,010	826,335	806,696	797,237	769,862	762,225	766,521	766,651	764,354
Texas	2,432,420	2,549,517	2,608,817	2,647,288	2,879,823	2,923,741	2,977,783	2,991,242	3,033,684
Utah	287,405	289,171	312,813	323,048	366,574	379,249	386,306	397,214	403,294
Vermont	97,772	98,015	95,045	90,884	85,734	85,875	85,985	87,760	88,532
Virginia	995,580	1,018,034	955,105	938,794	901,994	904,347	911,261	914,354	914,445
Washington	764,735	723,083	710,929	704,655	688,759	696,372	708,584	721,952	736,345
West Virginia	372,278	366,395	353,264	351,823	336,196	330,145	324,791	319,330	309,691
Wisconsin	880,609	858,407	770,554	743,505	696,071	694,351	682,560	698,963	700,389
Wyoming	81,293	82,147	89,471	91,381	94,583	95,547	94,176	92,434	91,515
Outlying areas									
American Samoa	—	7,461	—	—	10,580	10,816	10,559	10,579	11,222
Guam	20,315	26,318	—	22,343	23,632	23,220	23,409	23,172	23,203
Northern Marianas	—	—	—	—	5,548	4,921	5,071	5,851	—
Puerto Rico	—	669,400	656,709	671,661	649,651	636,268	629,922	621,731	608,945
Virgin Islands	—	21,793	—	23,312	—	23,811	22,814	22,103	21,159

[1] Data for California are not strictly comparable with those for other States because California's attendance figures include excused absences.

—Data not available.

SOURCE: U.S. Department of Education, National Center for Education Statistics, Revenues and Expenditures for Public Elementary and Secondary Education, *Statistics of State School Systems;* and Common Core of Data survey. (This table was prepared December 1990.)

Table 44.—Enrollment in public elementary and secondary schools, by race or ethnicity and State: Fall 1986 and fall 1989

State	Percent distribution, fall 1986						Percent distribution, fall 1989					
	Total	White [1]	Black [1]	Hispanic	Asian or Pacific Islander	American Indian/ Alaskan Native	Total	White [1]	Black [1]	Hispanic	Asian or Pacific Islander	American Indian/ Alaskan Native
1	2	3	4	5	6	7	8	9	10	11	12	13
United States	100.0	70.4	16.1	9.9	2.8	0.9	—	—	—	—	—	—
Alabama	100.0	62.0	37.0	0.1	0.4	0.5	100.0	62.9	35.7	0.2	0.5	0.7
Alaska	100.0	65.7	4.3	1.7	3.3	25.1	100.0	67.6	4.5	1.9	3.6	22.4
Arizona	100.0	62.2	4.0	26.4	1.3	6.1	100.0	64.1	4.1	23.7	1.5	6.6
Arkansas	100.0	74.7	24.2	0.4	0.6	0.2	100.0	74.8	24.0	0.4	0.6	0.2
California	100.0	53.7	9.0	27.5	9.1	0.7	100.0	47.1	8.7	33.0	10.4	0.8
Colorado	100.0	78.7	4.5	13.7	2.0	1.0	100.0	75.6	5.1	16.1	2.2	0.9
Connecticut	100.0	77.2	12.1	8.9	1.5	0.2	100.0	75.6	12.5	9.7	2.0	0.2
Delaware	100.0	68.3	27.7	2.5	1.4	0.2	100.0	68.7	26.9	2.6	1.5	0.1
District of Columbia	100.0	4.0	91.1	3.9	0.9	0.1	100.0	3.7	90.7	4.6	0.9	0.0
Florida	100.0	65.4	23.7	9.5	1.2	0.2	100.0	62.8	23.8	11.9	1.4	0.2
Georgia	100.0	60.7	37.9	0.6	0.8	(2)	—	—	—	—	—	—
Hawaii	100.0	23.5	2.3	2.2	71.7	0.3	100.0	23.0	2.6	2.3	71.7	0.3
Idaho	100.0	92.6	0.3	4.9	0.8	1.3	—	—	—	—	—	—
Illinois	100.0	69.8	18.7	9.2	2.3	0.1	100.0	66.0	21.9	9.3	2.6	0.1
Indiana	100.0	88.7	9.0	1.7	0.5	0.1	100.0	86.5	10.9	1.8	0.6	0.1
Iowa	100.0	94.6	3.0	0.9	1.2	0.3	100.0	94.5	2.7	1.1	1.3	0.3
Kansas	100.0	85.6	7.6	4.4	1.9	0.6	100.0	85.4	8.0	4.2	1.4	1.0
Kentucky	100.0	89.2	10.2	0.1	0.5	0.0	100.0	90.0	9.4	0.2	0.4	(2)
Louisiana	100.0	56.5	41.3	0.8	1.1	0.3	100.0	53.4	44.1	1.0	1.1	0.4
Maine	100.0	98.3	0.5	0.2	0.8	0.2	—	—	—	—	—	—
Maryland	100.0	59.7	35.3	1.7	3.1	0.2	100.0	61.7	32.7	2.1	3.3	0.2
Massachusetts	100.0	83.7	7.4	6.0	2.8	0.1	100.0	81.8	7.5	7.4	3.2	0.1
Michigan	100.0	76.4	19.8	1.8	1.2	0.8	100.0	77.8	17.8	2.3	1.2	0.9
Minnesota	100.0	93.9	2.1	0.9	1.7	1.5	100.0	91.1	3.1	1.2	2.9	1.6
Mississippi	100.0	43.9	55.5	0.1	0.4	0.1	100.0	48.7	50.6	0.1	0.4	0.1
Missouri	100.0	83.4	14.9	0.7	0.8	0.2	—	—	—	—	—	—
Montana	100.0	92.7	0.3	0.9	0.5	5.5	—	—	—	—	—	—
Nebraska	100.0	91.4	4.4	2.4	0.8	1.0	100.0	90.3	5.3	2.3	1.0	1.1
Nevada	100.0	77.4	9.6	7.5	3.2	2.3	100.0	75.6	9.2	9.8	3.3	2.0
New Hampshire	100.0	98.0	0.7	0.5	0.8	0.1	100.0	97.0	0.9	0.9	1.0	0.2
New Jersey	100.0	69.1	17.4	10.7	2.7	0.1	100.0	66.1	18.5	11.1	4.1	0.1
New Mexico	100.0	43.1	2.3	45.1	0.8	8.7	100.0	42.5	2.2	44.7	0.9	9.8
New York	100.0	68.4	16.5	12.3	2.7	0.2	100.0	62.1	20.5	13.2	3.9	0.3
North Carolina	100.0	68.4	28.9	0.4	0.6	1.7	100.0	66.5	30.4	0.7	0.8	1.6
North Dakota	100.0	92.4	0.6	1.1	0.8	5.0	100.0	92.0	0.6	0.6	0.7	6.1
Ohio	100.0	83.1	15.0	1.0	0.7	0.1	100.0	83.6	14.2	1.2	0.9	0.1
Oklahoma	100.0	79.0	7.8	1.6	1.0	10.6	100.0	75.0	9.9	2.6	1.1	11.4
Oregon	100.0	89.8	2.2	3.9	2.4	1.7	100.0	89.2	2.4	4.0	2.8	1.7
Pennsylvania	100.0	84.4	12.6	1.8	1.2	0.1	100.0	82.7	13.1	2.6	1.5	0.1
Rhode Island	100.0	87.9	5.6	3.7	2.4	0.3	100.0	84.1	6.4	5.9	3.2	0.4
South Carolina	100.0	54.6	44.5	0.2	0.6	0.1	100.0	57.9	41.1	0.3	0.6	0.1
South Dakota	100.0	90.6	0.5	0.6	0.7	7.6	—	—	—	—	—	—
Tennessee	100.0	76.5	22.6	0.2	0.6	(2)	100.0	76.6	22.4	0.3	0.7	(2)
Texas	100.0	51.0	14.4	32.5	2.0	0.2	100.0	50.3	14.6	33.1	1.9	0.2
Utah	100.0	93.7	0.4	3.0	1.5	1.5	100.0	92.6	0.5	3.7	1.8	1.4
Vermont	100.0	98.4	0.3	0.2	0.6	0.6	100.0	98.4	0.4	0.2	0.5	0.5
Virginia	100.0	72.6	23.7	1.0	2.6	0.1	—	—	—	—	—	—
Washington	100.0	84.5	4.2	3.8	5.1	2.3	100.0	82.9	4.1	5.2	5.3	2.4
West Virginia	100.0	95.9	3.7	0.1	0.3	0.0	100.0	95.5	3.9	0.2	0.4	0.0
Wisconsin	100.0	86.6	8.9	1.9	1.7	1.0	100.0	86.0	8.6	2.4	1.8	1.3
Wyoming	100.0	90.7	0.9	5.9	0.6	1.9	—	—	—	—	—	—
Outlying areas												
American Samoa	—	—	—	—	—	—	100.0	(2)	(2)	(2)	100.0	(2)
Guam	—	—	—	—	—	—	100.0	13.3	1.8	0.3	84.7	(2)
Northern Marianas	—	—	—	—	—	—	100.0	0.1	(2)	(2)	99.9	(2)
Puerto Rico	—	—	—	—	—	—	—	—	—	—	—	—
Virgin Islands	—	—	—	—	—	—	100.0	0.5	84.3	14.7	0.5	(2)

[1] Excludes persons of Hispanic origin.
[2] Less than 0.05 percent.
—Data not available.

NOTE.—The 1986-87 data were derived from the 1986 Elementary and Secondary School Civil Rights sample survey of public school districts. State estimates may differ from other data sources because of variations in survey methodology. Because of rounding, details may not add to totals.

SOURCE: U.S. Department of Education, Office for Civil Rights, *1986 State Summaries of Elementary and Secondary School Civil Rights Survey;* and National Center for Education Statistics, "Common Core of Data" survey. (This table was prepared March 1991.)

Table 45.—Enrollment of 3-, 4-, and 5-year-old children in preprimary programs, by level and control of program and by attendance status: October 1965 to October 1990

[In thousands]

Year and age	Total population, 3 to 5 years old	Enrollment by level and control						Enrollment by attendance		
		Total	Percent-age enrolled	Nursery school		Kindergarten		Full-day	Part-day	Percent full-day
				Public	Private	Public	Private			
1	2	3	4	5	6	7	8	9	10	11
Total, 3 to 5 years old										
1965	12,549	3,407	27.1	127	393	2,291	596	—	—	—
1970	10,949	4,104	37.5	332	762	2,498	511	698	3,405	17.0
1975	10,185	4,955	48.7	570	1,174	2,682	528	1,295	3,659	26.1
1979	9,119	4,664	51.1	633	1,228	2,381	421	1,454	3,210	31.2
1980	9,284	4,878	52.5	628	1,353	2,438	459	1,551	3,327	31.8
1981	9,421	4,937	52.4	—	—	—	—	1,472	3,465	29.8
1982	9,873	5,105	51.7	729	1,423	2,459	494	1,574	3,531	30.8
1983	10,254	5,384	52.5	809	1,538	2,416	623	—	—	—
1984	10,612	5,480	51.6	742	1,593	2,668	476	1,929	3,550	35.2
1985	10,733	5,865	54.6	846	1,631	2,847	541	2,144	3,722	36.6
1986	10,866	5,971	55.0	829	1,715	2,859	567	2,241	3,730	37.5
1987	10,872	5,931	54.6	819	1,736	2,842	534	2,090	3,841	35.2
1988	10,993	5,978	54.4	851	1,770	2,875	481	2,044	3,935	34.2
1989	11,039	6,026	54.6	930	1,894	2,704	497	2,238	3,789	37.1
1990	11,207	6,659	59.4	1,199	2,180	2,772	509	2,577	4,082	38.7
3 years old										
1965	4,149	203	4.9	41	153	5	4	—	—	—
1970	3,516	454	12.9	110	322	12	10	142	312	31.3
1975	3,177	683	21.5	179	474	11	18	259	423	37.9
1979	3,025	746	24.7	216	509	16	5	305	441	40.9
1980	3,143	857	27.3	221	604	16	17	321	536	37.5
1981	3,266	891	27.3	—	—	—	—	279	612	31.3
1982	3,387	928	27.4	312	578	27	10	280	648	30.2
1983	3,574	1,004	28.1	314	631	21	39	—	—	—
1984	3,609	1,004	27.8	295	658	30	22	401	603	39.9
1985	3,594	1,035	28.8	278	679	52	26	350	685	33.8
1986	3,607	1,041	28.9	257	737	26	21	399	642	38.3
1987	3,569	1,022	28.6	264	703	24	31	378	644	37.0
1988	3,719	1,027	27.6	298	678	24	26	369	658	35.9
1989	3,713	1,005	27.1	277	707	3	18	390	615	38.8
1990	3,692	1,205	32.6	347	840	11	7	447	758	37.1
4 years old										
1965	4,238	683	16.1	68	213	284	118	—	—	—
1970	3,620	1,007	27.8	176	395	318	117	230	776	22.8
1975	3,499	1,418	40.5	332	644	313	129	411	1,008	29.0
1979	3,070	1,393	45.4	359	664	247	123	421	972	30.2
1980	3,072	1,423	46.3	363	701	239	120	467	956	32.8
1981	2,985	1,442	48.3	—	—	—	—	431	1,011	29.9
1982	3,271	1,496	45.7	377	781	225	113	442	1,054	29.5
1983	3,414	1,619	47.4	402	813	231	173	—	—	—
1984	3,579	1,603	44.8	376	860	257	110	521	1,082	32.5
1985	3,598	1,766	49.1	496	859	276	135	643	1,123	36.4
1986	3,616	1,772	49.0	498	903	257	115	622	1,150	35.1
1987	3,597	1,717	47.7	431	881	280	125	548	1,169	31.9
1988	3,598	1,768	49.1	481	922	261	104	519	1,249	29.4
1989	3,692	1,882	51.0	524	1,055	202	100	592	1,290	31.4
1990	3,723	2,087	56.1	695	1,144	157	91	716	1,371	34.3
5 years old										
1965	4,162	2,521	60.6	18	27	2,002	474	—	—	—
1970	3,814	2,643	69.3	45	45	2,168	384	326	2,317	12.3
1975	3,509	2,854	81.3	59	57	2,358	381	625	2,228	21.9
1979	3,024	2,525	83.5	58	56	2,119	293	728	1,797	28.8
1980	3,069	2,598	84.7	44	48	2,183	322	763	1,835	29.4
1981	3,170	2,604	82.1	—	—	—	—	762	1,842	29.3
1982	3,215	2,681	83.4	40	64	2,207	370	852	1,829	31.8
1983	3,266	2,761	84.5	93	94	2,164	410	—	—	—
1984	3,423	2,872	83.9	72	76	2,381	344	1,007	1,865	35.1
1985	3,542	3,065	86.5	73	94	2,519	379	1,151	1,914	37.6
1986	3,643	3,157	86.7	75	75	2,576	432	1,220	1,937	38.6
1987	3,706	3,192	86.1	124	152	2,538	378	1,163	2,028	36.4
1988	3,676	3,184	86.6	72	170	2,590	351	1,155	2,028	36.3
1989	3,633	3,139	86.4	129	132	2,499	378	1,255	1,883	40.0
1990	3,792	3,367	88.8	157	196	2,604	411	1,414	1,953	42.0

—Data not available.

NOTE.—Data are based on sample surveys of the civilian noninstitutional population. Although cells with fewer than 75,000 children are subject to wide sampling variation, they are included in the table to permit various types of aggregations. Enrollment data for 5-year-olds include only those students in preprimary programs. Because of rounding, details may not add to totals.

SOURCE: U.S. Department of Education, National Center for Education Statistics, *Preprimary Enrollment,* various years; and U.S. Department of Commerce, Bureau of the Census, Current Population Survey, unpublished data. (This table was prepared May 1991.)

Table 46.—Public school pupils transported at public expense and current expenditures for transportation: 1929–30 to 1988–89

School year	Average daily attendance, all students [1]	Pupils transported at public expense		Expenditures for transportation	
		Number	Percent of total	Total [2] (in thousands)	Average for pupil transported
1	2	3	4	5	6
1929–30	25,678,015	1,902,826	7.4	$54,823	$29
1931–32	26,275,441	2,419,173	9.2	58,078	24
1933–34	26,434,193	2,794,724	10.6	53,908	19
1935–36	26,367,098	3,250,658	12.3	62,653	19
1937–38	25,975,108	3,769,242	14.5	75,637	20
1939–40	25,433,542	4,144,161	16.3	83,283	20
1941–42	24,562,473	4,503,081	18.3	92,922	21
1943–44	23,266,616	4,512,412	19.4	107,754	24
1945–46	23,299,941	5,056,966	21.7	129,756	26
1947–48	23,944,532	5,854,041	24.4	176,265	30
1949–50	25,111,427	6,947,384	27.7	214,504	31
1951–52	26,562,664	7,697,130	29.0	268,827	35
1953–54	25,643,871	8,411,719	32.8	307,437	37
1955–56	27,740,149	9,695,819	35.0	353,972	37
1957–58	29,722,275	10,861,689	36.5	416,491	38
1959–60	32,477,440	12,225,142	37.6	486,338	40
1961–62	34,682,340	13,222,667	38.1	576,361	44
1963–64	37,405,058	14,475,778	38.7	673,845	47
1965–66	39,154,497	15,536,567	39.7	787,358	51
1967–68	40,827,965	17,130,873	42.0	981,006	57
1969–70	41,934,376	18,198,577	43.4	1,218,557	67
1971–72	42,254,272	19,474,355	46.1	1,507,830	77
1973–74	41,438,054	21,347,039	51.5	1,858,141	87
1975–76	41,269,720	21,772,483	52.8	2,377,313	109
1977–78	40,079,590	[3]21,800,000	54.4	2,731,041	125
1979–80	38,288,911	21,713,515	56.7	3,833,145	177
1980–81	37,703,744	[3]22,272,000	59.1	[3]4,408,000	198
1981–82	37,094,652	[3]22,246,000	60.0	[3]4,793,000	215
1982–83	36,635,868	[3]22,199,000	60.6	[3]5,000,000	225
1983–84	36,362,978	[3]22,031,000	60.6	[3]5,284,000	240
1984–85	36,404,261	[3]22,320,000	61.3	[3]5,722,000	256
1985–86	36,523,103	[3]22,041,000	60.3	[3]6,123,000	278
1986–87	36,863,867	[3]22,397,000	60.8	[3]6,551,000	292
1987–88	37,050,707	[3]22,158,000	59.8	[3]6,799,000	307
1988–89	37,281,753	[3]22,635,000	60.7	[3]7,309,000	323

[1] Pupil data through 1951–52 are based on enrollment; data for 1953–54 and subsequent years are based on average daily attendance.

[2] Excludes capital outlay for years through 1979–80. Beginning in 1980–81, total transportation figures include capital outlay.

[3] Estimate based on data appearing in December–January issues of *School Bus Fleet.*

NOTE.—Some data have been revised from previously published figures.

SOURCE: U.S. Department of Education, National Center for Education Statistics, *Statistics of State School Systems; Revenues and Expenditures for Public Elementary and Secondary Education,* and unpublished data; and *School Bus Fleet,* © by Bobbit Publishing Co. December-January issues. (This table was prepared February 1991.)

Table 47.—Children 0 to 21 years old served in federally-supported special education programs, by type of handicap: 1976-77 to 1988-89

Type of handicap	1976–77	1977–78	1978–79	1979–80	1980–81	1981–82	1982–83	1983–84	1984–85	1985–86	1986–87	1987–88	1988–89
1	2	3	4	5	6	7	8	9	10	11	12	13	14

Number served,[1] in thousands

All conditions	3,692	3,751	3,889	4,005	4,142	4,198	4,255	4,298	4,315	4,317	4,374	4,447	4,544
Learning disabled	796	964	1,130	1,276	1,462	1,622	1,741	1,806	1,832	1,862	1,914	1,928	1,987
Speech impaired	1,302	1,223	1,214	1,186	1,168	1,135	1,131	1,128	1,126	1,125	1,136	953	967
Mentally retarded	959	933	901	869	829	786	757	727	694	660	643	582	564
Seriously emotionally disturbed	283	288	300	329	346	339	352	361	372	375	383	373	376
Hard of hearing and deaf	87	85	85	80	79	75	73	72	69	66	65	56	56
Orthopedically handicapped	87	87	70	66	58	58	57	56	56	57	57	47	47
Other health impaired	141	135	105	106	98	79	50	53	68	57	52	45	43
Visually handicapped	38	35	32	31	31	29	28	29	28	27	26	22	23
Multihandicapped	—	—	50	60	68	71	63	65	69	86	97	77	85
Deaf-blind	—	—	2	2	3	2	2	2	2	2	2	1	2
Preschool handicapped[2]	(3)	(3)	(3)	(3)	(3)	(3)	(3)	(3)	(3)	(3)	(3)	363	394

Percentage distribution of children served

All conditions	100.0	100.0	100.0	100.0	100.0	100.0	100.0	100.0	100.0	100.0	100.0	100.0	100.0
Learning disabled	21.6	25.7	29.1	31.9	35.3	38.6	40.9	42.0	42.4	43.1	43.8	43.4	43.6
Speech impaired	35.3	32.6	31.2	29.6	28.2	27.0	26.6	26.2	26.1	26.1	26.0	21.4	21.1
Mentally retarded	26.0	24.9	23.2	21.7	20.0	18.7	17.8	16.9	16.1	15.3	14.7	13.1	12.7
Seriously emotionally disturbed	7.7	7.7	7.7	8.2	8.4	8.1	8.3	8.4	8.6	8.7	8.8	8.4	8.3
Hard of hearing and deaf	2.4	2.3	2.2	2.0	1.9	1.8	1.7	1.7	1.6	1.5	1.5	1.3	1.3
Orthopedically handicapped	2.4	2.3	1.8	1.6	1.4	1.4	1.3	1.3	1.3	1.3	1.3	1.1	1.1
Other health impaired	3.8	3.6	2.7	2.6	2.4	1.9	1.2	1.2	1.6	1.3	1.2	1.0	1.0
Visually handicapped	1.0	0.9	0.8	0.8	(4)	0.7	0.7	0.7	0.7	0.6	0.6	0.5	0.5
Multihandicapped	—	—	1.3	1.5	1.6	1.7	1.5	1.5	1.6	2.0	2.2	1.7	1.8
Deaf-blind	—	—	0.1	(4)	0.1	(4)	(4)	0.1	(4)	(4)	(4)	(4)	(4)
Preschool handicapped[2]	(3)	(3)	(3)	(3)	(3)	(3)	(3)	(3)	(3)	(3)	(3)	8.2	8.7

Number served as a percent of total enrollment[5]

All conditions	8.33	8.61	9.14	9.62	10.12	10.48	10.75	10.95	11.00	10.95	11.00	11.11	11.30
Learning disabled	1.80	2.21	2.66	3.06	3.57	4.05	4.40	4.60	4.67	4.72	4.81	4.82	4.94
Speech impaired	2.94	2.81	2.85	2.85	2.85	2.84	2.86	2.87	2.87	2.85	2.86	2.38	2.41
Mentally retarded	2.16	2.14	2.12	2.09	2.03	1.96	1.91	1.85	1.77	1.68	1.62	1.45	1.40
Seriously emotionally disturbed	0.64	0.66	0.71	0.79	0.85	0.85	0.89	0.92	0.95	0.95	0.96	0.93	0.94
Hard of hearing and deaf	0.20	0.20	0.20	0.19	0.19	0.19	0.18	0.18	0.18	0.17	0.16	0.14	0.14
Orthopedically handicapped	0.20	0.20	0.16	0.16	0.14	0.14	0.14	0.14	0.14	0.14	0.14	0.12	0.12
Other health impaired	0.32	0.31	0.25	0.25	0.24	0.20	0.13	0.13	0.17	0.14	0.13	0.11	0.11
Visually handicapped	0.09	0.08	0.08	0.08	0.08	0.07	0.07	0.07	0.07	0.07	0.07	0.05	0.06
Multihandicapped	—	—	0.12	0.14	0.17	0.18	0.16	0.17	0.17	0.22	0.24	0.19	0.21
Deaf-blind	—	—	0.01	0.01	0.01	(6)	0.01	0.01	(6)	0.01	(6)	(6)	(6)
Preschool handicapped[2]	(3)	(3)	(3)	(3)	(3)	(3)	(3)	(3)	(3)	(3)	(3)	0.91	0.98

[1] Includes students served under Chapter I and Education of the Handicapped Act (EHA).

[2] Includes preschool children 3-5 years served under the EHA and 0-5 years served under Chapter I.

[3] Prior to 1987-88, these students were included in the counts by handicapping condition. Beginning in 1987-88, States are no longer required to report preschool handicapped students (0-5 years) by handicapping condition.

[4] Less than .05.

[5] Based on the enrollment in public schools, kindergarten through 12th grade, including a relatively small number of prekindergarten students.

[6] Less than .005.

—Data not available.

NOTE.—Counts are based on reports from the 50 States and District of Columbia only (i.e., figures from U.S. territories are not included). Increases since 1987-88 are due in part to new legislation enacted Fall 1986, which mandates public school special education services for all handicapped children ages 3 through 5 by the 1990-91 school year. Some data have been revised from previously published figures. Because of rounding, details may not add to totals.

SOURCE: U.S. Department of Education, Office of Special Education and Rehabilitative Services, *Annual Report to Congress on the Implementation of The Education of the Handicapped Act,* various years; National Center for Education Statistics, Common Core of Data survey. (This table was prepared March 1990.)

Table 48.—Percentage distribution of handicapped persons 6 to 21 years old receiving special education services, by educational environment: 1987–88

Type of handicap	All environments	Regular class	Resource room	Separate class	Public separate school facility	Private separate school facility	Public residential facility	Private residential facility	Homebound/ hospital environment
1	2	3	4	5	6	7	8	9	10
All conditions	**100.0**	**29.1**	**40.0**	**24.7**	**3.5**	**1.4**	**0.5**	**0.3**	**0.7**
Learning disabled	100.0	17.6	59.0	21.8	0.9	0.4	(1)	(1)	(1)
Speech impaired	100.0	74.9	19.7	3.8	0.3	1.1	(1)	(1)	(1)
Mentally retarded	100.0	5.8	23.5	57.9	10.3	1.1	0.6	(1)	(1)
Seriously emotionally disturbed	100.0	12.6	32.9	34.5	9.0	5.4	1.8	1.7	2.2
Hard of hearing and deaf .	100.0	30.5	1.9	43.4	8.6	4.5	9.6	1.2	0.2
Orthopedically handicapped	100.0	27.7	18.0	32.0	10.6	2.5	0.4	(1)	8.2
Other health impaired	100.0	30.6	20.8	18.7	7.8	1.7	0.4	0.4	19.5
Visually handicapped	100.0	37.9	25.2	21.0	3.6	1.7	8.8	1.3	0.4
Multihandicapped	100.0	6.5	13.6	46.6	20.7	7.1	2.7	1.3	1.6
Deaf-blind	100.0	8.9	6.3	36.8	18.8	2.6	22.6	3.0	1.0

[1] Less than .05 percent.

NOTE.—This table reflects a compilation of data reported by the States. There are some reporting variations, e.g., estimated or incomplete data and nonstandard definitions, from State to State. Data exclude U.S. Territories and schools operated by the Bureau of Indian Affairs. Data for 3– to 5–year old children are no longer collected by type of handicap. Because of rounding, details may not add to totals.

SOURCE: U.S. Department of Education, Office of Special Education and Rehabilitative Services, *Twelfth Annual Report to Congress on the Implementation of The Education of the Handicapped Act, 1989.* (This table was prepared April 1990.)

Table 49.—Number of children 3–5 years old served under The Education of the Handicapped Act, by State: 1986–87, 1987–88, and 1988–89

State	1986–87	1987–88	1988–89	Percent change 1986–87 to 1988–89	State	1986–87	1987–88	1988–89	Percent change 1986–87 to 1988–89
1	2	3	4	5	1	2	3	4	5
United States	**263,168**	**284,566**	**317,687**	**20.7**					
Alabama	2,666	6,987	8,243	209.2	Missouri	5,297	4,836	4,307	-18.7
Alaska	767	981	1,145	49.3	Montana	1,404	1,420	1,358	-3.3
Arizona	2,623	2,752	3,063	16.8	Nebraska	2,750	2,666	2,666	-3.1
Arkansas	2,505	2,534	3,101	23.8	Nevada	844	871	955	13.2
California	23,700	29,138	33,341	40.7	New Hampshire	1,105	1,118	1,187	7.4
Colorado	1,489	2,126	2,624	76.2	New Jersey	12,506	13,095	13,552	8.4
Connecticut	4,506	4,793	4,589	1.8	New Mexico	1,249	1,268	1,583	26.7
Delaware	709	822	845	19.2	New York	5,410	3,265	16,640	207.6
District of Columbia	370	398	301	-18.6	North Carolina	5,541	6,682	7,928	43.1
Florida	8,947	10,487	11,412	27.6	North Dakota	1,008	1,021	1,123	11.4
Georgia	4,442	4,981	6,295	41.7	Ohio	7,205	7,359	7,326	1.7
Hawaii	581	621	679	16.9	Oklahoma	5,635	5,388	5,317	-5.6
Idaho	1,270	974	1,138	-10.4	Oregon	1,177	1,297	1,205	2.4
Illinois	22,076	19,964	19,163	-13.2	Pennsylvania	7,134	9,533	13,339	87.0
Indiana	5,099	5,046	4,660	-8.6	Rhode Island	1,200	1,390	1,451	20.9
Iowa	4,929	5,072	5,137	4.2	South Carolina	5,671	6,973	7,334	29.3
Kansas	2,801	2,855	2,967	5.9	South Dakota	1,813	1,844	1,858	2.5
Kentucky	4,343	6,861	7,735	78.1	Tennessee	6,746	6,548	6,937	2.8
Louisiana	5,130	5,162	5,750	12.1	Texas	20,137	20,989	21,471	6.6
Maine	2,148	2,865	2,756	28.3	Utah	2,093	2,158	2,358	12.7
Maryland	5,971	6,150	6,423	7.6	Vermont	487	500	541	11.1
Massachusetts	8,041	8,034	9,455	17.6	Virginia	8,944	8,987	9,053	1.2
Michigan	12,517	12,268	13,133	4.9	Washington	6,562	7,259	8,252	25.8
Minnesota	8,731	8,934	8,443	-3.3	West Virginia	2,813	2,749	2,682	-4.7
Mississippi	2,841	4,854	5,060	78.1	Wisconsin	8,934	9,274	9,341	4.6
					Wyoming	301	417	465	54.5

NOTE.—The Education of the Handicapped Act was amended in October 1986 to extend the right to a free and appropriate education to handicapped children ages 3 through 5 years. The States have until the 1990–91 school year to fully implement the law.

SOURCE: U.S. Department of Education, Office of Special Education and Rehabilitative Services, *Twelfth Annual Report to Congress on the Implementation of The Education of the Handicapped Act.* (This table was prepared May 1990.)

Table 50.—State legislation on gifted and talented programs and number and percentage of students receiving services in public elementary and secondary schools, by State: 1986–87

State	State-mandated gifted and talented programs	Discretionary State-supported gifted and talented programs	Gifted and talented students receiving services	Gifted and talented students as a percent of enrollment	State	State-mandated gifted and talented programs	Discretionary State-supported gifted and talented programs	Gifted and talented students receiving services	Gifted and talented students as a percent of enrollment
1	2	3	4	5	1	2	3	4	5
Alabama	X		16,834	[1]2.3	Montana		X	[2]4,500	2.9
Alaska	X		[2]3,854	[3]3.7	Nebraska		X	[2]19,000	7.1
Arizona	X		[2]20,000	[3]3.4	Nevada		X	5,321	3.3
Arkansas	X		[2]19,928	4.6	New Hampshire			—	—
California		X	219,073	5.1	New Jersey		X	111,190	9.9
Colorado	X		—	—	New Mexico	X		[2]5,063	[1]1.8
Connecticut	([4])		[2]19,000	4.1	New York	X		[2]125,000	4.6
Delaware	([5])		3,815	4.1	North Carolina	X		62,329	4.5
Florida	X		47,463	3.0	North Dakota		X	1,365	0.7
Georgia	X		38,000	[1]3.5	Ohio		X	[2]50,000	2.8
Hawaii			[2]15,193	9.2	Oklahoma	X		38,084	6.4
Idaho	X		[3]2,510	1.2	Oregon		X	15,338	3.6
Illinois		X	[2]86,000	4.0	Pennsylvania	X		[2]78,000	[1]4.7
Indiana		X	[2]27,800	2.9	Rhode Island		X	[2]5,200	3.9
Iowa	X		[2]8,600	1.8	South Carolina	X		35,264	5.8
Kansas	X		[2]11,786	3.0	South Dakota	X		[2]4,791	3.8
Kentucky	X		[2]25,000	[1]3.9	Tennessee	X		13,852	1.7
Louisiana	X		[2]14,000	1.9	Texas		X	113,000	[1]3.5
Maine	X		—	—	Utah		X	22,000	5.5
Maryland		X	[2]54,000	8.1	Vermont			—	—
Massachusetts		X	—	—	Virginia	X		[6]81,741	8.5
Michigan		X	119,708	7.5	Washington		X	21,708	2.9
Minnesota		X	55,171	7.9	West Virginia	X		10,787	3.1
Mississippi		X	14,145	2.8	Wisconsin	X		—	—
Missouri		X	[2]16,000	2.0	Wyoming		X	[2]2,700	2.7

[1] Percent based on enrollment figures collected by the National Center for Education Statistics.

[2] Estimated by reporting State.

[3] Data for 1985–86.

[4] Legislation only mandates that all gifted and talented students be identified.

[5] Delaware does not have a State mandate for services to gifted and talented students, but it has gifted programs in all districts.

[6] Fiscal year 1986.

X=Indicates that legislation has been passed.

—Data not available.

NOTE.—The District of Columbia was not included in the survey.

SOURCE: Council of State Directors of Programs for the Gifted, *The 1987 State of the States Gifted and Talented Education Report*. (This table was prepared November 1987.)

Table 51.—Enrollment in grades 9 to 12 in public and private schools compared with population 14 to 17 years of age: 1889–90 to fall 1989

[Numbers in thousands]

Year	Enrollment, grades 9 to 12 [1]			Population 14 to 17 years of age [3]	Enrollment as a percent of population 14 to 17 years of age
	All schools	Public schools	Private schools [2]		
1	2	3	4	5	6
1889–90	298	203	95	5,355	5.6
1899–1900	630	519	111	6,152	10.2
1909–10	1,032	915	117	7,220	14.3
1919–20	2,414	2,200	214	7,736	31.2
1929–30	4,741	4,399	[4] 341	9,341	50.7
1939–40	7,059	6,601	[5] 458	9,720	72.6
1949–50	6,397	5,725	672	8,405	76.1
1951–52	6,538	5,882	656	8,516	76.8
1953–54	7,038	6,290	747	8,861	79.4
1955–56	7,696	6,873	823	9,207	83.6
1957–58	8,790	7,860	931	10,139	86.7
Fall 1959	9,306	8,271	1,035	11,155	83.4
Fall 1961	10,489	9,369	1,120	12,046	87.1
Fall 1963	12,170	10,883	1,287	13,492	90.2
Fall 1965	13,010	11,610	1,400	14,146	92.0
Fall 1966	13,294	11,894	1,400	14,398	92.3
Fall 1967	13,650	12,250	1,400	14,727	92.7
Fall 1968	14,118	12,718	1,400	15,170	93.1
Fall 1969	14,322	13,022	1,300	15,549	92.1
Fall 1970	14,643	13,332	1,311	15,921	92.0
Fall 1971	15,116	13,816	[6] 1,300	16,326	92.6
Fall 1972	15,213	13,913	[6] 1,300	16,637	91.4
Fall 1973	15,377	14,077	[6] 1,300	16,864	91.2
Fall 1974	15,432	14,132	[6] 1,300	17,033	90.6
Fall 1975	15,604	14,304	[6] 1,300	17,125	91.1
Fall 1976	15,671	14,311	1,360	17,117	91.6
Fall 1977	15,600	14,240	1,359	17,042	91.5
Fall 1978	15,576	14,223	1,353	16,944	91.9
Fall 1979	15,014	13,714	[6] 1,300	16,610	90.4
Fall 1980	14,581	13,242	1,339	16,140	90.3
Fall 1981	14,152	12,752	[6] 1,400	15,599	90.7
Fall 1982	13,807	12,407	[6] 1,400	15,040	91.8
Fall 1983	13,674	12,274	[6] 1,400	14,720	92.9
Fall 1984	13,708	12,308	[6] 1,400	14,705	93.2
Fall 1985	13,754	12,392	1,362	14,865	92.5
Fall 1986	13,669	12,333	[6] 1,336	14,797	92.4
Fall 1987	13,323	12,076	1,247	14,467	92.1
Fall 1988	12,893	11,686	[6] 1,206	13,983	92.2
Fall 1989	12,562	11,369	[6] 1,193	13,496	93.1

[1] Includes a relatively small number of secondary ungraded and postgraduate students.

[2] Data for most years are partly estimated.

[3] Data for 1890 through 1950 and for 1960 are from the decennial censuses of population. The other figures are Bureau of the Census estimates as of July 1 preceding the opening of the school year.

[4] Data are for 1927-28.

[5] Data are for 1940-41.

[6] Estimated.

NOTE.—Includes enrollment in public schools that are a part of State and local school systems and also in most nonprofit-making private schools, both religiously affiliated and nonsectarian. Excludes enrollment in subcollegiate departments of institutions of higher education, residential schools for exceptional children, and Federal schools. Because of rounding, details may not add to totals. Some data have been revised from previously published figures.

SOURCE: U.S. Department of Education, National Center for Education Statistics, *Statistics of State School Systems; Statistics of Public Elementary and Secondary School Systems; Statistics of Nonpublic Elementary and Secondary Schools;* Common Core of Data survey; and *Projections of Education Statistics to 2001.* (This table was prepared February 1991.)

Table 52.—Enrollment in foreign language courses compared with enrollment in grades 9 to 12 of public secondary schools: Fall 1948 to fall 1985

[In thousands]

Language	Fall 1948	Fall 1960	Fall 1965	Fall 1968	Fall 1970	Fall 1974	Fall 1976	Fall 1978	Fall 1982	Fall 1985	Percent change in enrollment	
											1965 to 1976	1976 to 1985
1	2	3	4	5	6	7	8	9	10	11	12	13
Total enrollment, grades 9 to 12	[1]5,602	8,589	11,610	12,718	13,332	14,132	14,311	14,125	12,407	12,392	23.3	−13.4
All foreign languages[2]												
Number enrolled	1,170	2,522	3,659	3,890	3,779	3,295	3,174	3,200	2,910	4,029	−13.3	26.9
Percent of all students	20.9	29.4	31.5	30.6	28.3	23.3	22.2	22.7	23.3	32.2	—	—
Modern foreign languages												
Number enrolled	741	1,867	3,068	3,518	3,514	3,127	3,023	3,048	2,740	3,852	−1.4	27.4
Percent of all students	13.2	21.7	26.4	27.7	26.4	22.1	21.1	21.6	21.9	30.9	—	—
Spanish												
Number enrolled	443	933	1,427	1,698	1,811	1,678	1,717	1,631	1,563	2,334	20.3	35.9
Percent of all students	7.9	10.9	12.3	13.4	13.6	11.9	12.0	11.5	12.5	18.7	—	—
French												
Number enrolled	254	744	1,251	1,328	1,231	978	888	856	858	1,134	−29.0	27.7
Percent of all students	4.5	8.7	10.8	10.4	9.2	6.9	6.2	6.1	6.9	9.1	—	—
German												
Number enrolled	43	151	328	423	411	393	353	331	267	312	7.5	−11.5
Percent of all students	0.8	1.8	2.8	3.3	3.1	2.8	2.5	2.3	2.1	2.5	—	—
Russian												
Number enrolled	—	10	27	24	20	15	11	9	6	6	−57.9	−46.7
Percent of all students	—	0.1	0.2	0.2	0.2	0.1	0.1	0.1	([3])	([3])	—	—
Italian												
Number enrolled	—	20	25	27	27	40	46	46	44	47	80.7	3.1
Percent of all students	—	0.2	0.2	0.2	0.2	0.3	0.3	0.3	0.4	0.4	—	—
Other modern foreign languages[4]												
Number enrolled	1	9	9	18	15	23	9	176	3	18	−9.0	—
Percent of all students	([3])	0.1	0.1	0.1	0.1	0.2	0.1	1.2	([3])	0.1	—	—
Latin												
Number enrolled	429	655	591	372	265	167	150	152	170	177	−74.6	17.6
Percent of all students	7.7	7.6	5.1	2.9	2.0	1.2	1.1	1.1	1.4	1.4	—	—

[1] Estimated.

[2] Includes enrollment in ancient Greek (not shown separately). Fewer than 1,000 students were enrolled in this language in each of the years shown.

[3] Less than 0.05 percent.

[4] Includes students enrolled in unspecified modern foreign languages. In 1978, a relatively large number of students were not identified by field of study.

—Data not reported, not available, or not applicable.

NOTE.—Because of rounding, details may not add to totals.

SOURCE: U.S. Department of Education, National Center for Education Statistics, Common Core of Data survey; American Council on the Teaching of Foreign Languages, "Report of Foreign Language Enrollment in Public Secondary Schools, Fall 1985." (This table was prepared October 1990.)

Table 53.—Student participation in school programs and services, by control, level, and community type of school: 1987–88

Control, level, and community type	Total students		Percent of students participating in program or service								
	Number	Percent distribution	Bilingual education	English as a second language	Remedial reading	Remedial mathematics	Programs for the handicapped	Programs for the gifted and talented	Vocational/ technical programs	Diagnostic and prescriptive	Extended day
1	2	3	4	5	6	7	8	9	10	11	12
Public total	**39,911,968**	**100.00**	**2.77**	**2.61**	**10.77**	**7.14**	**7.17**	**6.50**	**11.97**	**10.78**	**1.31**
School level[1]											
Elementary	23,947,579	60.00	3.71	3.15	12.40	7.24	7.00	6.20	2.55	11.13	1.80
Secondary	14,372,740	36.01	1.32	1.84	7.94	6.77	6.73	7.17	27.04	9.61	0.51
Combined	1,591,649	3.99	1.65	1.38	11.73	8.99	13.80	5.01	17.68	15.93	1.04
Community type											
Rural/farming	8,913,541	22.33	1.28	1.03	10.56	6.39	7.32	4.70	13.59	11.40	0.39
Small city/town	9,849,966	24.68	1.35	1.29	10.27	6.68	7.36	6.02	11.76	10.05	0.89
Suburban	8,744,360	21.91	1.73	2.21	8.40	5.52	6.99	7.41	10.71	10.78	1.25
Urban	12,129,222	30.39	5.63	4.96	13.01	9.21	7.02	7.62	12.01	10.84	2.37
Other	274,879	0.69	8.67	10.21	11.43	8.06	7.61	3.43	(2)	13.25	(2)
Private total	**5,479,368**	**100.00**	**1.72**	**1.12**	**6.31**	**4.37**	**2.12**	**6.85**	**1.74**	**7.60**	**6.95**
School level[1]											
Elementary	3,174,760	56.94	1.88	0.78	6.41	4.16	0.84	5.56	0.39	7.36	9.38
Secondary	896,478	17.16	(2)	1.00	3.67	3.31	0.95	8.12	3.41	2.78	(2)
Combined	1,408,132	25.90	2.18	1.96	7.81	5.51	5.71	8.83	3.62	11.32	5.99
Community type[3]											
Rural/farming	523,494	9.54	(2)	0.97	7.25	5.22	3.33	5.07	3.18	11.74	2.07
Small city/town	989,361	18.03	(2)	0.54	6.66	4.07	2.27	3.88	1.73	9.35	4.75
Suburban	1,446,736	26.04	0.50	0.77	5.68	3.93	1.75	8.79	1.07	6.30	6.79
Urban	2,504,081	46.09	0.93	1.38	6.17	4.36	2.00	7.32	1.82	6.81	8.96

[1] Elementary schools have grade 6 or lower or a low grade of ungraded and no grade higher than 8. Secondary schools have no grade lower than 7. Combined schools have grades lower than 7 and higher than 8.

[2] Too few sample cases (fewer than 30) for a reliable estimate.

[3] Other types of communities are included in the totals but are not shown separately.

NOTE.—Students may participate in more than one program or service. Totals differ from data appearing in other tables because of varying survey processing procedures and time period coverages.

SOURCE: U.S. Department of Education, National Center for Education Statistics, "Schools and Staffing Survey, 1987–88." (This table was prepared April 1990.)

Table 54.—Private elementary and secondary enrollment and schools, by selected characteristics: 1987–88

Selected characteristics	Kindergarten through 12th grade enrollment [1]				Schools			
	Total	Catholic	Other religious	Non-sectarian	Total	Catholic	Other religious	Non-sectarian
1	2	3	4	5	6	7	8	9
Total	**5,479,368**	**2,901,809**	**1,714,852**	**862,707**	**26,807**	**9,527**	**12,132**	**5,148**
School enrollment								
Less than 150	841,262	177,719	449,991	213,552	13,122	1,820	8,058	3,245
150 to 299	1,744,413	938,072	559,389	246,952	8,125	4,225	2,697	1,203
300 to 499	1,291,757	837,426	318,467	135,864	3,454	2,211	868	374
500 to 749	784,027	467,333	189,650	127,044	1,319	801	315	203
750 or more	817,908	481,259	197,354	(2)	758	470	193	(2)
Percent minority students								
Less than 5%	2,432,130	1,258,384	873,632	300,114	12,435	4,309	6,766	1,360
5%, but less than 20%	1,573,610	766,996	503,369	303,245	7,436	2,306	3,275	1,855
20%, but less than 50%	671,945	380,109	152,504	139,333	3,239	1,177	1,045	1,017
50% or more	801,682	496,320	185,346	120,015	3,697	1,736	1,046	915
Community type[3]								
Rural/farming	523,494	186,451	216,070	120,973	5,181	1,108	3,359	715
Small city/town	989,361	525,604	317,135	146,621	6,210	2,340	2,916	954
Suburban	1,446,736	786,635	429,390	230,711	5,257	1,925	2,137	1,194
Urban	2,504,081	1,401,756	751,986	350,339	10,150	4,141	3,717	2,292

[1] Only includes prekindergarten and kindergarten students that attend schools which offer first grade or above.

[2] Too few sample cases (fewer than 30) for reliable estimates.

[3] Other types of communities are included in the totals but are not shown separately.

NOTE.—Data are based upon a sample survey and may not be strictly comparable with data reported elsewhere. Includes only schools which offer first grade or above. Because of rounding and missing values in cells with too few sample cases, details may not add to totals.

SOURCE: U.S. Department of Education, National Center for Education Statistics, "Schools and Staffing Survey, 1987–88." (This table was prepared July 1990.)

Table 55.—Private elementary and secondary staff and student-staff ratios, by level and orientation of school: 1987–88

Orientation and type of staff	Full-time equivalent staff				Students per full-time equivalent staff member			
	Total	Elementary [1]	Secondary [2]	Combined [3]	Total	Elementary [1]	Secondary [2]	Combined [3]
1	2	3	4	5	6	7	8	9
Total	529,564	255,215	92,660	181,689	10.3	12.4	9.7	7.8
Principals and assistant principals	36,808	19,984	4,739	12,085	148.9	158.9	189.2	116.5
Teachers	352,648	172,306	63,980	116,362	15.5	18.4	14.0	12.1
Guidance counselors	8,514	1,728	3,737	3,049	643.5	1837.1	239.9	461.8
Librarians	11,911	5,984	2,432	3,495	460.0	530.5	368.7	402.9
Other professional staff	25,874	9,849	5,539	10,486	211.8	322.4	161.8	134.3
Teacher aides	40,188	22,787	1,027	16,374	136.3	139.3	872.6	86.0
Other noninstructional staff	53,620	22,578	11,204	19,838	102.2	140.6	80.0	71.0
Catholic								
Total	205,363	135,739	61,925	7,699	14.1	15.4	11.8	9.5
Principals and assistant principals	11,915	8,512	2,985	418	243.5	246.3	245.2	174.9
Teachers	146,792	97,761	43,870	5,161	19.8	21.4	16.7	14.2
Guidance counselors	4,090	1,069	2,872	148	709.5	1961.0	254.8	493.7
Librarians	6,027	4,114	1,665	248	481.5	509.6	439.7	294.9
Other professional staff	8,002	4,613	3,073	316	362.6	454.5	238.2	231.6
Teacher aides	9,217	8,097	759	360	314.8	258.9	964.4	202.9
Other noninstructional staff	19,321	11,571	6,701	1,048	150.2	181.2	109.2	69.8
Other religious orientation								
Total	185,295	80,651	14,367	90,276	9.3	9.5	6.5	9.5
Principals and assistant principals	16,200	7,901	973	7,327	105.9	97.3	95.7	116.5
Teachers	123,046	51,390	9,425	62,231	13.9	15.0	9.9	13.7
Guidance counselors	2,312	396	433	1,483	741.7	1939.8	215.0	575.5
Librarians	3,300	1,339	366	1,594	519.7	573.7	254.0	535.4
Other professional staff	7,733	2,676	925	4,132	221.8	287.1	100.6	206.6
Teacher aides	15,539	9,758	92	5,688	110.4	78.7	1007.8	150.0
Other noninstructional staff	17,164	7,191	2,153	7,821	99.9	106.9	43.2	109.1
Non-sectarian								
Total	138,907	38,824	16,368	83,714	6.2	8.0	4.4	5.8
Principals and assistant principals	8,693	3,571	782	4,340	99.2	86.7	91.4	111.0
Teachers	82,810	23,155	10,686	48,970	10.4	13.4	6.7	9.8
Guidance counselors	2,113	263	432	1,418	408.3	1178.2	165.6	339.6
Librarians	2,584	530	401	1,653	333.9	583.8	178.4	291.4
Other professional staff	10,138	2,559	1,541	6,038	85.1	121.0	46.4	79.8
Teacher aides	15,432	4,931	176	10,325	55.9	62.8	405.9	46.6
Other noninstructional staff	17,136	3,816	2,351	10,969	50.3	81.1	30.4	43.9
Unpaid volunteers [4]	290,919	212,829	33,583	44,507	—	—	—	—
Independent	31,224	14,519	682	16,022	—	—	—	—
Catholic	179,754	147,091	30,924	1,739	—	—	—	—
Other religious orientation	79,942	51,218	1,977	26,747	—	—	—	—

[1] Schools have grade 6 or lower or a low grade of ungraded and no grade higher than 8.
[2] Schools have no grade lower than 7.
[3] Schools have grades lower than 7 and higher than 8.
[4] Data represent total number of volunteers rather than full-time equivalents.
—Data not applicable.

NOTE.—Data are based upon a sample survey and may not be strictly comparable with data reported elsewhere. Includes only schools which offer first grade or above. Because of rounding and missing values in cells with too few sample cases, details may not add to totals.

SOURCE: U.S. Department of Education, National Center for Education Statistics, "Schools and Staffing Survey, 1987–88." (This table was prepared July 1990.)

Table 56.—Private elementary and secondary enrollment and schools, by amount of tuition, level, and orientation of school: 1987–88

Orientation and tuition	Kindergarten through 12th grade enrollment [1]				Schools				Average tuition paid by students			
	Total	Elementary	Second-ary	Combined	Total	Ele-menta-ry	Sec-ondary	Com-bined	Total	Ele-menta-ry	Sec-ondary	Com-bined
1	2	3	4	5	6	7	8	9	10	11	12	13
Total	5,479,368	3,174,760	896,478	1,408,132	26,807	17,087	2,425	7,296	$1,915	$1,357	$2,552	$2,767
Catholic	2,901,809	2,096,779	731,922	73,107	9,527	7,760	1,420	348	1,327	1,005	2,045	3,382
Less than $1,000	1,230,392	1,186,981	(2)	(2)	4,860	4,619	(2)	(2)	—	—	—	—
$1,000 to $2,499	1,456,418	881,701	556,150	(2)	4,113	3,017	1,037	(2)	—	—	—	—
$2,500 or more	214,998	(2)	(2)	(2)	554	(2)	(2)	(2)	—	—	—	—
Other religious	1,714,852	768,372	93,058	853,424	12,132	6,859	501	4,771	1,941	1,619	3,592	2,052
Less than $1,000	283,399	169,765	(2)	110,996	4,407	2,794	(2)	1,601	—	—	—	—
$1,000 to $2,499	1,034,471	480,903	(2)	537,175	6,377	3,497	(2)	2,751	—	—	—	—
$2,500 or more	396,984	117,704	74,027	205,253	1,347	568	360	419	—	—	—	—
Non-sectarian	862,707	309,609	71,498	481,601	5,148	2,468	504	2,177	3,839	3,091	6,391	3,941
Less than $1,000	96,326	(2)	(2)	74,401	805	(2)	(2)	619	—	—	—	—
$1,000 to $2,499	214,168	73,424	(2)	140,434	1,388	836	(2)	520	—	—	—	—
$2,500 or more	552,214	219,304	66,144	266,766	2,984	1,518	428	1,038	—	—	—	—

[1] Only includes prekindergarten and kindergarten students that attend schools which offer first grade or above.

[2] Too few sample cases (fewer than 30 schools) for reliable estimates.

—Data not applicable.

NOTE.—Data are based upon a sample survey and may not be strictly comparable with data reported elsewhere. Elementary schools have grade 6 or lower or a low grade of ungraded and no grade higher than 8. Secondary schools have no grade lower than 7. Combined schools have grades lower than 7 and higher than 8. Because of rounding and missing values in cells with too few sample cases, details may not add to totals.

SOURCE: U.S. Department of Education, National Center for Education Statistics, "Schools and Staffing Survey, 1987-88." (This table was prepared July 1990.)

Table 57.—Summary statistics on Catholic elementary and secondary schools, by level: 1919–20 to 1989–90

School year	Number of schools			Enrollment			Instructional staff [1]		
	Total	Elementary	Secondary	Total	Elementary	Secondary	Total	Elementary	Secondary
1	2	3	4	5	6	7	8	9	10
1919–20	8,103	6,551	1,552	1,925,521	1,795,673	129,848	49,516	41,592	7,924
1929–30	10,046	7,923	2,123	2,464,467	2,222,598	241,869	72,552	58,245	14,307
1939–40	10,049	7,944	2,105	2,396,305	2,035,182	361,123	81,057	60,081	20,976
1949–50	10,778	8,589	2,189	3,066,387	2,560,815	505,572	94,295	66,525	27,770
Fall 1960	12,893	10,501	2,392	5,253,791	4,373,422	880,369	151,902	108,169	43,733
1969–70	11,771	9,695	2,076	4,658,098	3,607,168	1,050,930	[2] 195,400	[2] 133,200	[2] 62,200
1970–71	11,350	9,370	1,980	4,363,566	3,355,478	1,008,088	166,208	112,750	53,458
1974–75	10,127	8,437	1,690	3,504,000	2,602,000	902,000	150,179	100,011	50,168
1975–76	9,993	8,340	1,653	3,415,000	2,525,000	890,000	149,276	99,319	49,957
1979–80	9,640	8,100	1,540	3,139,000	2,293,000	846,000	147,294	97,724	49,570
1980–81	9,559	8,043	1,516	3,106,000	2,269,000	837,000	145,777	96,739	49,038
1981–82	9,494	7,996	1,498	3,094,000	2,266,000	828,000	146,172	96,847	49,325
1982–83	9,432	7,950	1,482	3,026,000	2,225,000	801,000	146,460	97,337	49,123
1983–84	9,380	7,917	1,463	2,969,000	2,179,000	790,000	146,913	98,591	48,322
1984–85	9,325	7,876	1,449	2,903,000	2,119,000	784,000	149,888	99,820	50,068
1985–86	9,220	7,790	1,430	2,821,000	2,061,000	760,000	146,594	96,741	49,853
1986–87	9,102	7,693	1,409	2,726,000	1,998,000	728,000	141,930	93,554	48,376
1987–88	8,992	7,601	1,391	2,623,000	1,942,000	681,000	139,887	93,199	46,688
1988–89	8,867	7,505	1,362	2,551,000	1,912,000	639,000	137,700	93,154	44,546
1989–90	8,719	7,395	1,324	2,499,000	1,894,000	606,000	136,900	94,197	42,703

[1] Beginning in 1970–71, includes full-time teaching staff only.

[2] Includes estimates for the nonreporting schools.

NOTE.—Data reported by the National Catholic Educational Association and data reported by the National Center for Education Statistics are not directly comparable because survey procedures and definitions differ.

SOURCE: National Catholic Educational Association, *A Statistical Report on Catholic Elementary and Secondary Schools for the Years 1967–68 to 1969–70,* as compiled from the Official Catholic Directory (copyright © 1970 by the National Catholic Educational Association); *Catholic Schools in America* (1978 edition, copyright © 1978 by the Franklin Press); and *United States Catholic Elementary and Secondary Schools, 1989–90* (copyright © 1990 by the National Catholic Educational Association. All rights reserved.) (This table was prepared September 1990.)

Table 58.—Enrollment, teachers, and high school graduates in private elementary and secondary schools,[1] by State: Fall 1980 and 1979–80

State	Enrollment, fall 1980			Teachers, fall 1980			High school graduates, 1979–80		
	Total	Catholic	Other private	Total	Catholic	Other private	Total	Catholic	Other private
1	2	3	4	5	6	7	8	9	10
United States[2]	4,961,755	3,138,209	1,823,546	277,413	143,827	133,586	294,536	192,476	102,060
Alabama	62,669	14,720	47,949	3,625	668	2,957	3,877	668	3,209
Alaska	3,800	1,029	2,771	284	76	208	175	57	118
Arizona	40,261	18,306	21,955	2,291	778	1,513	1,802	992	810
Arkansas	18,423	7,223	11,200	1,119	376	743	1,114	493	621
California	513,709	262,690	251,019	26,913	10,097	16,816	24,862	15,910	8,952
Colorado	35,250	17,120	18,130	2,342	892	1,450	1,860	850	1,010
Connecticut	88,404	61,760	26,644	5,887	2,880	3,007	8,568	4,688	3,880
Delaware	23,374	14,725	8,649	1,361	668	693	1,466	1,080	386
District of Columbia	21,203	12,214	8,989	1,624	646	978	1,614	1,075	539
Florida	204,988	74,268	130,720	11,779	3,245	8,534	10,355	4,786	5,569
Georgia	82,505	13,297	69,208	5,302	617	4,685	5,272	841	4,431
Hawaii	37,147	15,059	22,088	2,051	626	1,425	2,628	921	1,707
Idaho	5,839	2,189	3,650	312	108	204	314	134	180
Illinois	349,463	278,240	71,223	17,126	12,075	5,051	20,338	17,684	2,654
Indiana	100,234	63,237	36,997	5,271	3,029	2,242	5,359	3,531	1,828
Iowa	55,227	44,790	10,437	3,059	2,405	654	3,837	3,307	530
Kansas	33,889	25,610	8,279	1,990	1,301	689	1,811	1,475	336
Kentucky	69,728	50,226	19,502	3,843	2,497	1,346	4,390	3,299	1,091
Louisiana	158,921	112,099	46,822	8,190	5,143	3,047	9,275	6,700	2,575
Maine	17,540	6,733	10,807	1,460	331	1,129	1,835	215	1,620
Maryland	106,447	68,168	38,279	6,541	3,442	3,099	6,851	4,645	2,206
Massachusetts	138,333	104,720	33,613	9,323	5,153	4,170	12,632	8,145	4,487
Michigan	211,871	129,992	81,879	10,050	5,517	4,533	13,063	8,296	4,767
Minnesota	88,966	64,418	24,548	4,876	3,264	1,612	4,403	3,004	1,399
Mississippi	50,116	11,342	38,774	3,032	605	2,427	3,722	572	3,150
Missouri	126,319	95,194	31,125	7,047	4,862	2,185	7,371	5,890	1,481
Montana	7,668	4,684	2,984	491	274	217	453	328	125
Nebraska	38,574	30,169	8,405	2,329	1,771	558	2,842	2,612	230
Nevada	6,599	4,305	2,294	316	171	145	299	288	11
New Hampshire	20,721	11,239	9,482	1,499	557	942	2,151	677	1,474
New Jersey	229,878	189,876	40,002	12,774	8,828	3,946	14,043	11,494	2,549
New Mexico	18,027	9,217	8,810	1,162	426	736	931	315	616
New York	579,670	425,981	153,689	31,618	18,285	13,333	32,366	24,643	7,723
North Carolina	58,078	9,323	48,755	3,919	417	3,502	2,781	310	2,471
North Dakota	10,659	8,230	2,429	645	479	166	714	575	139
Ohio	268,357	227,888	40,469	13,878	11,018	2,860	15,734	13,701	2,033
Oklahoma	16,335	7,381	8,954	1,126	403	723	1,035	491	544
Oregon	27,828	14,357	13,471	1,626	754	872	1,684	835	849
Pennsylvania	402,058	314,367	87,691	20,705	13,416	7,289	26,033	20,756	5,277
Rhode Island	29,875	25,015	4,860	1,748	1,132	616	2,102	1,685	417
South Carolina	49,619	7,555	42,064	3,218	367	2,851	2,693	332	2,361
South Dakota	10,898	6,882	4,016	815	437	378	639	400	239
Tennessee	71,617	15,185	56,432	4,623	817	3,806	5,226	1,241	3,985
Texas	148,534	79,766	68,768	9,242	4,165	5,077	7,089	3,929	3,160
Utah	5,555	3,055	2,500	309	121	188	479	210	269
Vermont	7,555	4,082	3,473	668	231	437	921	278	643
Virginia	75,069	23,060	52,009	5,208	1,135	4,073	4,473	1,252	3,221
Washington	55,950	27,356	28,594	3,168	1,265	1,903	3,097	1,566	1,531
West Virginia	12,608	8,466	4,142	742	467	275	850	597	253
Wisconsin	162,361	110,014	52,347	8,654	5,508	3,146	6,950	4,703	2,247
Wyoming	3,036	1,387	1,649	232	82	150	157	—	157

[1] Includes special education, vocational/technical, and alternative schools.

[2] Data represent an undercount because some schools were not included in the survey universe.

—Data not available.

NOTE.—Tabulation includes only schools which offer first grade or above.

SOURCE: U.S. Department of Education, National Center for Education Statistics, "Private Elementary and Secondary School Universe" survey. (This table was prepared May 1986.)

Table 59.—Public and private elementary and secondary teachers and pupil-teacher ratios, by level: Fall 1955 to fall 1991

Year	Public and private elementary and secondary schools			Public elementary and secondary schools			Private elementary and secondary schools		
	Kindergarten to grade 12	Elementary	Secondary	Kindergarten to grade 12	Elementary	Secondary	Kindergarten to grade 12	Elementary	Secondary
1	2	3	4	5	6	7	8	9	10
Number of teachers, in thousands									
1955	1,286	827	459	1,141	733	408	[1]145	[1]94	[1]51
1956	1,354	854	499	1,199	751	447	[1]155	[1]103	[1]52
1957	1,424	898	526	1,259	786	473	[1]165	[1]112	[1]53
1958	1,475	931	544	1,306	815	491	[1]169	[1]116	[1]53
1959	1,531	952	580	1,355	832	524	[1]176	[1]120	[1]56
1960	1,600	991	609	1,408	858	550	[1]192	[1]133	59
1961	1,643	992	651	1,461	869	592	182	123	[1]59
1962	1,708	1,021	686	1,508	886	621	[1]200	[1]135	[1]65
1963	1,790	1,050	739	1,578	908	669	[1]212	[1]142	[1]70
1964	1,865	1,086	779	1,648	940	708	[1]217	[1]146	[1]71
1965	1,933	1,112	822	1,710	965	746	223	147	76
1966	2,012	1,153	859	1,789	1,006	783	[1]223	[1]147	[1]76
1967	2,079	1,188	891	1,855	1,040	815	[1]224	[1]148	[1]76
1968	2,161	1,223	938	1,936	1,076	860	225	147	78
1969	2,242	1,258	985	2,013	1,107	907	[1]229	[1]151	[1]78
1970	2,288	1,281	1,007	2,055	1,128	927	233	153	80
1971	2,293	1,263	1,030	2,063	1,111	952	[1]230	[1]152	[1]78
1972	2,334	1,294	1,040	2,103	1,140	963	[1]231	[1]154	[1]77
1973	2,369	1,306	1,063	2,133	1,149	984	[1]236	[1]157	[1]79
1974	2,410	1,331	1,079	2,165	1,167	998	[1]245	[1]164	[1]81
1975	2,451	1,352	1,099	2,196	1,180	1,016	[1]255	[1]172	[1]83
1976	2,454	1,349	1,105	2,186	1,166	1,020	268	183	85
1977	2,488	1,375	1,113	2,209	1,185	1,024	279	190	89
1978	2,478	1,375	1,103	2,206	1,190	1,016	272	185	87
1979	2,459	1,378	1,081	2,183	1,190	993	[1]276	[1]188	[1]88
1980	2,485	1,401	1,084	2,184	1,189	995	301	212	89
1981	2,438	1,380	1,057	2,125	1,159	965	[1]313	[1]221	[1]92
1982	2,446	1,402	1,044	2,121	1,171	950	[1]325	[1]231	[1]94
1983	2,463	1,418	1,045	2,126	1,178	948	337	240	97
1984	2,508	1,448	1,060	2,168	1,205	963	[1]340	[1]243	[1]97
1985	2,550	1,483	1,067	2,207	1,237	970	343	246	97
1986	2,592	1,517	1,075	2,244	1,267	977	[1]348	[1]250	[1]98
1987	2,631	1,554	1,077	2,279	1,297	982	353	257	95
1988[2]	2,668	1,604	1,064	2,323	1,353	970	345	251	94
1989[2]	2,734	1,664	1,070	2,356	1,389	968	377	275	102
1990[3]	2,744	1,632	1,112	2,391	1,379	1,012	353	253	100
1991[4]	2,826	1,631	1,194	2,465	1,378	1,087	360	253	107
Pupil-teacher ratios									
1955	27.4	31.4	20.3	26.9	30.2	20.9	[1]31.7	[1]40.4	[1]15.7
1956	27.0	30.7	20.8	26.5	29.6	21.2	[1]31.6	[1]38.8	[1]17.3
1957	26.8	30.3	20.9	26.2	29.1	21.3	[1]31.5	[1]38.4	[1]17.0
1958	26.8	30.0	21.4	26.1	28.7	21.7	[1]32.5	[1]38.8	[1]18.9
1959	26.7	30.0	21.2	26.0	28.7	21.5	[1]32.2	[1]38.7	[1]18.5
1960	26.4	29.4	21.4	25.8	28.4	21.7	[1]30.7	[1]36.1	18.6
1961	26.4	29.6	21.5	25.6	28.3	21.7	[1]32.5	39.0	[1]19.0
1962	26.3	29.5	21.4	25.7	28.5	21.7	[1]30.5	[1]36.3	[1]18.5
1963	26.0	29.3	21.2	25.5	28.4	21.5	[1]29.7	[1]35.2	[1]18.6
1964	25.6	28.7	21.2	25.1	27.9	21.5	[1]29.0	[1]34.2	[1]18.3
1965	25.1	28.4	20.6	24.7	27.6	20.8	28.3	33.3	18.4
1966	24.5	27.7	20.2	24.1	26.9	20.3	[1]27.8	[1]32.7	[1]18.4
1967	24.0	26.9	20.1	23.7	26.3	20.3	[1]26.8	[1]31.1	[1]18.4
1968	23.5	26.0	20.2	23.2	25.4	20.4	25.8	29.9	17.9
1969	22.8	25.2	19.8	22.7	24.8	20.0	[1]24.0	[1]27.8	[1]16.7
1970	22.4	24.6	19.6	22.3	24.4	19.9	23.0	26.5	16.4
1971	22.4	25.0	19.1	22.3	24.9	19.3	[1]22.6	[1]25.7	[1]16.7
1972	21.7	24.0	19.0	21.8	24.0	19.1	[1]21.6	[1]24.0	[1]16.9
1973	21.3	23.1	19.1	21.3	23.0	19.3	[1]21.2	[1]23.6	[1]16.5
1974	20.8	22.6	18.5	20.8	22.6	18.7	[1]20.4	[1]22.6	[1]16.0
1975	20.3	21.7	18.6	20.4	21.7	18.8	[1]19.6	[1]21.5	[1]15.7
1976	20.2	21.7	18.3	20.3	21.8	18.5	19.3	20.9	15.8
1977	19.6	20.9	17.9	19.7	21.1	18.2	18.4	20.0	15.1
1978	19.2	20.9	17.1	19.3	21.0	17.3	18.7	20.2	15.6
1979	19.0	20.5	17.0	19.1	20.6	17.2	[1]18.1	[1]19.7	[1]14.8
1980	18.6	20.1	16.6	18.7	20.4	16.8	17.7	18.8	15.0
1981	18.7	20.4	16.4	18.8	20.8	16.5	[1]17.6	[1]18.6	[1]15.2
1982	18.5	20.0	16.4	18.7	20.3	16.6	[1]17.2	[1]18.2	[1]14.9
1983	18.3	19.9	16.0	18.5	20.3	16.1	17.0	18.0	14.4
1984	17.9	19.6	15.6	18.1	20.0	15.7	[1]16.8	[1]17.7	[1]14.4
1985	17.6	19.2	15.5	17.9	19.6	15.7	16.2	17.1	14.0
1986	17.4	18.6	15.8	17.7	19.1	16.0	[1]15.7	[1]16.5	[1]13.6
1987	17.3	18.4	15.7	17.6	18.7	16.0	15.5	16.4	13.1
1988[2]	17.0	17.7	16.0	17.3	18.0	16.3	[1]15.2	[1]16.1	[1]12.8
1989[2]	16.8	17.3	16.0	17.2	17.7	16.4	[1]14.2	[1]15.1	[1]11.7
1990[3]	16.8	18.2	14.9	17.2	18.6	15.2	[1]14.7	[1]16.1	[1]11.3
1991[4]	16.6	18.4	14.0	16.9	18.8	14.4	[1]14.6	[1]16.3	[1]10.7

[1] Estimated.

[2] Revised from previously published data.

[3] Data for public schools are estimated. Data for private schools are projected.

[4] Projected.

NOTE.—Data for teachers are expressed in full-time equivalents. Distribution of unclassified teachers by level is estimated. Distribution of elementary and secondary school teachers by level is determined by reporting units. Kindergarten includes a relatively small number of nursery school teachers and students. Some data have been revised from previously published figures. Because of rounding, details may not add to totals.

SOURCE: U.S. Department of Education, National Center for Education Statistics, *Statistics of Public Elementary and Secondary Day Schools*; Common Core of Data survey and *Projections of Education Statistics to 2002*. (This table was prepared April 1991.)

Table 60.—Public elementary and secondary teachers, by level and State: Fall 1985 to fall 1990

[In full-time equivalents]

State or other area	Number of teachers, fall 1985	Number of teachers, fall 1986	Number of teachers, fall 1987	Number of teachers, fall 1988 [1]				Number of teachers, fall 1989				Estimated number of teachers, 1990
				Total	Elementary	Secondary	Unclassified	Total	Elementary	Secondary	Unclassified	
1	2	3	4	5	6	7	8	9	10	11	12	13
United States	2,206,884	[2] 2,244,445	2,279,241	2,323,213	1,236,800	923,807	162,606	[2] 2,355,963	[2] 1,280,808	[2] 912,453	[2] 162,702	2,390,771
Alabama	36,138	36,971	37,716	38,845	21,123	17,722	—	39,928	22,211	17,717	—	40,100
Alaska	6,814	6,448	6,113	6,272	3,266	2,263	743	6,492	3,723	2,021	748	[3] 6,727
Arizona	27,935	29,104	30,707	31,617	22,873	8,744	—	32,134	23,458	8,676	—	31,799
Arkansas	24,767	24,944	25,572	27,730	12,536	12,821	2,373	25,585	13,204	12,242	139	[3] 25,632
California	184,151	190,484	195,864	203,342	143,689	54,883	4,770	212,687	151,019	56,258	5,410	215,799
Colorado	29,894	30,704	31,168	31,398	15,769	15,629	—	31,954	16,157	15,797	—	32,600
Connecticut	32,903	34,252	35,050	35,502	12,705	16,775	6,022	35,308	18,310	12,490	4,508	[4] 35,260
Delaware	5,745	5,883	5,951	5,898	2,936	2,962	—	5,968	2,935	3,033	—	[4] 5,951
District of Columbia	6,137	5,984	6,232	5,936	3,015	2,596	325	6,055	3,270	2,534	251	6,646
Florida	88,973	91,969	95,857	100,370	43,485	38,511	18,374	104,127	45,710	40,003	18,414	[4] 108,422
Georgia	57,374	57,881	62,280	59,916	36,645	23,271	—	61,487	41,319	20,168	—	65,067
Hawaii	7,276	7,291	7,684	8,737	4,524	3,272	941	8,866	4,692	3,130	1,044	8,956
Idaho	10,255	10,234	10,258	10,425	5,493	4,828	104	10,715	5,678	4,938	99	11,042
Illinois	102,657	104,609	105,217	105,097	59,144	29,500	16,453	106,183	60,439	28,973	16,771	106,320
Indiana	51,976	52,896	53,749	54,029	26,166	23,431	4,432	54,486	26,440	23,423	4,623	54,443
Iowa	31,770	30,958	30,873	30,327	16,766	12,558	1,003	30,423	17,303	12,058	1,062	[4] 31,843
Kansas	26,686	27,064	27,317	28,122	14,356	10,851	2,915	28,727	14,345	11,392	2,990	29,086
Kentucky	33,506	34,507	35,239	35,788	23,877	11,911	—	35,731	24,051	11,680	—	[4] 36,847
Louisiana	42,609	42,929	42,920	43,203	23,443	11,933	7,827	—	—	—	—	43,609
Maine	14,226	13,685	14,204	14,593	9,542	5,051	—	15,206	10,041	5,165	—	[3] 15,358
Maryland	38,433	39,491	40,093	40,899	20,790	20,109	—	41,646	21,536	20,110	—	44,373
Massachusetts	56,845	58,066	59,517	60,068	20,366	32,247	7,455	59,040	20,251	31,238	7,551	56,678
Michigan	82,193	83,130	79,972	79,847	31,073	39,637	9,137	80,150	31,662	39,285	9,203	[3] 80,307
Minnesota	41,314	40,957	42,132	42,750	22,593	20,157	—	43,101	23,137	19,964	—	43,771
Mississippi	26,102	26,219	26,930	27,283	15,615	10,563	1,105	27,591	16,087	10,562	942	[4] 27,691
Missouri	48,170	48,902	49,632	50,693	25,993	23,769	931	51,227	26,471	23,962	794	51,226
Montana	9,705	9,818	9,659	9,626	6,011	2,859	756	9,627	6,656	2,968	3	9,540
Nebraska	17,687	17,748	17,713	18,003	9,989	8,014	—	18,464	10,388	8,076	—	[4] 18,694
Nevada	7,751	7,908	8,348	8,699	4,874	3,825	—	9,175	4,646	3,464	1,065	9,642
New Hampshire	10,104	10,300	10,363	10,442	6,685	3,757	—	10,572	7,094	3,478	—	10,665
New Jersey	74,236	75,558	78,335	79,698	42,027	28,764	8,907	79,597	42,711	27,611	9,275	81,934
New Mexico	14,781	14,876	15,175	15,770	8,976	4,320	2,474	16,150	9,238	4,302	2,610	16,280
New York	165,573	168,940	170,236	172,807	80,897	66,615	25,295	174,610	82,769	65,857	25,984	174,500
North Carolina	57,638	58,103	59,771	61,933	31,781	21,152	9,000	63,160	32,667	20,858	9,635	64,331
North Dakota	7,796	7,779	7,632	7,731	5,048	2,683	—	7,809	5,171	2,638	—	[4] 6,593
Ohio	98,264	98,894	99,708	101,021	55,761	45,260	—	101,627	56,308	45,319	—	[4] 101,032
Oklahoma	35,752	35,041	34,515	35,116	16,399	15,050	3,667	35,631	16,747	15,122	3,762	36,600
Oregon	24,605	24,615	24,911	25,147	14,308	10,052	787	25,630	14,756	10,102	772	25,800
Pennsylvania	101,665	102,993	103,307	104,379	46,071	46,988	11,320	105,415	47,171	46,698	11,546	104,800
Rhode Island	8,844	8,916	8,934	9,216	4,208	3,775	1,233	9,369	4,293	3,820	1,256	[4] 9,450
South Carolina	34,645	35,349	35,701	35,877	23,416	12,461	—	36,337	24,034	12,303	—	36,670
South Dakota	8,340	8,031	8,172	8,260	4,521	3,082	657	8,191	4,465	3,029	697	[4] 8,333
Tennessee	40,023	41,103	42,082	42,657	26,507	16,150	—	42,824	26,979	15,845	—	44,491
Texas	181,051	186,385	187,159	196,616	103,542	93,074	—	199,397	106,196	93,201	—	206,399
Utah	17,126	17,752	17,124	17,602	9,274	6,350	1,978	17,611	9,277	6,258	2,076	18,300
Vermont	6,397	—	6,656	6,852	3,175	3,194	483	6,852	3,175	3,194	483	[3] 6,967
Virginia	57,339	58,141	59,928	60,883	34,942	25,464	477	62,138	36,420	25,191	527	62,796
Washington	36,202	37,065	38,344	38,780	19,359	15,745	3,676	40,279	21,101	15,391	3,787	41,219
West Virginia	22,733	22,931	22,702	22,177	10,359	8,104	3,714	21,653	10,289	7,741	3,623	21,251
Wisconsin	46,482	47,039	47,721	48,541	28,483	17,638	2,420	49,329	29,069	17,870	2,390	52,378
Wyoming	7,296	7,201	6,798	6,693	2,404	3,437	852	6,697	2,405	3,421	871	[4] 6,553
Outlying areas												
American Samoa	—	—	656	674	432	196	46	659	409	197	53	679
Guam	1,329	1,430	1,407	1,403	704	678	21	1,622	780	821	21	1,501
Northern Marianas	—	—	305	334	198	122	14	358	215	117	26	[3] 360
Puerto Rico	32,683	32,361	33,069	33,357	18,043	13,379	1,935	33,427	18,123	13,267	2,037	33,670
Virgin Islands	1,631	1,606	1,590	1,597	784	688	125	1,595	770	694	131	1,610

[1] Data have been revised from previously published figures.

[2] U.S. total includes imputation for nonreporting State or States.

[3] Estimated by the National Center for Education Statistics.

[4] Actual fall 1990 data.

—Data not available, not reported, or not applicable.

NOTE.—Distribution of elementary and secondary teachers determined by reporting units. Teachers reported in full-time equivalents.

SOURCE: U.S. Department of Education, National Center for Education Statistics, Common Core of Data surveys. (This table was prepared January 1991.)

Table 61.—Teachers, enrollment, and pupil-teacher ratios in public elementary and secondary schools, by State: Fall 1985 to fall 1989

State or other area	Pupil-teacher ratio, fall 1985	Pupil-teacher ratio, fall 1986	Fall 1987			Fall 1988 [1]			Fall 1989		
			Teachers	Enrollment	Pupil-teacher ratio	Teachers	Enrollment	Pupil-teacher ratio	Teachers	Enrollment	Pupil-teacher ratio
1	2	3	4	5	6	7	8	9	10	11	12
United States	17.9	[2] 17.7	2,279,241	40,007,946	17.6	2,323,213	40,188,690	17.3	2,355,963	40,526,372	[2] 17.2
Alabama	20.2	19.8	37,716	729,234	19.3	38,845	724,751	18.7	39,928	723,343	18.1
Alaska	15.8	16.7	6,113	105,678	17.3	6,272	106,481	17.0	6,492	109,280	16.8
Arizona	19.6	18.4	30,707	572,421	18.6	31,617	574,890	18.2	32,134	607,615	18.9
Arkansas	17.5	17.5	25,572	437,036	17.1	27,730	436,387	15.7	25,585	434,960	17.0
California	23.1	23.0	195,864	4,489,322	22.9	203,342	4,618,120	22.7	212,687	4,771,978	22.4
Colorado	18.4	18.2	31,168	560,236	18.0	31,398	560,081	17.8	31,954	562,755	17.6
Connecticut	14.0	13.7	35,050	465,465	13.3	35,502	460,637	13.0	35,308	461,560	13.1
Delaware	16.2	16.0	5,951	95,659	16.1	5,898	96,678	16.4	5,968	97,808	16.4
District of Columbia	14.2	14.3	6,232	86,435	13.9	5,936	84,792	14.3	6,055	81,301	13.4
Florida	17.6	17.5	95,857	1,664,774	17.4	100,370	1,720,930	17.1	104,127	1,772,349	17.0
Georgia	18.8	18.9	62,280	1,110,947	17.8	59,916	1,107,994	18.5	61,487	1,126,535	18.3
Hawaii	22.6	22.6	7,684	166,160	21.6	8,737	167,488	19.2	8,866	169,493	19.1
Idaho	20.3	20.4	10,258	212,444	20.7	10,425	214,615	20.6	10,715	214,932	20.1
Illinois	17.8	17.4	105,217	1,811,446	17.2	105,097	1,794,916	17.1	106,183	1,797,355	16.9
Indiana	18.6	18.3	53,749	964,129	17.9	54,029	960,994	17.8	54,486	954,165	17.5
Iowa	15.3	15.5	30,873	480,826	15.6	30,327	478,200	15.8	30,423	478,486	15.7
Kansas	15.4	15.4	27,317	421,112	15.4	28,122	426,596	15.2	28,727	430,864	15.0
Kentucky	19.2	18.6	35,239	642,696	18.2	35,788	637,627	17.8	35,731	630,688	17.7
Louisiana	18.5	18.5	42,920	793,093	18.5	43,203	786,683	18.2	—	783,025	—
Maine	14.5	15.5	14,204	211,817	14.9	14,593	212,902	14.6	15,206	213,775	14.1
Maryland	17.5	17.1	40,093	683,797	17.1	40,899	688,947	16.8	41,646	698,806	16.8
Massachusetts	14.9	14.4	59,517	825,320	13.9	60,068	823,428	13.7	59,040	825,588	14.0
Michigan	19.5	19.2	79,972	1,589,287	19.9	79,847	1,582,785	19.8	80,150	1,576,785	19.7
Minnesota	17.1	17.4	42,132	721,481	17.1	42,750	726,950	17.0	43,101	739,553	17.2
Mississippi	18.1	19.0	26,930	505,550	18.8	27,283	503,326	18.4	27,591	502,020	18.2
Missouri	16.5	16.4	49,632	802,060	16.2	50,693	806,639	15.9	51,227	807,934	15.8
Montana	15.9	15.6	9,659	152,207	15.8	9,626	152,191	15.8	9,627	151,265	15.7
Nebraska	15.0	15.1	17,713	268,100	15.1	18,003	269,434	15.0	18,464	270,920	14.7
Nevada	20.0	20.4	8,348	168,353	20.2	8,699	176,474	20.3	9,175	186,834	20.4
New Hampshire	15.9	15.9	10,363	166,045	16.0	10,442	169,413	16.2	10,572	171,696	16.2
New Jersey	15.0	14.7	78,335	1,092,982	14.0	79,698	1,080,871	13.6	79,597	1,076,005	13.5
New Mexico	18.8	19.0	15,175	287,229	18.9	15,770	292,425	18.5	16,150	296,057	18.3
New York	15.8	15.4	170,236	2,594,070	15.2	172,807	2,573,715	14.9	174,610	2,565,841	14.7
North Carolina	18.8	18.7	59,771	1,085,976	18.2	61,933	1,083,156	17.5	63,160	1,080,744	17.1
North Dakota	15.2	15.3	7,632	119,004	15.6	7,731	118,809	15.4	7,809	117,816	15.1
Ohio	18.3	18.1	99,708	1,793,431	18.0	101,021	1,778,544	17.6	101,627	1,767,159	17.4
Oklahoma	16.6	16.9	34,515	584,212	16.9	35,116	580,426	16.5	35,631	578,580	16.2
Oregon	18.2	18.3	24,911	455,895	18.3	25,147	461,752	18.4	25,630	472,394	18.4
Pennsylvania	16.6	16.3	103,307	1,668,542	16.2	104,379	1,659,714	15.9	105,415	1,655,279	15.7
Rhode Island	15.1	15.1	8,934	134,800	15.1	9,216	133,585	14.5	9,369	135,729	14.5
South Carolina	17.5	17.3	35,701	614,921	17.2	35,877	615,774	17.2	36,337	616,177	17.0
South Dakota	14.9	15.6	8,172	126,817	15.5	8,260	126,910	15.4	8,191	127,329	15.5
Tennessee	20.3	19.9	42,082	823,783	19.6	42,657	821,580	19.3	42,824	819,660	19.1
Texas	17.3	17.2	187,159	3,236,787	17.3	196,616	3,283,707	16.7	199,397	3,328,514	16.7
Utah	23.6	23.4	17,124	423,386	24.7	17,602	431,119	24.5	17,611	437,446	24.8
Vermont	14.1	—	6,656	92,755	13.9	6,852	93,381	13.6	6,852	94,779	13.8
Virginia	16.9	16.8	59,928	979,417	16.3	60,883	982,393	16.1	62,138	985,346	15.9
Washington	20.7	20.5	38,344	775,755	20.2	38,780	790,918	20.4	40,279	810,232	20.1
West Virginia	15.7	15.3	22,702	344,236	15.2	22,177	335,912	15.1	21,653	327,540	15.1
Wisconsin	16.5	16.3	47,721	772,363	16.2	48,541	774,857	16.0	49,329	782,905	15.9
Wyoming	14.1	14.0	6,798	98,455	14.5	6,693	97,793	14.6	6,697	97,172	14.5
Outlying areas											
American Samoa	—	—	656	11,248	17.1	674	11,764	17.5	659	12,258	18.6
Guam	19.6	18.0	1,407	25,936	18.4	1,403	26,041	18.6	1,622	26,493	16.3
Northern Marianas	—	—	305	5,819	19.1	334	6,079	18.2	358	6,101	17.0
Puerto Rico	21.0	21.0	33,069	672,837	20.3	33,357	661,693	19.8	33,427	651,225	19.5
Virgin Islands	15.6	15.2	1,590	24,020	15.1	1,597	23,492	14.7	1,595	21,193	13.3

[1] Some data have been revised from previously published figures.
[2] U.S. total includes imputation for nonreporting State.
—Data not available.

NOTE.—Teachers reported in full-time equivalents.

SOURCE: U.S. Department of Education, National Center for Education Statistics, Common Core of Data surveys. (This table was prepared March 1991.)

Table 62.—Teachers in public and private elementary and secondary schools, by selected characteristics: 1987–88

Selected characteristics	Total [1]	Percent of teachers, by highest degree earned						Percent of teachers, by years of full-time teaching experience			
		No degree	Associate	Bachelor's	Master's	Education specialist	Doctor's	Less than 3	3 to 9	10 to 20	Over 20
1	2	3	4	5	6	7	8	9	10	11	12
Public schools											
Total	2,323,204	0.2	0.4	52.2	40.0	6.3	0.9	8.0	26.0	44.5	21.4
Sex											
Men	681,161	0.6	1.2	44.2	44.9	7.5	1.6	6.2	19.5	44.3	29.9
Women	1,631,168	(2)	0.1	55.5	37.9	5.7	0.6	8.7	28.8	44.6	17.8
Race/ethnicity											
White	1,994,389	0.2	0.4	52.1	40.3	6.2	0.8	8.0	26.6	44.4	21.0
Black	187,836	(2)	(2)	49.7	42.4	0.6	(2)	6.1	19.4	46.3	28.2
Hispanic	67,084	(2)	(2)	84.5	29.9	6.7	(2)	11.9	33.2	40.9	13.9
Asian or Pacific Islander	20,709	(2)	(2)	52.8	28.7	13.5	(2)	11.2	22.1	43.0	23.7
American Indian or Alaskan Native	23,998	(2)	(2)	50.1	40.5	7.5	(2)	5.7	24.3	49.7	20.2
Age											
Less than 30	310,901	(2)	(2)	82.9	15.4	1.1	(2)	36.5	63.2	(2)	(2)
30 to 39	813,204	(2)	0.3	53.3	40.6	5.2	0.5	6.0	33.6	60.2	(2)
40 to 49	752,301	0.2	0.5	44.2	46.0	7.8	1.3	2.3	14.0	55.0	28.6
50 or more	416,857	0.5	0.8	42.3	45.5	9.3	1.6	1.2	5.7	27.9	65.0
Level											
Elementary	1,181,578	(2)	(2)	56.8	36.9	5.6	0.6	8.4	27.4	44.3	19.8
Secondary	1,141,626	0.4	0.9	47.3	43.2	7.0	1.3	7.6	24.6	44.7	23.0
Private schools											
Total	307,131	2.9	1.5	61.3	29.7	2.9	1.7	18.4	37.4	29.8	13.5
Sex											
Men	66,785	(2)	(2)	50.9	38.2	3.6	5.0	18.5	28.9	33.7	18.6
Women	239,975	3.2	1.7	64.2	27.4	2.7	0.8	18.4	39.8	28.8	12.1
Race/ethnicity											
White	281,152	2.9	1.3	61.2	30.3	2.7	1.6	18.4	37.7	30.2	13.8
Black	7,015	(2)	(2)	69.1	16.6	(2)	(2)	27.0	42.2	21.3	(2)
Hispanic	8,569	(2)	(2)	60.8	19.7	(2)	(2)	22.0	41.4	25.8	(2)
Asian or Pacific Islander	3,491	(2)	(2)	56.2	(2)	(2)	(2)	(2)	(2)	(2)	(2)
American Indian or Alaskan Native	2,747	(2)	(2)	93.7	(2)	(2)	(2)	(2)	(2)	(2)	(2)
Age											
Less than 30	65,843	3.5	(2)	83.4	11.4	(2)	(2)	47.3	51.4	(2)	(2)
30 to 39	104,287	2.6	2.2	59.3	31.4	3.1	(2)	15.6	45.4	38.2	(2)
40 to 49	83,021	2.4	(2)	51.9	39.1	3.1	2.6	8.0	31.6	44.0	15.4
50 or more	49,378	3.3	(2)	52.4	34.7	5.1	(2)	4.0	11.1	27.5	56.8
Level											
Elementary	159,893	3.8	1.8	70.9	21.0	2.1	(2)	18.4	40.5	28.7	11.8
Secondary	147,238	1.9	1.1	50.9	39.2	3.7	3.1	18.5	34.0	31.0	15.4

[1] Total differs from data appearing in other tables because of varying survey processing procedures and time period coverages.

[2] Too few sample cases (fewer than 30) for a reliable estimate.

SOURCE: U.S. Department of Education, National Center for Education Statistics, "Schools and Staffing Survey, 1987–88." (This table was prepared June 1990.)

Table 63.—Highest degree earned and number of years teaching experience for teachers in public elementary and secondary schools, by State: 1987–88

State	Total [1]	Percent of teachers, by highest degree [2]				Percent of teachers, by years of full-time teaching experience			
		Bachelor's	Master's	Education specialist	Doctor's	Less than 3	3 to 9	10 to 20	Over 20
1	2	3	4	5	6	7	8	9	10
United States	2,323,204	52.2	40.0	6.3	0.9	8.0	26.0	44.5	21.4
Alabama	38,678	40.5	50.8	6.7	—	7.5	26.6	47.3	18.5
Alaska	6,911	59.2	35.7	—	—	7.4	29.7	52.8	10.1
Arizona	29,858	56.3	38.4	4.6	—	10.7	32.9	41.6	14.7
Arkansas	27,543	66.5	30.0	—	—	8.7	34.4	43.6	13.4
California	183,784	55.3	31.4	11.6	1.5	8.9	24.0	39.9	27.1
Colorado	31,754	50.4	43.8	—	—	7.7	28.5	44.8	18.8
Connecticut	34,137	22.7	58.4	16.6	—	—	21.9	45.6	26.5
Delaware	5,335	65.2	27.6	—	—	—	24.9	45.6	23.9
District of Columbia	5,198	43.0	44.0	—	—	—	—	43.2	38.0
Florida	89,562	58.7	36.1	3.2	—	10.9	29.0	43.7	16.3
Georgia	62,897	45.4	47.1	5.5	—	8.8	32.0	46.2	13.0
Hawaii	8,691	53.6	16.1	27.1	—	13.4	15.3	37.9	33.4
Idaho	10,805	72.4	22.0	—	—	10.3	32.5	44.9	12.2
Illinois	102,000	51.4	42.0	5.7	—	6.6	22.6	43.5	27.1
Indiana	55,972	15.1	79.0	5.0	—	7.0	23.5	46.1	23.4
Iowa	40,991	65.6	31.2	—	—	7.6	24.2	39.9	28.3
Kansas	30,207	53.3	42.9	—	—	8.2	31.6	42.6	17.6
Kentucky	36,830	23.7	50.3	24.2	—	7.5	25.3	47.5	19.6
Louisiana	39,387	53.6	30.7	13.8	—	7.3	28.0	46.8	17.9
Maine	15,329	68.8	26.7	—	—	8.8	27.3	44.6	19.1
Maryland	38,557	41.0	50.8	—	—	9.8	18.4	48.7	22.8
Massachusetts	62,020	46.5	44.0	7.3	—	5.9	21.4	48.9	23.7
Michigan	81,517	39.8	55.6	4.0	—	7.2	16.9	48.7	27.2
Minnesota	43,682	64.6	31.3	—	—	7.4	22.6	41.4	28.3
Mississippi	28,740	56.9	36.8	5.1	—	8.1	28.2	46.3	17.4
Missouri	53,426	52.1	41.6	3.8	—	8.0	30.2	43.1	18.7
Montana	13,418	75.6	20.6	—	—	8.8	30.6	44.0	16.6
Nebraska	22,705	61.5	34.5	—	—	8.6	28.6	43.0	19.6
Nevada	8,631	47.0	41.8	9.9	—	9.3	26.3	43.8	20.6
New Hampshire	10,770	65.2	27.9	—	—	9.1	32.8	43.5	14.3
New Jersey	82,344	57.6	32.4	8.1	—	6.3	21.6	48.0	24.0
New Mexico	15,429	47.4	46.7	—	—	7.7	29.6	45.0	17.6
New York	174,828	32.0	57.4	8.8	1.3	7.1	23.9	44.1	24.8
North Carolina	58,237	66.9	29.6	—	—	6.3	26.8	45.9	20.7
North Dakota	9,031	82.2	15.9	—	—	11.2	34.1	35.8	18.7
Ohio	103,358	54.9	39.7	3.4	—	8.2	22.8	47.6	21.2
Oklahoma	40,988	55.0	39.0	5.3	—	7.5	35.7	43.1	13.6
Oregon	25,422	53.9	39.1	6.3	—	10.8	28.5	41.4	19.0
Pennsylvania	100,453	47.7	43.5	6.9	—	5.1	17.2	51.1	26.5
Rhode Island	8,886	37.1	53.5	—	—	—	16.1	55.0	23.5
South Carolina	36,069	50.0	43.0	4.8	—	10.2	29.2	43.3	17.3
South Dakota	10,434	82.4	15.9	—	—	11.3	34.6	36.5	17.5
Tennessee	43,747	52.2	38.5	7.3	—	8.4	26.7	45.0	19.8
Texas	183,443	64.4	29.6	4.1	—	9.7	34.8	40.6	14.8
Utah	16,385	73.8	20.0	—	—	15.8	35.1	33.9	15.1
Vermont	6,935	57.5	39.4	—	—	10.9	28.7	43.7	16.2
Virginia	60,435	61.6	34.1	—	—	7.4	27.4	45.5	19.6
Washington	39,401	69.2	25.4	4.0	—	6.8	25.1	45.6	22.4
West Virginia	22,943	51.9	38.8	7.6	—	7.2	29.6	46.8	16.4
Wisconsin	57,458	63.2	32.8	3.8	—	6.6	24.9	43.4	25.0
Wyoming	7,644	70.7	27.1	—	—	—	32.3	43.6	17.5

[1] Total differs from data appearing in other tables because of varying survey processing procedures and time period coverages.

[2] Excludes teachers with less than a bachelor's degree.

—Too few sample cases (fewer than 30) for a reliable estimate.

NOTE.—Details may not add to totals due to rounding or missing values in cells with too few sample cases, or item nonresponse. Cell entries may be underestimates due to item nonresponse.

SOURCE: U.S. Department of Education, National Center for Education Statistics, "Schools and Staffing Survey, 1987–88." (This table was prepared April 1990.)

Table 64.—Selected characteristics of public school teachers: Spring 1961 to spring 1986

Item	1961	1966	1971	1976	1981	1986
1	2	3	4	5	6	7
Number of teachers, in thousands	**1,408**	**1,710**	**2,055**	**2,196**	**2,184**	**2,207**
Sex (percent)						
Men	31.3	31.1	34.3	32.9	33.1	31.2
Women	68.7	69.0	65.7	67.0	66.9	68.8
Median age (years)						
All teachers	41	36	35	33	37	41
Men	34	33	33	33	38	42
Women	46	40	37	33	36	41
Race (percent)						
White	—	—	88.3	90.8	91.6	89.6
Black	—	—	8.1	8.0	7.8	6.9
Other	—	—	3.6	1.2	0.7	3.4
Marital status (percent)						
Single	22.3	22.0	19.5	20.1	18.5	12.9
Married	68.0	69.1	71.9	71.3	73.0	75.7
Widowed, divorced, or separated	9.7	9.0	8.6	8.6	8.5	11.4
Highest degree held (percent)						
Less than bachelor's	14.6	7.0	2.9	0.9	0.4	0.3
Bachelor's	61.9	69.6	69.6	61.6	50.1	48.3
Master's or specialist degree	23.1	23.2	27.1	37.1	49.3	50.7
Doctor's	0.4	0.1	0.4	0.4	0.3	0.7
College credits earned in last 3 years						
Percent who earned credits	—	—	60.7	63.2	56.1	53.1
Mean number of credits earned [1]	—	—	14	—	9	4
Median years of teaching experience	11	8	8	8	12	15
Teaching for first year (percent)	8.0	9.1	9.1	5.5	2.4	3.1
Average number of pupils per class						
Elementary teachers, not departmentalized ...	29	28	27	25	25	24
Elementary teachers, departmentalized	—	—	25	23	22	—
Secondary teachers	28	26	27	25	23	25
Mean number of students taught per day by secondary teachers	138	132	134	126	118	94
Average number of hours in required school day	7.4	7.3	7.3	7.3	7.3	7.3
Average number of hours per week spent on all teaching duties.						
All teachers	47	47	47	46	46	49
Elementary teachers	49	47	46	44	44	47
Secondary teachers	46	48	48	48	48	51
Average number of days of classroom teaching in school year	—	181	181	180	180	180
Average number of nonteaching days in school year ..	—	5	4	5	6	5
Average annual salary as classroom teacher	[2] $5,264	$6,253	$9,261	$12,005	$17,209	$24,504
Total income, including spouse's (if married)	—	—	$15,021	$19,957	$29,831	$43,413
Willingness to teach again (percent)						
Certainly would	49.9	52.6	44.9	37.5	21.8	22.7
Probably would	26.9	25.4	29.5	26.1	24.6	26.3
Chances about even	12.5	12.9	13.0	17.5	17.6	19.8
Probably would not	7.9	7.1	8.9	13.4	24.0	22.0
Certainly would not	2.8	2.0	3.7	5.6	12.0	9.3

[1] Measured in semester hours.
[2] Includes extra pay for extra duties.
—Data not available.

SOURCE: National Education Association, *Status of the American Public School Teacher, 1985–86.* (Copyright © 1987 by the National Education Association. All rights reserved.) (This table was prepared July 1987.)

NOTE.—Data are based upon sample surveys of public school teachers. Data differs from figures appearing in other tables because of varying procedures and time period coverages. Because of rounding, percents may not add to 100.0.

Table 65.—Public secondary school teachers, by subject taught: Spring 1966 to spring 1986

[Percentage distribution]

Teaching field in which largest portion of time was spent	1966	1971	1976	1981	1986
1	2	3	4	5	6
Total secondary school teachers, in thousands	**746**	**927**	**1,016**	**995**	**970**
All fields	100.0	100.0	100.0	100.0	100.0
Agriculture	1.6	0.6	0.6	1.1	0.6
Art	2.0	3.7	2.4	3.1	1.5
Business education	7.0	5.9	4.6	6.2	6.5
English	18.1	20.4	19.9	23.8	21.8
Foreign language	6.4	4.8	4.2	2.8	3.7
Health and physical education	6.9	8.3	7.9	6.5	5.6
Home economics	5.9	5.1	2.8	3.6	2.6
Industrial arts	5.1	6.2	3.9	5.2	2.2
Mathematics	13.9	14.4	18.2	15.3	19.2
Music	4.7	3.8	3.0	3.7	4.8
Science	10.8	10.6	13.1	12.1	11.0
Social studies	15.3	14.0	12.4	11.2	13.6
Special education	0.4	1.1	3.0	2.1	3.5
Other	1.9	1.0	4.0	3.3	3.4

NOTE.—Data are based upon sample surveys of public school teachers. Because of rounding, percents may not add to 100.0.

Table 66.—Teacher candidates' reasons for majoring in education and their perceptions of readiness to teach: Spring 1986 to 1988

Students' reasons for becoming teachers	Percent citing reason		Facet of teaching	Percent perceiving readiness		
	1986	1987		1986	1987	1988
1	2	3	4	5	6	7
Helping children grow and learn	90	95	Use proper teaching methods	83	63	—
Seems to be challenging field	63	65	Plan instruction	82	64	88
Like work conditions (e.g., job market, calendar, security) ...	54	52	Evaluate student learning	80	68	87
Inspired by favorite teachers	53	45	Responding to student differences	80	76	86
Sense of vocation and honor of teaching	52	52	Use materials properly	75	58	86
Could lead to other career	44	40	Develop materials	75	61	—
Could be admitted and would succeed	41	44	Work effectively with other teachers	74	66	82
Liked reputation of education campus	22	23	Diagnose learner needs	72	64	82
Friends are majoring in education	20	23	Manage classrooms	68	59	74
Inspired by parents	22	23	Develop curriculum	68	55	—
			Deal with misbehavior	56	52	—
			Teach with computers	29	28	32

Table 67.—Selected characteristics of public school teachers' current teaching assignments,[1] by State: 1987

State	Average number of students per class	Percent of teachers									Teaching subjects unqualified to teach
		Number of students per typical class			Feelings about most typical class size			Average number of hours per week spent on job[2]			
		19 or less	20 to 29	30 or more	Too large	About right	Too small	Less than 40	40 to 59	60 or more	
1	2	3	4	5	6	7	8	9	10	11	12
United States	23	20	64	16	36	62	1	11	78	11	20
Alabama	26	10	61	28	38	61	1	10	83	7	20
Alaska	21	33	60	7	25	74	2	6	80	15	29
Arizona	25	15	65	21	43	56	2	7	82	11	25
Arkansas	22	24	68	7	29	71	1	8	82	11	20
California	28	7	38	55	66	33	2	8	75	16	28
Colorado	23	21	69	11	31	67	2	9	78	13	23
Connecticut	20	40	60	0	26	74	0	21	72	7	15
Delaware	23	20	72	9	37	63	0	10	78	11	13
Florida	26	12	58	31	49	50	1	10	82	8	16
Georgia	25	11	74	16	37	63	1	6	80	14	24
Hawaii	26	12	61	28	55	44	1	14	72	14	29
Idaho	24	15	67	18	38	59	2	6	81	12	22
Illinois	23	24	59	16	31	67	2	10	76	14	18
Indiana	23	21	69	8	35	65	0	9	78	13	19
Iowa	21	36	58	7	20	79	1	7	78	15	18
Kansas	20	42	53	5	20	77	3	9	78	12	16
Kentucky	24	14	72	15	37	62	1	15	77	8	25
Louisiana	24	16	71	13	34	64	1	17	72	10	20
Maine	20	29	71	1	28	70	3	8	80	12	17
Maryland	25	11	66	23	41	59	1	7	79	15	20
Massachusetts	21	28	67	4	27	71	2	20	73	7	18
Michigan	25	11	66	22	47	52	1	14	79	7	22
Minnesota	25	13	69	18	44	55	1	8	81	11	25
Mississippi	24	12	71	17	32	66	2	10	81	9	17
Missouri	22	24	66	19	32	67	1	10	78	11	15
Montana	20	36	61	3	24	72	4	6	84	10	14
Nebraska	20	40	53	6	21	74	5	7	78	15	18
Nevada	26	13	61	27	48	50	2	13	76	11	20
New Hampshire	21	32	65	3	26	73	1	8	80	11	12
New Jersey	20	35	60	4	25	74	1	23	72	6	20
New Mexico	23	19	72	9	32	66	2	12	76	12	21
New York	22	23	69	8	31	67	2	19	72	9	14
North Carolina	25	7	83	10	47	53	1	5	82	13	20
North Dakota	19	45	51	4	19	74	7	9	78	13	18
Ohio	24	18	76	6	34	65	1	12	78	10	20
Oklahoma	21	34	59	6	25	72	3	10	77	13	21
Oregon	23	19	75	6	33	65	2	6	78	16	20
Pennsylvania	23	18	73	9	38	62	0	14	81	5	15
Rhode Island	22	20	78	2	33	66	0	28	70	2	16
South Carolina	23	20	73	6	29	70	2	11	80	9	17
South Dakota	19	42	55	3	20	77	3	8	77	15	21
Tennessee	25	12	65	23	53	45	1	9	80	11	19
Texas	22	28	61	11	24	74	1	6	79	16	19
Utah	28	6	49	45	58	41	1	10	79	11	30
Vermont	19	44	54	1	23	76	1	10	80	10	19
Virginia	22	21	71	8	33	67	1	9	80	11	22
Washington	25	13	68	19	44	54	2	6	83	10	30
West Virginia	21	26	71	4	20	78	2	12	75	12	23
Wisconsin	22	21	74	5	29	69	2	9	82	9	17
Wyoming	20	41	56	2	20	76	4	6	81	12	16

[1] As reported by the teachers.
[2] Includes time spent inside and outside of school.

NOTE.—Because of rounding, details may not add to totals.

SOURCE: The Carnegie Foundation for the Advancement of Teaching, *The Condition of Teaching: A State-by-State Analysis, 1988.* (This table was prepared January 1989.)

Table 68.—Percentage of teachers involved in making selected decisions, by State: 1987

State	Choosing textbooks	Shaping the curriculum	Tracking students into special classes	Setting promotion and retention policies	Deciding school budgets	Evaluating teacher per-formance	Selecting new teachers	Selecting new admin-istrators
1	2	3	4	5	6	7	8	9
United States	**79**	**63**	**45**	**34**	**20**	**10**	**7**	**7**
Alabama	71	51	47	38	19	8	4	3
Alaska	79	68	55	45	24	13	8	7
Arizona	78	61	47	43	18	17	12	9
Arkansas	88	51	44	39	9	12	4	3
California	74	62	40	41	35	8	17	11
Colorado	83	70	55	38	36	14	20	11
Connecticut	73	68	47	33	22	13	7	10
Delaware	84	71	40	30	21	8	5	12
District of Columbia	—	—	—	—	—	—	—	—
Florida	64	42	39	21	20	6	5	3
Georgia	74	54	52	35	19	20	3	4
Hawaii	91	69	53	37	57	14	9	2
Idaho	83	67	48	34	17	7	13	8
Illinois	86	62	45	39	12	11	4	5
Indiana	90	71	45	35	13	7	5	5
Iowa	90	75	48	37	15	7	6	10
Kansas	90	76	46	37	13	10	5	4
Kentucky	85	64	53	45	16	13	3	6
Louisiana	63	40	36	27	10	8	1	6
Maine	89	82	60	47	29	14	16	14
Maryland	61	44	44	24	18	8	4	4
Massachusetts	76	71	46	29	29	11	8	13
Michigan	87	66	42	41	15	7	7	8
Minnesota	88	79	63	45	20	14	17	12
Mississippi	81	59	50	36	11	17	4	5
Missouri	85	69	42	35	18	8	5	5
Montana	90	78	55	44	17	7	7	5
Nebraska	87	75	54	32	19	9	5	6
Nevada	73	46	38	25	27	6	5	1
New Hampshire	79	76	56	42	32	11	20	19
New Jersey	73	66	40	33	11	6	2	5
New Mexico	88	67	43	34	15	8	4	4
New York	78	62	44	36	18	7	9	11
North Carolina	76	53	43	36	28	17	4	4
North Dakota	92	71	48	43	8	7	4	4
Ohio	84	70	40	29	14	11	5	5
Oklahoma	92	62	46	37	10	8	3	3
Oregon	87	72	56	41	29	10	20	13
Pennsylvania	84	74	38	33	14	7	5	9
Rhode Island	68	70	40	31	17	6	5	7
South Carolina	87	61	46	30	23	16	4	3
South Dakota	90	76	55	49	10	9	8	8
Tennessee	71	55	45	38	16	13	3	4
Texas	78	62	42	24	20	8	4	3
Utah	76	63	46	26	23	20	10	4
Vermont	93	85	56	50	39	16	17	20
Virginia	82	61	41	30	16	14	4	3
Washington	78	68	53	36	25	7	18	12
West Virginia	67	43	39	27	12	11	4	2
Wisconsin	87	77	51	34	29	9	7	8
Wyoming	89	81	57	39	34	8	16	14

—Data not available.

SOURCE: The Carnegie Foundation for the Advancement of Teaching, *Teacher Involvement in Decisionmaking: A State-by-State Profile, September 1988.* (This table was prepared October 1988.)

Table 69.—Percentage of teachers reporting various problems in their school, by State: 1987

State	Disruptive classroom behavior	Student absentee-ism	Student apathy	Lack of parental support	Violence against students	Violence against teachers	Alcohol	Drugs other than alcohol	Abused/ neglected students	Poor health among students
1	2	3	4	5	6	7	8	9	10	11
United States	87	83	88	90	44	24	49	54	89	69
Alabama	92	84	87	89	40	22	44	52	83	65
Alaska	87	80	84	90	34	17	53	60	92	74
Arizona	87	89	90	91	45	22	38	51	90	76
Arkansas	90	88	91	92	46	24	53	59	90	74
California	90	89	87	90	49	26	42	48	90	74
Colorado	88	86	89	90	48	22	51	56	90	74
Connecticut	84	75	83	85	42	23	44	48	86	59
Delaware	92	86	90	95	54	28	50	54	91	76
District of Columbia	—	—	—	—	—	—	—	—	—	—
Florida	92	89	92	94	58	38	45	57	88	73
Georgia	91	84	91	90	48	28	39	45	89	71
Hawaii	93	91	93	95	76	44	45	53	89	74
Idaho	88	87	91	92	42	21	55	56	92	72
Illinois	79	74	85	89	34	18	39	42	84	62
Indiana	89	84	89	91	41	19	51	59	89	71
Iowa	80	78	86	87	35	16	63	63	88	61
Kansas	81	78	87	86	33	18	52	53	88	67
Kentucky	88	86	89	89	38	23	35	45	90	74
Louisiana	85	82	89	88	43	29	36	45	83	67
Maine	85	79	84	88	32	13	45	48	96	75
Maryland	90	78	86	89	50	27	43	49	85	64
Massachusetts	84	82	85	85	48	28	56	62	86	63
Michigan	87	80	89	89	50	24	45	50	91	72
Minnesota	86	80	88	89	39	19	61	59	94	68
Mississippi	81	80	82	89	37	22	41	50	77	62
Missouri	90	87	89	92	45	24	56	58	90	76
Montana	78	77	86	88	32	19	58	55	88	64
Nebraska	83	75	88	88	36	18	62	55	88	63
Nevada	88	85	92	92	50	30	51	54	92	71
New Hampshire	87	76	82	88	38	16	49	50	92	69
New Jersey	87	71	83	85	41	21	42	45	81	54
New Mexico	83	89	90	89	43	23	58	65	90	71
New York	91	82	90	90	46	26	59	64	91	66
North Carolina	91	87	92	94	48	32	45	50	89	76
North Dakota	81	65	81	85	22	11	57	52	83	53
Ohio	87	80	90	90	46	24	55	58	92	71
Oklahoma	85	84	90	90	37	23	56	63	91	70
Oregon	86	83	86	90	42	15	48	54	93	77
Pennsylvania	84	83	89	89	45	25	57	60	89	68
Rhode Island	91	83	85	89	53	22	47	54	88	67
South Carolina	87	76	85	93	46	27	39	45	86	72
South Dakota	74	68	82	84	28	16	55	49	88	64
Tennessee	88	88	90	91	41	26	39	47	91	76
Texas	81	85	89	92	41	24	51	61	89	71
Utah	87	82	86	88	44	18	43	48	86	64
Vermont	86	77	83	88	36	14	54	58	95	77
Virginia	91	82	88	91	43	25	41	46	88	70
Washington	88	87	91	91	44	19	56	62	95	79
West Virginia	87	86	88	91	39	21	41	45	89	76
Wisconsin	84	76	86	91	39	24	57	55	93	66
Wyoming	79	76	83	87	25	10	40	41	89	66

—Data not available.

SOURCE: The Carnegie Foundation for the Advancement of Teaching, *The Condition of Teaching: A State-by-State Analysis, 1988.* (This table was prepared January 1989.)

Table 70.—Average salaries for full-time teachers in public and private elementary and secondary schools, by selected characteristics: 1987–88

Selected characteristics	Total earned income	Base salary	Number of full-time teachers	School year supplemental contract		Supplemental contract during summer		Number of teachers with nonschool employment		
				Number of teachers	Supplemental salary	Number of teachers	Supplemental salary	School year only	Summer only	All year
1	2	3	4	5	6	7	8	9	10	11
Public schools										
Total	$28,189	$26,231	2,118,253	705,223	$2,134	361,360	$1,810	121,894	162,185	207,623
Men	32,436	28,244	628,799	355,374	2,691	135,044	2,152	59,682	71,389	126,863
Women	26,345	25,350	1,479,641	368,186	1,620	225,321	1,608	61,889	90,235	80,392
Race/ethnicity										
White, non-Hispanic	28,226	26,264	1,810,496	626,386	2,018	303,418	1,713	107,050	140,649	183,921
Black, non-Hispanic	27,786	25,976	177,055	39,144	3,184	34,880	2,227	8,752	12,176	13,619
Hispanic	27,234	25,103	63,129	19,271	2,877	13,356	2,581	2,595	4,578	4,432
Asian or Pacific Islander	30,262	28,499	19,314	5,514	2,331	3,563	1,990	(¹)	(¹)	1,432
American Indian or Alaskan Native	28,614	26,160	21,702	7,979	3,889	3,783	2,824	(¹)	1,939	2,355
Age										
Less than 30	21,228	19,257	284,016	117,832	1,881	54,067	1,880	16,176	52,688	35,262
30 to 39	26,359	24,447	735,299	260,051	2,127	132,525	1,761	40,452	54,132	71,656
40 to 49	30,635	28,556	686,838	231,417	2,142	122,413	1,779	43,900	38,565	71,582
50 or more	32,550	30,826	384,556	91,006	2,387	49,785	1,955	20,771	15,854	27,694
Level										
Elementary	26,660	25,578	1,067,475	206,247	1,818	155,180	1,646	44,222	66,852	68,816
Secondary	29,717	26,879	1,050,779	498,977	2,264	206,179	1,934	77,673	95,334	138,808
Private schools										
Total	18,318	16,562	250,524	48,559	2,026	39,231	2,163	18,046	29,708	29,999
Men	23,237	19,606	55,230	20,404	2,530	11,439	2,368	6,189	8,983	12,395
Women	16,924	15,693	195,065	28,156	1,662	27,792	2,079	11,857	20,725	17,605
Race/ethnicity										
White, non-Hispanic	18,244	16,521	229,429	45,357	2,035	34,054	2,124	16,659	27,592	28,292
Black, non-Hispanic	16,774	15,221	6,012	(¹)	(¹)	1,519	2,255	(¹)	(¹)	(¹)
Hispanic	18,360	16,385	6,157	(¹)	(¹)	(¹)	(¹)	(¹)	(¹)	(¹)
Asian or Pacific Islander	24,475	22,332	3,069	(¹)	(¹)	(¹)	(¹)	(¹)	(¹)	(¹)
American Indian or Alaskan Native	20,217	18,325	2,468	(¹)	(¹)	(¹)	(¹)	(¹)	(¹)	(¹)
Age										
Less than 30	15,708	13,755	58,179	13,330	1,289	11,064	1,922	3,270	14,605	11,512
30 to 39	18,340	16,719	83,101	17,520	1,862	14,057	2,328	5,865	9,670	10,139
40 to 49	20,044	18,271	66,312	12,864	2,507	9,497	2,369	5,133	3,340	6,105
50 or more	19,215	17,630	39,326	4,392	3,549	4,183	1,845	3,651	1,816	2,152
Level										
Elementary	16,122	14,957	138,230	13,183	1,828	16,494	2,234	7,999	16,801	12,292
Secondary	21,017	18,540	112,294	35,377	2,100	22,737	2,111	10,047	12,907	17,707

¹ Too few sample cases (fewer than 30) for a reliable estimate.

NOTE.—Details may not add to totals because of rounding or missing values in cells with too few cases or survey item nonresponse.

SOURCE: U.S. Department of Education, National Center for Education Statistics, "Schools and Staffing Survey, 1987–88." (This table was prepared July 1990.)

Table 71.—Job satisfaction of public school teachers: 1984 to 1989

Item	Percent of teachers					
	1984	1985	1986	1987	1988	1989
1	2	3	4	5	6	7
Satisfaction with job as a teacher in public schools:						
All teachers	100	—	100	100	100	100
Very satisfied	40	—	33	40	50	44
Somewhat satisfied	41	—	48	45	37	42
Somewhat dissatisfied	16	—	15	12	11	11
Very dissatisfied	2	—	4	2	2	3
Seriously considered leaving teaching to go into some other occupation	—	51	55	52	—	—
Likely to leave the teaching profession to go into some other occupation within the next 5 years	—	26	27	22	26	26

—Data not available.

NOTE.—Because of rounding, details may not add to totals.

SOURCE: Metropolitan Life/Louis Harris Associates, Inc., *The American Teacher, 1989,* copyrighted. (This table was prepared January 1990.)

Table 72.—Estimated average annual salary of teachers in public elementary and secondary schools: 1959–60 to 1990–91

School year	Current dollars			Constant 1990–91 dollars [1]		
	All teachers	Elementary teachers	Secondary teachers	All teachers	Elementary teachers	Secondary teachers
1	2	3	4	5	6	7
1959–60	$4,995	$4,815	$5,276	$22,773	$21,952	$24,054
1961–62	5,515	5,340	5,775	24,579	23,799	25,737
1963–64	5,995	5,805	6,266	26,039	25,213	27,216
1965–66	6,485	6,279	6,761	27,226	26,361	28,385
1967–68	7,423	7,208	7,692	29,240	28,393	30,299
1969–70	8,626	8,412	8,891	30,590	29,831	31,530
1970–71	9,268	9,021	9,568	31,253	30,420	32,265
1971–72	9,705	9,424	10,031	31,593	30,679	32,655
1972–73	10,174	9,893	10,507	31,837	30,958	32,880
1973–74	10,770	10,507	11,077	30,943	30,188	31,825
1974–75	11,641	11,334	12,000	30,109	29,315	31,038
1975–76	12,600	12,280	12,937	30,435	29,662	31,249
1976–77	13,354	12,989	13,776	30,479	29,646	31,442
1977–78	14,198	13,845	14,602	30,367	29,612	31,231
1978–79	15,032	14,681	15,450	29,397	28,710	30,214
1979–80	15,970	15,569	16,459	27,557	26,865	28,401
1980–81	17,644	17,230	18,142	27,285	26,645	28,055
1981–82	19,274	18,853	19,805	27,436	26,836	28,192
1982–83	20,695	20,227	21,291	28,245	27,607	29,059
1983–84	21,935	21,487	22,554	28,869	28,280	29,684
1984–85	23,600	23,200	24,187	29,891	29,384	30,634
1985–86	25,199	24,718	25,846	31,021	30,429	31,818
1986–87	26,565	26,051	27,247	31,992	31,373	32,814
1987–88	28,023	27,491	28,808	32,406	31,790	33,313
1988–89	29,570	29,017	30,253	32,685	32,074	33,440
1989–90	31,331	30,769	32,017	33,054	32,461	33,778
1990–91	33,015	32,448	33,701	33,015	32,448	33,701

[1] Based on the Consumer Price Index, prepared by the Bureau of Labor Statistics, U.S. Department of Labor.

NOTE.—Some data have been revised from previously published figures.

SOURCE: National Education Association, *Estimates of School Statistics;* and unpublished data. (Latest edition 1990–91. Copyright © 1991 by the National Education Association. All rights reserved.) (This table was prepared June 1991.)

Table 73.—Estimated average annual salary of teachers in public elementary and secondary schools, by State: 1969–70 to 1989–90

State	Current dollars						Constant 1989–90 dollars [1]					Percent change 1979–80 to 1989–90 in constant dollars
	1969–70	1979–80	1985–86 [2]	1987–88 [2]	1988–89	1989–90	1969–70	1979–80	1985–86	1987–88	1988–89	
1	2	3	4	5	6	7	8	9	10	11	12	13
United States	$8,626	$15,970	$25,199	$28,023	$29,570	$31,331	$28,995	$26,120	$29,404	$30,716	$30,981	19.9
Alabama	6,818	13,060	23,090	23,320	25,190	25,300	22,918	21,361	26,943	25,561	26,392	18.4
Alaska	10,560	27,210	39,115	40,424	41,754	43,153	35,496	44,504	45,642	44,309	43,746	3.0
Arizona	8,711	15,054	24,680	27,388	28,499	29,402	29,281	24,622	28,798	30,020	29,859	19.4
Arkansas	6,307	12,299	19,519	20,340	21,395	22,352	21,200	20,116	22,776	22,295	22,416	11.1
California	10,315	18,020	29,130	33,159	34,640	37,998	34,672	29,473	33,991	36,346	36,339	28.9
Colorado	7,761	16,205	25,892	28,651	29,558	30,758	26,087	26,505	30,213	31,405	30,968	16.0
Connecticut	9,262	16,229	26,610	33,487	37,343	40,461	31,133	26,544	31,050	36,705	39,125	52.4
Delaware	9,015	16,148	24,624	29,573	31,585	33,377	30,303	26,411	28,733	32,415	33,092	26.4
District of Columbia	10,285	22,190	33,211	34,705	36,290	37,950	34,571	36,294	38,753	38,040	38,022	4.6
Florida	8,412	14,149	22,250	25,198	26,974	28,803	28,276	23,142	25,963	27,620	28,261	24.5
Georgia	7,276	13,853	23,046	26,190	26,920	28,006	24,457	22,658	26,892	28,707	28,205	23.6
Hawaii	9,453	19,920	25,845	28,785	30,778	32,047	31,775	32,581	30,158	31,551	32,247	1.6
Idaho	6,890	13,611	20,969	22,242	22,734	23,861	23,160	22,262	24,468	24,380	23,819	7.2
Illinois	9,569	17,601	26,897	29,663	31,145	32,794	32,165	28,788	31,385	32,514	32,631	13.9
Indiana.	8,833	15,599	24,325	27,029	29,331	30,378	29,691	25,513	28,384	29,627	30,731	19.1
Iowa	8,355	15,203	21,663	24,842	25,778	26,747	28,084	24,866	25,278	27,229	27,008	7.6
Kansas	7,612	13,690	22,644	24,647	27,360	28,744	25,587	22,391	26,423	27,016	28,666	28.4
Kentucky	6,953	14,520	20,948	24,253	24,930	26,292	23,371	23,749	24,444	26,584	26,120	10.7
Louisiana	7,028	13,760	20,303	21,209	22,470	24,300	23,624	22,506	23,691	23,247	23,542	8.0
Maine	7,572	13,071	19,583	23,425	24,938	26,881	25,452	21,379	22,851	25,676	26,128	25.7
Maryland	9,383	17,558	26,800	30,933	33,895	36,601	31,540	28,718	31,272	33,906	35,512	27.5
Massachusetts	8,764	17,253	26,496	30,379	32,221	34,712	29,459	28,219	30,917	33,299	33,759	23.0
Michigan	9,826	19,663	30,067	33,151	34,823	[3]36,010	33,029	32,160	35,084	36,337	36,485	12.0
Minnesota	8,658	15,912	27,360	29,900	30,660	32,190	29,103	26,025	31,925	32,774	32,123	23.7
Mississippi	5,798	11,850	18,472	20,562	22,578	24,364	19,489	19,382	21,554	22,538	23,655	25.7
Missouri	7,799	13,682	21,945	24,709	26,006	27,229	26,215	22,378	25,607	27,084	27,247	21.7
Montana	7,606	14,537	22,482	23,798	24,421	25,081	25,566	23,776	26,234	26,085	25,586	5.5
Nebraska	7,375	13,516	20,939	22,683	23,845	25,522	24,790	22,107	24,433	24,863	24,983	15.5
Nevada	9,215	16,295	25,610	27,600	28,840	30,590	30,975	26,652	29,883	30,252	30,216	14.8
New Hampshire	7,771	13,017	20,263	24,019	26,702	28,986	26,121	21,290	23,644	26,327	27,976	36.1
New Jersey	9,130	17,161	27,170	30,720	33,037	35,676	30,689	28,068	31,704	33,672	34,613	27.1
New Mexico	7,796	14,887	21,982	23,804	23,897	25,120	26,205	24,349	25,650	26,092	25,037	3.2
New York	10,336	19,812	30,490	34,500	36,654	38,925	34,743	32,404	35,578	37,816	38,403	20.1
North Carolina	7,494	14,117	22,340	24,900	25,738	27,883	25,190	23,089	26,068	27,293	26,966	20.8
North Dakota	6,696	13,263	20,816	21,660	22,249	23,016	22,508	21,693	24,290	23,742	23,311	6.1
Ohio	8,300	15,269	24,518	27,606	29,671	31,218	27,899	24,974	28,609	30,259	31,087	25.0
Oklahoma	6,882	13,107	21,419	21,630	22,370	23,070	23,133	21,438	24,993	23,709	23,437	7.6
Oregon	8,818	16,266	25,660	28,060	29,390	30,840	29,640	26,604	29,942	30,757	30,792	15.9
Pennsylvania	8,858	16,515	25,853	29,177	31,248	33,338	29,775	27,012	30,167	31,981	32,739	23.4
Rhode Island	8,776	18,002	29,470	32,858	34,233	36,057	29,499	29,444	34,388	36,016	35,867	22.5
South Carolina	6,927	13,063	21,595	24,728	25,623	27,217	23,284	21,366	25,198	27,104	26,846	27.4
South Dakota	6,403	12,348	18,095	19,758	20,530	21,300	21,523	20,196	21,114	21,657	21,510	5.5
Tennessee	7,050	13,972	21,384	23,785	25,619	27,052	23,698	22,852	24,952	26,071	26,841	18.4
Texas	7,255	14,132	24,463	25,558	26,527	27,496	24,387	23,114	28,545	28,014	27,793	19.0
Utah	7,644	14,909	22,553	22,555	22,852	23,686	25,694	24,385	26,316	24,723	23,942	2.9
Vermont	7,968	12,484	20,796	24,519	27,092	28,798	26,783	20,419	24,266	26,875	28,385	41.0
Virginia	8,070	14,060	23,095	27,189	28,967	30,958	27,126	22,996	26,949	29,802	30,349	34.6
Washington	9,225	18,820	26,209	28,217	29,199	30,457	31,008	30,782	30,582	30,929	30,592	1.1
West Virginia	7,650	13,710	20,627	21,736	21,904	22,842	25,714	22,424	24,069	23,825	22,949	1.9
Wisconsin	8,963	16,006	26,347	29,122	30,779	31,921	30,128	26,179	30,743	31,921	32,248	21.9
Wyoming	8,232	16,012	27,224	27,134	27,685	28,188	27,671	26,189	31,767	29,742	29,006	7.6

[1] Based on the Consumer Price Index, prepared by the Bureau of Labor Statistics, U.S. Department of Labor. Price index does not account for different rates of change in the cost of living among States.
[2] Data revised from previously published figures.
[3] Estimated by the National Education Association.

SOURCE: National Education Association, *Estimates of School Statistics*; and unpublished data. (Latest edition 1990–91. Copyright © 1991 by the National Education Association. All rights reserved.) (This table was prepared June 1991.)

Table 74.—Minimum and average teacher salaries, by State: 1988–89 and 1989–90

State	1988–89				1989–90			Percent change, 1988–89 to 1989–90 [1]	
	Minimum (beginning) salary	Average salary	Minimum (beginning) salary in (1989–90 dollars) [1]	Average salary in (1989–90 dollars) [1]	Minimum (beginning) salary	Average salary	Minimum (beginning) salary as a percent of average salary	Minimum salary	Average salary
1	2	3	4	5	6	7	8	9	10
United States	$19,350	$29,636	$20,273	$31,050	$20,476	$31,315	65.4	1.0	0.9
Alabama	18,930	25,190	19,833	26,392	19,364	25,500	75.9	−2.4	−3.4
Alaska	27,310	41,752	28,613	43,744	29,763	43,097	69.1	4.0	−1.5
Arizona	[2] 20,300	28,499	21,268	29,859	[2] 21,100	29,402	71.8	−0.8	−1.5
Arkansas	16,444	21,955	17,228	23,002	[3] 16,673	[3] 22,471	74.2	−3.2	−2.3
California	21,491	35,495	22,516	37,188	[2] 22,780	[2] 37,625	60.5	1.2	1.2
Colorado	18,650	29,557	19,540	30,967	19,234	30,758	62.5	−1.6	−0.7
Connecticut	22,276	37,659	23,339	39,456	23,783	40,768	58.3	1.9	3.3
Delaware	19,008	31,585	19,915	33,092	20,123	33,377	60.3	1.0	0.9
District of Columbia	21,479	37,232	22,504	39,008	22,983	[2] 39,850	57.7	2.1	2.2
Florida	20,314	26,974	21,283	28,261	[2] 21,586	28,787	75.0	1.4	1.9
Georgia	17,823	26,920	18,673	28,204	[2] 18,892	28,013	67.4	1.2	−0.7
Hawaii	21,561	29,835	22,590	31,258	23,381	32,252	72.5	3.5	3.2
Idaho	15,252	22,732	15,980	23,816	16,214	23,861	68.0	1.5	0.2
Illinois	18,621	31,148	19,509	32,634	19,667	[3,4] 32,917	59.7	0.8	0.9
Indiana	18,437	29,330	19,317	30,729	[3] 19,847	[3] 30,978	64.1	2.7	0.8
Iowa	18,999	25,778	19,905	27,008	19,145	26,747	71.6	−3.8	−1.0
Kansas	18,362	25,926	19,238	27,163	[2,5] 19,348	[2,5] 27,220	71.1	0.6	0.2
Kentucky	16,672	24,933	17,467	26,122	17,530	26,275	66.7	0.4	0.6
Louisiana	15,648	22,469	16,394	23,541	16,544	24,300	68.1	0.9	3.2
Maine	15,814	24,938	16,568	26,128	16,599	[4] 26,881	61.7	0.2	2.9
Maryland	20,756	34,159	21,746	35,789	22,172	[3] 36,481	60.8	2.0	1.9
Massachusetts	19,783	32,221	20,727	33,758	20,295	34,175	59.4	−2.1	1.2
Michigan	[2] 20,150	34,128	21,111	35,756	[2] 21,575	36,427	59.2	2.2	1.9
Minnesota	20,152	30,661	21,113	32,124	21,157	[3] 32,190	65.7	0.2	0.2
Mississippi	[2] 17,500	22,579	18,335	23,656	[2] 18,750	24,365	77.0	2.3	3.0
Missouri	18,541	26,006	19,425	27,247	19,851	27,229	72.9	2.2	−0.1
Montana	[2] 17,200	24,421	18,021	25,586	[2] 17,750	25,081	70.8	−1.5	−2.0
Nebraska	16,519	23,841	17,307	24,978	17,690	25,522	69.3	2.2	2.2
Nevada	[2] 18,800	28,836	19,697	30,212	[2] 20,000	30,587	65.4	1.5	1.2
New Hampshire	17,416	26,703	18,247	27,977	19,126	28,986	66.0	4.8	3.6
New Jersey	21,500	33,037	22,526	34,613	22,500	35,676	63.1	−0.1	3.1
New Mexico	18,027	24,092	18,887	25,241	18,795	25,302	74.3	−0.5	0.2
New York	23,000	36,654	24,097	38,403	[6] 25,000	[6] 38,925	64.2	3.7	1.4
North Carolina	18,330	25,646	19,204	26,869	19,140	27,814	68.8	−0.3	3.5
North Dakota	15,318	22,249	16,049	23,310	15,882	23,016	69.0	−1.0	−1.3
Ohio	17,041	29,171	17,854	30,563	17,721	30,567	58.0	−0.7	0.0
Oklahoma	[2] 16,500	23,521	17,287	24,643	[2] 16,900	23,944	70.6	−2.2	−2.8
Oregon	18,915	29,387	19,817	30,789	19,418	30,842	63.0	−2.0	0.2
Pennsylvania	[2] 19,750	31,248	20,692	32,739	[2] 21,350	33,435	63.9	3.2	2.1
Rhode Island	18,417	34,233	19,296	35,866	19,635	[7] 36,057	54.5	1.8	0.5
South Carolina	18,025	25,185	18,885	26,386	19,039	26,638	71.5	0.8	1.0
South Dakota	15,354	20,525	16,086	21,504	15,820	21,300	74.3	−1.7	−0.9
Tennessee	[2] 18,600	25,619	19,487	26,841	[2] 19,800	27,052	73.2	1.6	0.8
Texas	[2] 19,100	26,513	20,011	27,778	[2] 20,000	[2] 27,400	73.0	−0.1	−1.4
Utah	15,409	22,852	16,144	23,942	16,040	[3] 23,652	67.8	−0.6	−1.2
Vermont	16,576	27,106	17,367	28,399	17,970	28,849	62.3	3.5	1.6
Virginia	19,500	28,976	20,430	30,358	21,217	30,926	68.6	3.9	1.9
Washington	18,148	29,200	19,014	30,593	[3] 18,965	[3] 30,475	62.2	−0.3	−0.4
West Virginia	15,055	21,904	15,773	22,949	15,778	22,842	69.1	0.0	−0.5
Wisconsin	19,235	31,046	20,153	32,527	20,000	[2] 32,600	61.3	−0.8	0.2
Wyoming	19,000	28,400	19,906	29,755	[2] 19,200	28,991	66.2	−3.5	−2.6

[1] Based on Consumer Price Index, prepared by the Bureau of Labor Statistics, U.S. Department of Labor. Price index does not account for different rates of change in the cost of living among States.

[2] Estimated by the American Federation of Teachers. See NOTE.

[3] Preliminary or State estimate.

[4] Includes extra duty and extracurricular pay.

[5] Estimated to exclude fringes.

[6] Median salary.

[7] Based on total gross salary.

NOTE.—Data in this table reflect results of surveys conducted by the American Federation of Teachers. Because of differing survey and estimation methods, these data are not entirely comparable with figures appearing in other tables.

SOURCE: American Federation of Teachers, *Survey and Analysis of Salary Trends,* 1989 and 1990. (This table was prepared September 1990.)

Table 75.—Average annual salary of instructional staff [1] in public elementary and secondary schools, by State: 1939-40 to 1989-90

State or other area	Current dollars								Constant 1989–90 dollars [2]			
	1939–40	1949–50	1959–60	1969–70	1979–80	1987–88 [3]	1988–89 [3]	1989–90	1969–70	1979–80	1987–88	1988–89
1	2	3	4	5	6	7	8	9	10	11	12	13
United States	$1,441	$3,010	$5,174	$9,047	$16,715	$29,235	[4] $30,969	$32,723	$30,410	$27,339	$32,045	$32,447
Alabama	744	2,111	4,002	6,954	13,338	24,210	26,150	26,700	23,375	21,815	26,537	27,398
Alaska	—	—	6,859	10,993	27,697	41,531	[4] 42,818	[4] 43,500	36,951	45,301	45,522	44,861
Arizona	1,544	3,556	5,590	8,975	16,180	30,550	31,985	33,592	30,168	26,464	33,486	33,511
Arkansas	584	1,801	3,295	6,461	12,704	21,097	22,193	22,693	21,718	20,778	23,125	23,252
California	2,351	—	[4] 6,600	10,950	18,626	34,304	35,882	[4] 39,309	36,807	30,464	37,601	37,594
Colorado	1,393	2,821	4,997	8,105	16,840	29,626	30,614	31,785	27,244	27,543	32,473	32,075
Connecticut	1,861	3,558	6,008	9,597	16,989	34,802	38,708	41,888	32,259	27,787	38,147	40,555
Delaware	1,684	3,273	[4] 5,800	9,387	16,845	30,614	32,736	34,620	31,553	27,551	33,556	34,298
District of Columbia .	2,350	3,920	6,280	10,700	23,027	39,616	42,310	43,637	35,966	37,663	43,423	44,329
Florida	1,012	2,958	5,080	8,785	14,875	27,052	28,697	30,275	29,529	24,329	29,652	30,066
Georgia	770	1,963	[5] 3,904	7,520	14,547	27,606	[4] 29,752	31,685	25,277	23,793	30,259	31,172
Hawaii	—	—	5,390	9,600	20,436	29,510	31,945	32,956	32,269	33,425	32,346	33,469
Idaho	1,057	2,481	4,216	7,081	14,110	23,105	23,640	24,758	23,802	23,078	25,326	24,768
Illinois	1,700	3,458	[6] 5,814	9,789	18,271	30,673	32,207	33,912	32,904	29,884	33,621	33,744
Indiana	1,433	3,401	5,542	9,239	16,256	27,188	30,357	31,300	31,056	26,588	29,801	31,806
Iowa	1,017	2,420	[4] 4,030	8,779	15,776	25,592	26,590	27,619	29,509	25,803	28,052	27,859
Kansas	1,014	2,628	[4] 4,450	7,811	14,513	26,309	29,248	30,154	26,256	23,737	28,837	30,644
Kentucky	826	1,936	3,327	7,325	15,350	25,327	26,026	27,482	24,622	25,106	27,761	27,268
Louisiana	1,006	2,983	4,978	7,264	14,020	21,802	23,150	25,036	24,417	22,931	23,897	24,255
Maine	894	2,115	3,694	8,059	13,743	24,161	25,779	27,831	27,089	22,478	26,483	27,009
Maryland	1,642	3,594	5,557	9,885	18,308	31,932	35,072	37,520	33,227	29,944	35,001	36,746
Massachusetts	2,037	3,338	[7] 5,545	9,347	18,900	35,327	38,419	40,175	31,419	30,912	38,722	40,252
Michigan	1,576	3,420	5,654	10,125	20,682	33,151	[4] 35,741	[4] 37,286	34,034	33,827	36,337	37,446
Minnesota	1,276	3,013	5,275	9,250	16,654	30,960	31,750	33,340	31,092	27,239	33,935	33,265
Mississippi	559	1,416	3,314	5,959	12,274	21,175	23,297	25,146	20,030	20,075	23,210	24,409
Missouri	1,159	2,581	4,536	8,064	14,543	25,666	27,020	28,381	27,106	23,786	28,133	28,309
Montana	1,184	2,962	[4] 4,425	7,875	15,080	28,042	28,415	29,526	26,471	24,665	30,737	29,771
Nebraska	829	2,292	3,876	7,633	14,236	24,100	25,335	27,024	25,657	23,284	26,416	26,544
Nevada	1,557	3,209	5,693	9,615	17,290	28,860	30,150	31,970	32,319	28,279	31,634	31,589
New Hampshire	1,258	2,712	4,455	8,016	13,508	24,690	[4] 27,448	[4] 28,958	26,945	22,093	27,063	28,758
New Jersey	2,093	3,511	5,871	9,650	18,851	32,110	34,627	37,485	32,437	30,832	35,196	36,279
New Mexico	1,144	3,215	5,382	10,021	15,406	24,797	25,003	25,790	33,684	25,198	27,180	26,196
New York	2,604	3,706	6,537	11,240	20,400	35,400	38,100	40,000	37,782	33,366	38,802	39,918
North Carolina	946	2,688	4,178	7,762	14,445	25,900	26,833	28,952	26,091	23,626	28,389	28,113
North Dakota	745	2,324	3,695	6,840	13,684	22,370	22,994	23,788	22,992	22,381	24,520	24,091
Ohio	1,587	3,088	5,124	8,594	16,100	29,322	30,934	32,467	28,887	26,333	32,140	32,410
Oklahoma	1,014	2,736	4,659	7,257	13,500	22,400	23,200	23,944	24,393	22,080	24,553	24,307
Oregon	1,333	3,323	5,535	9,200	16,996	29,300	30,680	32,100	30,924	27,798	32,116	32,144
Pennsylvania	1,640	3,006	5,308	8,899	17,060	29,881	31,555	34,110	29,913	27,903	32,753	33,061
Rhode Island	1,809	3,294	[8] 5,499	9,030	18,425	33,326	35,564	36,704	30,353	30,136	36,529	37,261
South Carolina	743	1,891	3,450	7,069	13,670	25,608	26,762	28,453	23,761	22,358	28,069	28,039
South Dakota	807	2,064	3,725	7,200	13,010	21,420	21,250	22,120	24,202	21,279	23,479	22,264
Tennessee	862	2,302	3,929	7,187	14,193	24,536	26,512	27,949	24,158	23,214	26,894	27,777
Texas	1,079	3,122	4,708	7,598	14,729	26,572	27,565	28,541	25,540	24,090	29,126	28,880
Utah	1,394	3,103	5,096	8,049	17,403	23,655	23,955	24,863	27,056	28,464	25,928	25,098
Vermont	981	2,348	4,466	8,225	13,300	25,525	[4] 27,265	[4] 29,982	27,647	21,753	27,978	28,566
Virginia	899	2,328	4,312	8,364	14,655	27,833	29,655	31,693	28,114	23,969	30,508	31,070
Washington	1,706	3,487	[8] 5,643	9,792	19,735	29,468	30,525	31,828	32,914	32,278	32,300	31,982
West Virginia	1,170	2,425	3,952	7,954	14,395	22,711	22,897	23,842	26,736	23,544	24,894	23,990
Wisconsin	1,379	3,007	[9] 4,870	9,150	16,335	30,958	32,500	32,445	30,756	26,717	33,933	34,051
Wyoming	1,169	2,798	4,937	8,496	16,830	28,327	28,844	29,308	28,558	27,527	31,049	30,220
Outlying areas												
American Samoa	—	—	852	5,130	—	—	—	—	17,244	—	—	—
Guam	—	—	4,107	7,800	—	—	—	—	26,219	—	—	—
Puerto Rico	—	—	[10] 2,360	—	—	—	—	—	—	—	—	—
Virgin Islands	—	—	3,407	—	—	—	—	—	—	—	—	—

[1] Includes supervisors, principals, classroom teachers, and other instructional staff.

[2] Based on the Consumer Price Index, prepared by the Bureau of Labor Statistics, U.S. Department of Labor. Price index does not account for different rates of change in the cost of living among States.

[3] Estimates revised from previously published data.

[4] Estimated.

[5] Excludes kindergarten teachers.

[6] Includes administrators.

[7] Includes clerical assistants to instructional personnel.

[8] Includes attendance personnel.

[9] Excludes vocational schools not operated as part of the regular public school system.

[10] Median salary.

—Data not available.

SOURCE: U.S. Department of Education, National Center for Education Statistics, *Statistics of State School Systems;* National Education Association, *Estimates of School Statistics;* and unpublished data. (Latest edition 1990–91. Copyright © 1991 by the National Education Association. All rights reserved.) (This table was prepared May 1991.)

Table 76.—Estimated average annual salary of instructional staff[1] in public elementary and secondary schools and average annual earnings of full-time employees in all industries: 1929–30 to 1990–91

School year	Current dollars		Constant 1990–91 dollars[2]		
	Average salary of instructional staff	Earnings per full-time employee working for wages or salary[3]	Average salary of instructional staff	Earnings per full-time working for wages or salary[3]	Ratio of instructional staff salary to salary for all full-time employees
1	2	3	4	5	6
1929–30	$1,420	$1,386	$11,113	$10,847	1.02
1931–32	1,417	1,198	13,166	11,132	1.18
1933–34	1,227	1,070	12,413	10,824	1.15
1935–36	1,283	1,160	12,507	11,308	1.11
1937–38	1,374	1,224	12,849	11,446	1.12
1939–40	1,441	1,282	13,813	12,289	1.12
1941–42	1,507	1,576	12,947	13,540	0.96
1943–44	1,728	2,030	13,284	15,606	0.85
1945–46	1,995	2,272	14,650	16,684	0.88
1947–48	2,639	2,692	15,172	15,477	0.98
1949–50	3,010	2,930	17,026	16,573	1.03
1951–52	3,450	3,322	17,584	16,932	1.04
1953–54	3,825	3,628	19,054	18,072	1.05
1955–56	4,156	3,924	20,710	19,553	1.06
1957–58	4,702	4,276	22,056	20,058	1.10
1959–60	5,174	4,632	23,589	21,118	1.12
1961–62	5,700	4,928	25,403	21,963	1.16
1963–64	6,240	5,373	27,103	23,337	1.16
1965–66	6,935	5,838	29,115	24,510	1.19
1967–68	7,630	6,444	30,055	25,383	1.18
1969–70	9,047	7,334	32,083	26,008	1.23
1970–71	9,698	7,815	32,703	26,353	1.24
1971–72	10,213	8,334	33,247	27,130	1.23
1972–73	10,634	8,858	33,277	27,719	1.20
1973–74	11,254	9,647	32,334	27,717	1.17
1974–75	12,167	10,420	31,470	26,951	1.17
1975–76	13,124	11,218	31,701	27,097	1.17
1976–77	13,840	11,991	31,589	27,368	1.15
1977–78	14,698	12,829	31,436	27,438	1.15
1978–79	15,764	13,851	30,828	27,087	1.14
1979–80	16,715	15,095	28,842	26,046	1.11
1980–81	18,404	16,495	28,460	25,508	1.12
1981–82	20,327	17,818	28,935	25,363	1.14
1982–83	21,641	18,883	29,536	25,772	1.15
1983–84	23,005	19,749	30,277	25,992	1.16
1984–85	24,666	20,626	31,241	26,124	1.20
1985–86	26,362	21,518	32,453	26,489	1.23
1986–87	27,707	22,432	33,368	27,015	1.24
1987–88	29,235	23,498	33,807	27,172	1.24
1988–89	30,969	24,483	34,231	27,062	1.26
1989–90	32,723	—	34,523	—	—
1990–91	34,456	—	34,456	—	—

[1] Includes supervisors, principals, classroom teachers, and other instructional staff.

[2] Based on the Consumer Price Index, prepared by the Bureau of Labor Statistics, U.S. Department of Labor.

[3] Calendar-year data from the U.S. Department of Commerce have been converted to a school-year basis by averaging the two appropriate calendar years in each case.

—Data not available.

NOTE.—Some data revised from previously published figures.

SOURCE: U.S. Department of Education, National Center for Education Statistics, *Statistics of State School Systems;* and unpublished data; National Education Association, *Estimates of School Statistics, 1990–91,* and unpublished data (Copyright © 1991 by the National Education Association. All rights reserved.); and U.S. Department of Commerce, *Survey of Current Business,* July issues. (This table was prepared June 1991.)

Table 77.—Staff employed in public elementary and secondary school systems, by functional area: 1949–50 to fall 1989

Year	Total	School district administrative staff					Instructional staff								Support staff						
		Total	Intermediate district staff	School district superintendents	Assistants to superintendents	Supervisors of instruction	Total	Principals and assistant principals	Teachers	Teachers aides	Librarians	Guidance counselors	Psychological personnel	Other instructional staff	Total	Secretarial and clerical personnel	Transportation staff	Food service	Plant operation and maintenance	Health	Recreational and other staff
1	2	3	4	5	6	7	8	9	10	11	12	13	14	15	16	17	18	19	20	21	22
1949–50	1,300,031	33,642	5,843	18,025	(1)	9,774	963,110	43,137	913,671	(2)	(2)	(2)	(2)	6,302	303,280	31,824	81,626	68,814	105,874	9,412	5,730
1959–60	2,089,283	42,423	9,901	13,361	5,386	13,775	1,457,329	63,554	1,353,372	(2)	17,363	14,643	2,121	6,277	589,531	75,930	113,111	161,925	192,655	16,104	29,807
1969–70	3,367,772	65,282	7,113	13,014	13,618	31,537	2,292,577	90,593	2,023,253	57,418	42,689	48,763	6,168	[3] 23,693	1,009,913	164,476	175,351	270,338	273,395	26,562	99,791
Fall 1980	4,167,608	78,784	—	13,269	[3] 44,961	[3] 20,554	2,858,895	107,061	2,183,538	325,755	48,018	63,973	14,033	[3] 116,517	1,229,929	223,647	(4)	(4)	(4)	(4)	[3] 1,006,282
Fall 1984	4,062,619	[3] 65,222	—	—	—	—	[3] 2,692,135	124,536	2,168,298	288,967	47,024	63,310	(5)	(5)	[3] 1,305,262	(5)	(5)	(5)	(5)	(5)	(5)
Fall 1985	4,160,521	[3] 67,404	—	—	—	—	[3] 2,757,129	129,297	2,206,884	306,860	47,442	66,646	(5)	(5)	[3] 1,335,988	(5)	(5)	(5)	(5)	(5)	(5)
Fall 1986	4,233,671	[3] 74,541	—	—	—	—	[3] 2,822,925	131,564	2,244,445	330,398	47,938	68,580	(5)	(5)	[3] 1,336,205	(5)	(5)	(5)	(5)	(5)	(5)
Fall 1987	4,311,941	[3] 74,191	—	—	—	—	[3] 2,859,626	125,927	2,279,241	335,991	48,185	70,282	(5)	(5)	[3] 1,378,124	(5)	(5)	(5)	(5)	(5)	(5)
Fall 1988	4,319,356	[3] 69,334	—	—	—	—	[3] 2,930,547	126,609	2,323,213	356,682	48,980	75,063	(5)	(5)	[3] 1,319,475	(5)	(5)	(5)	(5)	(5)	(5)
Fall 1989	4,420,553	371,220	—	—	—	—	[3] 2,986,119	128,272	2,355,963	373,221	49,744	78,919	(5)	(5)	[3] 1,363,214	(5)	(5)	(5)	(5)	(5)	(5)

Percentage distribution

Year	Total	3	4	5	6	7	8	9	10	11	12	13	14	15	16	17	18	19	20	21	22
1949–50	100.0	2.6	0.4	1.4	(1)	0.8	74.1	3.3	70.3	(2)	(2)	(2)	(2)	0.5	23.3	2.4	6.3	5.3	8.1	0.7	0.4
1959–60	100.0	2.0	0.5	0.6	0.3	0.7	69.8	3.0	64.8	(2)	0.8	0.7	0.1	0.3	28.2	3.6	5.4	7.8	9.2	0.8	1.4
1969–70	100.0	1.9	0.2	0.4	0.4	[3] 0.9	68.1	2.7	60.1	1.7	1.3	1.4	0.2	[3] 0.7	30.0	4.9	5.2	8.0	8.1	0.8	3.0
Fall 1980	100.0	1.9	—	0.3	[3] 1.1	[3] 0.5	68.6	2.6	52.4	7.8	1.2	1.5	0.3	[3] 2.8	29.5	5.4	(4)	(4)	(4)	(4)	[3] 24.1
Fall 1984	100.0	[3] 1.6	—	—	—	—	[3] 66.3	3.1	53.4	7.1	1.2	1.6	(5)	(5)	[3] 32.1	(5)	(5)	(5)	(5)	(5)	(5)
Fall 1985	100.0	[3] 1.6	—	—	—	—	[3] 66.3	3.1	53.0	7.4	1.1	1.6	(5)	(5)	[3] 32.1	(5)	(5)	(5)	(5)	(5)	(5)
Fall 1986	100.0	[3] 1.8	—	—	—	—	[3] 66.7	3.1	53.0	7.8	1.1	1.6	(5)	(5)	[3] 31.6	(5)	(5)	(5)	(5)	(5)	(5)
Fall 1987	100.0	[3] 1.7	—	—	—	—	[3] 66.3	2.9	52.9	7.8	1.1	1.6	(5)	(5)	[3] 32.0	(5)	(5)	(5)	(5)	(5)	(5)
Fall 1988	100.0	[3] 1.6	—	—	—	—	[3] 67.8	2.9	53.8	8.3	1.1	1.7	(5)	(5)	[3] 30.8	(5)	(5)	(5)	(5)	(5)	(5)
Fall 1989	100.0	[3] 1.6	—	—	—	—	[3] 67.6	2.9	53.3	8.4	1.1	1.8	(5)	(5)	[3] 3.08	(5)	(5)	(5)	(5)	(5)	(5)

Pupils per staff member

Year	Total	3	4	5	6	7	8	9	10	11	12	13	14	15	16	17	18	19	20	21	22
1949–50	19.3	746.4	4,297.7	1,393.1	6,532.2	2,569.2	26.1	582.1	27.5	(2)	2,026.3	2,402.7	16,589.1	3,984.7	82.8	789.1	307.6	364.9	237.2	2,668.0	4,382.4
1959–60	16.8	829.3	3,553.4	2,633.2	3,349.9	2,554.1	24.1	553.6	26.0	(2)	1,068.6	935.5	7,396.0	5,605.1	59.7	463.4	311.0	217.3	182.6	2,184.7	1,180.3
1969–70	13.5	698.8	6,413.4	3,505.3	[3] 910.1	[3] 1,446.5	19.9	503.6	22.5	794.5	852.1	639.6	2,915.9	[3] 1,925.4	45.2	277.4	260.2	168.7	166.9	1,717.4	457.1
Fall 1980	9.8	519.4	—	3,083.8	—	[3] 1,990.8	14.3	382.2	18.7	125.6	833.8	619.3	(5)	[3] 351.2	33.3	183.0	(4)	(4)	(4)	(4)	[3] 40.7
Fall 1984	9.7	[3] 601.2	—	—	—	—	[3] 14.6	314.8	18.1	135.7	831.0	591.5	(5)	(5)	[3] 30.0	(5)	(5)	(5)	(5)	(5)	(5)
Fall 1985	9.5	[3] 584.9	—	—	—	—	[3] 14.3	304.9	17.9	128.5	829.3	579.7	(5)	(5)	[3] 29.5	(5)	(5)	(5)	(5)	(5)	(5)
Fall 1986	9.4	[3] 533.3	—	—	—	—	[3] 14.1	302.2	17.7	120.3	830.3	569.2	(5)	(5)	[3] 29.8	(5)	(5)	(5)	(5)	(5)	(5)
Fall 1987	9.3	[3] 539.3	—	—	—	—	[3] 14.0	317.7	17.6	119.1	820.5	535.4	(5)	(5)	[3] 29.0	(5)	(5)	(5)	(5)	(5)	(5)
Fall 1988	9.3	[3] 579.6	—	—	—	—	[3] 13.7	317.4	17.3	112.7	814.7	513.5	(5)	(5)	[3] 30.5	(5)	(5)	(5)	(5)	(5)	(5)
Fall 1989	9.2	[3] 569.0	—	—	—	—	[3] 13.6	315.9	17.2	108.6			(5)	(5)	[3] 29.7	(5)	(5)	(5)	(5)	(5)	(5)

[1] Data included in column 5.
[2] Data included in column 10.
[3] Data not comparable with figures for years prior to 1984.
[4] Data included in column 22.
[5] Data included in column 16.
— Data not available.

NOTE: Some data have been revised from previously published figures. Because of variations in data collection instruments, some categories are only roughly comparable over time. Because of rounding, details may not add to totals.

SOURCE: U.S. Department of Education, National Center for Education Statistics, *Statistics of State School Systems*, Common Core of Data survey, and unpublished estimates. (This table was prepared December 1990.)

Table 78.—Staff employed in public school systems, by type of assignment and State: Fall 1989

[In full-time equivalents]

State or other area	Total	School district staff		School staff						Other support services staff
		Officials and administrators	Administrative support staff	School administrators	School and library support staff	Teachers	Instructional aides	Guidance counselors	Librarians	
1	2	3	4	5	6	7	8	9	10	11
United States [1]	4,420,553	71,220	135,739	128,272	187,745	2,355,963	373,221	78,919	49,744	1,039,730
Alabama	79,786	1,599	—	2,344	3,953	39,928	3,138	1,116	1,238	26,470
Alaska	13,438	855	546	393	947	6,492	1,450	201	165	2,389
Arizona	61,318	1,231	4,717	1,384	616	32,134	4,792	782	639	15,023
Arkansas	49,401	665	947	1,824	1,873	25,585	3,709	1,144	936	12,718
California	419,673	5,702	21,474	12,074	23,004	212,687	52,963	5,481	1,205	85,083
Colorado	60,603	932	2,188	2,479	3,972	31,954	4,016	1,006	732	13,324
Connecticut	57,423	1,161	275	1,506	—	35,308	6,048	2,134	653	10,338
Delaware	10,842	146	349	389	434	5,968	721	190	120	2,525
District of Columbia	10,619	435	464	581	226	6,055	638	217	196	1,807
Florida	206,351	3,016	—	5,945	—	104,127	20,380	4,348	2,467	66,068
Georgia	125,939	603	4,283	4,745	4,697	61,487	16,029	1,487	1,921	30,687
Hawaii	14,034	100	430	414	—	8,866	942	464	264	2,554
Idaho	17,160	311	356	553	623	10,715	1,123	294	176	3,009
Illinois	187,682	1,664	—	4,338	1,668	106,183	13,006	2,739	2,125	55,959
Indiana	107,094	1,606	455	2,684	7,076	54,486	11,174	1,566	1,055	26,992
Iowa	56,826	509	862	1,431	4,473	30,423	3,288	1,084	662	14,094
Kansas	50,175	472	2,114	1,537	2,062	28,727	2,977	1,135	930	10,221
Kentucky	71,377	1,567	5,109	1,701	2,602	35,731	5,522	1,017	1,085	17,043
Louisiana [2]	—	—	—	—	—	—	—	—	—	—
Maine	26,317	818	—	874	323	15,206	3,044	590	242	5,220
Maryland	76,623	322	2,176	2,342	3,545	41,646	5,585	1,504	1,070	18,433
Massachusetts	104,058	2,298	5,789	2,068	3,014	59,040	9,046	2,088	656	20,059
Michigan	170,889	1,658	1,704	4,595	11,046	80,150	11,240	2,842	1,575	56,079
Minnesota	76,268	1,650	3,291	1,745	3,052	43,101	7,712	861	767	14,089
Mississippi	56,361	880	1,572	1,326	2,035	27,591	8,301	698	681	13,277
Missouri	98,315	1,143	—	4,425	—	51,227	4,136	2,021	1,311	34,052
Montana [3]	12,543	276	—	489	—	9,627	1,131	324	312	384
Nebraska	33,325	656	1,602	1,070	—	18,464	2,563	578	520	7,872
Nevada [3]	10,311	194	—	434	—	9,175	0	333	175	—
New Hampshire	20,556	287	460	619	1,219	10,572	1,926	568	284	4,621
New Jersey	146,617	1,471	13,555	6,762	23,087	79,597	9,371	2,963	1,667	8,144
New Mexico	32,165	751	827	1,072	1,651	16,150	3,438	561	237	7,478
New York	345,072	4,211	24,910	7,027	8,782	174,610	24,490	6,198	3,387	91,457
North Carolina	122,470	2,227	—	3,800	—	63,160	18,388	2,361	2,137	30,397
North Dakota	14,132	350	349	374	471	7,809	1,033	171	172	3,403
Ohio	188,155	5,651	5,535	4,767	14,751	101,627	8,386	3,190	1,694	42,554
Oklahoma	65,076	668	797	1,654	3,573	35,631	4,009	1,020	705	17,019
Oregon	48,225	928	1,691	1,424	2,449	25,630	4,191	1,081	732	10,099
Pennsylvania	190,175	8,003	9,097	4,001	5,400	105,415	11,001	3,386	1,949	41,923
Rhode Island	15,184	156	710	549	537	9,369	1,003	346	231	2,283
South Carolina	63,333	818	2,312	2,059	3,463	36,337	4,816	1,267	1,084	11,177
South Dakota	14,129	326	647	504	320	8,191	1,298	254	174	2,415
Tennessee	86,049	603	—	4,355	4,136	42,824	8,555	1,125	1,330	23,121
Texas	332,948	5,324	4,244	11,121	15,239	199,397	29,762	8,000	3,811	56,050
Utah	31,351	304	484	810	1,664	17,611	3,284	385	252	6,557
Vermont	11,959	358	204	422	664	6,852	1,128	277	182	1,872
Virginia	120,203	1,930	648	3,183	5,676	62,138	9,291	2,918	1,771	32,648
Washington	72,517	1,041	2,239	2,249	3,809	40,279	5,814	1,327	1,150	14,609
West Virginia	39,407	494	1,613	1,193	682	21,653	2,761	541	381	10,089
Wisconsin	83,561	1,158	2,134	2,056	4,613	49,329	6,237	1,729	1,240	15,065
Wyoming	13,421	301	217	326	855	6,697	1,297	177	139	3,412
Outlying areas										
American Samoa	1,240	19	78	60	44	659	7	21	8	344
Guam	2,985	7	—	60	134	1,622	75	64	35	988
Northern Marianas	688	36	43	32	40	358	65	13	7	94
Puerto Rico	62,441	514	1,169	1,281	1,147	33,427	1,135	782	787	22,199
Virgin Islands	3,324	133	270	80	97	1,595	365	71	43	670

[1] U.S. totals include imputations for Louisiana, Montana, and Nevada, which are not reflected in State totals.

[2] Data not reported.

[3] Support staff underreported.

—Data not available or not applicable.

SOURCE: U.S. Department of Education, National Center for Education Statistics, Common Core of Data survey; and unpublished estimates. (This table was prepared December 1990.)

Table 79.—Staff employed in public school systems, by type of assignment and State: Fall 1988

[In full-time equivalents]

State or other area	Total	School district staff		School staff					Librarians	Other support services staff
		Officials and administrators	Administrative support staff	School administrators	School and library support staff	Teachers	Instructional aides	Guidance counselors		
1	2	3	4	5	6	7	8	9	10	11
United States [1]	4,319,356	69,334	127,299	126,609	187,557	2,323,213	356,682	75,063	48,980	1,004,619
Alabama	72,955	1,512	—	1,956	2,216	38,845	4,106	1,048	1,224	22,048
Alaska	13,500	520	597	420	1,977	6,272	1,537	178	169	1,830
Arizona	60,014	1,220	4,602	1,369	645	31,617	4,584	756	611	14,610
Arkansas	50,734	550	633	1,626	2,177	27,730	3,456	990	756	12,816
California	404,769	5,495	20,734	11,503	22,518	203,342	51,468	5,295	1,139	83,275
Colorado	59,814	1,015	1,988	2,534	3,992	31,398	4,040	996	724	13,127
Connecticut [2]	40,870	1,100	—	1,490	—	35,502	—	2,134	644	—
Delaware	10,766	146	349	389	434	5,898	719	188	119	2,524
District of Columbia	10,157	435	464	581	226	5,936	639	273	185	1,418
Florida	197,403	2,802	—	5,729	—	100,370	19,113	4,152	2,424	62,813
Georgia	120,669	623	4,138	4,340	4,444	59,916	14,094	1,379	1,871	29,864
Hawaii	20,730	187	—	420	—	8,737	1,800	448	258	8,880
Idaho	16,558	303	350	532	588	10,425	994	247	174	2,945
Illinois	186,235	1,689	—	4,278	1,641	105,097	12,340	2,708	2,115	56,367
Indiana	105,430	1,413	416	2,697	7,129	54,029	10,327	1,575	1,057	26,787
Iowa	56,220	531	872	1,442	4,361	30,327	3,243	1,006	675	13,763
Kansas	48,828	467	2,133	1,502	2,004	28,122	2,708	1,058	927	9,907
Kentucky	71,685	1,515	5,126	1,673	2,608	35,788	5,609	975	1,090	17,301
Louisiana	88,361	1,398	1,833	2,266	2,661	43,203	7,101	834	1,162	27,903
Maine	25,450	537	1,593	868	288	14,593	2,895	523	235	3,918
Maryland	75,229	307	2,072	2,369	3,383	40,899	5,480	1,470	1,051	18,198
Massachusetts	106,327	2,351	5,814	2,153	3,184	60,068	9,511	2,183	701	20,362
Michigan	169,610	1,694	1,798	4,507	10,071	79,847	10,783	2,800	1,564	56,546
Minnesota	75,885	1,655	3,182	1,680	3,035	42,750	7,556	877	785	14,365
Mississippi [3]	43,227	766	1,472	1,334	1,983	27,283	7,946	662	669	1,112
Missouri	97,946	1,131	—	4,311	—	50,693	3,930	1,965	1,303	34,613
Montana [3]	12,414	162	—	439	—	9,626	1,033	322	306	526
Nebraska	32,292	533	1,699	1,045	—	18,003	2,454	537	497	7,524
Nevada [3]	10,136	167	—	427	—	8,699	—	307	175	361
New Hampshire	19,185	148	584	578	1,080	10,442	1,981	526	222	3,624
New Jersey	144,051	1,498	12,680	6,201	22,683	79,698	8,789	2,932	1,635	7,935
New Mexico	30,159	363	668	736	1,763	15,770	3,067	528	229	7,035
New York	312,426	4,263	18,330	7,054	8,319	172,807	24,430	5,288	3,353	68,582
North Carolina	119,161	2,093	—	3,733	—	61,933	18,016	2,238	2,098	29,050
North Dakota	13,789	332	342	371	451	7,731	965	165	170	3,262
Ohio	186,631	5,600	5,487	4,759	14,585	101,021	8,031	3,103	1,707	42,338
Oklahoma	64,076	664	819	1,628	3,671	35,116	3,680	1,016	702	16,780
Oregon	47,317	915	1,615	1,419	2,420	25,147	4,048	1,072	726	9,955
Pennsylvania	188,279	7,889	7,131	3,955	7,026	104,379	10,624	3,307	1,940	42,028
Rhode Island	14,795	147	729	528	553	9,216	1,009	339	229	2,045
South Carolina	61,908	787	2,155	2,017	3,136	35,877	4,731	1,196	1,081	10,928
South Dakota	13,898	336	644	528	268	8,260	1,138	249	170	2,305
Tennessee	84,500	616	—	4,434	4,180	42,657	7,437	1,088	1,313	22,775
Texas	327,296	6,022	3,439	12,515	15,418	196,616	30,603	7,627	3,718	51,338
Utah	30,774	274	465	798	1,720	17,602	2,778	381	288	6,468
Vermont	11,959	358	204	422	664	6,852	1,128	277	182	1,872
Virginia	117,291	1,834	695	3,164	5,579	60,883	8,942	2,297	1,770	32,127
Washington	69,610	1,010	2,180	2,283	3,634	38,780	5,502	1,244	1,109	13,868
West Virginia	40,433	518	1,762	1,256	602	22,177	2,838	545	358	10,377
Wisconsin	82,307	1,118	2,063	2,029	4,497	48,541	6,232	1,587	1,230	15,010
Wyoming	13,275	325	239	321	849	6,693	1,247	172	140	3,289
Outlying areas										
American Samoa	1,255	19	73	60	49	674	23	20	8	329
Guam	2,778	8	—	54	123	1,403	60	56	29	1,045
Northern Marianas	643	—	18	36	39	334	97	13	8	98
Puerto Rico	62,322	476	1,485	1,259	1,039	33,357	2,358	785	752	20,811
Virgin Islands	3,322	135	270	79	119	1,597	353	73	46	650

[1] U.S. totals include imputations for Connecticut, Mississippi, Montana, and Nevada, which are not reflected in State totals.

[2] Support staff not reported.

[3] Support staff underreported.

— Data not available, not reported, or not applicable.

NOTE.—Some data have been revised from previously published figures.

SOURCE: U.S. Department of Education, National Center for Education Statistics, Common Core of Data survey; and unpublished estimates. (This table was prepared December 1990.)

Table 80.—Staff and teachers in public elementary and secondary schools, by State: Fall 1985 to fall 1989

State or other area	Teachers as a percent of staff, fall 1985	Teachers as a percent of staff, fall 1986	Fall 1987[1]			Fall 1988[1]			Fall 1989		
			Staff	Teachers	Teachers as a percent of staff	Staff	Teachers	Teachers as a percent of staff	Staff	Teachers	Teachers as a percent of staff
1	2	3	4	5	6	7	8	9	10	11	12
United States	[2]53.0	[2]53.0	[2]4,311,941	2,279,241	[2]52.9	[2]4,319,356	2,323,213	[2]53.8	[2]4,420,553	[2]2,355,963	[2]53.3
Alabama	52.1	52.1	70,655	37,716	53.4	72,955	38,845	53.2	79,786	39,928	50.0
Alaska	65.7	65.7	[3]7,285	6,113	[3]83.9	13,500	6,272	46.5	13,438	6,492	48.3
Arizona	51.8	51.8	59,095	30,707	52.0	60,014	31,617	52.7	61,318	32,134	52.4
Arkansas	53.8	53.8	47,741	25,572	53.6	50,734	27,730	54.7	49,401	25,585	51.8
California	49.4	49.4	392,299	195,864	49.9	404,769	203,342	50.2	419,673	212,687	50.7
Colorado	52.5	52.5	59,263	31,168	52.6	59,814	31,398	52.5	60,603	31,954	52.7
Connecticut	[4]87.2	[4]87.2	[4]40,214	35,050	[4]87.2	[4]40,870	35,502	[4]86.9	57,423	35,308	61.5
Delaware	55.5	55.5	10,790	5,951	55.2	10,766	5,898	54.8	10,842	5,968	55.0
District of Columbia .	50.1	50.1	11,130	6,232	56.0	10,157	5,936	58.4	10,619	6,055	57.0
Florida	51.8	51.8	184,608	95,857	51.9	197,403	100,370	50.8	206,351	104,127	50.5
Georgia	52.0	52.0	119,320	62,280	52.2	120,669	59,916	49.7	125,939	61,487	48.8
Hawaii	45.9	45.9	18,036	7,684	42.6	20,730	8,737	42.1	14,034	8,866	63.2
Idaho	63.8	63.8	16,205	10,258	63.3	16,558	10,425	63.0	17,160	10,715	62.4
Illinois	56.4	56.4	186,595	105,217	56.4	186,235	105,097	56.4	187,682	106,183	56.6
Indiana	50.6	50.6	105,326	53,749	51.0	105,430	54,029	51.2	107,094	54,486	50.9
Iowa	54.5	54.5	56,670	30,873	54.5	56,220	30,327	53.9	56,826	30,423	53.5
Kansas	57.3	57.3	47,569	27,317	57.4	48,828	28,122	57.6	50,175	28,727	57.3
Kentucky	51.0	51.0	69,192	35,239	50.9	71,685	35,788	49.9	71,377	35,731	50.1
Louisiana	48.5	48.5	88,794	42,920	48.3	88,361	43,203	48.9	—	—	—
Maine	59.6	59.6	24,410	14,204	58.2	25,450	14,593	57.3	26,317	15,206	57.8
Maryland	54.1	54.1	73,717	40,093	54.4	75,229	40,899	54.4	76,623	41,646	54.4
Massachusetts	57.0	57.0	103,471	59,517	57.5	106,327	60,068	56.5	104,058	59,040	56.7
Michigan	48.4	48.4	170,162	79,976	47.0	169,610	79,847	47.1	170,889	80,150	46.9
Minnesota	58.6	58.6	74,027	42,132	56.9	75,885	42,750	56.3	76,268	43,101	56.5
Mississippi	64.4	[3]64.4	[3]42,540	26,930	[3]63.3	[3]43,227	27,283	[3]63.1	56,361	27,591	49.0
Missouri	53.4	53.4	96,736	49,632	51.3	97,946	50,693	51.8	98,315	51,227	52.1
Montana	[3]77.8	[3]77.8	[3]12,477	9,659	[3]77.4	[3]12,414	9,626	[3]77.5	[3]12,543	9,627	[3]76.8
Nebraska	56.2	56.2	31,809	17,713	55.7	32,292	18,003	55.8	33,325	18,464	55.4
Nevada	[3]85.8	[3]85.8	[3]9,736	8,348	[3]85.7	[3]10,136	8,699	[3]85.8	[3]10,311	9,175	[3]89.0
New Hampshire	56.0	56.0	18,635	10,363	55.6	19,185	10,442	54.4	20,556	10,572	51.4
New Jersey	54.1	54.1	141,257	78,335	55.5	144,051	79,698	55.3	146,617	79,597	54.3
New Mexico	52.1	52.1	29,347	15,175	51.7	30,159	15,770	52.3	32,165	16,150	50.2
New York	53.2	53.2	327,428	170,236	52.0	312,426	172,807	55.3	345,072	174,610	50.6
North Carolina	52.5	52.5	114,243	59,771	52.3	119,161	61,933	52.0	122,470	63,160	51.6
North Dakota	56.8	56.8	13,533	7,632	56.4	13,789	7,731	56.1	14,132	7,809	55.3
Ohio	54.1	54.1	184,130	99,708	54.2	186,631	101,021	54.1	188,155	101,627	54.0
Oklahoma	53.7	53.7	63,822	34,515	54.1	64,076	35,116	54.8	65,076	35,631	54.8
Oregon	52.8	52.8	47,211	24,911	52.8	47,317	25,147	53.1	48,225	25,630	53.1
Pennsylvania	55.7	55.7	185,629	103,307	55.7	188,279	104,379	55.4	190,175	105,415	55.4
Rhode Island	62.3	62.3	14,569	8,934	61.3	14,795	9,216	62.3	15,184	9,369	61.7
South Carolina	57.2	57.2	62,557	35,701	57.1	61,908	35,877	58.0	63,333	36,337	57.4
South Dakota	57.8	57.8	14,202	8,172	57.5	13,898	8,260	59.4	14,129	8,191	58.0
Tennessee	50.8	50.8	83,256	42,082	50.5	84,500	42,657	50.5	86,049	42,824	49.8
Texas	49.7	49.7	377,240	187,159	49.6	327,296	196,616	60.1	332,948	199,397	59.9
Utah	58.2	58.2	29,976	17,124	57.1	30,774	17,602	57.2	31,351	17,611	56.2
Vermont	—	—	12,321	6,656	54.0	11,959	6,852	57.3	11,959	6,852	57.3
Virginia	53.6	53.6	114,439	59,928	52.4	117,291	60,883	51.9	120,203	62,138	51.7
Washington	56.2	56.2	68,405	38,344	56.1	69,610	38,780	55.7	72,517	40,279	55.5
West Virginia	55.1	55.1	41,415	22,702	54.8	40,433	22,177	54.8	39,407	21,653	54.9
Wisconsin	59.3	59.3	80,340	47,721	59.4	82,307	48,541	59.0	83,561	49,329	59.0
Wyoming	50.3	50.3	13,373	6,798	50.8	13,275	6,693	50.4	13,421	6,697	49.9
Outlying areas											
American Samoa	53.6	53.6	1,206	656	54.4	1,255	674	53.7	1,240	659	53.1
Guam	47.9	47.9	2,884	1,407	48.8	2,778	1,403	50.5	2,985	1,622	54.3
Northern Marianas ...	—	—	512	305	59.6	643	334	51.9	688	358	52.0
Puerto Rico	79.0	79.0	42,314	33,069	78.2	62,322	33,357	53.5	62,441	33,427	53.5
Virgin Islands	49.3	49.3	3,254	1,590	48.9	3,322	1,597	48.1	3,324	1,595	48.0

[1] Some data have been revised from previously published figures.
[2] U.S. totals include imputations for underreporting and nonreporting States.
[3] Support staff underreported.
[4] Support staff not reported.
—Data not available.

SOURCE: U.S. Department of Education, National Center for Education Statistics, Common Core of Data survey; and unpublished estimates. (This table as prepared December 1990.)

Table 81.—Staff, enrollment, and pupil-staff ratios in public elementary and secondary schools, by State: Fall 1985 to fall 1989

State or other area	Pupil-staff ratio, fall 1985	Pupil-staff ratio, fall 1986	Fall 1987			Fall 1988 [1]			Fall 1989		
			Staff	Enrollment	Pupil-staff ratio	Staff	Enrollment	Pupil-staff ratio	Staff	Enrollment	Pupil-staff ratio
1	2	3	4	5	6	7	8	9	10	11	12
United States	[2]9.5	[2]9.4	[2]4,311,941	40,007,946	[2]9.3	[2]4,319,356	40,188,690	[2]9.3	[2]4,420,553	40,526,372	[2]9.2
Alabama	10.6	10.3	70,655	729,234	10.3	72,955	724,751	9.9	79,786	723,343	9.1
Alaska	8.0	11.0	[3]7,285	105,678	[3]14.5	13,500	106,481	7.9	13,438	109,280	8.1
Arizona	10.2	9.5	59,095	572,421	9.7	60,014	574,890	9.6	61,318	607,615	9.9
Arkansas	9.3	9.4	47,741	437,036	9.2	50,734	436,387	8.6	49,401	434,960	8.8
California	11.2	11.4	392,299	4,489,322	11.4	404,769	4,618,120	11.4	419,673	4,771,978	11.4
Colorado	9.5	9.5	59,263	560,236	9.5	59,814	560,081	9.4	60,603	562,755	9.3
Connecticut	[4]12.2	[4]11.9	[4]40,214	465,465	[4]11.6	[4]40,870	460,637	[4]11.3	57,423	461,560	8.0
Delaware	9.0	8.9	10,790	95,659	8.9	10,766	96,678	9.0	10,842	97,808	9.0
District of Columbia .	8.3	7.2	11,130	86,435	7.8	10,157	84,792	8.3	10,619	81,301	7.7
Florida	9.1	9.0	184,608	1,664,774	9.0	197,403	1,720,930	8.7	206,351	1,772,349	8.6
Georgia	9.9	9.8	119,320	1,110,947	9.3	120,669	1,107,994	9.2	125,939	1,126,535	8.9
Hawaii	9.6	10.4	18,036	166,160	9.2	20,730	167,488	8.1	14,034	169,493	12.1
Idaho	13.0	13.0	16,205	212,444	13.1	16,558	214,615	13.0	17,160	214,932	12.5
Illinois	10.1	9.8	186,595	1,811,446	9.7	186,235	1,794,916	9.6	187,682	1,797,355	9.6
Indiana	9.4	9.3	105,326	964,129	9.2	105,430	960,994	9.1	107,094	954,165	8.9
Iowa	8.3	8.5	56,670	480,826	8.5	56,220	478,200	8.5	56,826	478,486	8.4
Kansas	8.8	8.8	47,569	421,112	8.9	48,828	426,596	8.7	50,175	430,864	8.6
Kentucky	9.8	9.5	69,192	642,696	9.3	71,685	637,627	8.9	71,377	630,688	8.8
Louisiana	8.9	9.0	88,794	793,093	8.9	88,361	786,683	8.9	—	783,025	—
Maine	8.9	9.2	24,410	211,817	8.7	25,450	212,902	8.4	26,317	213,775	8.1
Maryland	9.4	9.3	73,717	683,797	9.3	75,229	688,947	9.2	76,623	698,806	9.1
Massachusetts	8.6	8.2	103,471	825,320	8.0	106,327	823,428	7.7	104,058	825,588	7.9
Michigan	9.5	9.3	170,162	1,589,287	9.3	169,610	1,582,785	9.3	170,889	1,576,785	9.2
Minnesota	10.0	10.2	74,027	721,481	9.7	75,885	726,950	9.6	76,268	739,553	9.7
Mississippi	8.5	[3]12.3	[3]42,540	505,550	[3]11.9	[3]43,227	503,326	[3]11.6	56,361	502,020	8.9
Missouri	8.8	8.7	96,736	802,060	8.3	97,946	806,639	8.2	98,315	807,934	8.2
Montana	[3]12.1	[3]12.2	[3]12,477	152,207	[3]12.2	[3]12,414	152,191	[3]12.3	[3]12,543	151,265	[3]12.1
Nebraska	8.6	8.5	31,809	268,100	8.4	32,292	269,434	8.3	33,325	270,920	8.1
Nevada	[3]17.5	[3]17.5	[3]9,736	168,353	[3]17.3	[3]10,136	176,474	[3]17.4	[3]10,311	186,834	[3]18.1
New Hampshire	9.5	8.9	18,635	166,045	8.9	19,185	169,413	8.8	20,556	171,696	8.4
New Jersey	8.1	7.9	141,257	1,092,982	7.7	144,051	1,080,871	7.5	146,617	1,076,005	7.3
New Mexico	10.0	9.9	29,347	287,229	9.8	30,159	292,425	9.7	32,165	296,057	9.2
New York	8.4	8.2	327,428	2,594,070	7.9	312,426	2,573,715	8.2	345,072	2,565,841	7.4
North Carolina	9.9	9.8	114,243	1,085,976	9.5	119,161	1,083,156	9.1	122,470	1,080,744	8.8
North Dakota	8.7	8.7	13,533	119,004	8.8	13,789	118,809	8.6	14,132	117,816	8.3
Ohio	9.9	9.8	184,130	1,793,431	9.7	186,631	1,778,544	9.5	188,155	1,767,159	9.4
Oklahoma	8.9	9.1	63,822	584,212	9.2	64,076	580,426	9.1	65,076	578,580	8.9
Oregon	9.6	9.6	47,211	455,895	9.7	47,317	461,752	9.8	48,225	472,394	9.8
Pennsylvania	9.2	9.1	185,629	1,668,542	9.0	188,279	1,659,714	8.8	190,175	1,655,279	8.7
Rhode Island	9.6	9.4	14,569	134,800	9.3	14,795	133,585	9.0	15,184	135,729	8.9
South Carolina	9.9	9.9	62,557	614,921	9.8	61,908	615,774	9.9	63,333	616,177	9.7
South Dakota	8.5	9.0	14,202	126,817	8.9	13,898	126,910	9.1	14,129	127,329	9.0
Tennessee	10.4	10.1	83,256	823,783	9.9	84,500	821,580	9.7	86,049	819,660	9.5
Texas	8.8	8.6	377,240	3,236,787	8.6	327,296	3,283,707	—	332,948	3,328,514	10.0
Utah	13.7	13.6	29,976	423,386	14.1	30,774	431,119	14.0	31,351	437,446	14.0
Vermont	7.4	—	12,321	92,755	7.5	11,959	93,381	7.8	11,959	94,779	7.9
Virginia	9.2	9.0	114,439	979,417	8.6	117,291	982,393	8.4	120,203	985,346	8.2
Washington	11.7	11.5	68,405	775,755	11.3	69,610	790,918	11.4	72,517	810,232	11.2
West Virginia	8.7	8.4	41,415	344,236	8.3	40,433	335,912	8.3	39,407	327,540	8.3
Wisconsin	9.9	9.7	80,340	772,363	9.6	82,307	774,857	9.4	83,561	782,905	9.4
Wyoming	7.2	7.0	13,373	98,455	7.4	13,275	97,793	7.4	13,421	97,172	7.2
Outlying areas											
American Samoa	—	9.5	1,206	11,248	9.3	1,255	11,764	9.4	1,240	12,258	9.9
Guam	10.9	8.6	2,884	25,936	9.0	2,778	26,041	9.4	2,985	26,493	8.9
Northern Marianas ..	—	—	512	5,819	11.4	643	6,079	9.5	688	6,101	8.9
Puerto Rico	16.7	16.6	42,314	672,837	15.9	62,322	661,693	10.6	62,441	651,225	10.4
Virgin Islands	—	7.5	3,254	24,020	7.4	3,322	23,492	7.1	3,324	21,193	6.4

[1] Some data revised from previously published figures.
[2] U.S. totals include imputations for underreporting and nonreporting States.
[3] Support staff underreported.
[4] Support staff not reported.
—Data not available.

SOURCE: U.S. Department of Education, National Center for Education Statistics, Common Core of Data survey; and unpublished estimates. (This table was prepared December 1990.)

Table 82.—Principals in public and private elementary and secondary schools, by selected characteristics: 1987–88

Selected characteristics	Total [1]	Percent of principals, by highest degree earned [2]				Average years of experience				Average annual salary of principals, by length of work		
		Bachelor's	Master's	Education specialist	Doctor's and first-professional	As a principal	Other school position	As a teacher	Outside school position	10 months or less	11 months	12 months
1	2	3	4	5	6	7	8	9	10	11	12	13

Public schools

Selected characteristics	Total	Bachelor's	Master's	Education specialist	Doctor's	As a principal	Other school position	As a teacher	Outside school position	10 months or less	11 months	12 months
Total	77,890	2.4	53.4	35.1	8.9	10.0	3.8	9.8	1.0	$38,726	$41,563	$44,252
Sex												
Men	58,585	1.9	55.7	34.3	8.2	11.2	3.6	9.0	1.1	39,143	41,488	44,509
Women	19,118	3.9	46.6	37.8	11.3	6.1	4.0	12.3	1.0	37,643	41,562	43,241
Race/ethnicity												
White [3]	69,048	2.5	53.7	35.0	8.6	10.1	3.6	9.6	1.0	38,136	41,397	44,319
Black [3]	6,696	(5)	51.4	36.9	11.5	8.8	4.8	11.8	1.2	42,796	42,843	43,319
Hispanic [4]	2,483	(5)	54.2	30.2	(5)	6.6	5.4	9.8	1.3	40,394	42,235	46,770
Asian or Pacific Islander [3]	434	(5)	52.8	33.4	(5)	7.7	4.5	10.8	0.4	41,581	(5)	(5)
American Indian or Alaskan Native [3]	821	(5)	51.2	(5)	(5)	9.9	4.6	9.1	1.3	(5)	(5)	43,706
Age												
Under 40	14,430	3.6	54.7	33.7	(5)	4.3	2.5	7.8	0.7	34,901	37,885	39,359
40 to 44	17,755	2.0	49.0	39.7	9.2	6.8	3.7	9.2	1.0	37,872	40,225	43,351
45 to 49	16,408	0.0	52.8	35.8	9.6	10.0	4.0	10.3	0.9	39,004	42,316	45,249
50 to 54	14,936	2.2	56.6	33.2	7.9	13.2	4.3	10.6	1.3	40,377	43,454	45,884
55 or over	13,891	2.7	55.9	31.7	9.6	16.5	4.1	11.4	1.4	42,272	44,080	46,999

Private schools

Selected characteristics	Total	Bachelor's	Master's	Education specialist	Doctor's	As a principal	Other school position	As a teacher	Outside school position	10 months or less	11 months	12 months
Total	25,401	25.7	51.0	12.2	4.2	8.0	2.6	9.8	2.4	13,182	23,505	22,651
Sex												
Men	12,131	26.3	49.6	9.8	9.1	8.1	2.8	6.8	3.3	13,963	32,553	25,752
Women	13,243	25.2	52.3	14.4	3.8	7.8	2.5	12.5	1.5	12,784	18,863	18,693
Race/ethnicity												
White [3]	24,056	25.9	51.0	12.3	6.1	8.0	2.6	9.8	2.3	12,853	23,582	22,746
Black [3]	771	(5)	5.6	(5)	(5)	6.8	4.1	10.2	2.6	(5)	(5)	21,895
Hispanic [4]	629	(5)	(5)	(5)	(5)	8.0	3.5	11.1	2.2	(5)	(5)	23,101
Age												
Under 40	7,608	34.6	46.1	7.5	3.5	4.2	1.5	5.5	1.8	15,658	23,390	20,024
40 to 44	5,352	21.4	56.5	13.9	6.0	6.4	2.5	9.5	1.9	13,965	22,022	24,980
45 to 49	4,497	25.4	48.2	14.6	8.2	8.1	2.9	10.5	2.7	12,466	23,971	25,287
50 to 54	2,979	22.2	55.5	11.2	6.9	10.7	2.8	12.3	2.2	11,944	23,171	23,443
55 or over	4,703	18.3	54.0	15.4	9.2	14.1	4.3	14.4	3.7	10,465	25,565	22,197

[1] Total differs from data appearing in other tables because of varying survey processing procedures and time period coverages.

[2] Percentages for those with less than a bachelor's degree are not shown.

[3] Includes persons of Hispanic origin.

[4] Persons of Hispanic origin may be of any race.

[5] Too few sample cases (fewer than 30) for a reliable estimate.

NOTE.—Details may not add to 100 percent because of rounding and survey item nonresponse.

SOURCE: U.S. Department of Education, National Center for Education Statistics, "Schools and Staffing Survey, 1987–88." (This table was prepared May 1990.)

Table 83.—Secondary school principals' beliefs about educational issues and purposes: 1965, 1977, and 1987

Beliefs about educational issues	Percent agreeing with statement			School programs should include	Rank		
	1965	1977	1987		1965	1977	1987
1	2	3	4	5	6	7	8
School programs should include instruction on drug/alcohol abuse	—	—	92	Acquisition of basic skills	1	1	1
High schools should develop special programs for gifted students	19	92	92	Development of positive self-concept and good human relations	7	2	2
High schools should develop special programs for the handicapped, ethnic minority, and non-English-speaking	—	75	65	Development/practice of intellectual inquiry and problem solving	4	3	3
Computer competence is essential for all students	—	—	69	Preparation for a changing world	5	8	4
More stringent requirements are needed for all students in traditional academic subjects	—	—	63	Development of moral/spiritual values	2	4	5
Schools require far too little academic work of students	16	56	46	Career planning and training in specific entry-level occupational skills	—	5	6
Standardized testing in all subjects is necessary to improve instruction	—	—	40	Understanding of the American value system (political, economic, social)	3	7	7
Disinterested youth or those hostile toward school should not be required to attend high school	34	59	47	Development of skills to operate in a technological society	8	10	8
School attendance should be compulsory to high school graduation or age 18	39	15	34	Develop knowledge and skills in preparation for family life	—	6	9
The academic year should be lengthened	22	12	32	Physical fitness and useful leisure-time sports	6	9	10
				Appreciation for and experience with the fine arts	—	11	11

—Data not available.

SOURCE: National Association of Secondary School Principals, *High School Leaders and Their Schools*, Vol. I, 1988. (This table was prepared November 1988.)

Table 84.—Administrative roadblocks reported by secondary school principals: 1965, 1977, and 1987

Problem	Percent		
	1965	1977	1987
1	2	3	4
Time taken up by administrative detail	87	90	83
Lack of time	86	86	79
Inability to obtain funds	—	79	76
Apathetic or irresponsible parents	—	79	70
New State guidelines and requirements	—	—	69
Time to administer/supervise student activities	—	—	68
Variations in the ability of teachers	88	84	64
Inability to provide teachers time for professional development	83	59	62
Insufficient space and facilities	78	66	61
Resistance to change by staff	64	56	57
Problem students	—	76	55
Defective communications among administrative levels	41	54	55
Longstanding traditions	47	40	51

—Data not available.

SOURCE: National Association of Secondary School Principals, *High School Leaders and Their Schools*, Vol. I, 1988. (This table was prepared November 1988.)

Table 85.—Public school districts and public and private elementary and secondary schools: 1929–30 to 1989–90

School year	Public school districts [1]	Public schools [2]					Private schools [2,3]		
		Total, all schools [4]	Total, regular schools [5]	Elementary schools		Secondary schools	Total [4]	Elementary	Secondary
				Total	One-teacher				
1	2	3	4	5	6	7	8	9	10
1929–30	—	—	—	238,306	149,282	23,930	—	9,275	3,258
1937–38	119,001	—	—	221,660	121,178	25,467	—	9,992	3,327
1939–40	117,108	—	—	—	113,600	—	—	11,306	3,568
1945–46	101,382	—	—	160,227	86,563	24,314	—	9,863	3,294
1947–48	94,926	—	—	146,760	75,096	25,484	—	10,071	3,292
1949–50	83,718	—	—	128,225	59,652	24,542	—	10,375	3,331
1951–52	71,094	—	—	123,763	50,742	23,746	—	10,666	3,322
1953–54	63,057	—	—	110,875	42,865	25,637	—	11,739	3,913
1955–56	54,859	—	—	104,427	34,964	26,046	—	12,372	3,887
1957–58	47,594	—	—	95,446	25,341	25,507	—	13,065	3,994
1959–60	40,520	—	—	91,853	20,213	25,784	—	13,574	4,061
1961–62	35,676	—	—	81,910	13,333	25,350	—	14,762	4,129
1963–64	31,705	—	—	77,584	9,895	26,431	—	—	4,451
1965–66	26,983	—	—	73,216	6,491	26,597	17,849	15,340	4,606
1967–68	22,010	—	94,197	70,879	4,146	27,011	—	—	—
1970–71	17,995	—	89,372	65,800	1,815	25,352	—	14,372	3,770
1973–74	16,730	—	88,655	65,070	1,365	25,906	—	—	—
1975–76	16,376	88,597	87,034	63,242	1,166	25,330	—	—	—
1976–77	16,271	—	86,501	62,644	1,111	25,378	19,910	16,385	5,904
1978–79	16,014	—	84,816	61,982	1,056	24,504	19,489	16,097	5,766
1980–81	15,912	85,982	83,688	61,069	921	24,362	20,764	16,792	5,678
1982–83	15,824	84,740	82,039	59,656	798	23,988	—	—	—
1983–84	15,747	84,178	81,418	59,082	838	23,947	[6] 27,694	[6] 20,872	[6] 7,862
1984–85	—	84,007	81,147	58,827	825	23,916			
1985–86	—	—	—	—	—	—	[6] 25,616	[6] 20,252	[6] 7,387
1986–87	[7] 15,713	83,455	82,190	60,784	763	23,389	—	—	—
1987–88	[7] 15,577	83,248	82,248	61,490	729	22,937	[6] 26,836	[6] 22,959	[6] 8,418
1988–89	[7] 15,376	83,165	82,081	61,531	583	22,785	—	—	—
1989–90	[7] 15,367	83,425	82,396	62,037	630	22,639	—	—	—

[1] Includes operating and nonoperating districts.

[2] Schools with both elementary and secondary programs are included under elementary schools and also under secondary schools.

[3] Data for most years are partly estimated.

[4] Includes regular schools and special schools not classified by grade span.

[5] Includes elementary, secondary, and combined elementary/secondary schools.

[6] These data are from sample surveys and should not be compared directly with the data for earlier years.

[7] Because of expanded survey coverage, data are not directly comparable with figures for earlier years.

—Data not available.

SOURCE: U.S. Department of Education, National Center for Education Statistics, *Statistics of State School Systems; Statistics of Public Elementary and Secondary School Systems; Statistics of Nonpublic Elementary and Secondary Schools; Private Schools in American Education*; and, Common Core of Data survey. (This table was prepared December 1990.)

Table 86.—Public school districts and enrollment, by size of district: 1986–87 to 1989–90

Enrollment size of district	1986–87	1987–88			1988–89			1989–90		
	Number of districts	Number of districts	Percent of districts	Percent of students	Number of districts	Percent of districts	Percent of students	Number of districts	Percent of districts	Percent of students
1	2	3	4	5	6	7	8	9	10	11
Total	15,713	15,577	100.0	100.0	15,376	100.0	100.0	15,367	100.0	100.0
25,000 or more	173	171	1.1	27.3	177	1.2	27.8	179	1.2	28.0
10,000 to 24,999	447	464	3.0	17.4	473	3.1	17.6	479	3.1	17.7
5,000 to 9,999	915	937	6.0	16.5	924	6.0	16.1	913	5.9	15.8
2,500 to 4,999	1,823	1,912	12.3	16.8	1,907	12.4	16.7	1,937	12.6	16.8
1,000 to 2,499	3,504	3,561	22.9	14.7	3,529	23.0	14.5	3,547	23.1	14.4
600 to 999	1,754	1,796	11.5	3.6	1,813	11.8	3.6	1,801	11.7	3.5
300 to 599	2,257	2,290	14.7	2.5	2,266	14.7	2.5	2,283	14.9	2.5
1 to 299	4,071	4,041	25.9	1.3	3,984	25.9	1.3	3,910	25.4	1.3
Size not reported [1]	769	405	2.6	—	303	2.0	—	318	2.1	—

[1] Includes school districts reporting enrollment of 0.

—Data not reported.

NOTE.—Because of rounding, details may not add to totals.

SOURCE: U.S. Department of Education, National Center for Education Statistics, Common Core of Data survey. (This table was prepared December 1990.)

Table 87.—Number and percentage of public elementary and secondary education agencies, by State and type of agency: 1989–90

State or other area	Total agencies	Regular school districts, including supervisory union components		Regional education service agencies and supervisory union administrative centers		State-operated agencies		Federally-operated and other agencies	
		Number	Percent	Number	Percent	Number	Percent	Number	Percent
1	2	3	4	5	6	7	8	9	10
United States ...	16,962	15,367	90.6	1,297	7.6	185	1.1	113	0.7
Alabama	133	129	97.0	0	0.0	1	0.8	3	2.3
Alaska	55	54	98.2	0	0.0	1	1.8	0	0.0
Arizona	244	238	97.5	5	2.0	0	0.0	1	0.4
Arkansas	350	329	94.0	18	5.1	3	0.9	0	0.0
California	1,153	1,074	93.1	73	6.3	6	0.5	0	0.0
Colorado	196	176	89.8	20	10.2	0	0.0	0	0.0
Connecticut	176	166	94.3	6	3.4	4	2.3	0	0.0
Delaware	22	19	86.4	0	0.0	3	13.6	0	0.0
District of Columbia	1	1	100.0	0	0.0	0	0.0	0	0.0
Florida	67	67	100.0	0	0.0	0	0.0	0	0.0
Georgia	186	186	100.0	0	0.0	0	0.0	0	0.0
Hawaii	1	1	100.0	0	0.0	0	0.0	0	0.0
Idaho	115	115	100.0	0	0.0	0	0.0	0	0.0
Illinois	1,042	964	92.5	41	3.9	5	0.5	32	3.1
Indiana	331	303	91.5	24	7.3	3	0.9	1	0.3
Iowa	465	431	92.7	15	3.2	17	3.7	2	0.4
Kansas	304	304	100.0	0	0.0	0	0.0	0	0.0
Kentucky	256	177	69.1	0	0.0	77	30.1	2	0.8
Louisiana	83	66	79.5	0	0.0	6	7.2	11	13.3
Maine	326	282	86.5	43	13.2	1	0.3	0	0.0
Maryland	24	24	100.0	0	0.0	0	0.0	0	0.0
Massachusetts	438	352	80.4	86	19.6	0	0.0	0	0.0
Michigan	622	561	90.2	57	9.2	4	0.6	0	0.0
Minnesota	512	436	85.2	76	14.8	0	0.0	0	0.0
Mississippi	167	152	91.0	15	9.0	0	0.0	0	0.0
Missouri	544	543	99.8	1	0.2	0	0.0	0	0.0
Montana	631	548	86.8	79	12.5	3	0.5	1	0.2
Nebraska	957	838	87.6	112	11.7	7	0.7	0	0.0
Nevada	17	17	100.0	0	0.0	0	0.0	0	0.0
New Hampshire	233	170	73.0	63	27.0	0	0.0	0	0.0
New Jersey	616	603	97.9	13	2.1	0	0.0	0	0.0
New Mexico	96	88	91.7	0	0.0	8	8.3	0	0.0
New York	762	721	94.6	41	5.4	0	0.0	0	0.0
North Carolina	136	134	98.5	0	0.0	2	1.5	0	0.0
North Dakota	328	280	85.4	38	11.6	5	1.5	5	1.5
Ohio	794	613	77.2	179	22.5	2	0.3	0	0.0
Oklahoma	648	604	93.2	20	3.1	0	0.0	24	3.7
Oregon	341	303	88.9	29	8.5	8	2.3	1	0.3
Pennsylvania	602	501	83.2	98	16.3	3	0.5	0	0.0
Rhode Island	38	37	97.4	0	0.0	1	2.6	0	0.0
South Carolina	95	91	95.8	0	0.0	3	3.2	1	1.1
South Dakota	230	185	80.4	17	7.4	0	0.0	28	12.2
Tennessee	141	141	100.0	0	0.0	0	0.0	0	0.0
Texas	1,087	1,062	97.7	20	1.8	4	0.4	1	0.1
Utah	47	40	85.1	5	10.6	2	4.3	0	0.0
Vermont	336	276	82.1	60	17.9	0	0.0	0	0.0
Virginia	157	136	86.6	19	12.1	2	1.3	0	0.0
Washington	296	296	100.0	0	0.0	0	0.0	0	0.0
West Virginia	55	55	100.0	0	0.0	0	0.0	0	0.0
Wisconsin	448	429	95.8	19	4.2	0	0.0	0	0.0
Wyoming	58	49	84.5	5	8.6	4	6.9	0	0.0
Outlying areas									
American Samoa	1	0	0.0	0	0.0	1	100.0	0	0.0
Guam	1	0	0.0	0	0.0	1	100.0	0	0.0
Northern Marianas	1	1	100.0	0	0.0	0	0.0	0	0.0
Puerto Rico	1	1	100.0	0	0.0	0	0.0	0	0.0
Virgin Islands	1	0	0.0	0	0.0	1	100.0	0	0.0

SOURCE: U.S. Department of Education, National Center for Education Statistics, Common Core of Data survey. (This table was prepared December 1990.)

Table 88.—Selected statistics for public school districts enrolling more than 20,000 pupils, by State: 1989–90

Name of district, by State	State	Enrollment, fall 1989	Classroom teachers,[1] 1989	Pupils per teacher,[1] 1989	Percent minority pupils, 1989	Number of schools, 1989	Number of 1988–89 graduates	Revenue and expenditures[2] 1987–88 (in thousands of dollars)									Current expenditure per pupil 1987–88[3]
								Revenue receipts				Total expenditures	Current expenditures				
								Total	Federal	State	Local		Total	Instruction	Capital outlay	Interest on school debt	
1	2	3	4	5	6	7	8	9	10	11	12	13	14	15	16	17	18
Districts with more than 20,000 students	—	12,854,227	—	—	—	18,769	—	$56,864,993	$3,915,220	$28,154,337	$24,795,436	$55,507,558	$51,144,302	$30,041,604	$3,549,586	$813,670	$4,027
Birmingham City	Ala.	42,440	2,221	19.1	87.9	85	2,238	136,695	17,925	80,935	37,835	112,832	108,988	59,370	3,844	0	2,483
Huntsville City	Ala.	24,916	1,501	16.6	38.1	41	1,692	103,246	11,816	48,986	42,444	89,114	72,816	41,277	15,442	856	2,840
Jefferson County	Ala.	40,627	2,119	19.2	14.7	61	2,667	141,845	10,953	94,351	36,541	114,042	109,852	67,091	2,948	1,242	2,365
Mobile County	Ala.	67,620	3,337	20.3	47.0	86	3,675	178,709	21,258	119,532	37,919	152,071	144,027	84,100	5,525	2,519	2,099
Montgomery County	Ala.	36,004	1,924	18.7	60.5	55	1,767	99,932	10,622	64,240	25,070	87,511	80,823	46,612	6,688	0	3,072
Anchorage	Alaska	40,924	2,026	20.2	25.4	82	2,195	274,198	10,222	187,669	76,307	260,334	213,173	128,110	33,578	13,583	5,215
Mesa Unified	Ariz.	61,636	2,755	22.4	16.5	63	3,234	206,554	6,301	112,307	87,946	216,485	174,903	107,553	27,881	13,701	2,666
Paradise Valley Unified	Ariz.	25,969	1,234	21.0	6.4	30	1,628	101,214	1,963	44,947	54,304	104,229	80,771	50,092	17,144	6,314	2,960
Tucson Unified	Ariz.	56,115	2,497	22.5	48.8	104	3,242	217,648	10,953	105,645	101,050	248,533	219,104	129,301	26,823	2,606	3,579
Washington	Ariz.	21,871	1,127	19.4	12.6	32	—	78,488	2,844	40,364	35,280	73,893	69,259	46,402	3,547	1,087	3,151
Little Rock	Ark.	26,057	1,614	16.1	64.4	49	1,764	86,781	6,673	23,272	56,836	99,067	77,881	49,091	18,603	2,573	2,901
Pulaski County Special	Ark.	21,607	1,202	18.0	26.6	35	1,390	72,266	4,818	38,626	28,822	78,939	66,293	40,422	10,088	2,558	2,975
ABC Unified	Calif.	20,943	865	24.2	68.2	29	1,668	90,291	3,871	70,571	15,849	81,402	79,997	47,494	1,158	247	3,764
Anaheim Union High	Calif.	21,394	844	25.3	48.1	19	2,741	95,214	2,844	64,076	28,294	90,641	87,784	52,348	2,414	443	4,186
Bakersfield City Elementary	Calif.	23,585	1,003	23.5	62.9	32	—	76,752	6,061	58,331	12,360	76,302	74,899	45,159	1,403	0	3,613
Capistrano Unified	Calif.	24,846	1,038	23.9	16.9	27	1,443	92,952	1,312	38,153	53,487	78,973	73,058	44,341	5,004	911	3,379
Chino Unified	Calif.	22,127	907	24.4	38.8	25	931	89,265	1,155	56,121	31,989	71,237	64,820	39,286	5,345	1,072	3,425
Clovis Unified	Calif.	21,299	858	24.8	29.6	23	1,110	87,187	2,405	49,995	34,787	74,760	66,032	33,463	6,421	2,307	3,596
Compton Unified	Calif.	26,889	1,065	25.2	99.7	36	839	122,333	13,365	92,672	16,296	117,176	112,377	63,246	4,674	125	4,282
Corona-Norco Unified	Calif.	21,660	863	25.1	39.6	28	977	69,016	2,238	47,038	19,740	65,016	63,858	39,274	1,035	123	3,595
East Side Union High	Calif.	21,566	921	23.4	73.0	12	3,932	99,653	5,199	65,665	28,789	90,015	87,265	50,761	1,951	799	3,945
Elk Grove Unified	Calif.	24,390	981	24.9	42.6	31	1,293	82,931	2,586	62,590	17,755	70,718	66,180	39,929	4,110	428	3,413
Fontana Unified	Calif.	24,521	1,004	24.4	54.4	29	883	74,892	2,650	58,300	13,942	73,510	69,295	41,491	4,209	6	3,582
Fremont Unified	Calif.	26,913	1,180	22.8	35.0	40	1,710	101,365	3,074	72,945	25,346	96,362	95,054	58,188	1,206	102	3,679
Fresno Unified	Calif.	67,492	2,919	23.1	64.6	85	2,608	245,165	22,076	184,741	38,348	235,433	230,409	143,135	4,881	143	3,750
Garden Grove Unified	Calif.	36,725	1,473	24.9	60.6	58	2,307	149,690	7,710	93,381	48,599	136,221	132,619	82,263	3,446	156	3,713
Glendale Unified	Calif.	24,280	939	25.9	41.8	28	1,505	79,604	3,904	56,455	19,245	74,381	72,814	44,988	1,567	0	3,426
Hacienda La Puente Unified	Calif.	22,779	895	25.5	79.1	36	1,353	109,341	5,569	81,472	22,300	105,108	102,365	61,218	2,722	21	4,400
Lodi Unified	Calif.	23,230	950	24.5	40.4	31	1,239	84,919	10,535	58,708	15,676	79,042	72,987	45,055	5,511	544	3,512
Long Beach Unified	Calif.	68,292	2,750	24.8	80.6	80	3,221	273,651	22,330	197,325	53,996	275,394	262,113	148,780	13,281	0	4,066
Los Angeles Unified	Calif.	609,746	25,778	23.7	85.4	630	23,801	3,064,505	223,843	2,186,082	654,580	2,861,028	2,766,908	1,651,718	91,822	2,298	4,849
Montebello Unified	Calif.	32,362	1,214	26.7	93.3	28	1,474	134,115	9,849	107,796	16,470	135,558	123,071	72,297	12,249	238	3,814
Moreno Valley Unified	Calif.	26,630	1,070	24.9	41.4	29	969	96,139	2,695	82,240	11,204	74,748	67,398	39,461	7,294	56	3,329
Mt. Diablo Unified	Calif.	32,534	1,383	23.5	21.9	46	2,194	116,573	3,868	73,514	39,191	116,582	113,801	68,979	2,685	96	3,627
Oakland Unified	Calif.	50,741	2,079	24.4	91.2	90	2,030	226,198	22,817	173,657	29,724	226,531	222,206	130,144	2,945	1,380	4,545
Ontario-Montclair Elementary	Calif.	20,356	821	24.8	65.5	32	—	64,865	2,703	50,771	11,391	62,483	60,699	39,972	1,781	3	3,353
Orange Unified	Calif.	24,618	1,018	24.2	37.4	38	1,858	98,472	3,068	44,992	50,412	93,268	80,370	55,448	1,531	491	3,849
Pasadena Unified	Calif.	21,674	911	23.8	80.6	31	1,059	95,085	6,223	63,977	24,885	90,510	89,486	53,753	992	32	4,161
Placentia Unified	Calif.	21,216	865	24.5	30.7	29	1,318	76,050	1,713	39,231	35,106	65,880	61,898	35,435	2,611	1,371	3,549
Pomona Unified	Calif.	25,990	1,006	25.8	82.7	32	757	100,591	7,771	80,275	12,545	99,719	97,315	55,655	2,393	11	4,050
Poway Unified	Calif.	23,402	939	24.9	19.0	21	1,366	75,038	1,483	41,859	31,696	74,055	69,595	42,144	4,458	2	3,449
Richmond Unified	Calif.	31,102	1,425	21.8	67.7	52	1,565	123,759	7,486	75,886	40,387	115,296	113,803	66,122	1,470	23	4,107
Riverside Unified	Calif.	30,258	1,227	24.7	43.4	37	1,467	101,582	4,956	69,800	26,826	94,973	93,025	56,680	1,663	285	3,457
Sacramento City Unified	Calif.	48,061	2,057	23.4	63.7	72	1,993	190,443	17,245	134,777	38,421	177,310	174,005	105,683	2,957	348	3,854
Saddleback Valley Unified	Calif.	34,156	990	24.4	18.8	29	1,731	94,395	995	37,305	56,095	82,645	80,370	50,945	1,432	843	3,599
San Bernardino City Unified	Calif.	39,333	1,495	26.1	61.4	53	1,226	143,267	9,614	113,298	20,355	134,991	131,483	78,557	3,472	36	3,853
San Diego City Unified	Calif.	119,314	4,851	24.6	60.6	154	6,229	500,989	35,438	262,957	202,594	497,766	489,513	271,628	7,999	254	4,282
San Francisco Unified	Calif.	61,935	2,946	21.0	85.8	110	3,602	268,059	25,608	195,601	46,850	268,031	262,735	155,694	4,500	796	4,148
San Jose City Unified	Calif.	29,005	1,427	20.3	56.9	41	1,854	139,112	9,870	79,465	49,777	133,182	129,702	77,000	2,729	751	4,516
San Juan Unified	Calif.	46,640	2,063	22.6	16.3	86	2,977	179,191	7,312	131,101	40,778	176,147	173,237	104,002	2,729	181	3,780
Santa Ana Unified	Calif.	42,785	1,718	24.9	91.9	44	1,386	169,309	8,709	111,785	48,815	146,217	132,079	82,914	13,550	588	3,604
Stockton City Unified	Calif.	31,849	1,337	23.8	77.6	45	1,059	141,693	13,355	96,907	31,431	133,302	130,609	70,420	2,537	156	4,417
Sweetwater Union High	Calif.	27,265	1,082	25.2	75.0	20	3,409	115,581	5,330	82,815	27,436	119,495	111,434	63,829	7,986	75	4,400
Irvine Unified	Calif.	20,303	841	24.1	26.5	29	1,567	94,891	2,728	42,000	50,163	72,461	68,174	43,801	2,916	1,371	3,511
Adams-Arapahoe	Colo.	25,345	1,386	18.3	30.3	42	1,467	118,687	4,000	54,223	60,464	119,754	102,951	56,030	7,448	9,355	3,967
Boulder Valley	Colo.	21,013	1,170	18.0	14.1	42	1,475	98,936	2,037	24,911	71,988	94,174	84,285	50,004	7,397	2,492	4,045

Table 88.—Selected statistics for public school districts enrolling more than 20,000 pupils, by State: 1989–90—Continued

Name of district, by State	State	Enrollment, fall 1989	Classroom teachers, 1989	Pupils per teacher, 1989	Percent minority pupils, 1989	Number of schools, 1989	Number of 1988-89 graduates	Revenue and expenditures [2] 1987-88 (in thousands of dollars)									Current expenditure per pupil 1987-88 [3]
								Revenue receipts				Total expenditures	Current expenditures				
								Total	Federal	State	Local		Total	Instruction	Capital outlay	Interest on school debt	
1	2	3	4	5	6	7	8	9	10	11	12	13	14	15	16	17	18
Cherry Creek	Colo.	28,027	1,503	18.6	11.9	36	1,967	136,538	981	30,364	105,193	142,577	113,992	67,419	20,664	7,921	4,263
Colorado Springs	Colo.	29,931	1,654	18.1	21.8	56	1,886	116,821	5,269	54,281	57,271	122,362	114,590	68,249	7,772	0	3,732
Denver County	Colo.	58,299	3,641	16.0	65.4	113	2,854	313,967	24,103	59,690	230,174	270,722	256,050	164,557	14,035	637	4,308
Jefferson County	Colo.	75,164	3,565	21.1	10.9	121	4,960	356,705	7,071	140,825	208,809	383,931	329,842	204,927	49,754	4,335	4,378
Northglenn-Thornton	Colo.	20,692	1,120	18.5	19.5	35	1,317	94,280	2,564	45,161	46,555	107,834	72,798	43,670	27,799	7,237	3,534
Hartford	Conn.	24,682	1,671	14.8	91.7	31	817	154,109	12,417	89,850	51,842	147,263	142,049	91,120	4,230	984	5,669
D.C. Public Schools	D.C.	81,301	4,908	16.6	96.3	184	3,565	483,940	51,403	0	432,537	561,167	516,485	341,535	44,682	0	5,872
Alachua County	Fla.	25,495	1,366	18.7	37.5	39	1,281	103,983	8,024	65,862	30,097	104,132	92,112	46,219	9,942	2,078	3,850
Bay County	Fla.	21,002	1,267	16.6	19.2	34	1,204	88,925	7,603	53,195	28,127	89,658	81,691	45,115	7,874	93	3,792
Brevard Count	Fla.	53,615	3,037	17.5	17.5	73	3,268	205,033	10,148	111,243	83,642	201,736	185,637	101,451	15,436	663	3,749
Broward County	Fla.	148,803	8,022	18.5	41.1	176	7,584	709,193	33,482	325,830	349,881	666,621	598,768	295,865	65,407	2,446	4,359
Clay County	Fla.	20,861	1,164	17.9	9.8	24	1,214	76,034	3,627	53,944	18,463	72,514	65,393	35,917	6,783	338	3,297
Dade County	Fla.	279,420	15,388	18.2	80.2	301	13,086	1,265,522	89,254	719,335	456,933	1,269,476	1,169,124	641,656	96,806	3,546	4,608
Duval County	Fla.	106,593	5,695	18.7	40.5	147	5,035	436,897	28,580	268,523	139,794	414,683	392,124	214,256	18,564	3,995	3,733
Escambia County	Fla.	42,071	2,584	16.3	34.0	71	2,658	170,730	14,965	114,268	41,497	175,565	159,875	85,427	15,164	526	3,801
Hillsborough County	Fla.	119,810	7,161	16.7	34.5	173	6,201	535,699	43,722	297,376	194,601	521,448	461,139	246,649	49,294	11,015	3,902
Lake County	Fla.	20,096	1,218	16.5	22.1	41	1,031	80,988	5,493	50,277	25,218	77,646	74,390	38,083	2,801	455	3,899
Lee County	Fla.	40,569	2,271	17.9	22.3	62	2,069	177,987	10,016	70,897	97,074	184,798	152,964	75,409	30,706	1,128	4,057
Leon County	Fla.	26,211	1,678	15.6	37.7	44	1,414	114,860	7,723	74,080	33,057	111,943	102,678	49,128	8,644	621	4,154
Manatee County	Fla.	25,471	1,495	17.0	24.4	42	1,258	111,522	6,514	49,950	55,099	111,968	95,481	48,251	15,509	978	4,018
Marion County	Fla.	27,702	1,666	16.6	25.0	37	1,423	111,920	8,309	67,255	36,356	116,446	99,921	53,888	15,249	1,276	3,780
Okaloosa County	Fla.	25,410	1,481	17.2	17.5	35	1,716	98,271	7,794	61,241	29,236	92,545	88,650	46,392	3,427	468	3,595
Orange County	Fla.	96,244	5,984	16.1	37.6	138	4,452	413,688	22,338	206,914	184,436	413,868	363,899	185,944	49,023	946	4,094
Palm Beach County	Fla.	98,705	6,184	16.0	38.2	141	4,994	517,104	25,833	149,750	341,521	525,646	419,421	223,561	97,936	8,289	4,663
Pasco County	Fla.	32,164	1,901	16.9	8.4	42	1,540	139,439	8,136	76,181	55,122	134,789	116,711	61,171	16,611	1,467	3,851
Pinellas County	Fla.	91,393	5,548	16.5	20.8	130	5,436	446,018	19,478	196,065	204,475	409,041	368,323	194,951	39,369	1,349	4,145
Polk County	Fla.	63,932	3,769	17.0	27.2	103	3,184	240,840	18,377	153,654	74,809	236,121	224,831	122,849	10,629	661	3,662
Sarasota County	Fla.	27,541	1,683	16.4	14.4	35	1,614	141,526	6,952	43,667	90,907	143,239	125,993	61,973	16,246	1,000	4,823
Seminole County	Fla.	46,499	2,518	18.5	21.6	46	2,773	174,635	8,395	102,551	63,689	158,833	148,012	81,656	2,985	7,836	3,402
Saint Lucie County	Fla.	20,647	1,113	18.6	36.0	27	757	78,181	6,105	35,611	36,465	83,293	69,226	37,838	11,791	2,276	3,791
Volusia County	Fla.	45,775	2,665	17.2	20.9	65	2,166	192,869	9,631	94,486	88,752	210,681	159,932	85,524	36,656	14,093	3,823
Atlanta City	Ga.	61,373	4,412	13.9	—	116	3,428	424,171	45,806	180,518	197,847	367,911	326,215	178,931	41,696	0	4,987
Bibb County	Ga.	24,007	1,405	17.1	—	40	1,075	107,886	11,473	67,575	28,838	92,148	84,691	53,394	7,457	0	3,479
Chatham County	Ga.	33,407	1,980	16.9	—	45	1,294	161,049	13,691	89,736	57,622	140,192	120,138	72,202	20,054	0	3,683
Clayton County	Ga.	33,641	2,034	16.5	—	42	1,990	139,670	6,657	80,905	52,108	119,800	109,804	68,600	6,689	3,307	3,240
Cobb County	Ga.	66,668	3,992	16.7	—	78	4,322	279,462	7,083	149,825	122,554	243,814	205,785	132,390	29,208	8,821	3,207
DeKalb County	Ga.	72,865	4,610	15.8	—	102	5,289	380,184	17,006	169,598	193,580	329,921	304,458	203,930	22,624	2,839	4,122
Fulton County	Ga.	40,280	2,482	16.2	—	63	2,392	243,611	8,359	89,701	145,551	211,464	172,806	95,798	28,166	10,492	4,304
Gwinnett County	Ga.	62,196	3,421	18.2	—	58	3,464	237,489	3,799	131,311	102,379	226,348	183,599	115,638	36,663	6,086	3,353
Muscogee County	Ga.	29,569	1,757	16.8	—	53	1,642	182,113	13,076	81,125	87,912	165,433	149,332	65,257	14,886	1,215	4,885
Richmond County	Ga.	32,392	2,009	16.1	—	54	1,626	131,431	9,295	79,618	42,518	121,541	107,265	65,676	12,045	2,231	3,214
Hawaii Department of Education	Hawaii	169,493	8,830	19.2	77.0	234	10,404	709,591	79,334	604,582	25,675	630,273	551,318	340,657	78,955	0	3,324
Boise City ISD	Idaho	22,498	1,134	19.8	—	40	1,511	66,521	3,443	34,727	28,351	61,311	58,745	36,152	1,632	934	2,802
City of Chicago Schools	Ill.	408,442	22,177	18.4	88.0	608	17,890	1,812,031	218,579	903,703	689,749	1,712,591	1,640,782	913,645	63,420	8,389	3,911
Rockford	Ill.	26,757	1,562	17.1	29.5	47	1,589	102,277	6,050	46,219	50,008	106,419	99,817	58,314	3,803	2,799	3,609
School District 46	Ill.	26,767	1,317	20.3	28.1	49	1,565	90,751	4,182	38,223	48,346	93,834	89,707	57,810	2,506	1,621	3,432
Evansville-Vanderburgh Schools	Ind.	22,832	1,365	16.7	14.6	38	1,454	84,111	1,796	41,568	40,747	88,307	81,330	44,384	6,852	125	3,724
Fort Wayne Community Schools	Ind.	31,843	1,628	19.6	26.7	53	2,032	106,818	1,966	59,902	44,950	119,536	112,477	60,727	5,134	1,925	3,621
Gary Community Schools	Ind.	26,506	1,389	19.1	98.4	44	1,375	98,862	2,946	60,954	34,962	107,104	103,072	50,733	2,687	1,345	3,932
Indianapolis Public Schools	Ind.	48,805	2,985	16.4	51.3	89	1,699	227,002	8,165	133,952	84,885	222,843	205,616	101,486	16,831	396	3,756
South Bend Community Schools	Ind.	21,539	1,243	17.3	34.7	36	1,257	83,024	1,391	45,267	36,366	89,829	82,711	44,500	6,706	412	3,936
Des Moines Independent Community	Iowa	30,267	1,720	17.6	18.2	62	1,729	120,631	7,611	58,433	54,587	124,373	120,736	73,758	3,351	286	4,010
Kansas City	Kansas	22,543	1,207	18.7	58.7	50	1,212	86,555	4,153	52,040	30,362	83,840	81,264	53,212	2,258	318	3,497
Shawnee Mission Public Schools	Kansas	30,235	1,869	16.2	7.4	53	2,334	120,096	1,792	30,655	87,649	122,671	115,009	83,085	7,662	0	3,790
Wichita	Kansas	47,251	2,456	19.2	30.8	90	2,358	169,769	5,438	54,850	109,481	171,918	163,432	103,164	7,469	1,017	3,577

Table 88.—Selected statistics for public school districts enrolling more than 20,000 pupils, by State: 1989–90—Continued

Name of district, by State	State	Enrollment, fall 1989	Classroom teachers,[1] 1989	Pupils per teacher,[1] 1989	Percent minority pupils, 1989	Number of schools, 1989	Number of 1988–89 graduates	Revenue receipts[2] — Total	Federal	State	Local	Total expenditures	Current expenditures — Total	Instruction	Capital outlay	Interest on school debt	Current expenditure per pupil 1987–88[3]
1	2	3	4	5	6	7	8	9	10	11	12	13	14	15	16	17	18
Fayette County	Ky.	31,191	1,982	15.7	24.4	55	1,740	105,625	6,081	51,744	47,800	113,914	104,722	76,105	6,014	3,178	3,357
Jefferson County	Ky.	91,353	5,223	17.5	31.3	162	5,429	358,444	28,721	169,324	160,399	346,623	322,909	228,765	16,686	7,028	3,465
Caddo Parish School Board	La.	52,309	3,017	17.3	57.2	76	2,409	170,165	12,837	87,739	69,589	159,330	134,763	73,046	20,968	3,599	2,588
Calcasieu Parish School Board	La.	32,726	1,905	17.2	30.7	58	1,881	97,195	7,449	54,896	34,850	90,138	77,980	44,118	8,525	3,633	2,373
East Baton Rouge Parish School Board	La.	60,279	3,660	16.5	56.8	103	3,320	212,605	17,255	107,115	88,235	181,343	176,519	91,070	4,402	422	3,033
Jefferson Parish School Board	La.	57,663	3,342	17.3	45.3	84	2,340	216,419	17,565	97,339	101,515	187,866	167,944	93,783	9,558	10,364	2,887
Lafayette Parish School Board	La.	28,392	1,541	18.4	33.8	40	1,444	86,183	7,179	46,301	32,703	70,766	66,059	38,191	488	4,219	2,415
Orleans Parish School Board	La.	84,428	4,670	18.1	92.6	127	3,546	275,152	42,155	133,220	99,777	260,338	242,599	129,912	13,533	4,206	2,904
Rapides Parish School Board	La.	24,404	1,511	16.2	40.7	50	1,167	82,119	8,738	45,302	28,079	72,770	67,449	36,526	4,536	785	2,778
St. Tammany Parish School Board	La.	28,055	1,525	18.4	16.2	45	1,319	87,610	4,929	43,637	39,044	79,242	69,635	39,029	5,397	4,210	2,608
Terrebonne Parish School Board	La.	21,331	1,188	18.0	31.9	43	817	57,129	5,946	32,537	18,646	55,536	44,352	23,963	9,341	1,843	2,057
Anne Arundel County	Md.	64,104	3,564	18.0	17.9	114	4,609	318,411	11,879	123,022	183,510	274,700	250,038	144,998	24,024	638	3,773
Baltimore City	Md.	107,782	5,627	19.2	82.1	177	4,521	479,638	53,856	259,745	166,037	408,543	392,616	232,518	12,544	3,383	3,565
Baltimore County	Md.	84,133	5,032	16.7	21.4	146	5,735	448,718	12,415	140,356	295,947	380,262	364,855	207,537	13,265	2,142	4,397
Carroll County	Md.	21,244	1,010	21.0	3.0	32	1,599	87,123	2,915	42,137	42,071	76,552	69,789	42,835	6,666	97	3,292
Frederick County Board of Education	Md.	26,173	1,402	18.7	8.1	43	1,743	116,431	4,413	51,397	60,621	101,813	90,951	52,465	10,581	281	3,603
Harford County	Md.	30,217	1,704	17.7	14.4	42	1,998	122,088	6,572	56,780	58,736	105,543	101,612	62,007	3,509	422	3,509
Howard County	Md.	28,874	1,665	17.3	20.0	46	2,098	164,121	3,204	44,312	116,605	143,801	124,027	70,453	17,677	2,097	4,653
Montgomery County	Md.	100,261	5,927	16.9	36.6	166	7,190	727,892	14,476	144,176	569,240	630,607	517,408	316,495	106,314	6,885	5,374
Prince Georges County	Md.	106,974	5,853	18.3	70.9	172	7,500	525,229	27,232	221,888	276,109	472,818	449,955	241,113	21,323	1,540	4,309
Boston	Mass.	59,597	—	—	76.9	117	—	388,625	18,966	110,054	259,605	391,639	377,616	218,428	3,755	10,268	7,078
Springfield	Mass.	23,614	—	—	61.1	42	—	106,919	11,296	88,861	6,762	91,669	88,779	52,334	403	2,487	3,565
Worcester	Mass.	21,081	—	—	33.3	49	—	101,271	9,322	53,864	38,085	98,820	96,158	59,547	2,142	520	4,728
Detroit City	Mich.	175,436	9,631	18.2	91.6	259	7,510	785,684	76,516	448,073	261,095	804,313	774,139	431,415	20,184	9,990	4,016
Flint City	Mich.	28,599	1,873	15.3	70.1	42	1,444	140,071	10,623	59,509	69,939	140,662	139,751	62,592	911	0	4,354
Grand Rapids City	Mich.	26,039	2,268	11.5	47.1	72	1,065	163,283	15,190	57,464	95,629	131,724	125,460	58,150	4,441	1,823	3,937
Lansing City	Mich.	21,481	1,428	15.0	44.6	41	1,106	101,016	5,372	32,841	62,803	102,185	99,189	51,059	2,379	617	4,093
Utica Community Schools	Mich.	23,330	1,404	16.6	3.3	37	1,974	98,002	997	20,189	76,816	110,066	94,244	53,151	12,388	3,434	3,839
Anoka	Minn.	33,709	1,668	20.2	4.4	39	2,253	141,762	3,785	90,587	47,390	156,968	141,438	88,578	13,198	2,332	4,396
Minneapolis Special	Minn.	40,831	1,910	21.4	49.8	54	2,108	225,253	12,828	84,884	127,541	218,117	199,652	123,244	14,328	4,137	5,248
Saint Paul	Minn.	34,758	1,856	18.7	41.1	51	1,856	190,641	11,338	89,152	90,151	166,677	159,526	95,317	4,993	2,158	5,128
Jackson Public	Miss.	33,330	1,651	20.2	79.6	57	1,762	110,865	13,795	46,195	50,875	109,220	98,233	55,556	9,141	1,846	2,971
Kansas City	Mo.	34,640	2,500	13.9	58.6	78	1,415	241,970	15,787	82,291	143,892	230,532	193,491	94,850	37,041	0	5,505
Parkway	Mo.	22,379	1,235	18.1	6.4	25	1,890	101,250	1,022	23,458	76,770	94,232	90,975	55,865	1,702	1,555	4,012
Springfield	Mo.	23,248	1,334	17.4	—	56	1,494	83,072	4,289	27,976	50,807	77,537	71,677	42,260	5,212	648	3,087
St Louis City	Mo.	44,056	3,398	13.0	—	127	1,545	284,664	29,365	132,171	123,128	256,322	248,904	126,631	7,312	106	5,396
Lincoln	Neb.	27,356	1,700	16.1	7.7	46	1,619	96,540	5,225	18,492	72,823	105,343	100,020	54,819	5,323	0	3,917
Omaha	Neb.	41,251	2,432	17.0	33.7	80	2,201	176,596	12,883	34,787	128,926	173,470	163,618	78,816	9,852	0	4,058
Clark County	Nev.	111,460	5,252	15.2	29.3	137	5,678	383,625	13,472	246,944	123,209	375,819	331,503	198,370	41,751	2,565	3,314
Washoe County	Nev.	36,662	1,759	20.8	18.5	68	1,836	133,255	4,149	78,970	50,136	127,634	113,565	69,566	8,101	5,968	3,288
Jersey City	N.J.	27,788	1,826	15.2	87.4	37	992	190,605	15,695	111,172	63,738	199,928	167,474	107,010	28,665	3,789	5,606
Newark City	N.J.	48,573	3,413	14.2	90.2	82	1,908	354,248	34,811	248,105	71,332	333,888	326,785	189,936	5,259	1,844	6,173
Paterson City	N.J.	21,671	1,641	13.2	90.2	33	679	132,516	12,437	83,832	36,247	121,110	115,224	73,004	2,541	3,345	4,963
Albuquerque	N.M.	86,653	4,721	18.4	50.5	119	4,607	292,153	21,013	234,935	36,205	292,032	270,041	153,983	21,670	321	3,421
Buffalo City	N.Y.	46,694	3,082	15.2	58.6	75	2,416	294,911	34,575	166,456	93,880	280,421	271,103	168,502	6,631	2,687	6,117
New York City	N.Y.	930,440	54,969	16.9	73.7	998	36,841	5,828,357	434,349	2,421,391	2,972,617	5,827,616	5,589,465	3,412,527	164,589	73,562	6,030
Rochester City	N.Y.	31,941	2,253	14.2	72.0	53	1,141	235,679	20,604	116,012	99,063	236,650	226,227	140,661	8,352	2,071	7,096
Syracuse City	N.Y.	21,949	1,922	11.4	42.2	34	888	146,365	11,341	85,250	49,774	138,534	126,628	79,513	9,073	2,833	6,065
Cumberland County	N.C.	44,327	2,486	17.8	46.6	69	2,848	141,598	16,437	94,644	30,517	142,024	137,140	87,255	4,030	854	3,102
Buncombe County	N.C.	21,821	1,259	17.3	6.4	39	1,590	102,255	4,407	55,616	42,232	85,140	77,389	48,547	5,784	1,967	3,527
Forsyth County	N.C.	37,842	2,417	15.7	37.6	55	2,697	146,316	8,234	88,305	49,777	145,846	142,945	89,655	1,932	969	3,704
Gaston County	N.C.	30,064	1,880	16.0	18.9	54	1,889	99,350	5,501	69,187	24,662	97,211	92,081	62,562	4,053	1,077	2,950

Table 88.—Selected statistics for public school districts enrolling more than 20,000 pupils, by State: 1989–90—Continued

Name of district, by State	State	Enrollment, fall 1989	Classroom teachers, 1989	Pupils per teacher, 1989	Percent minority pupils, 1989	Number of schools, 1989	Number of 1988-89 graduates	Revenue and expenditures [2] 1987-88 (in thousands of dollars)									Current expenditure per pupil 1987-88 [3]
								Revenue receipts				Total expenditures	Current expenditures				
								Total	Federal	State	Local		Total	Instruction	Capital outlay	Interest on school debt	
1	2	3	4	5	6	7	8	9	10	11	12	13	14	15	16	17	18
Greensboro City	N.C.	20,342	1,274	16.0	54.5	38	1,398	91,840	4,580	50,755	36,505	85,824	83,469	52,496	2,355	0	3,993
Guilford County	N.C.	23,981	1,427	16.8	19.4	40	1,758	107,964	3,571	55,769	48,624	91,859	87,446	53,469	2,901	1,512	3,646
Mecklenburg County	N.C.	75,903	4,327	17.5	42.7	109	4,801	316,498	15,002	175,205	126,291	298,881	281,504	170,698	14,909	2,468	3,797
Robeson County	N.C.	23,658	1,375	17.2	75.2	44	1,292	54,608	7,301	32,770	14,537	46,852	44,660	27,926	1,428	764	3,076
Wake County	N.C.	62,474	3,041	20.5	30.3	83	3,980	259,067	10,222	134,073	114,772	248,529	213,665	130,952	29,949	4,915	3,580
Akron City	Ohio	33,230	1,838	18.1	40.7	58	2,158	142,710	12,594	65,707	64,409	157,843	151,690	81,653	5,798	355	4,389
Cincinnati City	Ohio	50,842	3,020	16.8	63.1	85	2,636	232,969	18,868	101,458	112,643	261,890	248,758	131,253	3,520	9,612	4,777
Cleveland City	Ohio	69,812	3,922	17.8	75.8	128	3,010	416,313	25,338	213,716	177,259	399,182	385,397	176,265	7,680	6,105	5,306
Columbus City	Ohio	64,051	3,785	16.9	49.7	137	3,070	319,104	25,986	127,532	165,586	331,585	323,590	162,057	5,277	2,718	4,936
Dayton City	Ohio	27,662	1,645	16.8	63.0	48	1,226	148,806	14,632	68,512	65,662	162,829	158,055	73,736	4,774	0	5,190
Toledo City	Ohio	40,944	2,259	18.1	43.1	61	2,309	186,729	14,161	90,482	82,086	198,029	187,221	96,830	9,459	1,349	4,297
Oklahoma City	Okla.	38,212	1,896	20.2	54.8	83	800	112,300	10,909	52,430	48,961	111,446	102,631	74,268	7,400	1,415	2,622
Tulsa City	Okla.	40,919	2,025	20.2	37.0	78	2,300	133,330	9,911	56,781	66,638	132,597	122,954	89,096	9,548	95	2,877
Beaverton	Oreg.	23,490	1,150	20.4	11.4	37	1,342	99,314	2,346	18,657	78,311	102,527	95,280	52,671	6,125	1,122	4,347
Portland	Oreg.	53,116	2,676	19.8	27.6	97	2,646	289,096	18,127	49,754	221,215	306,310	294,313	129,676	3,464	8,533	5,622
Salem/Keizer	Oreg.	26,930	1,160	23.2	9.6	48	1,468	110,645	5,395	34,765	70,485	114,214	107,654	55,322	3,803	2,757	4,185
Philadelphia City	Pa.	189,451	10,951	17.3	76.8	256	8,062	1,035,853	109,887	512,316	413,650	999,204	914,800	530,486	60,565	23,839	4,649
Pittsburgh	Pa.	39,559	2,493	15.9	53.3	82	2,590	283,377	20,574	92,041	170,762	291,739	266,398	146,336	19,660	5,681	6,673
Providence	R.I.	20,429	—	—	61.5	36	747	92,735	6,994	47,661	38,080	91,979	90,607	40,145	653	719	4,586
Aiken County	S.C.	23,283	1,219	19.1	35.5	36	1,378	76,984	5,064	44,417	27,503	76,351	66,222	38,918	8,153	1,976	2,991
Berkeley County	S.C.	27,071	1,410	19.2	33.3	36	1,401	81,622	7,204	48,416	26,002	79,082	72,445	43,386	3,828	2,809	2,891
Charleston County	S.C.	42,877	2,550	16.8	56.5	70	2,025	158,306	12,884	67,098	78,324	159,219	136,091	78,534	15,375	7,753	3,351
Greenville County	S.C.	50,849	2,975	17.1	27.7	92	3,066	174,139	10,084	91,276	72,779	171,726	158,714	93,340	8,283	4,729	3,233
Horry County	S.C.	23,701	1,423	16.7	30.5	38	1,440	88,382	6,636	33,721	48,025	127,547	77,131	44,893	44,972	5,444	3,465
Richland	S.C.	26,958	1,737	15.5	74.4	51	1,649	117,438	8,961	46,489	61,988	109,539	100,151	56,058	5,337	4,051	3,760
Chattanooga City	Tenn.	21,478	1,118	19.2	56.4	37	1,105	76,900	7,633	28,919	40,348	80,187	74,903	50,451	3,857	1,427	3,414
Hamilton County	Tenn.	22,348	1,209	18.5	4.4	39	996	59,265	2,945	26,408	29,912	61,843	59,040	41,377	1,465	1,338	2,672
Knox County	Tenn.	49,926	2,515	19.9	14.3	92	3,009	147,347	11,156	58,218	77,973	148,037	136,522	97,926	8,366	3,149	2,507
Memphis City	Tenn.	104,410	5,166	20.2	80.9	159	4,785	365,048	37,878	130,782	196,388	331,240	317,567	213,305	9,906	3,767	2,978
Nashville-Davidson County	Tenn.	68,473	4,197	16.3	40.3	120	2,574	236,357	16,958	80,134	139,265	284,243	241,037	165,765	36,893	6,313	3,580
Shelby County	Tenn.	36,254	1,742	20.8	16.4	37	1,919	85,256	4,461	37,544	43,251	78,203	78,387	55,756	9,268	548	2,240
Aldine ISD	Texas	38,245	2,178	17.6	63.7	37	1,681	114,892	6,462	54,461	53,969	110,781	102,611	63,271	5,747	2,423	2,440
Alief ISD	Texas	27,949	1,753	15.9	58.1	25	1,339	93,798	697	24,876	68,225	96,618	85,043	49,783	5,066	6,509	3,147
Amarillo ISD	Texas	26,146	1,563	16.7	32.9	46	1,647	88,468	4,797	42,699	40,972	106,453	71,650	39,222	31,716	3,087	2,364
Arlington ISD	Texas	42,651	2,328	18.3	24.4	50	2,536	145,764	3,664	35,232	106,868	146,307	121,912	75,097	17,412	6,983	2,761
Austin ISD	Texas	61,666	4,055	15.2	55.9	100	3,232	279,780	12,239	50,271	217,270	313,143	271,195	137,228	22,765	19,183	4,133
Beaumont ISD	Texas	20,132	1,248	16.1	64.5	39	1,008	76,023	6,803	29,290	39,930	79,468	74,252	42,401	5,053	163	3,616
Brownsville ISD	Texas	34,998	2,223	15.7	96.4	38	1,551	120,799	15,980	86,343	18,476	107,580	92,475	69,003	11,994	3,111	3,024
Clear Creek ISD	Texas	21,368	1,224	17.5	21.4	23	1,359	74,071	1,586	21,483	51,002	77,074	62,419	37,424	11,994	2,661	2,962
Conroe ISD	Texas	22,475	1,361	16.5	17.0	30	1,302	75,391	2,589	29,739	43,063	75,766	69,118	40,603	2,608	4,040	2,923
Corpus Christi ISD	Texas	42,054	2,359	17.8	74.7	61	2,141	137,650	11,985	74,873	50,792	145,093	127,616	77,454	14,073	3,404	3,049
Cypress-Fairbanks ISD	Texas	37,224	2,320	16.0	26.3	34	2,054	142,791	2,214	36,114	104,463	133,358	114,907	66,839	3,425	15,026	3,272
Dallas ISD	Texas	125,897	8,486	14.8	81.9	200	5,411	496,890	42,668	101,924	352,298	531,332	464,771	261,861	48,554	18,007	3,511
Ector County ISD	Texas	25,275	1,555	16.3	47.9	39	1,157	85,406	3,929	35,807	45,670	85,613	79,541	47,311	5,381	691	2,755
El Paso ISD	Texas	61,729	3,575	17.3	78.1	72	3,429	206,126	25,421	119,635	61,070	218,141	192,743	113,848	19,819	5,579	2,873
Fort Bend ISD	Texas	33,165	1,765	18.8	52.5	35	1,694	104,867	2,201	38,672	63,994	108,846	85,259	47,652	14,972	8,615	2,949
Fort Worth ISD	Texas	66,535	3,629	18.3	64.9	114	3,356	227,067	15,446	91,412	120,209	256,372	212,773	115,547	37,016	6,583	2,893
Garland ISD	Texas	36,029	1,882	19.1	28.7	55	2,013	122,320	3,610	45,459	73,251	135,709	100,487	58,845	24,573	10,649	2,701
Houston ISD	Texas	185,566	10,429	17.4	84.8	244	8,271	652,541	69,318	226,222	357,001	639,681	614,188	349,340	19,853	5,640	2,902
Irving ISD	Texas	22,504	1,291	17.4	35.7	31	1,281	72,860	2,891	18,383	51,586	89,853	73,126	41,299	14,753	1,974	3,100
Killeen ISD	Texas	21,013	1,284	16.4	51.4	30	959	63,180	13,200	40,290	9,690	64,732	59,488	35,874	4,702	542	2,730
Klein ISD	Texas	25,304	1,491	17.0	24.8	23	1,775	88,817	1,042	35,953	51,822	82,512	73,834	44,279	2,508	6,170	2,866
Laredo ISD	Texas	22,290	1,270	17.6	97.5	28	1,185	71,250	10,953	52,955	7,342	82,902	72,144	44,515	8,927	1,831	3,054
Lubbock ISD	Texas	30,854	1,980	15.6	51.1	59	1,648	108,173	8,642	53,976	45,555	109,543	106,349	63,455	2,429	765	3,228
McAllen ISD	Texas	20,958	1,219	19.1	87.2	29	1,077	67,470	8,447	41,698	17,325	65,405	61,405	38,954	1,614	2,386	2,868
Mesquite ISD	Texas	24,299	1,260	19.3	18.0	34	1,257	72,381	2,125	35,514	34,742	88,520	65,368	39,052	15,048	8,104	2,681

Table 88.—Selected statistics for public school districts enrolling more than 20,000 pupils, by State: 1989-90—Continued

Name of district, by State	State	Enrollment, fall 1989	Classroom teachers,[1] 1989	Pupils per teacher,[1] 1989	Percent minority pupils, 1989	Number of schools, 1989	Number of 1988-89 graduates	Revenue and expenditures[2] 1987-88 (in thousands of dollars)				Total expenditures	Current expenditures		Capital outlay	Interest on school debt	Current expenditure per pupil[3] 1987-88
								Revenue receipts									
								Total	Federal	State	Local		Total	Instruction			
1	2	3	4	5	6	7	8	9	10	11	12	13	14	15	16	17	18
North East ISD	Texas	40,644	2,276	17.9	37.5	43	2,892	125,268	4,636	39,580	81,052	123,450	120,182	69,727	2,135	1,133	2,917
Northside ISD	Texas	49,539	2,715	18.2	54.7	59	3,184	149,092	8,857	61,102	79,133	155,581	130,218	79,755	14,662	10,701	2,740
Pasadena ISD	Texas	35,251	1,954	18.0	47.2	46	1,630	120,078	7,105	55,937	57,036	121,357	111,529	66,781	8,557	1,271	2,849
Plano ISD	Texas	29,209	1,790	16.3	14.3	36	2,181	132,868	7,352	16,988	108,528	123,216	104,427	61,910	8,979	9,810	3,471
Richardson ISD	Texas	33,324	2,058	16.2	27.5	50	2,360	143,876	982	19,916	122,978	137,314	128,481	72,648	3,573	5,260	3,502
San Antonio ISD	Texas	58,720	3,503	16.8	93.3	101	2,825	219,534	28,524	127,556	63,454	246,979	217,533	132,707	24,945	4,501	3,233
Spring Branch ISD	Texas	25,807	1,704	15.1	49.4	36	2,074	101,992	4,421	21,151	76,420	103,190	98,147	51,954	236	4,807	3,338
Ysleta ISD	Texas	49,675	1,302	38.2	82.8	50	3,000	157,805	15,131	107,558	35,116	157,279	142,893	88,980	7,922	6,464	2,788
Alpine	Utah	38,246	1,463	26.1	3.9	45	1,736	90,181	4,740	62,982	22,459	90,870	83,561	49,802	3,204	4,105	2,276
Davis County	Utah	53,425	2,095	25.5	5.0	70	3,017	132,298	7,963	88,061	36,274	136,870	125,316	75,211	4,769	6,785	2,472
Granite	Utah	77,515	3,140	24.7	8.2	100	3,828	192,201	8,877	113,118	70,206	188,592	172,896	110,516	9,873	5,823	2,328
Jordan	Utah	63,605	2,593	24.5	5.2	69	3,283	156,003	7,606	99,264	49,133	159,089	144,698	87,626	10,333	4,058	2,323
Salt Lake City	Utah	24,569	1,174	20.9	22.7	43	1,051	78,955	7,232	24,353	47,370	78,829	76,793	43,000	1,343	693	3,158
Weber County	Utah	25,275	1,043	24.2	5.0	37	1,585	66,540	4,699	40,158	21,683	67,109	61,925	36,461	2,413	2,771	2,497
Chesapeake City	Va.	28,324	1,575	18.0	—	35	1,706	107,020	5,548	55,440	46,032	102,504	98,212	76,512	2,860	1,432	3,621
Chesterfield County	Va.	42,864	2,597	16.6	—	48	2,857	163,484	3,920	81,168	78,396	171,722	144,391	106,635	19,533	7,798	3,571
Fairfax County	Va.	126,790	7,643	16.6	—	188	10,424	700,813	17,278	186,081	497,454	751,583	663,963	465,892	75,590	12,030	5,197
Hampton City	Va.	20,788	1,259	16.5	—	34	1,307	82,034	5,881	41,068	35,085	80,431	78,544	59,406	1,463	424	3,808
Henrico County	Va.	31,963	1,947	16.4	—	51	2,270	138,566	4,095	53,768	80,703	138,618	123,858	88,936	13,197	1,563	3,976
Newport News City	Va.	28,313	1,548	18.3	—	34	1,554	113,056	8,235	55,151	49,670	114,947	105,799	77,867	7,998	1,150	3,909
Norfolk City	Va.	36,428	2,313	15.7	—	55	1,293	171,343	18,595	73,027	79,721	166,810	158,245	113,151	8,565	0	4,412
Prince William County	Va.	40,991	2,427	16.9	—	55	2,718	178,525	5,474	76,447	96,604	182,680	162,795	114,556	16,452	3,433	4,200
Richmond City	Va.	26,885	1,804	14.9	—	58	1,118	160,784	7,874	48,830	104,080	159,264	150,451	104,996	6,636	2,177	5,541
Virginia Beach City	Va.	68,348	3,790	18.0	—	71	3,649	259,364	17,506	119,436	122,422	238,190	200,919	157,879	29,928	7,343	3,115
Kent	Wash.	20,212	953	21.2	14.6	31	—	77,144	2,381	54,104	20,659	76,689	65,643	38,204	8,263	2,783	3,569
Lake Washington	Wash.	22,431	1,030	21.8	10.4	39	—	94,342	2,716	65,533	26,093	95,890	81,100	47,931	11,392	3,398	3,948
Seattle	Wash.	40,917	2,220	18.4	54.8	106	—	232,458	15,579	140,129	76,750	227,573	198,612	110,593	23,830	5,131	4,531
Spokane	Wash.	27,965	1,386	20.2	11.0	58	—	107,395	6,850	77,376	23,169	110,236	104,729	60,887	4,032	1,475	3,770
Tacoma	Wash.	29,465	1,620	18.2	33.0	66	—	154,407	10,156	101,687	42,564	154,468	139,670	80,984	11,058	3,740	4,737
Kanawha County	W.Va.	34,699	2,158	16.1	10.1	106	2,312	126,071	9,193	69,917	46,961	126,746	120,162	68,215	6,584	0	3,280
Madison Metropolitan Schools	Wis.	22,407	1,496	15.0	18.8	43	1,581	117,926	4,954	25,169	87,803	116,265	112,678	70,013	2,690	897	5,374
Milwaukee	Wis.	92,061	5,222	17.6	66.6	148	3,606	482,832	39,095	272,020	171,717	491,833	471,585	282,197	20,248	0	5,290
Racine	Wis.	21,749	1,390	15.6	32.5	37	1,209	101,996	4,807	54,631	42,558	105,650	102,558	63,582	1,725	1,367	4,939

—Data not available or not applicable.

[1] Data exclude teachers reported as working in school district offices rather than in schools.
[2] Expenditures by local school districts only. Excludes expenditures by State education agencies for local school districts.
[3] Current expenditure per pupil based on fall enrollment collected by the Bureau of the Census.
ISD— Independent school district.

SOURCE: U.S. Department of Education, National Center for Education Statistics, Common Core of Data survey; and U.S. Department of Commerce, "Survey of Local Government Finances." (This table was prepared March 1991.)

Table 89.—Enrollment of the 130 largest public school districts: Fall 1989

Name of school district	State	Rank order[1]	Enrollment, fall 1989	Name of school district	State	Rank order[1]	Enrollment, fall 1989
1	2	3	4	1	2	3	4
New York City	N.Y.	1	930,440	Ysleta ISD	Texas	66	49,675
Los Angeles Unified	Calif.	2	609,746	Northside ISD	Texas	67	49,539
City of Chicago Schools	Ill.	3	408,442	Indianapolis Public Schools	Ind.	68	48,805
Dade County	Fla.	4	279,420	Newark City	N.J.	69	48,573
Philadelphia City	Pa.	5	189,451	Sacramento City Unified	Calif.	70	48,061
Houston ISD	Texas	6	185,566	Wichita	Kansas	71	47,251
Detroit City	Mich.	7	175,436	Buffalo City	N.Y.	72	46,694
Hawaii Department of Education	Hawaii	8	169,493	San Juan Unified	Calif.	73	46,640
Broward County	Fla.	9	148,803	Seminole County	Fla.	74	46,499
Fairfax County	Va.	10	126,790	Volusia County	Fla.	75	45,775
Dallas ISD	Texas	11	125,897	Cumberland County	N.C.	76	44,327
Hillsborough County	Fla.	12	119,810	St. Louis City	Mo.	77	44,056
San Diego City Unified	Calif.	13	119,314	Charleston County	S.C.	78	42,877
Clark County	Nev.	14	111,460	Chesterfield County	Va.	79	42,864
Baltimore City	Md.	15	107,782	Santa Ana Unified	Calif.	80	42,785
Prince Georges County	Md.	16	106,974	Arlington ISD	Texas	81	42,651
Duval County	Fla.	17	106,593	Birmingham City	Ala.	82	42,440
Memphis City	Tenn.	18	104,410	Escambia County	Fla.	83	42,071
Montgomery County	Md.	19	100,261	Corpus Christi ISD	Texas	84	42,054
Palm Beach County	Fla.	20	98,705	Omaha	Neb.	85	41,251
Orange County	Fla.	21	96,244	Prince William County	Va.	86	40,991
Milwaukee	Wis.	22	92,061	Toledo City	Ohio	87	40,944
Pinellas County	Fla.	23	91,393	Anchorage	Alaska	88	40,924
Jefferson County	Ky.	24	91,353	Tulsa City	Okla.	89	40,919
Albuquerque	N.M.	25	86,653	Seattle	Wash.	90	40,917
Orleans Parish School Board	La.	26	84,428	Minneapolis Special	Minn.	91	40,831
Baltimore County	Md.	27	84,133	North East ISD	Texas	92	40,644
D.C. Public Schools	D.C.	28	81,301	Jefferson County	Ala.	93	40,627
Granite	Utah	29	77,515	Lee County	Fla.	94	40,569
Mecklenburg County	N.C.	30	75,903	Fulton County	Ga.	95	40,280
Jefferson County	Colo.	31	75,164	Pittsburgh	Pa.	96	39,559
DeKalb County	Ga.	32	72,865	San Bernardino City Unified	Calif.	97	39,033
Cleveland City	Ohio	33	69,812	Alpine	Utah	98	38,246
Nashville-Davidson County	Tenn.	34	68,473	Aldine ISD	Texas	99	38,245
Virginia Beach City	Va.	35	68,348	Oklahoma City	Okla.	100	38,212
Long Beach Unified	Calif.	36	68,292	Forsyth County	N.C.	101	37,842
Mobile County	Ala.	37	67,620	Cypress-Fairbanks ISD	Texas	102	37,224
Fresno Unified	Calif.	38	67,492	Garden Grove Unified	Calif.	103	36,725
Cobb County	Ga.	39	66,668	Washoe County	Nev.	104	36,662
Fort Worth ISD	Texas	40	66,535	Norfolk City	Va.	105	36,428
Anne Arundel County	Md.	41	64,104	Shelby County	Tenn.	106	36,254
Columbus City	Ohio	42	64,051	Garland ISD	Texas	107	36,029
Polk County	Fla.	43	63,932	Montgomery County	Ala.	108	36,004
Jordan	Utah	44	63,605	Pasadena ISD	Texas	109	35,251
Wake County	N.C.	45	62,474	Brownsville ISD	Texas	110	34,998
Gwinnett County	Ga.	46	62,196	Saint Paul	Minn.	111	34,758
San Francisco Unified	Calif.	47	61,935	Kanawha County	W.Va.	112	34,699
El Paso ISD	Texas	48	61,729	Kansas City	Mo.	113	34,640
Austin ISD	Texas	49	61,666	Anoka	Minn.	114	33,709
Mesa Unified	Ariz.	50	61,636	Clayton County	Ga.	115	33,641
Atlanta City	Ga.	51	61,373	Chatham County	Ga.	116	33,407
East Baton Rouge Parish School Board	La.	52	60,279	Jackson Public	Miss.	117	33,330
Boston	Mass.	53	59,597	Richardson ISD	Texas	118	33,324
San Antonio ISD	Texas	54	58,720	Akron City	Ohio	119	33,230
Denver County	Colo.	55	58,299	Fort Bend ISD	Texas	120	33,165
Jefferson Parish School Board	La.	56	57,663	Calcasieu Parish School Board	La.	121	32,726
Tucson Unified	Ariz.	57	56,115	Mt. Diablo Unified	Calif.	122	32,534
Brevard County	Fla.	58	53,615	Richmond County	Ga.	123	32,392
Davis County	Utah	59	53,425	Montebello Unified	Calif.	124	32,362
Portland	Oreg.	60	53,116	Pasco County	Fla.	125	32,164
Caddo Parish School Board	La.	61	52,309	Henrico County	Va.	126	31,963
Greenville County	S.C.	62	50,849	Rochester City	N.Y.	127	31,941
Cincinnati City	Ohio	63	50,842	Stockton City Unified	Calif.	128	31,849
Oakland Unified	Calif.	64	50,741	Fort Wayne Community Schools	Ind.	129	31,843
Knox County	Tenn.	65	49,926	Fayette County	Ky.	130	31,191

[1] Public school districts ranked by size of enrollment in fall 1989.
ISD=Independent School District.

SOURCE: U.S. Department of Education, National Center for Education Statistics, Common Core of Data survey. (This table was prepared March 1991.)

Table 90.—Public elementary and secondary schools, by type of school: 1967–68 to 1989–90

Year	Total, all public schools	Regular schools										Combined elementary/ secondary schools[6]	Other schools[7]
		Total[1]	Schools with elementary grades only				Schools with secondary grades only						
			Total[2]	Middle schools[3]	One-teacher schools	Other elementary schools	Total[4]	Junior high[5]	3-year or 4-year schools	5-year or 6-year schools	Other high schools		
1	2	3	4	5	6	7	8	9	10	11	12	13	14
1967–68	—	94,197	67,186	—	4,146	63,040	23,318	7,437	10,751	4,650	480	3,693	—
1970–71	—	89,372	64,020	2,080	1,815	60,125	23,572	7,750	11,265	3,887	670	1,780	—
1972–73	—	88,864	62,942	2,308	1,475	59,159	23,919	7,878	11,550	3,962	529	2,003	—
1974–75	—	87,456	61,759	3,224	1,247	57,288	23,837	7,690	11,480	4,122	545	1,860	—
1975–76	88,597	87,034	61,704	3,916	1,166	56,622	23,792	7,521	11,572	4,113	586	1,538	1,563
1976–77	—	86,501	61,123	4,180	1,111	55,832	23,857	7,434	11,658	4,130	635	1,521	—
1978–79	—	84,816	60,312	5,879	1,056	53,377	22,834	6,282	11,410	4,429	713	1,670	—
1980–81	85,982	83,688	59,326	6,003	921	52,402	22,619	5,890	10,758	4,193	1,778	1,743	2,294
1982–83	84,740	82,039	58,051	6,875	798	50,378	22,383	5,948	11,678	4,067	690	1,605	2,701
1983–84	84,178	81,418	57,471	6,885	838	49,748	22,336	5,936	11,670	4,046	684	1,611	2,760
1984–85	84,007	81,147	57,231	6,893	825	49,513	22,320	5,916	11,671	4,021	712	1,596	2,860
1986–87	83,455	82,190	58,801	7,452	763	50,586	21,406	5,142	11,453	4,197	614	1,983	1,265
1987–88	83,248	82,248	59,311	7,641	729	50,941	20,758	4,900	11,279	4,048	531	2,179	1,000
1988–89	83,165	82,081	59,296	7,957	583	50,756	20,550	4,687	11,350	3,994	519	2,235	1,084
1989–90	83,425	82,396	59,757	8,272	630	50,855	20,359	4,512	11,492	3,812	543	2,280	1,029

[1] Excludes special education, alternative, and other schools not classified by grade span.
[2] Includes schools beginning with grade 6 or below and with no grade higher than 8.
[3] Includes schools with grade spans beginning with 4, 5, or 6 and ending with grade 6, 7, or 8.
[4] Includes schools with no grade lower than 7.
[5] Includes schools with grades 7 and 8 or grades 7 through 9.
[6] Includes schools beginning with grade 6 or lower and ending with grade 9 or above.

[7] Includes special education, alternative, and other schools not classified by grade span.
—Data not available.

SOURCE: U.S. Department of Education, National Center for Education Statistics, *Statistics of State School Systems*; and Common Core of Data survey. (This table was prepared December 1990.)

Table 91.—Public elementary and secondary schools, by type and size of school: 1989–90

Enrollment size of school	Number of schools, by type					Enrollment, by type of school[1]				
	Total[2]	Elementary[3]	Secondary[4]	Combined elementary/ secondary[5]	Other[2]	Total[2]	Elementary[3]	Secondary[4]	Combined elementary/ secondary[5]	Other[2]
1	2	3	4	5	6	7	8	9	10	11
Total	83,425	59,757	20,359	2,280	1,029	40,501,948	25,783,590	13,646,932	917,175	154,251
Percent[6]	100.00	100.00	100.00	100.00	100.00	100.00	100.00	100.00	100.00	100.00
Under 100	8.92	6.56	11.10	26.32	60.93	0.92	0.74	0.94	2.97	17.33
100 to 199	10.88	10.59	10.96	14.61	17.01	3.32	3.66	2.41	5.23	16.08
200 to 299	12.23	13.45	9.16	10.09	9.14	6.23	7.69	3.39	6.16	14.53
300 to 399	14.53	17.08	8.29	9.17	5.15	10.30	13.54	4.32	7.98	11.86
400 to 499	13.70	16.00	8.29	8.16	2.53	12.46	16.26	5.57	9.04	7.45
500 to 599	11.49	13.16	7.65	7.54	1.07	12.74	16.32	6.27	10.22	4.00
600 to 699	8.31	9.01	7.03	5.35	0.68	10.88	13.17	6.81	8.59	2.94
700 to 799	5.65	5.74	5.84	3.99	0.58	8.54	9.69	6.53	7.42	2.90
800 to 999	6.37	5.46	9.24	6.58	0.97	11.45	10.91	12.31	14.55	5.68
1,000 to 1,499	5.41	2.71	13.26	6.27	1.55	13.08	7.06	24.09	18.46	12.35
1,500 to 1,999	1.60	0.21	5.70	1.40	0.29	5.56	0.78	14.59	5.89	3.25
2,000 to 2,999	0.80	0.03	3.08	0.39	0.10	3.78	0.15	10.76	2.29	1.63
3,000 or more	0.10	0.01	0.39	0.13	—	0.74	0.04	2.02	1.21	—
Average enrollment[6]	493	441	670	402	150	493	441	670	402	150

[1] These enrollment data should be regarded as approximations only. Totals differ from those reported in other tables because this table represents data reported by schools rather than by States or school districts.
[2] Includes special education, alternative, and other schools not classified by grade span.
[3] Includes schools beginning with grade 6 or below and with no grade higher than 8.
[4] Includes schools with no grade lower than 7.

[5] Includes schools with both elementary and secondary grades.
[6] Data by size of school for those schools reporting enrollment.
—Data not applicable.

NOTE.—Because of rounding, details may not add to totals.

SOURCE: U.S. Department of Education, National Center for Education Statistics, Common Core of Data survey. (This table was prepared December 1990.)

Table 92.—Public elementary and secondary schools, by type and State: 1987–88 to 1989–90

State or other area	Total, all schools,[1] 1987–88	Total, all schools,[1] 1988–89	Number of schools, 1989–90							
			Total[1]	Elementary schools[2]	Secondary schools[3]	Combined elementary/secondary schools[4]				Unclassified schools[5]
						Total	Prekindergarten, kindergarten, or first grade to grade 12	Other schools ending with grade 12	Other combined schools	
1	2	3	4	5	6	7	8	9	10	11
United States	83,248	83,165	83,425	59,757	20,359	2,280	1,336	477	467	1,029
Alabama	1,298	1,292	1,292	843	285	164	135	5	24	0
Alaska	456	453	495	207	96	192	142	2	48	0
Arizona	965	1,023	1,026	757	247	11	6	1	4	11
Arkansas	1,112	1,094	1,097	659	425	12	6	0	6	1
California	7,123	7,312	7,433	5,346	1,809	139	67	53	19	139
Colorado	1,323	1,339	1,337	954	352	12	3	6	3	19
Connecticut	970	973	983	731	223	14	8	2	4	15
Delaware	167	168	170	111	45	14	12	2	0	0
District of Columbia .	188	187	184	123	44	2	0	0	2	15
Florida	2,379	2,432	2,505	1,841	438	226	121	50	55	0
Georgia	1,724	1,728	1,732	1,324	355	53	16	26	11	0
Hawaii	229	231	234	172	51	9	8	0	1	2
Idaho	565	561	574	363	188	13	9	1	3	10
Illinois	4,263	4,225	4,225	3,086	939	25	18	4	3	175
Indiana	1,926	1,923	1,923	1,412	446	37	17	12	8	28
Iowa	1,633	1,622	1,607	1,081	503	16	1	11	4	7
Kansas	1,463	1,465	1,459	1,021	437	1	0	0	1	0
Kentucky	1,399	1,394	1,385	1,019	334	0	0	0	0	32
Louisiana	1,599	1,582	1,536	1,035	330	118	95	17	6	53
Maine	749	751	748	600	135	11	9	1	1	2
Maryland	1,206	1,217	1,217	971	222	20	11	7	2	4
Massachusetts	1,795	1,826	1,817	1,421	367	27	14	7	6	2
Michigan	3,620	3,284	3,314	2,419	763	61	35	16	10	71
Minnesota	1,570	1,559	1,564	1,032	516	16	6	6	4	0
Mississippi	955	957	954	617	234	92	67	14	11	11
Missouri	2,150	2,153	2,151	1,509	595	15	1	8	6	32
Montana	775	761	758	551	205	0	0	0	0	2
Nebraska	1,537	1,512	1,524	1,123	376	25	12	7	6	0
Nevada	305	315	331	243	77	8	3	5	0	3
New Hampshire	435	435	444	347	88	9	5	3	1	0
New Jersey	2,246	2,257	2,264	1,759	419	4	1	3	0	82
New Mexico	648	651	658	484	168	2	1	1	0	4
New York	3,971	3,983	3,996	2,794	957	160	96	29	35	85
North Carolina	1,952	1,949	1,952	1,444	444	42	19	11	12	22
North Dakota	691	681	679	426	244	9	5	3	1	0
Ohio	3,743	3,738	3,715	2,666	1,016	33	5	21	7	0
Oklahoma	1,889	1,832	1,859	1,195	657	0	0	0	0	7
Oregon	1,214	1,206	1,190	883	274	30	25	4	1	3
Pennsylvania	3,313	3,298	3,276	2,434	737	40	15	10	15	65
Rhode Island	298	302	294	230	59	2	2	0	0	3
South Carolina	1,103	1,103	1,103	831	257	15	7	5	3	0
South Dakota	790	792	799	493	291	0	0	0	0	15
Tennessee	1,578	1,565	1,535	1,122	339	55	39	3	13	19
Texas	5,787	5,856	5,937	4,194	1,359	384	219	92	73	0
Utah	725	730	718	476	211	10	3	2	5	21
Vermont	333	331	336	270	51	14	12	2	0	1
Virginia	1,761	1,765	1,779	1,359	363	21	6	7	8	36
Washington	1,852	1,870	1,858	1,298	486	74	44	15	15	0
West Virginia	1,084	1,065	1,035	753	235	27	7	0	20	20
Wisconsin	2,002	2,009	2,019	1,444	548	16	3	3	10	11
Wyoming	389	408	404	284	119	0	0	0	0	1
Outlying areas										
American Samoa	30	30	30	23	6	0	0	0	0	1
Guam	37	37	37	30	5	1	1	0	0	1
Northern Marianas ..	26	26	26	21	4	0	0	0	0	1
Puerto Rico	1,756	1,676	1,661	1,123	318	198	7	3	188	22
Virgin Islands	34	34	34	24	8	1	0	0	1	1

[1] Includes regular, special education, alternative, and other schools not classified by grade span.

[2] Includes schools beginning with grade 6 or below and with no grade higher than 8.

[3] Includes schools with no grade lower than 7.

[4] Includes schools beginning with grade 6 or below and ending grade 9 or above.

[5] Includes special education, alternative, and other schools not classified by grade span.

—Data not available.

SOURCE: U.S. Department of Education, National Center for Education Statistics, Common Core of Data survey. (This table was prepared December 1990.)

Table 93.—Public elementary schools by grade span, and average school size, by State: 1989–90

State or other area	Total	Schools, by grade span						Average number of students per school [1]
		Prekindergarten, kindergarten, or 1st grade to grades 3 or 4	Prekindergarten, kindergarten, or 1st grade to grade 5	Prekindergarten, kindergarten, or 1st grade to grade 6	Prekindergarten, kindergarten, or 1st grade to grade 8	Grades 4, 5, or 6 to 6, 7, or 8	Other grade spans	
1	2	3	4	5	6	7	8	9
United States	59,757	5,019	14,941	19,985	5,200	8,272	6,340	441
Alabama	843	78	218	226	88	158	75	487
Alaska	207	6	15	121	31	7	27	302
Arizona	757	43	79	356	143	75	61	541
Arkansas	659	70	63	394	6	74	52	384
California	5,346	233	1,101	2,659	515	534	304	574
Colorado	954	36	326	363	14	151	64	390
Connecticut	731	71	201	227	57	104	71	415
Delaware	111	43	5	12	1	25	25	557
District of Columbia	123	4	2	104	6	3	4	396
Florida	1,841	45	836	395	26	237	302	716
Georgia	1,324	78	484	221	42	244	255	573
Hawaii	172	1	17	134	9	9	2	595
Idaho	363	36	63	170	22	40	32	363
Illinois	3,086	331	494	746	761	404	350	385
Indiana	1,412	57	414	631	50	177	83	430
Iowa	1,081	147	276	347	30	192	89	279
Kansas	1,021	83	229	344	171	130	64	274
Kentucky	1,019	33	317	270	195	139	65	418
Louisiana	1,035	121	278	209	63	201	163	512
Maine	600	89	81	94	109	85	142	243
Maryland	971	23	473	238	13	149	75	498
Massachusetts	1,421	220	394	340	68	218	181	380
Michigan	2,419	215	780	764	57	381	222	417
Minnesota	1,032	111	140	556	19	91	115	444
Mississippi	617	70	50	189	50	86	172	532
Missouri	1,509	95	288	545	145	187	249	367
Montana	551	41	72	108	216	47	67	185
Nebraska	1,123	52	90	568	221	43	149	146
Nevada	243	7	70	111	17	22	16	498
New Hampshire	347	59	59	101	48	52	28	319
New Jersey	1,759	231	387	364	296	270	211	405
New Mexico	484	25	162	171	5	79	42	403
New York	2,794	250	661	1,140	63	390	290	563
North Carolina	1,444	118	438	353	151	268	116	481
North Dakota	426	14	5	288	44	10	65	182
Ohio	2,666	312	646	998	102	414	194	415
Oklahoma	1,195	108	218	321	312	167	69	320
Oregon	883	58	264	294	113	124	30	342
Pennsylvania	2,434	284	773	762	57	341	217	431
Rhode Island	230	38	31	100	5	25	31	361
South Carolina	831	94	265	134	28	175	135	525
South Dakota	493	30	61	188	109	49	56	164
Tennessee	1,122	103	233	310	241	143	92	473
Texas	4,194	430	1,386	817	144	826	591	534
Utah	476	12	101	311	3	37	12	561
Vermont	270	27	23	126	61	19	14	221
Virginia	1,359	104	491	288	2	208	266	491
Washington	1,298	54	319	503	56	152	214	435
West Virginia	753	68	112	389	49	63	72	268
Wisconsin	1,444	139	385	457	157	209	97	348
Wyoming	284	22	65	128	9	38	22	213
Outlying areas								
American Samoa	23	0	0	0	22	0	1	405
Guam	30	0	19	0	0	6	5	643
Northern Marianas	21	0	0	0	0	0	21	202
Puerto Rico	1,123	141	33	751	8	39	151	283
Virgin Islands	24	1	0	23	0	0	0	498

[1] Average for schools reporting enrollment data.

NOTE.—Schools beginning with grade 6 or below and no grade higher than 8. Excludes schools not reported by level, such as special education schools for the handicapped.

SOURCE: U.S. Department of Education, National Center for Education Statistics, Common Core of Data survey. (This table was prepared December 1990.)

Table 94.—Public secondary schools by grade span, and average school size, by State: 1989-90

State	Total	Schools, by grade span							Average number of students per school [1]
		Grades 7 to 8 and 7 to 9	Grades 7 to 12	Grades 8 to 12	Grades 9 to 12	Grades 10 to 12	Other spans ending with grade 12	Other grade spans	
1	2	3	4	5	6	7	8	9	10
United States	20,359	4,512	3,364	448	10,210	1,282	113	430	670
Alabama	285	31	77	13	141	12	2	9	705
Alaska	96	19	31	3	36	0	1	6	374
Arizona	247	86	6	2	141	8	0	4	863
Arkansas	425	76	228	3	44	62	0	12	407
California	1,809	494	89	36	987	135	9	59	918
Colorado	352	81	67	2	163	31	3	5	543
Connecticut	223	54	15	3	141	6	0	4	658
Delaware	45	12	6	2	22	3	0	0	781
District of Columbia	44	26	0	1	13	3	0	1	638
Florida	438	85	45	7	229	33	5	34	1,167
Georgia	355	53	19	64	204	7	1	7	942
Hawaii	51	19	8	0	24	0	0	0	1,202
Idaho	188	56	37	0	70	21	1	3	435
Illinois	939	261	21	7	625	6	7	12	624
Indiana	446	97	115	1	212	16	1	4	765
Iowa	503	96	137	2	241	27	0	0	336
Kansas	437	88	54	2	269	21	1	2	336
Kentucky	334	61	54	4	189	11	0	15	634
Louisiana	330	69	44	8	191	8	0	10	695
Maine	135	23	16	1	88	5	0	2	495
Maryland	222	45	8	3	155	4	1	6	964
Massachusetts	367	74	45	11	227	9	0	1	739
Michigan	763	151	127	23	412	37	0	13	689
Minnesota	516	85	265	9	111	42	1	3	538
Mississippi	234	52	47	8	90	26	1	10	640
Missouri	595	90	233	14	227	22	1	8	493
Montana	205	33	0	0	169	2	0	1	240
Nebraska	376	51	234	5	67	19	0	0	285
Nevada	77	21	22	1	28	5	0	0	842
New Hampshire	88	19	13	0	53	3	0	0	647
New Jersey	419	84	36	13	263	13	3	7	855
New Mexico	168	44	29	2	77	11	1	4	597
New York	957	214	214	16	432	51	0	30	914
North Carolina	444	114	30	3	233	53	1	10	831
North Dakota	244	18	186	8	17	12	2	1	193
Ohio	1,016	236	139	14	538	38	40	11	674
Oklahoma	657	162	0	0	331	142	6	16	294
Oregon	274	70	22	6	163	12	1	0	594
Pennsylvania	737	132	195	11	296	77	8	18	794
Rhode Island	59	19	6	2	28	4	0	0	833
South Carolina	257	49	23	13	144	14	1	13	793
South Dakota	291	112	0	0	164	9	4	2	163
Tennessee	339	81	38	5	186	26	0	3	804
Texas	1,359	256	167	26	821	33	7	49	748
Utah	211	71	26	2	59	46	1	6	789
Vermont	51	4	28	1	18	0	0	0	557
Virginia	363	76	17	62	174	23	0	11	926
Washington	486	120	62	19	225	49	1	10	582
West Virginia	235	87	36	2	65	41	1	3	545
Wisconsin	548	113	47	7	344	32	1	4	494
Wyoming	119	42	0	1	63	12	0	1	304
Outlying areas									
American Samoa	6	0	0	0	6	0	0	0	480
Guam	5	0	0	0	5	0	0	0	1,424
Northern Marianas	4	0	0	0	1	1	0	2	469
Puerto Rico	318	157	19	2	1	125	3	11	707
Virgin Islands	8	5	0	0	2	1	0	0	1,105

[1] Average for schools reporting enrollment data.

NOTE.—Schools with no grade lower than 7. Excludes schools not reported by level, such as special education schools for the handicapped.

SOURCE: U.S. Department of Education, National Center for Education Statistics, Common Core of Data survey. (This table was prepared December 1990.)

Table 95.—High school graduates compared with population 17 years of age: 1869–70 to 1990–91

[Numbers in thousands]

School year	Population 17 years old [1]	High school graduates					Graduates as a percent of 17-year-old population
		Total [2]	Sex		Control		
			Male	Female	Public [3]	Private [4]	
1	2	3	4	5	6	7	8
1869–70	815	16	7	9	—	—	2.0
1879–80	946	24	11	13	—	—	2.5
1889–90	1,259	44	19	25	22	22	3.5
1899–1900	1,489	95	38	57	62	33	6.4
1909–10	1,786	156	64	93	111	45	8.8
1919–20	1,855	311	124	188	231	80	16.8
1929–30	2,296	667	300	367	592	75	29.0
1939–40	2,403	1,221	579	643	1,143	78	50.8
1947–48	2,261	1,190	563	627	1,073	117	52.6
1949–50	2,034	1,200	571	629	1,063	136	59.0
1951–52	2,086	1,197	569	627	1,056	141	57.4
1953–54	2,135	1,276	613	664	1,129	147	59.8
1955–56	2,242	1,415	680	735	1,252	163	63.1
1956–57	2,272	1,434	690	744	1,270	164	63.1
1957–58	2,325	1,506	725	781	1,332	174	64.8
1958–59	2,458	1,627	784	843	1,435	192	66.2
1959–60	2,672	1,858	895	963	1,627	231	69.5
1960–61	2,892	1,964	955	1,009	1,725	239	67.9
1961–62	2,768	1,918	938	980	1,678	240	69.3
1962–63	2,740	1,943	956	987	1,710	233	70.9
1963–64	2,978	2,283	1,120	1,163	2,008	275	76.7
1964–65	3,684	2,658	1,311	1,347	2,360	298	72.1
1965–66	3,489	2,665	1,323	1,342	2,367	298	76.4
1966–67	3,500	2,672	1,328	1,344	2,374	298	76.3
1967–68	3,532	2,695	1,338	1,357	2,395	300	76.3
1968–69	3,659	2,822	1,399	1,423	2,522	300	77.1
1969–70	3,757	2,889	1,430	1,459	2,589	300	76.9
1970–71	3,872	2,937	1,454	1,483	2,637	300	75.9
1971–72	3,973	3,001	1,487	1,514	2,699	302	75.5
1972–73	4,049	3,036	1,500	1,536	2,730	306	75.0
1973–74	4,132	3,073	1,512	1,561	2,763	310	74.4
1974–75	4,256	3,133	1,542	1,591	2,823	310	73.6
1975–76	4,272	3,148	1,552	1,596	2,837	311	73.7
1976–77	4,272	3,155	1,548	1,607	2,840	315	73.9
1977–78	4,286	3,127	1,531	1,596	2,825	302	73.0
1978–79	4,327	3,117	1,523	1,594	2,817	300	72.0
1979–80	4,262	3,043	1,491	1,552	2,748	295	71.4
1980–81	4,207	3,020	1,483	1,537	2,725	295	71.8
1981–82	4,121	2,995	1,471	1,524	2,705	290	72.7
1982–83	3,939	2,888	1,437	1,451	2,598	290	73.3
1983–84	3,753	2,767	—	—	2,495	272	73.7
1984–85	3,658	2,677	—	—	2,414	263	73.2
1985–86	3,621	2,643	—	—	2,383	260	73.0
1986–87	3,697	2,694	—	—	2,429	265	72.9
1987–88	3,781	2,773	—	—	2,500	273	73.4
1988–89 [5]	3,761	2,724	—	—	2,456	268	72.4
1989–90 [6]	3,485	2,592	—	—	2,324	268	74.4
1990–91 [6]	3,325	2,508	—	—	2,253	255	75.4

[1] Derived from *Current Population Reports*, Series P–25. 17–year–old population adjusted to reflect October 17–year–old population.

[2] Includes graduates of public and private schools.

[3] Data for 1929–30 and preceding years are from *Statistics of Public High Schools* and exclude graduates of high schools which failed to report to the Office of Education.

[4] For most years, private school data have been estimated based on periodic private school surveys. For years through 1957–58, private includes data for subcollegiate departments of institutions of higher education and residential schools for exceptional children.

[5] Data have been revised from previously published figures.

[6] Public high school graduates based on State estimates.

—Data not available.

NOTE.—Includes graduates of regular day school programs. Excludes graduates of other programs, when separately reported, and recipients of high school equivalency certificates. Because of rounding, details may not add to totals.

SOURCE: U.S. Department of Education, National Center for Education Statistics, *Statistics of Public High Schools;* Biennial Survey of Education in the United States; *Statistics of State School Systems; Statistics of Nonpublic Elementary and Secondary Schools;* Common Core of Data surveys; and U.S. Department of Commerce, Bureau of the Census, *Current Population Reports,* Series P–25. (This table was prepared March 1991.)

Table 96.—Public high school graduates, by State: 1969–70 to 1990–91

State	1969–70	1974–75	1979–80	1980–81	1985–86	1986–87	1987–88	1988–89	Estimated 1989–90	Estimated 1990–91	Percent change, 1985–86 to 1990–91
1	2	3	4	5	6	7	8	9	10	11	12
United States	**2,588,639**	**2,822,638**	**2,747,678**	**2,725,285**	**[1]2,382,616**	**[1]2,428,803**	**2,500,192**	**[1]2,456,139**	**[1]2,324,035**	**[1]2,253,043**	**−5.4**
Alabama	45,286	46,633	45,190	44,894	39,620	42,463	43,799	43,437	[2]36,555	38,663	−2.4
Alaska	3,297	4,220	5,223	5,343	5,464	5,692	5,907	5,631	[3]5,437	[3]5,389	−1.4
Arizona	22,040	25,665	28,633	28,416	27,533	29,549	29,777	31,638	32,103	32,100	16.6
Arkansas	26,068	26,836	29,052	29,577	26,227	27,101	27,776	28,162	[2]27,343	26,587	1.4
California	260,908	273,411	249,217	242,172	229,026	237,414	249,617	244,629	229,353	228,319	−0.3
Colorado	30,312	34,963	36,804	35,897	32,621	34,200	35,977	35,520	[2]32,967	31,800	−2.5
Connecticut	34,755	[4]42,792	37,683	38,369	33,571	31,141	32,383	30,862	30,000	29,830	−11.1
Delaware	6,985	8,235	7,582	7,349	5,791	5,895	5,963	6,104	[2]6,111	6,230	7.6
District of Columbia[5]	4,980	5,367	4,959	4,848	3,875	3,842	3,882	3,565	[2]3,626	3,200	−17.4
Florida	70,478	86,481	87,324	88,755	83,029	82,184	89,206	90,759	[2]89,000	89,276	7.5
Georgia	56,859	59,803	61,621	62,963	59,082	60,018	61,765	61,937	[2]56,605	60,426	2.3
Hawaii	10,407	11,283	11,493	11,472	9,958	10,371	10,575	10,404	[3]9,905	[3]9,578	(6)
Idaho	12,296	12,631	13,187	12,679	12,059	12,243	12,445	12,520	[2]11,642	11,594	−3.9
Illinois	126,864	[4]141,316	135,579	136,795	114,319	116,075	119,090	116,660	[2]108,119	102,353	−10.5
Indiana	69,984	74,104	73,143	73,381	59,817	60,364	64,037	63,571	[2]59,415	56,520	−5.5
Iowa	44,063	43,005	43,445	42,635	34,279	34,580	35,218	34,294	[2]31,780	29,085	−15.2
Kansas	33,394	32,458	30,890	29,397	25,587	26,933	27,036	26,848	[2]25,108	24,094	−5.8
Kentucky	37,473	42,368	41,203	41,714	37,288	36,948	39,484	38,883	[2]38,693	36,200	−2.9
Louisiana	43,641	47,691	46,297	46,199	39,965	39,084	39,058	37,198	[2]35,899	38,803	−2.9
Maine	14,003	14,830	15,445	15,554	13,006	13,692	13,808	13,857	[2]13,323	12,754	−1.9
Maryland	46,462	55,408	54,270	54,050	46,700	46,107	47,175	45,791	[2]41,566	39,110	−16.3
Massachusetts	63,865	[4]79,000	73,802	74,831	[7]60,360	61,010	59,515	[3]54,892	54,954	50,866	−15.7
Michigan	121,000	135,509	124,316	124,372	101,042	102,725	106,151	101,784	93,000	[3]89,122	−11.8
Minnesota	60,480	66,535	64,908	64,166	51,988	53,533	54,645	53,122	48,502	45,980	−11.6
Mississippi	29,653	27,243	27,586	28,083	25,134	26,201	27,896	24,241	[2]25,039	22,535	−10.3
Missouri	55,315	62,375	62,265	60,359	49,204	50,840	51,316	51,968	48,457	46,297	−5.9
Montana	11,520	12,293	12,135	11,634	9,761	10,073	10,311	10,490	[2]9,375	9,000	−7.8
Nebraska	21,280	22,249	22,410	21,411	17,845	18,129	18,300	18,690	[2]18,556	[3]17,664	−1.0
Nevada	5,449	7,232	8,473	9,069	8,784	[7]9,506	9,404	9,464	[2]9,462	9,622	9.5
New Hampshire	8,516	11,050	11,722	11,552	10,648	10,796	11,685	11,340	[2]10,357	10,191	−4.3
New Jersey	86,498	[4]96,000	94,564	93,168	78,781	79,376	80,863	76,263	68,445	64,460	−18.2
New Mexico	16,060	18,438	18,424	17,915	15,468	15,701	15,868	15,481	[2]14,884	14,304	−7.5
New York	190,000	210,780	204,064	198,465	162,165	163,765	165,379	154,580	142,400	133,800	−17.5
North Carolina	68,886	70,094	70,862	69,395	65,865	65,421	67,836	69,300	[2]64,521	62,005	−5.9
North Dakota	11,150	10,690	9,928	9,924	7,610	7,821	8,432	8,077	[2]7,690	7,960	4.6
Ohio	142,248	158,179	144,169	143,503	119,561	121,121	124,503	125,036	[2]114,513	106,921	−10.6
Oklahoma	36,293	37,809	39,305	38,875	34,452	35,514	36,145	36,773	[2]35,606	36,000	4.5
Oregon	32,236	30,668	29,939	28,729	26,286	27,165	28,058	26,903	[2]25,564	25,100	−4.5
Pennsylvania	151,014	163,124	146,458	144,645	122,871	121,219	124,376	118,921	109,630	103,200	−16.0
Rhode Island	10,146	11,042	10,864	10,719	8,908	8,771	8,856	8,554	[2]7,708	7,523	−15.5
South Carolina	34,940	38,312	38,697	38,347	34,500	36,000	36,113	37,020	34,600	33,000	−4.3
South Dakota	11,757	11,725	10,689	10,385	7,870	8,074	8,415	8,181	[2]7,650	6,649	−15.5
Tennessee	49,000	49,363	49,845	50,648	43,263	44,731	47,904	48,553	47,500	[3]44,824	3.6
Texas	139,046	159,487	171,494	171,665	161,150	168,430	171,436	176,951	[2]182,057	184,060	14.2
Utah	18,395	19,668	20,035	19,886	19,774	20,930	22,226	22,934	[2]22,511	23,676	19.7
Vermont	6,095	6,455	6,733	6,424	5,794	5,968	6,177	5,963	[3]5,694	[3]5,436	−6.2
Virginia	58,562	65,570	66,621	67,126	63,113	65,008	65,688	65,004	[2]61,268	58,154	−7.9
Washington	50,425	50,990	50,402	50,046	45,805	49,873	51,754	49,425	46,872	45,086	−1.6
West Virginia	26,139	24,631	23,369	23,580	21,870	22,401	22,406	22,886	[2]21,854	21,256	−2.8
Wisconsin	66,753	70,979	69,332	67,743	58,340	56,872	58,428	54,994	[2]54,994	50,700	−13.1
Wyoming	5,363	5,648	6,072	6,161	5,587	5,933	6,148	6,079	[2]5,823	5,741	2.8
Outlying areas											
American Samoa	[8]367	448	—	—	608	647	633	569	560	535	−12.0
Guam	972	1,117	—	—	840	898	898	936	1,033	1,112	32.4
Northern Marianas	—	—	—	—	—	289	285	232	219	207	—
Puerto Rico	24,917	27,071	—	—	31,597	30,137	31,832	31,617	29,049	27,877	−11.8
Virgin Islands	[8]432	641	—	—	1,044	1,170	1,026	1,025	958	1,026	−1.7

[1] National total includes estimates for nonreporting States.
[2] Actual 1989–90 count.
[3] Data estimated by the National Center for Education Statistics (NCES).
[4] Data estimated by reported State.
[5] Beginning in 1985–86, graduates from adult programs are excluded.
[6] Less than .05 percent.
[7] Data from State Projections to 1993 published by NCES.
[8] Data are for 1970–71.
—Data not reported.

NOTE.—Data include graduates of regular day school programs, but exclude graduates of other programs and persons receiving high school equivalency certificates. They also exclude graduates of subcollegiate departments of institutions of higher education, Federal schools for American Indians and on Federal installations, and residential schools for exceptional children. Some data have been revised from previously published figures. All 1989–90 and 1990–91 data are State estimates unless otherwise indicated.

SOURCE: U.S. Department of Education, National Center for Education Statistics, Common Core of Data surveys and State Projections to 1993. (This table was prepared March 1991.)

Table 97.—General Educational Development (GED) credentials issued and age of test takers: 1974 to 1989

Year	Total, in thousands [1]	Percentage distribution of GED test takers, by age				
		19 years old or less	20- to 24-year-olds	25- to 29-year-olds	30- to 34-year-olds	35 years old or over
1	2	3	4	5	6	7
1974	294	35	27	13	9	17
1975	340	33	26	14	9	18
1976	333	31	28	14	10	17
1977	332	40	24	13	8	14
1978	381	31	27	13	10	18
1979	426	37	28	12	13	11
1980	479	37	27	13	8	15
1981	489	37	27	13	8	14
1982	486	37	28	13	8	15
1983	465	34	29	14	8	15
1984	427	32	28	15	9	16
1985	413	32	26	15	10	16
1986	428	32	26	15	10	17
1987	444	33	24	15	10	18
1988	410	35	22	14	10	18
1989	357	36	22	14	10	17

[1] Number of persons receiving high school equivalency certificates based on the GED test.

NOTE.—Because of rounding, details may not add to totals.

SOURCE: American Council on Education, General Educational Development Testing Service, GED Statistical Report, various years. (This table was prepared May 1990.)

Table 98.—Percentage of high school dropouts among persons 16 to 24 years old, [1] by sex and race/ethnicity: October 1967 to October 1990

Year	Total				Men				Women			
	All races	White [2]	Black [2]	Hispanic origin [3]	All races	White [2]	Black [2]	Hispanic origin [3]	All races	White [2]	Black [2]	Hispanic origin [3]
1	2	3	4	5	6	7	8	9	10	11	12	13
1967	17.0	15.4	28.6	—	16.5	14.7	30.6	—	17.3	16.1	26.9	—
1968	16.2	14.7	27.4	—	15.8	14.4	27.1	—	16.5	15.0	27.6	—
1969	15.2	13.6	26.7	—	14.3	12.6	26.9	—	16.0	14.6	26.7	—
1970	15.0	13.2	27.9	—	14.2	12.2	29.4	—	15.7	14.1	26.6	—
1971	14.7	13.4	23.7	—	14.2	12.6	25.5	—	15.2	14.2	22.1	—
1972	14.6	13.7	21.5	34.3	14.1	13.1	22.3	33.6	15.1	14.2	20.8	35.0
1973	14.1	12.9	22.3	33.7	13.7	12.5	21.6	30.7	14.5	13.3	22.9	36.4
1974	14.3	13.2	21.3	33.0	14.2	13.4	20.1	33.8	14.4	13.1	22.3	32.3
1975	13.9	12.6	22.8	29.2	13.3	12.0	22.8	26.6	14.5	13.2	22.8	31.5
1976	14.1	13.3	20.4	31.3	14.1	13.2	21.2	30.2	14.2	13.3	19.7	32.3
1977	14.1	13.4	19.7	32.9	14.5	13.9	19.5	31.5	13.8	12.8	20.0	34.2
1978	14.2	13.4	20.2	33.1	14.6	13.6	22.5	33.2	13.9	13.2	18.2	33.0
1979	14.6	13.6	21.2	33.8	15.0	14.0	22.5	33.0	14.2	13.1	20.0	34.5
1980	14.1	13.3	19.3	35.2	15.1	14.2	21.1	37.2	13.1	12.3	17.9	33.2
1981	13.9	13.8	18.5	33.1	15.1	14.5	20.0	35.9	12.8	13.2	17.2	30.4
1982	13.9	13.1	18.4	31.7	14.5	13.6	21.1	30.6	13.3	12.7	16.0	32.7
1983	13.7	12.9	18.1	31.5	14.9	14.1	19.8	34.3	12.5	11.7	16.5	29.1
1984	13.1	12.7	15.6	29.8	14.0	13.5	16.7	30.6	12.3	11.8	14.5	29.1
1985	12.6	12.2	15.7	27.6	13.4	13.0	16.1	29.8	11.8	11.3	15.3	25.2
1986	12.1	11.9	13.7	30.0	12.9	12.8	14.4	32.7	11.3	11.1	13.0	27.2
1987	12.7	12.5	14.5	28.6	13.3	13.0	15.7	29.0	12.2	12.0	13.5	28.1
1988	12.9	12.7	14.9	35.8	13.5	13.5	15.4	36.0	12.2	11.9	14.4	35.5
1989	12.6	12.4	13.8	33.0	13.6	13.4	14.9	34.4	11.7	11.4	12.9	31.6
1990	12.1	12.0	13.2	32.4	12.2	12.7	11.8	34.3	11.6	11.4	14.4	30.3

[1] "Status" dropouts.
[2] Includes persons of Hispanic origin.
[3] Persons of Hispanic origin may be of any race.
— Data not available.

NOTE.—"Status" dropouts are persons who are not enrolled in school and who are not high school graduates. People who have received GED credentials are counted as graduates. Data are based upon sample surveys of the civilian noninstitutional population.

SOURCE: U.S. Department of Commerce, Bureau of the Census, Current Population Survey, unpublished tabulations; and U.S. Department of Education, National Center for Education Statistics, "Dropout Rates in the United States." (This table was prepared June 1991.)

Table 99.—Percentage of high school dropouts among persons 14 to 34 years old, by age, race/ethnicity, and sex: October 1970 to October 1990

Year, race/ethnicity, and sex	Total, 14 to 34 years	14 and 15 years	16 and 17 yearts	18 and 19 years	20 and 21 years	22 to 24 years	25 to 29 years	30 to 34 years
1	2	3	4	5	6	7	8	9
October 1970								
All races	17.0	1.8	8.0	16.2	16.6	18.7	22.5	26.5
Male	16.2	1.7	7.1	16.0	16.1	17.9	21.4	26.2
Female	17.7	1.9	8.9	16.3	16.9	19.4	23.6	26.8
White [1]	15.2	1.7	7.3	14.1	14.6	16.3	19.9	24.6
Male	14.4	1.7	6.3	13.3	14.1	15.3	19.0	24.2
Female	16.0	1.8	8.4	14.8	15.1	17.2	20.7	24.9
Black [1]	30.0	2.4	12.8	31.2	29.6	37.8	44.4	43.5
Male	30.4	2.0	13.3	36.4	29.6	39.5	43.1	45.9
Female	29.5	2.8	12.4	26.6	29.6	36.4	45.6	41.5
October 1980								
All races	13.0	1.7	8.8	15.7	15.9	15.2	13.9	14.6
Male	13.2	1.3	8.9	16.9	17.8	16.4	13.8	14.0
Female	12.8	2.2	8.8	14.7	14.3	14.0	14.0	15.2
White [1]	12.1	1.7	9.2	14.9	14.5	13.9	12.7	13.4
Male	12.4	1.2	9.3	16.1	15.6	15.4	12.7	13.1
Female	11.8	2.1	9.2	13.8	13.4	12.6	12.7	13.6
Black [1]	18.8	2.0	6.9	21.2	24.8	24.0	22.6	23.5
Male	19.0	1.5	7.2	22.7	31.3	24.9	22.1	21.9
Female	18.7	2.5	6.6	19.8	19.6	23.3	22.9	24.8
Hispanic origin [2]	35.2	5.7	16.5	39.0	41.6	40.6	40.9	45.4
Male	35.6	3.3	18.1	43.1	41.4	42.9	40.1	43.9
Female	34.9	7.9	15.0	34.6	41.9	38.6	41.7	47.0
October 1988								
All races	12.2	1.1	6.7	14.6	14.6	14.6	13.9	12.8
Male	12.9	1.1	6.3	15.6	16.3	15.2	14.7	13.8
Female	11.5	1.0	7.1	13.5	13.0	14.0	13.2	11.8
White [1]	12.0	1.1	7.1	14.3	14.2	14.1	13.7	12.4
Male	12.8	1.1	6.8	15.5	16.1	14.8	14.8	13.4
Female	11.1	1.1	7.4	13.1	12.4	13.3	12.6	11.4
Black [1]	13.9	1.1	6.0	17.9	18.2	17.2	16.3	14.9
Male	14.1	1.0	5.1	18.0	21.7	17.7	15.2	16.6
Female	13.7	1.4	6.8	17.7	15.2	16.8	17.2	13.4
Hispanic origin [2]	34.9	1.1	19.7	31.2	43.2	42.6	40.8	39.5
Male	35.8	1.9	18.1	35.2	43.5	41.1	42.6	41.0
Female	33.9	0.3	21.4	27.3	42.7	44.2	39.0	38.0
October 1989								
All races	12.0	1.1	5.9	14.0	16.0	13.7	13.2	13.1
Male	12.6	0.7	5.9	14.6	18.1	15.1	13.9	13.6
Female	11.4	1.4	5.8	13.5	14.1	12.4	12.6	12.7
White [1]	11.6	1.1	6.1	13.6	15.6	13.4	12.6	12.3
Male	12.4	0.6	6.4	14.4	17.1	14.9	13.8	13.0
Female	10.8	1.7	5.7	12.8	14.2	12.0	11.5	11.6
Black [1]	14.6	0.4	5.6	18.0	16.9	14.9	17.3	18.8
Male	14.4	0.4	4.1	17.5	23.3	16.1	14.8	19.3
Female	14.8	0.5	7.1	18.5	11.2	14.0	19.3	18.3
Hispanic origin [2]	33.9	3.6	12.5	27.9	41.2	41.1	40.1	40.2
Male	35.1	2.0	9.6	25.9	45.8	44.9	41.9	41.0
Female	32.6	5.0	15.7	30.0	35.9	37.3	38.3	39.4
October 1990								
All races.								
Male	12.2	0.8	6.6	14.6	13.2	14.0	14.5	13.3
Female	11.6	1.0	6.1	13.8	12.4	13.6	13.4	12.5
White [1]	11.4	0.8	6.4	14.0	12.2	14.0	12.9	12.3
Male	12.0	0.7	6.9	14.8	13.5	14.4	13.7	12.9
Female	10.9	0.9	5.8	13.2	11.1	13.7	12.2	11.6
Black [1]	14.4	0.8	6.9	16.5	15.5	13.5	19.2	16.8
Male	13.4	0.3	6.1	15.3	12.5	13.3	18.9	16.4
Female	15.2	1.3	7.8	17.5	18.4	13.7	19.4	17.1
Hispanic origin [2]	34.3	1.1	12.9	34.2	31.6	42.8	41.7	42.4
Male	34.8	0.9	13.1	39.4	37.9	41.4	42.6	41.4
Female	33.8	1.3	12.5	29.4	25.0	44.4	40.7	43.5

[1] Includes persons of Hispanic origin.

[2] Persons of Hispanic origin may be of any race.

NOTE.—"Status" dropouts are persons who are not enrolled in school and who are not high school graduates. People who have received GED credentials are counted as graduates. Data are based upon sample surveys of the civilian noninstitutional population.

SOURCE: U.S. Department of Commerce, Bureau of the Census, *Current Population Reports*, Series P-20, Nos. 222 and 429; and unpublished data. (This table was prepared June 1991.)

Table 100.—Students with handicaps exiting the educational system, by age, handicapping condition, and basis of exit: United States and outlying areas, 1987–88

Student characteristics	Total exiting the system		Graduated with diploma		Graduated through certificate		Reached maximum age[1]		Dropped out[2]		Other reasons for exit[3]	
	Number	Percent	Number	Percent	Number	Percent	Number	Percent	Number	Percent	Number	Percent
1	2	3	4	5	6	7	8	9	10	11	12	13
Age group												
14 to 21+[4]	238,570	100.0	100,195	42.0	26,832	11.2	5,962	2.5	65,395	27.4	40,186	16.8
14	7,720	100.0	90	1.2	481	6.2	14	0.2	1,074	13.9	6,061	78.5
15	10,686	100.0	130	1.2	369	3.5	8	0.1	3,667	34.3	6,512	60.9
16	25,456	100.0	596	2.3	465	1.8	32	0.1	16,334	64.2	8,029	31.5
17	42,368	100.0	17,794	42.0	1,909	4.5	44	0.1	15,218	35.9	7,403	17.5
18	71,550	100.0	42,698	59.7	7,560	10.6	505	0.7	14,898	20.8	5,889	8.2
19	39,834	100.0	24,591	61.7	5,168	13.0	56	0.1	6,964	17.5	3,055	7.7
20	12,933	100.0	6,444	49.8	2,299	17.8	335	2.6	2,545	19.7	1,310	10.1
21	12,455	100.0	2,888	23.2	2,431	19.5	4,308	34.6	1,128	9.1	1,700	13.6
21+	1,991	100.0	400	20.1	593	29.8	660	33.1	111	5.6	227	11.4
Handicapping condition												
All conditions, 14 to 21+	236,481	100.0	98,442	41.6	26,829	11.3	5,971	2.5	65,274	27.6	39,965	16.9
Learning disabled	121,581	100.0	58,053	47.7	10,373	8.5	844	0.7	32,505	26.7	19,806	16.3
Speech impaired	10,605	100.0	3,719	35.1	854	8.1	140	1.3	1,881	17.7	4,011	37.8
Mentally retarded	53,141	100.0	18,335	34.5	11,419	21.5	3,241	6.1	14,241	26.8	5,905	11.1
Emotionally disturbed	34,091	100.0	10,552	31.0	1,702	5.0	498	1.5	13,683	40.1	7,656	22.5
Hard of hearing/deaf	4,489	100.0	2,541	56.6	506	11.3	256	5.7	664	14.8	522	11.6
Orthopedically impaired	3,384	100.0	1,645	48.6	418	12.4	121	3.6	556	16.4	644	19.0
Other health impaired	3,309	100.0	1,179	35.6	545	16.5	169	5.1	725	21.9	691	20.9
Visually handicapped	1,654	100.0	925	55.9	160	9.7	37	2.2	300	18.1	232	14.0
Multihandicapped	3,921	100.0	1,374	35.0	794	20.2	640	16.3	640	16.3	473	12.1
Deaf-blind	306	100.0	119	38.9	58	19.0	25	8.2	79	25.8	25	8.2

[1] Upper age limits for service eligibility vary by State.

[2] These figures reflect an estimate of those who were actually known to have dropped out and do not include youth who simply stopped coming to school or whose status was unknown.

[3] Includes students who died or no longer received special education services, but whose exit reason is unknown.

[4] Includes data for students not reported by specific age.

NOTE.—It can be assumed that a substantial proportion of the "Other" category includes students who are no longer in school and have neither graduated nor reached the maximum age. Therefore, the overall dropout figure probably exceeds 27 percent.

SOURCE: U.S. Department of Education, Office of Special Education and Rehabilitative Services, The Twelfth Annual Report to Congress on the Implementation of the Education of the Handicapped Act, 1989. (This table was prepared May 1990.)

Table 101.—Employment status, wages earned, and living arrangements of special education students out of high school more than 1 year: 1987[1]

Type of handicap	Percent of youth working for pay		Average hourly wage earned	Percent earning		Percent living	
	Full-time	Part-time		Less than $3.00	More than $5.00	Independently[2]	With parents
1	2	3	4	5	6	7	8
All conditions	**29.2**	**17.2**	**$4.35**	**11.9**	**21.0**	**17.3**	**68.9**
Learning disabled	37.9	19.3	4.63	7.6	25.0	22.0	66.6
Speech impaired	28.8	21.2	4.09	13.9	26.5	13.2	73.0
Mentally retarded	19.8	11.6	3.68	24.7	11.5	9.2	75.7
Emotionally disturbed	18.5	21.5	3.94	16.3	12.4	15.1	65.9
Hard of hearing	22.9	22.6	4.08	6.5	26.2	16.6	77.8
Deaf	23.6	14.7	4.08	3.4	6.6	20.2	71.6
Orthopedically impaired	1.3	12.6	(3)	(3)	(3)	11.8	76.8
Other health impaired	13.9	14.9	(3)	(3)	(3)	15.8	70.8
Visually handicapped	10.0	14.3	3.12	29.3	10.6	26.0	64.4
Multihandicapped	1.3	4.4	(3)	(3)	(3)	3.1	50.2
Deaf-blind	0.0	9.5	(3)	(3)	(3)	(3)	(3)

[1] Data based on students who completed, reached maximum age for services, or dropped out of high school during the 1985–86 school year.

[2] Living independently includes living alone, with a spouse or roommate, in military housing, or in a college dormitory.

[3] Too few cases to report.

SOURCE: U.S. Department of Education, Office of Special Education and Rehabilitative Services, The Eleventh Annual Report to Congress on the Implementation of The Education of the Handicapped Act, 1989. (This table was prepared December 1988.)

Table 102.—Student proficiency in reading, by age and selected characteristics of students: 1970–71 to 1987–88

Selected characteristics of students	9-year-olds				13-year-olds				17-year-olds [1]			
	1970–71	1979–80	1983–84	1987–88	1970–71	1979–80	1983–84	1987–88	1970–71	1979–80	1983–84	1987–88
1	2	3	4	5	6	7	8	9	10	11	12	13
Total	207.3	214.8	211.0	211.8	255.2	258.5	257.1	257.5	285.4	285.8	288.8	290.1
Sex												
Male	200.9	209.7	207.7	207.5	249.5	254.3	252.7	251.8	279.0	282.1	283.8	286.0
Female	213.7	220.0	214.2	216.3	260.9	262.7	261.7	263.0	291.5	289.5	293.9	293.8
Race/ethnicity												
White	213.8	221.3	218.3	217.7	260.9	264.4	262.6	261.3	291.4	293.1	295.6	294.7
Black	170.0	189.2	185.7	188.5	222.4	232.4	236.0	242.9	238.6	242.5	264.2	274.4
Hispanic	(2)	189.5	187.2	193.7	(2)	236.8	239.6	240.1	(2)	260.7	268.1	270.8
Television watched per day												
0 to 2 hours	—	219.9	219.3	217.0	—	263.3	268.1	264.3	—	291.0	297.4	295.6
3 to 5 hours	—	222.3	218.3	218.2	—	257.1	261.6	258.7	—	277.1	284.5	285.4
6 hours or more	—	211.0	198.9	198.1	—	243.2	244.2	245.5	—	257.7	267.8	268.6
Parental education												
Not high school graduate	188.4	193.9	195.1	192.5	238.5	238.5	240.1	246.5	261.6	261.9	269.3	267.4
Graduated high school	207.7	212.7	208.9	210.8	255.5	253.6	253.2	252.7	283.3	277.4	281.1	282.0
Post high school	223.7	225.9	222.9	220.0	270.2	270.9	267.7	265.3	302.3	299.3	301.2	299.5
Reading material in the home [3]												
0 to 2 items	186.2	197.7	196.4	198.5	226.6	235.8	238.4	242.9	246.2	257.6	264.1	268.8
3 items	207.9	216.6	216.6	214.8	248.9	253.1	254.3	255.6	273.9	278.5	283.0	287.1
4 items	222.8	227.9	227.1	223.0	266.5	268.5	266.1	264.2	295.6	295.6	296.3	295.8
Region												
Northeast	213.0	220.9	215.9	215.2	261.2	260.1	260.4	258.6	292.2	285.4	292.0	294.8
Southeast	194.3	210.2	204.3	207.2	245.0	252.7	256.4	257.6	270.8	281.0	284.6	285.5
Central	214.4	216.5	215.6	218.2	260.0	264.6	258.7	255.9	290.8	288.6	290.1	291.2
West	204.6	212.4	209.1	207.9	253.5	256.3	253.9	257.9	283.7	286.6	289.1	289.0

[1] All participants of this age were in school.
[2] Test scores of Hispanics were not tabulated separately.
[3] The 4 items for the scale were: (1) newspaper subscription; (2) magazine subscription; (3) more than 25 books in home; and (4) encyclopedia at home.
— Data not available.

NOTE.—The NAEP scores have been evaluated at certain performance levels. A score of 300 (adept) implies an ability to find, understand, summarize, and explain relatively complicated literary and informational material. A score of 250 (intermediate) im-

plies an ability to search for specific information, interrelate ideas, and make generalizations about literature, science, and social studies materials. A score of 200 (basic) implies an ability to understand, combine, and make inferences based on short uncomplicated passages about specific or sequentially related information. A score of 150 implies an ability to follow written directions and select phrases to describe pictures.

SOURCE: U.S. Department of Education, National Center for Education Statistics, National Assessment of Educational Progress, *The Reading Report Card, 1971–88,* by Educational Testing Service. (This table was prepared March 1990.)

Table 103.—Student proficiency in reading, by percentile and age: 1970–71 to 1987–88

Percentile	9-year-olds				13-year-olds				17-year-olds [1]			
	1970–71	1979–80	1983–84	1987–88	1970–71	1979–80	1983–84	1987–88	1970–71	1979–80	1983–84	1987–88
1	2	3	4	5	6	7	8	9	10	11	12	13
Average	207.3	214.8	211.0	211.8	255.2	258.5	257.1	257.5	285.4	285.8	288.8	290.1
Standard deviation	42.0	38.0	41.1	41.2	35.7	34.8	35.5	34.7	45.7	41.9	40.3	37.1
Percentiles												
5th	135.7	149.2	141.3	142.0	193.9	200.2	197.3	199.7	207.7	213.7	220.8	226.2
10th	152.1	165.4	157.2	156.8	208.5	213.3	210.6	213.0	226.4	231.1	236.6	241.5
25th	180.0	191.1	183.9	184.3	232.6	235.6	234.0	234.3	256.5	259.2	262.7	265.8
50th	209.2	217.2	212.7	213.7	257.1	259.7	258.3	257.9	288.1	288.0	290.4	291.1
75th	236.6	241.3	239.7	240.1	280.0	282.9	281.6	281.4	316.9	315.1	316.8	316.0
90th	260.3	261.6	262.9	263.0	299.6	302.4	301.7	301.6	341.9	337.8	339.6	336.9
95th	273.9	273.1	276.5	277.5	310.9	314.0	313.7	313.7	356.6	351.1	352.6	348.7

[1] All participants of this age were in school.

NOTE.—The NAEP scores have been evaluated at certain performance levels. A score of 300 (adept) implies an ability to find, understand, summarize, and explain relatively complicated literary and informational material. A score of 250 (intermediate) implies an ability to search for specific information, interrelate ideas, and make generalizations about literature, science, and social studies materials. A score of 200 (basic) im-

plies an ability to understand, combine ideas, and make inferences based on short uncomplicated passages about specific or sequentially related information. A score of 150 implies an ability to follow written directions and select phrases to describe pictures.

SOURCE: U.S. Department of Education, National Center for Education Statistics, National Assessment of Educational Progress, *The Reading Report Card, 1971–88,* by Educational Testing Service. (This table was prepared March 1990.)

Table 104.—Student proficiency in reading, by age, amount of time spent on homework and reading habits: 1979–80, 1983–84, and 1987–88

Age and year	Amount of time spend on homework						Reading of books, newspapers, and magazines [1]			
	Total	None	Did not do assigned homework	Less than 1 hour	1 to 2 hours	More than 2 hours	Total	Yearly or monthly	Weekly	Daily
1	2	3	4	5	6	7	8	9	10	11
Percent										
9-year-olds										
1983–84	100.0	35.6	4.1	41.5	12.7	6.1	100.0	58.7	30.5	10.7
1987–88	100.0	28.8	4.5	47.0	12.7	7.0	100.0	63.8	26.8	9.4
13-year-olds										
1979–80	100.0	31.6	6.0	31.3	23.9	7.2	—	—	—	—
1983–84	100.0	22.6	3.7	35.9	29.2	8.6	100.0	30.1	48.9	21.0
1987–88	100.0	17.1	4.4	37.4	30.4	10.7	100.0	32.9	47.7	19.4
17-year-olds [2]										
1979–80	100.0	31.0	12.6	23.9	22.8	9.7	—	—	—	—
1983–84	100.0	22.4	11.4	26.2	26.8	13.2	100.0	20.2	53.3	26.5
1987–88	100.0	20.8	13.4	27.8	26.0	12.0	100.0	24.4	54.3	21.3
Proficiency score										
9-year-olds										
1983–84	211.0	211.0	197.9	215.6	215.2	199.9	211.0	206.7	219.5	211.2
1987–88	211.8	212.4	195.0	215.3	213.4	199.8	211.8	209.7	219.8	212.9
13-year-old										
1979–80	258.5	253.5	251.3	259.8	264.4	261.9	—	—	—	—
1983–84	257.1	253.0	246.3	260.0	265.6	264.1	257.1	244.2	260.7	268.8
1987–88	257.5	251.0	248.1	258.9	262.3	263.9	257.5	249.7	264.0	267.5
17-year-olds [2]										
1979–80	285.8	276.2	285.8	288.4	292.5	298.2	—	—	—	—
1983–84	288.8	273.8	285.2	288.6	295.4	303.4	288.8	269.6	287.6	298.6
1987–88	290.1	277.2	287.5	289.4	296.8	304.0	290.1	273.2	291.8	301.8

[1] Reading in or out of school.

[2] All participants of this age were enrolled in school.

NOTE.—The NAEP scores have been evaluated at certain performance levels. A score of 300 (adept) implies an ability to find, understand, summarize, and explain relatively complicated literary and informational material. A score of 250 (intermediate) implies an ability to search for specific information, interrelate ideas, and make generalizations about literature, science, and social studies materials. A score of 200 (basic) im-plies an ability to understand, combine ideas, and make inferences based on short un-complicated passages about specific or sequentially related information. A score of 150 implies an ability to follow written directions and select phrases to describe pictures.

SOURCE: U.S. Department of Education, National Center for Education Statistics, National Assessment of Educational Progress, *The Reading Report Card, 1971–88,* by Educational Testing Service. (This table was prepared March 1990.)

Table 105.—Student reading in school, by type of reading material: 1983–84 and 1987–88

Type of reading	Percent of students reporting ever reading selected types of materials					
	9-year-olds		13-year-olds		17-year-olds	
	1983–84	1987–88	1983–84	1987–88	1983–84	1987–88
1	2	3	4	5	6	7
Biographies	45.1	44.0	62.2	65.8	58.9	64.1
Books about other times and places	79.0	80.4	83.4	81.1	81.4	78.7
Plays	55.6	52.8	59.2	66.6	63.4	70.3
Poems	70.4	69.2	68.4	74.9	76.0	81.7
Science books	84.0	89.8	89.8	92.8	69.6	74.6

[1] All participants of this age were in school.

SOURCE: U.S. Department of Education, National Center for Education Statistics, National Assessment of Educational Progress, *The Reading Report Card, 1971–88,* by Educational Testing Service. (This table was prepared April 1990.)

Table 106.—Percentage of students at or above selected reading proficiency levels, by race/ethnicity and age: 1970–71 to 1987–88

Year, sex, and race/ethnicity	9-year olds[1]					13-year olds[1]					17-year olds[2]				
	1970–71	1974–75	1979–80	1983–84	1987–88	1970–71	1974–75	1979–80	1983–84	1987–88	1970–71	1974–75	1979–80	1983–84	1987–88
1	2	3	4	5	6	7	8	9	10	11	12	13	14	15	16
Total															
Rudimentary[3]	90.5	93.2	94.6	92.5	93.0	99.8	99.7	99.9	99.8	99.8	99.6	99.7	99.8	100.0	100.0
Basic[4]	58.2	62.2	67.6	61.9	62.5	92.8	93.3	94.9	94.1	95.1	95.9	96.4	97.2	98.3	98.9
Intermediate[5]	15.3	14.6	17.2	17.0	17.0	57.9	58.6	60.9	59.1	58.0	78.5	80.4	81.0	83.1	86.2
Adept[6]	1.0	0.5	0.6	1.0	1.2	9.8	10.3	11.3	10.9	10.6	39.2	39.1	38.5	40.0	41.8
Advanced[7]	—	—	—	—	—	0.1	0.2	0.2	0.2	0.2	6.6	6.1	5.3	5.5	4.8
Male															
Rudimentary[3]	87.5	91.1	92.9	90.5	91.0	99.7	99.6	99.8	99.7	99.6	[2]	[2]	[2]	[2]	[2]
Basic[4]	52.0	56.3	62.2	58.6	58.1	90.3	91.0	93.4	92.5	93.5	94.5	95.4	96.2	97.7	98.4
Intermediate[5]	11.8	11.3	14.1	15.8	15.7	51.8	51.5	56.1	53.9	51.3	74.6	76.2	78.2	79.2	83.2
Adept[6]	0.8	0.3	0.4	0.8	0.6	7.3	7.0	9.1	8.9	8.2	34.0	33.9	35.7	35.4	37.3
Advanced[7]	—	—	—	—	—	—	—	—	—	—	5.0	5.2	4.6	4.7	3.9
Female															
Rudimentary[3]	93.4	95.4	96.4	94.5	95.0	99.9	99.9	99.9	99.9	100.0	[2]	[2]	[2]	[2]	[2]
Basic[4]	64.3	68.2	72.9	65.2	66.9	95.3	95.7	96.3	95.8	96.7	97.3	97.4	98.1	98.9	99.3
Intermediate[5]	18.7	17.9	20.2	18.1	18.4	64.0	65.7	65.6	64.1	64.6	82.2	84.3	83.9	87.0	89.0
Adept[6]	1.3	0.8	0.7	1.1	1.7	12.2	13.6	13.5	13.1	13.0	44.1	44.1	41.3	44.8	45.9
Advanced[7]	—	—	—	—	—	—	—	—	—	—	8.3	7.0	6.1	6.5	5.7
White[8]															
Rudimentary[3]	94.0	96.0	97.2	95.4	94.9	99.9	99.9	100.0	99.9	99.9	[2]	[2]	[2]	[2]	[2]
Basic[4]	64.4	68.8	74.3	69.1	68.3	96.0	96.4	97.2	96.3	96.6	97.7	98.6	99.1	99.1	99.5
Intermediate[5]	17.7	17.6	20.5	20.8	19.7	64.3	65.4	67.7	65.5	63.3	83.5	86.1	87.3	87.9	89.3
Adept[6]	1.2	0.6	0.7	1.2	1.4	11.3	12.0	13.6	13.3	12.3	43.3	44.0	44.1	46.3	46.3
Advanced[7]	—	—	—	—	—	—	—	—	—	—	7.5	7.0	6.3	6.5	5.7
Black[8]															
Rudimentary[3]	69.6	81.1	84.7	82.0	85.6	98.8	98.4	99.1	99.4	99.7	[2]	[2]	[2]	[2]	[2]
Basic[4]	21.9	33.2	40.8	35.7	39.2	74.4	77.4	84.0	85.5	90.7	82.0	81.1	84.9	95.8	97.1
Intermediate[5]	2.1	1.9	3.6	4.2	5.9	21.8	25.6	30.8	34.4	39.2	39.7	42.4	43.9	66.0	76.0
Adept[6]	—	—	—	—	0.1	0.9	1.7	1.5	2.1	4.0	7.5	7.9	6.7	16.3	25.8
Advanced[7]	—	—	—	—	—	—	—	—	—	—	0.3	0.3	0.2	0.9	1.9
Hispanic															
Rudimentary[3]	—	80.5	83.5	82.4	86.1	—	99.6	99.8	99.5	99.1	[2]	[2]	[2]	[2]	[2]
Basic[4]	—	35.9	40.9	39.9	46.9	—	82.3	87.3	86.4	86.3	—	88.3	93.2	95.6	96.4
Intermediate[5]	—	2.2	4.4	3.8	8.2	—	29.6	36.4	38.6	34.9	—	51.9	61.2	68.4	72.9
Adept[6]	—	—	—	—	—	—	2.3	1.9	3.9	3.1	—	12.9	14.9	20.6	24.3
Advanced[7]	—	—	—	—	—	—	—	—	—	—	—	1.1	1.3	1.9	1.3

[1] Virtually no students were able to read at the advanced level. All participants of this age were in school.
[2] Since virtually all 17-year olds read at the rudimentary level, details of this information by race and sex are not available.
[3] Able to follow brief written directions and select phrases to describe pictures.
[4] Able to understand combined ideas and make references based on short uncomplicated passages about specific or sequentially related information.
[5] Able to search for specific information, interrelate ideas, and make generalizations about literature, science, and social studies materials.
[6] Able to find, understand, summarize, and explain relatively complicated literary and informational material.

[7] Able to understand the links between ideas even when those links are not explicitly stated and to make appropriate generalizations even when the texts lack clear introductions or explanations.
[8] Data for 1970–71 include persons of Hispanic origin.
—Data not available.

SOURCE: U.S. Department of Education, National Center for Education Statistics, *National Assessment of Educational Progress, The Reading Report Card, 1971–88*, by Educational Testing Service. (This table was prepared September 1990.)

Table 107.—Writing performance of 4th, 8th, and 11th graders, by sex, race/ethnicity, and region: 1984 and 1988

Sex, race/ethnicity and region	4th graders		8th graders		11th graders	
	1984	1988	1984	1988	1984	1988
1	2	3	4	5	6	7
All students	**170.5**	**173.3**	**212.4**	**208.2**	**223.0**	**220.7**
Sex						
Male	165.0	164.3	204.5	197.9	211.9	211.1
Female	176.7	182.4	220.5	218.2	234.5	229.2
Race/ethnicity						
White	177.2	180.0	217.9	213.1	229.1	225.3
Black	148.2	150.7	188.3	190.1	204.2	206.9
Hispanic	157.9	162.2	194.2	197.2	200.6	202.0
Region						
Northeast	179.1	174.8	219.5	209.3	226.3	224.5
Southeast	168.7	171.3	211.8	209.7	222.1	221.3
Central	169.4	178.2	208.6	204.3	225.1	218.8
West	166.8	169.8	210.5	209.6	218.2	219.1

NOTE.—The writing scale score ranges from 0 to 400 and is defined as the average of a respondent's estimated scores on specific writing tasks. The average response method is used to estimate average writing achievement for each participant as if each had performed all 11 writing tasks.

SOURCE: U.S. Department of Education, National Center for Education Statistics, National Assessment of Educational Progress, *The Writing Report Card, 1984–88,* by Educational Testing Service. (This table was prepared April 1990.)

Table 108.—Student values and attitudes toward writing, by grade level: 1984 and 1988

Statements about writing	Percentage of students reporting the statement is true more than half the time, by grade level					
	Grade 4		Grade 8		Grade 11	
	1984	1988	1984	1988	1984	1988
1	2	3	4	5	6	7
Writing helps me think more clearly	—	—	44.5	44.0	52.4	46.8
Writing helps me tell others what I think	—	—	52.1	53.3	55.3	57.2
Writing helps tell others how I feel	—	—	50.1	54.1	55.4	58.2
Writing helps me understand my own feelings	—	—	40.2	44.7	47.3	48.5
Writing can help me get a good job	33.6	44.6	40.2	52.3	52.9	52.3
Writing helps me share my ideas	52.9	60.9	52.2	59.1	61.6	63.3
Writing helps me show people I know something	62.5	66.9	54.8	64.7	58.3	64.2
People who write well have a better chance of. getting good jobs	—	—	47.0	50.2	54.4	55.6
People who write well are more influential	—	—	49.2	54.5	54.2	58.3
I like to write	55.8	54.6	38.9	41.9	40.3	36.6
I am a good writer	60.0	59.7	41.5	43.7	38.6	40.5
People like what I write	53.4	53.2	38.1	38.0	35.7	37.0
I write on my own outside of school	47.7	44.1	36.4	36.5	31.0	26.4
I don't like to write things that will be graded	37.9	35.1	31.4	33.1	26.7	31.1
If I didn't have to write for school,. I wouldn't write anything	33.4	26.7	17.2	18.6	14.9	15.6

SOURCE: U.S. Department of Education, National Center for Education Statistics, National Assessment of Educational Progress, *The Writing Report Card, 1984–88,* by Educational Testing Service. (This table was prepared April 1990.)

Table 109.—Percentage of students writing at a minimal level or better,[1] by sex and race/ethnicity, by age: 1974, 1979, and 1984

Age, writing task, and year	All students	Sex		Race/ethnicity		
		Male	Female	White	Black	Hispanic
1	2	3	4	5	6	7
Age 9						
Informative writing						
1979	53.4	47.1	59.4	58.4	33.5	29.1
1984	55.7	50.9	60.7	59.7	36.0	51.9
Persuasive writing						
1979	63.7	58.8	68.7	68.0	44.1	45.4
1984	58.2	51.1	65.8	62.6	40.1	50.9
Imaginative writing						
1974	36.7	30.9	42.6	41.3	17.3	22.4
1979	41.4	36.8	46.1	43.6	29.9	36.6
1984	54.6	50.7	58.2	57.3	44.8	46.2
Age 13						
Informative writing						
1979	74.4	68.5	80.6	77.3	60.6	65.3
1984	81.4	78.6	84.2	84.9	64.4	78.8
Persuasive writing						
1979	27.8	27.8	27.9	30.1	18.2	18.6
1984	34.1	33.6	34.6	37.0	26.2	19.9
Imaginative writing						
1974	69.0	63.5	74.1	70.8	57.1	67.0
1979	60.7	55.8	65.9	62.3	53.1	58.3
1984	66.7	61.1	73.1	65.3	75.3	65.7
Age 17[2]						
Informative writing						
1979	87.1	81.6	91.8	89.4	72.8	78.1
1984	89.0	87.4	90.7	91.3	79.5	86.1
Persuasive writing						
1979	60.6	58.7	62.4	62.7	52.5	46.3
1984	63.8	62.3	65.4	67.2	55.7	52.9
Imaginative writing						
1974	76.4	72.1	80.1	77.6	70.3	67.8
1979	71.3	66.0	76.7	72.5	64.7	55.2
1984	75.1	70.6	79.5	76.4	68.4	76.2

[1] Standards for minimal performance level differ by grade level.
[2] All participants of this age group were in school.

NOTE.—Informative writing is used to share knowledge and convey messages, instructions, and ideas. Persuasive writing attempts to bring about some action or change. Imaginative writing provides a special way of sharing our experiences and understanding the world. Five levels of proficiency were defined for each task: non-rateable, unsatisfactory, minimal, adequate, and elaborated. Non-rateable responses included those that were blank, off-task, and unreadable. Unsatisfactory responses were those that failed to reflect a basic understanding of the purpose of the writing. Minimal responses recognized the elements needed to complete the task, but were not managed well enough to ensure that the intended purpose of the writing was achieved. Adequate responses included the features critical to accomplishing the purpose of the writing and were likely to have the intended effect. Elaborated responses went beyond the merely adequate, reflecting a higher level of coherence and elaboration.

SOURCE: U.S. Department of Education, Office of Educational Research and Improvement, National Assessment of Educational Progress, *Writing: Trends Across the Decade, 1974–1984*. (This table was prepared June 1987.)

Table 110.—Student writing in school, by type of writing assignment: 1983–84 and 1987–88

Type of writing assignment	Percent of students reporting at least one paper written for English class last week					
	9-year-olds		13-year-olds		17-year-olds [1]	
	1983–84	1987–88	1983–84	1987–88	1983–84	1987–88
1	2	3	4	5	6	7
Essay, composition, or theme	19.3	25.1	40.9	48.4	59.6	63.6
Book report	36.1	40.5	35.4	34.8	30.4	30.7
Other report	28.3	32.0	26.5	29.4	37.7	38.4
Letter	38.5	38.7	20.8	25.3	15.9	19.6
Story	37.2	43.3	41.6	48.9	39.7	39.7
Poem	25.7	29.7	14.7	14.7	18.3	20.9
Play	13.9	15.2	10.4	12.2	12.6	11.3

[1] All participants of this age were in school.

SOURCE: U.S. Department of Education, National Center for Education Statistics, National Assessment of Educational Progress, *The Writing Report Card, 1984–88,* by Educational Testing Service. (This table was prepared April 1990.)

Table 111.—Student proficiency in geography, U.S. history, and literature, by student characteristics: 1986 and 1988

Characteristic	Percentage distribution of 12th graders in 1988	Geography scores of 12th graders in 1988	History scores in 1988			Literature scores of 11th graders in 1986
			4th graders	8th graders	12th graders	
1	2	3	4	5	6	7
United States	100	293.1	220.6	263.9	295.0	285.0
Sex						
Male	48	301.2	222.9	266.2	298.5	282.8
Female	52	285.7	218.2	261.6	291.8	287.3
Race						
White	76	301.1	227.5	270.4	301.1	289.9
Black	14	258.4	199.5	246.0	274.4	267.5
Hispanic	7	271.8	202.7	244.3	273.9	264.8
Region						
Northeast	26	295.0	222.6	270.1	296.9	293.0
Southeast	23	283.3	215.5	258.0	289.2	282.6
Central	25	298.2	223.8	265.3	297.9	284.3
West	26	295.3	220.7	262.8	295.5	280.4
Size and type of community						
Rural	[1] 5	—	220.0	266.8	296.2	273.7
Urban disadvantaged	[1] 5	—	198.2	246.2	273.8	265.2
Urban advantaged	[1] 14	—	236.9	275.9	307.8	301.4
School program						
Academic	59	304.0	—	—	307.1	298.7
General	32	278.0	—	—	279.8	271.7
Vocational/technical	9	276.0	—	—	275.1	265.9
Hours of TV viewing each day						
0 to 2 hours	51	300.0	222.6	269.6	299.0	—
3 to 5 hours	44	289.0	225.5	265.0	293.3	—
6 or more hours	6	266.0	210.8	251.1	276.7	—

Characteristic	Percentage distribution of 12th graders in 1988	Geography scores of 12th graders in 1988	History scores in 1988			Literature scores of 11th graders in 1986
			4th graders	8th graders	12th graders	
1	2	3	4	5	6	7
Hours spent on homework each day.						
None assigned	8	277.0	223.6	253.4	280.7	—
Did not do it	9	289.0	209.0	247.2	291.6	—
½ hour or less	21	295.0	221.6	264.2	295.4	—
1 hour	34	294.0	223.2	265.7	295.6	—
2 hours	17	295.0	—	267.9	299.4	—
More than 2 hours	10	299.0	—	267.2	302.4	—
Parents' level of education.						
Not high school diploma	8	267.0	202.7	244.9	274.2	266.2
Graduated high school	24	283.5	214.1	256.1	285.3	273.4
Some college	23	294.2	228.0	269.1	296.8	288.3
Graduated college	43	305.3	231.4	274.9	306.0	297.6
Reading materials in the home.						
0 to 2 types	13	273.0	207.7	246.6	275.0	—
0 to 3 types	—	—	—	—	—	265.4
3 types	24	287.0	220.2	261.3	289.3	—
4 types	63	300.0	231.1	272.0	302.0	279.3
5 types	—	—	—	—	—	291.7
Parents living at home.						
Both	78	297.0	223.1	268.1	298.9	290.3
One parent	17	285.0	212.2	255.1	289.7	282.1
Neither	5	274.0	202.0	248.3	273.2	271.6
Mothers working outside the home.						
Full-time	55	293.0	—	265.3	296.3	288.1
Part-time	17	299.0	—	267.4	299.9	292.5
Not at all	25	295.0	—	264.2	295.3	286.2

[1] Data are for 11th graders in 1986.

—Data not available.

NOTE.—As with the NAEP reading scale, these scales range from 0 to 500. However, the distribution of scores varies by subject. Therefore, avoid direct score comparisons among the subjects.

SOURCE: U.S. Department of Education, National Center for Education Statistics, National Assessment of Educational Progress, Literature and U.S. History, *The U.S. History Report Card,* and *The Geography Learning of High-School Seniors,* prepared by Educational Testing Service. (This table was prepared in October 1990.)

Table 112.—Percentage of students at or above selected history proficiency levels, by age, sex, race/ethnicity, and region: 1988

Sex, region, and race/ethnicity	4th graders [1]			8th graders				12th graders			
	Simple historical facts [2]	Beginning historical information and interpretation [3]	Basic historical terms and relationships [4]	Simple historical facts [2]	Beginning historical information and interpretation [3]	Basic historical terms and relationships [4]	Interprets historical information an ideas [5]	Simple historical facts [2]	Beginning historical information and interpretation [3]	Basic historical terms and relationships [4]	Interprets historical information an ideas [5]
1	2	3	4	5	6	7	8	9	10	11	12
All students	**76.0**	**15.9**	**0.2**	**96.0**	**67.7**	**12.7**	**0.1**	**99.4**	**88.9**	**45.9**	**4.6**
Female	77.1	19.0	0.3	95.6	69.2	15.7	0.2	99.2	88.3	50.8	6.5
Male	74.9	12.7	0.1	96.5	66.2	9.8	(6)	99.6	89.4	41.4	2.8
White	84.8	19.8	0.3	97.4	75.9	15.7	0.1	99.6	92.7	52.8	5.5
Black	49.0	4.2	(6)	93.2	44.9	3.5	(6)	99.0	77.3	21.2	0.5
Hispanic	54.3	4.2	(6)	91.2	43.8	4.1	(6)	98.4	76.1	23.2	1.4
Region											
Northeast	77.1	18.8	0.1	97.2	73.7	17.2	0.2	99.3	89.9	48.6	6.2
Southeast	69.2	13.0	0.1	94.9	61.0	8.9	0.1	99.1	87.4	37.7	3.0
Central	82.0	17.7	0.2	96.5	69.5	12.9	0.1	99.7	90.8	49.9	4.7
West	76.4	14.7	0.4	95.7	66.9	12.1	(6)	99.6	87.4	46.6	4.2

[1] Virtually no students were able to interpret historical information and ideas.

[2] Score of 200 or more. Know some historical facts of the type learned from everyday experiences and able to read simple timelines, graphs, and maps.

[3] Score of 250 or more. Know a variety of historical facts of the type learned from historical studies. Developing sense of chronology.

[4] Score of 300 or more. Demonstrate broad knowledge of historical terms, facts, regions, and ideas. Some knowledge of content of primary texts in U.S. political history.

[5] Score of 350 or more. Detailed understanding of historical vocabulary, facts, regions, and ideas. Able to relate social science concepts to historical themes and can evaluate causal relationships.

[6] Virtually no students were able to perform at this level.

SOURCE: U.S. Department of Education, National Center for Education Statistics, National Assessment of Educational Progress, *The U.S. History Report Card*, prepared by Educational Testing Service. (This table was prepared April 1990.)

Table 113.—Average percentage of students responding correctly to history questions, by time period and grade: 1988

Area of test	Average percent correct			Area of test	Average percent correct		
	Grade 4	Grade 8	Grade 12		Grade 4	Grade 8	Grade 12
1	2	3	4	1	2	3	4
All items	**61.1**	**60.2**	**60.3**				
Exploration and colonization, up to 1763				Rise of modern America and World War I, 1877-1920			
All items given at a grade	70.2	75.8	64.6	All items given at a grade	60.1	50.7	57.1
14 items given at grades 4 and 8	70.2	85.8	—	14 items given at grades 8 and 12	—	37.5	54.6
6 items given at grades 8 and 12	—	55.9	71.3				
Revolutionary era, Constitution and New Republic, 1763 to 1815				United States, 1920-1941			
All items given at a grade	54.3	61.0	58.8	All items given at a grade	46.4	51.7	59.2
13 items given at grades 4 and 8	54.3	75.1	—	7 items given at grades 8 and 12	—	42.6	62.9
15 items given at grades 8 and 12	—	51.0	62.9	World War II and postwar era, 1931-1968			
Economic and social development of antebellum republic, 1790-1861				All items given at a grade	62.2	54.8	59.6
All items given at a grade	56.5	64.1	62.6	9 items given at grades 8 and 12	—	46.9	61.3
8 items given at grades 8 and 12	—	60.4	71.4	Modern post-industrial era, 1968 to present			
Crisis of the Union: Origins, Civil War and Reconstruction, 1850-1877				All items given at a grade	61.3	54.7	61.7
All items given at a grade	63.5	59.7	61.2	9 items given at grades 8 and 12	—	50.2	68.4
12 items given at grades 8 and 12	—	55.7	68.8				

—Not applicable.

SOURCE: U.S. Department of Education, National Center for Education Statistics, National Assessment of Educational Progress, *The U.S. History Report Card*, prepared by Educational Testing Service. (This table was prepared in April 1990.)

Table 114.—Mathematics proficiency, by age and by selected characteristics of students: 1977–78, 1981–82, and 1985–86

Selected characteristics of students	9-year-olds			13-year-olds			17-year-olds[1]		
	1977–78	1981–82	1985–86	1977–78	1981–82	1985–86	1977–78	1981–82	1985–86
1	2	3	4	5	6	7	8	9	10
All students	**219**	**219**	**222**	**264**	**269**	**269**	**300**	**299**	**302**
Sex									
Male	217	217	222	264	269	270	304	302	305
Female	220	221	222	265	268	268	297	296	299
Race/ethnicity									
White	224	224	227	272	274	274	306	304	308
Black	192	195	202	230	240	249	268	272	279
Hispanic	203	204	205	238	252	254	276	277	283
Television watched per day									
0 to 2 hours	—	218	222	—	273	276	305	303	310
3 to 5 hours	—	227	229	—	269	271	296	294	299
6 or more hours	—	215	213	—	256	255	279	280	282
Reading materials in the home [1]									
0 to 2 items	201	203	208	239	250	255	277	281	281
3 items	221	221	224	260	267	266	296	295	297
4 items	231	231	234	275	279	276	308	306	309

[1] All participants of this age were in school.

[2] The 4 items in the scale were: newspaper subscription; magazine subscription; more than 25 books in the home; and encyclopedia in the home.

—Data not available.

NOTE.—Performers at the 150 level know some basic addition and subtraction facts, and most can add two-digit numbers without regrouping. They recognize simple situations in which addition and subtraction apply. Performers at the 200 level have considerable understanding of two-digit numbers and know some basic multiplication and division facts. Performers at the 250 level have an initial understanding of the four basic operations. They can also compare information from graphs and charts, and are developing an ability to analyze simple logical relations. Performers at the 300 level can compute decimals, simple fractions, and percents. They can identify geometric figures, measure simple fractions, and percents. They can identify geometric figures, measure lengths and angles, and calculate areas of rectangles. They are developing the skills to operate with signed numbers, exponents, and square roots. Performers at the 350 level can apply a range of reasoning skills to solve multi-step problems. They can solve routine problems involving fractions and percents, recognize properties of basic geometric figures, and work with exponents and square roots.

SOURCE: U.S. Department of Education, National Center for Education Statistics, National Assessment of Educational Progress, *The Mathematics Report Card*, prepared by Educational Testing Service. (This table was prepared January 1989.)

Table 115.—Percentage of students at or above five mathematics proficiency levels, by race/ethnicity and age: 1977–78, 1981–82, and 1985–86

Year and race/ethnicity	9-year-old [1]				13-year-olds [2]				17-year-olds [2]			
	Simple arithmetic facts	Beginning skills and understanding	Basic operations and beginning problem solving	Moderately complex procedures and reasoning	Beginning skills and understanding	Basic operations and beginning problem solving	Moderately complex procedures and reasoning	Multistep problems and algebra	Beginning skills and understanding	Basic operations and beginning problem solving	Moderately complex procedures and reasoning	Multistep problems and algebra
1	2	3	4	5	6	7	8	9	10	11	12	13
1977–78												
All students	**96.5**	**70.3**	**19.4**	**0.8**	**94.5**	**64.9**	**17.9**	**0.9**	**99.8**	**92.1**	**51.4**	**7.4**
White	98.3	76.0	22.5	0.9	97.5	72.9	21.4	1.1	100.0	95.8	57.3	8.6
Black	87.8	42.5	4.3	(3)	79.5	28.9	2.1	(3)	98.7	70.0	18.0	0.4
Hispanic	93.5	54.3	10.8	0.5	85.9	35.6	3.4	0.1	99.3	77.4	22.1	1.1
1981–82												
All students	**97.2**	**71.5**	**18.7**	**0.6**	**97.6**	**71.6**	**17.8**	**0.5**	**99.9**	**92.9**	**48.3**	**5.4**
White	98.6	76.9	21.5	0.7	99.1	78.5	20.9	0.6	100.0	96.3	54.5	6.3
Black	90.4	46.7	4.5	(3)	89.0	38.1	3.3	(3)	99.6	75.3	17.3	0.6
Hispanic	95.0	55.0	9.2	(3)	96.1	54.2	6.2	0.2	99.9	81.3	20.6	0.5
1985–86												
All students	**97.8**	**73.9**	**20.8**	**0.6**	**98.5**	**73.1**	**15.9**	**0.4**	**99.9**	**96.0**	**51.1**	**6.4**
White	98.9	79.2	24.5	0.7	99.2	78.7	18.6	0.5	99.9	98.3	58.0	7.6
Black	93.0	53.3	5.4	(3)	95.5	49.4	4.0	0.1	100.0	86.0	21.7	0.3
Hispanic	96.4	58.7	8.0	(3)	96.1	55.2	5.4	0.3	98.9	90.8	26.8	1.2

[1] Virtually no students were able to perform multi-step problems and algebra.

[2] Virtually all students knew simple arithmetic facts. Data are only for students enrolled in school.

[3] Virtually no students were able to perform at this level.

SOURCE: U.S. Department of Education, National Center for Education Statistics, National Assessment of Educational Progress, *The Mathematics Report Card*, prepared by Educational Testing Service. (This table was prepared January 1989.)

Table 116.—Average proficiency in mathematics content areas for 8th graders in public schools, by region and State: 1990

Region and selected States	Average proficiency in content areas						Percentage of students at or above		
	Average proficiency, all areas	Numbers and operations	Measurement	Geometry	Data analysis, statistics, and probability	Algebra and functions	Level 200 [1]	Level 250 [2]	Level 300 [3]
1	2	3	4	5	6	7	8	9	10
United States	**261**	**266**	**258**	**259**	**262**	**260**	**97**	**64**	**12**
Region									
Northest	269	271	266	268	273	267	99	72	16
Southeast	253	259	246	249	250	254	94	52	8
Central	265	270	263	262	265	263	98	70	12
West	261	264	258	260	262	259	97	63	12
State									
Alabama	252	259	247	248	251	251	96	52	7
Arizona	259	264	257	256	258	258	98	61	10
Arkansas	256	262	253	253	254	253	97	57	7
California	256	259	252	255	254	256	95	56	11
Colorado	267	269	265	266	269	266	99	72	14
Connecticut	270	273	269	266	272	268	98	72	19
Delaware	261	265	258	256	261	260	97	60	13
District of Columbia	231	238	221	229	222	235	86	23	2
Florida	255	260	251	251	255	255	96	54	10
Georgia	258	263	252	256	260	257	96	59	12
Hawaii	251	256	249	252	242	249	93	49	10
Idaho	272	274	270	269	274	269	100	79	15
Illinois	260	265	256	256	262	260	96	64	12
Indiana	267	271	263	264	269	265	99	71	14
Iowa	278	283	277	275	281	274	100	84	21
Kentucky	256	261	253	253	257	256	98	57	8
Louisiana	246	253	241	242	243	245	94	43	4
Maryland	260	264	256	256	260	263	96	61	14
Michigan	264	268	260	262	264	264	98	67	13
Minnesota	276	279	272	273	279	274	99	82	20
Montana	280	282	279	280	282	278	100	88	23
Nebraska	276	279	274	273	279	273	99	81	21
New Hampshire	273	275	272	272	276	271	100	79	17
New Jersey	269	274	267	266	270	268	99	72	19
New Mexico	256	258	253	257	253	256	98	56	8
New York	261	263	255	259	263	260	96	62	13
North Carolina	250	255	241	249	247	251	94	49	7
North Dakota	281	286	280	278	286	275	100	88	24
Ohio	264	268	259	260	266	262	98	67	12
Oklahoma	263	268	258	259	264	262	99	67	10
Oregon	271	273	269	270	274	270	99	76	18
Pennsylvania	266	270	265	263	268	265	98	69	15
Rhode Island	260	264	256	256	258	261	96	61	12
Texas	258	262	253	258	256	256	97	58	10
Virginia	264	268	259	261	264	265	98	64	15
West Virginia	256	260	252	254	256	254	98	56	7
Wisconsin	274	278	273	272	277	271	99	80	20
Wyoming	272	275	270	270	274	270	100	80	15
Outlying areas									
Guam	231	239	227	236	213	230	81	28	3
Virgin Islands	218	227	214	222	196	218	76	11	0

[1] Indicates ability to perform simple additive reasoning and problem solving.

[2] Indicates ability to perform simple multiplicative reasoning and 2-step problem solving.

[3] Indicates ability to perform reasoning and problem solving involving fractions, decimals, percents, elementary geometry, and simple algebra.

SOURCE: U.S. Department of Education, National Center for Education Statistics, National Assessment of Educational Progress, *The State of Mathematics Achievement*, prepared by Educational Testing Service. (This table was prepared June 1991.)

Table 117.—Selected characteristics of 8th grade students in public schools, by region and State: 1990 [1]

Region and selected States	Math units required for gradua-tion, 1989	Passing competency test in math required for gradua-tion in 1989	Length of school year in 1989	Teachers' reports on average hours of math instruction provided each week	Percent of students reporting					
					Spending more than 30 minutes on math homework	Spending 1 or 2 hours on all homework	Spending more than 2 hours on all homework	Positive attitudes towards math [2]	Both parents living at home	Watching 6 or more hours of tele-vision each day
1	2	3	4	5	6	7	8	9	10	11
Total	—	—	—	3.5	60	59	7	76	75	16
Region										
Northest	—	—	—	3.4	57	64	7	79	78	15
Southeast	—	—	—	3.8	64	57	10	75	69	18
Central	—	—	—	3.3	59	60	5	75	77	14
West	—	—	—	3.4	57	58	8	75	78	16
State										
Alabama	2	Yes	175	3.7	64	61	7	78	75	18
Arizona	2	No	175	3.3	67	60	7	74	75	12
Arkansas [3]	3	Yes	178	3.4	63	56	6	76	77	20
California	2	Yes	180	3.5	64	62	11	76	78	11
Colorado	(4)	No	180	3.3	63	61	7	77	78	9
Connecticut	3	No	180	3.5	59	69	8	80	79	12
Delaware	2	No	180	3.5	56	63	6	77	75	18
District of Columbia	2	No	190	3.5	68	62	9	86	47	33
Florida	3	No	180	3.5	57	53	6	77	75	19
Georgia	2	Yes	180	3.8	60	59	7	79	73	17
Hawaii	2	Yes	183	3.4	70	55	12	72	78	23
Idaho	2	No	180	3.1	57	56	5	78	84	7
Illinois	2	No	180	3.3	64	64	10	79	78	14
Indiana	2	No	180	3.3	61	63	6	79	81	11
Iowa	(4)	No	180	3.2	61	63	5	81	83	8
Kentucky	3	No	175	3.6	62	57	7	78	79	14
Louisiana	3	Yes	180	3.7	61	61	10	79	73	19
Maryland	3	Yes	180	3.7	58	64	8	81	75	19
Michigan	(4)	No	180	3.3	63	63	6	80	77	14
Minnesota	1	No	175	3.4	57	59	5	77	83	7
Montana	2	No	180	3.6	62	63	6	80	83	6
Nebraska	(4)	Yes	(4)	3.2	63	61	6	82	85	9
New Hampshire	2	No	180	3.3	61	69	8	81	83	7
New Jersey	3	Yes	180	3.6	60	68	8	79	79	13
New Mexico	3	No	180	3.3	65	60	7	77	77	11
New York	2	Yes	180	3.4	56	65	9	78	76	17
North Carolina	2	Yes	180	3.8	63	60	9	80	74	21
North Dakota	2	No	180	3.5	61	60	5	79	85	6
Ohio	2	No	182	3.2	58	65	6	80	79	11
Oklahoma	2	No	175	3.0	67	59	8	80	78	14
Oregon	2	Yes	175	3.3	55	59	6	77	81	9
Pennsylvania	3	No	180	3.4	54	62	5	77	80	10
Rhode Island	2	No	180	3.6	61	62	8	77	78	12
Texas	3	Yes	175	3.3	61	56	8	79	77	15
Virginia [3]	3	No	180	3.4	62	64	7	79	78	16
West Virginia	2	No	180	3.4	55	56	6	78	82	16
Wisconsin	2	No	180	3.5	55	60	7	83	81	8
Wyoming	(4)	No	175	3.2	61	59	6	78	85	7
Outlying areas										
Guam	—	—	—	3.6	69	47	12	70	81	20
Virgin Islands	—	—	—	3.0	60	46	15	84	63	27

[1] Data are for 1990 unless otherwise specified.

[2] Percent of students agreeing or strongly agreeing with positive statements about mathematics.

[3] A unit of science may be substituted for one unit of mathematics.

[4] No statewide policy.

—Data not available.

SOURCE: U.S. Department of Education, National Center for Education Statistics, National Assessment of Educational Progress, *The State of Mathematics Achievement,* by Educational Testing Service; and Council of Chief State School Officers, *State Education Indicators.* (This table was prepared June 1991.)

Table 118.—Average proficiency in mathematics, by content area, grade, sex, and race/ethnicity: 1990

Grade, sex, and race/ethnicity	Percent of students	Overall mathematics proficiency, by content area						Percentage of students at or above anchor points			
		Average proficiency, all areas	Numbers and operations	Measurement	Geometry	Data analysis, statistics, and probability	Algebra and functions	Level 200 [1]	Level 250 [2]	Level 300 [3]	Level 350 [4]
1	2	3	4	5	6	7	8	9	10	11	12
Grade 4	100.0	215.8	212.9	221.5	217.1	—	215.6	71.8	11.0	0.0	0.0
Male	51.7	216.7	213.3	224.6	217.2	—	215.4	72.6	11.7	0.0	0.0
Female	48.3	214.9	212.5	218.3	217.0	—	215.9	71.0	10.2	0.0	0.0
White	70.2	222.7	219.6	229.3	223.4	—	222.2	81.4	14.1	0.0	0.0
Black	15.3	194.1	192.1	195.4	197.3	—	195.4	40.5	1.4	0.0	0.0
Hispanic	10.7	200.5	197.5	206.1	202.9	—	199.6	51.7	3.1	0.0	0.0
Asian [5]	2.0	228.2	225.9	234.0	227.1	—	228.6	85.0	22.5	0.0	0.0
Indian [6]	1.7	210.5	206.2	216.7	213.1	—	213.8	65.7	3.4	0.0	0.0
Grade 8	100.0	265.0	268.6	261.4	261.8	266.3	264.3	97.7	67.4	14.2	0.2
Male	50.0	265.5	268.4	265.4	262.6	266.3	263.8	97.8	66.7	15.9	0.3
Female	50.0	264.4	268.9	257.3	261.0	266.3	264.8	97.6	68.2	12.5	0.1
White	70.6	272.1	274.9	269.9	268.5	275.2	271.1	99.3	76.8	17.6	0.2
Black	15.1	240.8	248.1	232.2	238.3	237.2	241.4	91.9	36.0	2.7	0.0
Hispanic	10.0	247.9	252.6	242.0	246.9	245.0	248.3	94.9	46.5	4.1	0.0
Asian [5]	2.7	284.8	288.3	281.0	281.1	286.9	284.5	98.8	85.9	32.4	1.9
Indian [6]	1.4	247.9	249.7	247.4	250.2	245.7	245.0	96.9	47.3	3.6	0.0
Grade 12	100.0	295.3	293.8	294.3	296.3	295.3	296.7	99.9	90.5	45.4	4.7
Male	48.8	297.7	296.2	299.1	299.2	297.5	297.1	100.0	91.7	47.6	6.3
Female	51.2	293.1	291.5	289.8	293.6	293.2	296.3	99.9	89.4	43.3	3.2
White	73.9	301.1	298.8	300.8	302.6	302.3	301.8	100.0	94.6	52.1	5.6
Black	14.0	270.2	272.7	263.9	269.3	267.4	273.9	99.9	73.7	15.9	0.2
Hispanic	7.9	277.6	276.8	278.1	277.5	275.0	280.0	99.6	78.9	25.0	1.3
Asian [5]	3.4	315.0	311.8	318.3	317.1	306.3	320.0	100.0	97.3	69.7	13.3
Indian [6]	0.8	290.4	290.1	289.7	288.9	291.7	291.6	99.0	92.0	39.0	0.0

[1] Indicates ability to perform simple additive reasoning and problem solving.

[2] Indicates ability to perform simple multiplicative reasoning and 2-step problem solving.

[3] Indicates ability to perform reasoning and problem solving involving fractions, decimals, percents, elementary geometry, and simple algebra.

[4] Indicates ability to perform reasoning and problem solving involving geometry, algebra, and beginning statistics and probability.

[5] Asian/Pacific Islanders.

[6] American Indian/Alaskan Native.

—Data not available.

SOURCE: U.S. Department of Education, National Center for Education Statistics, National Assessment of Educational Progress, *The State of Mathematics Achievement,* prepared by Educational Testing Service. (This table was prepared June 1991.)

Table 119.—Percentage of students at or above five science proficiency levels, by race/ethnicity and age: 1976–77, 1981–82, and 1985–86

Year, age, and race/ethnicity	9-year-olds [1]				13-year-olds [2]				17-year-olds [2]			
	Know every-day science facts	Understand simple scientific principles	Apply basic scientific information	Analyze scientific procedures and data	Understand simple scientific principles	Apply basic scientific information	Analyze scientific procedures and data	Integrate specialized scientific information	Understand simple scientific principles	Apply basic scientific information	Analyze scientific procedures and data	Integrate specialized scientific information
1	2	3	4	5	6	7	8	9	10	11	12	13
1976–77												
Total	93.6	67.9	26.2	3.5	85.9	49.2	10.9	0.7	97.2	81.8	41.7	8.5
White	97.8	76.5	31.3	4.3	91.9	56.7	13.1	0.9	99.2	88.4	47.4	9.9
Black	73.1	27.7	3.8	0.1	57.1	15.1	1.2	(3)	84.5	40.9	8.3	0.6
Hispanic	83.1	42.1	8.5	0.5	63.1	19.1	2.3	0.2	92.7	61.7	19.1	2.0
1981–82												
Total	95.0	70.4	24.8	2.2	89.6	51.5	9.4	0.4	95.8	76.8	37.5	7.2
White	98.1	78.0	30.1	2.7	94.5	58.7	11.2	0.4	98.7	85.0	44.0	8.8
Black	81.2	38.7	3.8	0.4	66.8	18.6	0.8	(3)	81.0	36.5	6.7	0.1
Hispanic	84.6	41.8	4.4	(3)	74.5	25.8	2.4	(3)	86.1	46.6	12.5	1.4
1985–86												
Total	96.3	71.4	27.6	3.4	91.8	53.4	9.4	0.2	96.7	80.8	41.4	7.5
White	98.5	78.4	32.6	4.3	96.4	61.9	11.8	0.3	98.6	87.6	48.8	9.0
Black	87.5	45.1	8.8	0.4	74.3	20.2	0.9	(3)	89.8	52.9	12.3	1.0
Hispanic	89.6	49.1	10.7	0.2	76.1	27.6	1.6	(3)	92.9	61.6	15.5	0.5

[1] Virtually no students were able to integrate specialized scientific information.
[2] Virtually all students knew everyday science facts. Data are only for students enrolled in school.
[3] Virtually no students were able to perform at this level.

SOURCE: U.S. Department of Education, National Center for Education Statistics, *The Science Report Card, 1988,* by Educational Testing Service. (This table was prepared April 1990.)

Table 120.—Science proficiency, by age and by selected characteristics of students: 1976–77, 1981–82, and 1985–86

Selected characteristics of students	9-year-olds			13-year-olds			17-year-olds[1]		
	1976–77	1981–82	1985–86	1976–77	1981–82	1985–86	1976–77	1981–82	1985–86
1	2	3	4	5	6	7	8	9	10
All students	**219.9**	**220.9**	**224.3**	**247.4**	**250.2**	**251.4**	**289.6**	**283.3**	**288.5**
Sex									
Male	222.1	221.0	227.3	251.1	255.7	256.1	297.1	291.9	294.9
Female	217.7	220.7	221.3	243.8	245.0	246.9	282.3	275.2	282.3
Race/ethnicity									
White	229.6	229.1	231.9	256.1	257.3	259.2	297.7	293.2	297.5
Black	174.9	187.1	196.2	208.1	217.2	221.6	240.3	234.8	252.8
Hispanic	191.9	189.0	199.4	213.4	225.5	226.1	262.3	248.7	259.3
Region									
Northeast	224.5	221.8	228.2	255.3	254.1	257.6	296.4	284.4	292.2
Southeast	205.1	214.0	218.8	235.1	238.7	247.1	276.4	276.2	283.5
Central	225.3	226.3	227.9	253.8	253.9	249.4	294.1	289.3	294.4
West	220.9	219.9	222.1	243.0	252.4	252.3	286.6	280.9	283.2
Parental education									
Not high school graduate	198.5	198.2	203.6	223.5	225.4	229.4	265.4	258.6	257.5
Graduated high school	223.0	218.1	219.6	245.4	243.2	244.8	284.4	275.3	277.0
Some college	237.2	229.2	235.8	260.3	258.9	257.8	295.7	290.1	295.1
Graduated college	232.3	230.6	235.2	266.5	263.5	264.4	309.3	300.2	303.8

[1] All participants of this age were in school.

NOTE.—Performers at the 150 level know some general scientific facts of the type that could be learned from everyday experiences. Performers at the 200 level are developing some understanding of simple scientific principles, particularly in the life sciences. Performers at the 250 level can interpret data from simple tables and make inferences about the outcomes of experimental procedures. They exhibit knowledge and understanding of the life sciences, and also demonstrate some knowledge of basic information from the physical sciences. Performers at the 300 level can evaluate the appropriateness of the design of an experiment and have the skill to apply their scientific knowledge in

interpreting information from text and graphs. These students also exhibit a growing understanding of principles from the physical sciences. Performers at the 350 level can infer relationships and draw conclusions using detailed scientific knowledge from the physical sciences, particularly chemistry. They also can apply basic principles of genetics and interpret the societal implications of research in this field.

SOURCE: U.S. Department of Education, National Center for Education Statistics, National Assessment of Educational Progress, *The Science Report Card, 1988,* prepared by Educational Testing Service. (This table was prepared January 1989.)

Table 121.—Student proficiency in civics, by sex, race/ethnicity, and age: 1976, 1982, and 1988

Sex and race/ethnicity	Percent correct						Percent understanding the nature of political institutions,[2] 1988			Percent understanding specific government structures and functions,[3] 1988		
	13-year-olds			17-year-olds[1]			Grade 4	Grade 8	Grade 12	Grade 4	Grade 8	Grade 12
	1976	1982	1988	1976	1982	1988						
1	2	3	4	5	6	7	8	9	10	11	12	13
All students	**49.1**	**49.1**	**50.0**	**61.7**	**61.3**	**59.6**	**9.6**	**61.4**	**89.2**	**0.1**	**12.7**	**49.0**
Male	49.7	50.1	50.5	63.5	63.1	61.2	10.3	59.7	88.0	0.2	14.1	52.5
Female	48.5	48.2	49.5	60.0	59.6	58.2	8.9	63.1	90.4	([4])	11.4	45.8
White	50.7	50.7	51.2	63.4	63.6	61.4	12.3	69.3	92.8	0.1	16.3	55.4
Black	42.1	42.0	45.7	52.5	51.6	53.1	2.2	41.2	76.8	([4])	4.0	23.2
Hispanic	41.1	43.9	45.5	51.5	52.3	53.8	3.8	41.0	78.6	([4])	3.4	29.5

[1] All participants of this age were in school.

[2] Knowledge of government responsibilities; the interrelationships of citizens and government; and individual rights.

[3] Knowledge of the structures, functions, and powers of American government as described in the Constitution; and principles of government such as separation of powers or checks and balances.

[4] Virtually no students performed at this level.

SOURCE: U.S. Department of Education, National Center for Education Statistics, National Assessment of Educational Progress, *The Civics Report Card*, by Educational Testing Service. (This table was prepared April 1990.)

Table 122.—Eighth graders' achievement on history, mathematics, reading, and science tests: 1988

Achievement test	Sex		Race/ethnicity					Socioeconomic status[1]			Control of school		
	Male	Female	White	Black	Hispanic	Asian	American Indian	Low	Middle	High	Public	Catholic	Other private
1	2	3	4	5	6	7	8	9	10	11	12	13	14
Eighth graders' achievement, by standardized score[2]													
History	50.4	49.7	51.6	45.0	45.9	51.9	44.2	44.7	50.0	55.4	49.5	53.6	54.7
Mathematics	50.2	49.9	51.8	43.8	45.7	53.6	44.7	44.5	49.7	56.1	49.6	51.9	55.7
Reading	48.9	51.1	51.7	44.6	46.0	51.2	44.3	44.8	49.9	55.4	49.5	53.3	55.6
Science	50.6	49.5	51.8	43.9	46.1	51.8	43.9	45.0	49.9	55.2	49.7	51.7	54.6
Distribution of eighth graders' achievement, by score quartile[3]													
History	100.0	100.0	100.0	100.0	100.0	100.0	100.0	100.0	100.0	100.0	100.0	100.0	100.0
Lower quartile	25.3	25.3	19.6	41.9	40.4	21.7	43.1	44.4	23.5	9.8	27.1	12.6	11.2
Lower middle quartile	22.2	26.8	23.0	31.9	26.2	19.9	31.0	28.2	26.5	16.9	25.1	21.0	18.5
Upper middle quartile	25.3	26.0	28.2	17.4	20.1	26.4	18.4	18.1	27.9	28.5	25.0	31.3	28.5
Upper quartile	27.3	21.8	29.2	8.8	13.3	32.1	7.4	9.2	22.1	44.8	22.8	35.1	41.8
Mathematics	100.0	100.0	100.0	100.0	100.0	100.0	100.0	100.0	100.0	100.0	100.0	100.0	100.0
Lower quartile	25.4	25.0	18.3	49.0	39.2	18.8	46.3	44.3	23.8	9.3	26.8	16.9	8.3
Lower middle quartile	24.4	26.0	24.1	28.7	30.1	19.7	29.1	30.8	26.9	16.1	25.6	24.7	17.6
Upper middle quartile	24.4	24.3	27.0	15.1	19.9	22.3	16.3	17.0	27.0	26.2	23.7	28.6	28.4
Upper quartile	25.8	24.8	30.6	7.2	10.8	39.2	8.3	7.9	22.3	48.5	23.8	29.7	45.7
Reading	100.0	100.0	100.0	100.0	100.0	100.0	100.0	100.0	100.0	100.0	100.0	100.0	100.0
Lower quartile	30.4	21.3	19.9	45.0	38.2	23.5	44.9	44.0	24.2	11.1	27.7	13.8	10.4
Lower middle quartile	25.0	25.0	23.5	29.4	30.5	22.6	30.0	29.1	27.0	16.9	25.6	23.1	16.6
Upper middle quartile	22.7	25.6	26.2	16.6	20.1	24.6	18.5	18.5	25.8	26.3	23.7	28.2	25.8
Upper quartile	21.9	28.2	30.4	9.0	11.2	29.3	6.6	8.4	23.0	45.7	23.0	34.9	47.2
Science	100.0	100.0	100.0	100.0	100.0	100.0	100.0	100.0	100.0	100.0	100.0	100.0	100.0
Lower quartile	25.4	25.9	19.2	47.7	37.8	22.0	46.9	42.3	24.7	11.1	27.2	17.2	11.0
Lower middle quartile	21.7	26.7	22.4	30.1	30.7	23.0	27.4	29.2	25.5	16.9	24.3	25.3	21.1
Upper middle quartile	25.7	26.0	28.8	15.9	20.6	24.6	17.4	19.3	27.3	29.4	25.2	31.3	29.4
Upper quartile	27.1	21.4	29.6	6.3	10.9	30.3	8.3	9.1	22.6	42.5	23.4	26.1	38.5

[1] Socioeconomic status was measured by a composite score on parental education and occupations, and family income. The "Low" SES group is the lowest quartile; the "Middle" SES group is the middle two quartiles; and the "High" SES group is the upper quartile.

[2] Standardized scores with a mean of 50 and standard deviation of 10.

[3] Twenty-five percent of all students fall into each one of the quartile groupings.

NOTE.—Because of rounding, details may not add to totals.

SOURCE: U.S. Department of Education, National Center for Education Statistics, "National Education Longitudinal Study of 1988" survey. (This table was prepared April 1991.)

Table 123.—Scholastic Aptitude Test score averages for college-bound high school seniors, by sex: 1966–67 to 1989–90

School year	Verbal score			Mathematical score		
	Total	Male	Female	Total	Male	Female
1	2	3	4	5	6	7
1966–67	466	463	468	492	514	467
1967–68	466	464	466	492	512	470
1968–69	463	459	466	493	513	470
1969–70	460	459	461	488	509	465
1970–71	455	454	457	488	507	466
1971–72	453	454	452	484	505	461
1972–73	445	446	443	481	502	460
1973–74	444	447	442	480	501	459
1974–75	434	437	431	472	495	449
1975–76	431	433	430	472	497	446
1976–77	429	431	427	470	497	445
1977–78	429	433	425	468	494	444
1978–79	427	431	423	467	493	443
1979–80	424	428	420	466	491	443
1980–81	424	430	418	466	492	443
1981–82	426	431	421	467	493	443
1982–83	425	430	420	468	493	445
1983–84	426	433	420	471	495	449
1984–85	431	437	425	475	499	452
1985–86	431	437	426	475	501	451
1986–87	430	435	425	476	500	453
1987–88	428	435	422	476	498	455
1988–89	427	434	421	476	500	454
1989–90	424	429	419	476	499	455

NOTE.—Possible scores on each part of the SAT range from 200 to 800. Data for the years 1966–67 through 1970–71 are estimates derived from the test scores of all participants.

SOURCE: College Entrance Examination Board, *National Report on College-Bound Seniors*, various years. (Copyright © 1990 by the College Entrance Examination Board. All rights reserved.) (This table was prepared September 1990.)

Table 124.—Scholastic Aptitude Test score averages, by race/ethnicity: 1975–76 to 1989–90

Racial/ethnic background	1975–76	1976–77	1977–78	1978–79	1979–80	1980–81	1981–82	1982–83	1983–84	1984–85	1986–87	1987–88	1988–89	1989–90
1	2	3	4	5	6	7	8	9	10	11	12	13	14	15
SAT-Verbal														
All students	431	429	429	427	424	424	426	425	426	431	430	428	427	424
White	451	448	446	444	442	442	444	443	445	449	447	445	446	442
Black	332	330	332	330	330	332	341	339	342	346	351	353	351	352
Mexican-American	371	370	370	370	372	373	377	375	376	382	379	382	381	380
Puerto Rican	364	355	349	345	350	353	360	358	358	368	360	355	360	359
Asian-American	414	405	401	396	396	397	398	395	398	404	405	408	409	410
American Indian	388	390	387	386	390	391	388	388	390	392	393	393	384	388
Other	410	402	399	393	394	388	392	386	388	391	405	410	414	410
SAT-Mathematical														
All students	472	470	468	467	466	466	467	468	471	475	476	476	476	476
White	493	489	485	483	482	483	483	484	487	490	489	490	491	491
Black	354	357	354	358	360	362	366	369	373	376	377	384	386	385
Mexican-American	410	408	402	410	413	415	416	417	420	426	424	428	430	429
Puerto Rican	401	397	388	388	394	398	403	403	405	409	400	402	406	405
Asian-American	518	514	510	511	509	513	513	514	519	518	521	522	525	528
American Indian	420	421	419	421	426	425	424	425	427	428	432	435	428	437
Other	458	457	450	447	449	447	449	446	450	448	455	460	467	467

NOTE.—Possible scores on each part of the SAT range from 200 to 800. No race/ethnic group data are available prior to 1975–76. No data are available for 1985–86 due to changes in the Student Descriptive Questionnaire completed when students registered for the test.

SOURCE: College Entrance Examination Board, *National Report on College-Bound Seniors*, various years. (Copyright © 1990 by the College Entrance Examination Board. All rights reserved.) (This table was prepared September 1990.)

Table 125.—Distribution of Scholastic Aptitude Test scores, by sex of student: 1975–76 to 1989–90

Year	Number of test takers	Percent of students with specified scores											
		200 or higher	250 or higher	300 or higher	350 or higher	400 or higher	450 or higher	500 or higher	550 or higher	600 or higher	650 or higher	700 or higher	750 or higher
1	2	3	4	5	6	7	8	9	10	11	12	13	14

Verbal

Total

Year	Number of test takers	200	250	300	350	400	450	500	550	600	650	700	750
1975–76	999,809	100.00	96.26	89.26	77.47	60.27	43.01	28.11	15.58	8.20	3.55	1.23	0.25
1980–81	994,046	100.00	95.46	87.32	75.34	58.44	40.64	25.76	13.87	7.00	3.01	1.03	0.21
1984–85	977,361	100.00	95.96	88.81	77.22	60.62	43.23	27.38	15.33	7.88	3.55	1.16	0.19
1985–86	1,000,748	100.00	95.81	88.92	77.55	61.77	43.17	28.03	15.75	7.87	3.25	0.99	0.14
1986–87	1,080,426	100.00	96.08	88.57	76.62	60.18	43.02	27.85	15.44	8.14	3.42	1.07	0.13
1987–88	1,134,364	100.00	95.81	88.62	76.44	60.53	42.38	26.91	14.94	7.32	3.22	0.92	0.09
1988–89	1,088,223	100.00	95.72	88.21	75.39	59.55	42.17	26.77	14.85	7.76	3.16	0.87	0.10
1989–90	1,025,523	100.00	95.20	87.44	74.97	58.70	40.67	25.11	14.41	7.43	3.13	1.00	0.12

Male

Year	Number of test takers	200	250	300	350	400	450	500	550	600	650	700	750
1975–76	494,626	100.00	96.39	89.54	77.90	60.90	43.65	28.69	16.04	8.49	3.69	1.29	0.26
1980–81	478,448	100.00	95.97	88.50	77.16	60.73	42.89	27.53	15.03	7.67	3.30	1.13	0.23
1984–85	471,992	100.00	96.30	89.71	78.69	62.58	45.35	29.21	16.71	8.79	4.06	1.34	0.21
1985–86	481,477	100.00	96.19	89.87	79.10	63.74	45.17	29.77	17.02	8.71	3.68	1.11	0.15
1986–87	520,326	100.00	96.23	89.12	77.72	61.79	44.91	29.71	16.93	9.22	4.02	1.26	0.15
1987–88	544,065	100.00	96.14	89.54	78.21	62.92	45.04	29.25	16.70	8.44	3.82	1.13	0.11
1988–89	521,229	100.00	96.00	89.06	77.04	61.86	44.81	29.15	16.63	8.93	3.75	1.07	0.12
1989–90	490,420	100.00	95.40	88.00	76.04	60.19	42.62	27.05	15.91	8.40	3.60	1.15	0.14

Female

Year	Number of test takers	200	250	300	350	400	450	500	550	600	650	700	750
1975–76	505,183	100.00	96.14	88.97	77.05	59.65	42.38	27.55	15.13	7.92	3.42	1.17	0.24
1980–81	515,598	100.00	94.99	86.23	73.66	56.32	38.56	24.11	12.80	6.39	2.73	0.94	0.18
1984–85	505,369	100.00	95.64	87.96	75.86	58.79	41.26	25.66	14.04	7.02	3.07	0.98	0.16
1985–86	519,271	100.00	95.46	88.04	76.11	59.95	41.31	26.42	14.57	7.09	2.85	0.88	0.12
1986–87	560,100	100.00	95.93	88.07	75.60	58.67	41.26	26.13	14.05	7.14	2.87	0.90	0.11
1987–88	590,299	100.00	95.50	87.76	74.82	58.33	39.93	24.76	13.32	6.29	2.66	0.74	0.06
1988–89	566,994	100.00	95.45	87.42	73.88	57.42	39.75	24.58	13.21	6.68	2.61	0.69	0.08
1989–90	535,103	100.00	95.01	86.93	73.98	57.34	38.88	23.34	13.04	6.53	2.70	0.86	0.10

Mathematical

Total

Year	Number of test takers	200	250	300	350	400	450	500	550	600	650	700	750
1975–76	999,776	100.00	98.78	93.65	83.55	70.87	57.16	41.82	26.94	16.34	8.49	3.75	1.16
1980–81	993,672	100.00	98.85	92.99	82.77	70.48	55.57	40.59	25.98	14.45	7.08	2.71	0.66
1984–85	977,361	100.00	99.15	93.99	83.83	71.85	57.98	43.36	29.33	17.08	8.63	3.58	0.82
1985–86	1,000,747	100.00	98.91	93.63	84.64	71.98	57.41	42.32	29.29	17.95	9.56	4.08	1.01
1986–87	1,080,426	100.00	98.91	93.30	84.22	71.61	57.40	42.37	29.67	18.32	9.94	3.86	1.02
1987–88	1,134,364	100.00	99.08	93.93	84.62	72.17	57.43	43.03	29.55	17.60	9.26	3.78	0.91
1988–89	1,088,223	100.00	99.08	94.04	84.57	71.97	57.94	42.81	29.33	18.01	10.07	4.27	1.11
1989–90	1,025,523	100.00	98.89	93.77	84.21	71.57	57.71	43.20	29.59	18.41	10.14	4.23	1.18

Male

Year	Number of test takers	200	250	300	350	400	450	500	550	600	650	700	750
1975–76	494,619	100.00	99.13	95.37	87.63	77.29	65.30	50.65	34.93	22.71	12.70	6.02	1.99
1980–81	478,301	100.00	99.20	94.98	87.17	77.17	63.99	49.45	33.92	20.38	10.75	4.46	1.17
1984–85	471,995	100.00	99.37	95.53	87.73	78.05	65.78	51.80	37.09	23.09	12.59	5.65	1.41
1985–86	481,477	100.00	99.24	95.38	88.49	78.26	65.53	51.16	37.47	24.49	14.00	6.44	1.73
1986–87	520,326	100.00	99.16	94.91	87.75	77.36	64.90	50.74	37.66	24.82	14.47	6.15	1.75
1987–88	544,065	100.00	99.31	95.37	87.91	77.48	64.40	50.71	36.91	23.63	13.43	5.96	1.57
1988–89	521,229	100.00	99.30	95.45	88.00	77.62	65.19	50.91	37.13	24.43	14.62	6.70	1.89
1989–90	490,420	100.00	99.16	95.17	87.70	77.13	64.71	50.81	36.85	24.40	14.41	6.53	2.00

Female

Year	Number of test takers	200	250	300	350	400	450	500	550	600	650	700	750
1975–76	505,157	100.00	98.45	91.96	79.56	64.59	49.20	33.17	19.12	10.11	4.37	1.53	0.34
1980–81	515,371	100.00	98.53	91.14	78.69	64.27	47.76	32.37	18.60	8.94	3.66	1.09	0.19
1984–85	505,366	100.00	98.95	92.56	80.19	66.06	50.70	35.48	22.08	11.46	4.94	1.65	0.26
1985–86	519,270	100.00	98.61	92.01	81.07	66.16	49.87	34.12	21.70	11.88	5.45	1.89	0.34
1986–87	560,100	100.00	98.67	91.80	80.93	66.26	50.44	34.59	22.25	12.29	5.74	1.73	0.33
1987–88	590,299	100.00	98.87	92.60	81.58	67.28	51.00	35.94	22.78	12.05	5.42	1.77	0.30
1988–89	566,994	100.00	98.87	92.75	81.42	66.77	51.27	35.37	22.15	12.11	5.90	2.03	0.39
1989–90	535,103	100.00	98.65	92.50	81.01	66.47	51.30	36.22	22.94	12.92	6.22	2.12	0.44

NOTE.—Possible scores on each part of the SAT range from 200 to 800. In some years, mathematics and verbal test results were not available for each student.

SOURCE: College Entrance Examination Board, *National Report on College-Bound Seniors*, various years. (Copyright © 1990 by the College Entrance Examination Board. All rights reserved.) (This table was prepared September 1990.)

Table 126.—Scholastic Aptitude Test score averages, by intended area of study:[1] 1977–78 to 1989–90

Test and year	Intended area of study[2]									
	Arts and human-ities	Biological sciences and related areas	Business commerce, and commu-nications	Computer and infor-mation sciences	Educa-tion	Engi-neering	Mathe-matics	Physical sciences	Social sciences and related areas	Miscella-neous[3]
1	2	3	4	5	6	7	8	9	10	11
Verbal										
1977–78	439	436	409	420	396	448	464	499	448	422
1978–79	436	435	408	419	392	445	459	498	446	420
1979–80	434	433	406	417	389	444	455	495	448	419
1980–81	434	433	406	416	391	446	456	498	446	420
1981–82	436	434	409	417	394	449	455	496	450	424
1982–83	438	432	409	413	394	448	453	496	451	421
1983–84	440	434	410	411	398	453	457	501	451	423
1984–85	445	439	414	413	404	453	459	506	454	429
1986–87	447	438	415	403	408	456	475	507	452	410
1987–88	444	434	414	400	407	453	468	500	447	409
1988–89	445	433	414	396	406	452	473	504	447	410
1989–90	441	430	410	392	406	449	473	503	441	408
Change, 1979–80 to 1989–89 ..	7	–3	4	–25	17	5	18	8	–7	–11
Mathematical										
1977–78	454	474	448	499	422	540	585	566	464	461
1978–79	452	472	448	498	420	536	580	561	463	458
1979–80	452	472	446	496	418	535	577	560	463	459
1980–81	453	472	446	492	418	534	572	558	463	459
1981–82	452	470	446	489	419	537	569	558	464	461
1982–83	454	470	445	484	418	539	572	560	466	460
1983–84	456	475	449	483	425	543	578	564	467	463
1984–85	462	480	455	488	432	545	578	569	471	469
1986–87	469	482	459	476	437	554	602	576	472	453
1987–88	471	482	462	470	442	547	596	568	472	455
1988–89	473	481	465	472	440	551	606	577	473	459
1989–90	475	481	465	468	442	550	609	577	471	460
Change, 1979–80 to 1989–90 ..	23	9	19	–28	24	15	32	17	8	1

[1] Students indicated their first and second choices of fields of study. Only their first choices are reported here.

[2] Based on classifications reported by College Entrance Examination Board.

[3] Includes "trade and vocational," "other," and "undecided" through 1984–85. Data for 1986–87 to 1989–90 exclude "other."

NOTE.—Possible scores on each part of the SAT range from 200 to 800. No data are available for 1985–86 due to changes in the Student Descriptive Questionnaire completed when students registered for the test.

SOURCE: College Entrance Examination Board, *National Report on College-Bound Seniors*, various years. (Copyright © 1990 by the College Entrance Examination Board. All rights reserved.) (This table was prepared September 1990.)

Table 127.—Scholastic Aptitude Test score averages, by State: 1974–75, 1979–80, 1980–81, and 1985–86 to 1989–90

State	1974–75 Verbal	1974–75 Mathematical	1979–80 Verbal	1979–80 Mathematical	1980–81 Verbal	1980–81 Mathematical	1985–86 Verbal	1985–86 Mathematical	1987–88 Verbal	1987–88 Mathematical	1988–89 Verbal	1988–89 Mathematical	1989–90 Verbal	1989–90 Mathematical	Percent of graduates taking SAT 1990[1]
1	2	3	4	5	6	7	8	9	10	11	12	13	14	15	16
United States	434	472	424	466	424	466	431	475	428	476	427	476	424	476	40
Alabama	426	457	448	482	457	488	476	514	480	520	482	520	470	514	8
Alaska	461	481	450	482	449	486	445	479	441	475	443	480	438	476	42
Arizona	496	525	475	516	476	514	466	509	455	500	452	500	445	497	25
Arkansas	482	510	480	514	477	510	482	519	479	516	471	515	470	511	6
California	435	473	424	472	426	475	423	481	424	484	422	484	419	484	45
Colorado	479	515	468	515	467	513	466	514	460	511	458	508	456	513	28
Connecticut	442	471	431	466	430	463	440	474	436	472	435	473	430	471	74
Delaware	439	476	431	469	429	470	442	475	433	466	435	468	433	470	58
District of Columbia	—	—	—	—	—	—	413	439	405	434	407	439	409	441	68
Florida	441	474	424	464	424	463	426	469	422	468	420	467	418	466	44
Georgia	397	427	389	425	390	426	402	440	404	444	402	445	401	443	57
Hawaii	414	478	396	472	390	464	403	477	408	480	406	482	404	481	52
Idaho	493	524	482	518	486	523	475	512	467	501	465	500	466	502	17
Illinois	460	510	459	507	459	508	466	519	464	520	462	520	466	528	16
Indiana	418	463	407	450	406	451	415	459	412	458	412	459	408	459	54
Iowa	523	568	508	554	515	566	519	576	513	577	512	572	511	577	5
Kansas	503	540	497	538	502	542	498	544	494	541	495	545	492	548	10
Kentucky	470	507	471	507	474	509	483	519	475	515	477	519	473	521	10
Louisiana	456	491	462	499	461	494	474	507	476	513	473	513	476	517	9
Maine	437	471	427	467	426	465	434	466	430	466	431	466	423	463	60
Maryland	436	471	422	463	423	461	436	475	433	475	434	480	430	478	59
Massachusetts	434	469	423	464	422	462	436	473	432	474	432	473	427	473	72
Michigan	451	498	452	505	456	508	462	514	457	513	458	514	454	514	12
Minnesota	506	552	491	544	486	539	482	540	470	531	474	532	477	542	14
Mississippi	477	503	481	508	473	502	485	516	482	519	472	516	477	519	4
Missouri	465	500	458	508	462	504	476	519	471	519	471	518	473	522	12
Montana	500	547	488	544	485	539	485	541	471	529	469	523	464	523	20
Nebraska	459	507	484	539	489	537	493	549	487	545	487	543	484	546	10
Nevada	465	497	445	485	445	487	445	485	440	486	439	487	434	487	24
New Hampshire	449	485	441	485	439	479	450	485	446	487	447	485	442	486	67
New Jersey	424	454	415	452	414	450	424	465	424	469	423	471	418	473	69
New Mexico	486	516	482	524	474	510	489	527	478	524	483	532	480	527	12
New York	441	484	424	465	427	471	427	471	420	469	419	471	412	470	70
North Carolina	399	428	393	429	391	427	399	436	401	440	397	439	401	440	55
North Dakota	510	554	499	549	494	544	508	556	498	555	500	567	505	564	6
Ohio	456	499	455	499	457	500	460	503	452	499	451	497	450	499	22
Oklahoma	480	514	478	518	485	526	487	521	483	522	479	522	478	523	9
Oregon	440	468	428	465	431	469	444	486	441	482	443	484	439	484	49
Pennsylvania	430	470	423	463	421	459	429	465	424	462	423	463	420	463	64
Rhode Island	432	469	417	458	415	452	432	466	431	469	429	466	422	461	62
South Carolina	382	412	375	409	374	406	395	431	400	438	399	439	397	437	54
South Dakota	523	561	500	551	519	561	531	567	511	559	498	543	506	555	5
Tennessee	477	511	480	513	475	514	486	521	485	524	486	523	483	525	12
Texas	431	467	416	455	415	455	419	458	417	462	415	462	413	461	42
Utah	516	553	515	546	511	548	506	541	498	536	499	537	492	539	5
Vermont	439	476	432	468	427	467	442	474	437	472	435	470	431	466	62
Virginia	431	463	423	460	424	461	435	473	430	472	430	472	425	470	58
Washington	489	522	476	521	472	517	461	502	448	494	448	491	437	486	44
West Virginia	462	502	462	499	458	495	462	502	451	496	448	491	443	490	15
Wisconsin	492	544	472	533	477	533	478	536	473	534	477	536	476	543	11
Wyoming	506	548	484	525	478	528	484	534	474	527	462	516	458	519	13

[1] Based on the number of high school graduates in 1990 as projected by the Western Interstate Commission for Higher Education, and number of 1990 seniors who took the SAT.

—Data not available.

NOTE.—Possible scores on each part of the SAT range from 200 to 800. Rankings of States based on SAT scores alone are invalid because of the varying proportions of students in each State taking the tests.

SOURCE: College Entrance Examination Board, "SAT Verbal Scores Decline for Fourth Straight Year, but Class of 1990 Math Scores Remain Steady." (Copyright 1990 by the College Entrance Examination Board. All rights reserved.) (This table was prepared September 1990.)

Table 128.—Profile of Scholastic Aptitude Test takers: 1989–90

	SAT takers		Percent distribution			Verbal mean	Math mean
	Number	Percent	Total	Male	Female		
1	2	3	4	5	6	7	8
Total	**1,025,523**	**100**	**100**	**48**	**52**	**424**	**476**
Type of high school							
Public	803,838	82	100	47	53	421	475
Religiously affiliated	129,241	13	100	49	51	436	473
Independent	50,323	5	100	55	45	469	523
Not known	42,121	(1)	—	—	—	—	—
Location of high school							
Large city	229,476	23	100	47	53	412	466
Medium-sized city	131,985	13	100	47	53	426	476
Small city or town	191,245	20	100	48	52	424	472
Suburban	317,537	32	100	48	52	439	495
Rural	110,170	11	100	46	54	416	460
Not known	45,110	(1)	—	—	—	—	—
Size of senior class							
More than 1,000	4,745	(2)	100	50	50	447	513
750–1,000	18,132	2	100	47	53	420	478
500–749	131,107	13	100	47	53	423	484
250–499	412,088	42	100	48	52	424	479
100–249	285,277	29	100	48	52	425	473
Fewer than 100	126,453	13	100	46	54	434	475
Not known	47,721	—	—	—	—	—	—

[1] Not known category has been distributed into other categories.
[2] Less than 0.5 percent.
—Not applicable.

SOURCE: College Entrance Examination Board, *National Report on College-Bound Seniors*, various years. (Copyright © 1990 by College Entrance Board. All rights reserved.) (This table was prepared September 1990.)

Table 129.—American College Testing (ACT) score [1] averages, by sex: 1969–70 to 1988–89

Type of test and sex	1969–70	1974–75	1976–77	1977–78	1978–79	1979–80	1980–81	1981–82	1982–83	1983–84	1984–85	1985–86	1986–87	1987–88	1988–89
1	2	3	4	5	6	7	8	9	10	11	12	13	14	15	16
Composite, total	**19.9**	**18.6**	**18.4**	**18.5**	**18.6**	**18.5**	**18.5**	**18.4**	**18.3**	**18.5**	**18.6**	**18.8**	**18.7**	**18.8**	**18.6**
Male	20.3	19.5	19.2	19.3	19.3	19.3	19.3	19.2	19.1	19.3	19.4	19.6	19.5	19.6	19.3
Female	19.4	17.8	17.8	17.8	17.9	17.9	17.8	17.8	17.6	17.9	17.9	18.1	18.1	18.1	18.0
English, total ...	18.5	17.7	17.7	17.9	17.9	17.9	17.8	17.9	17.8	18.1	18.1	18.5	18.4	18.5	18.4
Male	17.6	17.1	17.0	17.4	17.4	17.3	17.3	17.3	17.3	17.5	17.6	17.9	17.9	18.0	17.8
Female	19.4	18.3	18.2	18.3	18.4	18.3	18.2	18.4	18.2	18.6	18.6	18.9	18.9	19.0	18.9
Math, total	20.0	17.6	17.4	17.5	17.5	17.4	17.3	17.2	16.9	17.3	17.2	17.3	17.2	17.2	17.1
Male	21.1	19.3	18.9	19.1	19.1	18.9	18.9	18.6	18.4	18.6	18.6	18.8	18.6	18.4	18.3
Female	18.8	16.2	16.1	16.2	16.2	16.2	16.0	16.0	15.7	16.1	16.0	16.0	16.1	16.1	16.1
Social studies, total	19.7	17.4	17.3	17.1	17.2	17.2	17.2	17.3	17.1	17.3	17.4	17.6	17.5	17.4	17.2
Male	20.3	18.7	18.2	18.0	18.1	18.2	18.3	18.1	18.0	18.1	18.3	18.6	18.4	18.4	18.1
Female	19.0	16.4	16.5	16.4	16.4	16.4	16.4	16.6	16.4	16.5	16.6	16.9	16.7	16.6	16.4
Natural science, total	20.8	21.1	20.9	20.9	21.1	21.1	21.0	20.8	20.9	21.0	21.2	21.4	21.4	21.4	21.2
Male	21.6	22.4	22.3	22.3	22.3	22.4	22.3	22.2	22.4	22.4	22.6	22.7	22.8	22.8	22.6
Female	20.0	20.0	19.6	19.8	20.2	20.0	20.0	19.7	19.6	19.9	20.0	20.2	20.1	20.2	20.0

[1] Scores on each test range from 1 to 36.

SOURCE: The American College Testing Program, *High School Profile Report, 1987* and "ACT News," September 12, 1989. (This table was prepared November 1989.)

Table 130.—Average number of Carnegie units earned by high school graduates in various subject fields, by student characteristics: 1982 and 1987

Student characteristics	Total	English	History/ social studies	Math	Computer science	Science	Foreign language	Voca- tional educa- tion [1]	Arts	Physical educa- tion	Other [2]
1	2	3	4	5	6	7	8	9	10	11	12
1982 graduates											
All students	**21.2**	**3.80**	**3.10**	**2.54**	**0.11**	**2.19**	**1.05**	**3.98**	**1.39**	**1.93**	**1.14**
Sex											
Male	21.0	3.76	3.09	2.61	0.13	2.25	0.86	3.91	1.23	2.06	1.06
Female	21.5	3.84	3.12	2.46	0.10	2.13	1.23	4.05	1.55	1.81	1.20
Race/ethnicity											
White	21.4	3.78	3.15	2.59	0.12	2.27	1.13	3.89	1.45	1.89	1.12
Black	20.5	3.90	2.97	2.44	0.10	1.99	0.73	4.15	1.18	1.98	1.07
Hispanic	20.8	3.79	2.94	2.22	0.07	1.79	0.78	4.55	1.27	2.13	1.25
Asian	22.0	3.94	3.04	3.11	0.19	2.56	1.81	2.56	1.22	2.21	1.34
Academic track											
Academic	22.6	4.17	3.52	3.34	0.15	3.01	1.71	2.16	1.39	1.92	1.18
Vocational	20.8	3.48	2.69	1.74	0.06	1.43	0.35	7.54	0.96	1.80	0.78
Both	24.7	4.41	3.74	2.99	0.12	2.58	0.55	6.66	0.89	2.01	0.77
Neither	19.4	3.44	2.71	1.91	0.09	1.53	0.70	3.96	1.70	2.00	1.32
Control											
Public	21.1	3.77	3.05	2.46	0.11	2.14	0.94	4.21	1.42	1.98	0.98
Private	22.7	4.10	3.52	3.16	0.08	2.57	1.95	2.09	1.20	1.50	2.51
1987 graduates											
All students	**23.0**	**4.03**	**3.33**	**2.97**	**0.43**	**2.59**	**1.46**	**3.65**	**1.43**	**1.97**	**1.14**
Sex											
Male	22.9	4.01	3.31	3.03	0.47	2.66	1.29	3.67	1.24	2.13	1.07
Female	23.1	4.05	3.35	2.92	0.40	2.53	1.63	3.64	1.60	1.81	1.21
Race/ethnicity											
White	23.1	3.99	3.30	2.98	0.45	2.64	1.50	3.69	1.48	1.94	1.11
Black	22.5	4.14	3.31	2.90	0.35	2.39	1.12	4.01	1.20	2.01	1.11
Hispanic	22.9	4.23	3.23	2.77	0.36	2.33	1.27	3.57	1.35	2.40	1.37
Asian	24.5	4.31	3.64	3.72	0.57	3.17	2.17	2.08	1.12	2.57	1.14
Academic track											
Academic	23.8	4.24	3.62	3.46	0.50	3.10	1.95	2.23	1.50	1.94	1.21
Vocational	22.1	3.61	2.73	1.99	0.24	1.65	0.49	7.74	0.94	1.91	0.83
Both	24.2	4.22	3.47	3.00	0.34	2.46	0.83	6.40	0.79	1.88	0.79
Neither	20.7	3.57	2.76	2.07	0.40	1.68	0.89	4.08	1.83	2.12	1.29
Control											
Public	22.9	4.01	3.31	2.92	0.43	2.57	1.37	3.88	1.44	2.06	0.94
Private	23.7	4.25	3.53	3.44	0.44	2.81	2.37	1.52	1.26	1.08	2.96

[1] Includes non-occupational vocational education, vocational general introduction, agriculture, business, marketing, health, occupational home economics, trade and industry, and technical courses.

[2] Includes personal and social courses, religion and theology, and all other courses not included in the other subject fields.

NOTE.—The Carnegie unit is a standard of measurement that represents one credit for the completion of a 1-year course.

SOURCE: U.S. Department of Education, National Center for Education Statistics, "1987 High School Transcript Study." (This table was prepared December 1988.)

Table 131.—Average number of Carnegie units earned by high school graduates in vocational education courses, by student characteristics: 1982 and 1987

Student characteristics	Total	Non-occupational vocational education	Vocational general introduction	Agriculture	Business	Marketing	Health	Occupational home economics	Trade and industry	Technical
1	2	3	4	5	6	7	8	9	10	11
1982 graduates										
All students	**3.98**	**1.84**	**0.37**	**0.17**	**0.78**	**0.08**	**0.04**	**0.09**	**0.60**	**0.01**
Sex										
Male	3.91	1.75	0.36	0.29	0.29	0.07	0.02	0.04	1.07	0.02
Female	4.05	1.93	0.38	0.06	1.23	0.09	0.06	0.14	0.15	0.01
Race/ethnicity										
White	3.89	1.78	0.36	0.18	0.80	0.08	0.03	0.09	0.55	0.02
Black	4.15	1.96	0.41	0.06	0.74	0.10	0.10	0.10	0.67	0.01
Hispanic	4.55	2.17	0.43	0.18	0.73	0.07	0.05	0.10	0.81	0.01
Asian	2.56	1.37	0.18	0.05	0.45	0.03	0.03	0.03	0.41	0.01
Academic track										
Academic	2.16	1.28	0.18	0.04	0.37	0.03	0.02	0.04	0.19	0.01
Vocational	7.54	2.13	0.77	0.51	1.83	0.18	0.08	0.17	1.85	0.02
Both	6.66	1.95	0.54	0.54	1.78	0.21	0.12	0.14	1.37	0.01
Neither	3.96	2.34	0.36	0.09	0.59	0.08	0.03	0.11	0.34	0.02
Control										
Public	4.21	1.94	0.39	0.18	0.81	0.09	0.04	0.10	0.65	0.01
Private	2.09	1.03	0.20	0.04	0.55	0.03	0.02	0.03	0.18	0.01
1987 graduates										
All students	**3.65**	**1.64**	**0.34**	**0.17**	**0.68**	**0.10**	**0.05**	**0.10**	**0.56**	**0.01**
Sex										
Male	3.67	1.61	0.31	0.28	0.34	0.07	0.03	0.05	0.96	0.02
Female	3.64	1.67	0.37	0.06	1.01	0.12	0.07	0.15	0.18	0.01
Race/ethnicity										
White	3.69	1.66	0.33	0.20	0.69	0.10	0.04	0.09	0.57	0.01
Black	4.01	1.83	0.44	0.09	0.74	0.11	0.09	0.19	0.50	0.02
Hispanic	3.57	1.64	0.30	0.06	0.70	0.11	0.05	0.09	0.62	0.00
Asian	2.08	1.01	0.20	0.01	0.44	0.08	0.03	0.05	0.25	0.01
Academic track										
Academic	2.23	1.29	0.20	0.04	0.42	0.03	0.02	0.04	0.18	0.01
Vocational	7.74	2.22	0.72	0.58	1.54	0.31	0.13	0.28	1.95	0.01
Both	6.40	1.67	0.58	0.59	1.49	0.23	0.13	0.23	1.46	0.02
Neither	4.08	2.35	0.40	0.10	0.58	0.10	0.04	0.12	0.38	0.01
Control										
Public	3.88	1.74	0.36	0.19	0.71	0.11	0.05	0.11	0.60	0.01
Private	1.52	0.73	0.15	0.01	0.43	0.01	0.01	0.00	0.17	0.01

NOTE.—The Carnegie unit is a standard of measurement that represents one credit for the completion of a 1-year course.

SOURCE: U.S. Department of Education, National Center for Education Statistics, "1987 High School Transcript Study." (This table was prepared December 1988.)

Table 132.—Percentage of high school graduates earning minimum credits in selected combinations of academic courses: 1982 and 1987

Year of graduation and course combinations taken [1]	All students	Sex		Race/ethnicity			
		Male	Female	White	Black	Hispanic	Asian
1	2	3	4	5	6	7	8
1982 graduates							
4 Eng., 3 S.S., 3 Sci., 3 Math, .5 Comp., & 2 F.L. [2]	1.9	2.0	1.7	2.2	0.7	0.5	6.0
4 Eng., 3 S.S., 3 Sci., 3 Math, & .5 Comp. [3]	2.7	3.3	2.1	3.1	1.0	0.9	7.1
4 Eng., 3 S.S., 3 Sci., 3 Math, & 2 F.L.	8.8	8.5	9.2	10.1	5.2	3.5	17.0
4 Eng., 3 S.S., 3 Sci., & 3 Math	13.4	14.3	12.6	14.9	10.1	6.3	21.0
4 Eng., 3 S.S., 2 Sci., & 2 Math	29.2	29.1	29.3	30.2	28.1	23.5	34.5
1987 graduates							
4 Eng., 3 S.S., 3 Sci., 3 Math, .5 Comp., & 2 F.L. [2]	12.0	13.3	10.9	12.7	8.3	5.5	24.3
4 Eng., 3 S.S., 3 Sci., 3 Math, & .5 Comp. [3]	16.3	18.4	14.4	17.2	11.7	8.6	28.1
4 Eng., 3 S.S., 3 Sci., 3 Math, & 2 F.L.	20.9	20.9	20.9	21.8	16.1	11.8	41.9
4 Eng., 3 S.S., 3 Sci., & 3 Math	28.6	30.1	27.2	29.7	24.3	17.9	48.3
4 Eng., 3 S.S., 2 Sci., & 2 Math	54.6	54.6	54.7	53.5	57.2	55.1	71.8

Increase from 1982 to 1987, in percentage points

Difference from 1982 to 1987							
4 Eng., 3 S.S., 3 Sci., 3 Math, .5 Comp., & 2 F.L. [2]	10.2	11.2	9.2	10.5	7.6	5.0	18.2
4 Eng., 3 S.S., 3 Sci., 3 Math, & .5 Comp. [3]	13.6	15.1	12.3	14.1	10.7	7.7	21.0
4 Eng., 3 S.S., 3 Sci., 3 Math, & 2 F.L.	12.1	12.4	11.8	11.7	10.9	8.4	24.9
4 Eng., 3 S.S., 3 Sci., & 3 Math	15.2	15.8	14.7	14.8	14.2	11.6	27.2
4 Eng., 3 S.S., 2 Sci., & 2 Math	25.4	25.5	25.4	23.4	29.1	31.6	37.3

[1] Eng. = English; S.S. = Social Studies; Sci. = Science; Comp. = Computer Science; and F.L. = Foreign Language.

[2] The National Commission on Excellence in Education recommended that all college-bound high school students follow these courses as a minimum.

[3] The National Commission on Excellence in Education recommended that all high school students follow these courses as a minimum.

NOTE.—Calculations based on unrounded figures.

SOURCE: U.S. Department of Education, National Center for Education Statistics, "1987 High School Transcript Study," unpublished tabulations. (This table was prepared December 1988.)

Table 133.—High school courses taken by persons age 18 and over,[1] by sex, race, and age: Spring 1984

[Numbers in thousands]

Courses taken	Total	Sex		Race		Age					
		Men	Women	White	Black	16 to 24 years old	25 to 34 years old	35 to 44 years old	45 to 54 years old	55 to 64 years old	65 years old and over
1	2	3	4	5	6	7	8	9	10	11	12
Persons over 18 who have attended 12 years of school or more	129,856	62,334	67,522	114,366	12,180	25,512	35,177	25,716	16,634	14,380	12,438

Number of persons completing courses

Algebra	102,696	50,837	51,859	90,689	9,272	20,106	27,554	20,314	12,882	11,437	10,404
Trigonometry or geometry	71,429	37,456	33,973	63,582	5,662	13,764	19,804	14,409	8,105	7,685	7,662
Chemistry or physics	62,352	33,812	28,540	54,268	5,922	11,771	17,111	12,714	7,579	6,979	6,197
English, 3 years or more	121,383	57,852	63,531	107,092	11,486	24,262	32,638	24,291	15,407	13,268	11,519
Foreign language, 2 years or more	56,855	24,384	32,471	50,493	4,456	10,187	16,093	11,622	6,422	5,867	6,665
Industrial arts, shop, or home economics, 2 years or more	73,883	36,243	37,640	63,758	8,230	15,300	20,708	14,896	9,874	7,701	5,404
Business courses, 2 years or more	54,297	16,043	38,254	47,865	5,190	10,967	14,165	11,280	7,315	6,184	4,386

Percentage of persons completing courses

Algebra	79.1	81.6	76.8	79.3	76.1	78.8	78.3	79.0	77.4	79.5	83.6
Trigonometry or geometry	55.0	60.1	50.3	55.6	46.5	54.0	56.3	56.0	48.7	53.4	61.6
Chemistry or physics	48.0	54.2	42.3	47.5	48.6	46.1	48.6	49.4	45.6	48.5	49.8
English, 3 years or more	93.5	92.8	94.1	93.6	94.3	95.1	92.8	94.5	92.6	92.3	92.6
Foreign language, 2 years or more	43.8	39.1	48.1	44.2	36.6	39.9	45.7	45.2	38.6	40.8	53.6
Industrial arts, shop, or home economics, 2 years or more	56.9	58.1	55.7	55.7	67.6	60.0	58.9	57.9	59.4	53.6	43.4
Business courses, 2 years or more	41.8	25.7	56.7	41.9	42.6	43.0	40.3	43.9	44.0	43.0	35.3

[1] Includes only persons completing 12 years of school or more.

NOTE.—Data are based on sample surveys of the civilian noninstitutional population.

SOURCE: U.S. Department of Commerce, Bureau of the Census, Current Population Reports, Series P–70, No. 11, "Educational Background and Economic Status: Spring 1984." (This table was prepared October 1987.)

Table 134.—Eighth graders' attitudes about selected classes, by selected student and school characteristics: 1988

Class subject and attitude	All 8th graders	Sex		Race/ethnicity					Socioeconomic status [1]			Control of school attended		
		Male	Female	White	Black	Hispanic	Asian	American Indian	Low	Middle	High	Public	Catholic	Other private
1	2	3	4	5	6	7	8	9	10	11	12	13	14	15
Mathematics class														
Look forward to	56.6	58.7	54.6	52.8	69.2	64.2	67.6	63.7	62.7	55.9	52.3	57.0	53.8	53.8
Afraid to ask questions ...	20.9	18.6	23.2	19.3	22.0	28.6	23.1	32.5	25.7	20.3	17.7	21.4	19.0	14.8
Useful in my future	88.0	89.0	86.9	87.4	89.3	89.7	90.4	85.1	88.0	87.8	88.3	88.0	88.3	86.6
English class														
Look forward to	56.9	52.0	61.6	52.2	72.8	67.5	63.6	66.0	62.7	55.7	53.8	57.8	46.4	56.9
Afraid to ask questions ...	15.4	15.6	15.3	14.2	16.7	20.7	17.4	19.6	19.4	15.5	11.5	15.7	15.2	11.0
Useful in my future	84.1	80.6	87.6	82.9	87.9	88.1	88.0	80.7	83.3	83.4	86.4	84.1	84.0	85.1
Social studies class														
Look forward to	58.5	62.1	55.0	56.0	67.6	63.3	64.0	60.2	58.5	57.8	59.9	59.0	54.0	55.8
Afraid to ask questions ...	15.1	14.1	16.1	13.7	16.5	20.8	19.1	22.2	19.4	15.2	10.7	15.4	13.6	12.1
Useful in my future	59.1	61.0	57.3	56.9	66.7	63.0	64.7	64.3	61.2	57.2	60.9	59.3	55.4	61.5
Science class														
Look forward to	61.3	65.1	57.5	59.0	68.3	66.6	67.2	64.3	62.9	60.5	61.2	61.7	54.7	63.4
Afraid to ask questions ...	14.9	14.2	15.5	13.5	16.0	20.8	16.2	25.6	18.7	14.8	11.5	15.2	14.0	11.0
Useful in my future	68.7	72.3	65.2	67.6	71.7	70.4	74.5	67.6	68.1	67.6	71.4	68.9	64.3	70.6

[1] Socioeconomic status was measured by a composite score on parental education and occupations and family income. The "Low" SES group is the lowest quartile; the "Middle" SES group is the middle two quartiles; and the "High" SES group is the upper quartile.

SOURCE: U.S. Department of Education, National Center for Education Statistics, "National Education Longitudinal Study of 1988" survey. (This table was prepared June 1989.)

Table 135.—Expected occupations of 8th graders at age 30, by selected student and school characteristics: 1988

Expected occupation at age 30	All 8th graders	Sex		Race/ethnicity					Socioeconomic status [1]			Control of school attended		
		Male	Female	White	Black	Hispanic	Asian	American Indian	Low	Middle	High	Public	Catholic	Other private
1	2	3	4	5	6	7	8	9	10	11	12	13	14	15
Total	100.0	100.0	100.0	100.0	100.0	100.0	100.0	100.0	100.0	100.0	100.0	100.0	100.0	100.0
Craftsperson or operator	4.2	7.6	0.9	4.3	3.2	5.3	3.6	6.6	7.1	4.3	1.4	4.5	2.4	2.0
Farmer or farm manager	1.0	1.7	0.3	1.2	0.1	0.6	0.6	0.3	1.0	1.2	0.5	1.0	0.3	1.0
Housewife/homemaker	2.3	0.2	4.4	2.5	0.9	2.9	1.1	3.1	3.2	1.9	2.2	2.2	2.1	3.8
Laborer or farm worker	0.6	1.0	0.1	0.5	0.6	0.8	0.7	0.2	1.1	0.4	0.3	0.6	0.2	0.1
Military, police, or security officer	9.6	14.9	4.3	9.0	11.4	11.0	7.0	17.0	11.5	10.2	6.5	10.0	6.4	6.0
Professional, business, or managerial	28.6	19.6	37.6	28.7	29.3	26.0	34.9	23.0	20.1	27.6	38.9	27.6	36.2	36.9
Business owner	6.2	6.8	5.6	6.3	5.8	5.7	6.4	5.7	4.7	6.4	7.2	6.0	7.6	8.0
Technical	6.2	8.3	4.2	5.7	8.0	7.3	7.6	6.5	6.4	6.6	5.1	6.4	5.6	4.2
Salesperson, clerical, or office worker	2.8	1.2	4.5	2.7	2.9	3.8	2.3	2.3	3.8	2.9	1.7	2.9	2.1	1.8
Science or engineering professional	5.9	8.5	3.3	6.1	4.2	4.8	9.7	6.4	3.4	5.3	9.4	5.6	7.5	7.6
Service worker	4.9	2.1	7.7	4.9	6.4	3.9	2.3	3.4	7.2	5.0	2.5	5.1	3.2	3.0
Other employment	17.0	17.6	16.5	17.7	16.3	15.1	13.4	11.9	15.7	17.9	16.6	17.0	17.7	16.4
Don't know	10.5	10.4	10.6	10.2	10.4	12.5	10.5	13.5	14.3	10.1	7.5	10.8	8.3	9.1

[1] Socioeconomic status was measured by a composite score on parental education and occupations and family income. The "Low" SES group is the lowest quartile; the "Middle" SES group is the middle two quartiles; and the "High" SES group is the upper quartile.

SOURCE: U.S. Department of Education, National Center for Education Statistics, "National Education Longitudinal Study of 1988" survey. (This table was prepared June 1989.)

Table 136.—Eighth graders' attitudes about school climate, by student and school characteristics: 1988

Statements about school climate	All 8th grad- ers	Percentage who strongly agree or agree with statement												
		Sex		Race/ethnicity					Socioeconomic status [1]			Control of school attended		
		Male	Fe- male	White	Black	His- panic	Asian	Amer- ican Indian	Low	Mid- dle	High	Pub- lic	Catho- lic	Other pri- vate
1	2	3	4	5	6	7	8	9	10	11	12	13	14	15
Students get along well with teachers	67.1	67.6	66.5	68.1	60.5	66.4	73.0	65.2	64.3	66.2	71.5	65.6	75.4	80.5
There is real school spirit	68.6	67.2	69.9	69.8	65.0	64.9	66.7	67.4	67.9	68.9	68.7	68.1	70.5	74.0
Rules for behavior are strict	68.5	70.9	66.1	68.5	68.7	68.4	67.3	65.4	68.2	68.1	69.4	67.1	78.4	77.2
Discipline is fair	69.1	67.3	70.9	69.7	65.0	70.7	72.5	63.5	67.1	68.3	72.7	68.9	69.4	72.7
Other students often disrupt class	77.9	78.2	77.5	77.3	80.5	79.1	76.1	79.0	79.1	78.5	75.6	79.0	70.8	67.8
Teaching is good	80.2	78.9	81.5	80.0	80.0	81.3	83.4	76.7	78.8	79.5	83.0	79.6	82.9	88.4
Teachers are interested in students	75.2	74.9	75.6	74.7	76.6	76.8	78.6	68.5	74.0	74.8	77.3	73.9	83.0	88.2
Teachers praise my effort when I work hard	63.3	63.0	63.5	60.3	72.1	70.7	70.8	63.3	66.8	61.7	63.0	62.3	66.9	74.8
I often feel "put down" by my teachers	21.8	23.4	20.1	21.7	21.5	22.6	17.1	30.5	23.7	21.9	19.6	21.8	22.4	19.3
Teachers listen to what I have to say	68.4	66.9	69.9	67.1	73.2	70.6	74.9	62.1	68.9	66.9	70.9	67.5	73.3	78.2
I don't feel safe at this school	11.8	13.3	10.3	9.9	18.0	16.1	12.2	17.4	15.3	12.1	7.9	12.5	7.6	5.8
Disruptions by other students interfere with my learning	39.6	39.3	39.9	35.7	54.9	44.9	45.1	55.2	48.0	39.4	32.1	41.0	31.8	28.0
Misbehaving students often get away with it	52.8	57.5	48.0	51.9	53.4	55.7	55.3	59.0	52.7	52.2	53.9	53.3	50.5	45.9

[1] Socioeconomic status was measured by a composite score on parental education and occupations and family income. The "Low" SES group is the lowest quartile; the "Middle" SES group is the middle two quartiles; and the "High" SES group is the upper quartile.

SOURCE: U.S. Department of Education, National Center for Education Statistics, "National Education Longitudinal Study of 1988" survey. (This table was prepared June 1989.)

Table 137.—Sex education in public and private schools: 1986

[Percent of all teenagers]

Sex education, by grade level and content of class	All teen- agers	Age of student responding			Region			
		12–13 years	14–15 years	16–17 years	East	Midwest	South	West
1	2	3	4	5	6	7	8	9
Ever had sex education course or class ..	**59**	**42**	**60**	**73**	**65**	**54**	**45**	**80**
Beginning in								
1st to 4th grade	6	13	4	4	7	7	2	6
5th grade	20	40	19	10	16	20	20	23
6th grade	18	21	19	16	28	13	12	20
7th grade	18	19	22	14	23	12	14	22
8th grade	13	5	13	17	14	9	13	15
9th grade	15	—	17	21	5	24	25	6
10th grade or later	7	—	(¹)	16	4	6	10	8
In one grade or more								
Just one grade	49	52	46	50	43	50	62	42
In more than one grade	49	44	52	49	56	46	38	55
Contents of sex education class								
Biological facts about reproduction	52	83	89	92	97	82	89	88
Coping with sexual development	46	66	83	83	85	76	84	71
Different types of birth control	39	48	63	79	71	55	74	65
Preventing sexual abuse	32	56	55	53	46	49	61	62
Facts about abortion	32	39	57	59	57	45	54	60
Where to get contraceptives	30	31	45	67	55	45	60	44
Percent who have had comprehensive sex education [2]	35	40	60	70	64	49	64	62

[1] Less than 0.5 percent.

[2] "Comprehensive" sex education includes at least four of the six content areas listed above.

—Data not applicable.

SOURCE: Planned Parenthood Federation of America, Inc., Louis Harris and Associates, Inc., *American Teens Speak: Sex, Myths, TV, and Birth Control*, September–October 1986. (This table was prepared November 1988.)

Table 138.—Participation of high school seniors in extracurricular activities, by selected student characteristics: 1972 and 1982

Student characteristics	Percentage of seniors participating in activities								
	Athletics [1]	Debating, drama, band, chorus [2]	Subject-matter clubs	Vocational education clubs	Newspaper, magazine, or yearbook clubs	Student council, government, political clubs	Hobby clubs	Cheerleaders, pep club, majorettes	Honorary clubs
1	2	3	4	5	6	7	8	9	10
All 1972 seniors	**44.5**	**32.9**	**25.8**	**23.0**	**20.4**	**19.6**	**18.7**	**17.3**	**14.8**
Sex									
Male	58.2	26.9	20.4	16.0	14.7	18.6	23.7	5.3	11.1
Female	32.1	39.8	31.2	29.8	26.7	21.0	13.3	29.6	19.4
Race									
White	44.5	32.6	25.0	21.9	20.7	19.2	18.3	17.3	15.7
Black	49.7	40.6	33.1	33.1	21.2	25.5	19.7	20.5	11.6
Father's highest level of education									
Less than high school ...	39.3	31.1	24.1	30.0	19.4	15.4	16.9	15.6	12.5
High school graduate [3] ..	46.7	32.9	25.7	21.9	21.4	20.2	18.0	19.6	16.1
College graduate [4]	51.4	40.2	28.6	12.4	24.2	27.6	20.8	17.5	23.1
High school curriculum									
General	43.3	33.0	22.3	24.3	17.5	15.5	19.4	15.5	7.0
Academic	53.4	39.7	29.6	14.8	25.7	26.7	17.7	20.2	25.2
Vocational	31.3	21.9	22.9	37.2	15.4	12.1	18.7	15.2	6.6
All 1982 seniors	**51.5**	**34.6**	**20.6**	**23.6**	**18.3**	**16.3**	**20.0**	**13.7**	**15.6**
Sex									
Male	61.7	25.8	16.4	20.2	13.3	13.1	23.5	4.1	12.1
Female	41.8	42.9	24.6	26.7	23.1	19.3	16.7	22.8	18.8
Race									
White	51.1	34.0	19.7	22.2	19.1	15.6	19.1	13.5	16.8
Black	54.5	43.1	23.9	30.0	16.0	19.7	19.5	16.8	12.5
Father's highest level of education									
Less than high school ...	43.4	29.4	21.2	31.0	14.6	12.2	18.4	11.8	10.6
High school graduate [3] ..	52.4	33.8	19.8	24.1	17.9	15.9	19.9	14.6	14.9
College graduate [4]	62.6	42.4	23.1	13.4	25.9	24.1	21.0	14.4	26.8
High school curriculum									
General	49.5	33.1	16.7	22.9	15.0	11.6	20.8	12.6	7.7
Academic	61.1	41.9	25.4	12.7	25.5	24.7	19.6	15.7	28.4
Vocational	40.7	26.0	18.7	40.2	12.4	10.5	19.5	12.4	7.7

[1] In 1972, includes participation in team athletics, intramurals, letterman's clubs, and sports clubs. In 1982, includes varsity athletic teams and other athletic teams—in or out of school.
[2] In 1972, includes debating, drama, band, and chorus. In 1982, includes debating, drama, band, orchestra, chorus, and dance.
[3] Includes attendance at a vocational, trade or business school, or 2-year college, or attendance at a 4-year college resulting in less than a bachelor's degree.

[4] Includes those with a bachelor's or higher-level degree.

SOURCE: U.S. Department of Education, National Center for Education Statistics, "National Longitudinal Study of 1972" and High School and Beyond surveys. (This table was prepared August 1987.)

Table 139.—Incidence of student infractions, disciplinary actions, and perceived changes in amount of classroom disruption in public secondary schools, by school characteristics: 1983–84

Disruption or disciplinary action	All public secondary schools	Type [1]		School size			Metropolitan status			District size		
		Junior high	Senior high	Less than 400	400 to 999	1,000 or more	Rural	Sub-urban	Urban	Less than 1,000	1,000 to 24,999	25,000 or more
1	2	3	4	5	6	7	8	9	10	11	12	13

Percentage of schools with occurrences

Student infractions												
Student caught selling illegal drugs at school	35	31	39	10	38	63	21	46	51	11	40	48
Theft of personal item reported to school [2]	82	80	84	71	85	93	79	84	89	72	84	87
Law violations reported to police by school authorities	72	70	75	62	71	88	64	76	88	61	73	85
Disciplinary actions												
Suspension for disciplinary reasons	96	97	95	89	98	99	92	98	100	88	97	99
In-school alternative to suspension	69	75	66	63	71	75	66	75	65	57	74	66
Expulsion	37	31	42	29	35	51	35	35	45	27	37	50
Transfer to special school for disruptive students	33	39	30	14	38	50	19	43	52	12	34	56

Occurrences per 100 students [3]

Student infractions												
Student caught selling illegal drugs at school	0.2	0.2	0.2	0.2	0.2	0.2	0.1	0.2	0.5	0.1	0.2	0.4
Theft of personal item reported to school [2]	1.2	0.8	1.4	1.7	0.9	1.1	1.4	1.0	1.3	2.0	1.0	1.1
Law violations reported to police by school authorities	0.8	0.7	0.8	1.0	0.7	0.9	0.7	0.8	1.5	0.9	0.7	1.2
Disciplinary actions												
Suspension for disciplinary reasons	10.0	10.2	9.9	7.1	10.1	13.7	6.6	10.9	18.8	4.7	10.4	15.3
In-school alternative to suspension	9.9	10.1	9.9	6.0	10.9	13.1	7.1	12.1	12.9	4.9	11.2	11.3
Expulsion	0.3	0.2	0.3	0.4	0.2	0.2	0.2	0.2	0.6	0.3	0.2	0.5
Transfer to special school for disruptive students	0.3	0.3	0.4	0.2	0.3	0.6	0.1	0.4	0.9	0.1	0.2	0.9

Percentage of school administrators

Perceived change in amount of classroom disruption between 1980 and 1985 [4]												
Less	66	59	73	60	69	68	65	71	58	66	66	66
Same	22	28	18	27	20	19	24	20	22	22	23	17
More	12	13	10	13	11	13	12	9	20	11	11	16

[1] Some schools have both elementary and secondary grades. These schools are not shown separately because their number is small. These schools are included in the totals and in analyses by other school characteristics.

[2] Includes only thefts of items valued at $10 or more reported by students to school authorities.

[3] Based on all schools, including those reporting no occurrences.

[4] School authorities compared current disruptive classroom behavior with that of 5 years ago on a 5-point scale ranging from "much less now" to "much more now." Percents have been adjusted for "don't know" responses. Because of rounding, details may not add to totals.

SOURCE: U.S. Department of Education, National Center for Education Statistics, "Discipline in Public Secondary Schools." (This table was prepared October 1986.)

Table 140.—Teacher perceptions of changes in disruptive student behavior, by school characteristics: 1986–87

School characteristics	Percent of teachers indicating that compared to 5 years ago disruptive behavior is—				
	Much less now	Somewhat less now	About the same	Somewhat more now	Much more now
1	2	3	4	5	6
All teachers	**10**	**17**	**28**	**25**	**19**
School level [1]					
Elementary	8	12	27	29	24
Middle school and junior high	13	22	24	22	20
Senior high school	12	23	32	22	12
School enrollment					
Less than 400	11	16	28	25	21
400 to 999	10	17	28	26	19
1,000 or more	10	19	30	24	17
Metropolitan status					
Urban [2]	15	16	20	23	26
Suburban [3]	8	16	32	26	18
Rural [4]	11	19	28	26	16

[1] Elementary schools include all schools in which the lowest grade is less than 6 and the highest grade is less than 9; middle schools and junior high schools include all schools in which the lowest grade is greater than 5 and the highest grade is less than 10; Senior high schools include all schools in which the lowest grade is greater than 6 and the highest grade is greater than 9. The small number of combined schools, which offer elementary and secondary-level education, are not shown by level of school, but are included in other totals.

[2] Within Standard Metropolitan Statistical Areas, inside central city.

[3] Within Standard Metropolitan Statistical Areas, outside central city.

[4] Outside of Standard Metropolitan Statistical Areas.

NOTE.—Because of rounding, details may not add to totals.

SOURCE: U.S. Department of Education, National Center for Education Statistics, Fast Response Survey System, "Public School Teacher Perspectives on School Discipline." (This table was prepared December 1987.)

Table 141.—Percentage of teachers rating selected factors as limiting their ability to maintain order, by school level and metropolitan status: 1986–87

Factors rated as limiting teachers much or very much [1]	All teachers	School level [2]			Metropolitan status		
		Elementary school	Middle and junior high school	Senior high school	Urban [3]	Suburban [4]	Rural [5]
1	2	3	4	5	6	7	8
Lack of or inadequate alternative placements/programs for disruptive students	39	43	39	35	52	36	36
Lack of student interest in learning	38	31	43	47	45	37	36
School or district restrictions on the use of strict penalties	22	21	25	23	34	21	17
Lack of administrative support	20	19	20	23	26	18	19
Likelihood of complaint from parents	19	23	17	14	23	18	18
Principal/administrator fear of being sued for disciplining students	18	19	15	18	21	17	18
Teacher fear of being sued for disciplining students	18	22	14	14	21	15	21
Lack of or inadequate teacher training in discipline procedures and school law	15	15	17	13	20	13	13
Court decisions on student misconduct	15	13	19	17	24	14	11
Teacher fear of being viewed as unable to control students	15	15	16	15	22	12	13
Fear of student reprisal	6	5	5	6	11	3	5
Lack of or inadequate security personnel	6	3	7	10	14	5	4

[1] Teachers responded on a 6-point scale with 0="not at all"; 1="very little"; 4="much"; and 5="very much." Percents are based on teachers who indicated the factor limited them "much" or "very much."

[2] Elementary schools include all schools in which the lowest grade is less than 6 and the highest grade is less than 9; middle schools and junior high schools include all schools in which the lowest grade is greater than 5 and the highest grade is less than 10; senior high schools include all schools in which the lowest grade is greater than 6 and the highest grade is greater than 9. The small number of combined schools, which offer both elementary and secondary-level education, are not shown by level of school but are included in other totals.

[3] Within Standard Metropolitan Statistical Areas, inside central city.

[4] Within Standard Metropolitan Statistical Areas, outside central city.

[5] Outside of Standard Metropolitan Statistical Areas.

NOTE.—Because of rounding, details may not add to totals.

SOURCE: U.S. Department of Education, National Center for Education Statistics, Fast Response Survey System, "Public School Teacher Perspectives on School Discipline." (This table was prepared December 1987.)

Table 142.—Trends in drug use among high school seniors, by type of drug and frequency of use: 1975 to 1989

Type of drug and frequency of use	Class of 1975	Class of 1976	Class of 1977	Class of 1978	Class of 1979	Class of 1980	Class of 1981	Class of 1982	Class of 1983	Class of 1984	Class of 1985	Class of 1986	Class of 1987	Class of 1988	Class of 1989
1	2	3	4	5	6	7	8	9	10	11	12	13	14	15	16

Percentage reporting having ever used drugs

Alcohol	90.4	91.9	92.5	93.1	93.0	93.2	92.6	92.8	92.6	92.6	92.2	91.3	92.2	92.0	90.7
Any illicit drug abuse	55.2	58.3	61.6	64.1	65.1	65.4	65.6	64.4	62.9	61.6	60.6	57.6	56.6	53.9	50.9
Marijuana only	19.0	22.9	25.8	27.6	27.7	26.7	22.8	23.3	22.5	21.3	20.9	19.9	20.8	21.4	19.5
Any illicit drug other than marijuana[1]	36.2	35.4	35.8	36.5	37.4	38.7	42.8	41.1	40.4	40.3	39.7	37.7	35.8	32.5	31.4
Use of selected drugs															
Cocaine	9.0	9.7	10.8	12.9	15.4	15.7	16.5	16.0	16.2	16.1	17.3	16.9	15.2	12.1	10.3
Heroin	2.2	1.8	1.8	1.6	1.1	1.1	1.1	1.2	1.2	1.3	1.2	1.1	1.2	1.1	1.3
LSD	11.3	11.0	9.8	9.7	9.5	9.3	9.8	9.6	8.9	8.0	7.5	7.2	8.4	7.7	8.3
Marijuana/hashish	47.3	52.8	56.4	59.2	60.4	60.3	59.5	58.7	57.0	54.9	54.2	50.9	50.2	47.2	43.7
PCP	—	—	—	—	12.8	9.6	7.8	6.0	5.6	5.0	4.9	4.8	3.0	2.9	3.9

Percentage reporting use of drugs in the past 12 months

Alcohol	84.8	85.7	87.0	87.7	88.1	87.9	87.0	86.8	87.3	86.0	85.6	84.5	85.7	85.3	82.7
Any illicit drug abuse	45.0	48.1	51.1	53.8	54.2	53.1	52.1	49.4	47.4	45.8	46.3	44.3	41.7	38.5	35.4
Marijuana only	18.8	22.7	25.1	26.7	26.0	22.7	18.1	19.3	19.0	17.8	18.9	18.4	17.6	17.4	15.4
Any illicit drug other than marijuana[1]	26.2	25.4	26.0	27.1	28.2	30.4	34.0	30.1	28.4	28.0	27.4	25.9	24.1	21.1	20.0
Use of selected drugs															
Cocaine	5.6	6.0	7.2	9.0	12.0	12.3	12.4	11.5	11.4	11.6	13.1	12.7	10.3	7.9	6.5
Heroin	1.0	0.8	0.8	0.8	0.5	0.5	0.5	0.6	0.6	0.5	0.6	0.5	0.5	0.5	0.6
LSD	7.2	6.4	5.5	6.3	6.6	6.5	6.5	6.1	5.4	4.7	4.4	4.5	5.2	4.8	4.9
Marijuana/hashish	40.0	44.5	47.6	50.2	50.8	48.8	46.1	44.3	42.3	40.0	40.6	38.8	36.3	33.1	29.6
PCP	—	—	—	—	7.0	4.4	3.2	2.2	2.6	2.3	2.9	2.4	1.3	1.2	2.4

Percentage reporting use of drugs in the past 30 days

Alcohol	68.2	68.3	71.2	72.1	71.8	72.0	70.7	69.7	69.4	67.2	65.9	65.3	66.4	63.9	60.0
Any illicit drug abuse	30.7	34.2	37.6	38.9	38.9	37.2	36.9	32.5	30.5	29.2	29.7	27.1	24.7	21.3	19.7
Marijuana only	15.3	20.3	22.4	23.8	22.2	18.8	15.2	15.5	15.1	14.1	14.8	13.9	13.1	11.3	10.6
Any illicit drug other than marijuana[1]	15.4	13.9	15.2	15.1	16.8	18.4	21.7	17.0	15.4	15.1	14.9	13.2	11.6	10.0	9.1
Use of selected drugs															
Cocaine	1.9	2.0	2.9	3.9	5.7	5.2	5.8	5.0	4.9	5.8	6.7	6.2	4.3	3.4	2.8
Heroin	0.4	0.2	0.3	0.3	0.2	0.2	0.2	0.2	0.2	0.3	0.3	0.2	0.2	0.2	0.3
LSD	2.3	1.9	2.1	2.1	2.4	2.3	2.5	2.4	1.9	1.5	1.6	1.7	1.8	1.8	1.8
Marijuana/hashish	27.1	32.2	35.4	37.1	36.5	33.7	31.6	28.5	27.0	25.2	25.7	23.4	21.0	18.0	16.7
PCP	—	—	—	—	2.4	1.4	1.4	1.0	1.3	1.0	1.6	1.3	0.6	0.3	1.4

[1] Other illicit drugs include any use of hallucinogens, cocaine, and heroin, or any use of other opiates, stimulants, sedatives, or tranquilizers not under a doctor's orders.

—Data not available.

NOTE.—A revised questionnaire was used in 1982 and later years to reduce the inappropriate reporting of nonprescription stimulants. This slightly reduced the positive responses for some types of drug abuse.

SOURCE: U.S. Department of Health and Human Services, Alcohol, Drug Abuse, and Mental Health Administration, *Drug Use Among American High School Students and Other Young Adults, National Trends Through 1987* and press release dated February 1990. (This table was prepared May 1990.)

Table 143.—Ages for compulsory school attendance and compulsory provision of services for special education students, by State: 1989–90

State	Compulsory attendance (November 1989)	Compulsory provision of services for special education (1989–90)	State	Compulsory attendance (November 1989)	Compulsory provision of services for special education (1989–90)
1	2	3	1	2	3
Alabama	7 to 16	5 to 20	Missouri	7 to 16	5 to 20
Alaska	[1] 7 to 16	3 to 21	Montana	[6] 7 to 16	6 to 18
Arizona	8 to 16	[2] 5 to 21	Nebraska	7 to 16	Birth to 20
Arkansas	5 to 17	5 to 20	Nevada	7 to 17	5 to 21
California	6 to 16	[2] 5 to 21	New Hampshire	6 to 16	3 to 20
Colorado	7 to 16	[2] 5 to 20	New Jersey	6 to 16	3 to 21
Connecticut	7 to 16	3 to 21	New Mexico	6 to 18	3 to 21
Delaware	5 to 16	3 to 20	New York	[7] 6 to 16	[3] 3 to 21
District of Columbia	7 to 17	[3] 3 to 21	North Carolina	7 to 16	5 to 20
Florida	6 to 16	5 to 18	North Dakota	7 to 16	3 to 20
Georgia	7 to 16	5 to 21	Ohio	6 to 18	5 to 21
Hawaii	6 to 18	3 to 20	Oklahoma	7 to 18	4 to 21
Idaho	7 to 16	3 to 20	Oregon	7 to 18	5 to 20
Illinois	7 to 16	3 to 21	Pennsylvania	8 to 17	[2] 5 to 21
Indiana	7 to 16	5 to 17	Rhode Island	6 to 16	3 to 20
Iowa	7 to 16	Birth to 20	South Carolina	[8] 5 to 17	5 to 20
Kansas	7 to 16	5 to 21	South Dakota	[6] 7 to 16	3 to 20
Kentucky	[4] 6 to 16	5 to 20	Tennessee	7 to 17	4 to 21
Louisiana	7 to 17	3 to 21	Texas	[9] 7 to 17	3 to 21
Maine	7 to 17	5 to 19	Utah	6 to 18	[3] 3 to 21
Maryland	6 to 16	Birth to 20	Vermont	7 to 16	[2] 5 to 21
Massachusetts	6 to 16	3 to 21	Virginia	5 to 17	2 to 21
Michigan	6 to 16	Birth to 25	Washington	8 to 18	3 to 21
Minnesota	[5] 7 to 18	Birth to 20	West Virginia	6 to 16	5 to 22
Mississippi	6 to 14	5 to 20	Wisconsin	6 to 18	3 to 20
			Wyoming	7 to 16	3 to 20

[1] Ages 7 to 16 or high school graduation.

[2] State or local discretion determines at what point in the year children become eligible for services.

[3] State has established two points in the program year by which children must be 3 years of age to be eligible for services.

[4] Must have parental signature for leaving school between ages of 16 and 18.

[5] Takes effect in the year 2000. Currently 7 to 16.

[6] May leave after completion of eighth grade.

[7] The ages are 6 to 17 for New York City and Buffalo.

[8] Permits parental waiver of kindergarten at age 5.

[9] Must complete academic year in which 16th birthday occurs.

NOTE.—The Education of the Handicapped Act (EHA) Amendments of 1986 make it mandatory for all States receiving EHA funds to serve all 5- to 18-year-old handicapped children at present and all 3- to 5-year-old handicapped children by 1991.

SOURCE: U.S. Department of Education, Office of Special Education and Rehabilitative Services, *The Twelfth Annual Report to Congress on the Implementation of the Education of the Handicapped Act, 1990;* Education Commission of the States; "Compulsory School Age Requirements, March 1987," and unpublished revisions. (This table was prepared March 1991.)

Table 144.—Eighth graders' attendance patterns, by student and school characteristics: 1988

Attendance pattern	All 8th grad- ers	Sex		Race/ethnicity					Socioeconomic status [1]			Control of school attended		
		Male	Fe- male	White	Black	His- panic	Asian	American Indian	Low	Middle	High	Public	Catholic	Other private
1	2	3	4	5	6	7	8	9	10	11	12	13	14	15
Number of days missed over the past 4 weeks														
None	45.2	49.2	41.3	44.6	50.0	41.8	57.9	32.6	39.4	46.0	49.2	44.1	53.5	52.8
1 or 2 days	33.7	32.2	35.3	35.1	27.8	31.9	28.5	35.1	32.9	33.5	35.0	33.9	32.8	32.5
3 or 4 days	13.3	11.7	15.0	13.0	13.8	16.1	7.3	21.0	16.2	13.4	10.4	13.9	8.5	9.5
5 or more days	7.7	6.9	8.5	7.2	8.4	10.2	6.2	11.2	11.4	7.1	5.4	8.1	5.1	5.2
Number of times late over the past 4 weeks														
None	63.1	62.5	63.7	66.3	53.8	52.4	66.2	52.9	59.1	63.9	65.4	62.8	69.3	57.8
1 or 2 days	25.2	25.4	25.1	24.2	28.6	28.1	23.5	28.9	26.3	24.7	25.3	25.3	22.6	28.8
3 or more days	11.7	12.1	11.2	9.5	17.6	19.5	10.3	18.2	14.6	11.5	9.3	11.9	8.1	13.3
Cut classes														
Never or almost never	91.1	89.4	92.9	92.0	91.0	85.6	91.7	87.3	88.3	91.3	93.6	90.6	95.8	94.2
At least sometimes ..	8.9	10.6	7.1	8.0	9.0	14.4	8.3	12.7	11.7	8.7	6.4	9.4	4.2	5.8

[1] Socioeconomic status was measured by a composite score on parental education and occupations and family income. The "Low" SES group is the lowest quartile; the "Middle" SES group is the middle two quartiles; and the "High" SES group is the upper quartile.

SOURCE: U.S. Department of Education, National Center for Education Statistics, "National Education Longitudinal Study of 1988" survey. (This table was prepared June 1989.)

Table 145.—Average number of days per school year, classes per day, hours of class per day, and minutes per class in public high schools, by selected school characteristics: 1984–85

School characteristic	Days per school year	Credit classes per day	Hours of class per day	Minutes per class
1	2	3	4	5
United States average	**178.0**	**6.1**	**5.14**	**51.1**
District enrollment size				
Less than 2,500	177.5	6.1	5.22	51.0
2,500 to 9,999	179.0	5.8	4.92	50.9
10,000 or more	179.1	5.9	5.19	53.2
Metropolitan status				
In SMSA,[1] inside central city	179.0	5.9	4.98	51.2
In SMSA,[1] outside central city	179.0	5.9	4.92	49.7
Outside SMSA [1]	177.4	6.1	5.26	51.8
Region				
North Atlantic	180.2	6.0	4.45	44.8
Great Lakes and Plains	177.8	6.0	5.10	51.2
Southeast	177.9	5.8	5.33	54.9
West and Southwest	176.7	6.3	5.61	53.2

[1] Standard Metropolitan Statistical Area.

SOURCE: U.S. Department of Education, National Center for Education Statistics, Fast Response Survey System, "Public High School Graduation Requirements." (This table was prepared January 1988.)

Table 146.—State requirements for high school graduation, in Carnegie units: 1980 and 1990

State	1980 All courses	1989 All courses	English/ language arts	Social studies	Mathematics	Science	Physical education/ health	Electives	Other courses	First graduating class to which these requirements apply	Notes
1	2	3	4	5	6	7	8	9	10	11	12
Alabama											
Standard	20	22	4	3	2	2	1.5	9.5		1989	Must become computer literate through related coursework. Minimum competency test is required for graduation.
Advanced	—	22	4	4	3	3	1.5	4	2 foreign languages, .5 home/personal management		
Alaska	19	21	4	3	2	2	1	9		1991	Minimum competency test is required for graduation.
Arizona	16	20	4	2.5	2	2	—	9	.5 free enterprise		
Arkansas	16	20	4	3	3	2	1	6.5	.5 fine arts	1988	Social studies options: 3 or 2 units social studies and 1 practical arts.
California											
Standard	(1)	13	3	3	2	2	2	—	1 fine arts or foreign language	—	The State board has published "Model Graduation Requirements" to be used as a guide by local districts. These include specifics in core subjects plus computer studies and foreign language. Dept. of Education has test and cut-off standards for early exit with parental approval. State has suggested model of curriculum to guide local districts advising students on requirements for college entry. Minimum competency test is required for graduation.
Advanced	—	16	3	3	3	2	2	—	2 in same foreign language, 1 fine arts	—	
Colorado	—	(2)	(2)	(2)	(2)	(2)	(2)	(2)		—	State has constitutional prohibition against State requirements. School accreditation requirements total 30 units appropriately covering language arts, social studies, science, math, foreign language, fine/vocational/ practical arts, health/safety, and physical education.
Connecticut	(2)18	20	4	3	3	2	1	6	1 arts or vocational education	1988	
Delaware	18	19	4	3	2	2	1.5	6.5		1987	Minimum competency test is required for graduation.
District of Columbia	18	20.5	4	2	2	2	1.5	7	1 foreign language; 1 life skills	1985	Electives must include life skills seminar or passage of a test.
Florida											
Standard	(2)	24	4	3	3	3	0.5	9	.5 practical/exploratory vocational education; .5 performing arts or speech & debate; .5 life management skills	1989	2 of science units must include labs. Beginning with 1989 class, students must have 1.5 GPA to graduate. Junior and senior students may receive dual credits for college coursework. Vocational students may substitute certain sequences of vocational courses to satisfy up to 2 of required credits in each of the areas of English, math, and science. Minimum competency test is required for graduation.
Georgia											
Academic scholars	—	26	4	2	2	2	1.5	1.5	2 foreign languages; 1 fine arts	1989	
Standard	20	21	4	3	2	2	1	8	1 computer technology and/or fine arts and/or vocational education and/or junior ROTC	1988	Students who completed 4 units of required for graduation receive a State seal of endorsement. Minimum competency test is required for graduation.
Advanced	—	21	4	3	3	3	1	4	2 foreign languages; 1 fine arts, vocational education, computer technology, or ROTC	1988	
Hawaii	20	20	4	4	2	2	1.5	6	.5 guidance	—	

Table 146.—State requirements for high school graduation, in Carnegie units: 1980 and 1990—Continued

State	1980 All courses	1989 All courses	English/ language arts	Social studies	Mathematics	Science	Physical education/ health	Electives	Other courses	First graduating class to which these requirements apply	Notes
1	2	3	4	5	6	7	8	9	10	11	12
Idaho	18	21	4	2	2	2	1.5	6	.5 each: reading, speech, and consumer education; 2 humanities	1989	Practical arts may substitute for 1 unit of humanities. State requires a C average, demonstrated competency in core curriculum on a junior class competency test, or adherence to local district's achievement plan for graduation. State level minimum competency test is an option of the local districts. If passed, students receive special proficiency endorsement on their diploma.
Illinois	16	16	3	2	2	1	4.5	2.25	.25 consumer education; 1 art, foreign technology. 1 year of social language, music, or vocational education	1988	1 year of math may be computer technology. One year of social studies must be U.S. history or half U.S. history and half American government. Beginning 1985–86, the school boards were allowed to excuse 11–12th grade pupils from physical education to: 1)participate in interscholastic athletics or 2)enroll in academic class required for college admission or to graduate from high school. Beginning 1986–1987, 9–12th grade pupils may elect to take a SBE developed consumer education proficiency test; if passed, they are excused from requirement.
Indiana Standard	16	19.5	4	2	2	2	1.5	4 or 5	3 or 4 in foreign languages (3 in 1 or 2 years each in 2)	1989	State does not use standard Carnegie units.
Academic honors		24	4	3	4	4	1	8		1990	
Iowa	—	—	—	—	—	—	1	—		1989	Legislative requirements in effect for many years. Local districts determine remaining requirements. State allows junior and senior students to receive dual credits for college coursework.
Kansas	17	21	4	3	2	2	1	9		1989	
Kentucky Standard	18	20	4	2	3	2	1	7	1 additional math, science, social studies, or vocational education	1987	
Commonwealth		22	5	2	—	—	1	7	1 foreign language in advance placement; 6 units in math and science	1986	7 electives are determined by the local school board.
Louisiana Standard	20	23	4	3	3	3	2	7.5	.5 computer literacy	1989	
Louisiana scholar program		23	4	3	3	3	2	7.5	.5 computer literacy	1987	Students with ACT score of 29 or above, 3.5 GPA with no semester grade lower than a B, no unexcused absences and no suspensions receive a Scholar Program seal on diploma. Minimum competency test is required for graduation.
Regents' scholar program		24	4	3.5	3	3	2	4.5	3 foreign languages, 1 fine arts	1983	American history is required. All students must pass computer proficiency standards. 1 of science units must include lab study.
Maine	(3)	16	4	2	2	2	1.5	3.5	1 fine arts	1989	
Maryland	20	20	4	3	3	2	1	5	1 fine arts; 1 industrial arts/technology education, home economics, vocational education or computer studies	1989	After grade 11, 4 credits must be earned. Students earn statewide certificate of merit with fulfillment of additional requirements or a special education program. Minimum competency test, writing test, and passage of quiz on citizenship are required for graduation.
Massachusetts	—	—	—	1	—	—	4	—		—	Legislative requirements in effect for many years. American history is required. Local boards determine additional requirements.

Table 146.—State requirements for high school graduation, in Carnegie units: 1980 and 1990—Continued

	1980	1989								First graduating class to which these requirements apply	Notes
	All courses	All courses	English/language arts	Social studies	Mathematics	Science	Physical education/health	Electives	Other courses		
State			Subject areas								
1	2	3	4	5	6	7	8	9	10	11	12
Michigan Standard	—	—	4	3	3	2	1	—	2 foreign languages, fine or performing arts, or vocational education; .5 computer education	—	Local legislative requirements in effect for many years. Local boards determine additional requirements. The State board, in January 1984, published graduation requirement guidelines which local districts are urged to incorporate. Included in the recommendations are a minimum of 15.5 units, which includes an option of 2 units picked from: foreign language, fine or performing arts, vocational education, and .5 computer education; and a modified academic classwork for college-bound students.
College preparatory		—	4	3	3	2	1	—		1982	Junior and senior students may receive dual credits for college coursework.
Minnesota	15	20	4	3	1	1	1.5	9.5	At least 2 years foreign language		
Mississippi	16	18	4	2	2	2	—	8		1989	At least 1 of science units must include a lab. Minimum competency test is required for graduation.
Missouri Standard	20	22	3	2	2	2	1	10	1 practical arts; 1 fine arts	1988	The college preparation diploma became available to qualifying graduates in 1985. For college preparation, specific core subjects must be taken.
College preparatory	20	24	4	3	3	3	1	8	1 practical arts; 1 fine arts	1988	
Montana	16	20	4	1.5	2	1	1	10.5		1989	Core requirements in effect for several years. State board raised the total — 1985 graduates needed 19 units; 1986 graduates needed 20. Social studies requirement has 2 alternatives. Effective 7/92, requirements will be changed to 2 units of science, 1 unit of fine arts, and 1 unit of vocational/ practical arts.
Nebraska	—	—	—	—	—	—	—	—		1991	For graduation, 200 credit hours required, with at least 80 percent in core curriculum courses. The State board is conducting hearings to define core courses.
Nevada	19	22.5	4	2	2	2	2.5	8.5	1 arts/humanities; .5 computer literacy	1992	Computer literacy may be waived by demonstration of competency. Minimum competency test is required for graduation.
New Hampshire	16	19.75	4	2.5	2	2	1.25	4	.5 arts; .5 computer science; 3 units from 2 of the following: arts, foreign language, practical arts, or vocational education	1989	Minimum competency test for high school graduation is an option of the local districts.
New Jersey	—	21.5	4	3	3	2	4	4	1 fine, practical, or performing arts; .5 career exploration	1990	92 credit hours are required for graduation. State does not use standard Carnegie units. Increased math requirement becomes effective for 9th grade class entering in 1990–1991 academic year. Minimum competency test is required for graduation.
New Mexico	20	23	4	3	3	2	1	9	1 communication skills	1990	State board requires student computer literacy prior to graduation. Languages other than English can satisfy communication skills requirement. Students preparing for college have an advanced curriculum. State level minimum competency test is an option of the local districts; if passed, students receive a special proficiency endorsement on their diploma.
New York Local diploma	16	18.5	4	4	2	2	.5	0 to 2	1 art and/or music; .5 health; 2 noncredit units of physical education beyond the total.	1989	3–5 units from a sequence of specific courses must be chosen by the Regents' diploma students and is an additional requirement for local. Minimum competency test is required for graduation. Comprehensive tests are required.

Table 146.—State requirements for high school graduation, in Carnegie units: 1980 and 1990—Continued

State	1980 All courses	1989 All courses	English/ language arts	Social studies	Mathe- matics	Science	Physical education/ health	Electives	Other courses	First graduating class to which these requirements apply	Notes
1	2	3	4	5	6	7	8	9	10	11	12
Regents' diploma	18	18.5	4	4	2	2	.5	0 to 2		1989	
North Carolina Standard	16	20	4	2	2	2	1	9		1987	1 science class must include a lab. Minimum competency test is required for graduation.
Scholars program	—	22	4	3	3	3	1	4	2 foreign languages; 2 additional: English, science, math, social science, or foreign language	1994	
North Dakota	17	17	4	3	2	2	1	5		1984	1 unit of higher level foreign language may be substituted for the 4th unit of English; 1 unit math may be business math. Although 17 units are required, the local education agencies are urged to require a minimum of 20 units.
Ohio	17	18	3	2	2	1	1	9		1988	By 1990, minimum competency test will be required for graduation.
Oklahoma High school graduation	18	20	4	2	2	2	—	10	4 from: math, history, computer science, economics, English, geography, government, foreign language, sociology, science, speech, psychology	1987	If foreign language is elected, 2 years in same language. Total hour requirement is less but more rigorous and restrictive for college preparatory path.
College preparatory	10.5	15	4	2	3	2	—	—		1988	
Oregon	21	22	3	3.5	2	2	2	8	.5 career development; 1 applied arts, fine arts, or foreign language	1988	Beginning 1992, minimum competency test will be required for graduation. Beginning 1988, 3.5 GPA students receive an honors seal on their diploma.
Pennsylvania	13	21	4	3	3	3	1	5	2 arts/humanities	1989	Computer science can be an option instead of arts and humanities. State has prescribed learning objectives and curriculum guidelines for 12 goals of quality education.
Rhode Island Standard	16	16	4	2	2	2	—	6		1989	
College preparatory	16	18	4	2	3	3	—	4	2 foreign languages; .5 arts; .5 computer literacy	1989	
South Carolina Standard	18	20	4	3	3	2	1	7		1987	If approved, 1 unit of computer science can count for a math requirement. 1 unit of science and 6 or more in a specific occupational service area can fulfill the service requirements. Junior and senior students may receive dual credits for college coursework. Beginning 1990, minimum competency test will be required for graduation.
South Dakota Academic achievement honors	—	22	4	3	3	2	1	7	2 foreign languages	1986	
South Dakota	16	20	4	3	2	3	—	7	.5 computer studies; .5 fine arts	1989	Beginning 1990, requirements include 3 science courses and 7 electives.
Tennessee Standard	18	20	4	1	2	2	1.5	9	.5 economics	1989	Economics requirement may include: 1 semester in economics, out-of-school experiences through Junior Achievement, or marketing education. Minimum competency test is required for graduation.
Honors, general education	—	20.5	4	3	3	3	1.5	2	2 in same foreign language; 2 fine/visual or performing arts		
Honors, vocation education	—	20.5	4	3	3	3	1.5	2	4 in same vocational education program	1989	

Table 146.—State requirements for high school graduation, in Carnegie units: 1980 and 1990—Continued

State	1980 All courses	1989 All courses	English/ language arts	Social studies	Mathe- matics	Science	Physical education/ health	Electives	Other courses	First graduating class to which these requirements apply	Notes
1	2	3	4	5	6	7	8	9	10	11	12
Texas Standard	18	21	4	2.5	3	2	1.5/.5	7	.5 economics/free enterprise	1988	1.5 units of physical education and .5 of health are required for either program. Minimum competency test is required for graduation. Junior and senior students can receive dual credits for college coursework.
College preparatory	18	22	4	2.5	3	3	1.5/.5	3	.5 economics/free enterprise; 2 foreign languages; 1 computer science; 1 fine arts	1988	
Utah	15	24	3	3	2	2	2	9.0	1.5 arts; 1 vocational education; optional .5 computer science	1988	State board makes specific course recommendations for college entry, vocational, etc.
Vermont	—	15.5	4	4	0 to 5	0 to 5	1.5	—	1 arts; 5 units in math and science	1989	
Virginia Standard	18	21	4	3	2	2	2	6	1 additional math or science; 1 fine or practical arts	1989	An appropriate vocational education class or ROTC may satisfy math or science. B average or better earns an State seal on the diploma. Junior and senior students can receive dual credits for college coursework. Minimum competency test is required for graduation.
Advanced studies	18	23	4	3	3	3	2	4	3 foreign languages; 1 fine or practical arts		
Washington	—	19	3	2.5	2	2	2	5.5	1 occupational education; 1 fine/ visual or performing arts	1991	Beginning 1980, 45 hours required for graduation. An additional credit required for 1991 graduates.
West Virginia	18	21	4	3	2	2	2	7	1 applied arts, fine or performing arts, or foreign language	1989	State has approved, but not implemented, an advance studies certificate.
Wisconsin	(2)	13	4	3	2	2	2	—		1989	Electives are the option of local districts. State recommends that districts require a total of 22 units.
Wyoming	18	18	(2)	1	(2)	(2)	(2)	(2)	Local board determines remaining requirements	—	Requirements in effect for a number of years. Accreditation standards indicated 4 units of English/ language arts, 3 social studies, 2 math courses and 2 science courses.

1 State permits local board to set minimum academic standards.
2 Local boards determine requirements.
3 State requires four credits in English/language arts. Local boards determine remaining requirements.
—Data not available or not applicable.

NOTE.—Local school districts frequently have other graduation requirements in addition to State requirements.

SOURCE: Education Commission of the States, Clearingho "Minimum High School Graduation Requirements: Standard Diplomas," 1980 and July 1990. (This table was prepared September 1990.)

Table 147.—States using minimum-competency testing, by government level setting standards, grade levels assessed, and expected uses of standards: November 1985

States using minimum-competency testing	Government level setting standards	Grade levels assessed	Expected uses					First graduating class assessed
			Grade promotion	High school graduation	Early exit	Remediation	Other	
1	2	3	4	5	6	7	8	9
Alabama	State	3,6,9,11		X		X	X	1985
Arizona	State/local	8,12	(^{1})	X				1976
Arkansas	State	3,4,6,8				X		
California	State/local	4–11,16 yr. old+	X	X	X	X		1979
Colorado	Local	9,12		(^{2})				
Connecticut[3]	State	4,6,8				X	X	
Delaware	State	1–8,11		X			X	1981
Florida	State/local	3,5,8,11	X	X	X			1983
Georgia	State	K,1,3,6,8,10	(^{4})	X		X	X	1985
Hawaii[5]	State	3,9–12		X		X	X	1983
Idaho	State	8–12				X	X	1982
Illinois	Local	Local option					(^{2})	
Indiana	Local	3,6,8,10				X	X	
Kansas[6]	State	2,4,6,8,10					(^{2})	
Kentucky[7]		K–12	X	X		X		
Louisiana[8]	State	2,3,4,5	X			X		
Maryland	State	7,9		X		X	X	1982
Massachusetts	Local	Local option				X		
Michigan	State	4,7,10				X	(^{2})	
Mississippi	State	3,5,8,11		X			X	[9]1987
Missouri	State	8+					X	
Nebraska	Local	5+					X	
Nevada	State	3,6,9,11		X		X		1982
New Hampshire[10]	State	4,8,12	(^{2})	(^{2})			(^{2})	
New Jersey	State	9–12		X		X	X	1985
New Mexico	State	Local option, 10–12					X	1981
New York	State	3,5,6,8–12		X		X		1979
North Carolina[11]	State	3,6,8,10		X			X	1980
Ohio	Local	Local option[12]					(^{2})	1990
Oklahoma[13]	None	3,6,9,12					X	
Oregon	Local	Local option		X				1978
Pennsylvania	State	3,5,8				X		
South Carolina[14]	State	1,2,3,6,8,11	X	X		X	X	1990
Tennessee[15]	State/local	3,6,8,9–12	X	X		X	X	1982
Texas[16]	State	1,3,5,7,9,11,12		X		X		1987
Utah	Local	Local option				X	X	1988
Vermont	State	1–8	(^{17})			X	X	1981
Virginia	State/local	K–6,10–12		X			X	1981
Wisconsin	Local	1–4,5–8,9–10	(^{2})	(^{2})		X		
Wyoming	Local	Local option				X		

[1] Legislation in 1983 called for development of a minimum course of study and criteria for high school graduation standards and for grade-to-grade promotion. Local school districts were to implement standards.

[2] Local option.

[3] A new program of State testing for grade 4 began in 1985 and expanded to grades 6 and 8 in 1986. The ninth grade State proficiency test, begun in 1980, was administered for the final time in 1986.

[4] Beginning in fall 1985, third grade students had to demonstrate acceptable performance on criterion-referenced tests in mathematics and reading before promotion to the fourth grade. Beginning in 1988–89 school year, students must pass school readiness test to be eligible for first grade.

[5] Students have three options: paper-and-pencil test; performance test; or course. First time taken (grade 9) must be paper-and-pencil test.

[6] The Kansas Minimum Competency Assessment (MCA) was re-established by 1984 legislative action (SB 473). The MCA will be in effect for 5 school years, 1984–85 through 1988–89.

[7] Legislation in 1984 required the State superintendent to recommend process of using test results for promotion and graduation to the 1986 legislature.

[8] Grade 8 was added beginning with 1986–87 school year.

[9] Although first class assessed graduated in 1987, the first class required to pass for graduation will be the class of 1989.

[10] Students are tested in elementary, middle, and high school. Some local districts test at grades other than 4, 8, and 12.

[11] Grades 3, 6, and 8 are given an annual standardized achievement test. Local school districts use the results as a diagnostic tool.

[12] Locally-based tests in the areas of English composition, mathematics, and reading are required at least once in grades 1–4. Tests in grades 5–8 and 9–11 will be implemented no later than 1989–90.

[13] Test was given in Oklahoma during the 1978–79 school year. There has been no followup to the program. However, a plan for Statewide testing was submitted for legislative action in January 1985.

[14] The South Carolina Education Improvement Act of 1984 specified that the 11th-grade test being used to gather baseline data be replaced in 1985–86 school year with an exit examination in the 10th grade. All students graduating in 1990 and after must pass the examination.

[15] Local districts use the State-designated tests at grades 3, 6, and 8 for remediation and to advise on grade retention. The Tennessee high school test, first taken at grade 9, is required for graduation.

[16] Texas HB 72 (1984) mandated the new testing program. New requirements became effective in 1985–86 school year.

[17] Vermont Basic Competency Program requires students to master the basics before they complete eighth grade.

NOTE.—Some States have dates for assessing the first high school graduating class but do not expect to use the results to determine whether students will graduate.

SOURCE: Education Commission of the States, *Clearinghouse Notes*, "State Activity—Minimum Competency Testing, as of November 1985." (This table was prepared September 1986.)

Table 148.—States requiring testing for initial certification of teachers, by authorization, year enacted, year effective, and test used: 1987 and 1989

State	1987				1989	
	Authority [1]	Enacted	Effective	Test used [2]	Effective	Test used [2]
1	2	3	4	5	6	7
Alabama	St. Bd.	1980	1981	State	1988	none required
Arizona	Leg.	1980	1980	State	1980	State
Arkansas	Leg.	1979	1983	NTE	1983	NTE
California	Leg.	1981	1982	State	([3])	NTE
Colorado	Leg.	1981	1983	California Achievement	1990	NTE
Connecticut	St. Bd.	1982	1985	State	1988	NTE
Delaware	St. Bd.	1982	1983	P–P.S.T.	1983	P–P.S.T.
District of Columbia	—	—	—	—	1989	NTE
Florida	Leg.	1978	1980	State	1988	State; NTE
Georgia	St. Bd.	1975	1980	State	1980	State
Hawaii	St. Bd.	1986	1986	NTE	1986	NTE
Idaho	Leg.	1987	1988	NTE	1988	NTE
Illinois	Leg.	1985	1988	State	1988	State
Indiana	Leg.	1984	1985	NTE	1985	State; NTE
Iowa	—	—	—	—	([3])	NTE; P–P.S.T.
Kansas	Leg.	1984	1986	To be determined	1986	NTE; P–P.S.T.
Kentucky	Leg.	1984	1985	NTE	1985	NTE
Louisiana	Leg.	1977	1978	NTE	1978	NTE
Maine	Leg.	1984	1988	NTE	1988	NTE
Maryland	St. Bd.	1986	1986	NTE	1986	NTE
Massachusetts	Leg.	1985	([3])	To be determined	([3])	NTE; State
Michigan	Leg.	1986	1991	To be determined [4]	1991	To be determined
Minnesota	—	—	—	—	1988	P–P.S.T.
Mississippi	Leg.	1975	1977	NTE	1977	NTE
Missouri	Leg.	1985	1988	To be determined	1988	To be determined
Montana	B.P.E.	1985	1986	NTE	1986	NTE
Nebraska	Leg.	1984	1989	To be determined [4]	1989	To be determined
Nevada	St. Bd.	1984	([3])	To be determined	1988	NTE
New Hampshire	St. Bd.	1984	1985	NTE	([3])	P–P.S.T.
New Jersey	St. Bd.	1984	1985	NTE	1985	NTE
New Mexico	St. Bd.	1981	1983	NTE	1983	NTE
New York	St. Bd.	1980	1984	NTE	([3])	NTE
North Carolina	St. Bd.	1964	1964	NTE	1964	NTE
Ohio [5]	St. Bd.	1986	1987	NTE	1987	NTE or P–P.S.T.
Oklahoma	Leg.	1980	1982	State	1982	State
Oregon	O.T.S.P.C.	1984	1985	C.B.E.S.T.	1985	C.B.E.S.T.
Pennsylvania	St. Bd.	1985	1987	State	1987	State
Rhode Island	St. Bd.	1985	1986	NTE	1986	NTE
South Carolina	Leg.	1979	1982	NTE and State	1982	NTE
South Dakota	St. Bd.	1985	1986	NTE	1988	Use of NTE repealed
Tennessee	St. Bd.	1980	1981	NTE	1981	NTE
Texas	Leg.	1981	1986	State	1986	State
Virginia	Leg.	1979	1980	NTE	1980	NTE
Washington	St. Bd.	1984	([3])	To be determined [6]	1993	To be determined [6]
West Virginia [7]	St. Bd.	1982	1985	State	([3])	N.E.S.
Wisconsin	S.P.I.	1986	1990	To be determined	1991	To be determined

[1] St. Bd. = State Board of Education; Leg. = Legislature; B.P.E. = Board of Public Education; O.T.S.P.C. = Oregon Teacher Standards and Practice Commission; S.P.I. = Superintendent of Public Instruction.

[2] NTE = National Teacher Examination; State = State developed test; C.B.E.S.T. = California Basic Education Skills Test; N.E.S. = National Education Service; P–P.S.T. = Preprofessional Skills Test.

[3] Effective year is yet to be determined.

[4] For basic skills and subject-matter competencies.

[5] Test requirements set by local school districts.

[6] State and undetermined tests will be used.

[7] Required for individuals entering West Virginia-approved education programs as of fall 1985.

—Data not available or not applicable.

SOURCE: Education Commission of the States, Clearinghouse Notes, "States Requiring Testing for Initial Certification of Teachers, April 1987;" and "State Education Leader, Winter 1989." (This table was prepared January 1990.)

Table 149.—Percentage of public high schools having or strengthening various policies, programs, or practices: 1987–88

Policy, program, or practice	In operation in 1987–88								Instituted or last strengthened since 1982–83			
	Total	District status			School enrollment				Total	District status		
		Rural	Sub-ur-ban	Urban	Less than 300	300 to 799	800 to 1,499	1,500 or more		Rural	Sub-ur-ban	Urban
1	2	3	4	5	6	7	8	9	10	11	12	13
Strict sanctions for disruptive students	98	98	99	95	97	97	98	98	49	55	40	51
Minimum academic standards for participation in athletics	96	97	96	97	96	96	97	96	47	44	49	53
Special recognition for academically outstanding students[1]	92	91	93	97	87	92	96	97	59	62	55	57
Programs to reduce absenteeism or tardiness	90	91	88	96	90	89	91	95	66	68	63	68
Instruction of students in study skills	77	76	76	84	72	78	77	83	61	61	60	66
Required in-service training of teachers in effective use of class time	73	76	68	75	77	72	72	68	65	71	59	53
Measures to reduce administrative burden on teachers	73	69	77	74	66	72	74	82	63	67	59	63
Nonfinancial recognition for outstanding teachers	70	66	72	85	56	73	75	85	54	54	54	56
Policy/guidelines on amount of required homework	47	42	48	65	38	47	50	58	52	50	50	63
Financial recognition for outstanding teachers	20	17	21	25	18	17	19	29	82	79	87	80

[1] Besides honor roll.

SOURCE: U.S. Department of Education, National Center for Education Statistics, "Public High School Principals' Perceptions of Academic Reform, May 1988." (This table was prepared November 1988.)

Table 150.—States requiring education, minimum curriculum standards, and teacher certification on substance abuse education, by State: 1986–87

State	State requires substance abuse education	Minimum curriculum standards provided	Certification requirement for all teachers	State	State requires substance abuse education	Minimum curriculum standards provided	Certification requirement for all teachers
1	2	3	4	1	2	3	4
Total number with requirement	**39**	**32**	**11**				
Alabama	X	X		Missouri			X
Alaska		X		Montana			
Arizona	X	X		Nebraska	X		
Arkansas	X	X	X	Nevada	X	X	X
California	X	X		New Hampshire	X	X	
Colorado	X	X		New Jersey	X		X
Connecticut	X			New Mexico	X	X	
Delaware	X	X		New York	X	X	X
District of Columbia	X	X	X	North Carolina			
Florida	X	X		North Dakota	X		
Georgia	X	X		Ohio	X		X
Hawaii		X		Oklahoma			
Idaho	X			Oregon	X		
Illinois	X	X	X	Pennsylvania	X	X	
Indiana	X		X	Rhode Island	X	X	
Iowa	X	X		South Carolina	X		
Kansas				South Dakota			
Kentucky	X	X	X	Tennessee		X	
Louisiana	X	X		Texas	X	X	
Maine	X	X		Utah	X	X	
Maryland	X	X		Vermont	X	X	
Massachusetts	X			Virginia	X	X	
Michigan		X		Washington	X	X	
Minnesota	X	X	X	West Virginia	X	X	
Mississippi				Wisconsin	X	X	
				Wyoming			

SOURCE: U.S. Department of Education, National Center for Education Statistics, "State Efforts in Substance Abuse Education." (This table was prepared August 1988.)

Table 151.—Revenues for public elementary and secondary schools, by source of funds: 1919–20 to 1988–89

School year	In thousands				Percentage distribution			
	Total	Federal	State	Local (including intermediate)[1]	Total	Federal	State	Local (including intermediate)[1]
1	2	3	4	5	6	7	8	9
1919–20	$970,121	$2,475	$160,085	$807,561	100.0	0.3	16.5	83.2
1929–30	2,088,557	7,334	353,670	1,727,553	100.0	0.4	16.9	82.7
1939–40	2,260,527	39,810	684,354	1,536,363	100.0	1.8	30.3	68.0
1941–42	2,416,580	34,305	759,993	1,622,281	100.0	1.4	31.4	67.1
1943–44	2,604,322	35,886	859,183	1,709,253	100.0	1.4	33.0	65.6
1945–46	3,059,845	41,378	1,062,057	1,956,409	100.0	1.4	34.7	63.9
1947–48	4,311,534	120,270	1,676,362	2,514,902	100.0	2.8	38.9	58.3
1949–50	5,437,044	155,848	2,165,689	3,115,507	100.0	2.9	39.8	57.3
1951–52	6,423,816	227,711	2,478,596	3,717,507	100.0	3.5	38.6	57.9
1953–54	7,866,852	355,237	2,944,103	4,567,512	100.0	4.5	37.4	58.1
1955–56	9,686,677	441,442	3,828,886	5,416,350	100.0	4.6	39.5	55.9
1957–58	12,181,513	486,484	4,800,368	6,894,661	100.0	4.0	39.4	56.6
1959–60	14,746,618	651,639	5,768,047	8,326,932	100.0	4.4	39.1	56.5
1961–62	17,527,707	760,975	6,789,190	9,977,542	100.0	4.3	38.7	56.9
1963–64	20,544,182	896,956	8,078,014	11,569,213	100.0	4.4	39.3	56.3
1965–66	25,356,858	1,996,954	9,920,219	13,439,686	100.0	7.9	39.1	53.0
1967–68	31,903,064	2,806,469	12,275,536	16,821,063	100.0	8.8	38.5	52.7
1969–70	40,266,923	3,219,557	16,062,776	20,984,589	100.0	8.0	39.9	52.1
1970–71	44,511,292	3,753,461	17,409,086	23,348,745	100.0	8.4	39.1	52.5
1971–72	50,003,645	4,467,969	19,133,256	26,402,420	100.0	8.9	38.3	52.8
1972–73	52,117,930	4,525,000	20,843,520	26,749,412	100.0	8.7	40.0	51.3
1973–74	58,230,892	4,930,351	24,113,409	29,187,132	100.0	8.5	41.4	50.1
1974–75	64,445,239	5,811,595	27,211,116	31,422,528	100.0	9.0	42.2	48.8
1975–76	71,206,073	6,318,345	31,776,101	33,111,627	100.0	8.9	44.6	46.5
1976–77	75,322,532	6,629,498	32,688,903	36,004,134	100.0	8.8	43.4	47.8
1977–78	81,443,160	7,694,194	35,013,266	38,735,700	100.0	9.4	43.0	47.6
1978–79	87,994,143	8,600,116	40,132,136	39,261,891	100.0	9.8	45.6	44.6
1979–80	96,881,165	9,503,537	45,348,814	42,028,813	100.0	9.8	46.8	43.4
1980–81	105,949,087	9,768,262	50,182,659	45,998,166	100.0	9.2	47.4	43.4
1981–82	110,191,257	8,186,466	52,436,435	49,568,356	100.0	7.4	47.6	45.0
1982–83	117,497,502	8,339,990	56,282,157	52,875,354	100.0	7.1	47.9	45.0
1983–84	126,055,419	8,576,547	60,232,981	57,245,892	100.0	6.8	47.8	45.4
1984–85	137,294,678	9,105,569	67,168,684	61,020,425	100.0	6.6	48.9	44.4
1985–86	149,127,779	9,975,622	73,619,575	65,532,582	100.0	6.7	49.4	43.9
1986–87	158,523,693	10,146,013	78,830,437	69,547,243	100.0	6.4	49.7	43.9
1987–88 [2]	169,561,974	10,716,687	84,004,415	74,840,873	100.0	6.3	49.5	44.1
1988–89	191,210,310	11,872,419	91,158,363	88,179,529	100.0	6.2	47.7	46.1

[1] Includes a relatively small amount from nongovernmental sources (gifts and tuition and transportation fees from patrons). These sources accounted for 0.4 percent of total revenues in 1967–68.

[2] Revised from previously published figures.

NOTE.—Beginning in 1980–81, revenues for State education agencies are excluded. Data for 1988–89 reflect new survey collection procedures and may not be entirely comparable to figures for earlier years. Because of rounding, details may not add to totals.

SOURCE: U.S. Department of Education, National Center for Education Statistics, *Statistics of State School Systems; Revenues and Expenditures for Public Elementary and Secondary Education;* and Common Core of Data survey. (This table was prepared January 1991.)

Table 152.—Revenues for public elementary and secondary schools, by source and State: 1988–89

[Amounts in thousands of dollars]

State or other area	Total	Revenues, by source					
		Federal		State		Local and other[1]	
		Amount	Percent of total	Amount	Percent of total	Amount	Percent of total
1	2	3	4	5	6	7	8
United States	$191,210,310	$11,872,419	6.2	$91,158,363	47.7	$88,179,529	46.1
Alabama	2,552,053	273,066	10.7	1,574,361	61.7	704,626	27.6
Alaska	864,292	99,822	11.5	549,468	63.6	215,001	24.9
Arizona	2,589,909	209,066	8.1	1,165,043	45.0	1,215,801	46.9
Arkansas	1,473,751	143,066	9.7	826,797	56.1	503,888	34.2
California	22,208,938	1,553,408	7.0	14,755,475	66.4	5,900,054	26.6
Colorado	2,477,978	126,856	5.1	965,623	39.0	1,385,499	55.9
Connecticut	3,116,060	81,120	2.6	1,407,684	45.2	1,627,256	52.2
Delaware	500,642	37,149	7.4	342,391	68.4	121,102	24.2
District of Columbia	521,094	54,604	10.5	0	0.0	466,490	89.5
Florida	8,396,809	542,291	6.5	4,340,627	51.7	3,513,891	41.8
Georgia	4,693,011	290,497	6.2	2,507,354	53.4	1,895,160	40.4
Hawaii	682,202	69,910	10.2	594,173	87.1	18,119	2.7
Idaho	651,165	52,281	8.0	387,951	59.6	210,932	32.4
Illinois	8,023,607	500,087	6.2	2,553,080	31.8	4,970,441	61.9
Indiana	4,372,707	201,396	4.6	2,429,991	55.6	1,741,320	39.8
Iowa	2,072,991	98,577	4.8	1,011,858	48.8	962,556	46.4
Kansas	1,920,927	98,304	5.1	836,531	43.5	986,092	51.3
Kentucky	2,071,522	206,637	10.0	1,409,846	68.1	455,039	22.0
Louisiana	2,787,869	293,594	10.5	1,471,391	52.8	1,022,884	36.7
Maine	1,027,134	56,575	5.5	546,008	53.2	424,551	41.3
Maryland	3,804,336	188,043	4.9	1,450,137	38.1	2,166,156	56.9
Massachusetts	4,847,275	221,281	4.6	1,987,808	41.0	2,638,185	54.4
Michigan	7,700,991	442,346	5.7	2,096,556	27.2	5,162,089	67.0
Minnesota	3,665,226	156,262	4.3	1,965,963	53.6	1,543,001	42.1
Mississippi	1,440,070	231,988	16.1	827,323	57.5	380,760	26.4
Missouri	3,442,018	198,500	5.8	1,365,067	39.7	1,878,451	54.6
Montana	662,104	59,186	8.9	308,486	46.6	294,432	44.5
Nebraska	1,214,451	75,690	6.2	244,802	20.2	893,959	73.6
Nevada	757,861	32,111	4.2	277,869	36.7	447,881	59.1
New Hampshire	803,925	3,281	0.4	68,265	8.5	732,378	91.1
New Jersey	7,992,886	310,480	3.9	3,362,505	42.1	4,319,900	54.0
New Mexico	1,142,068	139,300	12.2	839,141	73.5	163,628	14.3
New York	18,764,256	868,961	4.6	8,101,488	43.2	9,793,807	52.2
North Carolina	4,279,584	286,944	6.7	2,828,086	66.1	1,164,554	27.2
North Dakota	466,586	43,170	9.3	217,072	46.5	206,343	44.2
Ohio	8,222,796	449,803	5.5	3,613,306	43.9	4,159,688	50.6
Oklahoma	2,127,862	117,939	5.5	1,188,411	55.9	821,512	38.6
Oregon	2,315,476	152,751	6.6	585,464	25.3	1,577,261	68.1
Pennsylvania	9,154,167	508,355	5.6	3,797,265	41.5	4,848,548	53.0
Rhode Island	753,042	40,056	5.3	324,392	43.1	388,593	51.6
South Carolina	2,453,008	200,598	8.2	1,227,429	50.0	1,024,982	41.8
South Dakota	468,658	54,420	11.6	118,752	25.3	295,487	63.0
Tennessee	2,731,861	249,546	9.1	1,257,920	46.0	1,224,395	44.8
Texas	13,110,312	979,357	7.5	5,670,469	43.3	6,460,485	49.3
Utah	1,203,017	81,073	6.7	686,016	57.0	435,927	36.2
Vermont	507,918	25,317	5.0	171,522	33.8	311,078	61.2
Virginia	4,636,663	240,850	5.2	1,568,895	33.8	2,826,918	61.0
Washington	3,775,985	231,901	6.1	2,672,206	70.8	871,878	23.1
West Virginia	1,290,156	100,868	7.8	831,153	64.4	358,135	27.8
Wisconsin	3,904,897	167,690	4.3	1,556,530	39.9	2,180,678	55.8
Wyoming	566,196	26,046	4.6	272,412	48.1	267,738	47.3
Outlying areas							
American Samoa	24,385	16,918	69.4	7,425	30.4	42	0.2
Guam	104,724	10,225	9.8	0	0.0	94,499	90.2
Northern Marianas	—	—	—	—	—	—	—
Puerto Rico	1,096,135	383,469	35.0	707,466	64.5	5,200	0.5
Virgin Islands	132,329	25,784	19.5	—	—	106,545	80.5

[1] Includes revenues from local and intermediate sources, gifts, and tuition and fees from patrons.

—Data not available or not applicable.

NOTE.—Excludes revenues for State education agencies. Because of rounding, details may not add to totals.

SOURCE: U.S. Department of Education, National Center for Education Statistics, Common Core of Data survey. (This table was prepared December 1990.)

Table 153.—Revenues for public elementary and secondary schools, by source and State: 1987–88

[In thousands of dollars]

State or other area	Total	Revenues, by source					
		Federal		State		Local and other[1]	
		Amount	Percent of total	Amount	Percent of total	Amount	Percent of total
1	2	3	4	5	6	7	8
United States[2]	$169,561,974	$10,716,687	6.3	$84,004,415	49.5	$74,840,873	44.1
Alabama	2,171,704	257,108	11.8	1,398,658	64.4	515,937	23.8
Alaska	777,086	87,302	11.2	491,540	63.3	198,244	25.5
Arizona	2,361,006	185,845	7.9	1,100,795	46.6	1,074,366	45.5
Arkansas	1,211,164	133,222	11.0	681,964	56.3	395,978	32.7
California	17,884,769	1,312,836	7.3	12,554,882	70.2	4,017,051	22.5
Colorado	2,443,132	119,942	4.9	953,857	39.0	1,369,333	56.0
Connecticut	2,890,957	105,469	3.6	1,220,872	42.2	1,564,616	54.1
Delaware	464,318	35,410	7.6	318,037	68.5	110,871	23.9
District of Columbia	484,717	51,404	10.6	2,873	0.6	430,440	88.8
Florida	7,466,975	497,684	6.7	4,104,897	55.0	2,864,394	38.4
Georgia	3,715,388	272,309	7.3	2,120,595	57.1	1,322,484	35.6
Hawaii	623,136	82,157	13.2	540,441	86.7	538	0.1
Idaho	580,432	49,945	8.6	369,979	63.7	160,508	27.7
Illinois	6,452,386	338,715	5.2	2,377,115	36.8	3,736,555	57.9
Indiana	3,825,865	186,699	4.9	2,144,522	56.1	1,494,643	39.1
Iowa	1,958,184	100,755	5.1	927,099	47.3	930,330	47.5
Kansas	1,773,743	88,013	5.0	765,478	43.2	920,252	51.9
Kentucky	1,819,222	212,093	11.7	1,185,928	65.2	421,201	23.2
Louisiana	2,541,690	284,048	11.2	1,406,639	55.3	851,002	33.5
Maine	886,378	52,547	5.9	459,028	51.8	374,803	42.3
Maryland	3,464,182	173,331	5.0	1,342,091	38.7	1,948,760	56.3
Massachusetts	4,485,247	198,121	4.4	1,894,326	42.2	2,392,800	53.3
Michigan	7,650,004	432,045	5.6	2,699,032	35.3	4,518,927	59.1
Minnesota	3,298,933	139,507	4.2	1,842,218	55.8	1,317,208	39.9
Mississippi	1,135,053	112,512	9.9	744,429	65.6	278,112	24.5
Missouri	3,069,758	179,700	5.9	1,248,175	40.7	1,641,883	53.5
Montana	636,045	49,956	7.9	301,888	47.5	284,201	44.7
Nebraska	1,034,017	74,610	7.2	229,261	22.2	730,146	70.6
Nevada	660,290	24,811	3.8	255,584	38.7	379,895	57.5
New Hampshire	748,214	24,630	3.3	56,753	7.6	666,831	89.1
New Jersey	7,250,514	292,569	4.0	3,079,410	42.5	3,878,535	53.5
New Mexico	1,028,708	118,600	11.5	781,229	75.9	128,879	12.5
New York	17,094,990	774,715	4.5	7,416,745	43.4	8,903,530	52.1
North Carolina	3,789,548	286,457	7.6	2,529,307	66.7	973,784	25.7
North Dakota	433,358	38,664	8.9	222,567	51.4	172,127	39.7
Ohio	6,611,187	338,434	5.1	3,206,767	48.5	3,065,985	46.4
Oklahoma	1,750,530	104,480	6.0	1,151,783	65.8	494,267	28.2
Oregon	1,942,303	132,639	6.8	537,547	27.7	1,272,117	65.5
Pennsylvania	8,781,585	461,503	5.3	4,026,972	45.9	4,293,110	48.9
Rhode Island	682,486	30,299	4.4	298,372	43.7	353,816	51.8
South Carolina	2,175,842	184,820	8.5	1,184,466	54.4	806,557	37.1
South Dakota	434,761	47,359	10.9	114,914	26.4	272,488	62.7
Tennessee	2,233,442	233,465	10.5	993,897	44.5	1,006,080	45.0
Texas	12,612,869	977,742	7.8	5,573,372	44.2	6,061,755	48.1
Utah	1,183,399	73,494	6.2	660,195	55.8	449,710	38.0
Vermont	493,874	21,806	4.4	165,006	33.4	307,062	62.2
Virginia	(3)	(3)	(3)	(3)	(3)	(3)	(3)
Washington	3,218,732	193,211	6.0	2,428,119	75.4	597,402	18.6
West Virginia	1,268,654	103,357	8.1	853,419	67.3	311,878	24.6
Wisconsin	3,552,430	154,347	4.3	1,464,187	41.2	1,933,897	54.4
Wyoming	568,402	22,121	3.9	279,751	49.2	266,530	46.9
Outlying areas							
American Samoa	21,047	13,295	63.2	—	—	7,753	36.8
Guam	88,106	11,580	13.1	—	—	76,526	86.9
Northern Marianas	17,876	5,733	32.1	12,143	67.9	—	—
Puerto Rico	942,179	277,253	29.4	—	—	664,926	70.6
Virgin Islands	106,533	19,483	18.3	—	—	87,050	81.7

[1] Includes revenues from local and intermediate sources, gifts, and tuition and fees from patrons.

[2] Includes estimates for the nonreporting State.

[3] Data not reported.

—Data not available or not applicable.

NOTE.—Excludes revenues for State education agencies. Some data have been revised from previously published figures. Because of rounding, details may not add to totals.

SOURCE: U.S. Department of Education, National Center for Education Statistics, Common Core of Data survey. (This table was prepared January 1991.)

Table 154.—Current expenditures for public elementary and secondary education, by State: 1959–60 to 1990–91

[In thousands of dollars]

State or other area	1959–60	1969–70	1979–80	1980–81	1981–82	1982–83	1983–84
1	2	3	4	5	6	7	8
United States	$12,329,389	$34,217,773	$86,984,142	$94,321,093	$101,108,524	$108,267,717	$115,392,342
Alabama	171,130	422,730	1,146,713	1,393,137	1,423,748	1,486,521	1,396,804
Alaska	20,641	81,374	377,947	476,368	550,784	625,818	692,418
Arizona	104,054	281,941	949,753	1,075,362	1,152,564	1,242,928	1,326,552
Arkansas	83,896	235,083	666,949	709,394	755,680	801,194	903,510
California	[5]1,481,908	3,831,595	9,172,158	9,936,642	10,727,266	11,050,354	12,143,642
Colorado	136,760	369,218	1,243,049	1,369,883	1,500,214	1,605,885	1,697,085
Connecticut	185,336	588,710	1,227,892	1,440,881	1,543,483	1,711,013	1,818,683
Delaware	33,425	108,747	269,108	270,439	275,210	294,222	323,760
District of Columbia	45,617	141,138	298,448	295,155	312,940	340,027	371,113
Florida	276,506	961,273	2,766,468	3,336,657	3,552,127	3,747,760	4,071,134
Georgia	208,096	599,371	1,608,028	1,688,714	1,976,268	2,123,586	2,301,496
Hawaii	42,499	141,324	351,889	395,038	425,342	484,858	500,554
Idaho	42,719	103,107	313,927	352,912	371,290	398,996	417,426
Illinois	663,849	1,896,067	4,579,355	4,773,179	4,928,668	5,108,290	5,332,566
Indiana	318,073	809,105	1,851,292	1,898,194	2,133,789	2,239,069	2,434,738
Iowa	197,768	527,086	1,186,659	1,337,504	1,400,580	1,474,443	1,532,171
Kansas	153,346	362,593	830,133	958,281	1,044,483	1,131,758	1,209,537
Kentucky	132,068	353,265	1,054,459	1,096,472	1,157,496	1,233,797	1,354,120
Louisiana	230,402	503,217	1,303,902	1,767,692	1,857,207	1,908,595	1,950,869
Maine	51,465	155,907	385,492	401,355	447,360	484,744	540,351
Maryland	209,606	721,794	1,783,056	1,937,159	2,062,775	2,118,972	2,322,690
Massachusetts	324,408	907,341	2,638,734	2,794,762	2,673,115	2,792,653	2,898,355
Michigan	605,048	1,799,945	4,642,847	5,196,249	5,221,346	5,351,620	5,386,329
Minnesota	267,376	781,243	1,786,768	1,900,322	2,035,842	2,075,572	2,253,402
Mississippi	100,020	262,760	756,018	716,878	753,648	869,764	982,605
Missouri	242,447	642,030	1,504,988	1,643,258	1,715,761	1,772,111	1,965,436
Montana	54,079	127,176	358,118	380,092	418,027	456,519	502,290
Nebraska	87,692	231,612	581,615	629,017	699,487	759,197	813,214
Nevada	23,770	87,273	281,901	287,752	338,208	364,766	374,201
New Hampshire	33,185	101,370	295,400	340,518	372,027	402,307	431,288
New Jersey	459,413	1,343,564	3,638,533	3,648,914	4,080,209	4,340,960	4,666,185
New Mexico	73,396	183,736	515,451	560,213	647,867	713,599	721,641
New York	1,383,706	4,111,839	8,760,500	9,259,948	10,258,454	10,985,481	11,879,638
North Carolina	238,059	676,193	1,880,862	2,112,417	2,191,269	2,206,325	2,353,506
North Dakota	46,254	97,895	228,483	254,197	307,659	318,784	337,961
Ohio	632,932	1,639,805	3,836,576	4,149,858	4,357,731	4,600,475	5,051,057
Oklahoma	151,181	339,105	1,055,844	1,193,373	1,461,497	1,560,103	1,581,443
Oregon	154,691	403,844	1,126,812	1,292,624	1,352,825	1,417,393	1,475,990
Pennsylvania	732,486	1,912,644	4,584,320	4,955,115	5,158,103	5,506,931	5,843,492
Rhode Island	48,686	145,443	362,046	395,389	394,485	454,062	486,328
South Carolina	116,939	367,689	997,984	1,006,088	1,096,871	1,158,595	1,314,792
South Dakota	47,899	109,375	238,332	242,215	273,794	292,102	314,627
Tennessee	175,152	473,226	1,319,303	1,429,938	1,488,430	1,577,915	1,627,147
Texas	605,577	1,518,181	4,997,689	5,310,181	5,939,849	7,442,159	7,642,784
Utah	69,755	179,981	518,251	587,648	626,218	702,162	730,904
Vermont	24,132	78,921	189,811	224,901	247,035	267,530	290,206
Virginia	207,399	704,677	1,881,519	2,045,412	2,191,853	2,414,130	2,584,005
Washington	239,069	699,984	1,825,782	1,791,477	1,844,060	2,206,231	2,373,841
West Virginia	108,673	249,404	678,386	754,889	904,080	957,707	988,532
Wisconsin	254,626	777,288	1,908,523	2,035,879	2,142,172	2,305,552	2,455,671
Wyoming	32,175	69,584	226,067	271,153	317,328	382,182	424,251
Outlying areas							
American Samoa	308	—	—	—	—	—	—
Guam	3,020	16,652	—	—	50,000	51,173	54,251
Northern Marianas						7,714	5,534
Puerto Rico	54,375	—	—	713,000	670,000	745,360	822,589
Trust Territory of the Pacific	—	—	—	—	—	—	—
Virgin Islands	1,662	—	—	—	62,000	70,975	70,411

Table 154.—Current expenditures for public elementary and secondary education, by State: 1959–60 to 1990–91—Continued

[In thousands of dollars]

State or other area	1984–85	1985–86	1986–87	1987–88[1]	1988–89	Estimated 1989–90[2]	Estimated 1990–91[2]
1	9	10	11	12	13	14	15
United States	**$126,337,491**	**$137,164,965**	**$146,364,922**	**$157,097,951**	[3]**$172,932,385**	[3]**$185,249,661**	[3]**$198,864,363**
Alabama	1,590,856	1,761,154	1,775,997	1,873,390	2,188,020	2,234,432	2,452,406
Alaska	754,967	818,219	769,015	756,577	739,020	[4]805,828	[4]877,038
Arizona	1,436,844	1,649,832	1,836,908	2,002,395	2,143,148	2,416,350	2,518,000
Arkansas	1,005,347	1,085,943	1,118,904	1,211,156	1,319,370	[4]1,397,212	[4]1,481,732
California	13,477,768	15,040,898	16,512,668	17,402,063	19,370,242	[4]21,266,023	[4]23,457,031
Colorado	1,868,058	2,018,579	2,129,964	2,172,563	2,266,667	2,380,000	2,449,200
Connecticut	2,117,798	2,144,094	2,414,708	2,748,567	2,984,542	3,110,000	3,290,000
Delaware	353,191	391,558	418,116	440,631	479,327	562,136	593,317
District of Columbia	387,918	406,910	441,135	489,357	584,035	546,248	570,265
Florida	4,589,068	5,092,668	5,650,083	6,288,977	7,245,515	[6]8,287,905	8,897,191
Georgia	2,629,681	2,979,980	3,254,786	3,549,038	4,006,069	4,241,718	4,657,999
Hawaii	521,692	575,456	576,749	608,264	643,319	680,182	719,156
Idaho	467,532	492,092	513,011	532,274	571,159	[6]646,021	731,870
Illinois	5,662,354	6,066,390	6,463,564	6,923,298	7,655,153	8,664,858	8,968,128
Indiana	2,696,072	2,851,080	3,106,616	3,330,525	3,779,468	4,044,031	4,327,113
Iowa	1,599,674	1,644,359	1,708,440	1,859,173	1,925,623	2,002,648	2,102,780
Kansas	1,315,469	1,423,225	1,486,814	1,568,041	1,712,260	1,840,680	1,925,351
Kentucky	1,384,722	1,434,962	1,583,158	1,741,799	1,918,741	1,999,328	2,399,194
Louisiana	2,191,478	2,333,748	2,260,393	2,289,241	2,468,307	2,654,471	2,759,271
Maine	599,189	688,673	760,446	839,860	921,931	1,019,656	1,121,621
Maryland	2,446,771	2,634,209	2,845,404	3,128,165	3,505,018	3,722,880	4,059,187
Massachusetts	3,139,486	3,403,505	3,744,131	4,098,062	4,522,119	4,554,406	4,554,000
Michigan	5,735,303	6,184,767	6,427,556	6,913,261	7,493,266	7,942,861	8,340,005
Minnesota	2,461,571	2,637,722	2,818,390	2,981,209	3,282,296	3,465,711	3,774,159
Mississippi	1,023,720	1,058,301	1,112,535	1,221,560	1,372,290	[6]1,457,123	1,529,979
Missouri	2,106,539	2,277,576	2,515,846	2,747,234	3,096,666	3,066,000	3,271,116
Montana	538,245	567,901	583,861	590,226	592,454	635,000	679,000
Nebraska	870,019	911,983	948,149	995,235	1,105,009	[4]1,180,517	[4]1,266,813
Nevada	397,254	495,147	513,014	555,272	615,161	[6]830,859	879,445
New Hampshire	473,151	522,604	589,850	677,507	733,230	932,181	1,059,890
New Jersey	4,697,534	5,735,895	6,099,473	6,621,860	7,309,147	[4]7,730,812	[4]8,248,418
New Mexico	784,442	808,036	865,789	916,305	975,552	[4]1,049,372	[4]1,126,672
New York	12,681,301	13,686,039	14,724,687	16,073,392	17,127,584	17,900,000	19,600,000
North Carolina	2,674,774	2,991,747	3,193,337	3,424,194	3,892,971	4,021,104	4,099,566
North Dakota	365,341	379,470	374,941	385,427	431,814	483,631	502,977
Ohio	5,504,161	5,856,999	6,114,426	6,446,903	7,425,194	[6]8,067,933	8,519,737
Oklahoma	1,575,467	1,740,981	1,707,396	1,692,283	1,833,743	1,819,000	2,044,000
Oregon	1,560,242	1,662,372	1,747,125	1,944,657	2,123,241	2,174,000	2,385,000
Pennsylvania	6,660,369	6,750,520	7,176,886	7,679,986	8,597,355	9,199,000	9,843,000
Rhode Island	525,824	569,935	608,318	663,800	736,942	[6]809,345	882,186
South Carolina	1,556,552	1,708,603	1,814,160	1,932,502	2,118,732	[4]2,252,570	[4]2,410,539
South Dakota	338,800	360,832	368,266	389,436	427,522	[6]452,611	475,241
Tennessee	1,836,012	1,990,889	2,167,026	2,352,183	2,668,341	2,443,076	2,597,356
Texas	8,996,476	9,642,812	10,152,521	10,791,854	11,761,447	12,505,272	13,480,942
Utah	813,817	906,484	932,740	974,666	1,040,104	1,070,000	1,110,000
Vermont	313,026	346,164	378,264	456,992	485,226	[4]523,258	[4]563,218
Virginia	2,845,540	3,183,707	3,444,952	3,793,475	4,151,050	4,498,761	4,723,699
Washington	2,565,957	2,702,652	2,808,636	3,005,980	3,204,265	[6]3,677,921	4,111,028
West Virginia	1,090,514	1,164,882	1,229,069	1,231,966	1,202,486	1,365,420	1,410,000
Wisconsin	2,655,729	2,893,797	3,086,878	3,318,247	3,688,311	4,119,609	4,508,826
Wyoming	453,874	488,616	489,825	466,921	491,930	499,700	509,700
Outlying areas							
American Samoa	13,348	14,997	19,497	20,186	22,314	[6]22,273	[4]23,977
Guam	58,815	78,545	78,278	76,359	94,368	[6]86,325	86,325
Northern Marianas	9,394	12,556	15,714	19,694	—	—	—
Puerto Rico	856,743	842,827	872,050	935,392	1,030,387	1,091,714	[4]1,146,612
Trust Territory of the Pacific	34,002	—	—	—	—	—	—
Virgin Islands	—	76,751	97,585	89,217	111,750	115,409	127,291

[1] Data revised from previously published figures.

[2] Data estimated by State education agencies.

[3] U.S. total includes National Center for Education Statistics imputations for nonreporting States.

[4] Estimated by the National Center for Education Statistics.

[5] Includes an estimated $144,942,000 for summer schools, adult education, and community colleges.

[6] Actual count.

NOTE.—Beginning in 1980-81, expenditures for State administration are excluded. Some data have been revised from previously published figures. Because of rounding, details may not add to totals.

SOURCE: U.S. Department of Education, National Center for Education Statistics, *Statistics of State School Systems;* and Common Core of Data survey. (This table was prepared January 1991.)

Table 155.—Summary of expenditures for public elementary and secondary education, by purpose: 1919–20 to 1979–80

Purpose of expenditures	1919–20	1929–30	1939–40	1949–50	1959–60	1969–70	1971–72	1973–74	1975–76	1979–80
1	2	3	4	5	6	7	8	9	10	11

Amounts in thousands of dollars

Total expenditures, all schools ..	**$1,036,151**	**$2,316,790**	**$2,344,049**	**$5,837,643**	**$15,613,255**	**$40,683,429**	**$48,050,283**	**$56,970,355**	**$70,600,573**	**$95,961,561**
Current expenditures, all schools ...	864,396	1,853,377	1,955,166	4,722,887	12,461,955	34,853,578	42,213,093	50,477,845	62,607,754	87,581,727
Public elementary and secondary schools	861,120	1,843,552	1,941,799	4,687,274	12,329,389	34,217,773	41,817,782	50,024,638	62,054,105	86,984,142
Administration	36,752	78,680	91,571	220,050	528,408	1,606,646	1,875,504	2,275,726	2,808,956	4,263,757
Instruction	632,556	1,317,727	1,403,285	3,112,340	8,350,738	23,270,158	28,148,306	32,608,652	39,687,404	53,257,937
Plant operation	115,707	216,072	194,365	427,587	1,085,036	2,537,257	3,145,231	3,815,224	[1]6,675,499	[1]9,744,785
Plant maintenance	30,432	78,810	73,321	214,164	422,586	974,941	1,179,540	1,476,349	([1])	([1])
Fixed charges	9,286	50,270	50,116	261,469	909,323	3,266,920	4,096,404	5,626,662	7,321,317	11,793,934
Other school services [2]	36,387	101,993	129,141	451,663	1,033,297	2,561,856	3,372,790	4,222,025	5,560,928	7,923,729
Summer schools	([3])	([3])	([3])	([3])	13,263	106,481	90,554	93,829	101,319	24,753
Adult education [3]	3,277	9,825	13,367	35,614	26,858	128,778	—	—	—	—
Community colleges	([3])	([3])	([3])	([3])	34,492	138,813	—	—	—	—
Community services	([2])	([2])	([2])	([2])	57,953	261,731	304,765	359,378	452,330	572,832
Capital outlay [4]	153,543	370,878	257,974	1,014,176	2,661,786	4,659,072	4,458,949	4,978,976	6,146,435	6,506,167
Interest on school debt	18,212	92,536	130,909	100,578	489,514	1,170,782	1,378,236	1,513,534	1,846,384	1,873,666

Percentage distribution

Total expenditures, all schools ..	**100.0**	**100.0**	**100.0**	**100.0**	**100.0**	**100.0**	**100.0**	**100.0**	**100.0**	**100.0**
Current expenditures, all schools ...	83.4	80.0	83.4	80.9	79.8	85.7	87.9	88.6	88.7	91.2
Public elementary and secondary schools	83.1	79.6	82.8	80.3	79.0	84.1	87.0	87.8	87.9	90.6
Administration	3.5	3.4	3.9	3.8	3.4	3.9	3.9	4.0	4.0	4.4
Instruction	61.0	56.9	59.9	53.3	53.5	57.2	58.6	57.2	56.2	55.5
Plant operation	11.2	9.3	8.3	7.3	6.9	6.2	6.5	6.7	[1]9.5	[1]10.2
Plant maintenance	2.9	3.4	3.1	3.7	2.7	2.4	2.5	2.6	([1])	([1])
Fixed charges	0.9	2.2	2.1	4.5	5.8	8.0	8.5	9.9	10.4	12.3
Other school services [2]	3.5	4.4	5.5	7.7	6.6	6.3	7.0	7.4	7.9	8.3
Summer schools	([3])	([3])	([3])	([3])	0.1	0.3	0.2	0.2	0.1	([5])
Adult education [3]	0.3	0.4	0.6	0.6	0.2	0.3	—	—	—	—
Community colleges	([3])	([3])	([3])	([3])	0.2	0.3	—	—	—	—
Community services	([2])	([2])	([2])	([2])	0.4	0.6	0.6	0.6	0.6	0.6
Capital outlay [4]	14.8	16.0	11.0	17.4	17.0	11.5	9.3	8.7	8.7	6.8
Interest on school debt	1.8	4.0	5.6	1.7	3.1	2.9	2.9	2.7	2.6	2.0

[1] Plant operation also includes plant maintenance.

[2] Prior to 1959–60, items included under "other school services" were listed under "auxiliary services," a more comprehensive classification which also included community services.

[3] Prior to 1959–60, data shown for adult education represent combined expenditures for adult education, summer schools, and community colleges.

[4] Prior to 1969–70, excludes capital outlay by State and local schoolhousing authorities.

[5] Less than 0.05 percent.

—Data not available.

NOTE.—Beginning in 1959–60, includes Alaska and Hawaii. Because of rounding, details may not add to totals.

SOURCE: U.S. Department of Education, National Center for Education Statistics, *Statistics of State School Systems;* and Common Core of Data survey. (This table was prepared March 1986.)

Table 156.—Current expenditures for public elementary and secondary education, by function and State: 1988–89

[Amounts in thousands of dollars]

State or other area	Total	Current expenditures, by function							
		Instruction		Support services		Noninstructional		Direct support [1]	
		Amount	Percent of total	Amount	Percent of total	Amount	Percent of total	Amount	Percent of total
1	2	3	4	5	6	7	8	9	10
United States	$172,932,385	$101,125,731	58.5	$58,122,930	33.6	$7,670,692	4.4	$6,013,032	3.5
Alabama	2,188,020	1,356,302	62.0	638,344	29.2	193,374	8.8	0	0.0
Alaska	739,020	407,576	55.2	310,129	42.0	21,315	2.9	0	0.0
Arizona	2,143,148	1,257,114	58.7	779,544	36.4	102,229	4.8	4,261	0.2
Arkansas	1,319,370	706,746	53.6	392,742	29.8	112,617	8.5	107,265	8.1
California	19,370,242	10,900,575	56.3	7,236,178	37.4	718,414	3.7	515,076	2.7
Colorado	2,266,667	1,406,152	62.0	776,823	34.3	83,692	3.7	0	0.0
Connecticut	2,984,542	1,668,161	55.9	928,386	31.1	29,801	1.0	358,195	12.0
Delaware	479,327	326,043	68.0	143,985	30.0	9,300	1.9	0	0.0
District of Columbia	584,035	261,071	44.7	226,227	38.7	26,637	4.6	70,100	12.0
Florida	7,245,515	4,197,417	57.9	2,663,508	36.8	384,067	5.3	523	0.0
Georgia	4,006,069	2,501,278	62.4	1,207,998	30.2	243,073	6.1	53,721	1.3
Hawaii	643,319	379,505	59.0	217,871	33.9	45,944	7.1	0	0.0
Idaho	571,159	333,462	58.4	176,749	30.9	28,138	4.9	32,810	5.7
Illinois	7,655,153	4,210,421	55.0	2,772,007	36.2	278,530	3.6	394,196	5.1
Indiana	3,779,468	2,179,617	57.7	1,220,461	32.3	183,750	4.9	195,640	5.2
Iowa	1,925,623	1,160,702	60.3	682,764	35.5	82,156	4.3	0	0.0
Kansas	1,712,260	993,827	58.0	589,189	34.4	88,381	5.2	40,863	2.4
Kentucky	1,918,741	1,012,270	52.8	612,454	31.9	79,328	4.1	214,690	11.2
Louisiana	2,468,307	1,403,606	56.9	811,203	32.9	211,634	8.6	41,864	1.7
Maine	921,931	534,059	57.9	270,121	29.3	23,967	2.6	93,784	10.2
Maryland	3,505,018	1,831,985	52.3	1,129,794	32.2	127,382	3.6	415,858	11.9
Massachusetts	4,522,119	2,531,406	56.0	1,588,459	35.1	142,254	3.1	260,000	5.7
Michigan	7,493,266	3,888,833	51.9	2,752,386	36.7	232,922	3.1	619,124	8.3
Minnesota	3,282,296	2,077,372	63.3	1,061,709	32.3	139,137	4.2	4,079	0.1
Mississippi	1,372,290	865,661	63.1	390,193	28.4	109,991	8.0	6,444	0.5
Missouri	3,096,666	1,880,487	60.7	1,079,031	34.8	137,148	4.4	0	0.0
Montana	592,454	371,217	62.7	197,595	33.4	23,642	4.0	0	0.0
Nebraska	1,105,009	668,484	60.5	325,550	29.5	107,806	9.8	3,169	0.3
Nevada	615,161	377,118	61.3	227,885	37.0	10,159	1.7	0	0.0
New Hampshire	733,230	452,444	61.7	253,662	34.6	27,124	3.7	0	0.0
New Jersey	7,309,147	3,912,748	53.5	2,456,512	33.6	197,533	2.7	742,354	10.2
New Mexico	975,552	564,833	57.9	364,254	37.3	46,465	4.8	0	0.0
New York	17,127,584	11,332,843	66.2	5,261,695	30.7	533,045	3.1	0	0.0
North Carolina	3,892,971	2,432,251	62.5	1,191,243	30.6	269,478	6.9	0	0.0
North Dakota	431,814	272,254	63.0	139,350	32.3	20,210	4.7	0	0.0
Ohio	7,425,194	4,273,710	57.6	2,757,176	37.1	394,308	5.3	0	0.0
Oklahoma	1,833,743	1,045,356	57.0	530,715	28.9	103,261	5.6	154,411	8.4
Oregon	2,123,241	1,247,158	58.7	804,678	37.9	71,406	3.4	0	0.0
Pennsylvania	8,597,355	5,037,143	58.6	2,757,765	32.1	324,686	3.8	477,761	5.6
Rhode Island	736,942	463,762	62.9	218,133	29.6	2,002	0.3	53,046	7.2
South Carolina	2,118,732	1,220,036	57.6	646,873	30.5	201,670	9.5	50,152	2.4
South Dakota	427,522	263,660	61.7	139,197	32.6	24,665	5.8	0	0.0
Tennessee	2,668,341	1,563,334	58.6	725,250	27.2	200,651	7.5	179,106	6.7
Texas	11,761,447	6,553,099	55.7	3,750,292	31.9	664,000	5.6	794,056	6.8
Utah	1,040,104	668,651	64.3	305,203	29.3	66,251	6.4	0	0.0
Vermont	485,226	287,790	59.3	163,450	33.7	14,987	3.1	19,000	3.9
Virginia	4,151,050	2,743,186	66.1	1,249,466	30.1	158,398	3.8	0	0.0
Washington	3,204,265	1,867,444	58.3	1,177,740	36.8	159,081	5.0	0	0.0
West Virginia	1,202,486	628,989	52.3	384,809	32.0	77,200	6.4	111,487	9.3
Wisconsin	3,688,311	2,311,298	62.7	1,255,693	34.0	121,320	3.3	0	0.0
Wyoming	491,930	295,275	60.0	180,491	36.7	16,164	3.3	0	0.0
Outlying areas									
American Samoa	22,314	10,710	48.0	8,321	37.3	3,282	14.7	0	0.0
Guam	94,368	49,979	53.0	34,663	36.7	4,486	4.8	5,240	5.6
Northern Marianas	—	—	—	—	—	—	—	—	—
Puerto Rico	1,030,387	719,931	69.9	177,721	17.2	132,735	12.9	0	0.0
Virgin Islands	111,750	56,440	50.5	49,329	44.1	5,981	5.4	—	—

[1] State payments to support local school activities, predominantly through employee benefits.

—Data not available or not applicable.

NOTE.—Excludes expenditures for State education agencies. Because of rounding, details may not add to totals.

SOURCE: U.S. Department of Education, National Center for Education Statistics, Common Core of Data survey. (This table was prepared December 1990.)

Table 157.—Current expenditures for public elementary and secondary education, by function and State: 1987–88

[Amounts in thousands of dollars]

State or other area	Total	Current expenditures, by function					
		Instruction		Support services		Noninstructional	
		Amount	Percent of total	Amount	Percent of total	Amount	Percent of total
1	2	3	4	5	6	7	8
United States	$157,097,951	$96,966,550	61.7	$54,941,056	35.0	$5,190,345	3.3
Alabama	1,873,390	1,192,924	63.7	571,442	30.5	109,024	5.8
Alaska	756,577	463,235	61.2	279,223	36.9	14,119	1.9
Arizona	2,002,395	1,170,636	58.5	785,548	39.2	46,210	2.3
Arkansas	1,211,156	747,173	61.7	407,622	33.7	56,361	4.7
California	17,402,063	10,303,057	59.2	6,575,734	37.8	523,272	3.0
Colorado	2,172,563	1,297,046	59.7	829,251	38.2	46,266	2.1
Connecticut	2,748,567	1,782,708	64.9	914,662	33.3	51,197	1.9
Delaware	440,631	295,425	67.0	134,819	30.6	10,386	2.4
District of Columbia	489,357	341,535	69.8	119,801	24.5	28,021	5.7
Florida	6,288,977	3,616,668	57.5	2,464,879	39.2	207,431	3.3
Georgia	3,549,038	2,288,898	64.5	1,187,172	33.5	72,969	2.1
Hawaii	608,264	376,493	61.9	201,417	33.1	30,355	5.0
Idaho	532,274	330,274	62.0	176,129	33.1	25,871	4.9
Illinois	6,923,298	4,172,325	60.3	2,520,666	36.4	230,308	3.3
Indiana	3,330,525	2,076,217	62.3	1,180,747	35.5	73,561	2.2
Iowa	1,859,173	1,099,170	59.1	708,431	38.1	51,573	2.8
Kansas	1,568,041	919,817	58.7	591,361	37.7	56,863	3.6
Kentucky	1,741,799	1,291,621	74.2	367,667	21.1	82,510	4.7
Louisiana	2,289,241	1,308,574	57.2	798,808	34.9	181,859	7.9
Maine	839,860	586,469	69.8	232,160	27.6	21,231	2.5
Maryland	3,128,165	1,944,238	62.2	1,121,857	35.9	62,071	2.0
Massachusetts	4,098,062	2,660,673	64.9	1,328,106	32.4	109,282	2.7
Michigan	6,913,261	3,938,089	57.0	2,817,145	40.7	158,028	2.3
Minnesota	2,981,209	1,863,654	62.5	981,165	32.9	136,389	4.6
Mississippi	1,221,560	769,899	63.0	355,006	29.1	96,654	7.9
Missouri	2,747,234	1,684,123	61.3	992,462	36.1	70,649	2.6
Montana	590,226	364,028	61.7	189,791	32.2	36,407	6.2
Nebraska	995,235	643,270	64.6	327,290	32.9	24,675	2.5
Nevada	555,272	340,619	61.3	206,345	37.2	8,308	1.5
New Hampshire	677,507	435,836	64.3	232,792	34.4	8,879	1.3
New Jersey	6,621,860	4,238,134	64.0	2,199,891	33.2	183,835	2.8
New Mexico	916,305	526,459	57.5	342,102	37.3	47,744	5.2
New York	16,073,392	10,505,139	65.4	5,070,355	31.5	497,898	3.1
North Carolina	3,424,194	2,229,418	65.1	1,061,545	31.0	133,232	3.9
North Dakota	385,427	237,172	61.5	132,139	34.3	16,116	4.2
Ohio	6,446,903	3,759,496	58.3	2,485,029	38.5	202,378	3.1
Oklahoma	1,692,283	1,159,773	68.5	468,039	27.7	64,471	3.8
Oregon	1,944,657	1,090,681	56.1	786,417	40.4	67,559	3.5
Pennsylvania	7,679,986	4,712,060	61.4	2,711,644	35.3	256,282	3.3
Rhode Island	663,800	446,057	67.2	200,711	30.2	17,032	2.6
South Carolina	1,932,502	1,192,878	61.7	640,406	33.1	99,218	5.1
South Dakota	389,436	232,666	59.7	134,068	34.4	22,702	5.8
Tennessee	2,352,183	1,668,783	70.9	528,199	22.5	155,201	6.6
Texas	10,791,854	6,511,715	60.3	3,853,872	35.7	426,267	3.9
Utah	974,666	642,954	66.0	294,622	30.2	37,089	3.8
Vermont	456,992	305,266	66.8	145,102	31.8	6,624	1.4
Virginia	3,793,475	2,480,178	65.4	1,218,721	32.1	94,577	2.5
Washington	3,005,980	1,761,402	58.6	1,143,564	38.0	101,013	3.4
West Virginia	1,231,966	595,078	48.3	575,459	46.7	61,429	5.0
Wisconsin	3,318,247	2,085,505	62.8	1,171,981	35.3	60,761	1.8
Wyoming	466,921	281,044	60.2	177,690	38.1	8,186	1.8
Outlying areas							
American Samoa	20,186	10,717	53.1	5,780	28.6	3,690	18.3
Guam	76,359	55,426	72.6	17,638	23.1	3,295	4.3
Northern Marianas	19,694	8,015	40.7	8,858	45.0	2,821	14.3
Puerto Rico	935,392	632,791	67.6	157,027	16.8	145,575	15.6
Virgin Islands	89,217	48,174	54.0	34,038	38.2	7,005	7.9

NOTE.—Excludes expenditures for State education agencies. Some data have been revised from previously published figures. Because of rounding, details may not add to totals.

SOURCE: U.S. Department of Education, National Center for Education Statistics, Common Core of Data survey. (This table was prepared January 1991.)

Table 158.—Total and current expenditure per pupil in public elementary and secondary schools: 1919–20 to 1990–91

School year	Expenditures per pupil in average daily attendance				Expenditure per pupil in fall enrollment [1]			
	Unadjusted dollars		Constant 1990–1991 [2] dollars		Unadjusted dollars		Constant 1990–91 [2]	
	Total expenditure	Current expenditure	Total expenditure	Current expenditure	Total expenditure	Current expenditure	Total expenditure	Current expenditure
1	2	3	4	5	6	7	8	9
1919–20	$64	$53	$449	$375	$48	$40	$336	$280
1929–30	108	87	849	678	90	72	703	562
1931–32	97	81	900	753	82	69	762	638
1933–34	76	67	771	682	65	57	655	580
1935–36	88	74	857	724	74	63	725	612
1937–38	100	84	932	784	86	72	800	673
1939–40	106	88	1,013	844	92	76	878	732
1941–42	110	98	945	844	94	84	809	723
1943–44	125	117	958	899	105	99	807	758
1945–46	146	136	1,071	1,001	124	116	912	853
1947–48	205	181	1,177	1,043	179	158	1,028	911
1949–50	260	210	1,472	1,189	231	187	1,306	1,055
1951–52	314	246	1,602	1,254	275	215	1,403	1,098
1953–54	351	265	1,748	1,319	312	236	1,554	1,173
1955–56	387	294	1,928	1,466	354	269	1,762	1,340
1957–58	447	341	2,098	1,600	408	311	1,914	1,459
1959–60	471	375	2,147	1,710	440	350	2,005	1,597
1961–62	517	419	2,304	1,867	485	393	2,162	1,752
1963–64	559	460	2,426	1,999	520	428	2,258	1,860
1965–66	654	538	2,744	2,257	607	499	2,548	2,095
1967–68	786	658	3,097	2,592	732	612	2,881	2,411
1969–70	955	816	3,386	2,893	878	750	3,112	2,659
1970–71	1,049	911	3,538	3,071	970	842	3,270	2,839
1971–72	1,128	990	3,670	3,221	1,034	907	3,366	2,953
1972–73	1,211	1,077	3,787	3,369	1,116	993	3,492	3,106
1973–74	1,364	1,207	3,917	3,467	1,244	1,101	3,573	3,163
1974–75	1,545	1,365	3,994	3,528	1,424	1,258	3,681	3,252
1975–76	1,697	1,504	4,099	3,631	1,564	1,385	3,776	3,345
1976–77	1,816	1,638	4,144	3,736	1,673	1,509	3,818	3,443
1977–78	2,002	1,823	4,281	3,897	1,842	1,677	3,938	3,585
1978–79	2,210	2,020	4,320	3,950	2,029	1,855	3,968	3,627
1979–80	2,491	2,272	4,296	3,919	2,290	2,089	3,950	3,603
1980–81	[3]2,762	2,502	[3]4,269	3,867	[3]2,540	2,301	[3]3,927	3,558
1981–82	[3]2,997	2,726	[3]4,265	3,879	[3]2,773	2,521	[3]3,946	3,588
1982–83	[3]3,232	2,955	[3]4,410	4,032	[3]2,987	2,730	[3]4,075	3,725
1983–84	[3]3,506	3,173	[3]4,613	4,175	[3]3,240	2,932	[3]4,263	3,858
1984–85	[3]3,763	3,470	[3]4,765	4,394	[3]3,486	3,215	[3]4,414	4,071
1985–86	[3]4,069	3,756	[3]5,007	4,622	[3]3,761	3,472	[3]4,629	4,273
1986–87	[3]4,365	3,970	[3]5,255	4,780	[3]4,047	3,682	[3]4,873	4,433
1987–88	[3]4,654	[4]4,240	[3]5,380	4,902	[3]4,310	[4]3,927	[3]4,983	4,539
1988–89	[3]5,091	4,639	[3]5,626	[4]5,126	[3]4,723	4,303	[3]5,219	[4]4,755
1989–90	[3]5,421	[3]4,939	[3]5,717	[3]5,209	[3]5,017	[3]4,571	[3]5,292	[3]4,821
1990–91	[3]5,748	[3]5,237	[3]5,748	[3]5,237	[3]5,320	[3]4,847	[3]5,320	[3]4,847

[1] Data for 1919–20 to 1953–54 are based on school-year enrollment.

[2] Based on the Consumer Price Index, prepared by the Bureau of Labor Statistics, U.S. Department of Labor, adjusted to a school year basis.

[3] Estimated.

[4] Revised from previously published data.

NOTE.—Beginning in 1980–81, two changes in definitions were made. State administration expenditures are excluded from both "total" and "current" expenditures, and "other programs" such as summer schools and community services are included in both "total" and "current" expenditures. Beginning in 1988–89, extensive changes were made in the data collection procedures. Some data have been revised from previously published figures.

SOURCE: U.S. Department of Education, National Center for Education Statistics, *Statistics of State School Systems; Revenues and Expenditures for Public Elementary and Secondary Education;* and Common Core of Data survey. (This table was prepared July 1991.)

Table 159.—Current expenditure per pupil in average daily attendance in public elementary and secondary schools, by State: 1959–60 to 1988–89

State or other area	Unadjusted dollars											
	1959–60	1969–70	1974–75	1979–80	1980–81	1982–83	1983–84	1984–85	1985–86	1986–87	1987–88 [2]	1988–89
1	2	3	4	5	6	7	8	9	10	11	12	13
United States	$375	$816	$1,365	$2,272	$2,502	$2,955	$3,173	$3,470	$3,756	$3,970	$4,240	$4,639
Alabama	241	544	931	1,612	1,985	2,177	2,055	2,325	2,565	2,573	2,718	3,197
Alaska	546	1,123	2,439	4,728	5,688	7,325	8,627	7,843	8,304	8,010	7,971	7,716
Arizona	404	720	1,216	1,971	2,258	2,597	2,751	3,009	3,336	3,544	3,744	3,902
Arkansas	225	568	893	1,574	1,701	1,971	2,235	2,482	2,658	2,733	2,989	3,273
California	[3] 424	867	1,367	2,268	2,475	2,733	2,963	3,256	3,543	3,728	3,840	4,121
Colorado	396	738	1,287	2,421	2,693	3,171	3,373	3,697	3,975	4,147	4,220	4,408
Connecticut	436	951	1,556	2,420	2,876	3,636	4,023	4,738	4,743	5,435	6,230	6,857
Delaware	456	900	1,514	2,861	3,018	3,456	3,849	4,184	4,610	4,825	5,017	5,422
District of Columbia	431	1,018	1,779	3,259	3,441	4,260	4,766	5,103	5,337	5,742	6,132	7,850
Florida	318	732	1,304	1,889	2,401	2,739	2,932	3,241	3,529	3,794	4,092	4,563
Georgia	253	588	1,055	1,625	1,708	2,169	2,352	2,657	2,966	3,181	3,434	3,852
Hawaii	325	841	1,378	2,322	2,604	3,239	3,334	3,465	3,807	3,787	3,919	4,121
Idaho	290	603	1,016	1,659	1,856	2,070	2,146	2,362	2,484	2,585	2,667	2,838
Illinois	438	909	1,516	2,587	2,704	3,100	3,298	3,538	3,781	4,106	4,369	4,906
Indiana	369	728	1,114	1,882	2,010	2,480	2,725	3,051	3,275	3,556	3,794	4,284
Iowa	368	844	1,259	2,326	2,668	3,095	3,274	3,467	3,619	3,770	4,124	4,285
Kansas	348	771	1,270	2,173	2,559	3,058	3,284	3,560	3,829	3,933	4,076	4,443
Kentucky	233	545	905	1,701	1,784	2,100	2,311	2,390	2,486	2,733	3,011	3,347
Louisiana	372	648	1,130	1,792	2,469	2,691	2,694	2,990	3,187	3,069	3,138	3,317
Maine	283	692	1,108	1,824	1,934	2,458	2,700	3,024	3,472	3,850	4,258	4,744
Maryland	393	918	1,565	2,598	2,914	3,445	3,858	4,102	4,447	4,777	5,201	5,758
Massachusetts	409	859	1,481	2,819	2,940	3,378	3,595	4,026	4,562	5,145	5,471	5,979
Michigan	415	904	1,524	2,640	3,037	3,307	3,556	3,848	4,176	4,353	4,692	5,116
Minnesota	425	904	1,544	2,387	2,673	3,085	3,395	3,674	3,941	4,180	4,386	4,755
Mississippi	206	501	877	1,664	1,605	1,979	2,244	2,350	2,362	2,350	2,548	2,874
Missouri	344	709	1,149	1,936	2,172	2,468	2,748	2,958	3,189	3,472	3,786	4,263
Montana	411	782	1,351	2,476	2,683	3,289	3,604	3,847	4,091	4,194	4,246	4,293
Nebraska	337	736	1,271	2,150	2,384	2,984	3,221	3,471	3,634	3,756	3,943	4,360
Nevada	430	769	1,188	2,088	2,078	2,613	2,690	2,829	3,440	3,440	3,623	3,791
New Hampshire	347	723	1,180	1,916	2,265	2,750	2,980	3,271	3,542	3,933	4,457	4,807
New Jersey	388	1,016	1,783	3,191	3,254	4,007	4,496	4,504	5,570	5,953	6,564	7,549
New Mexico	363	707	1,114	2,034	2,329	2,902	2,928	3,153	3,195	3,558	3,691	3,473
New York	562	1,327	2,308	3,462	3,741	4,686	5,117	5,492	6,011	6,497	7,151	7,663
North Carolina	237	612	1,092	1,754	2,001	2,138	2,303	2,625	2,948	3,129	3,368	3,874
North Dakota	367	690	1,111	1,920	2,275	2,852	3,028	3,339	3,483	3,437	3,519	3,952
Ohio	365	730	1,167	2,075	2,303	2,676	2,982	3,285	3,527	3,673	3,998	4,649
Oklahoma	311	604	1,027	1,926	2,199	2,805	2,859	2,850	3,146	3,099	3,093	3,379
Oregon	448	925	1,561	2,692	3,100	3,504	3,677	3,889	4,141	4,337	4,789	5,182
Pennsylvania	409	882	1,514	2,535	2,824	3,354	3,648	4,237	4,325	4,616	4,989	5,609
Rhode Island	413	891	1,604	2,601	2,927	3,570	3,938	4,287	4,667	4,985	5,329	5,976
South Carolina	220	613	1,032	1,752	1,734	2,017	2,183	2,783	3,058	3,214	3,408	3,736
South Dakota	347	690	1,071	1,908	1,991	2,486	2,685	2,892	3,051	3,097	3,249	3,581
Tennessee	238	566	991	1,635	1,794	2,027	2,101	2,385	2,612	2,827	3,068	3,491
Texas	332	624	1,063	1,916	2,006	2,731	2,784	3,124	3,298	3,409	3,608	3,877
Utah	322	626	1,024	1,657	1,819	2,014	2,053	2,220	2,390	2,415	2,454	2,579
Vermont	344	807	1,366	1,997	2,475	3,061	3,359	3,651	4,031	4,399	5,207	5,481
Virginia	274	708	1,200	1,970	2,179	2,656	2,870	3,155	3,520	3,780	4,149	4,539
Washington	420	915	1,395	2,568	2,542	3,211	3,465	3,725	3,881	3,964	4,164	4,352
West Virginia	258	670	1,047	1,920	2,146	2,765	2,879	3,244	3,528	3,784	3,858	3,883
Wisconsin	413	883	1,409	2,477	2,738	3,233	3,513	3,815	4,168	4,523	4,747	5,266
Wyoming	450	856	1,426	2,527	2,967	4,045	4,523	4,799	5,114	5,201	5,051	5,375
Outlying areas												
American Samoa	—	—	880	—	—	—	—	1,262	1,387	1,846	1,908	1,988
Guam	236	820	1,820	—	—	2,186	2,301	2,489	3,383	3,344	3,295	4,067
Northern Marianas	—	—	—	—	—	—	1,731	1,142	1,693	2,552	3,099	3,366	—
Puerto Rico	106	—	742	—	—	1,112	1,247	1,319	1,325	1,384	1,504	1,692
Trust Territory	—	—	—	—	—	—	—	792	—	—	—	—
Virgin Islands	271	—	1,542	—	—	2,757	2,710	—	3,223	4,277	4,036	5,281

Table 159.—Current expenditure per pupil in average daily attendance in public elementary and secondary schools, by State: 1959–60 to 1988–89—Continued

State or other area	Constant 1988–89 dollars [1]											
	1959–60	1969–70	1974–75	1979–80	1980–81	1982–83	1983–84	1984–85	1985–86	1986–87	1987–88	1988–89
1	14	15	16	17	18	19	20	21	22	23	24	25
United States	$1,547	$2,618	$3,193	$3,546	$3,500	$3,649	$3,778	$3,977	$4,183	$4,326	$4,436	$4,639
Alabama	995	1,745	2,178	2,516	2,777	2,688	2,447	2,664	2,856	2,803	2,843	3,197
Alaska	2,253	3,601	5,706	7,380	7,958	9,045	10,272	8,987	9,248	8,727	8,339	7,716
Arizona	1,665	2,310	2,845	3,077	3,160	3,206	3,276	3,448	3,716	3,862	3,917	3,902
Arkansas	929	1,821	2,090	2,458	2,380	2,433	2,661	2,844	2,960	2,978	3,127	3,273
California	1,749	2,782	3,198	3,540	3,463	3,375	3,528	3,731	3,946	4,061	4,018	4,121
Colorado	1,634	2,367	3,011	3,779	3,767	3,915	4,016	4,236	4,427	4,519	4,415	4,408
Connecticut	1,799	3,052	3,642	3,778	4,023	4,490	4,790	5,429	5,282	5,922	6,518	6,857
Delaware	1,880	2,888	3,542	4,466	4,222	4,267	4,583	4,795	5,134	5,257	5,249	5,422
District of Columbia	1,778	3,267	4,162	5,088	4,814	5,260	5,675	5,847	5,944	6,256	6,415	7,850
Florida	1,310	2,349	3,052	2,949	3,360	3,381	3,491	3,713	3,931	4,134	4,281	4,563
Georgia	1,045	1,886	2,468	2,537	2,390	2,679	2,800	3,045	3,303	3,466	3,593	3,852
Hawaii	1,339	2,697	3,224	3,624	3,643	3,999	3,970	3,970	4,239	4,126	4,100	4,121
Idaho	1,195	1,935	2,378	2,590	2,597	2,557	2,555	2,707	2,766	2,817	2,790	2,838
Illinois	1,808	2,918	3,548	4,038	3,783	3,827	3,927	4,054	4,211	4,474	4,570	4,906
Indiana	1,521	2,336	2,607	2,939	2,812	3,063	3,245	3,496	3,648	3,874	3,969	4,284
Iowa	1,517	2,708	2,945	3,632	3,732	3,822	3,898	3,973	4,031	4,108	4,314	4,285
Kansas	1,434	2,474	2,972	3,392	3,580	3,776	3,910	4,079	4,265	4,285	4,265	4,443
Kentucky	961	1,749	2,117	2,656	2,496	2,593	2,752	2,738	2,769	2,978	3,150	3,347
Louisiana	1,534	2,079	2,645	2,798	3,455	3,323	3,208	3,426	3,550	3,344	3,283	3,317
Maine	1,166	2,222	2,593	2,847	2,705	3,035	3,214	3,465	3,867	4,194	4,455	4,744
Maryland	1,620	2,946	3,663	4,056	4,076	4,254	4,593	4,700	4,953	5,205	5,442	5,758
Massachusetts	1,687	2,756	3,465	4,401	4,113	4,171	4,281	4,613	5,081	5,606	5,724	5,979
Michigan	1,712	2,900	3,567	4,122	4,248	4,083	4,234	4,409	4,651	4,743	4,908	5,116
Minnesota	1,754	2,899	3,613	3,726	3,740	3,809	4,042	4,210	4,389	4,554	4,588	4,755
Mississippi	849	1,607	2,051	2,597	2,246	2,444	2,672	2,693	2,630	2,560	2,666	2,874
Missouri	1,419	2,273	2,688	3,023	3,039	3,048	3,272	3,389	3,552	3,782	3,961	4,263
Montana	1,694	2,508	3,162	3,866	3,754	4,061	4,291	4,408	4,556	4,570	4,442	4,293
Nebraska	1,390	2,363	2,974	3,356	3,336	3,684	3,835	3,977	4,047	4,092	4,125	4,360
Nevada	1,775	2,469	2,780	3,260	2,907	3,226	3,203	3,242	3,831	3,748	3,791	3,791
New Hampshire	1,432	2,320	2,761	2,991	3,169	3,395	3,548	3,748	3,944	4,285	4,663	4,807
New Jersey	1,598	3,260	4,171	4,982	4,553	4,948	5,353	5,160	6,203	6,486	6,868	7,549
New Mexico	1,496	2,268	2,607	3,175	3,259	3,583	3,486	3,613	3,559	3,876	3,862	3,473
New York	2,316	4,257	5,401	5,405	5,234	5,787	6,092	6,293	6,695	7,079	7,482	7,663
North Carolina	979	1,965	2,555	2,739	2,800	2,640	2,742	3,008	3,283	3,409	3,523	3,874
North Dakota	1,512	2,212	2,600	2,998	3,182	3,521	3,605	3,826	3,879	3,745	3,682	3,952
Ohio	1,506	2,342	2,732	3,239	3,222	3,305	3,551	3,764	3,928	4,002	4,182	4,649
Oklahoma	1,284	1,939	2,403	3,007	3,076	3,464	3,404	3,265	3,504	3,376	3,236	3,379
Oregon	1,849	2,967	3,652	4,202	4,337	4,327	4,378	4,457	4,612	4,725	5,010	5,182
Pennsylvania	1,689	2,829	3,543	3,957	3,951	4,142	4,343	4,855	4,817	5,030	5,220	5,609
Rhode Island	1,705	2,859	3,754	4,060	4,095	4,407	4,689	4,912	5,198	5,432	5,575	5,976
South Carolina	908	1,965	2,416	2,735	2,426	2,491	2,600	3,189	3,406	3,501	3,565	3,736
South Dakota	1,430	2,213	2,506	2,978	2,785	3,070	3,197	3,314	3,398	3,375	3,399	3,581
Tennessee	982	1,816	2,318	2,553	2,509	2,503	2,502	2,733	2,909	3,080	3,210	3,491
Texas	1,371	2,002	2,489	2,991	2,806	3,372	3,315	3,580	3,673	3,715	3,774	3,877
Utah	1,330	2,009	2,396	2,586	2,545	2,486	2,444	2,544	2,662	2,631	2,567	2,579
Vermont	1,419	2,590	3,196	3,118	3,462	3,779	3,999	4,184	4,489	4,793	5,448	5,481
Virginia	1,131	2,271	2,807	3,075	3,048	3,279	3,417	3,615	3,921	4,119	4,340	4,539
Washington	1,734	2,937	3,264	4,009	3,557	3,965	4,126	4,269	4,322	4,319	4,356	4,352
West Virginia	1,066	2,149	2,450	2,998	3,002	3,414	3,428	3,717	3,930	4,123	4,036	3,883
Wisconsin	1,704	2,832	3,297	3,867	3,831	3,992	4,183	4,372	4,642	4,927	4,967	5,266
Wyoming	1,858	2,746	3,337	3,944	4,151	4,994	5,385	5,499	5,695	5,667	5,285	5,375
Outlying areas												
American Samoa	—	—	2,059	—	—	—	—	1,446	1,544	2,012	1,996	1,988
Guam	975	2,630	4,259	—	—	2,699	2,740	2,852	3,767	3,643	3,447	4,067
Northern Marianas	—	—	—	—	—	2,137	1,360	1,940	2,842	3,376	3,521	—
Puerto Rico	438	—	1,736	—	—	1,373	1,485	1,511	1,475	1,508	1,574	1,692
Trust Territory	—	—	—	—	—	—	—	908	—	—	—	—
Virgin Islands	1,116	—	3,608	—	—	3,404	3,227	—	3,590	4,660	4,223	5,281

[1] Based on the Consumer Price Index, prepared by the Bureau of Labor Statistics, U.S. Department of Labor, adjusted to a school year basis. These data do not reflect differences in inflation rates from State to State.

[2] Some data revised from previously published figures.

[3] Estimated by the National Center for Education Statistics.

—Data not available or not applicable.

SOURCE: U.S. Department of Education, National Center for Education Statistics, *Statistics of State School Systems;* and Common Core of Data survey. (This table was prepared January 1991.)

CHAPTER 3
Postsecondary Education

A salient characteristic of postsecondary education in this country is its diversity. American colleges and universities offer a wide range and great variety of programs. For example, a junior college usually offers vocational training or the first 2 years of training at the college level, but a university normally offers a full undergraduate course leading to a bachelor's degree as well as first-professional and graduate programs leading to advanced degrees. Vocational and technical institutions offer training programs which are designed to prepare students for specific careers. Other types of postsecondary education providers, such as community groups, churches, and businesses, offer learning opportunities to adults. Postsecondary institutions serve a wide scope of individual needs but pose many problems of coverage and definition for researchers.

In recent decades, postsecondary education has become more accessible to all segments of the population. The growth of public junior colleges and low-cost institutions means that the student costs of attendance can be held to a minimum. Federal student financial aid and other aid programs also have attracted many students who otherwise would have found it difficult to finance a college education.

The National Center for Education Statistics (NCES) has expanded postsecondary data collection through the Integrated Postsecondary Education Data System (IPEDS). IPEDS obtains data from each college and university on its enrollment; State residence of freshmen; staff; faculty and faculty salaries; degrees conferred; and finances, including revenues, expenditures, and property. This annual study provides a comprehensive overview of postsecondary education by instituting a survey system with a consistent set of definitions and survey forms for 2-year, 4-year and other types of postsecondary institutions. The Center gathers detailed characteristics about college and university faculty through the National Survey of Postsecondary Faculty. Additional data on the packaging of student loans and grants are collected through the National Postsecondary Student Aid Survey.

This chapter provides an overview of the latest statistics from the IPEDS surveys. To maintain comparability over time, most of the data in the *Digest* are for higher education institutions, which include only 2- and 4-year colleges. This chapter highlights historical data that enable the reader to observe long-range trends in American higher education. In addition, it presents summary data from the Bureau of the Census on the characteristics and the majors of college students; and from the Equal Employment Opportunity Commission on the race/ethnicity, academic rank, and sex of college faculty members.

Additional data on other postsecondary institutions from the survey, "Participation in Adult Education," compare adult learning activities by demographic characteristics of participants. Data on price indexes and on the number of degrees held by the general population are in chapter 1. Chapter 4 contains tabulations on Federal funding for postsecondary education. Information on employment outcomes for college graduates is in chapter 5. Chapter 7 contains data on college libraries and use of computers by young adults. Further information on survey methodologies is in the "Guide to Sources" in the appendix and in the publications cited in the source notes.

Highlights

- Higher education enrollment increased 41 percent between 1970 and 1980. Since 1980, enrollments have risen more slowly. Between 1980 and 1989, enrollment increased about 11 percent, from 12.1 million to a record 13.5 million. Much of this growth was in part-time enrollment. Between 1980 and 1989, the number of men enrolled rose only 5 percent, while the number of women increased by 17 percent. (Table 161)

- The number of older students has been growing more rapidly than the number of younger students. Between 1980 and 1990, the enrollment of students under age 25 increased by 7 percent. During the same period, enrollment of persons 25 and over rose by 34 percent. From 1990 to 1997, the NCES projects a rise of 16 percent in enrollments of persons over 25, and an increase of only 5 percent in the number under 25. (Table 163)

- Some differing enrollment trends are seen at the undergraduate, graduate, and first-professional levels. Undergraduate enrollment increased rapidly during the 1970s, but fell between 1983 and 1985. Between 1985 and 1989, undergraduate enrollment rose about 10 percent. Graduate enrollment had been steady at about 1.3 million in the late 1970s and early 1980s, but rose about 10 percent between 1985 and 1989. Enrollment in first-professional programs has shown small fluctuations, dropping by less than 2 percent between 1984 and 1989. (Tables 175, 176, and 177)

- Since 1984, the number of women in graduate schools has exceeded the number of men. Between 1983 and 1989, the number of male full-time graduate students increased by 8 percent compared with 25 percent for full-time women. Among part-time graduate students, men increased by only 3 percent compared with 21 percent for women. (Table 176)

- The proportion of college students who were minorities rose between 1978 and 1988. In 1978, 16.3 percent were minorities compared with 18.9 percent in 1988. Much of the change can be attributed to sharply rising numbers of Hispanic and Asian students. However, the proportion of students who were black fell from 9.6 percent in 1978 to 8.9 percent in 1988. The drop in the proportion of black students reflected the declining enrollments of black males and the relatively slow increase in enrollments of black women. (Table 195)

- Despite the sizable numbers of small colleges, most students attend the larger colleges. In fall 1989, 38 percent of higher education institutions had fewer than 1,000 students; yet altogether, these institutions enrolled only 4 percent of college students. On the other hand, though only 11 percent of the colleges enrolled over 10,000 students each, they accounted for 51 percent of total college enrollment. (Table 203)

- The student/staff ratio at colleges and universities dropped from 5.4 in 1976 to 4.8 in 1987. The proportion of staff who were administrative and other nonteaching professional staff rose from 15.0 percent in 1976 to 20.7 percent in 1987, while the proportion of staff identified as nonprofessional declined from 42.4 percent to 38.5 percent. (Table 208)

- Approximately 2.3 million persons were employed in colleges and universities in the fall of 1987, including 1.4 million professional and .9 million nonprofessional staff. About 41 percent of the staff were teachers or teaching assistants, 21 percent were other nonteaching professionals, 19 percent were clerical or secretarial, and the remaining 20 percent were technical, paraprofessional, skilled crafts, service, and maintenance staff. (Table 209)

- Colleges differ widely in their practices of employing part-time and full-time staff. Only 56 percent of the employees at public 2-year colleges were employed full-time compared with 76 percent at public and private 4-year colleges. More of the faculty at public 4-year colleges were employed full-time (80 percent) than at private 4-year colleges (67 percent) or public 2-year colleges (46 percent). (Table 210)

- About 10 percent of full-time faculty in colleges and universities were minorities in 1987–88. Four percent of the faculty were Asian/Pacific Islanders, 3 percent were black, 2 percent were Hispanic, 1 percent was American Indian. (Table 214)

- College faculty generally suffered losses in the purchasing power of their salaries from 1972–73 to 1980–81, when average salaries fell 17 percent after adjustment for inflation. However, between 1980–81 and 1989–90, the average salaries rose by 17 percent, recouping most of the losses. Average salaries for men in 1989–90 ($42,629) were considerably higher than the average for women ($33,936) and have increased at a faster rate since 1980–81. (Table 218)

- The proportion of faculty with tenure has remained relatively stable in recent years. About 64 percent of full-time faculty had tenure in 1989–90, but a large difference existed between the proportion of men and women with tenure. Seventy percent of men compared with 48 percent of women had tenure in 1989–90. About 66 percent of the faculty at public institutions had tenure compared with 57 percent of faculty at private institutions. (Table 223)

- During the 1989–90 academic year, 10,606 institutions offered postsecondary education. This included 2,127 4-year colleges; 1,408 2-year colleges; and 7,071 vocational and technical institutions. (Tables 226 and 335)

- The total number of bachelor's degrees increased slowly in the 10-year period between 1978–79 and 1988–89, but there were notable shifts for men and women. Between 1978–79 and 1988–89, the number of bachelor's degrees awarded to men increased by 1 percent, while the number of degrees awarded to women rose by 20 percent. (Table 228)

- Between 1978–79 and 1988–89, the number of associate, bachelor's, master's, and doctor's degrees rose. Associate degrees increased by 8 percent, bachelor's increased by 10 percent, master's degrees increased by 3 percent, and doctor's degrees increased by 9 percent during this period. Although the number of first-professional degrees rose by 3 percent over the entire 1978–79 to

1988–89 period, they declined in the last years of the time period. (Table 228)

- Of the 1,017,667 bachelor's degrees conferred in 1988–89, the largest numbers of degrees were conferred in the fields of business and management (246,659), social sciences (107,714), education (96,998), engineering and engineering technology (85,273), and health professions (59,111). At the master's degree level, the largest fields were education (82,238) and business and management (73,154). The largest fields at the doctor's degree level were education (6,783), engineering and engineering technology (4,533), physical sciences (3,852), and life sciences (3,533). (Tables 235, 236, and 237)

- The pattern of bachelor's degrees by field of study has shifted significantly in recent years. The pace of growth in such areas as business and management has subsided and declines are significant in male majority fields such as engineering and computer and information sciences. The number of degrees conferred in business and management rose by 34 percent between 1978–79 and 1983–84, but by only 7 percent during the following 5-year period. Engineering and engineering technologies rose 51 percent between 1978–79 and 1983–84 but declined 10 percent between 1983–84 and 1988–89. Computer and information sciences had been showing spectacular growth, but dropped 27 percent between 1985–86 and 1988–89. In contrast, some fields such as social sciences and letters that had been declining began to increase. For example, the number of degrees conferred in social sciences dropped by 14 percent between 1978–79 and 1983–84, but rose 16 percent over the next 5 years. Letters declined by 2 percent between 1978–79 and 1983–84, but increased by 28 percent between 1983–84 and 1988–89. Psychology fell by 6 percent during the first 5-year period and rose by 22 percent between 1983–84 and 1988–89. In 1987–88, the number of degrees conferred in education rose for the first time since 1972–73. To some extent, these shifts during the 1983–84 and 1988–89 period highlight the increased female majority on college campuses by reflecting significant increases in predominantly female fields and

decreases in predominantly male fields. (Tables 235, 254, 256, 257, 258, 269, and 271)

- Only about half of the students who enrolled full-time in a 4-year college in 1980 graduated with a bachelor's degree by 1986, according to a recent High School and Beyond survey. About 55 percent of the students who enrolled in private 4-year colleges earned a bachelor's or higher degree by 1986 compared with 46 percent in public 4-year colleges. (Table 287)

- For the 1989–90 academic year, annual undergraduate charges for tuition, room, and board are estimated at $4,520 at public colleges and $12,057 at private colleges. Between 1979–80 and 1989–90, charges at public colleges have risen by 109 percent and charges at private colleges by 145 percent. These increases substantially surpassed the rise in the Consumer Price Index, which was about 64 percent during the same 10-year period. (Table 292)

- Trend data show some increases in the expenditures per student of institutions of higher education. After adjustment for inflation at colleges and universities, current-fund expenditures per student rose about 17 percent between 1977–78 and 1987–88. Expenditures increased more quickly at private institutions (23 percent) than at public institutions (13 percent). (Table 310)

- Administrative expenditures (institutional support and academic support, less libraries) have been rising more rapidly than most other types of college expenditures. At public universities, between 1980–81 and 1987–88, inflation adjusted administration expenditures per full-time-equivalent student rose 24 percent compared with 11 percent for instruction expenditures per student. At private universities during the same period, the per student administrative costs rose 40 percent, and the instruction costs rose by 27 percent. (Tables 316 and 319)

- Endowments of colleges and universities have risen rapidly in recent years. Between 1980–81 and 1985–86, the market value of endowments rose by 114 percent, from $23.5 billion to $50.3 billion. (Table 326)

Figure 13.--Enrollment, degrees conferred, and expenditures in institutions of higher education: 1960-61 to 1990-91

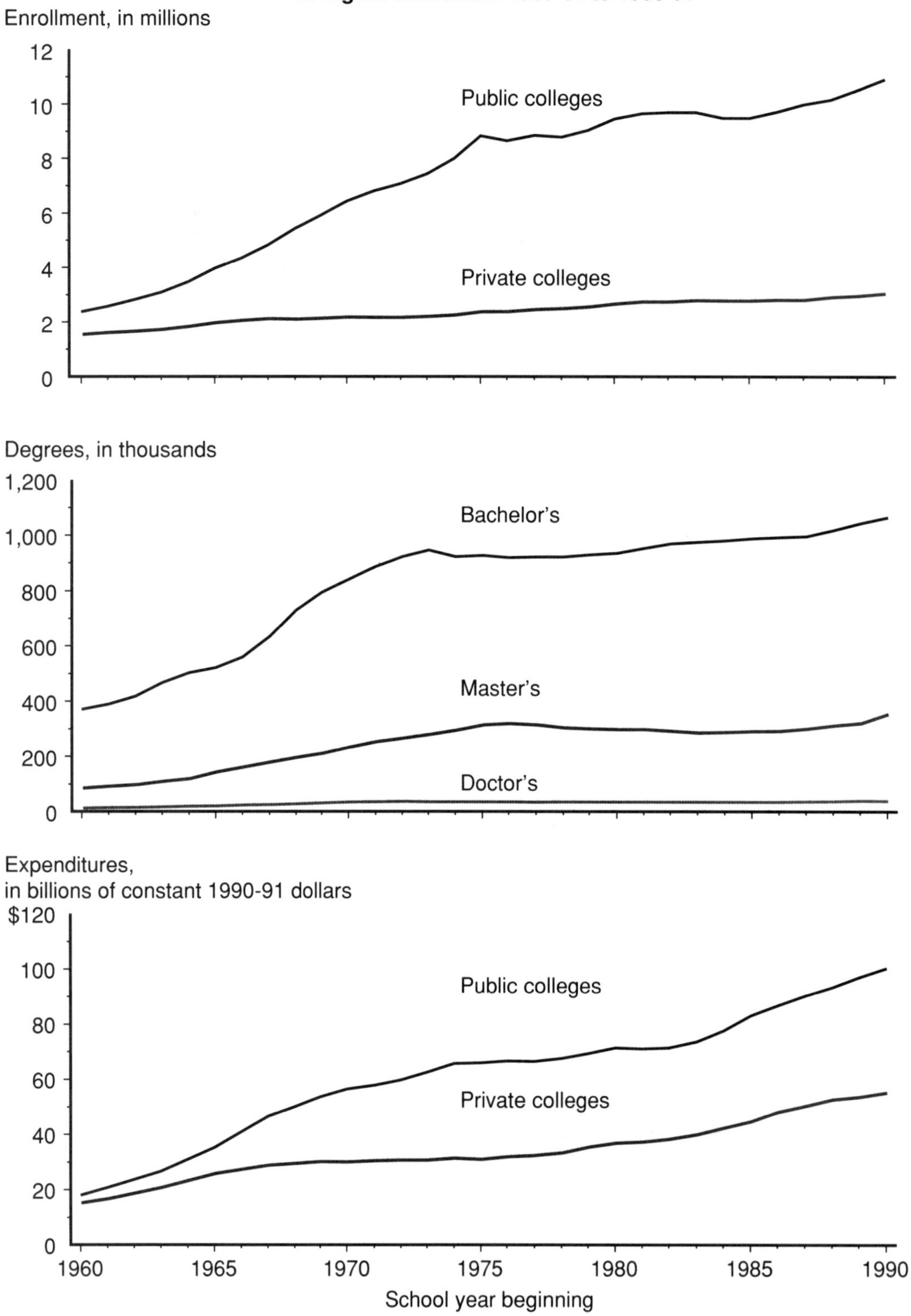

Enrollment, in millions

Degrees, in thousands

Expenditures,
in billions of constant 1990-91 dollars

School year beginning

SOURCE: U.S. Department of Education, National Center for Education Statistics, "Fall Enrollment in Institutions of Higher Education," "Degrees and Other Formal Awards Conferred," "Financial Statistics of Institutions of Higher Education" surveys, and Integrated Postsecondary Education Data System (IPEDS), "Fall Enrollment" and "Completions" surveys.

Figure 14.--Percentage change in total enrollment in institutions of higher education: by State: Fall 1984 to fall 1989

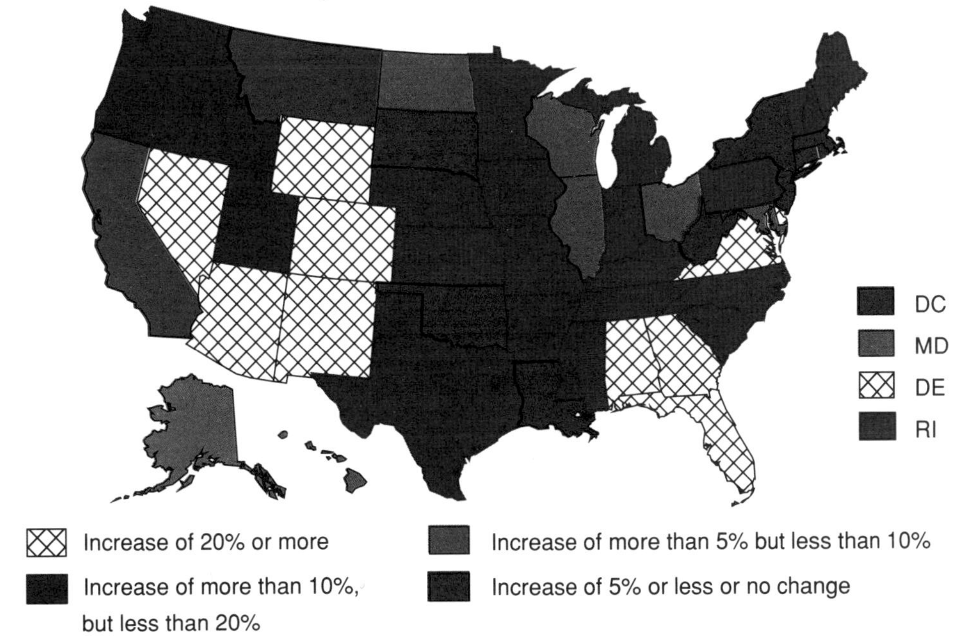

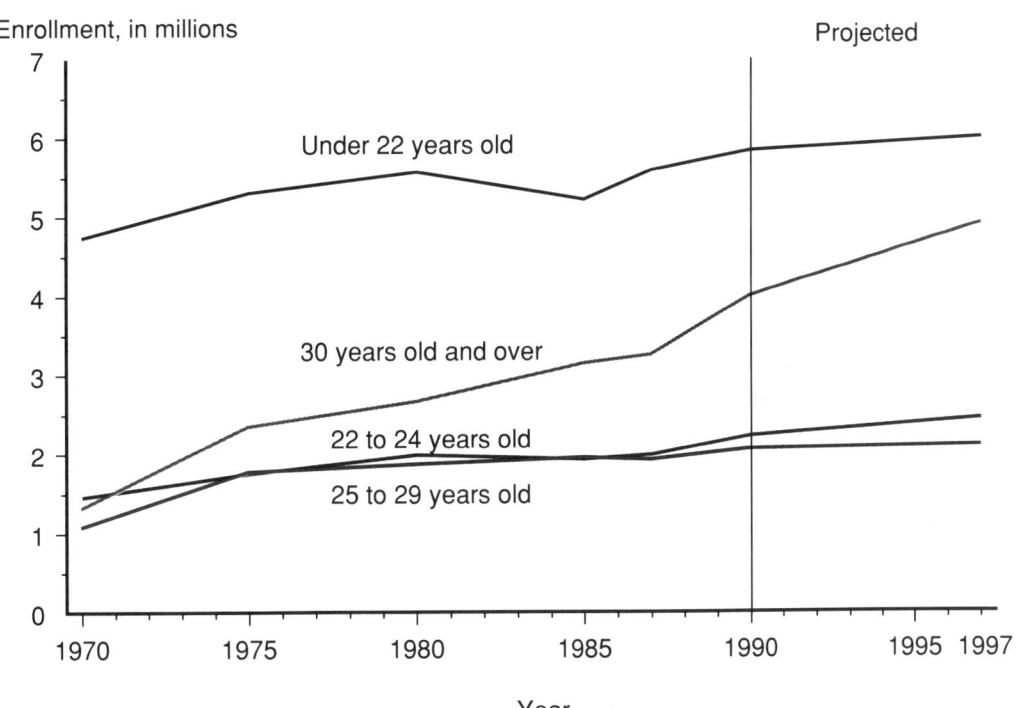

■	DC
▨	MD
⊠	DE
■	RI

⊠ Increase of 20% or more   ▨ Increase of more than 5% but less than 10%

■ Increase of more than 10%,   ■ Increase of 5% or less or no change
  but less than 20%

SOURCE: U.S. Department of Education, National Center for Education Statistics, "Fall Enrollment in Institutions of Higher Education" surveys, and Integrated Postsecondary Education Data System (IPEDS), "Fall Enrollment" surveys.

Figure 15.--Enrollment in institutions of higher education, by age: Fall 1970 to fall 1997

Enrollment, in millions   Projected

Under 22 years old

30 years old and over

22 to 24 years old

25 to 29 years old

Year

SOURCE: U.S. Department of Education, National Center for Education Statistics, "Fall Enrollment in Institutions of Higher Education" surveys; Integrated Postsecondary Education Data System (IPEDS), "Fall Enrollment" surveys; and *Projections of Education Statistics to 2002;* *and* U.S. Department of Commerce, Bureau of the Census, *Current Population Reports,* Series P–20, "Social and Economic Characteristics of Students," various years.

Figure 16.--Full-time-equivalent students per staff member in public and private institutions of higher education: 1976 and 1987

FTE students
per FTE staff

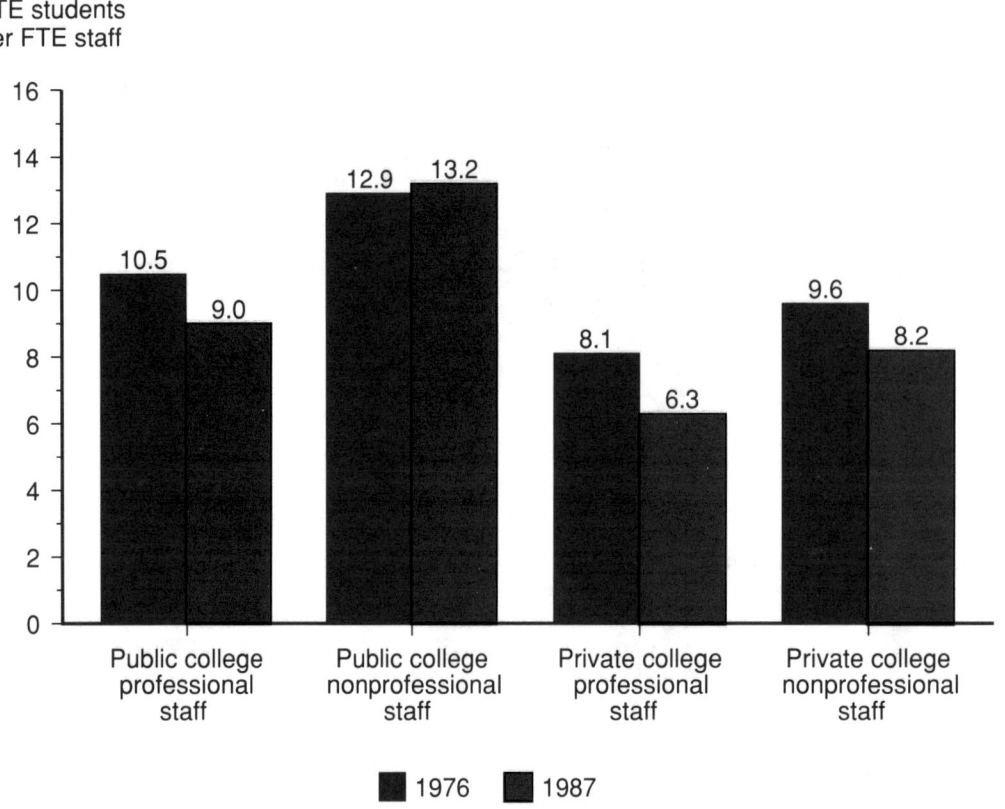

■ 1976 ■ 1987

SOURCE: U.S. Department of Education, National Center for Education Statistics, Higher Education General Information Survey (HEGIS), "Staff, 1976" survey, and Integrated Postsecondary Education Data System (IPEDS), "Staff, 1987" and "Fall Enrollment, 1987" surveys.

Figure 17.--Trends in bachelor's degrees conferred in selected fields of study: 1977-78, 1982-83, and 1988-89

Fields of study

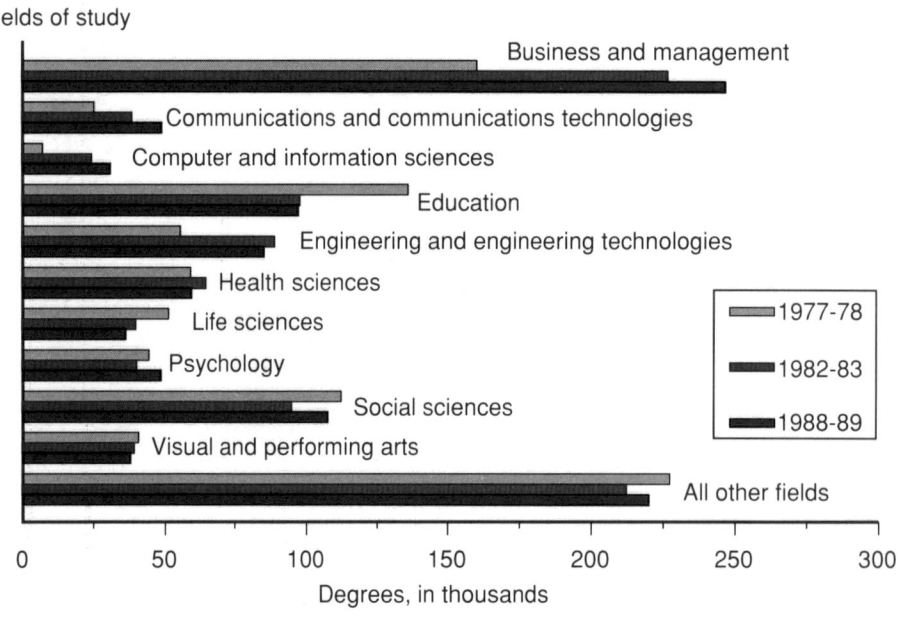

Degrees, in thousands

SOURCE: U.S. Department of Education, National Center for Education Statistics, Integrated Postsecondary Education Data System (IPEDS), "Finances, FY 1988" survey.

**Figure 18.--Sources of current-fund revenue for public
institutions of higher education: 1987-88**

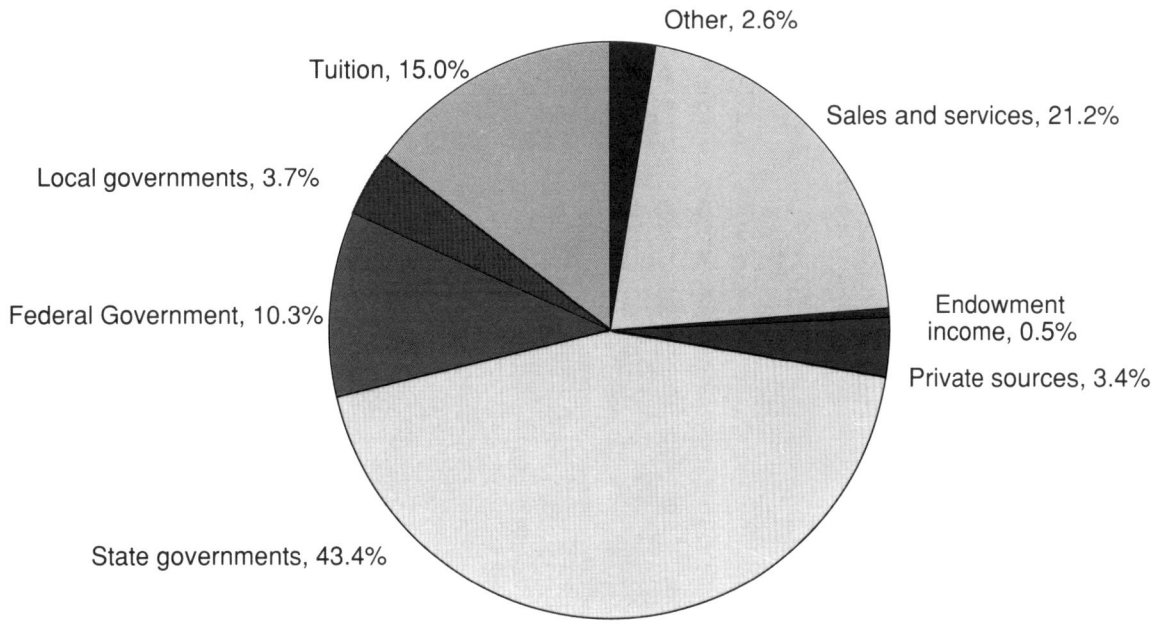

Other, 2.6%

Tuition, 15.0%

Sales and services, 21.2%

Local governments, 3.7%

Federal Government, 10.3%

Endowment
income, 0.5%

Private sources, 3.4%

State governments, 43.4%

Total revenues = $74.8 billion

SOURCE: U.S. Department of Education, National Center for Education Statistics, Integrated Postsecondary Education Data System (IPEDS), "Finance, FY 1988" survey.

**Figure 19.--Sources of current-fund revenue for private
institutions of higher education: 1987-88**

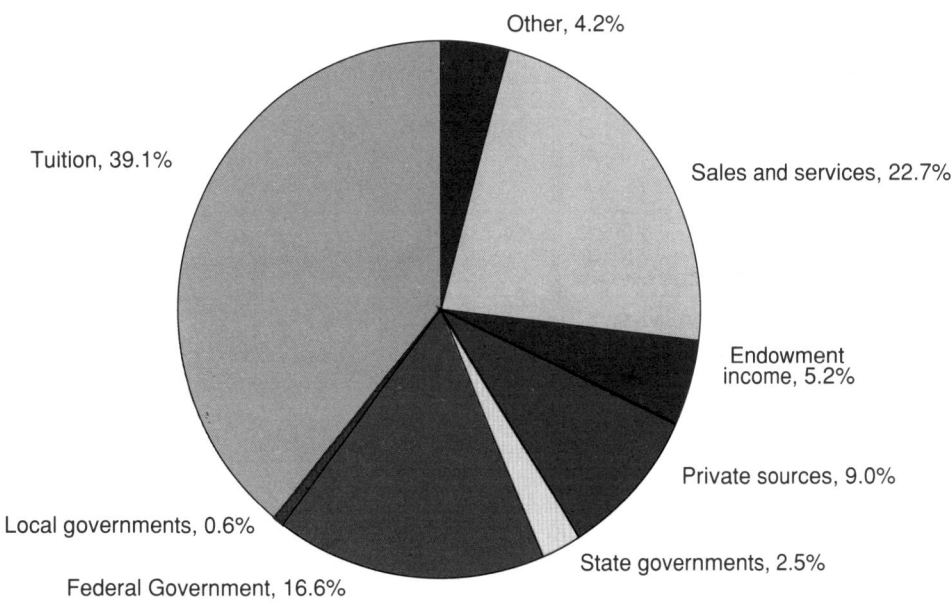

Other, 4.2%

Tuition, 39.1%

Sales and services, 22.7%

Endowment
income, 5.2%

Private sources, 9.0%

Local governments, 0.6%

State governments, 2.5%

Federal Government, 16.6%

Total revenues = $42.5 billion

SOURCE: U.S. Department of Education, National Center for Education Statistics, Integrated Postsecondary Education Data System (IPEDS), "Finance, FY 1988" survey.

Table 160.—Historical summary of faculty, students, degrees, and finances in institutions of higher education: 1869–70 to 1988–89

Item	1869–70	1879–80	1889–90	1899–1900	1909–10	1919–20	1929–30	1939–40	1949–50	1959–60	1969–70	1979–80	1986–87	1987–88	1988–89
1	2	3	4	5	6	7	8	9	10	11	12	13	14	15	16
Total institutions[1]	563	811	998	977	951	1,041	1,409	1,708	1,851	2,008	2,525	3,152	3,406	3,587	3,565
Total faculty[2]	[3]5,553	[3]11,522	[3]15,809	23,868	36,480	48,615	82,386	146,929	246,722	380,554	[4]450,000	[4]675,000	[4]722,000	[5]793,070	—
Men	[3]4,887	[3]7,328	[3]12,704	19,151	29,132	35,807	60,017	106,328	186,189	296,773	[4]346,000	[4]479,000	—	[5]529,413	—
Women	[3]666	[3]4,194	[3]3,105	4,717	7,348	12,808	22,369	40,601	60,533	83,781	[4]104,000	[4]196,000	—	[5]263,657	—
Total fall enrollment[6]	[3]52,286	[3]115,817	[3]156,756	237,592	[3]355,213	597,880	1,100,737	1,494,203	2,659,021	3,639,847	8,004,660	11,569,899	12,503,511	12,766,642	13,055,337
Men	[3]41,160	[3]77,972	[3]100,453	152,254	[3]214,648	314,938	619,935	893,250	1,833,068	2,332,617	4,746,201	5,682,877	5,884,515	5,932,056	6,001,896
Women	[3]11,126	[3]37,845	[3]56,303	85,338	[3]140,565	282,942	480,802	600,953	805,953	1,307,230	3,258,459	5,887,022	6,618,996	6,834,586	7,053,441
Earned degrees conferred															
Associate, total	—	—	—	—	—	—	—	—	—	—	206,023	400,910	437,137	435,085	435,210
Men	—	—	—	—	—	—	—	—	—	—	117,432	183,737	191,525	190,047	185,406
Women	—	—	—	—	—	—	—	—	—	—	88,591	217,173	245,612	245,038	249,804
Bachelor's,[7] total	9,371	12,896	15,539	27,410	37,199	48,622	122,484	186,500	432,058	392,440	792,656	929,417	991,339	994,829	1,017,667
Men	7,993	10,411	12,857	22,173	28,762	31,980	73,615	109,546	328,841	254,063	451,380	473,611	480,854	477,203	483,097
Women	1,378	2,485	2,682	5,237	8,437	16,642	48,869	76,954	103,217	138,377	341,276	455,806	510,485	517,626	534,570
Master's,[8] total	0	879	1,015	1,583	2,113	4,279	14,969	26,731	58,183	74,435	208,291	298,081	289,557	299,317	309,762
Men	0	868	821	1,280	1,555	2,985	8,925	16,508	41,220	50,898	125,624	150,749	141,363	145,163	148,982
Women	0	11	194	303	558	1,294	6,044	10,223	16,963	23,537	82,667	147,332	148,194	154,154	160,780
First-professional,[7] total	[7]	[7]	[7]	[7]	[7]	[7]	[7]	[7]	[7]	[7]	34,578	70,131	72,750	70,735	70,758
Men	[7]	[7]	[7]	[7]	[7]	[7]	[7]	[7]	[7]	[7]	32,794	52,716	47,460	45,484	45,067
Women	[7]	[7]	[7]	[7]	[7]	[7]	[7]	[7]	[7]	[7]	1,784	17,415	25,290	25,251	25,691
Doctor's, total	1	54	149	382	443	615	2,299	3,290	6,420	9,829	29,866	32,615	34,120	34,870	35,759
Men	1	51	147	359	399	522	1,946	2,861	5,804	8,801	25,890	22,943	22,099	22,615	22,705
Women	0	3	2	23	44	93	353	429	616	1,028	3,976	9,672	12,021	12,255	13,054
Finances, in thousands															
Current-fund revenue	—	—	—	$35,084	$76,883	$199,922	$554,511	$715,211	$2,374,645	$5,785,537	$21,515,242	$58,519,982	$108,809,827	[9]$117,301,141	—
Educational and general income	—	—	$21,464	—	67,917	172,929	483,065	571,288	1,833,845	4,688,352	16,486,177	—	—	—	—
Current-fund expenditures	—	—	—	—	—	—	507,142	674,688	2,245,661	5,601,376	21,043,113	56,193,588	105,763,557	[9]113,760,219	—
Educational and general expenditures	—	—	—	—	—	—	377,903	521,990	1,706,444	4,513,208	15,788,699	44,542,843	—	—	—
Value of physical property	—	—	95,426	253,599	460,532	741,333	2,065,050	[10]2,753,780	4,799,964	13,448,548	42,093,580	83,733,387	82,955,555	[9]89,132,803	—
Endowment funds[11]	—	—	78,788	194,998	323,661	569,071	1,512,023	1,764,604	2,644,323	5,571,121	[12]10,853,616	[12]18,561,472	—	—	—

[1] Prior to 1979–80, excludes branch campuses.
[2] Total number of different individuals (not reduced to full-time equivalent). Beginning in 1959–60, data are for the first term of the academic year. Beginning in 1969–70, data include only instructional faculty with the rank of instructor or above.
[3] Estimated.
[4] Estimated number of senior instructional staff. Excludes graduate assistants.
[5] Because of revised survey procedures, data may not be directly comparable with figures for earlier years.
[6] Data for 1869–70 to 1949–50 are for resident degree-credit students who enrolled at any time during the academic year.
[7] From 1869–70 to 1959–60, first-professional degrees included under bachelor's degrees.
[8] Figures for years prior to 1969–70 are not precisely comparable with later data.
[9] Preliminary data.
[10] Includes unexpended plant funds.
[11] Book value. Includes other nonexpendable funds.
[12] Endowment funds only.
— Data not available.

NOTE.—Some data have been revised from previously published figures.

SOURCE: U.S. Department of Education, National Center for Education Statistics, Biennial Survey of Education in the United States; Education Directory, Colleges and Universities; Faculty and Other Professional Staff in Institutions of Higher Education; Fall Enrollment in Colleges and Universities; Earned Degrees Conferred; Financial Statistics of Institutions of Higher Education; and "Fall Enrollment in Institutions of Higher Education," "Degrees and Other Formal Awards Conferred," and "Financial Statistics of Institutions of Higher Education" surveys; and Integrated Postsecondary Education Data System (IPEDS), "Fall Enrollment," "Completions," and "Finance" surveys. (This table was prepared February 1991.)

Table 161.—Total enrollment in institutions of higher education, by attendance status, sex of student, and control of institution: Fall 1947 to fall 1989

Year	Total enrollment	Attendance status		Sex of student		Control of institution			
		Full-time	Part-time	Men	Women	Public	Private		
							Total	Nonprofit	Proprietary
1	2	3	4	5	6	7	8	9	10
1947[1]	2,338,226	—	—	1,659,249	678,977	1,152,377	1,185,849	—	—
1948[1]	2,403,396	—	—	1,709,367	694,029	1,185,588	1,217,808	—	—
1949[1]	2,444,900	—	—	1,721,572	723,328	1,207,151	1,237,749	—	—
1950[1]	2,281,298	—	—	1,560,392	720,906	1,139,699	1,141,599	—	—
1951[1]	2,101,962	—	—	1,390,740	711,222	1,037,938	1,064,024	—	—
1952[1]	2,134,242	—	—	1,380,357	753,885	1,101,240	1,033,002	—	—
1953[1]	2,231,054	—	—	1,422,598	808,456	1,185,876	1,045,178	—	—
1954[1]	2,446,693	—	—	1,563,382	883,311	1,353,531	1,093,162	—	—
1955[1]	2,653,034	—	—	1,733,184	919,850	1,476,282	1,176,752	—	—
1956[1]	2,918,212	—	—	1,911,458	1,006,754	1,656,402	1,261,810	—	—
1957	3,323,783	—	—	2,170,765	1,153,018	1,972,673	1,351,110	—	—
1959	3,639,847	2,421,016	[2]1,218,831	2,332,617	1,307,230	2,180,982	1,458,865	—	—
1961	4,145,065	2,785,133	[2]1,359,932	2,585,821	1,559,244	2,561,447	1,583,618	—	—
1963	4,779,609	3,183,833	[2]1,595,776	2,961,540	1,818,069	3,081,279	1,698,330	—	—
1964	5,280,020	3,573,238	[2]1,706,782	3,248,713	2,031,307	3,467,708	1,812,312	—	—
1965	5,920,864	4,095,728	[2]1,825,136	3,630,020	2,290,844	3,969,596	1,951,268	—	—
1966	6,389,872	4,438,606	[2]1,951,266	3,856,216	2,533,656	4,348,917	2,040,955	—	—
1967	6,911,748	4,793,128	[2]2,118,620	4,132,800	2,778,948	4,816,028	2,095,720	—	—
1968	7,513,091	5,210,155	2,302,936	4,477,649	3,035,442	5,430,652	2,082,439	—	—
1969	8,004,660	5,498,883	2,505,777	4,746,201	3,258,459	5,896,868	2,107,792	—	—
1970	8,580,887	5,816,290	2,764,597	5,043,642	3,537,245	6,428,134	2,152,753	—	—
1971	8,948,644	6,077,232	2,871,412	5,207,004	3,741,640	6,804,309	2,144,335	—	—
1972	9,214,860	6,072,389	3,142,471	5,238,757	3,976,103	7,070,635	2,144,225	—	—
1973	9,602,123	6,189,493	3,412,630	5,371,052	4,231,071	7,419,516	2,182,607	—	—
1974	10,223,729	6,370,273	3,853,456	5,622,429	4,601,300	7,988,500	2,235,229	—	—
1975	11,184,859	6,841,334	4,343,525	6,148,997	5,035,862	8,834,508	2,350,351	—	—
1976	11,012,137	6,717,058	4,295,079	5,810,828	5,201,309	8,653,477	2,358,660	2,314,298	44,362
1977	11,285,787	6,792,925	4,492,862	5,789,016	5,496,771	8,846,993	2,438,794	2,386,652	52,142
1978	11,260,092	6,667,657	4,592,435	5,640,998	5,619,094	8,785,893	2,474,199	2,408,331	65,868
1979	11,569,899	6,794,039	4,775,860	5,682,877	5,887,022	9,036,822	2,533,077	2,461,773	71,304
1980	12,096,895	7,097,958	4,998,937	5,874,374	6,222,521	9,457,394	2,639,501	2,527,787	[3]111,714
1981	12,371,672	7,181,250	5,190,422	5,975,056	6,396,616	9,647,032	2,724,640	2,572,405	[3]152,235
1982	12,425,780	7,220,618	5,205,162	6,031,384	6,394,396	9,696,087	2,729,693	2,552,739	[3]176,954
1983	12,464,661	7,261,050	5,203,611	6,023,725	6,440,936	9,682,734	2,781,927	2,589,187	192,740
1984	12,241,940	7,098,388	5,143,552	5,863,574	6,378,366	9,477,370	2,764,570	2,574,419	190,151
1985	12,247,055	7,075,221	5,171,834	5,818,450	6,428,605	9,479,273	2,767,782	2,571,791	195,991
1986	12,503,511	7,119,550	5,383,961	5,884,515	6,618,996	9,713,893	2,789,618	2,572,479	[4]217,139
1987	12,766,642	7,231,085	5,535,557	5,932,056	6,834,586	9,973,254	2,793,388	2,602,350	[4]191,038
1988[5]	13,055,337	7,436,768	5,618,569	6,001,896	7,053,441	10,161,388	2,893,949	2,673,567	[4]220,382
1989[6]	13,457,855	7,627,172	5,830,683	6,155,484	7,302,371	10,514,973	2,942,882	2,717,641	[4]225,241

[1] Degree-credit enrollment only.

[2] Includes part-time resident students and all extension students.

[3] Large increases are due to the addition of schools accredited by the National Association of Trade and Technical Schools.

[4] Because of imputation techniques, data are not consistent with figures for other years.

[5] Revised from previously published data.

[6] Preliminary data.

—Data not available.

SOURCE: U.S. Department of Education, National Center for Education Statistics, "Fall Enrollment in Colleges and Universities"; and Integrated Postsecondary Education Data System (IPEDS), "Fall Enrollment" surveys. (This table was prepared February 1991.)

Table 162.—Total enrollment in institutions of higher education, by control and type of institution: Fall 1963 to fall 1989

Year	All institutions					Public institutions					Private institutions				
	Total	4-year			2-year	Total	4-year			2-year	Total	4-year			2-year
		Total	University	Other 4-year			Total	University	Other 4-year			Total	University	Other 4-year	
1	2	3	4	5	6	7	8	9	10	11	12	13	14	15	16
1963[1]	4,779,609	3,929,248	—	—	850,361	3,081,279	2,341,468	—	—	739,811	1,698,330	1,587,780	—	—	110,550
1964[1]	5,280,020	4,291,094	—	—	988,926	3,467,708	2,592,929	—	—	874,779	1,812,312	1,698,165	—	—	114,147
1965[1]	5,920,864	4,747,912	—	—	1,172,952	3,969,596	2,928,332	—	—	1,041,264	1,951,268	1,819,580	—	—	131,688
1966[1]	6,389,872	5,063,902	—	—	1,325,970	4,348,917	3,159,748	—	—	1,189,169	2,040,955	1,904,154	—	—	136,801
1967[1]	6,911,748	5,398,986	—	—	1,512,762	4,816,028	3,443,975	—	—	1,372,053	2,095,720	1,955,011	—	—	140,709
1968[1]	7,513,091	5,720,795	—	—	1,792,296	5,430,652	3,784,178	—	—	1,646,474	2,082,439	1,936,617	—	—	145,822
1969[1]	8,004,660	6,028,002	—	—	1,976,658	5,896,868	4,050,144	—	—	1,846,724	2,107,792	1,977,858	—	—	129,934
1970[1]	8,580,887	6,261,502	—	—	2,319,385	6,428,134	4,232,722	—	—	2,195,412	2,152,753	2,028,780	—	—	123,973
1971[1]	8,948,644	6,462,733	—	—	2,485,911	6,804,309	4,438,442	—	—	2,365,867	2,144,335	2,024,291	—	—	120,044
1972[1]	9,214,860	6,458,674	—	—	2,756,186	7,070,635	4,429,696	—	—	2,640,939	2,144,225	2,028,978	—	—	115,247
1973	9,602,123	6,592,074	—	—	3,010,049	7,419,516	4,529,895	—	—	2,889,621	2,182,607	2,062,179	—	—	120,428
1974	10,223,729	6,819,735	—	—	3,403,994	7,988,500	4,703,018	—	—	3,285,482	2,235,229	2,116,717	—	—	118,512
1975	11,184,859	7,214,740	2,838,266	4,376,474	3,970,119	8,834,508	4,998,142	2,124,221	2,873,921	3,836,366	2,350,351	2,216,598	714,045	1,502,553	133,753
1976	11,012,137	7,128,816	2,780,289	4,348,527	3,883,321	8,653,477	4,901,691	2,079,929	2,821,762	3,751,786	2,358,660	2,227,125	700,360	1,526,765	131,535
1977	11,285,787	7,242,845	2,793,418	4,449,427	4,042,942	8,846,993	4,945,224	2,070,032	2,875,192	3,901,769	2,438,794	2,297,621	723,386	1,574,235	141,173
1978	11,260,092	7,231,951	2,780,729	4,451,222	4,028,141	8,785,893	4,912,203	2,062,295	2,849,908	3,873,690	2,474,199	2,319,748	718,434	1,601,314	154,451
1979	11,569,899	7,353,233	2,839,582	4,513,651	4,216,666	9,036,822	4,980,012	2,099,525	2,880,487	4,056,810	2,533,077	2,373,221	740,057	1,633,164	159,856
1980	12,096,895	7,570,608	2,902,014	4,668,594	4,526,287	9,457,394	5,128,612	2,154,283	2,974,329	4,328,782	2,639,501	2,441,996	747,731	1,694,265	[2]197,505
1981	12,371,672	7,655,461	2,901,344	4,754,117	4,716,211	9,647,032	5,166,324	2,152,474	3,013,850	4,480,708	2,724,640	2,489,137	748,870	1,740,267	[2]235,503
1982	12,425,780	7,654,074	2,883,735	4,770,339	4,771,706	9,696,087	5,176,434	2,152,547	3,023,887	4,519,653	2,729,693	2,477,640	731,188	1,746,452	252,053
1983	12,464,661	7,741,195	2,888,813	4,852,382	4,723,466	9,682,734	5,223,404	2,154,790	3,068,614	4,459,330	2,781,927	2,517,791	734,023	1,783,768	264,136
1984	12,241,940	7,711,167	2,870,329	4,840,838	4,530,773	9,477,370	5,198,273	2,138,621	3,059,652	4,279,097	2,764,570	2,512,894	731,708	1,781,186	251,676
1985	12,247,055	7,715,978	2,870,692	4,845,286	4,531,077	9,479,273	5,209,540	2,141,112	3,068,428	4,269,733	2,767,782	2,506,438	729,580	1,776,858	261,344
1986	12,503,511	7,823,963	2,897,207	4,926,756	4,679,548	9,713,893	5,300,202	2,160,646	3,139,556	4,413,691	2,789,618	2,523,761	736,561	1,787,200	[4]265,857
1987[3]	12,766,642	7,990,420	2,929,327	5,061,093	4,776,222	9,973,254	5,432,200	2,188,008	3,244,192	4,541,054	2,793,388	2,558,220	741,319	1,816,901	[4]235,168
1988[4]	13,055,337	8,180,182	2,975,593	5,204,589	4,875,155	10,161,388	5,545,901	2,229,868	3,316,033	4,615,487	2,893,949	2,634,281	745,725	1,888,556	[4]259,668
1989[5]	13,457,855	8,374,394	3,018,166	5,356,228	5,083,461	10,514,973	5,694,202	2,265,658	3,428,544	4,820,771	2,942,882	2,680,192	752,508	1,927,684	[4]262,690

[1] Data for 2-year branch campuses of 4-year institutions are included with the 4-year institutions.
[2] Large increases are due to the addition of schools accredited by the National Association of Trade and Technical Schools in 1980 and 1981.
[3] Because of imputation techniques, data are not consistent with figures for other years.
[4] Revised from previously published figures.
[5] Preliminary data.

—Data not available.

SOURCE: U.S. Department of Education, National Center for Education Statistics, "Fall Enrollment in Colleges and Universities", and Integrated Postsecondary Education Data System (IPEDS), "Fall Enrollment" surveys. (This table was prepared February 1991.)

Table 163.—Total enrollment in institutions of higher education, by attendance status, sex, and age: Fall 1970 to fall 1997

[In thousands]

Sex and age	1970			1975			1980			1985			1987			1990 (estimated)			1997 (projected)		
	Total	Full-time	Part-time	Total	Full-time	Part-time	Total	Full-time	Part-time	Total	Full-time	Part-time	Total	Full-time	Part-time	Total	Full-time	Part-time	Total	Full-time	Part-time
1	2	3	4	5	6	7	8	9	10	11	12	13	14	15	16	17	18	19	20	21	22
Men and women, total	8,581	5,815	2,766	11,185	6,841	4,344	12,097	7,098	4,999	12,247	7,075	5,172	12,767	7,231	5,536	13,951	7,932	6,019	14,978	8,212	6,766
14 to 17 years old	259	242	17	278	242	36	247	216	31	235	203	32	237	142	95	173	143	30	196	162	34
18 and 19 years old	2,600	2,406	194	2,786	2,510	276	2,901	2,580	320	2,600	2,322	278	2,847	2,488	359	3,034	2,682	343	3,010	2,637	374
20 and 21 years old	1,880	1,647	233	2,243	1,854	390	2,423	2,060	364	2,383	1,975	408	2,504	2,024	480	2,575	2,130	444	2,616	2,143	473
22 to 24 years old	1,457	881	576	1,754	1,008	746	1,989	1,174	815	1,933	1,227	705	1,989	1,223	766	2,130	1,338	792	2,208	1,375	833
25 to 29 years old	1,074	407	668	1,774	692	1,082	1,871	610	1,261	1,953	695	1,258	1,930	693	1,237	2,062	720	1,340	2,035	666	1,370
30 to 34 years old	487	100	388	967	279	687	1,243	264	979	1,261	310	951	1,266	293	972	1,396	368	1,029	1,371	369	1,001
35 years old and over	823	134	689	1,383	256	1,127	1,422	193	1,229	1,885	345	1,540	1,993	367	1,626	2,591	549	2,041	3,541	858	2,682
Men, total	5,044	3,505	1,540	6,149	3,926	2,222	5,874	3,689	2,185	5,818	3,608	2,211	5,932	3,611	2,321	6,342	3,868	2,456	6,691	3,924	2,767
14 to 17 years old	130	124	5	126	109	17	99	84	15	121	102	19	114	69	46	68	56	13	78	63	15
18 and 19 years old	1,349	1,265	84	1,397	1,269	128	1,375	1,229	146	1,230	1,108	122	1,363	1,190	173	1,447	1,313	134	1,410	1,258	153
20 and 21 years old	1,095	990	105	1,245	1,053	192	1,259	1,104	154	1,216	1,027	189	1,258	1,029	229	1,253	1,044	209	1,300	1,071	229
22 to 24 years old	964	650	314	1,047	686	362	1,064	687	377	1,048	730	318	1,003	669	334	1,058	701	357	1,046	680	367
25 to 29 years old	783	327	456	1,122	474	649	993	379	615	991	395	596	964	371	593	996	394	602	946	353	594
30 to 34 years old	308	72	236	557	184	373	576	129	447	574	149	424	541	146	395	607	167	440	586	158	429
35 years old and over	415	75	340	654	152	502	507	77	430	639	97	542	690	138	552	896	193	702	1,324	342	982
Women, total	3,537	2,311	1,225	5,036	2,915	2,120	6,223	3,409	2,814	6,429	3,468	2,961	6,835	3,620	3,214	7,626	4,064	3,563	8,287	4,288	3,999
14 to 17 years old	129	117	12	152	133	19	148	132	17	113	101	12	123	73	50	104	87	17	118	99	19
18 and 19 years old	1,250	1,140	110	1,389	1,241	147	1,526	1,352	174	1,370	1,214	156	1,484	1,298	186	1,578	1,369	209	1,600	1,379	221
20 and 21 years old	786	657	128	998	800	198	1,165	955	209	1,166	948	218	1,246	995	251	1,322	1,086	236	1,316	1,072	244
22 to 24 years old	493	231	262	706	322	384	925	487	438	885	497	388	986	554	432	1,072	637	435	1,162	696	466
25 to 29 years old	291	80	212	652	218	433	878	232	646	962	299	662	966	323	643	1,066	327	739	1,089	313	776
30 to 34 years old	179	28	151	410	95	315	667	135	531	687	161	527	725	147	578	790	201	589	784	212	573
35 years old and over	409	59	349	729	105	625	914	115	799	1,246	248	998	1,303	229	1,074	1,695	357	1,338	2,217	516	1,700

NOTE.—Distribution by age is based on samples of the civilian noninstitutional population. Because of rounding, details may not add to totals.

SOURCE: U.S. Department of Education, National Center for Education Statistics. "Fall Enrollment in Institutions of Higher Education" surveys, Integrated Postsecondary Education Data System (IPEDS). "Fall Enrollment" surveys, and Projections of Education Statistics to 2002; and U.S. Department of Commerce, Bureau of the Census, Current Population Reports, "Social and Economic Characteristics of Students," various years. (This table was prepared May 1991.)

Table 164.—Total enrollment in institutions of higher education, by level, sex, age, and attendance status of student: Fall 1987

Attendance status and age of student	All levels			Undergraduate			First-professional			Graduate		
	Total	Men	Women	Total	Men	Women	Total	Men	Women	Total	Men	Women
1	2	3	4	5	6	7	8	9	10	11	12	13
All students	12,766,642	5,932,056	6,834,586	11,046,235	5,068,457	5,977,778	268,332	170,129	98,203	1,452,075	693,470	758,605
Under 18	207,085	87,168	119,917	206,271	86,732	119,539	47	33	14	767	403	364
18 and 19	2,696,652	1,253,984	1,442,668	2,695,892	1,253,615	1,442,277	194	106	88	566	263	303
20 and 21	2,392,038	1,168,820	1,223,218	2,375,398	1,160,289	1,215,109	7,269	4,102	3,167	9,371	4,429	4,942
22 to 24	2,025,725	1,078,235	947,490	1,724,576	915,014	809,562	99,644	63,181	36,463	201,505	100,040	101,465
25 to 29	1,839,916	926,756	913,160	1,327,828	639,577	688,251	95,381	63,701	31,680	416,707	223,478	193,229
30 to 34	1,242,344	558,441	683,903	921,165	386,317	534,848	33,065	20,691	12,374	288,114	151,433	136,681
35 to 39	882,763	337,774	544,989	647,596	231,380	416,216	16,159	9,368	6,791	219,008	97,026	121,982
40 to 49	872,120	288,231	583,889	654,007	209,118	444,889	9,898	4,959	4,939	208,215	74,154	134,061
50 to 64	291,698	98,263	193,435	238,029	80,086	157,943	2,078	1,114	964	51,591	17,063	34,528
65 and over	102,641	38,507	64,134	94,875	33,904	60,971	272	156	116	7,494	4,447	3,047
Age unknown	213,660	95,877	117,783	160,598	72,425	88,173	4,325	2,718	1,607	48,737	20,734	28,003
Full-time	7,231,085	3,610,888	3,620,197	6,462,549	3,163,676	3,298,873	241,807	153,668	88,139	526,729	293,544	233,185
Under 18	113,938	48,513	65,425	113,659	48,348	65,311	45	31	14	234	134	100
18 and 19	2,331,202	1,088,972	1,242,230	2,330,703	1,088,703	1,242,000	190	103	87	309	166	143
20 and 21	1,919,332	948,534	970,798	1,905,791	941,234	964,557	7,170	4,037	3,133	6,371	3,263	3,108
22 to 24	1,251,794	716,088	535,706	1,034,268	590,066	444,202	96,885	61,446	35,439	120,641	64,576	56,065
25 to 29	727,279	412,056	315,223	462,354	246,357	215,997	86,390	57,807	28,583	178,535	107,892	70,643
30 to 34	371,825	181,798	190,027	248,644	107,274	141,370	26,779	16,682	10,097	96,402	57,842	38,560
35 to 39	217,470	90,852	126,618	148,050	53,779	94,271	12,130	6,968	5,162	57,290	30,105	27,185
40 to 49	170,162	62,796	107,366	119,511	41,946	77,565	6,737	3,296	3,441	43,914	17,554	26,360
50 to 64	38,224	14,556	23,668	27,116	10,122	16,994	1,261	683	578	9,847	3,751	6,096
65 and over	9,330	5,463	3,867	6,565	3,209	3,356	197	113	84	2,568	2,141	427
Age unknown	80,529	41,260	39,269	65,888	32,638	33,250	4,023	2,502	1,521	10,618	6,120	4,498
Part-time	5,535,557	2,321,168	3,214,389	4,583,686	1,904,781	2,678,905	26,525	16,461	10,064	925,346	399,926	525,420
Under 18	93,147	38,655	54,492	92,612	38,384	54,228	2	2	0	533	269	264
18 and 19	365,450	165,012	200,438	365,189	164,912	200,277	4	3	1	257	97	160
20 and 21	472,706	220,286	252,420	469,607	219,055	250,552	99	65	34	3,000	1,166	1,834
22 to 24	773,931	362,147	411,784	690,308	324,948	365,360	2,759	1,735	1,024	80,864	35,464	45,400
25 to 29	1,112,637	514,700	597,937	865,474	393,220	472,254	8,991	5,894	3,097	238,172	115,586	122,586
30 to 34	870,519	376,643	493,876	672,521	279,043	393,478	6,286	4,009	2,277	191,712	93,591	98,121
35 to 39	665,293	246,922	418,371	499,546	177,601	321,945	4,029	2,400	1,629	161,718	66,921	94,797
40 to 49	701,958	225,435	476,523	534,496	167,172	367,324	3,161	1,663	1,498	164,301	56,600	107,701
50 to 64	253,474	83,707	169,767	210,913	69,964	140,949	817	431	386	41,744	13,312	28,432
65 and over	93,311	33,044	60,267	88,310	30,695	57,615	75	43	32	4,926	2,306	2,620
Age unknown	133,131	54,617	78,514	94,710	39,787	54,923	302	216	86	38,119	14,614	23,505

Percentage distribution

Attendance status and age of student	All levels			Undergraduate			First-professional			Graduate		
All students	100.0	100.0	100.0	100.0	100.0	100.0	100.0	100.0	100.0	100.0	100.0	100.0
Under 18	1.6	1.5	1.8	1.9	1.7	2.0	(1)	(1)	(1)	0.1	0.1	(1)
18 and 19	21.1	21.1	21.1	24.4	24.7	24.1	0.1	0.1	0.1	(1)	(1)	(1)
20 and 21	18.7	19.7	17.9	21.5	22.9	20.3	2.7	2.4	3.2	0.6	0.6	0.7
22 to 24	15.9	18.2	13.9	15.6	18.1	13.5	37.1	37.1	37.1	13.9	14.4	13.4
25 to 29	14.4	15.6	13.4	12.0	12.6	11.5	35.5	37.4	32.3	28.7	32.2	25.5
30 to 34	9.7	9.4	10.0	8.3	7.6	8.9	12.3	12.2	12.6	19.8	21.8	18.0
35 to 39	6.9	5.7	8.0	5.9	4.6	7.0	6.0	5.5	6.9	15.1	14.0	16.1
40 to 49	6.8	4.9	8.5	5.9	4.1	7.4	3.7	2.9	5.0	14.3	10.7	17.7
50 to 64	2.3	1.7	2.8	2.2	1.6	2.6	0.8	0.7	1.0	3.6	2.5	4.6
65 and over	0.8	0.6	0.9	0.9	0.7	1.0	0.1	0.1	0.1	0.5	0.6	0.4
Age unknown	1.7	1.6	1.7	1.5	1.4	1.5	1.6	1.6	1.6	3.4	3.0	3.7
Full-time	100.0	100.0	100.0	100.0	100.0	100.0	100.0	100.0	100.0	100.0	100.0	100.0
Under 18	1.6	1.3	1.8	1.8	1.5	2.0	(1)	(1)	(1)	(1)	(1)	(1)
18 and 19	32.2	30.2	34.3	36.1	34.4	37.6	0.1	0.1	0.1	0.1	0.1	0.1
20 and 21	26.5	26.3	26.8	29.5	29.8	29.2	3.0	2.6	3.6	1.2	1.1	1.3
22 to 24	17.3	19.8	14.8	16.0	18.7	13.5	40.1	40.0	40.2	22.9	22.0	24.0
25 to 29	10.1	11.4	8.7	7.2	7.8	6.5	35.7	37.6	32.4	33.9	36.8	30.3
30 to 34	5.1	5.0	5.2	3.8	3.4	4.3	11.1	10.9	11.5	18.3	19.7	16.5
35 to 39	3.0	2.5	3.5	2.3	1.7	2.9	5.0	4.5	5.9	10.9	10.3	11.7
40 to 49	2.4	1.7	3.0	1.8	1.3	2.4	2.8	2.1	3.9	8.3	6.0	11.3
50 to 64	0.5	0.4	0.7	0.4	0.3	0.5	0.5	0.4	0.7	1.9	1.3	2.6
65 and over	0.1	0.2	0.1	0.1	0.1	0.1	0.1	0.1	0.1	0.5	0.7	0.2
Age unknown	1.1	1.1	1.1	1.0	1.0	1.0	1.7	1.6	1.7	2.0	2.1	1.9
Part-time	100.0	100.0	100.0	100.0	100.0	100.0	100.0	100.0	100.0	100.0	100.0	100.0
Under 18	1.7	1.7	1.7	2.0	2.0	2.0	(1)	(1)	(1)	0.1	0.1	0.1
18 and 19	6.6	7.1	6.2	8.0	8.7	7.5	(1)	(1)	(1)	(1)	(1)	(1)
20 and 21	8.5	9.5	7.9	10.2	11.5	9.4	0.4	0.4	0.3	0.3	0.3	0.3
22 to 24	14.0	15.6	12.8	15.1	17.1	13.6	10.4	10.5	10.2	8.7	8.9	8.6
25 to 29	20.1	22.2	18.6	18.9	20.6	17.6	33.9	35.8	30.8	25.7	28.9	23.3
30 to 34	15.7	16.2	15.4	14.7	14.6	14.7	23.7	24.4	22.6	20.7	23.4	18.7
35 to 39	12.0	10.6	13.0	10.9	9.3	12.0	15.2	14.6	16.2	17.5	16.7	18.0
40 to 49	12.7	9.7	14.8	11.7	8.8	13.7	11.9	10.1	14.9	17.8	14.2	20.5
50 to 64	4.6	3.6	5.3	4.6	3.7	5.3	3.1	2.6	3.8	4.5	3.3	5.4
65 and over	1.7	1.4	1.9	1.9	1.6	2.2	0.3	0.3	0.3	0.5	0.6	0.5
Age unknown	2.4	2.4	2.4	2.1	2.1	2.1	1.1	1.3	0.9	4.1	3.7	4.5

[1] Less than .05 percent.

NOTE.—Because of rounding, details may not add to 100.0 percent.

SOURCE: U.S. Department of Education, National Center for Education Statistics, Integrated Postsecondary Education Data System, "Fall Enrollment, 1987" survey. (This table was prepared March 1990.)

Table 165.—Total enrollment in institutions of higher education, by type and control of institution, and age and attendance status of student: Fall 1987

Attendance status and age of student	All institutions			Public institutions			Private institutions		
	Total	4-year	2-year	Total	4-year	2-year	Total	4-year	2-year
1	2	3	4	5	6	7	8	9	10
All students	**12,766,642**	**7,990,420**	**4,776,222**	**9,973,254**	**5,432,200**	**4,541,054**	**2,793,388**	**2,558,220**	**235,168**
Under 18	207,085	114,510	92,575	154,713	66,232	88,481	52,372	48,278	4,094
18 and 19	2,696,652	1,761,544	935,108	2,056,871	1,191,350	865,521	639,781	570,194	69,587
20 and 21	2,392,038	1,735,485	656,553	1,817,443	1,198,031	619,412	574,595	537,454	37,141
22 to 24	2,025,725	1,409,564	616,161	1,609,102	1,028,462	580,640	416,623	381,102	35,521
25 to 29	1,839,916	1,107,823	732,093	1,439,550	740,906	698,644	400,366	366,917	33,449
30 to 34	1,242,344	676,718	565,626	991,389	447,802	543,587	250,955	228,916	22,039
35 to 39	882,763	474,892	407,871	707,179	312,430	394,749	175,584	162,462	13,122
40 to 49	872,120	428,264	443,856	709,539	274,526	435,013	162,581	153,738	8,843
50 to 64	291,698	107,484	184,214	249,182	67,226	181,956	42,516	40,258	2,258
65 and over	102,641	22,430	80,211	93,232	13,636	79,596	9,409	8,794	615
Age unknown	213,660	151,706	61,954	145,054	91,599	53,455	68,606	60,107	8,499
Full-time	7,231,085	5,522,416	1,708,669	5,267,062	3,736,150	1,530,912	1,964,023	1,786,266	177,757
Under 18	113,938	85,645	28,293	74,740	49,720	25,020	39,198	35,925	3,273
18 and 19	2,331,202	1,669,573	661,629	1,715,151	1,118,159	596,992	616,051	551,414	64,637
20 and 21	1,919,332	1,578,277	341,055	1,387,303	1,075,616	311,687	532,029	502,661	29,368
22 to 24	1,251,794	1,039,003	212,791	940,892	754,172	186,720	310,902	284,831	26,071
25 to 29	727,279	552,098	175,181	520,746	367,539	153,207	206,533	184,559	21,974
30 to 34	371,825	253,351	118,474	272,375	167,717	104,658	99,450	85,634	13,816
35 to 39	217,470	145,171	72,299	155,825	91,330	64,495	61,645	53,841	7,804
40 to 49	170,162	107,981	62,181	121,602	63,858	57,744	48,560	44,123	4,437
50 to 64	38,224	22,305	15,919	26,189	11,199	14,990	12,035	11,106	929
65 and over	9,330	5,989	3,341	5,394	2,121	3,273	3,936	3,868	68
Age unknown	80,529	63,023	17,506	46,845	34,719	12,126	33,684	28,304	5,380
Part-time	5,535,557	2,468,004	3,067,553	4,706,192	1,696,050	3,010,142	829,365	771,954	57,411
Under 18	93,147	28,865	64,282	79,973	16,512	63,461	13,174	12,353	821
18 and 19	365,450	91,971	273,479	341,720	73,191	268,529	23,730	18,780	4,950
20 and 21	472,706	157,208	315,498	430,140	122,415	307,725	42,566	34,793	7,773
22 to 24	773,931	370,561	403,370	668,210	274,290	393,920	105,721	96,271	9,450
25 to 29	1,112,637	555,725	556,912	918,804	373,367	545,437	193,833	182,358	11,475
30 to 34	870,519	423,367	447,152	719,014	280,085	438,929	151,505	143,282	8,223
35 to 39	665,293	329,721	335,572	551,354	221,100	330,254	113,939	108,621	5,318
40 to 49	701,958	320,283	381,675	587,937	210,668	377,269	114,021	109,615	4,406
50 to 64	253,474	85,179	168,295	222,993	56,027	166,966	30,481	29,152	1,329
65 and over	93,311	16,441	76,870	87,838	11,515	76,323	5,473	4,926	547
Age unknown	133,131	88,683	44,448	98,209	56,880	41,329	34,922	31,803	3,119

Percentage distribution

Attendance status and age of student	Total	4-year	2-year	Total	4-year	2-year	Total	4-year	2-year
All students	**100.0**	**100.0**	**100.0**	**100.0**	**100.0**	**100.0**	**100.0**	**100.0**	**100.0**
Under 18	1.6	1.4	1.9	1.6	1.2	1.9	1.9	1.9	1.7
18 and 19	21.1	22.0	19.6	20.6	21.9	19.1	22.9	22.3	29.6
20 and 21	18.7	21.7	13.7	18.2	22.1	13.6	20.6	21.0	15.8
22 to 24	15.9	17.6	12.9	16.1	18.9	12.8	14.9	14.9	15.1
25 to 29	14.4	13.9	15.3	14.4	13.6	15.4	14.3	14.3	14.2
30 to 34	9.7	8.5	11.8	9.9	8.2	12.0	9.0	8.9	9.4
35 to 39	6.9	5.9	8.5	7.1	5.8	8.7	6.3	6.4	5.6
40 to 49	6.8	5.4	9.3	7.1	5.1	9.6	5.8	6.0	3.8
50 to 64	2.3	1.3	3.9	2.5	1.2	4.0	1.5	1.6	1.0
65 and over	0.8	0.3	1.7	0.9	0.3	1.8	0.3	0.3	0.3
Age unknown	1.7	1.9	1.3	1.5	1.7	1.2	2.5	2.3	3.6
Full-time	100.0	100.0	100.0	100.0	100.0	100.0	100.0	100.0	100.0
Under 18	1.6	1.6	1.7	1.4	1.3	1.6	2.0	2.0	1.8
18 and 19	32.2	30.2	38.7	32.6	29.9	39.0	31.4	30.9	36.4
20 and 21	26.5	28.6	20.0	26.3	28.8	20.4	27.1	28.1	16.5
22 to 24	17.3	18.8	12.5	17.9	20.2	12.2	15.8	15.9	14.7
25 to 29	10.1	10.0	10.3	9.9	9.8	10.0	10.5	10.3	12.4
30 to 34	5.1	4.6	6.9	5.2	4.5	6.8	5.1	4.8	7.8
35 to 39	3.0	2.6	4.2	3.0	2.4	4.2	3.1	3.0	4.4
40 to 49	2.4	2.0	3.6	2.3	1.7	3.8	2.5	2.5	2.5
50 to 64	0.5	0.4	0.9	0.5	0.3	1.0	0.6	0.6	0.5
65 and over	0.1	0.1	0.2	0.1	0.1	0.2	0.2	0.2	(1)
Age unknown	1.1	1.1	1.0	0.9	0.9	0.8	1.7	1.6	3.0
Part-time	100.0	100.0	100.0	100.0	100.0	100.0	100.0	100.0	100.0
Under 18	1.7	1.2	2.1	1.7	1.0	2.1	1.6	1.6	1.4
18 and 19	6.6	3.7	8.9	7.3	4.3	8.9	2.9	2.4	8.6
20 and 21	8.5	6.4	10.3	9.1	7.2	10.2	5.1	4.5	13.5
22 to 24	14.0	15.0	13.1	14.2	16.2	13.1	12.7	12.5	16.5
25 to 29	20.1	22.5	18.2	19.5	22.0	18.1	23.4	23.6	20.0
30 to 34	15.7	17.2	14.6	15.3	16.5	14.6	18.3	18.6	14.3
35 to 39	12.0	13.4	10.9	11.7	13.0	11.0	13.7	14.1	9.3
40 to 49	12.7	13.0	12.4	12.5	12.4	12.5	13.7	14.2	7.7
50 to 64	4.6	3.5	5.5	4.7	3.3	5.5	3.7	3.8	2.3
65 and over	1.7	0.7	2.5	1.9	0.7	2.5	0.7	0.6	1.0
Age unknown	2.4	3.6	1.4	2.1	3.4	1.4	4.2	4.1	5.4

[1] Less than .05 percent.

NOTE.—Because of rounding, details may not add to 100.0 percent.

SOURCE: U.S. Department of Education, National Center for Education Statistics, Integrated Postsecondary Education Data System, "Fall Enrollment, 1987" survey. (This table was prepared March 1990.)

Table 166.—Total enrollment in institutions of higher education, by level of enrollment, sex, attendance status, and type and control of institution: Fall 1988 and fall 1989 [1]

Attendance status, and type and control of institution	Total			Undergraduate			First-professional			Graduate		
	Total	Men	Women	Total	Men	Women	Total	Men	Women	Total	Men	Women
1	2	3	4	5	6	7	8	9	10	11	12	13

Fall 1988

Total	13,055,337	6,001,896	7,053,441	11,316,548	5,137,644	6,178,904	267,109	166,912	100,197	1,471,680	697,340	774,340
Full-time	7,436,768	3,661,779	3,774,989	6,642,428	3,206,442	3,435,986	241,228	151,045	90,183	553,112	304,292	248,820
Part-time	5,618,569	2,340,117	3,278,452	4,674,120	1,931,202	2,742,918	25,881	15,867	10,014	918,568	393,048	525,520
Total 4-year	8,180,182	3,912,207	4,267,975	6,441,393	3,047,955	3,393,438	267,109	166,912	100,197	1,471,680	697,340	774,340
Full-time	5,693,176	2,843,186	2,849,990	4,898,836	2,387,849	2,510,987	241,228	151,045	90,183	553,112	304,292	248,820
Part-time	2,487,006	1,069,021	1,417,985	1,542,557	660,106	882,451	25,881	15,867	10,014	918,568	393,048	525,520
Total 2-year	4,875,155	2,089,689	2,785,466	4,875,155	2,089,689	2,785,466	—	—	—	—	—	—
Full-time	1,743,592	818,593	924,999	1,743,592	818,593	924,999	—	—	—	—	—	—
Part-time	3,131,563	1,271,096	1,860,467	3,131,563	1,271,096	1,860,467	—	—	—	—	—	—
Public, total	10,161,388	4,608,958	5,552,430	9,103,146	4,113,497	4,989,649	108,939	66,196	42,743	949,303	429,265	520,038
Full-time	5,410,348	2,656,238	2,754,110	4,949,950	2,399,490	2,550,460	104,847	63,886	40,961	355,551	192,862	162,689
Part-time	4,751,040	1,952,720	2,798,320	4,153,196	1,714,007	2,439,189	4,092	2,310	1,782	593,752	236,403	357,349
Public 4-year	5,545,901	2,632,158	2,913,743	4,487,659	2,136,697	2,350,962	108,939	66,196	42,743	949,303	429,265	520,038
Full-time	3,842,375	1,910,326	1,932,049	3,381,977	1,653,578	1,728,399	104,847	63,886	40,961	355,551	192,862	162,689
Part-time	1,703,526	721,832	981,694	1,105,682	483,119	622,563	4,092	2,310	1,782	593,752	236,403	357,349
Public 2-year	4,615,487	1,976,800	2,638,687	4,615,487	1,976,800	2,638,687	—	—	—	—	—	—
Full-time	1,567,973	745,912	822,061	1,567,973	745,912	822,061	—	—	—	—	—	—
Part-time	3,047,514	1,230,888	1,816,626	3,047,514	1,230,888	1,816,626	—	—	—	—	—	—
Private, total	2,893,949	1,392,938	1,501,011	2,213,402	1,024,147	1,189,255	158,170	100,716	57,454	522,377	268,075	254,302
Full-time	2,026,420	1,005,541	1,020,879	1,692,478	806,952	885,526	136,381	87,159	49,222	197,561	111,430	86,131
Part-time	867,529	387,397	480,132	520,924	217,195	303,729	21,789	13,557	8,232	324,816	156,645	168,171
Private 4-year	2,634,281	1,280,049	1,354,232	1,953,734	911,258	1,042,476	158,170	100,716	57,454	522,377	268,075	254,302
Full-time	1,850,801	932,860	917,941	1,516,859	734,271	782,588	136,381	87,159	49,222	197,561	111,430	86,131
Part-time	783,480	347,189	436,291	436,875	176,987	259,888	21,789	13,557	8,232	324,816	156,645	168,171
Private 2-year	259,668	112,889	146,779	259,668	112,889	146,779	—	—	—	—	—	—
Full-time	175,619	72,681	102,938	175,619	72,681	102,938	—	—	—	—	—	—
Part-time	84,049	40,208	43,841	84,049	40,208	43,841	—	—	—	—	—	—

Fall 1989 [1]

Total	13,457,855	6,155,484	7,302,371	11,665,643	5,277,774	6,387,869	273,728	168,480	105,248	1,518,484	709,230	809,254
Full-time	7,627,172	3,727,823	3,899,349	6,808,366	3,266,721	3,541,645	247,434	152,419	95,015	571,372	308,683	262,689
Part-time	5,830,683	2,427,661	3,403,022	4,857,277	2,011,053	2,846,224	26,294	16,061	10,233	947,112	400,547	546,565
Total 4-year	8,374,394	3,968,627	4,405,767	6,582,182	3,090,917	3,491,265	273,728	168,480	105,248	1,518,484	709,230	809,254
Full-time	5,795,330	2,867,131	2,928,199	4,976,524	2,406,029	2,570,495	247,434	152,419	95,015	571,372	308,683	262,689
Part-time	2,579,064	1,101,496	1,477,568	1,605,658	684,888	920,770	26,294	16,061	10,233	947,112	400,547	546,565
Total 2-year	5,083,461	2,186,857	2,896,604	5,083,461	2,186,857	2,896,604	—	—	—	—	—	—
Full-time	1,831,842	860,692	971,150	1,831,842	860,692	971,150	—	—	—	—	—	—
Part-time	3,251,619	1,326,165	1,925,454	3,251,619	1,326,165	1,925,454	—	—	—	—	—	—
Public, total	10,514,973	4,747,899	5,767,074	9,424,536	4,243,303	5,181,233	112,638	67,548	45,090	977,799	437,048	540,751
Full-time	5,588,063	2,723,230	2,864,833	5,112,608	2,462,515	2,650,093	108,753	65,366	43,387	366,702	195,349	171,353
Part-time	4,926,910	2,024,669	2,902,241	4,311,928	1,780,788	2,531,140	3,885	2,182	1,703	611,097	241,699	369,398
Public 4-year	5,694,202	2,680,946	3,013,256	4,603,765	2,176,350	2,427,415	112,638	67,548	45,090	977,799	437,048	540,751
Full-time	3,934,197	1,937,785	1,996,412	3,458,742	1,677,070	1,781,672	108,753	65,366	43,387	366,702	195,349	171,353
Part-time	1,760,005	743,161	1,016,844	1,145,023	499,280	645,743	3,885	2,182	1,703	611,097	241,699	369,398
Public 2-year	4,820,771	2,066,953	2,753,818	4,820,771	2,066,953	2,753,818	—	—	—	—	—	—
Full-time	1,653,866	785,445	868,421	1,653,866	785,445	868,421	—	—	—	—	—	—
Part-time	3,166,905	1,281,508	1,885,397	3,166,905	1,281,508	1,885,397	—	—	—	—	—	—
Private, total	2,942,882	1,407,585	1,535,297	2,241,107	1,034,471	1,206,636	161,090	100,932	60,158	540,685	272,182	268,503
Full-time	2,039,109	1,004,593	1,034,516	1,695,758	804,206	891,552	138,681	87,053	51,628	204,670	113,334	91,336
Part-time	903,773	402,992	500,781	545,349	230,265	315,084	22,409	13,879	8,530	336,015	158,848	177,167
Private 4-year	2,680,192	1,287,681	1,392,511	1,978,417	914,567	1,063,850	161,090	100,932	60,158	540,685	272,182	268,503
Full-time	1,861,133	929,346	931,787	1,517,782	728,959	788,823	138,681	87,053	51,628	204,670	113,334	91,336
Part-time	819,059	358,335	460,724	460,635	185,608	275,027	22,409	13,879	8,530	336,015	158,848	177,167
Private 2-year	262,690	119,904	142,786	262,690	119,904	142,786	—	—	—	—	—	—
Full-time	177,976	75,247	102,729	177,976	75,247	102,729	—	—	—	—	—	—
Part-time	84,714	44,657	40,057	84,714	44,657	40,057	—	—	—	—	—	—

[1] Preliminary data.
—Not applicable.

SOURCE: U.S. Department of Education, National Center for Education Statistics, Integrated Postsecondary Education Data System (IPEDS), "Fall Enrollment" survey. (This table was prepared February 1991.)

Table 167.—Total enrollment in institutions of higher education, by type and control of institution, attendance status, and sex of student: Fall 1970 to fall 1988

Type and control of institution, sex and attendance status of student	1970	1975	1980	1983	1984	1985	1986	1987	1988[1]	1989[2]
1	2	3	4	5	6	7	8	9	10	11
Total	8,580,887	11,184,859	12,096,895	12,464,661	12,241,940	12,247,055	12,503,511	12,766,642	13,055,337	13,457,855
Full-time	5,816,290	6,841,334	7,097,958	7,261,050	7,098,388	7,075,221	7,119,550	7,231,085	7,436,768	7,627,172
Men	3,504,095	3,926,753	3,689,244	3,759,787	3,647,509	3,607,720	3,599,047	3,610,888	3,661,779	3,727,823
Women	2,312,195	2,914,581	3,408,714	3,501,263	3,450,879	3,467,501	3,520,503	3,620,197	3,774,989	3,899,349
Part-time	2,764,597	4,343,525	4,998,937	5,203,611	5,143,552	5,171,834	5,383,961	5,535,557	5,618,569	5,830,683
Men	1,539,547	2,222,244	2,185,130	2,263,938	2,216,065	2,210,730	2,285,468	2,321,168	2,340,117	2,427,661
Women	1,225,050	2,121,281	2,813,807	2,939,673	2,927,487	2,961,104	3,098,493	3,214,389	3,278,452	3,403,022
4-year, total	6,261,502	7,214,740	7,570,608	7,741,195	7,711,167	7,715,978	7,823,963	7,990,420	8,180,182	8,374,394
Full-time	4,587,379	5,080,256	5,344,163	5,434,249	5,394,599	5,384,614	5,423,289	5,522,416	5,693,176	5,795,330
Men	2,732,796	2,891,192	2,809,528	2,845,083	2,806,161	2,781,412	2,774,496	2,790,721	2,843,186	2,867,131
Women	1,854,583	2,189,064	2,534,635	2,589,166	2,588,438	2,603,202	2,648,793	2,731,695	2,849,990	2,928,199
Part-time	1,674,123	2,134,484	2,226,445	2,306,946	2,316,568	2,331,364	2,400,674	2,468,004	2,487,006	2,579,064
Men	936,189	1,092,461	1,017,813	1,047,533	1,040,813	1,034,804	1,049,087	1,068,512	1,069,021	1,101,496
Women	737,934	1,042,023	1,208,632	1,259,413	1,275,755	1,296,560	1,351,587	1,399,492	1,417,985	1,477,568
Public 4-year	4,232,722	4,998,142	5,128,612	5,223,404	5,198,273	5,209,540	5,300,202	5,432,200	5,545,901	5,694,202
Full-time	3,086,491	3,469,821	3,592,193	3,665,325	3,629,275	3,623,341	3,656,940	3,736,150	3,842,375	3,934,197
Men	1,813,584	1,947,823	1,873,397	1,910,181	1,880,078	1,863,689	1,864,507	1,882,064	1,910,326	1,937,785
Women	1,272,907	1,521,998	1,718,796	1,755,144	1,749,197	1,759,652	1,792,433	1,854,086	1,932,049	1,996,412
Part-time	1,146,231	1,528,321	1,536,419	1,558,079	1,568,998	1,586,199	1,643,262	1,696,050	1,703,526	1,760,005
Men	609,422	760,469	685,051	697,652	694,506	693,115	706,133	722,562	721,832	743,161
Women	536,809	767,852	851,368	860,427	874,492	893,084	937,129	973,488	981,694	1,016,844
Private 4-year	2,028,780	2,216,598	2,441,996	2,517,791	2,512,894	2,506,438	2,523,761	2,558,220	2,634,281	2,680,192
Full-time	1,500,888	1,610,435	1,751,970	1,768,924	1,765,324	1,761,273	1,766,349	1,786,266	1,850,801	1,861,133
Men	919,212	943,369	936,131	934,902	926,083	917,723	909,989	908,657	932,860	929,346
Women	581,676	667,066	815,839	834,022	839,241	843,550	856,360	877,609	917,941	931,787
Part-time	527,892	606,163	690,026	748,867	747,570	745,165	757,412	771,954	783,480	819,059
Men	326,767	331,992	332,762	349,881	346,307	341,689	342,954	345,950	347,189	358,335
Women	201,125	274,171	357,264	398,986	401,263	403,476	414,458	426,004	436,291	460,724
2-year, total	2,319,385	3,970,119	4,526,287	4,723,466	4,530,773	4,531,077	4,679,548	4,776,222	4,875,155	5,083,461
Full-time	1,228,911	1,761,078	1,753,795	1,826,801	1,703,789	1,690,607	1,696,261	1,708,669	1,743,592	1,831,842
Men	771,299	1,035,561	879,716	914,704	841,348	826,308	824,551	820,167	818,593	860,692
Women	457,612	725,517	874,079	912,097	862,441	864,299	871,710	888,502	924,999	971,150
Part-time	1,090,474	2,209,041	2,772,492	2,896,665	2,826,984	2,840,470	2,983,287	3,067,553	3,131,563	3,251,619
Men	603,358	1,129,783	1,167,317	1,216,405	1,175,252	1,175,926	1,236,381	1,252,656	1,271,096	1,326,165
Women	487,116	1,079,258	1,605,175	1,680,260	1,651,732	1,664,544	1,746,906	1,814,897	1,860,467	1,925,454
Public 2-year	2,195,412	3,836,366	4,328,782	4,459,330	4,279,097	4,269,733	4,413,691	4,541,054	4,615,487	4,820,771
Full-time	1,129,165	1,662,621	1,595,493	1,633,790	1,518,331	1,496,905	1,505,873	1,530,912	1,567,973	1,653,866
Men	720,440	988,701	811,871	826,886	762,112	742,673	741,973	744,110	745,912	785,445
Women	408,725	673,920	783,622	806,904	756,219	754,232	763,900	786,802	822,061	868,421
Part-time	1,066,247	2,173,745	2,733,289	2,825,540	2,760,766	2,772,828	2,907,818	3,010,142	3,047,514	3,166,905
Men	589,439	1,107,680	1,152,268	1,175,319	1,137,816	1,138,011	1,192,965	1,224,730	1,230,888	1,281,508
Women	476,808	1,066,065	1,581,021	1,650,221	1,622,950	1,634,817	1,714,853	1,785,412	1,816,626	1,885,397
Private 2-year	123,973	133,753	[3]197,505	264,136	251,676	261,344	[4]265,857	[4]235,168	259,668	262,690
Full-time	99,746	98,457	[3]158,302	193,011	185,458	193,702	[4]190,388	[4]177,757	175,619	177,976
Men	50,859	46,860	[3]67,845	87,818	79,236	83,635	[4]82,578	[4]76,057	72,681	75,247
Women	48,887	51,597	[3]90,457	105,193	106,222	110,067	[4]107,810	[4]101,700	102,938	102,729
Part-time	24,227	35,296	[3]39,203	71,125	66,218	67,642	[4]75,469	[4]57,411	84,049	84,714
Men	13,919	22,103	[3]15,049	41,086	37,436	37,915	[4]43,416	[4]27,926	40,208	44,657
Women	10,308	13,193	[3]24,154	30,039	28,782	29,727	[4]32,053	[4]29,485	43,841	40,057

[1] Data revised from previously published figures.
[2] Preliminary data.
[3] Large increase is due to the addition of schools accredited by the National Association of Trade and Technical Schools.
[4] Because of imputation techniques, data are not consistent with figures for other years.

SOURCE: U.S. Department of Education, National Center for Education Statistics, "Fall Enrollment in Colleges and Universities," and Integrated Postsecondary Education Data Systems (IPEDS), "Fall Enrollment" surveys. (This table was prepared February 1991.)

Table 168.—Enrollment and number of institutions of higher education, by affiliation[1] of institution: Fall 1980 to fall 1985

| Affiliation | Enrollment | | | | | | | | Number of institutions[2] | |
| | Total, fall 1980 | Total, fall 1983 | Total, fall 1984 | Fall 1985 Total | Full-time Men | Full-time Women | Part-time Men | Part-time Women | Fall 1980 | Fall 1985 |
1	2	3	4	5	6	7	8	9	10	11
All institutions	**12,096,895**	**12,464,661**	**12,241,940**	**12,247,055**	**3,607,720**	**3,467,501**	**2,210,730**	**2,961,104**	**3,226**	**3,301**
Public institutions	9,457,394	9,682,734	9,477,370	9,479,273	2,606,362	2,513,884	1,831,126	2,527,901	1,493	1,493
Federal	50,989	54,800	54,358	55,787	48,741	6,331	539	176	12	12
State	5,879,057	5,964,595	5,883,571	5,924,118	1,963,955	1,884,583	887,272	1,188,308	881	881
State and local	2,360,972	2,538,044	2,465,058	2,439,409	389,989	421,901	668,889	958,630	379	397
State-related	154,964	149,385	145,992	148,094	58,644	47,325	19,852	22,273	31	31
Local	1,011,412	975,910	928,391	911,865	145,033	153,744	254,574	358,514	190	172
Private institutions	2,639,501	2,781,927	2,764,570	2,767,782	1,001,358	953,617	379,604	433,203	1,733	1,808
Independent nonprofit	1,521,614	1,554,187	1,528,571	1,529,779	562,590	497,668	226,639	242,882	795	811
Organized as profit making	111,714	192,740	190,151	195,991	76,400	74,321	32,650	12,620	164	211
Religiously affiliated	**1,006,173**	**1,035,000**	**1,045,848**	**1,042,012**	**362,368**	**381,628**	**120,315**	**177,701**	**774**	**786**
Advent Christian Church	143	142	126	103	48	46	6	3	1	1
African Methodist Episcopal Zion Church	1,091	939	836	702	416	278	5	3	3	2
African Methodist Episcopal	4,541	3,715	3,404	3,473	1,401	1,837	96	139	6	6
American Baptist	6,131	7,477	8,554	8,307	2,506	2,815	1,133	1,853	11	12
American Lutheran and Lutheran Church in America	3,092	2,999	2,770	2,730	913	798	406	613	3	3
American Lutheran	21,608	20,746	21,100	21,258	7,974	9,740	1,555	1,989	13	12
Assemblies of God Church	7,814	7,745	7,972	7,899	3,685	3,154	587	473	10	11
Baptist	38,231	39,559	39,152	41,163	16,958	16,316	4,020	3,869	33	36
Brethren Church	3,925	4,391	4,463	4,664	1,795	1,186	898	785	3	3
Brethren in Christ Church	1,301	1,612	1,761	1,846	650	1,117	27	52	1	1
Christian and Missionary Alliance Church	1,705	1,854	1,831	1,740	765	691	167	117	3	3
Christian Church (Disciples of Christ)	14,913	15,413	15,132	15,311	4,847	5,458	2,536	2,470	12	11
Christian Churches and Churches of Christ	1,342	1,457	1,591	1,543	757	521	150	115	7	10
Christian Methodist Episcopal	2,486	1,972	1,845	1,661	813	705	60	83	4	3
Christian Reformed Church	5,408	5,291	5,313	5,268	2,461	2,447	192	168	3	3
Church of Christ (Scientist)	2,773								6	—
Church of God of Prophecy		270	246	245	96	119	20	10	—	1
Church of God	6,082	6,091	6,187	5,990	2,407	2,463	598	522	9	9
Church of New Jerusalem	170	164	156	155	72	64	5	14	1	1
Church of the Brethren	8,482	8,699	9,302	8,684	2,590	2,880	1,471	1,743	6	6
Church of the Nazarene	11,716	11,140	10,834	10,757	4,258	4,609	843	1,047	10	10
Churches of Christ	9,343	11,775	11,486	10,945	4,674	4,617	895	759	9	13
Cumberland Presbyterian	594	659	684	636	277	221	65	73	2	2
Evangelical Congregational Church	80	60	53	71	13	0	48	10	1	1
Evangelical Convent Church of America	1,401	1,545	1,491	1,539	542	698	104	195	1	1
Evangelical Free Church of America	833	935	1,563	1,613	758	270	429	156	1	2
Evangelical Lutheran Church	743	724	575	589	339	136	107	7	3	3
Free Methodist	5,543	5,552	5,602	5,643	1,865	2,419	543	816	5	5
Free Will Baptist Church	1,132	1,198	1,242	1,191	436	442	183	130	4	3
Friends United Meeting	1,109	1,443	—	—	—	—	—	—	1	—
Friends	5,157	4,889	6,962	7,077	3,323	2,701	443	610	5	7
General Conference Mennonite Church	820	1,369	1,321	1,303	567	541	73	122	2	3
Greek Orthodox	204	303	219	161	126	22	11	2	1	1
Interdenominational	1,254	1,565	1,598	1,438	662	426	178	172	4	6
Jewish	5,738	5,191	5,444	5,472	4,226	735	278	233	24	22
Latter-Day Saints	39,172	39,277	38,973	39,406	15,900	14,324	4,551	4,631	4	4

Table 168.—Enrollment and number of institutions of higher education, by affiliation[1] of institution: Fall 1980 to fall 1985—Continued

Affiliation	Total, fall 1980	Total, fall 1983	Total, fall 1984	Enrollment Fall 1985					Number of institutions[2]	
				Total	Full-time		Part-time		Fall 1980	Fall 1985
					Men	Women	Men	Women		
1	2	3	4	5	6	7	8	9	10	11
Lutheran Church—Missouri Synod	11,727	12,209	11,940	11,507	5,029	4,983	468	1,027	15	15
Lutheran Church in America	23,877	22,977	23,108	22,659	9,158	9,640	1,368	2,493	20	20
Mennonite Brethren Church	1,344	1,510	1,561	1,548	450	432	224	442	3	3
Mennonite Church	4,008	2,794	2,632	2,490	993	1,234	108	155	6	5
Missionary Church Inc.	487	543	550	573	142	164	38	229	1	1
Moravian Church	2,434	2,545	2,436	2,352	655	1,086	238	373	2	2
Multiple Protestant Denominations	5,526	4,982	5,083	4,964	1,616	2,679	273	396	8	7
North American Baptist	155	147	138	133	62	19	35	17	1	1
Pentecostal Holiness Church	767	402	469	470	214	217	17	22	3	3
Presbyterian U.S. and United Presbyterian	47,144	51,483	50,679	52,290	20,499	20,960	4,642	6,189	57	58
Protestant Episcopal	5,396	5,258	5,323	5,344	2,344	2,626	151	223	12	13
Protestant, other	4,072	3,564	2,765	2,390	1,151	797	229	213	11	8
Reformed Church in America	2,713	5,149	5,284	5,238	2,142	2,572	264	260	4	5
Reformed Episcopal Church	67	—	—	—	—	—	—	—	1	—
Reformed Presbyterian Church	2,014	1,292	1,225	1,191	608	388	112	83	4	1
Reorganized Latter-Day Saints Church	4,274	4,237	4,265	4,517	1,923	1,251	879	464	2	2
Roman Catholic	422,842	445,030	456,936	452,992	132,519	151,173	61,954	107,346	229	234
Russian Orthodox	47	43	47	36	34	0	2	0	1	1
Seventh-Day Adventists	19,168	17,525	17,131	15,993	6,380	6,314	1,341	1,958	11	11
Southern Baptist	85,281	88,556	88,837	88,869	33,956	32,760	10,250	11,903	54	56
Unitarian Universalist	87	91	86	88	40	36	8	4	2	2
United Brethren Church	545	448	366	447	204	181	39	23	1	1
United Church of Christ	14,169	13,911	12,180	12,568	4,295	4,455	1,547	2,271	16	14
United Methodist	127,099	127,064	127,281	127,238	46,787	50,606	12,823	17,022	91	94
Wesleyan Church	3,583	2,584	2,516	2,394	918	1,067	174	235	5	4
Wisconsin Evangelical Lutheran Synod	808	629	559	520	173	344	2	1	1	1
Other religiously affiliated	462	1,866	2,663	2,618	956	848	446	368	1	7

[1] Affiliation as reported by institutions of higher education.
[2] Includes only institutions which reported enrollment.
—Data not applicable or not reported.

SOURCE: U.S. Department of Education, National Center for Education Statistics, "Fall Enrollment in Colleges and Universities" surveys. (This table was prepared August 1986.)

Table 169.—Total first-time freshmen enrollment in institutions of higher education, by sex of student, attendance status, and type and control of institution: Fall 1955 to fall 1989

[In thousands]

Year	Total, all freshmen	Men			Women			Type of institution, by control			
		Total	Full-time	Part-time	Total	Full-time	Part-time	4-year		2-year	
								Public	Private	Public	Private
1	2	3	4	5	6	7	8	9	10	11	12
1955[1]	670	416	—	—	254	—	—	[2]283	[2]247	[2]117	[2]23
1956[1]	718	443	—	—	275	—	—	[2]293	[2]262	[2]137	[2]25
1957[1]	724	442	—	—	282	—	—	[2]294	[2]263	[2]141	[2]27
1958[1]	775	465	—	—	310	—	—	[2]328	[2]272	[2]146	[2]29
1959[1]	822	488	—	—	334	—	—	[2]348	[2]292	[2]153	[2]28
1960[1]	923	540	—	—	384	—	—	[2]396	[2]313	[2]182	[2]32
1961[1]	1,018	592	—	—	426	—	—	[2]438	[2]336	[2]210	[2]34
1962[1]	1,031	598	—	—	432	—	—	[2]445	[2]325	[2]225	[2]36
1963[1]	1,046	604	—	—	442	—	—	—	—	—	—
1964[1]	1,225	702	—	—	523	—	—	[2]539	[2]363	[2]275	[2]47
1965[1]	1,442	829	—	—	613	—	—	[2]642	[2]399	[2]348	[2]53
1966	1,554	890	—	—	665	—	—	[2]626	[2]383	[2]478	[2]67
1967	1,641	931	761	170	710	574	136	[2]645	[2]368	[2]561	[2]67
1968	1,893	1,082	847	235	810	624	187	[2]725	[2]378	[2]718	[2]72
1969	1,967	1,118	876	242	849	649	200	[2]737	[2]393	[2]776	[2]61
1970	2,063	1,152	896	256	911	691	221	[2]754	[2]397	[2]854	[2]58
1971	2,119	1,171	896	275	949	710	238	[2]738	[2]386	[2]937	[2]58
1972	2,153	1,158	858	299	995	716	279	680	381	1,037	55
1973	2,226	1,182	867	315	1,044	740	304	699	379	1,089	59
1974	2,366	1,244	896	348	1,122	777	345	746	386	1,176	58
1975	2,515	1,328	942	386	1,187	821	366	772	395	1,284	64
1976	2,347	1,170	855	316	1,177	808	369	717	414	1,153	63
1977	2,394	1,156	840	316	1,239	841	398	737	405	1,186	67
1978	2,390	1,142	817	324	1,248	834	414	737	407	1,174	73
1979	2,503	1,180	840	340	1,323	866	457	760	415	1,254	74
1980	2,588	1,219	862	357	1,369	887	481	765	418	1,314	91
1981	2,595	1,218	852	366	1,378	886	492	754	419	1,318	104
1982	2,505	1,199	837	362	1,306	851	455	731	404	1,254	116
1983	2,444	1,159	825	334	1,285	853	431	728	404	1,190	122
1984	2,357	1,112	786	326	1,245	827	418	714	403	1,130	110
1985	2,292	1,076	775	301	1,216	827	389	717	399	1,060	116
1986	2,219	1,047	769	278	1,173	821	352	720	392	991	[3]117
1987	2,246	1,047	779	267	1,200	847	352	758	405	980	104
1988[4]	2,379	1,100	807	293	1,279	892	387	783	426	1,049	121
1989[5]	2,353	1,099	798	300	1,255	875	379	762	411	1,042	139

[1] Excludes first-time freshmen in occupational programs not creditable towards a bachelor's degree.

[2] Data for 2-year branches of 4-year college systems are aggregated with the 4-year institutions.

[3] Because of imputation techniques, data are not consistent with figures for other years.

[4] Data have been revised from previously published figures.

[5] Preliminary data.

—Data not available.

NOTE.—Alaska and Hawaii are included in all years. Because of rounding, details may not add to totals.

SOURCE: U.S. Department of Education, National Center for Education Statistics, *Fall Enrollment in Higher Education,* various years; "Fall Enrollment in Colleges and Universities"; and Integrated Postsecondary Education Data System (IPEDS), "Fall Enrollment" surveys. (This table was prepared February 1991.)

Table 170.—Total first-time freshmen enrollment in institutions of higher education, by attendance status, sex, control of institution, and State: Fall 1987 to fall 1989

State or other area	Fall 1987	Fall 1988 [1]	Fall 1989 [2]							Public insti-tutions	Private institu-tions
			Total	Full-time			Part-time				
				Total	Men	Women	Total	Men	Women		
1	2	3	4	5	6	7	8	9	10	11	12
United States	2,246,359	2,378,803	2,353,236	1,673,941	798,467	875,474	679,295	300,191	379,104	1,803,779	549,457
Alabama	40,181	43,218	44,003	35,425	16,196	19,229	8,578	3,828	4,750	38,374	5,629
Alaska	759	2,201	2,397	2,025	942	1,083	372	130	242	2,116	281
Arizona	56,345	64,174	61,241	25,076	13,396	11,680	36,165	16,836	19,329	58,394	2,847
Arkansas	16,772	18,579	18,398	15,919	7,264	8,655	2,479	913	1,566	15,004	3,394
California	277,766	281,561	273,783	134,035	65,731	68,304	139,748	63,565	76,183	251,441	22,342
Colorado	30,026	31,121	35,002	22,834	11,375	11,459	12,168	5,171	6,997	30,596	4,406
Connecticut	30,244	29,551	28,393	18,813	9,052	9,761	9,580	3,613	5,967	18,968	9,425
Delaware	7,186	7,905	8,227	6,043	2,644	3,399	2,184	850	1,334	6,788	1,439
District of Columbia	9,705	9,751	9,030	7,285	3,074	4,211	1,745	691	1,054	1,785	7,245
Florida	75,808	79,592	69,357	48,787	23,939	24,848	20,570	9,251	11,319	52,697	16,660
Georgia	[3] 45,922	50,728	50,914	39,598	18,385	21,213	11,316	5,024	6,292	38,430	12,484
Hawaii	8,427	8,405	8,675	5,972	2,768	3,204	2,703	1,384	1,319	6,116	2,559
Idaho	9,863	11,474	10,360	9,233	4,384	4,849	1,127	470	657	5,979	4,381
Illinois	109,599	125,320	125,519	76,193	37,768	38,425	49,326	20,765	28,561	102,610	22,909
Indiana	50,420	54,441	54,891	44,293	21,752	22,541	10,598	4,270	6,328	39,910	14,981
Iowa	35,439	37,125	37,583	31,083	15,455	15,628	6,500	2,351	4,149	28,957	8,626
Kansas	26,506	27,079	26,915	19,028	9,627	9,401	7,887	3,460	4,427	24,105	2,810
Kentucky	28,156	29,846	31,242	26,563	12,108	14,455	4,679	1,784	2,895	23,600	7,642
Louisiana	30,631	30,957	29,415	26,085	11,135	14,950	3,330	1,296	2,034	24,011	5,404
Maine	9,370	9,648	9,484	8,537	4,186	4,351	947	270	677	6,249	3,235
Maryland	30,763	31,699	31,486	21,635	10,218	11,417	9,851	3,865	5,986	27,000	4,486
Massachusetts	77,906	75,646	70,780	57,945	26,332	31,613	12,835	5,127	7,708	30,651	40,129
Michigan	94,593	96,211	93,725	62,599	29,154	33,445	31,126	13,952	17,174	77,342	16,383
Minnesota	46,716	48,104	49,123	36,129	17,131	18,998	12,994	4,763	8,231	39,449	9,674
Mississippi	27,067	28,349	27,244	23,362	10,647	12,715	3,882	1,416	2,466	24,566	2,678
Missouri	36,375	39,631	41,544	34,527	16,237	18,290	7,017	2,659	4,358	30,639	10,905
Montana	5,365	5,994	6,365	5,647	2,733	2,914	718	288	430	5,521	844
Nebraska	16,644	17,320	21,786	14,340	6,788	7,552	7,446	3,117	4,329	18,497	3,289
Nevada	6,655	8,192	8,455	3,563	1,750	1,813	4,892	2,189	2,703	8,360	95
New Hampshire	11,330	12,201	10,425	8,680	4,415	4,265	1,745	786	959	5,281	5,144
New Jersey	41,634	44,449	48,241	36,767	17,393	19,374	11,474	4,553	6,921	39,911	8,330
New Mexico	9,012	11,242	11,378	8,207	4,051	4,156	3,171	1,331	1,840	11,122	256
New York	163,900	170,592	162,398	140,617	65,399	75,218	21,781	9,087	12,694	102,088	60,310
North Carolina	62,157	65,625	66,320	54,757	25,266	29,491	11,563	5,538	6,025	50,753	15,567
North Dakota	8,249	9,107	8,558	7,656	4,159	3,497	902	420	482	7,985	573
Ohio	98,903	111,267	108,393	75,165	35,829	39,336	33,228	21,245	11,983	71,405	36,988
Oklahoma	31,424	30,526	30,031	20,778	10,128	10,650	9,253	3,448	5,805	25,200	4,831
Oregon	26,387	27,343	27,233	18,938	9,435	9,503	8,295	3,772	4,523	24,085	3,148
Pennsylvania	113,999	122,008	148,334	108,661	51,251	57,410	39,673	16,325	23,348	63,661	84,673
Rhode Island	13,700	13,419	13,308	11,445	5,718	5,727	1,863	831	1,032	5,506	7,802
South Carolina	32,124	34,311	33,752	27,001	12,334	14,667	6,751	2,883	3,868	25,894	7,858
South Dakota	6,623	6,085	6,390	5,699	2,615	3,084	691	260	431	4,570	1,820
Tennessee	34,492	37,486	37,846	32,809	15,066	17,743	5,037	2,265	2,772	25,008	12,838
Texas	134,478	150,065	132,051	87,372	43,038	44,334	44,679	19,452	25,227	115,419	16,632
Utah	15,285	19,138	20,374	15,453	7,179	8,274	4,921	2,405	2,516	14,916	5,458
Vermont	6,578	6,839	6,642	6,141	3,070	3,071	501	147	354	3,570	3,072
Virginia	48,972	50,546	47,098	40,286	18,175	22,111	6,812	3,154	3,658	35,978	11,120
Washington	68,450	72,576	66,853	39,528	19,252	20,276	27,325	12,008	15,317	62,066	4,787
West Virginia	15,568	16,773	18,318	15,000	7,386	7,614	3,318	1,070	2,248	15,324	2,994
Wisconsin	51,357	53,409	54,348	42,266	19,758	22,508	12,082	5,326	6,756	46,861	7,487
Wyoming	5,837	6,019	5,890	4,426	2,468	1,958	1,464	586	878	5,303	587
U.S. Service Schools	4,691	3,955	3,718	3,715	2,911	804	3	1	2	3,718	—
Outlying areas	29,768	33,544	35,653	30,943	12,788	18,155	4,710	1,987	2,723	13,652	22,001
American Samoa	461	582	753	353	223	130	400	237	163	753	—
Federated States of Micronesia	—	—	396	108	61	47	288	131	157	396	—
Guam	341	410	520	389	167	222	131	61	70	520	—
Northern Marianas	96	90	162	42	20	22	120	62	58	162	—
Palau	—	—	339	288	116	172	51	25	26	339	—
Puerto Rico	28,243	31,423	32,868	29,510	12,127	17,383	3,358	1,380	1,978	10,867	22,001
Trust Territory of the Pacific	383	524	—	—	—	—	—	—	—	—	—
Virgin Islands	244	515	615	253	74	179	362	91	271	615	—

[1] Data have been revised from previously published figures.

[2] Preliminary data.

[3] Part of the 1987 increase is due to the inclusion of additional public 2-year institutions in the survey.

—Data not available or not applicable.

SOURCE: U.S. Department of Education, National Center for Education Statistics, Integrated Postsecondary Education Data System, "Fall Enrollment" surveys. (This table was prepared February 1991.)

Table 171.—College enrollment rates of high school graduates, by race/ethnicity: 1960 to 1989

[Numbers in thousands]

Year	High school graduates				Enrolled in college [1]								
	Total	White [2]	Black [2,3]	Hispanic [3]	Total		White [2]		Black [2,3]		Hispanic [3]	
					Number	Percent	Number	Percent	Number	Percent	Number	Percent
1	2	3	4	5	6	7	8	9	10	11	12	13
1960	1,679	1,565	—	—	758	45.1	717	45.8	—	—	—	—
1961	1,763	1,612	—	—	847	48.0	798	49.5	—	—	—	—
1962	1,838	1,660	—	—	900	49.0	840	50.6	—	—	—	—
1963	1,741	1,615	—	—	784	45.0	736	45.6	—	—	—	—
1964	2,145	1,964	—	—	1,037	48.3	967	49.2	—	—	—	—
1965	2,659	2,417	—	—	1,354	50.9	1,249	51.7	—	—	—	—
1966	2,612	2,403	—	—	1,309	50.1	1,243	51.7	—	—	—	—
1967	2,525	2,267	—	—	1,311	51.9	1,202	53.0	—	—	—	—
1968	2,606	2,303	—	—	1,444	55.4	1,304	56.6	—	—	—	—
1969	2,842	2,538	—	—	1,516	53.3	1,402	55.2	—	—	—	—
1970	2,757	2,461	—	—	1,427	51.8	1,280	52.0	—	—	—	—
1971	2,872	2,596	—	—	1,535	53.4	1,402	54.0	—	—	—	—
1972	2,961	2,614	—	—	1,457	49.2	1,292	49.4	—	—	—	—
1973	3,059	2,707	—	—	1,425	46.6	1,302	48.1	—	—	—	—
1974	3,101	2,736	—	—	1,474	47.5	1,288	47.1	—	—	—	—
1975	3,186	2,825	—	—	1,615	50.7	1,446	51.2	—	—	—	—
1976	2,987	2,640	320	152	1,458	48.8	1,291	48.9	134	41.9	80	52.6
1977	3,140	2,768	335	156	1,590	50.6	1,403	50.7	166	49.6	80	51.3
1978	3,161	2,750	352	133	1,584	50.1	1,378	50.1	161	45.7	57	42.9
1979	3,160	2,776	324	154	1,559	49.3	1,376	49.6	147	45.4	69	44.8
1980	3,089	2,682	361	129	1,524	49.3	1,339	49.9	151	41.8	68	52.7
1981	3,053	2,626	359	146	1,646	53.9	1,434	54.6	154	42.9	76	52.1
1982	3,100	2,644	384	174	1,568	50.6	1,376	52.0	140	36.5	75	43.1
1983	2,964	2,496	392	138	1,562	52.7	1,372	55.0	151	38.5	75	54.3
1984	3,012	2,514	438	185	1,662	55.2	1,455	57.9	176	40.2	82	44.3
1985	2,666	2,241	333	141	1,539	57.7	1,332	59.4	141	42.3	72	51.1
1986	2,786	2,307	386	169	1,499	53.8	1,292	56.0	141	36.5	75	44.4
1987	2,647	2,207	337	176	1,503	56.8	1,249	56.6	175	51.9	59	33.5
1988	2,673	2,187	382	179	1,575	58.9	1,328	60.7	172	45.0	102	57.0
1989	2,454	2,051	337	168	1,463	59.6	1,238	60.4	178	52.8	93	55.4

[1] Enrollment in college as of October of each year for individuals age 16 to 24 who graduated from high school during the preceding 12 months.

[2] Includes persons of Hispanic origin.

[3] Due to the small sample size, data are subject to relatively large sampling errors.

—Data not available.

NOTE.—Data are based upon sample surveys of the civilian population. High school graduate data in this table differ from figures appearing in other tables because of varying survey procedures and coverage.

SOURCE: American College Testing Program, unpublished tabulations, 1987, derived from statistics collected by the U.S. Bureau of the Census; and U.S. Department of Labor, unpublished tabulations. (This table was prepared February 1991.)

Table 172.—College enrollment rates of high school graduates, by sex: 1960 to 1989

[Numbers in thousands]

Year	Total high school graduates			Enrolled in college [1]					
				Total		Males		Females	
	Total	Males	Females	Number	Percent	Number	Percent	Number	Percent
1	2	3	4	5	6	7	8	9	10
1960	1,679	756	923	758	45.1	408	54.0	350	37.9
1961	1,763	790	973	847	48.0	445	56.3	402	41.3
1962	1,838	872	966	900	49.0	480	55.0	420	43.5
1963	1,741	794	947	784	45.0	415	52.3	369	39.0
1964	2,145	997	1,148	1,037	48.3	570	57.2	467	40.7
1965	2,659	1,254	1,405	1,354	50.9	718	57.3	636	45.3
1966	2,612	1,207	1,405	1,309	50.1	709	58.7	600	42.7
1967	2,525	1,142	1,383	1,311	51.9	658	57.6	653	47.2
1968	2,606	1,184	1,422	1,444	55.4	748	63.2	696	48.9
1969	2,842	1,352	1,490	1,516	53.3	812	60.1	704	47.2
1970	2,757	1,343	1,414	1,427	51.8	741	55.2	686	48.5
1971	2,872	1,369	1,503	1,535	53.4	788	57.6	747	49.7
1972	2,961	1,420	1,541	1,457	49.2	749	52.7	708	45.9
1973	3,059	1,458	1,601	1,425	46.6	730	50.1	695	43.4
1974	3,101	1,491	1,610	1,474	47.5	736	49.4	738	45.8
1975	3,186	1,513	1,673	1,615	50.7	796	52.6	819	49.0
1976	2,987	1,450	1,537	1,458	48.8	685	47.2	773	50.3
1977	3,140	1,482	1,658	1,590	50.6	773	52.2	817	49.3
1978	3,161	1,485	1,676	1,584	50.1	758	51.0	826	49.3
1979	3,160	1,474	1,686	1,559	49.3	743	50.4	816	48.4
1980	3,089	1,500	1,589	1,524	49.3	701	46.7	823	51.8
1981	3,053	1,490	1,563	1,646	53.9	816	54.8	830	53.1
1982	3,100	1,508	1,592	1,568	50.6	739	49.0	829	52.1
1983	2,964	1,390	1,574	1,562	52.7	721	51.9	841	53.4
1984	3,012	1,429	1,583	1,662	55.2	800	56.0	862	54.5
1985	2,666	1,286	1,380	1,539	57.7	754	58.6	785	56.9
1986	2,786	1,331	1,455	1,499	53.8	744	55.9	755	51.9
1987	2,647	1,278	1,369	1,503	56.8	746	58.4	757	55.3
1988	2,673	1,334	1,339	1,575	58.9	761	57.0	814	60.8
1989	2,454	1,208	1,245	1,463	59.6	696	57.6	767	61.6

[1] Enrollment in college as of October of each year for individuals age 16 to 24 who graduated from high school during the preceding 12 months.

NOTE.—Data are based upon sample surveys of the civilian population. High school graduate data in this table differ from figures appearing in other tables because of varying survey procedures and coverage.

SOURCE: American College Testing Program, unpublished tabulations, 1987, derived from statistics collected by the U.S. Bureau of the Census; and U.S. Department of Labor, unpublished data. (This table was prepared February 1991.)

Table 173.—Graduation, college preparation, and college application rates of 12th graders, by selected school characteristics: 1987–88

Selected school characteristics	Public schools				Private schools			
	Number of schools with 12th graders	1987 graduation rate of fall 1986 12th graders	Percent of 12th graders in college preparatory courses, 1987–88	Average college application rate of 12th graders	Number of schools with 12th graders	1987 graduation rate of fall 1986 12th graders	Percent of 12th graders in college preparatory courses, 1987–88	Average college application rate of 12th graders
1	2	3	4	5	6	7	8	9
Total	17,736	91.5	49.8	48.3	7,294	97.5	74.6	73.4
School enrollment								
Less than 150	2,386	81.0	40.4	37.5	3,298	92.0	60.9	59.0
150 to 299	2,949	91.4	48.2	49.0	1,719	98.0	80.5	76.6
300 to 499	3,243	90.9	48.3	45.2	985	97.3	86.9	86.3
500 to 749	2,811	90.6	48.3	47.4	657	98.1	91.6	88.4
750 or more	6,346	91.9	55.5	54.0	634	98.3	92.5	90.0
Percent minority students								
Less than 5%	7,369	92.3	52.1	51.8	3,295	98.5	72.0	68.9
5% to 19%	4,115	91.4	51.7	50.8	2,307	98.4	82.2	77.1
20% to 49%	2,947	90.6	47.1	45.0	1,001	93.8	73.9	77.5
50% or more	3,304	91.2	44.7	40.3	691	97.6	62.7	74.9
Community type [1]								
Rural/farming	8,230	91.7	49.2	48.5	1,442	97.3	77.6	69.3
Small city/town	3,723	91.4	46.6	46.4	1,788	97.9	65.1	64.8
Suburban	2,653	93.0	56.7	54.4	1,403	97.8	81.8	81.3
Urban	2,939	90.0	49.7	45.3	2,647	97.3	75.3	76.8

[1] Excludes other.

NOTE.—Data are based upon a sample survey and may not be strictly comparable with data reported elsewhere. Because of rounding and missing values in cells with too few sample cases, details may not add to totals.

SOURCE: U.S. Department of Education, National Center for Education Statistics, "Schools and Staffing Survey, 1987–88." (This table was prepared July 1990.)

Table 174.—Enrollment rates of 18- to 24-year-olds in institutions of higher education, by race/ethnicity: 1967 to 1989

Year	All students		White		Black		Hispanic origin [1]	
	Enrollment as a percent of 18- to 24-year-olds	Enrollment as a percent of high school graduates	Enrollment as a percent of 18- to 24-year-olds	Enrollment as a percent of high school graduates	Enrollment as a percent of 18- to 24-year-olds	Enrollment as a percent of high school graduates	Enrollment as a percent of 18- to 24-year-olds	Enrollment as a percent of high school graduates
1	2	3	4	5	6	7	8	9
1967	25.5	33.7	26.9	34.5	13.0	23.3	—	—
1968	26.0	34.2	27.5	34.9	14.5	25.2	—	—
1969	27.3	35.0	28.7	35.6	16.0	27.2	—	—
1970	25.7	32.7	27.1	33.2	15.5	26.0	—	—
1971	26.2	33.2	27.2	33.5	18.2	29.2	—	—
1972	25.5	31.9	26.4	32.3	18.1	27.1	13.4	25.8
1973	24.0	29.7	25.0	30.2	16.0	24.0	16.0	29.1
1974	24.6	30.5	25.8	30.5	17.6	26.2	18.0	32.3
1975	26.3	32.5	27.4	32.3	20.4	31.5	20.4	35.5
1976	26.7	33.1	27.6	32.8	22.5	33.4	20.0	35.9
1977	26.1	32.5	27.2	32.3	21.1	31.3	17.2	31.5
1978	25.3	31.4	26.5	31.3	20.1	29.6	15.2	27.2
1979	25.0	31.2	26.3	31.3	19.8	29.4	16.7	30.2
1980	25.7	31.8	27.3	32.1	19.4	27.6	16.1	29.9
1981	26.2	32.5	27.7	32.7	19.9	28.0	16.6	29.9
1982	26.6	33.0	28.1	33.3	19.9	28.1	16.8	29.2
1983	26.2	32.5	28.0	33.0	19.2	27.0	17.3	31.5
1984	27.1	33.2	28.9	34.0	20.3	27.2	17.9	29.9
1985	27.8	33.7	30.0	34.9	19.6	26.0	16.9	26.8
1986	27.9	34.0	29.7	34.5	21.9	28.6	17.6	29.4
1987	29.7	36.4	31.9	37.5	23.0	30.0	17.7	28.6
1988	30.2	37.2	33.1	38.6	21.1	28.0	17.1	30.9
1989	30.9	38.1	34.2	39.8	23.4	30.8	16.0	28.6

—Data not available.

NOTE.—Data are based upon sample surveys of the civilian noninstitutional population.

SOURCE: U.S. Department of Commerce, Bureau of the Census, *Current Population Reports,* unpublished data. (This table was prepared June 1991.)

Table 175.—Total undergraduate enrollment [1] in institutions of higher education, by sex of student, attendance status, and control of institution: Fall 1969 to fall 1989

[In thousands]

Year	Total	Full-time	Part-time	Men	Women	Men		Women		Men		Women	
						Full-time	Part-time	Full-time	Part-time	Public	Private	Public	Private
1	2	3	4	5	6	7	8	9	10	11	12	13	14
1969	6,884	4,991	1,893	4,008	2,876	2,952	1,056	2,039	837	2,997	1,011	2,162	714
1970	7,376	5,280	2,096	4,254	3,122	3,097	1,157	2,183	939	3,241	1,013	2,387	735
1971	7,743	5,512	2,231	4,418	3,325	3,201	1,217	2,311	1,014	3,427	991	2,580	745
1972	7,941	5,488	2,453	4,429	3,512	3,121	1,308	2,367	1,145	3,467	962	2,756	756
1973	8,261	5,580	2,681	4,538	3,723	3,135	1,403	2,445	1,278	3,579	959	2,943	780
1974	8,798	5,726	3,072	4,765	4,033	3,191	1,574	2,535	1,498	3,799	966	3,232	801
1975	9,679	6,169	3,510	5,257	4,422	3,459	1,798	2,710	1,712	4,245	1,012	3,581	841
1976	9,429	6,030	3,399	4,902	4,527	3,242	1,660	2,788	1,739	3,949	953	3,668	859
1977	9,717	6,094	3,623	4,897	4,820	3,188	1,709	2,906	1,914	3,937	960	3,906	914
1978	9,691	5,967	3,724	4,766	4,925	3,072	1,694	2,895	2,030	3,812	954	3,974	951
1979	9,998	6,080	3,919	4,821	5,178	3,087	1,734	2,993	2,185	3,865	956	4,181	995
1980	10,475	6,362	4,113	5,000	5,475	3,227	1,773	3,135	2,340	4,014	985	4,427	1,048
1981	10,755	6,449	4,306	5,109	5,646	3,261	1,848	3,188	2,458	4,090	1,018	4,558	1,088
1982	10,825	6,484	4,341	5,170	5,655	3,299	1,871	3,184	2,470	4,140	1,031	4,573	1,081
1983	10,846	6,514	4,332	5,158	5,688	3,304	1,854	3,210	2,478	4,117	1,042	4,580	1,107
1984	10,618	6,348	4,270	5,007	5,611	3,195	1,812	3,153	2,459	3,990	1,017	4,504	1,107
1985	10,597	6,320	4,277	4,962	5,635	3,156	1,806	3,163	2,471	3,953	1,010	4,525	1,110
1986	10,798	6,352	4,446	5,018	5,780	3,146	1,871	3,206	2,575	4,002	1,015	4,658	1,122
1987	11,046	6,463	4,584	5,068	5,978	3,164	1,905	3,299	2,679	4,076	992	4,842	1,136
1988 [2]	11,317	6,642	4,674	5,138	6,179	3,206	1,931	3,436	2,743	4,113	1,024	4,990	1,189
1989 [3]	11,666	6,808	4,857	5,278	6,388	3,267	2,011	3,542	2,846	4,243	1,034	5,181	1,207

[1] Includes unclassified undergraduate students.
[2] Data have been revised from previously published figures.
[3] Preliminary data.

NOTE.—Because of rounding, details may not add to totals.

SOURCE: U.S. Department of Education, National Center for Education Statistics, "Fall Enrollment in Colleges and Universities"; and Integrated Postsecondary Education Data System (IPEDS), "Fall Enrollment" surveys. (This table was prepared February 1991.)

Table 176.—Total graduate enrollment [1] in institutions of higher education, by sex of student, attendance status, and control of institution: Fall 1969 to fall 1989

[In thousands]

Year	Total	Full-time	Part-time	Men	Women	Men		Women		Men		Women	
						Full-time	Part-time	Full-time	Part-time	Public	Private	Public	Private
1	2	3	4	5	6	7	8	9	10	11	12	13	14
1969	955	363	593	590	366	252	338	111	255	393	197	273	93
1970	1,031	379	651	630	400	264	366	115	285	423	207	301	99
1971	1,012	388	621	615	394	269	346	119	275	415	200	296	100
1972	1,066	394	671	626	439	268	358	126	313	427	199	330	109
1973	1,123	410	715	648	477	273	375	137	340	442	206	358	119
1974	1,190	427	762	663	526	276	387	151	375	454	209	398	128
1975	1,263	453	810	700	563	290	410	163	400	481	219	425	138
1976	1,333	463	870	714	619	287	427	176	443	477	237	454	165
1977	1,319	473	845	700	617	289	411	184	434	458	243	443	174
1978	1,312	468	844	682	630	280	402	188	442	441	241	453	177
1979	1,309	476	833	669	640	280	389	196	444	427	242	457	182
1980	1,343	485	860	675	670	281	394	204	466	426	247	474	195
1981	1,343	484	859	674	669	277	397	207	462	419	255	468	201
1982	1,322	485	838	670	653	280	390	205	447	417	253	453	200
1983	1,340	497	843	677	663	286	391	211	452	418	259	454	209
1984	1,345	501	844	672	673	286	386	215	459	411	261	459	215
1985	1,376	509	867	677	700	289	388	220	479	414	263	477	223
1986	1,435	522	913	693	742	294	399	228	514	433	260	508	234
1987	1,452	527	925	693	759	294	400	233	525	429	264	516	243
1988 [2]	1,472	553	919	697	774	304	393	249	526	429	268	520	254
1989 [3]	1,518	571	947	709	809	309	401	263	547	437	272	541	269

[1] Includes unclassified postbaccalaureate students.
[2] Revised from previously published data.
[3] Preliminary data.

NOTE.—Because of rounding, details may not add to totals.

SOURCE: U.S. Department of Education, National Center for Education Statistics, "Fall Enrollment in Colleges and Universities"; and Integrated Postsecondary Education Data System (IPEDS), "Fall Enrollment" surveys. (This table was prepared February 1991.)

Table 177.—Total first-professional enrollment in institutions of higher education, by sex of student, attendance status, and control of institution: Fall 1969 to fall 1989

Year	Total	Full-time	Part-time	Men	Women	Men		Women		Men		Women	
						Full-time	Part-time	Full-time	Part-time	Public	Private	Public	Private
1	2	3	4	5	6	7	8	9	10	11	12	13	14
1969	164,737	143,081	21,656	148,926	15,811	131,368	17,558	11,713	4,098	64,241	84,685	8,354	7,457
1970	173,411	157,384	16,027	158,649	14,762	144,270	14,379	13,114	1,648	68,956	89,693	6,501	8,261
1971	192,668	176,224	16,444	174,058	18,610	159,386	14,672	16,838	1,772	98,233	75,825	9,430	9,180
1972	206,659	190,039	16,620	183,443	23,216	168,990	14,453	21,049	2,167	79,723	103,720	10,842	12,374
1973	218,990	201,663	17,327	186,297	32,693	171,731	14,566	29,932	2,761	81,811	104,486	16,138	16,555
1974	235,452	216,329	19,123	194,079	41,373	178,926	15,153	37,403	3,970	84,271	109,808	20,085	21,288
1975	242,267	219,886	22,381	192,100	50,167	177,117	14,983	42,769	7,398	79,240	112,860	23,557	26,610
1976	244,292	220,124	24,168	189,810	54,482	171,967	17,843	48,157	6,325	77,873	111,937	23,468	31,014
1977	251,357	226,318	25,039	191,451	59,906	173,165	18,286	53,153	6,753	78,189	113,262	24,901	35,005
1978	256,904	232,540	24,364	192,221	64,683	174,906	17,315	57,634	7,049	77,748	114,473	26,839	37,844
1979	263,404	238,949	24,455	193,363	70,041	176,394	16,969	62,555	7,486	77,122	116,241	29,026	41,015
1980	277,767	251,359	26,408	199,344	78,423	181,448	17,896	69,911	8,512	81,022	118,322	33,415	45,008
1981	274,595	248,328	26,267	192,936	81,659	175,414	17,522	72,914	8,745	77,562	115,374	34,177	47,482
1982	278,425	252,108	26,317	191,200	87,225	173,941	17,259	78,167	9,058	76,273	114,927	37,183	50,042
1983	278,529	249,636	28,893	188,096	90,433	169,071	19,025	80,565	9,868	74,938	113,158	38,484	51,949
1984	278,598	249,708	28,890	184,949	93,649	166,286	18,663	83,422	10,227	73,722	111,227	40,186	53,463
1985	274,200	246,619	27,581	179,792	94,408	162,368	17,424	84,251	10,157	71,373	108,419	40,435	53,973
1986	270,401	245,647	24,754	173,851	96,550	158,557	15,294	87,090	9,460	70,326	103,525	41,699	54,851
1987	268,332	241,807	26,525	170,129	98,203	153,668	16,461	88,139	10,064	68,089	102,040	41,947	56,256
1988 [1]	267,109	241,228	25,881	166,912	100,197	151,045	15,867	90,183	10,014	66,196	100,716	42,743	57,454
1989 [2]	273,728	247,434	26,294	168,480	105,248	152,419	16,061	95,015	10,233	67,548	100,932	45,090	60,158

[1] Revised from previously published figures.
[2] Preliminary data.

NOTE.—Because of rounding, details may not add to totals.

SOURCE: U.S. Department of Education, National Center for Education Statistics, "Fall Enrollment in Colleges and Universities"; and Integrated Postsecondary Education Data System (IPEDS), "Fall Enrollment" surveys. (This table was prepared February 1991.)

Table 178.—Total enrollment in institutions of higher education, by State: Fall 1970 to fall 1989

State or other area	Fall 1970	Fall 1975	Fall 1980	Fall 1984	Fall 1985	Fall 1986	Fall 1987	Fall 1988[1]	Fall 1989[2]	Percent change, 1984 to 1989
1	2	3	4	5	6	7	8	9	10	11
United States	8,580,887	11,184,859	12,096,895	12,241,940	12,247,055	12,503,511	12,766,642	13,055,337	13,457,855	9.9
Alabama	103,936	164,700	164,306	171,631	179,343	181,443	183,348	197,352	208,562	21.5
Alaska	9,471	13,998	21,296	26,991	27,479	27,477	26,937	28,983	28,627	6.1
Arizona	109,619	173,542	202,716	210,029	216,854	226,595	237,233	258,792	252,614	20.3
Arkansas	52,039	65,547	77,607	78,777	77,958	79,182	79,273	84,562	88,572	12.4
California	1,257,245	1,787,932	1,790,993	1,665,155	1,650,439	1,727,295	1,788,170	1,754,478	1,744,879	4.8
Colorado	123,395	149,814	162,916	164,394	161,314	177,333	183,583	186,912	201,114	22.3
Connecticut	124,700	148,491	159,632	161,576	159,348	158,278	162,382	165,677	169,438	4.9
Delaware	25,260	32,389	32,939	31,872	31,883	33,895	36,637	38,261	40,562	27.3
District of Columbia	77,158	84,190	86,675	79,750	78,868	77,645	77,566	79,310	79,800	0.1
Florida	235,525	344,267	411,891	444,062	451,392	[3]483,958	489,964	516,508	573,712	29.2
Georgia	126,511	173,585	184,159	196,869	196,826	195,124	[4]224,066	230,893	239,208	21.5
Hawaii	36,562	46,671	47,181	49,981	49,937	51,697	52,291	52,297	54,188	8.4
Idaho	34,567	39,075	43,018	43,303	42,668	45,260	45,567	46,338	48,969	13.1
Illinois	452,146	584,089	644,245	661,114	678,689	692,018	686,954	689,326	709,937	7.4
Indiana	192,668	213,820	247,253	249,957	250,567	250,176	256,264	267,905	275,821	10.3
Iowa	108,902	121,678	140,449	153,069	152,897	155,369	158,230	162,098	169,901	11.0
Kansas	102,485	120,833	136,605	141,916	141,359	143,205	146,439	152,822	158,497	11.7
Kentucky	98,591	125,253	143,066	143,555	141,724	144,560	153,351	160,208	166,014	15.6
Louisiana	120,728	153,213	160,058	179,988	177,176	171,332	173,229	176,051	179,927	(5)
Maine	34,134	40,443	43,264	52,714	52,201	46,229	46,992	48,360	58,230	10.5
Maryland	149,607	205,570	225,526	234,302	231,649	233,492	239,362	249,079	255,326	9.0
Massachusetts	303,809	384,485	418,415	418,966	421,175	417,540	423,916	426,603	426,476	1.8
Michigan	392,726	496,405	520,131	505,334	507,293	520,392	535,486	544,399	560,320	10.9
Minnesota	160,788	184,756	206,691	215,566	221,162	226,558	237,212	244,612	253,097	17.4
Mississippi	73,967	99,962	102,364	104,339	101,180	101,104	105,510	111,262	116,370	11.5
Missouri	183,930	223,115	234,421	240,920	241,146	246,185	251,778	262,391	278,505	15.6
Montana	30,062	30,843	35,177	37,061	35,958	35,238	35,882	35,777	37,660	1.6
Nebraska	66,915	74,705	89,488	97,422	97,769	100,401	100,828	104,879	108,844	11.7
Nevada	13,669	30,187	40,455	43,007	43,656	46,796	48,063	48,831	56,471	31.3
New Hampshire	29,400	41,030	46,794	53,049	52,283	53,882	56,163	57,410	58,600	10.5
New Jersey	216,121	297,114	321,610	305,330	297,658	295,271	294,433	302,881	314,091	2.9
New Mexico	44,461	51,944	58,283	66,507	68,295	80,271	83,074	79,135	81,350	22.3
New York	806,479	1,005,063	992,237	1,007,770	1,000,098	1,000,817	992,544	1,006,494	1,018,130	1.0
North Carolina	171,925	251,786	287,537	309,249	327,288	322,980	321,251	332,226	345,401	11.7
North Dakota	31,495	29,743	34,069	37,585	37,939	37,309	36,259	38,489	40,350	7.4
Ohio	376,267	436,052	489,145	518,435	514,745	520,479	518,464	543,980	550,729	6.2
Oklahoma	110,155	146,613	160,295	168,034	169,173	170,840	172,730	176,308	175,855	4.7
Oregon	122,177	145,281	157,458	141,810	137,967	144,785	152,657	156,158	161,822	14.1
Pennsylvania	411,044	470,536	507,716	528,669	533,198	545,921	554,370	573,552	610,357	15.5
Rhode Island	45,898	64,479	66,869	69,145	69,927	69,567	71,708	74,847	76,503	10.6
South Carolina	69,518	133,023	132,476	131,479	131,902	134,115	140,841	148,168	145,730	10.8
South Dakota	30,639	30,260	32,761	32,473	32,772	30,935	31,755	31,461	32,666	0.6
Tennessee	135,103	181,435	204,581	200,937	194,845	197,071	202,006	206,367	218,866	8.9
Texas	442,225	624,390	701,391	795,337	769,692	776,023	801,771	847,310	877,859	10.4
Utah	81,687	87,323	93,987	101,863	103,994	106,218	106,792	108,631	114,815	12.7
Vermont	22,209	29,095	30,628	30,786	31,416	32,460	33,242	34,403	35,946	16.8
Virginia	151,915	244,671	280,504	283,109	292,416	308,318	319,026	320,931	344,284	21.6
Washington	183,544	227,168	303,603	230,667	231,553	242,379	245,872	254,051	255,760	10.9
West Virginia	63,153	78,619	81,973	79,000	76,659	76,781	77,256	80,540	82,455	4.4
Wisconsin	202,058	240,701	269,086	270,865	275,069	283,653	281,717	286,456	290,672	7.3
Wyoming	15,220	18,078	21,147	23,424	24,204	24,357	26,062	26,540	29,159	24.5
U.S. Service Schools	17,079	36,897	49,808	52,788	54,052	53,302	60,136	44,033	54,814	3.8
Outlying areas	67,237	104,270	137,749	158,452	164,890	165,620	156,809	163,449	163,348	3.1
American Samoa	—	689	976	871	758	759	897	908	1,011	16.1
Federated States of Micronesia	—	—	—	—	—	—	—	—	838	—
Guam	2,719	3,800	3,217	4,432	4,601	4,477	4,072	3,819	4,350	−1.9
Northern Marianas	—	—	—	431	318	514	366	352	419	−2.8
Palau	—	—	—	—	—	—	—	—	1,037	—
Puerto Rico	63,073	97,517	131,184	149,102	155,917	156,580	147,706	154,712	152,996	2.6
Trust Territory of the Pacific	—	185	224	796	724	795	1,223	1,187	—	—
Virgin Islands	1,445	2,079	2,148	2,820	2,572	2,495	2,545	2,471	2,697	−4.4

[1] Some data have been revised from previously published figures.

[2] Preliminary data.

[3] Because of imputation techniques, data are not consistent with figures for other years.

[4] Part of the 1987 increase is due to the inclusion of additional public 2-year institutions in the survey.

[5] Less than .05 percent.

—Data not reported or not applicable.

SOURCE: U.S. Department of Education, National Center for Education Statistics, "Fall Enrollment in Colleges and Universities"; and Integrated Postsecondary Education Data System (IPEDS), "Fall Enrollment" surveys. (This table was prepared February 1991.)

Table 179.—Total enrollment in public institutions of higher education, by State: Fall 1970 to fall 1989

State or other area	Fall 1970	Fall 1975	Fall 1980	Fall 1984	Fall 1985	Fall 1986	Fall 1987	Fall 1988[1]	Fall 1989[2]	Percent change, 1984 to 1989
1	2	3	4	5	6	7	8	9	10	11
United States	6,428,134	8,834,508	9,457,394	9,477,370	9,479,273	9,713,893	9,973,254	10,161,388	10,514,973	10.9
Alabama	87,884	145,698	143,674	149,579	158,688	160,432	162,278	173,736	187,575	25.4
Alaska	8,563	13,218	20,561	26,005	26,510	26,354	25,991	27,168	26,274	1.0
Arizona	107,315	168,666	194,034	196,537	202,036	213,568	228,552	242,699	239,314	21.8
Arkansas	43,599	56,127	66,068	66,753	66,123	68,760	68,313	71,954	76,416	14.5
California	1,123,529	1,617,558	1,599,838	1,459,579	1,444,207	1,521,681	1,580,532	1,542,351	1,534,209	5.1
Colorado	108,562	136,370	145,598	144,885	142,031	157,463	161,594	162,956	175,850	21.4
Connecticut	73,391	93,567	97,788	100,754	98,616	98,828	102,561	106,419	109,697	8.9
Delaware	21,151	27,082	28,325	27,422	27,933	28,894	29,647	31,646	33,037	20.5
District of Columbia	12,194	15,159	13,900	13,450	12,747	11,800	10,851	12,109	12,439	−7.5
Florida	189,450	287,745	334,349	354,156	362,241	385,433	405,292	420,378	480,869	35.8
Georgia	101,900	142,593	140,158	150,035	148,956	147,269	[3]174,355	177,852	186,776	24.5
Hawaii	32,963	43,278	43,269	43,806	43,246	42,593	42,746	42,529	43,644	−0.4
Idaho	27,072	31,298	34,491	34,918	33,666	35,532	34,791	35,856	38,447	10.1
Illinois	315,634	444,458	491,274	504,549	520,224	530,509	521,117	521,718	536,643	6.4
Indiana	136,739	159,453	189,224	192,618	193,833	194,132	201,457	209,236	216,433	12.4
Iowa	68,390	83,572	97,454	109,800	109,765	110,439	112,007	113,268	116,889	6.5
Kansas	88,215	107,761	121,987	127,211	127,220	129,841	133,383	138,702	145,134	14.1
Kentucky	77,240	105,265	114,884	112,702	110,836	115,056	122,019	129,442	137,297	21.8
Louisiana	101,127	132,054	136,703	154,846	153,173	146,297	148,492	149,351	151,733	−2.0
Maine	25,405	31,092	31,878	33,436	33,188	34,459	34,597	36,325	40,511	21.2
Maryland	118,988	176,544	195,051	201,894	198,992	199,433	203,711	212,322	217,562	7.8
Massachusetts	116,127	173,564	183,765	183,084	185,602	178,603	187,091	188,844	187,772	2.6
Michigan	339,625	436,655	454,147	433,134	434,270	445,731	459,313	466,091	479,714	10.8
Minnesota	130,567	148,630	162,379	168,726	173,984	178,790	186,096	191,192	198,610	17.7
Mississippi	64,968	89,919	90,661	92,641	90,704	89,925	93,284	98,394	103,035	11.2
Missouri	132,540	158,196	165,179	170,092	168,829	168,883	171,246	178,729	192,322	13.1
Montana	27,287	27,798	31,178	32,716	32,032	31,192	31,858	31,292	33,197	1.5
Nebraska	51,454	61,240	73,509	80,221	81,202	84,262	84,901	88,043	91,337	13.9
Nevada	13,576	30,010	40,280	42,700	43,368	46,490	47,791	48,644	56,184	31.6
New Hampshire	15,979	24,205	24,119	27,323	26,669	28,731	30,899	30,724	32,889	20.4
New Jersey	145,373	227,764	247,028	243,388	237,297	235,734	235,408	243,961	253,544	4.2
New Mexico	40,795	47,605	55,077	64,261	66,059	78,566	81,298	77,079	79,359	23.5
New York	449,437	613,842	563,251	567,151	563,251	565,244	567,046	583,850	600,587	5.9
North Carolina	123,761	201,288	228,154	249,417	267,044	262,638	258,930	267,070	277,062	11.1
North Dakota	30,192	27,954	31,709	34,441	34,802	34,898	33,555	35,622	37,501	8.9
Ohio	281,099	336,931	381,765	381,610	379,164	384,789	391,831	402,823	412,073	8.0
Oklahoma	91,438	124,372	137,188	145,822	146,827	149,043	148,906	151,410	151,410	3.8
Oregon	108,483	129,785	140,102	123,231	119,612	125,864	133,458	136,606	141,311	14.7
Pennsylvania	232,982	287,436	292,499	301,172	300,523	304,190	311,210	323,489	335,101	11.3
Rhode Island	25,527	32,311	35,052	34,507	35,389	35,507	36,317	38,993	40,604	17.7
South Carolina	47,101	107,690	107,683	105,213	105,854	108,191	113,352	120,386	118,639	12.8
South Dakota	23,936	21,925	24,328	24,023	23,339	24,036	24,147	23,899	25,075	4.4
Tennessee	98,897	139,526	156,835	152,797	147,951	149,445	154,104	155,610	167,056	9.3
Texas	365,522	542,212	613,552	703,717	677,192	685,544	709,255	753,145	782,495	11.2
Utah	49,588	56,536	59,598	67,215	69,426	73,072	74,453	74,434	79,623	18.5
Vermont	12,536	17,145	17,984	18,192	18,844	18,734	19,360	19,967	20,925	15.0
Virginia	123,279	215,253	246,500	245,104	250,754	265,687	275,583	270,372	287,624	17.3
Washington	162,718	202,531	276,028	200,857	201,532	212,268	214,207	219,290	221,362	10.2
West Virginia	51,363	68,117	71,228	68,384	66,531	67,078	67,959	70,381	72,478	6.0
Wisconsin	170,374	210,535	235,179	235,084	238,735	244,948	240,533	243,087	245,968	4.6
Wyoming	15,220	18,078	21,121	23,424	24,204	23,735	25,441	25,911	28,553	21.9
U.S. Service Schools	17,079	36,897	49,808	52,788	54,052	53,302	60,136	44,033	54,814	3.8
Outlying areas	46,680	59,923	60,692	65,134	65,411	67,979	66,785	67,433	67,449	3.6
American Samoa	—	689	976	871	758	759	897	908	1,011	16.1
Federated States of Micronesia	—	—	—	—	—	—	—	—	838	—
Guam	2,719	3,800	3,217	4,432	4,601	4,477	4,072	3,819	4,350	−1.9
Northern Marianas	—	—	—	431	318	514	366	352	419	−2.8
Palau	—	—	—	—	—	—	—	—	1,037	—
Puerto Rico	42,516	53,170	54,127	55,784	56,438	58,939	57,682	58,696	57,097	2.4
Trust Territory of the Pacific	—	185	224	796	724	795	1,223	1,187	—	—
Virgin Islands	1,445	2,079	2,148	2,820	2,572	2,495	2,545	2,471	2,697	−4.4

[1] Some data have been revised from previously published figures.

[2] Preliminary data.

[3] Part of the 1987 increase is due to the inclusion of additional public 2-year institutions in the survey.

—Data not reported or not applicable.

SOURCE: U.S. Department of Education, National Center for Education Statistics, "Fall Enrollment in Colleges and Universities"; and Integrated Postsecondary Education Data System (IPEDS), "Fall Enrollment" surveys. (This table was prepared February 1991.)

Table 180.—Total enrollment in private institutions of higher education, by State: Fall 1970 to fall 1989

State or other area	Fall 1970	Fall 1975	Fall 1980	Fall 1984	Fall 1985	Fall 1986	Fall 1987	Fall 1988[1]	Fall 1989[2]	Percent change, 1984 to 1989
1	2	3	4	5	6	7	8	9	10	11
United States	2,152,753	2,350,351	2,639,501	2,764,570	2,767,782	2,789,618	2,793,388	2,893,949	2,942,882	6.4
Alabama	16,052	19,002	20,632	22,052	20,655	21,011	21,070	23,616	20,987	−4.8
Alaska	908	780	735	986	969	1,123	946	1,815	2,353	138.6
Arizona	2,304	4,876	8,682	13,492	14,818	13,027	8,681	16,093	13,300	−1.4
Arkansas	8,440	9,420	11,539	12,024	11,835	10,422	10,960	12,608	12,156	1.1
California	133,716	170,374	191,155	205,576	206,232	205,614	207,638	212,127	210,670	2.5
Colorado	14,833	13,444	17,318	19,509	19,283	19,870	21,989	23,956	25,264	29.5
Connecticut	51,309	54,924	61,844	60,822	60,732	59,450	59,821	59,258	59,741	−1.8
Delaware	4,109	5,307	4,614	4,450	3,950	5,001	6,990	6,615	7,525	69.1
District of Columbia	64,964	69,031	72,775	66,300	66,121	65,845	66,715	67,201	67,361	1.6
Florida	46,075	56,522	77,542	89,906	89,151	3 98,525	84,672	96,130	92,843	3.3
Georgia	24,611	30,992	44,001	46,834	47,870	47,855	49,711	53,041	52,432	12.0
Hawaii	3,599	3,393	3,912	6,175	6,691	9,104	9,545	9,768	10,544	70.8
Idaho	7,495	7,777	8,527	8,385	9,002	9,728	10,776	10,482	10,522	25.5
Illinois	136,512	139,631	152,971	156,565	158,465	161,509	165,837	167,608	173,294	10.7
Indiana	55,929	54,367	58,029	57,339	56,734	56,044	54,807	58,669	59,388	3.6
Iowa	40,512	38,106	42,995	43,269	43,132	44,930	46,223	48,830	53,012	22.5
Kansas	14,270	13,072	14,618	14,705	14,139	13,364	13,056	14,120	13,363	−9.1
Kentucky	21,351	19,988	28,182	30,853	30,888	29,504	31,332	30,766	28,717	−6.9
Louisiana	19,601	21,159	23,355	25,142	24,003	25,035	24,737	26,700	28,194	12.1
Maine	8,729	9,351	11,386	19,278	19,013	11,770	12,395	12,035	17,719	−8.1
Maryland	30,619	29,026	30,475	32,408	32,657	34,059	35,651	36,757	37,764	16.5
Massachusetts	187,682	210,921	234,650	235,882	235,573	238,937	236,825	237,759	238,704	1.2
Michigan	53,101	59,750	65,984	72,200	73,023	74,661	76,173	78,308	80,606	11.6
Minnesota	30,221	36,126	44,312	46,840	47,178	47,768	51,116	53,420	54,487	16.3
Mississippi	8,999	10,043	11,703	11,698	10,476	11,179	12,226	12,868	13,335	14.0
Missouri	51,390	64,919	69,242	70,828	72,317	77,302	80,532	83,662	86,183	21.7
Montana	2,775	3,045	3,999	4,345	3,926	4,046	4,024	4,485	4,463	2.7
Nebraska	15,461	13,465	15,979	17,201	16,567	16,139	15,927	16,836	17,507	1.8
Nevada	93	177	175	307	288	306	272	187	287	−6.5
New Hampshire	13,421	16,825	22,675	25,726	25,614	25,151	25,264	26,686	25,711	−0.1
New Jersey	70,748	69,350	74,582	61,942	60,361	59,537	59,025	58,920	60,547	−2.3
New Mexico	3,666	4,339	3,206	2,246	2,236	1,705	1,776	2,056	1,991	−11.4
New York	357,042	391,221	428,986	440,619	436,847	435,573	425,498	422,644	417,543	−5.2
North Carolina	48,164	50,498	59,383	59,832	60,244	60,342	62,321	65,156	68,339	14.2
North Dakota	1,303	1,789	2,360	3,144	3,137	2,411	2,704	2,867	2,849	−9.4
Ohio	95,168	99,121	107,380	136,825	135,581	135,690	126,633	141,157	138,656	1.3
Oklahoma	18,717	22,241	23,107	22,212	22,346	21,797	23,824	24,898	24,445	10.1
Oregon	13,694	15,496	17,356	18,579	18,355	18,921	19,199	19,552	20,511	10.4
Pennsylvania	178,062	183,100	215,217	227,497	232,675	241,731	243,160	250,063	275,256	21.0
Rhode Island	20,371	32,168	31,817	34,638	34,538	34,060	35,391	35,854	35,899	3.6
South Carolina	22,417	25,333	24,793	26,266	26,048	25,924	27,489	27,782	27,091	3.1
South Dakota	6,703	8,335	8,433	8,450	9,433	6,899	7,608	7,562	7,591	−10.2
Tennessee	36,206	41,909	47,746	48,140	46,894	47,626	47,902	50,757	51,810	7.6
Texas	76,703	82,178	87,839	91,620	92,500	90,479	92,516	94,165	95,364	4.1
Utah	32,099	30,787	34,389	34,648	34,568	33,146	32,339	34,197	35,192	1.6
Vermont	9,673	11,950	12,644	12,594	12,572	13,726	13,882	14,436	15,021	19.3
Virginia	28,636	29,418	34,004	38,005	41,662	42,631	43,443	50,559	56,660	49.1
Washington	20,826	24,637	27,575	29,810	30,021	30,111	31,665	34,761	34,398	15.4
West Virginia	11,790	10,502	10,745	10,745	10,625	10,128	9,703	9,297	10,159	9,977	−6.1
Wisconsin	31,684	30,166	33,907	35,781	36,334	38,705	41,184	43,369	44,704	24.9
Wyoming	—	—	26	—	—	622	621	629	606	(4)
Outlying areas	20,557	44,347	77,057	93,318	99,479	97,641	90,024	96,016	95,899	2.8
American Samoa	—	—	—	—	—	—	—	—	—	—
Federated States of Micronesia	—	—	—	—	—	—	—	—	—	—
Guam	—	—	—	—	—	—	—	—	—	—
Northern Marianas	—	—	—	—	—	—	—	—	—	—
Palau	—	—	—	—	—	—	—	—	—	—
Puerto Rico	20,557	44,347	77,057	93,318	99,479	97,641	90,024	96,016	95,899	2.8
Trust Territory of the Pacific	—	—	—	—	—	—	—	—	—	—
Virgin Islands	—	—	—	—	—	—	—	—	—	—

[1] Some data have been revised from previously published figures.

[2] Preliminary data.

[3] Because of imputation techniques, data are not consistent with figures for other years.

[4] Percentage not shown because of introduction of a new institution in 1986.

—Data not reported or not applicable.

SOURCE: U.S. Department of Education, National Center for Education Statistics, "Fall Enrollment in Colleges and Universities"; and Integrated Postsecondary Education Data System (IPEDS), "Fall Enrollment" surveys. (This table was prepared February 1991.)

Table 181.—Total enrollment in all institutions of higher education, by attendance status, sex, and State: Fall 1988 and fall 1989

State or other area	Fall 1988 [1]					Fall 1989 [2]				
	Total	Full-time		Part-time		Total	Full-time		Part-time	
		Men	Women	Men	Women		Men	Women	Men	Women
1	2	3	4	5	6	7	8	9	10	11
United States	13,055,337	3,661,779	3,774,989	2,340,117	3,278,452	13,457,855	3,727,823	3,899,349	2,427,661	3,403,022
Alabama	197,352	64,037	70,964	28,586	33,765	208,562	66,990	76,942	28,138	36,492
Alaska	28,983	4,673	5,723	7,518	11,069	28,627	4,840	5,684	6,720	11,383
Arizona	258,792	57,664	51,967	63,522	85,639	252,614	56,565	51,958	62,660	81,431
Arkansas	84,562	27,863	32,300	8,906	15,493	88,572	28,889	34,352	9,222	16,109
California	1,754,478	381,779	390,984	426,523	555,192	1,744,879	381,543	390,922	423,133	549,281
Colorado	186,912	58,002	55,041	30,718	43,151	201,114	59,826	59,005	34,978	47,305
Connecticut	165,677	40,741	43,101	31,451	50,384	169,438	41,075	44,085	32,590	51,688
Delaware	38,261	10,355	13,195	5,991	8,720	40,562	11,087	13,733	6,481	9,261
District of Columbia	79,310	23,194	26,101	14,149	15,866	79,800	23,148	27,002	13,702	15,948
Florida	516,508	125,428	128,104	109,340	153,636	573,712	131,803	136,560	127,645	177,704
Georgia	230,893	74,341	78,999	33,283	44,270	239,208	76,498	81,987	33,570	47,153
Hawaii	52,297	14,516	15,714	10,005	12,062	54,188	14,686	16,076	10,336	13,090
Idaho	46,338	16,130	16,424	5,803	7,981	48,969	16,356	17,227	6,239	9,147
Illinois	689,326	174,692	172,036	140,827	201,771	709,937	178,001	178,057	146,570	207,309
Indiana	267,905	87,250	85,702	40,686	54,267	275,821	89,861	89,588	41,126	55,246
Iowa	162,098	60,748	56,205	17,360	27,785	169,901	60,897	58,281	18,981	31,742
Kansas	152,822	45,094	42,512	24,936	40,280	158,497	45,827	44,331	25,838	42,501
Kentucky	160,208	47,636	54,910	20,880	36,782	166,014	48,707	57,456	21,633	38,218
Louisiana	176,051	60,981	67,471	18,411	29,188	179,927	60,476	69,796	18,686	30,969
Maine	48,360	14,360	15,446	7,041	11,513	58,230	15,216	16,328	8,636	18,050
Maryland	249,079	55,310	59,617	53,995	80,157	255,326	56,287	60,870	54,992	83,177
Massachusetts	426,603	126,490	141,862	64,312	93,939	426,476	125,761	139,265	65,643	95,807
Michigan	544,399	133,571	143,403	112,816	154,609	560,320	136,837	147,715	117,790	157,978
Minnesota	244,612	72,484	75,407	38,248	58,473	253,097	74,144	78,925	39,822	60,206
Mississippi	111,262	39,503	45,042	9,745	16,972	116,370	40,305	47,782	10,381	17,902
Missouri	262,391	74,930	75,548	46,162	65,751	278,505	78,170	80,522	49,103	70,710
Montana	35,777	13,114	12,713	3,933	6,017	37,660	13,723	14,106	4,082	5,749
Nebraska	104,879	29,455	28,930	19,142	27,352	108,844	30,225	30,540	19,048	29,031
Nevada	48,831	7,740	7,612	14,363	19,116	56,471	8,466	8,790	16,287	22,928
New Hampshire	57,410	17,905	19,063	8,343	12,099	58,600	17,019	16,784	10,359	14,438
New Jersey	302,881	73,889	77,599	62,452	88,941	314,091	76,243	80,566	64,400	92,882
New Mexico	79,135	21,780	21,801	14,184	21,370	81,350	21,951	22,505	14,769	22,125
New York	1,006,494	301,430	329,533	146,808	228,723	1,018,130	299,460	330,534	151,882	236,254
North Carolina	332,226	96,485	111,624	49,844	74,273	345,401	100,766	118,117	51,364	75,154
North Dakota	38,489	16,609	14,228	3,404	4,248	40,350	17,176	15,243	3,602	4,329
Ohio	543,980	161,737	166,862	103,070	112,311	550,729	160,926	169,899	104,322	115,582
Oklahoma	176,308	50,676	50,359	30,978	44,295	175,855	50,645	49,917	31,003	44,290
Oregon	156,158	46,291	44,816	27,510	37,541	161,822	46,074	45,236	29,769	40,743
Pennsylvania	573,552	185,035	183,623	78,936	125,958	610,357	195,269	200,203	86,364	128,521
Rhode Island	74,847	22,941	23,735	10,930	17,241	76,503	22,961	23,779	11,626	18,137
South Carolina	148,168	46,770	53,383	18,402	29,613	145,730	46,463	52,220	17,951	29,096
South Dakota	31,461	11,301	11,639	2,973	5,548	32,666	11,404	12,145	3,217	5,900
Tennessee	206,367	66,539	70,907	28,611	40,310	218,866	68,373	75,462	31,398	43,633
Texas	847,310	232,049	229,078	167,898	218,285	877,859	236,372	238,551	173,629	229,307
Utah	108,631	37,136	32,838	19,761	18,896	114,815	38,861	35,347	20,328	20,279
Vermont	34,403	11,399	12,202	3,295	7,507	35,946	11,910	12,636	3,664	7,736
Virginia	320,931	85,301	97,237	55,959	82,434	344,284	88,621	102,181	64,362	89,120
Washington	254,051	71,167	74,800	42,673	65,411	255,760	71,240	76,191	43,048	65,281
West Virginia	80,540	26,275	26,702	9,579	17,984	82,455	27,398	28,383	9,214	17,460
Wisconsin	286,456	90,285	96,936	41,951	57,284	290,672	90,349	97,087	42,754	60,482
Wyoming	26,540	8,071	7,613	3,897	6,959	29,159	8,520	7,935	4,486	8,218
U.S. Service Schools	44,033	38,627	5,378	7	21	54,814	43,613	10,543	118	540
Outlying areas	163,449	48,928	76,856	14,017	23,648	163,348	49,074	75,543	14,609	24,122
American Samoa	908	236	184	233	255	1,011	280	178	329	224
Federated States of Micronesia	—	—	—	—	—	838	198	137	238	265
Guam	3,819	748	928	1,115	1,028	4,350	792	1,008	1,298	1,252
Northern Marianas	352	67	47	101	137	419	70	59	124	166
Palau	—	—	—	—	—	1,037	257	478	115	187
Puerto Rico	154,712	47,269	74,885	11,884	20,674	152,996	47,236	73,063	12,053	20,644
Trust Territory of the Pacific	1,187	423	246	250	268	—	—	—	—	—
Virgin Islands	2,471	185	566	434	1,286	2,697	241	620	452	1,384

[1] Data have been revised from previously published figures.

[2] Preliminary data.

—Data not reported or not applicable.

SOURCE: U.S. Department of Education, National Center for Education Statistics, Integrated Postsecondary Education Data System (IPEDS), "Fall Enrollment" surveys. (This table was prepared February 1991.)

Table 182.—Total enrollment in public institutions of higher education, by attendance status, sex, and State: Fall 1988 and fall 1989

State or other area	Fall 1988[1]					Fall 1989[2]				
	Total	Full-time		Part-time		Total	Full-time		Part-time	
		Men	Women	Men	Women		Men	Women	Men	Women
1	2	3	4	5	6	7	8	9	10	11
United States	10,161,388	2,656,238	2,754,110	1,952,720	2,798,320	10,514,973	2,723,230	2,864,833	2,024,669	2,902,241
Alabama	173,736	55,163	60,674	26,745	31,154	187,575	59,244	67,235	26,720	34,376
Alaska	27,168	4,392	4,790	7,191	10,795	26,274	4,434	5,034	6,374	10,432
Arizona	242,699	48,493	47,588	62,658	83,960	239,314	50,037	48,747	61,084	79,446
Arkansas	71,954	22,659	26,499	8,395	14,401	76,416	23,772	28,609	8,770	15,265
California	1,542,351	302,954	318,030	394,499	526,868	1,534,209	304,544	319,671	390,139	519,855
Colorado	162,956	49,142	46,980	26,877	39,957	175,850	51,409	50,596	30,499	43,346
Connecticut	106,419	22,747	25,371	20,793	37,508	109,697	22,800	26,005	22,049	38,843
Delaware	31,646	9,028	11,310	4,704	6,604	33,037	9,371	11,590	5,098	6,978
District of Columbia	12,109	2,001	2,004	3,586	4,518	12,439	1,795	2,369	3,601	4,674
Florida	420,378	88,225	97,784	94,192	140,177	480,869	95,799	108,649	112,462	163,959
Georgia	177,852	53,781	57,001	28,323	38,747	186,776	55,904	60,731	28,616	41,525
Hawaii	42,529	11,072	12,714	8,019	10,724	43,644	11,298	13,087	7,901	11,358
Idaho	35,856	12,102	11,209	5,356	7,189	38,447	12,481	11,891	5,786	8,289
Illinois	521,718	118,252	118,334	114,536	170,596	536,643	120,495	122,295	120,156	173,697
Indiana	209,236	62,155	62,845	36,929	47,307	216,433	64,090	66,249	37,489	48,605
Iowa	113,268	42,404	38,518	13,006	19,340	116,889	43,762	40,107	12,954	20,066
Kansas	138,702	39,863	37,217	23,542	38,080	145,134	40,920	39,137	24,482	40,595
Kentucky	129,442	36,880	43,059	18,096	31,407	137,297	39,130	46,053	19,153	32,961
Louisiana	149,351	50,905	56,610	15,961	25,875	151,733	50,305	58,083	16,177	27,168
Maine	36,325	10,287	10,166	6,220	9,652	40,511	10,968	10,811	7,227	11,505
Maryland	212,322	45,883	48,878	46,829	70,732	217,562	46,457	49,950	47,885	73,270
Massachusetts	188,844	46,343	54,754	33,990	53,757	187,772	45,634	53,740	34,251	54,147
Michigan	466,091	111,478	116,280	101,495	136,838	479,714	115,399	120,610	105,036	138,669
Minnesota	191,192	52,829	53,039	33,572	51,752	198,610	54,396	55,930	35,067	53,217
Mississippi	98,394	35,779	39,970	8,208	14,437	103,035	36,358	42,278	8,851	15,548
Missouri	178,729	49,496	51,633	30,422	47,178	192,322	52,082	55,656	32,787	51,797
Montana	31,292	12,005	11,079	3,182	5,026	33,197	12,604	12,500	3,406	4,687
Nebraska	88,043	23,729	22,694	17,512	24,108	91,337	24,285	23,713	17,428	25,911
Nevada	48,644	7,633	7,575	14,341	19,095	56,184	8,339	8,726	16,256	22,863
New Hampshire	30,724	8,952	10,080	4,814	6,878	32,889	8,025	8,687	6,771	9,406
New Jersey	243,961	55,564	60,394	52,164	75,839	253,544	57,793	62,841	54,006	78,904
New Mexico	77,079	21,184	21,196	13,659	21,040	79,359	21,388	21,869	14,386	21,716
New York	583,850	155,694	180,926	94,350	152,880	600,587	157,864	184,351	99,071	159,301
North Carolina	267,070	70,111	83,049	45,870	68,040	277,062	73,369	87,600	47,378	68,715
North Dakota	35,622	15,523	13,027	3,205	3,867	37,501	16,202	13,939	3,419	3,941
Ohio	402,823	119,197	124,052	67,932	91,642	412,073	119,043	128,825	69,337	94,868
Oklahoma	151,410	40,866	41,675	27,883	40,986	151,410	40,866	41,675	27,883	40,986
Oregon	136,606	37,880	37,314	25,948	35,464	141,311	37,496	37,317	28,024	38,474
Pennsylvania	323,489	103,208	103,227	46,173	70,881	335,101	105,430	107,453	47,501	74,717
Rhode Island	38,993	8,612	10,998	6,646	12,737	40,604	8,813	11,242	7,069	13,480
South Carolina	120,386	36,189	40,070	16,759	27,368	118,639	36,073	39,481	16,262	26,823
South Dakota	23,899	9,291	8,452	2,256	3,900	25,075	9,424	8,896	2,476	4,279
Tennessee	155,610	46,282	48,806	25,340	35,182	167,056	47,903	52,532	28,250	38,371
Texas	753,145	196,164	194,785	155,442	206,754	782,495	200,387	202,897	161,388	217,823
Utah	74,434	24,369	20,547	15,226	14,292	79,623	25,379	22,227	16,105	15,912
Vermont	19,967	6,187	6,485	2,321	4,974	20,925	6,475	6,631	2,522	5,297
Virginia	270,372	68,770	75,792	50,307	75,503	287,624	71,961	79,449	56,163	80,051
Washington	219,290	60,067	61,426	37,851	59,946	221,362	60,302	63,008	38,380	59,672
West Virginia	70,381	22,843	22,982	8,523	16,033	72,478	24,185	24,584	8,194	15,515
Wisconsin	243,087	75,533	81,234	36,968	49,352	245,968	75,209	80,803	37,776	52,180
Wyoming	25,911	7,445	7,610	3,897	6,959	28,553	7,918	7,931	4,486	8,218
U.S. Service Schools	44,033	38,627	5,378	7	21	54,814	43,613	10,543	118	540
Outlying areas	67,433	19,822	31,236	5,635	10,740	67,449	19,408	30,034	6,218	11,789
American Samoa	908	236	184	233	255	1,011	280	178	329	224
Federated States of Micronesia	—	—	—	—	—	838	198	137	238	265
Guam	3,819	748	928	1,115	1,028	4,350	792	1,008	1,298	1,252
Northern Marianas	352	67	47	101	137	419	70	59	124	166
Palau	—	—	—	—	—	1,037	257	478	115	187
Puerto Rico	58,696	18,163	29,265	3,502	7,766	57,097	17,570	27,554	3,662	8,311
Trust Territory of the Pacific	1,187	423	246	250	268	—	—	—	—	—
Virgin Islands	2,471	185	566	434	1,286	2,697	241	620	452	1,384

[1] Data have been revised from previously published figures.

[2] Preliminary data.

—Data not reported or not applicable.

SOURCE: U.S. Department of Education, National Center for Education Statistics, Integrated Postsecondary Education Data System (IPEDS), "Fall Enrollment" surveys. (This table was prepared February 1991.)

Table 183.—Total enrollment in private institutions of higher education, by attendance status, sex, and State: Fall 1988 and fall 1989

State or other area	Fall 1988[1]					Fall 1989[2]				
	Total	Full-time		Part-time		Total	Full-time		Part-time	
		Men	Women	Men	Women		Men	Women	Men	Women
1	2	3	4	5	6	7	8	9	10	11
United States	2,893,949	1,005,541	1,020,879	387,397	480,132	2,942,882	1,004,593	1,034,516	402,992	500,781
Alabama	23,616	8,874	10,290	1,841	2,611	20,987	7,746	9,707	1,418	2,116
Alaska	1,815	281	933	327	274	2,353	406	650	346	951
Arizona	16,093	9,171	4,379	864	1,679	13,300	6,528	3,211	1,576	1,985
Arkansas	12,608	5,204	5,801	511	1,092	12,156	5,117	5,743	452	844
California	212,127	78,825	72,954	32,024	28,324	210,670	76,999	71,251	32,994	29,426
Colorado	23,956	8,860	8,061	3,841	3,194	25,264	8,417	8,409	4,479	3,959
Connecticut	59,258	17,994	17,730	10,658	12,876	59,741	18,275	18,080	10,541	12,845
Delaware	6,615	1,327	1,885	1,287	2,116	7,525	1,716	2,143	1,383	2,283
District of Columbia	67,201	21,193	24,097	10,563	11,348	67,361	21,353	24,633	10,101	11,274
Florida	96,130	37,203	30,320	15,148	13,459	92,843	36,004	27,911	15,183	13,745
Georgia	53,041	20,560	21,998	4,960	5,523	52,432	20,594	21,256	4,954	5,628
Hawaii	9,768	3,444	3,000	1,986	1,338	10,544	3,388	2,989	2,435	1,732
Idaho	10,482	4,028	5,215	447	792	10,522	3,875	5,336	453	858
Illinois	167,608	56,440	53,702	26,291	31,175	173,294	57,506	55,762	26,414	33,612
Indiana	58,669	25,095	22,857	3,757	6,960	59,388	25,771	23,339	3,637	6,641
Iowa	48,830	18,344	17,687	4,354	8,445	53,012	17,135	18,174	6,027	11,676
Kansas	14,120	5,231	5,295	1,394	2,200	13,363	4,907	5,194	1,356	1,906
Kentucky	30,766	10,756	11,851	2,784	5,375	28,717	9,577	11,403	2,480	5,257
Louisiana	26,700	10,076	10,861	2,450	3,313	28,194	10,171	11,713	2,509	3,801
Maine	12,035	4,073	5,280	821	1,861	17,719	4,248	5,517	1,409	6,545
Maryland	36,757	9,427	10,739	7,166	9,425	37,764	9,830	10,920	7,107	9,907
Massachusetts	237,759	80,147	87,108	30,322	40,182	238,704	80,127	85,525	31,392	41,660
Michigan	78,308	22,093	27,123	11,321	17,771	80,606	21,438	27,105	12,754	19,309
Minnesota	53,420	19,655	22,368	4,676	6,721	54,487	19,748	22,995	4,755	6,989
Mississippi	12,868	3,724	5,072	1,537	2,535	13,335	3,947	5,504	1,530	2,354
Missouri	83,662	25,434	23,915	15,740	18,573	86,183	26,088	24,866	16,316	18,913
Montana	4,485	1,109	1,634	751	991	4,463	1,119	1,606	676	1,062
Nebraska	16,836	5,726	6,236	1,630	3,244	17,507	5,940	6,827	1,620	3,120
Nevada	187	107	37	22	21	287	127	64	31	65
New Hampshire	26,686	8,953	8,983	3,529	5,221	25,711	8,994	8,097	3,588	5,032
New Jersey	58,920	18,325	17,205	10,288	13,102	60,547	18,450	17,725	10,394	13,978
New Mexico	2,056	596	605	525	330	1,991	563	636	383	409
New York	422,644	145,736	148,607	52,458	75,843	417,543	141,596	146,183	52,811	76,953
North Carolina	65,156	26,374	28,575	3,974	6,233	68,339	27,397	30,517	3,986	6,439
North Dakota	2,867	1,086	1,201	199	381	2,849	974	1,304	183	388
Ohio	141,157	42,540	42,810	35,138	20,669	138,656	41,883	41,074	34,985	20,714
Oklahoma	24,898	9,810	8,684	3,095	3,309	24,445	9,779	8,242	3,120	3,304
Oregon	19,552	8,411	7,502	1,562	2,077	20,511	8,578	7,919	1,745	2,269
Pennsylvania	250,063	81,827	80,396	32,763	55,077	275,256	89,839	92,750	38,863	53,804
Rhode Island	35,854	14,329	12,737	4,284	4,504	35,899	14,148	12,537	4,557	4,657
South Carolina	27,782	10,581	13,313	1,643	2,245	27,091	10,390	12,739	1,689	2,273
South Dakota	7,562	2,010	3,187	717	1,648	7,591	1,980	3,249	741	1,621
Tennessee	50,757	20,257	22,101	3,271	5,128	51,810	20,470	22,930	3,148	5,262
Texas	94,165	35,885	34,293	12,456	11,531	95,364	35,985	35,654	12,241	11,484
Utah	34,197	12,767	12,291	4,535	4,604	35,192	13,482	13,120	4,223	4,367
Vermont	14,436	5,212	5,717	974	2,533	15,021	5,435	6,005	1,142	2,439
Virginia	50,559	16,531	21,445	5,652	6,931	56,660	16,660	22,732	8,199	9,069
Washington	34,761	11,100	13,374	4,822	5,465	34,398	10,938	13,183	4,668	5,609
West Virginia	10,159	3,432	3,720	1,056	1,951	9,977	3,213	3,799	1,020	1,945
Wisconsin	43,369	14,752	15,702	4,983	7,932	44,704	15,140	16,284	4,978	8,302
Wyoming	629	626	3	0	0	606	602	4	0	0
Outlying areas	96,016	29,106	45,620	8,382	12,908	95,899	29,666	45,509	8,391	12,333
American Samoa	—	—	—	—	—	—	—	—	—	—
Federated States of Micronesia	—	—	—	—	—	—	—	—	—	—
Guam	—	—	—	—	—	—	—	—	—	—
Northern Marianas	—	—	—	—	—	—	—	—	—	—
Palau	—	—	—	—	—	—	—	—	—	—
Puerto Rico	96,016	29,106	45,620	8,382	12,908	95,899	29,666	45,509	8,391	12,333
Trust Territory of the Pacific	—	—	—	—	—	—	—	—	—	—
Virgin Islands	—	—	—	—	—	—	—	—	—	—

[1] Data have been revised from previously published figures.
[2] Preliminary data.
—Data not reported or not applicable.

SOURCE: U.S. Department of Education, National Center for Education Statistics, Integrated Postsecondary Education Data System (IPEDS), "Fall Enrollment" surveys. (This table was prepared February 1991.)

Table 184.—Total enrollment in institutions of higher education, by control and type of institution and State: Fall 1988 and fall 1989

State or other area	Fall 1988 [1]				Fall 1989 [2]			
	Public 4-year	Public 2-year	Private 4-year	Private 2-year	Public 4-year	Public 2-year	Private 4-year	Private 2-year
1	2	3	4	5	6	7	8	9
United States	5,545,901	4,615,487	2,634,281	259,668	5,694,202	4,820,771	2,680,192	262,690
Alabama	112,944	60,792	18,886	4,730	121,155	66,420	17,526	3,461
Alaska	22,138	5,030	1,207	608	26,274	—	2,064	289
Arizona	94,317	148,382	14,104	1,989	96,276	143,038	11,371	1,929
Arkansas	55,353	16,601	9,823	2,785	58,662	17,754	9,916	2,240
California	484,181	1,058,170	200,657	11,470	494,099	1,040,110	201,938	8,732
Colorado	105,302	57,654	18,348	5,608	107,324	68,526	19,756	5,508
Connecticut	64,501	41,918	57,467	1,791	65,427	44,270	58,068	1,673
Delaware	22,328	9,318	6,615	—	23,080	9,957	7,525	—
District of Columbia	12,109	—	67,201	—	12,439	—	67,361	—
Florida	157,549	262,829	91,308	4,822	168,576	312,293	87,818	5,025
Georgia	129,693	48,159	42,554	10,487	136,239	50,537	42,284	10,148
Hawaii	22,550	19,979	9,768	—	23,111	20,533	10,544	—
Idaho	30,516	5,340	2,295	8,187	33,093	5,354	2,315	8,207
Illinois	193,442	328,276	158,008	9,600	194,913	341,730	164,985	8,309
Indiana	173,499	35,737	55,431	3,238	181,286	35,147	56,433	2,955
Iowa	68,872	44,396	45,339	3,491	68,221	48,668	50,955	2,057
Kansas	87,368	51,334	12,806	1,314	89,180	55,954	12,461	902
Kentucky	98,112	31,330	23,289	7,477	102,332	34,965	22,261	6,456
Louisiana	133,832	15,519	24,183	2,517	133,856	17,877	25,859	2,335
Maine	30,198	6,127	10,965	1,070	34,233	6,278	16,277	1,442
Maryland	109,281	103,041	35,882	875	110,167	107,395	37,043	721
Massachusetts	112,854	75,990	223,547	14,212	112,222	75,550	225,041	13,663
Michigan	249,484	216,607	73,402	4,906	255,555	224,159	75,567	5,039
Minnesota	133,905	57,287	48,681	4,739	134,896	63,714	49,381	5,106
Mississippi	54,272	44,122	10,251	2,617	56,716	46,319	10,329	3,006
Missouri	116,420	62,309	80,940	2,722	121,045	71,277	83,468	2,715
Montana	27,405	3,887	3,305	1,180	28,461	4,736	3,231	1,232
Nebraska	57,108	30,935	16,370	466	59,221	32,116	16,824	683
Nevada	25,179	23,465	161	26	27,085	29,099	264	23
New Hampshire	24,047	6,677	24,170	2,516	24,688	8,201	24,432	1,279
New Jersey	133,289	110,672	55,983	2,937	135,101	118,443	56,648	3,899
New Mexico	47,176	29,903	2,056	—	47,591	31,768	1,991	—
New York	352,559	231,291	393,027	29,617	358,538	242,049	394,521	23,022
North Carolina	140,025	127,045	59,265	5,891	144,413	132,649	63,205	5,134
North Dakota	27,932	7,690	2,659	208	29,718	7,783	2,672	177
Ohio	279,579	123,244	106,850	34,307	284,356	127,717	108,132	30,524
Oklahoma	94,688	56,722	18,434	6,464	94,688	56,722	18,497	5,948
Oregon	68,432	68,174	19,220	332	66,775	74,536	20,225	286
Pennsylvania	229,235	94,254	212,800	37,263	234,784	100,317	214,270	60,986
Rhode Island	24,278	14,715	35,854	—	25,204	15,400	35,899	—
South Carolina	79,252	41,134	22,980	4,802	79,252	39,387	22,490	4,601
South Dakota	23,899	—	7,180	382	25,075	—	7,232	359
Tennessee	103,791	51,819	45,075	5,682	107,780	59,276	45,666	6,144
Texas	391,942	361,203	89,969	4,196	410,392	372,103	90,771	4,593
Utah	52,633	21,801	33,171	1,026	54,444	25,179	34,164	1,028
Vermont	15,762	4,205	12,319	2,117	16,127	4,798	12,921	2,100
Virginia	154,165	116,207	47,766	2,793	158,260	129,364	54,389	2,271
Washington	78,174	141,116	33,011	1,750	78,387	142,975	32,455	1,943
West Virginia	60,733	9,648	7,488	2,671	62,227	10,251	7,196	2,781
Wisconsin	151,146	91,941	42,211	1,158	151,146	94,822	43,551	1,153
Wyoming	10,773	15,138	—	629	12,335	16,218	—	606
U.S. Service Schools	17,679	26,354	—	—	17,777	37,037	—	—
Outlying areas	57,792	9,641	86,164	9,852	57,019	10,430	85,727	10,172
American Samoa	—	908	—	—	—	1,011	—	—
Federated States of Micronesia	—	—	—	—	—	838	—	—
Guam	2,096	1,723	—	—	2,385	1,965	—	—
Northern Marianas	—	352	—	—	—	419	—	—
Palau	—	—	—	—	—	1,037	—	—
Puerto Rico	53,225	5,471	86,164	9,852	51,937	5,160	85,727	10,172
Trust Territory of the Pacific	—	1,187	—	—	—	—	—	—
Virgin Islands	2,471	—	—	—	2,697	—	—	—

[1] Data have been revised from previously published figures.

[2] Preliminary data.

—Data not reported or not applicable.

SOURCE: U.S. Department of Education, National Center for Education Statistics, Integrated Postsecondary Education Data System (IPEDS), "Fall Enrollment" surveys. (This table was prepared February 1991.)

Table 185.—Total enrollment in institutions of higher education, by level of enrollment and State: Fall 1987 to fall 1989

State or other area	Fall 1987 [1]			Fall 1988 [1]				Fall 1989 [2]			
	Under-graduate	First-pro-fessional	Graduate	Total	Under-graduate	First-pro-fessional	Graduate	Total	Under-graduate	First-pro-fessional	Graduate
1	2	3	4	5	6	7	8	9	10	11	12
United States	11,046,235	268,332	1,452,075	13,055,337	11,316,548	267,109	1,471,680	13,457,855	11,665,643	273,728	1,518,484
Alabama	164,041	3,009	16,298	197,352	176,712	3,160	17,480	208,562	185,592	3,049	19,921
Alaska	25,694	—	1,243	28,983	27,966	—	1,017	28,627	27,518	—	1,109
Arizona	213,799	1,451	21,983	258,792	231,266	1,476	26,050	252,614	226,120	1,435	25,059
Arkansas	72,089	1,315	5,869	84,562	77,280	1,416	5,866	88,572	80,962	1,415	6,195
California	1,588,445	29,567	170,158	1,754,478	1,561,783	30,097	162,598	1,744,879	1,546,687	31,516	166,676
Colorado	158,146	3,003	22,434	186,912	165,374	2,988	18,550	201,114	178,680	2,986	19,448
Connecticut	128,126	3,363	30,893	165,677	130,931	3,266	31,480	169,438	134,354	3,273	31,811
Delaware	32,711	1,029	2,897	38,261	34,066	1,180	3,015	40,562	35,757	1,528	3,277
District of Columbia	46,267	8,587	22,712	79,310	48,689	8,434	22,187	79,800	49,611	8,195	21,994
Florida	438,128	7,232	44,604	516,508	461,555	7,229	47,724	573,712	515,560	7,434	50,718
Georgia	189,718	7,437	26,911	230,893	196,406	7,445	27,042	239,208	202,793	8,127	28,288
Hawaii	47,100	475	4,716	52,297	46,080	432	5,785	54,188	47,361	438	6,389
Idaho	39,906	296	5,365	46,338	40,912	404	5,022	48,969	42,489	466	6,014
Illinois	587,099	17,022	82,833	689,326	591,240	17,157	80,929	709,937	607,274	17,211	85,452
Indiana	221,107	5,312	29,845	267,905	231,921	5,260	30,724	275,821	239,557	5,330	30,934
Iowa	135,016	6,094	17,120	162,098	138,695	5,919	17,484	169,901	142,936	5,747	21,218
Kansas	125,625	2,219	18,595	152,822	131,556	2,118	19,148	158,497	137,164	2,199	19,134
Kentucky	131,422	4,484	17,445	160,208	138,093	4,553	17,562	166,014	145,315	3,392	17,307
Louisiana	147,524	5,466	20,239	176,051	150,786	5,719	19,546	179,927	154,376	5,672	19,879
Maine	43,624	550	2,818	48,360	44,212	575	3,573	58,230	53,275	629	4,326
Maryland	204,581	3,776	31,005	249,079	212,645	3,940	32,494	255,326	216,118	4,379	34,829
Massachusetts	342,575	13,169	68,172	426,603	343,595	12,982	70,026	426,476	341,563	13,012	71,901
Michigan	471,061	9,602	54,823	544,399	479,516	9,789	55,094	560,320	492,910	11,052	56,358
Minnesota	207,882	5,702	23,628	244,612	214,190	5,621	24,801	253,097	222,852	5,571	24,674
Mississippi	95,206	1,631	8,673	111,262	99,390	1,716	10,156	116,370	104,352	2,170	9,848
Missouri	210,717	9,415	31,646	262,391	221,304	8,308	32,779	278,505	236,742	8,634	33,129
Montana	32,340	217	3,325	35,777	32,253	210	3,314	37,660	34,008	211	3,441
Nebraska	87,803	2,633	10,392	104,879	91,891	2,631	10,357	108,844	95,189	2,629	11,026
Nevada	44,058	185	3,820	48,831	44,516	183	4,132	56,471	51,610	195	4,666
New Hampshire	48,181	745	7,237	57,410	49,522	637	7,251	58,600	50,714	650	7,236
New Jersey	249,369	6,183	38,881	302,881	256,311	6,118	40,452	314,091	266,876	6,140	41,075
New Mexico	71,939	625	10,510	79,135	68,459	627	10,049	81,350	70,425	615	10,310
New York	812,195	26,202	154,147	1,006,494	818,689	27,098	160,707	1,018,130	828,344	26,761	163,025
North Carolina	287,980	6,088	27,183	332,226	298,340	5,948	27,938	345,401	307,980	6,799	30,622
North Dakota	33,670	407	2,182	38,489	35,640	425	2,424	40,350	36,334	1,145	2,871
Ohio	449,360	12,078	57,026	543,980	473,740	11,908	58,332	550,729	478,698	11,842	60,189
Oklahoma	148,293	3,672	20,765	176,308	151,996	3,502	20,810	175,855	151,543	3,502	20,810
Oregon	133,594	3,340	15,723	156,158	137,362	3,339	15,457	161,822	143,093	3,624	15,105
Pennsylvania	471,730	13,950	68,690	573,552	489,083	13,623	70,846	610,357	523,380	13,819	73,158
Rhode Island	62,814	288	8,606	74,847	65,961	291	8,595	76,503	66,920	297	9,286
South Carolina	120,988	2,496	17,357	148,168	127,897	2,381	17,890	145,730	125,407	2,431	17,892
South Dakota	28,178	423	3,154	31,461	28,308	423	2,730	32,666	28,851	495	3,320
Tennessee	175,569	5,247	21,190	206,367	180,117	5,429	20,821	218,866	192,321	5,237	21,308
Texas	693,351	15,374	93,046	847,310	739,091	15,385	92,834	877,859	766,863	15,509	95,487
Utah	95,676	1,276	9,840	108,631	98,181	1,213	9,237	114,815	104,394	1,230	9,191
Vermont	29,492	369	3,381	34,403	30,527	355	3,521	35,946	31,510	602	3,834
Virginia	276,121	6,084	36,821	320,931	276,054	6,048	38,829	344,284	297,369	6,097	40,818
Washington	224,660	3,054	18,158	254,051	232,324	3,010	18,717	255,760	234,974	2,922	17,864
West Virginia	67,415	1,232	8,609	80,540	70,304	1,288	8,948	82,455	72,115	1,449	8,891
Wisconsin	251,259	3,706	26,752	286,456	257,585	3,647	25,224	290,672	261,620	3,589	25,463
Wyoming	24,149	206	1,707	26,540	24,694	206	1,640	29,159	26,148	204	2,807
U.S. Service Schools	58,442	1,046	648	44,033	41,540	0	2,493	54,814	51,039	874	2,901
Outlying areas	145,196	2,312	9,301	163,449	150,661	2,959	9,829	163,348	151,606	2,236	9,506
American Samoa	897	—	—	908	908	—	—	1,011	1,011	—	—
Federated States of Micronesia	—	—	—	—	—	—	—	838	838	—	—
Guam	3,808	—	264	3,819	3,604	—	215	4,350	4,125	—	225
Northern Marianas	366	—	—	352	352	—	—	419	419	—	—
Palau	—	—	—	—	—	—	—	1,037	1,037	—	—
Puerto Rico	136,541	2,312	8,853	154,712	142,341	2,959	9,412	152,996	141,756	2,236	9,004
Trust Territory of the Pacific	1,223	—	—	1,187	1,187	—	—	—	—	—	—
Virgin Islands	2,361	—	184	2,471	2,269	—	202	2,697	2,420	—	277

[1] Data have been revised from previously published figures.
[2] Preliminary data.
—Data not reported or not applicable.

SOURCE: U.S. Department of Education, National Center for Education Statistics, Integrated Postsecondary Education Data System (IPEDS), "Fall Enrollment" surveys. (This table was prepared February 1991.)

Table 186.—Total enrollment in institutions of higher education, by control, level of enrollment, and State: Fall 1989 [1]

State or other area	Public					Private				
	Undergraduate			First-professional	Graduate	Undergraduate			First-professional	Graduate
	Total	4-year	2-year			Total	4-year	2-year		
1	2	3	4	5	6	7	8	9	10	11
United States	9,424,536	4,603,765	4,820,771	112,638	977,799	2,241,107	1,978,417	262,690	161,090	540,685
Alabama	166,613	100,193	66,420	2,192	18,770	18,979	15,518	3,461	857	1,151
Alaska	25,335	25,335	—	—	939	2,183	1,894	289	—	170
Arizona	216,463	73,425	143,038	1,434	21,417	9,657	7,728	1,929	1	3,642
Arkansas	69,025	51,271	17,754	1,415	5,976	11,937	9,697	2,240	—	219
California	1,429,363	389,253	1,040,110	7,778	97,068	117,324	108,592	8,732	23,738	69,608
Colorado	160,290	91,764	68,526	1,615	13,945	18,390	12,882	5,508	1,371	5,503
Connecticut	93,197	48,927	44,270	1,216	15,284	41,157	39,484	1,673	2,057	16,527
Delaware	30,294	20,337	9,957	—	2,743	5,463	5,463	—	1,528	534
District of Columbia	11,452	11,452	—	—	987	38,159	38,159	—	8,195	21,007
Florida	444,480	132,187	312,293	3,063	33,326	71,080	66,055	5,025	4,371	17,392
Georgia	161,208	110,671	50,537	2,950	22,618	41,585	31,437	10,148	5,177	5,670
Hawaii	37,620	17,087	20,533	438	5,586	9,741	9,741	—	—	803
Idaho	32,647	27,293	5,354	466	5,334	9,842	1,635	8,207	—	680
Illinois	490,317	148,587	341,730	4,239	42,087	116,957	108,648	8,309	12,972	43,365
Indiana	187,734	152,587	35,147	3,288	25,411	51,823	48,868	2,955	2,042	5,523
Iowa	101,346	52,678	48,668	2,698	12,845	41,590	39,533	2,057	3,049	8,373
Kansas	124,638	68,684	55,954	2,017	18,479	12,526	11,624	902	182	655
Kentucky	119,541	84,576	34,965	2,544	15,212	25,774	19,318	6,456	848	2,095
Louisiana	133,340	115,463	17,877	2,669	15,724	21,036	18,701	2,335	3,003	4,155
Maine	36,823	30,545	6,278	263	3,425	16,452	15,010	1,442	366	901
Maryland	193,200	85,805	107,395	3,530	20,832	22,918	22,197	721	849	13,997
Massachusetts	168,144	92,594	75,550	418	19,210	173,419	159,756	13,663	12,594	52,691
Michigan	422,504	198,345	224,159	7,144	50,066	70,406	65,367	5,039	3,908	6,292
Minnesota	178,840	115,126	63,714	2,351	17,419	44,012	38,906	5,106	3,220	7,255
Mississippi	93,059	46,740	46,319	1,579	8,397	11,293	8,287	3,006	591	1,451
Missouri	172,491	101,214	71,277	2,511	17,320	64,251	61,536	2,715	6,123	15,809
Montana	29,640	24,904	4,736	211	3,346	4,368	3,136	1,232	—	95
Nebraska	79,641	47,525	32,116	1,286	10,410	15,548	14,865	683	1,343	616
Nevada	51,340	22,241	29,099	195	4,649	270	247	23	—	17
New Hampshire	30,219	22,018	8,201	—	2,670	20,495	19,216	1,279	650	4,566
New Jersey	223,748	105,305	118,443	3,373	26,423	43,128	39,229	3,899	2,767	14,652
New Mexico	68,548	36,780	31,768	615	10,196	1,877	1,877	—	—	114
New York	533,507	291,458	242,049	4,931	62,149	294,837	271,815	23,022	21,830	100,876
North Carolina	251,031	118,382	132,649	2,497	23,534	56,949	51,815	5,134	4,302	7,088
North Dakota	33,642	25,859	7,783	1,145	2,714	2,692	2,515	177	—	157
Ohio	360,450	232,733	127,717	7,566	44,057	118,248	87,724	30,524	4,276	16,132
Oklahoma	131,018	74,296	56,722	2,035	18,357	20,525	14,577	5,948	1,467	2,453
Oregon	127,542	53,006	74,536	1,179	12,590	15,551	15,265	286	2,445	2,515
Pennsylvania	294,934	194,617	100,317	4,217	35,950	228,446	167,460	60,986	9,602	37,208
Rhode Island	35,003	19,603	15,400	6	5,595	31,917	31,917	—	291	3,691
South Carolina	100,365	60,978	39,387	1,864	16,410	25,042	20,441	4,601	567	1,482
South Dakota	21,557	21,557	—	430	3,088	7,294	6,935	359	65	232
Tennessee	148,103	88,827	59,276	2,502	16,451	44,218	38,074	6,144	2,735	4,857
Texas	692,474	320,371	372,103	9,644	80,377	74,389	69,796	4,593	5,865	15,110
Utah	72,348	47,169	25,179	761	6,514	32,046	31,018	1,028	469	2,677
Vermont	18,882	14,084	4,798	359	1,684	12,628	10,528	2,100	243	2,150
Virginia	249,354	119,990	129,364	4,255	34,015	48,015	45,744	2,271	1,842	6,803
Washington	208,345	65,370	142,975	1,623	11,394	26,629	24,686	1,943	1,299	6,470
West Virginia	62,760	52,509	10,251	1,269	8,449	9,355	6,574	2,781	180	442
Wisconsin	223,540	128,718	94,822	1,779	20,649	38,080	36,927	1,153	1,810	4,814
Wyoming	25,542	9,324	16,218	204	2,807	606	—	606	—	—
U.S. Service Schools	51,039	14,002	37,037	874	2,901	—	—	—	—	—
Outlying areas	62,165	51,735	10,430	532	4,752	89,441	79,269	10,172	1,704	4,754
American Samoa	1,011	—	1,011	—	—	—	—	—	—	—
Federated States of Micronesia	838	—	838	—	—	—	—	—	—	—
Guam	4,125	2,160	1,965	—	225	—	—	—	—	—
Northern Marianas	419	—	419	—	—	—	—	—	—	—
Palau	1,037	—	1,037	—	—	—	—	—	—	—
Puerto Rico	52,315	47,155	5,160	532	4,250	89,441	79,269	10,172	1,704	4,754
Virgin Islands	2,420	2,420	—	—	277	—	—	—	—	—

[1] Preliminary data.

—Data not reported or not applicable.

SOURCE: U.S. Department of Education, National Center for Education Statistics, Integrated Postsecondary Education Data System (IPEDS), "Fall Enrollment, 1989" survey. (This table was prepared February 1991.)

Table 187.—Total enrollment in institutions of higher education, by control, level of enrollment, and State: Fall 1988

State or other area	Public					Private				
	Undergraduate			First-pro-fessional	Graduate	Undergraduate			First-pro-fessional	Graduate
	Total	4-year	2-year			Total	4-year	2-year		
1	2	3	4	5	6	7	8	9	10	11
United States	9,103,146	4,487,659	4,615,487	108,939	949,303	2,213,402	1,953,734	259,668	158,170	522,377
Alabama	155,257	94,465	60,792	2,099	16,380	21,455	16,725	4,730	1,061	1,100
Alaska	26,336	21,306	5,030	—	832	1,630	1,022	608	—	185
Arizona	220,022	71,640	148,382	1,475	21,202	11,244	9,255	1,989	1	4,848
Arkansas	65,107	48,506	16,601	1,327	5,520	12,173	9,388	2,785	89	346
California	1,440,425	382,255	1,058,170	7,845	94,081	121,358	109,888	11,470	22,252	68,517
Colorado	147,828	90,174	57,654	1,578	13,550	17,546	11,938	5,608	1,410	5,000
Connecticut	90,197	48,279	41,918	1,218	15,004	40,734	38,943	1,791	2,048	16,476
Delaware	29,125	19,807	9,318	—	2,521	4,941	4,941	—	1,180	494
District of Columbia	10,886	10,886	—	—	1,223	37,803	37,803	—	8,434	20,964
Florida	386,874	124,045	262,829	3,033	30,471	74,681	69,859	4,822	4,196	17,253
Georgia	153,381	105,222	48,159	2,904	21,567	43,025	32,538	10,487	4,541	5,475
Hawaii	36,982	17,003	19,979	432	5,115	9,098	9,098	—	—	670
Idaho	30,984	25,644	5,340	404	4,468	9,928	1,741	8,187	—	554
Illinois	475,634	147,358	328,276	4,253	41,831	115,606	106,006	9,600	12,904	39,098
Indiana	180,387	144,650	35,737	3,222	25,627	51,534	48,296	3,238	2,038	5,097
Iowa	97,800	53,404	44,396	2,655	12,813	40,895	37,404	3,491	3,264	4,671
Kansas	118,132	66,798	51,334	2,021	18,549	13,424	12,110	1,314	97	599
Kentucky	112,206	80,876	31,330	2,577	14,659	25,887	18,410	7,477	1,976	2,903
Louisiana	130,674	115,155	15,519	2,713	15,964	20,112	17,595	2,517	3,006	3,582
Maine	33,030	26,903	6,127	208	3,087	11,182	10,112	1,070	367	486
Maryland	189,790	86,749	103,041	3,022	19,510	22,855	21,980	875	918	12,984
Massachusetts	169,931	93,941	75,990	407	18,506	173,664	159,452	14,212	12,575	51,520
Michigan	410,187	193,580	216,607	6,299	49,605	69,329	64,423	4,906	3,490	5,489
Minnesota	170,852	113,565	57,287	2,409	17,931	43,338	38,599	4,739	3,212	6,870
Mississippi	88,755	44,633	44,122	1,193	8,446	10,635	8,018	2,617	523	1,710
Missouri	159,458	97,149	62,309	2,529	16,742	61,846	59,124	2,722	5,779	16,037
Montana	27,841	23,954	3,887	210	3,241	4,412	3,232	1,180	—	73
Nebraska	77,030	46,095	30,935	1,293	9,720	14,861	14,395	466	1,338	637
Nevada	44,329	20,864	23,465	183	4,132	187	161	26	—	—
New Hampshire	27,680	21,003	6,677	—	3,044	21,842	19,326	2,516	637	4,207
New Jersey	214,771	104,099	110,672	3,298	25,892	41,540	38,603	2,937	2,820	14,560
New Mexico	66,488	36,585	29,903	627	9,964	1,971	1,971	—	—	85
New York	517,819	286,528	231,291	4,983	61,048	300,870	271,253	29,617	22,115	99,659
North Carolina	242,202	115,157	127,045	2,448	22,420	56,138	50,247	5,891	3,500	5,518
North Dakota	32,943	25,253	7,690	425	2,254	2,697	2,489	208	—	170
Ohio	352,659	229,415	123,244	7,653	42,511	121,081	86,774	34,307	4,255	15,821
Oklahoma	131,018	74,296	56,722	2,035	18,357	20,978	14,514	6,464	1,467	2,453
Oregon	122,297	54,123	68,174	1,181	13,128	15,065	14,733	332	2,158	2,329
Pennsylvania	285,019	190,765	94,254	4,249	34,221	204,064	166,801	37,263	9,374	36,625
Rhode Island	34,037	19,322	14,715	4	4,952	31,924	31,924	—	287	3,643
South Carolina	102,112	60,978	41,134	1,864	16,410	25,785	20,983	4,802	517	1,480
South Dakota	21,014	21,014	—	354	2,531	7,294	6,912	382	69	199
Tennessee	137,231	85,412	51,819	2,482	15,897	42,886	37,204	5,682	2,947	4,924
Texas	665,643	304,440	361,203	9,605	77,897	73,448	69,252	4,196	5,780	14,937
Utah	67,048	45,247	21,801	756	6,630	31,133	30,107	1,026	457	2,607
Vermont	18,039	13,834	4,205	355	1,573	12,488	10,371	2,117	—	1,948
Virginia	233,897	117,690	116,207	4,202	32,273	42,157	39,364	2,793	1,846	6,556
Washington	204,970	63,854	141,116	1,637	12,683	27,354	25,604	1,750	1,373	6,034
West Virginia	60,555	50,907	9,648	1,287	8,539	9,749	7,078	2,671	1	409
Wisconsin	220,659	128,718	91,941	1,779	20,649	36,926	35,768	1,158	1,868	4,575
Wyoming	24,065	8,927	15,138	206	1,640	629	—	629	—	—
U.S. Service Schools	41,540	15,186	26,354	—	2,493	—	—	—	—	—
Outlying areas	60,946	51,305	9,641	1,268	5,219	89,715	79,863	9,852	1,691	4,610
American Samoa	908	—	908	—	—	—	—	—	—	—
Guam	3,604	1,881	1,723	—	215	—	—	—	—	—
Northern Marianas	352	—	352	—	—	—	—	—	—	—
Puerto Rico	52,626	47,155	5,471	1,268	4,802	89,715	79,863	9,852	1,691	4,610
Trust Territory of the Pacific	1,187	—	1,187	—	—	—	—	—	—	—
Virgin Islands	2,269	2,269	—	—	202	—	—	—	—	—

—Data not reported or not applicable.

NOTE.—Some data have been revised from previously published figures.

SOURCE: U.S. Department of Education, National Center for Education Statistics, Integrated Postsecondary Education Data System (IPEDS), "Fall Enrollment, 1988" survey. (This table was prepared February 1991.)

Table 188.—Full-time-equivalent enrollment in institutions of higher education, by control and type of institution: Fall 1970 to fall 1989

Year	All institutions			Public institutions			Private institutions		
	Total	4-year	2-year	Total	4-year	2-year	Total	4-year	2-year
1	2	3	4	5	6	7	8	9	10
1970 [1]	6,737,819	5,219,855	1,517,964	4,953,144	3,540,559	1,412,585	1,784,675	1,679,296	105,379
1971 [1]	7,148,575	5,429,703	1,718,872	5,344,356	3,731,009	1,613,347	1,804,219	1,698,694	105,525
1972	7,253,739	5,406,821	1,846,918	5,452,848	3,706,239	1,746,609	1,800,891	1,700,582	100,309
1973	7,453,448	5,439,218	2,014,230	5,629,555	3,721,031	1,908,524	1,823,893	1,718,187	105,706
1974	7,805,453	5,606,249	2,199,204	5,944,804	3,847,550	2,097,254	1,860,649	1,758,699	101,950
1975	8,479,685	5,900,401	2,579,284	6,522,310	4,056,500	2,465,810	1,957,375	1,843,901	113,474
1976	8,312,502	5,848,001	2,464,501	6,349,903	3,998,450	2,351,453	1,962,599	1,849,551	113,048
1977	8,415,339	5,935,076	2,480,263	6,396,476	4,039,071	2,357,405	2,018,863	1,896,005	122,858
1978	8,348,482	5,932,573	2,415,909	6,279,199	3,996,126	2,283,073	2,069,283	1,936,447	132,836
1979	8,487,317	6,016,072	2,471,245	6,392,617	4,059,304	2,333,313	2,094,700	1,956,768	137,932
1980	8,819,013	6,161,372	2,657,641	6,642,294	4,158,267	2,484,027	2,176,719	2,003,105	[2]173,614
1981	9,014,521	6,249,847	2,764,674	6,781,300	4,208,506	2,572,794	2,233,221	2,041,341	[2]191,880
1982	9,091,648	6,248,923	2,842,725	6,850,589	4,220,648	2,629,941	2,241,059	2,028,275	212,784
1983	9,166,399	6,325,223	2,841,176	6,881,480	4,265,808	2,615,672	2,284,919	2,059,415	225,504
1984	8,951,695	6,292,711	2,658,984	6,684,664	4,237,895	2,446,769	2,267,031	2,054,816	212,215
1985	8,943,433	6,294,339	2,649,094	6,667,781	4,239,622	2,428,159	2,275,652	2,054,717	220,935
1986	9,064,168	6,360,324	2,703,844	6,778,046	4,295,495	2,482,551	2,286,122	2,064,829	[3]221,293
1987	9,229,736	6,486,510	2,743,225	6,937,690	4,395,731	2,541,958	2,292,046	2,090,779	201,267
1988 [4]	9,466,878	6,665,271	2,801,607	7,097,072	4,505,501	2,591,571	2,369,806	2,159,770	210,036
1989 [5]	9,733,727	6,803,495	2,930,232	7,336,939	4,619,374	2,717,565	2,396,788	2,184,121	212,667

[1] Data for 2-year branch campuses of 4-year systems are included with the 4-year institutions.

[2] Large increases are due to the addition of schools accredited by the National Association of Trade and Technical Schools in 1980 and 1981.

[3] Because of imputation techniques, data are not consistent with figures for other years.

[4] Data have been revised from previously published figures.

[5] Preliminary data.

NOTE.—Because of a revision in data compilation procedures, figures for 1986 to 1989 are not directly comparable with data for earlier years.

SOURCE: U.S. Department of Education, National Center for Education Statistics, "Fall Enrollment in Colleges and Universities"; and Integrated Postsecondary Education Data System (IPEDS), "Fall Enrollment" surveys. (This table was prepared February 1991.)

Table 189.—Full-time-equivalent enrollment in institutions of higher education, by control, type of institution, and State: Fall 1987 to fall 1989

State or other area	Public 4-year			Public 2-year			Private 4-year			Private 2-year		
	1987	1988[1]	1989[2]	1987	1988[1]	1989[2]	1987	1988[1]	1989[2]	1987	1988[1]	1989[2]
1	2	3	4	5	6	7	8	9	10	11	12	13
United States	4,395,731	4,505,501	4,619,374	2,541,958	2,591,571	2,717,565	2,090,779	2,159,770	2,184,121	201,267	210,036	212,667
Alabama	87,892	93,695	100,003	41,310	43,299	48,841	15,733	16,769	15,760	3,332	4,168	3,092
Alaska	8,022	13,999	16,227	6,265	2,124	—	739	842	1,313	—	608	255
Arizona	71,834	76,177	77,868	64,400	70,536	69,537	6,189	12,549	9,494	1,793	1,989	1,638
Arkansas	45,862	47,310	50,018	9,099	10,245	11,228	8,231	8,958	9,158	1,757	2,682	2,213
California	413,474	405,135	413,500	544,184	532,273	523,402	158,191	165,112	165,046	10,365	10,769	8,172
Colorado	89,982	90,031	93,143	28,214	30,079	35,082	14,307	14,288	14,983	3,741	5,407	5,165
Connecticut	46,728	48,396	48,688	19,963	20,629	21,955	43,846	43,559	44,223	1,295	1,357	1,268
Delaware	18,193	18,963	19,525	4,738	5,497	5,833	4,926	4,613	5,371	—	—	—
District of Columbia	6,455	7,239	7,475	—	—	—	53,108	53,991	54,471	—	—	—
Florida	114,505	120,978	129,019	140,240	146,970	171,739	64,043	74,110	70,224	4,021	4,605	4,995
Georgia	100,976	104,955	110,175	30,057	30,666	32,451	36,977	37,737	37,420	7,043	8,989	8,666
Hawaii	18,188	18,368	18,792	12,200	12,053	12,404	7,390	7,753	8,018	—	—	—
Idaho	23,216	24,324	25,877	3,549	3,751	3,850	2,137	1,876	1,832	7,516	7,859	7,896
Illinois	161,655	159,444	160,735	174,451	175,399	183,260	122,325	124,345	129,694	8,466	8,535	7,305
Indiana	130,757	136,242	142,702	19,882	20,594	20,265	45,327	49,336	50,492	3,065	2,867	2,702
Iowa	59,859	59,776	59,876	31,878	32,713	35,714	36,201	37,738	40,361	2,993	3,315	1,872
Kansas	68,978	70,397	72,406	26,721	28,723	30,840	9,954	10,752	10,581	1,124	1,197	813
Kentucky	74,863	78,663	82,354	17,486	19,645	22,119	18,921	19,242	18,307	7,253	6,628	5,741
Louisiana	114,219	113,977	114,008	8,664	9,377	10,739	20,247	20,833	22,078	1,135	2,432	2,331
Maine	21,854	22,773	25,097	3,466	3,771	3,917	9,688	9,510	11,747	838	905	1,164
Maryland	82,738	84,008	84,236	48,760	52,481	55,157	25,382	25,853	26,734	764	773	627
Massachusetts	87,240	86,806	85,934	44,520	46,079	45,445	182,274	185,110	184,812	11,459	10,079	9,759
Michigan	197,775	202,042	206,687	108,373	109,648	115,183	56,089	57,124	57,632	2,948	3,808	3,839
Minnesota	98,395	100,046	101,144	35,667	37,800	42,152	40,919	42,528	43,102	4,390	4,093	4,368
Mississippi	44,628	47,895	50,463	34,323	35,975	36,865	7,777	7,940	8,215	2,137	2,459	2,771
Missouri	91,051	94,799	98,734	32,395	34,278	39,360	58,267	60,244	62,240	3,041	2,610	2,621
Montana	23,384	23,821	24,660	2,600	2,333	3,494	2,522	2,625	2,589	436	814	832
Nebraska	43,993	45,111	46,761	15,650	16,329	16,856	12,789	13,490	14,047	402	400	593
Nevada	16,227	17,331	19,173	9,795	9,843	11,761	194	135	206	25	26	23
New Hampshire	18,604	19,476	18,348	4,326	3,900	4,431	18,381	19,526	19,206	1,624	1,853	1,269
New Jersey	97,755	98,765	100,389	59,252	63,235	67,939	42,547	42,490	42,817	2,008	2,282	2,977
New Mexico	37,313	37,902	38,269	17,190	16,898	17,875	1,362	1,538	1,511	—	—	—
New York	260,835	268,209	271,141	153,672	159,124	165,807	318,565	318,594	318,285	27,392	26,144	20,424
North Carolina	114,125	117,798	121,568	72,946	75,435	80,248	50,087	53,377	57,066	6,497	5,624	4,963
North Dakota	23,639	24,902	26,448	5,741	6,284	6,464	2,227	2,306	2,325	214	208	177
Ohio	222,912	231,376	234,679	68,833	69,853	72,815	85,069	88,023	89,114	13,770	19,662	16,120
Oklahoma	75,585	76,205	76,205	29,927	30,933	30,933	15,799	15,841	15,892	4,242	5,243	4,727
Oregon	53,550	57,104	55,775	37,920	39,671	42,319	16,526	17,020	17,802	329	331	285
Pennsylvania	188,138	194,106	198,499	50,690	54,603	58,477	169,959	172,339	173,619	31,157	24,688	45,748
Rhode Island	18,127	18,814	19,433	7,174	7,762	7,988	29,977	30,516	30,302	—	—	—
South Carolina	61,931	64,759	64,759	25,547	27,419	26,364	20,304	20,871	20,391	4,752	4,569	4,316
South Dakota	19,903	20,155	20,954	—	—	—	5,734	5,866	5,915	475	267	249
Tennessee	83,023	85,700	88,581	30,571	31,251	35,880	37,846	40,531	41,033	5,219	5,184	5,736
Texas	301,826	316,064	329,223	188,611	203,016	208,486	74,905	75,705	76,617	3,406	3,973	4,423
Utah	40,644	40,910	42,414	14,769	15,089	17,160	26,235	27,783	29,096	965	875	890
Vermont	13,241	13,414	13,735	1,812	1,924	2,215	10,173	10,536	11,110	1,698	1,773	1,738
Virginia	126,016	129,165	132,868	61,874	59,548	66,180	36,759	40,278	43,970	1,306	2,626	2,207
Washington	70,316	70,990	71,245	80,880	83,986	85,666	25,012	26,813	26,258	1,372	1,706	1,898
West Virginia	46,677	49,071	51,116	5,936	6,029	6,594	6,115	6,328	6,020	1,560	2,024	2,175
Wisconsin	130,128	130,638	130,638	55,977	56,967	57,433	32,501	34,527	35,622	1,323	1,001	1,018
Wyoming	9,104	9,615	10,433	9,153	9,180	9,805	—	—	—	621	629	606
U.S. Service Schools	19,393	17,662	17,374	40,310	26,354	37,037	—	—	—	—	—	—
Outlying areas	49,548	49,887	48,546	7,046	7,430	7,751	70,271	74,148	74,223	8,723	9,023	9,172
American Samoa	—	—	—	556	584	644	—	—	—	—	—	—
Federated States of Micronesia	—	—	—	—	—	504	—	—	—	—	—	—
Guam	1,702	1,661	1,848	845	777	860	—	—	—	—	—	—
Northern Marianas	—	—	—	196	194	226	—	—	—	—	—	—
Palau	—	—	—	—	—	836	—	—	—	—	—	—
Puerto Rico	46,358	46,789	45,108	4,582	5,032	4,681	70,271	74,148	74,223	8,723	9,023	9,172
Trust Territory of the Pacific	—	—	—	867	843	—	—	—	—	—	—	—
Virgin Islands	1,488	1,437	1,590	—	—	—	—	—	—	—	—	—

[1] Data revised from previously published figures.
[2] Preliminary data.
—Data not reported or not applicable.

SOURCE: U.S. Department of Education, National Center for Education Statistics, Integrated Postsecondary Education Data System (IPEDS), ''Fall Enrollment'' surveys. (This table was prepared February 1991.)

Table 190.—Full-time-equivalent enrollment in institutions of higher education, by control and State: Fall 1980 to fall 1989

State or other area	Total					Public			Private		
	1980	1985	1987	1988 [1]	1989 [2]	1987	1988 [1]	1989 [2]	1987	1988 [1]	1989 [2]
1	2	3	4	5	6	7	8	9	10	11	12
United States	18,819,013	8,943,433	9,229,736	9,466,878	9,733,727	6,937,690	7,097,072	7,336,939	2,292,046	2,369,806	2,396,788
Alabama	138,910	149,895	148,267	157,931	167,696	129,203	136,994	148,844	19,065	20,937	18,852
Alaska	10,073	14,098	15,026	17,573	17,795	14,287	16,123	16,227	739	1,450	1,568
Arizona	127,114	134,954	144,217	161,251	158,537	136,235	146,713	147,405	7,982	14,538	11,132
Arkansas	64,307	63,230	64,948	69,195	72,617	54,961	57,555	61,246	9,987	11,640	11,371
California	1,099,559	1,062,439	1,126,215	1,113,289	1,110,120	957,658	937,408	936,902	168,556	175,881	173,218
Colorado	123,589	121,804	136,243	139,805	148,373	118,196	120,110	128,225	18,048	19,695	20,148
Connecticut	112,612	107,803	111,831	113,941	116,134	66,691	69,025	70,643	45,141	44,916	45,491
Delaware	26,284	25,750	27,857	29,073	30,729	22,931	24,460	25,358	4,926	4,613	5,371
District of Columbia	62,126	59,198	59,563	61,230	61,946	6,455	7,239	7,475	53,108	53,991	54,471
Florida	290,647	308,315	322,809	346,663	375,977	254,746	267,948	300,758	68,063	78,715	75,219
Georgia	152,369	161,952	[3] 175,052	182,347	188,712	131,033	135,621	142,626	44,019	46,726	46,086
Hawaii	35,859	36,986	37,778	38,174	39,214	30,388	30,421	31,196	7,390	7,753	8,018
Idaho	33,938	32,649	36,418	37,810	39,455	26,765	28,075	29,727	9,653	9,735	9,728
Illinois	432,365	450,504	466,897	467,723	480,994	336,106	334,843	343,995	130,791	132,880	136,999
Indiana	193,445	195,630	199,031	209,039	216,161	150,639	156,836	162,967	48,392	52,203	53,194
Iowa	120,083	128,492	130,931	133,542	137,823	91,737	92,489	95,590	39,194	41,053	42,233
Kansas	101,147	100,807	106,777	111,069	114,640	95,699	99,120	103,246	11,078	11,949	11,394
Kentucky	113,709	110,539	118,522	124,178	128,521	92,348	98,308	104,473	26,174	25,870	24,048
Louisiana	132,780	148,983	144,265	146,619	149,156	122,884	123,354	124,747	21,382	23,265	24,409
Maine	34,471	37,993	35,846	36,959	41,925	25,320	26,544	29,014	10,527	10,415	12,911
Maryland	149,202	148,091	157,644	163,115	166,754	131,498	136,489	139,393	26,146	26,626	27,361
Massachusetts	315,937	321,022	325,493	328,074	325,950	131,760	132,885	131,379	193,733	195,189	194,571
Michigan	366,058	354,690	365,184	372,622	383,341	306,147	311,690	321,870	59,036	60,932	61,471
Minnesota	162,559	170,958	179,371	184,467	190,766	134,062	137,846	143,296	45,309	46,621	47,470
Mississippi	85,621	86,846	88,865	94,269	98,314	78,951	83,870	87,328	9,914	10,399	10,986
Missouri	180,156	178,090	184,754	191,931	202,955	123,446	129,077	138,094	61,308	62,854	64,861
Montana	29,428	29,992	28,943	29,593	31,575	25,984	26,154	28,154	2,959	3,439	3,421
Nebraska	68,505	70,778	72,834	75,330	78,257	59,643	61,440	63,617	13,191	13,890	14,640
Nevada	22,467	23,093	26,241	27,335	31,163	26,022	27,174	30,934	219	161	229
New Hampshire	39,456	41,733	42,936	44,755	43,254	22,930	23,376	22,779	20,006	21,379	20,475
New Jersey	218,838	201,270	201,563	206,772	214,122	157,007	162,000	168,328	44,556	44,772	45,794
New Mexico	43,722	47,169	55,865	56,338	57,655	54,503	54,800	56,144	1,362	1,538	1,511
New York	760,305	763,596	760,465	772,071	775,657	414,507	427,333	436,948	345,957	344,738	338,709
North Carolina	235,266	249,901	243,654	252,234	263,845	187,070	193,233	201,816	56,584	59,001	62,029
North Dakota	30,188	32,456	31,821	33,700	35,414	29,380	31,186	32,912	2,441	2,514	2,502
Ohio	369,342	383,898	390,584	408,914	412,728	291,745	301,229	307,494	98,840	107,685	105,234
Oklahoma	115,701	126,691	125,553	128,222	127,757	105,512	107,138	107,138	20,041	21,084	20,619
Oregon	110,649	102,247	108,325	114,126	116,181	91,469	96,775	98,094	16,855	17,351	18,087
Pennsylvania	404,192	422,349	439,943	445,736	476,343	238,828	248,709	256,976	201,115	197,027	219,367
Rhode Island	50,628	53,016	55,279	57,092	57,723	25,302	26,576	27,421	29,977	30,516	30,302
South Carolina	109,346	109,303	112,534	117,618	115,830	87,478	92,178	91,123	25,056	25,440	24,707
South Dakota	27,873	26,988	26,112	26,288	27,118	19,903	20,155	20,954	6,210	6,133	6,164
Tennessee	161,058	152,967	156,659	162,666	171,230	113,594	116,951	124,461	43,065	45,715	46,769
Texas	527,724	566,736	568,749	598,758	618,749	490,437	519,080	537,709	78,312	79,678	81,040
Utah	78,199	84,095	82,613	84,657	89,560	55,413	55,999	59,574	27,200	28,658	29,986
Vermont	25,572	25,649	26,924	27,647	28,798	15,053	15,338	15,950	11,871	12,309	12,848
Virginia	199,549	204,928	225,954	231,617	245,225	187,890	188,713	199,048	38,064	42,904	46,177
Washington	194,440	171,668	177,580	183,495	185,067	151,196	154,976	156,911	26,384	28,519	28,156
West Virginia	60,394	58,438	60,287	63,452	65,905	52,613	55,100	57,710	7,675	8,352	8,195
Wisconsin	206,790	211,749	219,930	223,133	224,711	186,106	187,605	188,071	33,825	35,528	36,640
Wyoming	14,725	17,037	18,877	19,424	20,844	18,256	18,795	20,238	621	629	606
U.S. Service Schools	49,736	53,968	59,703	44,016	54,411	59,703	44,016	54,411	—	—	—
Outlying areas	117,637	145,530	135,588	140,488	139,692	56,594	57,317	56,297	78,994	83,171	83,395
American Samoa	824	497	556	584	644	556	584	644	—	—	—
Federated States of Micronesia	—	—	—	—	504	—	—	504	—	—	—
Guam	2,115	3,049	2,547	2,438	2,708	2,547	2,438	2,708	—	—	—
Northern Marianas	—	183	196	194	226	196	194	226	—	—	—
Palau	—	—	—	—	836	—	—	836	—	—	—
Puerto Rico	113,285	139,627	129,935	134,992	133,184	50,940	51,821	49,789	78,994	83,171	83,395
Trust Territory of the Pacific	195	680	867	843	—	867	843	—	—	—	—
Virgin Islands	1,218	1,494	1,488	1,437	1,590	1,488	1,437	1,590	—	—	—

[1] Data have been revised from previously published figures.

[2] Preliminary data.

[3] Part of the 1987 increase is due to inclusion of additional public 2-year institutions in the survey.

—Data not reported or not applicable.

SOURCE: U.S. Department of Education, National Center for Education Statistics, Integrated Postsecondary Education Data System (IPEDS), "Fall Enrollment" surveys. (This table was prepared February 1991.)

Table 191.—Residence and migration of all new undergraduate students [1] in institutions of higher education, by State: Fall 1988

| State or other area | Students enrolled in State [2] | Student residents of State [3] | Students remaining in State [4] | Ratio of students remaining to— | | Migration of students | | |
				Students enrolled	Student residents	Out of	Into	Net (column 8– column 7) [5]
1	2	3	4	5	6	7	8	9
United States	2,337,354	2,337,354	1,895,942	0.81	0.81	441,412	441,412	0
Alabama	41,827	35,685	32,855	0.79	0.92	2,830	8,972	6,142
Alaska	1,615	2,965	1,266	0.78	0.43	1,699	349	−1,350
Arizona	69,614	62,577	60,338	0.87	0.96	2,239	9,276	7,037
Arkansas	17,065	16,769	14,463	0.85	0.86	2,306	2,602	296
California	283,290	268,770	255,962	0.90	0.95	12,808	27,328	14,520
Colorado	30,932	30,158	24,234	0.78	0.80	5,924	6,698	774
Connecticut	29,086	36,491	22,620	0.78	0.62	13,871	6,466	−7,405
Delaware	7,961	6,137	4,568	0.57	0.74	1,569	3,393	1,824
District of Columbia	9,674	3,489	1,733	0.18	0.50	1,756	7,941	6,185
Florida	71,524	67,131	55,704	0.78	0.83	11,427	15,820	4,393
Georgia	48,301	46,811	38,786	0.80	0.83	8,025	9,515	1,490
Hawaii	7,804	8,932	6,906	0.88	0.77	2,026	898	−1,128
Idaho	9,891	7,444	5,836	0.59	0.78	1,608	4,055	2,447
Illinois	123,073	132,931	113,039	0.92	0.85	19,892	10,034	−9,858
Indiana	50,414	42,834	37,814	0.75	0.88	5,020	12,600	7,580
Iowa	37,243	35,066	30,818	0.83	0.88	4,248	6,425	2,177
Kansas	26,274	24,082	21,557	0.82	0.90	2,525	4,717	2,192
Kentucky	34,702	33,582	30,387	0.88	0.90	3,195	4,315	1,120
Louisiana	29,191	27,899	24,327	0.83	0.87	3,572	4,864	1,292
Maine	9,209	9,370	6,546	0.71	0.70	2,824	2,663	−161
Maryland	39,595	43,935	32,819	0.83	0.75	11,116	6,776	−4,340
Massachusetts	72,194	61,761	48,798	0.68	0.79	12,963	23,396	10,433
Michigan	98,891	92,227	83,888	0.85	0.91	8,339	15,003	6,664
Minnesota	46,743	45,814	37,617	0.80	0.82	8,197	9,126	929
Mississippi	28,396	26,771	24,699	0.87	0.92	2,072	3,697	1,625
Missouri	38,393	35,603	30,156	0.79	0.85	5,447	8,237	2,790
Montana	5,533	6,536	4,738	0.86	0.72	1,798	795	−1,003
Nebraska	17,496	17,670	15,082	0.86	0.85	2,588	2,414	−174
Nevada	9,167	9,459	8,128	0.89	0.86	1,331	1,039	−292
New Hampshire	11,470	9,612	5,610	0.49	0.58	4,002	5,860	1,858
New Jersey	44,323	65,328	38,088	0.86	0.58	27,240	6,235	−21,005
New Mexico	11,503	11,793	9,704	0.84	0.82	2,089	1,799	−290
New York	178,311	142,764	114,131	0.64	0.80	28,633	64,180	35,547
North Carolina	63,403	54,974	51,422	0.81	0.94	3,552	11,981	8,429
North Dakota	9,049	7,603	6,384	0.71	0.84	1,219	2,665	1,446
Ohio	90,960	90,017	78,335	0.86	0.87	11,682	12,625	943
Oklahoma	27,708	28,190	25,309	0.91	0.90	2,881	2,399	−482
Oregon	38,911	34,677	31,815	0.82	0.92	2,862	7,096	4,234
Pennsylvania	99,050	92,302	76,073	0.77	0.82	16,229	22,977	6,748
Rhode Island	12,890	8,092	5,693	0.44	0.70	2,399	7,197	4,798
South Carolina	30,412	27,424	24,307	0.80	0.89	3,117	6,105	2,988
South Dakota	6,124	6,063	4,385	0.72	0.72	1,678	1,739	61
Tennessee	35,574	33,022	27,952	0.79	0.85	5,070	7,622	2,552
Texas	159,608	155,522	147,079	0.92	0.95	8,443	12,529	4,086
Utah	18,699	13,372	12,014	0.64	0.90	1,358	6,685	5,327
Vermont	6,832	4,654	2,950	0.43	0.63	1,704	3,882	2,178
Virginia	49,019	42,843	33,298	0.68	0.78	9,545	15,721	6,176
Washington	71,759	69,114	63,877	0.89	0.92	5,237	7,882	2,645
West Virginia	17,009	14,106	12,051	0.71	0.85	2,055	4,958	2,903
Wisconsin	54,253	51,656	45,634	0.84	0.88	6,022	8,619	2,597
Wyoming	5,389	5,134	4,147	0.77	0.81	987	1,242	255
State unknown [6]	—	130,193	—	—	—	130,193	—	−130,193

[1] Includes students who are enrolled at the reporting institution for the first time at the undergraduate level.

[2] "Students enrolled in State" are all of the new students reported by the institutions in that State; i.e., all inmigrants and "remaining" students.

[3] "Student residents of State" are all students from a State in which they were residing when first admitted to an institution in any State at the current student level.

[4] "Students remaining in State" are students who attend institutions in their home State.

[5] Net migration is overestimated because students who are not identified by State are not counted as out migrants from their appropriate States.

[6] Students are reported in "State unknown" when an institution is unable to determine the student's home State.

—Not applicable.

NOTE.—Data for U.S. Service Schools are included in State totals. Excludes students from foreign countries and the outlying areas.

SOURCE: U.S. Department of Education, National Center for Education Statistics, Integrated Postsecondary Education Data System (IPEDS), "Residence of First-Time Students" survey, 1988. (This table was prepared May 1990.)

Table 192.—Residence and migration of all freshmen students [1] graduating from high school in the past 12 months, by State: Fall 1988

| State or other area | Students enrolled in State [2] | Student residents of State [3] | Students remaining in State [4] | Ratio of students remaining to— | | Migration of students | | |
				Students enrolled	Student residents	Out of	Into	Net (column 8– column 7) [5]
1	2	3	4	5	6	7	8	9
United States	1,328,604	1,328,604	1,094,671	0.82	0.82	233,933	233,933	0
Alabama	26,404	22,620	20,640	0.78	0.91	1,980	5,764	3,784
Alaska	541	1,619	477	0.88	0.29	1,142	64	−1,078
Arizona	19,759	17,482	15,977	0.81	0.91	1,505	3,782	2,277
Arkansas	12,431	11,932	10,253	0.82	0.86	1,679	2,178	499
California	158,585	158,936	150,381	0.95	0.95	8,555	8,204	−351
Colorado	17,728	16,720	12,515	0.71	0.75	4,205	5,213	1,008
Connecticut	14,888	19,832	9,922	0.67	0.50	9,910	4,966	−4,944
Delaware	5,065	3,163	1,969	0.39	0.62	1,194	3,096	1,902
District of Columbia	5,116	1,708	460	0.09	0.27	1,248	4,656	3,408
Florida	42,186	42,216	33,811	0.80	0.80	8,405	8,375	−30
Georgia	31,567	31,765	25,943	0.82	0.82	5,822	5,624	−198
Hawaii	4,872	5,960	4,521	0.93	0.76	1,439	351	−1,088
Idaho	5,785	4,105	3,134	0.54	0.76	971	2,651	1,680
Illinois	62,927	73,211	57,326	0.91	0.78	15,885	5,601	−10,284
Indiana	37,165	30,905	27,396	0.74	0.89	3,509	9,769	6,260
Iowa	24,230	22,303	19,021	0.79	0.85	3,282	5,209	1,927
Kansas	16,893	15,157	13,407	0.79	0.88	1,750	3,486	1,736
Kentucky	24,610	23,007	20,903	0.85	0.91	2,104	3,707	1,603
Louisiana	20,935	19,674	17,216	0.82	0.88	2,458	3,719	1,261
Maine	2,499	3,446	1,396	0.56	0.41	2,050	1,103	−947
Maryland	20,526	24,851	16,223	0.79	0.65	8,628	4,303	−4,325
Massachusetts	45,167	36,562	27,577	0.61	0.75	8,985	17,590	8,605
Michigan	55,236	57,751	52,045	0.94	0.90	5,706	3,191	−2,515
Minnesota	27,778	29,155	22,320	0.80	0.77	6,835	5,458	−1,377
Mississippi	15,329	15,119	13,541	0.88	0.90	1,578	1,788	210
Missouri	26,252	25,501	21,351	0.81	0.84	4,150	4,901	751
Montana	2,728	3,548	2,376	0.87	0.67	1,172	352	−820
Nebraska	12,051	12,286	10,244	0.85	0.83	2,042	1,807	−235
Nevada	3,829	4,091	3,245	0.85	0.79	846	584	−262
New Hampshire	7,140	5,422	3,049	0.43	0.56	2,373	4,091	1,718
New Jersey	19,441	39,020	17,562	0.90	0.45	21,458	1,879	−19,579
New Mexico	6,659	6,975	5,479	0.82	0.79	1,496	1,180	−316
New York	80,029	88,315	67,203	0.84	0.76	21,112	12,826	−8,286
North Carolina	44,682	37,408	34,974	0.78	0.93	2,434	9,708	7,274
North Dakota	6,681	5,121	4,540	0.68	0.89	581	2,141	1,560
Ohio	57,363	57,550	48,692	0.85	0.85	8,858	8,671	−187
Oklahoma	11,991	12,017	10,033	0.84	0.83	1,984	1,958	−26
Oregon	16,293	15,575	13,533	0.83	0.87	2,042	2,760	718
Pennsylvania	68,391	64,002	51,724	0.76	0.81	12,278	16,667	4,389
Rhode Island	5,267	4,765	3,003	0.57	0.63	1,762	2,264	502
South Carolina	19,605	18,175	15,743	0.80	0.87	2,432	3,862	1,430
South Dakota	3,622	3,714	2,565	0.71	0.69	1,149	1,057	−92
Tennessee	25,883	24,358	20,433	0.79	0.84	3,925	5,450	1,525
Texas	89,534	89,966	83,741	0.94	0.93	6,225	5,793	−432
Utah	6,077	6,119	5,235	0.86	0.86	884	842	−42
Vermont	4,906	3,624	2,416	0.49	0.67	1,208	2,490	1,282
Virginia	34,972	33,536	26,051	0.74	0.78	7,485	8,921	1,436
Washington	25,624	26,525	23,260	0.91	0.88	3,265	2,364	−901
West Virginia	12,224	9,620	8,161	0.67	0.85	1,459	4,063	2,604
Wisconsin	35,977	33,967	29,326	0.82	0.86	4,641	6,651	2,010
Wyoming	3,161	2,955	2,358	0.75	0.80	597	803	206
State unknown [6]	—	5,250	—	—	—	5,250	—	−5,250

[1] Freshmen students who are enrolled at the reporting institution for the first time.

[2] "Students enrolled in State" are all of the new students reported by the institutions in that State; i.e., all inmigrants and "remaining" students.

[3] "Student residents of State" are all students from a State in which they were residing when first admitted to an institution in any State at the current student level.

[4] "Students remaining in State" are students who attend institutions in their home State.

[5] Net migration is overestimated because students who are not identified by State are not counted as out migrants from their appropriate States.

[6] Students are reported in "State unknown" when an institution is unable to determine the student's home State.

—Not applicable.

NOTE.—Data for U.S. Service Schools are included in State totals. Excludes students from foreign countries and the outlying areas.

SOURCE: U.S. Department of Education, National Center for Education Statistics, Integrated Postsecondary Education Data System (IPEDS), "Residence of First-Time Students" survey, 1988. (This table was prepared May 1990.)

Table 193.—Residence and migration of all freshmen students [1] in 4-year colleges graduating from high school in the past 12 months, by State: Fall 1988

State or other area	Students enrolled in State [2]	Student residents of State [3]	Students remaining in State [4]	Ratio of students remaining to—		Migration of students		
				Students enrolled	Student residents	Out of	Into	Net (column 8– column 7) [5]
1	2	3	4	5	6	7	8	9
United States	865,384	865,384	654,055	0.76	0.76	211,329	211,329	0
Alabama	16,298	12,842	11,089	0.68	0.86	1,753	5,209	3,456
Alaska	520	1,447	469	0.90	0.32	978	51	−927
Arizona	6,647	5,339	4,072	0.61	0.76	1,267	2,575	1,308
Arkansas	10,325	9,559	8,335	0.81	0.87	1,224	1,990	766
California	56,785	59,562	51,787	0.91	0.87	7,775	4,998	−2,777
Colorado	15,619	14,103	10,488	0.67	0.74	3,615	5,131	1,516
Connecticut	10,439	14,624	5,743	0.55	0.39	8,881	4,696	−4,185
Delaware	5,065	3,097	1,969	0.39	0.64	1,128	3,096	1,968
District of Columbia	5,116	1,624	460	0.09	0.28	1,164	4,656	3,492
Florida	21,163	22,042	14,341	0.68	0.65	7,701	6,822	−879
Georgia	24,357	24,299	19,007	0.78	0.78	5,292	5,350	58
Hawaii	2,494	3,463	2,162	0.87	0.62	1,301	332	−969
Idaho	2,421	2,717	1,860	0.77	0.68	857	561	−296
Illinois	35,981	45,698	30,590	0.85	0.67	15,108	5,391	−9,717
Indiana	33,375	26,857	23,809	0.71	0.89	3,048	9,566	6,518
Iowa	15,176	13,561	10,530	0.69	0.78	3,031	4,646	1,615
Kansas	11,241	10,226	8,622	0.77	0.84	1,604	2,619	1,015
Kentucky	15,837	14,279	12,355	0.78	0.87	1,924	3,482	1,558
Louisiana	19,697	17,914	15,989	0.81	0.89	1,925	3,708	1,783
Maine	1,707	2,499	641	0.38	0.26	1,858	1,066	−792
Maryland	10,574	14,993	6,612	0.63	0.44	8,381	3,962	−4,419
Massachusetts	35,195	27,264	18,738	0.53	0.69	8,526	16,457	7,931
Michigan	34,935	37,332	32,041	0.92	0.86	5,291	2,894	−2,397
Minnesota	20,224	21,584	15,190	0.75	0.70	6,394	5,034	−1,360
Mississippi	3,943	4,166	2,758	0.70	0.66	1,408	1,185	−223
Missouri	21,704	20,969	17,202	0.79	0.82	3,767	4,502	735
Montana	2,407	2,946	2,071	0.86	0.70	875	336	−539
Nebraska	9,690	9,828	8,060	0.83	0.82	1,768	1,630	−138
Nevada	3,244	3,288	2,676	0.82	0.81	612	568	−44
New Hampshire	6,106	4,237	2,182	0.36	0.51	2,055	3,924	1,869
New Jersey	9,036	27,980	7,309	0.81	0.26	20,671	1,727	−18,944
New Mexico	4,875	5,282	4,029	0.83	0.76	1,253	846	−407
New York	54,334	62,237	42,107	0.77	0.68	20,130	12,227	−7,903
North Carolina	31,745	24,988	22,754	0.72	0.91	2,234	8,991	6,757
North Dakota	5,114	3,718	3,249	0.64	0.87	469	1,865	1,396
Ohio	47,901	47,678	39,406	0.82	0.83	8,272	8,495	223
Oklahoma	9,407	9,260	7,643	0.81	0.83	1,617	1,764	147
Oregon	9,726	8,966	7,208	0.74	0.80	1,758	2,518	760
Pennsylvania	55,681	51,482	39,963	0.72	0.78	11,519	15,718	4,199
Rhode Island	3,734	3,184	1,571	0.42	0.49	1,613	2,163	550
South Carolina	13,761	12,386	10,127	0.74	0.82	2,259	3,634	1,375
South Dakota	3,608	3,525	2,551	0.71	0.72	974	1,057	83
Tennessee	20,088	18,447	14,774	0.74	0.80	3,673	5,314	1,641
Texas	52,244	53,406	47,676	0.91	0.89	5,730	4,568	−1,162
Utah	3,779	3,482	3,108	0.82	0.89	374	671	297
Vermont	3,663	2,534	1,504	0.41	0.59	1,030	2,159	1,129
Virginia	27,157	25,522	18,595	0.68	0.73	6,927	8,562	1,635
Washington	11,628	12,528	9,831	0.85	0.78	2,697	1,797	−900
West Virginia	10,776	8,216	6,956	0.65	0.85	1,260	3,820	2,560
Wisconsin	27,358	25,116	20,824	0.76	0.83	4,292	6,534	2,242
Wyoming	1,484	1,451	1,022	0.69	0.70	429	462	33
State unknown [6]	—	1,637	—	—	—	1,637	—	−1,637

[1] Freshmen students who are enrolled at the reporting institution for the first time.

[2] "Students enrolled in State" are all of the new students reported by the institutions in that State; i.e., all inmigrants and "remaining" students.

[3] "Student residents of State" are all students from a State in which they were residing when first admitted to an institution in any State at the current student level.

[4] "Students remaining in State" are students who attend institutions in their home State.

[5] Net migration is overestimated because students who are not identified by State are not counted as out migrants from their appropriate States.

[6] Students are reported in "State unknown" when an institution is unable to determine the student's home State.

—Not applicable.

NOTE.—Data for U.S. Service Schools are included in State totals. Excludes students from foreign countries and the outlying areas.

SOURCE: U.S. Department of Education, National Center for Education Statistics, Integrated Postsecondary Education Data System (IPEDS), "Residence of First-Time Students" survey, 1988. (This table was prepared May 1990.)

Table 194.—Total enrollment in institutions of higher education, by type and control of institution and race/ethnicity of student: Fall 1976 to fall 1988

Type and control of institution and race/ethnicity of student	Number, in thousands							Percent distribution by type and control [1]					
	1976	1978	1980	1982	1984	1986	1988	1976	1980	1982	1984	1986	1988
1	2	3	4	5	6	7	8	9	10	11	12	13	14
All students													
Total	10,985.6	11,231.2	12,086.8	12,387.9	12,233.0	12,503.5	13,043.1	100.0	100.0	100.0	100.0	100.0	100.0
White, non-Hispanic	9,076.1	9,194.0	9,833.0	9,997.1	9,814.7	9,920.6	10,283.2	84.3	83.5	82.9	82.5	81.6	81.1
Total minority	1,690.8	1,784.6	1,948.8	2,059.5	2,083.8	2,238.2	2,398.8	15.7	16.5	17.1	17.5	18.4	18.9
Black, non-Hispanic	1,033.0	1,054.4	1,106.8	1,101.5	1,075.8	1,082.3	1,129.6	9.6	9.4	9.1	9.0	8.9	8.9
Hispanic	383.8	417.3	471.7	519.3	534.9	618.0	680.0	3.6	4.0	4.3	4.5	5.1	5.4
Asian or Pacific Islander	197.9	235.1	286.4	351.0	389.5	447.8	496.7	1.8	2.4	2.9	3.3	3.7	3.9
American Indian/Alaskan Native	76.1	77.9	83.9	87.7	83.6	90.1	92.5	0.7	0.7	0.7	0.7	0.7	0.7
Nonresident alien	218.7	252.6	305.0	331.3	334.6	344.7	361.2	—	—	—	—	—	—
4-year													
Total	7,106.5	7,202.4	7,565.4	7,648.0	7,706.1	7,824.0	8,175.0	100.0	100.0	100.0	100.0	100.0	100.0
White, non-Hispanic	5,999.0	6,027.1	6,274.5	6,305.6	6,300.4	6,337.0	6,581.6	86.6	85.7	85.5	84.9	84.1	83.6
Total minority	931.0	974.7	1,049.9	1,072.7	1,123.6	1,194.9	1,291.8	13.4	14.3	14.5	15.1	15.9	16.4
Black, non-Hispanic	603.7	611.8	634.3	612.3	617.0	615.1	656.3	8.7	8.7	8.3	8.3	8.2	8.3
Hispanic	173.6	190.4	216.6	228.7	246.1	278.4	296.0	2.5	3.0	3.1	3.3	3.7	3.8
Asian or Pacific Islander	118.7	137.8	162.1	193.1	222.4	261.8	297.4	1.7	2.2	2.6	3.0	3.5	3.8
American Indian/Alaskan Native	35.0	34.8	36.9	38.6	38.1	39.6	42.1	0.5	0.5	0.5	0.5	0.5	0.5
Nonresident alien	176.5	200.5	240.9	269.8	282.1	292.1	301.5	—	—	—	—	—	—
Public	4,892.9	4,896.1	5,127.6	5,175.5	5,196.0	5,300.2	5,544.0	69.1	68.0	68.0	67.7	68.0	68.1
White, non-Hispanic	4,120.2	4,085.1	4,243.0	4,257.9	4,229.9	4,275.1	4,454.8	59.5	57.9	57.7	57.0	56.8	56.6
Total minority	666.7	691.4	740.8	756.1	795.9	849.6	907.7	9.6	10.1	10.2	10.7	11.3	11.5
Black, non-Hispanic	421.8	424.9	438.2	420.7	426.7	423.7	448.5	6.1	6.0	5.7	5.7	5.6	5.7
Hispanic	129.3	140.2	156.4	164.1	178.8	205.9	215.8	1.9	2.1	2.2	2.4	2.7	2.7
Asian or Pacific Islander	87.5	99.1	117.2	140.3	160.3	188.2	210.2	1.3	1.6	1.9	2.2	2.5	2.7
American Indian/Alaskan Native	28.2	27.2	29.0	30.9	30.1	31.7	33.3	0.4	0.4	0.4	0.4	0.4	0.4
Nonresident alien	106.0	119.5	143.8	161.4	170.1	175.5	181.4	—	—	—	—	—	—
Private	2,213.6	2,306.3	2,437.8	2,472.6	2,510.2	2,523.8	2,631.0	30.9	32.0	32.0	32.3	32.0	31.9
White, non-Hispanic	1,878.8	1,942.0	2,031.5	2,047.7	2,070.5	2,061.9	2,126.8	27.1	27.7	27.8	27.9	27.4	27.0
Total minority	264.3	283.3	309.2	316.6	327.7	345.3	384.1	3.8	4.2	4.3	4.4	4.6	4.9
Black, non-Hispanic	182.0	186.9	196.1	191.6	190.4	191.4	207.8	2.6	2.7	2.6	2.6	2.5	2.6
Hispanic	44.3	50.1	60.2	64.5	67.3	72.6	80.2	0.6	0.8	0.9	0.9	1.0	1.0
Asian or Pacific Islander	31.2	38.7	44.9	52.8	62.1	73.5	87.2	0.5	0.6	0.7	0.8	1.0	1.1
American Indian/Alaskan Native	6.8	7.6	7.9	7.6	7.9	7.8	8.8	0.1	0.1	0.1	0.1	0.1	0.1
Nonresident alien	70.5	81.0	97.1	108.4	112.0	116.6	120.1	—	—	—	—	—	—
2-year													
Total	3,879.1	4,028.8	4,521.4	4,739.8	4,526.9	4,679.5	4,868.1	100.0	100.0	100.0	100.0	100.0	100.0
White, non-Hispanic	3,077.1	3,166.9	3,558.5	3,691.5	3,514.3	3,583.6	3,701.5	80.2	79.8	78.9	78.5	77.5	77.0
Total minority	759.8	809.9	898.9	986.8	960.1	1,043.4	1,106.9	19.8	20.2	21.1	21.5	22.5	23.0
Black, non-Hispanic	429.3	442.6	472.5	489.2	458.7	467.2	473.3	11.2	10.6	10.5	10.3	10.1	9.8
Hispanic	210.2	226.9	255.1	290.6	288.8	339.6	383.9	5.5	5.7	6.2	6.5	7.3	8.0
Asian or Pacific Islander	79.2	97.2	124.3	157.9	167.1	186.0	199.3	2.1	2.8	3.4	3.7	4.0	4.1
American Indian/Alaskan Native	41.2	43.1	47.0	49.1	45.5	50.5	50.4	1.1	1.1	1.1	1.0	1.1	1.0
Nonresident alien	42.2	52.0	64.1	61.5	52.5	52.6	59.6	—	—	—	—	—	—
Public	3,748.1	3,873.7	4,328.8	4,519.7	4,260.4	4,413.7	4,612.4	96.7	95.8	95.4	94.1	94.3	94.7
White, non-Hispanic	2,974.3	3,051.0	3,413.1	3,526.8	3,312.5	3,378.8	3,509.0	77.5	76.6	75.4	74.0	73.0	73.0
Total minority	734.5	774.5	855.4	935.6	899.0	986.0	1,047.0	19.1	19.2	20.0	20.1	21.3	21.8
Black, non-Hispanic	409.5	414.6	437.9	452.4	417.3	430.1	432.6	10.7	9.8	9.7	9.3	9.3	9.0
Hispanic	207.5	222.3	249.8	281.5	277.3	326.0	371.1	5.4	5.6	6.0	6.2	7.0	7.7
Asian or Pacific Islander	78.2	96.3	122.5	155.3	162.4	182.5	195.5	2.0	2.7	3.3	3.6	3.9	4.1
American Indian/Alaskan Native	39.3	41.3	45.2	46.4	42.0	47.4	47.8	1.0	1.0	1.0	0.9	1.0	1.0
Nonresident alien	39.2	48.2	60.3	57.2	48.9	48.9	56.4	—	—	—	—	—	—
Private	131.0	155.1	192.6	220.2	266.4	265.9	255.7	3.3	4.2	4.6	5.9	5.7	5.3
White, non-Hispanic	102.8	115.9	145.4	164.8	201.8	204.8	192.6	2.7	3.3	3.5	4.5	4.4	4.0
Total minority	25.3	35.4	43.5	51.1	61.2	57.3	60.0	0.7	1.0	1.1	1.4	1.2	1.2
Black, non-Hispanic	19.8	28.0	34.6	36.8	41.4	37.1	40.7	0.5	0.8	0.8	0.9	0.8	0.8
Hispanic	2.6	4.6	5.3	9.1	11.6	13.6	12.9	0.1	0.1	0.2	0.3	0.3	0.3
Asian or Pacific Islander	0.9	0.9	1.8	2.6	4.7	3.5	3.8	(2)	(2)	0.1	0.1	0.1	0.1
American Indian/Alaskan Native	1.8	1.9	1.8	2.7	3.5	3.1	2.7	(2)	(2)	0.1	0.1	0.1	0.1
Nonresident alien	3.0	3.8	3.7	4.3	3.5	3.7	3.2	—	—	—	—	—	—

[1] Distribution for U.S. citizens only.
[2] Less than .05 percent.
—Not applicable.

NOTE.—Because of underreporting and nonreporting of racial/ethnic data, figures are slightly lower than corresponding data in other tables. Because of rounding, details may not add to totals.

SOURCE: U.S. Department of Education, National Center for Education Statistics, "Fall Enrollment in Colleges and Universities"; and Integrated Postsecondary Education Data System (IPEDS), "Fall Enrollment" surveys. (This table was prepared February 1990.)

Table 195.—Total enrollment in institutions of higher education, by level of study and race/ethnicity of student: Fall 1976 to fall 1988

Level of study, sex, and race/ethnicity of student	Number, in thousands							Percent distribution by level of study [1]					
	1976	1978	1980	1982	1984	1986	1988	1976	1980	1982	1984	1986	1988
1	2	3	4	5	6	7	8	9	10	11	12	13	14
All students													
Men	5,794.4	5,621.5	5,868.1	5,999.2	5,858.3	5,884.5	5,998.2	52.4	48.0	47.8	47.3	46.5	45.4
White, non-Hispanic	4,813.7	4,613.1	4,772.9	4,830.4	4,689.9	4,647.1	4,711.6	44.7	40.5	40.1	39.4	38.2	37.2
Total minority	826.6	828.9	884.4	938.6	937.9	1,004.7	1,051.3	7.7	7.5	7.8	7.9	8.3	8.3
Black, non-Hispanic	469.9	453.3	463.7	457.9	436.8	436.1	442.7	4.4	3.9	3.8	3.7	3.6	3.5
Hispanic	209.7	212.5	231.6	251.8	253.8	290.1	310.3	1.9	2.0	2.1	2.1	2.4	2.4
Asian or Pacific Islander	108.4	126.3	151.3	189.0	210.0	239.1	259.2	1.0	1.3	1.6	1.8	2.0	2.0
American Indian/Alaskan Native	38.5	36.8	37.8	39.9	37.4	39.4	39.1	0.4	0.3	0.3	0.3	0.3	0.3
Nonresident alien	154.1	179.5	210.8	230.3	230.4	232.7	235.3	—	—	—	—	—	—
Women	5,191.2	5,609.6	6,218.7	6,388.6	6,374.7	6,619.0	7,044.9	47.6	52.0	52.2	52.7	53.5	54.6
White, non-Hispanic	4,262.4	4,580.9	5,060.1	5,166.7	5,124.7	5,273.5	5,571.6	39.6	42.9	42.9	43.1	43.4	43.9
Total minority	864.2	955.7	1,064.4	1,120.9	1,145.8	1,233.5	1,347.4	8.0	9.0	9.3	9.6	10.1	10.6
Black, non-Hispanic	563.1	601.1	643.0	643.6	639.0	646.2	686.9	5.2	5.5	5.3	5.4	5.3	5.4
Hispanic	174.1	204.7	240.1	267.5	281.2	327.9	369.6	1.6	2.0	2.2	2.4	2.7	2.9
Asian or Pacific Islander	89.4	108.7	135.2	162.0	179.5	208.7	237.5	0.8	1.1	1.3	1.5	1.7	1.9
American Indian/Alaskan Native	37.6	41.0	46.1	47.8	46.1	50.6	53.4	0.3	0.4	0.4	0.4	0.4	0.4
Nonresident alien	64.6	73.1	94.2	101.0	104.1	112.0	125.9	—	—	—	—	—	—
Undergraduate													
Total	9,419.0	9,665.8	10,469.1	10,788.7	10,610.8	10,798.0	11,304.2	100.0	100.0	100.0	100.0	100.0	100.0
White, non-Hispanic	7,740.5	7,870.6	8,480.7	8,676.1	8,484.0	8,557.6	8,906.7	83.4	82.7	82.1	81.6	80.8	80.2
Total minority	1,535.3	1,625.1	1,778.5	1,889.3	1,911.0	2,035.9	2,192.4	16.6	17.3	17.9	18.4	19.2	19.8
Black, non-Hispanic	943.4	966.5	1,018.8	1,019.7	994.9	996.2	1,038.0	10.2	9.9	9.7	9.6	9.4	9.4
Hispanic	352.9	384.0	433.1	480.1	495.2	563.2	631.2	3.8	4.2	4.5	4.8	5.3	5.7
Asian or Pacific Islander	169.3	202.8	248.7	308.2	343.0	393.0	436.6	1.8	2.4	2.9	3.3	3.7	3.9
American Indian/Alaskan Native	69.7	71.9	77.9	81.3	77.8	83.5	85.9	0.8	0.8	0.8	0.7	0.8	0.8
Nonresident alien	143.2	170.1	209.9	223.2	215.8	204.5	205.0	—	—	—	—	—	—
Women	4,522.1	4,915.0	5,471.7	5,649.0	5,608.4	5,780.5	6,170.4	48.2	52.7	52.8	53.2	53.9	54.9
White, non-Hispanic	3,688.3	3,986.8	4,425.8	4,542.2	4,478.9	4,579.8	4,852.9	39.8	43.1	43.0	43.1	43.2	43.7
Total minority	787.0	874.5	975.8	1,032.8	1,056.0	1,126.3	1,236.5	8.5	9.5	9.8	10.2	10.6	11.1
Black, non-Hispanic	512.7	550.2	590.6	595.0	590.2	593.7	630.6	5.5	5.8	5.6	5.7	5.6	5.7
Hispanic	161.2	189.8	221.8	248.1	261.3	299.2	344.0	1.7	2.2	2.3	2.5	2.8	3.1
Asian or Pacific Islander	78.2	96.1	120.2	145.1	161.4	186.4	212.2	0.8	1.2	1.4	1.6	1.8	1.9
American Indian/Alaskan Native	34.9	38.4	43.1	44.6	43.2	47.0	49.7	0.4	0.4	0.4	0.4	0.4	0.4
Nonresident alien	46.8	53.7	70.1	74.0	73.5	74.4	81.1	—	—	—	—	—	—
Graduate													
Total	1,322.5	1,310.4	1,340.9	1,320.8	1,343.7	1,435.1	1,471.9	100.0	100.0	100.0	100.0	100.0	100.0
White, non-Hispanic	1,115.6	1,094.1	1,104.7	1,074.7	1,087.3	1,132.5	1,153.2	89.2	88.5	88.4	88.5	87.2	87.3
Total minority	134.5	136.8	144.0	141.1	141.1	166.6	167.2	10.8	11.5	11.6	11.5	12.8	12.7
Black, non-Hispanic	78.5	76.4	75.1	68.9	67.4	72.0	76.5	6.3	6.0	5.7	5.5	5.5	5.8
Hispanic	26.4	28.0	32.1	31.7	31.7	45.8	39.5	2.1	2.6	2.6	2.6	3.5	3.0
Asian or Pacific Islander	24.5	27.5	31.6	35.0	37.1	43.4	45.7	2.0	2.5	2.9	3.0	3.3	3.5
American Indian/Alaskan Native	5.1	4.9	5.2	5.4	4.8	5.5	5.6	0.4	0.4	0.4	0.4	0.4	0.4
Nonresident alien	72.4	79.5	92.2	105.0	115.3	136.0	151.4	—	—	—	—	—	—
Women	614.6	630.2	668.7	652.4	672.6	742.0	774.1	47.8	51.7	51.5	52.3	54.3	55.3
White, non-Hispanic	526.5	537.9	566.2	549.2	566.0	613.3	636.8	42.1	45.3	45.2	46.1	47.2	48.2
Total minority	70.8	73.5	79.0	76.9	76.9	92.2	93.9	5.7	6.3	6.3	6.3	7.1	7.1
Black, non-Hispanic	46.5	46.5	46.9	42.8	42.5	45.8	49.1	3.7	3.8	3.5	3.5	3.5	3.7
Hispanic	11.8	13.5	16.4	17.0	17.1	25.3	22.0	0.9	1.3	1.4	1.4	1.9	1.7
Asian or Pacific Islander	10.1	11.1	13.0	14.2	14.7	17.9	19.5	0.8	1.0	1.2	1.2	1.4	1.5
American Indian/Alaskan Native	2.4	2.4	2.7	2.9	2.6	3.2	3.3	0.2	0.2	0.2	0.2	0.2	0.2
Nonresident alien	17.3	18.7	23.5	26.3	29.7	36.5	43.4	—	—	—	—	—	—
First-professional													
Total	244.1	255.0	276.8	278.3	278.5	270.4	267.1	100.0	100.0	100.0	100.0	100.0	100.0
White, non-Hispanic	220.0	229.3	247.7	246.2	243.4	230.5	223.2	91.3	90.4	89.5	88.5	86.6	85.1
Total minority	21.1	22.6	26.3	29.0	31.7	35.7	39.1	8.7	9.6	10.5	11.5	13.4	14.9
Black, non-Hispanic	11.2	11.4	12.8	12.9	13.4	14.1	14.3	4.6	4.7	4.7	4.9	5.3	5.5
Hispanic	4.5	5.4	6.5	7.4	8.0	9.1	9.3	1.9	2.4	2.7	2.9	3.4	3.6
Asian or Pacific Islander	4.1	4.8	6.1	7.7	9.3	11.4	14.4	1.7	2.2	2.8	3.4	4.3	5.5
American Indian/Alaskan Native	1.3	1.1	0.8	0.9	1.0	1.1	1.1	0.5	0.3	0.3	0.4	0.4	0.4
Nonresident alien	3.1	3.0	2.9	3.1	3.4	4.1	4.7	—	—	—	—	—	—
Women	54.5	64.5	78.4	87.2	93.6	96.6	100.4	22.4	28.4	31.4	33.7	35.8	37.7
White, non-Hispanic	47.6	56.3	68.1	75.3	79.8	80.4	82.0	19.7	24.9	27.4	29.0	30.2	31.2
Total minority	6.4	7.6	9.6	11.2	12.9	15.0	17.1	2.6	3.5	4.1	4.7	5.6	6.5
Black, non-Hispanic	3.9	4.4	5.5	5.7	6.3	6.8	7.2	1.6	2.0	2.1	2.3	2.5	2.7
Hispanic	1.0	1.4	1.9	2.4	2.8	3.4	3.6	0.4	0.7	0.9	1.0	1.3	1.4
Asian or Pacific Islander	1.1	1.5	2.0	2.7	3.5	4.4	5.8	0.5	0.7	1.0	1.3	1.6	2.2
American Indian/Alaskan Native	0.2	0.3	0.3	0.3	0.4	0.5	0.5	0.1	0.1	0.1	0.1	0.2	0.2
Nonresident alien	0.5	0.6	0.6	0.8	0.9	1.1	1.4	—	—	—	—	—	—

[1] Distribution for U.S. citizens only.

—Not applicable.

NOTE.—Because of underreporting and nonreporting of racial/ethnic data, figures are slightly lower than corresponding data in other tables. Because of rounding, details may not add to totals.

SOURCE: U.S. Department of Education, National Center for Education Statistics, "Fall Enrollment in Colleges and Universities"; and Integrated Postsecondary Education Data System (IPEDS), "Fall Enrollment, 1986" survey and unpublished tabulations. (This table was prepared February 1990.)

Table 196.—Total enrollment in institutions of higher education, by race/ethnicity of student and by State: Fall 1988

State or other area	Total	White non-Hispanic	Minority enrollment, by race/ethnicity						Nonresident alien
			Total	Percent minority [1]	Black, non-Hispanic	Hispanic	Asian/Pacific Islander	American Indian/Alaskan Native	
1	2	3	4	5	6	7	8	9	10
United States	13,043,118	10,283,176	2,398,764	18.9	1,129,580	679,962	496,688	92,534	361,178
Alabama	199,813	153,884	42,133	21.5	38,978	1,121	1,596	438	3,796
Alaska	28,361	23,613	4,587	16.3	1,048	522	784	2,233	161
Arizona	257,786	203,748	46,986	18.7	7,263	26,082	5,340	8,301	7,052
Arkansas	84,550	70,180	12,775	15.4	11,361	366	668	380	1,595
California	1,753,564	1,131,731	556,314	33.0	114,388	215,397	205,929	20,600	65,519
Colorado	186,288	157,982	24,234	13.3	5,078	13,452	4,050	1,654	4,072
Connecticut	165,677	143,934	17,680	10.9	8,930	4,824	3,528	398	4,063
Delaware	38,260	32,315	5,282	14.0	4,313	356	545	68	663
District of Columbia	79,089	41,348	28,668	40.9	23,926	2,114	2,494	134	9,073
Florida	515,590	386,687	113,749	22.7	48,396	54,513	9,331	1,509	15,154
Georgia	230,762	176,235	49,030	21.8	43,029	2,336	3,237	428	5,497
Hawaii	52,297	15,700	33,003	67.8	957	844	31,008	194	3,594
Idaho	45,717	42,695	1,847	4.1	280	653	541	373	1,175
Illinois	688,974	521,510	153,644	22.8	83,090	40,784	27,798	1,972	13,820
Indiana	267,902	239,057	22,342	8.5	14,723	3,686	3,329	604	6,503
Iowa	161,174	147,933	7,426	4.8	3,511	1,402	2,056	457	5,815
Kansas	152,847	134,878	13,125	8.9	6,300	2,910	2,089	1,826	4,844
Kentucky	159,868	146,703	11,484	7.3	9,296	683	1,078	427	1,681
Louisiana	176,031	123,362	47,627	27.9	41,213	3,283	2,507	624	5,042
Maine	47,903	46,748	893	1.9	263	135	260	235	262
Maryland	249,079	188,900	54,507	22.4	39,530	4,327	9,962	688	5,672
Massachusetts	426,620	362,797	44,293	10.9	17,777	11,628	13,731	1,157	19,530
Michigan	542,580	458,194	70,941	13.4	51,494	7,718	8,607	3,122	13,445
Minnesota	244,706	229,422	10,441	4.4	3,274	1,507	3,929	1,731	4,843
Mississippi	112,872	79,451	31,624	28.5	30,367	316	604	337	1,797
Missouri	261,667	228,721	27,482	10.7	20,110	2,610	3,922	840	5,464
Montana	35,772	32,472	2,613	7.4	141	269	135	2,068	687
Nebraska	104,617	97,630	5,313	5.2	2,520	1,220	948	625	1,674
Nevada	48,832	41,304	6,836	14.2	2,242	2,324	1,603	667	692
New Hampshire	55,334	52,433	1,989	3.7	611	647	541	190	912
New Jersey	302,640	232,047	58,768	20.2	28,831	17,894	11,196	847	11,825
New Mexico	79,450	50,647	27,363	35.1	1,667	20,221	929	4,546	1,440
New York	1,007,411	742,572	229,401	23.6	111,000	70,739	44,043	3,619	35,438
North Carolina	332,521	260,563	67,489	20.6	58,267	2,249	4,353	2,620	4,469
North Dakota	38,293	35,231	2,050	5.5	215	137	212	1,486	1,012
Ohio	541,737	478,222	50,094	9.5	38,130	4,552	6,140	1,272	13,421
Oklahoma	176,307	145,486	25,112	14.7	11,777	2,534	2,787	8,014	5,709
Oregon	156,159	138,077	12,180	8.1	2,013	2,572	6,055	1,540	5,902
Pennsylvania	573,927	504,972	56,055	10.0	38,415	6,139	10,583	918	12,900
Rhode Island	74,839	68,139	5,002	6.8	2,185	1,197	1,402	218	1,698
South Carolina	147,757	113,939	31,634	21.7	29,247	863	1,288	236	2,184
South Dakota	31,460	28,526	2,305	7.5	226	69	122	1,888	629
Tennessee	206,406	170,510	31,792	15.7	28,494	1,166	1,728	404	4,104
Texas	847,192	597,400	227,654	27.6	75,478	125,778	23,642	2,756	22,138
Utah	107,538	97,575	5,186	5.0	619	1,743	1,736	1,088	4,777
Vermont	34,467	32,953	1,016	3.0	277	234	407	98	498
Virginia	321,216	257,686	57,717	18.3	44,164	3,783	9,032	738	5,813
Washington	253,088	219,643	28,270	11.4	6,504	4,830	13,492	3,444	5,175
West Virginia	80,379	75,128	3,907	4.9	2,876	335	577	119	1,344
Wisconsin	285,227	261,147	18,487	6.6	9,060	3,497	4,033	1,897	5,593
Wyoming	26,540	24,668	1,371	5.3	267	646	82	376	501
U.S. Service Schools	44,032	36,478	7,043	16.2	5,459	755	699	130	511
Outlying areas	163,441	630	161,766	99.6	1,867	154,677	5,184	38	1,045
American Samoa	759	0	622	100.0	0	0	607	15	137
Guam	3,819	335	3,060	90.1	26	43	2,976	15	424
Northern Marianas	352	24	270	91.8	0	0	270	0	58
Puerto Rico	154,739	19	154,559	100.0	17	154,536	6	0	161
Trust Territory of the Pacific	1,301	0	1,301	100.0	0	0	1,301	0	0
Virgin Islands	2,471	252	1,954	88.6	1,824	98	24	8	265

[1] Percent minority based on U.S. citizen enrollment (total enrollment less enrollment of nonresident aliens).

NOTE.—Because of adjustments to underreported and nonreported racial/ethnic data, figures are slightly different from corresponding data in other tables.

SOURCE: U.S. Department of Education, National Center for Education Statistics, Integrated Postsecondary Education Data System (IPEDS), "Fall Enrollment, 1988" survey. (This table was prepared March 1990.)

Table 197.—Disabled students enrolled in postsecondary institutions, by type of disability: Fall 1986

Type of disability	Disabled students		Percent of disabled students by condition
	Enrollment	Percent of all students	
1	2	3	4
Disabled students	1,319,229	10.5	—
Specific learning disability	160,878	1.3	12.2
Visual handicap	514,681	4.1	39.0
Hard of hearing	265,484	2.1	20.1
Deafness	80,910	0.6	6.1
Speech disability	62,525	0.5	4.7
Orthopedic handicap	231,491	1.8	17.5
Health impairment	320,272	2.5	24.3

NOTE.—Disabled students are students who reported that they had one or more of the following conditions: a specific learning disability, a visual handicap, hard of hearing, deafness, a speech disability, an orthopedic handicap, or a health impairment.

SOURCE: U.S. Department of Education, National Center for Education Statistics, "The 1987 National Postsecondary Student Aid Study." (This table was prepared April 1991.)

Table 198.—Percentage of students enrolled in postsecondary institutions, by disability status and selected student characteristics: Fall 1986

Selected student characteristics	Disabled students [1]	Nondisabled students	Selected student characteristics	Disabled students [1]	Nondisabled students
1	2	3	1	2	3
Sex	100.0	100.0	Level of study	100.0	100.0
Male	50.7	44.7	Undergraduate	91.6	88.8
Female	49.3	55.3	Graduate	6.6	8.7
			First-professional	1.8	2.5
Race/ethnicity	100.0	100.0			
White, non-Hispanic	78.7	78.2	Undergraduate	100.0	100.0
Black, non-Hispanic	7.9	9.0	Arts and humanities	6.4	5.9
Hispanic	7.4	6.5	Business	22.9	27.3
Asian American	4.1	5.5	Education	8.2	7.8
American Indian	1.9	.8	Engineering	9.4	9.0
			Health	7.8	9.4
Age	100.0	100.0	Liberal/general studies	6.4	6.1
15 to 23	49.8	55.8	Natural sciences [2]	10.3	10.0
24 to 29	17.5	19.8	Social sciences	4.2	3.9
30 or older	32.7	24.4	Trade/industrial	4.7	3.5
			All other	19.8	17.0
Veteran status	100.0	100.0			
Veteran	11.4	6.0	Graduate	100.0	100.0
Not a veteran	88.6	94.0	Arts and humanities	9.7	8.9
			Business	13.5	19.7
Dependency status	100.0	100.0	Education	25.3	22.4
Dependent	56.9	59.5	Engineering	4.1	6.1
Independent	43.1	40.5	Natural sciences [2]	9.6	11.3
			Social sciences	8.9	9.0
Housing status	100.0	100.0	All other	28.9	22.6
School-owned	19.1	18.9			
Off-campus, not with parents	55.2	53.5	First-professional	100.0	100.0
With parents	25.7	27.6	Law	46.5	37.4
			Medicine	28.0	39.1
Attendance status	100.0	100.0	Other medical [3]	21.1	19.0
Full-time	62.6	61.0	Theology	4.4	4.5
Part-time	37.4	39.0			

[1] Disabled students are those who reported that they had one or more of the following conditions: a specific learning disability, a visual handicap, hard of hearing, deafness, a speech disability, an orthopedic handicap, or a health impairment.

[2] Includes students who majored in life sciences, physical sciences, mathematics, or computer sciences.

[3] Includes chiropractic medicine, dentistry, optometry, osteopathic medicine, pharmacy, podiatry, and veterinary medicine.

NOTE.—Because of rounding, details may not add to totals.

SOURCE: U.S. Department of Education, National Center for Education Statistics, "The 1987 National Postsecondary Student Aid Study." (This table was prepared April 1991.)

Table 199.—Enrollment of persons 14 to 34 years of age [1] in institutions of higher education, by race/ethnicity, sex, and year of college: October 1965 to October 1990

Characteristic	1965	1970	1975	1979	1980	1981[2]	1982	1983	1984	1985	1986	1987	1988	1989	1990
1	2	3	4	5	6	7	8	9	10	11	12	13	14	15	16

Numbers in thousands

	1965	1970	1975	1979	1980	1981[2]	1982	1983	1984	1985	1986	1987	1988	1989	1990
All students	5,675	7,413	9,697	9,978	10,181	10,734	10,919	10,825	10,858	10,863	10,605	10,919	10,937	11,068	11,303
White, non-Hispanic[3]															
Total	5,317	6,759	8,141	8,293	8,453	8,680	8,850	8,741	8,764	8,781	8,284	8,519	8,616	8,786	8,892
Men	3,326	4,066	4,566	4,188	4,225	4,376	4,439	4,477	4,487	4,361	4,158	4,221	4,155	4,220	4,298
Women	1,991	2,693	3,576	4,104	4,228	4,304	4,411	4,265	4,277	4,420	4,126	4,299	4,461	4,565	4,594
Black, non-Hispanic[3]															
Total	274	522	927	988	996	1,122	1,119	1,088	1,124	1,036	1,126	1,162	1,096	1,116	1,167
Men	126	253	433	427	431	500	480	488	538	458	484	505	423	425	508
Women	148	269	494	561	565	622	639	600	586	578	642	657	674	690	659
Hispanic origin															
Total	—	—	411	440	443	510	493	523	524	579	677	667	654	640	617
Men	—	—	219	226	222	258	216	253	232	280	331	369	313	311	297
Women	—	—	192	214	221	252	278	270	292	299	346	298	341	330	321
Year of college															
First	1,861	2,212	2,886	2,885	2,958	3,096	2,990	2,987	3,023	2,956	2,965	2,915	3,131	2,983	3,109
Second	1,256	1,739	2,376	2,291	2,411	2,559	2,617	2,624	2,454	2,585	2,564	2,745	2,598	2,680	2,798
Third	896	1,248	1,491	1,653	1,716	1,800	1,814	1,805	1,981	1,931	1,803	2,011	1,979	2,017	1,958
Fourth	803	1,074	1,354	1,458	1,403	1,598	1,688	1,595	1,599	1,642	1,640	1,556	1,631	1,676	1,817
Fifth or higher	859	1,140	1,590	1,691	1,692	1,681	1,810	1,814	1,802	1,749	1,633	1,690	1,598	1,711	1,620

Percentage distribution

	1965	1970	1975	1979	1980	1981[2]	1982	1983	1984	1985	1986	1987	1988	1989	1990
All students	100.0	100.0	100.0	100.0	100.0	100.0	100.0	100.0	100.0	100.0	100.0	100.0	100.0	100.0	100.0
White, non-Hispanic[3]															
Total	93.7	91.2	84.0	83.1	83.0	80.9	81.1	80.8	80.7	80.8	78.1	78.0	78.8	79.4	78.7
Men	58.6	54.8	47.1	42.0	41.5	40.8	40.7	41.4	41.3	40.1	39.2	38.7	38.0	38.1	38.0
Women	35.1	36.3	36.9	41.1	41.5	40.1	40.4	39.4	39.4	40.7	38.9	39.4	40.8	41.2	40.6
Black, non-Hispanic[3]															
Total	4.8	7.0	9.6	9.9	9.8	10.5	10.2	10.1	10.4	9.5	10.6	10.6	10.0	10.1	10.3
Men	2.2	3.4	4.5	4.3	4.2	4.7	4.4	4.5	5.0	4.2	4.6	4.6	3.9	3.8	4.5
Women	2.6	3.6	5.1	5.6	5.5	5.8	5.9	5.5	5.4	5.3	6.1	6.0	6.2	6.2	5.8
Hispanic origin															
Total	—	—	4.2	4.4	4.4	4.8	4.5	4.8	4.8	5.3	6.4	6.1	6.0	5.8	5.5
Men	—	—	2.3	2.3	2.2	2.4	2.0	2.3	2.1	2.6	3.1	3.4	2.9	2.8	2.6
Women	—	—	2.0	2.1	2.2	2.3	2.5	2.5	2.7	2.8	3.3	2.7	3.1	3.0	2.8
Year of college															
First	32.8	29.8	29.8	28.9	29.1	28.8	27.4	27.6	27.8	27.2	28.0	26.7	28.6	27.0	27.5
Second	22.1	23.5	24.5	23.0	23.7	23.8	24.0	24.2	22.6	23.8	24.2	25.1	23.8	24.2	24.8
Third	15.8	16.8	15.4	16.6	16.9	16.8	16.6	16.7	18.2	17.8	17.0	18.4	18.1	18.2	17.3
Fourth	14.1	14.5	14.0	14.6	13.8	14.9	15.5	14.7	14.7	15.1	15.5	14.3	14.9	15.1	16.1
Fifth or higher	15.1	15.4	16.4	17.0	16.6	15.7	16.6	16.8	16.6	16.1	15.4	15.5	14.6	15.5	14.3

[1] Totals differ from those shown in other tables. This table presents data collected in sample surveys of households rather than surveys of institutions. Excludes persons age 35 and over.

[2] Data for 1981 and later years are controlled to 1980 census base.

[3] Data for 1965 and 1970 include persons of Hispanic origin.

—Data not available.

NOTE.—Data are based upon sample surveys of the civilian noninstitutional population. Because of rounding, details may not add to totals.

SOURCE: U.S. Department of Commerce, Bureau of the Census, Current Population Reports, Series P–20, No. 403, and unpublished data. (This table was prepared May 1991.)

Table 200.—Total enrollment in selected major fields of study in 4-year institutions of higher education, by sex: Fall 1976 to fall 1988

Selected major fields of study	1976 Total	1978[1] Total	1978[1] Men	1978[1] Women	1980 Total	1980 Men	1980 Women	1984[2] Total	1984[2] Men	1984[2] Women	1986 Total	1986 Men	1986 Women	1988[3] Total	1988[3] Men	1988[3] Women
1	2	3	4	5	6	7	8	9	10	11	12	13	14	15	16	17
Total enrollment Enrollment	7,126,515	7,230,380	3,754,579	3,475,801	7,570,608	3,827,341	3,743,267	7,622,667	3,797,607	3,825,060	7,823,963	3,823,583	4,000,380	8,180,182	3,912,207	4,267,975
Percent	**100.0**	**100.0**	**51.9**	**48.1**	**100.0**	**50.6**	**49.4**	**100.0**	**49.8**	**50.2**	**100.0**	**48.9**	**51.1**	**100.0**	**47.8**	**52.2**
Agriculture and natural resources Enrollment	124,903	125,312	88,235	37,077	113,376	78,158	35,218	—	—	—	—	—	—	—	—	—
Percent	100.0	100.0	70.4	29.6	100.0	68.9	31.1	—	—	—	—	—	—	—	—	—
Architecture and environmental design Enrollment	58,149	57,673	42,106	15,567	59,660	42,302	17,358	56,896	37,632	19,264	56,756	36,878	19,878	63,296	39,410	23,886
Percent	100.0	100.0	73.0	27.0	100.0	70.9	29.1	100.0	66.1	33.9	100.0	65.0	35.0	100.0	62.3	37.7
Business and management Enrollment	951,945	1,112,511	728,011	384,500	1,240,258	742,859	497,399	1,292,868	715,415	577,453	1,270,187	690,588	579,599	1,369,943	749,222	620,721
Percent	100.0	100.0	65.4	34.6	100.0	59.9	40.1	100.0	55.3	44.7	100.0	54.4	45.6	100.0	54.7	45.3
Dentistry Enrollment	20,272	21,793	18,735	3,058	22,668	18,812	3,856	19,997	15,217	4,780	17,773	12,916	4,857	16,296	11,293	5,003
Percent	100.0	100.0	86.0	14.0	100.0	83.0	17.0	100.0	76.1	23.9	100.0	72.7	27.3	100.0	69.3	30.7
Engineering Enrollment	374,815	440,038	392,871	47,167	503,960	441,965	61,995	514,257	439,444	74,813	485,857	414,973	70,884	457,939	390,191	67,748
Percent	100.0	100.0	89.3	10.7	100.0	87.7	12.3	100.0	85.5	14.5	100.0	85.4	14.6	100.0	85.2	14.8
Law Enrollment	119,581	118,298	82,302	35,996	118,993	78,569	40,424	117,673	71,443	46,230	105,965	62,789	43,176	117,548	67,934	49,614
Percent	100.0	100.0	69.6	30.4	100.0	66.0	34.0	100.0	60.7	39.3	100.0	59.3	40.7	100.0	57.8	42.2
Life sciences Enrollment	289,906	272,560	154,971	117,589	241,807	132,067	109,740	233,333	118,651	114,682	218,001	108,044	109,957	227,057	111,352	115,705
Percent	100.0	100.0	56.9	43.1	100.0	54.6	45.4	100.0	50.9	49.1	100.0	49.6	50.4	100.0	49.0	51.0
Mathematics Enrollment	—	—	—	—	—	—	—	96,772	56,041	40,731	89,434	51,086	38,348	83,366	47,151	36,215
Percent	—	—	—	—	—	—	—	100.0	57.9	42.1	100.0	57.1	42.9	100.0	56.6	43.4
Medicine Enrollment	58,085	66,713	51,241	15,472	74,132	55,060	19,072	67,877	46,492	21,385	65,462	43,680	21,782	65,430	42,576	22,854
Percent	100.0	100.0	76.8	23.2	100.0	74.3	25.7	100.0	68.5	31.5	100.0	66.7	33.3	100.0	65.1	34.9
Physical sciences Enrollment	146,025	148,432	114,166	34,266	154,092	114,919	39,173	143,514	105,412	38,102	128,979	92,483	36,496	122,970	87,496	35,474
Percent	100.0	100.0	76.9	23.1	100.0	74.6	25.4	100.0	73.5	26.5	100.0	71.7	28.3	100.0	71.2	28.8
Veterinary medicine Enrollment	6,126	7,186	4,762	2,424	8,164	4,980	3,184	9,190	4,762	4,428	8,707	4,092	4,615	8,504	3,661	4,843
Percent	100.0	100.0	66.3	33.7	100.0	61.0	39.0	100.0	51.8	48.2	100.0	47.0	53.0	100.0	43.1	56.9
All other Enrollment	[4]4,976,708	[4]4,859,864	[4]2,077,179	[4]2,782,685	[4]5,033,498	[4]2,117,650	[4]2,915,848	[4]5,070,290	[4]2,187,098	[4]2,883,192	[4]5,376,842	[4]2,306,054	[4]3,070,788	[4]5,647,833	[4]2,361,921	[4]3,285,912
Percent	100.0	100.0	42.7	57.3	100.0	42.1	57.9	100.0	43.1	56.9	100.0	42.9	57.1	100.0	41.8	58.2

[1] Excludes approximately 0.1 percent of students whose major field of study was not reported.
[2] Excludes approximately 1.2 percent of students whose major field of study was not reported.
[3] Revised from previously published data.
[4] Includes students whose major field of study was not reported.
—Data not available.

SOURCE: U.S. Department of Education, National Center for Education Statistics, "Fall Enrollment in Institutions of Higher Education"; and Integrated Postsecondary Education Data System (IPEDS), "Fall Enrollment" surveys. (This table was prepared February 1991.)

Table 201.—Total enrollment in selected major fields of study in 4-year institutions of higher education, by level, sex, and attendance status: Fall 1988 [1]

Level, sex, and attendance status of student	All fields	Architecture and environmental design	Business and management	Dentistry	Engineering	Law	Life sciences	Mathematics	Medicine	Physical sciences	Veterinary medicine	All other fields [2]
1	2	3	4	5	6	7	8	9	10	11	12	13
All students	**8,180,182**	**63,296**	**1,369,943**	**16,296**	**457,939**	**117,548**	**227,057**	**83,366**	**65,430**	**122,970**	**8,504**	**5,647,833**
Men	3,912,207	39,410	749,222	11,293	390,191	67,934	111,352	47,151	42,576	87,496	3,661	2,361,921
Full-time	2,843,186	33,923	527,895	11,244	306,322	57,674	93,878	36,778	42,188	69,363	3,625	1,660,296
Part-time	1,069,021	5,487	221,327	49	83,869	10,260	17,474	10,373	388	18,133	36	701,625
Women	4,267,975	23,886	620,721	5,003	67,748	49,614	115,705	36,215	22,854	35,474	4,843	3,285,912
Full-time	2,849,990	19,146	413,465	4,977	54,337	42,160	96,013	28,960	22,632	28,135	4,795	2,135,370
Part-time	1,417,985	4,740	207,256	26	13,411	7,454	19,692	7,255	222	7,339	48	1,150,542
Undergraduate students	6,441,393	51,352	1,133,000	—	360,847	—	184,282	66,309	—	80,800	—	4,564,803
Men	3,047,955	31,790	599,201	—	305,575	—	87,699	35,789	—	55,583	—	1,932,318
Full-time	2,387,849	27,804	475,179	—	260,601	—	77,202	29,645	—	46,727	—	1,470,691
Part-time	660,106	3,986	124,022	—	44,974	—	10,497	6,144	—	8,856	—	461,627
Women	3,393,438	19,562	533,799	—	55,272	—	96,583	30,520	—	25,217	—	2,632,485
Full-time	2,510,987	15,736	387,509	—	47,979	—	83,410	25,983	—	21,239	—	1,929,131
Part-time	882,451	3,826	146,290	—	7,293	—	13,173	4,537	—	3,978	—	703,354
Graduate students	1,471,680	11,944	236,943	—	97,092	—	42,775	17,057	—	42,170	—	1,023,699
Men	697,340	7,620	150,021	—	84,616	—	23,653	11,362	—	31,913	—	388,155
Full-time	304,292	6,119	52,716	—	45,721	—	16,676	7,133	—	22,636	—	153,291
Part-time	393,048	1,501	97,305	—	38,895	—	6,977	4,229	—	9,277	—	234,864
Women	774,340	4,324	86,922	—	12,476	—	19,122	5,695	—	10,257	—	635,544
Full-time	248,820	3,410	25,956	—	6,358	—	12,603	2,977	—	6,896	—	190,620
Part-time	525,520	914	60,966	—	6,118	—	6,519	2,718	—	3,361	—	444,924
First-professional students	267,109	—	—	16,296	—	117,548	—	—	65,430	—	8,504	59,331
Men	166,912	—	—	11,293	—	67,934	—	—	42,576	—	3,661	41,448
Full-time	151,045	—	—	11,244	—	57,674	—	—	42,188	—	3,625	36,314
Part-time	15,867	—	—	49	—	10,260	—	—	388	—	36	5,134
Women	100,197	—	—	5,003	—	49,614	—	—	22,854	—	4,843	17,883
Full-time	90,183	—	—	4,977	—	42,160	—	—	22,632	—	4,795	15,619
Part-time	10,014	—	—	26	—	7,454	—	—	222	—	48	2,264

[1] Revised from previously published data.

[2] Includes students whose major field of study was not reported.

—Data not reported or not applicable.

SOURCE: U.S. Department of Education, National Center for Education Statistics, Integrated Postsecondary Education Data System (IPEDS), "Fall Enrollment, 1988" survey. (This table was prepared February 1991.)

Table 202.—Graduate enrollment in science and engineering programs in institutions of higher education, by field of study: United States and outlying areas, 1981 to 1989

Field of engineering or science	1981	1982	1983	1984 [1]	1985 [1]	1986 [1]	1987 [1]	1988	1989	Percent change, 1981 to 1989
1	2	3	4	5	6	7	8	9	10	11
Total, all fields	378,104	385,056	394,048	398,178	407,942	419,338	425,358	429,831	440,983	16.6
Engineering, total	80,479	84,594	91,952	93,659	96,968	103,093	104,717	103,816	104,922	30.4
Aerospace	1,883	1,941	2,408	2,445	2,658	2,924	3,121	3,318	3,505	86.1
Agricultural	802	875	969	954	941	1,054	1,063	1,039	1,031	28.6
Biomedical	1,057	1,116	1,244	1,345	1,373	1,549	1,689	1,755	1,919	81.6
Chemical	6,496	7,189	7,563	7,373	7,150	7,012	7,111	6,618	6,411	−1.3
Civil	14,515	14,523	15,314	15,584	15,265	15,379	14,957	15,077	15,073	3.8
Electrical	20,193	22,017	25,213	26,306	28,128	30,008	31,339	31,960	33,306	64.9
Engineering science	1,965	2,130	2,261	2,153	2,098	2,362	2,359	2,408	2,092	6.5
Industrial	10,026	9,870	9,621	9,820	11,104	12,160	12,750	11,940	11,750	17.2
Mechanical	10,618	11,467	12,911	13,885	14,157	15,740	16,304	16,233	16,184	52.4
Metallurgical/materials	3,125	3,124	3,447	3,657	3,938	4,170	4,309	4,272	4,546	45.5
Mining	462	449	524	502	489	512	513	489	449	−2.8
Nuclear	1,283	1,301	1,203	1,234	1,220	1,265	1,279	1,303	1,323	3.1
Petroleum	521	586	737	744	782	747	818	742	665	27.6
Other engineering	7,533	8,006	8,537	7,687	7,665	8,211	7,105	6,662	6,668	−11.5
All sciences, total	297,625	300,462	302,096	304,519	310,974	316,245	320,641	326,015	336,061	12.9
Physical sciences, total	27,382	28,199	29,466	30,064	30,995	32,260	32,738	32,972	33,584	22.6
Astronomy	597	632	618	639	671	689	722	731	789	32.2
Chemistry	16,347	17,015	17,801	17,756	18,309	18,745	18,824	18,578	18,806	15.0
Physics	10,150	10,306	10,811	11,335	11,677	12,443	12,810	13,312	13,627	34.3
Other physical sciences	288	246	236	334	338	383	382	351	362	25.7
Environmental sciences, total	14,422	15,174	15,544	15,612	15,545	15,163	14,522	14,032	13,812	−4.2
Atmospheric sciences	882	889	896	907	964	961	952	940	912	3.4
Geosciences	8,808	9,621	10,321	10,370	10,294	9,819	8,998	8,495	8,043	−8.7
Oceanography	2,082	2,091	2,063	2,102	2,081	2,128	2,127	2,033	2,198	5.6
Other environmental sciences	2,650	2,573	2,264	2,233	2,206	2,255	2,445	2,564	2,659	0.3
Mathematical sciences, total	15,915	17,199	17,397	17,478	17,613	17,990	18,602	19,193	19,473	22.4
Computer sciences, total	16,437	19,812	23,616	25,810	29,844	31,425	32,137	32,787	32,914	100.2
Life sciences, total	103,124	102,889	102,795	104,336	105,116	107,278	108,091	110,775	115,077	11.6
Agricultural sciences, total	12,100	12,314	12,290	12,062	11,380	11,329	11,004	11,000	11,039	−8.8
Biological sciences, total	46,979	46,310	46,055	46,171	46,538	47,216	47,401	48,273	49,662	5.7
Anatomy	1,072	1,074	1,037	1,029	993	973	1,027	1,068	1,109	3.5
Biochemistry	4,061	4,124	4,234	4,490	4,691	4,909	4,848	4,958	5,169	27.3
Biology	14,203	13,397	13,071	12,905	12,732	12,707	12,508	12,602	12,988	−8.6
Biometry/epidemiology	1,182	1,166	1,156	1,004	1,360	1,441	1,506	1,631	1,677	41.9
Biophysics	463	440	450	433	441	547	591	592	655	41.5
Botany	3,498	3,644	3,450	3,404	3,335	3,290	3,140	3,083	2,998	−14.3
Cell biology	1,018	1,143	1,182	1,256	1,429	1,716	1,978	2,083	2,215	117.6
Ecology	1,101	1,051	1,007	1,088	1,028	1,012	963	1,028	1,109	0.7
Entomology/parasitology	1,664	1,540	1,475	1,438	1,342	1,306	1,244	1,240	1,181	−29.0
Genetics	937	990	1,035	1,059	1,120	1,262	1,314	1,289	1,365	45.7
Microbiology	4,070	4,130	4,262	4,326	4,447	4,374	4,492	4,810	4,857	19.3
Nutrition	4,355	4,359	4,351	4,277	4,314	4,321	4,288	4,244	4,277	−1.8
Pathology	1,444	1,460	1,462	1,468	1,355	1,398	1,442	1,400	1,452	0.6
Pharmacology	2,024	2,084	2,140	2,122	2,181	2,159	2,154	2,210	2,349	16.1
Physiology	2,144	2,058	1,994	2,160	2,211	2,220	2,213	2,220	2,206	2.9
Zoology	2,625	2,503	2,430	2,303	2,135	2,083	2,113	2,034	2,089	−20.4
Other biosciences	1,118	1,147	1,319	1,409	1,424	1,498	1,580	1,781	1,966	75.8
Health sciences, total	44,045	44,265	44,450	46,103	47,198	48,733	49,686	51,502	54,376	23.5
Dentistry	942	836	776	850	835	938	1,057	1,085	1,157	22.8
Neurology	191	204	261	317	337	383	494	605	690	261.3
Nursing	15,703	16,254	16,945	17,987	17,962	18,424	18,479	18,987	19,882	26.6
Pharmaceutical sciences	2,549	2,519	2,570	2,447	2,479	2,603	2,530	2,535	2,771	8.7
Preventive medicine and community health	7,226	6,816	6,679	6,841	7,292	7,226	7,560	7,671	7,744	7.2
Speech pathology/audiology	8,596	8,683	7,970	7,897	8,136	8,066	7,607	7,844	8,269	−3.8
Veterinary sciences	481	471	466	557	637	630	731	752	801	66.5
Other clinical medicine	1,610	1,747	1,644	1,570	1,732	1,709	1,797	1,879	1,882	16.9
Other health related	6,747	6,735	7,139	7,637	7,788	8,754	9,431	10,144	11,180	65.7
Psychology, total	40,691	40,098	41,039	41,074	41,308	41,551	42,785	44,277	46,248	13.7
Social sciences, total	79,654	77,091	72,239	70,145	70,553	70,578	71,766	71,979	74,953	−5.9
Agricultural economics	2,262	2,267	2,295	2,279	2,268	2,248	2,203	2,259	2,276	0.6
Anthropology	6,118	5,948	5,644	5,590	5,621	5,795	5,825	5,935	6,154	0.6
Economics (except agricultural)	13,344	13,735	13,162	12,599	12,502	12,198	12,153	12,174	12,291	−7.9
Geography	3,187	3,166	3,060	3,035	2,936	3,055	3,223	3,208	3,504	9.9
History and philosophy of science	248	256	253	274	272	266	294	288	314	26.6
Linguistics	3,139	2,803	3,022	3,160	3,055	3,109	3,282	3,255	3,355	6.9
Political science	30,791	29,907	28,069	25,939	27,035	27,310	27,667	27,875	29,321	−4.8
Sociology	7,816	7,246	6,920	6,740	6,567	6,504	6,945	7,058	7,352	−5.9
Sociology/anthropology	1,110	1,133	1,200	1,075	1,034	1,021	982	991	1,022	−7.9
Other social sciences	11,639	10,630	8,614	9,454	9,263	9,072	9,192	8,936	9,364	−19.5

[1] Includes estimated data for master's degree-granting institutions, which were surveyed on a sample basis from 1984 through 1987.

NOTE.—Figures have been revised from previously published data. Because of rounding, details may not add to totals.

SOURCE: National Science Foundation, Division of Science Resources Studies, *Academic Science/Engineering: Graduate Enrollment and Support, Fall 1989.* (This table was prepared March 1991.)

Table 203.—Institutions of higher education and branches, by type, control, and size of enrollment: Fall 1989[1]

Control of institution and size of total enrollment	All institutions		Universities		All other 4-year institutions		2-year institutions	
	Number[2]	Enrollment	Number[2]	Enrollment	Number[2]	Enrollment	Number[2]	Enrollment
1	2	3	4	5	6	7	8	9
Public and private institutions ...	**3,487**	**13,457,855**	**156**	**3,018,166**	**1,953**	**5,356,228**	**1,378**	**5,083,461**
Under 200	434	43,828	0	0	289	30,665	145	13,163
200 to 499	427	145,357	0	0	246	83,295	181	62,062
500 to 999	460	329,413	0	0	292	211,051	168	118,362
1,000 to 2,499	890	1,446,588	0	0	559	885,466	331	561,122
2,500 to 4,999	489	1,713,452	5	20,485	253	881,962	231	811,005
5,000 to 9,999	408	2,884,523	31	241,068	189	1,311,512	188	1,331,943
9,000 to 19,999	260	3,586,338	53	758,145	94	1,428,949	93	1,399,244
20,000 to 29,999	85	2,047,760	42	1,048,468	18	427,691	25	571,601
30,000 or more	34	1,260,596	25	950,000	3	95,637	6	214,959
Public institutions	**1,543**	**9,514,973**	**94**	**2,265,658**	**497**	**3,428,544**	**952**	**4,820,771**
Under 200	7	1,058	0	0	0	0	7	1,058
200 to 499	33	12,207	0	0	9	3,350	24	8,857
500 to 999	114	86,436	0	0	26	20,497	88	65,939
1,000 to 2,499	390	677,287	0	0	93	180,481	287	496,806
2,500 to 4,999	332	1,178,143	0	0	94	377,687	228	800,456
5,000 to 9,999	330	2,355,504	6	51,006	137	980,339	187	1,324,159
9,000 to 19,999	228	3,165,036	29	439,196	97	1,342,862	92	1,382,978
20,000 to 29,999	78	1,874,811	37	921,561	18	427,691	23	525,559
30,000 or more	31	1,164,491	22	853,895	3	95,637	6	214,959
Private institutions	**1,944**	**2,942,882**	**62**	**752,508**	**1,456**	**1,927,684**	**426**	**262,690**
Under 200	427	42,770	0	0	289	30,665	138	12,95
200 to 499	394	133,150	0	0	237	79,945	157	53,205
500 to 999	346	242,977	0	0	266	190,554	80	52,423
1,000 to 2,499	500	769,301	0	0	456	704,985	44	64,316
2,500 to 4,999	157	535,309	5	20,485	149	504,275	3	9,549
5,000 to 9,999	78	529,019	25	190,062	52	331,173	1	7,784
9,000 to 19,999	32	421,302	24	318,949	7	86,087	1	16,266
20,000 to 29,999	7	172,949	5	126,907	0	0	2	46,042
30,000 or more	3	96,95	3	96,95	0	0	0	0

[1] These preliminary data represent the institutions and enrollments reported in the "Fall Enrollment" survey.

[2] Because some institutions do not report enrollment data, counts of institutions in this table are somewhat lower than figures appearing in other tables.

SOURCE: U.S. Department of Education, National Center for Education Statistics, Integrated Postsecondary Education Data System (IPEDS), "Fall Enrollment, 1989" survey. (This table was prepared January 1991.)

Table 204.—Selected statistics for college and university campuses enrolling more than 14,600 students in 1989

Institution	State	Con-trol [1]	Type [2]	Total enrollment, fall 1985	Total enrollment, fall 1987	Total enrollment, fall 1988	Total enrollment, fall 1989	Enrollment, by sex, fall 1989		Enrollment, by attendance status, fall 1989	
								Men	Women	Full-time	Part-time
1	2	3	4	5	6	7	8	9	10	11	12
United States, all institutions	—	—	—	12,247,055	12,766,642	13,055,337	13,457,855	6,155,484	7,302,371	7,627,172	5,830,683
Colleges with enrollment over 14,600	—	—	—	4,388,318	4,560,733	4,717,654	4,887,220	2,372,198	2,515,022	2,893,749	1,993,471
Auburn University, Main Campus	Ala.	1	1	19,056	19,363	20,553	21,701	12,249	9,452	18,862	2,839
University of Alabama	Ala	1	1	15,577	17,166	18,510	19,765	9,675	10,090	16,580	3,185
University of Alabama at Birmingham	Ala.	1	1	13,511	13,479	13,886	14,692	6,580	8,112	8,451	6,241
University of Alaska Anchorage	Alaska	1	1	4,371	4,616	13,448	15,942	6,380	9,562	5,404	10,538
Arizona State University	Ariz.	1	1	40,529	42,968	43,426	43,550	22,070	21,480	27,815	15,735
Glendale Community College	Ariz.	1	2	13,377	15,826	19,200	18,241	8,118	10,123	5,037	13,204
Mesa Community College	Ariz.	1	2	16,789	19,443	19,627	19,094	8,635	10,459	5,621	13,473
Northern Arizona University	Ariz.	1	1	12,726	13,396	16,166	16,050	7,080	8,970	11,922	4,128
Pima Community College	Ariz.	1	2	20,801	24,866	26,810	26,747	11,991	14,756	6,294	20,453
University of Arizona	Ariz.	1	1	30,864	33,009	34,725	36,676	18,964	17,712	26,684	9,992
American River College	Calif.	1	2	17,413	19,318	18,716	18,716	8,090	10,626	3,926	14,790
Calif. Polytechnic State U., Obispo	Calif.	1	1	15,968	16,049	15,912	16,721	9,467	7,254	14,232	2,489
California State Polytechnic U., Pomona	Calif.	1	1	17,024	18,317	17,905	18,507	10,596	7,911	12,750	5,757
California State University, Fresno	Calif.	1	1	16,454	18,364	17,467	18,222	8,454	9,768	13,268	4,954
California State University, Fullerton	Calif.	1	1	23,034	24,317	23,376	23,588	10,503	13,085	14,121	9,467
California State University, Long Beach	Calif.	1	1	31,124	34,926	33,179	30,665	14,071	16,594	18,520	12,145
California State University, Los Angeles	Calif.	1	1	19,576	20,977	17,960	18,472	7,799	10,673	9,923	8,549
California State University, Northridge	Calif.	1	1	28,144	29,719	29,401	28,604	12,287	16,317	17,302	11,302
California State University, Chico	Calif.	1	1	14,196	15,434	14,979	15,847	7,777	8,070	13,271	2,576
California State University, Sacramento	Calif.	1	1	22,483	24,128	23,478	23,337	10,066	13,271	15,667	7,670
Cerritos College	Calif.	1	2	17,416	18,110	15,886	15,886	6,985	8,901	3,839	12,047
Chabot College	Calif.	1	2	17,882	19,417	19,705	19,705	9,226	10,479	4,622	15,083
City College of San Francisco	Calif.	1	2	(5)	(5)	(5)	24,408	10,980	13,428	6,667	17,741
De Anza College	Calif.	1	2	23,743	25,036	21,948	21,948	10,127	11,821	6,439	15,509
Diablo Valley College	Calif.	1	2	16,668	20,043	20,255	20,255	8,770	11,485	6,456	13,799
El Camino College	Calif.	1	2	24,179	25,485	25,789	25,789	11,770	14,019	5,523	20,266
Fresno City College	Calif.	1	2	13,240	15,177	14,710	14,710	6,637	8,073	5,188	9,522
Fullerton College	Calif.	1	2	16,596	17,235	17,548	17,548	8,494	9,054	4,364	13,184
Grossmont College	Calif.	1	2	14,214	15,715	15,357	15,357	6,601	8,756	4,973	10,384
Long Beach City College	Calif.	1	2	22,245	20,585	18,378	18,378	8,479	9,899	3,704	14,674
Los Angeles Pierce College	Calif.	1	2	17,135	18,316	16,970	16,970	8,052	8,918	5,095	11,875
Los Angeles Valley College	Calif.	1	2	16,046	18,139	16,457	16,457	7,275	9,182	3,695	12,762
Mount San Antonio College	Calif.	1	2	20,314	19,840	20,563	20,563	9,600	10,963	5,965	14,598
Orange Coast College	Calif.	1	2	21,925	24,167	22,365	22,365	11,204	11,161	7,022	15,343
Palomar College	Calif.	1	2	15,261	15,404	16,707	16,707	7,479	9,228	3,953	12,754
Pasadena City College	Calif.	1	2	17,818	20,178	19,581	19,581	9,039	10,542	6,088	13,493
Rancho Santiago College	Calif.	1	2	20,843	20,606	20,532	20,532	9,908	10,624	3,521	17,011
Riverside Community College	Calif.	1	2	13,647	15,033	15,683	15,683	6,495	9,188	2,728	12,955
San Diego Mesa College	Calif.	1	2	17,989	21,336	23,410	23,410	10,790	12,620	7,173	16,237
San Diego State University	Calif.	1	1	33,898	36,280	34,155	33,406	15,353	18,053	21,625	11,781
San Francisco State University	Calif.	1	1	24,170	26,002	24,138	25,656	10,482	15,174	15,767	9,889
San Joaquin Delta College	Calif.	1	2	14,430	14,988	14,792	14,792	6,485	8,307	4,517	10,275
San Jose State University	Calif.	1	1	24,843	27,549	26,456	27,650	13,266	14,384	17,495	10,155
Santa Monica College	Calif.	1	2	19,270	17,413	18,108	18,108	8,083	10,025	3,618	14,490
Santa Rosa Junior College	Calif.	1	2	16,804	21,305	20,479	20,479	8,525	11,954	4,619	15,860
Stanford University	Calif.	2	1	13,758	14,132	14,387	14,723	9,275	5,448	12,015	2,708
University of California, Berkeley	Calif.	1	1	31,007	32,055	30,102	29,674	16,238	13,436	26,261	3,413
University of California, Davis	Calif.	1	1	19,534	20,847	20,733	21,388	10,773	10,615	19,274	2,114
University of California, Irvine	Calif.	1	1	12,684	15,139	14,772	15,074	7,629	7,445	13,929	1,145
University of California, Los Angeles	Calif.	1	1	34,501	35,435	34,371	34,993	17,831	17,162	31,417	3,576
University of California, San Diego	Calif.	1	1	14,295	16,589	16,410	16,700	9,269	7,431	15,635	1,065
University of California, Santa Barbara	Calif.	1	1	16,935	17,879	17,743	18,193	9,092	9,101	17,152	1,041
University of Southern California	Calif.	2	1	30,373	30,504	29,657	29,657	17,681	11,976	19,842	9,815
Colorado State University	Colo.	1	1	18,084	19,192	19,192	19,994	10,357	9,637	18,106	1,888
Metropolitan State College	Colo.	1	1	14,614	15,710	15,741	16,840	7,862	8,978	9,126	7,714
University of Colorado at Boulder	Colo.	1	1	22,767	23,551	24,070	24,589	13,315	11,274	22,152	2,437
University of Connecticut	Conn.	1	1	23,063	24,552	25,374	25,634	12,236	13,398	17,745	7,889
University of Delaware	Del.	1	1	18,162	19,067	19,818	20,477	9,296	11,181	15,324	5,153
George Washington University	D.C.	2	1	18,790	19,500	19,236	18,949	10,057	8,892	10,322	8,627
Brevard Community College	Fla.	1	2	10,696	12,284	12,375	19,248	7,722	11,526	4,641	14,607
Broward Community College	Fla.	1	2	19,324	21,621	21,682	23,547	9,433	14,114	7,803	15,744
Florida Community College, Jacksonville	Fla.	1	2	14,533	11,998	16,778	21,381	9,048	12,333	4,944	16,437
Florida International University	Fla.	1	1	16,966	16,619	18,128	20,222	8,594	11,628	8,685	11,537
Florida State University	Fla.	1	1	21,537	23,826	25,907	27,975	13,186	14,789	22,187	5,788
Hillsborough Community College	Fla.	1	2	12,503	14,246	15,573	17,554	7,442	10,112	4,552	13,002
Miami-Dade Community College	Fla.	1	2	37,082	42,663	43,880	47,330	20,002	27,328	15,910	31,420
Palm Beach Community College	Fla.	1	2	12,253	13,084	13,121	21,191	9,361	11,830	4,508	16,683
Saint Petersburg Junior College	Fla.	1	2	16,064	18,764	18,870	18,680	7,300	11,380	6,916	11,764
University of Central Florida	Fla.	1	1	16,519	17,527	18,342	20,345	9,689	10,656	10,797	9,548
University of Florida	Fla.	1	1	35,334	33,568	33,282	34,098	18,410	15,688	28,461	5,637
University of South Florida	Fla.	1	1	28,032	29,069	29,912	31,566	13,829	17,737	16,125	15,441
Valencia Community College	Fla.	1	2	12,158	13,773	14,840	14,840	6,460	8,380	4,756	10,084
Georgia State University	Ga.	1	1	21,612	22,070	22,176	23,004	9,819	13,185	10,042	12,962
University of Georgia	Ga.	1	1	25,408	26,547	27,176	27,448	12,752	14,696	23,229	4,219
University of Hawaii at Manoa	Hi.	1	1	19,606	18,382	18,424	18,546	8,501	10,045	13,302	5,244
City College of Chicago - Truman College	Ill.	1	2	15,185	14,258	12,977	15,137	7,347	7,790	4,140	10,997
College of Du Page	Ill.	1	2	22,537	24,474	26,493	28,037	12,039	15,998	7,848	20,189
Depaul University	Ill.	2	1	12,836	13,688	14,699	15,387	7,551	7,836	8,407	6,980

Table 204.—Selected statistics for college and university campuses enrolling more than 14,600 students in 1989—Continued

Enrollment, by level, fall 1989		Earned degrees conferred, 1988–89					Financial statistics, 1987–88,[3] in thousands			Full-time-equivalent enrollment, fall 1988	Full-time-equivalent enrollment, fall 1989
Undergradu-ate	Postbacca-laureate	Associate	Bachelor's	First professional	Master's	Doctor's	Current-fund revenues	Current-fund expenditures	Educational and general expenditures		
13	14	15	16	17	18	19	20	21	22	23	24
11,665,643	1,792,212	435,210	1,017,667	70,758	309,762	35,759	$117,301,141	$113,760,219	$89,132,803	9,466,878	9,733,727
14,050,745	836,475	87,339	436,850	25,747	143,125	24,148	47,404,599	48,910,029	37,361,070	3,516,979	3,621,579
18,998	2,703	—	3,571	79	443	114	234,895	242,334	206,203	18,909	19,956
15,910	3,855	—	2,135	148	609	126	173,028	178,196	141,802	16,820	17,791
10,616	4,076	—	1,313	230	840	75	481,055	498,538	248,060	10,384	10,903
15,615	327	440	430	—	89	—	61,290	60,858	57,252	8,239	9,647
32,610	10,940	—	5,462	155	1,394	194	342,200	350,719	295,418	33,583	33,865
18,241	—	614	—	—	—	—	23,334	23,011	20,873	9,657	9,472
19,094	—	679	—	—	—	—	25,833	25,658	23,087	10,191	10,146
12,561	3,489	—	1,659	—	582	39	100,610	106,471	87,320	13,718	13,480
26,747	—	955	—	—	—	—	45,385	45,500	42,653	13,069	13,164
28,254	8,422	—	4,020	265	1,182	326	503,106	515,347	413,673	28,875	30,523
18,716	—	827	—	—	—	—	41,234	41,987	37,981	8,894	8,894
15,717	1,004	—	2,587	—	225	0	133,241	142,744	117,688	14,411	15,216
16,672	1,835	—	2,414	—	280	0	111,436	125,877	104,562	14,482	15,017
14,832	3,390	—	2,644	—	363	0	121,910	118,923	112,725	14,549	15,186
19,759	3,829	—	3,608	—	602	0	112,936	125,454	105,437	17,615	17,829
25,096	5,569	—	4,085	—	678	0	170,889	186,777	157,539	25,248	23,259
13,771	4,701	—	1,783	—	650	3	118,718	134,002	110,139	12,844	13,227
22,844	5,760	—	3,350	—	650	0	144,310	161,393	131,615	22,515	21,692
13,949	1,898	—	2,597	—	180	0	104,112	117,162	97,747	13,458	14,273
18,484	4,853	—	3,598	—	654	0	128,387	141,433	118,571	18,683	18,642
15,886	—	837	—	—	—	—	41,453	42,357	38,686	7,885	7,885
19,705	—	825	—	—	—	—	[4]39,943	[4]37,312	[4]35,084	9,688	9,688
24,408	—	1,012	—	—	—	—	[5]	[5]	[5]	12,626	12,626
21,948	—	746	—	—	—	—	[5]	[5]	[5]	11,648	11,648
20,255	—	683	—	—	—	—	42,124	45,922	37,547	11,091	11,091
25,789	—	1,071	—	—	—	—	51,167	51,731	45,594	12,330	12,330
14,710	—	988	—	—	—	—	31,261	33,202	27,942	8,386	8,386
17,548	—	1,099	—	—	—	—	37,304	36,156	33,018	8,792	8,792
15,357	—	735	—	—	—	—	29,948	30,793	29,329	8,461	8,461
18,378	—	796	—	—	—	—	46,622	46,725	46,278	8,633	8,633
16,970	—	749	—	—	—	—	38,493	42,168	35,051	9,084	9,084
16,457	—	629	—	—	—	—	33,300	37,059	30,085	7,982	7,982
20,563	—	1,095	—	—	—	—	42,568	45,518	42,198	10,868	10,868
22,365	—	1,131	—	—	—	—	[6]	[6]	[6]	12,175	12,175
16,707	—	496	—	—	—	—	36,471	36,990	33,080	8,237	8,237
19,581	—	722	—	—	—	—	46,737	48,497	46,737	10,620	10,620
20,532	—	364	—	—	—	—	50,388	52,115	47,615	9,235	9,235
15,683	—	753	—	—	—	—	29,468	31,747	26,278	7,079	7,079
23,410	—	650	—	—	—	—	27,543	40,607	23,635	12,627	12,627
27,078	6,328	—	4,513	—	1,000	2	197,148	219,475	177,099	26,768	26,217
19,604	6,052	—	3,245	—	809	5	140,359	139,217	128,050	18,585	19,617
14,792	—	873	—	—	—	—	37,130	37,747	34,253	7,968	7,968
21,693	5,957	—	3,408	—	923	0	158,305	170,392	139,153	20,473	21,438
18,108	—	622	—	—	—	—	38,697	41,438	38,697	8,485	8,485
20,479	—	729	—	—	—	—	37,093	40,346	35,626	9,946	9,946
6,580	8,143	—	1,621	266	1,693	540	1,083,542	1,141,926	745,317	12,833	13,074
20,842	8,832	—	5,332	370	1,839	838	652,756	665,340	614,577	28,051	27,591
16,393	4,995	—	3,203	334	533	221	683,117	709,353	460,495	19,383	20,111
12,343	2,731	—	2,196	93	208	84	461,328	469,068	278,027	14,132	14,383
23,627	11,366	—	4,832	420	1,824	459	1,247,059	1,309,361	859,450	32,441	32,805
13,533	3,167	—	2,333	106	282	189	641,175	681,964	424,712	15,773	16,058
16,143	2,050	—	3,015	—	375	106	250,678	258,282	215,826	17,219	17,557
16,113	13,544	—	3,119	566	3,236	429	602,095	615,669	538,969	23,621	23,621
16,918	3,076	—	2,814	122	752	173	238,456	243,611	206,519	17,820	18,851
16,840	0	—	1,846	—	0	0	39,367	40,898	39,367	11,532	12,239
20,038	4,551	—	3,710	160	819	221	285,018	299,465	242,325	22,593	23,094
18,239	7,395	0	2,908	208	978	198	251,807	255,640	225,428	20,830	20,784
18,026	2,451	15	2,726	—	431	114	225,006	240,652	196,096	16,908	17,359
7,894	11,055	89	1,620	590	1,978	161	415,472	407,643	217,411	13,666	13,697
19,248	—	1,289	—	—	—	—	32,235	31,375	31,587	7,080	9,547
23,547	—	1,538	—	—	—	—	49,140	47,545	45,452	12,216	13,091
21,381	—	1,377	—	—	—	—	54,520	53,401	54,520	8,949	10,465
16,256	3,966	—	2,378	—	463	3	99,136	101,411	89,876	11,751	13,216
22,106	5,869	492	4,008	171	945	246	230,803	239,995	199,121	22,758	24,417
17,554	—	1,281	—	—	—	—	29,940	30,493	27,764	8,238	8,919
47,330	—	4,260	—	—	—	—	132,552	139,691	124,679	25,388	26,463
21,191	—	1,281	—	—	—	—	25,415	29,510	25,415	6,759	10,111
18,680	—	2,125	—	—	—	—	36,866	39,016	36,783	10,707	10,867
16,659	3,686	273	2,958	—	507	21	105,987	108,761	89,306	13,041	14,524
25,664	8,434	1,793	5,394	653	1,218	342	599,233	608,151	548,881	30,112	30,632
23,742	7,824	284	4,178	93	1,144	72	255,912	260,068	234,466	21,086	22,120
14,840	—	1,561	—	—	—	—	34,858	35,859	32,201	8,143	8,143
16,197	6,807	30	2,166	144	1,312	107	125,757	126,409	124,723	14,494	15,146
21,494	5,954	1	3,822	280	1,038	340	412,918	419,755	379,374	24,779	24,860
12,821	5,725	108	2,404	119	833	162	268,408	276,736	238,445	15,176	15,295
15,137	—	220	—	—	—	—	25,648	26,377	25,648	6,413	7,834
28,037	—	1,409	—	—	—	—	44,978	50,318	42,058	13,705	14,629
9,416	5,971	0	1,407	245	1,105	11	81,463	84,274	71,577	9,901	11,166

Table 204.—Selected statistics for college and university campuses enrolling more than 14,600 students in 1989—Continued

Institution	State	Control [1]	Type [2]	Total enrollment, fall 1985	Total enrollment, fall 1987	Total enrollment, fall 1988	Total enrollment, fall 1989	Enrollment, by sex, fall 1989		Enrollment, by attendance status, fall 1989	
								Men	Women	Full-time	Part-time
1	2	3	4	5	6	7	8	9	10	11	12
Illinois State University	Ill.	1	1	21,178	23,141	22,330	23,107	10,225	12,882	19,210	3,897
Northern Illinois University	Ill.	1	1	24,311	25,455	24,255	24,443	10,841	13,602	17,093	7,350
Northwestern University	Ill.	2	1	15,845	16,437	16,592	16,807	8,939	7,868	13,341	3,466
Southern Illinois University, Carbondale	Ill.	1	1	22,553	24,160	24,227	24,596	14,856	9,740	19,272	5,324
Triton College	Ill.	1	2	18,888	18,022	17,691	16,625	7,938	8,687	5,084	11,541
University of Illinois at Chicago	Ill.	1	1	24,158	23,924	23,993	24,050	12,414	11,636	17,610	6,440
University of Illinois, Urbana Campus	Ill.	1	1	35,997	38,970	38,347	37,481	21,184	16,297	31,835	5,646
William Rainey Harper College	Ill.	1	2	16,511	16,034	16,121	16,685	6,922	9,763	4,731	11,954
Ball State University	Ind.	1	1	17,033	19,080	18,732	19,724	8,923	10,801	16,147	3,577
Indiana University, Bloomington	Ind.	1	1	32,816	33,421	33,776	34,863	16,427	18,436	29,352	5,511
Indiana U. - Purdue U. at Indianapolis	Ind.	1	1	23,430	23,618	24,808	26,649	11,347	15,302	10,786	15,863
Purdue University, Main Campus	Ind.	1	1	32,822	34,069	36,517	37,459	21,829	15,630	31,361	6,098
Iowa State University	Iowa	1	1	27,182	26,600	26,475	26,038	15,355	10,683	22,277	3,761
University of Iowa	Iowa	1	1	30,611	29,995	30,001	29,674	15,033	14,641	22,829	6,845
Kansas State U. of Agr. and App. Sci.	Kans.	1	1	17,570	18,049	19,301	20,110	10,800	9,310	16,261	3,849
University of Kansas, Main Campus	Kans.	1	1	24,774	26,306	26,020	26,320	12,956	13,364	20,517	5,803
Wichita State University	Kans.	1	1	16,309	16,407	16,673	16,765	7,880	8,885	7,844	8,921
University of Kentucky	Ky.	1	1	20,421	21,869	22,230	22,407	10,766	11,641	16,929	5,478
University of Louisville	Ky.	1	1	19,603	20,497	21,313	22,555	10,581	11,974	12,527	10,028
Western Kentucky University	Ky.	1	1	11,223	13,466	14,056	14,721	5,983	8,738	10,552	4,169
Louisiana State University	La.	1	1	29,727	28,011	27,350	26,750	13,276	13,474	21,829	4,921
University of New Orleans	La.	1	1	15,987	16,109	16,076	15,559	6,934	8,625	9,245	6,314
University of Southwestern Louisiana	La.	1	1	16,275	15,419	15,033	15,461	7,026	8,435	11,461	4,000
Towson State University	Md.	1	1	14,987	15,542	15,169	14,958	5,733	9,225	9,472	5,486
University of Maryland, College Park	Md.	1	1	38,679	38,058	36,681	35,825	18,702	17,123	26,577	9,248
U. of Maryland, University College	Md.	1	1	12,512	13,132	14,263	14,614	7,138	7,476	1,400	13,214
Boston University	Mass.	2	1	27,181	28,308	28,555	28,529	13,766	14,763	21,276	7,253
Harvard University	Mass.	2	1	20,711	23,691	24,195	24,509	13,211	11,298	17,448	7,061
Northeastern University	Mass.	2	1	35,271	33,042	32,389	32,809	17,632	15,177	17,609	15,200
University of Lowell	Mass.	1	1	15,261	14,334	14,507	14,622	9,202	5,420	8,561	6,061
University of Massachusetts at Amherst	Mass.	1	1	27,852	28,118	27,921	27,298	13,332	13,966	20,888	6,410
Central Michigan University	Mich.	1	1	17,070	19,141	19,024	19,195	7,999	11,196	14,998	4,197
Eastern Michigan University	Mich.	1	1	20,166	22,375	23,077	23,288	9,292	13,996	13,067	10,221
Henry Ford Community College	Mich.	1	2	15,577	15,261	15,791	16,126	8,197	7,929	3,424	12,702
Lansing Community College	Mich.	1	2	19,548	21,153	21,474	21,716	9,686	12,030	6,031	15,685
Macomb Community College	Mich.	1	2	29,491	32,141	31,466	31,670	15,034	16,636	6,124	25,546
Michigan State University	Mich.	1	1	42,746	43,960	44,480	44,423	21,416	23,007	36,198	8,225
Oakland Community College	Mich.	1	2	26,553	26,251	26,855	27,504	11,490	16,014	5,826	21,678
University of Michigan, Ann Arbor	Mich.	1	1	34,456	35,623	36,003	36,474	20,374	16,100	32,452	4,022
Wayne State University	Mich.	1	1	28,424	30,377	30,751	32,477	15,108	17,369	15,101	17,376
Western Michigan University	Mich.	1	1	20,963	23,336	24,861	26,315	11,922	14,393	16,671	9,644
Mankato State University	Minn.	1	1	14,195	15,385	15,944	16,200	7,554	8,646	11,872	4,328
Saint Cloud State University	Minn.	1	1	12,973	15,520	16,252	16,551	7,514	9,037	12,688	3,863
University of Minnesota, Twin Cities	Minn.	1	1	63,067	62,223	61,556	58,815	29,302	29,513	25,874	32,941
Saint Louis Community College	Mo.	1	2	6,773	6,110	30,221	31,847	13,234	18,613	8,321	23,526
Southwest Missouri State University	Mo.	1	1	15,511	16,085	17,006	18,427	8,425	10,002	13,678	4,749
University of Missouri, Columbia	Mo.	1	1	23,047	22,958	23,568	24,344	12,438	11,906	20,133	4,211
University of Missouri, Saint Louis	Mo.	1	1	11,444	13,162	13,932	14,635	6,180	8,455	5,956	8,679
University of Nebraska at Omaha	Nebr.	1	1	13,789	14,210	14,985	15,475	7,157	8,318	7,518	7,957
University of Nebraska, Lincoln	Nebr.	1	1	24,020	23,469	23,985	23,926	12,927	10,999	18,593	5,333
University of Nevada-Las Vegas	Nev.	1	1	12,011	13,476	14,673	16,163	7,543	8,620	7,510	8,653
Rutgers University, New Brunswick	N.J.	1	1	33,524	33,157	32,911	33,020	15,505	17,515	24,135	8,885
University of New Mexico, Main Campus	N.Mex.	1	1	26,628	24,856	24,214	24,645	11,483	13,162	15,290	9,355
Columbia University, New York	N.Y.	2	1	17,523	18,066	17,296	17,532	9,527	8,005	13,683	3,849
CUNY Bernard Baruch College	N.Y.	1	1	15,753	16,587	16,463	16,467	7,217	9,250	9,454	7,013
CUNY Brooklyn College	N.Y.	1	1	14,426	14,961	15,933	16,298	6,472	9,826	8,120	8,178
CUNY Hunter College	N.Y.	1	1	18,606	19,657	20,754	19,894	5,344	14,550	8,935	10,959
CUNY Queens College	N.Y.	1	1	16,243	16,613	16,942	17,708	6,748	10,960	8,985	8,723
Nassau Community College	N.Y.	1	2	20,320	19,692	20,130	20,677	8,851	11,826	10,085	10,592
New York University	N.Y.	2	1	32,266	31,691	30,753	31,083	14,004	17,079	19,229	11,854
Saint John's University New York	N.Y.	2	1	19,248	19,234	19,143	18,969	9,074	9,895	14,126	4,843
SUNY at Albany	N.Y.	1	1	15,978	16,219	16,561	16,628	7,957	8,671	12,371	4,257
SUNY at Buffalo	N.Y.	1	1	22,896	24,449	28,005	27,406	14,923	12,483	19,214	8,192
SUNY at Stony Brook	N.Y.	1	1	14,360	14,524	16,728	17,012	8,112	8,900	12,360	4,652
Syracuse University, Main Campus	N.Y.	2	1	20,980	21,334	22,086	22,196	10,990	11,206	16,495	5,701
University of the State of N.Y. Regents	N.Y.	1	1	17,221	14,829	16,476	16,476	8,171	8,305	4,021	12,455
Central Piedmont Community College	N.C.	1	2	26,550	16,186	16,442	16,235	7,077	9,158	4,492	11,743
East Carolina University	N.C.	1	1	15,267	15,901	16,501	16,954	7,096	9,858	12,780	4,174
North Carolina State U. at Raleigh	N.C.	1	1	24,294	24,349	25,725	26,870	16,506	10,364	17,409	9,461
University of North Carolina, Chapel Hill	N.C.	1	1	22,066	22,958	23,626	23,619	10,293	13,326	19,409	4,210
Bowling Green State U., Main Campus	Ohio	1	1	17,691	17,960	18,345	18,584	7,678	10,906	15,896	2,688
Cleveland Institute of Electronics	Ohio	2	2	(5)	(5)	23,373	23,373	22,205	1,168	0	23,373
Cleveland State University	Ohio	1	1	17,540	17,714	17,353	18,534	9,272	9,262	10,014	8,520
Cuyahoga Community College District	Ohio	1	2	24,159	22,825	22,014	22,548	7,978	14,570	6,397	16,151
Kent State University, Main Campus	Ohio	1	1	20,406	21,521	22,753	23,746	10,029	13,717	17,867	5,879
Miami University, Oxford Campus	Ohio	1	1	15,761	15,980	16,028	16,143	7,533	8,610	14,614	1,529
Ohio State University, Main Campus	Ohio	1	1	53,199	53,115	53,669	52,895	27,926	24,969	41,473	11,422
Ohio University, Main Campus	Ohio	1	1	15,217	16,693	17,836	17,864	8,838	9,026	16,351	1,513

Table 204.—Selected statistics for college and university campuses enrolling more than 14,600 students in 1989—Continued

Enrollment, by level, fall 1989		Earned degrees conferred, 1988–89					Financial statistics, 1987–88,[3] in thousands			Full-time-equivalent enrollment, fall 1988	Full-time-equivalent enrollment, fall 1989
Undergraduate	Postbaccalaureate	Associate	Bachelor's	First professional	Master's	Doctor's	Current-fund revenues	Current-fund expenditures	Educational and general expenditures		
13	14	15	16	17	18	19	20	21	22	23	24
20,147	2,960	—	3,703	—	562	41	134,627	133,091	107,237	19,942	20,700
18,029	6,414	—	3,823	81	1,207	97	164,248	163,298	125,507	19,769	19,832
9,404	7,403	0	1,983	434	2,033	358	395,092	438,520	370,201	14,506	14,690
20,428	4,168	596	4,600	160	674	149	226,781	229,014	197,793	21,088	21,302
16,625	—	842	—	—	—	—	39,535	40,003	35,927	9,288	8,960
16,045	8,005	—	2,698	535	1,211	161	528,896	532,641	367,211	19,727	20,079
27,529	9,952	0	6,422	272	2,084	647	612,569	613,231	533,012	34,807	33,990
16,685	—	1,230	—	—	—	—	39,138	41,006	33,189	8,377	8,746
17,364	2,360	221	2,556	—	852	76	148,898	163,052	130,309	16,621	17,526
27,136	7,727	60	4,604	258	1,677	313	416,185	414,937	317,658	30,532	31,459
20,087	6,562	986	1,812	539	589	22	429,393	448,282	234,313	15,753	17,067
31,247	6,212	607	4,989	79	1,186	420	476,226	493,583	396,412	32,948	33,735
21,349	4,689	—	4,041	106	676	257	374,135	375,934	287,227	23,864	23,712
20,309	9,365	—	3,942	434	1,324	287	562,405	641,665	341,987	25,517	25,436
16,610	3,500	7	2,588	91	627	137	183,067	188,010	156,231	16,750	17,740
19,260	7,060	—	3,192	163	1,029	224	213,900	227,883	174,378	22,506	22,686
13,537	3,228	234	1,388	—	486	18	80,689	82,411	72,581	11,085	11,332
17,202	5,205	—	2,606	294	732	181	441,599	463,614	313,888	18,987	19,045
17,761	4,794	185	1,697	308	696	47	240,543	247,022	206,472	15,376	16,471
12,589	2,132	271	1,297	—	493	0	79,396	79,313	67,882	11,506	12,162
21,646	5,104	—	3,149	285	743	207	315,617	318,934	255,437	24,323	23,750
12,609	2,950	3	1,312	—	386	15	67,604	68,468	58,623	12,116	11,699
13,815	1,646	101	1,742	—	259	15	69,762	69,967	56,342	12,717	13,028
13,464	1,494	—	2,423	—	204	0	78,366	81,267	58,685	12,078	11,632
26,863	8,962	0	5,655	—	1,294	393	425,589	468,250	358,900	30,824	30,104
12,288	2,326	89	1,571	—	172	0	30,712	32,108	30,712	6,521	6,639
18,758	9,771	6	3,390	713	2,341	304	494,110	504,178	418,640	24,019	24,104
10,814	13,695	20	1,741	735	2,650	461	865,010	865,615	762,727	19,994	20,203
27,860	4,949	354	3,251	139	1,165	63	225,281	236,653	209,016	23,486	23,585
11,727	2,895	73	1,429	—	584	23	83,444	83,476	83,444	10,810	10,925
20,667	6,631	91	4,336	—	984	329	320,570	334,752	263,400	24,091	23,313
16,008	3,187	0	2,977	—	2,036	6	122,247	128,749	95,837	16,419	16,579
18,328	4,960	—	2,527	—	1,182	0	127,247	120,781	108,392	16,847	17,010
16,126	—	1,037	—	—	—	—	36,185	31,887	33,768	7,472	7,690
21,716	—	1,371	—	—	—	—	52,835	49,326	52,113	11,030	11,299
31,670	—	2,369	—	—	—	—	58,077	52,479	54,437	14,410	14,704
34,951	9,472	0	6,839	322	1,702	434	596,347	627,588	496,859	39,212	39,325
27,504	—	1,781	—	—	—	—	[7]61,904	[7]54,181	[7]57,884	12,659	13,107
23,285	13,189	0	5,356	679	2,628	527	1,162,676	1,311,061	673,126	33,493	33,966
20,592	11,885	0	2,300	463	1,479	193	278,569	301,692	270,579	20,754	21,833
19,928	6,387	—	3,109	—	1,053	52	155,155	162,428	121,196	19,227	20,340
13,783	2,417	73	2,002	—	392	—	68,568	67,797	58,238	13,236	13,546
14,891	1,660	81	2,069	—	207	—	66,244	66,093	55,568	13,927	14,187
45,491	13,324	157	5,422	672	2,020	543	1,035,211	1,095,722	743,303	40,855	38,917
31,847	—	1,880	—	—	—	—	77,661	79,548	72,054	15,305	16,223
17,037	1,390	33	1,916	—	259	—	[7]76,223	[7]80,176	[7]63,417	14,313	15,545
18,196	6,148	—	3,366	311	1,068	236	411,569	427,417	261,569	20,969	21,721
12,126	2,509	—	1,527	42	445	18	52,878	55,638	48,406	8,947	9,374
13,146	2,329	—	1,331	—	464	—	53,228	54,072	48,041	10,266	10,649
19,791	4,135	28	2,783	138	716	236	[7]243,400	[7]247,758	[7]194,610	20,483	20,662
13,905	2,258	64	1,077	—	218	7	73,137	75,824	66,719	9,796	10,921
25,277	7,743	—	5,234	—	1,308	327	550,801	584,376	485,121	27,450	27,507
17,474	7,171	83	2,023	181	917	137	186,917	195,698	159,080	18,456	18,880
5,721	11,811	0	1,313	531	3,787	615	701,019	700,771	672,574	15,249	15,168
13,666	2,801	—	1,561	—	482	0	78,795	78,538	78,795	12,120	12,197
11,825	4,473	—	802	—	356	0	92,512	92,577	92,512	10,980	11,250
15,355	4,539	—	1,255	—	854	0	98,565	98,302	98,565	13,799	13,197
14,232	3,476	—	1,634	—	628	0	97,563	96,625	97,006	11,807	12,373
20,677	—	2,769	—	—	—	—	82,927	80,513	82,927	13,349	13,643
14,906	16,177	283	2,691	704	3,700	392	897,625	917,505	603,328	23,196	23,811
14,154	4,815	497	2,750	351	753	50	105,370	115,259	100,543	16,217	16,059
11,834	4,794	—	2,483	—	1,076	122	172,848	181,290	150,520	14,121	13,971
18,888	8,518	275	2,993	495	1,452	274	324,127	330,169	301,569	22,988	22,368
11,109	5,903	—	2,076	127	834	190	452,263	447,146	262,234	14,152	14,111
15,095	7,101	15	2,656	234	1,591	170	288,017	300,368	226,281	18,460	18,705
13,666	2,810	1,770	2,191	—	0	0	3,778	4,042	3,778	8,985	8,985
16,235	—	577	—	—	—	—	36,420	36,554	33,531	8,239	8,436
13,767	3,187	—	2,104	67	533	5	175,323	183,984	156,080	14,076	14,371
22,709	4,161	73	3,252	71	622	224	375,860	384,752	329,359	20,463	21,119
15,490	8,129	—	3,527	458	1,269	299	551,529	568,253	479,397	20,991	20,976
15,978	2,606	13	2,820	—	609	47	142,525	142,738	108,072	16,795	16,921
23,373	—	67	—	—	—	—	8,139	9,093	8,139	9,571	9,571
13,408	5,126	—	1,575	258	583	11	97,899	98,213	92,214	12,441	13,350
22,548	—	1,784	—	—	—	—	82,557	85,531	77,490	11,704	11,822
19,012	4,734	—	2,715	—	772	132	[7]153,418	[7]161,670	[7]115,550	18,994	20,118
14,456	1,687	188	3,381	—	469	37	143,729	149,572	109,449	15,117	15,198
40,122	12,773	168	6,717	721	2,263	608	[7]910,436	[7]895,792	[7]634,163	46,703	45,875
15,106	2,758	33	2,833	102	847	95	161,506	167,572	132,608	16,865	16,940

Table 204.—Selected statistics for college and university campuses enrolling more than 14,600 students in 1989—Continued

Institution	State	Con-trol[1]	Type[2]	Total enrollment, fall 1985	Total enrollment, fall 1987	Total enrollment, fall 1988	Total enrollment, fall 1989	Enrollment, by sex, fall 1989		Enrollment, by attendance status, fall 1989	
								Men	Women	Full-time	Part-time
1	2	3	4	5	6	7	8	9	10	11	12
Sinclair Community College	Ohio	1	2	14,483	16,344	16,632	17,433	6,772	10,661	4,182	13,251
University of Akron, Main Campus	Ohio	1	1	26,025	27,069	27,818	28,967	14,346	14,621	17,314	11,653
University of Cincinnati, Main Campus	Ohio	1	1	30,205	31,233	32,726	30,787	16,018	14,769	20,085	10,702
University of Toledo	Ohio	1	1	21,238	21,740	22,806	23,928	11,661	12,267	15,642	8,286
Wright State University, Main Campus	Ohio	1	1	15,424	16,123	16,149	16,516	7,819	8,697	10,165	6,351
Youngstown State University	Ohio	1	1	15,026	14,675	14,710	14,864	7,001	7,863	9,621	5,243
Oklahoma State University, Main Campus	Okla.	1	1	21,639	21,082	21,258	21,258	11,494	9,764	16,562	4,696
Tulsa Junior College	Okla.	1	2	15,210	16,011	16,778	16,778	6,494	10,284	3,465	13,313
University of Oklahoma, Norman Campus	Okla.	1	1	21,748	22,352	22,225	22,225	12,290	9,935	15,789	6,436
Oregon State University	Oreg.	1	1	15,217	15,749	16,042	16,056	9,177	6,879	14,387	1,669
Portland Community College	Oreg.	1	2	17,915	20,492	20,904	21,578	9,955	11,623	6,169	15,409
Portland State University	Oreg.	1	1	14,768	17,316	17,316	16,750	7,597	9,153	8,115	8,635
University of Oregon	Oreg.	1	1	16,375	18,195	18,840	18,565	8,811	9,754	15,245	3,320
Center for Degree Studies	Pa.	2	2	5,821	13,486	17,738	22,669	10,096	12,573	(5)	22,669
Community College of Allegheny County	Pa.	1	2	(5)	(5)	18,211	18,211	7,783	10,428	7,590	10,621
International Correspondence Schools	Pa.	2	2	(5)	(5)	(5)	16,266	6,994	9,272	16,266	—
Pennsylvania State U., Main Campus	Pa.	1	1	(5)	37,269	37,718	37,718	21,419	16,299	33,383	4,335
Temple University	Pa.	1	1	30,277	30,431	32,139	32,713	16,146	16,567	21,584	11,129
University of Pennsylvania	Pa.	2	1	21,870	21,875	22,169	22,016	12,124	9,892	18,007	4,009
University of Pittsburgh, Main Campus	Pa.	1	1	28,710	28,364	28,524	28,362	14,689	13,673	18,603	9,759
Community College of Rhode Island	R.I.	1	2	12,617	13,107	14,718	15,400	5,477	9,923	4,240	11,160
University of Rhode Island	R.I.	1	1	14,235	15,170	15,847	16,254	7,493	8,761	10,958	5,296
Clemson University	S.C.	1	1	12,893	13,865	14,794	14,794	8,351	6,443	12,542	2,252
University of South Carolina, Columbia	S.C.	1	1	23,263	25,504	26,435	26,435	11,539	14,896	16,570	9,865
Memphis State University	Tenn.	1	1	20,749	20,470	20,267	20,605	9,441	11,164	12,788	7,817
University of Tennessee, Knoxville	Tenn.	1	1	25,397	25,986	24,985	25,512	13,226	12,286	19,134	6,378
Austin Community College	Tex.	1	2	17,549	19,905	21,418	23,067	10,734	12,333	5,685	17,382
El Paso Community College	Tex.	1	2	13,612	14,878	14,820	16,566	6,676	9,890	7,522	9,044
Houston Community College	Tex.	1	2	25,415	27,196	30,236	32,536	14,390	18,146	6,642	25,894
San Antonio College	Tex.	1	2	22,041	21,816	21,593	20,037	8,485	11,552	6,673	13,364
Southwest Texas State University	Tex.	1	1	19,268	20,039	20,505	20,800	9,828	10,972	15,525	5,275
Tarrant County Junior College District	Tex.	1	2	24,135	24,490	25,946	27,109	12,255	14,854	6,906	20,203
Texas A&M University	Tex.	1	1	35,675	39,079	39,163	40,492	23,556	16,936	36,108	4,384
Texas Tech University	Tex.	1	1	23,457	23,564	24,605	25,027	13,139	11,888	20,608	4,419
University of Houston-University Park	Tex.	1	1	29,944	28,907	30,372	32,289	16,434	15,855	18,653	13,636
University of North Texas	Tex.	1	1	20,996	22,379	24,498	26,523	12,625	13,898	17,884	8,639
University of Texas at Arlington	Tex.	1	1	23,109	22,760	23,383	23,871	13,078	10,793	13,538	10,333
University of Texas at Austin	Tex.	1	1	47,838	47,743	50,106	50,245	27,100	23,145	43,489	6,756
University of Texas at El Paso	Tex.	1	1	14,110	14,056	10,491	15,707	7,436	8,271	9,678	6,029
Brigham Young University	Utah	2	1	29,800	29,674	31,317	32,213	16,578	15,635	24,871	7,342
University of Utah	Utah	1	1	24,770	24,124	23,758	23,883	13,336	10,547	15,644	8,239
George Mason University	Va.	1	1	17,094	18,112	18,965	19,747	8,816	10,931	10,770	8,977
Liberty University	Va.	2	1	7,288	6,351	10,902	16,607	8,935	7,672	6,064	10,543
Northern Virginia Community College	Va.	1	2	32,282	34,884	31,896	34,539	15,549	18,990	8,746	25,793
Old Dominion University	Va.	1	1	15,865	15,640	16,364	16,239	7,799	8,440	10,522	5,717
Tidewater Community College	Va.	1	2	13,926	16,818	16,557	18,349	7,914	10,435	4,511	13,838
University of Virginia, Main Campus	Va.	1	1	17,417	21,268	20,802	20,879	10,142	10,737	16,518	4,361
Virginia Commonwealth University	Va.	1	1	19,556	20,485	20,645	21,391	8,768	12,623	13,403	7,988
Virginia Polytechnic Institute	Va.	1	1	24,193	24,977	24,280	24,926	14,780	10,146	21,455	3,471
University of Washington	Wash.	1	1	34,086	33,302	33,460	33,238	17,119	16,119	26,709	6,529
Washington State University	Wash.	1	1	16,139	16,484	16,405	17,138	9,554	7,584	15,573	1,565
West Virginia University	W.Va.	1	1	18,031	17,270	18,746	19,997	10,460	9,537	16,571	3,426
Milwaukee Area Voc./Tech. District	Wisc.	1	2	23,173	20,781	19,693	20,671	9,533	11,138	5,546	15,125
University of Wisconsin, Madison	Wisc.	1	1	45,050	43,368	43,364	43,364	22,204	21,160	36,617	6,747
University of Wisconsin, Milwaukee	Wisc.	1	1	26,213	25,210	25,212	25,212	11,805	13,407	13,452	11,760
Community College of the Air Force	U.S.	1	2	35,212	40,310	26,354	37,037	31,852	5,185	37,037	—

Table 204.—Selected statistics for college and university campuses enrolling more than 14,600 students in 1989—Continued

Enrollment, by level, fall 1989		Earned degrees conferred, 1988–89					Financial statistics, 1987–88,[3] in thousands			Full-time-equivalent enrollment, fall 1988	Full-time-equivalent enrollment, fall 1989
Undergraduate	Postbaccalaureate	Associate	Bachelor's	First professional	Master's	Doctor's	Current-fund revenues	Current-fund expenditures	Educational and general expenditures		
13	14	15	16	17	18	19	20	21	22	23	24
17,433	—	1,035	—	—	—	—	35,213	38,711	32,240	8,263	8,633
23,872	5,095	755	2,549	153	595	85	[7]136,956	[7]143,582	[7]125,130	21,057	21,900
24,263	6,524	495	2,949	318	892	182	513,597	532,150	303,698	26,519	24,289
20,691	3,237	611	2,110	207	472	56	128,264	126,559	112,712	17,889	18,914
13,042	3,474	—	1,560	85	735	37	120,454	117,652	112,064	12,276	12,624
13,647	1,217	393	1,420	—	253	—	71,504	71,987	63,724	11,605	11,691
16,278	4,980	43	2,872	69	713	211	196,786	195,846	157,831	18,326	18,326
16,778	—	947	—	—	—	—	31,092	31,077	27,847	7,937	7,937
16,464	5,761	—	2,219	220	864	114	220,225	227,196	129,026	18,233	18,233
13,128	2,928	—	2,620	36	691	142	235,584	237,222	213,275	14,879	15,027
21,578	—	940	—	—	—	—	54,607	58,367	50,445	11,015	11,345
12,590	4,160	—	1,851	—	668	35	76,557	75,533	67,306	11,778	11,471
13,907	4,658	0	2,643	164	837	196	150,168	153,943	122,956	16,949	16,515
22,669	—	211	—	—	—	—	3,182	5,015	3,182	7,264	9,283
18,211	—	1,915	—	—	—	—	61,956	58,738	58,974	11,157	11,157
16,266	—	—	—	—	—	—	(5)	(5)	(5)	(5)	16,266
31,621	6,097	57	7,234	—	1,151	417	[7]569,146	[7]593,810	[7]469,939	34,539	35,052
22,669	10,044	84	3,438	649	1,115	285	516,488	523,732	284,795	25,436	25,845
11,660	10,356	43	2,385	523	1,788	414	980,805	994,862	548,517	19,546	19,570
18,805	9,557	0	3,053	446	1,798	367	515,934	523,056	393,943	22,332	22,356
15,400	—	1,019	—	—	—	—	38,529	38,105	36,159	7,762	7,988
12,646	3,608	14	1,909	0	490	75	159,692	161,801	135,532	12,799	12,994
11,774	3,020	—	2,099	—	569	56	212,294	218,082	176,789	13,383	13,383
15,962	10,473	25	2,910	307	1,505	169	240,925	249,406	210,161	20,269	20,269
16,306	4,299	—	1,842	118	773	68	124,510	128,390	109,487	15,545	15,832
19,068	6,444	—	3,175	190	1,149	209	347,245	347,515	295,158	21,266	21,570
23,067	—	638	—	—	—	—	31,884	40,693	31,557	10,532	11,523
16,566	—	714	—	—	—	—	39,093	38,903	38,949	9,629	10,560
32,536	—	666	—	—	—	—	59,966	67,150	59,925	14,045	15,339
20,037	—	930	—	—	—	—	43,611	46,373	43,127	11,862	11,162
18,187	2,613	18	2,749	—	442	—	93,818	102,681	69,597	17,482	17,576
27,109	—	1,215	—	—	—	—	49,645	49,613	44,168	13,099	13,692
32,951	7,541	—	5,892	168	1,143	420	578,699	573,632	493,744	36,534	37,794
20,749	4,278	—	2,859	173	577	141	198,229	203,819	159,073	21,477	22,321
24,558	7,731	—	2,490	417	1,279	126	212,304	215,537	183,832	22,527	24,028
19,970	6,553	—	2,338	—	1,079	150	126,557	131,190	102,430	19,456	21,200
18,129	5,742	—	2,519	—	707	69	120,749	112,102	102,414	17,246	17,559
38,118	12,127	—	6,725	551	1,958	583	580,286	534,990	499,338	46,023	46,155
13,232	2,475	—	1,205	—	335	4	68,648	69,373	54,196	8,065	12,038
29,449	2,764	95	4,729	151	902	118	193,919	196,036	155,532	26,612	27,761
19,633	4,250	1	2,806	225	746	174	452,969	479,392	283,441	18,621	18,926
13,354	6,393	—	2,032	173	698	28	98,407	100,498	79,793	13,447	14,215
13,141	3,466	13	813	—	131	—	41,568	41,814	31,032	7,680	10,204
34,539	—	1,667	—	—	—	—	59,425	59,497	59,425	15,676	17,409
11,526	4,713	—	2,082	—	554	43	96,120	98,641	80,163	12,784	12,671
18,349	—	915	—	—	—	—	27,414	27,258	27,414	8,315	9,159
12,222	8,657	—	2,799	520	1,273	242	528,351	546,568	294,203	17,993	18,145
15,632	5,759	10	2,003	241	836	89	486,131	494,369	216,838	15,776	16,497
18,620	6,306	53	3,611	77	1,194	303	353,724	358,656	318,475	22,161	22,740
24,442	8,796	—	5,408	346	1,716	403	773,945	799,194	599,497	29,509	29,277
14,802	2,336	—	2,662	92	437	151	244,424	250,565	204,226	15,477	16,181
14,984	5,013	—	2,277	234	970	112	212,867	218,594	177,802	16,462	17,854
20,671	—	1,414	—	—	—	—	88,528	88,520	83,350	10,642	10,626
32,142	11,222	—	6,000	524	1,983	667	901,290	913,632	692,475	39,262	39,262
20,686	4,526	—	2,474	—	947	54	169,323	170,676	148,010	18,057	18,057
37,037	—	6,412	—	—	—	—	(5)	(5)	(5)	26,354	37,037

[1] Publicly controlled institutions are identified by a "1"; privately controlled, by a "2."

[2] The types of institutions are identified as follows: "1", 4-year institutions; "2", 2-year institutions.

[3] Totals for the United States and the colleges enrolling more than 14,600 students include estimates for nonrespondents.

[4] Data not reported, imputed based on prior year's response.

[5] Data not reported.

[6] Data not reported, imputed.

[7] Includes data for more than one campus.

—Not applicable.

SOURCE: U.S. Department of Education, National Center for Education Statistics, "Financial Statistics of Institutions of Higher Education," "Fall Enrollment in Institutions of Higher Education" surveys; and Integrated Postsecondary Education Data System (IPEDS), "Completions" and "Fall Enrollment" surveys. (This table was prepared April 1991.)

Table 205.—Enrollment of the 120 largest college and university campuses: [1] Fall 1989

Institution	State	Rank	Control[2]	Type[3]	Total enrollment, fall 1989	Institution	State	Rank	Control[2]	Type[3]	Total enrollment, fall 1989
1	2	3	4	5	6	1	2	3	4	5	6
University of Minnesota, Twin Cities	Minn.	1	1	1	58,815	University of Connecticut	Conn.	61	1	1	25,634
Ohio State University, Main Campus	Ohio	2	1	1	52,895	University of Tennessee-Knoxville	Tenn.	62	1	1	25,512
University of Texas at Austin	Tex.	3	1	1	50,245	University of Wisconsin-Milwaukee	Wisc.	63	1	1	25,512
Miami-Dade Community College	Fla.	4	1	2	47,330	Texas Tech University	Tex.	64	1	1	25,027
Michigan State University	Mich.	5	1	1	44,423	Virginia Polytechnic Institute	Va.	65	1	1	24,926
Arizona State University	Ariz.	6	1	1	43,550	University of New Mexico, Main Campus	N. Mex.	66	1	1	24,645
University of Wisconsin-Madison	Wisc.	7	1	1	43,364	Southern Illinois University-Carbondale	Ill.	67	1	1	24,596
Texas A&M University	Tex.	8	1	1	40,492	University of Colorado at Boulder	Colo.	68	1	1	24,589
Pennsylvania State U., Main Campus	Pa.	9	1	1	37,718	Harvard University	Mass.	69	2	1	24,509
University of Illinois, Urbana Campus	Ill.	10	1	1	37,481	Northern Illinois University	Ill.	70	1	1	24,443
Purdue University, Main Campus	Ind.	11	1	1	37,459	City College of San Francisco	Calif.	71	1	2	24,408
Community College of the Air Force	U.S.	12	1	2	37,037	University of Missouri-Columbia	Mo.	72	1	1	24,344
University of Arizona	Ariz.	13	1	1	36,676	University of Illinois at Chicago	Ill.	73	1	1	24,050
University of Michigan, Ann Arbor	Mich.	14	1	1	36,474	University of Toledo	Ohio	74	1	1	23,928
University of Maryland, College Park	Md.	15	1	1	35,825	University of Nebraska-Lincoln	Nebr.	75	1	1	23,926
University of California, Los Angeles	Calif.	16	1	1	34,993	University of Utah	Utah	76	1	1	23,883
Indiana University, Bloomington	Ind.	17	1	1	34,863	University of Texas at Arlington	Tex.	77	1	1	23,871
Northern Virginia Community College	Va.	18	1	2	34,539	Kent State University, Main Campus	Ohio	78	1	1	23,746
University of Florida	Fla.	19	1	1	34,098	University of North Carolina, Chapel Hill	N.C.	79	1	1	23,619
San Diego State University	Calif.	20	1	1	33,406	California State University, Fullerton	Calif.	80	1	1	23,588
University of Washington	Wash.	21	1	1	33,238	Broward Community College	Fla.	81	1	2	23,547
Rutgers University, New Brunswick	N.J.	22	1	1	33,020	San Diego Mesa College	Calif.	82	1	2	23,410
Northeastern University	Mass.	23	2	1	32,809	Cleveland Institute of Electronics	Ohio	83	2	2	23,373
Temple University	Pa.	24	1	1	32,713	California State University-Sacramento	Calif.	84	1	1	23,337
Houston Community College	Tex.	25	1	2	32,536	Eastern Michigan University	Mich.	85	1	1	23,288
Wayne State University	Mich.	26	1	1	32,477	Illinois State University	Ill.	86	1	1	23,107
University of Houston-University Park	Tex.	27	1	1	32,289	Austin Community College	Tex.	87	1	2	23,067
Brigham Young University	Utah	28	2	1	32,213	Georgia State University	Ga.	88	1	1	23,004
Saint Louis Community College	Mo.	29	1	2	31,847	Center For Degree Studies	Pa.	89	2	2	22,669
Macomb Community College	Mich.	30	1	2	31,670	University of Louisville	Ky.	90	1	1	22,555
University of South Florida	Fla.	31	1	1	31,566	Cuyahoga Community College District	Ohio	91	1	2	22,548
New York University	N.Y.	32	2	1	31,083	University of Kentucky	Ky.	92	1	1	22,407
University of Cincinnati, Main Campus	Ohio	33	1	1	30,787	Orange Coast College	Calif.	93	1	2	22,365
California State University, Long Beach	Calif.	34	1	1	30,665	University of Oklahoma, Norman Campus	Okla.	94	1	1	22,225
University of Iowa	Iowa	35	1	1	29,674	Syracuse University, Main Campus	N.Y.	95	2	1	22,196
University of California-Berkeley	Calif.	36	1	1	29,674	University of Pennsylvania	Pa.	96	2	1	22,016
University of Southern California	Calif.	37	2	1	29,657	De Anza College	Calif.	97	1	2	21,948
University of Akron, Main Campus	Ohio	38	1	1	28,967	Lansing Community College	Mich.	98	1	2	21,716
California State University, Northridge	Calif.	39	1	1	28,604	Auburn University, Main Campus	Ala.	99	1	1	21,701
Boston University	Mass.	40	2	1	28,529	Portland Community College	Oreg.	100	1	2	21,578
University of Pittsburgh, Main Campus	Pa.	41	1	1	28,362	Virginia Commonwealth University	Va.	101	1	1	21,391
College of Du Page	Ill.	42	1	2	28,037	University of California-Davis	Calif.	102	1	1	21,388
Florida State University	Fla.	43	1	1	27,975	Florida Community College, Jacksonville	Fla.	103	1	2	21,381
San Jose State University	Calif.	44	1	1	27,650	Oklahoma State University, Main Campus	Okla.	104	1	1	21,258
Oakland Community College	Mich.	45	1	2	27,504	Palm Beach Community College	Fla.	105	1	2	21,191
University of Georgia	Ga.	46	1	1	27,448	University of Virginia, Main Campus	Va.	106	1	1	20,879
SUNY at Buffalo	N.Y.	47	1	1	27,406	Southwest Texas State University	Tex.	107	1	1	20,800
University of Massachusetts at Amherst	Mass.	48	1	1	27,298	Nassau Community College	N.Y.	108	1	2	20,677
Tarrant County Junior College District	Tex.	49	1	2	27,109	Milwaukee Area Voc./Tech. District	Wisc.	109	1	2	20,671
North Carolina State U. at Raleigh	N.C.	50	1	1	26,870	Memphis State University	Tenn.	110	1	1	20,605
Louisiana State University	La.	51	1	1	26,750	Mount San Antonio College	Calif.	111	1	2	20,563
Pima Community College	Ariz.	52	1	2	26,747	Rancho Santiago College	Calif.	112	1	2	20,532
Indiana U.-Purdue U. at Indianapolis	Ind.	53	1	1	26,649	Santa Rosa Junior College	Calif.	113	1	2	20,479
University of North Texas	Tex.	54	1	1	26,523	University of Delaware	Del.	114	1	1	20,477
University of South Carolina, Columbia	S.C.	55	1	1	26,435	University of Central Florida	Fla.	115	1	1	20,345
University of Kansas, Main Campus	Kans.	56	1	1	26,320	Diablo Valley College	Calif.	116	1	2	20,255
Western Michigan University	Mich.	57	1	1	26,315	Florida International University	Fla.	117	1	1	20,222
Iowa State University	Iowa	58	1	1	26,038	Kansas State U. of Agr. and App. Sci.	Kans.	118	1	1	20,110
El Camino College	Calif.	59	1	2	25,789	San Antonio College	Tex.	119	1	2	20,037
San Francisco State University	Calif.	60	1	1	25,656	West Virginia University	W. Va.	120	1	1	19,997

[1] College and university campuses ranked in fall 1989. Data are preliminary.

[2] Publicly controlled institutions are identified by a "1." Privately controlled, by a "2."

[3] The types of institutions are identified as follows: "1," 4-year institutions: "2," 2-year institutions.

NOTE.—Institutions which did not report or which did report enrollment data for branch campuses were excluded from this tabulation.

SOURCE: U.S. Department of Education, National Center for Education Statistics, integrated Postsecondary Education Data System (IPEDS), "Fall Enrollment, 1989" survey. (This table was prepared April 1991.)

Table 206.—Selected statistics on historically black colleges and universities [1] of higher education: 1980, 1988, and 1989

Item	Total	Public		Private	
		4-year	2-year	4-year	2-year
1	2	3	4	5	6
Number of institutions, fall 1989	**106**	**40**	**11**	**49**	**6**
Total enrollment, fall 1980	233,557	155,085	13,132	62,924	2,416
Men	106,387	70,236	6,758	28,352	1,041
Men, black	81,818	53,654	2,781	24,412	971
Women	127,170	84,849	6,374	34,572	1,375
Women, black	109,171	70,582	4,644	32,589	1,356
Total enrollment, fall 1988	239,755	158,606	15,066	64,644	1,439
Men	100,561	66,097	6,772	27,219	473
Men, black	78,268	50,545	3,192	24,081	450
Women	139,194	92,509	8,294	37,425	966
Women, black	115,883	73,893	5,894	35,145	951
Total enrollment, fall 1989	249,178	166,481	14,670	66,491	1,536
Men	102,534	68,383	6,319	27,334	498
Women	146,644	98,098	8,351	39,157	1,038
Full-time enrollment, fall 1989	189,126	118,744	8,576	60,501	1,305
Men	79,793	50,939	3,545	24,843	466
Women	109,333	67,805	5,031	35,658	839
Part-time enrollment, fall 1989	60,052	47,737	6,094	5,990	231
Men	22,741	17,444	2,774	2,491	32
Women	37,311	30,293	3,320	3,499	199
Earned degrees conferred, 1988–89					
Associate	2,526	1,101	1,146	120	159
Men	963	379	484	54	46
Men, black	476	168	220	42	46
Women	1,563	722	662	66	113
Women, black	1,011	306	536	57	112
Bachelor's	19,748	13,002	—	6,746	—
Men	7,895	5,415	—	2,480	—
Men, black	5,982	3,894	—	2,088	—
Women	11,853	7,587	—	4,266	—
Women, black	9,943	6,072	—	3,871	—
Master's	3,916	3,147	—	769	—
Men	1,477	1,178	—	299	—
Men, black	730	581	—	149	—
Women	2,439	1,969	—	470	—
Women, black	1,638	1,304	—	334	—
Doctor's	190	62	—	128	—
Men	105	31	—	74	—
Men, black	55	11	—	44	—
Women	85	31	—	54	—
Women, black	57	14	—	43	—
First-professional	843	347	—	496	—
Men	493	199	—	294	—
Men, black	273	54	—	219	—
Women	350	148	—	202	—
Women, black	205	49	—	156	—
Financial statistics, 1987–88, in thousands of dollars					
Current-fund revenues	$2,263,263	$1,232,677	$63,653	$958,580	$8,353
Tuition and fees	456,227	198,159	8,015	247,617	2,435
Federal Government [2]	435,540	153,440	9,763	270,271	2,066
State governments [2]	663,192	609,503	33,193	20,024	471
Local governments [2]	87,883	77,154	7,424	3,054	250
Private gifts, grants, and contracts	111,161	10,669	928	97,951	1,613
Endowment income	24,084	2,279	262	21,543	0
Sales and services	442,977	160,052	2,210	279,503	1,213
Other sources	42,199	21,420	1,857	18,618	305
Current-fund expenditures	2,222,412	1,211,293	61,399	941,298	8,422
Educational and general expenditures	1,812,838	1,051,819	59,229	693,535	8,255
Auxiliary enterprises	233,986	159,474	2,170	72,175	167
Hospitals	174,441	0	0	174,441	0
Independent operations	1,147	0	0	1,147	0

[1] Most institutions are in the southern and border States and were established prior to 1954.

[2] Includes appropriations, grants, and contracts. —Not applicable.

NOTE.—Enrollment data for fall 1989, degree data for 1988–89, and financial statistics for 1987–88 are preliminary. Because of rounding, details may not add to totals.

SOURCE: U.S. Department of Education, National Center for Education Statistics, "Fall Enrollment in Institutions of Higher Education"; and Integrated Postsecondary Education Data System (IPEDS), "Fall Enrollment," "Completions," and "Finance" surveys. (This table was prepared April 1991.)

Table 207.—Enrollment in historically black colleges and universities, by type and control of institution: Fall 1976 to fall 1989

Year	Total enrollment	Type of institution		Public institutions			Private institutions		
		4-year	2-year	Total	4-year	2-year	Total	4-year	2-year
1	2	3	4	5	6	7	8	9	10
1976	222,613	206,676	15,937	156,836	143,528	13,308	65,777	63,148	2,629
1977	226,062	209,898	16,164	158,823	145,450	13,373	67,239	64,448	2,791
1978	227,797	211,651	16,146	163,237	150,168	13,069	64,560	61,483	3,077
1979	230,124	214,147	15,977	166,315	153,139	13,176	63,809	61,008	2,801
1980	233,557	218,009	15,548	168,217	155,085	13,132	65,340	62,924	2,416
1981	232,460	217,152	15,308	166,991	154,269	12,722	65,469	62,883	2,586
1982	228,371	212,017	16,354	165,871	151,472	14,399	62,500	60,545	1,955
1983	234,446	217,909	16,537	170,051	155,665	14,386	64,395	62,244	2,151
1984	227,519	212,844	14,675	164,116	151,289	12,827	63,403	61,555	1,848
1985	225,801	210,648	15,153	163,677	150,002	13,675	62,124	60,646	1,478
1986	223,275	207,231	16,044	162,048	147,631	14,417	61,227	59,600	1,627
1987	227,994	211,654	16,340	165,486	150,560	14,926	62,508	61,094	1,414
1988	239,755	223,250	16,505	173,672	158,606	15,066	66,083	64,644	1,439
1989 [1]	249,178	232,972	16,206	181,151	166,481	14,670	68,027	66,491	1,536

[1] Preliminary.

SOURCE: U.S. Department of Education, National Center for Education Statistics, "Fall Enrollment in Colleges and Universities"; and Integrated Postsecondary Education Data System (IPEDS), "Fall Enrollment" surveys. (This table was prepared February 1991.)

Table 208.—Employees in institutions of higher education, by primary occupation, employment status, and control of institution: Fall 1976 and fall 1987

Primary occupation and control of institution	Fall 1976						Fall 1987					
	Total staff				Full-time equivalent staff		Total staff				Full-time equivalent staff	
	Number	Percent	Full-time	Part-time	Total	FTE students per FTE staff	Number	Percent	Full-time	Part-time	Total	FTE students per FTE staff
1	2	3	4	5	6	7	8	9	10	11	12	13
Total, all institutions	1,863,790	100.0	1,339,911	523,879	1,541,339	5.4	2,337,534	100.0	1,689,069	648,465	1,937,334	4.8
Professional staff	1,073,119	57.6	709,400	363,719	845,456	9.8	1,437,975	61.5	947,733	490,242	1,131,266	8.2
Executive/administrative/managerial	101,263	5.4	97,003	4,260	98,972	84.0	133,719	5.7	128,809	4,910	131,075	70.4
Faculty (instruction and research)	633,210	34.0	434,071	199,139	500,533	16.6	793,070	33.9	523,420	269,650	613,319	15.0
Instruction and research assistants	160,086	8.6	28,007	132,079	82,684	100.5	161,464	6.9	—	161,464	66,718	138.3
Non-faculty professionals	178,560	9.6	150,319	28,241	163,267	50.9	349,722	15.0	295,504	54,218	320,154	28.8
Nonprofessional staff	790,671	42.4	630,511	160,160	695,883	11.9	899,559	38.5	741,336	158,223	806,068	11.5
Public, total	1,329,122	100.0	946,354	382,768	1,092,558	5.8	1,586,261	100.0	1,119,759	466,502	1,296,802	5.3
Professional staff	769,836	57.9	502,325	267,511	601,942	10.5	997,226	62.9	633,942	363,284	769,264	9.0
Executive/administrative/managerial	60,733	4.6	58,649	2,084	59,579	106.6	74,170	4.7	71,660	2,510	72,780	95.3
Faculty (instruction and research)	448,733	33.8	313,367	135,366	357,761	17.7	552,749	34.8	364,157	188,592	426,007	16.3
Instruction and research assistants	127,925	9.6	19,076	108,849	63,420	100.1	136,370	8.6	—	136,370	55,556	124.9
Non-faculty professionals	132,445	10.0	111,233	21,212	121,182	52.4	233,937	14.7	198,125	35,812	214,922	32.3
Nonprofessional staff	559,286	42.1	444,029	115,257	490,616	12.9	589,035	37.1	485,817	103,218	527,538	13.2
Private, total	534,668	100.0	393,557	141,111	448,781	4.4	751,273	100.0	569,310	181,963	640,532	3.6
Professional staff	303,283	56.7	207,075	96,208	243,514	8.1	440,749	58.7	313,791	126,958	362,002	6.3
Executive/administrative/managerial	40,530	7.6	38,354	2,176	39,393	49.8	59,549	7.9	57,149	2,400	58,295	39.3
Faculty (instruction and research)	184,477	34.5	120,704	63,773	142,772	13.7	240,321	32.0	159,263	81,058	187,312	12.2
Instruction and research assistants	32,161	6.0	8,931	23,230	19,264	101.9	25,094	3.3	—	25,094	11,162	205.3
Non-faculty professionals	46,115	8.6	39,086	7,029	42,085	46.6	115,785	15.4	97,379	18,406	105,232	21.8
Nonprofessional staff	231,385	43.3	186,482	44,903	205,267	9.6	310,524	41.3	255,519	55,005	278,530	8.2

—Not applicable.

NOTE.—Because of rounding, details may not add to totals.

SOURCE: U.S. Department of Education, National Center for Education Statistics, Higher Education General Information Survey (HEGIS), "Staff, 1976" survey; and Integrated Postsecondary Education Data System (IPEDS), "Staff, 1987" survey. (This table was prepared May 1990.)

Table 209.—Employees in institutions of higher education, by primary occupation, employment status, sex, and by type or control of institution: Fall 1987

Primary occupation and type and control of institution	Full-time and part-time					Full-time				Part-time		
	Total		Men	Women		Total		Men	Women	Total	Men	Women
	Number	Percent		Number	Percent women	Number	Percent full-time					
1	2	3	4	5	6	7	8	9	10	11	12	13
Total, all institutions	2,337,534	100.0	1,164,067	1,173,467	50.2	1,689,069	72.3	840,237	848,832	648,465	323,830	324,635
Professional staff	1,437,975	61.5	850,451	587,524	40.9	947,733	65.9	576,028	371,705	490,242	274,423	215,819
Executive/administrative/managerial	133,719	5.7	82,882	50,837	38.0	128,809	96.3	80,524	48,285	4,910	2,358	2,552
Faculty (instruction and research)	793,070	33.9	529,413	263,657	33.2	523,420	66.0	373,546	149,874	269,650	155,867	113,783
Instruction and research assistants	161,464	6.9	98,608	62,856	38.9	—	—	—	—	161,464	98,608	62,856
Non-faculty professionals	349,722	15.0	139,548	210,174	60.1	295,504	84.5	121,958	173,546	54,218	17,590	36,628
Nonprofessional staff	899,559	38.5	313,616	585,943	65.1	741,336	82.4	264,209	477,127	158,223	49,407	108,816
Technical and paraprofessionals	167,377	7.2	68,390	98,987	59.1	136,034	81.3	57,152	78,882	31,343	11,238	20,105
Clerical and secretarial	435,434	18.6	44,270	391,164	89.8	350,129	80.4	28,597	321,532	85,305	15,673	69,632
Skilled crafts	60,511	2.6	57,204	3,307	5.5	57,884	95.7	55,363	2,521	2,627	1,841	786
Service and maintenance	236,237	10.1	143,752	92,485	39.1	197,289	83.5	123,097	74,192	38,948	20,655	18,293
Public, total	1,586,261	100.0	804,882	781,379	49.3	1,119,759	70.6	571,486	548,273	466,502	233,396	233,106
Professional staff	997,226	62.9	594,896	402,330	40.3	633,942	63.6	393,560	240,382	363,284	201,336	161,948
Executive/administrative/managerial	74,170	4.7	50,164	24,006	32.4	71,660	96.6	48,868	22,792	2,510	1,296	1,214
Faculty (instruction and research)	552,749	34.8	366,127	186,622	33.8	364,157	65.9	260,114	104,043	188,592	106,013	82,579
Instruction and research assistants	136,370	8.6	82,579	53,791	39.4	—	—	—	—	136,370	82,579	53,791
Non-faculty professionals	233,937	14.7	96,026	137,911	59.0	198,125	84.7	84,578	113,547	35,812	11,448	24,364
Nonprofessional staff	589,035	37.1	209,986	379,049	64.4	485,817	82.5	177,926	307,891	103,218	32,060	71,158
Technical and paraprofessionals	110,612	7.0	46,589	64,023	57.9	88,220	79.8	38,397	49,823	22,392	8,192	14,200
Clerical and secretarial	281,159	17.7	27,370	253,789	90.3	224,692	79.9	16,971	207,721	56,467	10,399	46,068
Skilled crafts	43,417	2.7	40,846	2,571	5.9	41,404	95.4	39,430	1,974	2,013	1,416	597
Service and maintenance	153,847	9.7	95,181	58,666	38.1	131,501	85.5	83,128	48,373	22,346	12,053	10,293
Private, total	751,273	100.0	359,185	392,088	52.2	569,310	75.8	268,751	300,559	181,963	90,434	91,529
Professional staff	440,749	58.7	255,555	185,194	42.0	313,791	71.2	182,468	131,323	126,958	73,087	53,871
Executive/administrative/managerial	59,549	7.9	32,718	26,831	45.1	57,149	96.0	31,656	25,493	2,400	1,062	1,338
Faculty (instruction and research)	240,321	32.0	163,286	77,035	32.1	159,263	66.3	113,432	45,831	81,058	49,854	31,204
Instruction and research assistants	25,094	3.3	16,029	9,065	36.1	—	—	—	—	25,094	16,029	9,065
Non-faculty professionals	115,785	15.4	43,522	72,263	62.4	97,379	84.1	37,380	59,999	18,406	6,142	12,264
Nonprofessional staff	310,524	41.3	103,630	206,894	66.6	255,519	82.3	86,283	169,236	55,005	17,347	37,658
Technical and paraprofessionals	56,765	7.6	21,801	34,964	61.6	47,814	84.2	18,755	29,059	8,951	3,046	5,905
Clerical and secretarial	154,275	20.5	16,900	137,375	89.0	125,437	81.3	11,626	113,811	28,838	5,274	23,564
Skilled crafts	17,094	2.3	16,358	736	4.3	16,480	96.4	15,933	547	614	425	189
Service and maintenance	82,390	11.0	48,571	33,819	41.0	65,788	79.8	39,969	25,819	16,602	8,602	8,000
4-year, total	1,905,408	100.0	945,193	960,215	50.4	1,444,094	75.8	713,763	730,331	461,314	231,430	229,884
Professional staff	1,130,054	59.3	673,700	456,354	40.4	791,715	70.1	480,768	310,947	338,339	192,932	145,407
Executive/administrative/managerial	112,274	5.9	68,871	43,403	38.7	108,523	96.7	67,094	41,429	3,751	1,777	1,974
Faculty (instruction and research)	547,505	28.7	385,257	162,248	29.6	409,899	74.9	301,095	108,804	137,606	84,162	53,444
Instruction and research assistants	150,499	7.9	92,352	58,147	38.6	—	—	—	—	150,499	92,352	58,147
Non-faculty professionals	319,776	16.8	127,220	192,556	60.2	273,293	85.5	112,579	160,714	46,483	14,641	31,842
Nonprofessional staff	775,354	40.7	271,493	503,861	65.0	652,379	84.1	232,995	419,384	122,975	38,498	84,477
Technical and paraprofessionals	143,951	7.6	59,435	84,516	58.7	119,894	83.3	50,793	69,101	24,057	8,642	15,415
Clerical and secretarial	371,243	19.5	38,283	332,960	89.7	306,496	82.6	26,611	279,885	64,747	11,672	53,075
Skilled crafts	54,125	2.8	51,635	2,490	4.6	52,511	97.0	50,339	2,172	1,614	1,296	318
Service and maintenance	206,035	10.8	122,140	83,895	40.7	173,478	84.2	105,252	68,226	32,557	16,888	15,669
2-year, total	432,126	100.0	218,874	213,252	49.3	244,975	56.7	126,474	118,501	187,151	92,400	94,751
Professional staff	307,921	71.3	176,751	131,170	42.6	156,018	50.7	95,260	60,758	151,903	81,491	70,412
Executive/administrative/managerial	21,445	5.0	14,011	7,434	34.7	20,286	94.6	13,430	6,856	1,159	581	578
Faculty (instruction and research)	245,565	56.8	144,156	101,409	41.3	113,521	46.2	72,451	41,070	132,044	71,705	60,339
Instruction and research assistants	10,965	2.5	6,256	4,709	42.9	—	—	—	—	10,965	6,256	4,709
Non-faculty professionals	29,946	6.9	12,328	17,618	58.8	22,211	74.2	9,379	12,832	7,735	2,949	4,786
Nonprofessional staff	124,205	28.7	42,123	82,082	66.1	88,957	71.6	31,214	57,743	35,248	10,909	24,339
Technical and paraprofessionals	23,426	5.4	8,955	14,471	61.8	16,140	68.9	6,359	9,781	7,286	2,596	4,690
Clerical and secretarial	64,191	14.9	5,987	58,204	90.7	43,633	68.0	1,986	41,647	20,558	4,001	16,557
Skilled crafts	6,386	1.5	5,569	817	12.8	5,373	84.1	5,024	349	1,013	545	468
Service and maintenance	30,202	7.0	21,612	8,590	28.4	23,811	78.8	17,845	5,966	6,391	3,767	2,624

—Not applicable.

SOURCE: U.S. Department of Education, National Center for Education Statistics, Integrated Postsecondary Education Data System (IPEDS), "Staff" survey. (This table was prepared May 1990.)

Table 210.—Employees in institutions of higher education, by primary occupation, employment status, sex, and by type and control of institution: Fall 1987

Primary occupation and type and control of institution	Full-time and part-time					Full-time				Part-time		
	Total		Men	Women		Total		Men	Women	Total	Men	Women
	Number	Percent		Number	Percent woman	Number	Percent full-time					
1	2	3	4	5	6	7	8	9	10	11	12	13
Total, all employees	**2,337,534**	**100.0**	**1,164,067**	**1,173,467**	**50.2**	**1,689,069**	**72.3**	**840,237**	**848,832**	**648,465**	**323,830**	**324,635**
Professional staff	1,437,975	61.5	850,451	587,524	40.9	947,733	65.9	576,028	371,705	490,242	274,423	215,819
Executive/administrative/managerial	133,719	5.7	82,882	50,837	38.0	128,809	96.3	80,524	48,285	4,910	2,358	2,552
Faculty (instruction and research)	793,070	33.9	529,413	263,657	33.2	523,420	66.0	373,546	149,874	269,650	155,867	113,783
Instruction and research assistants	161,464	6.9	98,608	62,856	38.9	—	—	—	—	161,464	98,608	62,856
Non-faculty professionals	349,722	15.0	139,548	210,174	60.1	295,504	84.5	121,958	173,546	54,218	17,590	36,628
Nonprofessional staff	899,559	38.5	313,616	585,943	65.1	741,336	82.4	264,209	477,127	158,223	49,407	108,816
Technical and paraprofessionals	167,377	7.2	68,390	98,987	59.1	136,034	81.3	57,152	78,882	31,343	11,238	20,105
Clerical and secretarial	435,434	18.6	44,270	391,164	89.8	350,129	80.4	28,597	321,532	85,305	15,673	69,632
Skilled crafts	60,511	2.6	57,204	3,307	5.5	57,884	95.7	55,363	2,521	2,627	1,841	786
Service and maintenance	236,237	10.1	143,752	92,485	39.1	197,289	83.5	123,097	74,192	38,948	20,655	18,293
Public 4-year, total	1,184,934	100.0	598,891	586,043	49.5	896,095	75.6	453,858	442,237	288,839	145,033	143,806
Professional staff	711,714	60.1	428,579	283,135	39.8	492,591	69.2	305,143	187,448	219,123	123,436	95,687
Executive/administrative/managerial	55,967	4.7	37,792	18,175	32.5	54,473	97.3	37,018	17,455	1,494	774	720
Faculty (instruction and research)	322,635	27.2	229,626	93,009	28.8	259,112	80.3	191,977	67,135	63,523	37,649	25,874
Instruction and research assistants	125,603	10.6	76,422	49,181	39.2	—	—	—	—	125,603	76,422	49,181
Non-faculty professionals	207,509	17.5	84,739	122,770	59.2	179,006	86.3	76,148	102,858	28,503	8,591	19,912
Nonprofessional staff	473,220	39.9	170,312	302,908	64.0	403,504	85.3	148,715	254,789	69,716	21,597	48,119
Technical and paraprofessionals	88,386	7.5	37,977	50,409	57.0	72,997	82.6	32,311	40,686	15,389	5,666	9,723
Clerical and secretarial	221,095	18.7	21,623	199,472	90.2	184,372	83.4	15,152	169,220	36,723	6,471	30,252
Skilled crafts	37,376	3.2	35,562	1,814	4.9	36,343	97.2	34,676	1,667	1,033	886	147
Service and maintenance	126,363	10.7	75,150	51,213	40.5	109,792	86.9	66,576	43,216	16,571	8,574	7,997
Public 2-year, total	401,327	100.0	205,991	195,336	48.7	223,664	55.7	117,628	106,036	177,663	88,363	89,300
Professional staff	285,512	71.1	166,317	119,195	41.7	141,351	49.5	88,417	52,934	144,161	77,900	66,261
Executive/administrative/managerial	18,203	4.5	12,372	5,831	32.0	17,187	94.4	11,850	5,337	1,016	522	494
Faculty (instruction and research)	230,114	57.3	136,501	93,613	40.7	105,045	45.6	68,137	36,908	125,069	68,364	56,705
Instruction and research assistants	10,767	2.7	6,157	4,610	42.8	—	—	—	—	10,767	6,157	4,610
Non-faculty professionals	26,428	6.6	11,287	15,141	57.3	19,119	72.3	8,430	10,689	7,309	2,857	4,452
Nonprofessional staff	115,815	28.9	39,674	76,141	65.7	82,313	71.1	29,211	53,102	33,502	10,463	23,039
Technical and paraprofessionals	22,226	5.5	8,612	13,614	61.3	15,223	68.5	6,086	9,137	7,003	2,526	4,477
Clerical and secretarial	60,064	15.0	5,747	54,317	90.4	40,320	67.1	1,819	38,501	19,744	3,928	15,816
Skilled crafts	6,041	1.5	5,284	757	12.5	5,061	83.8	4,754	307	980	530	450
Service and maintenance	27,484	6.8	20,031	7,453	27.1	21,709	79.0	16,552	5,157	5,775	3,479	2,296
Private 4-year, total	720,474	100.0	346,302	374,172	51.9	547,999	76.1	259,905	288,094	172,475	86,397	86,078
Professional staff	418,340	58.1	245,121	173,219	41.4	299,124	71.5	175,625	123,499	119,216	69,496	49,720
Executive/administrative/managerial	56,307	7.8	31,079	25,228	44.8	54,050	96.0	30,076	23,974	2,257	1,003	1,254
Faculty (instruction and research)	224,870	31.2	155,631	69,239	30.8	150,787	67.1	109,118	41,669	74,083	46,513	27,570
Instruction and research assistants	24,896	3.5	15,930	8,966	36.0	—	—	—	—	24,896	15,930	8,966
Non-faculty professionals	112,267	15.6	42,481	69,786	62.2	94,287	84.0	36,431	57,856	17,980	6,050	11,930
Nonprofessional staff	302,134	41.9	101,181	200,953	66.5	248,875	82.4	84,280	164,595	53,259	16,901	36,358
Technical and paraprofessionals	55,565	7.7	21,458	34,107	61.4	46,897	84.4	18,482	28,415	8,668	2,976	5,692
Clerical and secretarial	150,148	20.8	16,660	133,488	88.9	122,124	81.3	11,459	110,665	28,024	5,201	22,823
Skilled crafts	16,749	2.3	16,073	676	4.0	16,168	96.5	15,663	505	581	410	171
Service and maintenance	79,672	11.1	46,990	32,682	41.0	63,686	79.9	38,676	25,010	15,986	8,314	7,672
Private 2-year, total	30,799	100.0	12,883	17,916	58.2	21,311	69.2	8,846	12,465	9,488	4,037	5,451
Professional staff	22,409	72.8	10,434	11,975	53.4	14,667	65.5	6,843	7,824	7,742	3,591	4,151
Executive/administrative/managerial	3,242	10.5	1,639	1,603	49.4	3,099	95.6	1,580	1,519	143	59	84
Faculty (instruction and research)	15,451	50.2	7,655	7,796	50.5	8,476	54.9	4,314	4,162	6,975	3,341	3,634
Instruction and research assistants	198	0.6	99	99	50.0	—	—	—	—	198	99	99
Non-faculty professionals	3,518	11.4	1,041	2,477	70.4	3,092	87.9	949	2,143	426	92	334
Nonprofessional staff	8,390	27.2	2,449	5,941	70.8	6,644	79.2	2,003	4,641	1,746	446	1,300
Technical and paraprofessionals	1,200	3.9	343	857	71.4	917	76.4	273	644	283	70	213
Clerical and secretarial	4,127	13.4	240	3,887	94.2	3,313	80.3	167	3,146	814	73	741
Skilled crafts	345	1.1	285	60	17.4	312	90.4	270	42	33	15	18
Service and maintenance	2,718	8.8	1,581	1,137	41.8	2,102	77.3	1,293	809	616	288	328

—Data not available or not applicable.

SOURCE: U.S. Department of Education, National Center for Education Statistics, Integrated Postsecondary Education Data System (IPEDS), "Staff" survey. (This table was prepared May 1990.)

Table 211.—Full-time and part-time senior instructional faculty [1] in institutions of higher education, by employment status and control and type of institution: Fall 1970 to fall 1990

[In thousands]

Year	Total	Employment status		Control		Type	
		Full-time	Part-time	Public	Private	4-year	2-year
1	2	3	4	5	6	7	8
1970	474	369	104	314	160	382	92
1971 [2]	492	379	113	333	159	387	105
1972	500	380	120	343	157	384	116
1973 [2]	527	389	138	365	162	401	126
1974 [2]	567	406	161	397	170	427	140
1975 [2]	628	440	188	443	185	467	161
1976	633	434	199	450	183	467	166
1977	678	448	230	492	186	485	193
1979 [2]	675	445	230	488	187	494	182
1980 [2]	686	450	236	495	191	494	192
1981	705	461	244	509	196	493	212
1982 [2]	710	462	248	506	204	493	217
1983	724	471	254	512	212	504	220
1984 [2]	717	462	255	505	212	504	213
1985 [2]	715	459	256	503	212	504	211
1986 [2]	722	459	263	510	212	506	216
1987 [3]	793	523	270	553	240	548	246
1988 [4]	741	—	—	524	217	—	—
1989 [4]	755	—	—	534	221	—	—
1990 [4]	762	—	—	539	223	—	—

[1] Includes faculty members with the title of professor, associate professor, assistant professor, instructor, lecturer, assisting professor, adjunct professor, or interim professor (or the equivalent). Excluded are graduate students with titles such as graduate or teaching fellow who assist senior faculty.

[2] Estimated on the basis of enrollment.

[3] Because of revised survey methods, data are not directly comparable to figures for other years.

[4] Estimated.

—Data not available.

NOTE.—Data exclude faculty employed by system offices. Some data have been revised from previously published figures. For methodological details on estimates, see *Projections of Education Statistics to 2000*. Because of rounding, details may not add to totals.

SOURCE: U.S. Department of Education, National Center for Education Statistics, *Employees in Institutions of Higher Education*, various years; *Projections of Education Statistics to 2000*; Integrated Postsecondary Education Data System (IPEDS), "Staff, 1987" survey; and U.S. Equal Employment Opportunity Commission, *Higher Education Staff Information Report File, 1977, 1981, and 1983*. (This table was prepared March 1991.)

Table 212.—Full-time instructional faculty in institutions of higher education, by race/ethnicity, academic rank, and sex: Fall 1985

Academic rank and sex	Total	Race/ethnicity				
		White non-Hispanic	Black non-Hispanic	Hispanic	Asian or Pacific Islander	American Indian/Alaskan Native
1	2	3	4	5	6	7
Men and women, all ranks	**464,072**	**417,036**	**19,227**	**7,704**	**18,370**	**1,735**
Professors	129,269	119,868	2,859	1,455	4,788	299
Associate professors	111,092	100,630	4,201	1,727	4,130	404
Assistant professors	111,308	97,496	5,895	1,968	5,469	480
Instructors	75,411	66,799	4,572	1,798	1,806	436
Lecturers	9,766	8,477	631	251	360	47
Other faculty	27,226	23,766	1,069	505	1,817	69
Men, all ranks	**336,009**	**303,953**	**10,456**	**5,360**	**14,846**	**1,394**
Professors	114,258	106,335	2,058	1,206	4,395	264
Associate professors	85,156	77,483	2,595	1,280	3,451	347
Assistant professors	71,463	62,582	2,923	1,316	4,240	402
Instructors	43,251	38,592	2,107	1,141	1,105	306
Lecturers	5,098	4,436	304	117	212	29
Other faculty	16,783	14,525	469	300	1,443	46
Women, all ranks	**128,063**	**113,083**	**8,771**	**2,344**	**3,524**	**341**
Professors	15,011	13,533	801	249	393	35
Associate professors	25,936	23,147	1,606	447	679	57
Assistant professors	39,845	34,914	2,972	652	1,229	78
Instructors	32,160	28,207	2,465	657	701	130
Lecturers	4,668	4,041	327	134	148	18
Other faculty	10,443	9,241	600	205	374	23

NOTE.—Data exclude faculty employed by system offices. Totals may differ from figures reported on other tables because of varying survey methodologies.

SOURCE: U.S. Equal Employment Opportunity Commission, *Higher Education Staff Information Report File, 1985,* unpublished data. (This table was prepared June 1989.)

Table 213.—Full-time regular instructional faculty in institutions of higher education, by selected characteristics and type and control of institution: Fall 1987

Selected characteristics	Number in thousands	Percent total	Public research	Private research	Public doctoral	Private doctoral	Public compre-hensive	Private compre-hensive	Liberal arts	Public 2-year	Private 2-year	Medical	Other
1	2	3	4	5	6	7	8	9	10	11	12	13	14
Total (in thousands)	**489**	—	**96**	**39**	**36**	**15**	**93**	**35**	**39**	**91**	**4**	**25**	**15**
Percent	—	**100.0**	**19.7**	**8.0**	**7.3**	**3.0**	**19.0**	**7.2**	**8.0**	**18.7**	**0.8**	**5.2**	**3.0**

Percent distribution

Total	—	100.0	100.0	100.0	100.0	100.0	100.0	100.0	100.0	100.0	100.0	100.0	100.0
Sex													
Male	356	72.7	79.3	80.5	74.5	77.3	71.1	72.5	70.9	62.1	64.2	75.7	78.7
Female	133	27.3	20.7	19.5	25.5	22.7	28.9	27.5	29.1	37.9	35.8	24.3	21.3
Race													
White, non-Hispanic	438	89.5	90.4	85.4	92.0	91.3	88.0	91.2	86.9	91.0	94.1	85.3	95.1
Black, non-Hispanic	16	3.2	1.6	6.1	1.8	0.1	3.5	1.7	8.0	3.0	3.1	3.0	2.3
Hispanic	11	2.3	2.4	5.0	1.1	2.2	2.1	1.6	1.2	3.5	2.3	(1)	1.6
Asian	21	4.2	4.8	3.5	4.5	5.9	5.8	4.4	2.7	1.6	0.5	10.3	1.0
American Indian	3	0.7	0.7	(1)	0.6	0.5	0.6	1.1	1.2	0.9	(1)	1.4	(1)
Age													
29 or younger	8	1.6	1.1	0.6	1.8	1.3	1.6	2.1	2.2	1.9	9.5	0.7	1.2
30–34	41	8.3	7.1	11.5	10.2	4.5	7.9	6.2	8.5	5.6	6.7	22.1	5.7
35–39	72	14.7	16.5	21.4	14.8	17.9	12.5	16.3	14.4	12.2	4.6	10.7	17.0
40–44	82	16.7	15.2	17.6	14.0	11.4	15.7	18.4	19.8	18.1	36.3	16.9	17.0
45–49	92	18.9	18.5	15.1	18.7	17.3	21.2	18.0	19.9	21.2	3.3	13.5	18.2
50–54	74	15.1	14.8	12.3	15.9	18.4	15.3	16.9	9.9	18.2	19.8	10.5	15.6
55–59	59	12.0	12.1	8.6	13.2	10.7	13.2	10.2	13.6	13.5	12.8	8.6	9.1
60 or older	62	12.7	14.7	12.8	11.5	18.5	12.6	11.9	11.7	9.3	6.8	17.0	16.3
Highest degree													
Doctoral	263	54.7	72.1	69.1	73.0	74.4	62.7	64.0	60.3	17.5	13.8	25.9	40.6
Professional	61	12.7	18.3	23.9	5.4	14.9	6.2	8.1	1.8	1.5	3.2	62.7	27.8
Master's	134	27.9	8.5	6.2	19.2	10.7	29.9	24.3	34.6	64.9	58.1	9.8	26.5
Graduate work, no degree	7	1.5	0.2	0.7	1.0	(1)	0.6	1.2	2.0	4.8	6.1	(1)	1.8
Bachelor's	11	2.2	0.9	0.2	0.9	(1)	0.6	1.8	1.3	7.7	10.9	(1)	2.9
Less than bachelor's	4	0.9	(1)	(1)	0.5	(1)	(1)	0.6	(1)	3.7	8.0	1.5	0.5
Academic rank													
Professor	162	33.1	45.3	39.2	35.6	35.4	37.2	30.8	29.4	15.6	12.5	31.6	34.3
Associate professor	116	23.7	28.1	25.3	30.1	34.3	26.5	29.5	23.0	9.5	4.6	26.9	22.4
Assistant professor	111	22.8	21.2	29.1	25.9	28.3	23.4	32.7	31.2	10.9	21.9	29.0	16.3
Instructor	56	11.5	2.7	3.1	6.7	2.0	8.7	6.1	9.3	33.3	25.0	11.8	9.1
Lecturer	8	1.6	2.7	2.4	1.4	(1)	3.0	0.4	0.5	0.7	0.5	(1)	(1)
Other	4	0.9	0.1	0.8	0.3	(1)	1.2	0.3	0.6	1.7	0.6	0.7	3.2
No rank	32	6.5	(1)	0.1	(1)	0.1	(1)	0.2	5.9	28.3	34.9	(1)	14.6
Base salary													
Less than $20,000	24	5.0	2.2	3.2	5.3	4.1	3.6	7.8	15.1	3.0	30.0	0.8	18.4
$20,000–24,999	50	10.2	3.4	2.1	11.9	4.2	10.2	18.3	21.7	15.2	19.9	1.3	10.6
$25,000–29,999	72	14.8	8.1	8.4	14.5	15.2	17.5	17.7	22.3	19.5	35.7	3.6	15.8
$30,000–34,999	76	15.6	9.4	7.0	15.8	17.7	16.9	20.0	17.2	22.9	8.3	15.8	11.1
$35,000–39,999	67	13.8	12.5	11.7	15.6	10.9	15.4	15.0	10.0	17.6	2.7	8.7	12.1
$40,000–49,999	96	19.7	25.0	20.5	24.8	17.7	22.2	12.7	9.7	19.6	1.9	10.8	18.5
$50,000–74,999	78	15.9	30.5	29.8	9.7	21.4	12.5	7.5	4.0	2.3	1.0	40.5	13.5
$75,000 or more	24	4.9	9.0	17.2	2.4	8.9	1.6	1.0	(1)	(1)	0.4	18.5	(1)

[1] Less than .05 percent.
—Data not applicable.

NOTE.—Data may not add to totals because of rounding or missing data.

SOURCE: U.S. Department of Education, National Center for Education Statistics, National Survey of Postsecondary Faculty (NSOPF), 1988. (This table was prepared June 1990.)

Table 214.—Full-time regular instructional faculty in institutions of higher education, by faculty characteristics and by field: 1987–88

Faculty characteristics	Number in thousands	All fields	Agriculture and home economics	Business	Education	Engineering	Fine arts	Health	Humanities	Natural sciences	Social sciences	Other
1	2	3	4	5	6	7	8	9	10	11	12	13
Total, in thousands	**489**	—	**13**	**37**	**35**	**25**	**32**	**85**	**62**	**84**	**53**	**64**
Percentage	—	**100**	**3**	**7**	**7**	**5**	**7**	**17**	**13**	**17**	**11**	**13**

Percentage distribution

Faculty characteristics	Number in thousands	All fields	Agriculture and home economics	Business	Education	Engineering	Fine arts	Health	Humanities	Natural sciences	Social sciences	Other
Total	**489**	**100**	**100**	**100**	**100**	**100**	**100**	**100**	**100**	**100**	**100**	**100**
Sex												
Male	356	73	63	72	55	98	74	61	67	83	78	77
Female	133	27	37	28	45	2	26	39	33	17	22	23
Race/ethnicity												
White, non-Hispanic	438	90	94	88	88	87	92	88	90	91	90	89
Asian	21	4	2	6	1	11	1	7	2	6	2	3
Black, non-Hispanic	16	3	0	4	6	(¹)	3	2	3	2	5	5
Hispanic	11	2	3	1	4	2	3	1	5	1	3	2
American Indian	4	1	1	1	1	(¹)	(¹)	1	1	(¹)	1	1
Age												
34 or younger	48	10	11	10	8	10	13	13	5	9	7	12
35–39	72	15	22	16	11	13	14	17	13	15	15	14
40–44	82	17	16	18	16	13	19	16	14	17	21	15
45–49	92	19	21	17	19	18	18	18	20	22	20	16
50–54	74	15	11	17	18	14	16	13	16	17	14	14
55–59	59	12	12	12	15	17	9	9	15	11	10	14
60 and older	62	13	7	9	13	14	11	15	16	9	13	14
Degree												
Less than bachelor's	4	1	2	(¹)	(¹)	(¹)	1	1	(¹)	1	(¹)	4
Bachelor's	11	2	2	4	1	4	2	2	(¹)	1	(¹)	7
Graduate work no degree	7	2	(¹)	1	(¹)	2	3	1	1	2	1	3
Master's	134	28	26	39	38	29	51	20	26	24	18	30
Professional	48	10	2	6	1	1	4	44	1	1	2	8
Doctoral	276	57	67	50	59	64	40	32	71	71	79	49
Rank												
Professor	162	33	35	21	28	41	30	31	38	38	36	30
Associate professor	116	24	23	21	24	24	26	24	25	23	26	20
Assistant professor	111	23	22	27	22	23	22	29	19	18	22	23
Instructor	56	12	12	19	12	7	10	11	8	9	6	20
Lecturer	8	2	3	3	1	1	1	1	3	2	1	1
Other	3	1	(¹)	(¹)	2	1	(¹)	(¹)	(¹)	(¹)	1	1
No rank	34	7	4	8	11	3	10	4	8	9	8	5

¹ Less than 0.5 percent —Not applicable.

NOTE.—Because of rounding and survey item nonresponse, details may not add to totals.

SOURCE: U.S. Department of Education, *National Survey of Postsecondary Faculty (NSOPF), 1987–88.* (This table was prepared April 1991)

Table 215.—Total regular and temporary instructional faculty in institutions of higher education, by selected characteristics and type and control of institution: Fall 1987

Selected characteristics	Number in thousands	Percent total	Public research	Private research	Public doctoral	Private doctoral	Public comprehensive	Private comprehensive	Liberal arts	Public 2-year	Private 2-year	Medical	Other
1	2	3	4	5	6	7	8	9	10	11	12	13	14
Total (in thousands)	770	—	119	53	45	27	130	130	130	201	6	35	32
Percent	—	100	16	7	6	4	17	17	17	26	1	5	4

Percent distribution

Total	—	100	100	100	100	100	100	100	100	100	100	100	100
Sex													
Male	521	68	77	75	69	77	66	66	66	61	53	71	72
Female	248	32	23	25	31	23	34	34	34	39	47	29	28
Race													
White, non-Hispanic	690	90	91	85	93	91	88	88	88	91	90	82	92
Black, non-Hispanic	25	3	1	7	2	(1)	3	3	3	3	4	2	4
Hispanic	18	2	2	5	1	4	2	2	2	4	2	(1)	1
Asian	30	4	4	4	4	4	6	6	6	2	2	15	4
American Indian	6	1	1	(1)	1	1	1	1	1	1	2	1	(1)
Type of employment													
Temporary	105	14	11	10	10	17	12	12	12	14	6	13	17
Regular	665	86	89	90	90	83	88	88	88	86	94	87	84

[1] Less than 0.5 percent.
—Not applicable.

NOTE.—Data may not add to totals because of rounding or missing data.

SOURCE: U.S. Department of Education, National Center for Education Statistics, National Survey of Postsecondary Faculty (NSOPF), 1988. (This table was prepared June 1990.)

Table 216.—Part-time regular instructional faculty in institutions of higher education, by selected characteristics and type and control of institution: Fall 1987

Selected characteristics	Number in thousands	Percent total	Public research	Private research	Public doctoral	Private doctoral	Public comprehensive	Private comprehensive	Liberal arts	Public 2-year	Private 2-year	Medical	Other
1	2	3	4	5	6	7	8	9	10	11	12	13	14
Total (in thousands)	174	—	10	9	5	8	22	10	13	81	2	5	11
Percent	—	100	6	5	3	5	12	6	7	46	1	3	6

Percent distribution

Total	—	100	100	100	100	100	100	100	100	100	100	100	100
Sex													
Male	99	57	67	58	36	87	50	49	39	58	(1)	(1)	77
Female	75	43	33	42	64	13	50	52	61	42	(1)	(1)	23
Race													
White, non-Hispanic	156	90	98	83	94	91	84	97	82	92	(1)	(1)	97
Black, non-Hispanic	6	4	1	12	2	(2)	2	(2)	14	3	(1)	(1)	1
Hispanic	4	3	(2)	2	2	9	2	3	2	3	(1)	(1)	(2)
Asian	6	3	(2)	2	(2)	(2)	9	0	(2)	2	(1)	(1)	1
American Indian	2	1	1	2	2	(2)	4	(2)	1	0	(1)	(1)	(2)
Age													
29 or younger	9	5	5	10	8	(2)	6	10	2	4	(1)	(1)	11
30–34	17	10	11	3	19	7	11	5	6	13	(1)	(1)	3
35–39	39	22	16	20	21	28	27	16	23	22	(1)	(1)	21
40–44	34	19	18	20	10	13	16	15	11	22	(1)	(1)	21
45–49	25	14	12	21	16	12	12	9	20	13	(1)	(1)	29
50–54	19	11	4	10	11	29	12	13	10	11	(1)	(1)	3
55–59	12	7	9	2	7	6	12	12	6	6	(1)	(1)	3
60 or older	19	11	26	16	9	7	5	19	22	9	(1)	(1)	10
Degree													
Doctoral	26	15	27	34	17	27	27	19	17	7	(1)	(1)	17
Professional	22	13	29	38	14	19	9	9	9	4	(1)	(1)	25
Master's	70	42	31	20	47	23	49	58	50	46	(1)	(1)	29
Graduate work, no degree	13	8	7	5	2	6	5	7	4	10	(1)	(1)	13
Bachelor's	28	17	4	2	21	23	10	8	19	22	(1)	(1)	14
Less than bachelor's	9	5	2	1	(2)	3	(2)	(2)	1	10	(1)	(1)	1

[1] Too few cases for reliable estimates
[2] Less than 0.5 percent.
—Not applicable.

NOTE.—Data may not add to totals because of rounding or missing data.

SOURCE: U.S. Department of Education, National Center for Education Statistics, National Survey of Postsecondary Faculty (NSOPF), 1988. (This table was prepared June 1990.)

Table 217.—Salaries of full-time regular instructional faculty in institutions of higher education, by type and control of institution and by field of instruction: 1987–88

Field of instruction	Public									Private							
	All 4-year institutions								All 2-year institutions	All 4-year institutions							All 2-year institutions
	Total	Research	Doctoral	Comprehensive	Liberal arts	Medical	Other			Total	Research	Doctoral	Comprehensive	Liberal arts	Medical	Other	
1	2	3	4	5	6	7	8	9	10	11	12	13	14	15	16	17
Number of faculty, in thousands	**251**	96	36	97	1	18	2	88	147	39	15	35	38	8	13	3
Mean salary																
All fields	**$39,200**	$43,800	$35,600	$35,800	$27,700	$57,000	$37,300	$32,900	$35,500	$47,400	$40,400	$31,500	$29,400	$53,400	$32,500	$26,500
Agriculture and home economics	39,500	45,100	35,800	34,300	—	—	—	31,600	32,800	47,900	28,000	24,100	24,300	—	—	13,700
Business	39,200	45,300	39,100	34,800	—	—	—	33,600	38,300	53,500	40,900	38,100	25,300	—	32,700	33,700
Education	36,800	39,700	36,400	35,100	27,000	38,400	—	33,700	30,200	40,600	40,100	29,500	25,300	—	28,300	41,700
Engineering	44,300	48,400	43,200	39,100	—	—	39,100	30,600	43,800	56,000	46,700	41,900	37,900	—	32,000	27,300
Fine arts	33,900	37,300	32,800	32,600	—	—	31,500	32,600	30,400	34,600	37,000	28,700	29,600	56,800	24,700	10,500
Health	53,500	58,400	41,100	39,800	—	59,100	—	30,200	50,900	63,600	46,500	35,400	25,600	—	41,900	26,400
Humanities	36,800	39,600	33,000	36,300	28,400	—	38,900	35,800	33,100	39,300	39,600	30,800	30,800	38,100	29,100	22,700
Natural sciences	41,000	45,800	39,300	37,000	24,500	46,200	40,000	32,900	37,000	49,400	39,800	31,500	29,700	—	29,100	23,300
Social sciences	38,200	41,200	36,200	35,600	27,600	62,000	40,000	34,100	35,400	44,800	39,300	28,500	29,800	—	35,400	19,300
Other	36,700	42,000	35,400	34,400	27,400	—	40,500	31,300	35,700	57,100	37,000	30,200	27,500	—	38,700	21,800
Median salary																
All fields	37,000	41,600	35,000	35,000	27,600	53,000	38,000	32,000	32,200	43,000	38,000	30,000	28,000	46,000	29,700	22,300
Agriculture and home economics	39,000	42,000	35,000	33,000	—	—	—	30,000	28,000	48,500	28,000	23,400	24,200	—	—	14,000
Business	40,000	45,000	41,600	35,000	—	—	—	32,800	38,000	50,000	42,500	35,500	25,000	—	27,200	21,000
Education	36,000	38,100	32,800	34,000	27,000	38,400	—	34,000	28,000	39,500	41,000	28,500	24,000	—	29,000	43,200
Engineering	43,800	48,000	40,500	36,000	—	—	45,600	33,000	42,000	52,000	48,600	41,000	36,000	—	32,500	27,300
Fine arts	32,000	35,500	32,000	30,000	—	—	32,000	33,000	30,000	34,000	36,100	30,000	27,800	55,000	18,500	10,500
Health	47,000	54,000	32,500	30,000	—	55,000	—	29,400	44,000	62,500	35,000	34,300	25,500	—	42,000	27,600
Humanities	35,500	38,000	33,200	35,900	28,400	—	—	35,500	31,000	35,000	39,000	30,000	30,000	38,100	28,900	27,100
Natural sciences	39,900	45,000	36,000	36,900	24,500	50,000	40,000	32,600	34,800	45,000	37,500	30,000	29,800	—	28,000	22,000
Social sciences	38,000	40,000	36,000	36,000	27,600	64,000	40,000	34,600	31,900	40,000	36,700	29,000	29,400	—	33,500	18,500
Other	34,800	38,900	34,600	33,800	27,500	—	40,500	30,400	29,000	54,000	34,500	27,300	25,000	—	36,000	24,000

—Data not available.

NOTE.—Because of rounding, details may not add to totals.

SOURCE: U.S. Department of Education, National Center for Education Statistics, National Survey of Postsecondary Faculty (NSOPF), 1987–88. (This table was prepared April 1991.)

Table 218.—Average salary of full-time instructional faculty in institutions of higher education, by academic rank and sex: 1972–73 to 1989–90

Academic year and sex	All ranks	Professor	Associate professor	Assistant professor	Instructor	Lecturer	Undesignated or no academic rank
1	2	3	4	5	6	7	8

Current dollars

Total

Academic year and sex	All ranks	Professor	Associate professor	Assistant professor	Instructor	Lecturer	Undesignated or no academic rank
1972–73	$13,850	$19,182	$14,572	$12,029	$10,737	$11,637	$12,676
1975–76	16,634	22,611	17,026	13,966	13,682	12,887	15,201
1979–80	21,367	28,371	21,431	17,459	14,021	16,151	20,479
1980–81	23,302	30,753	23,214	18,901	15,178	17,301	22,334
1981–82	25,449	33,437	25,278	20,608	16,450	18,756	24,331
1982–83	27,196	35,540	26,921	22,056	17,601	20,072	25,557
1984–85	30,447	39,743	29,945	24,668	20,230	22,334	27,683
1985–86	32,392	42,268	31,787	26,277	20,918	23,770	29,088
1987–88	35,897	47,040	35,231	29,110	22,728	25,977	31,532
1989–90	39,965	52,809	39,381	32,694	25,001	28,973	32,794

Men

Academic year and sex	All ranks	Professor	Associate professor	Assistant professor	Instructor	Lecturer	Undesignated or no academic rank
1972–73	14,415	19,405	14,714	12,190	11,147	12,105	13,047
1975–76	17,388	22,866	17,167	14,154	14,440	13,577	15,764
1979–80	22,423	28,653	21,627	17,712	14,321	16,987	21,247
1980–81	24,499	31,082	23,451	19,227	15,545	18,281	23,170
1981–82	26,796	33,799	25,553	21,025	16,906	19,721	25,276
1982–83	28,664	35,956	27,262	22,586	18,160	21,225	26,541
1984–85	32,182	40,269	30,392	25,330	21,159	23,557	28,670
1985–86	34,294	42,833	32,273	27,094	21,693	25,238	30,267
1987–88	38,112	47,735	35,823	30,086	23,645	27,652	32,747
1989–90	42,629	53,646	40,128	33,783	25,891	31,102	34,069

Women

Academic year and sex	All ranks	Professor	Associate professor	Assistant professor	Instructor	Lecturer	Undesignated or no academic rank
1972–73	11,925	17,122	13,827	11,510	10,099	10,775	11,913
1975–76	14,292	20,257	16,336	13,506	12,580	11,870	14,098
1979–80	18,395	25,910	20,642	16,971	13,749	15,142	19,069
1980–81	19,996	27,959	22,295	18,302	14,854	16,168	20,843
1981–82	21,802	30,438	24,271	19,866	16,054	17,676	22,672
1982–83	23,261	32,221	25,738	21,130	17,102	18,830	23,855
1984–85	25,941	35,824	28,517	23,575	19,362	21,004	26,050
1985–86	27,576	38,252	30,300	24,966	20,237	22,273	27,171
1987–88	30,499	42,371	33,528	27,600	21,962	24,370	29,605
1989–90	33,936	47,673	37,440	31,099	24,302	27,031	31,019

Constant 1989–90 dollars [1]

Total

Academic year and sex	All ranks	Professor	Associate professor	Assistant professor	Instructor	Lecturer	Undesignated or no academic rank
1972–73	41,081	56,897	43,223	35,680	31,848	34,517	37,599
1975–76	38,085	51,769	38,982	31,976	31,326	29,506	34,804
1979–80	34,947	46,403	35,052	28,556	22,932	26,416	33,495
1980–81	34,156	45,078	34,027	27,705	22,248	25,360	32,737
1981–82	34,337	45,115	34,106	27,805	22,195	25,306	32,829
1982–83	35,183	45,977	34,827	28,533	22,770	25,967	33,063
1984–85	36,552	47,712	35,949	29,614	24,286	26,812	33,234
1985–86	37,797	49,321	37,091	30,662	24,409	27,736	33,942
1987–88	39,347	51,561	38,617	31,908	24,912	28,473	34,563
1989–90	39,965	52,809	39,381	32,694	25,001	28,973	32,794

Men

Academic year and sex	All ranks	Professor	Associate professor	Assistant professor	Instructor	Lecturer	Undesignated or no academic rank
1972–73	42,757	57,558	43,644	36,157	33,064	35,905	38,699
1975–76	39,811	52,353	39,305	32,407	33,061	31,085	36,093
1979–80	36,675	46,864	35,373	28,969	23,423	27,784	34,751
1980–81	35,911	45,560	34,374	28,183	22,786	26,796	33,963
1981–82	36,154	45,603	34,477	28,368	22,810	26,609	34,104
1982–83	37,082	46,516	35,268	29,219	23,493	27,458	34,336
1984–85	38,635	48,344	36,486	30,409	25,402	28,281	34,419
1985–86	40,017	49,980	37,658	31,615	25,313	29,449	35,318
1987–88	41,774	52,322	39,266	32,978	25,917	30,310	35,894
1989–90	42,629	53,646	40,128	33,783	25,891	31,102	34,069

Women

Academic year and sex	All ranks	Professor	Associate professor	Assistant professor	Instructor	Lecturer	Undesignated or no academic rank
1972–73	35,371	50,786	41,013	34,140	29,955	31,960	35,336
1975–76	32,723	46,380	37,402	30,923	28,803	27,177	32,278
1979–80	30,086	42,378	33,762	27,757	22,488	24,766	31,189
1980–81	29,310	40,982	32,680	26,827	21,773	23,699	30,552
1981–82	29,416	41,068	32,748	26,804	21,661	23,849	30,590
1982–83	30,092	41,684	33,297	27,336	22,125	24,360	30,861
1984–85	31,143	43,007	34,235	28,302	23,244	25,216	31,273
1985–86	32,178	44,635	35,356	29,132	23,614	25,990	31,705
1987–88	33,431	46,443	36,750	30,253	24,072	26,712	32,450
1989–90	33,936	47,673	37,440	31,099	24,302	27,031	31,019

[1] Data adjusted, using the Consumer Price Index prepared by the Bureau of Labor Statistics, averaged on an academic year time frame.

NOTE.—Data for 1972–73, 1975–76, 1987–88, and 1989–90 are for faculty on 9- to 10-month contracts; data for 1979–80 to 1985–86 are for faculty on 9-month contracts. Data for 1987–88 and 1989–90 include imputations for nonrespondent institutions.

SOURCE: U.S. Department of Education, National Center for Education Statistics, *Faculty Salaries, Tenure, and Benefits;* and Integrated Postsecondary Education Data System (IPEDS), "Salaries, Tenure, and Fringe Benefits of Full-Time Instructional Faculty" surveys. (This table was prepared February 1991.)

Table 219.—Average salary of full-time instructional faculty on 9-month contracts in institutions of higher education, by academic rank and sex and by type and control of institution: 1980–81, 1985–86, 1987–88, and 1989–90

Academic year, control, and type of institution	Average salary, all faculty	Average salary, by rank						Average salary, by sex	
		Professor	Associate professor	Assistant professor	Instructor	Lecturer	No academic rank	Men	Women
1	2	3	4	5	6	7	8	9	10
1980–81									
All institutions	$23,302	$30,753	$23,214	$18,901	$15,178	$17,301	$22,334	$24,499	$19,996
4-year	23,693	31,016	23,265	18,867	15,056	17,375	17,380	24,909	19,809
University	25,949	33,622	24,392	19,684	15,530	17,327	17,856	27,206	20,736
Other 4-year	22,230	28,798	22,558	18,398	14,887	17,425	17,334	23,271	19,372
2-year	21,898	26,528	22,750	19,166	15,621	16,222	22,615	22,736	20,434
Public institutions	23,745	31,077	23,772	19,431	15,613	17,620	22,820	24,873	20,673
4-year	24,373	31,442	23,898	19,442	15,486	17,712	19,240	25,509	20,608
University	25,571	32,945	24,268	19,637	15,305	17,426	17,358	26,788	20,564
Other 4-year	23,500	30,097	23,639	19,315	15,567	17,997	19,798	24,499	20,633
2-year	22,177	26,880	22,947	19,370	15,928	16,458	22,875	22,965	20,778
Private institutions	22,093	29,994	21,833	17,767	14,192	15,899	15,946	23,493	18,073
4-year	22,325	30,089	21,887	17,816	14,316	15,971	16,706	23,669	18,326
University	26,897	35,227	24,730	19,792	16,197	16,956	18,933	28,251	21,176
Other 4-year	19,996	26,173	20,502	16,939	13,905	14,741	16,617	21,040	17,342
2-year	15,065	18,645	17,685	14,663	12,155	12,441	14,993	16,075	13,892
1985–86									
All institutions	32,392	42,268	31,787	26,277	20,918	23,770	29,088	34,294	27,576
4-year	33,270	42,803	31,940	26,335	20,383	23,805	24,055	35,174	27,696
University	36,837	46,994	33,704	28,242	20,784	23,807	24,139	38,841	29,243
Other 4-year	31,078	39,610	30,864	25,314	20,253	23,802	24,043	32,688	26,994
2-year	29,259	36,076	30,483	25,823	22,434	23,154	29,420	30,490	27,294
Public institutions	32,750	42,328	32,367	26,951	21,553	23,839	29,597	34,528	28,299
4-year	34,033	43,044	32,642	27,100	20,895	23,862	25,142	35,786	28,680
University	35,835	45,322	33,133	27,887	20,226	23,557	23,706	37,771	28,567
Other 4-year	32,757	41,170	32,296	26,597	21,180	24,101	25,705	34,260	28,742
2-year	29,590	36,418	30,733	26,162	22,818	23,500	29,712	30,758	27,693
Private institutions	31,402	42,118	30,400	24,891	19,314	23,477	21,577	33,656	25,523
4-year	31,732	42,260	30,486	24,987	19,483	23,574	23,394	33,900	25,889
University	39,519	51,355	35,307	29,125	22,743	24,540	26,603	41,680	31,106
Other 4-year	28,198	36,455	28,365	23,412	18,910	22,093	23,295	29,882	24,280
2-year	19,436	24,519	22,291	19,297	16,419	9,231	18,783	20,412	18,504
1987–88 [1]									
All institutions	35,897	47,040	35,231	29,110	22,728	25,977	31,532	38,112	30,499
4-year	36,967	47,656	35,399	29,210	22,255	26,000	26,501	39,185	30,755
University	41,476	53,096	37,702	31,784	22,779	26,408	28,203	43,834	32,966
Other 4-year	34,285	43,684	34,024	27,878	22,093	25,654	26,219	36,132	29,772
2-year	31,904	39,049	33,610	28,136	24,326	25,551	31,905	33,236	29,864
Public institutions	36,231	47,073	35,956	29,832	23,269	26,029	32,034	38,314	31,215
4-year	37,840	47,917	36,272	30,037	22,637	26,057	27,195	39,898	31,820
University	40,106	50,865	37,011	31,206	21,909	26,060	25,645	42,405	31,986
Other 4-year	36,286	45,615	35,756	29,312	22,936	26,055	28,077	38,042	31,729
2-year	32,209	39,443	33,901	28,523	24,661	25,627	32,148	33,477	30,228
Private institutions	35,049	46,964	33,653	27,750	21,522	25,773	24,676	37,603	28,621
4-year	35,346	47,113	33,738	27,845	21,645	25,793	26,190	37,817	28,946
University	44,814	58,332	39,482	33,128	25,463	27,271	37,672	47,262	35,497
Other 4-year	31,089	40,010	31,237	25,869	20,968	23,441	25,664	32,941	26,970
2-year	21,867	26,796	24,288	21,481	18,613	16,566	21,169	22,641	21,215
1989–90									
All institutions	39,965	52,809	39,381	32,694	25,001	28,973	32,794	42,629	33,936
4-year	41,441	53,515	39,647	32,827	24,618	28,964	29,401	44,041	34,674
University	46,732	59,750	42,480	35,809	25,508	29,544	31,116	49,461	37,511
Other 4-year	38,320	48,977	37,960	31,304	24,361	28,466	29,159	40,483	33,427
2-year	34,062	44,050	36,680	31,281	26,296	29,156	33,079	35,571	31,996
Public institutions	40,161	52,863	40,169	33,480	25,364	28,659	33,289	42,745	34,459
4-year	42,355	53,860	40,637	33,741	24,820	28,630	30,975	44,827	35,704
University	44,958	57,269	41,568	34,945	24,040	28,235	30,932	47,656	36,145
Other 4-year	40,567	51,211	39,975	32,989	25,123	28,915	30,996	42,714	35,464
2-year	34,404	44,496	37,041	31,685	26,593	29,156	33,351	35,888	32,346
Private institutions	39,505	52,694	37,814	31,296	24,184	30,003	26,989	42,363	32,641
4-year	39,860	52,859	37,918	31,388	24,285	30,010	28,682	42,647	33,002
University	50,787	65,012	44,692	37,778	30,576	32,393	32,049	53,482	40,920
Other 4-year	34,987	45,069	35,031	29,081	23,318	26,410	28,579	37,048	30,650
2-year	24,601	30,468	26,366	24,788	22,334	29,146	23,451	25,218	24,000

[1] Data revised from previously published figures.

NOTE.—Data for 1987–88 and 1989–90 include imputations for nonrespondent institutions.

SOURCE: U.S. Department of Education, National Center for Education Statistics, *Faculty Salaries, Tenure, and Benefits, 1980–81*; and Integrated Postsecondary Education Data System (IPEDS), "Salaries, Tenure, and Fringe Benefits of Full-Time Instructional Faculty" survey. (This table was prepared February 1991.)

Table 220.—Average salary of full-time instructional faculty on 9-month contracts in institutions of higher education, by type and control of institution and by State: 1989–90

State or other area	Average, all institutions	Public institutions					Private institutions				
		Total	4-year institutions			2-year	Total	4-year institutions			2-year
			Total	University	Other 4-year			Total	University	Other 4-year	
1	2	3	4	5	6	7	8	9	10	11	12
United States	$39,965	$40,161	$42,355	$44,958	$40,567	$34,404	$39,505	$39,860	$50,787	$34,987	$24,601
Alabama	33,308	34,148	35,386	38,711	32,956	30,644	29,305	29,760	—	29,760	23,961
Alaska	44,789	45,280	45,280	44,828	45,552	—	37,976	37,976	—	37,976	—
Arizona	40,903	41,386	43,465	44,856	36,893	37,413	32,987	32,987	—	32,987	—
Arkansas	31,588	32,194	33,369	37,902	31,869	25,471	28,044	28,116	—	28,116	23,969
California	46,476	47,194	52,765	59,945	51,396	35,482	43,846	44,071	56,997	37,461	33,148
Colorado	38,450	38,216	41,043	46,063	37,184	27,701	40,380	40,380	41,219	39,263	—
Connecticut	47,232	47,709	49,978	54,203	45,453	41,081	46,667	46,894	59,192	41,721	27,639
Delaware	40,682	41,248	42,074	43,547	32,733	35,401	36,537	36,537	—	36,537	—
District of Columbia	44,708	42,195	42,195	—	42,195	—	45,186	45,186	46,524	34,453	—
Florida	38,027	38,557	41,741	45,130	39,362	34,100	36,103	36,225	46,298	32,852	22,834
Georgia	36,261	36,912	38,118	40,468	37,439	30,925	34,317	35,198	48,112	30,833	23,326
Hawaii	39,917	40,847	43,535	44,984	36,729	35,317	25,466	25,466	—	25,466	—
Idaho	32,118	33,784	34,430	37,920	32,793	29,090	25,042	26,893	—	26,893	24,436
Illinois	40,546	40,065	41,180	43,712	38,725	38,201	41,466	41,728	53,081	34,066	24,667
Indiana	37,442	37,357	39,556	41,342	35,445	25,442	37,635	34,668	54,402	33,020	28,825
Iowa	38,028	41,229	45,619	47,892	38,613	29,047	32,406	32,499	40,177	31,261	26,936
Kansas	34,185	36,023	38,668	40,275	34,476	29,453	23,871	24,238	—	24,238	19,878
Kentucky	32,714	34,018	35,739	39,998	33,145	26,596	28,008	28,287	—	28,287	17,797
Louisiana	33,275	32,114	32,579	38,633	30,865	26,641	38,664	38,664	44,748	27,499	—
Maine	36,794	36,780	38,389	40,705	36,590	28,683	36,828	36,923	—	36,923	27,740
Maryland	41,877	42,087	44,000	48,442	41,661	38,560	41,077	41,126	55,798	34,358	20,076
Massachusetts	46,113	43,952	47,079	53,044	44,590	36,110	47,384	48,138	54,245	40,843	25,912
Michigan	41,270	42,820	44,081	49,745	39,285	39,648	33,502	33,757	37,886	33,362	23,095
Minnesota	39,376	41,204	42,342	49,879	38,650	38,119	34,952	35,303	—	35,303	25,670
Mississippi	30,595	30,747	33,602	36,245	31,925	26,972	29,434	30,290	—	30,290	17,156
Missouri	35,621	36,274	37,006	41,330	36,168	33,514	34,337	34,573	46,136	28,755	23,706
Montana	29,780	30,671	31,305	32,629	28,456	26,029	25,140	25,871	—	25,871	24,048
Nebraska	34,745	35,827	38,069	43,430	34,097	24,603	31,236	31,514	37,726	27,993	19,936
Nevada	39,414	39,483	41,104	42,479	40,116	33,411	29,110	27,454	—	27,454	33,250
New Hampshire	38,783	37,116	39,166	42,233	34,344	28,982	41,045	41,379	—	41,379	16,851
New Jersey	45,136	44,524	46,741	52,314	44,796	39,293	46,510	46,510	56,335	39,756	—
New Mexico	34,661	34,913	37,099	38,412	32,912	27,328	29,226	29,226	—	29,226	—
New York	44,557	46,766	49,452	53,364	48,847	41,741	42,473	42,631	51,237	37,973	21,911
North Carolina	37,207	38,753	40,473	45,466	38,216	24,915	34,050	34,592	45,404	29,616	25,709
North Dakota	30,907	31,696	32,768	33,781	30,541	27,642	23,832	24,897	—	24,897	17,948
Ohio	40,141	42,323	44,721	45,821	40,865	33,091	34,793	34,799	50,068	33,197	32,177
Oklahoma	34,508	34,234	35,665	37,590	33,978	29,554	35,598	36,182	40,977	34,303	20,775
Oregon	34,342	34,362	35,504	36,801	33,981	32,887	34,257	34,257	—	34,257	—
Pennsylvania	41,177	41,891	42,983	47,060	40,687	36,545	40,364	40,832	53,088	36,807	24,894
Rhode Island	43,971	42,442	44,559	47,341	39,862	36,018	45,566	45,566	—	45,566	—
South Carolina	34,017	35,312	38,343	42,133	34,211	26,117	29,041	29,755	—	29,755	24,209
South Dakota	29,437	31,351	31,351	31,848	30,663	—	24,917	24,928	—	24,928	21,000
Tennessee	36,126	37,160	39,158	43,378	37,606	29,094	33,857	34,157	51,787	27,450	21,336
Texas	37,615	37,449	40,233	44,696	35,920	32,469	38,339	38,444	46,116	32,324	22,529
Utah	38,319	34,181	36,404	39,185	29,953	27,109	43,647	43,684	44,271	27,414	33,596
Vermont	36,018	38,796	39,891	42,454	30,697	28,138	33,397	34,828	—	34,828	23,680
Virginia	40,984	43,328	46,232	49,697	43,846	34,370	33,743	33,861	—	33,861	24,068
Washington	36,675	37,024	41,097	43,742	36,576	31,435	35,120	35,120	—	35,120	—
West Virginia	29,758	30,426	30,975	35,759	28,490	24,471	26,303	26,583	—	26,583	21,295
Wisconsin	38,463	38,973	40,920	49,175	37,952	35,501	36,133	36,133	43,531	33,650	—
Wyoming	34,438	34,438	39,468	39,468	—	28,961	—	—	—	—	—
U.S. Service Schools	42,924	42,924	42,924	—	42,924	—	—	—	—	—	—
Outlying areas	22,364	26,677	26,345	25,519	27,530	28,747	9,863	9,663	—	9,663	10,598
American Samoa	20,694	20,694	—	—	—	20,694	—	—	—	—	—
Guam	36,263	36,263	39,966	—	39,966	30,809	—	—	—	—	—
Northern Marianas	—	—	—	—	—	—	—	—	—	—	—
Palau	30,873	30,873	—	—	—	30,873	—	—	—	—	—
Puerto Rico	19,961	24,383	24,190	25,519	21,374	27,950	9,863	9,663	—	9,663	10,598
Virgin Islands	40,888	40,888	40,888	—	40,888	—	—	—	—	—	—

—Data not reported or not applicable.

NOTE.—Data include imputations for nonrespondent institutions.

SOURCE: U.S. Department of Education, National Center for Education Statistics, Integrated Postsecondary Education Data System (IPEDS), "Salaries, Tenure, and Fringe Benefits of Full-Time Instructional Faculty, 1989–90" survey. (This table was prepared February 1991.)

Table 221.—Average salary of full-time instructional faculty on 9-month contracts in institutions of higher education, by type and control of institution and by State: 1987-88 [1]

State or other area	Average, all institutions	Public institutions					Private institutions				
		Total	4-year institutions			2-year	Total	4-year institutions			2-year
			Total	University	Other 4-year			Total	University	Other 4-year	
1	2	3	4	5	6	7	8	9	10	11	12
United States	$35,897	$36,231	$37,840	$40,106	$36,286	$32,209	$35,049	$35,346	$44,814	$31,089	$21,867
Alabama	31,328	31,806	32,953	36,307	30,422	28,269	29,024	29,234	—	29,234	23,355
Alaska	41,045	41,649	40,617	40,310	40,997	43,608	33,311	33,311	—	33,311	—
Arizona	38,080	38,674	41,074	41,828	37,035	33,975	27,796	28,259	—	28,259	18,035
Arkansas	28,911	29,520	30,572	34,266	29,292	23,165	25,354	25,411	—	25,411	14,600
California	42,611	43,026	47,696	53,307	46,585	37,266	40,472	40,756	50,491	34,117	24,375
Colorado	34,373	34,452	36,397	40,249	33,253	26,174	33,813	33,813	34,358	33,202	—
Connecticut	41,437	42,073	44,374	48,379	40,322	35,428	40,688	40,867	51,780	36,392	23,855
Delaware	35,706	36,545	37,624	38,933	29,372	29,661	29,951	29,951	—	29,951	—
District of Columbia	39,028	36,743	36,743	—	36,743	—	39,515	39,515	40,794	29,292	—
Florida	34,375	35,313	37,552	40,607	35,284	31,066	31,494	31,580	40,220	28,680	21,980
Georgia	33,171	34,251	35,342	37,378	34,727	28,176	30,040	30,538	43,750	26,770	21,346
Hawaii	35,489	36,289	38,449	39,747	32,331	31,526	22,900	22,900	—	22,900	—
Idaho	30,825	31,300	31,846	35,013	30,330	27,348	25,966	25,966	—	25,966	—
Illinois	35,509	34,804	35,258	38,453	32,330	34,067	36,909	37,154	46,880	30,435	21,983
Indiana	33,716	33,891	35,748	37,338	31,856	22,753	33,315	33,343	47,477	29,305	22,964
Iowa	31,894	33,935	37,162	38,541	32,995	25,698	28,276	28,371	31,828	27,928	22,440
Kansas	29,957	31,465	32,885	34,031	29,890	27,594	21,573	22,135	—	22,135	17,151
Kentucky	30,257	31,632	32,950	37,030	30,489	25,083	25,383	25,925	—	25,925	17,855
Louisiana	30,463	29,691	29,963	34,955	28,562	25,636	34,227	34,227	39,747	24,113	—
Maine	31,836	31,531	32,900	34,959	31,358	24,710	32,552	32,637	—	32,637	24,664
Maryland	36,874	36,543	37,886	41,867	35,600	34,109	38,077	38,114	54,324	30,760	22,421
Massachusetts	40,273	38,489	41,949	47,780	39,461	30,327	41,419	42,002	47,324	35,924	24,096
Michigan	36,947	38,456	39,294	44,038	35,246	36,211	28,888	28,990	32,820	28,582	23,914
Minnesota	34,719	36,199	36,911	44,272	32,901	34,129	31,276	31,496	—	31,496	25,370
Mississippi	26,763	27,223	29,828	31,866	28,529	23,566	22,052	22,841	—	22,841	16,670
Missouri	31,979	32,660	33,260	36,696	32,574	30,400	30,541	30,730	41,782	24,818	22,312
Montana	28,746	29,404	29,648	30,665	27,421	26,793	23,488	23,782	—	23,782	22,076
Nebraska	29,747	30,380	31,641	35,934	28,475	24,106	27,661	27,820	33,010	24,895	20,975
Nevada	36,250	36,306	37,654	38,469	36,963	31,157	31,381	31,381	—	31,381	—
New Hampshire	34,333	33,334	35,124	37,147	31,762	25,874	35,469	35,764	—	35,764	13,618
New Jersey	40,151	40,084	42,197	46,906	40,591	34,768	40,307	40,307	47,615	35,713	—
New Mexico	31,086	31,284	33,100	34,067	30,189	25,360	26,496	26,496	—	26,496	—
New York	39,727	40,658	42,708	47,695	42,028	35,922	38,666	38,916	45,215	34,384	20,786
North Carolina	32,908	34,889	36,514	40,697	34,495	22,802	28,616	29,136	33,417	27,171	22,512
North Dakota	28,591	29,156	29,959	30,813	28,111	26,591	22,758	23,272	—	23,272	19,547
Ohio	36,026	37,907	40,061	40,887	36,972	29,765	31,206	31,218	43,554	29,781	19,676
Oklahoma	30,461	30,670	31,763	33,719	30,089	27,143	29,609	29,947	35,903	27,018	20,449
Oregon	31,608	31,933	33,981	34,966	32,737	29,289	30,165	30,165	—	30,165	—
Pennsylvania	36,148	36,359	37,233	40,816	35,220	32,137	35,904	36,330	46,741	32,871	21,669
Rhode Island	36,907	36,408	38,127	40,658	33,874	31,108	37,306	37,306	—	37,306	—
South Carolina	30,382	31,288	34,051	37,015	30,726	22,484	27,603	28,045	—	28,045	23,090
South Dakota	27,388	28,958	28,958	29,592	28,103	—	22,608	22,753	—	22,753	19,330
Tennessee	32,935	33,759	35,396	38,979	33,984	26,660	31,022	31,373	45,469	25,454	19,106
Texas	33,990	33,955	35,963	39,990	32,291	29,972	34,136	34,221	40,696	29,048	21,241
Utah	32,208	32,342	34,060	36,346	28,574	26,460	25,557	25,557	—	25,557	—
Vermont	32,013	34,878	35,520	37,675	27,913	27,525	29,440	30,345	—	30,345	22,235
Virginia	35,987	37,760	40,038	43,708	37,372	30,747	29,628	29,758	—	29,758	20,173
Washington	33,182	33,824	37,295	39,663	33,299	29,267	30,417	30,417	—	30,417	—
West Virginia	28,287	29,223	29,825	33,929	27,888	23,644	23,296	23,520	—	23,520	19,248
Wisconsin	35,034	35,765	37,780	45,832	35,116	32,285	31,090	31,090	38,949	27,965	—
Wyoming	32,819	32,819	37,053	37,053		27,889	—	—	—	—	—
U.S. Service Schools	42,299	42,299	42,436	—	42,436	42,158	—	—	—	—	—
Outlying areas	17,346	22,411	22,294	22,804	21,410	24,736	7,750	8,657		—	6,321
American Samoa	—	—	—	—	—	—	—	—	—	—	—
Guam	9,336	9,336	9,336	—	9,336	—	—	—	—	—	—
Northern Marianas	—	—	—	—	—	—	—	—	—	—	—
Puerto Rico	16,717	21,771	21,593	22,804	19,045	25,190	7,750	8,657	—	8,657	6,321
Trust Territory of the Pacific	12,468	12,468	—	—	—	12,468	—	—	—	—	—
Virgin Islands	33,500	33,500	33,500	—	33,500	—	—	—	—	—	—

[1] Data have been revised from previously published figures.

—Data not reported or not applicable.

NOTE.—Data include imputations for nonrespondent institutions.

SOURCE: U.S. Department of Education, National Center for Education Statistics, Integrated Postsecondary Education Data System (IPEDS), "Salaries, Tenure, and Fringe Benefits of Full-Time Instructional Faculty, 1987-88" survey. (This table was prepared February 1991.)

Table 222.—Average salary of full-time instructional faculty on 9-month contracts in 4-year institutions of higher education, by type and control of institution and rank of faculty and by State: 1989–90

State or other area	Public university			Public other 4-year			Private university			Private other 4-year		
	Professor	Associate professor	Assistant professor	Professor	Associate professor	Assistant professor	Professor	Associate professor	Assistant professor	Professor	Associate professor	Assistant professor
1	2	3	4	5	6	7	8	9	10	11	12	13
United States	$57,269	$41,568	$34,945	$51,211	$39,975	$32,989	$65,012	$44,692	$37,778	$45,069	$35,031	$29,081
Alabama	50,844	38,269	32,255	42,817	34,406	30,150	—	—	—	38,235	30,430	26,414
Alaska	57,975	48,783	39,281	54,834	47,984	37,987	—	—	—	61,739	36,891	32,415
Arizona	56,672	41,536	35,621	47,202	37,844	31,295	—	—	—	38,931	35,403	29,375
Arkansas	49,323	36,941	31,849	41,026	34,111	29,112	—	—	—	33,090	27,935	24,723
California	71,627	46,048	40,322	58,997	44,909	37,163	70,566	48,990	40,881	47,082	35,248	30,555
Colorado	53,380	41,262	36,372	44,414	36,676	31,415	50,859	37,891	34,197	49,162	36,886	30,094
Connecticut	65,061	47,897	39,497	54,615	44,450	36,082	77,730	47,702	36,936	53,044	40,335	33,462
Delaware	58,787	42,535	34,665	43,324	34,348	30,479	—	—	—	41,549	42,118	30,692
District of Columbia	—	—	—	52,056	41,242	33,497	61,615	42,945	34,974	48,661	36,340	30,110
Florida	55,257	38,648	34,834	49,106	38,299	33,801	57,708	41,603	37,146	42,633	33,548	27,957
Georgia	54,836	38,469	33,204	47,945	37,856	31,980	64,070	44,589	34,440	40,288	31,738	26,174
Hawaii	55,858	42,058	36,647	45,013	37,551	32,328	—	—	—	31,667	26,916	22,739
Idaho	44,099	35,296	33,421	38,039	32,728	28,896	—	—	—	29,640	—	—
Illinois	57,212	41,035	34,501	46,862	37,956	33,063	68,356	45,296	39,287	41,693	34,898	29,186
Indiana	53,336	40,362	32,670	47,513	37,281	30,942	69,142	47,039	40,783	40,083	32,755	28,078
Iowa	60,840	44,920	37,292	49,628	41,178	33,955	48,676	37,846	32,628	38,415	31,519	27,015
Kansas	50,335	38,034	32,006	42,513	34,110	29,490	—	—	—	29,315	24,959	22,206
Kentucky	49,851	36,474	32,110	40,088	34,022	28,776	—	—	—	35,955	29,122	24,522
Louisiana	53,246	38,255	32,996	38,623	32,421	28,356	56,858	42,877	35,015	35,311	27,957	25,377
Maine	52,313	39,870	33,820	45,100	36,506	30,640	—	—	—	51,078	36,578	29,588
Maryland	64,459	45,831	38,123	54,514	43,893	36,445	68,072	45,232	38,494	44,133	36,178	29,968
Massachusetts	62,303	48,799	37,625	51,227	44,190	35,898	71,241	46,934	39,769	53,846	39,862	33,066
Michigan	61,409	45,791	39,405	47,599	39,500	33,113	46,146	37,495	31,743	43,444	32,460	26,990
Minnesota	59,402	42,455	37,086	47,824	38,582	31,798	—	—	—	46,024	35,251	29,589
Mississippi	44,851	36,229	32,541	42,035	34,074	28,918	—	—	—	39,018	31,693	24,494
Missouri	50,859	37,445	34,569	45,594	37,333	31,591	57,632	40,530	35,754	36,276	29,740	25,238
Montana	37,495	31,527	27,967	35,133	28,990	25,066	—	—	—	31,400	27,146	22,829
Nebraska	54,124	40,066	35,302	42,280	34,909	30,115	53,978	37,353	30,171	34,512	28,144	25,361
Nevada	53,434	41,528	35,573	54,059	43,398	35,227	—	—	—	—	—	—
New Hampshire	53,212	41,206	32,883	42,114	34,457	28,927	—	—	—	56,700	36,920	31,781
New Jersey	69,550	48,413	38,378	56,058	44,855	35,630	72,654	46,658	38,025	49,333	39,662	31,599
New Mexico	47,669	36,405	32,621	40,033	33,798	28,824	—	—	—	30,191	27,162	23,864
New York	67,796	49,431	37,846	61,774	47,273	37,618	65,335	45,722	37,678	49,152	37,970	31,160
North Carolina	60,564	42,551	36,291	48,448	39,534	33,702	56,951	43,969	35,445	36,716	32,092	25,658
North Dakota	42,103	34,710	30,081	36,651	32,491	27,568	—	—	—	32,106	28,226	24,636
Ohio	58,301	43,644	35,745	53,759	41,538	33,461	63,022	44,399	38,188	41,995	33,428	27,991
Oklahoma	47,743	37,733	31,761	40,961	36,546	32,470	52,664	39,158	32,085	46,004	35,437	28,336
Oregon	46,209	36,276	30,314	40,444	33,116	28,358	—	—	—	43,213	32,556	27,578
Pennsylvania	59,986	44,071	36,735	52,388	41,738	33,639	67,308	47,162	39,669	48,338	36,465	30,534
Rhode Island	55,304	42,984	37,213	46,657	39,540	33,642	—	—	—	59,759	41,922	34,145
South Carolina	54,456	39,545	34,604	43,187	36,195	29,553	—	—	—	37,806	30,786	25,547
South Dakota	39,054	31,838	27,799	38,400	33,238	27,367	—	—	—	33,465	27,225	24,804
Tennessee	52,077	39,196	33,504	46,209	37,862	31,875	67,683	44,766	38,785	35,003	27,916	24,271
Texas	58,930	40,899	34,500	45,660	37,460	31,771	60,821	42,554	36,161	39,689	32,304	27,205
Utah	48,707	35,578	31,695	36,707	30,191	26,710	49,100	37,774	36,391	32,313	28,820	24,768
Vermont	56,015	40,506	34,252	37,255	31,928	26,518	—	—	—	47,698	34,848	29,769
Virginia	65,172	45,983	38,021	55,226	43,856	36,179	—	—	—	43,604	33,828	28,021
Washington	54,286	38,603	35,059	41,475	35,119	29,676	—	—	—	42,481	34,336	30,028
West Virginia	44,575	35,239	29,430	35,546	29,825	23,851	—	—	—	31,905	26,622	24,023
Wisconsin	57,140	41,910	36,526	45,583	36,975	32,453	57,987	43,526	36,684	43,172	33,600	27,739
Wyoming	47,944	36,943	33,733	—	—	—	—	—	—	—	—	—
U.S. Service Schools	—	—	—	53,022	41,484	32,856	—	—	—	—	—	—
Outlying areas	32,779	26,724	22,355	46,628	31,700	25,583	—	—	—	30,034	20,583	20,906
American Samoa	—	—	—	—	—	—	—	—	—	—	—	—
Guam	—	—	—	54,041	43,972	34,252	—	—	—	—	—	—
Northern Marianas	—	—	—	—	—	—	—	—	—	—	—	—
Puerto Rico	32,779	26,724	22,355	33,755	24,900	20,977	—	—	—	30,034	20,583	20,906
Trust Territory of the Pacific	—	—	—	—	—	—	—	—	—	—	—	—
Virgin Islands	—	—	—	52,027	43,659	36,159	—	—	—	—	—	—

—Data not reported or not applicable.

NOTE.—Data include imputations for nonrespondent institutions.

SOURCE: U.S. Department of Education, National Center for Education Statistics, Integrated Postsecondary Education Data System (IPEDS), "Salaries, Tenure, and Fringe Benefits of Full-Time Instructional Faculty, 1989–90" survey. (This table was prepared February 1991.)

Table 223.—Full-time instructional faculty with tenure for institutions reporting tenure status, by academic rank, sex, and type and control of institution: 1980–81, 1985–86, 1987–88, and 1989–90

Academic year, type, and control of institution	Percent with tenure, by rank							Percent with tenure, by sex	
	All ranks	Professor	Associate professor	Assistant professor	Instructor	Lecturer	No academic rank	Men	Women
1	2	3	4	5	6	7	8	9	10
1980–81									
All institutions	64.8	95.8	82.9	27.9	9.2	11.9	77.4	70.0	49.7
4-year	62.7	95.8	82.2	24.1	6.6	10.7	24.7	68.3	44.0
University	64.5	96.7	83.7	15.3	5.4	4.3	3.5	70.0	41.0
Other 4-year	61.3	94.9	81.2	29.7	7.1	17.8	32.4	67.0	45.5
2-year	74.5	95.6	89.2	58.9	19.8	34.8	81.1	78.8	66.6
Public institutions	68.0	96.6	85.9	32.5	11.8	14.3	79.4	72.8	54.0
4-year	65.7	96.6	85.3	27.6	8.7	12.8	12.2	71.1	47.5
University	66.0	96.9	86.5	16.8	6.1	4.9	4.5	71.3	42.8
Other 4-year	65.5	96.3	84.4	35.5	10.0	21.4	17.2	70.9	50.2
2-year	75.2	95.9	89.5	59.5	20.3	35.8	81.8	79.3	67.5
Private institutions	55.9	93.8	75.2	17.5	3.0	1.5	43.4	62.2	37.2
4-year	56.0	93.8	75.2	17.4	2.8	1.5	37.5	62.2	37.2
University	60.4	96.3	75.8	11.5	3.5	1.8	0.6	66.3	36.5
Other 4-year	53.6	92.0	74.9	20.2	2.6	1.2	43.4	59.8	37.4
2-year	49.5	84.7	77.3	35.2	8.8	—	52.2	57.3	39.5
1985–86									
All institutions	66.0	95.8	82.2	25.1	10.7	9.3	75.3	71.3	51.7
4-year	64.1	95.8	81.5	21.5	5.7	8.3	20.0	69.9	46.4
University	66.8	97.0	85.0	13.0	5.0	3.2	0.3	72.3	45.4
Other 4-year	62.2	94.8	79.2	26.6	6.0	13.0	27.0	68.1	46.8
2-year	75.1	95.1	88.5	56.4	27.3	28.6	80.4	79.1	68.5
Public institutions	68.9	96.5	85.4	29.1	13.4	10.9	77.2	73.9	55.6
4-year	66.9	96.6	84.9	24.4	7.3	9.7	11.1	72.5	49.3
University	68.1	97.1	87.8	14.0	5.8	3.4	0.3	73.5	46.4
Other 4-year	66.0	96.2	82.7	31.8	8.0	15.0	18.3	71.6	51.1
2-year	75.7	95.2	89.0	57.4	28.0	28.7	80.8	79.5	69.2
Private institutions	57.6	93.8	73.8	16.0	2.7	2.1	40.3	63.9	40.3
4-year	57.7	93.9	73.9	15.9	2.5	2.1	32.1	64.0	40.3
University	63.0	96.7	76.6	10.1	2.2	2.8	0.0	68.4	42.7
Other 4-year	55.1	92.0	72.6	18.3	2.5	1.0	34.6	61.6	39.5
2-year	48.4	89.9	63.6	24.9	9.3	—	57.5	56.1	39.3
1987–88[1]									
All institutions	65.4	95.7	81.5	22.8	7.1	8.8	73.5	71.2	50.2
4-year	64.0	95.8	81.0	19.9	4.6	7.8	20.6	70.2	46.1
University	66.7	97.0	84.8	11.5	3.8	3.2	1.1	72.5	45.1
Other 4-year	62.1	94.9	78.4	24.9	4.9	11.7	33.3	68.4	46.6
2-year	74.4	94.2	87.3	55.5	18.4	32.9	80.1	78.7	67.7
Public institutions	67.9	96.2	84.2	26.5	8.8	10.3	75.6	73.5	53.4
4-year	66.4	96.4	83.8	22.7	5.8	9.1	11.7	72.4	48.3
University	68.0	97.2	87.6	12.4	4.3	3.1	0.8	73.9	45.8
Other 4-year	65.1	95.7	80.8	29.8	6.4	13.3	23.1	71.1	49.7
2-year	74.9	94.3	87.7	56.5	18.7	33.1	80.6	79.1	68.5
Private institutions	58.6	94.5	74.8	14.7	2.3	2.6	41.6	65.0	41.5
4-year	58.7	94.5	74.9	14.6	2.1	2.6	35.0	65.1	41.6
University	63.1	96.6	76.8	9.1	1.9	3.3	2.4	68.6	43.2
Other 4-year	56.4	93.0	73.8	17.0	2.1	1.3	43.3	63.0	41.0
2-year	49.3	91.0	63.3	27.7	10.0	—	56.7	57.6	40.7
1989–90									
All institutions	63.5	95.6	81.0	19.7	6.9	7.8	68.7	69.7	48.5
4-year	62.3	95.7	80.6	17.0	4.5	6.7	17.9	68.8	44.6
University	65.0	96.9	85.0	9.7	3.8	2.5	0.3	71.2	43.6
Other 4-year	60.4	94.7	77.7	21.2	4.7	10.5	29.4	67.0	45.1
2-year	71.6	94.2	85.6	52.0	17.1	36.6	75.7	76.7	64.4
Public institutions	65.9	96.2	83.9	22.9	8.7	9.3	70.3	71.9	51.4
4-year	64.6	96.4	83.7	19.3	5.8	8.0	10.2	71.0	46.7
University	66.0	97.1	87.9	10.3	4.2	2.6	0.3	72.2	44.4
Other 4-year	63.5	95.9	80.4	25.5	6.5	12.2	20.7	70.1	48.0
2-year	72.0	94.4	85.9	52.9	17.5	36.8	76.0	77.0	65.0
Private institutions	57.0	93.9	73.8	12.7	1.7	1.6	41.4	63.7	40.3
4-year	57.1	93.9	73.8	12.5	1.6	1.6	32.8	63.7	40.3
University	62.2	96.3	75.9	8.3	2.1	2.1	—	68.2	41.3
Other 4-year	54.6	92.3	72.8	14.3	1.5	0.8	39.1	61.2	39.9
2-year	51.5	87.9	70.4	27.3	6.8	—	63.3	61.1	41.8

[1] Some data have been revised from previously published figures.

—Data not available or not applicable.

NOTE.—Data exclude tenure imputations for nonrespondent institutions.

SOURCE: U.S. Department of Education, National Center for Education Statistics, Faculty Salaries, Tenure, and Benefits; and Integrated Postsecondary Education Data System (IPEDS), "Salaries, Tenure, and Fringe Benefits of Full-Time Instructional Faculty" survey. (This table was prepared February 1991.)

Table 224.—Institutions of higher education, by control and type of institution: 1949–50 to 1989–90

Year	All institutions			Public			Private		
	Total	4-year	2-year	Total	4-year	2-year	Total	4-year	2-year
1	2	3	4	5	6	7	8	9	10
Excluding branch campuses									
1949–50	1,851	1,327	524	641	344	297	1,210	983	227
1950–51	1,852	1,312	540	636	341	295	1,216	971	245
1951–52	1,832	1,326	506	641	350	291	1,191	976	215
1952–53	1,882	1,355	527	639	349	290	1,243	1,006	237
1953–54	1,863	1,345	518	662	369	293	1,201	976	225
1954–55	1,849	1,333	516	648	353	295	1,201	980	221
1955–56	1,850	1,347	503	650	360	290	1,200	987	213
1956–57	1,878	1,355	523	656	359	297	1,222	996	226
1957–58	1,930	1,390	540	666	366	300	1,264	1,024	240
1958–59	1,947	1,394	553	673	366	307	1,274	1,028	246
1959–60	2,004	1,422	582	695	367	328	1,309	1,055	254
1960–61	2,021	1,431	590	700	368	332	1,321	1,063	258
1961–62	2,033	1,443	590	718	374	344	1,315	1,069	246
1962–63	2,093	1,468	625	740	376	364	1,353	1,092	261
1963–64	2,132	1,499	633	760	386	374	1,372	1,113	259
1964–65	2,175	1,521	654	799	393	406	1,376	1,128	248
1965–66	2,230	1,551	679	821	401	420	1,409	1,150	259
1966–67	2,329	1,577	752	880	403	477	1,449	1,174	275
1967–68	2,374	1,588	786	934	414	520	1,440	1,174	266
1968–69	2,483	1,619	864	1,011	417	594	1,472	1,202	270
1969–70	2,525	1,639	886	1,060	426	634	1,465	1,213	252
1970–71	2,556	1,665	891	1,089	435	654	1,467	1,230	237
1971–72	2,606	1,675	931	1,137	440	697	1,469	1,235	234
1972–73	2,665	1,701	964	1,182	449	733	1,483	1,252	231
1973–74	2,720	1,717	1,003	1,200	440	760	1,520	1,277	243
1974–75	2,747	1,744	1,003	1,214	447	767	1,533	1,297	236
1975–76	2,765	1,767	998	1,219	447	772	1,546	1,320	226
1976–77	2,785	1,783	1,002	1,231	452	779	1,554	1,331	223
1977–78	2,826	1,808	1,018	1,241	454	787	1,585	1,354	231
1978–79	2,954	1,843	1,111	1,308	463	845	1,646	1,380	266
1979–80	2,975	1,863	1,112	1,310	464	846	1,665	1,399	266
1980–81	3,056	1,861	1,195	1,334	465	869	1,722	1,396	[1]326
1981–82	3,083	1,883	1,200	1,340	471	869	1,743	1,412	[1]331
1982–83	3,111	1,887	1,224	1,336	472	864	1,775	1,415	[1]360
1983–84	3,117	1,914	1,203	1,325	474	851	1,792	1,440	352
1984–85	3,146	1,911	1,235	1,329	461	868	1,817	1,450	367
1985–86	3,155	1,915	1,240	1,326	461	865	1,829	1,454	375
Including branch campuses									
1974–75	3,004	1,866	1,138	1,433	537	896	1,571	1,329	242
1975–76	3,026	1,898	1,128	1,442	545	897	1,584	1,353	231
1976–77	3,046	1,913	1,133	1,455	550	905	1,591	1,363	228
1977–78	3,095	1,938	1,157	1,473	552	921	1,622	1,386	236
1978–79	3,134	1,941	1,193	1,474	550	924	1,660	1,391	269
1979–80	3,152	1,957	1,195	1,475	549	926	1,677	1,408	269
1980–81	3,231	1,957	1,274	1,497	552	945	1,734	1,405	[1]329
1981–82	3,253	1,979	1,274	1,498	558	940	1,755	1,421	[1]334
1982–83	3,280	1,984	1,296	1,493	560	933	1,787	1,424	[1]363
1983–84	3,284	2,013	1,271	1,481	565	916	1,803	1,448	355
1984–85	3,331	2,025	1,306	1,501	566	935	1,830	1,459	371
1985–86	3,340	2,029	1,311	1,498	566	932	1,842	1,463	379
1986–87 [2]	3,406	2,070	1,336	1,533	573	960	1,873	1,497	376
1987–88 [2]	3,587	2,135	1,452	1,591	599	992	1,996	1,536	460
1988–89 [2]	3,565	2,129	1,436	1,582	598	984	1,983	1,531	452
1989–90 [2]	3,535	2,127	1,408	1,563	595	968	1,972	1,532	440

[1] Large increases are due to the addition of schools accredited by the National Association of Trade and Technical Schools in 1980 and 1981.

[2] Because of revised survey procedures, data are not entirely comparable with figures prior to 1986–87. The number of branch campuses reporting separately has increased.

SOURCE: U.S. Department of Education, National Center for Education Statistics, *Education Directory, Colleges and Universities;* "Fall Enrollment in Higher Education" and "Institutional Characteristics of Colleges and Universities" surveys; Integrated Postsecondary Education Data System, "Institutional Characteristics" survey. (This table was prepared June 1990.)

Table 225.—Institutions of higher education and branches, by control of institution, highest level of offering, and sex of student body: 1985–86

Highest level of offering and sex of student body	Total	Public					Private				
		Federal[1]	State	Local (city, county, or district)	State and local	State-related	Independent nonprofit	Organized as profit making	Religious group		
									Protestant	Catholic	Other[2]
1	2	3	4	5	6	7	8	9	10	11	12
All institutions	**3,340**	**13**	**883**	**173**	**398**	**31**	**828**	**220**	**524**	**235**	**35**
Coeducational	3,126	13	881	173	398	31	726	218	505	168	13
Men only	99	0	1	0	0	0	47	0	3	30	18
Women only	102	0	1	0	0	0	48	2	14	34	3
Coordinate[3]	13	0	0	0	0	0	7	0	2	3	1
Less than 4 years beyond high school	1,309	3	356	170	383	20	121	190	43	20	3
Coeducational	1,282	3	356	170	383	20	107	188	40	13	2
Men only	6	0	0	0	0	0	4	0	0	2	0
Women only	20	0	0	0	0	0	9	2	3	5	1
Coordinate[3]	1	0	0	0	0	0	1	0	0	0	0
4- or 5-year baccalaureate degree	707	5	73	1	5	2	242	19	286	70	4
Coeducational	627	5	72	1	5	2	209	19	275	37	2
Men only	31	0	1	0	0	0	10	0	2	16	2
Women only	46	0	0	0	0	0	22	0	8	16	0
Coordinate[3]	3	0	0	0	0	0	1	0	1	1	0
First-professional degree	93	0	9	0	0	0	67	2	11	2	2
Coeducational	80	0	9	0	0	0	58	2	10	1	0
Men only	12	0	0	0	0	0	9	0	0	1	2
Women only	1	0	0	0	0	0	0	0	1	0	0
Coordinate[3]	0	0	0	0	0	0	0	0	0	0	0
Master's degree	566	2	148	1	0	3	196	5	103	105	3
Coeducational	525	2	148	1	0	3	181	5	100	82	3
Men only	12	0	0	0	0	0	4	0	0	8	0
Women only	24	0	0	0	0	0	9	0	2	13	0
Coordinate[3]	5	0	0	0	0	0	2	0	1	2	0
Beyond master's but less than doctorate	153	0	100	0	4	0	25	0	13	9	2
Coeducational	146	0	100	0	4	0	22	0	13	7	0
Men only	5	0	0	0	0	0	1	0	0	2	2
Women only	2	0	0	0	0	0	2	0	0	0	0
Coordinate[3]	0	0	0	0	0	0	0	0	0	0	0
Doctoral	473	3	197	1	6	6	153	1	68	29	9
Coeducational	462	3	196	1	6	6	148	1	67	28	6
Men only	4	0	0	0	0	0	0	0	1	1	2
Women only	3	0	1	0	0	0	2	0	0	0	0
Coordinate[3]	4	0	0	0	0	0	3	0	0	0	1
Undergraduate nondegree-granting	15	0	0	0	0	0	11	1	0	0	3
Coeducational	2	0	0	0	0	0	1	1	0	0	0
Men only	7	0	0	0	0	0	6	0	0	0	1
Women only	6	0	0	0	0	0	4	0	0	0	2
Coordinate[3]	0	0	0	0	0	0	0	0	0	0	0
Graduate nondegree-granting	22	0	0	0	0	0	13	0	0	0	9
Coeducational	0	0	0	0	0	0	0	0	0	0	0
Men only	22	0	0	0	0	0	13	0	0	0	9
Women only	0	0	0	0	0	0	0	0	0	0	0
Coordinate[3]	0	0	0	0	0	0	0	0	0	0	0

[1] Includes 10 U.S. Service Schools, Haskell Indian Junior College, Institute of American Indian Arts, and Oglala Sioux Community College.

[2] Includes Jewish, Latter-Day Saints, Greek Orthodox, Russian Orthodox, and Unitarian.

[3] Institutions with separate colleges for men and women.

SOURCE: U.S. Department of Education, National Center for Education Statistics, "Institutional Characteristics of Colleges and Universities, 1985–86" survey. (This table was prepared September 1986.)

Table 226.—Institutions of higher education and branches, by type, control of institution, and State: 1989–90

State or other area	Total	All institutions		4-year institutions							2-year institutions		
		Public	Private	All 4-year institutions			Universities		Other 4-year institutions		Total	Public	Private
				Total	Public	Private	Public	Private	Public	Private			
1	2	3	4	5	6	7	8	9	10	11	12	13	14
United States	3,535	1,563	1,972	2,127	595	1,532	93	62	502	1,470	1,408	968	440
Alabama	87	55	32	36	18	18	2	0	16	18	51	37	14
Alaska	8	3	5	7	3	4	1	0	2	4	1	0	1
Arizona	37	20	17	17	3	14	2	0	1	14	20	17	3
Arkansas	37	20	17	20	10	10	1	0	9	10	17	10	7
California	310	138	172	171	31	140	2	4	29	136	139	107	32
Colorado	54	28	26	30	13	17	2	1	11	16	24	15	9
Connecticut	48	24	24	28	7	21	1	1	6	20	20	17	3
Delaware	10	5	5	7	2	5	1	0	1	5	3	3	0
District of Columbia	17	2	15	17	2	15	0	5	2	10	0	0	0
Florida	95	38	57	53	10	43	2	1	8	42	42	28	14
Georgia	95	47	48	51	19	32	1	1	18	31	44	28	16
Hawaii	14	9	5	8	3	5	1	0	2	5	6	6	0
Idaho	11	6	5	7	4	3	1	0	3	3	4	2	2
Illinois	166	59	107	103	12	91	3	4	9	87	63	47	16
Indiana	78	28	50	55	14	41	4	1	10	40	23	14	9
Iowa	58	18	40	37	3	34	2	1	1	33	21	15	6
Kansas	54	29	25	30	8	22	3	0	5	22	24	21	3
Kentucky	59	22	37	32	8	24	2	0	6	24	27	14	13
Louisiana	34	20	14	24	14	10	1	2	13	8	10	6	4
Maine	31	13	18	21	8	13	1	0	7	13	10	5	5
Maryland	57	33	24	35	14	21	1	1	13	20	22	19	3
Massachusetts	117	30	87	85	14	71	1	7	13	64	32	16	16
Michigan	97	44	53	63	15	48	3	1	12	47	34	29	5
Minnesota	81	36	45	44	10	34	1	0	9	34	37	26	11
Mississippi	47	29	18	21	9	12	2	0	7	12	26	20	6
Missouri	89	27	62	65	13	52	1	2	12	50	24	14	10
Montana	19	13	6	9	6	3	2	0	4	3	10	7	3
Nebraska	36	20	16	21	7	14	1	1	6	13	15	13	2
Nevada	8	6	2	3	2	1	1	0	1	1	5	4	1
New Hampshire	29	12	17	17	5	12	1	0	4	12	12	7	5
New Jersey	62	33	29	39	14	25	1	2	13	23	23	19	4
New Mexico	26	22	4	10	6	4	2	0	4	4	16	16	0
New York	326	90	236	228	42	186	2	12	40	174	98	48	50
North Carolina	126	74	52	53	16	37	2	2	14	35	73	58	15
North Dakota	20	15	5	10	6	4	2	0	4	4	10	9	1
Ohio	152	61	91	90	25	65	8	1	17	64	62	36	26
Oklahoma	47	28	19	27	14	13	2	1	12	12	20	14	6
Oregon	46	21	25	32	8	24	2	0	6	24	14	13	1
Pennsylvania	217	61	156	146	43	103	2	4	41	99	71	18	53
Rhode Island	11	3	8	10	2	8	1	0	1	8	1	1	0
South Carolina	64	33	31	32	12	20	2	0	10	20	32	21	11
South Dakota	19	7	12	17	7	10	2	0	5	10	2	0	2
Tennessee	86	24	62	52	10	42	1	1	9	41	34	14	20
Texas	174	107	67	96	40	56	6	4	34	52	78	67	11
Utah	14	9	5	6	4	2	2	1	2	1	8	5	3
Vermont	22	6	16	17	4	13	1	0	3	13	5	2	3
Virginia	78	39	39	48	15	33	3	0	12	33	30	24	6
Washington	55	33	22	26	6	20	2	0	4	20	29	27	2
West Virginia	28	16	12	21	12	9	1	0	11	9	7	4	3
Wisconsin	61	30	31	41	13	28	1	1	12	27	20	17	3
Wyoming	9	8	1	1	1	0	1	0	0	0	8	7	1
U.S. Service Schools	9	9	0	8	8	0	0	0	8	0	1	1	0
Outlying areas[1]	63	23	40	44	14	30	1	0	13	30	19	9	10
American Samoa	1	1	0	0	0	0	0	0	0	0	1	1	0
Guam	2	2	0	1	1	0	0	0	1	0	1	1	0
Northern Marianas	1	1	0	0	0	0	0	0	0	0	1	1	0
Palau	2	2	0	0	0	0	0	0	0	0	2	2	0
Puerto Rico	55	15	40	41	11	30	1	0	10	30	14	4	10
Virgin Islands	2	2	0	2	2	0	0	0	2	0	0	0	0

[1] Excludes Federated States of Micronesia.

NOTE.—Because of revised survey procedures, data are not entirely comparable with figures for earlier years. The number of branch campuses reporting separately has increased.

SOURCE: U.S. Department of Education, National Center for Education Statistics, Integrated Postsecondary Education Data System (IPEDS), "Institutional Characteristics, 1989–90" survey. (This table was prepared June 1990.)

Table 227.—Institutions of higher education that have closed their doors, by control and type of institution: 1960–61 to 1989–90

Year	All institutions			Public			Private		
	Total	4-year	2-year	Total	4-year	2-year	Total	4-year	2-year
1	2	3	4	5	6	7	8	9	10
Excluding branch campuses:									
Total, 1960–61 to 1989–90	323	168	155	38	1	37	285	167	118
1960–61	8	1	7	1	—	1	7	1	6
1961–62	2	1	1	—	—	—	2	1	1
1962–63	—	—	—	—	—	—	—	—	—
1963–64	7	1	6	1	—	1	6	1	5
1964–65	8	1	7	4	—	4	4	1	3
1965–66	8	2	6	4	—	4	4	2	2
1966–67	9	2	7	3	—	3	6	2	4
1967–68	14	6	8	—	—	—	14	6	8
1968–69	21	11	10	1	—	1	20	11	9
1969–70	18	8	10	3	—	3	15	8	7
1970–71	32	9	23	9	—	9	23	9	14
1971–72	12	3	9	3	—	3	9	3	6
1972–73	19	12	7	2	—	2	17	12	5
1973–74	18	11	7	—	—	—	18	11	7
1974–75	17	13	4	3	—	3	14	13	1
1975–76	8	6	2	2	1	1	6	5	1
1976–77	8	5	3	—	—	—	8	5	3
1977–78	12	9	3	—	—	—	12	9	3
1978–79	9	4	5	—	—	—	9	4	5
1979–80	6	5	1	—	—	—	6	5	1
1980–81	4	3	1	—	—	—	4	3	1
1981–82	7	6	1	—	—	—	7	6	1
1982–83	7	4	3	—	—	—	7	4	3
1983–84	4	4	—	—	—	—	4	4	—
1984–85	4	4	—	—	—	—	4	4	—
1985–86	10	6	4	1	—	1	9	6	3
1986–87 and 1987–88	25	19	6	1	—	1	24	19	5
1988–89	14	6	8	—	—	—	14	6	8
1989–90	12	6	6	—	—	—	12	6	6
Including branch campuses:									
Total, 1969–70 to 1989–90	275	156	119	33	4	29	242	152	90
1969–70	24	10	14	5	1	4	19	9	10
1970–71	35	10	25	11	—	11	24	10	14
1971–72	14	5	9	3	—	3	11	5	6
1972–73	21	12	9	4	—	4	17	12	5
1973–74	20	12	8	1	—	1	19	12	7
1974–75	18	13	5	4	—	4	14	13	1
1975–76	9	7	2	2	1	1	7	6	1
1976–77	9	6	3	—	—	—	9	6	3
1977–78	12	9	3	—	—	—	12	9	3
1978–79	9	4	5	—	—	—	9	4	5
1979–80	6	5	1	—	—	—	6	5	1
1980–81	4	3	1	—	—	—	4	3	1
1981–82	7	6	1	—	—	—	7	6	1
1982–83	7	4	3	—	—	—	7	4	3
1983–84	5	5	—	1	1	—	4	4	—
1984–85	4	4	—	—	—	—	4	4	—
1985–86	12	8	4	1	1	—	11	7	4
1986–87 and 1987–88	26	19	7	1	—	1	25	19	6
1988–89	14	6	8	—	—	—	14	6	8
1989–90	19	8	11	—	—	—	19	8	11

—Data not applicable or not available.

NOTE.—This table indicates the year in which the institution closed.

SOURCE: U.S. Department of Education, National Center for Education Statistics, *Education Directory, Higher Education,* 1960–61 to 1974–75; *Education Directory,* *Colleges and Universities,* 1975–76 to 1983–84; *1982–83 Supplement to the Education Directory, Colleges and Universities*; and Integrated Postsecondary Education Data System, "Institutional Characteristics" survey, 1987, unpublished data. (This table was prepared April 1990.)

Table 228.—Earned degrees conferred by institutions of higher education, by level of degree and sex of student: 1869–70 to 1999–2000

Year	Associate degrees			Bachelor's degrees			Master's degrees			First-professional degrees			Doctor's degrees		
	Total	Men	Women	Total	Men	Women	Total	Men	Women	Total	Men	Women	Total	Men	Women
1	2	3	4	5	6	7	8	9	10	11	12	13	14	15	16
1869–70	—	—	—	[1]9,371	[1]7,993	[1]1,378	0	0	0	[2]	[2]	[2]	1	1	0
1879–80	—	—	—	[1]12,896	[1]10,411	[1]2,485	879	868	11	[2]	[2]	[2]	54	51	3
1889–90	—	—	—	[1]15,539	[1]12,857	[1]2,682	1,015	821	194	[2]	[2]	[2]	149	147	2
1899–1900	—	—	—	[1]27,410	[1]22,173	[1]5,237	1,583	1,280	303	[2]	[2]	[2]	382	359	23
1909–10	—	—	—	[1]37,199	[1]28,762	[1]8,437	2,113	1,555	558	[2]	[2]	[2]	443	399	44
1919–20	—	—	—	[1]48,622	[1]31,980	[1]16,642	4,279	2,985	1,294	[2]	[2]	[2]	615	522	93
1929–30	—	—	—	[1]122,484	[1]73,615	[1]48,869	14,969	8,925	6,044	[2]	[2]	[2]	2,299	1,946	353
1939–40	—	—	—	[1]186,500	[1]109,546	[1]76,954	26,731	16,508	10,223	[2]	[2]	[2]	3,290	2,861	429
1949–50	—	—	—	[1]432,058	[1]328,841	[1]103,217	58,183	41,220	16,963	[2]	[2]	[2]	6,420	5,804	616
1959–60	—	—	—	[1]392,440	[1]254,063	[1]138,377	74,435	50,898	23,537	[2]	[2]	[2]	9,829	8,801	1,028
1960–61	—	—	—	369,995	228,500	141,495	81,690	55,267	26,423	25,253	24,577	676	10,575	9,463	1,112
1961–62	—	—	—	388,680	234,671	154,009	88,414	59,710	28,704	25,607	24,836	771	11,622	10,377	1,245
1962–63	—	—	—	416,928	246,129	170,799	95,470	64,198	31,272	26,590	25,753	837	12,822	11,448	1,374
1963–64	—	—	—	466,944	270,319	196,625	105,551	70,339	35,212	27,209	26,357	852	14,490	12,955	1,535
1964–65	—	—	—	501,713	289,003	212,710	117,152	77,544	39,608	28,290	27,283	1,007	16,467	14,692	1,775
1965–66	111,607	63,779	47,828	520,923	299,871	221,052	140,548	93,063	47,485	30,124	28,982	1,142	18,237	16,121	2,116
1966–67	139,183	78,356	60,827	558,852	322,948	235,904	157,707	103,092	54,615	31,695	30,401	1,294	20,617	18,163	2,454
1967–68	159,441	90,317	69,124	632,758	358,105	274,653	176,749	113,519	63,230	33,939	32,402	1,537	23,089	20,183	2,906
1968–69	183,279	105,661	77,618	729,071	410,785	318,286	193,756	121,531	72,225	35,114	33,595	1,519	26,188	22,752	3,436
1969–70	206,023	117,432	88,591	792,656	451,380	341,276	208,291	125,624	82,667	34,578	32,794	1,784	29,866	25,890	3,976
1970–71	252,610	144,395	108,215	839,730	475,594	364,136	230,509	138,146	92,363	37,946	35,544	2,402	32,107	27,530	4,577
1971–72	292,119	166,317	125,802	887,273	500,590	386,683	251,633	149,550	102,083	43,411	40,723	2,688	33,363	28,090	5,273
1972–73	316,174	175,413	140,761	922,362	518,191	404,171	263,371	154,468	108,903	50,018	46,489	3,529	34,777	28,571	6,206
1973–74	343,924	188,591	155,333	945,776	527,313	418,463	277,033	157,842	119,191	53,816	48,530	5,286	33,816	27,365	6,451
1974–75	360,171	191,017	169,154	922,933	504,841	418,092	292,450	161,570	130,880	55,916	48,956	6,960	34,083	26,817	7,266
1975–76	391,454	209,996	181,458	925,746	504,925	420,821	311,771	167,248	144,523	62,649	52,892	9,757	34,064	26,267	7,797
1976–77	406,377	210,842	195,535	919,549	495,545	424,004	317,164	167,783	149,381	64,359	52,374	11,985	33,232	25,142	8,090
1977–78	412,246	204,718	207,528	921,204	487,347	433,857	311,620	161,212	150,408	66,581	52,270	14,311	32,131	23,658	8,473
1978–79	402,702	192,091	210,611	921,390	477,344	444,046	301,079	153,370	147,709	68,848	52,652	16,196	32,730	23,541	9,189
1979–80	400,910	183,737	217,173	929,417	473,611	455,806	298,081	150,749	147,332	70,131	52,716	17,415	32,615	22,943	9,672
1980–81	416,377	188,638	227,739	935,140	469,883	465,257	295,739	147,043	148,696	71,956	52,792	19,164	32,958	22,711	10,247
1981–82	434,515	196,939	237,576	952,998	473,364	479,634	295,546	145,532	150,014	72,032	52,223	19,809	32,707	22,224	10,483
1982–83	456,441	207,141	249,300	969,510	479,140	490,370	289,921	144,697	145,224	73,136	51,310	21,826	32,775	21,902	10,873
1983–84	452,416	202,762	249,654	974,309	482,319	491,990	284,263	143,595	140,668	74,407	51,334	23,073	33,209	22,064	11,145
1984–85	454,712	202,932	251,780	979,477	482,528	496,949	286,251	143,390	142,861	75,063	50,455	24,608	32,943	21,700	11,243
1985–86	446,047	196,166	249,881	987,823	485,923	501,900	288,567	143,508	145,059	73,910	49,261	24,649	33,653	21,819	11,834
1986–87	437,137	191,525	245,612	991,339	480,854	510,485	289,557	141,363	148,194	72,750	47,460	25,290	34,120	22,099	12,021
1987–88 [3]	435,085	190,047	245,038	994,829	477,203	517,626	299,317	145,163	154,154	70,735	45,484	25,251	34,870	22,615	12,255
1988–89 [4]	435,210	185,406	249,804	1,017,667	483,097	534,570	309,762	148,982	160,780	70,758	45,067	25,691	35,759	22,705	13,054
1989–90 [5]	445,000	185,000	260,000	1,043,000	485,000	558,000	319,000	149,000	170,000	71,000	43,000	28,000	38,000	24,000	14,000
1990–91 [6]	470,000	200,000	270,000	1,064,000	492,000	572,000	327,000	150,000	177,000	73,800	44,200	29,600	38,700	24,200	14,500
1991–92 [6]	477,000	205,000	272,000	1,081,000	495,000	586,000	338,000	157,000	181,000	80,100	49,000	31,100	39,300	24,300	15,000
1992–93 [6]	476,000	204,000	272,000	1,101,000	514,000	587,000	343,000	159,000	184,000	82,600	50,400	32,200	39,800	24,400	15,400
1993–94 [6]	478,000	204,000	274,000	1,100,000	511,000	589,000	350,000	162,000	188,000	85,500	51,500	34,000	40,000	24,100	15,900
1994–95 [6]	480,000	203,000	277,000	1,100,000	510,000	590,000	354,000	165,000	189,000	87,800	52,500	35,300	40,200	23,800	16,400
1995–96 [6]	487,000	204,000	283,000	1,098,000	507,000	591,000	354,000	164,000	190,000	88,100	52,800	35,300	40,400	23,600	16,800
1996–97 [6]	491,000	205,000	286,000	1,100,000	505,000	595,000	355,000	164,000	191,000	88,100	52,800	35,300	40,600	23,400	17,200
1997–98 [6]	500,000	208,000	292,000	1,102,000	503,000	599,000	357,000	165,000	192,000	89,100	53,500	35,600	40,900	23,300	17,600
1998–99 [6]	507,000	209,000	298,000	1,114,000	507,000	607,000	362,000	168,000	194,000	90,900	54,600	36,300	41,100	23,200	17,900
1999–2000 [6]	519,000	213,000	306,000	1,129,000	509,000	620,000	368,000	173,000	195,000	92,200	55,300	36,900	41,200	22,900	18,300

[1] Includes first-professional degrees.

[2] First-professional degrees are included with bachelor's degrees.

[3] Revised from previously published data.

[4] Preliminary data.

[5] Estimated.

[6] Projected.

—Data not available.

NOTE.—Some data have been revised from previously published figures. Because of rounding, details may not add to totals.

SOURCE: U.S. Department of Education, National Center for Education Statistics, *Earned Degrees Conferred; Projections of Education Statistics to 2002;* and Integrated Postsecondary Education Data System (IPEDS), "Completions" survey. (This table was prepared April 1991.)

Table 229.—Earned degrees conferred by institutions of higher education, by level of degree and by State: 1987-88 and 1988-89

State or other area	1987–88					1988–89 [1]				
	Associate degrees	Bachelor's degrees	First-professional degrees	Master's degrees	Doctor's degrees (Ph.D., Ed.D., etc.)	Associate degrees	Bachelor's degrees	First-professional degrees	Master's degrees	Doctor's degrees (Ph.D., Ed.D., etc.)
1	2	3	4	5	6	7	8	9	10	11
United States	435,085	994,829	70,735	299,317	34,870	435,210	1,017,667	70,758	309,762	35,759
Alabama	5,974	16,270	817	4,559	289	5,877	16,508	787	4,233	341
Alaska	661	927	—	318	15	606	1,011	—	286	14
Arizona	5,466	12,348	404	4,970	495	6,167	13,767	420	4,884	559
Arkansas	2,412	7,017	369	1,746	101	2,432	7,300	343	1,801	96
California	47,503	88,553	7,889	31,506	4,116	48,018	91,508	7,651	33,060	4,209
Colorado	5,825	15,144	872	4,397	667	5,943	15,561	873	4,574	665
Connecticut	4,781	13,680	918	5,892	496	4,703	13,525	920	6,022	553
Delaware	1,131	3,527	284	649	107	1,138	3,414	317	691	114
District of Columbia	391	6,933	2,437	5,126	542	407	7,482	2,467	5,123	503
Florida	30,666	32,406	1,984	9,849	1,200	32,244	34,244	2,051	10,563	1,201
Georgia	6,653	19,481	1,875	5,883	737	7,126	19,883	1,846	6,099	800
Hawaii	2,309	3,724	126	969	116	2,120	3,628	119	1,017	172
Idaho	2,600	3,043	71	703	63	2,589	3,017	67	706	60
Illinois	24,720	47,958	4,353	17,783	2,152	23,141	48,865	4,404	18,666	2,176
Indiana	8,949	26,408	1,422	7,079	941	8,902	26,874	1,442	7,514	962
Iowa	7,013	16,747	1,518	3,001	658	8,145	16,859	1,489	3,218	574
Kansas	4,759	11,891	628	2,983	376	5,171	12,189	590	3,132	379
Kentucky	4,915	12,074	1,161	3,333	313	4,938	12,337	1,167	3,491	332
Louisiana	2,532	16,367	1,400	3,941	346	2,542	16,210	1,505	3,859	384
Maine	2,069	5,168	157	548	25	1,884	5,173	139	633	36
Maryland	7,061	17,334	1,081	5,414	717	6,938	17,928	1,124	5,970	711
Massachusetts	13,047	41,801	3,721	15,692	1,937	13,016	42,500	3,605	16,967	1,986
Michigan	19,249	38,939	2,341	11,904	1,238	20,168	40,767	2,212	12,720	1,333
Minnesota	7,591	21,167	1,560	3,839	549	6,947	21,901	1,486	4,114	568
Mississippi	4,448	8,486	473	2,082	241	4,810	8,227	414	2,108	245
Missouri	6,711	23,024	2,264	7,920	531	6,891	23,700	2,300	8,569	621
Montana	714	4,170	78	724	65	683	3,887	59	674	57
Nebraska	2,546	8,288	706	1,722	248	2,734	8,406	727	1,776	248
Nevada	857	1,943	46	434	28	885	2,023	46	502	35
New Hampshire	2,377	6,803	172	1,635	69	2,334	6,797	154	1,754	87
New Jersey	9,379	22,327	1,723	6,397	824	9,337	22,898	1,613	7,024	747
New Mexico	1,760	4,778	164	1,798	222	1,698	4,959	181	1,868	217
New York	46,888	87,981	6,628	34,360	3,497	45,465	87,719	7,046	34,442	3,579
North Carolina	10,333	25,688	1,594	5,938	796	9,894	26,981	1,632	5,872	724
North Dakota	1,886	4,110	114	584	66	1,797	4,287	115	579	61
Ohio	17,656	43,909	3,199	12,287	1,434	18,827	45,141	3,225	12,791	1,652
Oklahoma	5,341	13,173	1,031	4,118	349	6,172	13,617	950	4,112	358
Oregon	4,823	11,251	845	2,869	409	4,456	11,823	906	3,120	414
Pennsylvania	18,283	58,348	3,637	13,791	1,882	16,823	58,890	3,575	14,587	2,027
Rhode Island	3,659	7,934	84	1,625	237	3,663	8,493	80	1,774	222
South Carolina	4,776	12,136	683	3,535	302	4,949	12,524	738	3,269	266
South Dakota	831	3,627	121	756	51	783	3,698	130	793	48
Tennessee	5,906	17,175	1,348	4,423	541	5,605	17,398	1,343	4,840	582
Texas	21,993	55,575	3,999	17,559	2,067	22,595	56,987	4,146	17,163	2,113
Utah	3,552	10,820	378	2,574	418	3,572	10,682	376	2,345	367
Vermont	1,149	4,273	98	830	45	1,136	4,193	85	991	49
Virginia	8,192	25,149	1,699	6,056	746	7,438	26,028	1,695	6,545	764
Washington	11,664	17,552	898	4,262	576	12,284	18,118	809	4,275	583
West Virginia	2,419	7,260	308	1,824	131	2,640	7,033	315	1,691	112
Wisconsin	8,570	25,057	988	5,479	812	8,658	25,604	1,017	5,398	771
Wyoming	1,386	1,631	69	343	73	1,507	1,647	57	335	73
U.S. Service Schools	8,709	3,454	—	1,308	14	6,412	3,456	—	1,222	9
Outlying areas	5,556	12,671	729	1,358	58	4,846	12,504	560	1,288	32
American Samoa	—	—	—	—	—	89	—	—	—	—
Federated States of Micronesia	—	—	—	—	—	10	—	—	—	—
Guam	64	227	—	35	—	65	186	—	40	—
Northern Marianas	23	—	—	—	—	23	—	—	—	—
Palau	—	—	—	—	—	16	—	—	—	—
Puerto Rico	5,324	12,298	729	1,291	58	4,587	12,200	560	1,215	32
Trust Territory of the Pacific	71	—	—	—	—	—	—	—	—	—
Virgin Islands	74	146	—	32	—	56	118	—	33	—

[1] Revised from previously published data.
[2] Preliminary data.
—Data not available or not applicable.

SOURCE: U.S. Department of Education, National Center for Education Statistics, Integrated Postsecondary Education Data System (IPEDS), "Completions" survey. (This table was prepared February 1991.)

Table 230.—1- to 4-year awards and associate degrees, by field of study: 1984–85 to 1988–89

Field of study	1- to 4-year awards					Associate degrees				
	1984–85	1985–86	1986–87	1987–88 [1]	1988–89 [2]	1984–85	1985–86	1986–87	1987–88 [1]	1988–89 [2]
1	2	3	4	5	6	7	8	9	10	11
Total	123,680	120,380	109,613	106,672	104,233	454,712	446,047	437,137	435,085	435,210
Agriculture and natural resources, total	2,969	2,891	1,640	1,359	1,344	6,554	5,741	5,428	5,029	4,740
Agricultural business and agricultural production	2,216	2,087	1,389	1,116	1,116	4,175	3,651	3,655	3,003	2,889
Agricultural science	583	591	107	107	68	1,393	1,096	806	1,015	975
Renewable natural resources	170	213	144	136	160	986	994	967	1,011	876
Architecture and environmental design	411	550	593	653	598	1,490	1,432	1,662	1,809	1,815
Area and ethnic studies	20	64	208	124	117	32	33	19	18	15
Business and management	39,014	38,716	34,886	34,514	32,533	120,731	117,358	115,197	110,971	106,579
Accounting	680	748	776	805	656	5,527	5,094	5,253	4,894	4,380
Business and management, general	685	642	836	733	906	12,887	12,163	12,363	12,458	11,899
Business administration and management	682	825	723	899	1,069	19,530	18,988	20,401	22,266	24,876
Business and management, other	6,579	5,984	1,993	2,081	1,804	11,307	11,268	11,351	11,395	8,580
Business data processing	4,363	4,179	3,213	3,135	2,711	18,835	15,926	13,294	10,255	9,673
Secretarial and related programs	15,160	15,130	14,015	13,802	14,741	21,845	21,095	20,019	18,741	17,599
Business and office, other	3,408	3,475	3,881	3,750	1,840	14,378	15,373	14,877	15,073	14,860
Marketing and distribution	2,736	3,144	4,552	4,392	4,198	15,624	16,553	16,938	15,063	13,909
Consumer and personal services	4,721	4,589	4,897	4,917	4,608	798	898	701	826	803
Communications	154	119	461	461	402	1,846	2,055	1,590	1,919	1,779
Communications technologies	232	314	283	289	297	2,270	1,929	1,947	1,476	1,965
Computer and information sciences	2,453	1,889	1,977	1,800	1,534	12,677	10,704	9,098	8,628	7,914
Education	561	573	661	559	817	7,580	7,391	7,309	7,219	7,330
Engineering	233	465	113	227	832	3,881	5,256	4,518	3,850	2,682
Engineering technologies	31,212	28,419	28,297	27,541	23,311	59,951	58,083	58,191	58,377	53,176
Mechanics and repairers	14,795	13,418	12,308	12,834	11,011	8,666	10,996	11,023	10,430	7,739
Construction trades	3,499	3,289	3,204	3,185	3,090	2,341	2,131	2,082	2,020	1,695
Engineering technologies, other	12,918	11,712	12,785	11,522	9,210	48,944	44,956	45,086	45,927	43,742
Foreign languages	39	63	13	15	15	388	437	426	418	332
Health sciences	27,220	25,789	22,310	21,083	22,654	68,453	66,559	62,545	59,711	59,328
Dental assisting	2,912	2,623	2,595	2,494	2,188	4,160	4,051	4,017	3,675	3,599
Emergency medical technician-ambulance	573	721	668	410	891	74	88	63	79	51
Emergency medical technician-paramedic	596	546	454	770	562	211	267	307	277	299
Medical lab technician	33	110	64	43	69	2,788	2,609	2,205	1,839	1,703
Medical assisting	1,786	1,653	2,094	1,687	1,795	2,196	2,004	1,881	1,701	1,774
Nursing assisting	3,067	3,096	1,200	383	341	133	33	24	8	12
Practical nursing	12,322	10,570	8,748	8,834	9,862	1,252	991	607	561	591
Nursing, general	581	674	745	981	1,188	40,334	38,610	37,613	36,344	35,851
Health sciences, other	5,350	5,796	5,742	5,481	5,758	17,305	17,906	15,828	15,227	15,448
Home economics	3,762	4,099	3,603	3,659	3,396	9,611	9,469	9,311	9,739	10,430
Law	781	819	755	821	1,589	2,060	2,259	2,501	3,139	3,742
Letters	54	226	14	46	44	617	548	508	484	526
Liberal/general studies	1,343	1,754	907	869	1,006	106,396	107,672	108,207	113,048	118,463
Library and archival sciences	89	66	63	63	66	128	126	117	70	103
Life sciences	82	81	6	5	5	1,121	998	907	854	970
Mathematics	18	99	19	12	9	789	602	667	684	654
Military sciences	11	970	959	3	0	23	30	50	138	164
Multi/interdisciplinary studies	139	134	36	122	99	8,525	9,586	9,796	10,837	11,312
Parks and recreation	113	147	99	68	52	728	634	556	621	615
Philosophy and religion	65	161	80	21	69	138	114	100	94	81
Physical sciences	101	120	107	77	93	2,193	2,107	2,059	1,890	1,947
Science technologies	73	101	99	59	85	1,138	1,054	934	743	887
Physical sciences, other	28	19	8	18	8	1,055	1,053	1,125	1,147	1,060
Protective services	1,832	2,066	2,141	3,050	2,156	12,305	12,096	11,960	11,829	11,655
Criminal justice administration and studies	444	510	597	656	741	5,533	5,579	5,803	5,044	4,695
Law enforcement and security services	870	1,019	502	749	503	4,211	4,167	3,860	4,343	4,386
Fire control and safety	373	394	380	450	340	1,724	1,666	1,449	1,397	1,488
Protective services, other	145	143	662	1,195	572	837	684	848	1,045	1,086
Psychology	38	54	53	71	37	983	939	1,011	1,000	1,085
Public affairs	1,069	614	548	762	711	3,675	3,649	3,553	3,651	4,482
Transportation and material moving	734	296	277	548	484	1,561	1,338	1,284	1,327	2,090
Public affairs, other	335	318	271	214	227	2,114	2,311	2,269	2,324	2,392
Social sciences	15	179	127	174	122	2,587	2,540	2,620	2,709	2,700
Theology	724	559	460	607	677	701	705	578	627	568
Visual and performing arts	8,926	8,380	7,962	7,221	6,567	13,742	13,961	14,560	13,884	12,794
Fine arts, general	76	69	47	55	82	1,033	924	1,011	1,123	1,084
Graphic arts technician	215	237	193	158	128	1,686	1,855	721	766	529
Precision production	8,199	7,609	7,333	6,651	6,082	8,711	9,104	9,204	9,357	9,018
Visual and performing arts, other	436	465	389	357	275	2,312	2,078	3,624	2,638	2,163
Undistributed	0	0	232	396	3,081	2,537	1,034	146	362	5,264

[1] Revised from previously published data.
[2] Preliminary data.

SOURCE: U.S. Department of Education, National Center for Education Statistics, "Degrees and Other Formal Awards Conferred" surveys, and Integrated Postsecondary Education Data System (IPEDS), "Completions" survey. (This table was prepared February 1991.)

Table 231.—Associate degrees and other subbaccalaureate awards,[1] by length of curriculum, sex of student, and field of study: 1988–89

Field of study	Less than 1-year awards			1- to less than 4-year awards			Associate degrees		
	Total	Men	Women	Total	Men	Women	Total	Men	Women
1	2	3	4	5	6	7	8	9	10
Total	57,057	31,509	25,548	104,233	44,456	59,777	435,210	185,406	249,804
Agriculture and natural resources, total	1,423	1,165	258	1,344	904	440	4,740	3,074	1,666
Agricultural business and agricultural production	1,145	911	234	1,116	741	375	2,889	1,921	968
Agricultural science	222	203	19	68	37	31	975	418	557
Renewable natural resources	56	51	5	160	126	34	876	735	141
Architecture and environmental design	41	5	36	598	57	541	1,815	256	1,559
Area and ethnic studies	75	38	37	117	37	80	15	8	7
Business and management	11,212	2,547	8,665	32,533	4,961	27,572	106,579	33,121	73,458
Accounting	184	50	134	656	157	499	4,380	1,118	3,262
Business and management, general	437	196	241	906	324	582	11,899	4,969	6,930
Business administration and management	655	299	356	1,069	429	640	24,876	10,670	14,206
Business and management, other	1,072	606	466	1,804	743	1,061	8,580	4,202	4,378
Business data processing	1,536	445	1,091	2,711	771	1,940	9,673	4,169	5,504
Secretarial and related programs	3,261	148	3,113	14,741	166	14,575	17,599	204	17,395
Business and office, other	1,452	331	1,121	1,840	886	954	14,860	4,149	10,711
Marketing and distribution	1,913	422	1,491	4,198	864	3,334	13,909	3,231	10,678
Consumer and personal services	702	50	652	4,608	621	3,987	803	409	394
Communications	220	136	84	402	278	124	1,779	821	958
Communications technologies	638	219	419	297	153	144	1,965	1,292	673
Computer and information sciences	833	456	377	1,534	531	1,003	7,914	4,005	3,909
Education	106	30	76	817	128	689	7,330	2,132	5,198
Engineering	56	43	13	832	761	71	2,682	2,369	313
Engineering technologies	13,806	13,324	482	23,311	21,846	1,465	53,176	48,190	4,986
Mechanics and repairers	3,920	3,670	250	11,011	10,573	438	7,739	7,345	394
Construction trades	1,264	1,236	28	3,090	2,958	132	1,695	1,620	75
Engineering technologies, other	8,622	8,418	204	9,210	8,315	895	43,742	39,225	4,517
Foreign languages	290	139	151	15	6	9	332	112	220
Health sciences	13,759	3,589	10,170	22,654	3,322	19,332	59,328	6,977	52,351
Dental assisting	109	8	101	2,188	75	2,113	3,599	219	3,380
Emergency medical technician-ambulance	2,142	1,582	560	891	590	301	51	39	12
Emergency medical technician-paramedic	746	516	230	562	379	183	299	216	83
Medical lab technician	11	2	9	69	15	54	1,703	375	1,328
Medical assisting	615	72	543	1,795	39	1,756	1,774	93	1,681
Nursing assisting	5,764	653	5,111	341	34	307	12	1	11
Practical nursing	400	45	355	9,862	730	9,132	591	52	539
Nursing, general	62	1	61	1,188	98	1,090	35,851	2,493	33,358
Health sciences, other	3,910	710	3,200	5,758	1,362	4,396	15,448	3,489	11,959
Home economics	1,362	472	890	3,396	655	2,741	10,430	3,304	7,126
Law	737	159	578	1,589	590	999	3,742	471	3,271
Letters	60	22	38	44	19	25	526	164	362
Liberal/general studies	161	55	106	1,006	417	589	118,463	49,161	69,302
Library and archival sciences	35	0	35	66	3	63	103	12	91
Life sciences	61	58	3	5	1	4	970	412	558
Mathematics	1	0	1	9	4	5	654	415	239
Military sciences	0	0	0	0	0	0	164	133	31
Multi/interdisciplinary studies	33	6	27	99	53	46	11,312	5,135	6,177
Parks and recreation	16	7	9	52	36	16	615	303	312
Philosophy and religion	2	1	1	69	26	43	81	58	23
Physical sciences	23	18	5	93	51	42	1,947	1,135	812
Science technologies	13	12	1	85	44	41	887	555	332
Physical sciences, other	10	6	4	8	7	1	1,060	580	480
Protective services	3,854	3,199	655	2,156	1,644	512	11,655	8,370	3,285
Criminal justice administration and studies	579	485	94	741	542	199	4,695	3,083	1,612
Law enforcement and security services	1,537	1,295	242	503	413	90	4,386	3,211	1,175
Fire control and safety	698	650	48	340	324	16	1,488	1,409	79
Protective services, other	1,040	769	271	572	365	207	1,086	667	419
Psychology	16	1	15	37	9	28	1,085	280	805
Public affairs	3,457	3,020	437	711	485	226	4,482	2,266	2,216
Transportation and material moving	3,315	2,926	389	484	440	44	2,090	1,750	340
Public affairs, other	142	94	48	227	45	182	2,392	516	1,876
Social sciences	99	26	73	122	63	59	2,700	1,174	1,526
Theology	105	55	50	677	348	329	568	320	248
Visual and performing arts	1,835	1,435	400	6,567	5,234	1,333	12,794	7,439	5,355
Fine arts, general	6	4	2	82	34	48	1,084	381	703
Graphic arts technician	57	29	28	128	60	68	529	197	332
Precision production	1,685	1,391	294	6,082	4,984	1,098	9,018	5,899	3,119
Visual and performing arts, other	87	11	76	275	156	119	2,163	962	1,201
Undistributed	2,741	1,284	1,457	3,081	1,834	1,247	5,264	2,497	2,767

[1] Preliminary data

SOURCE: U.S. Department of Education, National Center for Education Statistics, Integrated Postsecondary Education Data System (IPEDS), "Completions" survey. (This table was prepared November 1990.)

Table 232.—Associate degrees and other subbaccalaureate awards,[1] by length of curriculum, sex of student, and field of study: 1987-88

Field of study	Less than 1-year awards			1- to less than 4-year awards			Associate degrees		
	Total	Men	Women	Total	Men	Women	Total	Men	Women
1	2	3	4	5	6	7	8	9	10
Total	**54,981**	**29,504**	**25,477**	**106,672**	**47,653**	**59,019**	**435,085**	**190,047**	**245,038**
Agriculture and natural resources, total	2,384	1,786	598	1,359	934	425	5,029	3,371	1,658
Agricultural business and agricultural production	1,711	1,275	436	1,116	757	359	3,003	2,043	960
Agricultural science	579	426	153	107	59	48	1,015	472	543
Renewable natural resources	94	85	9	136	118	18	1,011	856	155
Architecture and environmental design	54	4	50	653	95	558	1,809	218	1,591
Area and ethnic studies	30	13	17	124	6	118	18	4	14
Business and management	12,283	3,274	9,009	34,514	5,575	28,939	110,971	35,131	75,840
Accounting	134	33	101	805	193	612	4,894	1,321	3,573
Business and management, general	438	206	232	733	258	475	12,458	5,163	7,295
Business administration and management	653	292	361	899	337	562	22,266	9,563	12,703
Business and management, other	1,340	726	614	2,081	909	1,172	11,395	5,841	5,554
Business data processing	1,778	622	1,156	3,135	1,040	2,095	10,255	4,376	5,879
Secretarial and related programs	3,365	94	3,271	13,802	377	13,425	18,741	262	18,479
Business and office, other	1,265	348	917	3,750	757	2,993	15,073	4,222	10,851
Marketing and distribution	2,530	881	1,649	4,392	989	3,403	15,063	3,939	11,124
Consumer and personal services	780	72	708	4,917	715	4,202	826	444	382
Communications	210	140	70	461	318	143	1,919	1,004	915
Communications technologies	45	34	11	289	148	141	1,476	903	573
Computer and information sciences	1,471	711	760	1,800	800	1,000	8,628	4,474	4,154
Education	162	27	135	559	41	518	7,219	2,315	4,904
Engineering	149	103	46	227	159	68	3,850	3,437	413
Engineering technologies	13,576	12,893	683	27,541	25,915	1,626	58,377	53,127	5,250
Mechanics and repairers	3,987	3,712	275	12,834	12,275	559	10,430	9,875	555
Construction trades	1,255	1,174	81	3,185	3,045	140	2,020	1,956	64
Engineering technologies, other	8,334	8,007	327	11,522	10,595	927	45,927	41,296	4,631
Foreign languages	151	59	92	15	3	12	418	225	193
Health sciences	13,373	3,269	10,104	21,083	2,976	18,107	59,711	6,938	52,773
Dental assisting	115	9	106	2,494	108	2,386	3,675	250	3,425
Emergency medical technician-ambulance	2,349	1,654	695	410	236	174	79	61	18
Emergency medical technician-paramedic	430	254	176	770	550	220	277	185	92
Medical lab technician	59	6	53	43	7	36	1,839	403	1,436
Medical assisting	704	46	658	1,687	36	1,651	1,701	42	1,659
Nursing assisting	4,740	463	4,277	383	48	335	8	2	6
Practical nursing	435	24	411	8,834	671	8,163	561	39	522
Nursing, general	90	3	87	981	82	899	36,344	2,556	33,788
Health sciences, other	4,451	810	3,641	5,481	1,238	4,243	15,227	3,400	11,827
Home economics	1,696	586	1,110	3,659	755	2,904	9,739	2,938	6,801
Law	702	68	634	821	126	695	3,139	369	2,770
Letters	40	8	32	46	16	30	484	163	321
Liberal/general studies	44	23	21	869	397	472	113,048	48,074	64,974
Library and archival sciences	32	1	31	63	9	54	70	8	62
Life sciences	121	101	20	5	3	2	854	348	506
Mathematics	1	0	1	12	7	5	684	435	249
Military sciences	0	0	0	3	3	0	138	118	20
Multi/interdisciplinary studies	94	9	85	122	65	57	10,837	4,921	5,916
Parks and recreation	28	14	14	68	46	22	621	291	330
Philosophy and religion	3	2	1	21	6	15	94	64	30
Physical sciences	28	20	8	77	50	27	1,890	1,112	778
Science technologies	25	18	7	59	35	24	743	435	308
Physical sciences, other	3	2	1	18	15	3	1,147	677	470
Protective services	2,980	2,445	535	3,050	2,472	578	11,829	8,672	3,157
Criminal justice administration and studies	1,235	1,013	222	656	481	175	5,044	3,418	1,626
Law enforcement and security services	757	636	121	749	601	148	4,343	3,254	1,089
Fire control and safety	420	379	41	450	404	46	1,397	1,344	53
Protective services, other	568	417	151	1,195	986	209	1,045	656	389
Psychology	26	1	25	71	15	56	1,000	299	701
Public affairs	2,594	2,242	352	762	521	241	3,651	1,620	2,031
Transportation and material moving	2,413	2,139	274	548	480	68	1,327	1,125	202
Public affairs, other	181	103	78	214	41	173	2,324	495	1,829
Social sciences	28	13	15	174	91	83	2,709	1,153	1,556
Theology	83	37	46	607	292	315	627	388	239
Visual and performing arts	1,942	1,499	443	7,221	5,696	1,525	13,884	7,816	6,068
Fine arts, general	31	9	22	55	26	29	1,123	381	742
Graphic arts technician	85	22	63	158	71	87	766	232	534
Precision production	1,741	1,461	280	6,651	5,416	1,235	9,357	6,031	3,326
Visual and performing arts, other	85	7	78	357	183	174	2,638	1,172	1,466
Undistributed	651	122	529	396	113	283	362	111	251

[1] Preliminary data.

SOURCE: U.S. Department of Education, National Center for Education Statistics, Integrated Postsecondary Education Data System (IPEDS), "Completions" survey. (This table was prepared March 1990.)

Table 233.—Bachelor's, master's, and doctor's degrees conferred [1] by institutions of higher education, by sex of student and field of study: 1988–89

Field of study	Bachelor's degrees requiring 4 or 5 years			Master's degrees			Doctor's degrees (Ph.D., Ed.D., etc.)		
	Total	Men	Women	Total	Men	Women	Total	Men	Women
1	2	3	4	5	6	7	8	9	10
All fields	1,017,667	483,097	534,570	309,762	148,982	160,780	35,759	22,705	13,054
Agriculture and natural resources, total	13,488	9,295	4,193	3,245	2,231	1,014	1,184	952	232
Agribusiness and agricultural production, total	4,736	3,577	1,159	654	495	159	203	162	41
Agricultural business and management, total	3,448	2,669	779	510	396	114	160	129	31
Agricultural business and management, general	339	270	69	27	19	8	1	1	0
Agricultural business	1,222	951	271	24	20	4	0	0	0
Agricultural economics	1,750	1,329	421	452	351	101	159	128	31
Agricultural business and management, other	137	119	18	7	6	1	0	0	0
Agricultural mechanics	233	230	3	15	14	1	0	0	0
Agricultural production	93	72	21	26	23	3	13	12	1
Horticulture	339	236	103	37	18	19	17	13	4
International agriculture	24	15	9	12	11	1	0	0	0
Agribusiness and agricultural production, other	599	355	244	54	33	21	13	8	5
Agricultural sciences, total	5,920	3,555	2,365	1,684	1,104	580	752	600	152
Agricultural sciences, general	976	686	290	176	121	55	21	17	4
Animal sciences, total	2,814	1,507	1,307	465	287	178	211	168	43
Animal sciences, general	2,380	1,234	1,146	347	208	139	161	124	37
Animal breeding and genetics	14	8	6	4	2	2	7	6	1
Animal health	15	3	12	12	5	7	2	2	0
Animal nutrition	1	1	0	8	7	1	13	10	3
Dairy	152	120	32	40	26	14	14	13	1
Fisheries science	0	0	0	0	0	0	0	0	0
Poultry	97	77	20	27	22	5	6	5	1
Animal sciences, other	155	64	91	27	17	10	8	8	0
Food sciences	558	230	328	300	141	159	112	82	30
Plant sciences, total	1,372	984	388	587	444	143	317	258	59
Plant sciences, general	205	143	62	66	54	12	33	24	9
Agronomy	548	480	68	287	231	56	196	166	30
Horticulture science	495	275	220	155	99	56	63	47	16
Ornamental horticulture	0	0	0	0	0	0	0	0	0
Plant breeding and genetics	0	0	0	0	0	0	0	0	0
Plant pathology (applied)	0	0	0	0	0	0	0	0	0
Plant protection (pest management)	20	16	4	19	12	7	0	0	0
Range management	67	44	23	50	40	10	18	15	3
Plant sciences, other	37	26	11	10	8	2	7	6	1
Soil sciences	103	81	22	108	76	32	57	49	8
Agricultural sciences, other	97	67	30	48	35	13	34	26	8
Renewable natural resources, total	2,832	2,163	669	907	632	275	229	190	39
Renewable natural resources, general	698	471	227	190	115	75	33	25	8
Conservation and regulation	195	143	52	22	18	4	0	0	0
Fishing and fisheries	135	112	23	92	66	26	28	24	4
Forestry production and processing	213	184	29	34	27	7	16	16	0
Forestry and related sciences	820	684	136	420	299	121	119	101	18
Wildlife management	670	497	173	118	86	32	15	9	6
Renewable natural resources, other	101	72	29	31	21	10	18	15	3
Architecture and environmental design, total	9,191	5,580	3,611	3,378	2,191	1,187	86	63	23
Architecture and environmental design, general	523	375	148	117	77	40	3	2	1
Architecture	4,681	3,396	1,285	1,675	1,201	474	30	19	11
City, community, and regional planning	310	228	82	987	620	367	39	30	9
Environmental design	734	487	247	64	32	32	4	4	0
Interior design	1,721	192	1,529	41	12	29	1	1	0
Landscape architecture	884	648	236	280	141	139	0	0	0
Urban design	1	1	0	83	53	30	0	0	0
Architecture and environmental design, other	337	253	84	131	55	76	9	7	2
Area and ethnic studies, total	3,949	1,613	2,336	978	497	481	110	57	53
Area studies, total	2,969	1,164	1,805	766	368	398	95	51	44
African studies	23	10	13	11	4	7	1	1	0
American studies	1,248	445	803	208	88	120	60	26	34
Asian studies	721	305	416	199	111	88	17	13	4
European studies	350	169	181	27	13	14	2	0	2
Latin American studies	211	80	131	157	65	92	1	0	1
Middle Eastern studies	48	19	29	59	36	23	10	8	2
Russian and Slavic studies	256	126	130	94	46	48	1	1	0
Area studies, other	112	10	102	11	5	6	3	2	1
Ethnic studies, total	856	395	461	108	47	61	6	3	3
Afro-American (black) studies	185	74	111	35	15	20	0	0	0
Hispanic-American studies	59	22	37	13	2	11	0	0	0
Ethnic studies, other	612	299	313	60	30	30	6	3	3
Area and ethnic studies, other	124	54	70	104	82	22	9	3	6

Table 233.—Bachelor's, master's, and doctor's degrees conferred [1] by institutions of higher education, by sex of student and field of study: 1988–89—Continued

Field of study	Bachelor's degrees requiring 4 or 5 years			Master's degrees			Doctor's degrees (Ph.D., Ed.D., etc.)		
	Total	Men	Women	Total	Men	Women	Total	Men	Women
1	2	3	4	5	6	7	8	9	10
Business and management, business and office, and marketing and distribution	246,659	131,419	115,240	73,154	48,557	24,597	1,150	844	306
Business and management, total	238,699	128,871	109,828	72,961	48,444	24,517	1,150	844	306
Business and management, general	41,024	21,990	19,034	12,936	8,663	4,273	188	143	45
Accounting	43,454	20,243	23,211	3,067	1,727	1,340	68	47	21
Banking and finance	26,485	17,534	8,951	4,850	3,443	1,407	51	42	9
Business administration and management	69,069	38,031	31,038	38,433	25,987	12,446	547	395	152
Business economics	3,452	2,246	1,206	176	125	51	33	24	9
Human resources development	1,622	777	845	770	335	435	6	2	4
Institutional management	5,632	2,945	2,687	367	203	164	5	5	0
Insurance and risk management	509	312	197	33	23	10	8	7	1
International business management	1,458	626	832	1,776	1,108	668	26	19	7
Investments and securities	257	157	100	183	144	39	0	0	0
Labor/industrial relations	993	467	526	659	281	378	16	11	5
Management information systems	3,053	1,787	1,266	1,009	764	245	6	4	2
Management science, total	2,480	1,478	1,002	1,107	833	274	55	42	13
Business statistics	0	0	0	0	0	0	0	0	0
Operations research (quantitative methods)	1,373	810	563	746	548	198	51	39	12
Management science, other	1,107	668	439	361	285	76	4	3	1
Marketing management and research	30,040	14,865	15,175	2,093	1,101	992	38	28	10
Organizational behavior	768	358	410	137	60	77	31	18	13
Personnel management	1,754	819	935	204	108	96	2	1	1
Real estate	1,058	764	294	223	178	45	1	1	0
Small business management and ownership	103	77	26	6	5	1	0	0	0
Taxation	0	0	0	829	526	303	0	0	0
Trade and industrial supervision and management	905	717	188	72	63	9	0	0	0
Consumer and personal services	106	77	29	0	0	0	0	0	0
Business and management, other	4,477	2,601	1,876	4,031	2,767	1,264	69	55	14
Business and office, total	2,774	636	2,138	23	15	8	0	0	0
Accounting, bookkeeping, and related programs	285	120	165	18	12	6	0	0	0
Business data processing and related programs	475	277	198	4	3	1	0	0	0
Office supervision and management	1,292	157	1,135	0	0	0	0	0	0
Secretarial and related programs	595	51	544	0	0	0	0	0	0
Business and office, other	127	31	96	1	0	1	0	0	0
Marketing and distribution, total	5,186	1,912	3,274	170	98	72	0	0	0
Apparel and accessories marketing	1,683	82	1,601	0	0	0	0	0	0
Business and personal services marketing	837	468	369	0	0	0	0	0	0
General marketing	1,967	1,035	932	44	16	28	0	0	0
Transportation and travel marketing	185	43	142	53	24	29	0	0	0
Marketing and distribution, other	514	284	230	73	58	15	0	0	0
Communications and communications technologies, total	48,625	19,263	29,362	4,233	1,710	2,523	248	137	111
Communications, total	47,385	18,567	28,818	3,926	1,540	2,386	242	135	107
Communications, general	22,399	8,423	13,976	1,501	563	938	163	94	69
Advertising	2,651	939	1,712	204	77	127	2	2	0
Communications, research	130	38	92	29	7	22	13	5	8
Journalism (mass communications)	11,522	4,191	7,331	1,270	485	785	29	17	12
Public relations	1,711	517	1,194	92	21	71	0	0	0
Radio/television news broadcasting	834	344	490	47	29	18	0	0	0
Radio television, general	5,542	2,983	2,559	232	123	109	20	10	10
Communications, other	2,596	1,132	1,464	551	235	316	15	7	8
Communications technologies, total	1,240	696	544	307	170	137	6	2	4
Motion picture technology	36	32	4	0	0	0	0	0	0
Photographic technology	25	12	13	0	0	0	0	0	0
Radio and television technology	1,111	614	497	236	139	97	1	1	0
Communications technologies, other	68	38	30	71	31	40	5	1	4
Computer and information sciences, total	30,637	21,221	9,416	9,392	6,769	2,623	538	457	81
Computer and information sciences, general	24,155	17,107	7,048	7,756	5,716	2,040	504	441	63
Computer programming	348	268	80	130	109	21	0	0	0
Data processing	506	294	212	30	17	13	0	0	0
Information science and systems	4,092	2,529	1,563	1,061	617	444	28	11	17
Systems analysis	274	173	101	108	84	24	0	0	0
Computer and information sciences, other	1,262	850	412	307	226	81	6	5	1
Education, total	96,988	21,662	75,326	82,238	20,286	61,952	6,783	2,894	3,889
Education, general	2,238	418	1,820	8,780	2,222	6,558	1,046	413	633
Bilingual/bicultural education	95	8	87	158	54	104	48	27	21
Curriculum and instruction	424	35	389	4,543	970	3,573	747	264	483
Education administration, total	74	22	52	9,802	4,162	5,640	1,911	967	944
Education administration, general	68	19	49	6,055	2,696	3,359	1,355	723	632
Administration of special education	0	0	0	11	1	10	11	2	9

Table 233.—Bachelor's, master's, and doctor's degrees conferred [1] by institutions of higher education, by sex of student and field of study: 1988–89—Continued

Field of study	Bachelor's degrees requiring 4 or 5 years			Master's degrees			Doctor's degrees (Ph.D., Ed.D., etc.)		
	Total	Men	Women	Total	Men	Women	Total	Men	Women
1	2	3	4	5	6	7	8	9	10
Adult and continuing education administration	2	0	2	173	41	132	53	20	33
Educational supervision	0	0	0	810	258	552	35	16	19
Elementary and secondary education administration	1	1	0	1,861	805	1,056	51	23	28
Higher education administration	2	2	0	258	87	171	280	131	149
Community college education administration	0	0	0	57	28	29	10	4	6
Educational administration, other	1	0	1	577	246	331	116	48	68
Educational media	29	9	20	776	208	568	40	18	22
Evaluation and research, total	14	5	9	161	62	99	130	56	74
Evaluation and research, general	0	0	0	48	20	28	45	18	27
Educational statistics and research	0	0	0	41	28	13	38	13	25
Educational testing, evaluation, and measurement	0	0	0	54	10	44	30	17	13
Elementary and secondary research	14	5	9	7	1	6	0	0	0
Higher education research	0	0	0	11	3	8	17	8	9
School psychology	173	19	154	1,389	343	1,046	458	183	275
Social foundations	0	0	0	204	77	127	134	50	84
Special education, total	6,671	441	6,230	8,872	1,043	7,829	253	46	207
Special education, general	4,385	286	4,099	6,537	777	5,760	200	37	163
Education of the deaf and hearing impaired	190	4	186	180	17	163	3	1	2
Education of the gifted and talented	2	0	2	167	17	150	4	0	4
Education of the emotionally handicapped	188	18	170	251	44	207	1	0	1
Education of the mentally handicapped	600	45	555	200	25	175	7	2	5
Education of the multiple handicapped	61	5	56	116	17	99	0	0	0
Education of the physically handicapped	53	1	52	29	3	26	3	0	3
Education of the visually handicapped	15	1	14	28	5	23	0	0	0
Remedial education	0	0	0	40	6	34	4	1	3
Special learning disabilities	295	29	266	731	62	669	11	2	9
Speech correction	592	27	565	220	15	205	0	0	0
Special education, other	290	25	265	373	55	318	20	3	17
Student counseling and personnel services	81	18	63	9,569	2,219	7,350	409	178	231
Teacher education, general programs, total	52,691	4,812	47,879	18,749	2,811	15,938	405	137	268
Adult and continuing education	89	30	59	620	198	422	143	44	99
Elementary education	43,326	3,138	40,188	11,356	1,024	10,332	94	17	77
Junior high/middle school education	766	140	626	519	71	448	0	0	0
Pre-elementary education	4,480	56	4,424	1,490	23	1,467	23	4	19
Secondary education	3,647	1,413	2,234	3,487	1,191	2,296	80	44	36
Teacher education, general programs, other	383	35	348	1,277	304	973	65	28	37
Teacher education, specific subject areas, total	33,594	15,636	17,958	15,755	5,165	10,590	911	427	484
Agricultural education	573	482	91	525	240	285	26	19	7
Art education	1,021	188	833	554	104	450	50	27	23
Business education	1,885	387	1,498	557	108	449	35	11	24
Driver and safety education	48	40	8	65	47	18	0	0	0
English education	1,674	329	1,345	475	91	384	13	2	11
Foreign languages education	326	64	262	140	33	107	11	4	7
Health education	1,538	342	1,196	811	190	621	111	33	78
Home economics education	530	4	526	195	3	192	16	2	14
Industrial arts education	1,935	1,672	263	662	512	150	36	26	10
Marketing and distributive education	265	105	160	14	3	11	0	0	0
Mathematics education	1,690	639	1,051	669	212	457	41	17	24
Music education	2,846	1,213	1,633	847	390	457	80	47	33
Physical education	12,449	6,559	5,890	3,538	1,724	1,814	203	113	90
Reading education	251	24	227	3,560	171	3,389	82	13	69
Science education	1,446	639	807	734	300	434	36	20	16
Social science education	840	393	447	118	45	73	2	1	1
Social studies education	1,494	909	585	240	129	111	8	6	2
Technical education	302	220	82	158	96	62	39	18	21
Trade and industrial education	1,199	861	338	544	277	267	46	30	16
Teacher education, other	1,282	566	716	1,349	490	859	76	38	38
Teaching English as a second language	28	6	22	869	215	654	1	0	1
Education, other	876	233	643	2,611	735	1,876	290	128	162
Engineering and engineering technologies, total	85,273	73,651	11,622	24,541	21,355	3,186	4,533	4,133	400
Engineering, total	66,296	56,234	10,062	23,713	20,633	3,080	4,521	4,121	400
Engineering, general	2,570	2,180	390	958	848	110	254	236	18
Aerospace, aeronautical, and astronautical engineering	2,944	2,643	301	855	791	64	154	147	7
Agricultural engineering	461	414	47	167	153	14	96	90	6
Architectural engineering	512	423	89	63	60	3	5	5	0
Bioengineering and biomedical engineering	672	448	224	369	282	87	81	61	20
Ceramic engineering	275	203	72	101	73	28	25	23	2
Chemical engineering	3,684	2,581	1,103	1,097	885	212	599	520	79
Civil engineering	7,316	6,278	1,038	2,902	2,536	366	503	455	48
Computer engineering	2,198	1,871	327	823	697	126	74	65	9
Electrical, electronics, and communications engineering	21,909	19,078	2,831	7,024	6,234	790	1,002	936	66
Engineering mechanics	188	172	16	182	159	23	97	89	8
Engineering physics	337	303	34	68	58	10	44	41	3
Engineering science	262	215	47	283	238	45	51	46	5
Environmental health engineering	104	67	37	324	248	76	34	26	8

Table 233.—Bachelor's, master's, and doctor's degrees conferred[1] by institutions of higher education, by sex of student and field of study: 1988–89—Continued

Field of study	Bachelor's degrees requiring 4 or 5 years			Master's degrees			Doctor's degrees (Ph.D., Ed.D., etc.)		
	Total	Men	Women	Total	Men	Women	Total	Men	Women
1	2	3	4	5	6	7	8	9	10
Geological engineering	127	95	32	45	41	4	4	3	1
Geophysical engineering	24	22	2	16	16	0	0	0	0
Industrial engineering	3,973	2,767	1,206	1,823	1,465	358	203	177	26
Materials engineering	421	305	116	453	346	107	245	208	37
Mechanical engineering	14,883	13,229	1,654	3,517	3,214	303	634	610	24
Metallurgical engineering	418	345	73	253	208	45	96	86	10
Mining and mineral engineering	99	90	9	77	70	7	33	32	1
Naval architecture and marine engineering	332	315	17	52	50	2	9	8	1
Nuclear engineering	287	252	35	246	219	27	83	78	5
Ocean engineering	97	81	16	71	65	6	15	14	1
Petroleum engineering	452	405	47	218	202	16	32	31	1
Surveying and mapping sciences, total	122	103	19	34	31	3	5	4	1
Systems engineering	285	229	56	269	224	45	21	19	2
Textile engineering	33	21	12	21	17	4	0	0	0
Engineering, other	1,311	1,099	212	1,402	1,203	199	122	111	11
Engineering and related technologies, total	18,977	17,417	1,560	828	722	106	12	12	0
Architectural technologies	791	733	58	22	20	2	0	0	0
Civil technologies	709	641	68	0	0	0	0	0	0
Electrical and electronic technologies	5,191	4,824	367	46	41	5	0	0	0
Electromechanical instrumentation and maintenance technologies	252	240	12	7	7	0	0	0	0
Environmental control technologies	140	113	27	74	52	22	4	4	0
Industrial production technologies	4,828	4,350	478	183	167	16	5	5	0
Quality control and safety technologies	272	209	63	179	157	22	0	0	0
Mechanical and related technologies	2,408	2,255	153	0	0	0	0	0	0
Mining and petroleum technologies	52	47	5	0	0	0	0	0	0
Mechanics and repairers	197	190	7	0	0	0	0	0	0
Construction trades	30	28	2	0	0	0	0	0	0
Engineering and related technologies, other	4,107	3,787	320	317	278	39	3	3	0
Foreign languages, total	10,774	2,879	7,895	1,911	602	1,309	422	169	253
Foreign languages, multiple emphasis	721	181	540	244	73	171	42	18	24
African (non-Semitic) languages	2	2	0	2	1	1	3	3	0
Asiatic languages, total	343	149	194	65	27	38	21	13	8
Chinese	140	57	83	27	14	13	8	7	1
Japanese	162	75	87	14	1	13	4	1	3
Asiatic languages, other	41	17	24	24	12	12	9	5	4
Baltic-Slavic languages, total	533	214	319	124	59	65	16	8	8
Slavic languages (other than Russian)	57	24	33	66	36	30	6	4	2
Russian languages	467	185	282	55	21	34	6	3	3
Balto-Slavic languages, other	9	5	4	3	2	1	4	1	3
Germanic languages, total	1,478	521	957	279	91	188	68	28	40
German	1,429	507	922	261	86	175	59	23	36
Scandinavian languages	32	7	25	7	2	5	2	2	0
Germanic languages, other	17	7	10	11	3	8	7	3	4
Greek (classical)	32	18	14	15	11	4	2	0	2
Indic languages	1	0	1	1	0	1	9	5	4
Italic languages, total	7,428	1,716	5,712	1,118	306	812	221	70	151
French	3,286	633	2,653	462	115	347	81	15	66
Italian	242	55	187	43	13	30	16	7	9
Latin	82	35	47	15	8	7	1	1	0
Portuguese	28	16	12	3	2	1	0	0	0
Spanish	3,750	971	2,779	550	158	392	103	41	62
Italic languages, other	40	6	34	45	10	35	20	6	14
Semitic languages, total	67	21	46	22	13	9	15	10	5
Arabic	6	1	5	2	1	1	1	0	1
Hebrew	55	17	38	15	8	7	3	2	1
Semitic languages, other	6	3	3	5	4	1	11	8	3
Foreign languages, other	169	57	112	41	21	20	25	14	11
Allied health and health sciences, total	59,111	8,926	50,185	19,255	4,210	15,045	1,439	612	827
Allied health, total	12,572	2,553	10,019	3,275	785	2,490	54	29	25
Dental services	731	7	724	24	4	20	0	0	0
Diagnostic and treatment services	759	281	478	39	24	15	0	0	0
Medical laboratory technologies	1,814	376	1,438	24	5	19	1	0	1
Mental health/human services	956	172	784	1,164	307	857	23	12	11
Miscellaneous allied health services	795	324	471	140	37	103	0	0	0
Nursing-related services	124	10	114	47	28	19	0	0	0
Rehabilitative services	6,701	1,201	5,500	1,543	307	1,236	14	4	10
Occupational therapy	1,995	146	1,849	337	30	307	2	0	2
Physical therapy	3,514	790	2,724	757	194	563	3	1	2
Speech-language pathology/audiology	55	1	54	18	1	17	3	2	1
Rehabilitative services, other	1,137	264	873	431	82	349	6	1	5
Allied health, other	692	182	510	294	73	221	16	13	3

Table 233.—Bachelor's, master's, and doctor's degrees conferred [1] by institutions of higher education, by sex of student and field of study: 1988–89—Continued

Field of study	Bachelor's degrees requiring 4 or 5 years			Master's degrees			Doctor's degrees (Ph.D., Ed.D., etc.)		
	Total	Men	Women	Total	Men	Women	Total	Men	Women
1	2	3	4	5	6	7	8	9	10
Health sciences, total	46,539	6,373	40,166	15,980	3,425	12,555	1,385	583	802
Audiology and speech pathology	2,486	107	2,379	2,763	147	2,616	87	24	63
Basic clinical health sciences	216	79	137	116	49	67	125	73	52
Chiropractic	0	0	0	0	0	0	0	0	0
Dentistry, total	156	87	69	385	289	96	17	15	2
Epidemiology	0	0	0	0	0	0	0	0	0
Health services administration, total	3,271	695	2,576	2,911	981	1,930	27	13	14
Health services administration	2,451	612	1,839	2,407	808	1,599	21	12	9
Health care planning	17	4	13	247	91	156	5	1	4
Medical records administration	626	36	590	1	0	1	0	0	0
Health services administration, other	177	43	134	256	82	174	1	0	1
Medical laboratory	759	147	612	86	31	55	1	0	1
Medicine, total	216	99	117	239	121	118	140	85	55
Nursing	30,086	1,582	28,504	6,466	536	5,930	371	27	344
Optometry	216	129	87	13	7	6	5	5	0
Osteopathic medicine	5	5	0	0	0	0	0	0	0
Pharmacy	5,486	2,238	3,248	251	144	107	178	114	64
Pre-dentistry	85	52	33	0	0	0	0	0	0
Pre-medicine	531	358	173	0	0	0	2	1	1
Pre-veterinary	53	27	26	2	2	0	0	0	0
Public health	312	114	198	1,804	727	1,077	200	75	125
Veterinary medicine	241	103	138	112	69	43	68	42	26
Health sciences, other	2,420	551	1,869	832	322	510	164	109	55
Home economics and vocational home economics, total	14,717	1,380	13,337	2,174	311	1,863	263	59	204
Home economics, total	13,416	1,034	12,382	2,099	290	1,809	236	52	184
Home economics, general	3,239	177	3,062	353	19	334	33	2	31
Business home economics	193	8	185	0	0	0	0	0	0
Family and community services	170	14	156	46	12	34	0	0	0
Family/consumer resource management	747	198	549	41	2	39	12	2	10
Food sciences and human nutrition	2,613	256	2,357	602	64	538	62	19	43
Human environment and housing	646	66	580	50	18	32	6	0	6
Individual and family development	2,584	141	2,443	835	151	684	109	29	80
Textiles and clothing	3,018	158	2,860	100	12	88	13	0	13
Home economics, other	206	16	190	72	12	60	1	0	1
Vocational home economics, total	1,301	346	955	75	21	54	27	7	20
Consumer and homemaking education	601	78	523	35	11	24	15	7	8
Institutional, home management, and supporting services	94	37	57	9	0	9	2	0	2
Vocational home economics, other	606	231	375	31	10	21	10	0	10
Law, total	1,976	785	1,191	2,098	1,491	607	76	46	30
Law	657	354	303	1,195	835	360	71	44	27
Pre-law	316	166	150	0	0	0	0	0	0
Legal assisting	523	76	447	3	0	3	0	0	0
Law, other	480	189	291	900	656	244	5	2	3
Letters, total	43,323	14,237	29,086	6,608	2,272	4,336	1,238	559	679
English, general	30,293	9,566	20,727	4,077	1,363	2,714	730	318	412
Classics	464	210	254	117	68	49	51	32	19
Comparative literature	687	199	488	228	73	155	92	47	45
Composition	164	59	105	9	2	7	11	3	8
Creative writing	592	238	354	511	208	303	4	2	2
Linguistics	442	133	309	579	211	368	165	71	94
Literature, American	34	8	26	4	2	2	1	0	1
Literature, English	1,600	557	1,043	252	74	178	43	18	25
Rhetoric	0	0	0	0	0	0	0	0	0
Speech, debate, and forensics	7,878	2,889	4,989	557	178	379	107	56	51
Technical and business writing	134	38	96	83	21	62	0	0	0
Letters, other	1,035	340	695	191	72	119	34	12	22
Liberal/general studies, total	23,459	10,051	13,408	1,408	495	913	32	16	16
Liberal arts and sciences	12,997	5,791	7,206	1,204	438	766	19	9	10
Liberal/general studies, other	10,462	4,260	6,202	204	57	147	13	7	6
Library and archival sciences, total	122	16	106	3,940	816	3,124	61	27	34
Library and archival sciences, general	5	0	5	971	175	796	3	0	3
Library science	113	14	99	2,897	625	2,272	58	27	31
Library and archival sciences, other	4	2	2	72	16	56	0	0	0
Life sciences, total	36,079	17,970	18,109	4,933	2,484	2,449	3,533	2,235	1,298
Biology, general	26,251	12,871	13,380	2,120	1,058	1,062	529	349	180
Biochemistry and biophysics	1,976	1,101	875	223	122	101	555	354	201
Botany, total	239	115	124	333	164	169	251	158	93

Table 233.—Bachelor's, master's, and doctor's degrees conferred [1] by institutions of higher education, by sex of student and field of study: 1988–89—Continued

Field of study	Bachelor's degrees requiring 4 or 5 years			Master's degrees			Doctor's degrees (Ph.D., Ed.D., etc.)		
	Total	Men	Women	Total	Men	Women	Total	Men	Women
1	2	3	4	5	6	7	8	9	10
Botany, general	184	89	95	187	90	97	149	87	62
Bacteriology	25	10	15	17	6	11	8	8	0
Plant pathology	13	7	6	100	53	47	60	39	21
Botany, other	17	9	8	29	15	14	34	24	10
Cell and molecular biology, total	693	396	297	91	56	35	208	134	74
Cell biology	54	30	24	31	20	11	46	30	16
Molecular biology	383	226	157	39	29	10	117	79	38
Cell and molecular biology, other	256	140	116	21	7	14	45	25	20
Microbiology	1,755	834	921	369	165	204	351	221	130
Miscellaneous specialized areas, total	1,460	713	747	827	357	470	562	336	226
Anatomy	123	67	56	54	34	20	100	65	35
Biometrics and biostatistics	16	3	13	96	44	52	40	18	22
Ecology	418	245	173	202	121	81	68	51	17
Marine biology	267	158	109	72	39	33	18	16	2
Neurosciences	111	63	48	25	15	10	82	54	28
Nutritional sciences	217	36	181	240	38	202	102	39	63
Toxicology	72	35	37	41	23	18	64	41	23
Miscellaneous specialized areas, other	236	106	130	97	43	54	88	52	36
Zoology	2,768	1,435	1,333	822	474	348	866	559	307
Zoology, general	2,109	1,101	1,008	248	144	104	143	102	41
Entomology	50	38	12	148	100	48	135	110	25
Genetics, human and animal	189	94	95	101	37	64	114	59	55
Pathology, human and animal	15	6	9	50	26	24	116	71	45
Pharmacology, human and animal	18	10	8	46	23	23	169	94	75
Physiology, human and animal	387	186	201	229	144	85	187	122	65
Zoology, other	0	0	0	0	0	0	2	1	1
Life sciences, other	937	505	432	148	88	60	211	124	87
Mathematics, total	15,237	8,221	7,016	3,424	2,058	1,366	882	711	171
Mathematics, general	13,023	6,880	6,143	2,299	1,390	909	585	480	105
Actuarial sciences	201	108	93	42	28	14	0	0	0
Applied mathematics	986	592	394	352	223	129	100	82	18
Pure mathematics	112	76	36	23	18	5	20	18	2
Statistics	425	246	179	640	355	285	170	125	45
Mathematics, other	490	319	171	68	44	24	7	6	1
Military sciences and military technologies, total	419	378	41	0	0	0	0	0	0
Military sciences, total	250	234	16	0	0	0	0	0	0
Military technologies, total	169	144	25	0	0	0	0	0	0
Multi/interdisciplinary studies, total	18,213	8,419	9,794	3,225	1,966	1,259	257	158	99
Biological and physical sciences	2,009	1,125	884	207	109	98	24	13	11
Engineering and other disciplines	267	211	56	185	135	50	48	37	11
Humanities and social sciences	2,895	1,141	1,754	399	185	214	40	16	24
Systems science	24	14	10	981	797	184	4	3	1
Women's studies	157	1	156	12	0	12	1	0	1
Multi/interdisciplinary studies, other	12,861	5,927	6,934	1,441	740	701	140	89	51
Parks and recreation, total	4,171	1,709	2,462	460	213	247	36	28	8
Parks and recreation, general	1,657	600	1,057	156	63	93	16	10	6
Outdoor recreation	108	54	54	17	12	5	0	0	0
Parks and recreation management	1,882	808	1,074	198	90	108	11	9	2
Water resources	49	43	6	41	29	12	5	5	0
Parks and recreation, other	475	204	271	48	19	29	4	4	0
Philosophy and religion, total	6,411	4,122	2,289	1,274	755	519	464	341	123
Philosophy	3,854	2,633	1,221	522	357	165	255	191	64
Religion	2,284	1,321	963	587	341	246	204	145	59
Philosophy and religion, other	273	168	105	165	57	108	5	5	0
Physical sciences and science technologies, total	17,204	12,097	5,107	5,737	4,204	1,533	3,852	3,093	759
Physical sciences, total	17,141	12,064	5,077	5,684	4,166	1,518	3,847	3,089	758
Physical sciences, general	422	298	124	56	35	21	0	0	0
Astronomy	113	88	25	80	67	13	53	42	11
Astrophysics	51	39	12	16	15	1	16	12	4
Atmospheric science and meteorology	330	278	52	206	174	32	67	60	7
Chemistry, total	8,654	5,312	3,342	1,785	1,121	664	2,034	1,518	516
Chemistry, general	8,443	5,183	3,260	1,678	1,055	623	1,870	1,396	474
Analytical chemistry	0	0	0	13	9	4	12	9	3
Inorganic chemistry	0	0	0	5	2	3	6	3	3
Organic chemistry	17	11	6	12	8	4	11	11	0
Pharmaceutical chemistry	7	6	1	32	19	13	63	42	21
Chemistry, other	187	112	75	45	28	17	72	57	15
Geological sciences, total	2,249	1,682	567	1,408	1,027	381	358	288	70

Table 233.—Bachelor's, master's, and doctor's degrees conferred [1] by institutions of higher education, by sex of student and field of study: 1988–89—Continued

Field of study	Bachelor's degrees requiring 4 or 5 years			Master's degrees			Doctor's degrees (Ph.D., Ed.D., etc.)		
	Total	Men	Women	Total	Men	Women	Total	Men	Women
1	2	3	4	5	6	7	8	9	10
Geology	2,109	1,570	539	1,171	855	316	271	217	54
Geochemistry	7	6	1	18	11	7	11	8	3
Geophysics and seismology	54	42	12	95	72	23	46	41	5
Geological sciences, other	79	64	15	124	89	35	30	22	8
Miscellaneous physical sciences, total	638	444	194	310	210	100	157	120	37
Metallurgy	0	0	0	8	7	1	9	9	0
Oceanography	144	107	37	102	64	38	89	64	25
Earth science	451	310	141	103	72	31	45	33	12
Miscellaneous physical sciences, other	43	27	16	97	67	30	14	14	0
Physics, total	4,339	3,697	642	1,736	1,445	291	1,111	1,009	102
Physics, general	4,190	3,577	613	1,636	1,365	271	1,025	930	95
Physics, other	149	120	29	100	80	20	86	79	7
Physical sciences, other	345	226	119	87	72	15	51	40	11
Science technologies, total	63	33	30	53	38	15	5	4	1
Protective services, total	14,626	9,074	5,552	1,046	722	324	27	19	8
Criminal justice, total	14,466	8,922	5,544	1,019	697	322	27	19	8
Correctional administration	265	155	110	31	23	8	0	0	0
Corrections	386	167	219	56	30	26	0	0	0
Criminal justice administration	3,735	2,395	1,340	294	195	99	0	0	0
Criminal justice studies	7,316	4,413	2,903	511	367	144	26	18	8
Criminal justice technology	28	15	13	0	0	0	0	0	0
Forensic studies	362	187	175	27	12	15	1	1	0
Law enforcement	1,315	952	363	56	42	14	0	0	0
Law enforcement administration	158	113	45	13	10	3	0	0	0
Criminal justice, other	901	525	376	31	18	13	0	0	0
Fire protection	144	138	6	27	25	2	0	0	0
Protective services, other	16	14	2	0	0	0	0	0	0
Psychology, total	48,516	14,181	34,335	8,579	2,799	5,780	3,263	1,429	1,834
Psychology, general	45,196	13,100	32,096	3,993	1,325	2,668	1,661	724	937
Clinical psychology	104	27	77	828	229	599	1,017	433	584
Counseling psychology	148	28	120	2,189	621	1,568	201	82	119
Developmental psychology	287	31	256	65	16	49	26	11	15
Experimental psychology	173	49	124	44	16	28	78	39	39
Industrial and organizational psychology	163	56	107	467	220	247	41	25	16
Physiological psychology	98	37	61	5	1	4	23	10	13
Psychometrics and quantitative psychology	2	2	0	11	3	8	4	2	2
Social psychology	698	283	415	58	17	41	38	18	20
Psychology, other	1,647	568	1,079	919	351	568	174	85	89
Public affairs, total	15,254	4,948	10,306	17,928	6,398	11,530	417	208	209
Public affairs, general	764	436	328	530	279	251	16	11	5
Community services	832	177	655	120	40	80	10	2	8
International public service	207	90	117	148	85	63	0	0	0
Public administration	1,570	869	701	5,168	2,893	2,275	126	88	38
Public policy studies	206	104	102	476	262	214	47	30	17
Public works	0	0	0	0	0	0	0	0	0
Social work, total	9,129	1,316	7,813	10,013	1,868	8,145	195	68	127
Social work, general	8,674	1,236	7,438	9,310	1,718	7,592	183	65	118
Medical social work	60	6	54	58	15	43	0	0	0
Social work, other	395	74	321	645	135	510	12	3	9
Transportation and material moving	1,841	1,650	191	692	655	37	0	0	0
Public affairs, other	705	306	399	781	316	465	23	9	14
Social sciences, total	107,714	59,924	47,790	10,854	6,493	4,361	2,878	1,939	939
Social sciences, general	5,132	2,221	2,911	407	191	216	39	32	7
Anthropology	3,066	1,132	1,934	704	285	419	318	166	152
Archeology	65	20	45	21	5	16	13	5	8
Criminology	1,080	600	480	57	37	20	2	1	1
Demography	0	0	0	24	12	12	11	7	4
Economics	23,502	15,871	7,631	1,870	1,338	532	834	675	159
Geography	3,013	2,116	897	548	369	179	121	94	27
History	20,098	12,474	7,624	2,110	1,286	824	480	310	170
International relations	4,186	1,762	2,424	1,516	972	544	50	34	16
Political science and government	30,348	17,937	12,411	1,593	1,074	519	451	335	116
Sociology	14,329	4,463	9,866	1,143	494	649	450	221	229
Urban studies	547	286	261	353	202	151	41	19	22
Social sciences, other	2,348	1,042	1,306	508	228	280	68	40	28
Theology, total	5,322	4,108	1,214	4,625	3,003	1,622	1,165	1,022	143
Biblical languages	19	17	2	8	8	0	2	1	1
Bible studies	1,748	1,410	338	341	289	52	20	20	0
Missionary studies	307	211	96	203	136	67	30	29	1

Table 233.—Bachelor's, master's, and doctor's degrees conferred [1] by institutions of higher education, by sex of student and field of study: 1988–89—Continued

Field of study	Bachelor's degrees requiring 4 or 5 years			Master's degrees			Doctor's degrees (Ph.D., Ed.D., etc.)		
	Total	Men	Women	Total	Men	Women	Total	Men	Women
1	2	3	4	5	6	7	8	9	10
Religious education	821	512	309	933	489	444	41	32	9
Religious music	203	114	89	108	72	36	6	6	0
Theological studies	1,389	1,124	265	2,277	1,521	756	835	731	104
Theology, other	835	720	115	755	488	267	231	203	28
Visual and performing arts, total	37,781	14,558	23,223	8,234	3,598	4,636	755	443	312
Visual and performing arts, general	1,889	675	1,214	219	98	121	8	3	5
Crafts	412	100	312	108	33	75	0	0	0
Dance	694	105	589	203	34	169	3	0	3
Design	4,713	1,945	2,768	341	156	185	0	0	0
Dramatic arts	4,612	1,935	2,677	1,070	515	555	61	39	22
Film arts, total	1,561	926	635	219	116	103	6	4	2
Cinematography/film	653	423	230	136	70	66	6	4	2
Photography	840	467	373	82	46	36	0	0	0
Film arts, other	68	36	32	1	0	1	0	0	0
Fine arts, total	16,172	5,222	10,950	2,762	1,019	1,743	162	50	112
Fine arts, general	10,225	3,442	6,783	1,451	603	848	36	14	22
Art history and appreciation	2,228	405	1,823	420	89	331	108	30	78
Arts management	85	15	70	74	24	50	0	0	0
Painting	715	253	462	195	82	113	0	0	0
Fine arts, other	2,919	1,107	1,812	622	221	401	18	6	12
Graphic arts technology	0	0	0	0	0	0	0	0	0
Music, total	6,580	3,140	3,440	3,243	1,588	1,655	514	347	167
Music, general	3,295	1,479	1,816	1,046	513	533	222	143	79
Music history and appreciation	65	27	38	62	27	35	32	22	10
Music performance	2,318	1,074	1,244	1,697	791	906	172	114	58
Music theory and composition	177	119	58	163	102	61	47	36	11
Music, other	725	441	284	275	155	120	41	32	9
Precision production	515	251	264	0	0	0	0	0	0
Visual and performing arts, other	633	259	374	69	39	30	1	0	1
Not classified by field of study	2,428	1,410	1,018	890	496	394	67	54	13

[1] Preliminary data.

NOTE.—Aggregations by field of study derived from the *Classification of Instructional Programs* developed by the National Center for Education Statistics.

SOURCE: U.S. Department of Education, National Center for Education Statistics, Integrated Postsecondary Education Data System (IPEDS), "Completions" survey. (This table was prepared October 1990.)

Table 234.—Bachelor's, master's, and doctor's degrees conferred [1] by institutions of higher education, by sex of student and field of study: 1987–88

Field of study	Bachelor's degrees requiring 4 or 5 years			Master's degrees			Doctor's degrees (Ph.D., Ed.D., etc.)		
	Total	Men	Women	Total	Men	Women	Total	Men	Women
1	2	3	4	5	6	7	8	9	10
All fields	**994,829**	**477,203**	**517,626**	**299,317**	**145,163**	**154,154**	**34,870**	**22,615**	**12,255**
Agriculture and natural resources, total	14,222	9,744	4,478	3,479	2,427	1,052	1,142	926	216
Agribusiness and agricultural production, total	4,800	3,648	1,152	710	536	174	199	162	37
Agricultural business and management, total	3,542	2,770	772	566	443	123	164	132	32
Agricultural business and management, general	423	334	89	38	29	9	1	1	0
Agricultural business	1,235	996	239	46	41	5	0	0	0
Agricultural economics	1,758	1,331	427	467	359	108	163	131	32
Agricultural business and management, other	126	109	17	15	14	1	0	0	0
Agricultural mechanics	237	230	7	7	7	0	1	1	0
Agricultural production	109	86	23	17	11	6	11	9	2
Horticulture	356	231	125	43	28	15	12	11	1
International agriculture	20	10	10	16	6	10	0	0	0
Agribusiness and agricultural production, other	536	321	215	61	41	20	11	9	2
Agricultural sciences, total	6,392	3,869	2,523	1,762	1,204	558	726	588	138
Agricultural sciences, general	1,045	737	308	209	150	59	0	0	0
Animal sciences, total	3,034	1,617	1,417	529	365	164	190	157	33
Animal sciences, general	2,547	1,302	1,245	363	240	123	139	115	24
Animal breeding and genetics	0	0	0	12	12	0	8	8	0
Animal health	21	10	11	20	13	7	5	2	3
Animal nutrition	0	0	0	9	9	0	7	6	1
Dairy	210	163	47	52	38	14	13	10	3
Fisheries science	0	0	0	0	0	0	0	0	0
Poultry	101	70	31	39	26	13	9	8	1
Animal sciences, other	155	72	83	34	27	7	9	8	1
Food sciences	589	270	319	247	109	138	114	85	29
Plant sciences, total	1,573	1,146	427	668	493	175	336	273	63
Plant sciences, general	240	169	71	72	53	19	25	18	7
Agronomy	638	543	95	333	262	71	226	191	35
Horticulture science	565	341	224	162	101	61	57	41	16
Ornamental horticulture	0	0	0	0	0	0	0	0	0
Plant breeding and genetics	0	0	0	0	0	0	0	0	0
Plant pathology (applied)	0	0	0	0	0	0	0	0	0
Plant protection (pest management)	26	15	11	24	18	6	1	1	0
Range management	87	66	21	66	51	15	23	18	5
Plant sciences, other	17	12	5	11	8	3	4	4	0
Soil sciences	102	75	27	94	78	16	78	68	10
Agricultural sciences, other	49	24	25	15	9	6	8	5	3
Renewable natural resources, total	3,030	2,227	803	1,007	687	320	217	176	41
Renewable natural resources, general	798	523	275	236	145	91	29	23	6
Conservation and regulation	218	148	70	22	14	8	1	0	1
Fishing and fisheries	146	124	22	127	94	33	33	25	8
Forestry production and processing	226	180	46	28	21	7	10	7	3
Forestry and related sciences	955	780	175	440	309	131	126	106	20
Wildlife management	580	411	169	108	74	34	14	13	1
Renewable natural resources, other	107	61	46	46	30	16	4	2	2
Architecture and environmental design, total	8,603	5,271	3,332	3,159	2,042	1,117	98	66	32
Architecture and environmental design, general	649	463	186	109	80	29	6	2	4
Architecture	4,266	3,131	1,135	1,637	1,166	471	26	21	5
City, community, and regional planning	274	199	75	864	535	329	59	38	21
Environmental design	672	473	199	45	30	15	2	2	0
Interior design	1,540	174	1,366	37	5	32	0	0	0
Landscape architecture	814	554	260	284	137	147	2	2	0
Urban design	1	1	0	49	34	15	0	0	0
Architecture and environmental design, other	387	276	111	134	55	79	3	1	2
Area and ethnic studies, total	3,453	1,390	2,063	903	490	413	140	71	69
Area studies, total	3,114	1,252	1,862	720	353	367	120	59	61
African studies	13	6	7	16	5	11	10	7	3
American studies	1,181	449	732	189	63	126	59	21	38
Asian studies	626	270	356	176	105	71	17	11	6
European studies	343	122	221	45	22	23	6	3	3
Latin American studies	242	90	152	126	72	54	6	3	3
Middle Eastern studies	63	34	29	60	25	35	16	11	5
Russian and Slavic studies	245	136	109	85	46	39	3	2	1
Area studies, other	401	145	256	23	15	8	3	1	2
Ethnic studies, total	244	97	147	48	19	29	8	5	3
Afro-American (black) studies	155	61	94	25	12	13	3	1	2
Hispanic-American studies	53	25	28	11	3	8	0	0	0
Ethnic studies, other	36	11	25	12	4	8	5	4	1
Area and ethnic studies, other	95	41	54	135	118	17	12	7	5

Table 234.—Bachelor's, master's, and doctor's degrees conferred [1] by institutions of higher education, by sex of student and field of study: 1987–88—Continued

Field of study	Bachelor's degrees requiring 4 or 5 years			Master's degrees			Doctor's degrees (Ph.D., Ed.D., etc.)		
	Total	Men	Women	Total	Men	Women	Total	Men	Women
1	2	3	4	5	6	7	8	9	10
Business and management, business and office, and marketing and distribution	243,725	129,948	113,777	69,655	46,305	23,350	1,109	853	256
Business and management, total	235,910	127,602	108,308	69,455	46,207	23,248	1,108	853	255
Business and management, general	41,102	22,372	18,730	11,626	7,897	3,729	210	174	36
Accounting	42,962	20,341	22,621	3,096	1,737	1,359	57	35	22
Banking and finance	26,148	17,014	9,134	5,258	3,703	1,555	43	36	7
Business administration and management	68,784	37,785	30,999	37,640	25,401	12,239	541	417	124
Business economics	3,448	2,306	1,142	175	120	55	36	28	8
Human resources development	1,350	653	697	810	414	396	10	5	5
Institutional management	5,083	2,696	2,387	253	163	90	1	0	1
Insurance and risk management	562	354	208	31	21	10	4	4	0
International business management	1,255	525	730	1,709	1,128	581	6	5	1
Investments and securities	235	141	94	167	120	47	0	0	0
Labor/industrial relations	1,065	530	535	609	309	300	11	8	3
Management information systems	3,250	1,875	1,375	1,055	761	294	4	3	1
Management science, total	2,279	1,302	977	634	471	163	56	51	5
Business statistics	0	0	0	0	0	0	0	0	0
Operations research (quantitative methods)	896	511	385	454	339	115	46	43	3
Management science, other	1,383	791	592	180	132	48	10	8	2
Marketing management and research	30,256	14,944	15,312	1,942	1,002	940	47	32	15
Organizational behavior	584	262	322	141	57	84	24	14	10
Personnel management	1,777	815	962	236	131	105	6	3	3
Real estate	835	595	240	195	151	44	1	1	0
Small business management and ownership	56	38	18	8	7	1	0	0	0
Taxation	0	0	0	832	559	273	0	0	0
Trade and industrial supervision and management	804	641	163	62	50	12	0	0	0
Consumer and personal services	39	34	5	0	0	0	0	0	0
Business and management, other	4,036	2,379	1,657	2,976	2,005	971	51	37	14
Business and office, total	2,927	708	2,219	51	27	24	0	0	0
Accounting, bookkeeping, and related programs	315	159	156	43	27	16	0	0	0
Business data processing and related programs	560	331	229	0	0	0	0	0	0
Office supervision and management	1,287	131	1,156	6	0	6	0	0	0
Secretarial and related programs	649	52	597	1	0	1	0	0	0
Business and office, other	116	35	81	1	0	1	0	0	0
Marketing and distribution, total	4,888	1,638	3,250	149	71	78	1	0	1
Apparel and accessories marketing	1,790	94	1,696	2	0	2	1	0	1
Business and personal services marketing	775	428	347	0	0	0	0	0	0
General marketing	1,594	779	815	45	21	24	0	0	0
Transportation and travel marketing	225	41	184	58	17	41	0	0	0
Marketing and distribution, other	504	296	208	44	33	11	0	0	0
Communications and communications technologies, total	46,726	18,592	28,134	3,925	1,568	2,357	234	134	100
Communications, total	45,410	17,857	27,553	3,678	1,446	2,232	230	132	98
Communications, general	21,340	8,040	13,300	1,430	552	878	164	91	73
Advertising	2,745	957	1,788	222	89	133	1	0	1
Communications, research	111	30	81	22	10	12	8	5	3
Journalism (mass communications)	11,052	3,926	7,126	1,035	400	635	22	15	7
Public relations	1,453	481	972	94	22	72	0	0	0
Radio/television news broadcasting	937	419	518	42	21	21	0	0	0
Radio television, general	5,404	3,004	2,400	238	113	125	15	12	3
Communications, other	2,368	1,000	1,368	595	239	356	20	9	11
Communications technologies, total	1,316	735	581	247	122	125	4	2	2
Motion picture technology	77	65	12	0	0	0	0	0	0
Photographic technology	28	16	12	1	1	0	0	0	0
Radio and television technology	1,136	605	531	182	96	86	3	1	2
Communications technologies, other	75	49	26	64	25	39	1	1	0
Computer and information sciences, total	34,523	23,331	11,192	9,197	6,726	2,471	428	380	48
Computer and information sciences, general	27,122	18,792	8,330	7,607	5,684	1,923	405	365	40
Computer programming	303	246	57	120	94	26	0	0	0
Data processing	700	410	290	25	16	9	0	0	0
Information science and systems	4,491	2,677	1,814	1,067	662	405	17	10	7
Systems analysis	383	220	163	93	72	21	1	0	1
Computer and information sciences, other	1,524	986	538	285	198	87	5	5	0
Education, total	91,287	21,028	70,259	77,867	19,437	58,430	6,553	2,949	3,604
Education, general	2,113	407	1,706	7,739	2,022	5,717	949	417	532
Bilingual/bicultural education	308	119	189	387	137	250	55	30	25
Curriculum and instruction	329	17	312	3,605	704	2,901	663	245	418
Education administration, total	9	0	9	9,586	4,008	5,578	1,870	956	914
Education administration, general	1	0	1	6,048	2,623	3,425	1,310	687	623
Administration of special education	3	0	3	16	3	13	11	2	9

Table 234.—Bachelor's, master's, and doctor's degrees conferred [1] by institutions of higher education, by sex of student and field of study: 1987–88—Continued

Field of study	Bachelor's degrees requiring 4 or 5 years			Master's degrees			Doctor's degrees (Ph.D., Ed.D., etc.)		
	Total	Men	Women	Total	Men	Women	Total	Men	Women
1	2	3	4	5	6	7	8	9	10
Adult and continuing education administration	0	0	0	142	44	98	38	18	20
Educational supervision	0	0	0	805	251	554	29	9	20
Elementary and secondary education administration	5	0	5	1,684	723	961	51	32	19
Higher education administration	0	0	0	268	100	168	299	138	161
Community college education administration	0	0	0	98	49	49	5	1	4
Educational administration, other	0	0	0	525	215	310	127	69	58
Educational media	22	10	12	827	213	614	28	14	14
Evaluation and research, total	19	5	14	149	44	105	130	63	67
Evaluation and research, general	0	0	0	67	21	46	55	19	36
Educational statistics and research	5	3	2	27	11	16	32	19	13
Educational testing, evaluation, and measurement	0	0	0	50	10	40	29	15	14
Elementary and secondary research	14	2	12	0	0	0	0	0	0
Higher education research	0	0	0	5	2	3	14	10	4
School psychology	184	41	143	1,308	330	978	493	210	283
Social foundations	0	0	0	175	57	118	136	60	76
Special education, total	6,573	478	6,095	8,581	1,026	7,555	217	55	162
Special education, general	4,267	346	3,921	6,546	793	5,753	194	48	146
Education of the deaf and hearing impaired	201	4	197	180	17	163	1	0	1
Education of the gifted and talented	3	0	3	175	15	160	1	0	1
Education of the emotionally handicapped	166	12	154	200	37	163	1	0	1
Education of the mentally handicapped	620	41	579	160	21	139	3	2	1
Education of the multiple handicapped	54	2	52	109	18	91	0	0	0
Education of the physically handicapped	24	2	22	36	1	35	0	0	0
Education of the visually handicapped	22	1	21	44	13	31	0	0	0
Remedial education	0	0	0	24	1	23	2	1	1
Special learning disabilities	340	22	318	570	46	524	6	1	5
Speech correction	513	22	491	263	14	249	0	0	0
Special education, other	363	26	337	274	50	224	9	3	6
Student counseling and personnel services	76	25	51	9,277	2,211	7,066	442	193	249
Teacher education, general programs, total	48,261	4,514	43,747	18,261	2,715	15,546	430	162	268
Adult and continuing education	92	42	50	612	172	440	110	53	57
Elementary education	39,547	2,830	36,717	11,053	918	10,135	97	23	74
Junior high/middle school education	693	123	570	455	56	399	0	0	0
Pre-elementary education	4,071	82	3,989	1,514	47	1,467	24	3	21
Secondary education	3,532	1,390	2,142	3,408	1,202	2,206	102	45	57
Teacher education, general programs, other	326	47	279	1,219	320	899	97	38	59
Teacher education, specific subject areas, total	32,550	15,150	17,400	15,005	5,143	9,862	839	412	427
Agricultural education	575	445	130	292	230	62	21	20	1
Art education	1,022	220	802	441	93	348	33	13	20
Business education	1,941	404	1,537	541	93	448	24	16	8
Driver and safety education	41	34	7	95	80	15	3	3	0
English education	1,477	302	1,175	453	124	329	33	11	22
Foreign languages education	266	42	224	143	30	113	35	9	26
Health education	1,627	358	1,269	690	149	541	77	25	52
Home economics education	539	4	535	198	0	198	12	0	12
Industrial arts education	2,111	1,884	227	627	507	120	41	27	14
Marketing and distributive education	242	87	155	13	3	10	1	0	1
Mathematics education	1,646	588	1,058	626	201	425	21	7	14
Music education	2,919	1,208	1,711	859	369	490	64	40	24
Physical education	12,216	6,395	5,821	3,501	1,765	1,736	211	118	93
Reading education	189	14	175	3,153	171	2,982	55	8	47
Science education	1,415	677	738	800	334	466	38	23	15
Social science education	697	330	367	138	46	92	2	1	1
Social studies education	1,265	736	529	180	99	81	6	4	2
Technical education	287	209	78	163	90	73	40	17	23
Trade and industrial education	1,164	905	259	579	290	289	56	36	20
Teacher education, other	911	308	603	1,513	469	1,044	66	34	32
Teaching English as a second language	33	8	25	617	150	467	5	1	4
Education, other	810	254	556	2,350	677	1,673	296	131	165
Engineering and engineering technologies, total	88,706	76,538	12,168	23,388	20,477	2,911	4,191	3,898	293
Engineering, total	69,461	58,813	10,648	22,655	19,861	2,794	4,181	3,888	293
Engineering, general	2,590	2,111	479	1,050	922	128	275	261	14
Aerospace, aeronautical, and astronautical engineering	3,092	2,794	298	797	734	63	141	134	7
Agricultural engineering	460	423	37	185	167	18	60	57	3
Architectural engineering	461	397	64	31	29	2	0	0	0
Bioengineering and biomedical engineering	642	434	208	306	217	89	77	63	14
Ceramic engineering	332	229	103	96	73	23	25	24	1
Chemical engineering	3,917	2,864	1,053	1,088	901	187	579	526	53
Civil engineering	7,488	6,429	1,059	2,836	2,512	324	481	455	26
Computer engineering	2,115	1,799	316	760	660	100	77	71	6
Electrical, electronics, and communications engineering	23,597	20,425	3,172	6,688	5,974	714	860	818	42
Engineering mechanics	286	253	33	182	166	16	81	77	4
Engineering physics	340	302	38	54	50	4	24	24	0
Engineering science	306	240	66	268	245	23	42	29	13
Environmental health engineering	135	97	38	267	184	83	39	29	10

Table 234.—Bachelor's, master's, and doctor's degrees conferred [1] by institutions of higher education, by sex of student and field of study: 1987–88—Continued

Field of study	Bachelor's degrees requiring 4 or 5 years			Master's degrees			Doctor's degrees (Ph.D., Ed.D., etc.)		
	Total	Men	Women	Total	Men	Women	Total	Men	Women
1	2	3	4	5	6	7	8	9	10
Geological engineering	170	129	41	68	58	10	6	5	1
Geophysical engineering	52	36	16	17	15	2	1	1	0
Industrial engineering	4,082	2,886	1,196	1,815	1,491	324	162	140	22
Materials engineering	418	305	113	410	317	93	226	204	22
Mechanical engineering	14,900	13,182	1,718	3,329	3,050	279	596	571	25
Metallurgical engineering	453	353	100	221	186	35	104	97	7
Mining and mineral engineering	227	199	28	82	81	1	11	11	0
Naval architecture and marine engineering	371	349	22	41	40	1	4	4	0
Nuclear engineering	296	264	32	212	196	16	97	94	3
Ocean engineering	95	80	15	90	85	5	22	22	0
Petroleum engineering	667	611	56	216	198	18	35	33	2
Surveying and mapping sciences, total	81	71	10	28	24	4	7	7	0
Systems engineering	313	245	68	242	191	51	24	19	5
Textile engineering	21	12	9	20	12	8	2	2	0
Engineering, other	1,554	1,294	260	1,256	1,083	173	123	110	13
Engineering and related technologies, total	19,245	17,725	1,520	733	616	117	10	10	0
Architectural technologies	808	749	59	20	16	4	0	0	0
Civil technologies	672	597	75	2	2	0	0	0	0
Electrical and electronic technologies	5,323	5,009	314	46	38	8	0	0	0
Electromechanical instrumentation and maintenance technologies	171	159	12	6	6	0	1	1	0
Environmental control technologies	150	114	36	34	22	12	0	0	0
Industrial production technologies	4,898	4,400	498	180	150	30	6	6	0
Quality control and safety technologies	245	199	46	156	127	29	0	0	0
Mechanical and related technologies	2,611	2,465	146	0	0	0	0	0	0
Mining and petroleum technologies	41	39	2	4	3	1	3	3	0
Mechanics and repairers	197	190	7	0	0	0	0	0	0
Construction trades	47	40	7	0	0	0	0	0	0
Engineering and related technologies, other	4,082	3,764	318	285	252	33	0	0	0
Foreign languages, total	10,045	2,732	7,313	1,844	591	1,253	411	180	231
Foreign languages, multiple emphasis	694	202	492	237	75	162	44	18	26
African (non-Semitic) languages	0	0	0	0	0	0	3	3	0
Asiatic languages, total	316	141	175	61	25	36	17	9	8
Chinese	103	44	59	31	11	20	9	3	6
Japanese	144	60	84	9	4	5	1	1	0
Asiatic languages, other	69	37	32	21	10	11	7	5	2
Baltic-Slavic languages, total	536	205	331	117	49	68	15	7	8
Slavic languages (other than Russian)	62	32	30	63	28	35	6	1	5
Russian languages	472	173	299	54	21	33	8	5	3
Balto-Slavic languages, other	2	0	2	0	0	0	1	1	0
Germanic languages, total	1,395	505	890	260	95	165	74	33	41
German	1,350	487	863	244	90	154	71	31	40
Scandinavian languages	31	10	21	10	2	8	1	1	0
Germanic languages, other	14	8	6	6	3	3	2	1	1
Greek (classical)	33	19	14	10	5	5	0	0	0
Indic languages	3	2	1	2	1	1	3	2	1
Italic languages, total	6,890	1,595	5,295	1,086	296	790	205	72	133
French	3,082	589	2,493	437	102	335	89	29	60
Italian	224	50	174	45	18	27	7	3	4
Latin	88	44	44	17	8	9	0	0	0
Portuguese	20	7	13	2	1	1	0	0	0
Spanish	3,416	898	2,518	553	159	394	93	32	61
Italic languages, other	60	7	53	32	8	24	16	8	8
Semitic languages, total	44	22	22	49	31	18	22	18	4
Arabic	9	6	3	4	2	2	0	0	0
Hebrew	28	13	15	30	18	12	11	9	2
Semitic languages, other	7	3	4	15	11	4	11	9	2
Foreign languages, other	134	41	93	22	14	8	28	18	10
Allied health and health sciences, total	60,754	8,985	51,769	18,665	4,059	14,606	1,261	548	713
Allied health, total	12,339	2,429	9,910	2,675	628	2,047	43	23	20
Dental services	727	7	720	12	2	10	0	0	0
Diagnostic and treatment services	794	272	522	33	23	10	0	0	0
Medical laboratory technologies	1,990	412	1,578	43	13	30	0	0	0
Mental health/human services	953	150	803	864	221	643	19	10	9
Miscellaneous allied health services	734	269	465	116	29	87	0	0	0
Nursing-related services	136	9	127	40	26	14	0	0	0
Rehabilitative services	6,402	1,147	5,255	1,381	261	1,120	16	8	8
Occupational therapy	1,963	147	1,816	332	23	309	2	0	2
Physical therapy	3,402	753	2,649	664	154	510	5	3	2
Speech-language pathology/audiology	28	0	28	11	0	11	1	0	1
Rehabilitative services, other	1,009	247	762	374	84	290	8	5	3
Allied health, other	603	163	440	186	53	133	8	5	3

Table 234.—Bachelor's, master's, and doctor's degrees conferred [1] by institutions of higher education, by sex of student and field of study: 1987–88—Continued

Field of study	Bachelor's degrees requiring 4 or 5 years			Master's degrees			Doctor's degrees (Ph.D., Ed.D., etc.)		
	Total	Men	Women	Total	Men	Women	Total	Men	Women
1	2	3	4	5	6	7	8	9	10
Health sciences, total	48,415	6,556	41,859	15,990	3,431	12,559	1,218	525	693
Audiology and speech pathology	2,483	107	2,376	2,820	158	2,662	81	29	52
Basic clinical health sciences	156	52	104	105	46	59	109	65	44
Chiropractic	0	0	0	0	0	0	0	0	0
Dentistry, total	150	79	71	416	314	102	17	9	8
Epidemiology	0	0	0	0	0	0	0	0	0
Health services administration, total	3,243	638	2,605	2,873	1,038	1,835	33	15	18
Health services administration	2,326	522	1,804	2,370	888	1,482	21	9	12
Health care planning	35	13	22	275	88	187	8	4	4
Medical records administration	701	40	661	0	0	0	0	0	0
Health services administration, other	181	63	118	228	62	166	4	2	2
Medical laboratory	835	179	656	66	20	46	1	0	1
Medicine, total	148	69	79	203	109	94	101	57	44
Nursing	31,793	1,640	30,153	6,500	482	6,018	283	27	256
Optometry	214	112	102	3	1	2	5	3	2
Osteopathic medicine	1	0	1	1	0	1	0	0	0
Pharmacy	5,360	2,282	3,078	244	142	102	178	118	60
Pre-dentistry	105	83	22	0	0	0	0	0	0
Pre-medicine	591	405	186	1	0	1	0	0	0
Pre-veterinary	80	39	41	0	0	0	0	0	0
Public health	305	96	209	1,794	717	1,077	213	81	132
Veterinary medicine	330	144	186	132	70	62	69	43	26
Health sciences, other	2,621	631	1,990	832	334	498	128	78	50
Home economics and vocational home economics, total	14,855	1,226	13,629	2,053	246	1,807	309	82	227
Home economics, total	13,604	949	12,655	1,962	229	1,733	253	70	183
Home economics, general	3,639	156	3,483	405	11	394	36	4	32
Business home economics	182	10	172	0	0	0	0	0	0
Family and community services	181	17	164	28	6	22	0	0	0
Family/consumer resource management	660	142	518	40	3	37	16	7	9
Food sciences and human nutrition	2,852	251	2,601	611	55	556	58	17	41
Human environment and housing	677	71	606	36	10	26	0	0	0
Individual and family development	2,414	147	2,267	715	139	576	117	39	78
Textiles and clothing	2,858	149	2,709	99	1	98	13	1	12
Home economics, other	141	6	135	28	4	24	13	2	11
Vocational home economics, total	1,251	277	974	91	17	74	56	12	44
Consumer and homemaking education	586	47	539	33	7	26	22	8	14
Institutional, home management, and supporting services	77	24	53	18	3	15	0	0	0
Vocational home economics, other	588	206	382	40	7	33	34	4	30
Law, total	1,303	413	890	1,880	1,386	494	89	66	23
Law	3	1	2	1,000	752	248	31	25	6
Pre-law	275	159	116	0	0	0	0	0	0
Legal assisting	471	61	410	2	1	1	0	0	0
Law, other	554	192	362	878	633	245	58	41	17
Letters, total	39,551	13,158	26,393	6,194	2,124	4,070	1,172	530	642
English, general	27,768	8,897	18,871	3,878	1,288	2,590	687	302	385
Classics	405	192	213	98	53	45	53	30	23
Comparative literature	555	149	406	196	74	122	123	48	75
Composition	182	66	116	4	1	3	5	1	4
Creative writing	481	185	296	451	183	268	3	2	1
Linguistics	476	129	347	527	200	327	138	72	66
Literature, American	35	18	17	3	1	2	6	3	3
Literature, English	1,296	416	880	189	66	123	65	23	42
Rhetoric	0	0	0	0	0	0	0	0	0
Speech, debate, and forensics	7,137	2,696	4,441	587	182	405	69	37	32
Technical and business writing	117	36	81	69	17	52	0	0	0
Letters, other	1,099	374	725	192	59	133	23	12	11
Liberal/general studies, total	21,790	9,499	12,291	1,354	518	836	31	16	15
Liberal arts and sciences	12,831	5,870	6,961	1,197	483	714	19	8	11
Liberal/general studies, other	8,959	3,629	5,330	157	35	122	12	8	4
Library and archival sciences, total	123	17	106	3,713	790	2,923	46	22	24
Library and archival sciences, general	13	2	11	820	177	643	2	1	1
Library science	105	15	90	2,828	598	2,230	42	19	23
Library and archival sciences, other	5	0	5	65	15	50	2	2	0
Life sciences, total	36,755	18,245	18,510	4,784	2,423	2,361	3,629	2,349	1,280
Biology, general	26,838	13,187	13,651	1,981	1,011	970	576	359	217
Biochemistry and biophysics	2,060	1,144	916	248	142	106	533	362	171
Botany, total	273	138	135	343	174	169	291	204	87

Table 234.—Bachelor's, master's, and doctor's degrees conferred [1] by institutions of higher education, by sex of student and field of study: 1987–88—Continued

Field of study	Bachelor's degrees requiring 4 or 5 years			Master's degrees			Doctor's degrees (Ph.D., Ed.D., etc.)		
	Total	Men	Women	Total	Men	Women	Total	Men	Women
1	2	3	4	5	6	7	8	9	10
Botany, general	216	113	103	176	91	85	153	97	56
Bacteriology	31	13	18	19	7	12	7	3	4
Plant pathology	11	7	4	94	48	46	72	55	17
Botany, other	15	5	10	54	28	26	59	49	10
Cell and molecular biology, total	657	374	283	77	42	35	192	124	68
Cell biology	60	23	37	25	13	12	52	36	16
Molecular biology	345	207	138	39	23	16	113	72	41
Cell and molecular biology, other	252	144	108	13	6	7	27	16	11
Microbiology	1,983	909	1,074	338	158	180	379	230	149
Miscellaneous specialized areas, total	1,352	605	747	808	326	482	590	366	224
Anatomy	47	23	24	61	35	26	109	62	47
Biometrics and biostatistics	26	9	17	103	39	64	41	28	13
Ecology	370	200	170	147	82	65	85	58	27
Marine biology	234	132	102	68	40	28	38	30	8
Neurosciences	112	65	47	14	10	4	82	51	31
Nutritional sciences	229	31	198	258	40	218	98	42	56
Toxicology	88	38	50	44	20	24	55	44	11
Miscellaneous specialized areas, other	246	107	139	113	60	53	82	51	31
Zoology	2,786	1,455	1,331	818	479	339	902	596	306
Zoology, general	2,095	1,095	1,000	224	133	91	190	139	51
Entomology	92	68	24	155	117	38	137	109	28
Genetics, human and animal	206	96	110	93	23	70	116	65	51
Pathology, human and animal	22	8	14	52	29	23	103	64	39
Pharmacology, human and animal	21	13	8	44	21	23	191	120	71
Physiology, human and animal	350	175	175	250	156	94	161	98	63
Zoology, other	0	0	0	0	0	0	4	1	3
Life sciences, other	806	433	373	171	91	80	166	108	58
Mathematics, total	15,904	8,523	7,381	3,442	2,066	1,376	750	625	125
Mathematics, general	13,499	7,095	6,404	2,326	1,386	940	502	417	85
Actuarial sciences	192	115	77	29	14	15	0	0	0
Applied mathematics	1,095	639	456	429	273	156	83	74	9
Pure mathematics	108	68	40	24	15	9	14	13	1
Statistics	440	246	194	580	340	240	140	111	29
Mathematics, other	570	360	210	54	38	16	11	10	1
Military sciences and military technologies, total	350	328	22	49	48	1	0	0	0
Military sciences, total	350	328	22	49	48	1	0	0	0
Military technologies, total	0	0	0	0	0	0	0	0	0
Multi/interdisciplinary studies, total	17,353	8,188	9,165	3,098	1,801	1,297	261	167	94
Biological and physical sciences	2,151	1,261	890	253	133	120	17	10	7
Engineering and other disciplines	260	195	65	187	140	47	59	50	9
Humanities and social sciences	2,484	888	1,596	460	169	291	35	23	12
Systems science	29	10	19	891	738	153	7	6	1
Women's studies	148	2	146	8	0	8	2	0	2
Multi/interdisciplinary studies, other	12,281	5,832	6,449	1,299	621	678	141	78	63
Parks and recreation, total	4,078	1,681	2,397	461	205	256	29	19	10
Parks and recreation, general	1,619	638	981	157	59	98	15	10	5
Outdoor recreation	151	70	81	40	26	14	0	0	0
Parks and recreation management	1,946	793	1,153	198	85	113	9	5	4
Water resources	40	40	0	31	18	13	1	1	0
Parks and recreation, other	322	140	182	35	17	18	4	3	1
Philosophy and religion, total	5,963	3,855	2,108	1,099	677	422	405	306	99
Philosophy	3,565	2,411	1,154	465	339	126	222	172	50
Religion	2,173	1,297	876	532	298	234	176	128	48
Philosophy and religion, other	225	147	78	102	40	62	7	6	1
Physical sciences and science technologies, total	17,806	12,389	5,417	5,733	4,324	1,409	3,809	3,123	686
Physical sciences, total	17,706	12,326	5,380	5,642	4,270	1,372	3,797	3,114	683
Physical sciences, general	477	331	146	36	20	16	1	1	0
Astronomy	92	77	15	64	49	15	76	63	13
Astrophysics	33	29	4	21	19	2	20	18	2
Atmospheric science and meteorology	348	291	57	191	155	36	76	64	12
Chemistry, total	9,052	5,452	3,600	1,708	1,158	550	1,995	1,552	443
Chemistry, general	8,826	5,304	3,522	1,567	1,060	507	1,847	1,440	407
Analytical chemistry	0	0	0	8	6	2	9	6	3
Inorganic chemistry	0	0	0	6	4	2	15	10	5
Organic chemistry	9	6	3	20	14	6	20	15	5
Pharmaceutical chemistry	9	4	5	37	24	13	51	38	13
Chemistry, other	208	138	70	70	50	20	53	43	10

Table 234.—Bachelor's, master's, and doctor's degrees conferred [1] by institutions of higher education, by sex of student and field of study: 1987–88—Continued

Field of study	Bachelor's degrees requiring 4 or 5 years			Master's degrees			Doctor's degrees (Ph.D., Ed.D., etc.)		
	Total	Men	Women	Total	Men	Women	Total	Men	Women
1	2	3	4	5	6	7	8	9	10
Geological sciences, total	2,551	1,930	621	1,523	1,146	377	350	287	63
Geology	2,374	1,788	586	1,283	968	315	273	223	50
Geochemistry	3	2	1	13	8	5	4	3	1
Geophysics and seismology	84	71	13	101	79	22	44	42	2
Geological sciences, other	90	69	21	126	91	35	29	19	10
Miscellaneous physical sciences, total	701	521	180	310	210	100	134	106	28
Metallurgy	8	4	4	22	21	1	8	7	1
Oceanography	145	118	27	99	69	30	85	65	20
Earth science	509	369	140	100	58	42	27	23	4
Miscellaneous physical sciences, other	39	30	9	89	62	27	14	11	3
Physics, total	4,100	3,488	612	1,675	1,423	252	1,093	982	111
Physics, general	3,970	3,375	595	1,555	1,329	226	1,018	917	101
Physics, other	130	113	17	120	94	26	75	65	10
Physical sciences, other	352	207	145	114	90	24	52	41	11
Science technologies, total	100	63	37	91	54	37	12	9	3
Protective services, total	13,367	8,352	5,015	1,024	727	297	32	23	9
Criminal justice, total	13,206	8,207	4,999	1,022	725	297	32	23	9
Correctional administration	221	150	71	40	31	9	0	0	0
Corrections	301	105	196	59	32	27	0	0	0
Criminal justice administration	3,385	2,121	1,264	312	222	90	0	0	0
Criminal justice studies	6,844	4,200	2,644	500	364	136	32	23	9
Criminal justice technology	26	15	11	0	0	0	0	0	0
Forensic studies	239	102	137	18	10	8	0	0	0
Law enforcement	1,268	940	328	43	23	20	0	0	0
Law enforcement administration	69	54	15	30	30	0	0	0	0
Criminal justice, other	853	520	333	20	13	7	0	0	0
Fire protection	130	127	3	2	2	0	0	0	0
Protective services, other	31	18	13	0	0	0	0	0	0
Psychology, total	45,003	13,497	31,506	7,872	2,593	5,279	2,987	1,363	1,624
Psychology, general	42,204	12,618	29,586	3,886	1,302	2,584	1,565	753	812
Clinical psychology	72	11	61	767	240	527	858	373	485
Counseling psychology	167	48	119	1,884	534	1,350	177	85	92
Developmental psychology	249	24	225	58	13	45	33	13	20
Experimental psychology	186	60	126	41	17	24	92	38	54
Industrial and organizational psychology	132	56	76	410	205	205	37	18	19
Physiological psychology	123	49	74	6	3	3	30	11	19
Psychometrics and quantitative psychology	1	1	0	9	3	6	2	0	2
Social psychology	585	229	356	44	16	28	32	11	21
Psychology, other	1,284	401	883	767	260	507	161	61	100
Public affairs, total	14,294	4,545	9,749	17,290	6,359	10,931	470	238	232
Public affairs, general	784	412	372	481	256	225	15	6	9
Community services	997	251	746	146	50	96	8	4	4
International public service	147	60	87	112	72	40	0	0	0
Public administration	1,529	837	692	5,188	3,066	2,122	106	72	34
Public policy studies	208	102	106	433	229	204	93	59	34
Public works	0	0	0	3	3	0	0	0	0
Social work, total	8,518	1,170	7,348	9,476	1,766	7,710	226	89	137
Social work, general	8,021	1,098	6,923	8,783	1,629	7,154	204	85	119
Medical social work	47	7	40	75	21	54	0	0	0
Social work, other	450	65	385	618	116	502	22	4	18
Transportation and material moving	1,715	1,555	160	679	635	44	0	0	0
Public affairs, other	396	158	238	772	282	490	22	8	14
Social sciences, total	100,288	56,297	43,991	10,294	6,237	4,057	2,781	1,849	932
Social sciences, general	4,766	2,062	2,704	449	212	237	29	19	10
Anthropology	2,909	1,072	1,837	696	295	401	304	149	155
Archeology	88	28	60	45	19	26	20	13	7
Criminology	1,180	687	493	76	49	27	2	2	0
Demography	14	7	7	30	13	17	9	7	2
Economics	22,911	15,412	7,499	1,847	1,377	470	770	619	151
Geography	2,944	2,045	899	569	361	208	135	99	36
History	18,207	11,388	6,819	2,090	1,268	822	517	325	192
International relations	4,228	1,896	2,332	1,213	807	406	63	50	13
Political science and government	27,207	16,297	10,910	1,579	1,056	523	391	305	86
Sociology	13,024	4,065	8,959	984	424	560	452	210	242
Urban studies	548	285	263	292	159	133	40	20	20
Social sciences, other	2,262	1,053	1,209	424	197	227	49	31	18
Theology, total	5,563	4,173	1,390	4,814	3,199	1,615	1,199	1,072	127
Biblical languages	19	19	0	15	13	2	0	0	0
Bible studies	1,922	1,483	439	306	252	54	28	28	0

Table 234.—Bachelor's, master's, and doctor's degrees conferred [1] by institutions of higher education, by sex of student and field of study: 1987–88—Continued

Field of study	Bachelor's degrees requiring 4 or 5 years			Master's degrees			Doctor's degrees (Ph.D., Ed.D., etc.)		
	Total	Men	Women	Total	Men	Women	Total	Men	Women
1	2	3	4	5	6	7	8	9	10
Missionary studies	242	164	78	193	135	58	26	25	1
Religious education	915	516	399	909	475	434	38	26	12
Religious music	181	97	84	100	63	37	5	4	1
Theological studies	1,514	1,245	269	2,125	1,483	642	891	801	90
Theology, other	770	649	121	1,166	778	388	211	188	23
Visual and performing arts, total	36,638	14,127	22,511	7,937	3,445	4,492	725	424	301
Visual and performing arts, general	1,739	628	1,111	191	66	125	3	0	3
Crafts	388	101	287	96	35	61	0	0	0
Dance	623	79	544	174	23	151	6	1	5
Design	4,586	1,786	2,800	289	132	157	0	0	0
Dramatic arts	4,574	1,883	2,691	1,084	546	538	73	36	37
Film arts, total	1,356	802	554	202	118	84	1	0	1
Cinematography/film	630	415	215	130	74	56	1	0	1
Photography	657	342	315	70	43	27	0	0	0
Film arts, other	69	45	24	2	1	1	0	0	0
Fine arts, total	15,498	5,056	10,442	2,641	966	1,675	139	51	88
Fine arts, general	9,809	3,253	6,556	1,484	560	924	28	14	14
Art history and appreciation	1,908	372	1,536	386	84	302	97	31	66
Arts management	91	18	73	70	26	44	1	0	1
Painting	711	243	468	173	81	92	0	0	0
Fine arts, other	2,979	1,170	1,809	528	215	313	13	6	7
Graphic arts technology	0	0	0	0	0	0	0	0	0
Music, total	6,708	3,263	3,445	3,183	1,517	1,666	502	335	167
Music, general	3,248	1,493	1,755	1,030	471	559	209	132	77
Music history and appreciation	64	30	34	55	30	25	33	21	12
Music performance	2,382	1,126	1,256	1,628	764	864	166	111	55
Music theory and composition	203	132	71	125	77	48	54	39	15
Music, other	811	482	329	345	175	170	40	32	8
Precision production	531	255	276	5	3	2	0	0	0
Visual and performing arts, other	635	274	361	72	39	33	1	1	0
Not classified by field of study	1,801	1,131	670	4,144	1,873	2,271	579	336	243

[1] Revised from previously published data.

NOTE.—Aggregations by field of study derived from the *Classification of Instructional Programs* developed by the National Center for Education Statistics.

SOURCE: U.S. Department of Education, National Center for Education Statistics, Integrated Postsecondary Education Data System (IPEDS), "Completions" survey. (This table was prepared February 1991.)

Table 235.—Bachelor's degrees conferred by institutions of higher education, by discipline division: 1970–71 to 1988–89

Discipline division	1970–71	1974–75	1975–76	1976–77	1977–78	1978–79	1979–80	1980–81	1981–82	1982–83	1983–84	1984–85	1985–86	1986–87	1987–88 [1]	1988–89 [2]
1	2	3	4	5	6	7	8	9	10	11	12	13	14	15	16	17
Total	839,730	922,933	925,746	919,549	921,204	921,390	929,417	935,140	952,998	969,510	974,309	979,477	987,823	991,339	994,829	1,017,667
Agriculture and natural resources	12,672	17,528	19,402	21,467	22,650	23,134	22,802	21,886	21,029	20,909	19,317	18,107	16,823	14,991	14,222	13,488
Architecture and environmental design	5,570	8,226	9,146	9,222	9,250	9,273	9,132	9,455	9,728	9,823	9,186	9,325	9,119	8,922	8,603	9,191
Area and ethnic studies	2,582	3,544	3,577	3,450	3,257	3,006	2,840	2,887	2,862	2,971	2,879	2,867	3,060	3,340	3,453	3,949
Business and management	114,865	133,010	142,379	150,964	160,187	171,764	185,361	199,338	214,001	226,893	230,031	233,351	238,160	241,156	243,725	246,659
Communications	10,324	18,156	20,045	21,698	23,873	24,906	26,927	29,428	32,428	36,954	38,586	40,358	41,666	43,969	45,410	47,385
Communications technologies	478	1,092	1,237	1,516	1,527	1,551	1,689	1,854	1,794	1,648	1,579	1,725	1,425	1,439	1,316	1,240
Computer and information sciences	2,388	5,033	5,652	6,407	7,201	8,719	11,154	15,121	20,267	24,510	32,172	38,878	41,889	39,664	34,523	30,637
Education	176,614	167,015	154,807	143,722	136,141	126,109	118,169	108,309	101,113	97,991	92,382	88,161	87,221	87,115	91,287	96,988
Engineering	44,898	39,388	38,388	40,936	46,869	53,021	58,402	63,287	67,021	72,248	75,732	77,154	76,333	73,797	69,461	66,296
Engineering technologies	5,148	7,464	7,943	8,347	8,785	9,354	10,491	11,713	12,984	17,022	18,712	18,951	19,620	19,277	19,245	18,977
Foreign languages	19,945	17,606	15,471	13,944	12,730	11,825	11,133	10,319	9,841	9,685	9,479	9,954	10,102	10,184	10,045	10,774
Health sciences	25,190	48,858	53,813	57,122	59,168	61,819	63,607	63,348	63,385	64,614	64,338	64,513	64,535	63,206	60,754	59,111
Home economics	11,167	16,772	17,409	17,439	17,621	18,300	18,411	18,370	17,872	16,705	16,316	15,555	15,288	14,942	14,855	14,717
Law	545	436	531	559	653	678	683	776	846	1,099	1,272	1,157	1,197	1,178	1,303	1,976
Letters	64,933	48,534	43,019	38,849	36,365	34,557	33,497	33,208	34,334	32,743	33,739	34,091	35,434	37,133	39,551	43,323
Liberal/general studies	5,461	13,032	14,736	16,763	19,694	19,524	20,069	18,596	18,145	18,524	18,815	19,191	19,248	21,365	21,790	23,459
Library and archival sciences	1,013	1,069	843	781	693	558	398	375	307	258	255	202	157	139	123	122
Life sciences	35,743	51,741	54,275	53,605	51,502	48,846	46,370	43,216	41,639	39,982	38,640	38,445	38,524	38,114	36,755	36,079
Mathematics	24,801	18,181	15,984	14,196	12,569	11,806	11,378	11,078	11,599	12,453	13,211	15,146	16,306	16,489	15,904	15,237
Military sciences	357	340	1,177	933	386	347	251	305	283	267	195	299	256	383	350	419
Multi/interdisciplinary studies	8,306	15,185	17,707	17,149	15,944	14,630	14,404	15,895	17,651	17,282	16,734	15,727	15,700	16,402	17,353	18,213
Parks and recreation	1,621	4,518	5,182	5,514	5,623	5,981	5,753	5,729	5,335	5,198	4,752	4,593	4,433	4,107	4,078	4,171
Philosophy and religion	8,146	8,997	8,447	8,158	7,907	7,347	7,069	6,776	6,309	6,483	6,435	6,400	6,239	5,976	5,963	6,411
Physical sciences	21,412	20,778	21,465	22,497	22,986	23,207	23,410	23,952	24,052	23,405	23,671	23,732	21,731	19,974	17,806	17,204
Protective services	2,045	9,956	12,507	14,530	14,889	14,803	15,015	13,707	12,438	12,579	12,654	12,510	12,704	12,930	13,707	14,626
Psychology	37,880	50,988	49,908	47,373	44,559	42,461	41,962	40,833	41,031	40,364	39,872	39,811	40,521	42,868	45,003	48,516
Public affairs	6,252	14,730	16,751	17,627	18,078	18,882	18,422	18,714	18,739	16,290	14,396	13,838	13,878	14,161	14,294	15,254
Social sciences	155,236	135,165	126,287	116,879	112,827	107,922	103,519	100,345	99,545	95,088	93,212	91,461	93,703	96,185	100,288	107,714
Theology	3,744	4,809	5,520	6,109	6,319	6,091	6,207	5,841	5,998	6,053	5,914	6,039	5,602	5,710	5,563	5,322
Visual and performing arts	30,394	40,782	42,138	41,793	40,951	40,969	40,892	40,479	40,422	39,469	39,833	37,936	36,949	36,223	36,638	37,781
Not classified by field of study	0	0	0	0	0	0	0	0	0	0	0	0	0	0	1,801	2,428

[1] Revised from previously published data.

[2] Preliminary data.

NOTE.—Beginning in 1982–83, the taxonomy used to collect data on earned degrees by major field of study was revised. The figures for earlier years have been reclassified when necessary to make them conform to the new taxonomy. To facilitate trend comparisons, certain aggregations have been made of the degree fields as reported in the IPEDS "Completions" survey: "Agriculture and natural resources" includes Agribusiness and agriculture production, Agricultural sciences, and Renewable natural resources; "Business and management" includes Business and management, Business and office, Marketing and distribution, and Consumer and personal services; "Engineering and related technologies" includes Engineering and related technologies, Mechanics and repairers, and Construction trades; "Physical sciences" includes: Physical sciences and Science technologies; "Public affairs" includes: Public affairs, and Transportation and material moving; "Visual and performing arts" includes: Visual and performing arts and Precision production.

SOURCE: U.S. Department of Education, National Center for Education Statistics, "Degrees and Other Formal Awards Conferred" surveys, and Integrated Postsecondary Education Data System (IPEDS), "Completions" survey. (This table was prepared February 1991.)

Table 236.—Master's degrees conferred by institutions of higher education, by discipline division: 1970–71 to 1988–89

Discipline division	1970–71	1974–75	1975–76	1976–77	1977–78	1978–79	1979–80	1980–81	1981–82	1982–83	1983–84	1984–85	1985–86	1986–87	1987–88[1]	1988–89[2]
1	2	3	4	5	6	7	8	9	10	11	12	13	14	15	16	17
Total	230,509	292,450	311,771	317,164	311,620	301,079	298,081	295,739	295,546	289,921	284,263	286,251	288,567	289,557	299,317	309,762
Agriculture and natural resources	2,457	3,067	3,340	3,724	4,023	3,994	3,976	4,003	4,163	4,254	4,178	3,928	3,801	3,523	3,479	3,245
Architecture and environmental design	1,705	2,938	3,215	3,213	3,115	3,113	3,139	3,153	3,327	3,357	3,223	3,275	3,260	3,142	3,159	3,378
Area and ethnic studies	1,032	1,166	995	1,052	981	853	852	804	809	826	888	879	927	851	903	978
Business and management	26,481	36,247	42,512	46,420	48,326	50,372	55,006	57,898	61,299	65,319	66,653	67,527	67,137	67,496	69,655	73,154
Communications	1,770	2,644	2,961	2,870	3,077	2,654	2,911	2,896	3,104	3,502	3,513	3,460	3,500	3,666	3,678	3,926
Communications technologies	86	150	165	221	219	228	171	209	223	102	143	209	323	271	247	307
Computer and information sciences	1,588	2,299	2,603	2,798	3,038	3,055	3,647	4,218	4,935	5,321	6,190	7,101	8,070	8,491	9,197	9,392
Education	88,952	120,169	128,417	126,825	119,038	111,995	103,951	98,938	93,757	84,853	77,187	76,137	76,353	75,501	77,867	82,238
Engineering	16,309	15,127	16,014	15,961	16,038	15,227	15,904	16,386	17,526	18,830	20,094	20,926	21,059	22,081	22,655	23,713
Engineering technologies	134	221	328	284	360	268	339	323	413	520	567	631	602	612	733	828
Foreign languages	4,755	3,807	3,531	3,147	2,726	2,426	2,236	2,104	2,008	1,759	1,773	1,721	1,721	1,746	1,844	1,911
Health sciences	5,445	9,901	11,885	12,323	13,619	14,781	15,068	16,004	15,942	17,068	17,443	17,383	18,624	18,426	18,665	19,255
Home economics	1,452	1,901	2,179	2,334	2,613	2,510	2,690	2,570	2,355	2,406	2,422	2,383	2,298	2,070	2,053	2,174
Law	955	1,245	1,442	1,574	1,786	1,647	1,817	1,832	1,893	2,091	1,802	1,796	1,924	1,943	1,880	2,098
Letters	11,148	10,068	9,468	8,701	8,306	7,289	6,807	6,515	6,421	5,767	5,818	5,934	6,291	6,123	6,194	6,608
Liberal/general studies	549	1,630	1,758	1,492	1,387	1,251	1,373	1,085	1,094	889	1,173	1,180	1,154	1,126	1,354	1,408
Library and archival sciences	7,001	8,091	8,037	7,572	6,914	5,906	5,374	4,859	4,506	3,979	3,805	3,893	3,626	3,815	3,713	3,940
Life sciences	5,728	6,550	6,582	7,114	6,806	6,831	6,510	5,978	5,874	5,696	5,406	5,059	5,013	4,954	4,784	4,933
Mathematics	5,191	4,327	3,857	3,695	3,373	3,036	2,860	2,567	2,727	2,837	2,741	2,882	3,159	3,321	3,442	3,424
Military sciences	2	0	0	43	45	38	46	43	49	110	127	119	83	83	49	0
Multi/interdisciplinary studies	1,157	1,938	2,033	3,006	3,100	3,335	3,579	3,434	3,884	2,930	3,148	3,184	3,104	3,041	3,098	3,225
Parks and recreation	218	604	571	609	574	755	647	643	526	565	555	544	495	476	461	460
Philosophy and religion	1,326	1,402	1,356	1,300	1,249	1,143	1,204	1,229	1,152	1,091	1,153	1,167	1,163	1,108	1,099	1,274
Physical sciences	6,367	5,807	5,466	5,331	5,561	5,451	5,219	5,284	5,514	5,290	5,576	5,796	5,902	5,652	5,733	5,737
Protective services	194	993	1,197	1,681	1,902	1,729	1,805	1,538	1,336	1,300	1,219	1,235	1,074	1,019	1,024	1,046
Psychology	4,431	7,066	7,811	8,301	8,160	8,003	7,806	7,998	7,791	8,378	8,000	8,408	8,293	8,204	7,872	8,579
Public affairs	8,215	14,610	16,117	17,917	18,341	18,300	18,413	18,524	18,216	16,245	15,372	16,045	16,300	17,032	17,290	17,928
Social sciences	16,476	16,892	15,824	15,395	14,578	12,807	12,101	11,855	11,892	11,112	10,465	10,380	10,428	10,397	10,294	10,854
Theology	2,710	3,228	3,290	3,625	3,329	3,558	3,922	4,220	4,064	4,782	5,106	4,352	4,467	4,881	4,814	4,625
Visual and performing arts	6,675	8,362	8,817	8,636	9,036	8,524	8,708	8,629	8,746	8,742	8,520	8,714	8,416	8,506	7,937	8,234
Not classified by field of study	0	0	0	0	0	0	0	0	0	0	0	0	0	0	0	890

[1] Revised from previously published data.
[2] Preliminary data.

NOTE.—Beginning in 1982–83, the taxonomy used to collect data on earned degrees by major field of study was revised. The figures for earlier years have been reclassified when necessary to make them conform to the new taxonomy. To facilitate trend comparisons, certain aggregations have been made of the degree fields as reported in the IPEDS "Completions" survey: "Agriculture and natural resources" includes Agribusiness and agriculture production, Agricultural sciences, and Renewable natural resources; "Business and management" includes Business and management, Business and office, Marketing and distribution, and Consumer and personal services; "Engineering and related technologies" includes Engineering and related technologies, Mechanics and repairers, and Construction trades; "Physical sciences" includes: Physical sciences and Science technologies; "Public affairs" includes: Public affairs, and Transportation and material moving; "Visual and performing arts" includes: Visual and performing arts and Precision production.

SOURCE: U.S. Department of Education, National Center for Education Statistics, "Degrees and Other Formal Awards Conferred" surveys, and Integrated Postsecondary Education Data System (IPEDS), "Completions" survey. (This table was prepared February 1991.)

Table 237.—Doctor's degrees conferred by institutions of higher education, by discipline division: 1970–71 to 1988–89

Discipline division	1970-71	1974-75	1975-76	1976-77	1977-78	1978-79	1979-80	1980-81	1981-82	1982-83	1983-84	1984-85	1985-86	1986-87	1987-88[1]	1988-89[2]
1	2	3	4	5	6	7	8	9	10	11	12	13	14	15	16	17
Total	**32,107**	**34,083**	**34,064**	**33,232**	**32,131**	**32,730**	**32,615**	**32,958**	**32,707**	**32,775**	**33,209**	**32,943**	**33,653**	**34,120**	**34,870**	**35,759**
Agriculture and natural resources	1,086	991	928	893	971	950	991	1,067	1,079	1,149	1,172	1,213	1,158	1,049	1,142	1,184
Architecture and environmental design	36	69	82	73	73	96	79	93	80	97	84	89	92	73	98	86
Area and ethnic studies	144	165	188	153	145	135	151	162	102	153	139	137	157	132	140	110
Business and management	807	1,009	953	863	866	860	792	842	855	809	977	866	969	1,098	1,109	1,150
Communications	145	162	196	162	179	182	182	171	182	205	215	228	212	273	230	242
Communications technologies	0	3	8	9	12	10	11	11	18	9	4	6	11	2	4	6
Computer and information sciences	128	213	244	216	196	236	240	252	251	262	251	248	344	374	428	538
Education	6,403	7,446	7,778	7,963	7,595	7,736	7,941	7,900	7,680	7,551	7,473	7,151	7,110	6,909	6,553	6,783
Engineering	3,637	3,106	2,819	2,583	2,437	2,500	2,502	2,551	2,621	2,822	2,979	3,221	3,400	3,809	4,181	4,521
Engineering technologies	1	2	2	3	3	6	5	10	15	9	2	9	10	11	10	12
Foreign languages	781	857	864	752	649	641	549	588	536	488	462	437	448	441	411	422
Health sciences	459	609	577	538	638	705	771	827	910	1,155	1,163	1,199	1,241	1,213	1,261	1,439
Home economics	123	156	178	160	203	219	192	247	247	255	279	276	311	297	309	263
Law	20	21	76	60	39	46	40	60	22	72	121	105	54	120	89	76
Letters	1,857	1,951	1,884	1,723	1,616	1,504	1,500	1,380	1,313	1,176	1,215	1,239	1,215	1,181	1,172	1,238
Liberal/general studies	11	16	36	33	55	264	106	23	35	55	48	53	38	29	31	32
Library and archival sciences	39	56	71	75	67	70	73	71	84	52	74	87	62	57	46	61
Life sciences	3,645	3,384	3,392	3,397	3,309	3,542	3,636	3,718	3,743	3,341	3,437	3,432	3,358	3,423	3,629	3,533
Mathematics	1,199	975	856	823	805	730	724	728	681	698	695	699	742	725	750	882
Military sciences	0	0	0	0	0	0	0	0	0	0	0	0	0	0	0	0
Multi/interdisciplinary studies	80	254	237	271	246	445	295	256	358	387	378	285	319	276	261	257
Parks and recreation	2	14	15	15	10	25	21	42	33	33	27	36	39	32	29	36
Philosophy and religion	554	544	554	468	444	415	374	410	364	404	442	468	477	422	405	464
Physical sciences	4,390	3,626	3,431	3,341	3,133	3,102	3,089	3,141	3,286	3,269	3,306	3,403	3,551	3,672	3,809	3,852
Protective services	1	11	9	10	17	15	18	21	24	38	31	33	21	18	32	27
Psychology	1,782	2,442	2,581	2,761	2,587	2,662	2,768	2,955	2,780	3,108	2,973	2,908	3,088	3,123	2,987	3,263
Public affairs	185	271	298	316	385	344	372	388	389	347	421	431	385	398	470	417
Social sciences	3,659	4,209	4,154	3,784	3,583	3,358	3,219	3,114	3,061	2,931	2,911	2,851	2,955	2,916	2,781	2,878
Theology	312	872	1,033	1,125	1,160	1,232	1,319	1,276	1,288	1,208	1,202	1,140	1,183	1,236	1,199	1,165
Visual and performing arts	621	649	620	662	708	700	655	654	670	692	728	693	722	792	725	755
Not classified by field of study	0	0	0	0	0	0	0	0	0	0	0	0	0	0	579	67

[1] Revised from previously published data.
[2] Preliminary data.

NOTE.—Beginning in 1982–83, the taxonomy used to collect data on earned degrees by major field of study was revised. The figures for earlier years have been reclassified when necessary to make them conform to the new taxonomy. To facilitate trend comparisons, certain aggregations have been made of the degree fields as reported in the IPEDS "Completions" survey: "Agriculture and natural resources" includes Agribusiness and agriculture production, Agricultural sciences, and Renewable natural resources; "Business and management" includes Business and management, Business and office, Marketing and distribution, and Consumer and personal services; "Engineering and related technologies" includes Engineering and related technologies, Mechanics and repairers, and Construction trades; "Physical sciences" includes: Physical sciences and Science technologies; "Public affairs" includes: Public affairs, and Transportation and material moving; "Visual and performing arts" includes: Visual and performing arts and Precision production.

SOURCE: U.S. Department of Education, National Center for Education Statistics, "Degrees and Other Formal Awards Conferred" surveys, and Integrated Postsecondary Education Data System (IPEDS), "Completions" survey. (This table was prepared October 1990.)

Table 238.—Degrees conferred by institutions of higher education, by control of institution: 1973–74 to 1988–89

Year	Public institutions					Private institutions				
	Associate	Bachelor's	Master's	Doctor's	First-professional	Associate	Bachelor's	Master's	Doctor's	First-professional
1	2	3	4	5	6	7	8	9	10	11
1973–74	303,188	651,544	184,632	21,810	23,208	40,736	294,232	92,401	12,006	30,608
1974–75	318,474	634,785	193,804	22,176	23,612	41,697	288,148	98,646	11,907	32,304
1975–76	345,006	635,161	206,298	21,751	25,766	46,448	290,585	105,473	12,313	36,883
1976–77	355,650	630,463	208,901	21,229	26,344	50,727	289,086	108,263	12,003	38,015
1977–78	358,874	627,903	202,099	20,456	27,097	53,372	293,301	109,521	11,675	39,484
1978–79	346,808	621,666	192,016	20,817	27,785	55,894	299,724	109,063	11,913	41,063
1979–80	344,536	624,084	187,499	20,608	27,942	56,374	305,333	110,582	12,007	42,189
1980–81	352,391	626,452	184,384	20,895	29,128	63,986	308,688	111,355	12,063	42,828
1981–82	[1] 366,700	636,475	182,295	20,889	29,611	[1] 67,800	316,523	113,251	11,818	42,421
1982–83	—	646,317	176,246	21,186	29,757	—	323,193	113,675	11,589	43,379
1983–84	[1] 379,000	646,013	170,693	21,141	29,586	[1] 73,000	328,296	113,570	12,068	44,821
1984–85	377,625	652,246	170,000	21,337	30,152	77,087	327,231	116,251	11,606	44,911
1985–86	369,052	658,586	169,903	21,433	29,568	76,995	329,237	118,664	12,220	44,342
1986–87	358,893	659,240	167,803	21,872	29,346	78,244	332,099	121,754	12,248	43,404
1987–88 [2]	354,180	658,491	173,778	22,488	29,153	80,905	336,338	125,539	12,382	41,582
1988–89 [3]	356,388	674,750	178,164	22,978	28,985	78,822	342,917	131,598	12,781	41,773

[1] Data are approximations
[2] Revised from previously published data.
[3] Preliminary data.
—Data not available.

SOURCE: U.S. Department of Education, National Center for Education Statistics, "Degrees and Other Formal Awards Conferred" surveys, and Integrated Postsecondary Education Data System (IPEDS), "Completions" survey. (This table was prepared February 1991.)

Table 239.—Earned degrees conferred by institutions of higher education, by control of institution, level of degree, and discipline division: 1988–89 [1]

Discipline division	Public institutions				Private institutions			
	Associate degrees	Bachelor's degrees	Master's degrees	Doctor's degrees	Associate degrees	Bachelor's degrees	Master's degrees	Doctor's degrees
1	2	3	4	5	6	7	8	9
Total	**356,388**	**674,750**	**178,164**	**22,978**	**78,822**	**342,917**	**131,598**	**12,781**
Agriculture and natural resources	4,475	13,032	3,077	1,170	265	456	168	14
Architecture and environmental design	746	6,692	2,233	51	1,069	2,499	1,145	35
Area and ethnic studies	8	1,482	560	48	7	2,467	418	62
Business and management	81,373	156,865	28,977	824	25,206	89,794	44,177	326
Communications	1,385	33,716	2,186	177	394	13,669	1,740	65
Communications technologies	1,575	566	37	5	390	674	270	1
Computer and information sciences	5,299	19,484	4,749	327	2,615	11,153	4,643	211
Education	6,616	76,028	57,704	4,915	714	20,960	24,534	1,868
Engineering	2,243	48,265	15,440	2,947	439	18,031	8,273	1,574
Engineering technologies	35,928	13,342	653	12	17,248	5,635	175	0
Foreign languages	173	6,251	1,283	251	159	4,523	628	171
Health sciences	53,555	38,511	11,268	1,044	5,773	20,600	7,987	395
Home economics	6,380	12,703	1,542	235	4,050	2,014	632	28
Law	2,913	1,286	411	31	829	690	1,687	45
Letters	474	27,215	4,843	853	52	16,108	1,765	385
Liberal/general studies	108,421	17,312	621	13	10,042	6,147	787	19
Library and archival sciences	101	108	3,131	58	2	14	809	3
Life sciences	908	22,491	3,679	2,483	62	13,588	1,254	1,050
Mathematics	629	10,038	2,780	575	25	5,199	644	307
Military sciences	22	241	0	0	142	178	0	0
Multi/interdisciplinary studies	11,110	13,277	1,423	178	202	4,936	1,802	79
Parks and recreation	523	3,714	418	35	92	457	42	1
Philosophy and religion	33	1,975	367	155	48	4,436	907	309
Physical sciences	1,860	11,060	4,203	2,638	87	6,144	1,534	1,214
Protective services	11,299	11,816	726	25	356	2,810	320	2
Psychology	985	30,343	3,928	1,565	100	18,173	4,651	1,698
Public affairs	3,828	10,157	10,558	182	654	5,097	7,370	235
Social sciences	2,441	65,196	6,567	1,722	259	42,518	4,287	1,156
Theology	2	1	0	0	566	5,321	4,625	1,165
Visual and performing arts	8,738	21,559	4,784	459	4,056	16,222	3,450	296
Not classified by field of study	2,345	24	16	0	2,919	2,404	874	67

[1] Preliminary data.

NOTE.—To facilitate trend comparisons, certain aggregations have been made of the degree fields as reported in the IPEDS "Completions" survey: "Agriculture and natural resources" includes Agribusiness and agriculture production, Agricultural sciences, and Renewable natural resources; "Business and management" includes Business and management, Business and office, Marketing and distribution, and Consumer and personal services; "Engineering and related technologies" includes Engineering and related technologies, Mechanics and repairers, and Construction trades; "Physical sciences" includes Physical sciences and Science technologies; "Public affairs" includes Public affairs and Transportation and material moving; and "Visual and performing arts" includes Visual and performing arts and Precision production.

SOURCE: U.S. Department of Education, National Center for Education Statistics, Integrated Postsecondary Education Data System (IPEDS), "Completions" survey. (This table was prepared November 1990.)

Table 240.—Earned degrees conferred by institutions of higher education, by control of institution, level of degree, and discipline division: 1987–88 [1]

Discipline division	Public institutions				Private institutions			
	Associate degrees	Bachelor's degrees	Master's degrees	Doctor's degrees	Associate degrees	Bachelor's degrees	Master's degrees	Doctor's degrees
1	2	3	4	5	6	7	8	9
Total	354,180	658,491	173,778	22,488	80,905	336,338	125,539	12,382
Agriculture and natural resources	4,741	13,694	3,318	1,124	288	528	161	18
Architecture and environmental design	685	6,313	2,246	57	1,124	2,290	913	41
Area and ethnic studies	11	1,319	529	63	7	2,134	374	77
Business and management	84,289	155,501	27,538	816	26,682	88,224	42,117	293
Communications	1,581	32,546	2,138	173	338	12,864	1,540	57
Communications technologies	1,112	649	38	1	364	667	209	3
Computer and information sciences	5,530	21,753	4,687	267	3,098	12,770	4,510	161
Education	6,384	71,480	55,889	4,986	835	19,807	21,978	1,567
Engineering	3,191	50,456	14,919	2,723	659	19,005	7,736	1,458
Engineering technologies	38,692	13,403	601	10	19,685	5,842	132	0
Foreign languages	337	5,852	1,304	255	81	4,193	540	156
Health sciences	53,704	38,634	11,225	945	6,007	22,120	7,440	316
Home economics	6,275	12,727	1,525	240	3,464	2,128	528	69
Law	2,513	837	380	8	626	466	1,500	81
Letters	443	24,744	4,765	770	41	14,807	1,429	402
Liberal/general studies	103,183	15,829	615	9	9,865	5,961	739	22
Library and archival sciences	60	106	2,956	40	10	17	757	6
Life sciences	797	22,852	3,579	2,667	57	13,903	1,205	962
Mathematics	656	10,419	2,744	512	28	5,485	698	238
Military sciences	39	337	49	0	99	13	0	0
Multi/interdisciplinary studies	10,658	12,750	1,487	174	179	4,603	1,611	87
Parks and recreation	521	3,585	393	29	100	493	68	0
Philosophy and religion	34	1,851	340	136	60	4,112	759	269
Physical sciences	1,801	11,376	4,315	2,638	89	6,430	1,418	1,171
Protective services	11,482	10,652	689	29	347	2,715	335	3
Psychology	919	28,177	3,769	1,508	81	16,826	4,103	1,479
Public affairs	3,009	9,375	10,451	191	642	4,919	6,839	279
Social sciences	2,380	60,255	6,483	1,654	329	40,033	3,811	1,127
Theology	2	2	0	0	625	5,561	4,814	1,199
Visual and performing arts	8,918	21,016	4,806	463	4,966	15,622	3,131	262
Not classified by field of study	233	1	0	0	129	1,800	4,144	579

[1] Revised from previously published data.

NOTE.—To facilitate trend comparisons, certain aggregations have been made of the degree fields as reported in the IPEDS "Completions" survey: "Agriculture and natural resources" includes Agribusiness and agriculture production, Agricultural sciences, and Renewable natural resources; "Business and management" includes Business and management, Business and office, Marketing and distribution, and Consumer and personal services; "Engineering and related technologies" includes Engineering and related tech-

nologies, Mechanics and repairers, and Construction trades; "Physical sciences" includes Physical sciences and Science technologies; "Public affairs" includes Public affairs and Transportation and material moving; and "Visual and performing arts" includes Visual and performing arts and Precision production.

SOURCE: U.S. Department of Education, National Center for Education Statistics, Integrated Postsecondary Education Data System (IPEDS), "Completions" survey. (This table was prepared February 1991.)

Table 241.—Number of institutions of higher education conferring degrees,[1] by level of degree and discipline division: 1988–89

Discipline division	Total number of institutions awarding degrees				Number of public institutions awarding degrees				Number of private institutions awarding degrees			
	Associate degrees	Bachelor's degrees	Master's degrees	Doctor's degrees	Associate degrees	Bachelor's degrees	Master's degrees	Doctor's degrees	Associate degrees	Bachelor's degrees	Master's degrees	Doctor's degrees
1	2	3	4	5	6	7	8	9	10	11	12	13
Total	2,100	1,804	1,241	453	1,203	545	479	207	897	1,259	762	246
Agriculture and natural resources	390	194	99	58	359	149	90	53	31	45	9	5
Architecture and environmental design	144	214	116	18	92	116	85	11	52	98	31	7
Area and ethnic studies	10	300	89	32	7	132	51	16	3	168	38	16
Business and management	1,590	1,318	669	108	1,058	485	347	73	532	833	322	35
Communications	223	827	203	39	187	341	140	30	36	486	63	9
Communications technologies	142	51	12	2	124	17	3	1	18	34	9	1
Computer and information sciences	634	1,045	299	95	440	426	192	63	194	619	107	32
Education	389	1,184	751	196	300	452	407	134	89	732	344	62
Engineering	262	374	252	155	238	205	163	106	24	169	89	49
Engineering technologies	1,062	297	52	3	889	206	43	3	173	91	9	0
Foreign languages	66	798	186	73	61	341	124	44	5	457	62	29
Health sciences	1,142	918	464	126	904	410	270	92	238	508	194	34
Home economics	539	382	165	34	471	227	130	27	68	155	35	7
Law	258	108	62	13	195	43	26	4	63	65	36	9
Letters	112	1,195	414	134	99	467	285	87	13	728	129	47
Liberal/general studies	1,208	526	96	8	915	229	36	5	293	297	60	3
Library and archival sciences	36	32	87	16	35	27	69	14	1	5	18	2
Life sciences	149	1,197	438	218	133	456	305	144	16	741	133	74
Mathematics	128	1,118	334	136	121	460	245	94	7	658	89	42
Military sciences	3	11	0	0	1	8	0	0	2	3	0	0
Multi/interdisciplinary studies	206	655	195	57	180	281	128	40	26	374	67	17
Parks and recreation	96	267	69	14	86	183	61	13	10	84	8	1
Philosophy and religion	78	336	238	101	2	1	0	0	76	335	238	101
Physical sciences	146	1,203	467	217	126	450	278	123	20	753	189	94
Protective services	265	1,047	348	197	212	446	240	129	53	601	108	68
Psychology	722	397	100	7	669	236	76	5	53	161	24	2
Public affairs	308	658	336	66	253	298	222	35	55	360	114	31
Social sciences	28	811	178	88	15	255	81	45	13	556	97	43
Theology	211	1,267	420	158	172	476	286	102	39	791	134	56
Visual and performing arts	697	1,146	362	90	571	430	225	56	126	716	137	34
Unknown	32	24	8	4	5	2	1	0	27	22	7	4

[1] Preliminary data.

NOTE.—To facilitate trend comparisons, certain aggregations have been made of the degree fields as reported in the IPEDS "Completions" survey: "Agriculture and natural resources" includes Agribusiness and agriculture production, Agricultural sciences, and Renewable natural resources; "Business and management" includes Business and management, Business and office, Marketing and distribution, and Consumer and personal services; "Engineering and related technologies" includes Engineering and related tech-

nologies, Mechanics and repairers, and Construction trades; "Physical sciences" includes Physical sciences and Science technologies; "Public affairs" includes Public affairs and Transportation and material moving; and "Visual and performing arts" includes Visual and performing arts and Precision production.

SOURCE: U.S. Department of Education, National Center for Education Statistics, Integrated Postsecondary Education Data System (IPEDS), "Completions" survey. (This table was prepared February 1991.)

Table 242.—First-professional degrees conferred in dentistry, medicine, and law, by sex: 1949–50 to 1988–89

Year	Dentistry (D.D.S. or D.M.D.)				Medicine (M.D.)				Law (LL.B. or J.D.)			
	Number of institutions conferring degrees	Degrees conferred			Number of institutions conferring degrees	Degrees conferred			Number of institutions conferring degrees	Degrees conferred		
		Total	Men	Women		Total	Men	Women		Total	Men	Women
1	2	3	4	5	6	7	8	9	10	11	12	13
1949–50	40	2,579	2,561	18	72	5,612	5,028	584	(1)	(1)	(1)	(1)
1951–52	41	2,918	2,895	23	72	6,201	5,871	330	(1)	(1)	(1)	(1)
1953–54	42	3,102	3,063	39	73	6,712	6,377	335	(1)	(1)	(1)	(1)
1955–56	42	3,009	2,975	34	73	6,810	6,464	346	131	8,262	7,974	288
1957–58	43	3,065	3,031	34	75	6,816	6,469	347	131	9,394	9,122	272
1959–60	45	3,247	3,221	26	79	7,032	6,645	387	134	9,240	9,010	230
1961–62	46	3,183	3,166	17	81	7,138	6,749	389	134	9,364	9,091	273
1963–64	46	3,180	3,168	12	82	7,303	6,878	425	133	10,679	10,372	307
1965–66	47	3,178	3,146	32	84	7,673	7,170	503	136	13,246	12,776	470
1967–68	48	3,422	3,375	47	85	7,944	7,318	626	138	16,454	15,805	649
1969–70	48	3,718	3,684	34	86	8,314	7,615	699	145	14,916	14,115	801
1970–71	48	3,745	3,703	42	89	8,919	8,110	809	147	17,421	16,181	1,240
1971–72	48	3,862	3,819	43	92	9,253	8,423	830	147	21,764	20,266	1,498
1972–73	51	4,047	3,992	55	97	10,307	9,388	919	152	27,205	25,037	2,168
1973–74	52	4,440	4,355	85	99	11,356	10,093	1,263	151	29,326	25,986	3,340
1974–75	52	4,773	4,627	146	104	12,447	10,818	1,629	154	29,296	24,881	4,415
1975–76	56	5,425	5,187	238	107	13,426	11,252	2,174	166	32,293	26,085	6,208
1976–77	57	5,138	4,764	374	109	13,461	10,891	2,570	169	34,104	26,447	7,657
1977–78	57	5,189	4,623	566	109	14,279	11,210	3,069	169	34,402	25,457	8,945
1978–79	58	5,434	4,794	640	109	14,786	11,381	3,405	175	35,206	25,180	10,026
1979–80	58	5,258	4,558	700	112	14,902	11,416	3,486	179	35,647	24,893	10,754
1980–81	58	5,460	4,672	788	116	15,505	11,672	3,833	176	36,331	24,563	11,768
1981–82	59	5,282	4,467	815	119	15,814	11,867	3,947	180	35,991	23,965	12,026
1982–83	59	5,585	4,631	954	118	15,484	11,350	4,134	177	36,853	23,550	13,303
1983–84	60	5,353	4,302	1,051	119	15,813	11,359	4,454	179	37,012	23,382	13,630
1984–85	59	5,339	4,233	1,106	120	16,041	11,167	4,874	181	37,491	23,070	14,421
1985–86	59	5,046	3,907	1,139	120	15,938	11,022	4,916	181	35,844	21,874	13,970
1986–87	58	4,741	3,603	1,138	122	15,620	10,566	5,054	180	36,172	21,643	14,529
1987–88[2]	57	4,477	3,300	1,177	122	15,358	10,278	5,080	180	35,397	21,067	14,330
1988–89[3]	58	4,247	3,139	1,108	124	15,454	10,326	5,128	182	35,567	21,048	14,519

[1] Data prior to 1955–56 are not shown because they lack comparability with the figures for subsequent years.

[2] Revised from previously published data.

[3] Preliminary data.

SOURCE: U.S. Department of Education, National Center for Education Statistics, "Degrees and Other Formal Awards Conferred" surveys, and Integrated Postsecondary Education Data System (IPEDS), "Completions" surveys. (This table was prepared February 1991.)

Table 243.—First-professional degrees [1] conferred by institutions of higher education, by sex of student, control of institution, and field of study: 1981–82 to 1988–89

Control of institution and field of study	1981–82 Total	1982–83 Total	1983–84 Total	1984–85 Total	1985–86 Total	1985–86 Men	1985–86 Women	1986–87 Total	1986–87 Men	1986–87 Women	1987–88 [2] Total	1987–88 [2] Men	1987–88 [2] Women	1988–89 [3] Total	1988–89 [3] Men	1988–89 [3] Women
	2	3	4	5	6	7	8	9	10	11	12	13	14	15	16	17
Total, all institutions	**72,032**	**73,136**	**74,407**	**75,063**	**73,910**	**49,261**	**24,649**	**72,750**	**47,460**	**25,290**	**70,735**	**45,484**	**25,251**	**70,758**	**45,067**	**25,691**
Dentistry (D.D.S. or D.M.D.)	5,282	5,585	5,353	5,339	5,046	3,907	1,139	4,741	3,603	1,138	4,477	3,300	1,177	4,247	3,139	1,108
Medicine (M.D.)	15,814	15,484	15,813	16,041	15,938	11,022	4,916	15,620	10,566	5,054	15,358	10,278	5,080	15,454	10,326	5,128
Optometry (O.D.)	1,110	1,116	1,086	1,115	1,029	744	285	1,082	697	385	1,023	672	351	1,093	683	410
Osteopathic medicine (D.O.)	1,047	1,319	1,515	1,489	1,547	1,159	388	1,618	1,206	412	1,544	1,123	421	1,635	1,183	452
Pharmacy (D.Phar.)	625	705	709	861	903	432	471	861	351	510	962	389	573	1,074	422	652
Podiatry (Pod.D. or D.P.) or podiatric medicine (D.P.M.)	598	631	607	582	612	488	124	590	468	122	645	495	150	636	487	149
Veterinary medicine (D.V.M.)	2,038	2,060	2,269	2,178	2,270	1,191	1,079	2,230	1,150	1,080	2,235	1,117	1,118	2,157	981	1,176
Chiropractic (D.C. or D.C.M.)	2,626	2,889	3,105	2,661	3,395	2,554	841	2,655	1,982	673	2,628	1,963	665	2,890	2,159	731
Law, general (LL.B. or J.D.)	35,991	36,853	37,012	37,491	35,844	21,874	13,970	36,172	21,643	14,529	35,397	21,067	14,330	35,567	21,048	14,519
Theological professions, general (B.D., M.Div., M.H.L.)	6,901	6,494	6,878	7,221	7,283	5,865	1,418	7,181	5,794	1,387	6,466	5,080	1,386	6,005	4,639	1,366
Other	0	0	60	85	43	25	18	0	0	0	0	0	0	0	0	0
Total, public institutions	**29,611**	**29,757**	**29,586**	**30,152**	**29,568**	**19,119**	**10,449**	**29,346**	**18,610**	**10,736**	**29,153**	**18,291**	**10,862**	**28,985**	**18,188**	**10,797**
Dentistry (D.D.S. or D.M.D.)	3,154	3,438	3,174	3,051	2,827	2,170	657	2,655	2,004	651	2,524	1,846	678	2,518	1,893	625
Medicine (M.D.)	9,706	9,569	9,674	10,071	9,991	6,908	3,083	9,711	6,639	3,072	9,557	6,435	3,122	9,480	6,421	3,059
Optometry (O.D.)	430	427	384	456	441	302	139	454	272	182	429	285	144	451	273	178
Osteopathic medicine (D.O.)	364	386	537	455	486	355	131	480	344	136	434	304	130	500	362	138
Pharmacy (D.Phar.)	328	366	356	416	473	219	254	475	196	279	615	240	375	679	260	419
Podiatry (Pod.D. or D.P.) or podiatric medicine (D.P.M.)	0	0	0	0	0	0	0	0	0	0	0	0	0	0	0	0
Veterinary medicine (D.V.M.)	1,889	1,828	2,060	1,963	1,931	1,008	923	2,003	1,056	947	2,014	1,018	996	1,943	900	1,043
Chiropractic (D.C. or D.C.M.)	0	0	0	0	0	0	0	0	0	0	0	0	0	0	0	0
Law, general (LL.B. or J.D.)	13,740	13,743	13,380	13,695	13,419	8,157	5,262	13,568	8,099	5,469	13,580	8,163	5,417	13,414	8,079	5,335
Theological professions, general (B.D., M.Div., M.H.L.)	0	0	0	2	0	0	0	0	0	0	0	0	0	0	0	0
Other	0	0	0	43	0	0	0	0	0	0	0	0	0	0	0	0
Total, private institutions	**42,421**	**43,379**	**44,821**	**44,911**	**44,342**	**30,142**	**14,200**	**43,404**	**28,850**	**14,554**	**41,582**	**27,193**	**14,389**	**41,773**	**26,879**	**14,894**
Dentistry (D.D.S. or D.M.D.)	2,128	2,147	2,179	2,288	2,219	1,737	482	2,086	1,599	487	1,953	1,454	499	1,729	1,246	483
Medicine (M.D.)	6,108	5,915	6,139	5,970	5,947	4,114	1,833	5,909	3,927	1,982	5,801	3,843	1,958	5,974	3,905	2,069
Optometry (O.D.)	680	689	702	659	588	442	146	628	425	203	594	387	207	642	410	232
Osteopathic medicine (D.O.)	683	933	978	1,034	1,061	804	257	1,138	862	276	1,110	819	291	1,135	821	314
Pharmacy (D.Phar.)	297	339	353	445	430	213	217	386	155	231	347	149	198	395	162	233
Podiatry (Pod.D. or D.P.) or podiatric medicine (D.P.M.)	598	631	607	582	612	488	124	590	468	122	645	495	150	636	487	149
Veterinary medicine (D.V.M.)	149	232	209	215	339	183	156	227	94	133	221	99	122	214	81	133
Chiropractic (D.C. or D.C.M.)	2,626	2,889	3,105	2,661	3,395	2,554	841	2,655	1,982	673	2,628	1,963	665	2,890	2,159	731
Law, general (LL.B. or J.D.)	22,251	23,110	23,632	23,796	22,425	13,717	8,708	22,604	13,544	9,060	21,817	12,904	8,913	22,153	12,969	9,184
Theological professions, general (B.D., M.Div., M.H.L.)	6,901	6,494	6,878	7,219	7,283	5,865	1,418	7,181	5,794	1,387	6,466	5,080	1,386	6,005	4,639	1,366
Other	0	0	39	42	43	25	18	0	0	0	0	0	0	0	0	0

[1] Includes degrees which require at least 6 years of college work for completion (including at least 2 years of preprofessional training).
[2] Revised from previously published data.
[3] Preliminary data.

SOURCE: U.S. Department of Education, National Center for Education Statistics, "Degrees and Other Formal Awards Conferred" surveys, and Integrated Postsecondary Education Data System (IPEDS), "Completions" survey. (This table was prepared February 1991.)

Table 244.—Associate degrees conferred by institutions of higher education, by racial/ethnic group, major field of study, and sex of student: 1988–89

Major field of study and sex of student	Total	White non-Hispanic	Black non-Hispanic	Hispanic	Asian/ Pacific Islander	American Indian/ Alaskan Native	Nonresident alien
1	2	3	4	5	6	7	8
All fields, total [1]	**429,946**	**353,122**	**34,411**	**20,294**	**12,433**	**3,318**	**6,368**
Men	182,909	150,073	12,826	9,172	6,320	1,315	3,203
Women	247,037	203,049	21,585	11,122	6,113	2,003	3,165
Agriculture and natural resources, total	4,740	4,474	42	109	22	35	58
Men	3,074	2,913	24	50	13	29	45
Women	1,666	1,561	18	59	9	6	13
Architecture and environmental design, total	1,815	1,546	68	81	62	4	54
Men	256	191	13	17	15	2	18
Women	1,559	1,355	55	64	47	2	36
Area and ethnic studies, total	15	3	5	0	1	6	0
Men	8	1	4	0	1	2	0
Women	7	2	1	0	0	4	0
Business and management, total	106,579	85,505	10,981	4,743	3,011	782	1,557
Men	33,121	26,753	3,057	1,455	1,041	193	622
Women	73,458	58,752	7,924	3,288	1,970	589	935
Communications, total	3,744	3,151	306	126	50	22	89
Men	2,113	1,792	168	74	27	13	39
Women	1,631	1,359	138	52	23	9	50
Computer and information sciences, total	7,914	6,045	871	376	357	63	202
Men	4,005	3,180	315	199	170	24	117
Women	3,909	2,865	556	177	187	39	85
Education, total	7,330	5,813	727	454	103	127	106
Men	2,132	1,584	253	157	46	42	50
Women	5,198	4,229	474	297	57	85	56
Engineering, total	2,682	2,114	127	134	206	13	88
Men	2,369	1,884	103	111	180	11	80
Women	313	230	24	23	26	2	8
Engineering technologies, total	53,176	43,842	3,511	2,412	2,366	396	649
Men	48,190	39,909	2,970	2,224	2,151	349	587
Women	4,986	3,933	541	188	215	47	62
Foreign languages, total	332	256	11	35	8	10	12
Men	112	90	2	7	4	5	4
Women	220	166	9	28	4	5	8
Health sciences, total	59,328	50,382	4,908	2,052	1,147	410	429
Men	6,977	5,624	534	442	227	50	100
Women	52,351	44,758	4,374	1,610	920	360	329
Home economics, total	10,430	8,501	1,005	455	271	76	122
Men	3,304	2,910	193	65	90	15	31
Women	7,126	5,591	812	390	181	61	91
Law, total	3,742	3,216	258	133	42	36	57
Men	471	378	44	28	2	8	11
Women	3,271	2,838	214	105	40	28	46
Letters, total	526	406	46	23	13	16	22
Men	164	119	22	6	4	7	6
Women	362	287	24	17	9	9	16
Liberal/general studies, total	118,463	97,083	8,138	6,686	3,335	908	2,313
Men	49,161	39,817	3,431	2,887	1,483	358	1,185
Women	69,302	57,266	4,707	3,799	1,852	550	1,128
Library and archival science, total	103	88	5	5	2	3	0
Men	12	10	0	1	0	1	0
Women	91	78	5	4	2	2	0
Life sciences, total	970	728	67	62	56	20	37
Men	412	310	18	26	31	8	19
Women	558	418	49	36	25	12	18
Mathematics, total	654	482	26	50	68	9	19
Men	415	301	17	33	45	6	13
Women	239	181	9	17	23	3	6
Military sciences, total	164	133	22	9	0	0	0
Men	133	109	17	7	0	0	0
Women	31	24	5	2	0	0	0
Multi/interdisciplinary studies, total	11,312	9,992	568	357	267	49	79
Men	5,135	4,504	290	170	119	14	38
Women	6,177	5,488	278	187	148	35	41
Parks and recreation, total	615	528	45	30	6	1	5
Men	303	249	25	19	5	1	4
Women	312	279	20	11	1	0	1

Table 244.—Associate degrees conferred by institutions of higher education, by racial/ethnic group, major field of study, and sex of student: 1988–89—Continued

Major field of study and sex of student	Total	White non-Hispanic	Black non-Hispanic	Hispanic	Asian/ Pacific Islander	American Indian/ Alaskan Native	Nonresident alien
1	2	3	4	5	6	7	8
Philosophy and religion, total	81	70	0	2	3	2	4
Men	58	50	0	1	3	1	3
Women	23	20	0	1	0	1	1
Physical sciences, total	1,947	1,626	82	92	95	3	49
Men	1,135	932	39	60	69	1	34
Women	812	694	43	32	26	2	15
Protective services, total	11,655	9,640	1,032	701	138	93	51
Men	8,370	7,109	561	480	123	61	36
Women	3,285	2,531	471	221	15	32	15
Psychology, total	1,085	853	83	95	14	13	27
Men	280	210	30	24	5	5	6
Women	805	643	53	71	9	8	21
Public affairs, total	4,482	3,547	493	217	97	70	58
Men	2,266	1,871	134	141	47	31	42
Women	2,216	1,676	359	76	50	39	16
Social sciences, total	2,700	1,957	325	206	114	44	54
Men	1,174	840	162	88	41	15	28
Women	1,526	1,117	163	118	73	29	26
Theology, total	568	510	24	17	8	2	7
Men	320	286	18	9	2	0	5
Women	248	224	6	8	6	2	2
Visual and performing arts, total	12,794	10,631	635	632	571	105	220
Men	7,439	6,147	382	391	376	63	80
Women	5,355	4,484	253	241	195	42	140

[1] Reported racial/ethnic distributions of students by level of degree, field of degree, and sex were used to estimate race/ethnicity for students whose race/ethnicity was not reported. Excludes 2,497 men and 2,767 women whose racial/ethnic group and field of study were not available.

NOTE.—To facilitate trend comparisons, certain aggregations have been made of the degree fields as reported in the IPEDS "Completions" survey: "Agriculture and natural resources" includes Agribusiness and agriculture production, Agricultural sciences, and Renewable natural resources; "Business and management" includes Business and management, Business and office, Marketing and distribution, and Consumer and personal services; "Engineering and related technologies" includes Engineering and related technologies, Mechanics and repairers, and Construction trades; "Physical sciences" includes Physical sciences and Science technologies; "Public affairs" includes Public affairs and Transportation and material moving; and "Visual and performing arts" includes Visual and performing arts and Precision production.

SOURCE: U.S. Department of Education, National Center for Education Statistics, Integrated Postsecondary Education Data System (IPEDS), "Completions" survey. (This table was prepared November 1990.)

Table 245.—Bachelor's degrees conferred by institutions of higher education, by racial/ethnic group and sex of student: 1976–77 to 1988–89

Year and sex of student	Total	White non-Hispanic	Black non-Hispanic	Hispanic	Asian or Pacific Islander	American Indian/Alaskan Native	Non-resident alien
1	2	3	4	5	6	7	8
Number of degrees conferred							
1976–77							
Total [1]	917,900	807,688	58,636	18,743	13,793	3,326	15,714
Men	494,424	438,161	25,147	10,318	7,638	1,804	11,356
Women	423,476	369,527	33,489	8,425	6,155	1,522	4,358
1978–79							
Total [2]	919,540	802,542	60,246	20,096	15,407	3,410	17,839
Men	476,065	418,215	24,659	10,418	8,261	1,736	12,776
Women	443,475	384,327	35,587	9,678	7,146	1,674	5,063
1980–81							
Total [3]	934,800	807,319	60,673	21,832	18,794	3,593	22,589
Men	469,625	406,173	24,511	10,810	10,107	1,700	16,324
Women	465,175	401,146	36,162	11,022	8,687	1,893	6,265
1984–85							
Total [4]	968,311	826,106	57,473	25,874	25,395	4,246	29,217
Men	476,148	405,085	23,018	12,402	13,554	1,998	20,091
Women	492,163	421,021	34,455	13,472	11,841	2,248	9,126
1986–87							
Total [5]	991,260	841,820	56,555	26,990	32,618	3,971	29,306
Men	480,780	406,751	22,499	12,864	17,249	1,819	19,598
Women	510,480	435,069	34,056	14,126	15,369	2,152	9,708
1988–89							
Total [6]	1,015,239	858,186	58,016	29,800	38,219	4,046	26,972
Men	481,687	406,656	22,365	13,920	19,537	1,768	17,441
Women	533,552	451,530	35,651	15,880	18,682	2,278	9,531
Percentage distribution of degrees conferred							
1976–77							
Total [1]	100.0	88.0	6.4	2.0	1.5	0.4	1.7
Men	100.0	88.6	5.1	2.1	1.5	0.4	2.3
Women	100.0	87.3	7.9	2.0	1.5	0.4	1.0
1978–79							
Total [2]	100.0	87.3	6.6	2.2	1.7	0.4	1.9
Men	100.0	87.8	5.2	2.2	1.7	0.4	2.7
Women	100.0	86.7	8.0	2.2	1.6	0.4	1.1
1980–81							
Total [3]	100.0	86.4	6.5	2.3	2.0	0.4	2.4
Men	100.0	86.5	5.2	2.3	2.2	0.4	3.5
Women	100.0	86.2	7.8	2.4	1.9	0.4	1.3
1984–85							
Total [4]	100.0	85.3	5.9	2.7	2.6	0.4	3.0
Men	100.0	85.1	4.8	2.6	2.8	0.4	4.2
Women	100.0	85.5	7.0	2.7	2.4	0.5	1.9
1986–87							
Total [5]	100.0	84.9	5.7	2.7	3.3	0.4	3.0
Men	100.0	84.6	4.7	2.7	3.6	0.4	4.1
Women	100.0	85.2	6.7	2.8	3.0	0.4	1.9
1988–89							
Total [6]	100.0	84.5	5.7	2.9	3.8	0.4	2.7
Men	100.0	84.4	4.6	2.9	4.1	0.4	3.6
Women	100.0	84.6	6.7	3.0	3.5	0.4	1.8

[1] Excludes 1,121 men and 528 women whose racial/ethnic group was not available.

[2] Excludes 1,279 men and 571 women whose racial/ethnic group was not available.

[3] Excludes 258 men and 82 women whose racial/ethnic group was not available.

[4] Excludes 6,380 men and 4,786 women whose racial/ethnic group was not available.

[5] Reported racial/ethnic distributions of students by level of degree, field of degree, and sex were used to estimate race/ethnicity for students whose race/ethnicity was not reported. Excludes 74 men and 5 women whose racial/ethnic group and field of study were not available.

[6] Reported racial/ethnic distributions of students by level of degree, field of degree, and sex were used to estimate race/ethnicity for students whose race/ethnicity was not reported. Excludes 1,410 men and 1,018 women whose racial/ethnic group and field of study were not available.

SOURCE: U.S. Department of Education, National Center for Education Statistics, "Degrees and Other Formal Awards Conferred" surveys, and Integrated Postsecondary Education Data System (IPEDS), "Completions" survey. (This table was prepared November 1990.)

Table 246.—Bachelor's degrees conferred by institutions of higher education, by racial/ethnic group, major field of study, and sex of student: 1988–89

Major field of study and sex of student	Total	White non-Hispanic	Black non-Hispanic	Hispanic	Asian/ Pacific Islander	American Indian/ Alaskan Native	Nonresident alien
1	2	3	4	5	6	7	8
All fields, total [1]	**1,015,239**	**858,186**	**58,016**	**29,800**	**38,219**	**4,046**	**26,972**
Men	481,687	406,656	22,365	13,920	19,537	1,768	17,441
Women	533,552	451,530	35,651	15,880	18,682	2,278	9,531
Agriculture and natural resources, total	13,488	12,248	311	222	240	70	397
Men	9,295	8,494	174	158	114	45	310
Women	4,193	3,754	137	64	126	25	87
Architecture and environmental design, total	9,191	7,421	281	359	430	39	661
Men	5,580	4,448	187	233	225	28	459
Women	3,611	2,973	94	126	205	11	202
Area and ethnic studies, total	3,949	3,055	237	171	333	25	128
Men	1,613	1,237	99	61	142	7	67
Women	2,336	1,818	138	110	191	18	61
Business and management, total	246,659	207,824	15,088	6,987	8,039	824	7,897
Men	131,419	112,938	6,051	3,483	3,669	359	4,919
Women	115,240	94,886	9,037	3,504	4,370	465	2,978
Communications, total	48,625	42,472	3,202	1,169	992	137	653
Men	19,263	16,920	1,151	461	383	60	288
Women	29,362	25,552	2,051	708	609	77	365
Computer and information sciences, total	30,637	22,515	2,557	902	2,355	94	2,214
Men	21,221	16,314	1,244	571	1,466	60	1,566
Women	9,416	6,201	1,313	331	889	34	648
Education, total	96,988	88,152	4,233	2,293	1,127	537	646
Men	21,662	19,203	1,149	580	273	170	287
Women	75,326	68,949	3,084	1,713	854	367	359
Engineering, total	66,296	50,783	2,094	1,937	6,159	179	5,144
Men	56,234	43,402	1,417	1,598	5,008	143	4,666
Women	10,062	7,381	677	339	1,151	36	478
Engineering technologies, total	18,977	15,726	1,143	521	853	106	628
Men	17,417	14,555	934	465	762	96	605
Women	1,560	1,171	209	56	91	10	23
Foreign languages, total	10,774	8,778	319	964	403	36	274
Men	2,879	2,337	63	263	144	6	66
Women	7,895	6,441	256	701	259	30	208
Health sciences, total	59,111	51,011	3,973	1,386	1,733	245	763
Men	8,926	7,513	462	265	407	48	231
Women	50,185	43,498	3,511	1,121	1,326	197	532
Home economics, total	14,717	12,846	894	284	462	51	180
Men	1,380	1,173	106	32	33	5	31
Women	13,337	11,673	788	252	429	46	149
Law, total	1,976	1,725	127	57	54	5	8
Men	785	668	46	37	26	4	4
Women	1,191	1,057	81	20	28	1	4
Letters, total	43,323	38,898	1,862	969	1,048	158	388
Men	14,237	12,935	504	304	314	50	130
Women	29,086	25,963	1,358	665	734	108	258
Liberal/general studies, total	23,459	19,699	1,721	1,064	544	157	274
Men	10,051	8,592	721	368	191	54	125
Women	13,408	11,107	1,000	696	353	103	149
Library and archival science, total	122	105	8	2	3	0	4
Men	16	12	1	0	1	0	2
Women	106	93	7	2	2	0	2
Life sciences, total	36,079	28,896	1,944	1,254	2,951	147	887
Men	17,970	14,634	710	655	1,467	70	434
Women	18,109	14,262	1,234	599	1,484	77	453
Mathematics, total	15,237	12,487	801	310	1,034	54	551
Men	8,221	6,724	380	189	537	39	352
Women	7,016	5,763	421	121	497	15	199
Military sciences, total	419	356	37	12	4	0	10
Men	378	325	31	8	4	0	10
Women	41	31	6	4	0	0	0
Multi/interdisciplinary studies, total	18,213	15,454	1,097	539	695	79	349
Men	8,419	7,182	456	240	301	41	199
Women	9,794	8,272	641	299	394	38	150
Parks and recreation, total	4,171	3,768	197	90	58	23	35
Men	1,709	1,499	110	44	28	7	21
Women	2,462	2,269	87	46	30	16	14

Table 246.—Bachelor's degrees conferred by institutions of higher education, by racial/ethnic group, major field of study, and sex of student: 1988–89—Continued

Major field of study and sex of student	Total	White non-Hispanic	Black non-Hispanic	Hispanic	Asian/ Pacific Islander	American Indian/ Alaskan Native	Nonresident alien
1	2	3	4	5	6	7	8
Philosophy and religion, total	6,411	5,713	224	160	174	25	115
Men	4,122	3,677	136	100	111	17	81
Women	2,289	2,036	88	60	63	8	34
Physical sciences, total	17,204	14,502	708	384	936	63	611
Men	12,097	10,359	371	275	636	45	411
Women	5,107	4,143	337	109	300	18	200
Protective services, total	14,626	11,501	2,106	686	182	74	77
Men	9,074	7,426	1,031	399	130	36	52
Women	5,552	4,075	1,075	287	52	38	25
Psychology, total	48,516	41,584	2,815	1,773	1,605	214	525
Men	14,181	12,229	661	541	514	61	175
Women	34,335	29,355	2,154	1,232	1,091	153	350
Public affairs, total	15,254	12,053	1,974	613	287	133	194
Men	4,948	4,019	486	200	121	36	86
Women	10,306	8,034	1,488	413	166	97	108
Social sciences, total	107,714	90,929	6,498	3,618	3,992	431	2,246
Men	59,924	51,657	2,874	1,876	1,962	220	1,335
Women	47,790	39,272	3,624	1,742	2,030	211	911
Theology, total	5,322	4,779	185	96	121	12	129
Men	4,108	3,674	162	69	94	8	101
Women	1,214	1,105	23	27	27	4	28
Visual and performing arts, total	37,781	32,906	1,380	978	1,405	128	984
Men	14,558	12,510	648	445	474	53	428
Women	23,223	20,396	732	533	931	75	556

[1] Reported racial/ethnic distributions of students by level of degree, field of degree, and sex were used to estimate race/ethnicity for students whose race/ethnicity was not reported. Excludes 1,410 men and 1,018 women whose racial/ethnic group and field of study were not available.

NOTE.—To facilitate trend comparisons, certain aggregations have been made of the degree fields as reported in the IPEDS "Completions" survey: "Agriculture and natural resources" includes Agribusiness and agriculture production, Agricultural sciences, and Renewable natural resources; "Business and management" includes Business and management, Business and office, Marketing and distribution, and Consumer and personal services; "Engineering and related technologies" includes Engineering and related technologies, Mechanics and repairers, and Construction trades; "Physical sciences" includes Physical sciences and Science technologies; "Public affairs" includes Public affairs and Transportation and material moving; and "Visual and performing arts" includes Visual and performing arts and Precision production.

SOURCE: U.S. Department of Education, National Center for Education Statistics, Integrated Postsecondary Education Data System (IPEDS), "Completions" survey. (This table was prepared November 1990.)

Table 247.—Master's degrees conferred by institutions of higher education, by racial/ethnic group and sex of student: 1976–77 to 1988–89

Year and sex of student	Total	White non-Hispanic	Black non-Hispanic	Hispanic	Asian or Pacific Islander	American Indian/Alaskan Native	Non-resident alien
1	2	3	4	5	6	7	8

Number of degrees conferred

1976–77							
Total [1]	316,602	266,061	21,037	6,071	5,122	967	17,344
Men	167,396	139,210	7,781	3,268	3,123	521	13,493
Women	149,206	126,851	13,256	2,803	1,999	446	3,851
1978–79							
Total [2]	300,255	249,360	19,418	5,555	5,496	999	19,427
Men	152,637	124,058	7,070	2,786	3,325	495	14,903
Women	147,618	125,302	12,348	2,769	2,171	504	4,524
1980–81							
Total [3]	294,183	241,216	17,133	6,461	6,282	1,034	22,057
Men	145,666	115,562	6,158	3,085	3,773	501	16,587
Women	148,517	125,654	10,975	3,376	2,509	533	5,470
1984–85							
Total [4]	280,421	223,628	13,939	6,864	7,782	1,256	26,952
Men	139,417	106,059	5,200	3,059	4,842	583	19,674
Women	141,004	117,569	8,739	3,805	2,940	673	7,278
1986–87							
Total [5]	289,341	228,870	13,867	7,044	8,558	1,104	29,898
Men	141,264	105,573	5,151	3,330	5,238	517	21,455
Women	148,077	123,297	8,716	3,714	3,320	587	8,443
1988–89							
Total [6]	308,872	241,607	14,076	7,270	10,714	1,133	34,072
Men	148,486	109,184	5,200	3,360	6,247	500	23,995
Women	160,386	132,423	8,876	3,910	4,467	633	10,077

Percentage distribution of degrees conferred

1976–77							
Total [1]	100.0	84.0	6.6	1.9	1.6	0.3	5.5
Men	100.0	83.2	4.6	2.0	1.9	0.3	8.1
Women	100.0	85.0	8.9	1.9	1.3	0.3	2.6
1978–79							
Total [2]	100.0	83.0	6.5	1.9	1.8	0.3	6.5
Men	100.0	81.3	4.6	1.8	2.2	0.3	9.8
Women	100.0	84.9	8.4	1.9	1.5	0.3	3.1
1980–81							
Total [3]	100.0	82.0	5.8	2.2	2.1	0.4	7.5
Men	100.0	79.3	4.2	2.1	2.6	0.3	11.4
Women	100.0	84.6	7.4	2.3	1.7	0.4	3.7
1984–85							
Total [4]	100.0	79.7	5.0	2.4	2.8	0.4	9.6
Men	100.0	76.1	3.7	2.2	3.5	0.4	14.1
Women	100.0	83.4	6.2	2.7	2.1	0.5	5.2
1986–87							
Total [5]	100.0	79.1	4.8	2.4	3.0	0.4	10.3
Men	100.0	74.7	3.6	2.4	3.7	0.4	15.2
Women	100.0	83.3	5.9	2.5	2.2	0.4	5.7
1988–89							
Total [6]	100.0	78.2	4.6	2.4	3.5	0.4	11.0
Men	100.0	73.5	3.5	2.3	4.2	0.3	16.2
Women	100.0	82.6	5.5	2.4	2.8	0.4	6.3

[1] Excludes 387 men and 175 women whose racial/ethnic group was not available.

[2] Excludes 733 men and 91 women whose racial/ethnic group was not available.

[3] Excludes 1,377 men and 179 women whose racial/ethnic group was not available.

[4] Excludes 3,973 men and 1,857 women whose racial/ethnic group was not available.

[5] Reported racial/ethnic distributions of students by level of degree, field of degree, and sex were used to estimate race/ethnicity for students whose race/ethnicity was not reported. Excludes 99 men and 117 women whose racial/ethnic group and field of study were not available.

[6] Reported racial/ethnic distributions of students by level of degree, field of degree, and sex were used to estimate race/ethnicity for students whose race/ethnicity was not reported. Excludes 496 men and 394 women whose racial/ethnic group and field of study were not available.

SOURCE: U.S. Department of Education, National Center for Education Statistics, "Degrees and Other Formal Awards Conferred" surveys, and Integrated Postsecondary Education Data System (IPEDS), "Completions" survey. (This table was prepared November 1990.)

Table 248.—Master's degrees conferred by institutions of higher education, by racial/ethnic group, major field of study, and sex of student: 1988–89

Major field of study and sex of student	Total	White non-Hispanic	Black non-Hispanic	Hispanic	Asian/ Pacific Islander	American Indian/ Alaskan Native	Nonresident alien
1	2	3	4	5	6	7	8
All fields, total [1]	**308,872**	**241,607**	**14,076**	**7,270**	**10,714**	**1,133**	**34,072**
Men	148,486	109,184	5,200	3,360	6,247	500	23,995
Women	160,386	132,423	8,876	3,910	4,467	633	10,077
Agriculture and natural resources, total	3,245	2,222	53	56	53	6	855
Men	2,231	1,464	41	39	31	6	650
Women	1,014	758	12	17	22	0	205
Architecture and environmental design, total	3,378	2,350	98	90	118	9	713
Men	2,191	1,461	54	68	73	3	532
Women	1,187	889	44	22	45	6	181
Area and ethnic studies, total	978	667	30	57	48	7	169
Men	497	358	16	21	24	5	73
Women	481	309	14	36	24	2	96
Business and management, total	73,154	57,445	3,077	1,581	2,962	197	7,892
Men	48,557	38,013	1,746	982	1,886	125	5,805
Women	24,597	19,432	1,331	599	1,076	72	2,087
Communications, total	4,233	3,328	215	70	99	14	507
Men	1,710	1,329	82	24	47	3	225
Women	2,523	1,999	133	46	52	11	282
Computer and information sciences, total	9,392	5,290	218	152	987	43	2,702
Men	6,769	3,809	132	107	628	40	2,053
Women	2,623	1,481	86	45	359	3	649
Education, total	82,238	70,827	5,272	2,157	1,064	386	2,532
Men	20,286	17,046	1,105	591	278	121	1,145
Women	61,952	53,781	4,167	1,566	786	265	1,387
Engineering, total	23,713	13,575	375	472	2,108	35	7,148
Men	20,633	11,538	278	396	1,803	31	6,587
Women	3,080	2,037	97	76	305	4	561
Engineering technologies, total	828	631	49	10	38	2	98
Men	722	548	37	8	36	1	92
Women	106	83	12	2	2	1	6
Foreign languages, total	1,911	1,271	21	158	46	3	412
Men	602	399	8	51	10	1	133
Women	1,309	872	13	107	36	2	279
Health sciences, total	19,255	16,235	854	398	563	85	1,120
Men	4,210	3,203	179	102	168	21	537
Women	15,045	13,032	675	296	395	64	583
Home economics, total	2,174	1,820	67	45	54	10	178
Men	311	240	12	12	5	1	41
Women	1,863	1,580	55	33	49	9	137
Law, total	2,098	1,050	73	41	62	4	868
Men	1,491	751	43	29	41	1	626
Women	607	299	30	12	21	3	242
Letters, total	6,608	5,469	125	125	187	24	678
Men	2,272	1,863	30	40	51	8	280
Women	4,336	3,606	95	85	136	16	398
Liberal/general studies, total	1,408	1,248	31	39	24	6	60
Men	495	423	13	9	12	2	36
Women	913	825	18	30	12	4	24
Library and archival science, total	3,940	3,444	129	61	113	19	174
Men	816	708	25	11	29	4	39
Women	3,124	2,736	104	50	84	15	135
Life sciences, total	4,933	3,791	128	113	230	17	654
Men	2,484	1,882	61	59	108	8	366
Women	2,449	1,909	67	54	122	9	288
Mathematics, total	3,424	2,123	61	29	186	6	1,019
Men	2,058	1,220	33	20	122	5	658
Women	1,366	903	28	9	64	1	361
Military sciences, total	0	0	0	0	0	0	0
Men	0	0	0	0	0	0	0
Women	0	0	0	0	0	0	0
Multi/interdisciplinary studies, total	3,225	2,741	125	76	99	7	177
Men	1,966	1,656	69	45	72	5	119
Women	1,259	1,085	56	31	27	2	58
Parks and recreation, total	460	376	24	5	15	1	39
Men	213	158	14	4	11	0	26
Women	247	218	10	1	4	1	13

Table 248.—Master's degrees conferred by institutions of higher education, by racial/ethnic group, major field of study, and sex of student: 1988–89—Continued

Major field of study and sex of student	Total	White non-Hispanic	Black non-Hispanic	Hispanic	Asian/ Pacific Islander	American Indian/ Alaskan Native	Nonresident alien
1	2	3	4	5	6	7	8
Philosophy and religion, total	1,274	1,054	51	32	36	2	99
Men	755	598	43	21	22	0	71
Women	519	456	8	11	14	2	28
Physical sciences, total	5,737	3,962	82	77	292	18	1,306
Men	4,204	2,888	59	53	187	12	1,005
Women	1,533	1,074	23	24	105	6	301
Protective services, total	1,046	826	138	15	12	1	54
Men	722	573	80	11	7	1	50
Women	324	253	58	4	5	0	4
Psychology, total	8,579	7,420	414	301	137	35	272
Men	2,799	2,402	126	108	46	13	104
Women	5,780	5,018	288	193	91	22	168
Public affairs, total	17,928	14,337	1,626	594	417	100	854
Men	6,398	4,871	508	235	168	33	583
Women	11,530	9,466	1,118	359	249	67	271
Social sciences, total	10,854	7,678	397	247	329	53	2,150
Men	6,493	4,457	200	148	192	31	1,465
Women	4,361	3,221	197	99	137	22	685
Theology, total	4,625	3,767	146	99	148	9	456
Men	3,003	2,376	103	74	107	4	339
Women	1,622	1,391	43	25	41	5	117
Visual and performing arts, total	8,234	6,660	197	170	287	34	886
Men	3,598	2,950	103	92	83	15	355
Women	4,636	3,710	94	78	204	19	531

[1] Reported racial/ethnic distributions of students by level of degree, field of degree, and sex were used to estimate race/ethnicity for students whose race/ethnicity was not reported. Excludes 496 men and 394 women whose racial/ethnic group and field of study were not available

NOTE.—To facilitate trend comparisons, certain aggregations have been made of the degree fields as reported in the IPEDS "Completions" survey: "Agriculture and natural resources" includes Agribusiness and agriculture production, Agricultural sciences, and Renewable natural resources; "Business and management" includes Business and management, Business and office, Marketing and distribution, and Consumer and personal

services; "Engineering and related technologies" includes Engineering and related technologies, Mechanics and repairers, and Construction trades; "Physical sciences" includes Physical sciences and Science technologies; "Public affairs" includes Public affairs and Transportation and material moving; and "Visual and performing arts" includes Visual and performing arts and Precision production.

SOURCE: U.S. Department of Education, National Center for Education Statistics, Integrated Postsecondary Education Data System (IPEDS), "Completions" survey. (This table was prepared November 1990.)

Table 249.—Doctor's degrees [1] conferred by institutions of higher education, by racial/ethnic group and sex of student: 1976–77 to 1988–89

Year and sex of student	Total	White non-Hispanic	Black non-Hispanic	Hispanic	Asian or Pacific Islander	American Indian/Alaskan Native	Non-resident alien
1	2	3	4	5	6	7	8

Number of degrees conferred

1976–77							
Total [2]	33,126	26,851	1,253	522	658	95	3,747
Men	25,036	20,032	766	383	540	67	3,248
Women	8,090	6,819	487	139	118	28	499
1978–79							
Total [3]	32,675	26,138	1,268	439	811	104	3,915
Men	23,488	18,433	734	294	646	69	3,312
Women	9,187	7,705	534	145	165	35	603
1980–81							
Total [4]	32,839	25,908	1,265	456	877	130	4,203
Men	22,595	17,310	694	277	655	95	3,564
Women	10,244	8,598	571	179	222	35	639
1984–85							
Total [5]	32,307	23,934	1,154	677	1,106	119	5,317
Men	21,296	15,017	561	431	802	64	4,421
Women	11,011	8,917	593	246	304	55	896
1986–87							
Total [6]	34,033	24,435	1,060	750	1,097	104	6,587
Men	22,059	14,813	488	439	795	58	5,466
Women	11,974	9,622	572	311	302	46	1,121
1988–89							
Total [7]	35,692	24,895	1,071	625	1,337	84	7,680
Men	22,651	14,568	497	352	954	49	6,231
Women	13,041	10,327	574	273	383	35	1,449

Percentage distribution of degrees conferred

1976–77							
Total [2]	100.0	81.1	3.8	1.6	2.0	0.3	11.3
Men	100.0	80.0	3.1	1.5	2.2	0.3	13.0
Women	100.0	84.3	6.0	1.7	1.5	0.3	6.2
1978–79							
Total [3]	100.0	80.0	3.9	1.3	2.5	0.3	12.0
Men	100.0	78.5	3.1	1.3	2.8	0.3	14.1
Women	100.0	83.9	5.8	1.6	1.8	0.4	6.6
1980–81							
Total [4]	100.0	78.9	3.9	1.4	2.7	0.4	12.8
Men	100.0	76.6	3.1	1.2	2.9	0.4	15.8
Women	100.0	83.9	5.6	1.7	2.2	0.3	6.2
1984–85							
Total [5]	100.0	74.1	3.6	2.1	3.4	0.4	16.5
Men	100.0	70.5	2.6	2.0	3.8	0.3	20.8
Women	100.0	81.0	5.4	2.2	2.8	0.5	8.1
1986–87							
Total [6]	100.0	71.8	3.1	2.2	3.2	0.3	19.4
Men	100.0	67.2	2.2	2.0	3.6	0.3	24.8
Women	100.0	80.4	4.8	2.6	2.5	0.4	9.4
1988–89							
Total [7]	100.0	69.7	3.0	1.8	3.7	0.2	21.5
Men	100.0	64.3	2.2	1.6	4.2	0.2	27.5
Women	100.0	79.2	4.4	2.1	2.9	0.3	11.1

[1] Includes Ph.D., Ed.D, and comparable degrees at the doctoral level. Excludes first-professional degrees.

[2] Excludes 106 men whose racial/ethnic group was not available.

[3] Excludes 53 men and 2 women whose racial/ethnic group was not available.

[4] Excludes 116 men and 3 women whose racial/ethnic group was not available.

[5] Excludes 404 men and 232 women whose racial/ethnic group was not available.

[6] Reported racial/ethnic distributions of students by level of degree, field of degree, and sex were used to estimate race/ethnicity for students whose race/ethnicity was not reported. Excludes 40 men and 47 women whose racial/ethnic group and field of study were not available.

[7] Reported racial/ethnic distributions of students by level of degree, field of degree, and sex were used to estimate race/ethnicity for students whose race/ethnicity was not reported. Excludes 54 men and 13 women whose racial/ethnic group and field of study were not available.

SOURCE: U.S. Department of Education, National Center for Education Statistics, "Degrees and Other Formal Awards Conferred" surveys, and Integrated Postsecondary Education Data System (IPEDS), "Completions" survey. (This table was prepared November 1990.)

Table 250.—Doctor's degrees conferred by institutions of higher education, by racial/ethnic group, major field of study, and sex of student: 1988–89

Major field of study and sex of student	Total	White non-Hispanic	Black non-Hispanic	Hispanic	Asian/ Pacific Islander	American Indian/ Alaskan Native	Nonresident alien
1	2	3	4	5	6	7	8
All fields, total [1]	35,692	24,895	1,071	625	1,337	84	7,680
Men	22,651	14,568	497	352	954	49	6,231
Women	13,041	10,327	574	273	383	35	1,449
Agriculture and natural resources, total	1,184	677	15	20	30	0	442
Men	952	519	12	17	22	0	382
Women	232	158	3	3	8	0	60
Architecture and environmental design, total	86	34	2	2	6	1	41
Men	63	25	0	1	4	1	32
Women	23	9	2	1	2	0	9
Area and ethnic studies, total	110	82	2	4	2	1	19
Men	57	39	1	3	0	0	14
Women	53	43	1	1	2	1	5
Business and management, total	1,150	746	20	14	57	2	311
Men	844	491	17	12	52	2	270
Women	306	255	3	2	5	0	41
Communications, total	248	177	16	4	2	0	49
Men	137	97	2	2	1	0	35
Women	111	80	14	2	1	0	14
Computer and information sciences, total	538	285	2	4	42	0	205
Men	457	233	0	1	37	0	186
Women	81	52	2	3	5	0	19
Education, total	6,783	5,445	450	162	128	25	573
Men	2,894	2,255	174	68	58	11	328
Women	3,889	3,190	276	94	70	14	245
Engineering, total	4,521	1,939	30	43	326	3	2,180
Men	4,121	1,679	27	37	300	3	2,075
Women	400	260	3	6	26	0	105
Engineering technologies, total	12	8	0	0	0	0	4
Men	12	8	0	0	0	0	4
Women	0	0	0	0	0	0	0
Foreign languages, total	422	282	14	32	7	0	87
Men	169	107	5	10	3	0	44
Women	253	175	9	22	4	0	43
Health sciences, total	1,439	1,107	39	15	47	2	229
Men	612	424	11	5	29	1	142
Women	827	683	28	10	18	1	87
Home economics, total	263	207	12	2	6	0	36
Men	59	50	0	0	2	0	7
Women	204	157	12	2	4	0	29
Law, total	76	24	4	0	2	0	46
Men	46	13	0	0	2	0	31
Women	30	11	4	0	0	0	15
Letters, total	1,238	1,000	29	24	24	3	158
Men	559	449	7	9	10	3	81
Women	679	551	22	15	14	0	77
Liberal/general studies, total	32	25	6	0	0	0	1
Men	16	15	1	0	0	0	0
Women	16	10	5	0	0	0	1
Library and archival science, total	61	42	1	0	3	0	15
Men	27	15	1	0	1	0	10
Women	34	27	0	0	2	0	5
Life sciences, total	3,533	2,677	58	47	174	10	567
Men	2,235	1,678	35	36	95	6	385
Women	1,298	999	23	11	79	4	182
Mathematics, total	882	413	8	7	33	1	420
Men	711	321	5	5	24	0	356
Women	171	92	3	2	9	1	64
Military sciences, total	0	0	0	0	0	0	0
Men	0	0	0	0	0	0	0
Women	0	0	0	0	0	0	0
Multi/interdisciplinary studies, total	257	207	5	5	5	1	34
Men	158	121	3	3	4	0	27
Women	99	86	2	2	1	1	7
Parks and recreation, total	36	24	2	0	0	0	10
Men	28	20	0	0	0	0	8
Women	8	4	2	0	0	0	2

Table 250.—Doctor's degrees conferred by institutions of higher education, by racial/ethnic group, major field of study, and sex of student: 1988–89—Continued

Major field of study and sex of student	Total	White non-Hispanic	Black non-Hispanic	Hispanic	Asian/ Pacific Islander	American Indian/ Alaskan Native	Nonresident alien
1	2	3	4	5	6	7	8
Philosophy and religion, total	464	377	9	9	12	0	57
Men	341	271	7	7	11	0	45
Women	123	106	2	2	1	0	12
Physical sciences, total	3,852	2,436	32	54	185	13	1,132
Men	3,093	1,926	26	43	149	9	940
Women	759	510	6	11	36	4	192
Protective services, total	27	24	3	0	0	0	0
Men	19	18	1	0	0	0	0
Women	8	6	2	0	0	0	0
Psychology, total	3,263	2,876	113	89	61	8	116
Men	1,429	1,263	40	37	26	3	60
Women	1,834	1,613	73	52	35	5	56
Public affairs, total	417	297	36	10	16	1	57
Men	208	130	17	4	8	0	49
Women	209	167	19	6	8	1	8
Social sciences, total	2,878	1,874	108	60	101	10	725
Men	1,939	1,172	62	36	68	8	593
Women	939	702	46	24	33	2	132
Theology, total	1,165	984	44	10	35	2	90
Men	1,022	863	35	10	32	2	80
Women	143	121	9	0	3	0	10
Visual and performing arts, total	755	626	11	8	33	1	76
Men	443	366	8	6	16	0	47
Women	312	260	3	2	17	1	29

[1] Reported racial/ethnic distributions of students by level of degree, field of degree, and sex were used to estimate race/ethnicity for students whose race/ethnicity was not reported. Excludes 54 men and 13 women whose racial/ethnic group and field of study were not available.

NOTE.—To facilitate trend comparisons, certain aggregations have been made of the degree fields as reported in the IPEDS "Completions" survey: "Agriculture and natural resources" includes Agribusiness and agriculture production, Agricultural sciences, and Renewable natural resources; "Business and management" includes Business and management, Business and office, Marketing and distribution, and Consumer and personal services; "Engineering and related technologies" includes Engineering and related technologies, Mechanics and repairers, and Construction trades; "Physical sciences" includes Physical sciences and Science technologies; "Public affairs" includes Public affairs and Transportation and material moving; and "Visual and performing arts" includes Visual and performing arts and Precision production.

SOURCE: U.S. Department of Education, National Center for Education Statistics, Integrated Postsecondary Education Data System (IPEDS), "Completions" survey. (This table was prepared November 1990.)

Table 251.—First-professional degrees conferred by institutions of higher education, by racial/ethnic group, major field of study, and sex of student: 1988–89

Year and sex of student	Total	White non-Hispanic	Black non-Hispanic	Hispanic	Asian or Pacific Islander	American Indian/Alaskan Native	Non-resident alien
1	2	3	4	5	6	7	8
All fields, total [1]	**70,758**	**61,188**	**3,101**	**2,254**	**2,967**	**268**	**980**
Men	45,067	39,448	1,608	1,367	1,811	149	684
Women	25,691	21,740	1,493	887	1,156	119	296
Dentistry (D.D.S. or D.M.D.), total	4,247	3,280	179	201	418	13	156
Men	3,139	2,515	101	134	284	7	98
Women	1,108	765	78	67	134	6	58
Medicine (M.D.), total	15,454	12,790	779	565	1,147	61	112
Men	10,326	8,726	380	369	742	31	78
Women	5,128	4,064	399	196	405	30	34
Optometry (O.D.), total	1,093	936	30	27	79	4	17
Men	683	606	16	12	37	3	9
Women	410	330	14	15	42	1	8
Osteopathic medicine (D.O), total	1,635	1,465	41	58	55	9	7
Men	1,183	1,065	27	39	40	8	4
Women	452	400	14	19	15	1	3
Pharmacy (D.Phar.), total	1,074	735	51	31	210	2	45
Men	422	289	19	14	80	1	19
Women	652	446	32	17	130	1	26
Podiatry (Pod.D. or D.P.) or podiatric medicine (D.P.M.), total	636	541	40	15	18	2	20
Men	487	427	21	12	11	2	14
Women	149	114	19	3	7	0	6
Veterinary medicine (D.V.M.), total	2,157	2,029	32	44	29	14	9
Men	981	924	11	25	7	8	6
Women	1,176	1,105	21	19	22	6	3
Chiropractic medicine (D.C. or D.C.M.), total	2,890	2,614	24	73	52	4	123
Men	2,159	1,958	15	55	37	4	90
Women	731	656	9	18	15	0	33
Law, general (LL.B. or J.D.), total	35,567	31,679	1,586	1,146	793	146	217
Men	21,048	19,011	770	636	426	81	124
Women	14,519	12,668	816	510	367	65	93
Theological professions, general (B.D., M.Div., Rabbi), total	6,005	5,119	339	94	166	13	274
Men	4,639	3,927	248	71	147	4	242
Women	1,366	1,192	91	23	19	9	32

[1] Data are preliminary

SOURCE: U.S. Department of Education, National Center for Education Statistics, Integrated Postsecondary Education Data System (IPEDS), "Completions" survey. (This table was prepared October 1990.)

Table 252.—Earned degrees in agriculture and natural resources [1] conferred by institutions of higher education, by level of degree and sex of student: 1970–71 to 1988–89

Year	Bachelor's degrees			Master's degrees			Doctor's degrees		
	Total	Men	Women	Total	Men	Women	Total	Men	Women
1	2	3	4	5	6	7	8	9	10
1970–71	12,672	12,136	536	2,457	2,313	144	1,086	1,055	31
1971–72	13,516	12,779	737	2,680	2,490	190	971	945	26
1972–73	14,756	13,661	1,095	2,807	2,588	219	1,059	1,031	28
1973–74	16,253	14,684	1,569	2,928	2,640	288	930	897	33
1974–75	17,528	15,061	2,467	3,067	2,703	364	991	958	33
1975–76	19,402	15,845	3,557	3,340	2,862	478	928	867	61
1976–77	21,467	16,690	4,777	3,724	3,177	547	893	831	62
1977–78	22,650	17,069	5,581	4,023	3,268	755	971	909	62
1978–79	23,134	16,854	6,280	3,994	3,187	807	950	877	73
1979–80	22,802	16,045	6,757	3,976	3,082	894	991	879	112
1980–81	21,886	15,154	6,732	4,003	3,061	942	1,067	940	127
1981–82	21,029	14,443	6,586	4,163	3,114	1,049	1,079	925	154
1982–83	20,909	14,085	6,824	4,254	3,129	1,125	1,149	1,004	145
1983–84	19,317	13,206	6,111	4,178	2,989	1,189	1,172	1,001	171
1984–85	18,107	12,477	5,630	3,928	2,846	1,082	1,213	1,036	177
1985–86	16,823	11,544	5,279	3,801	2,701	1,100	1,158	966	192
1986–87	14,991	10,314	4,677	3,523	2,461	1,062	1,049	871	178
1987–88	14,222	9,744	4,478	3,479	2,427	1,052	1,142	926	216
1988–89 [2]	13,488	9,295	4,193	3,245	2,231	1,014	1,184	952	232

[1] Includes degrees in agribusiness and agricultural production, agricultural sciences, and renewable natural resources.

[2] Preliminary data.

SOURCE: U.S. Department of Education, National Center for Education Statistics, "Degrees and Other Formal Awards Conferred" surveys, and Integrated Postsecondary Education Data System (IPEDS), "Completions" survey. (This table was prepared October 1990.)

Table 253.—Earned degrees in architecture and environmental design [1] conferred by institutions of higher education, by level of degree and sex of student: 1949–50 to 1988–89

Year	Bachelor's degrees			Master's degrees			Doctor's degrees		
	Total	Men	Women	Total	Men	Women	Total	Men	Women
1	2	3	4	5	6	7	8	9	10
1949–50	2,563	2,441	122	166	159	7	1	1	—
1959–60	1,801	1,744	57	319	305	14	17	17	—
1967–68	3,057	2,931	126	1,021	953	68	15	15	—
1969–70	4,105	3,888	217	1,427	1,260	167	35	33	2
1970–71	5,570	4,906	664	1,705	1,469	236	36	33	3
1971–72	6,440	5,667	773	1,899	1,626	273	50	43	7
1972–73	6,962	6,042	920	2,307	1,943	364	58	54	4
1973–74	7,822	6,665	1,157	2,702	2,208	494	69	65	4
1974–75	8,226	6,791	1,435	2,938	2,343	595	69	58	11
1975–76	9,146	7,396	1,750	3,215	2,545	670	82	69	13
1976–77	9,222	7,249	1,973	3,213	2,489	724	73	62	11
1977–78	9,250	7,054	2,196	3,115	2,304	811	73	57	16
1978–79	9,273	6,876	2,397	3,113	2,226	887	96	74	22
1979–80	9,132	6,596	2,536	3,139	2,245	894	79	66	13
1980–81	9,455	6,800	2,655	3,153	2,234	919	93	73	20
1981–82	9,728	6,825	2,903	3,327	2,242	1,085	80	58	22
1982–83	9,823	6,403	3,420	3,357	2,224	1,133	97	74	23
1983–84	9,186	5,895	3,291	3,223	2,197	1,026	84	62	22
1984–85	9,325	6,019	3,306	3,275	2,148	1,127	89	66	23
1985–86	9,119	5,824	3,295	3,260	2,129	1,131	73	56	17
1986–87	8,922	5,590	3,332	3,142	2,073	1,069	92	66	26
1987–88 [2]	8,603	5,271	3,332	3,159	2,042	1,117	98	66	32
1988–89 [3]	9,191	5,580	3,611	3,378	2,191	1,187	86	63	23

[1] Prior to 1965–66, includes degrees in architecture. From 1965–66, includes degrees in environmental design, general; architecture; interior design; landscape architecture; urban architecture; city, community, and regional planning; and other architecture and environmental design.

[2] Revised from previously published data.

[3] Preliminary data.

—Data not reported.

SOURCE: U.S. Department of Education, National Center for Education Statistics, "Degrees and Other Formal Awards Conferred" surveys, and Integrated Postsecondary Education Data System (IPEDS), "Completions" survey. (This table was prepared February 1991.)

Table 254.—Earned degrees in business and management [1] conferred by institutions of higher education, by level of degree and sex of student: 1955–56 to 1988–89

Year	Bachelor's degrees			Master's degrees			Doctor's degrees		
	Total	Men	Women	Total	Men	Women	Total	Men	Women
1	2	3	4	5	6	7	8	9	10
1955–56	42,813	38,706	4,107	3,280	3,118	162	129	127	2
1957–58	51,991	48,063	3,928	4,223	4,072	151	110	105	5
1959–60	52,110	48,265	3,845	4,814	4,645	169	138	136	2
1961–62	52,139	48,236	3,903	5,401	5,221	180	232	227	5
1963–64	59,198	54,692	4,506	6,513	6,310	203	281	274	7
1965–66	63,639	58,376	5,263	13,142	12,806	336	402	385	17
1967–68	80,138	73,147	6,991	18,048	17,431	617	456	442	14
1969–70	105,580	96,346	9,234	21,561	20,792	769	620	610	10
1970–71	114,865	104,404	10,461	26,481	25,443	1,038	807	784	23
1971–72	121,360	109,776	11,584	30,367	29,166	1,201	896	876	20
1972–73	126,263	112,897	13,366	31,007	29,481	1,526	923	871	52
1973–74	131,766	114,850	16,916	32,644	30,491	2,153	981	931	50
1974–75	133,010	111,411	21,599	36,247	33,185	3,062	1,009	968	41
1975–76	142,379	114,267	28,112	42,512	37,559	4,953	953	901	52
1976–77	150,964	115,526	35,438	46,420	39,766	6,654	863	809	54
1977–78	160,187	116,579	43,608	48,326	40,150	8,176	866	794	72
1978–79	171,764	119,227	52,537	50,372	40,701	9,671	860	760	100
1979–80	185,361	122,897	62,464	55,006	42,722	12,284	792	677	115
1980–81	199,338	125,795	73,543	57,898	43,394	14,504	842	717	125
1981–82	214,001	129,668	84,333	61,299	44,243	17,056	855	704	151
1982–83	226,893	131,718	95,175	65,319	46,457	18,862	809	673	136
1983–84	230,031	129,909	100,122	66,653	46,565	20,088	977	775	202
1984–85	233,351	128,032	105,319	67,527	46,624	20,903	866	718	148
1985–86	238,160	129,271	108,889	67,137	46,288	20,849	969	759	210
1986–87	241,156	128,958	112,198	67,496	45,211	22,285	1,098	839	259
1987–88 [2]	243,725	129,948	113,777	69,655	46,305	23,350	1,109	853	256
1988–89 [3]	246,659	131,419	115,240	73,154	48,557	24,597	1,150	844	306

[1] Includes degrees in business and management, business and office, marketing and distribution, and consumer and personal services.
[2] Revised from previously published data.
[3] Preliminary data.

SOURCE: U.S. Department of Education, National Center for Education Statistics, "Degrees and Other Formal Awards Conferred" surveys, and Integrated Postsecondary Education Data System (IPEDS), "Completions" survey. (This table was prepared October 1990.)

Table 255.—Earned degrees in communications [1] conferred by institutions of higher education, by level of degree and sex of student: 1970–71 to 1988–89

Year	Bachelor's degrees			Master's degrees			Doctor's degrees		
	Total	Men	Women	Total	Men	Women	Total	Men	Women
1	2	3	4	5	6	7	8	9	10
1970–71	10,802	6,989	3,813	1,856	1,214	642	145	126	19
1971–72	12,340	7,964	4,376	2,200	1,443	757	111	96	15
1972–73	14,317	9,074	5,243	2,406	1,546	860	139	114	25
1973–74	17,096	10,536	6,560	2,640	1,668	972	175	146	29
1974–75	19,248	11,455	7,793	2,794	1,618	1,176	165	119	46
1975–76	21,282	12,458	8,824	3,126	1,818	1,308	204	154	50
1976–77	23,214	12,932	10,282	3,091	1,719	1,372	171	130	41
1977–78	25,400	13,480	11,920	3,296	1,673	1,623	191	138	53
1978–79	26,457	13,266	13,191	2,882	1,483	1,399	192	138	54
1979–80	28,616	13,656	14,960	3,082	1,527	1,555	193	121	72
1980–81	31,282	14,179	17,103	3,105	1,448	1,657	182	107	75
1981–82	34,222	14,917	19,305	3,327	1,578	1,749	200	136	64
1982–83	38,602	16,185	22,417	3,604	1,661	1,943	214	126	88
1983–84	40,165	16,647	23,518	3,656	1,600	2,056	219	131	88
1984–85	42,083	17,238	24,845	3,669	1,576	2,093	234	143	91
1985–86	43,091	17,647	25,444	3,823	1,610	2,213	223	116	107
1986–87	45,408	18,155	27,253	3,937	1,606	2,331	275	158	117
1987–88 [2]	46,726	18,592	28,134	3,925	1,568	2,357	234	134	100
1988–89 [3]	48,625	19,263	29,362	4,233	1,710	2,523	248	137	111

[1] Includes degrees in communications, general; journalism; radio–television; advertising; communications media; and other communications.
[2] Revised from previously published data.
[3] Preliminary data.

SOURCE: U.S. Department of Education, National Center for Education Statistics, "Degrees and Other Formal Awards Conferred" surveys, and Integrated Postsecondary Education Data System (IPEDS), "Completions" survey. (This table was prepared February 1991.)

Table 256.—Earned degrees in computer and information sciences [1] conferred by institutions of higher education, by level of degree and sex of student: 1970–71 to 1988–89

Year	Bachelor's degrees			Master's degrees			Doctor's degrees		
	Total	Men	Women	Total	Men	Women	Total	Men	Women
1	2	3	4	5	6	7	8	9	10
1970–71	2,388	2,064	324	1,588	1,424	164	128	125	3
1971–72	3,402	2,941	461	1,977	1,752	225	167	155	12
1972–73	4,304	3,664	640	2,113	1,888	225	196	181	15
1973–74	4,756	3,976	780	2,276	1,983	293	198	189	9
1974–75	5,033	4,080	953	2,299	1,961	338	213	199	14
1975–76	5,652	4,534	1,118	2,603	2,226	377	244	221	23
1976–77	6,407	4,876	1,531	2,798	2,332	466	216	197	19
1977–78	7,201	5,349	1,852	3,038	2,471	567	196	181	15
1978–79	8,719	6,272	2,447	3,055	2,480	575	236	206	30
1979–80	11,154	7,782	3,372	3,647	2,883	764	240	213	27
1980–81	15,121	10,202	4,919	4,218	3,247	971	252	227	25
1981–82	20,267	13,218	7,049	4,935	3,625	1,310	251	230	21
1982–83	24,510	15,606	8,904	5,321	3,813	1,508	262	228	34
1983–84	32,172	20,246	11,926	6,190	4,379	1,811	251	225	26
1984–85	38,878	24,579	14,299	7,101	5,064	2,037	248	223	25
1985–86	41,889	26,923	14,966	8,070	5,658	2,412	344	299	45
1986–87	39,664	25,929	13,735	8,491	5,995	2,496	374	322	52
1987–88 [2]	34,523	23,331	11,192	9,197	6,726	2,471	428	380	48
1988–89 [3]	30,637	21,221	9,416	9,392	6,769	2,623	538	457	81

[1] Includes degrees in computer and information sciences, general; information sciences and systems; data processing; computer programming; systems analysis; and other information sciences.
[2] Revised from previously published data.
[3] Preliminary data.

SOURCE: U.S. Department of Education, National Center for Education Statistics, "Degrees and Other Formal Awards Conferred" surveys, and Integrated Postsecondary Education Data System (IPEDS), "Completions" survey. (This table was prepared February 1991.)

Table 257.—Earned degrees in education conferred by institutions of higher education, by level of degree and sex of student: 1949–50 to 1988–89

Year	Bachelor's degrees			Master's degrees			Doctor's degrees		
	Total	Men	Women	Total	Men	Women	Total	Men	Women
1	2	3	4	5	6	7	8	9	10
1949–50	61,472	31,398	30,074	20,069	12,025	8,044	953	797	156
1959–60	89,421	25,838	63,583	33,512	18,126	15,386	1,590	1,281	309
1967–68	134,905	32,492	102,413	63,503	30,798	32,705	4,079	3,249	830
1969–70	165,453	41,347	124,106	79,349	35,451	43,898	5,894	4,698	1,196
1970–71	176,614	45,094	131,520	88,952	38,977	49,975	6,403	5,045	1,358
1971–72	191,220	49,537	141,683	98,143	41,816	56,327	7,044	5,384	1,660
1972–73	194,229	51,441	142,788	105,565	44,128	61,437	7,318	5,504	1,814
1973–74	185,225	49,160	136,065	112,610	45,124	67,486	7,293	5,316	1,977
1974–75	167,015	44,557	122,458	120,169	45,421	74,748	7,446	5,147	2,299
1975–76	154,807	42,070	112,737	128,417	45,796	82,621	7,778	5,179	2,599
1976–77	143,722	39,941	103,781	126,825	43,288	83,537	7,963	5,189	2,774
1977–78	136,141	37,484	98,657	119,038	38,413	80,625	7,595	4,634	2,961
1978–79	126,109	33,819	92,290	111,995	35,143	76,852	7,736	4,472	3,264
1979–80	118,169	30,922	87,247	103,951	31,020	72,931	7,941	4,419	3,522
1980–81	108,309	27,076	81,233	98,938	28,256	70,682	7,900	4,164	3,736
1981–82	101,113	24,402	76,711	93,757	25,953	67,804	7,680	3,950	3,730
1982–83	97,991	23,670	74,321	84,853	23,232	61,621	7,551	3,764	3,787
1983–84	92,382	22,215	70,167	77,187	21,581	55,606	7,473	3,703	3,770
1984–85	88,161	21,264	66,897	76,137	20,945	55,192	7,151	3,419	3,732
1985–86	87,221	20,986	66,235	76,353	20,719	55,634	7,110	3,315	3,795
1986–87	87,115	20,770	66,345	75,501	19,642	55,859	6,900	3,117	3,792
1987–88 [1]	91,287	21,028	70,259	77,867	19,437	58,430	6,553	2,949	3,604
1988–89 [2]	96,988	21,662	75,326	82,238	20,286	61,952	6,783	2,894	3,889

[1] Revised from previously published data.
[2] Preliminary data.

SOURCE: U.S. Department of Education, National Center for Education Statistics, "Degrees and Other Formal Awards Conferred" surveys, and Integrated Postsecondary Education Data System (IPEDS), "Completions" survey. (This table was prepared February 1991.)

Table 258.—Earned degrees in engineering [1] conferred by institutions of higher education, by level of degree and sex of student: 1949–50 to 1988–89

Year	Bachelor's degrees			Master's degrees			Doctor's degrees		
	Total	Men	Women	Total	Men	Women	Total	Men	Women
1	2	3	4	5	6	7	8	9	10
1949–50	52,246	52,071	175	4,496	4,481	15	417	416	1
1959–60	37,679	37,537	142	7,159	7,133	26	786	783	3
1963–64	35,013	34,862	151	10,827	10,793	34	1,693	1,686	7
1965–66	35,615	35,472	143	13,675	13,599	76	2,304	2,295	9
1967–68	37,368	37,159	209	15,182	15,083	99	2,932	2,920	12
1969–70 [2]	49,678	49,296	382	15,723	15,547	176	3,691	3,667	24
1970–71	50,046	49,646	400	16,443	16,258	185	3,638	3,615	23
1971–72	51,164	50,638	526	16,960	16,688	272	3,671	3,649	22
1972–73	51,265	50,652	613	16,619	16,341	278	3,492	3,438	54
1973–74	50,286	49,490	796	15,379	15,023	356	3,312	3,257	55
1974–75	46,852	45,838	1,014	15,348	14,973	375	3,108	3,042	66
1975–76	46,331	44,871	1,460	16,342	15,760	582	2,821	2,755	66
1976–77	49,283	47,065	2,218	16,245	15,525	720	2,586	2,513	73
1977–78	55,654	51,945	3,709	16,398	15,533	865	2,440	2,383	57
1978–79	62,375	57,201	5,174	15,495	14,544	951	2,506	2,423	83
1979–80	68,893	62,488	6,405	16,243	15,101	1,142	2,507	2,412	95
1980–81	75,000	67,301	7,699	16,709	15,347	1,362	2,561	2,457	104
1981–82	80,005	70,899	9,106	17,939	16,311	1,628	2,636	2,496	140
1982–83	89,270	78,316	10,954	19,350	17,553	1,797	2,831	2,706	125
1983–84	94,444	82,309	12,135	20,661	18,504	2,157	2,981	2,816	165
1984–85	96,105	83,453	12,652	21,557	19,249	2,308	3,230	3,022	208
1985–86	95,953	83,372	12,581	21,661	19,168	2,493	3,410	3,181	229
1986–87	93,074	80,347	12,727	22,693	19,841	2,852	3,820	3,557	263
1987–88 [2]	88,706	76,538	12,168	23,388	20,477	2,911	4,191	3,898	293
1988–89 [3]	85,273	73,651	11,622	24,541	21,355	3,186	4,533	4,133	400

[1] Includes degrees in engineering and engineering technologies from 1969–70 through 1988–89.
[2] Revised from previously published data.
[3] Preliminary data.

SOURCE: U.S. Department of Education, National Center for Education Statistics, "Degrees and Other Formal Awards Conferred" surveys, and Integrated Postsecondary Education Data System (IPEDS), "Completions" survey. (This table was prepared February 1991.)

Table 259.—Earned degrees in chemical, civil, and electrical engineering conferred by institutions of higher education, by level of degree: 1970–71 to 1988–89

Year	Chemical engineering			Civil engineering [1]			Electrical engineering		
	Bachelor's	Master's	Doctor's	Bachelor's	Master's	Doctor's	Bachelor's	Master's	Doctor's
1	2	3	4	5	6	7	8	9	10
1970–71	3,579	1,100	406	6,526	2,425	446	12,198	4,282	879
1971–72	3,625	1,154	394	6,803	2,487	415	12,101	4,206	824
1972–73	3,578	1,051	397	7,390	2,627	397	12,313	3,895	791
1973–74	3,399	1,044	400	8,017	2,652	368	11,316	3,499	705
1974–75	3,070	990	346	7,651	2,769	356	10,161	3,469	701
1975–76	3,140	1,031	308	7,923	2,999	370	9,791	3,774	649
1976–77	3,524	1,086	291	8,228	2,964	309	9,936	3,788	566
1977–78	4,569	1,235	259	9,135	2,685	277	11,133	3,740	503
1978–79	5,568	1,149	304	9,809	2,646	253	12,338	3,591	586
1979–80	6,320	1,270	284	10,326	2,683	270	13,821	3,836	525
1980–81	6,527	1,267	300	10,678	2,891	325	14,938	3,901	535
1981–82	6,740	1,285	311	10,524	2,995	329	16,455	4,462	526
1982–83	7,185	1,368	319	9,989	3,074	340	18,049	4,531	550
1983–84	7,475	1,514	330	9,693	3,146	369	19,943	5,078	585
1984–85	7,146	1,544	418	9,162	3,172	377	21,691	5,153	660
1985–86	5,877	1,361	446	8,679	2,926	395	23,742	5,534	722
1986–87	4,983	1,184	497	8,147	2,901	451	24,563	6,234	726
1987–88 [2]	3,917	1,088	579	7,488	2,836	481	23,597	6,688	860
1988–89 [3]	3,684	1,097	599	7,316	2,902	503	21,909	7,024	1,002

[1] From 1970–71 to 1981–82 includes "construction and transportation engineering."
[2] Revised from previously published data.
[3] Preliminary data.

NOTE.—Degrees in engineering technologies are not included in this tabulation.

SOURCE: U.S. Department of Education, National Center for Education Statistics, "Degrees and Other Formal Awards Conferred" surveys, and Integrated Postsecondary Education Data System (IPEDS), "Completions" survey. (This table was prepared February 1991.)

Table 260.—Earned degrees in English and literature[1] conferred by institutions of higher education, by level of degree and sex of student: 1949–50 to 1988–89

Year	Bachelor's degrees			Master's degrees			Doctor's degrees		
	Total	Men	Women	Total	Men	Women	Total	Men	Women
1	2	3	4	5	6	7	8	9	10
1949–50	17,240	8,221	9,019	2,259	1,320	939	230	181	49
1959–60	20,128	7,580	12,548	2,931	1,458	1,473	397	314	83
1967–68	47,977	15,700	32,277	7,916	3,434	4,482	977	717	260
1969–70	56,400	18,644	37,756	8,480	3,309	5,171	1,205	832	373
1970–71	57,026	19,000	38,026	8,935	3,485	5,450	1,441	1,021	420
1971–72	55,991	19,169	36,822	8,714	3,356	5,358	1,591	1,056	535
1972–73	52,478	18,544	33,934	8,151	3,203	4,948	1,631	1,040	591
1973–74	47,343	17,091	30,252	7,906	3,192	4,714	1,616	1,006	610
1974–75	40,297	14,727	25,570	7,620	2,932	4,688	1,507	884	623
1975–76	35,432	13,252	22,180	7,217	2,775	4,442	1,511	856	655
1976–77	31,996	11,816	20,180	6,513	2,436	4,077	1,318	718	600
1977–78	29,732	10,837	18,895	6,351	2,292	4,059	1,265	670	595
1978–79	27,720	9,776	17,944	5,522	2,015	3,507	1,137	600	537
1979–80	26,638	9,032	17,606	5,122	1,857	3,265	1,131	594	537
1980–81	26,006	8,788	17,218	4,948	1,793	3,155	1,047	494	553
1981–82	26,152	8,692	17,460	4,809	1,698	3,111	974	455	519
1982–83	25,632	8,550	17,082	4,350	1,538	2,812	890	416	474
1983–84	26,419	8,723	17,696	4,403	1,566	2,837	941	421	520
1984–85	26,536	8,862	17,674	4,571	1,590	2,981	943	426	517
1985–86	27,360	9,150	18,210	4,923	1,740	3,183	937	405	532
1986–87	28,822	9,576	19,246	4,876	1,743	3,133	896	387	509
1987–88[2]	30,839	9,959	20,880	4,888	1,683	3,205	942	409	533
1988–89[3]	33,968	10,875	23,093	5,281	1,811	3,470	932	420	512

[1] Includes degrees conferred in general English, English literature, comparative literature, classics, creative writing, composition, American literature, and technical and business writing.
[2] Revised from previously published data.
[3] Preliminary data.

SOURCE: U.S. Department of Education, National Center for Education Statistics, "Degrees and Other Formal Awards Conferred" surveys, and Integrated Postsecondary Education Data System (IPEDS), "Completions" survey. (This table was prepared February 1991.)

Table 261.—Earned degrees in modern foreign languages[1] conferred by institutions of higher education, by level of degree and sex of student: 1949–50 to 1988–89

Year	Bachelor's degrees			Master's degrees			Doctor's degrees		
	Total	Men	Women	Total	Men	Women	Total	Men	Women
1	2	3	4	5	6	7	8	9	10
1949–50	4,477	1,746	2,731	919	456	463	168	135	33
1959–60	4,527	1,548	2,979	832	392	440	150	100	50
1967–68	17,499	4,450	13,049	3,911	1,555	2,356	491	336	155
1969–70	19,457	4,921	14,536	4,154	1,476	2,678	590	369	221
1970–71	19,057	4,734	14,323	4,410	1,494	2,916	704	425	279
1971–72	18,140	4,446	13,694	4,278	1,450	2,828	754	467	287
1972–73	18,234	4,348	13,886	3,994	1,407	2,587	891	521	370
1973–74	18,256	4,279	13,977	3,795	1,254	2,541	876	488	388
1974–75	17,118	3,914	13,204	3,674	1,180	2,494	829	442	387
1975–76	15,081	3,496	11,585	3,365	1,100	2,265	831	429	402
1976–77	13,630	3,226	10,404	2,992	890	2,102	733	352	381
1977–78	12,449	2,938	9,511	2,658	771	1,887	636	290	346
1978–79	11,533	2,706	8,827	2,342	687	1,655	627	288	339
1979–80	10,816	2,583	8,233	2,160	631	1,529	524	218	306
1980–81	10,052	2,402	7,650	2,023	659	1,364	561	262	299
1981–82	9,577	2,279	7,298	1,917	573	1,344	502	224	278
1982–83	9,335	2,343	6,992	1,605	533	1,072	454	185	269
1983–84	9,158	2,400	6,758	1,641	513	1,128	429	191	238
1984–85	9,675	2,529	7,146	1,613	505	1,108	389	158	231
1985–86	9,810	2,686	7,124	1,656	482	1,174	427	174	253
1986–87	9,847	2,656	7,191	1,694	492	1,202	406	165	241
1987–88[2]	9,790	2,628	7,162	1,795	564	1,231	383	162	221
1988–89[3]	10,491	2,769	7,722	1,840	562	1,278	394	154	240

[1] Includes degrees conferred in a single language or a combination of modern foreign languages. Excludes degrees in linguistics, Latin, classical Greek, and "other" foreign languages.
[2] Revised from previously published data.
[3] Preliminary data.

SOURCE: U.S. Department of Education, National Center for Education Statistics, "Degrees and Other Formal Awards Conferred" surveys, and Integrated Postsecondary Education Data System (IPEDS), "Completions" survey. (This table was prepared February 1991.)

Table 262.—Earned degrees in French, German, and Spanish conferred by institutions of higher education, by level of degree: 1949–50 to 1988–89

Year	French			German			Spanish		
	Bachelor's	Master's	Doctor's	Bachelor's	Master's	Doctor's	Bachelor's	Master's	Doctor's
1	2	3	4	5	6	7	8	9	10
1949–50	1,471	299	53	540	121	40	2,122	373	34
1959–60	1,927	316	58	659	126	21	1,610	261	31
1967–68	7,068	1,301	152	2,368	771	117	6,381	1,188	123
1969–70	7,624	1,409	181	2,652	669	118	7,226	1,372	139
1970–71	7,306	1,437	192	2,601	690	144	7,068	1,456	168
1971–72	6,822	1,421	193	2,477	608	167	6,847	1,421	152
1972–73	6,705	1,277	203	2,520	598	176	7,209	1,298	206
1973–74	6,263	1,195	213	2,425	550	149	7,250	1,217	203
1974–75	5,745	1,077	200	2,289	480	147	6,719	1,228	202
1975–76	4,783	914	190	1,983	471	164	5,984	1,080	176
1976–77	4,228	875	177	1,820	394	126	5,359	930	153
1977–78	3,708	692	155	1,647	357	101	4,832	822	113
1978–79	3,558	576	143	1,524	344	106	4,563	720	118
1979–80	3,285	513	128	1,466	309	94	4,331	685	103
1980–81	3,178	460	115	1,286	294	79	3,870	592	131
1981–82	3,054	485	92	1,327	324	76	3,633	568	140
1982–83	2,871	360	106	1,367	281	68	3,349	506	129
1983–84	2,876	418	86	1,292	241	63	3,254	537	102
1984–85	2,991	385	74	1,411	240	58	3,415	505	115
1985–86	3,015	409	86	1,396	249	73	3,385	521	95
1986–87	3,057	421	85	1,363	234	70	3,445	504	104
1987–88 [1]	3,082	437	89	1,350	244	71	3,416	553	93
1988–89 [2]	3,286	462	81	1,429	261	59	3,750	550	103

[1] Revised from previously published data.
[2] Preliminary data.

SOURCE: U.S. Department of Education, National Center for Education Statistics, "Degrees and Other Formal Awards Conferred" surveys, and Integrated Postsecondary Education Data System (IPEDS), "Completions" survey. (This table was prepared February 1991.)

Table 263.—Earned degrees in the health professions[1] conferred by institutions of higher education, by level of degree and sex of student: 1970–71 to 1988–89

Year	Bachelor's degrees			Master's degrees			Doctor's degrees		
	Total	Men	Women	Total	Men	Women	Total	Men	Women
1	2	3	4	5	6	7	8	9	10
1970–71	25,190	5,764	19,426	5,445	2,401	3,044	459	384	75
1971–72	28,570	6,990	21,580	6,875	2,987	3,888	425	351	74
1972–73	33,523	7,744	25,779	7,879	3,304	4,575	643	483	160
1973–74	41,394	9,365	32,029	9,090	3,533	5,557	568	439	129
1974–75	48,858	10,855	38,003	9,901	3,710	6,191	609	437	172
1975–76	53,813	11,412	42,401	11,885	3,955	7,930	577	411	166
1976–77	57,122	11,887	45,235	12,323	3,910	8,413	538	366	172
1977–78	59,168	11,548	47,620	13,619	3,990	9,629	638	393	245
1978–79	61,819	11,161	50,658	14,781	4,223	10,558	705	447	258
1979–80	63,607	11,336	52,271	15,068	4,131	10,937	771	424	347
1980–81	63,348	10,464	52,884	16,004	4,151	11,853	827	469	358
1981–82	63,385	10,064	53,321	15,942	3,843	12,099	910	499	411
1982–83	64,614	10,204	54,410	17,068	4,232	12,836	1,155	649	506
1983–84	64,338	10,079	54,259	17,443	4,269	13,174	1,163	573	590
1984–85	64,513	9,786	54,727	17,383	4,135	13,248	1,199	565	634
1985–86	64,535	9,683	54,852	18,624	4,460	14,164	1,241	604	637
1986–87	63,206	9,177	54,029	18,426	3,887	14,539	1,213	564	649
1987–88 [2]	60,754	8,985	51,769	18,665	4,059	14,606	1,261	548	713
1988–89 [3]	59,111	8,926	50,185	19,255	4,210	15,045	1,439	612	827

[1] Includes degrees in health professions, general; hospital and health care administration; nursing; dental specialties; medical specialties; occupational therapy; optometry; pharmacy; physical therapy; dental hygiene; public health; medical record librarianship; podiatry or podiatric medicine; biomedical communication; veterinary medicine specialties; speech pathology and audiology; chiropractic; medical laboratory technologies; dental technologies; radiologic technologies; and other health professions. Excludes first-professional degrees that require at least 6 years for completion (including at least 2 years of preprofessional training) in dentistry, medicine, optometry, osteopathic medicine, pharmacy, podiatry or podiatric medicine, veterinary medicine, and chiropractic.

[2] Revised from previously published data.
[3] Preliminary data.

SOURCE: U.S. Department of Education, National Center for Education Statistics, "Degrees and Other Formal Awards Conferred" surveys, and Integrated Postsecondary Education Data System (IPEDS), "Completions" survey. (This table was prepared February 1991.)

Table 264.—Earned degrees in the life sciences[1] conferred by institutions of higher education, by level of degree and sex of student: 1951–52 to 1988–89

Year	Bachelor's degrees			Master's degrees			Doctor's degrees		
	Total	Men	Women	Total	Men	Women	Total	Men	Women
1	2	3	4	5	6	7	8	9	10
1951–52	11,094	8,212	2,882	2,307	1,908	399	764	680	84
1953–54	9,279	6,710	2,569	1,610	1,287	323	1,077	977	100
1955–56	12,423	9,515	2,908	1,759	1,379	380	1,025	908	117
1957–58	14,308	11,159	3,149	1,852	1,448	404	1,125	987	138
1959–60	15,576	11,654	3,922	2,154	1,668	486	1,205	1,086	119
1961–62	16,915	12,136	4,779	2,642	1,982	660	1,338	1,179	159
1963–64	22,723	16,321	6,402	3,296	2,348	948	1,625	1,432	193
1965–66	26,916	19,368	7,548	4,232	3,085	1,147	2,097	1,792	305
1967–68	31,826	22,986	8,840	5,506	3,959	1,547	2,784	2,345	439
1969–70	37,389	27,004	10,385	5,800	3,975	1,825	3,289	2,820	469
1970–71	35,743	25,333	10,410	5,728	3,805	1,923	3,645	3,050	595
1971–72	37,293	26,323	10,970	6,101	4,087	2,014	3,653	3,031	622
1972–73	42,233	29,636	12,597	6,263	4,354	1,909	3,636	2,926	710
1973–74	48,340	33,245	15,095	6,552	4,555	1,997	3,439	2,740	699
1974–75	51,741	34,612	17,129	6,550	4,587	1,963	3,384	2,641	743
1975–76	54,275	35,520	18,755	6,582	4,497	2,085	3,392	2,663	729
1976–77	53,605	34,218	19,387	7,114	4,718	2,396	3,397	2,671	726
1977–78	51,502	31,705	19,797	6,806	4,400	2,406	3,309	2,511	798
1978–79	48,846	29,191	19,655	6,831	4,265	2,566	3,542	2,636	906
1979–80	46,370	26,828	19,542	6,510	4,098	2,412	3,636	2,690	946
1980–81	43,216	24,149	19,067	5,978	3,654	2,324	3,718	2,666	1,052
1981–82	41,639	22,754	18,885	5,874	3,426	2,448	3,743	2,654	1,089
1982–83	39,982	21,564	18,418	5,696	3,214	2,482	3,341	2,266	1,075
1983–84	38,640	20,558	18,082	5,406	2,996	2,410	3,437	2,381	1,056
1984–85	38,445	20,064	18,381	5,059	2,647	2,412	3,432	2,307	1,125
1985–86	38,524	19,993	18,531	5,013	2,616	2,397	3,358	2,229	1,129
1986–87	38,114	19,641	18,473	4,954	2,539	2,415	3,423	2,226	1,197
1987–88[2]	36,755	18,245	18,510	4,784	2,423	2,361	3,629	2,349	1,280
1988–89[3]	36,079	17,970	18,109	4,933	2,484	2,449	3,533	2,235	1,298

[1] Includes degrees in anatomy, bacteriology, biochemistry, biology, botany, entomology, physiology, zoology, and other biological sciences.
[2] Revised from previously published data.
[3] Preliminary data.

SOURCE: U.S. Department of Education, National Center for Education Statistics, "Degrees and Other Formal Awards Conferred" surveys, and Integrated Postsecondary Education Data System (IPEDS), "Completions" survey. (This table was prepared February 1991.)

Table 265.—Earned degrees in biology, zoology, and microbiology conferred by institutions of higher education, by level of degree: 1970–71 to 1988–89

Year	Biology, general			Zoology[1]			Microbiology		
	Bachelor's	Master's	Doctor's	Bachelor's	Master's	Doctor's	Bachelor's	Master's	Doctor's
1	2	3	4	5	6	7	8	9	10
1970–71	26,294	2,665	536	5,768	1,255	1,235	1,122	382	323
1971–72	27,473	2,943	580	5,570	1,260	1,228	1,263	416	326
1972–73	31,185	2,959	627	5,808	1,263	1,113	1,567	454	318
1973–74	36,188	3,186	657	6,238	1,347	1,012	1,907	448	348
1974–75	38,748	3,109	637	6,224	1,339	1,047	2,394	490	324
1975–76	40,163	3,177	624	6,214	1,268	1,030	2,485	529	336
1976–77	39,530	3,322	608	5,716	1,311	1,056	2,492	581	309
1977–78	37,598	3,094	664	5,236	1,296	978	2,355	530	338
1978–79	35,962	3,093	663	5,008	1,277	1,050	2,342	512	367
1979–80	33,523	2,911	718	4,447	1,202	1,079	2,347	545	348
1980–81	31,323	2,598	734	4,020	1,198	1,076	2,227	438	351
1981–82	29,651	2,579	678	3,770	1,135	1,059	2,215	430	338
1982–83	28,022	2,354	521	3,578	1,005	911	2,141	406	319
1983–84	27,379	2,313	617	3,440	960	928	2,214	413	351
1984–85	27,593	2,130	658	3,287	895	909	2,091	378	295
1985–86	27,618	2,173	574	3,140	936	930	2,164	342	328
1986–87	27,458	2,022	537	3,032	833	900	2,057	360	325
1987–88[2]	26,838	1,981	576	2,786	818	902	1,983	338	379
1988–89[3]	26,251	2,120	529	2,768	822	866	1,755	369	351

[1] Zoology includes general zoology, entomology, genetics, pathology, pharmacology, physiology, and zoology, other.
[2] Revised from previously published data.
[3] Preliminary data.

SOURCE: U.S. Department of Education, National Center for Education Statistics, "Degrees and Other Formal Awards Conferred" surveys, and Integrated Postsecondary Education Data System (IPEDS), "Completions" survey. (This table was prepared February 1991.)

Table 266.—Earned degrees in mathematics[1] conferred by institutions of higher education, by level of degree and sex of student: 1949–50 to 1988–89

Year	Bachelor's degrees			Master's degrees			Doctor's degrees		
	Total	Men	Women	Total	Men	Women	Total	Men	Women
1	2	3	4	5	6	7	8	9	10
1949–50	6,382	4,942	1,440	974	784	190	160	151	9
1959–60	11,399	8,293	3,106	1,757	1,422	335	303	285	18
1967–68	23,513	14,782	8,731	5,527	4,199	1,328	947	895	52
1969–70	27,442	17,177	10,265	5,636	3,966	1,670	1,236	1,140	96
1970–71	24,801	15,369	9,432	5,191	3,673	1,518	1,199	1,106	93
1971–72	23,713	14,454	9,259	5,198	3,655	1,543	1,128	1,039	89
1972–73	23,067	13,796	9,271	5,028	3,525	1,503	1,068	966	102
1973–74	21,635	12,791	8,844	4,834	3,337	1,497	1,031	931	100
1974–75	18,181	10,586	7,595	4,327	2,905	1,422	975	865	110
1975–76	15,984	9,475	6,509	3,857	2,547	1,310	856	762	94
1976–77	14,196	8,303	5,893	3,695	2,396	1,299	823	714	109
1977–78	12,569	7,398	5,171	3,373	2,228	1,145	805	681	124
1978–79	11,806	6,899	4,907	3,036	1,985	1,051	730	608	122
1979–80	11,378	6,562	4,816	2,860	1,828	1,032	724	624	100
1980–81	11,078	6,342	4,736	2,567	1,692	875	728	614	114
1981–82	11,599	6,593	5,006	2,727	1,821	906	681	587	94
1982–83	12,453	6,995	5,458	2,837	1,858	979	698	582	116
1983–84	13,211	7,366	5,845	2,741	1,791	950	695	569	126
1984–85	15,146	8,164	6,982	2,882	1,874	1,008	699	590	109
1985–86	16,306	8,725	7,581	3,159	2,047	1,112	742	618	124
1986–87	16,489	8,834	7,655	3,321	2,024	1,297	725	599	126
1987–88[2]	15,904	8,523	7,381	3,442	2,066	1,376	750	625	125
1988–89[3]	15,237	8,221	7,016	3,424	2,058	1,366	882	711	171

[1] Includes degrees conferred in statistics.
[2] Revised from previously published data.
[3] Preliminary data.

SOURCE: U.S. Department of Education, National Center for Education Statistics, "Degrees and Other Formal Awards Conferred" surveys, and Integrated Postsecondary Education Data System (IPEDS), "Completions" survey. (This table was prepared February 1991.)

Table 267.—Earned degrees in the physical sciences[1] conferred by institutions of higher education, by level of degree and sex of student: 1959–60 to 1988–89

Year	Bachelor's degrees			Master's degrees			Doctor's degrees		
	Total	Men	Women	Total	Men	Women	Total	Men	Women
1	2	3	4	5	6	7	8	9	10
1959–60	16,007	14,013	1,994	3,376	3,049	327	1,838	1,776	62
1967–68	19,380	16,739	2,641	5,499	4,869	630	3,593	3,405	188
1969–70	21,439	18,522	2,917	5,935	5,093	842	4,312	4,077	235
1970–71	21,412	18,459	2,953	6,367	5,521	846	4,390	4,144	246
1971–72	20,745	17,663	3,082	6,287	5,404	883	4,103	3,830	273
1972–73	20,696	17,626	3,070	6,257	5,414	843	4,006	3,738	268
1973–74	21,178	17,674	3,504	6,062	5,186	876	3,626	3,373	253
1974–75	20,778	16,992	3,786	5,807	4,969	838	3,626	3,325	301
1975–76	21,465	17,353	4,112	5,466	4,648	818	3,431	3,132	299
1976–77	22,497	17,996	4,501	5,331	4,450	881	3,341	3,022	319
1977–78	22,986	18,090	4,896	5,561	4,620	941	3,133	2,821	312
1978–79	23,207	17,985	5,222	5,451	4,461	990	3,102	2,752	350
1979–80	23,410	17,864	5,546	5,219	4,248	971	3,089	2,705	384
1980–81	23,952	18,064	5,888	5,284	4,200	1,084	3,141	2,765	376
1981–82	24,052	17,866	6,186	5,514	4,318	1,196	3,286	2,835	451
1982–83	23,405	17,016	6,389	5,290	4,157	1,133	3,269	2,811	458
1983–84	23,671	17,134	6,537	5,576	4,268	1,308	3,306	2,815	491
1984–85	23,732	17,095	6,637	5,796	4,452	1,344	3,403	2,851	552
1985–86	21,731	15,769	5,962	5,902	4,470	1,432	3,551	2,963	588
1986–87	19,974	14,302	5,672	5,652	4,243	1,409	3,672	3,038	634
1987–88[2]	17,806	12,389	5,417	5,733	4,324	1,409	3,809	3,123	686
1988–89[3]	17,204	12,097	5,107	5,737	4,204	1,533	3,852	3,093	759

[1] Includes degrees in astronomy, chemistry, geology, metallurgy, meteorology, physics, science technologies, and other physical sciences.
[2] Revised from previously published data.
[3] Preliminary data.

SOURCE: U.S. Department of Education, National Center for Education Statistics, "Degrees and Other Formal Awards Conferred" surveys, and Integrated Postsecondary Education Data System (iPEDS), "Completions" survey. (This table was prepared February 1991.)

Table 268.—Earned degrees in chemistry, physics, and geology conferred by institutions of higher education, by level of degree: 1970–71 to 1988–89

Year	Chemistry			Physics			Geology[1]		
	Bachelor's	Master's	Doctor's	Bachelor's	Master's	Doctor's	Bachelor's	Master's	Doctor's
1	2	3	4	5	6	7	8	9	10
1970–71	11,063	2,275	2,159	5,071	2,188	1,482	2,414	651	324
1971–72	10,590	2,248	1,971	4,634	2,033	1,344	2,573	841	310
1972–73	10,128	2,225	1,872	4,259	1,747	1,338	2,923	827	305
1973–74	10,438	2,125	1,823	3,952	1,655	1,115	3,253	938	315
1974–75	10,549	1,986	1,822	3,706	1,574	1,080	3,319	932	292
1975–76	11,022	1,783	1,621	3,544	1,451	997	3,358	1,003	313
1976–77	11,215	1,767	1,568	3,420	1,319	945	3,879	1,047	325
1977–78	11,315	1,886	1,521	3,330	1,294	873	4,342	1,239	268
1978–79	11,509	1,757	1,516	3,337	1,319	918	4,502	1,300	286
1979–80	11,232	1,723	1,545	3,396	1,192	830	4,597	1,295	313
1980–81	11,347	1,654	1,622	3,441	1,294	866	5,202	1,396	294
1981–82	11,025	1,618	1,595	3,472	1,282	863	5,538	1,540	282
1982–83	10,796	1,622	1,746	3,793	1,369	873	6,102	1,552	295
1983–84	10,704	1,667	1,744	3,907	1,532	953	6,549	1,514	315
1984–85	10,482	1,719	1,789	4,097	1,523	951	6,308	1,692	289
1985–86	10,116	1,754	1,908	4,180	1,501	1,010	4,974	1,767	271
1986–87	9,661	1,738	1,976	4,330	1,563	1,086	3,665	1,603	280
1987–88[2]	9,052	1,708	1,995	4,100	1,675	1,093	2,551	1,523	350
1988–89[3]	8,654	1,785	2,034	4,339	1,736	1,111	2,249	1,408	358

[1] Includes geology, geochemistry, and geophysics and seismology. Beginning in 1982–83, also includes other geological sciences.

[2] Revised from previously published data.

[3] Preliminary data.

SOURCE: U.S. Department of Education, National Center for Education Statistics, "Degrees and Other Formal Awards Conferred" surveys, and Integrated Postsecondary Education Data System (IPEDS), "Completions" survey. (This table was prepared February 1991.)

Table 269.—Earned degrees in psychology conferred by institutions of higher education, by level of degree and by sex of student: 1949–50 to 1988–89

Year	Bachelor's degrees			Master's degrees			Doctor's degrees		
	Total	Men	Women	Total	Men	Women	Total	Men	Women
1	2	3	4	5	6	7	8	9	10
1949–50	9,569	6,055	3,514	1,316	948	368	283	241	42
1959–60	8,061	4,773	3,288	1,406	981	425	641	544	97
1967–68	23,819	13,792	10,027	3,479	2,321	1,158	1,268	982	286
1969–70	33,606	19,042	14,564	4,111	2,549	1,562	1,668	1,296	372
1970–71	37,880	21,029	16,851	4,431	2,783	1,648	1,782	1,355	427
1971–72	43,093	23,159	19,934	5,289	3,259	2,030	1,881	1,414	467
1972–73	47,695	24,976	22,719	5,831	3,495	2,336	2,089	1,484	605
1973–74	51,821	25,705	26,116	6,588	3,971	2,617	2,336	1,645	691
1974–75	50,988	24,190	26,798	7,066	4,044	3,022	2,442	1,688	754
1975–76	49,908	22,832	27,076	7,811	4,171	3,640	2,581	1,762	819
1976–77	47,373	20,553	26,820	8,301	4,313	3,988	2,761	1,770	991
1977–78	44,559	18,348	26,211	8,160	3,919	4,241	2,587	1,621	966
1978–79	42,461	16,464	25,997	8,003	3,672	4,331	2,662	1,597	1,065
1979–80	41,962	15,419	26,543	7,806	3,376	4,430	2,768	1,602	1,166
1980–81	40,833	14,295	26,538	7,998	3,358	4,640	2,955	1,681	1,274
1981–82	41,031	13,623	27,408	7,791	3,209	4,582	2,780	1,518	1,262
1982–83	40,364	13,105	27,259	8,378	3,238	5,140	3,108	1,621	1,487
1983–84	39,872	12,792	27,080	8,002	2,961	5,041	2,973	1,517	1,456
1984–85	39,811	12,694	27,117	8,408	3,044	5,364	2,908	1,492	1,416
1985–86	40,521	12,578	27,943	8,293	2,923	5,370	3,088	1,497	1,591
1986–87	42,868	13,332	29,536	8,204	2,856	5,348	3,123	1,458	1,665
1987–88[1]	45,003	13,497	31,506	7,872	2,593	5,279	2,987	1,363	1,624
1988–89[2]	48,516	14,181	34,335	8,579	2,799	5,780	3,263	1,429	1,834

[1] Revised from previously published data.

[2] Preliminary data.

SOURCE: U.S. Department of Education, National Center for Education Statistics, "Degrees and Other Formal Awards Conferred" surveys, and Integrated Postsecondary Education Data System (IPEDS), "Completions" survey. (This table was prepared February 1991.)

Table 270.—Earned degrees in public affairs and services[1] conferred by institutions of higher education, by level of degree and sex of student: 1970–71 to 1988–89

Year	Bachelor's degrees			Master's degrees			Doctor's degrees		
	Total	Men	Women	Total	Men	Women	Total	Men	Women
1	2	3	4	5	6	7	8	9	10
1970–71	6,252	2,489	3,763	8,215	4,176	4,039	185	141	44
1971–72	8,221	3,260	4,961	9,183	4,780	4,403	219	170	49
1972–73	11,346	4,587	6,759	10,899	5,767	5,132	214	174	40
1973–74	12,671	4,890	7,781	12,077	6,455	5,622	214	165	49
1974–75	14,730	5,465	9,265	14,610	7,747	6,863	271	200	71
1975–76	16,751	6,776	9,975	16,117	8,421	7,696	298	198	100
1976–77	17,627	6,705	10,922	17,917	9,251	8,666	316	210	106
1977–78	18,082	6,146	11,936	18,341	9,033	9,308	385	256	129
1978–79	18,882	6,009	12,873	18,300	8,547	9,753	344	233	111
1979–80	18,422	5,650	12,772	18,413	8,261	10,152	372	241	131
1980–81	18,714	5,670	13,044	18,524	7,790	10,734	388	226	162
1981–82	18,739	5,733	13,006	18,216	7,314	10,902	389	210	179
1982–83	16,290	4,910	11,380	16,245	6,112	10,133	347	184	163
1983–84	14,396	4,592	9,804	15,373	5,869	9,504	421	231	190
1984–85	13,838	4,635	9,203	16,045	5,938	10,107	431	213	218
1985–86	13,878	4,670	9,208	16,300	6,108	10,192	385	174	211
1986–87	14,161	4,537	9,624	17,032	6,191	10,841	398	216	182
1987–88[2]	14,294	4,545	9,749	17,290	6,359	10,931	470	238	232
1988–89[3]	15,254	4,948	10,306	17,928	6,398	11,530	417	208	209

[1] Includes degrees in community services, general; public administration; management; social work and helping services; international public service; transportation and public utilities; clinical social work; and other public affairs and services.
[2] Revised from previously published data.
[3] Preliminary data.

SOURCE: U.S. Department of Education, National Center for Education Statistics, "Degrees and Other Formal Awards Conferred" surveys, and Integrated Postsecondary Education Data System (IPEDS), "Completions" survey. (This table was prepared February 1991.)

Table 271.—Earned degrees in the social sciences[1] conferred by institutions of higher education, by level of degree and sex of student: 1970–71 to 1988–89

Year	Bachelor's degrees			Master's degrees			Doctor's degrees		
	Total	Men	Women	Total	Men	Women	Total	Men	Women
1	2	3	4	5	6	7	8	9	10
1970–71	155,236	98,090	57,146	16,476	11,779	4,697	3,659	3,152	507
1971–72	158,037	100,879	57,158	17,416	12,517	4,899	4,078	3,480	598
1972–73	155,922	99,704	56,218	17,288	12,529	4,759	4,230	3,569	661
1973–74	150,298	95,637	54,661	17,249	12,289	4,960	4,123	3,382	741
1974–75	135,165	84,813	50,352	16,892	11,826	5,066	4,209	3,332	877
1975–76	126,287	78,623	47,664	15,824	10,831	4,993	4,154	3,259	895
1976–77	116,879	71,006	45,873	15,395	10,340	5,055	3,784	2,949	835
1977–78	112,827	67,144	45,683	14,578	9,751	4,827	3,583	2,713	870
1978–79	107,922	62,765	45,157	12,807	8,300	4,507	3,358	2,492	866
1979–80	103,519	58,434	45,085	12,101	7,746	4,355	3,219	2,347	872
1980–81	100,345	56,039	44,306	11,855	7,403	4,452	3,114	2,269	845
1981–82	99,545	55,111	44,434	11,892	7,408	4,484	3,061	2,237	824
1982–83	95,088	52,708	42,380	11,112	6,916	4,196	2,931	2,042	889
1983–84	93,212	52,102	41,110	10,465	6,496	3,969	2,911	2,030	881
1984–85	91,461	51,172	40,289	10,380	6,400	3,980	2,851	1,933	918
1985–86	93,703	52,654	41,049	10,428	6,339	4,089	2,955	1,970	985
1986–87	96,185	53,879	42,306	10,397	6,294	4,103	2,916	2,026	890
1987–88[2]	100,288	56,297	43,991	10,294	6,237	4,057	2,781	1,849	932
1988–89[3]	107,714	59,924	47,790	10,854	6,493	4,361	2,878	1,939	939

[1] Includes degrees in social sciences, general; anthropology; archeology; economics; history; geography; political science and government; sociology; criminology; international relations; urban studies; demography; and other social sciences.
[2] Revised from previously data.
[3] Preliminary data.

SOURCE: U.S. Department of Education, National Center for Education Statistics, "Degrees and Other Formal Awards Conferred" surveys, and Integrated Postsecondary Education Data System (IPEDS), "Completions" survey. (This table was prepared February 1991.)

Table 272.—Earned degrees in economics, history, political science and government, and sociology conferred by institutions of higher education, by level of degree: 1949–50 to 1988–89

Year	Economics			History			Political science and government [1]			Sociology		
	Bache-lor's	Master's	Doctor's	Bache-lor's	Master's	Doctor's	Bache-lor's	Master's	Doctor's	Bache-lor's	Master's	Doctor's
1	2	3	4	5	6	7	8	9	10	11	12	13
1949–50	14,568	921	200	13,542	1,801	275	6,336	710	127	7,870	552	98
1951–52	8,593	695	239	10,187	1,445	317	4,911	525	147	6,648	517	141
1953–54	6,719	609	245	9,363	1,220	355	5,314	534	153	5,692	440	184
1955–56	6,555	581	232	10,510	1,114	259	5,633	509	203	5,878	402	170
1957–58	7,457	669	239	12,840	1,397	297	6,116	665	170	6,568	397	150
1959–60	7,453	708	237	14,737	1,794	342	6,596	722	201	7,147	440	161
1961–62	8,366	853	268	17,340	2,163	343	8,326	839	214	8,120	578	173
1963–64	10,583	1,104	385	23,668	2,705	507	12,126	1,163	263	10,943	646	198
1965–66	11,555	1,522	458	28,612	3,883	599	15,242	1,429	336	15,038	981	244
1967–68	15,193	1,916	600	35,291	4,845	688	20,387	1,937	457	21,710	1,193	367
1969–70	17,197	1,988	794	43,386	5,049	1,038	25,713	2,105	525	30,436	1,813	534
1970–71	15,758	1,995	721	44,663	5,157	991	27,482	2,318	700	33,263	1,808	574
1971–72	15,231	2,224	794	43,695	5,217	1,133	28,135	2,451	758	35,216	1,944	636
1972–73	14,770	2,225	845	40,943	5,030	1,140	30,100	2,398	747	35,436	1,923	583
1973–74	14,285	2,141	788	37,049	4,533	1,114	30,744	2,448	766	35,491	2,196	632
1974–75	14,046	2,127	815	31,470	4,226	1,117	29,126	2,333	680	31,488	2,112	693
1975–76	14,741	2,087	763	28,400	3,658	1,014	28,302	2,191	723	27,634	2,009	729
1976–77	15,296	2,158	758	25,433	3,393	921	26,411	2,222	641	24,713	1,830	714
1977–78	15,661	1,995	706	23,004	3,033	813	26,069	2,069	636	22,750	1,611	599
1978–79	16,409	1,955	712	21,019	2,536	756	25,628	2,037	563	20,285	1,415	612
1979–80	17,863	1,821	677	19,301	2,367	712	25,457	1,938	535	18,881	1,341	583
1980–81	18,753	1,911	727	18,301	2,237	643	24,977	1,875	484	17,272	1,240	610
1981–82	19,876	1,964	677	17,146	2,210	636	25,658	1,954	513	16,042	1,145	558
1982–83	20,517	1,972	734	16,465	2,040	575	25,791	1,829	435	14,105	1,112	522
1983–84	20,719	1,891	729	16,642	1,937	561	25,719	1,769	457	13,145	1,008	520
1984–85	20,711	1,992	749	16,048	1,921	468	25,834	1,500	441	11,968	1,022	480
1985–86	21,602	1,937	789	16,413	1,959	497	26,439	1,704	439	12,271	965	504
1986–87	22,387	1,855	750	16,988	2,023	534	26,834	1,618	435	12,231	950	451
1987–88 [2]	22,911	1,847	770	18,207	2,090	517	27,207	1,579	391	13,024	984	452
1988–89 [3]	23,502	1,870	834	20,098	2,110	480	30,348	1,593	451	14,329	1,143	450

[1] Excludes degrees in public administration and international relations.
[2] Revised from previously published data.
[3] Preliminary data.

SOURCE: U.S. Department of Education, National Center for Education Statistics, "Degrees and Other Formal Awards Conferred" surveys, and Integrated Postsecondary Education Data System (IPEDS), "Completions" survey. (This table was prepared February 1991.)

Table 273.—Earned degrees in visual and performing arts [1] conferred by institutions of higher education, by level of degree and sex of student: 1970–71 to 1988–89

Year	Bachelor's degrees			Master's degrees			Doctor's degrees		
	Total	Men	Women	Total	Men	Women	Total	Men	Women
1	2	3	4	5	6	7	8	9	10
1970–71	30,394	12,256	18,138	6,675	3,510	3,165	621	483	138
1971–72	33,831	13,580	20,251	7,537	4,049	3,488	572	428	144
1972–73	36,017	14,267	21,750	7,254	4,005	3,249	616	449	167
1973–74	39,730	15,821	23,909	8,001	4,325	3,676	585	440	145
1974–75	40,782	15,532	25,250	8,362	4,448	3,914	649	446	203
1975–76	42,138	16,491	25,647	8,817	4,507	4,310	620	447	173
1976–77	41,793	16,166	25,627	8,636	4,211	4,425	662	447	215
1977–78	40,951	15,572	25,379	9,036	4,327	4,709	708	448	260
1978–79	40,969	15,380	25,589	8,524	3,933	4,591	700	454	246
1979–80	40,892	15,065	25,827	8,708	4,067	4,641	655	413	242
1980–81	40,479	14,798	25,681	8,629	4,056	4,573	654	396	258
1981–82	40,422	14,819	25,603	8,746	3,866	4,880	670	380	290
1982–83	39,469	14,699	24,770	8,742	4,011	4,731	692	404	288
1983–84	39,833	15,103	24,730	8,520	3,897	4,623	728	406	322
1984–85	37,936	14,506	23,430	8,714	3,897	4,817	693	407	286
1985–86	36,949	14,284	22,665	8,416	3,775	4,641	722	396	326
1986–87	36,223	13,783	22,440	8,506	3,757	4,749	792	447	345
1987–88 [2]	36,638	14,127	22,511	7,937	3,445	4,492	725	424	301
1988–89 [3]	37,781	14,558	23,223	8,234	3,598	4,636	755	443	312

[1] Includes degrees in fine arts, general; art; art history and appreciation; music (performing composition, theory); music (liberal arts program); music history and appreciation; dramatic arts; dance; applied design; cinematography; photography; and other fine and applied arts.
[2] Revised from previously published data.
[3] Preliminary data.

SOURCE: U.S. Department of Education, National Center for Education Statistics, "Degrees and Other Formal Awards Conferred" surveys, and Integrated Postsecondary Education Data System (IPEDS), "Completions" survey. (This table was prepared February 1991.)

Table 274.—Statistical profile of persons receiving doctor's degrees,[1] by field of study: 1988–89

Item	All fields	Field of Study								
		Education	Engineering	Humanities	Life sciences	Mathematics	Physical sciences[3]	Business and management	Social sciences and psychology	Other professional fields
1	2	3	4	5	6	7	8	9	10	11
Doctor's degrees conferred (number)	**34,319**	**6,265**	**4,536**	**3,558**	**6,343**	**861**	**5,460**	**1,071**	**5,955**	**1,131**
Sex (percent)										
Men	63.5	42.5	91.8	54.5	61.8	81.9	81.2	73.9	54.8	56.6
Women	36.5	57.5	8.2	45.5	38.2	18.1	18.8	26.1	45.2	43.4
Racial/ethnic group (percent)[2]										
American Indian	0.4	0.4	0.3	0.2	0.3	0.0	0.5	0.1	0.4	0.7
Asian	5.1	1.9	16.2	2.9	5.2	5.6	7.2	6.7	3.1	3.4
Black	3.8	8.0	1.4	2.8	2.1	1.9	1.3	2.2	4.3	6.4
Mexican-American	0.7	0.9	0.6	0.8	0.5	0.5	0.4	0.3	1.0	0.6
Puerto Rican	0.7	1.0	0.3	0.8	0.6	0.9	0.7	0.1	0.8	0.5
Other Hispanic	1.3	1.2	1.2	2.1	1.0	1.2	1.3	1.0	1.5	1.3
White	86.2	85.7	77.4	88.2	88.3	86.2	86.0	87.5	87.5	86.4
Other and unknown	1.8	0.9	2.5	2.3	2.0	3.7	2.6	2.1	1.6	0.9
Citizenship (percent)										
United States	67.5	82.9	40.9	76.4	71.1	45.6	59.0	61.5	70.4	73.3
Foreign	23.9	9.7	50.4	15.5	22.1	43.9	32.9	30.8	17.3	16.7
Unknown	8.6	7.4	8.8	8.1	6.9	10.5	8.0	7.7	12.2	9.9
Median age at doctorate (years)	33.8	41.1	31.1	35.7	32.2	30.7	30.2	35.1	33.9	38.5
Percent with bachelor's degree in same field as doctorate	54.2	38.5	76.2	55.5	53.4	68.5	66.2	34.2	52.3	23.5
Median time lapse from bachelor's to doctorate (years)										
Total time	10.5	17.3	8.1	12.5	9.1	7.8	7.3	11.7	10.3	14.7
Registered time	6.9	8.2	6.0	8.4	6.5	6.2	6.1	7.0	7.4	8.1
Postdoctoral activities (percent)										
Postdoctoral study plans	22.7	4.1	19.4	5.9	51.4	23.3	41.8	2.7	14.1	3.7
Fellowship	11.3	1.6	5.8	3.5	29.7	10.7	17.8	0.7	8.4	1.5
Research associateship	9.0	1.3	11.7	1.1	16.3	9.4	22.4	1.1	2.7	1.3
Traineeship	1.0	0.3	1.4	0.2	1.4	2.2	0.9	0.6	1.6	0.6
Other	1.5	0.9	0.5	1.1	4.1	1.0	0.8	0.3	1.3	0.4
Planned postdoctoral employment	65.8	85.8	67.8	82.7	39.4	62.8	47.5	86.9	71.1	83.8
Educational institution	39.0	63.3	23.1	67.6	20.5	49.5	20.0	75.7	36.7	52.7
Industry, business	13.5	6.0	34.6	4.3	8.3	7.4	20.9	7.9	11.2	8.9
Government	6.3	8.2	7.0	2.1	6.1	3.4	4.4	1.6	9.5	5.3
Nonprofit organization	4.2	5.0	1.2	4.9	2.6	0.7	0.6	0.6	9.0	14.0
Other and unknown	2.8	3.3	1.9	3.8	1.9	1.9	1.5	1.1	4.8	2.9
Postdoctoral status unknown	11.4	10.2	12.8	11.4	9.2	13.8	10.7	10.4	14.8	12.5
Definite postdoctoral study	16.9	2.2	11.7	3.4	41.3	16.4	32.3	1.8	9.7	2.3
Seeking postdoctoral study	5.8	1.8	7.7	2.4	10.1	7.0	9.5	0.9	4.3	1.4
Definite employment	48.5	65.5	46.8	56.9	29.3	45.2	36.0	72.7	51.6	64.5
Seeking employment	17.3	20.2	21.0	25.8	10.1	17.7	11.5	14.2	19.6	19.3
Primary activity (percent)										
Research and development	28.9	5.8	63.5	7.0	44.0	36.2	59.4	34.1	24.4	11.0
Teaching	36.9	36.3	20.0	72.4	28.5	53.0	26.8	54.0	29.8	50.6
Administration	12.6	36.7	1.7	4.5	6.1	2.1	2.1	3.0	6.2	12.2
Professional services	12.4	11.1	6.0	5.0	11.4	2.6	3.8	1.9	31.4	15.6
Other	3.1	2.8	2.4	5.2	4.0	0.8	2.4	1.8	2.5	4.3
Region of employment after doctorate (percent)										
New England	6.1	6.2	4.8	7.5	4.6	7.5	6.5	6.5	7.1	3.5
Middle Atlantic	14.4	15.1	13.9	13.8	10.5	11.8	17.4	13.0	14.9	13.7
East North Central	12.7	12.7	12.4	14.2	10.2	15.9	12.6	16.7	12.5	13.5
West North Central	6.3	7.9	4.1	5.5	7.1	5.4	5.0	6.3	6.6	7.1
South Atlantic	15.1	16.0	11.5	15.1	15.6	14.9	13.8	15.4	17.0	14.8
East South Central	4.6	5.4	3.2	5.1	4.8	4.1	3.9	7.7	3.1	5.9
West South Central	7.8	8.3	8.0	6.8	7.4	8.7	8.5	9.4	6.6	10.8
Mountain	5.0	5.7	5.2	4.6	4.3	3.9	4.8	4.5	4.6	5.0
Pacific and insular	10.6	8.7	13.4	10.7	10.7	8.5	13.6	9.1	10.2	7.3
Foreign	9.8	5.1	16.7	7.9	18.1	12.9	8.4	8.3	9.0	9.7
Region unknown	7.6	8.9	6.8	8.9	6.8	6.4	5.5	3.1	8.3	8.6

[1] Includes Ph.D., Ed.D., and comparable degrees at the doctoral level. Excludes first-professional degrees, such as M.D., D.D.S., and D.V.M.

[2] Includes 2,952 individuals who did not report their citizenship at time of doctorate.

[3] Includes mathematics, computer science, physics and astronomy, chemistry, and earth, atmospheric, and marine science.

NOTE.—The above classification of degrees by field differs somewhat from that in most publications of the National Center for Education Statistics (NCES). The major differences are that history is included under humanities rather than social sciences and that psychology is included under social sciences. The number of degrees also differs slightly from that reported in the NCES "Degrees and Other Formal Awards Conferred" survey. The above tabulation excludes some non-research doctorate degrees such as doctor's degrees in theology. Because of rounding, percents may not add to 100.0.

SOURCE: National Academy of Sciences, National Research Council, Office of Scientific and Engineering Personnel, *Summary Report 1989: Doctorate Recipients From United States Universities.* (This table was prepared February 1991.)

Table 275.—Statistical profile of persons receiving doctor's degrees in education: 1978–79 to 1988–89

Item	1978–79	1979–80	1980–81	1981–82	1982–83	1983–84	1984–85	1985–86	1986–87	1987–88	1988–89
1	2	3	4	5	6	7	8	9	10	11	12
Number of doctorates	7,370	7,576	7,489	7,226	7,147	6,780	6,717	6,602	6,447	6,349	6,265
Sex (percent)											
Men	57.9	55.5	52.8	51.2	49.6	49.0	48.2	45.6	44.9	44.8	42.5
Women	42.1	44.5	47.2	48.8	50.4	51.0	51.8	54.4	55.1	55.2	57.5
Racial/ethnic group (percent) [1]											
American Indian	0.9	0.8	0.6	0.5	0.7	0.5	0.7	0.5	0.7	0.6	0.4
Asian	1.3	1.3	1.8	1.7	1.9	1.5	1.7	1.6	1.7	2.4	1.9
Black	8.6	8.8	8.8	9.5	8.1	8.5	8.6	8.0	7.3	7.5	8.0
Mexican-American	(2)	0.8	1.1	1.2	1.3	1.2	1.2	1.4	1.3	1.2	0.9
Puerto Rican	(2)	0.4	0.6	0.7	0.7	0.6	1.0	0.9	0.9	0.8	1.0
Other Hispanic	(2)	1.1	0.7	1.0	0.9	0.8	1.0	1.3	1.3	0.9	1.2
White	81.7	83.1	83.1	83.6	84.8	85.1	84.5	84.8	85.1	85.3	85.7
Other and unknown	5.0	3.7	3.3	1.8	1.7	1.8	1.4	1.6	1.6	1.2	0.9
Citizenship (percent)											
United States	88.8	88.7	87.7	86.6	87.1	86.8	85.5	84.7	84.9	83.1	82.9
Foreign	8.1	8.2	8.8	9.9	9.8	9.8	10.4	9.6	9.2	10.2	9.7
Unknown	3.1	3.1	3.6	3.5	3.1	3.4	4.1	5.6	6.0	6.7	7.4
Median age at doctorate (years)	36.5	37.0	37.3	37.4	37.8	38.4	38.7	39.4	39.8	40.5	41.1
Percent with bachelor's degree in same field as doctorate	38.6	39.0	38.9	39.9	39.5	39.6	38.7	39.0	37.8	36.9	38.5
Median time lapse from bachelor's to doctorate (years)											
Total time	12.7	13.1	13.5	13.6	14.1	14.6	15.1	15.7	16.2	16.9	17.3
Registered time	6.6	6.9	7.0	7.2	7.4	7.6	7.6	7.8	7.9	8.1	8.2

[1] Longitudinal comparisons by race/ethnicity should be done with extreme care, due to periodic changes in the survey.
[2] Hispanic subcategories totaled 2.5 percent in 1978–79.

NOTE.—The National Research Council's classification of degrees by field differs somewhat from that in most publications of the National Center for Education Statistics (NCES). The number of degrees also differs slightly from that reported in the NCES "De-grees and Other Formal Awards Conferred" survey. Because of rounding, percents may not add to 100.0.

SOURCE: National Academy of Sciences, National Research Council, Office of Scientific and Engineering Personnel, *Doctorate Records File*. (This table was prepared March 1991.)

Table 276.—Statistical profile of persons receiving doctor's degrees in engineering: 1978–79 to 1988–89

Item	1978–79	1979–80	1980–81	1981–82	1982–83	1983–84	1984–85	1985–86	1986–87	1987–88	1988–89
1	2	3	4	5	6	7	8	9	10	11	12
Number of doctorates	2,494	2,479	2,528	2,644	2,780	2,915	3,165	3,376	3,716	4,190	4,536
Sex (percent)											
Men	97.5	96.4	96.1	95.3	95.5	94.8	93.7	93.3	93.5	93.2	91.8
Women	2.5	3.6	3.9	4.7	4.5	5.2	6.3	6.7	6.6	6.8	8.2
Racial/ethnic group (percent) [1]											
American Indian	0.2	0.2	0.3	0.2	0.1	0.2	0.1	0.3	0.4	0.2	0.3
Asian	18.9	17.9	19.2	16.8	16.7	16.5	17.6	15.2	17.1	15.5	16.2
Black	1.2	1.1	1.3	1.4	1.9	1.0	2.1	1.4	1.3	1.4	1.4
Mexican-American	(2)	0.1	0.1	0.3	0.3	0.4	0.4	0.3	0.4	0.5	0.6
Puerto Rican	(2)	0.2	0.3	0.7	0.4	0.5	0.3	0.6	0.2	0.6	0.3
Other Hispanic	(2)	1.5	0.6	1.4	1.3	1.4	0.7	1.1	1.1	1.8	1.2
White	71.4	73.5	74.4	75.2	76.1	76.4	74.5	78.3	76.2	77.0	77.4
Other and unknown	6.7	5.5	3.7	4.0	3.2	3.6	4.3	2.7	3.3	2.9	2.5
Citizenship (percent)											
United States	51.9	50.6	46.2	44.1	41.8	42.5	40.4	40.8	41.8	42.4	40.9
Foreign	45.6	46.3	49.1	50.1	53.5	52.9	54.6	50.8	50.7	49.8	50.4
Unknown	2.5	3.1	4.7	5.9	4.7	4.6	5.0	8.4	7.4	7.7	8.8
Median age at doctorate (years)	30.3	30.3	30.5	30.7	30.8	30.7	30.9	31.0	31.0	31.0	31.1
Percent with bachelor's degree in same field as doctorate	77.9	75.2	74.1	72.4	74.0	74.3	74.2	73.0	75.2	76.4	76.2
Median time lapse from bachelor's to doctorate (years)											
Total time	7.6	7.6	7.9	8.0	8.0	8.0	8.1	8.1	8.1	8.1	8.1
Registered time	5.5	5.6	5.6	5.8	5.7	5.8	5.8	5.9	5.9	5.9	6.0

[1] Longitudinal comparisons by race/ethnicity should be done with extreme care, due to periodic changes in the survey.
[2] Hispanic subcategories totaled 1.5 percent in 1978–79.

NOTE.—The National Research Council's classification of degrees by field differs somewhat from that in most publications of the National Center for Education Statistics (NCES). The number of degrees also differs slightly from that reported in the NCES "De-grees and Other Formal Awards Conferred" survey. Because of rounding, percents may not add to 100.0.

SOURCE: National Academy of Sciences, National Research Council, Office of Scientific and Engineering Personnel, *Doctorate Records File*. (This table was prepared March 1991.)

Table 277.—Statistical profile of persons receiving doctor's degrees in the humanities:
1978–79 to 1988–89

Item	1978–79	1979–80	1980–81	1981–82	1982–83	1983–84	1984–85	1985–86	1986–87	1987–88	1988–89
1	2	3	4	5	6	7	8	9	10	11	12
Number of doctorates	4,143	3,863	3,745	3,560	3,494	3,528	3,428	3,461	3,504	3,553	3,558
Sex (percent)											
Men	61.5	60.4	58.7	57.6	56.2	55.0	56.6	54.8	55.1	55.7	54.5
Women	38.5	39.6	41.3	42.4	43.8	45.0	43.4	45.2	44.9	44.3	45.5
Racial/ethnic group (percent) [1]											
American Indian	0.6	0.3	0.4	0.2	0.2	0.2	0.3	0.2	0.4	0.2	0.2
Asian	1.9	1.9	1.7	1.7	1.5	1.8	2.2	1.8	2.1	2.3	2.9
Black	3.4	2.9	2.8	3.3	2.5	3.3	2.5	2.8	2.8	3.0	2.8
Mexican-American	([2])	0.4	0.5	0.8	0.7	0.8	0.8	0.8	0.6	0.8	0.8
Puerto Rican	([2])	0.3	0.7	0.9	0.7	0.7	0.6	0.5	1.1	0.9	0.8
Other Hispanic	([2])	2.2	1.9	2.5	2.2	2.1	2.3	2.1	2.5	2.1	2.1
White	84.8	87.3	88.0	87.8	89.4	88.4	88.9	89.6	88.4	89.1	88.2
Other and unknown	5.9	4.6	4.1	2.8	2.7	2.7	2.4	2.2	2.2	1.6	2.2
Citizenship (percent)											
United States	88.2	87.3	85.7	84.7	85.3	83.7	83.1	78.8	78.0	78.4	76.4
Foreign	8.5	8.8	10.2	10.2	10.7	11.2	12.1	13.7	14.3	14.4	15.5
Unknown	3.3	3.9	4.1	5.1	4.0	5.2	4.8	7.4	7.7	7.1	8.1
Median age at doctorate (years)	33.0	33.4	33.5	34.0	34.0	34.5	34.7	35.0	35.0	35.4	35.7
Percent with bachelor's degree in same field as doctorate	62.3	64.2	61.0	61.1	58.4	60.2	58.8	58.2	58.5	56.7	55.5
Median time lapse from bachelor's to doctorate (years)											
Total time	10.3	10.6	10.8	11.2	11.1	11.5	11.7	12.1	12.0	12.2	12.5
Registered time	7.5	7.7	7.7	8.0	8.0	8.2	8.3	8.2	8.4	8.5	8.4

[1] Longitudinal comparisons by race/ethnicity should be done with extreme care, due to periodic changes in the survey.

[2] Hispanic subcategories totaled 3.4 percent in 1978–79.

NOTE.—The National Research Council's classification of degrees by field differs somewhat from that in most publications of the National Center for Education Statistics (NCES). The major differences are that history is included under humanities rather than social sciences and that psychology is included under social sciences. The number of degrees also differs slightly from that reported in the NCES "Degrees and Other Formal Awards Conferred" survey. Because of rounding, percents may not add to 100.0.

SOURCE: National Academy of Sciences, National Research Council, Office of Scientific and Engineering Personnel, *Doctorate Records File*. (This table was prepared March 1991.)

Table 278.—Statistical profile of persons receiving doctor's degrees in the life sciences:
1978–79 to 1988–89

Item	1978–79	1979–80	1980–81	1981–82	1982–83	1983–84	1984–85	1985–86	1986–87	1987–88	1988–89
1	2	3	4	5	6	7	8	9	10	11	12
Number of doctorates	5,076	5,325	5,461	5,565	5,540	5,745	5,748	5,720	5,742	6,143	6,343
Sex (percent)											
Men	76.6	74.8	73.6	72.3	69.0	68.9	67.7	66.0	64.8	63.2	61.8
Women	23.4	25.2	26.4	27.7	31.0	31.1	32.3	34.0	35.2	36.8	38.2
Racial/ethnic group (percent) [1]											
American Indian	0.4	0.2	0.2	0.3	0.2	0.3	0.4	0.5	0.4	0.4	0.3
Asian	5.3	5.0	4.6	4.5	5.2	4.6	4.6	4.8	5.6	4.9	5.2
Black	1.4	1.5	1.8	1.5	1.6	2.0	2.1	1.9	2.4	2.2	2.1
Mexican-American	([2])	0.2	0.3	0.4	0.2	0.3	0.4	0.4	0.4	0.4	0.5
Puerto Rican	([2])	0.1	0.2	0.3	0.3	0.3	0.4	0.4	0.6	0.6	0.6
Other Hispanic	([2])	0.7	0.8	0.8	0.7	0.8	1.1	1.3	1.0	1.3	1.0
White	85.9	86.7	87.6	89.1	89.5	89.1	89.0	88.9	87.3	88.5	88.3
Other and unknown	5.9	5.6	4.5	3.1	2.3	2.6	2.0	1.8	2.3	1.7	2.0
Citizenship (percent)											
United States	79.8	80.4	80.3	80.4	79.9	79.4	77.1	75.9	73.5	71.3	71.1
Foreign	17.4	17.6	17.1	16.6	17.4	17.6	19.3	18.8	20.5	22.2	22.1
Unknown	2.7	2.0	2.6	3.0	2.6	3.0	3.6	5.3	6.1	6.4	6.9
Median age at doctorate (years)	30.0	30.0	30.1	30.3	30.6	31.0	31.3	31.6	31.7	31.9	32.2
Percent with bachelor's degree in same field as doctorate	40.7	40.9	40.7	41.4	56.3	58.1	58.3	57.1	55.6	55.4	53.4
Median time lapse from bachelor's to doctorate (years)											
Total time	7.3	7.3	7.3	7.6	7.9	8.2	8.4	8.7	8.7	8.9	9.1
Registered time	5.7	5.8	5.9	6.0	6.1	6.3	6.3	6.4	6.5	6.5	6.5

[1] Longitudinal comparisons by race/ethnicity should be done with extreme care, due to periodic changes in the survey.

[2] Hispanic subcategories totaled 1.1 percent in 1978–79.

NOTE.—The National Research Council's classification of degrees by field differs somewhat from that in most publications of the National Center for Education Statistics (NCES). The number of degrees also differs slightly from that reported in the NCES "De- grees and Other Formal Awards Conferred" survey. Because of rounding, percents may not add to 100.0.

SOURCE: National Academy of Sciences, National Research Council, Office of Scientific and Engineering Personnel, *Doctorate Records File*. (This table was prepared March 1991.)

Table 279.—Statistical profile of persons receiving doctor's degrees in the physical sciences:[1] 1978–79 to 1988–89

Item	1978–79	1979–80	1980–81	1981–82	1982–83	1983–84	1984–85	1985–86	1986–87	1987–88	1988–89
1	2	3	4	5	6	7	8	9	10	11	12
Number of doctorates	3,321	3,151	3,208	3,348	3,438	3,459	3,531	3,679	3,837	4,046	3,987
Sex (percent)											
Men	89.4	87.7	88.7	86.3	86.4	85.4	83.7	83.6	83.3	82.6	80.9
Women	10.6	12.3	11.3	13.7	13.6	14.6	16.3	16.4	16.7	17.4	19.1
Racial/ethnic group (percent)[2]											
American Indian	0.5	0.2	0.1	0.2	0.3	0.2	0.1	0.2	0.3	0.3	0.6
Asian	6.9	7.2	6.5	6.0	6.4	6.4	6.7	6.9	6.8	5.5	6.6
Black	1.5	0.9	1.2	1.1	1.0	1.3	1.2	1.0	1.0	1.3	1.3
Mexican-American	(3)	0.2	0.1	0.2	0.2	0.3	0.5	0.5	0.4	0.6	0.5
Puerto Rican	(3)	0.1	0.4	0.3	0.3	0.4	0.2	0.5	1.0	0.8	0.7
Other Hispanic	(3)	0.7	0.7	0.7	0.8	1.2	0.9	1.0	0.9	1.1	1.3
White	82.6	83.7	85.3	88.5	87.4	87.0	87.0	86.5	86.6	87.3	86.8
Other and unknown	7.1	7.0	5.7	3.0	3.6	3.2	3.2	3.4	3.0	3.1	2.1
Citizenship (percent)											
United States	77.4	75.9	75.4	75.0	74.0	73.6	70.3	66.1	65.1	64.3	62.5
Foreign	20.6	21.6	21.3	21.9	23.1	23.5	25.5	27.8	28.5	28.8	29.8
Unknown	2.0	2.4	3.3	3.1	2.9	2.9	4.1	6.1	6.4	6.9	7.8
Median age at doctorate (years)	28.9	29.1	29.0	29.2	29.3	29.5	29.5	29.9	29.8	30.1	30.0
Percent with bachelor's degree in same field as doctorate	78.1	76.5	76.6	77.2	75.4	77.7	75.0	73.4	72.6	72.6	72.6
Median time lapse from bachelor's to doctorate (years)											
Total time	6.6	6.8	6.7	6.8	7.0	7.0	7.1	7.1	7.1	7.2	7.2
Registered time	5.6	5.7	5.7	5.8	5.9	6.0	6.0	6.0	5.9	6.1	6.0

[1] Includes physics and astronomy, chemistry, and earth, atmosphere, and marine science. Excludes mathematics and computer science.

[2] Longitudinal comparisons by race/ethnicity should be done with extreme care, due to periodic changes in the survey.

[3] Hispanic subcategories totaled 1.4 percent in 1978–79.

NOTE.—The National Research Council's classification of degrees by field differs somewhat from that in most publications of the National Center for Education Statistics (NCES). The number of degrees also differs slightly from that reported in the NCES "Degrees and Other Formal Awards Conferred" survey. Because of rounding, percents may not add to 100.0.

SOURCE: National Academy of Sciences, National Research Council, Office of Scientific and Engineering Personnel, *Doctorate Records File*. (This table was prepared March 1991.)

Table 280.—Statistical profile of persons receiving doctor's degrees in the social sciences: 1978–79 to 1988–89

Item	1978–79	1979–80	1980–81	1981–82	1982–83	1983–84	1984–85	1985–86	1986–87	1987–88	1988–89
1	2	3	4	5	6	7	8	9	10	11	12
Number of doctorates	6,379	6,253	6,505	6,250	6,055	5,895	5,720	5,841	5,718	5,769	5,955
Sex (percent)											
Men	67.0	65.4	64.4	63.3	60.7	59.2	58.9	57.6	57.2	55.0	54.8
Women	33.0	34.6	35.6	36.7	39.9	40.8	41.1	42.4	42.8	45.0	45.2
Racial/ethnic group (percent)[1]											
American Indian	0.6	0.3	0.2	0.4	0.2	0.2	0.4	0.4	0.5	0.3	0.4
Asian	2.3	2.7	2.4	2.4	2.1	2.4	2.5	2.5	3.1	3.2	3.1
Black	3.9	4.0	3.9	4.6	3.8	4.5	4.3	4.0	3.7	4.3	4.3
Mexican-American	(2)	0.4	0.8	0.9	0.9	0.8	0.9	1.0	1.0	1.0	1.0
Puerto Rican	(2)	0.3	0.3	0.6	0.4	0.6	0.5	0.6	0.5	0.7	0.8
Other Hispanic	(2)	1.2	1.1	1.1	1.6	1.3	1.4	1.6	2.0	1.5	1.5
White	85.5	86.5	87.6	87.8	88.2	88.0	87.6	87.9	87.3	87.3	87.5
Other and unknown	5.7	4.5	3.7	2.2	2.8	2.1	2.4	2.0	2.0	1.7	1.6
Citizenship (percent)											
United States	84.4	84.7	84.0	81.8	82.9	80.6	79.3	77.9	76.1	74.8	70.4
Foreign	11.6	11.6	11.9	12.6	12.5	14.1	15.3	15.3	15.7	16.1	17.3
Unknown	4.0	3.7	4.2	5.6	4.5	5.4	5.4	6.9	8.3	9.1	12.2
Median age at doctorate (years)	31.5	31.6	32.0	32.3	32.4	32.7	33.0	33.4	33.5	34.1	33.9
Percent with bachelor's degree in same field as doctorate	56.4	58.6	59.1	57.4	58.9	59.3	58.5	57.0	56.4	54.5	52.3
Median time lapse from bachelor's to doctorate (years)											
Total time	8.5	8.7	9.0	9.2	9.3	9.7	9.9	10.0	10.3	10.5	10.3
Registered time	6.2	6.4	6.5	6.7	6.8	7.1	7.1	7.2	7.4	7.4	7.4

[1] Longitudinal comparisons by race/ethnicity should be done with extreme care, due to periodic changes in the survey.

[2] Hispanic categories totaled 1.9 percent in 1978–79.

NOTE.—The National Research Council's classification of degrees by field differs somewhat from that in most publications of the National Center for Education Statistics (NCES). The major differences are that history is included under humanities rather than social sciences and that psychology is included under social sciences. The number of degrees also differs slightly from that reported in the NCES "Degrees and Other Formal Awards Conferred" survey. Because of rounding, percents may not add to 100.0.

SOURCE: National Academy of Sciences, National Research Council, Office of Scientific and Engineering Personnel, *Doctorate Records File*. (This table was prepared March 1991.)

Table 281.—Doctor's degrees [1] conferred by 60 large institutions of higher education: 1979-80 to 1988-89

Institution	Rank order [2]	Total, 1979–80 to 1988–89	1979–80	1980–81	1981–82	1982–83	1983–84	1984–85	1985–86	1986–87	1987–88 [3]	1988–89 [4]
1	2	3	4	5	6	7	8	9	10	11	12	13
United States, all institutions	—	335,609	32,615	32,958	32,707	32,775	33,209	32,943	33,653	34,120	34,870	35,759
Total, 60 large institutions	—	200,611	20,060	20,103	19,927	19,350	19,865	19,749	19,799	20,132	20,472	21,154
University of California, Berkeley	1	7,268	735	672	712	702	698	689	753	727	742	838
University of Wisconsin, Madison	2	6,500	665	623	690	594	630	674	606	667	684	667
Columbia University (N.Y.) [5]	3	5,969	630	610	587	529	603	625	610	593	567	615
University of Illinois, Urbana Campus	4	5,958	597	622	567	543	538	622	560	616	646	647
University of Michigan, Ann Arbor	5	5,933	569	552	605	584	738	607	598	589	564	527
Ohio State University, Main Campus	6	5,541	566	530	586	563	521	543	512	570	542	608
University of Minnesota, Minneapolis-St. Paul	7	5,072	485	518	459	466	495	515	556	508	527	543
Stanford University (Calif.)	8	5,059	458	495	469	451	497	497	530	562	560	540
University of Texas at Austin	9	4,949	432	452	418	418	427	474	545	612	588	583
University of California, Los Angeles	10	4,746	479	559	481	465	465	449	433	448	508	459
Harvard University (Mass.)	11	4,689	513	586	462	474	457	385	452	434	465	461
Michigan State University	12	4,491	474	485	488	481	395	405	438	464	427	434
Massachusetts Institute of Technology	13	4,421	387	406	416	429	415	447	455	458	516	492
Cornell University (N.Y.) [6]	14	4,391	419	424	405	442	432	433	456	445	454	481
New York University	15	4,040	438	432	435	344	418	391	377	392	421	392
Indiana University, Bloomington	16	3,921	451	436	448	413	417	397	353	374	319	313
University of Pittsburgh, Main Campus (Pa.)	17	3,901	383	357	426	407	389	398	390	394	390	367
Purdue University, Main Campus (Ind.)	18	3,855	387	396	377	388	383	389	379	370	366	420
University of Southern California	19	3,810	424	365	365	308	424	424	363	354	354	429
Pennsylvania State University, Main Campus	20	3,764	365	394	389	394	364	371	350	341	379	417
University of Washington	21	3,699	351	342	368	387	358	342	345	411	392	403
University of Maryland, College Park Campus	22	3,639	310	346	364	354	387	373	370	378	364	393
University of Pennsylvania	23	3,569	335	323	396	361	406	367	341	307	319	414
Rutgers University, New Brunswick (N.J.)	24	3,399	323	381	340	372	362	343	320	320	311	327
Texas A&M University, Main Campus	25	3,223	290	274	253	286	298	315	336	369	382	420
University of Chicago (Ill.)	26	3,196	296	340	349	315	329	291	329	319	318	310
Northwestern University (Ill.)	27	3,115	308	308	287	274	310	326	312	319	313	358
Boston University (Mass.)	28	3,056	338	316	314	324	333	276	307	299	245	304
University of Georgia	29	2,981	268	268	282	298	270	355	309	275	316	340
University of Florida	30	2,967	281	295	237	299	294	301	290	313	315	342
University of Massachusetts at Amherst	31	2,940	282	317	298	264	268	300	290	311	281	329
University of North Carolina at Chapel Hill	32	2,899	307	296	280	279	283	260	283	311	301	299
Yale University (Conn.)	33	2,870	286	265	292	281	299	276	259	305	290	317
Nova University (Fla.)	34	2,864	447	332	294	240	210	209	263	271	292	306
University of Iowa	35	2,808	274	270	315	248	273	284	258	287	312	287
Florida State University	36	2,791	370	336	316	293	273	257	224	226	250	246
University of Arizona	37	2,717	259	225	270	269	259	261	260	298	290	326
Temple University (Pa.)	38	2,590	260	230	237	227	243	264	277	290	277	285
Virginia Polytechnic Institute and State U.	39	2,568	194	211	227	246	271	260	274	295	287	303
Iowa State University of Science and Technology	40	2,549	239	256	249	214	228	245	256	296	309	257
Vanderbilt University (Tenn.)	41	2,423	250	282	267	228	232	239	259	252	196	218
University of California, Davis	42	2,420	247	270	204	290	253	224	245	228	238	221
University of Kansas, Main Campus	43	2,278	238	222	236	212	241	260	211	221	213	224
University of Tennessee, Knoxville	44	2,250	218	228	234	232	250	223	233	206	217	209
University of Colorado at Boulder	45	2,247	212	267	218	215	258	198	198	229	231	221
University of Missouri, Columbia	46	2,245	254	220	229	221	245	230	202	181	227	236
Princeton University (N.J.)	47	2,240	195	217	230	231	226	211	216	218	269	227
State U. of New York at Buffalo, Main Campus	48	2,224	234	208	238	213	208	194	206	209	240	274
City University of New York Graduate School and University Center	49	2,201	190	212	203	208	200	234	232	232	258	232
University of Virginia, Main Campus	50	2,199	229	227	202	224	190	221	217	218	229	242
Johns Hopkins University (Md.)	51	2,162	184	209	187	187	212	254	220	213	267	229
University of Nebraska, Lincoln	52	2,099	206	222	201	203	215	179	201	203	233	236
Oklahoma State University, Main Campus	53	2,000	193	198	187	197	197	220	224	189	184	211
North Carolina State University at Raleigh	54	1,987	164	159	191	177	210	204	219	200	239	224
University of Oregon	55	1,901	201	207	215	197	208	173	197	140	167	196
University of Cincinnati, Main Campus (Ohio)	56	1,858	183	193	181	189	202	171	187	182	188	182
University of Connecticut	57	1,847	194	205	168	159	195	181	174	193	180	198
University of Utah	58	1,837	208	193	181	168	162	175	188	179	209	174
University of Rochester (N.Y.)	59	1,784	191	160	164	179	154	168	195	198	167	208
Wayne State University (Mich.)	60	1,691	194	159	238	194	147	150	156	123	137	193

[1] Includes Ph.D., Ed.D., and comparable degrees at the doctoral level. Excludes first-professional degrees (e.g., M.D., D.D.S., and D.V.M.).

[2] Institutions are ranked by the total number of doctor's degrees conferred during the designated 10-year period.

[3] Some data have been revised from previously published figures.

[4] Preliminary data.

[5] Includes degrees conferred by the Main Division and Teachers College.

[6] Includes degrees conferred by the Endowed and Statutory Colleges.

—Not applicable.

SOURCE: U.S. Department of Education, National Center for Education Statistics, "Degrees and Other Formal Awards Conferred" surveys, and Integrated Postsecondary Education Data System (IPEDS), "Completions" surveys. (This table was prepared March 1991.)

Table 282.—Percentage of the high school class of 1980 enrolled in postsecondary education, by attendance status, sex, race/ethnicity, socioeconomic status, and ability level: Fall 1980 to fall 1985

Sex, race/ethnicity, socioeconomic status, and ability level	Fall 1980		Fall 1981		Fall 1982		Fall 1983		Fall 1984		Fall 1985	
	Full-time	Part-time	Full-time	Part-time	Full-time	Part-time	Full-time	Part-time	Full-time	Part-time	Full-time	Part-time
1	2	3	4	5	6	7	8	9	10	11	12	13
Total	46.1	5.8	43.1	6.6	34.1	9.9	33.3	6.8	17.1	7.5	10.4	7.6
Sex												
Male	43.2	5.4	42.4	6.0	33.9	9.0	34.0	6.4	18.3	6.7	11.6	7.5
Female	48.9	6.1	43.8	7.1	34.3	10.8	32.7	7.1	15.9	8.1	9.2	7.8
Race/ethnicity												
White, non-Hispanic	47.7	5.8	44.6	6.6	35.5	10.2	34.7	6.7	18.0	7.6	10.5	7.6
Black, non-Hispanic	42.0	4.1	39.8	4.8	29.8	8.1	28.3	6.0	12.7	5.4	8.9	6.2
Hispanic	34.9	7.8	30.5	9.4	23.6	10.6	22.9	8.0	11.6	8.0	10.0	8.3
American Indian	34.2	5.3	35.0	6.9	21.0	11.9	22.4	8.2	14.8	2.1	10.5	2.6
Asian	67.4	12.0	64.6	12.8	57.7	15.8	53.8	10.9	37.2	13.6	20.8	16.8
Socioeconomic status [1]												
Low	30.3	5.0	26.7	5.4	18.7	8.7	17.1	5.4	9.7	5.3	6.3	5.6
Low-middle	40.3	5.9	35.8	7.1	27.3	9.4	25.0	6.8	13.5	7.1	8.0	7.6
High-middle	51.9	7.0	48.5	7.2	38.0	11.7	36.7	8.0	18.2	8.6	10.5	7.8
High	70.2	5.6	68.4	6.9	59.3	11.0	60.1	7.8	29.2	9.5	18.5	9.0
Ability level [2]												
Low	22.2	4.9	19.6	5.6	13.0	7.8	12.8	4.6	7.2	3.3	5.2	2.9
Low-middle	38.4	6.4	34.8	7.7	25.5	10.7	23.7	8.0	13.8	8.0	8.0	7.4
High-middle	58.1	6.3	52.3	7.8	39.9	13.1	39.2	8.0	19.6	8.3	11.7	8.4
High	75.1	5.7	73.3	6.1	63.8	10.3	63.5	7.1	30.8	9.6	18.4	11.1

[1] Socioeconomic status quartiles as measured by a composite score on parental education, family income, father's occupation, and household characteristics in 1980.

[2] Ability level quartiles as measured by performance on a test battery administered as part of the High School and Beyond survey in 1980.

SOURCE: U.S. Department of Education, National Center for Education Statistics, High School and Beyond survey. (This table was prepared October 1988.)

Table 283.—Percentage of the high school class of 1980 enrolled in 4-year colleges, by attendance status, sex, race/ethnicity, socioeconomic status, and ability level: Fall 1980 to fall 1985

Sex, race/ethnicity, socioeconomic status, and ability level	Fall 1980		Fall 1981		Fall 1982		Fall 1983		Fall 1984		Fall 1985	
	Full-time	Part-time	Full-time	Part-time	Full-time	Part-time	Full-time	Part-time	Full-time	Part-time	Full-time	Part-time
1	2	3	4	5	6	7	8	9	10	11	12	13
Total	30.3	1.5	28.9	1.6	26.3	3.4	27.9	2.7	13.8	4.3	7.9	4.2
Sex												
Male	28.9	1.4	28.5	1.6	25.9	3.3	28.7	2.6	15.5	4.1	9.2	4.1
Female	31.6	1.5	29.3	1.6	26.6	3.5	27.2	2.7	12.3	4.6	6.7	4.3
Race/ethnicity												
White, non-Hispanic	31.8	1.5	30.6	1.6	28.0	3.5	29.8	2.7	14.7	4.4	8.3	4.2
Black, non-Hispanic	28.2	1.1	26.1	1.3	21.2	3.2	21.3	2.1	9.1	3.0	5.6	3.2
Hispanic	16.7	1.3	14.2	1.5	13.9	2.0	15.5	2.8	9.1	4.7	6.2	4.3
American Indian	14.5	1.3	14.4	1.8	13.2	2.7	15.7	2.3	9.8	1.0	6.6	1.0
Asian	44.6	4.0	43.1	4.0	42.6	6.6	46.4	4.7	34.0	8.5	18.3	8.3
Socioeconomic status [1]												
Low	15.5	1.1	14.8	0.9	12.3	2.2	12.2	1.4	6.6	2.4	4.0	2.3
Low-middle	23.2	1.3	20.9	1.4	19.1	2.7	19.7	2.3	10.0	4.0	5.6	4.0
High-middle	33.5	1.4	31.4	1.6	28.7	3.6	29.6	3.2	14.6	4.7	8.0	4.5
High	55.0	2.3	54.6	2.5	49.8	5.3	54.3	3.7	25.9	6.8	16.1	6.2
Ability level [2]												
Low	8.2	1.0	7.4	0.8	6.2	1.5	7.1	0.5	4.1	0.8	2.4	0.9
Low-middle	21.1	0.7	19.9	0.8	17.3	2.7	17.2	2.5	9.8	3.6	5.1	3.7
High-middle	35.8	1.7	32.9	2.3	29.6	4.5	32.5	3.6	15.5	5.6	9.2	4.5
High	62.9	2.3	61.5	2.6	56.8	5.2	58.8	3.8	28.6	7.3	17.0	8.0

[1] Socioeconomic status quartiles as measured by a composite score on parental education, family income, father's occupation, and household characteristics in 1980.

[2] Ability level quartiles as measured by performance on a test battery administered as part of the High School and Beyond survey in 1980.

SOURCE: U.S. Department of Education, National Center for Education Statistics, High School and Beyond survey. (This table was prepared October 1988.)

Table 284.—Mean number of semester credits completed by bachelor's degree recipients, by major and course area: 1972 to 1976 and 1980 to 1984

Selected college majors	Course areas									
	Total	Business	Computer science	Education	Engineering	Mathe-matics	Biological sciences	Physical sciences	Social sciences	Other
1	2	3	4	5	6	7	8	9	10	11
1972–76 [1]										
Mean, all majors	**124.0**	**7.8**	**1.0**	**9.7**	**2.3**	**7.4**	**7.6**	**9.0**	**30.3**	**48.8**
Business and management	124.4	41.2	2.3	0.5	0.4	10.2	2.5	4.8	30.4	32.0
Computer science	133.3	6.6	33.5	0.4	5.3	22.4	1.9	7.8	20.6	34.8
Education	126.4	0.9	0.3	40.2	—	5.0	5.5	4.3	23.9	46.4
Engineering	134.8	1.6	2.0	0.1	50.0	18.2	1.3	20.5	14.0	27.1
English	117.8	0.5	0.1	7.8	0.1	3.2	3.4	3.4	24.2	75.2
Fine arts	124.9	0.3	0.1	6.6	—	1.3	2.5	2.1	13.6	98.4
Life sciences	122.2	0.4	0.8	1.7	—	8.4	35.6	26.2	17.8	31.3
Physical sciences	122.7	0.8	1.4	0.9	1.9	16.2	9.6	49.5	13.1	29.2
Psychology	119.1	2.0	0.5	5.9	0.3	5.5	6.2	5.9	56.0	36.9
Social sciences	120.6	3.4	0.4	3.3	0.4	5.3	3.2	4.3	60.3	40.1
1980–84 [2]										
Mean, all majors	**123.5**	**12.8**	**3.3**	**6.2**	**4.6**	**8.4**	**5.3**	**8.1**	**27.5**	**47.2**
Business and management	122.8	41.2	4.5	0.6	1.1	8.9	2.2	3.9	27.5	32.7
Computer science	129.3	11.8	27.9	0.3	4.7	21.3	1.8	8.5	19.0	33.9
Education	127.4	0.7	0.3	45.5	0.1	4.4	4.4	3.8	20.8	47.3
Engineering	132.3	1.0	2.3	0.8	52.5	16.2	1.1	20.2	12.3	25.9
English	114.8	1.7	1.5	6.9	—	2.2	2.1	4.7	21.4	74.4
Fine arts	120.5	1.7	0.6	5.1	—	1.7	2.7	1.5	14.1	93.1
Life sciences	121.9	0.7	1.5	1.9	0.2	10.1	33.5	22.6	18.1	33.3
Physical sciences	124.3	0.2	4.9	0.1	2.0	14.1	12.9	48.7	11.6	30.0
Psychology	120.7	3.0	2.7	2.1	—	6.5	5.8	4.2	55.2	41.2
Social sciences	119.2	6.0	1.4	1.0	0.5	5.4	4.4	5.1	52.0	43.3

[1] Sample survey based on 1972 high school seniors who completed bachelor's degrees by 1976.

[2] Sample survey based on 1980 high school seniors who completed bachelor's degrees by 1984.

—Data not available.

NOTE.—Because of rounding, details may not add to totals.

SOURCE: U.S. Department of Education, National Center for Education Statistics, High School and Beyond survey. (This table was prepared April 1986.)

Table 285.—Colleges and universities offering remedial instruction or tutoring, by type and control of institution: 1980–81 to 1990–91

Type and control of institution	Percent of colleges offering remedial instruction or tutoring					Change in percentage points		
	1980–81	1984–85	1988–89	1989–90	1990–91	1980–81 to 1984–85	1984–85 to 1988–89	1988–89 to 1990–91
1	2	3	4	5	6	7	8	9
All 4-year colleges	**78.9**	**85.8**	**89.0**	**90.2**	**89.0**	**6.9**	**3.2**	**0.0**
All 2-year colleges	**83.8**	**93.4**	**93.8**	**94.9**	**94.1**	**9.6**	**0.4**	**0.3**
Public institutions								
4-year colleges	89.8	92.9	94.7	99.5	95.5	3.1	1.8	0.8
2-year colleges	89.6	97.2	98.9	99.0	98.8	7.6	1.7	−0.1
Private institutions								
4-year colleges	73.8	82.5	86.3	85.9	86.0	8.7	3.8	−0.3
2-year colleges	61.9	78.9	77.8	79.8	79.8	17.0	−1.1	2.0

SOURCE: College Entrance Examination Board, *Annual Survey of Colleges, 1986–87, Summary Statistics,* copyrighted, and unpublished tabulations. (This table was prepared March 1991.)

Table 286.—Highest level of education attained by 1980 high school seniors, by selected student and school characteristics: Spring 1986

Student and school characteristics	Highest educational attainment of 1980 high school seniors in 1986						
	Total	No high school diploma [1]	High school diploma	License [2]	Associate degree	Bachelor's degree	Graduate/ professional degree
1	2	3	4	5	6	7	8
Total	100.0	0.9	61.8	11.9	6.5	18.2	0.7
Sex							
Men	100.0	1.0	64.0	10.5	5.9	17.6	0.9
Women	100.0	0.8	59.6	13.3	7.0	18.8	0.6
Race/ethnicity							
White, non-Hispanic	100.0	0.8	60.0	11.5	6.6	20.2	0.9
Black, non-Hispanic	100.0	1.2	69.4	13.9	5.3	9.9	0.2
Hispanic	100.0	1.7	70.2	13.8	7.3	6.8	0.1
Asian	100.0	([3])	49.6	12.6	8.7	27.3	1.7
American Indian	100.0	([3])	61.3	18.6	9.3	10.8	([3])
Socioeconomic status group [4]							
Low	100.0	1.2	74.1	12.3	5.5	6.6	0.2
Low-middle	100.0	0.5	66.7	13.6	8.0	11.1	0.2
High-middle	100.0	0.1	58.4	12.9	7.7	20.4	0.6
High	100.0	([3])	45.7	8.7	6.3	37.1	2.2
High school program [5]							
General	100.0	0.8	69.7	12.6	6.5	10.2	0.2
Academic	100.0	0.1	45.6	8.8	7.2	36.6	1.8
Vocational	100.0	0.6	72.8	16.2	6.9	3.6	0.0
Postsecondary education plans [6]							
No plans	100.0	1.4	83.5	12.7	2.1	0.2	([3])
Attend vocational/technical school	100.0	0.3	72.5	17.7	8.4	1.1	([3])
Attend college less than 4 years ..	100.0	0.2	65.5	14.4	13.1	6.8	([3])
Earn bachelor's degree	100.0	([3])	48.3	8.2	6.9	35.8	0.7
Earn advanced degree	100.0	0.1	43.5	7.9	4.9	40.6	3.0
Type of high school							
Public	100.0	1.0	63.2	12.1	6.6	16.4	0.7
Catholic	100.0	([3])	47.4	11.9	6.4	32.8	1.6
Other private	100.0	([3])	52.3	7.0	3.9	36.7	0.1

[1] Seniors who dropped out of high school after spring 1980 survey and had not completed high school by 1986.

[2] Persons who earned a certificate for completing a program of study.

[3] Less than .05 percent.

[4] Socioeconomic status was measured by a composite score on parental education, family income, father's occupation, and household characteristics in 1980.

[5] Students' self-reported high school program.

[6] During their senior year of high school, students were asked about the highest level of education they planned to attain. Students who planned to get less than a high school education or a high school education only were classified as having no postsecondary education plans.

NOTE.—Because of rounding, percents may not add to 100.0.

SOURCE: U.S. Department of Education, National Center for Education Statistics, High School and Beyond survey. (This table was prepared September 1987.)

Table 287.—Highest level of education attained by 1980 high school seniors, by race/ethnicity and October 1980 postsecondary education attendance status: Spring 1986

Race/ethnicity and October 1980 postsecondary education attendance status	Highest educational attainment 1980 high school seniors in 1986						
	Total	No high school diploma [1]	High school diploma	License [2]	Associate degree	Bachelor's degree	Graduate/ professional degree
1	2	3	4	5	6	7	8
All students							
Part-time 2-year public college	100.0	0.7	66.4	17.7	8.8	6.5	([3])
Part-time 4-year public college	100.0	2.7	57.1	15.4	1.6	22.6	0.6
Full-time 2-year public college	100.0	([3])	49.5	11.7	20.7	17.6	0.5
Full-time 4-year public college	100.0	([3])	41.7	7.6	4.5	44.9	1.3
Full-time 4-year private college	100.0	([3])	31.1	8.8	5.1	51.9	3.0
Not a student	100.0	1.8	78.2	12.8	3.6	3.5	0.2
White							
Part-time 2-year public college	100.0	0.8	67.7	17.9	6.9	6.7	([3])
Part-time 4-year public college	100.0	3.4	54.8	14.5	0.3	27.0	([3])
Full-time 2-year public college	100.0	([3])	48.6	10.8	20.7	19.3	0.7
Full-time 4-year public college	100.0	([3])	39.0	6.8	4.8	48.0	1.5
Full-time 4-year private college	100.0	([3])	28.1	7.9	5.1	55.7	3.3
Not a student	100.0	1.6	78.5	12.7	3.5	3.5	0.2
Black							
Part-time 2-year public college	100.0	([3])	65.8	22.1	9.8	2.3	([3])
Part-time 4-year public college	100.0	([3])	58.5	25.1	6.0	8.5	1.8
Full-time 2-year public college	100.0	([3])	52.8	19.2	18.9	9.1	([3])
Full-time 4-year public college	100.0	([3])	59.4	11.2	3.4	25.6	0.5
Full-time 4-year private college	100.0	([3])	50.5	15.0	5.5	28.5	0.6
Not a student	100.0	2.2	78.1	13.3	3.6	2.8	([3])
Hispanic							
Part-time 2-year public college	100.0	([3])	57.4	14.9	23.4	4.4	([3])
Part-time 4-year public college	([4])	([4])	([4])	([4])	([4])	([4])	([4])
Full-time 2-year public college	100.0	([3])	53.9	14.9	22.7	8.5	([3])
Full-time 4-year public college	100.0	([3])	51.1	18.4	4.1	25.6	0.9
Full-time 4-year private college	100.0	([3])	46.8	19.4	6.1	26.8	1.0
Not a student	100.0	3.1	83.2	10.3	2.4	0.9	([3])

[1] Seniors who dropped out of high school after spring 1980 survey and had not completed high school by 1986.

[2] Includes persons who earned a certificate for completing a program of study.

[3] Less than .05 percent.

[4] Fewer than 30 cases available for analysis. Estimates are suppressed because they are unreliable.

NOTE.—Because of rounding, percents may not add to 100.0.

SOURCE: U.S. Department of Education, National Center for Education Statistics, High School and Beyond survey. (This table was prepared September 1987.)

Table 288.—Highest level of education attained by 1980 high school seniors, by socioeconomic status and race/ethnicity: Spring 1986

Socioeconomic status [1] in 1980 and race/ethnicity	Highest educational attainment of 1980 high school seniors in 1986						
	Total	No high school diploma [2]	High school diploma	License [3]	Associate degree	Bachelor's degree	Graduate/ professional degree
1	2	3	4	5	6	7	8
Lower 25 percent							
White, non-Hispanic	100.0	0.9	75.1	12.2	5.0	6.6	0.3
Black, non-Hispanic	100.0	1.4	73.0	12.7	5.1	7.7	0.1
Hispanic	100.0	1.6	73.9	11.8	7.8	4.9	([4])
Asian	100.0	([4])	53.4	17.3	15.7	12.0	1.6
Middle 50 percent							
White, non-Hispanic	100.0	0.3	62.0	13.0	8.0	16.3	0.4
Black, non-Hispanic	100.0	0.3	67.5	14.7	6.5	10.7	0.3
Hispanic	100.0	1.0	67.0	14.7	6.5	10.7	0.2
Asian	100.0	([4])	51.1	11.7	11.1	26.1	([4])
Upper 25 percent							
White, non-Hispanic	100.0	([4])	44.9	8.6	6.2	38.2	2.2
Black, non-Hispanic	100.0	([4])	56.3	12.4	5.4	25.5	0.4
Hispanic	100.0	0.3	60.0	11.4	9.6	18.0	0.7
Asian	100.0	([4])	42.9	6.5	4.8	40.0	5.9

[1] Socioeconomic status was measured by a composite score on parental education, family income, father's occupation, and household characteristics in 1980.

[2] Seniors who dropped out of high school after spring 1980 survey and had not completed high school by 1986.

[3] Includes persons who earned a certificate for completing a program of study.

[4] Less than .05 percent.

NOTE.—Because of rounding, percents may not add to 100.0.

SOURCE: U.S. Department of Education, National Center for Education Statistics, High School and Beyond survey. (This table was prepared September 1987.)

Table 289.—Cumulative percentage of 1972, 1980, and 1982 high school graduates completing college, by level of degree and selected student characteristics: 1976 to 1986

Student characteristics	1972 high school seniors												1980 high school seniors			1982 high school seniors 1 to 2-year degree[1]
	1 to 2-year degree,[1] by year of attainment						Bachelor's degree, by year of attainment						1 to 2-year degree[1]		Bachelor's degree	
	June 1976	June 1978	June 1980	June 1982	June 1984	June 1986	June 1976	June 1978	June 1980	June 1982	June 1984	June 1986	Feb. 1984	Feb. 1986	Feb. 1986	Feb. 1986
1	2	3	4	5	6	7	8	9	10	11	12	13	14	15	16	17
Total	**6.39**	**7.87**	**9.35**	**11.76**	**14.22**	**16.59**	**14.33**	**23.71**	**25.14**	**26.42**	**27.08**	**27.68**	**8.84**	**12.51**	**18.77**	**7.85**
Sex																
Male	5.57	7.09	8.58	10.84	13.69	15.81	13.32	25.64	27.47	28.71	29.57	30.09	7.70	10.84	18.35	5.94
Female	7.16	8.62	10.08	12.64	14.73	17.33	15.29	21.87	22.92	24.24	24.72	25.39	9.92	14.08	19.17	9.59
Race/ethnicity																
White	6.94	8.52	9.91	12.11	14.72	16.99	15.61	25.46	26.98	28.05	28.76	29.39	9.03	12.54	20.79	7.93
Black	2.14	3.48	4.89	9.36	11.09	14.61	7.75	13.49	14.69	18.29	18.66	19.18	6.37	10.42	10.14	7.14
Hispanic	3.29	4.01	6.59	9.07	10.99	13.69	3.09	9.13	9.70	10.44	10.81	10.88	9.16	14.71	6.75	9.49
American Indian	4.11	5.51	11.36	20.06	23.46	26.23	29.19	48.48	53.23	54.93	54.93	56.06	16.88	20.35	9.22	5.79
Asian	8.02	8.02	12.77	21.00	25.49	27.66	5.76	5.76	5.76	10.72	15.29	18.52	11.83	15.68	28.65	5.29
Ability level[2]																
Lower 25 percent	3.48	4.20	4.94	5.91	7.14	9.27	1.47	3.80	4.12	4.68	4.98	5.14	6.02	8.71	2.98	7.31
Middle 50 percent	8.23	9.84	11.83	14.73	17.15	19.15	8.70	17.75	19.15	20.77	21.54	22.05	10.83	15.06	15.53	9.36
Upper 25 percent	7.04	8.76	10.28	13.43	16.77	18.68	31.76	47.94	50.04	51.81	52.61	53.56	9.32	12.18	41.82	5.46
High school grades																
A	7.89	8.72	9.72	13.52	16.95	19.02	41.94	57.21	59.27	59.82	60.20	60.65	8.17	11.29	48.95	3.85
A to B	7.40	9.45	10.91	12.95	14.93	16.95	23.48	38.04	39.31	40.94	41.50	42.37	12.61	15.92	28.54	7.08
B	7.07	8.12	9.88	11.74	14.91	16.79	12.31	22.75	24.92	26.16	27.02	28.02	9.72	14.00	18.49	9.46
B to C	6.79	8.58	10.21	12.83	15.63	18.15	6.00	13.10	14.29	16.08	17.04	17.46	9.65	12.47	8.95	8.52
C	2.58	3.99	5.22	7.74	9.27	12.77	2.37	5.40	6.09	6.82	7.20	7.74	5.41	9.97	2.50	7.19
D[3]	3.22	3.51	5.04	6.97	8.00	9.74	1.08	2.81	3.61	4.26	4.51	4.51	2.96	7.63	1.26	[3]6.20
High school program																
General	5.43	6.90	8.04	10.07	11.91	14.68	5.57	10.77	11.96	13.12	13.73	14.21	8.50	12.04	9.96	8.49
Academic	7.96	9.79	11.64	15.00	18.50	20.88	27.50	43.56	45.58	47.42	48.21	49.08	10.24	13.96	37.40	6.77
Vocational/technical	4.71	5.53	6.78	7.88	9.22	10.93	1.29	3.69	4.29	4.68	5.15	5.39	9.08	12.60	3.44	9.22
Socioeconomic status[4]																
Lower 25 percent	4.19	5.30	6.72	8.19	9.91	12.38	5.02	8.89	10.08	11.00	11.55	11.97	7.12	10.06	6.84	7.99
Middle 50 percent	7.22	8.64	10.08	12.41	15.08	17.40	10.92	19.17	20.28	21.77	22.39	23.04	10.01	13.89	15.56	8.52
Upper 25 percent	6.73	8.67	10.28	13.69	16.40	18.75	29.15	45.61	47.86	49.10	49.93	50.58	9.88	13.36	38.25	6.35

[1] Includes licenses, awards, and associate degree programs of 1 to 2 years duration.
[2] Ability level as measured by a test battery administered as part of the High School and Beyond survey.
[3] Low C or D grade average.
[4] Socioeconomic status as measured by a composite score on parental education, family income, father's occupation, and household characteristics.

SOURCE: U.S. Department of Education, National Center for Education Statistics, High School and Beyond and National Longitudinal Study surveys, unpublished tabulations. (This table was prepared November 1988.)

Table 290.—Changes in scores on Graduate Record Examination (GRE) and professional school admission tests: 1964 to 1988 [1]

Magnitude of change and test	Change in standard deviation units [2]		GRE means for selected years								
	Long-term (1964–1987)	Short-term (1978–79) (1988–89)	1975–76	1977–78	1979–80	1981–82	1983–84	1985–86	1987–88	1988–89
1	2	3	4	5	6	7	8	9	10	11
Moderate increase (+0.20 to +0.39)										
Mathematics (GRE [3] area test)	0.37	0.26	693	692	696	696	711	714	720	720
LSAT [4] (1975–1982)	0.21	—	—	—	—	—	—	—	—	—
Small increase (+0.10 to +0.19)										
Biology (MCAT [5] subtest; 1977–1982)	0.15	—	—	—	—	—	—	—	—	—
Physics (GRE area test)	0.13	0.09	654	652	650	647	637	645	645	661
GRE quantitative	0.12	0.31	510	518	522	533	541	552	557	560
No change (–0.09 to +0.09)										
Chemistry (GRE area test)	0.01	0.17	627	624	618	616	619	628	631	642
Engineering (GRE area test)	0.01	0.29	594	594	590	593	604	616	622	626
Biology (GRE area test)	–0.01	–0.08	627	622	619	616	622	612	615	612
Chemistry (MCAT subtest; 1977–1982)	–0.06	—	—	—	—	—	—	—	—	—
Computer science	—	0.15	—	608	605	604	607	607	622	620
Small decline (–0.10 to –0.19)										
Economics (GRE area test)	–0.10	0.27	597	609	603	614	617	609	625	630
Reading (MCAT sub-test; 1977–1982)	–0.10	—	—	—	—	—	—	—	—	—
GMAT [6]	–0.16	—	—	—	—	—	—	—	—	—
Education (GRE area test)	–0.18	0.16	454	452	449	456	461	464	467	465
Moderate decline (–0.20 to –0.39)										
Psychology (GRE area test)	–0.21	0.08	531	529	534	532	543	542	537	538
MCAT quantitative (1977–1982)	–0.22	—	—	—	—	—	—	—	—	—
Music (GRE area test)	–0.22	0.03	498	502	500	494	498	490	492	498
Geology (GRE area test; 1967–1987)	–0.31	0.07	580	577	576	570	574	576	582	580
Large decline (–0.40 to –0.74)										
GRE verbal	–0.42	0.06	492	484	474	469	475	475	483	484
English literature (GRE area test)	–0.67	0.03	539	530	521	521	530	527	525	528
French (GRE area test; 1964–1979)	–0.68	—	519	514	503	512	510	509	519	—
History (GRE area test)	–0.74	–0.01	518	509	508	507	512	509	505	504
Extreme decline (–0.75 and below)										
Sociology (GRE area test)	–1.04	–0.10	457	450	438	433	434	430	434	425
Political science (GRE area test)	–1.14	–0.08	473	471	456	461	460	455	457	457

[1] Test score changes are for these years unless indicated otherwise.
[2] Computed as the change in scale points divided by the mean standard deviation for the entire period.
[3] GRE-Graduate Record Examination.
[4] LSAT-Law School Admissions Test.
[5] MCAT-Medical College Admission Test.
[6] GMAT-Graduate Management Admissions Test.

—Data not available or not applicable.

SOURCE: U.S. Department of Education, National Institute of Education, *The Standardized Test Scores of College Graduates, 1964–1982*, 1985; unpublished data; and National Center for Education Statistics, *The Condition of Education, 1988*. (This table was prepared June 1990.)

Table 291.—Average undergraduate tuition and fees and room and board rates[1] paid by students in institutions of higher education, by type and control of institution: 1964–65 to 1989–90

Year and control of institution	Total tuition, room and board					Tuition and required fees (in-State)					Dormitory rooms					Board (7-day basis)[1]				
	All insti-tutions	4-year institutions			2-year	All insti-tutions	4-year institutions			2-year	All insti-tutions	4-year institutions			2-year	All insti-tutions	4-year institutions			2-year
		All 4-year	Univer-sities	Other 4-year			All 4-year	Univer-sities	Other 4-year			All 4-year	Univer-sities	Other 4-year			All 4-year	Univer-sities	Other 4-year	
1	2	3	4	5	6	7	8	9	10	11	12	13	14	15	16	17	18	19	20	21
All institutions																				
1976–77	2,275	2,577	2,647	2,527	1,598	924	1,218	1,210	1,223	346	603	611	649	584	503	748	748	788	719	750
1977–78	2,411	2,725	2,777	2,685	1,703	984	1,291	1,269	1,305	378	645	654	691	628	525	781	780	818	752	801
1978–79	2,587	2,917	2,967	2,879	1,828	1,073	1,397	1,370	1,413	411	688	696	737	667	575	826	825	860	800	842
1979–80	2,809	3,167	3,223	3,124	1,979	1,163	1,513	1,484	1,530	451	751	759	803	729	628	895	895	936	865	900
1980–81	3,101	3,499	3,535	3,469	2,230	1,289	1,679	1,634	1,705	526	836	846	881	821	705	976	975	1,020	943	1,000
1981–82	3,489	3,951	4,005	3,908	2,476	1,457	1,907	1,860	1,935	590	950	961	1,023	919	793	1,083	1,082	1,121	1,055	1,094
1982–83	3,877	4,406	4,466	4,356	2,713	1,626	2,139	2,081	2,173	675	1,064	1,078	1,150	1,028	873	1,187	1,189	1,235	1,155	1,165
1983–84	4,167	4,747	4,793	4,712	2,854	1,783	2,344	2,300	2,368	730	1,145	1,162	1,211	1,130	916	1,239	1,242	1,282	1,214	1,208
1984–85	4,563	5,160	5,236	5,107	3,179	1,985	2,567	2,539	2,583	821	1,267	1,282	1,343	1,242	1,058	1,310	1,311	1,353	1,282	1,301
1985–86[2]	4,885	5,504	5,597	5,441	3,367	2,181	2,784	2,770	2,793	888	1,338	1,355	1,424	1,309	1,107	1,365	1,365	1,403	1,339	1,372
1986–87[3]	5,206	5,964	6,124	5,857	3,295	2,312	3,042	3,042	3,042	897	1,405	1,427	1,501	1,376	1,034	1,489	1,495	1,581	1,439	1,364
1987–88	5,494	6,272	6,339	6,226	3,263	2,458	3,201	3,168	3,220	809	1,488	1,516	1,576	1,478	1,017	1,549	1,555	1,596	1,529	1,437
1988–89	5,869	6,725	6,801	6,673	3,573	2,658	3,472	3,422	3,499	979	1,575	1,609	1,665	1,573	1,085	1,636	1,644	1,715	1,601	1,509
1989–90[4]	6,269	7,244	7,377	7,156	3,781	2,892	3,826	3,791	3,845	1,025	1,643	1,679	1,739	1,641	1,111	1,734	1,739	1,847	1,670	1,645
Public institutions																				
1964–65	950	—	1,051	867	638	243	—	298	224	99	271	—	291	241	178	436	—	462	402	361
1965–66	983	—	1,105	904	670	257	—	327	241	109	281	—	304	255	194	445	—	474	408	367
1966–67	1,026	—	1,171	947	710	275	—	360	259	121	294	—	321	271	213	457	—	490	417	376
1967–68	1,064	—	1,199	997	789	283	—	366	268	144	313	—	337	292	243	468	—	496	437	402
1968–69	1,117	—	1,245	1,063	883	295	—	377	281	170	337	—	359	318	278	485	—	509	464	435
1969–70	1,203	—	1,362	1,135	951	323	—	427	306	178	369	—	395	346	308	511	—	540	483	465
1970–71	1,287	—	1,477	1,206	998	351	—	478	332	187	401	—	431	375	338	535	—	568	499	473
1971–72	1,357	—	1,579	1,263	1,073	376	—	526	354	192	430	—	463	400	366	551	—	590	509	515
1972–73	1,458	—	1,668	1,460	1,197	407	—	566	455	233	476	—	500	455	398	575	—	602	550	566
1973–74	1,517	—	1,707	1,506	1,274	438	—	581	463	274	480	—	505	464	409	599	—	621	579	591
1974–75	1,563	—	1,760	1,558	1,339	432	—	599	448	277	506	—	527	497	424	625	—	634	613	638
1975–76	1,666	—	1,935	1,657	1,386	433	—	642	469	245	544	—	573	533	442	689	—	720	655	699
1976–77	1,789	1,935	2,067	1,827	1,491	479	617	689	564	283	582	592	614	572	465	728	727	763	692	742
1977–78	1,888	2,038	2,170	1,931	1,590	512	655	736	596	306	621	631	649	616	486	755	752	785	720	797
1978–79	1,994	2,145	2,289	2,027	1,691	543	688	777	622	327	655	664	689	641	527	796	793	823	764	837
1979–80	2,165	2,327	2,487	2,198	1,822	583	738	840	662	355	715	725	750	703	574	867	865	898	833	893
1980–81	2,373	2,550	2,712	2,421	2,027	635	804	915	722	391	799	811	827	796	642	940	936	969	904	994
1981–82	2,663	2,871	3,079	2,705	2,224	714	909	1,042	813	434	909	925	970	885	703	1,039	1,036	1,067	1,006	1,086
1982–83	2,945	3,196	3,403	3,032	2,390	798	1,031	1,164	936	473	1,010	1,030	1,072	993	755	1,136	1,134	1,167	1,103	1,162
1983–84	3,156	3,433	3,628	3,285	2,534	891	1,148	1,284	1,052	528	1,087	1,110	1,131	1,092	801	1,178	1,175	1,213	1,141	1,205
1984–85	3,408	3,682	3,899	3,518	2,807	971	1,228	1,386	1,117	584	1,196	1,217	1,237	1,200	921	1,241	1,237	1,276	1,201	1,302
1985–86[2]	3,571	3,859	4,146	3,637	2,981	1,045	1,318	1,536	1,157	641	1,242	1,263	1,290	1,240	960	1,285	1,278	1,320	1,240	1,380
1986–87[3]	3,805	4,138	4,469	3,891	2,989	1,106	1,414	1,651	1,248	660	1,301	1,323	1,355	1,295	979	1,398	1,401	1,464	1,348	1,349
1987–88	4,050	4,403	4,619	4,250	3,066	1,218	1,537	1,726	1,407	706	1,378	1,410	1,410	1,409	943	1,454	1,456	1,482	1,434	1,417
1988–89	4,274	4,678	4,905	4,526	3,183	1,285	1,646	1,846	1,515	730	1,457	1,496	1,483	1,506	965	1,533	1,536	1,576	1,504	1,488
1989–90[4]	4,520	4,979	5,289	4,758	3,324	1,367	1,781	2,006	1,631	758	1,516	1,558	1,563	1,554	958	1,638	1,640	1,720	1,572	1,609

Table 291.—Average undergraduate tuition and fees and room and board rates[1] paid by students in institutions of higher education, by type and control of institution: 1964–65 to 1989–90—Continued

Year and control of institution	Total tuition, room and board					Tuition and required fees (in-State)					Dormitory rooms					Board (7-day basis)[1]				
	All institutions	4-year institutions			2-year	All institutions	4-year institutions			2-year	All institutions	4-year institutions			2-year	All institutions	4-year institutions			2-year
		All 4-year	Universities	Other 4-year			All 4-year	Universities	Other 4-year			All 4-year	Universities	Other 4-year			All 4-year	Universities	Other 4-year	
1	2	3	4	5	6	7	8	9	10	11	12	13	14	15	16	17	18	19	20	21
Private institutions																				
1964–65	1,907	—	2,202	1,810	1,455	1,088	—	1,297	1,023	702	331	—	390	308	289	488	—	515	479	464
1965–66	2,005	—	2,316	1,899	1,557	1,154	—	1,369	1,086	768	356	—	418	330	316	495	—	529	483	473
1966–67	2,124	—	2,456	2,007	1,679	1,233	—	1,456	1,162	845	385	—	452	355	347	506	—	548	490	487
1967–68	2,205	—	2,545	2,104	1,762	1,297	—	1,534	1,237	892	392	—	455	366	366	516	—	556	501	504
1968–69	2,321	—	2,673	2,237	1,876	1,383	—	1,638	1,335	956	404	—	463	382	391	534	—	572	520	529
1969–70	2,530	—	2,920	2,420	1,993	1,533	—	1,809	1,468	1,034	436	—	503	409	413	561	—	608	543	546
1970–71	2,738	—	3,163	2,599	2,103	1,684	—	1,980	1,603	1,109	468	—	542	434	434	586	—	641	562	560
1971–72	2,917	—	3,375	2,748	2,186	1,820	—	2,133	1,721	1,172	494	—	576	454	449	603	—	666	573	565
1972–73	3,038	—	3,512	2,934	2,273	1,898	—	2,226	1,846	1,221	524	—	622	490	457	616	—	664	598	595
1973–74	3,164	—	3,717	3,040	2,410	1,989	—	2,375	1,925	1,303	533	—	622	502	483	642	—	720	613	624
1974–75	3,403	—	4,076	3,156	2,591	2,117	—	2,614	1,954	1,367	586	—	691	536	564	700	—	771	666	660
1975–76	3,663	—	4,467	3,385	2,711	2,272	—	2,881	2,084	1,427	636	—	753	583	572	755	—	833	718	712
1976–77	3,906	3,977	4,715	3,714	2,971	2,467	2,534	3,051	2,351	1,592	649	651	783	604	607	790	791	882	759	772
1977–78	4,158	4,240	5,033	3,967	3,148	2,624	2,700	3,240	2,520	1,706	698	702	850	648	631	836	838	943	800	811
1978–79	4,514	4,609	5,403	4,327	3,389	2,867	2,958	3,487	2,771	1,831	758	761	916	704	700	889	890	1,000	851	858
1979–80	4,912	5,013	5,891	4,700	3,751	3,130	3,225	3,811	3,020	2,062	827	831	1,001	768	766	955	957	1,078	912	923
1980–81	5,470	5,594	6,569	5,249	4,303	3,498	3,617	4,275	3,390	2,413	918	921	1,086	859	871	1,054	1,056	1,209	1,000	1,019
1981–82	6,166	6,330	7,443	5,947	4,746	3,953	4,113	4,887	3,853	2,605	1,038	1,039	1,229	970	1,022	1,175	1,178	1,327	1,124	1,119
1982–83	6,920	7,126	8,536	6,646	5,364	4,439	4,639	5,583	4,329	3,008	1,181	1,181	1,453	1,083	1,177	1,300	1,306	1,501	1,234	1,179
1983–84	7,508	7,759	9,308	7,244	5,571	4,851	5,093	6,217	4,726	3,099	1,278	1,279	1,531	1,191	1,253	1,380	1,387	1,559	1,327	1,219
1984–85	8,202	8,451	10,243	7,849	6,203	5,315	5,556	6,843	5,135	3,485	1,426	1,426	1,753	1,309	1,424	1,462	1,469	1,647	1,405	1,294
1985–86 [2]	8,885	9,228	11,034	8,551	6,512	5,789	6,121	7,374	5,641	3,672	1,553	1,557	1,940	1,420	1,500	1,542	1,551	1,720	1,490	1,340
1986–87 [3]	9,676	10,039	12,278	9,276	6,384	6,316	6,658	8,118	6,171	3,684	1,658	1,673	2,097	1,518	1,266	1,702	1,708	2,063	1,587	1,434
1987–88	10,512	10,659	13,075	9,854	7,078	6,988	7,116	8,771	6,574	4,161	1,748	1,760	2,244	1,593	1,380	1,775	1,783	2,060	1,687	1,537
1988–89	11,189	11,474	14,073	10,620	7,967	7,461	7,722	9,451	7,172	4,817	1,849	1,863	2,353	1,686	1,540	1,880	1,889	2,269	1,762	1,609
1989–90 [4]	12,057	12,348	15,165	11,423	8,772	8,174	8,446	10,400	7,815	5,324	1,931	1,945	2,420	1,783	1,648	1,951	1,957	2,345	1,825	1,800

[1] Data for 1986–87 through 1989–90 reflect 20 meals per week rather than meals 7 days per week.

[2] Room and board data are estimated.

[3] Because of revisions in data collection procedures, figures are not entirely comparable with those for previous years. In particular, data on board rates are somewhat higher than earlier years because they reflect a basis of 20 meals per week, rather than meals 7 days per week. Since many institutions serve fewer than 3 meals each day, the 1986–87 through 1989–90 data reflect a more accurate accounting of total board costs. Because of their low response rate, data for private 2-year colleges must be interpreted with caution.

[4] Preliminary data based on 1988 enrollment data.

NOTE.—Data are for the entire academic year and are average charges paid by students. Tuition and fees were weighted by the number of full-time-equivalent undergraduates but are not adjusted to reflect student residency. Room and board were based on full-time students. The data have not been adjusted for changes in the purchasing power of the dollar. Some data have been revised from previously published figures. Because of rounding, details may not add to totals.

SOURCE: U.S. Department of Education, National Center for Education Statistics, "Institutional Characteristics of Colleges and Universities," and "Fall Enrollment in Institutions of Higher Education," surveys; Integrated Postsecondary Education Data System (IPEDS), "Fall Enrollment" and "Institutional Characteristics" surveys. (This table was prepared July 1990.)

Table 292.—Average undergraduate tuition and fees and room and board rates [1] paid by students in institutions of higher education, by control of institution and by State: 1989–90

State or other area	Public 4-year				Private 4-year				2-year, tuition only	
	Total	Tuition (in-State)	Room	Board	Total	Tuition	Room	Board	Public	Private
1	2	3	4	5	6	7	8	9	10	11
United States	$4,979	$1,781	$1,558	$1,640	$12,348	$8,446	$1,945	$1,957	$758	$5,324
Alabama	4,119	1,522	1,236	1,361	8,212	5,484	1,136	1,592	662	3,703
Alaska	4,352	1,280	1,493	1,579	9,030	5,078	1,742	2,210	—	—
Arizona	5,595	1,362	1,416	2,817	6,432	4,127	1,026	1,279	519	11,007
Arkansas	4,187	1,376	1,387	1,424	6,110	3,715	994	1,401	644	6,102
California	5,547	1,123	2,182	2,242	14,245	9,489	2,423	2,333	112	7,664
Colorado	4,956	1,830	1,489	1,637	12,920	9,188	1,833	1,899	792	8,036
Connecticut	5,445	2,017	1,758	1,670	16,184	11,268	2,635	2,281	915	7,906
Delaware	6,196	2,768	1,613	1,815	8,776	5,388	1,821	1,567	882	—
District of Columbia	—	664	—	—	14,622	9,489	2,701	2,432	—	—
Florida	—	—	—	—	10,738	7,153	1,870	1,715	729	5,519
Georgia	4,308	1,631	1,193	1,484	10,244	7,076	1,511	1,657	852	3,194
Hawaii	4,529	1,293	1,242	1,994	6,997	4,008	1,399	1,590	410	—
Idaho	3,792	1,119	943	1,730	9,827	6,669	908	2,250	779	1,400
Illinois	5,495	2,370	1,553	1,572	12,209	8,281	2,021	1,907	871	5,505
Indiana	4,969	1,975	1,349	1,645	11,461	8,267	1,621	1,573	1,374	7,412
Iowa	4,347	1,823	1,239	1,285	10,769	7,945	1,293	1,531	1,225	6,423
Kansas	3,509	1,467	1,017	1,025	8,272	5,460	1,184	1,628	711	3,962
Kentucky	4,047	1,316	1,129	1,602	7,366	4,689	1,168	1,509	693	4,669
Louisiana	4,311	1,768	1,212	1,331	13,464	9,257	2,157	2,050	837	5,648
Maine	5,429	1,980	1,729	1,720	14,598	10,425	2,085	2,088	1,134	3,787
Maryland	6,437	2,120	2,230	2,087	14,621	9,914	2,463	2,244	1,172	8,393
Massachusetts	5,478	2,052	1,827	1,599	16,904	11,450	2,834	2,620	1,332	7,186
Michigan	5,854	2,484	1,493	1,877	9,764	6,520	1,481	1,763	1,047	6,400
Minnesota	4,670	2,063	1,262	1,345	11,891	8,776	1,535	1,580	1,499	5,181
Mississippi	4,241	1,858	1,111	1,272	7,208	4,828	1,062	1,318	680	3,602
Missouri	4,098	1,532	1,449	1,117	10,691	7,170	1,817	1,704	815	5,554
Montana	5,047	1,535	1,478	2,034	8,013	5,034	1,071	1,908	877	1,144
Nebraska	3,944	1,519	1,043	1,382	9,101	6,442	1,325	1,334	919	3,410
Nevada	4,007	1,100	1,481	1,426	—	5,400	2,000	—	522	—
New Hampshire	5,484	2,196	2,050	1,238	14,748	10,299	2,347	2,102	1,608	4,050
New Jersey	6,396	2,511	2,267	1,618	14,439	9,398	2,270	2,771	1,130	6,748
New Mexico	4,018	1,326	1,250	1,442	10,563	7,335	1,309	1,919	496	—
New York	5,094	1,460	2,014	1,620	14,076	9,517	2,341	2,218	1,412	5,544
North Carolina	3,790	1,015	1,293	1,482	10,412	7,373	1,345	1,694	288	4,880
North Dakota	4,360	1,604	847	1,909	7,939	5,149	1,308	1,482	1,286	2,100
Ohio	5,805	2,432	1,658	1,715	11,330	8,019	1,594	1,717	1,636	5,690
Oklahoma	3,754	1,309	1,096	1,349	8,119	5,133	1,308	1,678	840	5,382
Oregon	4,776	1,738	1,233	1,805	12,074	8,656	1,602	1,816	753	5,250
Pennsylvania	6,366	3,210	1,641	1,515	13,416	9,430	2,030	1,956	1,419	5,497
Rhode Island	6,340	2,281	2,140	1,919	14,126	10,143	1,935	2,048	1,004	—
South Carolina	5,089	2,162	1,367	1,560	8,771	5,914	1,356	1,501	807	4,898
South Dakota	4,236	1,718	873	1,645	8,595	6,224	1,106	1,265	—	2,447
Tennessee	4,172	1,406	1,287	1,479	9,642	6,530	1,572	1,540	803	3,395
Texas	4,168	959	1,585	1,624	9,402	6,047	1,526	1,829	455	5,112
Utah	4,342	1,429	1,449	1,464	4,970	1,975	1,169	1,826	1,136	2,768
Vermont	7,715	3,641	2,386	1,688	14,691	10,928	1,846	1,917	2,210	5,979
Virginia	5,983	2,532	1,851	1,600	10,342	7,238	1,472	1,632	813	4,409
Washington	4,634	1,710	1,534	1,390	11,229	8,096	1,618	1,515	802	7,045
West Virginia	5,128	1,591	1,857	1,680	10,058	7,197	1,287	1,574	803	2,554
Wisconsin	4,411	1,861	1,351	1,199	11,021	7,615	1,434	1,972	1,160	4,001
Wyoming	3,880	1,003	1,226	1,651	—	—	—	—	613	6,900

[1] Preliminary data based on fall 1988 enrollment weights.

—Data not reported or not applicable.

NOTE.—Data are for the entire academic year and are average charges. Tuition and fees were weighted by the number of full-time-equivalent undergraduates but are not adjusted to reflect student residency. Room and board are based on full-time students.

SOURCE: U.S. Department of Education, National Center for Education Statistics, Integrated Postsecondary Education Data System (IPEDS), "Fall Enrollment" and "Institutional Characteristics" surveys. (This table was prepared July 1990.)

Table 293.—Percentage of undergraduates enrolled in fall 1986 and average amount awarded in 1986–87 per student, by type and source of aid and selected student characteristics

Selected student characteristics	Enrollment of under-graduates,[1] in thousands	Any aid			Grants			Loans			Work study		
		Total[2]	Federal	Non-Federal	Total	Federal	Non-Federal	Total	Federal	Non-Federal	Total	Federal	Non-Federal
1	2	3	4	5	6	7	8	9	10	11	12	13	14
		Percent of all undergraduates receiving aid											
All undergraduates	11,185	48.6	34.5	32.7	36.4	24.6	25.9	24.1	23.0	1.7	6.1	4.3	2.1
Sex													
Men	5,012	47.7	33.7	31.8	35.3	23.5	25.0	23.4	28.9	1.5	5.6	3.8	2.0
Women	6,174	49.2	35.2	33.3	37.3	25.5	26.6	24.6	18.3	1.8	6.6	4.7	2.1
Race/ethnicity													
White, non-Hispanic	8,700	46.3	31.5	32.0	33.8	20.9	25.5	23.2	22.2	1.7	5.6	3.8	2.1
Black, non-Hispanic	1,047	66.7	55.5	37.6	55.7	47.0	30.1	34.9	32.6	2.8	9.8	8.1	2.1
Hispanic	759	51.8	40.9	31.6	39.9	33.1	24.6	24.0	23.4	1.1	5.8	4.3	1.5
Asian American	572	44.9	32.3	34.0	35.2	27.0	26.3	18.0	17.7	0.9	7.5	5.2	2.5
American Indian	106	53.0	40.4	34.7	38.8	34.6	23.7	19.1	18.0	1.1	6.8	4.3	3.1
Age													
23 years old or younger	6,754	52.9	38.7	37.0	40.1	26.4	30.5	28.6	27.5	1.9	8.4	5.9	2.9
24 to 29 years old	1,880	45.5	33.3	25.6	33.1	25.5	18.5	21.6	20.4	1.9	3.6	2.6	1.1
30 years old or over	2,551	39.4	24.4	26.3	28.9	19.1	19.1	13.9	13.2	1.0	2.0	1.3	0.7
Marital status													
Married	2,710	39.1	24.1	24.4	27.9	17.9	17.3	14.8	13.9	1.3	2.0	1.5	0.6
Not married[3]	8,475	51.6	37.8	35.3	39.1	26.7	28.6	27.0	25.9	1.8	7.4	5.2	2.6
Attendance status[4]													
Full-time	6,954	60.4	46.6	40.2	46.8	32.9	33.8	33.6	32.5	2.0	9.1	6.5	3.0
Part-time	4,226	29.1	14.7	20.2	19.2	10.9	12.8	8.3	7.5	1.2	1.3	0.7	0.6
Dependency status													
Dependent	7,048	47.8	33.0	34.2	34.8	21.4	27.4	24.7	23.6	1.7	7.3	4.9	2.7
Independent	4,138	49.9	37.1	29.9	39.1	30.1	23.3	23.0	22.0	1.6	4.2	3.3	1.1
Housing status													
School-owned	2,215	66.4	48.8	51.4	52.0	31.0	44.1	41.1	39.8	2.6	16.3	11.4	5.8
Off-campus, not with parents	5,633	45.4	32.1	28.5	33.6	23.8	21.7	21.6	20.5	1.6	4.0	2.9	1.2
With parents	3,337	42.1	29.0	27.3	30.8	21.7	20.8	16.9	16.1	1.2	2.9	1.9	1.1
		Average 1986–87 award for full-time, full-year undergraduates enrolled in fall 1986											
All full-time, full-year undergraduates	6,068	$3,674	$2,862	$2,130	$2,533	$1,538	$1,966	$2,349	$2,322	$1,690	$1,061	$962	$1,135
Sex													
Men	2,833	3,808	2,975	2,239	2,671	1,658	2,064	2,398	2,369	1,740	1,064	951	1,144
Women	3,235	3,565	2,771	2,044	2,423	1,444	1,889	2,310	2,282	1,656	1,059	969	1,129
Race/ethnicity													
White, non-Hispanic	4,793	3,573	2,850	2,066	2,434	1,488	1,893	2,372	2,334	1,811	1,025	926	1,082
Black, non-Hispanic	537	4,023	3,036	2,273	2,695	1,704	2,157	2,207	2,242	1,128	1,162	1,020	1,445
Hispanic	361	3,692	2,699	2,139	2,656	1,494	2,083	2,395	2,360	1,954	1,179	1,158	1,197
Asian American	332	4,257	2,800	2,661	3,200	1,648	2,407	2,261	2,249	1,133	1,183	1,042	1,374
American Indian	45	4,196	2,852	2,637	3,260	1,812	2,576	2,439	2,439	—	681	646	662
Age													
23 years old or younger	4,803	3,713	2,825	2,213	2,587	1,455	2,080	2,343	2,314	1,748	1,051	953	1,109
24 to 29 years old	667	3,591	3,017	1,866	2,343	1,734	1,521	2,311	2,299	1,344	1,161	1,052	1,361
30 years old or over	598	3,488	2,927	1,703	2,360	1,774	1,417	2,446	2,405	1,759	1,049	954	1,219
Marital status													
Married	704	3,354	2,927	1,765	2,260	1,701	1,558	2,424	2,411	1,307	1,042	997	1,094
Not married[3]	5,364	3,718	2,853	2,171	2,569	1,513	2,007	2,339	2,310	1,744	1,062	959	1,137
Dependency status													
Dependent	4,747	3,617	2,732	2,247	2,551	1,368	2,111	2,348	2,320	1,745	1,030	924	1,100
Independent	1,321	3,821	3,133	1,750	2,490	1,813	1,504	2,353	2,324	1,545	1,168	1,075	1,319
Housing status													
School-owned	1,979	4,528	3,155	2,812	3,160	1,603	2,591	2,406	2,346	2,083	1,014	873	1,134
Off-campus, not with parents	2,251	3,561	2,987	1,785	2,364	1,691	1,581	2,328	2,315	1,437	1,161	1,016	1,207
With parents	1,838	2,642	2,232	1,501	1,890	1,210	1,434	2,272	2,281	1,350	1,030	985	1,013
		Average 1986–87 award for other undergraduates enrolled in fall 1986											
All other undergraduates[5]	5,117	1,971	2,108	1,102	1,376	1,186	978	2,051	2,060	1,358	1,001	934	975
Sex													
Men	2,179	1,983	2,034	1,233	1,458	1,250	1,095	2,035	2,000	1,757	1,160	956	1,114
Women	2,938	1,962	2,159	1,007	1,318	1,144	897	2,061	2,097	1,090	905	923	836
Race/ethnicity													
White, non-Hispanic	3,907	1,848	2,024	1,083	1,298	1,134	960	2,037	2,023	1,477	1,009	899	1,000
Black, non-Hispanic	510	2,266	2,226	1,060	1,487	1,279	907	1,984	2,068	906	1,108	1,009	1,352
Hispanic	398	2,260	2,373	1,099	1,521	1,229	1,048	2,230	2,257	973	838	991	586
Asian American	240	2,523	2,381	1,621	1,817	1,356	1,365	2,251	2,168	3,041	989	1,029	949
American Indian	61	1,738	1,841	919	1,866	1,262	1,264	1,643	1,830	690	484	719	277
Age													
23 years old or younger	1,950	2,297	2,242	1,257	1,595	1,202	1,185	2,008	2,041	1,097	987	843	1,030
24 to 29 years old	1,213	1,737	1,945	936	1,168	1,120	760	1,977	2,004	1,230	1,021	1,082	804
30 years old or over	1,953	1,744	2,028	1,034	1,257	1,219	869	2,217	2,152	2,044	1,026	1,078	887

Table 293.—Percentage of undergraduates enrolled in fall 1986 and average amount awarded in 1986–87 per student, by type and source of aid and selected student characteristics—Continued

Selected student characteristics	Enrollment of under- graduates,[1] in thousands	Any aid			Grants			Loans			Work study		
		Total[2]	Federal	Non- Federal	Total	Federal	Non- Federal	Total	Federal	Non- Federal	Total	Federal	Non- Federal
1	2	3	4	5	6	7	8	9	10	11	12	13	14
Marital status													
Married	2,006	1,683	1,956	1,067	1,186	1,180	865	2,184	2,136	1,944	986	857	1,150
Not married[3]	3,111	2,127	2,170	1,123	1,479	1,189	1,043	2,005	2,034	1,083	1,004	949	946
Dependency status													
Dependent	2,300	2,097	2,121	1,281	1,503	1,124	1,191	1,988	2,013	1,154	1,016	897	1,076
Independent	2,817	1,885	2,099	974	1,301	1,222	840	2,104	2,098	1,554	981	973	812
Housing status													
School-owned	236	3,316	2,524	1,999	2,341	1,261	1,946	2,071	2,002	1,444	1,064	884	1,116
Off-campus, not with parents	3,381	1,818	2,059	982	1,250	1,184	820	2,065	2,077	1,417	900	926	754
With parents	1,499	1,942	2,080	1,084	1,390	1,168	1,002	2,012	2,048	1,128	1,179	1,075	1,249

[1] Numbers of undergraduates may not equal figures reported in other tables, since these data are based on a sample survey.

[2] Includes students who reported they were awarded aid, but did not specify the source or type of aid.

[3] Includes students who were single, separated, divorced, or widowed.

[4] Excludes persons whose attendance status was not reported.

[5] Enrollment data include persons whose attendance status was not reported.

—Data not available.

NOTE.—Because of rounding and/or the fact that some students receive aid from multiple sources, details may not add to totals. Data have been revised from previously published figures.

SOURCE: U.S. Department of Education, National Center for Education Statistics, *National Postsecondary Student Aid Study,* unpublished data. (This table was prepared June 1991.)

Table 294.—Undergraduates enrolled in fall 1986, by aid status and source of aid during 1986–87, and control and level of institution

Control and level of institution	Number of undergraduates, fall 1986[1] in thousands	Aid status, 1986–87, in percents					
		Nonaided	Receiving aid, by source				
			Any aid[2]	Federal	State	Institutional	Other[2]
1	2	3	4	5	6	7	8
All institutions	**11,185**	**51.4**	**48.6**	**34.5**	**14.7**	**17.7**	**7.8**
Public	8,558	58.6	41.4	28.2	12.5	12.8	6.9
4-year doctoral	2,565	50.5	49.5	34.7	13.9	17.9	8.1
Other 4-year	1,683	50.3	49.7	37.8	19.1	12.3	6.8
2-year	4,180	67.4	32.6	19.8	9.0	9.9	6.2
Less than 2-year	129	44.5	55.5	43.2	14.1	9.4	4.8
Private, nonprofit	2,026	31.9	68.1	47.7	25.5	42.3	12.6
4-year doctoral	756	35.2	64.8	44.5	21.3	41.3	12.6
Other 4-year	1,120	29.7	70.3	49.7	28.5	44.6	13.3
2-year	134	31.2	68.8	48.0	24.5	32.9	7.7
Less than 2-year	16	32.4	67.6	59.4	27.2	5.5	7.3
Private, proprietary	602	15.0	85.0	80.6	10.3	5.4	3.8
2-year and above	223	16.7	83.3	79.1	18.1	5.1	4.0
Less than 2-year	379	14.1	85.9	81.4	5.7	5.5	3.8

[1] Numbers of undergraduates may not equal figures reported in other tables, since these data are based on a sample survey.

[2] Includes students who reported they were awarded aid but did not specify the source of aid.

NOTE.—Because some students receive aid from multiple sources, details may not add to totals. Data have been revised from previously published figures.

SOURCE: U.S. Department of Education, National Center for Education Statistics, *National Postsecondary Student Aid Study,* unpublished data. (This table was prepared March 1991.)

Table 295.—Undergraduates enrolled in fall 1986, by type and source of aid received during 1986–87, and by control and level of institution

Control and level of institution	Number of undergraduates, fall 1986[1]	Type and source of aid, 1986–87, in percents											
		Any aid			Grants			Loans			Work-study		
		Total[2]	Federal	Non-Federal	Total	Federal	Non-Federal	Total	Federal	Non-Federal	Total	Federal[3]	Non-Federal
1	2	3	4	5	6	7	8	9	10	11	12	13	14
All institutions	**11,185,356**	**48.6**	**34.5**	**32.7**	**36.4**	**24.6**	**25.9**	**24.1**	**23.0**	**1.7**	**6.1**	**4.3**	**2.1**
Public	8,557,781	41.4	28.2	27.7	30.3	21.3	20.9	17.0	16.0	1.3	4.6	3.3	1.4
4-year doctoral	2,564,851	49.5	34.7	32.4	35.0	23.1	25.0	26.9	25.8	1.7	5.7	4.2	1.8
Other 4-year	1,683,448	49.7	37.8	33.2	36.6	27.9	26.6	24.6	23.7	1.4	8.1	5.6	2.7
2-year	4,180,263	32.6	19.8	22.7	24.4	17.0	16.1	7.7	6.7	1.2	2.4	1.9	0.6
Less than 2-year	129,219	55.5	43.2	25.9	42.9	34.7	18.6	19.6	19.4	0.5	3.4	2.5	0.9
Private, nonprofit	2,025,592	68.1	47.7	57.8	55.3	29.5	50.4	40.1	38.9	3.0	14.4	9.6	5.7
4-year doctoral	755,502	64.8	44.5	55.2	50.9	24.6	46.4	38.5	37.0	3.7	13.1	8.9	4.5
Other 4-year	1,119,871	70.3	49.7	60.6	58.6	32.2	54.3	41.8	40.7	2.5	16.4	10.7	7.1
2-year	133,779	68.8	48.0	51.2	53.3	32.4	42.8	35.8	34.4	2.5	5.7	5.2	0.4
Less than 2-year	16,441	67.6	59.4	37.3	55.1	45.2	33.1	40.4	38.9	1.9	5.0	4.0	1.7
Private, proprietary	601,983	85.0	80.6	18.4	60.0	55.6	14.6	70.7	70.0	2.2	0.8	0.5	0.3
2-year and above	223,448	83.3	79.1	25.2	54.7	48.9	22.4	69.3	68.5	2.1	1.2	0.7	0.6
Less than 2-year	378,535	85.9	81.4	14.4	63.1	59.6	10.0	71.5	70.9	2.2	0.5	0.5	0.1

[1] Numbers of undergraduates may not equal figures reported in other tables, since these data are based on a sample survey.

[2] Includes students who reported they were awarded aid but did not specify the source of aid.

[3] Prior to October 17, 1986, private, proprietary institutions were prohibited by law from spending CWS (College Work-Study) funds for on-campus work.

NOTE.—Because some students receive multiple types and sources of aid, details may not add to totals. Data have been revised from previously published figures.

SOURCE: U.S. Department of Education, National Center for Education Statistics, *Undergraduate Financing of Postsecondary Education: A Report of the 1987 National Postsecondary Student Aid Study.* (This table was prepared March 1991.)

Table 296.—Postbaccalaureate students enrolled in fall 1986, by aid status and source of aid during 1986–87, and by control and level of institution

Level of degree, control and type of institution	Number of postbaccalaureate students,[1] fall 1986	Aid status, 1986–87, in percents						
		Nonaided	Receiving aid, by source					
			Any aid[2]	Federal	State	Institutional	Employer	Other[3]
1	2	3	4	5	6	7	8	9
All institutions	**1,358**	**42.0**	**58.0**	**29.1**	**6.1**	**35.8**	**7.3**	**4.7**
Master's degree	843	51.6	48.4	18.1	3.3	29.1	9.7	3.0
Public	520	53.9	46.1	16.4	3.5	30.0	7.1	2.4
4-year doctoral	351	49.3	50.7	17.5	3.4	34.1	7.4	2.6
Other 4-year	169	63.4	36.6	14.2	3.7	21.5	6.5	1.8
Private	324	47.8	52.2	20.9	3.0	27.6	13.9	3.9
4-year doctoral	217	42.9	57.1	22.8	3.4	33.1	13.8	4.8
Other 4-year	107	57.7	42.3	16.9	2.1	16.5	14.1	2.2
Doctor's degree	194	26.2	73.8	21.2	4.5	61.0	6.3	4.9
Public	124	27.9	72.1	21.2	5.1	60.4	5.5	4.1
Private	70	23.1	76.9	21.0	3.3	61.9	7.6	6.4
First-professional	320	26.4	73.6	62.9	14.6	38.1	1.3	9.1
Public	110	27.6	72.4	61.4	13.8	31.9	1.5	9.4
Private	210	25.8	74.2	63.7	15.1	41.4	1.2	9.0

[1] Numbers of postbaccalaureate students may not equal figures reported in other tables, since these data are based on a sample survey of all postsecondary postbaccalaureate students.

[2] Includes students who reported they were awarded aid but did not specify the source of aid.

[3] Includes aid provided by corporations, unions, foundations, fraternal organizations, community organizations, etc.

NOTE.—Because some students receive aid from multiple sources, details may not add to totals. Data have been revised from previously published figures.

SOURCE: U.S. Department of Education, National Center for Education Statistics, *Student Financing of Graduate and Professional Education: A Report of the 1987 National Postsecondary Student Aid Study;* and unpublished data. (This table was prepared April 1991.)

Table 297.—Undergraduates enrolled in fall 1986, by Federal aid program and by control and level of institution: 1986–87

Control and level of institution	Number of undergraduates, fall 1986[1]	Type of Federal aid, 1986–87, in percents							
		Any Federal aid	Any Title IV aid[2]	Selected Title IV programs[3]					Any other Federal aid[6]
				Pell	SEOG	CWS[4]	NDSL	GSL[5]	
1	2	3	4	5	6	7	8	9	10
All institutions	11,213,432	34.9	30.8	17.5	5.0	4.3	5.6	20.5	4.0
Public	8,572,090	28.5	24.3	15.5	3.7	3.3	4.0	13.7	4.1
4-year doctoral	2,581,556	35.5	32.0	16.9	4.7	4.2	7.6	21.9	3.6
Other 4-year	1,681,052	38.4	34.6	21.1	5.5	5.7	6.8	19.8	3.7
2-year	4,180,263	19.9	15.1	12.0	2.5	1.9	0.6	6.0	4.3
Less than 2-year	129,219	41.9	33.1	25.6	2.3	2.5	2.4	18.0	9.4
Private, nonprofit	2,038,949	48.4	44.7	17.3	8.9	9.6	11.8	35.2	3.8
4-year doctoral	769,069	45.7	41.1	13.0	8.0	8.9	13.6	33.9	4.8
Other 4-year	1,119,661	50.1	46.8	19.0	9.9	10.7	11.6	36.4	3.2
2-year	133,779	47.9	45.6	25.6	4.9	5.2	4.2	32.1	2.7
Less than 2-year	16,441	59.4	56.1	33.6	7.6	4.0	0.9	37.6	5.8
Private, proprietary	602,394	80.6	75.5	46.9	9.6	0.5	7.7	67.3	4.9
2-year and above	223,859	79.2	74.8	39.5	9.5	0.7	7.9	65.8	4.4
Less than 2-year	378,535	81.4	75.9	51.3	9.8	0.5	7.5	68.1	5.2

[1] Numbers of undergraduates may not equal figures reported in other tables, since these data are based on a sample survey.

[2] Includes Pell, SEOG, CWS, NDSL, GSL, PLUS/ALAS (Parent Loans for Undergraduates and Auxiliary Loans to Assist Students) and the Federal portion of SSIG (State Student Incentive Grants) program.

[3] Selected types of Federal aid: SEOG=Supplemental Educational Opportunity Grants; CWS=College Work-Study; NDSL=National Direct Student Loans; GSL=Guaranteed Student Loans.

[4] Prior to October 17, 1986, private, proprietary institutions were prohibited by law from spending CWS funds for on-campus work.

[5] Does not include PLUS/ALAS.

[6] Includes aid from all Federal departments and agencies except Title IV aid.

NOTE.—Because some students receive aid from multiple sources, details may not add to totals.

SOURCE: U.S. Department of Education, National Center for Education Statistics, *Undergraduate Financing of Postsecondary Education: A Report of the 1987 National Postsecondary Student Aid Study.* (This table was prepared February 1989.)

Table 298.—Postbaccalaureate students enrolled in fall 1986, by type of aid received during 1986–87, by level of study and by control and level of institution

Level of degree, control and type of institution	Number of postbaccalaureate students,[1] fall 1986	Type of aid, 1986–87, in percents						
		Any aid[2]	Fellowships/ grants[3]	Tuition waivers	Assistantships[4]	Loans		
						Any loans	Guaranteed student loans	Other
All institutions	1,357,763	58.0	25.4	17.5	20.1	28.4	25.3	14.6
Master's degree	843,328	48.4	22.3	17.3	17.7	17.1	14.9	5.6
Public	519,787	46.1	17.6	20.2	20.6	15.0	13.0	4.1
4-year doctoral	350,909	50.7	19.6	23.1	24.4	16.5	14.3	4.5
Other 4-year	168,878	36.6	13.4	14.2	12.7	12.0	10.4	3.2
Private	323,541	52.2	29.9	12.7	13.0	20.5	17.8	7.9
4-year doctoral	216,609	57.1	32.9	16.3	16.3	22.3	19.5	9.5
Other 4-year	106,932	42.3	24.0	5.4	6.3	16.8	14.3	4.6
Doctor's degree	194,137	73.8	30.8	37.1	46.9	19.5	16.7	7.3
Public	124,252	72.1	24.5	37.2	50.2	19.4	17.2	5.8
Private	69,885	76.9	42.1	36.8	41.1	19.9	15.7	10.0
First-professional	320,298	73.6	30.0	6.0	10.4	63.6	58.1	42.9
Public	110,237	72.4	29.6	6.9	10.3	61.2	56.8	37.0
Private	210,061	74.2	30.2	5.5	10.5	64.8	58.7	45.9

[1] Numbers of postbaccalaureate students may not equal figures reported on other tables, since these data are based on a sample survey.

[2] Includes students who reported they were awarded aid but did not specify the type of aid.

[3] Includes students who received employer benefits.

[4] Includes students who received teaching or research assistantships and/or participated in work-study programs.

NOTE.—Because some students receive various types of aid, details may not add to totals. Data have been revised from previously published figures.

SOURCE: U.S. Department of Education, National Center for Education Statistics, *National Postsecondary Student Aid Study, unpublished data.* (This table was prepared April 1991.)

Table 299.—Scholarship and fellowship awards [1] of institutions of higher education, by control of institution: 1959–60 to 1987–88

[In thousands]

Year	Total scholarship and fellowship awards			Scholarship and fellowship awards from unrestricted funds			Scholarship and fellowship awards from restricted funds		
	All institutions	Public	Private	All institutions	Public	Private	All institutions	Public	Private
1	2	3	4	5	6	7	8	9	10
1959–60	$172,051	$59,673	$112,377	—	—	—	—	—	—
1961–62	228,765	78,255	150,510	—	—	—	—	—	—
1963–64	300,370	107,767	192,603	—	—	—	—	—	—
1965–66	425,524	153,256	272,269	—	—	—	—	—	—
1966–67	583,390	248,077	335,311	—	—	—	—	—	—
1967–68	712,425	326,915	385,510	—	—	—	—	—	—
1968–69	814,755	367,433	447,322	—	—	—	—	—	—
1969–70	984,594	456,977	527,617	—	—	—	—	—	—
1970–71	1,098,198	528,243	569,955	—	—	—	—	—	—
1971–72	1,241,372	621,387	619,986	—	—	—	—	—	—
1972–73	1,322,411	656,054	666,357	—	—	—	—	—	—
1973–74	1,396,488	705,691	690,797	—	—	—	—	—	—
1974–75	1,449,542	718,780	730,762	$631,801	$267,191	$364,610	$817,741	$451,589	$366,152
1975–76	1,635,859	798,515	837,343	686,604	276,334	410,269	949,255	522,181	427,074
1976–77	1,770,215	859,011	911,204	748,763	291,073	457,690	1,021,451	567,938	453,514
1977–78	1,839,298	840,666	998,632	818,101	305,563	512,537	1,021,197	535,102	486,095
1978–79	1,944,599	861,578	1,083,021	883,213	326,201	557,012	1,061,386	535,377	526,009
1979–80	2,200,468	970,363	1,230,106	904,876	324,224	580,652	1,295,592	646,138	649,454
1980–81	2,504,525	1,064,864	1,439,661	1,080,614	367,476	713,138	1,423,911	697,388	726,523
1981–82	2,684,945	1,088,717	1,596,228	1,236,081	374,632	861,449	1,448,864	714,085	734,779
1982–83	2,922,897	1,188,383	1,734,514	1,478,762	460,291	1,018,470	1,444,136	728,092	716,044
1983–84	3,301,673	1,276,644	2,025,028	1,738,188	518,626	1,219,562	1,563,485	758,018	805,466
1984–85	3,670,355	1,374,803	2,295,551	1,961,597	569,058	1,392,539	1,708,758	805,745	903,012
1985–86	4,160,174	1,575,909	2,584,266	2,285,116	696,973	1,588,143	1,875,059	878,935	996,123
1986–87	4,776,100	1,751,671	3,024,430	2,644,615	750,931	1,893,684	2,131,486	1,000,740	1,130,746
1987–88 [2]	5,324,933	1,941,390	3,383,543	2,940,929	830,195	2,110,734	2,384,003	1,111,194	1,272,809

[1] Includes Supplementary Educational Opportunity Grants and State Student Incentive Grants, but excludes Pell Grants.
[2] Preliminary data.
—Data not collected.

NOTE.—Because of rounding, details may not add to totals.

SOURCE: U.S. Department of Education, National Center for Education Statistics, "Financial Statistics of Institutions of Higher Education" surveys and Integrated Postsecondary Education Data System (IPEDS), "Finance" survey. (This table was prepared April 1991.)

Table 300.—Pell Grant revenue of institutions of higher education compared to current-fund revenue and tuition, by type and control of institution: 1983–84 to 1987–88

[Amounts in thousands]

Year and type of control of institution	Current-fund revenue		Pell Grant revenue	Pell Grants as a percent of current-fund revenue	Pell Grants as a percent of tuition	Distribution of Pell Grants
	Total	Tuition				
1	2	3	4	5	6	7
1983–84						
Total	84,417,287	19,714,884	2,119,716	2.5	10.8	100.0
4-year	73,827,400	17,399,381	1,478,158	2.0	8.5	69.7
2-year	10,589,887	2,315,503	641,558	6.1	27.7	30.3
Public	54,545,275	8,123,318	1,478,362	2.7	18.2	69.7
4-year	44,849,649	6,419,039	962,451	2.1	15.0	45.4
2-year	9,695,626	1,704,279	515,910	5.3	30.3	24.3
Private	29,872,012	11,591,566	641,354	2.1	5.5	30.3
4-year	28,977,751	10,980,342	515,706	1.8	4.7	24.3
2-year	894,261	611,224	125,648	14.1	20.6	5.9
1984–85						
Total	92,472,694	21,283,329	2,259,538	2.4	10.6	100.0
4-year	81,023,952	18,814,449	1,572,771	1.9	8.4	69.6
2-year	11,448,743	2,468,879	686,767	6.0	27.8	30.4
Public	59,794,159	8,647,637	1,607,965	2.7	18.6	71.2
4-year	49,325,939	6,849,480	1,052,350	2.1	15.4	46.6
2-year	10,468,220	1,798,157	555,615	5.3	30.9	24.6
Private	32,678,536	12,635,691	651,573	2.0	5.2	28.8
4-year	31,698,013	11,964,969	520,421	1.6	4.3	23.0
2-year	980,523	670,722	131,152	13.4	19.6	5.8
1985–86						
Total	100,437,616	23,116,605	2,565,048	2.6	11.1	100.0
4-year	88,144,386	20,498,399	1,770,042	2.0	8.6	69.0
2-year	12,293,231	2,618,206	795,006	6.5	30.4	31.0
Public	65,004,632	9,439,177	1,873,456	2.9	19.8	73.0
4-year	53,746,503	7,539,717	1,214,303	2.3	16.1	47.3
2-year	11,258,128	1,899,460	659,153	5.9	34.7	25.7
Private	35,432,985	13,677,429	691,592	2.0	5.1	27.0
4-year	34,397,882	12,958,683	555,739	1.6	4.3	21.7
2-year	1,035,102	718,746	135,853	13.1	18.9	5.3
1986–87						
Total	109,981,606	24,732,651	2,289,104	2.1	9.3	100.0
4-year	96,793,437	22,451,939	1,627,190	1.7	7.2	71.1
2-year	13,188,168	2,280,712	661,914	5.0	29.0	28.9
Public	71,408,764	10,198,633	1,795,475	2.5	17.6	78.4
4-year	58,810,417	8,200,747	1,165,978	2.0	14.2	50.9
2-year	12,598,347	1,997,886	629,497	5.0	31.5	27.5
Private	38,572,842	14,534,018	493,629	1.3	3.4	21.6
4-year	37,983,020	14,251,192	461,212	1.2	3.2	20.1
2-year	589,822	282,826	32,417	5.5	11.5	1.4
1987–88 [1]						
Total	118,840,747	27,028,579	2,399,125	2.0	8.9	100.0
4-year	104,720,559	24,543,137	1,695,693	1.6	6.9	70.7
2-year	14,120,187	2,485,442	703,432	5.0	28.3	29.3
Public	76,648,032	11,184,657	1,876,777	2.4	16.8	78.2
4-year	63,166,199	9,032,936	1,207,418	1.9	13.4	50.3
2-year	13,481,834	2,151,721	669,359	5.0	31.1	27.9
Private	42,192,715	15,843,922	522,348	1.2	3.3	21.8
4-year	41,554,361	15,510,201	488,274	1.2	3.1	20.4
2-year	638,354	333,721	34,073	5.3	10.2	1.4

[1] Preliminary data.

NOTE.—Pell Grants which are spent on campus for tuition, room, board or other college expenses are included in current-fund revenue. Because of rounding, details may not add to totals.

SOURCE: U.S. Department of Education, National Center for Education Statistics, "Financial Statistics of Institutions of Higher Education" surveys and Integrated Postsecondary Education Data System (IPEDS), "Finance" survey. (This table was prepared April 1991.)

Table 301.—State awards for need-based [1] undergraduate scholarship and grant programs, by State: 1983–84 to 1990–91

[In thousands]

State	1983–84	1984–85	1985–86	1986–87	1987–88	1988–89	1989–90	1990–91 [2]	Percent change, 1983–84 to 1990–91 [3]
1	2	3	4	5	6	7	8	9	10
United States	$1,024,206	$1,141,870	$1,222,112	$1,325,984	$1,377,996	$1,423,743	$1,539,182	$1,647,435	60.8
Alabama	1,731	2,242	2,242	2,120	2,260	2,196	2,984	4,308	148.9
Alaska	189	241	241	229	[4]240	234	228	464	145.5
Arizona	2,027	2,355	2,401	2,437	3,222	3,508	3,420	3,410	68.2
Arkansas	2,226	3,792	4,108	3,800	3,759	3,903	3,946	4,137	85.8
California	86,031	92,166	112,373	112,770	118,819	129,264	153,045	161,859	88.1
Colorado	7,341	8,779	9,282	9,491	9,327	[4]9,395	10,349	11,075	50.9
Connecticut	9,371	9,612	11,095	9,094	14,650	21,149	19,915	20,803	122.0
Delaware	548	536	756	875	807	829	956	1,243	126.8
District of Columbia	759	1,109	1,106	1,059	1,106	1,075	1,069	974	28.3
Florida	12,515	13,967	14,819	14,151	15,245	16,522	20,134	27,132	116.8
Georgia	3,683	4,040	4,510	4,946	4,599	5,197	4,607	5,174	40.5
Hawaii	493	493	604	595	563	[4]598	726	611	23.9
Idaho	378	509	509	487	343	348	346	342	9.5
Illinois	104,384	110,217	122,300	131,788	135,880	143,373	171,361	180,650	73.1
Indiana	20,380	25,007	26,448	30,512	45,408	35,692	41,874	46,488	128.1
Iowa	20,263	22,205	22,379	22,378	25,960	30,050	32,467	37,648	85.8
Kansas	4,664	4,841	5,609	5,250	5,337	5,540	6,478	6,585	41.2
Kentucky	7,886	8,242	8,758	12,139	12,161	12,522	12,605	19,393	145.9
Louisiana	1,693	1,931	2,003	1,818	[4]1,880	1,947	2,786	4,196	147.8
Maine	477	794	809	1,151	1,418	1,408	1,877	5,100	969.2
Maryland	5,459	7,361	6,859	7,822	8,737	12,841	14,800	15,076	176.2
Massachusetts	25,655	35,937	43,466	56,995	61,600	62,443	59,844	50,403	96.5
Michigan	30,753	32,866	57,645	66,864	70,099	75,467	70,721	69,919	127.4
Minnesota	46,600	44,900	45,486	65,473	63,300	68,293	58,136	76,074	63.2
Mississippi	1,015	1,297	1,288	1,287	1,230	1,251	1,243	1,136	11.9
Missouri	8,766	9,128	9,645	9,692	8,394	10,234	10,796	11,144	27.1
Montana	353	382	440	401	419	[4]420	415	383	8.5
Nebraska	860	1,089	1,093	1,042	1,094	1,052	2,037	2,196	155.3
Nevada	327	414	414	326	[4]352	[4]352	[4]352	[4]352	7.6
New Hampshire	536	582	660	623	810	886	918	774	44.4
New Jersey	47,980	57,579	65,173	63,978	70,298	76,204	84,347	94,821	97.6
New Mexico	695	1,025	1,461	1,461	4,107	[4]5,024	5,601	6,535	840.3
New York	327,320	380,390	363,949	391,989	372,363	355,192	382,655	396,090	21.0
North Carolina	3,974	4,449	4,440	4,386	4,559	[4]4,489	3,046	2,569	35.4
North Dakota	635	702	808	503	490	976	1,242	1,200	89.0
Ohio	41,974	44,800	45,000	47,846	49,200	50,865	53,848	52,770	25.7
Oklahoma	6,561	6,487	8,242	8,630	10,245	9,861	11,591	11,717	78.6
Oregon	8,546	8,936	9,514	9,204	9,959	10,108	10,092	11,748	37.5
Pennsylvania	83,474	88,002	96,800	103,401	110,992	118,986	132,344	145,057	73.8
Rhode Island	6,745	7,560	7,856	8,930	8,138	8,967	9,917	10,067	49.3
South Carolina	12,588	13,726	15,146	16,348	16,346	17,810	18,150	18,079	43.6
South Dakota	440	531	624	563	516	506	504	468	6.4
Tennessee	6,700	8,207	9,434	10,618	12,591	11,977	12,977	14,156	111.3
Texas	21,438	22,291	19,033	20,990	22,705	22,266	24,784	24,863	16.0
Utah	1,538	1,665	1,131	1,080	1,133	1,081	1,091	1,001	34.9
Vermont	7,039	7,218	7,724	8,088	8,414	9,264	11,137	10,807	53.5
Virginia	4,075	4,374	4,415	4,349	4,414	8,062	7,966	7,400	81.6
Washington	7,530	7,185	8,827	10,022	12,425	12,858	13,925	21,145	180.8
West Virginia	4,376	4,850	5,167	5,157	5,189	5,204	5,217	5,550	26.8
Wisconsin	23,011	24,655	27,816	30,622	34,653	35,842	38,072	42,102	83.0
Wyoming	204	204	204	204	240	212	241	[4]241	18.1

[1] In 1987–88, 1988–89, 1989–90, and 1990–91, need-based aid comprised 81.0, 78.2, 76.8, and 77.4 percent of all aid, respectively, compared with non-need-based aid or other types of aid.
[2] Estimated.
[3] Changes may reflect introduction of new programs or discontinuation of existing programs.

[4] Data are estimated based on prior year's report.

SOURCE: National Association of State Scholarship and Grant Programs, *Annual Survey Report*, various years. (This table was prepared March 1991.)

Table 302.—Current-fund revenue of institutions of higher education, by source: 1979–80 to 1987–88

Source	1979–80	1980–81	1981–82	1982–83	1983–84	1984–85	1985–86	1986–87	1987–88
1	2	3	4	5	6	7	8	9	10

In thousands

Source	1979–80	1980–81	1981–82	1982–83	1983–84	1984–85	1985–86	1986–87	1987–88
Total current-fund revenue	$58,519,982	$65,584,789	$72,190,856	$77,595,726	$84,417,287	$92,472,694	$100,437,616	$108,809,827	$117,301,141
Tuition and fees	11,930,340	13,773,259	15,774,038	17,776,041	19,714,884	21,283,329	23,116,605	25,705,827	27,800,180
Federal Government	8,902,843	9,747,586	9,591,805	9,631,097	10,406,166	11,509,125	12,704,750	13,904,049	14,771,894
Appropriations	1,223,429	1,346,835	1,297,832	1,347,259	1,426,539	1,570,590	1,617,510	1,656,245	1,664,054
Unrestricted grants and contracts	965,300	1,126,558	1,173,656	1,225,523	1,332,157	1,474,586	1,658,636	1,878,202	1,980,749
Restricted grants and contracts [1]	5,582,997	6,005,317	5,848,329	5,608,619	6,024,108	6,570,045	7,190,345	7,690,232	8,225,069
Independent operations (FFRDC) [2]	1,131,117	1,268,877	1,271,988	1,449,695	1,623,363	1,893,904	2,238,259	2,679,369	2,902,022
State governments	18,378,299	20,106,222	21,848,791	23,065,636	24,706,990	27,583,011	29,911,500	31,309,303	33,517,015
Appropriations	17,611,594	19,266,186	20,963,863	22,084,273	23,635,761	26,373,160	28,402,288	29,337,120	31,298,537
Unrestricted grants and contracts	91,892	84,848	107,630	101,155	120,546	135,139	154,109	213,461	217,208
Restricted grants and contracts	674,813	755,188	777,298	880,208	950,683	1,074,712	1,355,102	1,758,722	2,001,269
Local governments	1,587,552	1,790,740	1,937,669	2,031,353	2,192,275	2,387,212	2,544,506	2,799,321	3,006,263
Appropriations	1,314,368	1,482,536	1,603,904	1,693,399	1,826,590	1,973,284	2,153,160	2,294,133	2,470,439
Unrestricted grants and contracts	36,891	29,629	41,055	37,006	43,421	63,442	56,975	92,724	76,638
Restricted grants and contracts	236,293	278,575	292,710	300,948	322,264	350,485	334,371	412,465	459,186
Private gifts, grants, and contracts	2,808,075	3,176,670	3,563,558	4,052,649	4,415,275	4,896,325	5,410,905	5,952,682	6,359,282
Unrestricted	1,084,041	1,210,903	1,357,419	1,552,294	1,674,942	1,944,876	2,111,972	2,234,942	2,235,096
Restricted	1,724,034	1,965,766	2,206,140	2,500,355	2,740,333	2,951,448	3,298,933	3,717,741	4,124,186
Endowment income	1,176,627	1,364,443	1,596,813	1,720,677	1,873,945	2,096,298	2,275,898	2,377,958	2,586,441
Unrestricted	670,841	770,358	906,845	958,392	1,021,134	1,227,797	1,285,194	1,229,943	1,340,788
Restricted	505,785	594,085	689,968	762,285	852,811	868,501	990,704	1,148,015	1,245,654
Sales and services	12,094,281	13,677,366	15,543,098	17,024,567	18,467,779	19,701,912	21,274,265	23,283,927	25,490,497
Educational activities	1,239,439	1,409,730	1,582,922	1,723,484	1,970,747	2,126,927	2,373,494	2,641,906	2,918,090
Auxiliary enterprises	6,481,458	7,287,290	8,121,611	8,769,521	9,456,369	10,100,410	10,674,136	11,364,188	11,945,841
Hospitals	4,373,384	4,980,346	5,838,565	6,531,562	7,040,662	7,474,575	8,226,635	9,277,834	10,626,566
Other sources	1,641,965	1,948,503	2,335,084	2,293,706	2,639,973	3,015,483	3,199,186	3,476,760	3,769,570

Percentage distribution

Source	1979–80	1980–81	1981–82	1982–83	1983–84	1984–85	1985–86	1986–87	1987–88
Total current-fund revenue	100.0	100.0	100.0	100.0	100.0	100.0	100.0	100.0	100.0
Tuition and fees	20.4	21.0	21.9	22.9	23.4	23.0	23.0	23.6	23.7
Federal Government	15.2	14.9	13.3	12.4	12.3	12.4	12.6	12.8	12.6
Appropriations	2.1	2.1	1.8	1.7	1.7	1.7	1.6	1.5	1.4
Unrestricted grants and contracts	1.6	1.7	1.6	1.6	1.6	1.6	1.7	1.7	1.7
Restricted grants and contracts [1]	9.5	9.2	8.1	7.2	7.1	7.1	7.2	7.1	7.0
Independent operations (FFRDC) [2]	1.9	1.9	1.8	1.9	1.9	2.0	2.2	2.5	2.5
State governments	31.4	30.7	30.3	29.7	29.3	29.8	29.8	28.8	28.6
Appropriations	30.1	29.4	29.0	28.5	28.0	28.5	28.3	27.0	26.7
Unrestricted grants and contracts	0.2	0.1	0.1	0.1	0.1	0.1	0.2	0.2	0.2
Restricted grants and contracts	1.2	1.2	1.1	1.1	1.1	1.2	1.3	1.6	1.7
Local governments	2.7	2.7	2.7	2.6	2.6	2.6	2.5	2.6	2.6
Appropriations	2.2	2.3	2.2	2.2	2.2	2.1	2.1	2.1	2.1
Unrestricted grants and contracts	0.1	(3)	0.1	(3)	0.1	0.1	0.1	0.1	0.1
Restricted grants and contracts	0.4	0.4	0.4	0.4	0.4	0.4	0.3	0.4	0.4
Private gifts, grants, and contracts	4.8	4.8	4.9	5.2	5.2	5.3	5.4	5.5	5.4
Unrestricted	1.9	1.8	1.9	2.0	2.0	2.1	2.1	2.1	1.9
Restricted	2.9	3.0	3.1	3.2	3.2	3.2	3.3	3.4	3.5
Endowment income	2.0	2.1	2.2	2.2	2.2	2.3	2.3	2.2	2.2
Unrestricted	1.1	1.2	1.3	1.2	1.2	1.3	1.3	1.1	1.1
Restricted	0.9	0.9	1.0	1.0	1.0	0.9	1.0	1.1	1.1
Sales and services	20.7	20.9	21.5	21.9	21.9	21.3	21.2	21.4	21.7
Educational activities	2.1	2.1	2.2	2.2	2.3	2.3	2.4	2.4	2.5
Auxiliary enterprises	11.1	11.1	11.3	11.3	11.2	10.9	10.6	10.4	10.2
Hospitals	7.5	7.6	8.1	8.4	8.3	8.1	8.2	8.5	9.1
Other sources	2.8	3.0	3.2	3.0	3.1	3.3	3.2	3.2	3.2

[1] Excludes Pell Grants. Federally supported student aid that is received through students is included under tuition and auxiliary enterprises.

[2] Generally includes only those revenues associated with major federally funded research and development centers (FFRDC).

[3] Less than 0.05 percent.

NOTE.—Because of rounding, details may not add to totals.

SOURCE: U.S. Department of Education, National Center for Education Statistics, "Financial Statistics of Institutions of Higher Education" surveys, and Integrated Postsecondary Education Data System (IPEDS), "Finance" survey. (This table was prepared April 1991.)

Table 303.—Current-fund revenue of public institutions of higher education, by source: 1979–80 to 1987–88

Source	1979–80	1980–81	1981–82	1982–83	1983–84	1984–85	1985–86	1986–87	1987–88
1	2	3	4	5	6	7	8	9	10

In thousands

Source	1979–80	1980–81	1981–82	1982–83	1983–84	1984–85	1985–86	1986–87	1987–88
Total current-fund revenue	$38,824,207	$43,195,617	$47,270,822	$50,412,086	$54,545,275	$59,794,159	$65,004,632	$69,613,289	$74,771,255
Tuition and fees	4,860,162	5,570,404	6,394,813	7,295,879	8,123,318	8,647,637	9,439,177	10,198,633	11,184,657
Federal Government	5,073,481	5,540,101	5,373,330	5,351,137	5,719,602	6,309,818	6,852,370	7,227,995	7,714,261
Appropriations	1,025,663	1,128,101	1,087,493	1,142,486	1,215,616	1,349,183	1,401,367	1,434,295	1,434,906
Unrestricted grants and contracts	470,429	529,424	573,015	598,135	642,117	723,509	816,364	907,299	989,781
Restricted grants and contracts [1]	3,516,235	3,812,197	3,635,947	3,535,108	3,774,093	4,120,266	4,481,723	4,662,798	5,095,910
Independent operations (FFRDC) [2]	61,154	70,379	76,875	75,408	87,777	116,860	152,916	223,602	193,664
State governments	17,973,842	19,675,968	21,397,064	22,562,685	24,157,316	26,965,417	29,220,586	30,439,878	32,437,504
Appropriations	17,390,352	19,006,716	20,695,114	21,805,452	23,340,360	26,065,494	28,071,070	28,974,665	30,917,354
Unrestricted grants and contracts	48,740	45,390	63,570	54,547	66,000	71,113	88,779	139,059	113,204
Restricted grants and contracts	534,751	623,863	638,379	702,686	750,956	828,810	1,060,737	1,326,154	1,406,946
Local governments	1,436,474	1,622,938	1,757,007	1,845,517	1,984,184	2,178,761	2,325,844	2,535,014	2,731,862
Appropriations	1,310,360	1,478,001	1,599,110	1,691,259	1,824,430	1,970,829	2,150,459	2,289,420	2,465,172
Unrestricted grants and contracts	17,608	9,915	16,834	12,447	18,856	35,398	27,852	56,781	41,940
Restricted grants and contracts	108,505	135,022	141,064	141,811	140,898	172,534	147,533	188,813	224,751
Private gifts, grants, and contracts	978,697	1,100,084	1,277,049	1,498,319	1,621,468	1,845,606	2,109,782	2,292,985	2,517,422
Unrestricted	105,495	110,462	138,118	180,457	204,441	236,385	279,381	297,163	305,457
Restricted	873,202	989,622	1,138,931	1,317,861	1,417,027	1,609,220	1,830,401	1,995,822	2,211,966
Endowment income	191,037	214,561	244,070	274,113	315,109	342,833	398,603	349,779	361,545
Unrestricted	98,930	102,888	114,571	129,423	137,945	147,237	181,624	125,165	127,861
Restricted	92,107	111,673	129,499	144,690	177,165	195,596	216,979	224,614	233,684
Sales and services	7,442,992	8,455,449	9,620,314	10,392,946	11,262,071	11,967,500	12,990,670	14,775,531	15,851,714
Educational activities	819,154	943,737	1,071,743	1,158,594	1,279,212	1,424,896	1,596,946	1,771,760	1,948,679
Auxiliary enterprises	4,088,524	4,614,561	5,122,566	5,501,669	5,947,717	6,296,312	6,684,794	7,092,985	7,306,302
Hospitals	2,535,313	2,897,151	3,426,005	3,732,684	4,035,142	4,246,293	4,708,930	5,910,785	6,596,733
Other sources	867,523	1,016,110	1,207,176	1,191,491	1,362,205	1,536,586	1,667,600	1,793,474	1,972,290

Percentage distribution

Source	1979–80	1980–81	1981–82	1982–83	1983–84	1984–85	1985–86	1986–87	1987–88
Total current-fund revenue	100.0	100.0	100.0	100.0	100.0	100.0	100.0	100.0	100.0
Tuition and fees	12.5	12.9	13.5	14.5	14.9	14.5	14.5	14.7	15.0
Federal Government	13.1	12.8	11.4	10.6	10.5	10.6	10.5	10.4	10.3
Appropriations	2.6	2.6	2.3	2.3	2.2	2.3	2.2	2.1	1.9
Unrestricted grants and contracts	1.2	1.2	1.2	1.2	1.2	1.2	1.3	1.3	1.3
Restricted grants and contracts [1]	9.1	8.8	7.7	7.0	6.9	6.9	6.9	6.7	6.8
Independent operations (FFRDC) [2]	0.2	0.2	0.2	0.1	0.2	0.2	0.2	0.3	0.3
State governments	46.3	45.6	45.3	44.8	44.3	45.1	45.0	43.7	43.4
Appropriations	44.8	44.0	43.8	43.3	42.8	43.6	43.2	41.6	41.3
Unrestricted grants and contracts	0.1	0.1	0.1	0.1	0.1	0.1	0.1	0.2	0.2
Restricted grants and contracts	1.4	1.4	1.4	1.4	1.4	1.4	1.6	1.9	1.9
Local governments	3.7	3.8	3.7	3.7	3.6	3.6	3.6	3.6	3.7
Appropriations	3.4	3.4	3.4	3.4	3.3	3.3	3.3	3.3	3.3
Unrestricted grants and contracts	(3)	(3)	(3)	(3)	(3)	0.1	(3)	0.1	0.1
Restricted grants and contracts	0.3	0.3	0.3	0.3	0.3	0.3	0.2	0.3	0.3
Private gifts, grants, and contracts	2.5	2.5	2.7	3.0	3.0	3.1	3.2	3.3	3.4
Unrestricted	0.3	0.3	0.3	0.4	0.4	0.4	0.4	0.4	0.4
Restricted	2.2	2.3	2.4	2.6	2.6	2.7	2.8	2.9	3.0
Endowment income	0.5	0.5	0.5	0.5	0.6	0.6	0.6	0.5	0.5
Unrestricted	0.3	0.2	0.2	0.3	0.3	0.2	0.3	0.2	0.2
Restricted	0.2	0.3	0.3	0.3	0.3	0.3	0.3	0.3	0.3
Sales and services	19.2	19.6	20.4	20.6	20.6	20.0	20.0	21.2	21.2
Educational activities	2.1	2.2	2.3	2.3	2.3	2.4	2.5	2.5	2.6
Auxiliary enterprises	10.5	10.7	10.8	10.9	10.9	10.5	10.3	10.2	9.8
Hospitals	6.5	6.7	7.2	7.4	7.4	7.1	7.2	8.5	8.8
Other sources	2.2	2.4	2.6	2.4	2.5	2.6	2.6	2.6	2.6

[1] Excludes Pell Grants. Federally supported student aid that is received through students is included under tuition and auxiliary enterprises.

[2] Generally includes only those revenues associated with major federally funded research and development centers (FFRDC).

[3] Less than 0.05 percent.

NOTE.—Because of rounding, details may not add to totals.

SOURCE: U.S. Department of Education, National Center for Education Statistics, "Financial Statistics of Institutions of Higher Education" surveys and Integrated Postsecondary Education Data System (IPEDS), "Finance" survey. (This table was prepared April 1991.)

Table 304.—Current-fund revenue of private institutions of higher education, by source: 1979–80 to 1987–88

Source	1979–80	1980–81	1981–82	1982–83	1983–84	1984–85	1985–86	1986–87	1987–88
1	2	3	4	5	6	7	8	9	10
In thousands									
Total current-fund revenue	$19,695,774	$22,389,172	$24,920,034	$27,183,640	$29,872,012	$32,678,536	$35,432,985	$39,196,539	$42,529,887
Tuition and fees	7,070,178	8,202,855	9,379,225	10,480,163	11,591,566	12,635,691	13,677,429	15,507,194	16,615,523
Federal Government	3,829,362	4,207,485	4,218,475	4,279,960	4,686,564	5,199,307	5,852,380	6,676,054	7,057,633
Appropriations	197,766	218,733	210,339	204,774	210,923	221,407	216,143	221,950	229,148
Unrestricted grants and contracts	494,871	597,134	600,641	627,388	690,040	751,076	842,272	970,903	990,968
Restricted grants and contracts [1]	2,066,762	2,193,119	2,212,382	2,073,511	2,250,015	2,449,780	2,708,622	3,027,434	3,129,159
Independent operations (FFRDC) [2]	1,069,963	1,198,498	1,195,113	1,374,287	1,535,586	1,777,044	2,085,343	2,455,767	2,708,358
State governments	404,457	430,253	451,728	502,951	549,673	617,593	690,914	869,424	1,079,511
Appropriations	221,242	259,470	268,749	278,821	295,401	307,666	331,219	362,454	381,183
Unrestricted grants and contracts	43,153	39,458	44,060	46,609	54,546	64,026	65,330	74,402	104,004
Restricted grants and contracts	140,062	131,326	138,919	177,522	199,727	245,902	294,365	432,568	594,324
Local governments	151,078	167,801	180,661	185,836	208,091	208,451	218,662	264,307	274,400
Appropriations	4,008	4,535	4,794	2,140	2,160	2,455	2,701	4,713	5,267
Unrestricted grants and contracts	19,283	19,714	24,221	24,559	24,565	28,045	29,123	35,943	34,698
Restricted grants and contracts	127,788	143,552	151,646	159,137	181,366	177,951	186,838	223,651	234,435
Private gifts, grants, and contracts	1,829,378	2,076,585	2,286,510	2,554,331	2,793,807	3,050,719	3,301,124	3,659,697	3,841,860
Unrestricted	978,546	1,100,441	1,219,301	1,371,836	1,470,501	1,708,491	1,832,592	1,937,778	1,929,639
Restricted	850,832	976,144	1,067,209	1,182,494	1,323,306	1,342,228	1,468,532	1,721,919	1,912,220
Endowment income	985,590	1,149,883	1,352,742	1,446,564	1,558,836	1,753,465	1,877,295	2,028,179	2,224,896
Unrestricted	571,912	667,471	792,273	828,969	883,190	1,080,560	1,103,570	1,104,778	1,212,926
Restricted	413,678	482,412	560,469	617,595	675,646	672,905	773,725	923,400	1,011,970
Sales and services	4,651,289	5,221,917	5,922,784	6,631,620	7,205,708	7,734,412	8,283,595	8,508,396	9,638,783
Educational activities	420,285	465,993	511,179	564,890	691,535	702,032	776,548	870,145	969,411
Auxiliary enterprises	2,392,934	2,672,729	2,999,045	3,267,852	3,508,652	3,804,098	3,989,342	4,271,203	4,639,539
Hospitals	1,838,070	2,083,195	2,412,560	2,798,878	3,005,520	3,228,282	3,517,705	3,367,048	4,029,833
Other sources	774,442	932,392	1,127,908	1,102,215	1,277,768	1,478,897	1,531,586	1,683,287	1,797,280
Percentage distribution									
Total current-fund revenue	100.0	100.0	100.0	100.0	100.0	100.0	100.0	100.0	100.0
Tuition and fees	35.9	36.6	37.6	38.6	38.8	38.7	38.6	39.6	39.1
Federal Government	19.4	18.8	16.9	15.7	15.7	15.9	16.5	17.0	16.6
Appropriations	1.0	1.0	0.8	0.8	0.7	0.7	0.6	0.6	0.5
Unrestricted grants and contracts	2.5	2.7	2.4	2.3	2.3	2.3	2.4	2.5	2.3
Restricted grants and contracts [1]	10.5	9.8	8.9	7.6	7.5	7.5	7.6	7.7	7.4
Independent operations (FFRDC) [2]	5.4	5.4	4.8	5.1	5.1	5.4	5.9	6.3	6.4
State governments	2.1	1.9	1.8	1.9	1.8	1.9	1.9	2.2	2.5
Appropriations	1.1	1.2	1.1	1.0	1.0	0.9	0.9	0.9	0.9
Unrestricted grants and contracts	0.2	0.2	0.2	0.2	0.2	0.2	0.2	0.2	0.2
Restricted grants and contracts	0.7	0.6	0.6	0.7	0.7	0.8	0.8	1.1	1.4
Local governments	0.8	0.7	0.7	0.7	0.7	0.6	0.6	0.7	0.6
Appropriations	(3)	(3)	(3)	(3)	(3)	(3)	(3)	(3)	(3)
Unrestricted grants and contracts	0.1	0.1	0.1	0.1	0.1	0.1	0.1	0.1	0.1
Restricted grants and contracts	0.6	0.6	0.6	0.6	0.6	0.5	0.5	0.6	0.6
Private gifts, grants, and contracts	9.3	9.3	9.2	9.4	9.4	9.3	9.3	9.3	9.0
Unrestricted	5.0	4.9	4.9	5.0	4.9	5.2	5.2	4.9	4.5
Restricted	4.3	4.4	4.3	4.4	4.4	4.1	4.1	4.4	4.5
Endowment income	5.0	5.1	5.4	5.3	5.2	5.4	5.3	5.2	5.2
Unrestricted	2.9	3.0	3.2	3.0	3.0	3.3	3.1	2.8	2.9
Restricted	2.1	2.2	2.2	2.3	2.3	2.1	2.2	2.4	2.4
Sales and services	23.6	23.3	23.8	24.4	24.1	23.7	23.4	21.7	22.7
Educational activities	2.1	2.1	2.1	2.1	2.3	2.1	2.2	2.2	2.3
Auxiliary enterprises	12.1	11.9	12.0	12.0	11.7	11.6	11.3	10.9	10.9
Hospitals	9.3	9.3	9.7	10.3	10.1	9.9	9.9	8.6	9.5
Other sources	3.9	4.2	4.5	4.1	4.3	4.5	4.3	4.3	4.2

[1] Excludes Pell Grants. Federally supported student aid that is received through students is included under tuition and auxiliary enterprises.

[2] Generally includes only those revenues associated with major federally funded research and development centers (FFRDC).

[3] Less than 0.05 percent.

NOTE.—Because of rounding, details may not add to totals.

SOURCE: U.S. Department of Education, National Center for Education Statistics, "Financial Statistics of Institutions of Higher Education" surveys and Integrated Postsecondary Education Data System (IPEDS), "Finance" survey. (This table was prepared April 1991.)

Table 305.—Revenue of institutions of higher education, by source of funds: 1919–20 to 1987–88

[In thousands]

Item	1919-20	1929-30	1939-40	1949-50	1959-60	1969-70	1975-76	1977-78	1979-80	1981-82	1983-84	1985-86	1986-87	1987-88[1]
1	2	3	4	5	6	7	8	9	10	11	12	13	14	15
Current-fund revenue	$199,922	$554,511	$715,211	$2,374,645	$5,785,537	$21,515,242	$39,703,166	$47,034,032	$58,519,982	$72,190,856	$84,417,287	$100,437,616	$108,809,827	$117,301,141
Educational and general	172,929	483,065	571,288	1,833,845	4,688,352	—	—	—	—	—	—	—	—	—
Student tuition and fees[2]	42,255	144,126	200,897	394,610	1,157,482	4,419,845	8,171,942	9,855,270	11,930,340	15,774,038	19,714,884	23,116,605	25,705,827	27,800,180
Federal Government:[3]														
Veterans' tuition and fees[2]	—	—	—	307,325	3,422	—	—	—	—	—	—	—	—	—
Research[4]	—	—	—	216,994	827,263	4,130,066	6,477,179	6,968,501	8,902,844	9,591,805	10,406,166	12,704,750	13,904,049	14,771,894
Other purposes[5]	12,783	20,658	38,860	—	206,305	—	—	—	—	—	—	—	—	—
State governments[6]	61,690	150,847	151,222	491,636	1,374,476	5,873,626	12,260,886	14,746,166	18,378,299	21,848,791	24,706,990	29,911,500	31,309,303	33,517,015
Local governments	(6)	(6)	24,392	61,700	151,715	778,162	1,616,975	1,744,230	1,587,552	1,937,669	2,192,275	2,544,506	2,799,321	3,006,263
Endowment earnings	26,482	68,605	71,304	96,341	206,619	516,038	687,470	832,286	1,176,627	1,596,813	1,873,945	2,275,898	2,377,958	2,586,441
Private gifts and grants[7]	7,584	26,172	40,453	118,627	382,569	1,129,438	1,917,036	2,320,368	2,808,075	3,563,558	4,415,275	5,410,905	5,952,682	6,359,282
Sales and services of educational activities	—	—	32,777	111,987	102,525	612,777	645,420	882,715	1,239,439	1,582,922	1,970,747	2,373,494	2,641,906	2,918,090
Other educational and general	22,135	72,657	11,383	34,625	88,207	—	—	—	—	—	—	—	—	—
Auxiliary enterprises	26,993	60,419	143,923	511,265	1,004,283	2,900,390	4,547,622	5,327,821	6,481,458	8,121,611	9,456,369	10,674,136	11,364,188	11,945,841
Student-aid income[8]	—	—	—	16,288	92,902	619,578	2,494,340	3,268,956	4,373,384	5,838,565	7,040,662	8,226,635	9,277,834	10,626,566
Hospitals[9]	—	11,027	—	—	—	535,323	884,298	1,087,719	1,641,965	2,335,084	2,639,973	3,199,186	3,476,760	3,769,570
Other current income	—	—	—	13,247	187,769	—	—	—	—	—	—	—	—	—
Plant-fund receipts	19,194	82,078	66,209	528,747	1,308,506	—	7,286,363	6,761,466	8,853,540	10,247,333	11,727,629	16,213,426	—	—
Federal Government	11,294	30,621	22,987	12,358	57,599	—	6,400,819	5,738,021	7,546,010	8,695,342	9,703,180	13,661,547	—	—
State governments	—	—	18,404	283,920	319,513	—	—	—	—	—	—	—	—	—
Local governments	7,900	51,457	2,154	19,373	36,304	—	—	—	—	—	—	—	—	—
Private gifts and grants	—	—	22,663	72,620	196,408	—	—	—	—	—	—	—	—	—
Loans, noninstitutional sources	—	—	—	—	361,112	—	—	—	—	—	—	—	—	—
Loans, institutional sources	—	—	—	—	31,873	—	—	—	—	—	—	—	—	—
Transfers from other funds	—	—	—	60,582	228,576	—	885,544	1,023,445	1,307,530	1,551,991	2,024,449	2,551,879	—	—
Miscellaneous receipts	—	—	—	79,894	77,122	—	—	—	—	—	—	—	—	—
Other fund receipts	50,907	63,512	44,518	116,932[10]	498,950	—	1,312,947	1,438,793	2,612,488	3,351,273	3,646,719	7,794,247	—	—
Private gifts and grants	—	—	36,376	66,850	209,146	—	—	—	—	—	—	—	—	—
Other sources	—	—	8,142	50,082	289,804	—	—	—	—	—	—	—	—	—
Net increase in principal of funds	—	—	—	—	419,310	367,978	958,887	1,032,164	2,153,706	2,224,189	2,409,715	7,238,860	—	—
Endowment funds[11]	—	—	—	—	375,178	367,978	648,887	757,622	1,874,241	2,030,269	2,147,552	6,792,298	—	—
Annuity funds	—	—	—	—	11,854	—	52,963	45,420	64,466	48,604	69,429	234,611	—	—
Student loan funds	—	—	—	—	32,279	—	257,037	229,122	214,999	145,316	192,734	211,951	—	—

[1] Preliminary data.
[2] Tuition and fees received from veterans under Public Law 550 are reported under student fees and not under income from the Federal Government.
[3] Federally supported student aid that is received through students is included under tuition and auxiliary enterprises.
[4] Income from the Federal Government for research at agricultural experiment stations administered by land-grant institutions is included under Federal Government "other purposes," not under "research." Beginning in 1969–70, data include independent operations (Federally Funded Research and Development Centers.)
[5] Includes Federal aid received through State channels and regional compacts, through 1959–60.
[6] Income from State and local governments tabulated under "State governments."
[7] Beginning in 1969–70, the private grants represent nongovernmental revenue for sponsored research, student aid, and other sponsored programs.
[8] Specifically designated or earmarked funds.
[9] From 1939–40 to 1959–60, data for hospitals are included under sales and services of educational activities.
[10] Does not include interfund transfers.
[11] Includes funds functioning as endowment; increase calculated on book value.
— Data not available.

NOTE.—Data for years prior to 1969–70 are not entirely comparable with data for later years. Also, some details for 1969–70 through 1973–74 are not directly comparable with data for later years. Details for 1959–60 and 1969–70 have been revised from previously published figures. Because of rounding, details may not add to totals.

SOURCE: U.S. Department of Education, National Center for Education Statistics, "Financial Statistics of Institutions of Higher Education" surveys. (This table was prepared April 1991.)

Table 306.—Current-fund revenue for public institutions of higher education, by State: 1974–75 to 1987–88

[In thousands of dollars]

State	1974–75	1979–80	1980–81	1982–83	1983–84	1984–85	1985–86	1986–87	1987–88 [1]	Percent change, 1982–83 to 1987–88
1	2	3	4	5	6	7	8	9	10	11
United States	$24,004,864	$38,824,207	$43,195,617	$50,412,086	$54,545,275	$59,794,159	$65,004,632	$69,613,289	$74,771,255	48.32
Alabama	442,015	776,033	889,121	998,862	1,072,838	1,242,999	1,401,693	1,438,945	1,552,128	55.39
Alaska	67,714	152,628	159,446	221,703	233,675	235,069	221,837	211,186	220,393	-0.59
Arizona	353,049	613,135	719,835	818,508	904,621	941,769	1,049,493	1,119,516	1,221,641	49.25
Arkansas	182,032	325,144	350,597	400,265	437,714	498,689	539,185	566,317	652,029	62.90
California	3,413,325	5,191,945	5,906,729	6,502,822	6,859,043	7,913,216	8,739,396	9,506,244	9,995,464	53.71
Colorado	430,841	688,506	747,040	900,396	955,865	1,012,873	1,085,076	1,153,559	1,247,390	38.54
Connecticut	213,650	337,426	378,527	449,653	498,488	535,142	578,866	636,210	692,830	54.08
Delaware	92,865	149,921	168,522	197,453	208,974	229,561	251,677	275,473	294,347	49.07
District of Columbia	44,894	60,998	66,138	77,366	82,778	88,757	91,842	95,139	99,457	28.55
Florida	716,440	1,093,760	1,202,788	1,399,084	1,516,669	1,660,841	1,810,090	2,035,008	2,228,502	59.28
Georgia	413,777	677,184	765,826	933,495	1,065,777	1,157,711	1,267,472	1,421,979	1,528,997	63.79
Hawaii	136,457	196,229	219,633	264,780	277,039	295,228	316,246	323,030	358,754	35.49
Idaho	90,346	153,412	169,274	195,579	206,264	224,069	235,507	243,122	270,133	38.12
Illinois	1,064,843	1,613,720	1,809,981	1,973,690	2,113,033	2,312,046	2,560,241	2,722,913	2,812,875	42.52
Indiana	645,809	958,284	1,094,560	1,279,558	1,421,573	1,532,377	1,701,421	1,800,669	1,910,144	49.28
Iowa	409,377	724,259	784,950	916,667	960,380	1,052,891	1,109,681	1,210,284	1,321,697	44.19
Kansas	313,371	526,880	594,104	687,863	760,763	821,396	864,119	891,746	975,159	41.77
Kentucky	366,020	625,016	671,414	758,174	833,406	873,077	943,068	1,016,961	1,109,682	46.36
Louisiana	339,238	625,290	735,374	878,345	934,388	1,011,370	1,055,941	1,078,664	1,118,919	27.39
Maine	93,460	142,366	157,370	186,743	197,681	213,880	222,624	253,862	278,078	48.91
Maryland	444,926	706,082	818,850	896,886	946,923	1,061,354	1,144,230	1,233,023	1,397,950	55.87
Massachusetts	341,790	523,328	582,873	719,497	780,193	938,898	1,075,348	1,161,694	1,287,595	78.96
Michigan	1,240,622	1,954,179	2,094,394	2,354,487	2,577,386	2,785,058	3,071,172	3,348,947	3,699,398	57.12
Minnesota	528,074	815,673	894,236	1,084,583	1,189,622	1,290,356	1,373,436	1,530,623	1,631,838	50.46
Mississippi	279,372	500,578	543,209	593,801	645,674	667,078	734,813	729,024	802,055	35.07
Missouri	421,311	637,375	717,626	822,443	860,798	930,651	1,032,685	1,086,719	1,169,613	42.21
Montana	84,110	114,394	123,933	160,579	173,831	181,506	181,462	184,812	196,957	22.65
Nebraska	195,461	348,976	390,372	456,764	483,707	525,341	554,814	601,666	628,140	37.52
Nevada	51,428	104,307	113,298	131,343	143,191	156,918	184,883	201,941	221,740	68.82
New Hampshire	76,576	124,247	131,990	146,847	160,437	173,231	190,462	208,577	232,411	58.27
New Jersey	504,493	820,932	917,143	1,084,707	1,186,469	1,316,623	1,446,098	1,657,551	1,853,740	70.90
New Mexico	144,053	287,837	334,392	387,026	395,195	440,567	473,716	521,547	543,196	40.35
New York	1,752,173	2,361,836	2,519,437	3,103,322	3,314,699	3,647,741	3,830,119	4,321,209	4,553,725	46.74
North Carolina	650,621	1,005,891	1,146,931	1,312,435	1,492,216	1,679,156	1,857,124	2,005,207	2,138,818	62.97
North Dakota	92,824	166,947	196,267	239,551	251,284	270,401	286,550	304,304	303,700	26.78
Ohio	1,009,441	1,667,974	1,828,079	2,178,134	2,438,112	2,627,717	2,824,411	3,025,444	3,221,449	47.90
Oklahoma	277,533	509,968	588,936	763,352	757,856	776,181	873,446	846,389	862,152	12.94
Oregon	337,669	611,898	647,391	733,297	808,757	838,596	899,709	963,153	1,042,939	42.23
Pennsylvania	970,529	1,429,461	1,575,104	1,908,464	2,055,415	2,241,489	2,473,794	2,703,292	2,951,559	54.66
Rhode Island	90,414	144,100	156,451	175,876	189,272	200,477	213,859	227,564	247,546	40.78
South Carolina	317,651	565,851	630,966	691,528	752,972	868,386	957,771	997,857	1,096,800	58.61
South Dakota	87,694	123,244	127,839	137,562	140,806	136,859	147,699	154,582	160,019	16.33
Tennessee	367,747	602,981	675,770	797,319	851,895	976,132	1,104,118	1,226,302	1,346,786	68.91
Texas	1,297,669	2,549,922	2,858,725	3,664,882	4,062,329	4,327,624	4,558,275	4,437,640	4,814,275	31.36
Utah	210,779	375,015	431,294	523,194	549,220	621,338	686,817	729,349	794,630	51.88
Vermont	69,194	113,401	127,337	149,551	164,871	179,705	191,559	207,565	223,950	49.75
Virginia	547,234	1,051,493	1,159,453	1,387,444	1,477,897	1,702,464	1,876,151	2,054,766	2,245,676	61.86
Washington	544,965	926,782	998,146	1,083,799	1,244,046	1,348,070	1,445,849	1,552,662	1,627,937	50.21
West Virginia	137,390	305,115	318,915	370,754	411,385	364,577	385,170	398,943	415,387	12.04
Wisconsin	715,803	1,118,997	1,228,414	1,413,666	1,512,943	1,621,860	1,761,927	1,864,947	2,032,154	43.75
Wyoming	62,537	112,074	140,520	178,308	199,802	189,926	208,595	204,300	211,403	18.56
U.S. Service Schools	323,256	511,217	586,095	719,677	785,110	854,916	913,092	920,863	927,039	28.81
Outlying areas	195,332	250,469	242,380	368,690	422,108	420,641	451,734	446,110	508,034	37.79
American Samoa	1,159	1,266	1,305	1,784	1,990	2,313	2,413	2,568	2,791	56.51
Guam	11,808	14,575	14,291	25,868	21,034	26,555	31,139	29,447	35,943	38.94
Northern Marianas	—	—	—	—	1,212	1,293	1,350	1,484	774	
Puerto Rico	174,698	222,842	213,012	321,825	378,404	365,213	392,194	388,945	440,382	36.84
Trust Territory of the Pacific	707	1,253	1,669	4,121	4,352	7,208	5,681	4,523	4,862	18.01
Virgin Islands	6,960	10,533	12,103	15,093	15,117	18,059	18,957	19,143	23,281	54.26

[1] Preliminary data.

—Data not available or not applicable.

NOTE.—Because of rounding, details may not add to totals.

SOURCE: U.S. Department of Education, National Center for Education Statistics, "Financial Statistics of Institutions of Higher Education" surveys and Integrated Postsecondary Education Data System (IPEDS), "Finance" survey. (This table was prepared April 1991.)

Table 307.—Current-fund revenue for public institutions of higher education, by source of funds and State: 1987–88 [1]

[In thousands of dollars]

State	Total	Tuition and fees	Federal appropriations, grants, and contracts [2]	State appropriations, grants and contracts	Local appropriations, grants and contracts	Private gifts, grants, and contracts	Endowment income	Auxiliary enterprises	Hospitals	Educational activities and other
1	2	3	4	5	6	7	8	9	10	11
United States	$74,771,255	$11,184,657	$7,714,261	$32,437,504	$2,731,862	$2,517,422	$361,545	$7,306,302	$6,596,733	$3,920,973
Alabama	1,552,129	202,326	166,355	620,602	6,865	59,118	7,116	125,061	297,710	66,976
Alaska	220,393	18,526	22,918	147,630	1,644	4,153	74	12,339	—	13,109
Arizona	1,221,641	216,629	139,433	501,569	104,109	57,456	5,663	163,146	0	33,636
Arkansas	652,028	79,478	42,272	294,055	580	16,381	1,536	65,771	74,101	77,854
California	9,995,465	872,795	892,155	5,065,963	595,671	252,633	56,709	599,916	1,023,734	635,889
Colorado	1,247,390	283,402	181,284	367,737	29,100	40,912	6,620	138,126	129,547	70,662
Connecticut	692,829	111,112	54,024	329,612	909	18,559	431	69,459	96,521	12,202
Delaware	294,348	86,591	20,947	102,680	0	11,512	17,930	35,779	0	18,909
District of Columbia	99,457	6,441	14,545	0	74,395	77	977	614	0	2,408
Florida	2,228,501	296,771	166,089	1,378,946	16,590	80,709	129	188,001	—	101,266
Georgia	1,528,996	208,547	177,214	745,515	23,782	78,222	2,238	128,727	129,545	35,206
Hawaii	358,754	30,787	57,822	223,538	141	5,663	1,045	34,948	0	4,810
Idaho	270,133	36,041	23,314	140,795	6,011	11,371	5,593	28,219	0	18,789
Illinois	2,812,876	461,239	245,915	1,171,602	231,912	84,581	3,065	303,973	121,033	189,556
Indiana	1,910,143	359,937	137,488	737,498	1,350	72,029	6,150	293,824	186,516	115,351
Iowa	1,321,697	183,665	154,074	429,143	21,276	40,753	2,736	164,073	237,111	88,866
Kansas	975,158	139,581	94,282	367,083	77,503	18,613	17,557	102,685	109,075	48,779
Kentucky	1,109,681	151,202	65,800	541,418	5,227	22,710	5,250	103,425	119,298	95,351
Louisiana	1,118,920	198,306	69,938	497,924	2,459	23,212	393	156,028	83,975	86,685
Maine	278,077	45,363	26,444	138,995	1,167	9,845	1,239	38,072	—	16,952
Maryland	1,397,950	269,911	196,047	602,369	95,332	30,851	1,694	152,792	0	48,954
Massachusetts	1,287,595	140,619	99,520	678,073	1,628	36,180	583	116,779	127,111	87,102
Michigan	3,699,398	713,298	333,518	1,243,673	129,474	163,729	19,958	400,758	501,247	193,743
Minnesota	1,631,839	247,533	163,951	611,232	1,618	107,274	8,221	146,759	242,953	102,298
Mississippi	802,055	119,355	85,993	335,432	23,740	20,092	1,324	100,011	81,223	34,885
Missouri	1,169,613	217,130	58,489	497,587	33,879	33,862	6,758	122,436	112,334	87,138
Montana	196,958	29,750	17,780	96,274	5,419	8,327	111	33,439	0	5,858
Nebraska	628,141	83,622	50,124	229,678	32,815	30,245	2,293	70,282	103,760	25,322
Nevada	221,738	28,382	28,487	119,584	149	12,098	1,775	15,732	0	15,531
New Hampshire	232,411	78,920	36,793	65,549	931	4,983	1,717	32,642	—	10,876
New Jersey	1,853,740	322,984	85,539	885,010	107,535	44,159	7,137	146,708	187,121	67,547
New Mexico	543,195	58,591	88,860	235,919	28,201	21,244	11,047	57,908	0	41,425
New York	4,553,726	674,833	227,175	2,431,033	344,252	137,994	11,283	248,465	364,932	113,754
North Carolina	2,138,818	181,380	234,034	1,177,418	49,568	86,374	6,529	261,286	—	142,229
North Dakota	303,700	48,337	38,703	117,635	702	11,721	1,113	54,115	9,625	21,749
Ohio	3,221,451	733,411	185,785	1,181,016	45,911	105,751	23,918	306,093	479,838	159,728
Oklahoma	862,152	96,517	120,140	385,326	11,912	19,157	339	203,081	0	25,680
Oregon	1,042,939	143,002	142,793	332,763	105,883	43,684	3,352	95,560	134,846	41,056
Pennsylvania	2,951,559	774,270	281,538	881,053	59,719	107,170	29,850	335,773	397,143	85,043
Rhode Island	247,606	54,566	30,008	119,014	—	3,869	—	31,675	—	8,474
South Carolina	1,096,801	174,533	89,537	486,142	13,986	29,101	1,725	124,058	129,472	48,247
South Dakota	160,019	37,718	19,270	69,069	16	3,019	254	18,710	0	11,963
Tennessee	1,346,787	179,560	128,258	619,247	8,383	52,760	5,694	129,705	168,993	54,187
Texas	4,814,275	593,030	445,109	2,372,967	202,665	223,270	30,435	463,691	75,803	407,305
Utah	794,631	82,551	115,750	267,687	13,250	22,372	5,715	74,971	140,465	71,870
Vermont	223,951	80,326	32,742	40,753	164	14,812	3,285	30,859	0	21,010
Virginia	2,245,678	375,394	177,146	815,349	12,708	72,139	16,511	274,989	454,806	46,636
Washington	1,627,937	224,405	270,122	677,337	7,142	72,244	6,124	170,881	120,627	79,055
West Virginia	415,387	59,842	32,303	227,836	1,080	6,850	821	66,557	0	20,098
Wisconsin	2,032,154	355,949	236,616	717,349	182,771	74,935	7,101	201,240	154,842	101,351
Wyoming	211,404	15,903	25,497	115,825	10,332	7,878	2,429	27,563	—	5,977
U.S. Service Schools	927,039	296	884,321	—	—	769	—	38,599	1,428	1,626
Outlying areas	508,035	37,918	74,581	333,389	13,563	6,674	573	9,960	2,764	28,613
American Samoa	2,792	15	1,106	—	1,671	—	—	—	—	—
Guam	35,942	2,846	5,232	16,439	7,960	663	280	1,370	—	1,152
Northern Marianas	773	291	479	0	0	0	0	3	0	0
Puerto Rico	440,381	30,929	63,551	302,400	2,443	5,635	0	5,686	2,764	26,973
Trust Territory of the Pacific	4,863	1,812	1,308	825	0	0	0	808	0	110
Virgin Islands	23,284	2,025	2,905	13,725	1,489	376	293	2,093	0	378

[1] Preliminary data.

[2] Includes independent operations (federally-funded research and development centers).

—Data not available or not applicable.

NOTE.—Because of rounding, details may not add to totals.

SOURCE: U.S. Department of Education, National Center for Education Statistics, Integrated Postsecondary Education Data System (IPEDS), "Finance" survey. (This table was prepared April 1991.)

Table 308.—Current-fund revenue from State and local governments of institutions of higher education, by State: 1982–83 to 1987–88

[In thousands]

State	Current-fund revenue from State and local governments					Current-fund revenue from State and local governments, 1987–88 [1]					
	1982–83	1983–84	1984–85	1985–86	1986–87	Total	State appropriations for public institutions	Local appropriations for public institutions	State and local appropriations for private institutions	State and local grants and contracts for public institutions	State and local grants and contracts for private institutions
1	2	3	4	5	6	7	8	9	10	11	12
United States [2]	$25,096,989	$26,899,265	$29,970,223	$32,456,006	$34,108,623	$36,523,277	$30,917,354	$2,465,172	$386,450	$1,786,840	$967,461
Alabama	419,892	436,574	568,958	656,823	611,859	634,187	598,048	5,197	2,766	24,222	3,955
Alaska	155,172	163,355	171,888	159,781	142,721	149,725	143,067	225	0	5,982	451
Arizona	379,338	427,559	476,993	539,054	566,789	605,943	484,395	101,711	0	19,572	265
Arkansas	189,631	203,288	254,883	266,898	276,266	295,852	282,185	380	105	12,071	1,111
California	3,729,632	3,700,828	4,412,324	4,943,659	5,391,779	5,688,888	4,856,826	544,836	4,026	259,972	23,228
Colorado	331,247	349,241	369,073	391,468	370,248	398,399	343,799	14,700	0	38,338	1,562
Connecticut	217,493	238,376	254,872	280,012	302,120	348,070	319,918	0	3,183	10,603	14,366
Delaware	71,252	74,361	82,250	88,661	97,351	102,818	99,288	0	0	3,393	137
District of Columbia	61,261	62,980	67,530	71,761	75,469	77,675	—	71,667	0	2,728	3,280
Florida	906,555	1,005,790	1,088,802	1,172,112	1,315,327	1,456,447	1,296,776	0	12,585	98,761	48,325
Georgia	495,967	585,964	640,938	689,379	741,466	789,695	718,891	21,168	11,954	29,239	8,444
Hawaii	171,244	169,435	173,951	195,375	200,274	224,368	217,284	0	0	6,395	690
Idaho	100,551	105,590	114,422	125,338	132,512	146,882	135,368	5,898	0	5,540	76
Illinois	1,064,568	1,137,153	1,236,560	1,405,622	1,481,338	1,474,881	1,064,787	213,871	23,420	124,855	47,948
Indiana	463,199	541,573	584,351	645,880	712,596	753,620	704,993	888	103	32,967	14,669
Iowa	389,922	403,976	444,893	431,840	424,572	455,663	412,828	21,276	725	16,315	4,520
Kansas	358,529	369,380	403,293	422,278	401,232	447,097	355,311	74,066	398	15,208	2,114
Kentucky	396,569	442,320	454,739	483,027	504,005	548,415	507,632	3,493	0	35,520	1,770
Louisiana	501,611	519,896	572,680	562,205	495,535	505,630	463,469	1,862	8	35,052	5,239
Maine	75,010	79,537	92,212	103,724	129,041	140,933	134,645	1,167	202	4,350	569
Maryland	479,223	511,811	564,827	631,471	672,126	722,586	554,198	94,696	16,584	48,807	8,302
Massachusetts	349,706	385,980	534,697	589,876	727,276	778,790	639,895	100	753	39,705	98,336
Michigan	882,903	986,520	1,077,734	1,215,291	1,313,018	1,411,333	1,197,841	120,928	6,310	54,379	31,875
Minnesota	411,248	464,942	494,834	533,573	600,262	625,951	592,491	298	1,017	20,061	12,085
Mississippi	292,449	326,887	336,717	362,517	315,621	359,380	313,111	22,637	0	23,425	207
Missouri	377,295	392,407	433,052	506,246	503,088	534,552	474,304	32,471	0	24,691	3,085
Montana	89,311	97,172	99,092	97,672	94,857	101,856	91,806	4,567	0	5,319	164
Nebraska	219,831	231,625	250,531	248,544	264,576	263,866	219,130	30,195	15	13,167	1,358
Nevada	68,204	71,175	79,789	99,841	107,228	119,737	110,963	0	0	8,770	4
New Hampshire	37,054	42,624	45,254	52,393	58,533	67,943	62,933	112	28	3,436	1,435
New Jersey	604,873	656,209	749,962	837,214	927,137	1,040,339	796,478	103,396	13,573	92,671	34,221
New Mexico	178,189	184,746	218,286	221,094	248,985	264,522	214,766	23,971	382	25,383	20
New York	2,223,913	2,369,001	2,517,676	2,726,150	3,012,046	3,196,289	2,285,302	316,482	136,261	173,507	284,737
North Carolina	758,820	845,648	972,913	1,074,960	1,162,836	1,373,613	1,153,341	47,538	2,943	26,106	143,683
North Dakota	114,271	108,993	122,389	118,691	129,155	118,339	116,302	563	0	1,472	2
Ohio	781,208	919,630	1,030,246	1,132,678	1,219,687	1,260,720	1,131,119	40,573	11,075	55,235	22,717
Oklahoma	380,276	355,840	361,638	437,693	391,147	400,522	363,099	11,419	8	22,721	3,275
Oregon	304,287	356,271	363,528	394,899	415,405	441,470	313,870	99,139	626	25,637	2,198
Pennsylvania	766,530	808,788	888,715	961,089	1,031,785	1,086,048	822,271	51,527	79,526	66,974	65,750
Rhode Island	87,908	93,039	100,031	107,265	113,442	121,493	114,993	0	0	4,022	983
South Carolina	351,638	373,496	446,824	491,802	465,869	504,646	478,149	13,056	0	8,923	4,518
South Dakota	55,462	57,051	56,374	65,151	67,944	69,221	66,235	0	0	2,850	136
Tennessee	357,171	376,541	457,745	528,933	593,556	635,111	597,915	1,511	1,392	28,204	6,090
Texas	2,205,158	2,464,751	2,609,730	2,521,860	2,379,761	2,655,685	2,297,697	174,778	42,615	103,157	37,438
Utah	202,693	207,585	242,285	256,997	262,130	289,379	258,382	0	0	22,554	8,443
Vermont	30,705	32,779	34,006	35,334	38,904	42,027	35,953	164	0	4,800	1,110
Virginia	560,821	549,725	708,775	775,474	769,583	843,189	792,053	780	7,246	35,224	7,886
Washington	462,151	565,266	601,857	620,383	656,032	685,320	641,311	267	0	42,900	841
West Virginia	173,938	189,501	211,013	222,693	225,170	229,658	218,385	701	0	9,830	742
Wisconsin	695,149	741,097	778,723	825,610	841,995	908,349	709,565	180,928	5,126	9,627	3,103
Wyoming	115,962	114,990	115,366	127,714	126,973	126,156	113,986	9,971	0	2,200	0

[1] Preliminary data.

[2] Excludes U.S. Service Schools.

—Not applicable.

NOTE.—Because of rounding, details may not add to totals.

SOURCE: U.S. Department of Education, National Center for Education Statistics, "Financial Statistics of Institutions of Higher Education" surveys and Integrated Postsecondary Education Data System (IPEDS), "Finance" survey. (This table was prepared April 1991.)

Table 309.—Current-fund revenue received from the Federal Government by the 100 institutions of higher education receiving the largest amounts: 1986–87

[In thousands]

Institution	Rank order	Current-fund revenue from the Federal Government [1]	Institution	Rank order	Current-fund revenue from the Federal Government [1]
1	2	3	1	2	3
United States (all institutions)	—	$13,904,049			
California Institute of Technology	1	971,357	Oregon State University	51	58,963
Massachusetts Institute of Technology	2	561,500	Baylor College of Medicine (Tex.)	52	56,999
Johns Hopkins University (Md.)	3	505,237	University of Colorado at Boulder	53	56,998
University of Chicago (Ill.)	4	357,542	Iowa State University of Science and Technology	54	56,741
Stanford University (Calif.)	5	[2] 353,335	Vanderbilt University (Tenn.)	55	55,554
U.S. Air Force Academy (Colo.)	6	[2] 260,928	University of California, Davis	56	54,579
U.S. Military Academy (N.Y.)	7	[2] 244,141	Medical College of Wisconsin	57	[2] 53,529
Harvard University (Mass.)	8	[2] 201,533	University of Virginia, Main Campus	58	52,126
University of Washington	9	189,959	University of Oklahoma Health Science Center	59	52,099
University of Wisconsin, Madison	10	169,120	University of Georgia	60	51,765
Columbia University, Main Division (N.Y.)	11	162,940	University of Hawaii at Manoa	61	49,546
U.S. Naval Academy (Md.)	12	[2] 161,299	North Carolina State University, Raleigh	62	48,903
Howard University (D.C.)	13	159,214	University of Texas, Health Science Center at Dallas	63	48,591
University of Michigan, Ann Arbor	14	155,636	Uniformed Services University of the Health Sciences (Md.)	64	47,766
University of California, Los Angeles	15	151,532	Air Force Institute of Technology (Ohio)	65	47,282
University of California, San Diego	16	142,781	University of Tennessee, Knoxville	66	46,541
Princeton University (N.J.)	17	141,790	University of Texas Medical Branch at Galveston	67	46,310
University of Pennsylvania	18	136,748	Emory University (Ga.)	68	45,607
University of California, San Francisco	19	135,323	Gallaudet College (D.C.)	69	44,739
University of Minnesota, Minneapolis-St. Paul	20	134,617	Virginia Polytechnic Institute and State University	70	44,012
University of Illinois, Urbana Campus	21	133,025	Tufts University (Mass.)	71	43,132
Cornell University, Medical Center (N.Y.)	22	127,952	University of Illinois at Chicago	72	42,614
University of Miami (Fla.)	23	125,529	University of California, Irvine	73	42,201
University of North Carolina, Chapel Hill	24	124,113	Colorado State University	74	41,320
University of California, Berkeley	25	117,000	Cornell University Statutory Colleges (N.Y.)	75	39,069
University of Southern California	26	112,692	University of Cincinnati, Main Campus (Ohio)	76	39,014
Northwestern University (Ill.)	27	112,292	University of Massachusetts, Amherst Campus	77	38,276
Georgetown University (D.C.)	28	108,159	University of Colorado, Health Sciences Center	78	38,176
Virginia Commonwealth University	29	103,892	Rockefeller University (N.Y.)	79	37,983
University of Texas at Austin	30	94,693	Mayo Graduate School of Medicine (Minn.)	80	37,796
Cornell University, Endowed Colleges (N.Y.)	31	94,029	University of Kentucky	81	37,628
Washington University (Mo.)	32	87,479	Tulane University of Louisiana	82	36,989
University of Arizona	33	86,434	Brown University (R.I.)	83	36,466
University of Rochester (N.Y.)	34	86,393	Utah State University	84	35,943
New York University	35	85,599	Rochester Institute of Technology (N.Y.)	85	35,414
Rush University (Ill.)	36	83,900	University of Vermont and State Agricultural College	86	34,279
University of Pittsburgh, Main Campus (Pa.)	37	79,148	University of California, Santa Barbara	87	33,893
Michigan State University	38	74,504	Mount Sinai School of Medicine of City Univ. of New York	88	32,876
University of Maryland, College Park Campus	39	73,885	U.S. Coast Guard Academy (Conn.)	89	[2] 32,514
Carnegie-Mellon University (Pa.)	40	71,050	Washington State University	90	32,513
University of Iowa	41	69,829	University of Maryland, Baltimore Professional Schools	91	30,675
Purdue University (Ind.)	42	69,751	University of Missouri, Columbia	92	29,411
University of Florida	43	69,605	Florida State University	93	29,003
Yeshiva University (N.Y.)	44	66,345	Mississippi State University	94	27,508
Georgia Institute of Technology, Main Campus	45	65,028	Indiana University, Bloomington	95	27,342
Naval Postgraduate School (Calif.)	46	[2] 64,640	University of Texas Health Science Center	96	26,507
Boston University (Mass.)	47	63,941	University of New Mexico, Main Campus	97	26,414
University of Alabama at Birmingham	48	63,302	University of Dayton (Ohio)	98	26,318
University of Utah	49	62,667	Syracuse University, Main Campus (N.Y.)	99	26,093
Case Western Reserve University (Ohio)	50	61,453	University of Texas Health Science Center at San Antonio	100	25,635

[1] Excludes institutions which have not reported data for 1985–86 or 1986–87 or have submitted system-wide reports. Institutions which appeared in the 1985–86 listing, but have been excluded for 1986–87 for these reasons are: State University of New York at Stony Brook, Main Campus; U.S. Army Command and General Staff College (Kans.); Duke University (N.C.); New Mexico State University, Main Campus; Pennsylvania State University, Main Campus; Ohio State University, Main Campus; Yale University (Conn.). Federal current-fund revenue includes Federal appropriations, unrestricted and restricted Federal contracts and grants, and revenue for independent operations. Independent operations generally include only the revenues associated with major federally funded research and development centers. Excludes Pell Grants. Federally supported student aid that is received through students is excluded.

[2] NCES estimate based on 1985–86 data.

—Not applicable.

SOURCE: U.S. Department of Education, National Center for Education Statistics, Integrated Postsecondary Education Data System (IPEDS), "Finance" survey. (This table was prepared July 1990.)

Table 310.—Current-fund expenditures and expenditures per full-time-equivalent student in institutions of higher education, by type and control of institution: 1970–71 to 1987–88

Control of institution and year	All institutions			4-year institutions			2-year institutions		
	Current-fund expenditures, in millions		Current-fund expenditures per student, in constant 1987–88 dollars	Current-fund expenditures, in millions		Current-fund expenditures per student, in constant 1987–88 dollars	Current-fund expenditures, in millions		Current-fund expenditures per student, in constant 1987–88 dollars
	Unadjusted dollars	Constant 1987–88 dollars [1]		Unadjusted dollars	Constant 1987–88 dollars [1]		Unadjusted dollars	Constant 1987–88 dollars [1]	
1	2	3	4	5	6	7	8	9	10
All institutions									
1970–71	$23,375	$70,631	$10,483	$21,049	$63,601	$12,184	$2,327	$7,030	$4,631
1971–72	25,560	73,019	10,214	22,851	65,280	12,023	2,709	7,739	4,502
1972–73	27,956	75,897	10,463	24,653	66,930	12,379	3,303	8,966	4,855
1973–74	30,714	77,837	10,443	26,912	68,202	12,392	3,802	9,634	4,942
1974–75	35,058	81,910	10,494	30,596	71,486	12,751	4,461	10,423	4,740
1975–76	38,903	85,194	10,047	33,811	74,043	12,549	5,092	11,151	4,323
1976–77	42,600	87,640	10,543	37,052	76,226	13,034	5,548	11,414	4,631
1977–78	45,971	88,628	10,532	39,899	76,921	12,960	6,072	11,707	4,720
1978–79	50,721	90,821	10,879	44,163	79,078	13,330	6,558	11,743	4,861
1979–80	56,914	92,669	10,919	49,661	80,859	13,441	7,253	11,810	4,779
1980–81	64,053	94,169	10,678	55,840	82,095	13,324	8,212	12,074	4,543
1981–82	70,339	94,060	10,434	61,333	82,017	13,123	9,006	12,043	4,356
1982–83	75,936	95,451	10,499	66,238	83,262	13,324	9,697	12,190	4,288
1983–84 [2]	81,993	98,439	10,748	71,680	86,057	13,609	10,314	12,382	4,367
1984–85 [2]	89,951	102,324	11,439	78,744	89,576	14,238	11,207	12,749	4,799
1985–86 [2]	97,536	106,057	11,872	85,560	93,036	14,776	11,976	13,022	4,937
1986–87	105,764	110,419	12,182	92,985	97,078	15,263	12,779	13,342	4,934
1987–88	113,760	113,760	12,325	100,116	100,116	15,435	13,644	13,644	4,974
Public institutions									
1970–71	14,996	45,313	9,148	12,899	38,976	11,008	2,097	6,337	4,486
1971–72	16,484	47,093	8,812	14,014	40,035	10,730	2,470	7,057	4,374
1972–73	18,204	49,421	9,063	15,146	41,120	11,095	3,058	8,301	4,753
1973–74	20,336	51,538	9,155	16,802	42,581	11,252	3,534	8,957	4,854
1974–75	23,490	54,883	9,232	19,309	45,115	11,726	4,181	9,768	4,658
1975–76	26,184	57,340	8,791	21,392	46,846	11,548	4,792	10,494	4,256
1976–77	28,635	58,910	9,277	23,411	48,163	12,045	5,224	10,747	4,571
1977–78	30,725	59,235	9,261	25,013	48,223	11,939	5,712	11,012	4,671
1978–79	33,733	60,402	9,619	27,600	49,421	12,367	6,132	10,981	4,810
1979–80	37,768	61,495	9,620	30,979	50,441	12,426	6,789	11,054	4,738
1980–81	42,280	62,159	9,358	34,677	50,982	12,260	7,602	11,177	4,499
1981–82	46,219	61,806	9,114	37,890	50,667	12,039	8,330	11,139	4,329
1982–83	49,573	62,313	9,096	40,616	51,054	12,096	8,957	11,259	4,281
1983–84	53,087	63,734	9,262	43,588	52,331	12,268	9,499	11,404	4,359
1984–85 [2]	58,314	66,336	9,920	48,017	54,622	12,889	10,297	11,714	4,778
1985–86 [2]	63,194	68,715	10,298	52,184	56,744	13,384	11,010	11,972	4,928
1986–87	67,654	70,632	10,421	56,003	58,468	13,611	11,651	12,164	4,900
1987–88	72,641	72,641	10,471	60,137	60,137	13,681	12,505	12,505	4,919
Private institutions									
1970–71	8,379	25,319	14,187	8,150	24,625	14,664	230	694	6,582
1971–72	9,075	25,926	14,370	8,837	25,245	14,861	239	681	6,457
1972–73	9,752	26,475	14,701	9,507	25,810	15,177	245	665	6,630
1973–74	10,377	26,299	14,419	10,110	25,622	14,900	267	677	6,491
1974–75	11,568	27,027	14,526	11,287	26,372	14,995	280	655	6,425
1975–76	12,719	27,854	14,230	12,419	27,197	14,750	300	657	5,787
1976–77	13,965	28,730	14,639	13,641	28,063	15,173	324	667	5,899
1977–78	15,246	29,392	14,559	14,885	28,698	15,136	360	694	5,652
1978–79	16,988	30,419	14,700	16,563	29,657	15,315	425	762	5,735
1979–80	19,146	31,174	14,882	18,682	30,418	15,545	464	755	5,475
1980–81	21,773	32,010	14,706	21,163	31,113	15,533	610	897	5,166
1981–82	24,120	32,255	14,443	23,444	31,350	15,358	676	904	4,713
1982–83	26,363	33,138	14,787	25,623	32,208	15,879	740	930	4,373
1983–84 [2]	28,907	34,705	15,236	28,092	33,726	16,387	815	978	4,454
1984–85 [2]	31,637	35,989	15,933	30,727	34,954	17,022	910	1,035	5,043
1985–86 [2]	34,342	37,342	16,514	33,376	36,292	17,671	966	1,050	4,639
1986–87	38,110	39,787	17,404	36,982	38,610	16,870	1,128	1,177	5,321
1987–88	41,119	41,119	17,940	39,980	39,980	15,958	1,139	1,139	5,660

[1] Dollars adjusted by the Higher Education Price Index.

[2] Expenditure-per-student calculation includes only those institutions for which both finance and enrollment data were available.

NOTE.—Because of rounding, details may not add to totals.

SOURCE: U.S. Department of Education, National Center for Education Statistics, "Financial Statistics of Institutions of Higher Education" and "Fall Enrollment in Colleges and Universities" surveys; and Integrated Postsecondary Education Data System (IPEDS), "Fall Enrollment" and "Finance" surveys. (This table was prepared April 1991.)

Table 311.—Current-fund expenditures of institutions of higher education, by purpose: 1979–80 to 1987–88

Purpose	1979–80	1980–81	1981–82	1982–83	1983–84	1984–85	1985–86	1986–87	1987–88
1	2	3	4	5	6	7	8	9	10

In thousands

Purpose	1979–80	1980–81	1981–82	1982–83	1983–84	1984–85	1985–86	1986–87	1987–88
Total current-fund expenditures	$56,913,588	$64,052,938	$70,339,448	$75,935,749	$81,993,360	$89,951,263	$97,535,742	$105,763,557	$113,760,219
Educational and general expenditures	44,542,843	50,073,805	54,848,752	58,929,218	63,741,276	70,061,324	76,127,965	82,955,555	89,132,803
Instruction	18,496,717	20,733,166	22,962,527	24,673,293	26,436,308	28,777,183	31,032,099	33,711,146	35,819,684
Research	5,099,151	5,657,719	5,929,894	6,265,280	6,723,534	7,551,892	8,437,367	9,352,309	10,350,931
Public service	1,816,521	2,057,770	2,203,726	2,320,478	2,499,203	2,861,095	3,119,533	3,448,453	3,786,362
Academic support	3,876,388	4,273,286	4,656,454	5,086,892	5,531,152	6,074,253	6,667,392	7,575,451	8,141,175
Libraries	1,623,811	1,759,784	1,922,416	2,039,671	2,231,149	2,361,793	2,551,331	2,441,184	2,836,497
Student services	2,566,732	2,908,998	3,176,997	3,461,379	3,797,935	4,178,236	4,562,938	4,975,913	5,390,820
Institutional support	5,054,411	5,772,515	6,471,072	6,950,854	7,763,325	8,587,216	9,350,786	10,084,663	10,771,660
Operation and maintenance of plant	4,700,070	5,350,310	5,979,281	6,391,596	6,729,825	7,345,482	7,605,226	7,819,032	8,229,606
Scholarships and fellowships	2,200,468	2,504,525	2,684,945	2,922,897	3,301,673	3,670,355	4,160,174	4,776,100	5,324,933
From unrestricted funds	904,876	1,080,614	1,236,081	1,478,762	1,738,188	1,961,597	2,285,116	2,644,615	2,940,929
From restricted funds [1]	1,295,592	1,423,911	1,448,864	1,444,136	1,563,485	1,708,758	1,875,059	2,131,486	2,384,003
Mandatory transfers	732,385	815,516	783,854	856,548	958,321	1,015,613	1,192,449	1,212,488	1,317,633
Auxiliary enterprises	6,485,608	7,288,089	7,997,632	8,614,316	9,250,196	10,012,248	10,528,303	11,037,333	11,398,321
Mandatory transfers	468,044	508,377	524,166	543,105	576,066	597,344	617,171	633,461	629,370
Hospitals	4,757,409	5,433,111	6,234,287	6,986,089	7,379,654	8,010,141	8,692,113	9,173,014	10,406,463
Mandatory transfers	50,134	57,963	62,103	103,918	88,447	130,892	128,833	151,071	178,472
Independent operations (FFRDC) [2]	1,127,728	1,257,934	1,258,777	1,406,126	1,622,233	1,867,550	2,187,361	2,597,655	2,822,633
Mandatory transfers	1,178	643	1,376	1,470	2,110	1,899	3,432	2,292	4,161

Percentage distribution

Purpose	1979–80	1980–81	1981–82	1982–83	1983–84	1984–85	1985–86	1986–87	1987–88
Total current-fund expenditures	100.0	100.0	100.0	100.0	100.0	100.0	100.0	100.0	100.0
Educational and general expenditures	78.3	78.2	78.0	77.6	77.7	77.9	78.1	78.4	78.4
Instruction	32.5	32.4	32.6	32.5	32.2	32.0	31.8	31.9	31.5
Research	9.0	8.8	8.4	8.3	8.2	8.4	8.7	8.8	9.1
Public service	3.2	3.2	3.1	3.1	3.0	3.2	3.2	3.3	3.3
Academic support	6.8	6.7	6.6	6.7	6.7	6.8	6.8	7.2	7.2
Libraries	2.9	2.7	2.7	2.7	2.7	2.6	2.6	2.3	2.5
Student services	4.5	4.5	4.5	4.6	4.6	4.6	4.7	4.7	4.7
Institutional support	8.9	9.0	9.2	9.2	9.5	9.5	9.6	9.5	9.5
Operation and maintenance of plant	8.3	8.4	8.5	8.4	8.2	8.2	7.8	7.4	7.2
Scholarships and fellowships	3.9	3.9	3.8	3.8	4.0	4.1	4.3	4.5	4.7
From unrestricted funds	1.6	1.7	1.8	1.9	2.1	2.2	2.3	2.5	2.6
From restricted funds [1]	2.3	2.2	2.1	1.9	1.9	1.9	1.9	2.0	2.1
Mandatory transfers	1.3	1.3	1.1	1.1	1.2	1.1	1.2	1.1	1.2
Auxiliary enterprises	11.4	11.4	11.4	11.3	11.3	11.1	10.8	10.4	10.0
Mandatory transfers	0.8	0.8	0.7	0.7	0.7	0.7	0.6	0.6	0.6
Hospitals	8.4	8.5	8.9	9.2	9.0	8.9	8.9	8.7	9.1
Mandatory transfers	0.1	0.1	0.1	0.1	0.1	0.1	0.1	0.1	0.2
Independent operations (FFRDC) [2]	2.0	2.0	1.8	1.9	2.0	2.1	2.2	2.5	2.5
Mandatory transfers	(3)	(3)	(3)	(3)	(3)	(3)	(3)	(3)	(3)

[1] Excludes Pell Grants.

[2] Generally includes only those expenditures associated with major federally funded research and development centers (FFRDC).

[3] Less than 0.05 percent.

NOTE.—Because of rounding, details may not add to totals.

SOURCE: U.S. Department of Education, National Center for Education Statistics, "Financial Statistics of Institutions of Higher Education" surveys and Integrated Postsecondary Education Data System (IPEDS), "Finance" survey. (This table was prepared April 1991.)

Table 312.—Current-fund expenditures of public institutions of higher education, by purpose: 1979–80 to 1987–88

Purpose	1979–80	1980–81	1981–82	1982–83	1983–84	1984–85	1985–86	1986–87	1987–88
1	2	3	4	5	6	7	8	9	10

In thousands

Total current-fund expenditures	$37,767,970	$42,279,806	$46,219,134	$49,572,918	$53,086,644	$58,314,550	$63,193,853	$67,653,838	$72,641,305
Educational and general expenditures	30,627,436	34,173,013	37,170,551	39,707,421	42,593,562	46,873,546	50,872,962	54,359,434	58,639,470
Instruction	13,318,733	14,849,822	16,348,109	17,461,536	18,592,391	20,287,410	21,880,782	23,359,057	24,954,204
Research	3,408,633	3,813,350	4,004,955	4,254,947	4,559,531	5,119,191	5,705,144	6,258,625	6,976,925
Public service	1,512,843	1,718,924	1,812,148	1,901,541	2,049,032	2,316,270	2,515,734	2,727,593	2,986,164
Academic support	2,785,726	3,029,284	3,298,322	3,548,064	3,809,572	4,267,698	4,693,543	5,048,232	5,436,156
Libraries	1,114,447	1,187,116	1,287,812	1,338,026	1,463,500	1,557,489	1,685,052	1,619,353	1,853,410
Student services	1,754,757	1,950,566	2,085,796	2,252,985	2,460,204	2,684,343	2,921,758	3,158,991	3,482,112
Institutional support	3,135,496	3,563,194	3,957,315	4,185,089	4,679,824	5,191,693	5,667,144	6,042,593	6,470,163
Operation and maintenance of plant	3,267,409	3,681,921	4,104,249	4,390,420	4,577,702	5,040,869	5,177,254	5,308,631	5,601,733
Scholarships and fellowships	970,363	1,064,864	1,088,717	1,188,383	1,276,644	1,374,803	1,575,909	1,751,671	1,941,390
From unrestricted funds	324,224	367,476	374,632	460,291	518,626	569,058	696,973	750,931	830,195
From restricted funds [1]	646,138	697,388	714,085	728,092	758,018	805,745	878,935	1,000,740	1,111,194
Mandatory transfers	473,476	501,087	470,940	524,455	588,662	591,269	735,695	704,040	790,624
Auxiliary enterprises	4,131,944	4,658,140	5,069,948	5,473,341	5,901,869	6,431,577	6,830,235	7,135,393	7,237,867
Mandatory transfers	314,236	344,043	349,871	355,461	367,956	387,585	410,777	409,726	412,006
Hospitals	2,947,862	3,377,972	3,902,217	4,315,263	4,503,492	4,914,560	5,358,699	5,904,212	6,532,906
Mandatory transfers	25,458	26,613	27,736	60,187	37,003	69,072	75,569	102,623	106,181
Independent operations (FFRDC) [2]	60,728	70,681	76,418	76,892	87,720	94,867	131,956	254,799	231,063
Mandatory transfers	775	322	973	738	656	451	846	194	2,063

Percentage distribution

Total current-fund expenditures	100.0	100.0	100.0	100.0	100.0	100.0	100.0	100.0	100.0
Educational and general expenditures	81.1	80.8	80.4	80.1	80.2	80.4	80.5	80.3	80.7
Instruction	35.3	35.1	35.4	35.2	35.0	34.8	34.6	34.5	34.4
Research	9.0	9.0	8.7	8.6	8.6	8.8	9.0	9.3	9.6
Public service	4.0	4.1	3.9	3.8	3.9	4.0	4.0	4.0	4.1
Academic support	7.4	7.2	7.1	7.2	7.2	7.3	7.4	7.5	7.5
Libraries	3.0	2.8	2.8	2.7	2.8	2.7	2.7	2.4	2.6
Student services	4.6	4.6	4.5	4.5	4.6	4.6	4.6	4.7	4.8
Institutional support	8.3	8.4	8.6	8.4	8.8	8.9	9.0	8.9	8.9
Operation and maintenance of plant	8.7	8.7	8.9	8.9	8.6	8.6	8.2	7.8	7.7
Scholarships and fellowships	2.6	2.5	2.4	2.4	2.4	2.4	2.5	2.6	2.7
From unrestricted funds	0.9	0.9	0.8	0.9	1.0	1.0	1.1	1.1	1.1
From restricted funds [1]	1.7	1.6	1.5	1.5	1.4	1.4	1.4	1.5	1.5
Mandatory transfers	1.3	1.2	1.0	1.1	1.1	1.0	1.2	1.0	1.1
Auxiliary enterprises	10.9	11.0	11.0	11.0	11.1	11.0	10.8	10.5	10.0
Mandatory transfers	0.8	0.8	0.8	0.7	0.7	0.7	0.7	0.6	0.6
Hospitals	7.8	8.0	8.4	8.7	8.5	8.4	8.5	8.7	9.0
Mandatory transfers	0.1	0.1	0.1	0.1	0.1	0.1	0.1	0.2	0.1
Independent operations (FFRDC) [2]	0.2	0.2	0.2	0.2	0.2	0.2	0.2	0.4	0.3
Mandatory transfers	(3)	(3)	(3)	(3)	(3)	(3)	(3)	(3)	(3)

[1] Excludes Pell Grants.

[2] Generally includes only those expenditures associated with major federally funded research and development centers (FFRDC).

[3] Less than 0.05 percent.

NOTE.—Because of rounding, details may not add to totals.

SOURCE: U.S. Department of Education, National Center for Education Statistics, "Financial Statistics of Institutions of Higher Education" surveys and Integrated Postsecondary Education Data System (IPEDS), "Finance" survey. (This table was prepared April 1991.)

Table 313.—Current-fund expenditures of private institutions of higher education, by purpose: 1979–80 to 1987–88

Purpose	1979–80	1980–81	1981–82	1982–83	1983–84	1984–85	1985–86	1986–87	1987–88
1	2	3	4	5	6	7	8	9	10

In thousands

Total current-fund expenditures	$19,145,618	$21,773,132	$24,120,314	$26,362,831	$28,906,716	$31,636,713	$34,341,889	$38,109,719	$41,118,914
Educational and general expenditures	13,915,407	15,900,792	17,678,201	19,221,796	21,147,714	23,187,778	25,255,003	28,596,121	30,493,333
Instruction	5,177,984	5,883,343	6,614,419	7,211,757	7,843,917	8,489,773	9,151,318	10,352,089	10,865,480
Research	1,690,518	1,844,369	1,924,939	2,010,333	2,164,003	2,432,701	2,732,222	3,093,684	3,374,006
Public service	303,678	338,845	391,578	418,937	450,171	544,825	603,799	720,860	800,198
Academic support	1,090,662	1,244,002	1,358,133	1,538,828	1,721,580	1,806,555	1,973,849	2,527,219	2,705,019
Libraries	509,364	572,667	634,604	701,645	767,649	804,304	866,279	821,831	983,087
Student services	811,975	958,432	1,091,201	1,208,394	1,337,731	1,493,893	1,641,180	1,816,922	1,908,708
Institutional support	1,918,915	2,209,321	2,513,757	2,765,765	3,083,501	3,395,523	3,683,642	4,042,069	4,301,497
Operation and maintenance of plant	1,432,662	1,668,389	1,875,032	2,001,176	2,152,123	2,304,612	2,427,972	2,510,400	2,627,873
Scholarships and fellowships	1,230,106	1,439,661	1,596,228	1,734,514	2,025,028	2,295,551	2,584,266	3,024,430	3,383,543
From unrestricted funds	580,652	713,138	861,449	1,018,470	1,219,562	1,392,539	1,588,143	1,893,684	2,110,734
From restricted funds [1]	649,454	726,523	734,779	716,044	805,466	903,012	996,123	1,130,746	1,272,809
Mandatory transfers	258,909	314,429	312,914	332,093	369,659	424,344	456,754	508,448	527,009
Auxiliary enterprises	2,353,664	2,629,948	2,927,684	3,140,975	3,348,327	3,580,671	3,698,067	3,901,940	4,160,454
Mandatory transfers	153,808	164,335	174,295	187,644	208,110	209,760	206,394	223,736	217,364
Hospitals	1,809,547	2,055,139	2,332,070	2,670,826	2,876,161	3,095,581	3,333,414	3,268,802	3,873,557
Mandatory transfers	24,676	31,349	34,368	43,732	51,444	61,819	53,264	48,449	72,291
Independent operations (FFRDC) [2]	1,067,000	1,187,253	1,182,359	1,329,234	1,534,513	1,772,683	2,055,405	2,342,856	2,591,570
Mandatory transfers	404	321	403	731	1,454	1,449	2,586	2,098	2,098

Percentage distribution

Total current-fund expenditures	100.0	100.0	100.0	100.0	100.0	100.0	100.0	100.0	100.0
Educational and general expenditures	72.7	73.0	73.3	72.9	73.2	73.3	73.5	75.0	74.2
Instruction	27.0	27.0	27.4	27.4	27.1	26.8	26.6	27.2	26.4
Research	8.8	8.5	8.0	7.6	7.5	7.7	8.0	8.1	8.2
Public service	1.6	1.6	1.6	1.6	1.6	1.7	1.8	1.9	1.9
Academic support	5.7	5.7	5.6	5.8	6.0	5.7	5.7	6.6	6.6
Libraries	2.7	2.6	2.6	2.7	2.7	2.5	2.5	2.2	2.4
Student services	4.2	4.4	4.5	4.6	4.6	4.7	4.8	4.8	4.6
Institutional support	10.0	10.1	10.4	10.5	10.7	10.7	10.7	10.6	10.5
Operation and maintenance of plant	7.5	7.7	7.8	7.6	7.4	7.3	7.1	6.6	6.4
Scholarships and fellowships	6.4	6.6	6.6	6.6	7.0	7.3	7.5	7.9	8.2
From unrestricted funds	3.0	3.3	3.6	3.9	4.2	4.4	4.6	5.0	5.1
From restricted funds [1]	3.4	3.3	3.0	2.7	2.8	2.9	2.9	3.0	3.1
Mandatory transfers	1.4	1.4	1.3	1.3	1.3	1.3	1.3	1.3	1.3
Auxiliary enterprises	12.3	12.1	12.1	11.9	11.6	11.3	10.8	10.2	10.1
Mandatory transfers	0.8	0.8	0.7	0.7	0.7	0.7	0.6	0.6	0.5
Hospitals	9.5	9.4	9.7	10.1	9.9	9.8	9.7	8.6	9.4
Mandatory transfers	0.1	0.1	0.1	0.2	0.2	0.2	0.2	0.1	0.2
Independent operations (FFRDC)[2]	5.6	5.5	4.9	5.0	5.3	5.6	6.0	6.1	6.3
Mandatory transfers	(3)	(3)	(3)	(3)	(3)	(3)	(3)	(3)	(3)

[1] Excludes Pell Grants.

[2] Generally includes only those expenditures associated with major federally funded research and development centers (FFRDC).

[3] Less than 0.05 percent.

NOTE.—Because of rounding, details may not add to totals.

SOURCE: U.S. Department of Education, National Center for Education Statistics, "Financial Statistics of Institutions of Higher Education" surveys and Integrated Postsecondary Education Data System (IPEDS), "Finance" survey. (This table was prepared April 1991.)

Table 314.—Voluntary support for institutions of higher education, by source and purpose of support: 1949–50 to 1987–88

[In millions]

Source and purpose of support	1949–50	1959–60	1965–66	1970–71	1975–76	1980–81	1984–85	1985–86	1986–87	1987–88
1	2	3	4	5	6	7	8	9	10	11
Total voluntary support[1]	$240	$815	$1,440	$1,860	$2,410	$4,230	$6,320	$7,400	$8,500	$8,200
Sources										
Alumni	60	191	310	458	588	1,049	1,460	1,825	2,346	2,042
Nonalumni individuals	60	194	350	495	569	1,007	1,416	1,781	2,066	1,927
Corporations	28	130	230	259	379	778	1,574	1,702	1,819	1,853
Foundations	60	163	357	418	549	922	1,175	1,363	1,513	1,607
Religious organizations	16	80	108	104	130	140	208	211	204	197
Other	16	57	85	126	195	334	487	518	552	574
Purpose										
Current operations	101	385	675	1,050	1,480	2,590	3,800	4,022	4,420	4,666
Capital purposes	139	430	765	810	930	1,640	2,520	3,378	4,080	3,534
Voluntary support as a percent of total expenditures[2]	9.0	11.4	9.2	6.8	5.5	6.0	6.4	6.9	7.3	6.5

[1] Data are based on a sample survey of institutions of higher education.

[2] Total expenditures include current-fund expenditures and additions to plant value.

SOURCE: Council for Aid to Education, Research Report, "Contributions to Colleges Drop for First Time Since 1975." (This table was prepared April 1990.)

Table 315.—Expenditures of institutions of higher education: 1929–30 to 1973–74[1]

[In thousands]

Item	1929–30	1939–40	1949–50	1959–60	1969–70	1971–72	1973–74
1	2	3	4	5	6	7	8
Current-fund expenditures	$507,142	$674,688	$2,245,661	$5,601,376	$21,043,112	$25,559,560	$30,713,581
Educational and general	377,903	521,990	1,706,444	4,513,208	15,788,699	19,200,505	23,257,361
General administration and general expense	42,633	62,827	213,070	583,224	2,627,993	3,344,215	4,200,955
Instruction and departmental research	221,598	280,248	780,994	1,793,320	[2]7,653,097	[2]9,503,250	[2]11,574,145
Extension and public services	24,982	35,325	86,674	205,595	521,148	615,997	730,560
Libraries	9,654	19,487	56,147	135,384	652,596	764,481	939,023
Plant operation and maintenance	60,919	69,612	225,110	469,943	1,541,698	1,927,553	2,494,057
Separately organized research	18,117	27,266	225,341	1,022,353	2,144,076	2,265,282	2,480,451
Related activities	[3]	27,225	119,108	294,255	648,089	779,728	838,170
Other educational and general	[3]	[3]	[3]	[4]9,134	[3]	[3]	[3]
Auxiliary enterprises	[5]	124,184	476,401	916,117	2,769,276	3,178,272	3,613,256
Student-aid expenditures	[5]	[5]	[5]	172,050	984,594	1,241,372	1,396,488
Other current expenditures	129,239	28,514	62,816	—	[6]1,500,544	[6]1,939,411	[6]2,446,476
Gross additions to plant value[7]	125,106	83,765	416,831	1,314,717	4,232,526	4,162,626	4,312,142

[1] Refer to the preceding table for revised format for educational and general items. Includes scholarships and fellowships under educational and general. Student aid item previously reported has been dropped.

[2] Includes "other sponsored programs."

[3] Data not collected separately.

[4] Sales and services expenditures.

[5] Data not tabulated separately.

[6] "Major public service programs" previously reported in "separately organized research," "extension and public services," and "related activities."

[7] Includes expenditures from plant and current funds, gifts and grants of plant assets, and increases in value due to reappraisal and other adjustments.

—Data not available.

NOTE.—Beginning in 1959–60, data are for 50 States and the District of Columbia; data for earlier years are for 48 States and the District of Columbia. Because of rounding, details may not add to totals.

SOURCE: U.S. Department of Education, National Center for Education Statistics, "Financial Statistics of Institutions of Higher Education" surveys. (This table was prepared January 1986.)

Table 316.—Educational and general expenditures of public universities, by purpose: 1976–77 to 1987–88

Year	Educational and general expenditures									
	Total	Instruction	Admin-istration [1]	Student services	Research	Libraries	Public serv-ice	Operation and mainte-nance of plant	Scholar-ships and fellowships	Mandatory transfers
1	2	3	4	5	6	7	8	9	10	11

Expenditures, in thousands of current dollars

1976–77	$9,413,626	$3,670,554	$1,222,410	$346,906	$1,727,807	$331,614	$763,809	$857,677	**$377,749**	$115,099
1977–78	10,220,191	4,009,870	1,344,538	388,262	1,896,578	343,198	803,309	938,952	389,682	105,803
1978–79	11,284,191	4,408,025	1,478,568	419,231	2,136,135	363,875	920,726	1,046,740	396,356	114,533
1979–80	12,540,072	4,860,411	1,572,523	473,460	2,444,471	463,642	1,012,376	1,148,942	439,461	124,786
1980–81	13,951,029	5,374,271	1,795,504	525,891	2,743,145	451,978	1,158,512	1,270,339	492,225	139,164
1981–82	15,077,263	5,852,958	1,974,219	566,366	2,903,178	488,939	1,223,417	1,412,557	525,498	130,131
1982–83	16,089,168	6,247,358	2,107,933	604,657	3,086,846	528,470	1,300,353	1,512,947	562,903	137,702
1983–84	17,234,711	6,646,501	2,263,565	643,614	3,295,053	577,136	1,385,191	1,627,702	624,642	171,306
1984–85	18,960,810	7,257,618	2,598,784	701,451	3,682,755	609,365	1,519,324	1,745,825	677,533	168,155
1985–86	20,716,657	7,807,522	2,882,006	762,324	4,076,258	669,253	1,664,917	1,831,618	780,080	242,679
1986–87	22,023,792	8,368,187	3,088,348	819,829	4,399,405	677,531	1,725,613	1,829,880	847,733	267,266
1987–88	23,848,428	8,902,624	3,311,806	889,528	4,911,929	762,858	1,857,008	1,934,490	949,439	328,746

Percentage distribution

1976–77	100.0	39.0	13.0	3.7	18.4	3.5	8.1	9.1	4.0	1.2
1977–78	100.0	39.2	13.2	3.8	18.6	3.4	7.9	9.2	3.8	1.0
1978–79	100.0	39.1	13.1	3.7	18.9	3.2	8.2	9.3	3.5	1.0
1979–80	100.0	38.8	12.5	3.8	19.5	3.7	8.1	9.2	3.5	1.0
1980–81	100.0	38.5	12.9	3.8	19.7	3.2	8.3	9.1	3.5	1.0
1981–82	100.0	38.8	13.1	3.8	19.3	3.2	8.1	9.4	3.5	0.9
1982–83	100.0	38.8	13.1	3.8	19.2	3.3	8.1	9.4	3.5	0.9
1983–84	100.0	38.6	13.1	3.7	19.1	3.3	8.0	9.4	3.6	1.0
1984–85	100.0	38.3	13.7	3.7	19.4	3.2	8.0	9.2	3.6	0.9
1985–86	100.0	37.7	13.9	3.7	19.7	3.2	8.0	8.8	3.8	1.2
1986–87	100.0	38.0	14.0	3.7	20.0	3.1	7.8	8.3	3.8	1.2
1987–88	100.0	37.3	13.9	3.7	20.6	3.2	7.8	8.1	4.0	1.4

Expenditure per full-time-equivalent student in constant 1987–88 dollars

1976–77	$11,033	$4,302	$1,433	$407	$2,025	$389	$895	$1,005	$443	$135
1977–78	11,144	4,372	1,466	423	2,068	374	876	1,024	425	115
1978–79	11,510	4,496	1,508	428	2,179	371	939	1,068	404	117
1979–80	11,383	4,412	1,427	430	2,219	421	919	1,043	399	113
1980–81	11,203	4,315	1,442	422	2,203	363	930	1,020	395	112
1981–82	10,993	4,268	1,439	413	2,117	357	892	1,030	383	95
1982–83	10,981	4,264	1,439	413	2,107	361	887	1,033	384	94
1983–84	11,258	4,341	1,479	420	2,152	377	905	1,063	408	112
1984–85	11,808	4,520	1,618	437	2,294	379	946	1,087	422	105
1985–86	12,309	4,639	1,712	453	2,422	398	989	1,088	463	144
1986–87	12,500	4,750	1,753	465	2,497	385	979	1,039	481	152
1987–88	12,828	4,789	1,781	478	2,642	410	999	1,041	511	177

[1] Includes institutional and academic support less libraries.

NOTE.—Data in this table may differ slightly from data appearing in other tables. Data for 1976–77 through 1985–86 include only institutions which provided both enrollment and finance data. The Higher Education Price Index was used to convert the per student figures to constant dollars. Because of rounding, details may not add to totals.

SOURCE: U.S. Department of Education, National Center for Education Statistics, "Financial Statistics of Institutions of Higher Education" surveys. (This table was prepared April 1991.)

Table 317.—Educational and general expenditures of public 4-year colleges,[1] by purpose: 1976–77 to 1987–88

Year	Educational and general expenditures									
	Total	Instruction	Adminis-tration[2]	Student services	Research	Libraries	Public service	Operation and maintenance of plant	Scholarships and fellow-ships	Mandatory transfers
1	2	3	4	5	6	7	8	9	10	11

Expenditures, in thousands of current dollars

Year	Total	Instruction	Administration	Student services	Research	Libraries	Public service	Oper & maint	Scholarships	Mandatory transfers
1976–77	$8,682,538	$4,027,051	$1,445,651	$500,832	$607,235	$340,002	$250,152	$1,001,848	**$338,432**	$171,335
1977–78	9,568,977	4,423,487	1,598,092	572,193	677,414	369,408	274,314	1,118,393	332,899	202,777
1978–79	10,455,134	4,770,598	1,789,534	651,541	786,072	395,299	301,387	1,214,996	337,588	208,119
1979–80	11,750,398	5,271,621	2,029,327	733,557	937,874	448,190	359,467	1,375,308	383,036	212,019
1980–81	13,139,618	5,890,759	2,258,987	807,249	1,043,614	511,817	407,816	1,563,514	412,972	242,890
1981–82	14,321,586	6,537,888	2,518,182	834,225	1,086,146	536,080	440,736	1,738,210	403,069	227,050
1982–83	15,286,145	6,980,269	2,660,360	904,745	1,150,011	559,353	469,841	1,857,151	450,067	254,349
1983–84	16,538,128	7,464,035	3,013,666	1,041,488	1,246,289	622,879	513,732	1,873,628	473,503	288,908
1984–85	18,333,578	8,211,171	3,370,676	1,140,312	1,420,844	669,518	603,018	2,137,225	489,188	291,626
1985–86	19,860,947	8,945,373	3,658,627	1,235,418	1,618,737	712,112	648,178	2,118,522	569,841	354,139
1986–87	21,490,078	9,608,239	4,019,850	1,318,666	1,846,712	695,692	766,865	2,226,599	660,940	346,515
1987–88	23,124,456	10,310,532	4,261,441	1,434,726	2,053,638	774,274	864,347	2,340,495	711,704	373,299

Percentage distribution

Year	Total	Instruction	Administration	Student services	Research	Libraries	Public service	Oper & maint	Scholarships	Mandatory transfers
1976–77	100.0	46.4	16.7	5.8	7.0	3.9	2.9	11.5	3.9	2.0
1977–78	100.0	46.2	16.7	6.0	7.1	3.9	2.9	11.7	3.5	2.1
1978–79	100.0	45.6	17.1	6.2	7.5	3.8	2.9	11.6	3.2	2.0
1979–80	100.0	44.9	17.3	6.2	8.0	3.8	3.1	11.7	3.3	1.8
1980–81	100.0	44.8	17.2	6.1	7.9	3.9	3.1	11.9	3.1	1.8
1981–82	100.0	45.7	17.6	5.8	7.6	3.7	3.1	12.1	2.8	1.6
1982–83	100.0	45.7	17.4	5.9	7.5	3.7	3.1	12.1	2.9	1.7
1983–84	100.0	45.1	18.2	6.3	7.5	3.8	3.1	11.3	2.9	1.7
1984–85	100.0	44.8	18.4	6.2	7.7	3.7	3.3	11.7	2.7	1.6
1985–86	100.0	45.0	18.4	6.2	8.2	3.6	3.3	10.7	2.9	1.8
1986–87	100.0	44.7	18.7	6.1	8.6	3.2	3.6	10.4	3.1	1.6
1987–88	100.0	44.6	18.4	6.2	8.9	3.3	3.7	10.1	3.1	1.6

Expenditure per full-time-equivalent student in constant 1987–88 dollars

Year	Total	Instruction	Administration	Student services	Research	Libraries	Public service	Oper & maint	Scholarships	Mandatory transfers
1976–77	$8,045	$3,732	$1,340	$464	$563	$315	$232	$928	$314	$159
1977–78	8,124	3,755	1,357	486	575	314	233	949	283	172
1978–79	8,355	3,812	1,430	521	628	316	241	971	270	166
1979–80	8,445	3,789	1,458	527	674	322	258	988	275	152
1980–81	8,357	3,747	1,437	513	664	326	259	994	263	154
1981–82	8,278	3,779	1,456	482	628	310	255	1,005	233	131
1982–83	8,086	3,692	1,407	479	608	296	249	982	238	135
1983–84	8,178	3,691	1,490	515	616	308	254	927	234	143
1984–85	8,649	3,874	1,590	538	670	316	284	1,008	231	138
1985–86	8,963	4,037	1,651	558	731	321	293	956	257	160
1986–87	8,943	3,998	1,673	549	768	289	319	927	275	144
1987–88	9,116	4,065	1,680	566	810	305	341	923	281	147

[1] Excludes universities. See preceding table.

[2] Includes institutional and academic support less libraries.

NOTE.—Data in this table may differ slightly from data appearing in other tables. Data for 1976–77 through 1985–86 include institutions which provided both enrollment and finance data. The Higher Education Price Index was used to convert the per student figures to constant dollars. Because of rounding, details may not add to totals.

SOURCE: U.S. Department of Education, National Center for Education Statistics, "Financial Statistics of Institutions of Higher Education" surveys. (This table was prepared April 1991.)

Table 318.—Educational and general expenditures of public 2-year colleges, by purpose: 1976-77 to 1987-88

Year	Educational and general expenditures									
	Total	Instruction	Administration[1]	Student services	Research	Libraries	Public service	Operation and maintenance of plant	Scholarships and fellowships	Mandatory transfers
1	2	3	4	5	6	7	8	9	10	11

Expenditures, in thousands of current dollars

1976–77	$4,875,998	$2,490,274	$882,813	$409,217	$15,698	$171,409	$97,635	$547,515	$142,827	$118,610
1977–78	5,336,153	2,700,489	1,035,206	437,060	9,333	188,201	112,944	605,464	117,996	129,458
1978–79	5,734,611	2,877,651	1,119,840	482,323	21,289	193,703	110,918	650,447	127,633	150,807
1979–80	6,334,777	3,185,815	1,204,082	547,457	26,288	202,583	141,000	743,014	147,865	136,672
1980–81	7,063,474	3,575,743	1,347,020	615,869	26,591	222,391	152,597	844,781	159,474	119,008
1981–82	7,757,435	3,947,065	1,473,733	684,650	15,632	262,697	147,385	952,691	160,109	113,473
1982–83	8,292,446	4,218,388	1,620,644	741,179	18,090	248,682	123,722	1,016,267	175,069	130,403
1983–84	8,820,575	4,481,854	1,748,535	775,084	18,189	263,485	150,109	1,076,371	178,500	128,448
1984–85	9,560,507	4,806,050	1,929,968	841,101	15,591	278,363	193,903	1,156,074	207,975	131,482
1985–86	10,252,955	5,116,884	2,122,060	920,299	10,136	295,691	202,440	1,220,646	225,979	138,820
1986–87	10,845,969	5,382,631	2,363,275	1,020,496	12,508	246,131	235,115	1,252,152	243,402	90,258
1987–88	11,666,586	5,741,049	2,479,661	1,157,858	11,358	316,278	264,809	1,326,748	280,247	88,578

Percentage distribution

1976–77	100.0	51.1	18.1	8.4	0.3	3.5	2.0	11.2	2.9	2.4
1977–78	100.0	50.6	19.4	8.2	0.2	3.5	2.1	11.3	2.2	2.4
1978–79	100.0	50.2	19.5	8.4	0.4	3.4	1.9	11.3	2.2	2.6
1979–80	100.0	50.3	19.0	8.6	0.4	3.2	2.2	11.7	2.3	2.2
1980–81	100.0	50.6	19.1	8.7	0.4	3.1	2.2	12.0	2.3	1.7
1981–82	100.0	50.9	19.0	8.8	0.2	3.4	1.9	12.3	2.1	1.5
1982–83	100.0	50.9	19.5	8.9	0.2	3.0	1.5	12.3	2.1	1.6
1983–84	100.0	50.8	19.8	8.8	0.2	3.0	1.7	12.2	2.0	1.5
1984–85	100.0	50.3	20.2	8.8	0.2	2.9	2.0	12.1	2.2	1.4
1985–86	100.0	49.9	20.7	9.0	0.1	2.9	2.0	11.9	2.2	1.4
1986–87	100.0	49.6	21.8	9.4	0.1	2.3	2.2	11.5	2.2	0.8
1987–88	100.0	49.2	21.3	9.9	0.1	2.7	2.3	11.4	2.4	0.8

Expenditure per full-time-equivalent student in constant 1987–88 dollars

1976–77	$4,336	$2,215	$785	$364	$14	$152	$87	$487	$127	$105
1977–78	4,364	2,208	847	357	8	154	92	495	96	106
1978–79	4,498	2,257	878	378	17	152	87	510	100	118
1979–80	4,421	2,223	840	382	18	141	98	518	103	95
1980–81	4,235	2,144	808	369	16	133	91	506	96	71
1981–82	4,211	2,143	800	372	8	143	80	517	87	62
1982–83	3,988	2,029	779	356	9	120	60	489	84	63
1983–84	4,049	2,057	803	356	8	121	69	494	82	59
1984–85	4,445	2,234	897	391	7	129	90	537	97	61
1985–86	4,591	2,291	950	412	5	132	91	547	101	62
1986–87	4,657	2,311	1,015	438	5	106	101	538	105	39
1987–88	4,590	2,259	975	455	4	124	104	522	110	35

[1] Includes institutional and academic support less libraries.

NOTE.—Data in this table may differ slightly from data appearing in other tables. Data for 1976–77 through 1985–86 include only institutions which provided both enrollment and finance data. The Higher Education Price Index was used to convert the per student figures to constant dollars. Because of rounding, details may not add to totals.

SOURCE: U.S. Department of Education, National Center for Education Statistics, "Financial Statistics of Institutions of Higher Education" surveys. (This table was prepared April 1991.)

Table 319.—Educational and general expenditures of private (nonprofit) universities, by purpose: 1976–77 to 1987–88

Year	Educational and general expenditures									
	Total	Instruction	Admin-istration [1]	Student services	Research	Libraries	Public service	Operation and mainte-nance of plant	Scholarships and fellow-ships	Mandatory transfer
1	2	3	4	5	6	7	8	9	10	11

Expenditures, in thousands of current dollars

Year	Total	Instruction	Admin-istration	Student services	Research	Libraries	Public service	Oper. & maint.	Scholarships	Mandatory
1976–77	$4,694,593	$1,784,975	$621,733	$156,457	$988,656	$195,146	$105,011	$411,340	$380,821	$50,453
1977–78	5,120,125	1,943,031	683,988	172,261	1,063,906	215,068	108,201	447,743	427,907	58,019
1978–79	5,675,608	2,120,800	796,751	195,238	1,175,657	221,676	119,082	510,819	460,200	75,385
1979–80	6,408,288	2,426,312	908,580	215,646	1,315,469	236,184	148,028	568,806	507,257	82,006
1980–81	7,249,102	2,763,320	1,009,957	254,872	1,436,318	267,142	149,946	660,152	596,241	111,154
1981–82	7,951,934	3,105,731	1,100,088	289,398	1,505,340	294,523	160,496	752,673	650,285	93,401
1982–83	8,198,167	3,227,925	1,214,617	304,617	1,464,809	295,709	169,382	754,480	670,390	96,238
1983–84	9,491,967	3,660,650	1,445,910	350,096	1,683,020	360,238	187,615	859,065	833,108	112,266
1984–85	10,431,950	3,965,165	1,556,854	393,526	1,892,570	366,356	253,010	930,229	931,027	143,212
1985–86	11,407,571	4,308,432	1,711,155	438,678	2,108,731	397,745	271,271	981,131	1,040,677	149,751
1986–87	13,013,183	4,998,565	1,977,175	502,291	2,399,976	397,460	332,223	1,006,334	1,218,002	181,159
1987–88	13,876,587	5,209,101	2,107,206	529,262	2,597,435	484,987	340,475	1,073,880	1,328,776	205,464

Percentage distribution

Year	Total	Instruction	Admin-istration	Student services	Research	Libraries	Public service	Oper. & maint.	Scholarships	Mandatory
1976–77	100.0	38.0	13.2	3.3	21.1	4.2	2.2	8.8	8.1	1.1
1977–78	100.0	37.9	13.4	3.4	20.8	4.2	2.1	8.7	8.4	1.1
1978–79	100.0	37.4	14.0	3.4	20.7	3.9	2.1	9.0	8.1	1.3
1979–80	100.0	37.9	14.2	3.4	20.5	3.7	2.3	8.9	7.9	1.3
1980–81	100.0	38.1	13.9	3.5	19.8	3.7	2.1	9.1	8.2	1.5
1981–82	100.0	39.1	13.8	3.6	18.9	3.7	2.0	9.5	8.2	1.2
1982–83	100.0	39.4	14.8	3.7	17.9	3.6	2.1	9.2	8.2	1.2
1983–84	100.0	38.6	15.2	3.7	17.7	3.8	2.0	9.1	8.8	1.2
1984–85	100.0	38.0	14.9	3.8	18.1	3.5	2.4	8.9	8.9	1.4
1985–86	100.0	37.8	15.0	3.8	18.5	3.5	2.4	8.6	9.1	1.3
1986–87	100.0	38.4	15.2	3.9	18.4	3.1	2.6	7.7	9.4	1.4
1987–88	100.0	37.5	15.2	3.8	18.7	3.5	2.5	7.7	9.6	1.5

Expenditure per full-time-equivalent student in constant 1987–88 dollars

Year	Total	Instruction	Admin-istration	Student services	Research	Libraries	Public service	Oper. & maint.	Scholarships	Mandatory
1976–77	$17,080	$6,494	$2,262	$569	$3,597	$710	$382	$1,497	$1,386	$184
1977–78	16,897	6,412	2,257	568	3,511	710	357	1,478	1,412	191
1978–79	17,054	6,372	2,394	587	3,533	666	358	1,535	1,383	227
1979–80	17,293	6,548	2,452	582	3,550	637	399	1,535	1,369	221
1980–81	17,498	6,670	2,438	615	3,467	645	362	1,594	1,439	268
1981–82	17,351	6,777	2,400	631	3,285	643	350	1,642	1,419	204
1982–83	17,510	6,894	2,594	651	3,129	632	362	1,611	1,432	206
1983–84	18,811	7,255	2,865	694	3,335	714	372	1,702	1,651	222
1984–85	19,611	7,454	2,927	740	3,558	689	476	1,749	1,750	269
1985–86	20,420	7,712	3,063	785	3,775	712	486	1,756	1,863	268
1986–87	22,247	8,545	3,380	859	4,103	679	568	1,720	2,082	310
1987–88	22,497	8,445	3,416	858	4,211	786	552	1,741	2,154	333

[1] Includes institutional and academic support less libraries.

NOTE.—Data in this table may differ slightly from data appearing in other tables. Data for 1976–77 through 1985–86 include only institutions which provided both enrollment and finance data. The Higher Education Price Index was used to convert the per student figures to constant dollars. Because of rounding, details may not add to totals.

SOURCE: U.S. Department of Education, National Center for Education Statistics, "Financial Statistics of Institutions of Higher Education" surveys. (This table was prepared April 1991.)

Table 320.—Educational and general expenditures of private (nonprofit) 4-year colleges, [1] by purpose: 1976–77 to 1987–88

Year	Educational and general expenditures									
	Total	Instruction	Admin- istration [2]	Student services	Research	Libraries	Public service	Operation and mainte- nance of plant	Scholar- ships and fellow- ships	Mandatory transfers
1	2	3	4	5	6	7	8	9	10	11

Expenditures, in thousands of current dollars

Year	Total	Instruction	Admin.	Student services	Research	Libraries	Public service	Operation	Scholarships	Mandatory transfers
1976–77	$5,139,939	$1,919,574	$1,047,932	$381,428	$259,530	$200,844	$123,717	$574,910	$511,907	$120,097
1977–78	5,637,836	2,114,043	1,160,141	428,265	271,637	221,807	123,214	638,330	550,372	130,026
1978–79	6,263,692	2,328,418	1,299,063	483,031	328,042	240,098	136,861	704,180	598,487	145,513
1979–80	7,063,953	2,589,908	1,466,556	549,639	374,520	259,969	153,056	807,943	694,791	167,570
1980–81	8,061,774	2,907,255	1,703,307	639,795	407,622	289,944	186,399	930,075	811,636	185,741
1981–82	9,061,667	3,271,255	1,938,727	727,382	419,283	322,702	228,368	1,036,118	913,999	203,834
1982–83	9,805,459	3,552,387	2,124,446	804,943	437,286	356,768	236,142	1,092,836	983,887	216,764
1983–84	10,845,622	3,900,082	2,347,962	890,707	480,459	388,153	259,932	1,184,788	1,149,813	243,726
1984–85	11,835,351	4,213,485	2,564,844	980,416	539,322	416,539	289,124	1,251,490	1,312,673	267,459
1985–86	12,855,040	4,507,505	2,790,504	1,067,717	623,050	446,766	328,827	1,317,062	1,481,954	291,654
1986–87	14,166,507	4,857,389	3,234,202	1,181,305	691,231	408,636	383,386	1,380,745	1,711,783	317,830
1987–88	15,405,503	5,248,764	3,403,379	1,293,302	776,022	485,517	456,111	1,462,345	1,966,124	313,939

Percentage distribution

Year	Total	Instruction	Admin.	Student services	Research	Libraries	Public service	Operation	Scholarships	Mandatory transfers
1976–77	100.0	37.3	20.4	7.4	5.0	3.9	2.4	11.2	10.0	2.3
1977–78	100.0	37.5	20.6	7.6	4.8	3.9	2.2	11.3	9.8	2.3
1978–79	100.0	37.2	20.7	7.7	5.2	3.8	2.2	11.2	9.6	2.3
1979–80	100.0	36.7	20.8	7.8	5.3	3.7	2.2	11.4	9.8	2.4
1980–81	100.0	36.1	21.1	7.9	5.1	3.6	2.3	11.5	10.1	2.3
1981–82	100.0	36.1	21.4	8.0	4.6	3.6	2.5	11.4	10.1	2.2
1982–83	100.0	36.2	21.7	8.2	4.5	3.6	2.4	11.1	10.0	2.2
1983–84	100.0	36.0	21.6	8.2	4.4	3.6	2.4	10.9	10.6	2.2
1984–85	100.0	35.6	21.7	8.3	4.6	3.5	2.4	10.6	11.1	2.3
1985–86	100.0	35.1	21.7	8.3	4.8	3.5	2.6	10.2	11.5	2.3
1986–87	100.0	34.3	22.8	8.3	4.9	2.9	2.7	9.7	12.1	2.2
1987–88	100.0	34.1	22.1	8.4	5.0	3.2	3.0	9.5	12.8	2.0

Expenditure per full-time-equivalent student in constant 1987–88 dollars

Year	Total	Instruction	Admin.	Student services	Research	Libraries	Public service	Operation	Scholarships	Mandatory transfers
1976–77	$8,420	$3,145	$1,717	$625	$425	$329	$203	$942	$839	$197
1977–78	8,392	3,147	1,727	637	404	330	183	950	819	194
1978–79	8,466	3,147	1,756	653	443	325	185	952	809	197
1979–80	8,607	3,156	1,787	670	456	317	186	984	847	204
1980–81	8,645	3,117	1,826	686	437	311	200	997	870	199
1981–82	8,715	3,146	1,865	700	403	310	220	996	879	196
1982–83	8,907	3,227	1,930	731	397	324	214	993	894	197
1983–84	9,215	3,314	1,995	757	408	330	221	1,007	977	207
1984–85	9,566	3,406	2,073	792	436	337	234	1,012	1,061	216
1985–86	9,928	3,481	2,155	825	481	345	254	1,017	1,145	225
1986–87	10,447	3,582	2,385	871	510	301	283	1,018	1,262	234
1987–88	10,738	3,659	2,372	901	541	338	318	1,019	1,370	219

[1] Excludes universities. See preceding table.

[2] Includes institutional and academic support less libraries.

NOTE.—Data in this table may differ slightly from data appearing in other tables. Data for 1976–77 through 1985–86 include only institutions which provided both enrollment and finance data. The Higher Education Price Index was used to convert the per student figures to constant dollars. Because of rounding, details may not add to totals.

SOURCE: U.S. Department of Education, National Center for Education Statistics, "Financial Statistics of Institutions of Higher Education" surveys. (This table was prepared April 1991.)

Table 321.—Educational and general expenditures of private (nonprofit) 2-year colleges, by purpose: 1976–77 to 1987–88

| Year | Educational and general expenditures | | | | | | | | | |
	Total	Instruction	Admin-istration [1]	Student services	Research	Libraries	Public service	Operation and maintenance of plant	Scholarships and fellow-ships	Mandatory transfers
1	2	3	4	5	6	7	8	9	10	11

Expenditures, in thousands of current dollars

Year	Total	Instruction	Admin	Student services	Research	Libraries	Public service	Operation	Scholarships	Mandatory
1976–77	$234,112	$82,723	$59,152	$22,900	$1,022	$7,903	$2,890	$32,431	$17,912	$7,179
1977–78	246,542	86,456	64,390	25,406	266	8,478	2,698	33,606	18,598	6,644
1978–79	269,169	94,875	69,071	29,419	564	8,640	2,766	34,741	21,000	8,092
1979–80	293,743	102,298	77,312	31,182	425	9,237	2,284	37,617	24,644	8,742
1980–81	333,257	114,350	87,803	34,926	211	9,535	2,080	43,936	28,395	12,022
1981–82	365,142	127,315	100,413	39,120	239	10,244	2,030	46,639	28,170	10,973
1982–83	389,876	134,950	103,697	40,934	403	10,566	1,961	50,748	33,128	13,489
1983–84	411,779	138,487	111,931	44,410	102	11,085	2,103	55,014	37,576	11,070
1984–85	447,163	150,202	119,191	52,937	350	12,123	2,054	58,602	41,335	10,370
1985–86	467,445	158,873	124,941	56,471	70	12,413	1,936	60,189	43,167	9,385
1986–87	488,478	150,388	152,140	55,072	137	10,988	2,981	65,149	42,804	8,821
1987–88	527,833	177,196	149,336	59,011	510	10,969	3,587	65,026	54,796	7,402

Percentage distribution

Year	Total	Instruction	Admin	Student services	Research	Libraries	Public service	Operation	Scholarships	Mandatory
1976–77	100.0	35.3	25.3	9.8	0.4	3.4	1.2	13.9	7.7	3.1
1977–78	100.0	35.1	26.1	10.3	0.1	3.4	1.1	13.6	7.5	2.7
1978–79	100.0	35.2	25.7	10.9	0.2	3.2	1.0	12.9	7.8	3.0
1979–80	100.0	34.8	26.3	10.6	0.1	3.1	0.8	12.8	8.4	3.0
1980–81	100.0	34.3	26.3	10.5	0.1	2.9	0.6	13.2	8.5	3.6
1981–82	100.0	34.9	27.5	10.7	0.1	2.8	0.6	12.8	7.7	3.0
1982–83	100.0	34.6	26.6	10.5	0.1	2.7	0.5	13.0	8.5	3.5
1983–84	100.0	33.6	27.2	10.8	0.0	2.7	0.5	13.4	9.1	2.7
1984–85	100.0	33.6	26.7	11.8	0.1	2.7	0.5	13.1	9.2	2.3
1985–86	100.0	34.0	26.7	12.1	0.0	2.7	0.4	12.9	9.2	2.0
1986–87	100.0	30.8	31.1	11.3	0.0	2.2	0.6	13.3	8.8	1.8
1987–88	100.0	33.6	28.3	11.2	0.1	2.1	0.7	12.3	10.4	1.4

Expenditures per full-time-equivalent student in constant 1987–88 dollars

Year	Total	Instruction	Admin	Student services	Research	Libraries	Public service	Operation	Scholarships	Mandatory
1976–77	$5,315	$1,878	$1,343	$520	$23	$179	$66	$736	$407	$163
1977–78	5,025	1,762	1,312	518	5	173	55	685	379	135
1978–79	5,224	1,841	1,341	571	11	168	54	674	408	157
1979–80	5,174	1,802	1,362	549	7	163	40	663	434	154
1980–81	5,166	1,773	1,361	541	3	148	32	681	440	186
1981–82	4,982	1,737	1,370	534	3	140	28	636	384	150
1982–83	5,172	1,790	1,376	543	5	140	26	673	440	179
1983–84	5,166	1,737	1,404	557	1	139	26	690	471	139
1984–85	5,667	1,904	1,511	671	4	154	26	743	524	131
1985–86	5,732	1,948	1,532	693	1	152	24	738	529	115
1986–87	6,916	2,129	2,154	780	2	156	42	922	606	125
1987–88	7,077	2,376	2,002	791	7	147	48	872	735	99

[1] Includes institutional and academic support less libraries.

NOTE.—Data in this table may differ slightly from data appearing in other tables. Data for 1976–77 through 1985–86 include only institutions which provided both enrollment and finance data. The Higher Education Price Index was used to convert the per student figures to constant dollars. Because of rounding, details may not add to totals.

SOURCE: U.S. Department of Education, National Center for Education Statistics, "Financial Statistics of Institutions of Higher Education" surveys. (This table was prepared April 1991.)

Table 322.—Current-fund expenditures of public institutions of higher education, by State: 1974–75 to 1987–88

[In thousands of dollars]

State	1974–75	1979–80	1980–81	1982–83	1983–84	1984–85	1985–86	1986–87	1987–88 [1]	Percent change, 1982–83 to 1987–88
1	2	3	4	5	6	7	8	9	10	11
United States	$23,489,981	$37,767,970	$42,279,806	$49,572,918	$53,086,644	$58,314,550	$63,193,853	$67,653,838	$72,641,305	46.5
Alabama	423,231	751,398	839,366	955,520	1,040,356	1,191,478	1,324,774	1,351,761	1,511,246	58.2
Alaska	65,986	148,397	158,700	213,083	224,589	235,168	224,042	213,286	221,296	3.9
Arizona	341,338	595,852	691,481	819,504	889,573	934,587	1,017,203	1,098,146	1,193,765	45.7
Arkansas	175,584	306,206	340,621	393,679	425,497	485,363	528,831	543,200	622,442	58.1
California	3,259,945	5,019,441	5,775,482	6,390,339	6,630,635	7,705,638	8,515,440	9,079,890	9,493,900	48.6
Colorado	419,550	681,868	738,363	881,518	935,447	993,440	1,057,558	1,123,508	1,225,193	39.0
Connecticut	205,649	333,418	367,850	426,462	489,917	522,006	562,696	621,183	680,087	59.5
Delaware	87,129	140,990	158,332	181,356	190,636	207,584	229,377	255,335	279,084	53.9
District of Columbia	44,125	60,328	71,791	77,802	84,234	90,520	88,462	92,438	96,642	24.2
Florida	679,780	1,054,042	1,170,305	1,366,801	1,497,560	1,650,338	1,782,180	1,973,533	2,182,947	59.7
Georgia	410,458	669,134	754,060	921,021	1,054,899	1,142,836	1,255,964	1,404,747	1,507,960	63.7
Hawaii	135,403	195,758	222,718	267,258	273,105	288,217	312,248	317,294	349,791	30.9
Idaho	87,781	149,634	166,844	192,701	204,783	226,142	238,438	246,847	269,697	40.0
Illinois	1,062,946	1,591,213	1,780,403	1,951,623	2,079,772	2,320,251	2,571,409	2,707,123	2,789,932	43.0
Indiana	628,121	933,703	1,064,395	1,252,380	1,367,711	1,472,807	1,602,203	1,758,524	1,841,317	47.0
Iowa	400,536	713,898	767,590	909,647	944,211	1,027,080	1,092,542	1,162,266	1,229,142	35.1
Kansas	309,174	513,087	579,857	664,708	733,372	794,588	848,602	886,190	928,956	39.8
Kentucky	348,908	605,151	673,775	741,846	806,091	845,505	898,718	992,842	1,068,927	44.1
Louisiana	333,508	612,723	716,702	862,911	914,211	1,000,470	1,039,177	1,065,692	1,112,935	29.0
Maine	90,392	138,278	153,658	184,042	197,915	210,749	216,737	244,432	271,928	47.8
Maryland	447,411	704,407	795,100	886,798	901,569	1,021,140	1,064,430	1,144,897	1,302,127	46.8
Massachusetts	327,719	492,512	553,019	687,245	740,329	878,644	980,585	1,100,445	1,235,566	79.8
Michigan	1,235,651	1,904,616	2,053,795	2,356,196	2,512,255	2,706,362	2,946,336	3,094,481	3,507,141	48.8
Minnesota	524,107	786,017	876,632	1,043,667	1,110,870	1,220,404	1,324,691	1,427,227	1,565,491	50.0
Mississippi	273,799	488,894	539,222	582,401	628,647	660,816	706,380	701,795	775,821	33.2
Missouri	409,430	608,690	687,643	782,706	831,884	899,740	999,869	1,071,224	1,132,628	44.7
Montana	83,835	112,353	121,894	156,492	170,366	185,588	182,102	182,795	192,382	22.9
Nebraska	195,041	341,734	378,928	444,133	469,817	506,752	537,858	582,939	610,064	37.4
Nevada	49,810	99,675	111,347	132,724	140,646	156,584	180,107	198,714	217,330	63.7
New Hampshire	76,052	121,882	134,391	151,983	153,461	168,453	183,959	200,211	222,842	46.6
New Jersey	492,944	805,448	903,169	1,070,511	1,166,525	1,285,926	1,406,490	1,579,018	1,770,521	65.4
New Mexico	137,909	282,439	325,960	379,595	382,998	422,740	456,600	500,674	524,181	38.1
New York	1,739,842	2,337,898	2,519,104	3,132,439	3,359,316	3,636,384	3,802,602	4,227,556	4,494,943	43.5
North Carolina	642,140	988,975	1,128,383	1,284,630	1,439,145	1,633,304	1,799,173	1,955,910	2,076,493	61.6
North Dakota	94,401	167,202	192,046	232,038	254,455	263,909	288,214	309,961	303,762	30.9
Ohio	996,691	1,612,495	1,784,754	2,149,696	2,328,494	2,536,913	2,718,408	2,933,615	3,172,348	47.6
Oklahoma	274,536	501,400	583,174	747,590	728,923	765,599	844,829	826,461	844,428	13.0
Oregon	335,116	586,355	642,411	734,767	788,183	832,296	880,696	959,238	1,023,207	39.3
Pennsylvania	963,368	1,398,891	1,544,586	1,872,341	2,004,320	2,159,745	2,392,145	2,608,557	2,874,641	53.5
Rhode Island	91,446	144,002	158,365	175,371	187,412	197,849	213,253	225,033	246,258	40.4
South Carolina	313,200	553,866	617,963	683,829	743,385	853,452	951,848	980,264	1,079,002	57.8
South Dakota	82,967	123,662	124,103	135,637	141,986	140,885	149,092	152,274	157,736	16.3
Tennessee	364,942	582,038	665,885	781,885	839,477	958,612	1,081,052	1,275,950	1,311,921	67.8
Texas	1,246,924	2,391,570	2,736,276	3,538,762	3,847,623	4,087,570	4,375,082	4,451,215	4,771,023	34.8
Utah	207,032	359,536	405,314	515,087	533,836	595,755	669,714	700,774	757,976	47.2
Vermont	69,621	109,954	122,708	146,712	159,763	174,051	188,112	201,435	216,972	47.9
Virginia	538,067	1,018,187	1,143,755	1,367,587	1,465,098	1,681,173	1,825,156	2,003,090	2,201,018	60.9
Washington	544,422	905,936	993,171	1,088,315	1,205,410	1,331,849	1,399,780	1,512,376	1,575,333	44.7
West Virginia	132,736	298,859	317,482	364,875	404,735	357,335	376,293	392,671	406,170	11.3
Wisconsin	707,518	1,104,035	1,208,396	1,410,280	1,493,528	1,605,692	1,754,395	1,872,979	2,022,712	43.4
Wyoming	59,624	105,604	126,082	166,762	181,300	186,652	203,307	198,934	208,663	25.1
U.S. Service Schools	322,135	514,316	592,454	715,661	786,375	857,612	904,695	942,888	963,419	34.6
Outlying areas	192,195	239,769	268,310	361,327	419,255	418,141	451,370	429,481	491,892	36.1
American Samoa	1,159	1,424	1,609	1,399	1,369	1,092	1,092	1,162	1,257	−10.1
Guam	10,360	14,163	16,100	25,574	25,912	25,576	31,310	30,780	33,481	30.9
Northern Marianas	—	—	—	—	1,212	1,293	1,350	2,787	2,292	—
Puerto Rico	173,848	212,461	237,319	315,465	371,696	368,536	394,046	370,455	427,572	35.5
Trust Territory of the Pacific	655	1,227	1,447	3,960	4,038	5,525	5,992	5,444	6,455	63.0
Virgin Islands	6,173	10,494	11,835	14,929	15,028	16,120	17,580	18,853	20,834	39.6

[1] Preliminary data.

—Data not available or not applicable.

NOTE.—Because of rounding, details may not add to totals.

SOURCE: U.S. Department of Education, National Center for Education Statistics, "Financial Statistics of Institutions of Higher Education" surveys and Integrated Postsecondary Education Data System (IPEDS), "Finance" survey. (This table was prepared April 1991.)

Table 323.—Current-fund expenditures per full-time-equivalent student in institutions of higher education, by control and type of institution and purpose of expenditure: 1987–88

Item	Total				Public				Private			
	All insti-tutions	Univer-sities	Other 4-year	2-year	All insti-tutions	Univer-sities	Other 4-year	2-year	All insti-tutions	Univer-sities	Other 4-year	2-year
1	2	3	4	5	6	7	8	9	10	11	12	13
Total current-fund expenditures [1]	$12,325	$20,182	$12,504	$4,974	$10,471	$16,341	$11,731	$4,919	$17,940	$31,759	$13,834	$5,660
Educational and general expenditures	9,657	15,237	9,651	4,630	8,452	12,828	9,116	4,590	13,304	22,497	10,572	5,139
Instruction	3,881	5,700	3,896	2,217	3,597	4,789	4,065	2,259	4,741	8,445	3,606	1,693
Research	1,121	3,033	706	4	1,006	2,642	810	4	1,472	4,211	527	3
Public service	410	888	329	98	430	999	341	104	349	552	309	18
Academic support	882	1,367	847	495	784	1,197	870	395	1,180	1,882	807	1,765
Libraries	307	504	315	119	267	410	305	124	429	786	330	55
Student services	584	573	687	444	502	478	566	455	833	858	896	293
Institutional support	1,167	1,325	1,391	697	933	995	1,115	705	1,877	2,321	1,866	596
Operation and maintenance of plant	892	1,215	955	507	807	1,041	923	522	1,147	1,741	1,010	323
Scholarships and fellowships	577	920	669	132	280	511	281	110	1,476	2,154	1,338	411
From unrestricted funds	319	—	—	—	120	—	—	—	921	—	—	—
From restricted funds [2]	258	—	—	—	160	—	—	—	555	—	—	—
Mandatory transfers	143	216	171	35	114	177	147	35	230	333	213	37

[1] Includes expenditures for auxiliary enterprises, hospitals, and independent operations which are not shown separately.
[2] Excludes Pell Grants.
—Data not available.

NOTE.—Because of rounding, details may not add to totals.

SOURCE: U.S. Department of Education, National Center for Education Statistics, Integrated Postsecondary Education Data System (IPEDS), "Fall Enrollment" and "Finance" surveys. (This table was prepared April 1991.)

Table 324.—Additions to physical plant value of institutions of higher education, by type of addition and control of institution: 1969–70 to 1985–86

[In millions]

Year	Total all institutions	Public institutions				Private institutions			
		Total	Land	Buildings	Equipment	Total	Land	Buildings	Equipment
1	2	3	4	5	6	7	8	9	10
1969–70	$4,233	$2,985	$152	$2,185	$648	$1,248	$59	$967	$221
1970–71	4,165	3,032	128	2,241	663	1,134	41	895	198
1971–72	4,163	3,054	112	2,277	665	1,109	53	860	195
1972–73	3,967	2,940	126	2,077	737	1,028	53	750	225
1973–74	4,312	3,206	205	2,188	813	1,106	55	816	235
1974–75	4,761	3,476	263	2,246	967	1,284	67	860	357
1975–76	4,702	3,552	168	2,365	1,019	1,150	58	768	325
1976–77	4,623	3,362	128	2,208	1,026	1,261	58	838	366
1977–78	4,527	3,306	102	2,117	1,087	1,221	45	777	400
1978–79	4,576	3,377	154	1,944	1,279	1,199	52	763	383
1979–80	5,551	3,666	164	2,149	1,354	1,886	98	1,220	568
1980–81	6,471	4,279	146	2,555	1,579	2,192	104	1,398	690
1981–82	6,975	4,594	170	2,679	1,744	2,382	83	1,488	811
1982–83	7,421	4,765	374	2,396	1,994	2,656	106	1,666	884
1983–84	7,604	5,038	196	2,427	2,415	2,566	110	1,507	950
1984–85	8,306	5,390	202	2,455	2,733	2,916	135	1,671	1,110
1985–86	10,149	6,875	237	3,318	3,320	3,274	128	1,922	1,225

NOTE.—Because of rounding, details may not add to totals.

SOURCE: U.S. Department of Education, National Center for Education Statistics, "Financial Statistics of Institutions of Higher Education" surveys. (This table was prepared July 1987.)

Table 325.—Capital expenditures[1] for science and engineering programs in institutions of higher education, by field of study and source of funds: United States and outlying areas, 1976-77 to 1988-89

[In thousands]

Field of study and source of funds	1976-77	1978-79	1979-80	1980-81	1981-82	1982-83	1983-84	1984-85	1985-86	1986-87	1987-88	1988-89
1	2	3	4	5	6	7	8	9	10	11	12	13
Total from all sources	$960,014	$696,218	$794,512	$954,795	$964,596	$1,091,753	$1,174,646	$1,222,698	$1,493,503	$1,737,118	$1,954,626	$2,091,698
Engineering	87,718	87,128	89,297	105,768	146,996	136,835	146,884	183,598	314,149	379,785	365,315	371,825
Sciences, total	872,296	609,090	705,215	849,027	817,600	954,918	1,027,762	1,039,100	1,179,354	1,357,333	1,589,311	1,719,873
Physical sciences	65,216	64,685	77,154	89,106	83,296	97,864	110,134	115,653	143,667	156,849	204,919	237,669
Environmental sciences	28,351	25,153	36,208	36,834	44,006	42,174	36,218	54,574	48,945	54,063	58,676	72,673
Mathematical and computer sciences	25,136	27,282	32,318	31,913	35,651	54,206	48,921	77,209	90,603	82,651	95,412	67,518
Life sciences	642,493	428,293	459,057	592,020	578,398	667,367	716,602	691,149	768,281	908,977	1,050,025	1,161,851
Psychological sciences	12,702	7,060	17,982	11,183	12,956	16,705	31,317	12,807	17,816	9,669	12,130	13,893
Social sciences	31,798	21,358	35,073	45,742	31,344	40,898	46,941	60,720	49,919	55,207	80,709	77,483
Other sciences	66,600	35,259	47,423	42,229	31,949	35,704	37,629	26,988	60,123	89,917	87,440	88,787
Total from Federal sources	195,519	164,460	149,563	161,043	126,448	135,101	142,440	106,801	170,509	193,246	202,034	205,769
Engineering	17,219	20,927	20,438	19,150	20,931	18,390	30,640	16,793	37,536	49,344	47,010	43,340
Sciences, total	178,300	143,533	129,125	141,893	105,517	116,711	111,800	90,008	132,973	143,902	155,024	162,429
Physical sciences	21,894	32,186	22,463	26,693	21,966	19,482	20,713	31,497	38,108	40,130	33,140	40,250
Environmental sciences	9,307	8,220	8,033	8,352	6,006	4,639	4,828	4,128	8,168	15,199	13,455	18,985
Mathematical and computer sciences	1,882	2,983	5,653	5,649	5,049	5,516	8,697	8,918	17,516	12,228	19,529	7,336
Life sciences	137,369	90,796	86,105	90,767	67,319	79,357	72,685	40,315	57,823	57,954	71,203	77,030
Psychological sciences	2,398	1,740	2,002	1,784	1,205	1,082	1,035	871	1,739	989	2,184	1,654
Social sciences	2,109	2,076	1,528	7,150	2,213	5,277	3,209	2,493	3,618	4,834	7,985	8,178
Other sciences	3,341	5,532	3,341	1,498	1,759	1,358	633	1,786	6,001	12,568	7,528	8,997
Total from other sources	764,495	531,758	644,949	793,752	838,148	956,652	1,032,206	1,115,897	1,322,994	1,543,872	1,752,592	1,885,929
Engineering	70,499	66,201	68,859	86,618	126,065	118,445	116,244	166,805	276,613	330,441	318,305	328,485
Sciences, total	693,996	465,557	576,090	707,134	712,083	838,207	915,962	949,092	1,046,381	1,213,431	1,434,287	1,557,444
Physical sciences	43,322	32,499	54,691	62,413	61,330	78,382	89,421	84,156	105,559	116,719	171,779	197,419
Environmental sciences	19,044	16,933	28,175	28,482	38,000	37,535	31,390	50,446	40,777	38,864	45,221	53,688
Mathematical and computer sciences	23,254	24,299	26,665	26,264	30,602	48,690	40,224	68,291	73,087	70,423	75,883	60,182
Life sciences	505,124	337,497	372,952	501,253	511,079	588,010	643,917	650,834	710,458	851,023	978,822	1,084,821
Psychological sciences	10,304	5,320	15,980	9,399	11,751	15,623	30,282	11,936	16,077	8,680	9,946	12,239
Social sciences	29,689	19,282	33,545	38,592	29,131	35,621	43,732	58,227	46,301	50,373	72,724	69,305
Other sciences	63,259	29,727	44,082	40,731	30,190	34,346	36,996	25,202	54,122	77,349	79,912	79,790

[1] Includes expenditures for facilities and equipment for research, development, and instruction.

NOTE: Some data have been revised from previously published figures.

SOURCE: National Science Foundation, Division of Science Resources Studies, "Early Release of Summary Statistics on Academic Science/Engineering Resources," various years; and unpublished tabulations. (This table was prepared March 1991.)

Table 326.—Value of property and liabilities of institutions of higher education: 1899–1900 to 1985–86

[In thousands]

Academic year	Property value at end of year						Endowment (end of year market value) [1]	Liabilities of plant funds
	Total	Physical plant value				Endowment (book value) [1]		
		Total	Land	Buildings	Equipment			
1	2	3	4	5	6	7	8	9
1899–1900	$448,597	$253,599	—	—	—	[2] $194,998	—	—
1909–10	781,255	457,594	$92,359	$297,153	$68,082	[2] 323,661	—	—
1919–20	1,316,404	747,333	128,922	495,920	122,491	[2] 569,071	—	—
1929–30	3,437,117	2,065,049	304,114	1,490,014	270,921	[2] 1,372,068	—	—
1935–36	3,913,028	2,359,418	334,085	1,636,722	388,611	[2] 1,553,610	—	—
1937–38	4,208,695	2,556,075	313,665	1,811,309	431,101	1,652,620	—	—
1939–40	4,440,063	2,753,780	—	—	—	1,686,283	—	—
1941–42	4,525,925	2,759,261	—	—	—	[2] 1,766,664	—	—
1947–48	6,076,212	3,691,725	—	—	—	2,384,487	—	—
1949–50	7,401,187	4,799,964	—	—	—	[2] 2,601,223	—	—
1951–52	9,241,725	6,373,195	—	—	—	2,868,530	—	—
1953–54	10,717,082	7,523,193	—	—	—	3,193,889	—	—
1955–56	12,561,046	8,858,907	624,467	[3] 6,697,648	1,536,792	3,702,139	—	$894,383
1957–58	15,770,197	11,124,489	733,182	[3] 8,540,429	1,850,878	4,645,708	—	1,444,602
1959–60	18,870,628	13,548,548	842,664	[3] 10,472,478	2,233,407	5,322,080	—	1,964,306
1961–62	22,761,193	16,681,844	1,009,294	[3] 12,900,093	2,772,457	6,079,349	—	2,806,868
1963–64	28,232,362	21,279,346	1,292,691	[3] 16,460,867	3,525,788	6,953,016	—	4,190,189
1965–66	35,274,597	26,851,273	1,758,901	[3] 20,653,028	4,439,344	8,423,324	$11,126,831	6,071,750
1967–68	—	34,506,348	2,062,545	[3] 26,673,826	5,769,977	—	—	—
1969–70	52,930,923	42,093,580	3,076,751	31,865,179	7,151,649	10,837,343	11,206,632	9,384,731
1970–71	57,394,951	46,053,585	3,117,895	35,042,590	7,893,100	11,341,366	13,714,330	9,786,240
1971–72	62,136,459	50,153,251	3,287,326	38,131,339	8,734,586	11,983,208	15,180,934	10,291,095
1972–73	66,814,103	53,814,596	3,492,611	40,808,481	9,513,503	12,999,507	15,099,840	10,823,595
1973–74	71,305,817	58,002,777	3,888,372	43,701,491	10,412,914	13,303,040	13,168,076	11,400,916
1974–75	75,585,674	62,183,078	4,210,901	46,453,642	11,518,536	13,402,596	14,364,545	12,413,420
1975–76	80,300,595	66,348,304	4,345,232	49,349,224	12,653,847	13,952,291	15,488,265	12,687,015
1976–77	85,486,550	70,739,427	4,444,927	52,384,393	13,910,107	14,747,123	16,304,553	13,068,341
1977–78	90,337,044	74,770,804	4,621,071	55,188,603	14,961,131	15,566,240	16,840,129	13,437,861
1978–79	95,442,468	78,637,991	4,824,250	57,563,005	16,250,737	16,804,477	18,158,634	13,712,648
1979–80	102,294,859	83,733,387	5,037,172	60,847,097	17,849,119	18,561,472	20,743,045	14,181,991
1980–81	109,701,242	88,760,567	5,212,453	64,158,017	19,390,097	20,940,675	23,465,001	14,794,669
1981–82	117,601,954	94,516,512	5,402,339	67,794,877	21,319,297	23,085,442	24,415,245	15,487,618
1982–83	127,345,302	100,992,841	5,889,080	71,519,718	23,584,042	26,352,461	32,691,133	16,749,900
1983–84	137,141,741	107,640,113	6,109,746	75,220,765	26,309,602	29,501,629	32,975,610	18,277,315
1984–85	148,163,096	114,763,986	6,236,159	79,133,998	29,393,829	33,399,110	39,916,361	22,105,712
1985–86	160,959,517	122,261,355	6,573,923	82,886,012	32,801,419	38,698,162	50,280,775	25,699,408

[1] Includes funds functioning as endowment.

[2] Includes annuity funds.

[3] Includes improvements to land and equipment. These funds are included under appropriate categories after 1967–68.

— Data not available.

NOTE.—Because of rounding, details may not add to totals.

SOURCE: U.S. Department of Education, National Center for Education Statistics, "Financial Statistics of Institutions of Higher Education" surveys. (This table was prepared August 1987.)

Table 327.—Physical plant value and endowment funds per student in institutions of higher education, by type and control of institution: 1975–76 to 1985–86

Control and level of institution	Institutions		Plant value (end of year)		Market value of endowment funds (end of year)	
	Number [1]	Full-time-equivalent enrollment, in thousands	Total, in thousands of dollars	Per full-time-equivalent student	Total, in thousands of dollars	Per full-time-equivalent student
1	2	3	4	5	6	7
1975–76						
Total	3,026	8,480	$66,348,304	$7,824	$15,488,266	$1,827
4-year	1,898	5,900	57,333,509	9,717	15,337,285	2,599
2-year	1,128	2,579	9,014,795	3,495	150,981	59
Public	1,442	6,522	44,795,168	6,868	2,932,737	450
4-year	545	4,057	36,440,349	8,983	2,886,157	711
2-year	897	2,466	8,354,819	3,388	46,580	19
Private	1,584	1,957	21,553,136	11,011	12,555,529	6,414
4-year	1,353	1,844	20,893,160	11,331	12,451,128	6,753
2-year	231	113	659,976	5,816	104,401	920
1979–80						
Total	3,152	8,487	83,733,387	9,866	20,743,045	2,444
4-year	1,957	6,016	71,524,828	11,889	20,541,897	3,415
2-year	1,195	2,471	12,208,559	4,940	201,148	81
Public	1,475	6,393	56,970,126	8,912	3,708,329	580
4-year	549	4,059	45,523,288	11,215	3,628,794	894
2-year	926	2,333	11,446,838	4,906	79,535	34
Private	1,677	2,095	26,763,261	12,777	17,034,716	8,132
4-year	1,408	1,957	26,001,540	13,288	16,913,103	8,643
2-year	269	138	761,721	5,522	121,613	882
1983–84						
Total	3,284	9,166	107,640,113	11,743	32,975,610	3,597
4-year	2,013	6,324	92,237,794	14,585	32,644,125	5,162
2-year	1,271	2,842	15,402,318	5,419	331,486	117
Public	1,481	6,881	72,605,169	10,551	6,038,051	877
4-year	565	4,266	58,108,916	13,623	5,887,180	1,380
2-year	916	2,616	14,496,252	5,542	150,871	58
Private	1,803	2,285	35,034,944	15,333	26,937,560	11,789
4-year	1,448	2,059	34,128,878	16,577	26,756,944	12,997
2-year	355	226	906,066	4,006	180,615	799
1984–85						
Total	3,331	8,952	114,763,986	12,820	39,916,361	4,459
4-year	2,025	6,293	98,417,404	15,640	39,524,453	6,281
2-year	1,306	2,659	16,346,582	6,148	391,908	147
Public	1,501	6,685	77,314,401	11,566	7,344,312	1,099
4-year	566	4,238	61,924,903	14,612	7,172,486	1,692
2-year	935	2,447	15,389,498	6,290	171,826	70
Private	1,830	2,267	37,449,585	16,519	32,572,049	14,368
4-year	1,459	2,055	36,492,501	17,759	32,351,967	15,744
2-year	371	212	957,084	4,510	220,082	1,037
1985–86						
Total	3,340	8,943	122,261,355	13,671	50,280,775	5,622
4-year	2,029	6,294	105,074,835	16,694	49,806,974	7,913
2-year	1,311	2,649	17,186,520	6,488	473,801	179
Public	1,498	6,668	82,553,486	12,381	9,087,997	1,363
4-year	566	4,240	66,339,329	15,647	8,881,733	2,095
2-year	932	2,428	16,214,157	6,678	206,265	85
Private	1,842	2,276	39,707,869	17,449	41,192,778	18,102
4-year	1,463	2,055	38,735,506	18,852	40,925,241	19,918
2-year	379	221	972,363	4,401	267,536	1,211

[1] Includes main and branch campuses.

NOTE.—Because of rounding, details may not add to totals.

SOURCE: U.S. Department of Education, National Center for Education Statistics, "Financial Statistics of Institutions of Higher Education" and "Fall Enrollment in Colleges and Universities" surveys. (This table was prepared August 1987.)

Table 328.—Endowment funds of the 100 institutions of higher education with the largest amounts: Fiscal year 1987

Institution	Rank order [1]	Market value of endowment, in thousands of dollars (end of fiscal year)	Institution	Rank order [1]	Market value of endowment, in thousands of dollars (end of fiscal year)
1	2	3	1	2	3
United States (all institutions)	—	$58,199,243			
University of Texas at Austin	1	2,594,767	Oberlin College (Ohio)	51	217,952
Princeton University (N.J.)	2	1,892,091	George Washington University (D.C.)	52	217,392
Columbia University, Main Division (N.Y.)	3	1,387,056	Tulane University of Louisiana	53	213,198
Washington University (Missouri)	4	1,218,884	University of Cincinnati, Main Campus (Ohio)	54	209,388
Massachusetts Institute of Technology	5	1,169,740	Georgetown University (D.C.)	55	204,600
Rice University (Tex.)	6	893,027	Middlebury College (Vt.)	56	202,583
University of Chicago (Ill.)	7	889,268	Rensselaer Polytechnic Institute (N.Y.)	57	190,835
Emory University (Ga.)	8	849,247	Lehigh University (Penn.)	58	181,259
Northwestern University (Ill.)	9	823,303	Lafayette College (Penn.)	59	176,331
University of Pennsylvania	10	648,528	Boston College (Mass.)	60	176,214
Dartmouth College (N.H.)	11	590,204	Thomas Jefferson University (Penn.)	61	160,724
University of Rochester (N.Y.)	12	568,056	Boston University (Mass.)	62	159,192
Rockefeller University (N.Y.)	13	549,153	Mount Holyoke College (Mass.)	63	151,916
Cornell University, Endowed Colleges (N.Y.)	14	540,298	Carleton College (Minn.)	64	144,190
Johns Hopkins University (Md.)	15	534,965	St. Louis University, Main Campus (Missouri)	65	140,883
Vanderbilt University (Tenn.)	16	514,377	Bowdoin College (Maine)	66	138,579
New York University	17	511,220	CUNY Mount Sinai School of Medicine (N.Y.)	67	138,319
Mayo Graduate School of Medicine (Minn.)	18	466,479	Rochester Institute of Technology (N.Y.)	68	135,628
University of Notre Dame (Ind.)	19	456,099	University of Wisconsin at Madison	69	135,472
California Institute of Technology	20	418,235	University of North Carolina at Chapel Hill	70	128,619
University of Virginia, Main Campus	21	414,834	Syracuse University, Main Campus (N.Y.)	71	128,400
University of Southern California	22	401,170	Brandeis University (Mass.)	72	126,439
Brown University (R.I.)	23	345,369	Cornell University Medical Center (N.Y.)	73	126,412
Case Western Reserve University (Ohio)	24	340,561	Occidental College (Calif.)	74	126,317
Princeton Theological Seminary (N.J.)	25	322,090	Northeastern University (Mass.)	75	124,137
University of Michigan at Ann Arbor	26	321,427	Wabash College (Ind.)	76	121,600
Southern Methodist University (Tex.)	27	301,732	Purdue University (Ind.)	77	117,171
Wellesley College (Mass.)	28	297,958	Trinity College (Conn.)	78	115,324
Smith College (Mass.)	29	293,625	Colorado College	79	113,102
Swarthmore College (Penn.)	30	277,516	University of Miami (Fla.)	80	112,094
Williams College (Mass.)	31	275,188	Earlham College (Ind.)	81	111,304
Carnegie-Mellon University (Penn.)	32	265,893	Tufts University (Mass.)	82	110,795
Baylor College of Medicine (Tex.)	33	264,634	Bryn Mawr College (Penn.)	83	109,922
Texas Christian University	34	261,718	Rush University (Ill.)	84	109,721
University of Delaware	35	258,926	State University of New York at Buffalo, Main Campus	85	108,820
Wesleyan University (Conn.)	36	258,131	The Juilliard School (N.Y.)	86	108,260
Trinity University (Tex.)	37	248,788	New Mexico Military Institute	87	104,627
Amherst College (Mass.)	38	248,354	Colgate University (N.Y.)	88	104,527
Loyola University of Chicago (Ill.)	39	241,088	Hamilton College (N.Y.)	89	103,190
Loyola University in New Orleans (La.)	40	237,000	Southwestern University (Tex.)	90	101,406
University of Minnesota, Minneapolis-St. Paul	41	236,517	Yeshiva University (N.Y.)	91	100,111
Pomona College (Calif.)	42	232,675	University of Oklahoma, Norman Campus	92	95,831
University of Washington	43	231,945	Whitman College (Wash.)	93	90,295
University of Richmond (Va.)	44	228,761	Agnes Scott College (Ga.)	94	88,991
Grinnell College (Iowa)	45	226,932	Cooper Union (N.Y.)	95	87,863
Wake Forest University (N.C.)	46	226,072	University of The South (Tenn.)	96	87,396
Berea College (Ky.)	47	225,938	Union College (N.Y.)	97	87,063
Vassar College (N.Y.)	48	225,184	Claremont McKenna College (Calif.)	98	83,735
Baylor University (Tex.)	49	220,819	Radcliffe College (Mass.)	99	83,383
University of Pittsburgh, Main Campus (Penn.)	50	218,645	Bucknell University (Penn.)	100	82,388

[1] Institutions ranked by size of endowment. Excludes institutions which have not reported data for 1985–86 or 1986–87 or have submitted system-wide reports. Institutions which appeared in the 1985–86 listing, but have been excluded for 1986–87 for these reasons are: Pennsylvania State University, Main Campus; Harvard University (Mass.); Yale University (Conn.); Stanford University (Calif.); University of California at Berkeley; University of California at Los Angeles; University of California at Davis; University of California at Santa Barbara; Duke University (N.C.); Oral Roberts University (Oklahoma); Ohio State University, Main Campus;

—Not applicable.

SOURCE: U.S. Department of Education, National Center for Education Statistics, Integrated Postsecondary Education Data System (IPEDS), "Finances, 1986–87" survey. (This table was prepared July 1990.)

Table 329.—Characteristics of persons who ever received work-related training by Spring 1987

[Numbers in thousands]

Characteristic	Total	Sex		Race/ethnicity			Years of school completed		
		Male	Female	White	Black	Other	Less than 9 years	9 to 12 years	More than 12 years
1	2	3	4	5	6	7	8	9	10
All persons, 18 to 64 years old	148,137	72,366	75,771	126,496	16,847	4,793	11,089	78,373	58,675
Persons ever receiving work training	37,615	18,917	18,698	32,588	3,974	1,053	1,410	20,637	15,568
Uses training on current or most recent job	24,350	12,600	11,750	21,488	2,107	755	717	12,195	11,438
Percent of all persons	16.4	17.4	15.5	17.0	12.5	15.8	6.5	15.6	19.5
Provider of training									
Apprenticeship	1,266	1,069	196	1,162	43	61	59	871	336
Business/vocational school	8,975	3,684	5,291	7,984	837	155	210	5,906	2,859
2-year college	2,865	1,092	1,773	2,599	172	93	90	1,242	1,533
4-year college	2,111	1,087	1,024	1,930	98	83	8	269	1,833
High school vocational program	1,536	602	934	1,319	195	22	68	1,147	321
Training program at work	10,471	5,525	4,946	9,410	760	301	248	4,913	5,310
Military	1,702	1,506	196	1,549	145	8	51	939	712
Correspondence	707	415	291	651	30	26	9	371	327
Previous job	1,306	671	634	1,127	87	92	57	576	672
Sheltered workshop	254	168	86	254	—	—	48	126	80
Vocational rehabilitation center	557	236	321	438	119	—	96	320	142
Other	5,493	2,563	2,930	4,753	582	158	232	2,609	2,652
Length of training program (average number of weeks)	20	22	18	20	21	14	19	23	17
Program paid for by:									
Self or family	11,655	4,676	6,979	10,509	881	265	334	6,276	5,045
Employer	15,842	8,561	7,281	14,417	1,034	390	407	7,725	7,709
Federal, State, or local government	10,193	5,603	4,590	7,863	1,949	381	639	6,467	3,087
Someone else	1,226	679	547	998	176	52	91	733	401
Participated in government sponsored training program [1]	4,657	2,685	1,971	3,376	1,064	216	285	2,964	1,408

[1] Includes Job Training Partnership Act (JTPA), Comprehensive Employment Training Act (CETA), Work Incentive Program (WIN), Trade Adjustment Assistance Act, and Veteran's Training Programs.

—Less than 500.

NOTE.—Includes persons who received worker training at any time prior to Spring 1987.

SOURCE: U.S. Department of Commerce, Bureau of the Census, *What's it Worth? Educational Background and Economic Status: Spring 1987*. (This table was prepared April 1991.)

Table 330.—Selected characteristics of participants in adult education: 1984

[Numbers in thousands]

Characteristics of participants	Number of adults in population [1]	Participants in adult education [2]						
		Total		Full-time students in high school or college degree programs		Not full-time students in high school or college degree programs [3]		
		Number	Percent	Number	Percent	Number	Percent	
1	2	3	4	5	6	7	8	
Total	172,583	23,303	13.5	1,118	0.6	22,184	12.9	
Age								
17 to 34 years	71,891	11,704	16.3	948	1.3	10,756	15.0	
35 to 54 years	52,303	8,864	16.9	152	0.3	8,712	16.7	
55 years and over	48,388	2,735	5.7	18	(4)	2,717	5.6	
Sex								
Men	81,700	10,446	12.8	485	0.6	9,961	12.2	
Women	90,883	12,857	14.1	634	0.7	12,224	13.5	
Racial/ethnic group								
White, non-Hispanic	139,777	20,429	14.6	939	0.7	19,491	13.9	
Black, non-Hispanic	18,628	1,506	8.1	88	0.5	1,418	7.6	
Hispanic	9,706	796	8.2	63	0.6	733	7.6	
Other	4,472	571	12.8	28	0.6	543	12.1	
Highest level of education completed								
Less than 4 years of high school	47,297	1,890	4.0	315	0.7	1,574	3.3	
4 years of high school	66,224	6,991	10.6	193	0.3	6,799	10.3	
1 to 3 years of college	30,287	6,022	19.9	394	1.3	5,628	18.6	
4 or more years of college	28,775	8,400	29.2	217	0.8	8,184	28.4	
Labor force status								
In labor force	112,441	19,788	17.6	740	0.7	19,047	16.9	
Employed	104,464	18,929	18.1	654	0.6	18,275	17.5	
Unemployed	7,977	859	10.8	86	1.1	772	9.7	
Not in labor force	60,141	3,515	5.8	378	0.6	3,137	5.2	
Keeping house	31,131	2,178	7.0	22	0.1	2,156	6.9	
Going to school	6,866	524	7.6	330	4.8	195	2.8	
Other	22,144	813	3.7	26	0.1	786	3.5	
Annual family income								
Under $5,000	13,016	797	6.1	85	0.7	712	5.5	
$5,000 to $7,499	11,562	712	6.2	69	0.6	643	5.6	
$7,500 to $9,999	10,308	742	7.2	44	0.4	698	6.8	
$10,000 to $12,499	12,079	1,089	9.0	54	0.4	1,035	8.6	
$12,500 to $14,999	10,509	1,028	9.8	39	0.4	988	9.4	
$15,000 to $17,499	10,353	1,253	12.1	61	0.6	1,192	11.5	
$17,500 to $19,999	9,422	1,255	13.3	53	0.6	1,202	12.8	
$20,000 to $24,999	17,431	2,625	15.1	116	0.7	2,509	14.4	
$25,000 to $29,999	15,090	2,503	16.6	106	0.7	2,397	15.9	
$30,000 to $34,999	13,839	2,505	18.1	110	0.8	2,395	17.3	
$35,000 to $39,999	10,287	1,919	18.7	76	0.7	1,843	17.9	
$40,000 to $49,999	12,643	2,626	20.8	103	0.8	2,522	19.9	
$50,000 to $74,999	11,981	2,543	21.2	123	1.0	2,420	20.2	
$75,000 cr more	5,112	1,011	19.8	48	0.9	963	18.8	
Not reported	8,951	695	7.8	32	0.4	664	7.4	

[1] Persons 17 years of age and over on the date of the survey.

[2] Data are for the year ending in May 1984.

[3] On the date of the survey. Includes part-time undergraduate and graduate students who indicated that they were also adult education participants.

[4] Less than .05 percent.

NOTE.—Data are based upon a sample survey of the civilian noninstitutional population. Because of rounding, details may not add to totals.

SOURCE: U.S. Department of Education, National Center for Education Statistics, *Participation in Adult Education,* May 1984. (This table was prepared June 1986.)

Table 331.—Courses [1] taken by participants in adult education,[2] by sex, age, and field of study: Year ending May 1984

[In thousands]

Field of study	Total	Courses taken by men							Courses taken by women						
		Total	17 to 24 years	25 to 34 years	35 to 44 years	45 to 54 years	55 to 64 years	65 years and over	Total	17 to 24 years	25 to 34 years	35 to 44 years	45 to 54 years	55 to 64 years	65 years and over
1	2	3	4	5	6	7	8	9	10	11	12	13	14	15	16
Total courses	**40,752**	**17,770**	**2,574**	**6,509**	**4,622**	**2,324**	**1,328**	**413**	**22,981**	**3,563**	**7,907**	**5,900**	**2,994**	**1,796**	**822**
Agriculture and renewable natural resources	430	321	28	118	91	40	35	7	109	20	28	36	15	8	2
Arts, visual and performing	2,149	509	122	177	76	45	46	43	1,640	232	534	354	194	194	132
Business	8,981	4,329	507	1,601	1,175	643	352	52	4,652	772	1,616	1,360	631	238	33
Education	2,875	863	146	282	246	126	38	25	2,011	298	742	540	293	106	31
Engineering and engineering technology	5,899	4,030	552	1,613	1,059	547	227	32	1,869	243	572	567	324	138	25
Health care and health sciences	5,101	1,648	103	543	543	227	194	38	3,453	461	1,277	859	453	349	55
Health education	1,204	346	32	161	99	32	16	6	858	101	319	238	125	45	30
Home economics	947	66	5	26	17	7	11	0	882	60	285	228	128	99	82
Personal services occupations	842	302	59	123	73	22	20	6	540	97	204	165	36	33	5
Language, linguistics, and literature	2,167	828	198	327	167	52	54	30	1,338	292	468	239	157	107	76
Life sciences, physical sciences, and mathematical sciences	1,331	609	183	246	89	42	33	16	722	169	275	198	42	27	12
Philosophy, religion, and psychology	2,703	1,028	125	292	254	188	105	64	1,674	234	481	407	230	162	160
Physical education and leisure	2,324	684	148	241	126	75	45	48	1,640	293	600	329	162	158	97
Social sciences and social studies	2,080	1,230	180	448	336	152	91	23	850	142	278	199	131	58	41
Interdisciplinary studies	357	143	37	33	43	22	6	2	214	49	53	68	30	11	4
Unable to classify	1,362	833	148	278	228	105	54	20	529	98	174	113	45	62	37

[1] The total number of adult education courses taken between May 1983 and May 1984 was 43,192,000. However, only 40,752,000 course descriptions were obtained through the survey, which asked for information on up to 4 courses (the most recent courses if more than 4 courses were taken during the year). Five percent of participants took more than 4 courses during the year.

[2] Includes part-time undergraduate and graduate students who indicated they were also adult education participants.

NOTE.—Because of rounding, details may not add to totals.

SOURCE: U.S. Department of Education, National Center for Education Statistics, "Current Population Survey, May 1984, Survey of Adult Education," conducted by the Bureau of the Census, unpublished tabulations. (This table was prepared June 1986.)

Table 332.—Courses[1] taken by participants in adult education,[2] by sex, age, and reason for taking course: Year ending May 1984

[In thousands]

Main reason for taking course	Total	Courses taken by men							Courses taken by women						
		Total	17 to 24 years	25 to 34 years	35 to 44 years	45 to 54 years	55 to 64 years	65 years and over	Total	17 to 24 years	25 to 34 years	35 to 44 years	45 to 54 years	55 to 64 years	65 years and over
1	2	3	4	5	6	7	8	9	10	11	12	13	14	15	16
Total courses	**40,752**	**17,770**	**2,574**	**6,509**	**4,622**	**2,324**	**1,328**	**413**	**22,981**	**3,563**	**7,907**	**5,900**	**2,994**	**1,796**	**822**
Job-related reason	26,159	12,607	1,394	4,774	3,585	1,820	908	126	13,552	1,854	4,880	3,889	1,930	861	138
To get new job	4,802	1,824	502	790	307	154	56	15	2,978	866	1,033	748	264	59	9
In current occupation	984	395	40	218	77	37	19	4	589	128	196	185	54	24	1
In new occupation	3,818	1,428	462	571	230	117	37	11	2,390	738	836	563	210	34	8
To advance in job	19,703	10,004	835	3,665	3,035	1,567	797	105	9,699	880	3,495	2,934	1,537	727	125
Other job-related reason	1,654	779	58	319	244	99	55	5	875	108	352	207	128	76	5
Non-job-related reason	14,447	5,117	1,170	1,720	1,024	495	420	287	9,330	1,676	3,014	1,987	1,050	919	684
American citizenship	34	19	10	7	0	0	2	0	15	2	5	2	4	0	2
General education	3,358	1,447	595	503	206	74	43	27	1,911	673	633	317	150	85	52
Volunteer work	520	208	30	60	61	21	25	11	312	21	98	65	53	46	29
Personal or social	10,230	3,298	492	1,093	734	392	342	246	6,932	949	2,202	1,579	832	780	590
Other non-job-related	306	146	44	59	23	9	8	3	160	31	76	24	10	9	10
Not reported	145	46	9	15	13	10	0	0	99	32	13	24	15	15	0

[1] The total number of adult education courses taken between May 1983 and May 1984 was 43,192,000. However, only 40,752,000 course descriptions were obtained through the survey, which asked for information on up to 4 courses (the most recent courses of more than 4 courses were taken during the year). Five percent of participants took more than 4 courses during the year.

[2] Includes part-time undergraduate and graduate students who indicated they were adult education participants.

NOTE: Because of rounding, details may not add to totals.

SOURCE: U.S. Department of Education, National Center for Education Statistics, *Trends in Adult Education, 1969–1984*. (This table was prepared June 1986.)

Table 333.—Participants in adult basic and secondary education programs, by sex, level of enrollment, and State: Fiscal years 1980, 1984, and 1988

State or other area	1980 Total	1980 Adult basic education	1980 Adult secondary education	1980 Ungraded	1984 Total	1984 Adult basic education	1984 Adult secondary education	1988 Total	1988 Adult basic education	1988 Adult secondary education
1	2	3	4	5	6	7	8	9	10	11
United States	2,018,906	915,936	531,663	571,307	2,559,550	1,910,003	649,547	3,007,169	1,951,089	1,056,080
Alabama	51,599	36,726	12,372	2,501	44,126	28,034	16,092	37,154	24,430	12,724
Alaska	5,667	2,200	2,188	1,279	11,855	6,649	5,206	5,519	4,479	1,040
Arizona	9,996	9,968	22	6	15,836	11,480	4,356	27,122	20,102	7,020
Arkansas	8,583	7,308	1,275	—	9,000	7,603	1,397	24,182	10,001	14,181
California	267,625	60,385	—	207,240	632,938	632,938	—	845,023	603,243	241,780
Colorado	9,381	4,295	2,644	2,442	9,300	7,910	1,390	10,536	8,527	2,009
Connecticut	21,889	8,882	4,805	8,202	41,064	21,078	19,986	35,862	19,238	16,624
Delaware	1,797	1,110	503	184	1,858	[1] 1,263	[1] 595	2,259	1,910	349
District of Columbia	25,214	4,928	6,502	13,784	16,192	9,981	6,211	17,569	11,144	6,425
Florida	467,162	100,958	184,568	181,636	585,053	351,032	234,021	404,277	203,856	200,421
Georgia	50,820	26,734	17,008	7,078	54,257	36,996	17,261	47,344	32,406	14,938
Hawaii	16,457	16,457	—	—	22,219	[1] 22,219	—	46,900	26,692	20,208
Idaho	12,851	8,915	3,010	926	11,086	8,179	2,907	12,284	9,342	2,942
Illinois	76,456	59,314	17,142	—	58,726	50,080	8,646	77,628	61,477	16,151
Indiana	20,882	18,127	2,660	95	62,619	24,011	38,608	32,128	28,215	3,913
Iowa	25,851	16,928	5,153	3,770	23,319	18,118	5,201	32,623	26,840	5,783
Kansas	14,405	3,687	7,436	3,282	10,845	6,666	4,179	8,353	6,916	1,437
Kentucky	27,800	6,147	4,735	16,918	23,192	17,459	5,733	30,635	23,051	7,584
Louisiana	16,046	12,608	2,485	953	45,896	15,357	30,539	41,103	20,966	20,137
Maine	5,327	3,029	942	1,356	5,369	2,198	3,171	12,822	4,612	8,210
Maryland	34,572	23,421	6,043	5,108	29,732	26,555	3,177	31,659	28,829	2,830
Massachusetts	20,420	10,241	5,044	5,135	29,262	20,369	8,893	33,035	25,975	7,060
Michigan	40,973	29,945	—	11,028	60,561	60,561	—	160,797	47,334	113,463
Minnesota	10,826	8,627	877	1,322	23,912	12,610	11,302	31,146	22,006	9,140
Mississippi	14,317	10,340	2,918	1,059	13,533	9,279	4,254	16,520	11,556	4,964
Missouri	33,292	27,206	3,732	2,354	26,245	21,521	4,724	29,815	25,785	4,030
Montana	3,525	1,795	978	752	3,262	2,037	1,225	5,793	2,887	2,906
Nebraska	7,514	5,152	2,362	—	9,135	7,845	1,290	5,570	5,102	468
Nevada	3,063	845	82	2,136	2,381	2,381	—	2,872	2,872	0
New Hampshire	4,844	2,657	1,625	562	5,349	3,546	1,803	5,332	3,869	1,463
New Jersey	35,770	17,152	6,790	11,828	42,641	35,101	7,540	43,522	31,363	12,159
New Mexico	13,102	3,590	5,147	4,365	16,157	7,145	9,012	27,374	12,234	15,140
New York	94,574	57,217	20,002	17,355	78,195	59,238	18,957	122,942	96,732	26,210
North Carolina	84,252	33,854	46,679	3,719	49,600	49,600	—	101,401	56,816	44,585
North Dakota	2,810	1,963	538	309	1,741	1,221	520	3,300	2,708	592
Ohio	50,056	42,421	7,635	—	51,617	43,388	8,229	72,054	58,129	13,925
Oklahoma	14,701	6,983	5,697	2,021	14,801	12,951	1,850	18,629	15,418	3,211
Oregon	27,645	10,690	12,594	4,361	18,381	10,903	7,478	29,231	17,622	11,609
Pennsylvania	29,477	19,246	6,436	3,795	27,987	21,527	6,460	39,555	31,981	7,574
Rhode Island	5,844	2,266	1,357	2,221	6,315	4,508	1,807	7,110	4,876	2,234
South Carolina	69,659	27,959	35,165	6,535	71,436	32,846	38,590	74,614	36,714	37,900
South Dakota	4,067	2,080	1,109	878	5,279	4,070	1,209	4,359	3,485	874
Tennessee	26,268	17,079	3,244	5,945	26,199	24,452	1,747	28,320	23,398	4,922
Texas	157,349	94,245	51,126	11,978	155,932	84,271	71,661	216,931	133,461	83,470
Utah	18,541	3,756	14,785	—	21,695	6,325	15,370	20,025	3,766	16,259
Vermont	4,583	3,990	—	593	5,172	4,646	526	4,448	3,979	469
Virginia	21,525	10,480	3,804	7,241	23,388	21,767	1,621	17,903	17,218	685
Washington	16,286	7,245	3,894	5,147	18,450	15,299	3,151	24,834	21,335	3,499
West Virginia	14,628	9,743	3,672	1,213	15,618	[1] 10,706	[1] 4,912	20,738	[1] 10,758	9,980
Wisconsin	16,158	14,185	1,973	—	17,578	12,124	5,454	52,362	43,492	8,870
Wyoming	2,457	857	905	695	3,246	[1] 1,960	[1] 1,286	3,655	[1] 1,942	1,713
Outlying areas										
American Samoa	313	252	61	—	—	—	—	—	—	—
Northern Marianas	—	—	—	—	309	[1] 247	[1] 62	175	[1] 155	20
Guam	1,346	612	471	263	1,712	[1] 702	[1] 1,010	1,444	[1] 398	1,046
Puerto Rico	30,164	17,844	9,010	3,310	31,014	26,342	4,672	28,031	19,843	8,188
Trust Territory of the Pacific	3,753	2,138	699	916	—	—	—	—	—	—
Virgin Islands	3,500	1,002	859	1,639	3,959	1,883	2,076	2,611	857	1,754

[1] Estimated.

—Data not available or not applicable.

SOURCE: U.S. Department of Education, National Center for Education Statistics, "Women and Minority Groups Make Up Largest Segment of Adult Basic and Secondary Education Programs"; and Office of Vocational and Adult Education, unpublished data. (This table was prepared January 1990.)

Table 334.—Enrollment, mean charges, and mean number of hours required to complete selected programs in noncollegiate noncorrespondence postsecondary schools offering occupational programs, by control of school: United States and outlying areas, 1980–81

Selected program offerings	Enrollment [1]			Mean charges			Mean number of hours to complete program		
	Total	Public	Private	Total	Public	Private	Total	Public	Private
1	2	3	4	5	6	7	8	9	10
All programs [2]	1,687,097	451,430	1,235,667	$1,608	$593	$2,200	1,107	1,324	981
Agri-business									
Agri-mechanics	513	513	—	778	778	—	1,719	1,719	—
Agri-production	1,166	1,166	—	722	722	—	1,548	1,548	—
Agri-products	874	874	—	924	924	—	2,103	2,103	—
Agri-supplies/services	2,297	373	1,924	1,778	379	3,832	880	974	742
Horticulture	2,039	1,802	237	704	617	4,758	1,361	1,352	1,780
Business/office									
Accounting	40,746	13,887	26,859	2,254	488	2,893	1,077	1,238	1,019
Business administration	22,889	4,690	18,199	3,307	395	3,913	1,189	1,148	1,198
Clerk	24,378	11,358	13,020	1,284	507	1,870	843	924	783
Computer programmer	34,769	2,450	32,319	3,113	551	3,473	775	1,276	704
Data processing, not elsewhere classified	32,905	11,493	21,412	2,499	695	4,119	1,061	1,139	991
Office occupations, not elsewhere classified	23,025	14,506	8,519	1,284	413	2,222	1,022	1,281	742
Secretary	106,476	23,387	83,089	2,463	541	2,903	1,034	998	1,043
Typing	10,539	2,292	8,247	564	94	719	398	408	394
Health									
Dental assistant	9,047	2,110	6,937	1,914	747	2,590	767	1,112	568
Medical assistant (office)	20,950	1,762	19,188	2,326	820	2,787	766	1,046	680
Nurse (practical)	36,181	26,416	9,765	892	756	1,998	1,416	1,449	1,149
Radiology technician	6,018	986	5,032	758	918	705	3,244	2,779	3,397
Home economics									
Child care	2,244	2,194	50	256	247	325	1,108	1,003	1,900
Clothing management, product, and services	3,378	1,824	1,554	1,365	292	1,974	717	1,038	535
Dietician	1,240	906	334	522	454	665	1,342	1,253	1,529
Tailoring	2,046	567	1,479	2,099	321	2,512	866	1,269	773
Marketing/distribution									
Apparel	45,776	1,048	44,728	3,087	402	3,456	943	1,355	887
Banking	11,028	1,055	9,973	967	788	1,103	475	856	185
Entertainment services	35,122	308	34,814	714	808	709	232	1,834	134
Insurance sales	11,149	92	11,057	202	352	188	95	576	51
Merchandising	5,653	2,108	3,545	1,566	849	2,216	1,061	1,490	672
Real estate	100,745	891	99,854	202	238	201	58	419	53
Recreation/tourism	26,320	233	26,087	1,787	361	1,846	401	451	399
Technical									
Automotive technologies	9,571	1,430	8,141	2,756	993	4,541	1,436	1,503	1,369
Civil technologies	6,878	3,154	3,724	2,791	709	3,823	1,369	1,936	1,088
Communications technologies	15,924	1,951	13,973	2,460	1,199	2,848	937	1,848	657
Electronics technologies	45,152	8,996	36,156	2,600	697	4,870	1,610	1,706	1,497
Performing arts (music, dance, and drama)	20,969	113	20,856	2,144	88	2,412	752	275	815
Pilot	48,732	202	48,530	7,898	7,900	7,898	—	—	—
Trades/industry									
Auto mechanic	28,666	18,914	9,752	1,070	607	2,841	1,466	1,561	1,101
Commercial art occupations	19,956	3,155	16,801	3,166	943	4,082	1,259	1,640	1,102
Cosmetology	153,381	8,822	144,559	1,457	483	1,525	1,342	1,297	1,346
Drafting	15,937	9,215	6,722	1,489	518	3,102	1,510	1,652	1,275
Maritime occupations	15,664	3,051	12,613	909	662	971	458	979	328
Truck driver	34,800	1,845	32,955	1,357	489	1,497	187	516	134
Welding	46,804	23,052	23,752	925	455	1,527	756	1,076	347

[1] Includes proprietary (operated for profit) schools, independent (nonprofit) schools, and schools operated by religious groups.

[2] Includes programs not shown separately below.

—Data not available.

NOTE.—Includes students enrolled at any time during the 12-month period ending June 30, 1981.

SOURCE: U.S. Department of Education, National Center for Education Statistics, "Postsecondary Schools with Occupational Programs" survey. (This table was prepared June 1986.)

Table 335.—Number of noncollegiate institutions offering postsecondary education, by control and State: 1988–89 and 1989–90

State or other area	1988–89					1989–90				
	Total	Public	Private			Total	Public	Private		
			Total	Nonprofit	Proprietary			Total	Nonprofit	Proprietary
1	2	3	4	5	6	7	8	9	10	11
United States	7,824	587	7,237	1,434	5,803	7,071	557	6,514	1,286	5,228
Alabama	78	5	73	14	59	72	6	66	11	55
Alaska	54	7	47	10	37	40	5	35	8	27
Arizona	201	4	197	16	181	176	4	172	13	159
Arkansas	122	24	98	15	83	109	23	86	15	71
California	1,047	41	1,006	212	794	916	37	879	187	692
Colorado	129	7	122	18	104	119	7	112	15	97
Connecticut	133	4	129	29	100	122	4	118	25	93
Delaware	22	1	21	2	19	21	1	20	2	18
District of Columbia	33	1	32	11	21	31	1	30	12	18
Florida	355	45	310	62	248	320	38	282	60	222
Georgia	141	21	120	21	99	137	24	113	19	94
Hawaii	39	2	37	7	30	35	2	33	5	28
Idaho	39	1	38	4	34	39	1	38	4	34
Illinois	404	14	390	95	295	359	11	348	80	268
Indiana	145	11	134	16	118	135	9	126	14	112
Iowa	85	1	84	21	63	77	2	75	19	56
Kansas	82	16	66	16	50	76	16	60	13	47
Kentucky	133	15	118	13	105	131	15	116	12	104
Louisiana	206	53	153	13	140	196	52	144	7	137
Maine	27	1	26	10	16	22	1	21	8	13
Maryland	198	1	197	24	173	180	1	179	23	156
Massachusetts	201	18	183	63	120	177	18	159	55	104
Michigan	341	9	332	64	268	314	5	309	54	255
Minnesota	134	37	97	23	74	122	32	90	24	66
Mississippi	54	—	54	4	50	48	—	48	4	44
Missouri	226	28	198	35	163	203	24	179	34	145
Montana	46	5	41	9	32	45	5	40	9	31
Nebraska	54	1	53	9	44	48	—	48	8	40
Nevada	64	—	64	1	63	55	—	55	—	55
New Hampshire	33	—	33	5	28	28	—	28	4	24
New Jersey	222	5	217	52	165	192	7	185	48	137
New Mexico	38	3	35	5	30	39	3	36	5	31
New York	415	14	401	133	268	356	15	341	118	223
North Carolina	73	8	65	9	56	72	8	64	8	56
North Dakota	23	1	22	8	14	21	—	21	7	14
Ohio	327	36	291	67	224	310	38	272	61	211
Oklahoma	85	16	69	3	66	90	21	69	3	66
Oregon	137	1	136	6	130	113	1	112	4	108
Pennsylvania	410	11	399	123	276	366	13	353	119	234
Rhode Island	33	—	33	4	29	28	—	28	4	24
South Carolina	64	4	60	7	53	62	2	60	8	52
South Dakota	22	4	18	8	10	21	4	17	8	9
Tennessee	141	44	97	19	78	127	38	89	18	71
Texas	421	9	412	45	367	397	7	390	41	349
Utah	58	7	51	3	48	40	6	34	2	32
Vermont	13	3	10	4	6	11	3	8	3	5
Virginia	174	18	156	32	124	165	17	148	28	120
Washington	160	6	154	25	129	143	6	137	21	116
West Virginia	56	18	38	11	27	52	19	33	9	24
Wisconsin	111	4	107	27	80	99	4	95	26	69
Wyoming	15	2	13	1	12	14	1	13	1	12
Outlying areas [1]	134	6	128	23	105	107	6	101	20	81
American Samoa	—	—	—	—	—	1	—	1	—	1
Guam	1	—	1	—	1	1	—	1	—	1
Northern Marianas	—	—	—	—	—	—	—	—	—	—
Palau	—	—	—	—	—	—	—	—	—	—
Puerto Rico	133	6	127	23	104	106	6	100	20	80
Virgin Islands	—	—	—	—	—	—	—	—	—	—

[1] Excluedes Federated States of Micronesia.
—Data not available or not applicable.

SOURCE: U.S. Department of Education, National Center for Education Statistics, Integrated Postsecondary Education Data System (IPEDS), "Institutional Characteristics" surveys. (This table was prepared May 1990.)

CHAPTER 4
Federal Programs for Education and Related Activities

This chapter provides a summary of Federal funds for education to help describe the magnitude of the Federal fiscal effort and give some indication of the scope and variety of the education programs. Data in this chapter reflect outlays and obligations of Federal agencies. These tabulations differ from Federal receipts reported in other chapters because of numerous variations in the data collection systems. Federal appropriations are not necessarily spent by recipient institutions in the same year they are appropriated. In some cases, institutions cannot identify the source of Federal revenues because they flow through State agencies. Some types of revenues, such as tuition and fees, are reported as revenues from students even though they may be supported by Federal student aid programs. Some institutions that receive Federal education funds are not included in regular surveys conducted by the National Center for Education Statistics. Thus, the revenue data tabulated in this chapter are not comparable with figures reported in other chapters. Readers should be careful about comparing data on obligations shown on some tables with data on outlays appearing on others.

A capsule view of the history of Federal education activities is provided in the following list of selected legislation:

1787 *Northwest Ordinance* authorized land grants for the establishment of educational institutions.

1802 *An Act Fixing the Military Peace Establishment of the United States* established the U.S. Military Academy. (The U.S. Naval Academy was established in 1845 by the Secretary of the Navy.)

1862 *First Morrill Act* authorized public land grants to the States for the establishment and maintenance of agricultural and mechanical colleges.

1867 *Department of Education Act* authorized the establishment of the Department of Education.*

---

* The Department of Education as established in 1867 was later known as the Office of Education. In 1980, under P.L. 96–88, it became a cabinet-level department. Therefore, for purposes of consistency, it is referred to as the "Department of Education" even in those tables covering years when it was officially the Office of Education.

1876 *Appropriation Act, Department of the Treasury* established the U.S. Coast Guard Academy.

1890 *Second Morrill Act* provided for money grants for support of instruction in the agricultural and mechanical colleges.

1911 *State Marine School Act* authorized Federal funds to be used for the benefit of any nautical school in any of 11 specified State seaport cities.

1917 *Smith-Hughes Act* provided for grants to States for support of vocational education.

1918 *Vocational Rehabilitation Act* provided for grants for rehabilitation through training of World War I veterans.

1919 *An Act to Provide for Further Educational Facilities* authorized the sale by the Federal Government of surplus machine tools to educational institutions at 15 percent of acquisition cost.

1920 *Smith-Bankhead Act* authorized grants to States for vocational rehabilitation programs.

1935 *Bankhead-Jones Act* (Public Law 74–182) authorized grants to States for agricultural experiment stations.

Agricultural Adjustment Act (Public Law 74–320) authorized 30 percent of the annual customs receipts to be used to encourage the exportation and domestic consumption of agricultural commodities. Commodities purchased under this authorization began to be used in school lunch programs in 1936. The National School Lunch Act of 1946 continued and expanded this assistance.

1936 *An Act to Further the Development and Maintenance of an Adequate and Well-balanced American Merchant Marine* (Public Law 84–415) established the U.S. Merchant Marine Academy.

1937 *National Cancer Institute Act* established the Public Health Service fellowship program.

1941 *Amendment to Lanham Act of 1940* authorized Federal aid for construction, maintenance, and operation of schools in federally impacted areas. Such assistance was continued under Public Law 815 and Public Law 874, 81st Congress, in 1950.

1943 *Vocational Rehabilitation Act* (Public Law 78–16) provided assistance to disabled veterans.

School Lunch Indemnity Plan (Public Law 78–129) provided funds for local lunch food purchases.

1944 *Servicemen's Readjustment Act* (Public Law 78–346) provided assistance for the education of veterans.

Surplus Property Act (Public Law 78–457) authorized transfer of surplus property to educational institutions.

1946 *National School Lunch Act* (Public Law 79–396) authorized assistance through grants-in-aid and other means to States to assist in providing adequate foods and facilities for the establishment, maintenance, operation, and expansion of nonprofit school lunch programs.

George-Barden Act (Public Law 80–402) expanded Federal support of vocational education.

1948 *United States Information and Educational Exchange Act* (Public Law 80–402) provided for the interchange of persons, knowledge, and skills between the United States and other countries.

1949 *Federal Property and Administrative Services Act* (Public Law 81–152) provided for donation of surplus property to educational institutions and for other public purposes.

1950 *Financial Assistance for Local Educational Agencies Affected by Federal Activities* (Public Law 81–815 and P.L. 81–874) provided assistance for construction (Public Law 815) and operation (Public Law 874) of schools in federally affected areas.

Housing Act (Public Law 81–475) authorized loans for construction of college housing facilities.

1954 *An Act for the Establishment of the United States Air Force Academy and Other Purposes* (Public Law 83–325) established the U.S. Air Force Academy.

Cooperative Research Act (Public Law 83–531) authorized cooperative arrangements with universities, colleges, and State education agencies for educational research.

National Advisory Committee on Education Act (Public Law 83–532) established a National Advisory Committee on Education to recommend needed studies of national concern in the field of education and to propose appropriate action indicated by such studies.

School Milk Program Act (Public Law 83–597) provided funds for purchase of milk for school lunch programs.

1956 *Library Services Act* (Public Law 84–911) provided grants to States for extension and improvement of rural public library services.

1957 *Practical Nurse Training Act* (Public Law 84–911) provided grants to States for practical nurse training.

1958 *National Defense Education Act* (Public Law 85–865) provided assistance to State and local school systems for strengthening instruction in science, mathematics, modern foreign languages, and other critical subjects; improvement of State statistical services; guidance, counseling, and testing services and training institutes; higher education student loans and fellowships; foreign language study and training provided by colleges and universities; experimentation and dissemination of information on more effective utilization of television, motion pictures, and related media for educational purposes; and vocational education for technical occupations necessary to the national defense.

Education of Mentally Retarded Children Act (Public Law 85–926) authorized Federal assistance for training teachers of the handicapped.

Captioned Films for the Deaf Act (Public Law 85–905) authorized a loan service of captioned films for the deaf.

1961 *Area Redevelopment Act* (Public Law 87–27) included provisions for training or retraining of persons in redevelopment areas.

1962 *Manpower Development and Training Act* (Public Law 87–415) provided training in new and improved skills for the unemployed and underemployed.

Communications Act of 1934, Amendment (Public Law 87–447) provided grants for the construction of educational television broadcasting facilities.

Migration and Refugee Assistance Act of 1962 (Public Law 87–510) authorized loans, advances, and grants for education and training of refugees.

1963 *Health Professions Educational Assistance Act* (Public Law 88–129) provided funds to expand teaching facilities and for loans to students in the health professions.

Vocational Education Act of 1963 (Public Law 88–210) increased Federal support of vocational education schools; vocational work-study programs; and research, training, and demonstrations in vocational education.

Higher Education Facilities Act of 1963 (Public Law 88–204) authorized grants and loans for classrooms, libraries, and laboratories in public community colleges and technical institutes, as well as undergraduate and graduate facilities in other institutions of higher education.

1964 *Civil Rights Act of 1964* (Public Law 88–352) authorized the Commissioner of Education to arrange for support for institutions of higher education and school districts to provide in-service programs for assisting instructional staff in dealing with problems caused by desegregation.

Economic Opportunity Act of 1964 (Public Law 88–452) authorized grants for college work-study programs for students from low-income families; established a Job Corps program and authorized support for work-training programs to provide education and vocational training and work experience opportunities in welfare programs; authorized support of education and training activities and of community action programs, including Head Start, Follow Through, and Upward Bound; and authorized the establishment of Volunteers in Service to America (VISTA).

1965 *Elementary and Secondary Education Act* (Public Law 89–10) authorized grants for elementary and secondary school programs for children of low-income families; school library resources, textbooks, and other instructional materials for school children; supplementary educational centers and services; strengthening State education agencies; and educational research and research training.

Health Professions Educational Assistance Amendments (Public Law 89–290) authorized scholarships to aid needy students in the health professions.

Higher Education Act of 1965 (Public Law 89–329) provided grants for university community service programs, college library assistance, library training and research, strengthening developing institutions, teacher training programs, and undergraduate instructional equipment. Authorized insured student loans, established a National Teacher Corps, and provided for graduate teacher-training fellowships.

Medical Library Assistance Act (Public Law 89–291) provided assistance for construction and improvement of health sciences libraries.

National Foundation on the Arts and the Humanities Act (Public Law 89–209) authorized grants and loans for projects in the creative and performing arts, and for research, training, and scholarly publications in the humanities.

National Technical Institute for the Deaf Act (Public Law 89–36) provided for the establishment, construction, equipping, and operation of a residential school for postsecondary education and technical training of the deaf.

National Vocational Student Loan Insurance Act (Public Law 89–287) encouraged State and nonprofit private institutions and organizations to establish adequate loan insurance programs to assist students to attend postsecondary business, trade, technical, and other vocational schools.

Disaster Relief Act (Public Law 89–313) provided for assistance to local education agencies to help meet exceptional costs resulting from a major disaster.

1966 *International Education Act* (Public Law 89–698) provided grants to institutions of higher education for the establishment, strengthening, and operation of centers for research and training in international studies and the international aspects of other fields of study.

National Sea Grant College and Program Act (Public Law 89–688) authorized the establishment and operation of sea grant colleges and programs by initiating and supporting programs of education and research in the various fields relating to the development of marine resources.

Adult Education Act (Public Law 89–750) authorized grants to States for the encouragement and expansion of educational programs for adults, including training of teachers of adults and demonstrations in adult education (previously part of Economic Opportunity Act of 1964).

Model Secondary School for the Deaf Act (Public Law 89–694) authorized the establishment and operation, by Gallaudet College, of a model secondary school for the deaf.

Elementary and Secondary Education Amendments of 1966 (Public Law 89–750) in addition to modifying existing programs, authorized grants to assist States in the initiation, expansion, and improvement of programs and projects for the education of handicapped children.

1967 *Education Professions Development Act* (Public Law 90–35) amended the Higher Education Act of 1965 for the purpose of improving the quality of teaching and to help meet critical shortages of adequately trained educational personnel.

Public Broadcasting Act of 1967 (Public Law 90–129) established a corporation for Public Broadcasting to assume major responsibility in channeling Federal funds to noncommercial radio and television stations, program production groups, and ETV networks; conduct research, demonstration, or training in matters related to noncommercial broadcasting; and award grants for construction of educational radio and television facilities.

1968 *Elementary and Secondary Education Amendments of 1967* (Public Law 90–247) modified existing programs, authorized support of regional centers for education of handicapped children, model centers and services for deaf-blind children, recruitment of personnel and dissemination of information on education of the handicapped; technical assistance in education to rural areas; support of dropout prevention projects; and support of bilingual education programs.

Handicapped Children's Early Education Assistance Act (Public Law 90–538) authorized preschool and early education programs for handicapped children.

Vocational Education Amendments of 1968 (Public Law 90–576) modified existing programs and provided for a National Advisory Council on Vocational Education, and collection and dissemination of information for programs administered by the Commissioner of Education.

Higher Education Amendments of 1968 (Public Law 90–575) authorized new programs to assist disadvantaged college students through special counseling and summer tutorial programs, and programs to assist colleges to combine resources of cooperative programs

and to expand programs which provide clinical experiences to law students.

1970 *Elementary and Secondary Education Assistance Programs, Extension* (Public Law 91–230) authorized comprehensive planning and evaluation grants to State and local education agencies; provided for the establishment of a National Commission on School Finance.

National Commission on Libraries and Information Services Act (Public Law 91–345) established a National Commission on Libraries and Information Science to effectively utilize the Nation's educational resources.

Office of Education Appropriation Act (Public Law 91–380) provided emergency school assistance to desegregating local education agencies.

Environmental Education Act (Public Law 91–516) established an Office of Environmental Education to develop curriculum and initiate and maintain environmental education programs at the elementary-secondary levels; disseminate information; provide training programs for teachers and other educational, public, community, labor, and industrial leaders and employees; provide community education programs; and distribute material dealing with environment and ecology.

Drug Abuse Education Act of 1970 (Public Law 527) provided for development, demonstration, and evaluation of curriculums on the problems of drug abuse.

1971 *Comprehensive Health Manpower Training Act of 1971* (Public Law 92–257) amended Title VII of the Public Health Service Act, increasing and expanding provisions for health manpower training and training facilities.

Nurse Training Act of 1971 (Public Law 92–158) amended Title VIII, Nurse Training, of the Public Health Service Act, increasing and expanding provisions for nurse training facilities.

1972 *Drug Abuse Office and Treatment Act of 1972* (Public Law 92–255) established a Special Action Office for Drug Abuse Prevention to provide overall planning and policy for all Federal drug-abuse prevention functions; a National Advisory Council for Drug Abuse Prevention; community assistance grants for community mental health center for treatment and rehabilitation of persons with drug-abuse problems, and, in December 1974, a National Institute on Drug Abuse.

Education Amendments of 1972 (Public Law 92–318) established the Education Division in the U.S. Department of Health, Education, and Welfare and the National Institute of Education; general aid for institutions of higher education; Federal matching grants for State student incentive grants; a National Commission on Financing Postsecondary Education; State Advisory Councils on Community Colleges; a Bureau of Occupational and Adult Education and State grants for the design, establishment, and conduct of postsecondary occupational education; and a bureau-level Office of Indian Education. Amended current Office of Education programs to increase their effectiveness and better meet special needs. Prohibited sex bias in admission to vocational, professional, and graduate schools, and public institutions of undergraduate higher education.

1973 *Older Americans Comprehensive Services Amendment of 1973* (Public Law 93–29) made available to older citizens comprehensive programs of health, education, and social services.

Comprehensive Employment and Training Act of 1973 (Public Law 93–203) provided for opportunities for employment and training to unemployed and underemployed persons. Extended and expanded provisions in the Manpower Development and Training Act of 1962, Title I of the Economic Opportunity Act of 1962, Title I of the Economic Opportunity Act of 1964, and the Emergency Employment Act of 1971 as in effect prior to June 30, 1973.

1974 *Educational Amendments of 1974* (Public Law 93–380) provided for the consolidation of certain programs; and established a National Center for Education Statistics.

Juvenile Justice and Delinquency Prevention Act of 1974 (Public Law 93–415) provided for technical assistance, staff training, centralized research, and resources to develop and implement programs to keep students in elementary and secondary schools; and established, in the Department of Justice, a National Institute for Juvenile Justice and Delinquency Prevention.

1975 *Indian Self-Determination and Education Assistance Act* (Public Law 93–638) provided for increased participation of American Indians in the establishment and conduct of their education programs and services.

Harry S Truman Memorial Scholarship Act (Public Law 93–642) established the Harry S Truman Scholarship Foundation and created a perpetual education scholarship fund for young Americans to prepare and pursue careers in public service.

Indochina Migration and Refugee Assistance Act of 1975 (Public Law 94–23) authorized funds to be used for education and training of aliens who have fled from Cambodia or Vietnam.

Education of the Handicapped Act (Public Law 994–142) provided that all handicapped children have available to them a free appropriate education designed to meet their unique needs.

1976 *Educational Broadcasting Facilities and Telecommunications Demonstration Act of 1976* (Public Law 94–309) established a telecommunications demonstration program to promote the development of nonbroadcast telecommunications facilities and services for the transmission, distribution, and delivery of health, education, and public or social service information.

Education Amendments of 1976 (Public Law 94–482) extended and revised Federal programs for education assistance for higher education, vocational education, and a variety of other programs.

1977 *Youth Employment and Demonstration Projects Act of 1977* (Public Law 95–93) established a youth employment training program that includes, among other activities, promoting education-to-work transition, literacy training and bilingual training, and attainment of certificates of high school equivalency.

1978 *Career Education Incentive Act* (Public Law 95–207) authorized the establishment of a career education program for elementary and secondary schools.

Tribally Controlled Community College Assistance Act (Public Law 95–471) provided Federal funds for the operation and improvement of tribally controlled community colleges for American Indian students.

Education Amendments of 1978 (Public Law 95–561) established a comprehensive basic skills program aimed at improving pupil achievement (replaced the existing National Reading Improvement program); and established a community schools program to provide for the use of public buildings.

Middle Income Student Assistance Act (Public Law 95–566) modified the provisions for student financial assistance programs to allow middle income as well as low income students attending college or other postsecondary institutions to qualify for Federal education assistance.

1979 *Department of Education Organization Act* (Public Law 96–88) established a Department of Education containing functions from the Education Division of the Department of Health, Education, and Welfare along with other selected education programs from H.E.W., the Department of Justice, Department of Labor, and the National Science Foundation.

1980 *Asbestos School Hazard Protection and Control Act of 1980* (Public Law 96–270) established a program for inspection of schools for detection of hazardous asbestos materials and provided loans to assist educational agencies to contain or remove and replace such materials.

Amendments to the Higher Education Act (Public Law 96–374) provided for a new Commission on National Development in Postsecondary Education and a new Urban Grant University Program.

1981 *Education Consolidation and Improvement Act of 1981* (Public Law 97–35) consolidated 42 programs into 7 programs to be funded under the elementary and secondary block grant authority.

1983 *Student Loan Consolidation and Technical Amendments Act of 1983* (Public Law 98–79) established 8 percent interest rate for Guaranteed Student Loans and extended Family Contribution Schedule.

Challenge Grant Amendments of 1983 (Public Law 98–95) amended Title III, Higher Education Act, and added authorization of Challenge Grant program. The Challenge Grant program provides funds to eligible institutions on a matching basis as incentive to seek alternative sources of funding.

Education of Handicapped Act Amendments (Public Law 98–199) added Architectural Barrier amendment and clarified participation of handicapped children in private schools.

Education Consolidation and Improvement Act of 1981, Amendments (Public Law 98–211) added technical amendments for Chapter 1,

and provided for parental involvement and minor changes in other programs.

1984 *Rehabilitation Amendments of 1984* (Public Law 98–221) revised and extended the Rehabilitation Act of 1973. Provides for the Helen Keller National Center for Deaf-Blind.

Education for Economic Security Act (Public Law 98–377) added new science and mathematics programs for elementary, secondary, and postsecondary education. The new programs include magnet schools, excellence in education, and equal access.

Higher Education Act of 1965, Amendments (Public Law 98–312) amended Title III of the Higher Education Act of 1965 by creating a new method of funding the Challenge Grant program. The act also increased the level of authorization for the Office of the Inspector General and extended the Allen J. Ellender Fellowship program through fiscal year 1989.

Carl D. Perkins Vocational Education Act (Public Law 98–524) reauthorized Federal assistance for vocational education through fiscal year 1989. The act replaces the Vocational Education Act of 1963. It provides aid to the States to make vocational education programs accessible to all persons, including handicapped and disadvantaged, single parents and homemakers, and the incarcerated.

Human Services Reauthorization Act (Public Law 98–558) reauthorized the Head Start and Follow Through programs through fiscal year 1986. It also created a Carl D. Perkins scholarship program, a National Talented Teachers Fellowship program, a Federal Merit Scholarships program, and a Leadership in Educational Administration program.

1985 *Montgomery GI Bill—Active Duty* (Public Law–525), brought about a new GI Bill for individuals who initially entered active military duty on or after July 1, 1985.

Montgomery GI Bill—Selected Reserve (Public Law 98–525), is an education program for members of the Selected Reserve (which includes the National Guard) who enlist, reenlist, or extend an enlistment after June 30, 1985, for a 6-year period.

1986 *Education of the Deaf Act* (Public Law 99–371) places Gallaudet College and the National Technical Institute for the Deaf on a 5-year reauthorization cycle. Establishes an 18-month Commission to Study Deaf Education.

Handicapped Children's Protection Act (Public Law 99–372) allows parents of handicapped children to collect attorney's fees in cases brought under the Education of the Handicapped Act and provides that the Education of the Handicapped Act does not preempt other laws, such as Section 504 of the Rehabilitation Act.

Reauthorization of the Education of the Handicapped Act, Amendments (Public Law 99–457) reauthorizes for 3 years the discretionary programs under the Education of the Handicapped Act. Included are programs to provide demonstration projects for severely disabled individuals, research and technology activities, early childhood education, and a new State grant program to provide early intervention services for handicapped children from birth through age 2.

Reauthorization of the Higher Education Act of 1965 (Public Law 99–498) reauthorizes for 5 years the Higher Education Act of 1965, as amended. Provides increases in maximum Pell Grant and student loan amounts, institutes a new agency to provide college construction funding, cuts incentives to lenders involved in the student aid programs and extends the authorization for the Office of Educational Research and Improvement.

Reauthorization of the Rehabilitation Act (Public Law 99–506) authorizes for 5 years programs to provide vocational rehabilitation for disabled persons. Includes increasing the State/Federal match requirements and establishes a new State grant program for supported employment.

The Drug-Free Schools and Communities Act of 1986 (Public Law 99–570), part of the Anti-Drug Abuse Act of 1986, authorizes funding for fiscal years 1987–89. Establishes programs for drug abuse education and prevention, coordinated with related community efforts and resources, through the use of Federal financial assistance.

1987 *Higher Education Act Amendments of 1987* (Public Law 100–50) makes technical corrections, clarifications, or conforming amendments related to the enactment of the Higher Education Amendments of 1986.

1988 *The Augustus F. Hawkins-Robert T. Stafford Elementary and Secondary School Improvement Amendments of 1988* (Public Law 100–297) reauthorizes through 1993 major elementary and secondary education programs

including: Chapter 1, Chapter 2, Bilingual Education, Math-Science Education, Magnet Schools, Impact Aid, Indian Education, Adult Education, and other smaller education programs.

The Handicapped Programs Technical Amendments Act of 1988 (Public Law 100–360) makes certain technical and conforming amendments to the Education of the Handicapped Act and the Rehabilitation Act of 1973.

Technology-Related Assistance for Individuals with Disabilities Act of 1988 (Public Law 100–407) provides financial assistance to States to develop and implement consumer-responsive Statewide programs of technology-related assistance for persons of all ages with disabilities.

The Omnibus Trade and Competitiveness Act of 1988 (Public Law 100–418) authorizes new and expanded education programs. Title VI of the Act, Education and Training for American Competitiveness, authorizes new programs in literacy, math-science, foreign language, vocational training, international education, technology training, and technology transfer.

The Omnibus Drug Abuse Prevention Act of 1988 (Public Law 100–690) authorizes a new teacher training program under the Drug-Free Schools and Communities Act, an early childhood education program to be administered jointly by the Departments of Health and Human Services and Education, and a pilot program for the children of alcoholics.

Stewart B. McKinney Homeless Assistance Act (Public Law 100–628) extends for 2 additional years programs providing assistance to the homeless, including literacy training for homeless adults and education for homeless youths.

Tax Reform Technical Amendments (Public Law 100–647) authorizes an Education Savings Bond for the purpose of postsecondary educational expenses. The bill grants tax exclusion for interest earned on regular series EE savings bonds.

1989 *The Education and Training for a Competitive America Act of 1988* (Public Law 101–26) makes some technical corrections to the act.

The Head Start Supplemental Authorization Act of 1989 (Public Law 101–120) amends the Head Start Act to increase the amount authorized to be appropriated for fiscal year 1990.

The Children with Disabilities Temporary Care Reauthorization Act of 1989 (Public Law 101–127) revises and extends the programs established in the Temporary Child Care for Handicapped Children and Crises Nurseries Act of 1986.

The Drug-Free Schools and Communities Act Amendments of 1989 (Public Law 101–226) amends the Drug-Free Schools and Communities Act of 1986 to revise certain requirements relating to the provision of drug abuse education and prevention programs in elementary and secondary schools.

1990 *The Childhood Education and Development Act of 1989* (Public Law 101–239) authorized the appropriations to expand Head Start Programs and programs carried out under the Elementary and Secondary Education Act of 1965 to include child care services.

The Carl D. Perkins Vocational and Applied Technology Education Act Amendments of 1990 (Public Law 101–392) reauthorized and amends the Carl D. Perkins Vocational Education Act to extend the authorities contained in such Act through fiscal year 1995.

The Excellence in Mathematics, Science and Engineering Education Act of 1990 (Public Law 101–589) promotes excellence in American mathematics, science and engineering education by creating a national mathematics and science clearinghouse, establishing regional mathematics and science education consortia, establishing three new mathematics, science and engineering scholarships programs, and creating several other mathematics, science and engineering education programs.

The Individuals with Disabilities Education Act of 1990 (IDEA) (Public Law 101–476) reauthorized the Education of the Handicapped Act, which mandates a free public education for students with disabilities.

The Student Right-To-Know and Campus Security Act (Public Law 101–542) requires institutions of higher education receiving federal financial assistance to provide certain information with respect to the graduation rates of student-athletes at such institutions. The act also requires the institution to certify that it has a campus security policy and will annually submit a uniform crime report to the Federal Bureau of Investigation (FBI).

The Children's Television Act of 1990 (Public Law 101–437) requires the Federal Communications Commission to reinstate restrictions on advertising during children's television, and enforces the obligation of broadcasters to meet the educational and informational needs of the child audience.

The Elementary and Secondary Education Act of 1965 Amendments (Public Law 101–250) reauthorized certain school dropout demonstration programs.

The McKinney Homeless Assistance Amendments Act of 1990 (Public Law 101–645) reauthorized the Stewart B. McKinney Homeless Assistance Act programs of grants to State and local education agencies for the provision of support services to homeless children and youth.

The National Assessment of Chapter 1 Act (Public Law 101–305) requires the Secretary of Education to conduct a comprehensive national assessment of programs carried out with assistance under Chapter 1 of Title I of the Elementary and Secondary Education Act of 1965.

The Augustus F. Hawkins Human Services Reauthorization Act of 1990 (Public Law 101–501) authorized appropriations for fiscal years 1991–1994 to carry out the Head Start Act, the Follow Through Act, the Community Services Block Grant Act, and the Low-Income Home Energy Assistance Act of 1981.

The National and Community Service Act of 1989 (Public Law 101–610) increased school- and college-based community service opportunities and authorized the President's Points of Light Foundation.

The School Dropout Prevention and Basic Skills Improvement Act of 1990 (Public Law 101–600) improves secondary school programs for basic skills improvements and dropout reduction.

The Medical Residents Student Loan Amendments Act of 1989 (Enacted in Public Law 101–239, the Omnibus Budget Reconciliation Act of 1989) amended the Higher Education Act of 1965 to eliminate student loan deferments for medical students serving in internships or residency programs.

The Asbestos School Hazard Abatement Reauthorization Act of 1990 (Public Law 101–637) reauthorized the Asbestos School Hazard Abatement Act of 1984, which provided financial support to elementary and secondary schools to inspect for asbestos, and to develop and implement an asbestos management plan. In addition, the act provides for programs of information, technical and scientific assistance, and training.

The National Commission on Responsibilities for Financing Higher Education (Public Law 101–324) clarified the procedures of the National Commission on Responsibilities for Financing Higher Education.

The Eisenhower Exchange Fellowship Program (Public Law 101–454) provided a permanent endowment for the Eisenhower Exchange Fellowship Program.

The Tribally Controlled Community College Reauthorization (Public Law 101–477) reauthorized the Tribally Controlled Community College Assistance Act and the Navajo Community College Act.

The Environmental Education Act (Public Law 101–619) promotes environmental education by the establishment of an Office of Environmental Education in the Environmental Protection Agency and the creation of several environmental education programs.

The Anti-Drug Education Act of 1990 and the Drug Abuse Resistance Education (DARE) Act of 1990 (Both bills were enacted as part of Public Law 101–647, the Comprehensive Crime Control Act of 1990.) amends the Drug Free Schools and Communities Act and raises funding levels for school personnel training, funds the replication of successful drug education programs, helps local education agencies to cooperate with law enforcement agencies and allows funds to be used for after-school programs. The Drug Abuse Resistance Education Act establishes a program of grants to HHS for Drug Abuse Resistance Education (DARE) programs.

The Public Service Assistance Education Act (Enacted as part of Public Law 101–510, of the Department of Defense Authorization Act) gives Federal agencies authority to provide new educational benefits to employees by paying for an employee to obtain an academic degree for which there is an agency shortage of qualified personnel, and by repaying up to $6,000 per year of the student loan of a qualified employee in exchange for a 3-year commitment.

The 1990 Budget Reconciliation Act (Public Law 101–508) included a set of student aid provisions that were estimated to yield a savings of $2 billion over 5 years. These provisions included delayed Guaranteed Student Loan disbursements, tightened ability-to-benefit eligibility, and expanded pro rata refund policy and the elimination of student aid eligibility at high default schools.

Highlights

- Federal funding for education showed sizable growth between fiscal years 1965 and 1991, after adjustment for inflation. Particularly large increases occurred between 1965 and 1975. After a period of relative stability between 1975 and 1980, Federal funding for education, excluding estimated Federal tax expenditures for education, declined approximately 8 percent between 1980 and 1985. From 1985 to 1991, Federal funding for education increased by 12 percent. (Table 336)

- During the 1965 to 1975 period, after adjustment for inflation, Federal funds for elementary and secondary education rose by 189 percent, postsecondary education by 230 percent, and other education by 127 percent, but research funding fell by about 1 percent. Between 1975 and 1980, Federal funding for elementary and secondary education rose by 1 percent and research by 14 percent, but postsecondary education fell by 2 percent and other education by 35 percent. After dipping 20 percent between 1980 and 1985, Federal funding for elementary and secondary education programs rose by 17 percent between 1985 and 1991. Postsecondary education rose by 1 percent between 1985 and 1991, other education by 41 percent, and research by 17 percent, after adjustment for inflation. (Table 336)

- Total Federal support for education was $84.1 billion in fiscal year 1990, down 2 percent from fiscal year 1980, after adjustment for inflation. From fiscal year 1980 to fiscal year 1990, Federal program funds fell by 5 percent; non-Federal student aid funds generated by Federal programs rose 49 percent; and estimated Federal tax expenditures for education declined by 12 percent. (Table 336)

- According to fiscal year 1991 estimates, $24.9 billion or about 46 percent of the $54.6 billion dollars spent by the Federal Government on education came from the Department of Education. Large amounts of money also came from the Department of Health and Human Services ($8.0 billion), the Department of Agriculture ($7.0 billion), the Department of Defense ($3.5 billion), and the Department of Energy ($2.7 billion). (Table 337)

- In fiscal year 1991, Federal program funds for elementary/secondary education amounted to $24.4

billion; for higher education, $13.7 billion; for research at universities and related institutions, $12.8 billion; and for other programs, $3.7 billion. (Table 338)

- Between fiscal years 1980 and 1991, Department of Education obligations rose by about 27 percent, after adjustment for inflation. Funds for student financial assistance increased to $12.2 billion in 1991, a rise of 46 percent since 1980. Funds for elementary and secondary education stood at an estimated $8.1 billion in 1991, an increase of 17 percent since 1980. Funds for the handicapped increased by about 100 percent, to $5.1 billion, while funds for vocational education declined 30 percent, after adjustment for inflation. (Table 36 and 339)

- Of the $24.9 billion spent by the Department of Education in 1991, about $9.2 billion went to school districts, $3.8 billion to institutions of higher education, $3.8 billion to college students, and $2.8 billion to State education agencies. A large portion of the remaining $5.2 billion went to banks to subsidize student loans. (Table 340)

- About one in four elementary and secondary school students in the United States received publicly funded free or reduced price lunches in 1987–88. At public elementary schools, the participation rate was 34 percent compared with 18 percent for public secondary schools. Private school students were less likely to participate in school lunch programs; only 7 percent of elementary school students and 4 percent of the secondary school students participated in school lunch programs. (Table 350)

- About 10 percent of all elementary and secondary school children received Chapter 1 services in 1987–88. Federally sponsored Chapter 1 programs are designed to assist educationally disadvantaged children. Children in rural areas (12 percent) and urban areas (12 percent) were more likely to receive services than those in suburban areas (6 percent). (Table 351)

Figure 20.—Federal funds for education, by agency: Fiscal year 1991

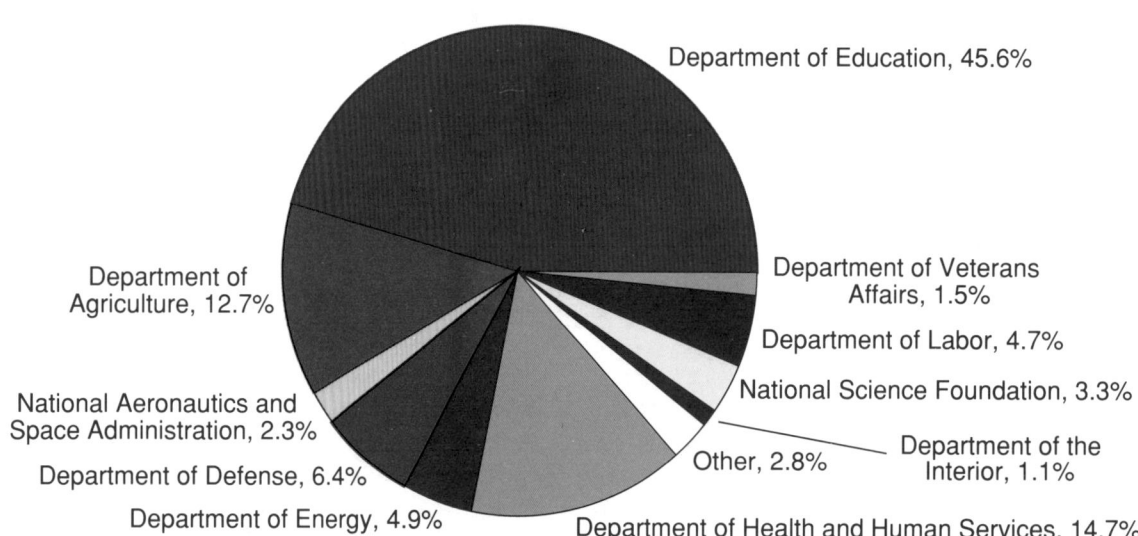

Department of Education, 45.6%

Department of Veterans Affairs, 1.5%

Department of Labor, 4.7%

National Science Foundation, 3.3%

Other, 2.8%

Department of the Interior, 1.1%

Department of Health and Human Services, 14.7%

Department of Energy, 4.9%

Department of Defense, 6.4%

National Aeronautics and Space Administration, 2.3%

Department of Agriculture, 12.7%

Total = $54.6 billion

SOURCE: U.S. Office of Management and Budget, *Budget of the U.S. Government,* Fiscal year 1992; and National Science Foundation, *Federal Funds for Research and Development, Fiscal years 1989, 1990, and 1991.*

Figure 21.—Federal on-budget funds for education, by level: 1965 to 1992

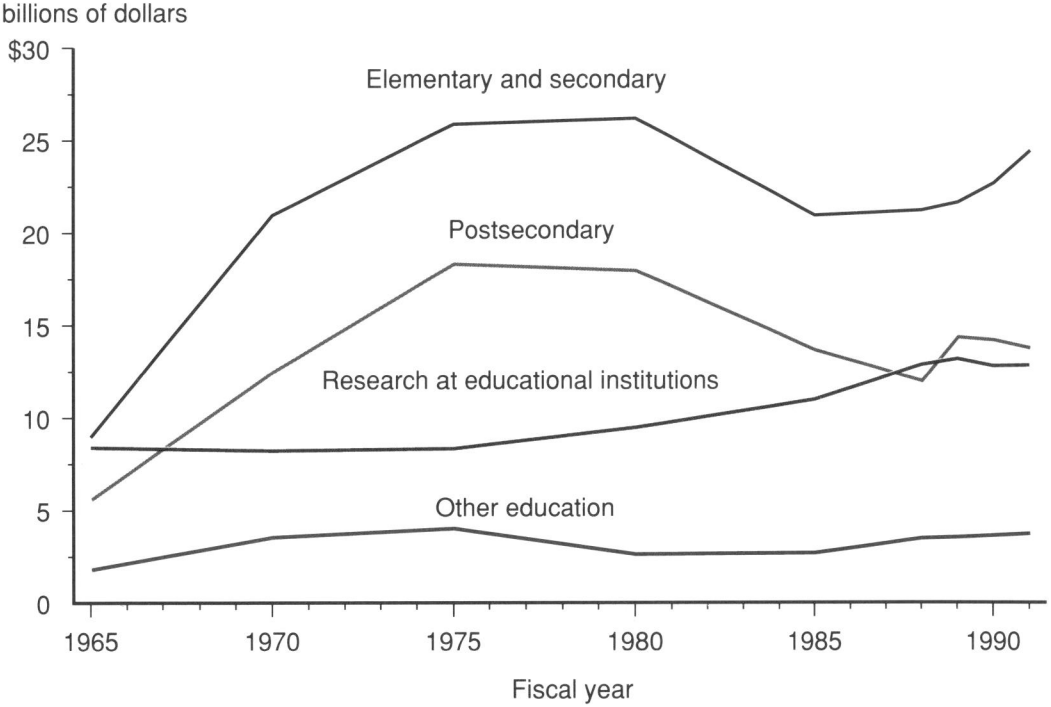

In billions of dollars

SOURCE: U.S. Office of Management and Budget, *Budget of the U.S. Government, Appendix,* fiscal years 1967 to 1991; National Science Foundation, *Federal Funds for Research and Development,* fiscal years 1965 to 1991; and unpublished data.

Figure 22.—Department of Education outlays, by type of recipient: Fiscal year 1991

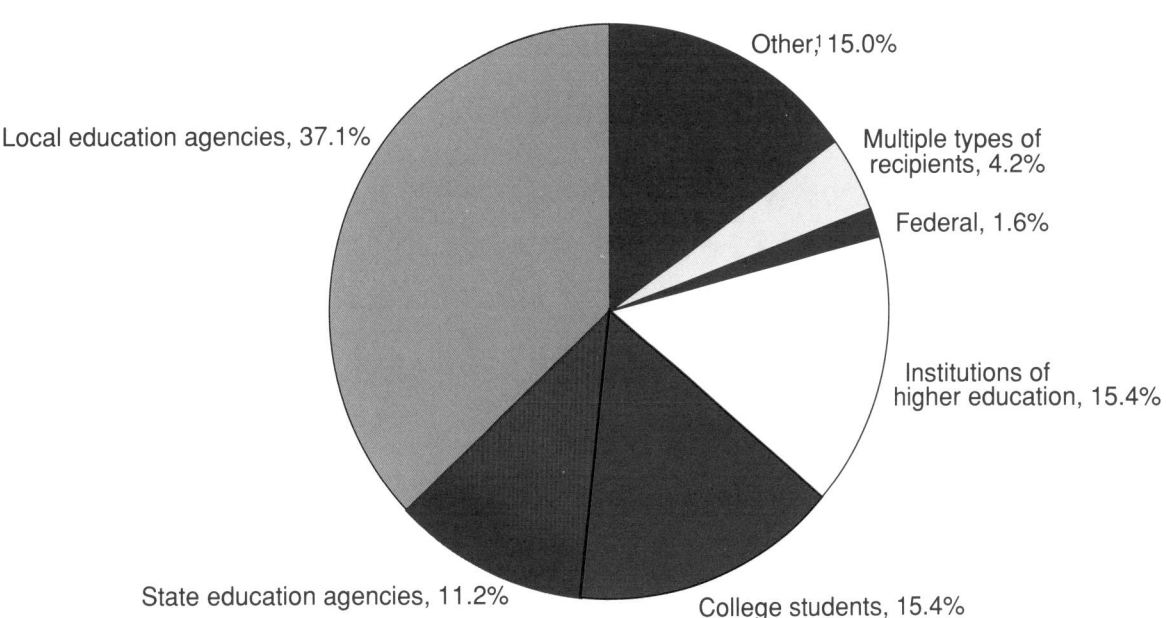

Total outlays = $24.9 billion

[1]Primarily private lending institutions and private nonprofit agencies.

SOURCE: U.S. Department of Education, National Center for Education Statistics, unpublished data.

Table 336.—Federal education support and estimated Federal tax expenditures, by category: Fiscal years 1965 to 1991

[In millions of dollars]

Fiscal year	Total on-budget support and non-Federal funds generated by Federal programs[1]	On-budget support[1]					Non-Federal funds generated by Federal programs							Estimated Federal tax expenditures for education[8]
		Total	Elementary and secondary	Post-secondary	Other education	Research at educational institutions	Total	Guaranteed student loans[2]	Perkins loans[3]	Income contingent loans[4]	State student incentive grants[5]	Supplemental educational opportunity grants[6]	Work-study aid[7]	
1	2	3	4	5	6	7	8	9	10	11	12	13	14	15

Current dollars

Fiscal year	2	3	4	5	6	7	8	9	10	11	12	13	14	15
1965	$5,354.7	$5,331.0	$1,942.6	$1,197.5	$374.7	$1,816.3	$23.7	—	$16.1	—	—	—	$7.6	—
1970	13,359.1	12,526.5	5,830.4	3,447.7	964.7	2,283.6	832.6	$770.0	21.0	—	—	—	41.6	—
1975	24,536.6	23,133.2	10,617.2	7,489.2	1,608.5	3,418.4	1,403.4	1,233.0	35.7	—	$20.0	—	114.7	$8,605.0
1980	39,172.8	34,317.1	16,027.7	10,939.5	1,548.7	5,801.2	4,855.7	4,598.0	31.8	—	76.5	—	149.4	13,320.0
1981	44,121.6	36,446.2	15,903.7	12,084.8	2,182.2	6,275.5	7,675.4	7,433.0	20.7	—	76.5	—	145.2	16,380.0
1982	40,142.2	34,304.7	14,839.2	10,872.8	1,995.1	6,597.4	5,837.5	5,597.0	19.8	—	72.0	—	148.7	16,180.0
1983	41,544.7	34,719.2	14,527.8	10,753.4	2,204.1	7,233.8	6,825.5	6,582.0	19.8	—	60.0	—	163.7	16,725.0
1984	43,875.9	36,104.5	15,292.4	10,163.2	2,710.4	7,938.6	7,771.4	7,520.0	17.9	—	76.0	—	157.5	17,090.0
1985	47,535.4	38,809.9	16,901.3	10,956.5	2,107.6	8,844.6	8,725.5	8,467.0	21.4	—	76.0	—	161.1	18,035.0
1986	48,139.4	39,745.0	17,049.9	11,065.6	2,620.0	9,009.4	8,394.4	8,142.0	20.2	—	72.7	—	159.5	19,460.0
1987	50,502.0	40,972.2	17,535.7	10,077.5	2,820.4	10,538.6	9,529.8	9,272.0	20.9	$0.6	76.0	—	160.4	19,590.0
1988	53,840.5	43,216.0	18,564.9	10,419.1	2,981.6	11,250.5	10,624.5	10,380.0	20.6	0.5	73.0	$22.0	150.4	16,190.0
1989	59,196.3	47,928.5	19,724.0	13,014.3	3,180.3	12,009.8	11,267.8	10,938.0	20.4	0.5	71.9	—	215.0	16,890.0
1990	61,676.7	50,439.5	21,525.1	13,399.1	3,382.9	12,132.4	11,237.2	10,871.0	15.0	5.5	59.2	48.8	237.7	18,140.0
1991[9]	66,026.1	54,638.1	24,436.2	13,702.0	3,670.5	12,829.4	11,388.0	10,979.0	17.3	5.4	63.5	87.7	235.0	—

Constant fiscal year 1991 dollars[10]

Fiscal year	2	3	4	5	6	7	8	9	10	11	12	13	14	15
1965	24,671.8	24,562.5	8,950.4	5,517.5	1,726.2	8,368.4	109.2	—	74.2	—	—	—	35.0	—
1970	48,010.6	45,018.4	20,953.8	12,390.5	3,467.1	8,207.1	2,992.2	2,767.3	75.4	—	—	—	149.5	—
1975	59,725.4	56,309.4	25,843.7	18,229.7	3,915.3	8,320.8	3,416.0	3,001.3	86.8	—	48.7	—	279.2	20,945.8
1980	63,970.3	56,040.9	26,173.7	17,864.5	2,529.1	9,473.5	7,929.5	7,508.7	51.9	—	124.9	—	244.0	21,752.0
1981	65,244.1	53,894.3	23,517.4	17,870.2	3,226.9	9,279.8	11,349.8	10,991.4	30.6	—	113.1	—	214.7	24,221.7
1982	55,412.1	47,353.9	20,484.0	15,008.8	2,754.0	9,107.1	8,058.1	7,726.1	27.4	—	99.4	—	205.3	22,334.9
1983	54,983.9	45,950.4	19,227.4	14,232.0	2,917.1	9,573.9	9,033.5	8,711.2	26.3	—	79.4	—	216.7	22,135.4
1984	56,038.5	46,112.9	19,531.5	12,980.5	3,461.7	10,139.2	9,925.6	9,604.6	22.9	—	97.1	—	201.2	21,827.4
1985	58,918.8	48,103.8	20,948.7	13,580.2	2,612.3	10,962.6	10,815.0	10,494.6	26.5	—	94.2	—	199.7	22,353.9
1986	58,250.0	48,092.5	20,630.9	13,389.7	3,170.3	10,901.6	10,157.5	9,852.0	24.4	—	88.0	—	193.0	23,547.1
1987	59,619.4	48,369.1	20,701.5	11,896.8	3,329.6	12,441.2	11,250.3	10,945.9	24.7	0.7	89.7	—	189.4	23,126.7
1988	61,519.3	49,379.5	21,212.6	11,905.1	3,406.8	12,855.6	12,139.8	11,860.4	23.6	0.5	83.4	24.1	171.9	18,499.0
1989	64,966.3	52,600.2	21,646.6	14,282.9	3,490.3	13,180.4	12,366.1	12,004.1	22.4	0.6	78.9	—	236.0	18,536.3
1990	64,991.2	53,150.1	22,681.9	14,119.2	3,564.7	12,784.4	11,841.1	11,455.2	15.8	5.8	62.4	51.4	250.5	19,114.9
1991[9]	66,026.1	54,638.1	24,436.2	13,702.0	3,670.5	12,829.4	11,388.0	10,979.0	17.3	5.4	63.5	87.7	235.0	—

[1] On-budget support includes Federal funds for education programs tied to appropriations.
[2] New student loans guaranteed by the Federal Government and disbursed to borrowers. Also known as off-budget support.
[3] Student loans created from institutional matching funds (1/9 of the Federal contribution). Excludes repayments of outstanding loans.
[4] Student loans created from institutional matching funds (1/9 of the Federal contribution). This is a demonstration project which involves only 10 institutions and has unsubsidized interest rates.
[5] Required State matching contributions.
[6] Institutions award grants to undergraduate students, and the Federal share of such grants may not exceed 85 percent of the total grant.
[7] Employer contributions to student earnings.
[8] Tax expenditures are the difference between current Federal tax receipts and what these receipts would be without

[10] Data adjusted by the Composite Deflator prepared by the Office of Management and Budget.
—Data not available or not applicable.

NOTE.—To the extent possible, Federal education funds data represent outlays rather than obligations. Because of rounding, details may not add to totals. Data have been revised from previously published figures.

SOURCE: U.S. Department of Education, National Center for Education Statistics, compiled from data appearing in U.S. Office of Management and Budget, *Budget of the U.S. Government*, fiscal years 1967 to 1992; National Science Foundation, *Federal Funds for Research and Development, fiscal years 1965 to 1991*; "Federal Tax Expenditures, FY 1980 to FY 1984," "Federal Tax Expenditures, FY 1984 to FY 1988," and "Federal Tax Expenditures, FY 1970 to FY 1990" by Stephen M. Barro, prepared for the National Center for Education Statistics; and unpublished data obtained from various Federal agencies. (This table was prepared April 1991.)

Table 337—Federal on-budget funds for education, by agency: Fiscal years 1965 to 1991

[In thousands of dollars]

Agency	1965	1970	1975	1980	1983	1984	1985	1986	1987	1988	1989	1990	1991 [1]
1	2	3	4	5	6	7	8	9	10	11	12	13	14
Total	$5,331,016	$12,526,499	$23,133,209	$34,317,114	$34,719,162	$36,104,529	$38,809,949	$39,744,958	$40,972,176	$43,216,013	$47,928,506	$50,439,481	$54,638,134
Department of Education	1,000,567	4,625,224	7,350,355	13,137,785	14,585,825	15,534,737	16,701,065	17,740,051	16,879,827	18,326,916	21,671,232	23,198,575	24,912,441
Department of Agriculture	768,927	960,910	2,219,352	4,562,467	4,340,869	4,616,372	4,782,274	5,041,317	5,189,779	5,481,976	5,793,616	6,258,734	6,965,449
Department of Commerce	9,347	13,990	38,967	135,561	55,090	55,160	55,114	64,613	38,896	38,553	47,586	50,712	40,400
Department of Defense	587,412	821,388	1,009,229	1,560,301	2,487,597	2,625,146	3,119,213	3,354,588	3,695,617	3,461,345	3,746,031	3,392,089	3,512,898
Department of Energy	442,434	551,527	764,676	1,605,558	1,933,068	2,042,881	2,247,822	2,181,391	2,256,799	2,385,966	2,563,978	2,523,865	2,653,830
Department of Health and Human Services	1,027,537	1,796,854	3,520,350	5,437,542	4,804,004	4,735,554	5,104,429	5,098,910	5,882,270	6,273,185	6,611,926	7,088,620	8,023,658
Department of Housing and Urban Development	221,256	114,709	−52,768	5,314	2,158	2,000	2,000	438	342	463	51	100	200
Department of the Interior	170,088	190,975	300,191	440,547	484,314	576,779	549,479	454,273	485,922	528,409	542,466	624,547	626,815
Department of Justice	10,252	15,728	61,542	60,721	68,700	62,282	66,802	72,191	79,815	83,405	88,129	99,217	119,231
Department of Labor	230,041	424,494	1,103,935	1,862,738	1,833,392	1,755,839	1,948,685	1,976,960	2,258,631	2,272,228	2,277,556	2,512,987	2,592,715
Department of State	64,200	59,742	89,433	25,188	23,813	23,086	23,820	23,401	24,288	38,671	45,848	50,906	50,646
Department of Transportation	—	27,534	52,290	54,712	82,139	83,931	82,035	66,214	75,360	65,134	90,840	78,578	75,885
Department of Treasury	8,240	18	1,118,840	1,247,463	287,300	287,905	290,276	41,257	19,279	32,768	39,511	41,688	46,927
Department of Veterans Affairs	97,237	1,032,918	4,402,212	2,351,233	1,672,348	1,445,049	1,289,849	1,055,948	1,002,109	966,549	896,435	757,476	826,590
Other agencies and programs:													
ACTION programs	63,329	88,034	7,081	2,833	1,830	4,975	1,761	1,368	3,368	4,110	4,800	8,472	8,960
Agency for International Development	—	—	78,896	176,770	173,629	236,983	198,807	198,929	240,827	242,650	227,864	229,671	213,936
Appalachian Regional Commission	—	37,838	45,786	19,032	2,855	4,919	4,745	6,582	5,445	6,468	6,145	93	93
Barry Goldwater Scholarship and Excellence in Education Foundation	—	—	—	—	—	—	—	—	—	—	753	1,033	2,033
Environmental Protection Agency	—	19,446	33,875	41,083	43,557	97,395	60,521	101,844	67,465	58,053	64,517	79,800	91,200
Estimated education share of Federal aid to the District of Columbia	11,350	33,019	55,487	81,847	97,526	43,700	107,340	69,718	126,942	122,366	103,764	104,940	100,844
Federal Emergency Management Agency	—	—	—	1,946	1,145	321	1,828	290	290	290	77	39	24
General Services Administration	4,013	14,775	22,532	34,800	44,200	50,894	—	—	—	—	—	—	—
Harry S Truman scholarship fund	—	—	—	−1,895	1,795	1,929	1,332	2,441	2,717	2,815	2,851	2,883	3,102
Institute of American Indian and Alaska Native Culture and Arts Development	—	—	—	—	—	—	—	—	—	13,200	3,094	4,305	5,447
James Madison Memorial Fellowship Foundation	—	—	—	—	—	—	—	235	3,225	3,004	10,005	191	711
Japanese-United States Friendship Commission	—	—	—	2,294	2,364	1,611	2,236	2,236	3,004	2,274	3,004	2,299	2,325
Library of Congress	15,111	29,478	63,766	151,871	154,198	164,080	169,310	166,130	160,835	160,505	177,954	189,827	215,094
National Aeronautics and Space Administration	208,788	258,366	197,901	255,511	367,763	354,528	487,624	490,948	787,391	899,897	978,778	1,095,500	1,238,600
National Archives and Records Administration	—	—	—	—	—	—	52,118	55,252	59,521	65,153	86,266	77,397	89,915
National Commission on Libraries and Information Science	—	—	449	2,090	681	733	723	781	512	522	839	3,281	2,797
National Endowment for the Arts	—	340	4,754	5,220	4,701	5,197	5,536	5,188	5,394	5,550	5,655	5,577	6,500
National Endowment for the Humanities	—	8,459	63,955	142,586	123,315	127,571	125,671	121,125	124,407	125,230	137,076	141,048	152,139
National Science Foundation	181,216	295,628	535,294	808,392	907,917	1,035,746	1,147,115	1,147,273	1,270,415	1,329,520	1,472,835	1,579,284	1,801,814
Nuclear Regulatory Commission	—	—	7,093	32,590	37,987	36,400	30,261	27,472	29,176	25,676	25,690	20,300	22,200
Office of Economic Opportunity	189,871	1,092,410	16,619	—	—	—	—	—	—	—	—	—	—
Smithsonian Institution	2,233	2,461	5,509	5,153	6,073	5,758	7,886	6,191	6,545	5,393	5,880	5,779	7,113
United States Arms Control Agency	—	100	—	661	157	—	395	276	3,244	2,633	1,619	(²)	100
United States Information Agency	7,512	8,423	9,405	66,210	86,556	83,768	143,007	170,514	179,653	183,206	185,521	201,547	216,021
United States Institute of Peace	—	—	—	—	—	—	—	230	4,083	3,476	7,232	7,621	8,781
Other agencies	10,055	1,421	5,913	990	296	1,300	432	715	1,666	1,870	947	500	700

[1] Estimated.
[2] Less than $50,000.
—Data not available or not applicable.

NOTE.—To the extent possible, funds data represent outlays, rather than obligations. Data revised from previously published figures.

SOURCE: U.S. Department of Education, National Center for Education Statistics, compiled from data appearing in U.S. Office of Management and Budget, Budget of the U.S. Government, fiscal years 1967 to 1992; National Science Foundation, Federal Funds for Research and Development, fiscal years 1965 to 1991; and unpublished data obtained from various Federal agencies. (This table was prepared April 1991.)

Table 338.—Federal on-budget funds for education, by level of education or activity, agency, and program: Fiscal years 1965 to 1991

[In thousands of dollars]

Level, agency, and program	1965	1970	1975	1980	1985	1988	1989	1990	1991 [1]
1	2	3	4	5	6	7	8	9	10
Total, all programs	$5,331,016	$12,526,499	$23,133,209	$34,317,114	$38,809,949	$43,216,013	$47,928,506	$50,439,481	$54,638,134
Elementary/secondary education programs	$1,942,577	$5,830,442	$10,617,195	$16,027,686	$16,901,334	$18,564,859	$19,724,017	$21,525,140	$24,436,218
Department of Education [2]	567,343	2,719,204	4,132,742	6,629,095	7,296,702	8,098,436	8,869,300	9,681,313	11,192,216
Grants for the disadvantaged	—	1,339,014	1,874,353	3,204,664	4,206,754	4,027,559	4,185,357	4,494,111	5,335,441
Impact aid program	349,671	656,372	618,711	690,170	647,402	707,539	755,477	816,366	815,311
School improvement programs	72,298	288,304	700,470	788,918	526,401	443,468	975,237	1,189,158	1,555,733
Indian education	—	—	40,036	93,365	82,328	18,339	65,683	69,451	69,080
Bilingual education	—	21,250	92,693	169,540	157,539	159,746	164,759	188,919	192,916
Education for the handicapped	13,849	79,090	151,244	821,777	1,017,964	1,465,985	1,880,751	1,616,623	2,317,248
Vocational and adult education	131,525	335,174	655,235	860,661	658,314	1,275,800	842,036	1,306,685	906,487
Department of Agriculture	623,014	760,477	1,884,345	4,064,497	4,134,906	4,806,766	5,104,502	5,528,950	6,186,460
Child nutrition programs	178,580	299,131	1,452,267	3,377,056	3,664,561	4,286,242	4,555,581	4,977,075	5,635,168
Agricultural Marketing Service--commodities [3]	340,073	341,597	248,839	388,000	336,502	349,670	342,071	350,441	350,900
Special milk program	86,609	83,800	122,858	159,293	15,993	18,342	18,544	18,707	22,899
Estimated education share of Forest Service permanent appropriations	17,752	35,949	60,381	140,148	117,850	152,512	188,306	182,727	177,493
Department of Commerce	—	—	—	54,816	—	—	—	—	—
Local public works program—school facilities [4]	—	—	—	54,816	—	—	—	—	—
Department of Defense	73,000	143,100	264,500	370,846	831,625	988,265	1,059,259	1,097,876	1,175,824
Junior ROTC	—	12,100	12,500	32,000	55,600	45,300	53,930	39,300	37,300
Overseas dependents schools	73,000	131,000	252,000	338,846	613,437	773,810	821,365	864,958	916,313
Section VI schools [5]	—	—	—	—	162,588	169,155	183,964	193,618	222,211
Department of Energy [6]	100	200	300	77,633	23,031	12,931	12,851	15,563	16,350
Energy conservation for school buildings [7]	—	—	—	77,240	22,731	12,611	12,442	15,213	15,000
Pre-engineering program	100	200	300	393	300	320	409	350	1,350
Department of Health and Human Services [8]	79,999	167,333	683,885	1,077,000	1,531,059	1,651,324	1,703,515	1,937,572	2,552,125
Head Start [9]	—	—	403,900	735,000	1,075,059	1,206,324	1,234,869	1,447,758	2,055,514
Social security student benefits [10]	79,999	167,333	279,985	342,000	456,000	445,000	468,646	489,814	496,611
Department of the Interior	130,096	140,705	220,392	318,170	389,810	379,645	379,381	445,267	429,383
Mineral Leasing Act and other funds:									
Payments to States—estimated education share	11,075	12,294	27,389	62,636	127,369	92,227	114,414	123,811	141,792
Payments to counties—estimated education share	10,731	16,359	29,494	48,953	59,016	34,922	54,804	102,522	47,111
Indian Education:									
Bureau of Indian Affairs schools	92,603	95,850	141,056	178,112	177,265	231,512	186,643	192,841	215,049
Johnson-O'Malley assistance [11]	15,534	16,080	22,251	28,081	25,675	20,400	23,000	25,556	24,931
Education expenses for children of employees, Yellowstone National Park	153	122	202	388	485	584	520	538	500
Department of Justice	6,402	8,237	9,822	23,890	36,117	50,679	58,523	65,997	82,652
Vocational training expenses for prisoners in Federal prison	1,466	2,720	3,039	4,966	8,292	8,679	6,933	2,066	3,167
Inmate programs [12]	4,936	5,517	6,783	18,924	27,825	42,000	51,590	63,931	79,485
Department of Labor	230,041	420,927	1,097,811	1,849,800	1,945,268	2,266,700	2,271,966	2,505,487	2,584,215
Job Corps [13]	—	—	175,000	469,800	604,748	712,218	771,966	739,376	800,238
Training programs—estimated funds for education programs [14]	230,041	420,927	922,811	1,380,000	1,340,520	1,554,482	1,500,000	1,766,111	1,783,977
Department of Transportation [15]	—	45	50	60	60	50	40	46	65
Tuition assistance for educational accreditation— Coast Guard personnel [16]	—	45	50	60	60	50	40	46	65
Department of the Treasury	32	—	847,139	935,903	273,728	—	—	—	—
Estimated education share of general revenue sharing— [17]									
State [18]	—	—	475,224	525,019	—	—	—	—	—
Local	—	—	371,915	410,884	273,728	—	—	—	—
Tuition assistance for educational accreditation— Coast Guard personnel [16]	32	—	—	—	—	—	—	—	—
Department of Veterans Affairs [19]	41,250	338,910	1,371,500	545,786	344,758	196,159	168,865	155,351	126,345
Noncollegiate and job training programs [20]	14,550	281,640	1,249,410	439,993	224,035	76,367	43,696	12,848	—
Vocational rehabilitation for disabled veterans [21]	17,400	41,700	73,100	87,980	107,480	112,058	118,749	136,780	120,919
Dependents' education [22]	9,300	15,570	48,990	17,813	13,243	7,734	6,420	5,723	5,426
Other agencies:									
Appalachian Regional Commission [23]	—	33,161	41,667	9,157	4,632	5,327	5,145	93	93
National Endowment for the Arts [24]	—	—	3,686	4,989	4,399	4,350	4,462	4,641	4,975
Arts in education	—	—	3,686	4,989	4,399	4,350	4,462	4,641	4,975
National Endowment for the Humanities [25]	—	20	149	330	321	826	698	404	436
Office of Economic Opportunity [26]	182,793	1,072,375	16,619	—	—	—	—	—	—
Head Start [27]	96,400	325,700		—	—	—	—	—	—
Other elementary and secondary programs [28]	20,000	42,809	16,612	—	—	—	—	—	—
Job Corps [29]	34,000	144,000		—	—	—	—	—	—
Youth Corps—and other training programs [30]	31,000	553,368	7	—	—	—	—	—	—
Volunteers in Service to America (VISTA) [31]	1,393	6,498		—	—	—	—	—	—

Table 338.—Federal on-budget funds for education, by level of education or activity, agency, and program: Fiscal years 1965 to 1991—Continued

[In thousands of dollars]

Level, agency, and program	1965	1970	1975	1980	1985	1988	1989	1990	1991 [1]
1	2	3	4	5	6	7	8	9	10
Other programs:									
Estimated education share of Federal aid to the District of Columbia	8,507	25,748	42,588	65,714	84,918	103,400	85,510	86,579	85,079
Higher education programs	**1,197,511**	**3,447,697**	**7,489,162**	**10,939,494**	**10,956,452**	**10,419,120**	**13,014,330**	**13,399,103**	**13,702,003**
Department of Education [2]	237,955	1,187,962	2,089,184	5,682,242	8,202,499	8,247,103	10,640,044	11,175,978	11,168,541
Student financial assistance [32]	—	—	—	3,682,789	4,162,695	5,219,916	5,859,774	5,920,328	5,970,200
Guaranteed student loans [32]	—	2,323	111,087	1,407,977	3,534,795	2,779,304	3,899,387	4,372,446	4,201,245
Higher education	218,264	1,029,131	1,838,066	399,787	404,511	411,775	606,849	659,492	599,262
Facilities—loans and insurance [33]	3,588	114,199	16,292	−19,031	5,307	−43,282	10,182	19,219	63,829
College housing loans [33][34]	—	—	—	14,082	−164,061	−372,778	−31,299	−57,167	7,766
Educational activities overseas	129	774	1,881	3,561	1,838	233	374	82	—
Gallaudet College and Howard University	15,974	38,559	111,971	176,829	229,938	224,781	258,519	230,327	284,451
National Technical Institute for the Deaf [35]	—	2,976	9,887	16,248	27,476	27,154	36,258	31,251	41,788
Department of Agriculture	—	—	6,450	10,453	17,741	27,799	27,799	31,273	32,302
Agriculture Extension Service, Second Morrill Act payments to agricultural and mechanical colleges and Tuskegee Institute [36]	—	—	6,450	10,453	17,741	27,799	27,799	31,273	32,302
Department of Commerce	5,081	8,277	14,973	29,971	2,163	2,420	2,765	3,312	3,700
Sea Grant Program [37]	—	—	1,886	3,123	2,163	2,420	2,765	3,312	3,700
Merchant Marine Academy [38]	3,570	6,160	10,152	14,809	—	—	—	—	—
State marine schools [38]	1,511	2,117	2,935	12,039	—	—	—	—	—
Department of Defense [39]	77,500	322,100	379,800	545,000	1,041,700	573,400	746,464	625,313	643,974
Tuition assistance for military personnel	—	57,500	86,800	([40]	77,100	134,500	236,089	106,100	99,500
Service academies [41]	77,500	78,700	86,200	106,100	196,400	109,100	115,150	120,613	132,074
Senior ROTC	—	108,100	116,500	([40]	354,000	179,200	198,325	174,600	154,800
Professional development education [42]	—	77,800	90,300	([40]	414,200	150,600	196,900	224,000	257,600
Department of Energy [6]	3,000	3,000	3,000	57,701	19,475	22,609	15,062	25,502	41,980
University laboratory cooperative program	3,000	3,000	3,000	2,800	6,500	13,571	5,929	9,402	20,920
Teacher development projects [43]	—	—	—	1,400	—	—	—	—	—
Graduate traineeship programs [44]	—	—	—	—	—	(26)	—	—	—
Energy conservation for buildings— higher education [7]	—	—	—	53,501	12,705	7,746	6,493	7,459	7,400
Minority honors vocational training [45]	—	—	—	—	150	598	720	—	—
Honors research program [45]	—	—	—	—	120	720	820	6,472	10,550
Pre-college science [46]	—	—	—	—	—	—	1,100	2,169	3,110
Department of Health and Human Services [8]	469,223	981,483	1,531,775	2,235,670	298,161	277,684	287,238	337,186	404,682
Health professions training programs	139,795	353,029	599,350	460,736	212,200	216,591	223,811	230,600	269,600
Indian health manpower [47]	—	—	—	7,187	5,577	5,998	5,972	9,508	13,542
National Health Service Corps scholarships	—	—	1,206	70,667	2,268	4,100	6,531	4,759	27,000
National Institute of Occupational Safety and Health training grants	4,327	8,088	7,182	12,899	8,760	9,718	10,095	10,461	10,472
Alcohol, drug abuse, and mental health training programs	85,101	118,366	83,727	122,103	43,617	40,726	40,301	81,353	83,587
Health teaching facilities [48]	—	—	353	3,078	739	551	528	505	481
Social security postsecondary students' benefits [49]	240,000	502,000	839,957	1,559,000	25,000	—	—	—	—
Department of Housing and Urban Development	220,744	114,199	−55,418	—	—	—	—	—	—
College housing loans [33][34]	220,744	114,199	−55,418	—	—	—	—	—	—
Department of the Interior	30,153	31,749	50,844	80,202	125,247	113,661	123,529	135,480	165,632
Shared revenues, Mineral Leasing Act and other receipts—estimated education share	6,260	6,949	15,480	35,403	71,991	52,117	64,669	69,980	80,143
Indian programs:									
Continuing education [50]	8,993	9,380	13,311	16,909	24,338	30,822	28,424	34,911	57,619
Higher education scholarships	14,900	15,420	22,053	27,890	28,918	30,722	30,436	30,589	27,870
Department of State	53,420	30,850	50,347	—	—	4,120	4,422	2,167	9,108
Educational exchange [51]	53,420	30,850	50,347	—	—	—	—	—	—
Mutual educational and cultural exchange activities ...	47,025	30,454	50,300	—	—	—	—	—	—
International educational exchange activities	6,395	396	47	—	—	—	—	—	—
Soviet-East European Research and Training [52]	—	—	—	—	—	4,120	4,422	2,167	9,108
Department of Transportation [15]	—	11,197	11,885	12,530	55,569	44,998	63,559	46,025	49,038
Merchant Marine Academy [38]	—	—	—	—	19,898	20,579	20,611	20,926	21,560
State marine schools [53]	—	—	—	—	19,777	7,961	26,062	8,269	8,872
Coast Guard Academy [16]	—	9,342	9,780	10,000	11,857	10,810	11,740	12,074	12,550
Postgraduate training for Coast Guard officers [54]	—	1,655	1,855	2,230	3,499	5,084	4,621	4,173	5,459
Tuition assistance to Coast Guard military personnel [16]	—	200	250	300	538	564	525	582	597
Department of the Treasury	8,208	—	268,605	296,750	—	—	—	—	—
General revenue sharing—estimated State share to higher education [17][18]	—	—	268,605	296,750	—	—	—	—	—
Coast Guard Academy [16]	6,815	—	—	—	—	—	—	—	—
Postgraduate training for Coast Guard officers [54]	1,293	—	—	—	—	—	—	—	—
Tuition assistance to Coast Guard military personnel [16]	100	—	—	—	—	—	—	—	—
Department of Veterans Affairs [19]	55,650	693,490	3,029,600	1,803,847	944,091	768,090	725,270	599,825	697,945
Vietnam-era veterans [55]	33,950	638,260	2,840,600	1,579,974	694,217	345,242	264,702	46,998	—
College student support	—	—	—	1,560,081	679,953	337,568	258,982	39,458	—
Work-study	—	—	—	19,893	14,264	7,674	5,720	7,540	—
Service persons college support [56]	—	18,900	74,690	46,617	35,630	33,472	34,399	8,911	—
Post-Vietnam veterans [57]	—	—	—	922	82,554	203,262	195,142	161,475	160,045

Table 338.—Federal on-budget funds for education, by level of education or activity, agency, and program: Fiscal years 1965 to 1991—Continued

[In thousands of dollars]

Level, agency, and program	1965	1970	1975	1980	1985	1988	1989	1990	1991 [1]
1	2	3	4	5	6	7	8	9	10
All-volunteer-force educational assistance [58]	—	—	—	—	196	73,731	122,222	269,947	423,237
Veterans [59]	—	—	—	—	—	8,386	43,423	183,765	311,874
Reservists [60]	—	—	—	—	196	65,345	78,799	86,182	95,850
Work-study	—	—	—	—	—	—	—	—	15,513
Veteran dependents' education [61]	21,700	36,330	114,310	176,334	131,494	100,883	96,805	100,494	102,663
Payments to State education agencies [62]	—	—	—	—	—	11,500	12,000	12,000	12,000
Other agencies:									
Appalachian Regional Commission [23]	—	4,105	2,545	1,751	—	1,141	825	—	—
National Endowment for the Humanities [25]	—	3,349	25,320	56,451	49,098	47,601	51,449	50,938	54,937
National Science Foundation	27,170	42,000	60,283	64,583	60,069	97,466	130,187	161,884	213,414
Science and engineering education programs	27,170	37,000	60,283	64,583	60,069	97,466	130,187	161,884	213,414
Sea Grant Program [37]	—	5,000	—	—	—	—	—	—	—
United States Information Agency [63]	7,512	8,423	9,405	51,095	124,041	160,447	164,807	181,172	193,403
Educational and cultural affairs	—	—	—	49,546	21,079	23,466	21,596	35,862	35,728
Educational and cultural exchange programs [64]	—	—	—	—	101,529	136,646	143,194	145,307	157,191
Educational exchange activities, international	—	—	—	1,549	1,433	335	17	3	484
Information center and library activities [65]	7,512	8,423	9,405	—	—	—	—	—	—
Other programs:									
Barry Goldwater Scholarship and Excellence in Education Foundation [66]	—	—	—	—	—	—	753	1,033	2,033
Estimated education share of Federal aid to the District of Columbia	1,895	5,513	10,564	13,143	15,266	14,566	14,207	14,637	12,054
Harry S Truman scholarship fund [33][67]	—	—	—	−1,895	1,332	2,815	2,851	2,883	3,102
Institute of American Indian and Alaska Native Culture and Arts Development [68]	—	—	—	—	—	—	3,094	4,305	5,447
James Madison Memorial Fellowship Foundation [69]	—	—	—	—	—	13,200	10,005	191	711
Other education programs	**374,652**	**964,719**	**1,608,478**	**1,548,730**	**2,107,588**	**2,981,571**	**3,180,334**	**3,382,855**	**3,670,549**
Department of Education [2]	182,021	630,235	1,045,659	747,706	1,173,055	1,938,998	2,071,574	2,251,801	2,450,220
Administration	17,732	47,456	108,372	187,317	284,900	295,615	301,260	328,293	365,491
Libraries	26,111	108,284	225,810	129,127	85,650	101,202	140,398	137,264	154,801
Rehabilitative services and handicapped research	137,313	473,091	709,483	426,886	798,298	1,536,905	1,623,255	1,780,360	1,921,076
American Printing House for the Blind	865	1,404	1,994	4,349	4,230	5,234	6,645	5,736	8,376
Trust funds	—	—	—	27	(23)	42	16	148	476
Department of Agriculture	87,551	135,637	220,395	271,112	336,375	342,523	347,021	352,511	382,687
Extension Service	85,924	131,734	215,523	263,584	325,986	330,164	333,571	337,907	366,176
National Agricultural Library	1,627	3,903	4,872	7,528	10,389	12,359	13,450	14,604	16,511
Department of Commerce	251	1,226	2,317	2,479	—	—	—	—	—
Maritime Administration:									
Training for private sector employees [38]	251	1,226	2,317	2,479	—	—	—	—	—
Department of Health and Human Services [8]	3,953	24,273	31,653	37,819	47,195	62,060	71,912	77,962	87,251
National Library of Medicine	3,953	24,273	31,653	37,819	47,195	62,060	71,912	77,962	87,251
Department of Housing and Urban Development	512	—	—	—	—	—	—	—	—
Urban mass transportation—managerial training grants [70]	512	—	—	—	—	—	—	—	—
Department of Justice	3,850	5,546	42,818	27,642	25,517	26,361	23,906	26,920	30,979
FBI National Academy	1,850	2,066	5,100	7,234	4,189	5,385	5,513	6,028	10,020
FBI—Field Police Academy	1,450	2,500	5,254	7,715	10,220	9,995	7,673	10,548	11,045
Narcotics and dangerous drug training	550	980	1,152	2,416	83	142	824	850	950
National Institute of Corrections [71]	—	—	31,312	10,277	11,025	10,839	9,896	9,494	8,964
Department of State	10,780	20,672	28,113	25,000	23,791	33,308	40,157	47,539	40,338
Foreign Service Institute	6,395	15,857	20,750	25,000	23,791	33,308	40,157	47,539	40,338
Center for Cultural and Technical Interchange [51]	4,385	4,815	7,363	—	—	—	—	—	—
Department of Transportation [15]	—	3,964	11,877	10,212	3,785	3,153	4,415	1,507	1,582
Highways training and education grants [72]	—	2,418	3,250	3,412	1,500	1,416	1,416	—	—
Maritime Administration:									
Training for private sector employees [38]	—	—	—	—	1,135	1,517	1,499	1,507	1,582
Urban mass transportation—managerial training grants [70]	—	1,546	2,627	500	1,150	220	1,500	—	—
Federal Aviation Administration [73] Air traffic controllers second career program [74]	—	—	6,000	6,300	—	—	—	—	—
Department of the Treasury	—	18	3,096	14,584	16,160	32,768	39,100	41,488	46,527
Federal Law Enforcement Training Center [75]	—	18	3,096	14,584	16,160	32,768	39,100	41,488	46,527
Other agencies:									
ACTION [76]	—	—	7,045	2,833	1,761	4,110	4,800	8,472	8,960
Estimated education funds [77]	—	—	7,045	2,833	1,761	4,110	4,800	8,472	8,960
Agency for International Development	63,329	88,034	78,896	99,707	141,847	193,115	182,839	170,371	167,536
Education and human resources	53,968	61,570	58,349	80,518	115,104	160,051	146,915	142,801	126,006
American schools and hospitals abroad	9,361	26,464	20,547	19,189	26,743	33,064	35,924	27,570	41,530
Appalachian Regional Commission [23]	—	572	1,574	8,124	113	—	175	—	—

Table 338.—Federal on-budget funds for education, by level of education or activity, agency, and program: Fiscal years 1965 to 1991—Continued

[In thousands of dollars]

Level, agency, and program	1965	1970	1975	1980	1985	1988	1989	1990	1991 [1]
1	2	3	4	5	6	7	8	9	10
Federal Emergency Management Agency [78]	—	290	290	281	405	290	77	39	24
Estimated architect/engineer student development program [79]	—	40	40	31	155	40	50	24	24
Estimated other training programs [80]	—	250	250	250	250	250	27	15	—
General Services Administration [81]									
Libraries and other archival activities	4,013	14,775	22,532	34,800	—	—	—	—	—
Japanese-United States Friendship Commission [82]	—	—	—	2,294	2,236	2,274	3,004	2,299	2,325
Library of Congress	15,111	29,478	63,766	151,871	169,310	160,505	177,954	189,827	215,094
Salaries and expenses	11,421	20,700	48,798	102,364	130,354	122,356	137,637	148,985	174,081
Books for the blind and the physically handicapped	2,317	6,195	11,908	31,436	32,954	36,245	38,233	37,473	37,501
Special foreign currency program	1,187	2,273	2,333	3,492	4,621	405	99	10	50
Furniture and furnishings	186	310	727	14,579	1,381	1,499	1,985	3,359	3,462
National Aeronautics and Space Administration Aerospace education services project	100	350	600	882	1,800	2,400	2,300	3,300	3,800
National Archives and Records Administration [83] Libraries and other archival activities	—	—	—	—	52,118	65,153	86,266	77,397	89,915
National Commission on Libraries and Information Science [84]	—	—	449	2,090	723	522	839	3,281	2,797
National Endowment for the Arts [24]	—	340	1,068	231	1,137	1,200	1,193	936	1,525
National Endowment for the Humanities [25]	—	5,090	38,486	85,805	76,252	76,803	84,929	89,706	96,766
Smithsonian Institution	2,233	2,461	5,509	5,153	7,886	5,393	5,880	5,779	7,113
Museum programs and related research	2,133	2,261	4,203	3,254	4,665	1,223	870	690	1,500
National Gallery of Art extension service	100	200	300	426	675	656	650	474	666
Woodrow Wilson International Center for Scholars	—	—	1,006	1,473	2,546	3,514	4,360	4,615	4,947
United States Information Agency—Center for Cultural and Technical Interchange [51]	—	—	—	15,115	18,966	22,759	20,714	20,375	22,618
United States Institute of Peace [85]	—	—	—	—	—	3,476	7,232	7,621	8,781
Other programs:									
Estimated education share of Federal aid for the District of Columbia	948	1,758	2,335	2,990	7,156	4,400	4,047	3,724	3,711
Research programs at universities and related institutions [86]	**1,816,276**	**2,283,641**	**3,418,374**	**5,801,204**	**8,844,575**	**11,250,464**	**12,009,825**	**12,132,383**	**12,829,364**
Department of Education [87]	13,248	87,823	82,770	78,742	28,809	42,379	90,314	89,483	101,464
Department of Agriculture	58,362	64,796	108,162	216,405	293,252	304,888	314,294	346,000	364,000
Department of Commerce	4,015	4,487	21,677	48,295	52,951	36,133	44,821	47,400	36,700
Department of Defense	436,912	356,188	364,929	644,455	1,245,888	1,899,680	1,940,308	1,668,900	1,693,100
Department of Energy	439,334	548,327	761,376	1,470,224	2,205,316	2,350,426	2,536,065	2,482,800	2,595,500
Department of Health and Human Services	474,362	623,765	1,273,037	2,087,053	3,228,014	4,282,117	4,549,261	4,735,900	4,979,600
Department of Housing and Urban Development	—	510	2,650	5,314	438	51	186	100	200
Department of the Interior	9,839	18,521	28,955	42,175	34,422	35,103	39,556	43,800	31,800
Department of Justice	—	1,945	8,902	9,189	5,168	6,365	5,700	6,300	5,600
Department of Labor	—	3,567	6,124	12,938	3,417	5,528	5,590	7,500	8,500
Department of State	—	8,220	10,973	188	29	1,243	1,269	1,200	1,200
Department of Transportation	—	12,328	28,478	31,910	22,621	16,933	22,826	31,000	25,200
Department of the Treasury	—	—	—	226	388	—	411	200	400
Department of Veterans Affairs	337	518	1,112	1,600	1,000	2,300	2,300	2,300	2,300
ACTION	—	—	36	—	—	—	—	—	—
Agency for International Development	—	—	—	77,063	56,960	49,535	45,025	59,300	46,400
Environmental Protection Agency	—	19,446	33,875	41,083	60,521	58,053	64,517	79,800	91,200
Federal Emergency Management Agency	—	—	—	1,665	1,423	—	—	—	—
National Aeronautics and Space Administration	208,688	258,016	197,301	254,629	485,824	897,497	976,478	1,092,200	1,234,800
National Science Foundation	154,046	253,628	475,011	743,809	1,087,046	1,232,054	1,342,648	1,417,400	1,588,400
Nuclear Regulatory Commission	—	—	7,093	32,590	30,261	25,676	25,690	20,300	22,200
Office of Economic Opportunity	7,078	20,035	—	—	—	—	—	—	—
U.S. Arms Control and Disarmament Agency	—	100	—	661	395	2,633	1,619	([88])	100
U.S. Information Agency	—	—	—	—	—	—	—	—	—
Other agencies	10,055	1,421	5,913	990	432	1,870	947	500	700

[1] Estimated.

[2] The U.S. Department of Education was created in May 1980. It formerly was the Office of Education in the U.S. Department of Health, Education, and Welfare.

[3] These commodities are purchased under Section 32 of the Act of August 24, 1935, for use in the child nutrition programs.

[4] This program assisted in the construction of public facilities, such as vocational schools, through grants or loans. No funds have been appropriated for this account since FY 77, and it was completely phased out in FY 84 after the monitoring of closeouts of projects was completed. Data are not available for previous years.

[5] This program was funded by the Department of Education in FYs 65 through 81 in the "Impact Aid" program. This program provides for education of dependents of Federal employees residing on Federal property in cases where free public education is unavailable in the nearby community.

[6] The U.S. Department of Energy was created in 1977. It formerly was the Energy Research and Development Administration and before that the Atomic Energy Commission.

[7] This program was established in 1979. Funds were appropriated for this program in FY 80.

[8] The U.S. Department of Health and Human Services was part of the U.S. Department of Health, Education, and Welfare until May 1980.

[9] The Head Start program was in the Office of Economic Opportunity, and funds were appropriated to the U.S. Department of Health, Education, and Welfare, Office of Child Development, beginning in 1972.

[10] After age 18, benefits terminate at the end of the school term or in 3 months, whichever is less.

[11] This program provides funding for supplemental programs for eligible Indian students in public schools.

[12] This program finances the cost of academic, social, and occupational education courses for inmates in Federal prisons.

[13] The Job Corps program was formerly in the Office of Economic Opportunity, and funds were appropriated to the U.S. Department of Labor beginning in 1971 and 1972.

[14] Some of the work and training programs included in this program were in the Office of Economic Opportunity and were transferred to the U.S. Department of Labor in 1971 and 1972.

[15] The U.S. Department of Transportation was created in 1967.

[16] This program was transferred from the U.S. Department of the Treasury to the U.S. Department of Transportation in 1967.

[17] This program was established in FY 72 and closed in FY 86.

[18] The States' share of revenue-sharing funds was not spent on education in FYs 81 through 86.

[19] The U.S. Department of Veterans Affairs, formerly the Veterans Administration, was created in March 1989.

[20] This program provides educational assistance allowances in order to restore lost educational opportunities to those individuals whose careers were interrupted or impeded by reason of active military service between January 31, 1955, and January 1, 1977. Includes "Readjustment Benefits," Chapter 34, for education other than college and also includes the Veterans Job Training Program for service persons and veterans. Chapter 34 program closed December 31, 1989. The Veterans Job Training Program were put in the program Payments to State Education Agencies. Veterans who were still eligible to receive benefits under Chapter 34 where put in Chapter 30 (The All-Volunteer-Force Educational Assistance program).

[21] This program is in "Readjustment Benefits" program, Chapter 31, and covers the costs of subsistence, tuition, books, supplies, and equipment for disabled veterans requiring vocational rehabilitation.

[22] This program is in the "Readjustment Benefits" program, Chapter 35, and provides benefits to children and spouses of veterans.

[23] This agency was established March 9, 1965. First year of appropriations was 1966. The outlays were larger in the years 1970 and 1975 for elementary and secondary education because of the construction of facilities for vocational schools.

[24] This agency was established in 1965. In 1970, $900,000 was appropriated through the Office of Education, U.S. Department of Health, Education, and Welfare, for the National Endowment for the Arts, Arts in Education program.

[25] This agency was established in 1965. First year of appropriations was 1966.

[26] The Economic Opportunity Act of 1964 authorized 10 major action programs, including Job Corps, Neighborhood Youth Corps, Adult Literacy, Work Experience, College Work-Study, and Community Action programs, including Head Start, Follow Through, and Upward Bound, and authorized the establishment of Volunteers in Service to America (VISTA). These programs were transferred to the U.S. Department of Health, Education, and Welfare, U.S. Department of Labor, and the Action Agency in the 1970's. An act on January 4, 1975 established the Community Services Administration as the successor agency to the Office of Economic Opportunity.

[27] Head Start program funds were transferred to the U.S. Department of Health, Education, and Welfare, Office of Child Development, in 1972.

[28] Most of these programs were transferred to the U.S. Department of Health, Education, and Welfare, Office of Education, in 1972.

[29] The Job Corps programs were transferred to the U.S. Department of Labor in 1971 and 1972.

[30] These programs were transferred to the U.S. Department of Labor in 1971 and 1972.

[31] These programs were transferred to the Action Agency in 1972.

[32] Similar programs were included in the "higher education" program in 1965 through 1975.

[33] Negative amounts occur when program receipts exceed outlays.

[34] This program was formerly in the U.S. Department of Housing and Urban Development and was transferred to the U.S. Department of Health, Education, and Welfare, Office of Education, in FY 79.

[35] First year of appropriations for this program was 1967.

[36] Program funds were first appropriated for Tuskeegee Institute in 1972.

[37] The Sea Grant College Program Act of 1966 established a matching fund grant program that provides for the establishment of a network of programs in fields related to development and preservation of the nations coastal and marine resources. One of the objectives is to provide trained personnel to utilize and manage these resources. This program was in the National Science Foundation and transferred to the U.S. Department of Commerce, October 1970. Appropriations began in 1968.

[38] This program was transferred to the U.S. Department of Transportation in FY 81 by Public Law 97–31, from the U.S. Department of Commerce.

[39] The Department of Defense funds for FYs 88 to 91 are lower than previous years because they exclude military pay and reserve accounts which were included in previous years. FY 65 data are not available except for service academies.

[40] Included in total above.

[41] Instructional costs only are included. These include academics, audiovisual, academic computing center, faculty training, military training, physical education, and libraries.

[42] Includes special education programs (military and civilian); legal education program; flight training; advanced degree program; college degree program (officers); and "Armed Forces Health Professions Scholarship" program.

[43] No funds have been appropriated for this program since FY 82.

[44] This program receives funds periodically.

[45] Appropriations began in FY 84.

[46] Appropriations began in FY 89.

[47] Appropriations began in FY 78.

[48] The amount reported in FY 83 was large because of a loan default.

[49] Postsecondary student benefits were ended by the Omnibus Budget Reconciliation Act of 1981 (Public Law 97–35) and were completely phased out by August 1985.

[50] Includes adult education, tribally controlled community colleges, other postsecondary schools, and in FY 91 also includes indirect administrative cost grants.

[51] This program was transferred to the International Communication Agency (I.C.A.) in the Reorganization Plan No. 2 of 1977, which consolidated the functions of the United States Information Agency (U.S.I.A.) and the Department of State's, Bureau of Educational and Cultural Affairs. In FY 82 the I.C.A. became the U.S.I.A.

[52] This program provides funds for advanced study and research projects of the Soviet Union and Eastern European countries by American institutions of higher education and private research firms. Appropriations began in FY 88.

[53] This program was transferred to the U.S. Department of Transportation in FY 81 by Public Law 97–31, from the U.S. Department of Commerce. FY 89 outlays are high because of the replacement of one of the training ships.

[54] Includes flight training. This program was in the U.S. Department of the Treasury in 1965 and was transferred to the U.S. Department of Transportation in 1967.

[55] Includes Vietnam-era veterans under Chapter 34 (GI Bill) of the "Readjustment Benefits" education and training program. This program provides educational assistance allowances, primarily on a monthly basis, in order to restore lost educational opportunities to those individuals whose careers were interrupted or impeded by reason of active mili-

tary service between January 31, 1955, and January 1, 1977. This program closed December 31, 1989. Some veterans who were still eligible were put in Chapter 30 (the All-Volunteer-Force Educational Assistance program).

[56] Includes service persons under Chapter 34 (GI Bill) of the "Readjustment Benefits" education and training program. Service persons with over 180 days of active duty, any part of which was before January 1, 1977, are eligible to participate in this program.

[57] Includes post-Vietnam-era veterans, under Chapter 32, of the post-Vietnam-era "Veterans Education Account." Provides education and training assistance payments to veterans and service persons with no active duty time before January 1, 1977. Funding is provided through participants' contributions while on active duty and through transfers from the U.S. Department of Defense (DOD). Participants' contributions, up to a maximum of $2,700, are deposited to the fund prior to discharge. When the participant enters training, the monthly disbursement from his or her account is matched two for one from funds provided by DOD. Additional amounts in the form of incentive bonuses may also be provided by DOD funds. The U.S. Department of Veterans Affairs funds are not appropriated for this program so these data represent obligations.

[58] Public Law 98–525, enacted October 19, 1984 (New GI Bill), established two new peacetime educational programs: An assistance program for veterans who enter active duty during the period beginning July 1, 1985, and ending on June 30, 1988, and an assistance program for certain members of the Selected Reserve.

[59] Chapter 30, also called the Montgomery Bill, and the new GI Bill are for eligible veterans who have agreed to have their military pay reduced $100 per month for their first 12 months of active duty in order to participate in this program. The "Readjustment Benefits" account under the U.S. Department of Veterans Affairs pays only the basic allowance, up to a maximum of $300 per month, for full-time training. "Supplemental Benefits" are paid by the U.S. Department of Defense (DOD).

[60] Chapter 106 is for members of the Selected Reserve. The reserve components include the Army, Navy, Air Force, Marine Corps Reserve, Army National Guard and Air National Guard under the U.S. Department of Defense (DOD), and the Coast Guard Reserve, which is under the U.S. Department of Transportation (DOT), when it is not operating as a service in the Navy. Eligible persons can receive up to $140 per month for full-time training. The DOD and DOT pay for this program, and the U.S. Department of Veterans Affairs administers it.

[61] Includes dependents of veterans under Chapter 35, the "Readjustment Benefits" education and training program. Provides education and training benefits to dependents of veterans who died of a service-connected disability or whose service-connected disability is rated permanent and total.

[62] These payments have been made to State education agencies for years but they were not available as a separate budget item until FY 88.

[63] The U.S.I.A. was called the "International Communication Agency" in FYs 80 and 81.

[64] This program was in the "Educational and Cultural Affairs" program in FYs 80 through 83, and became an independent program in FY 84.

[65] This program was combined with the "educational and cultural affairs" program in FY 77.

[66] Public Law 99–661 established this program to operate the scholarship program in tribute to the former Senator from Arizona. The Foundation will award scholarships and fellowships to outstanding graduate and undergraduate students who intend to pursue careers or advanced degrees in science or mathematics. The Foundation may also award honoraria to outstanding individuals who have made significant contributions to improve the instruction of science and mathematics in secondary schools.

[67] Appropriations for this program began in FY 76.

[68] Public Law 99–498 established this Institute as an independent non-profit corporation administered by a Board of Trustees. The Institute provides Native Americans with an opportunity to obtain a postsecondary education in various fields of Indian art and culture.

[69] Public Laws 99–500 and 99–591 established the James Madison Memorial Fellowship Foundation to operate a fellowship program to encourage graduate study of the American Constitution. First year of appropriations was FY 88.

[70] This program was transferred to the U.S. Department of Transportation in FY 68 from the U.S. Department of Housing and Urban Development.

[71] This program was established by the Juvenile Justice and Delinquency Prevention Act of 1974 to provide education and training and to provide leadership in improving correctional programs and practices in prisons. FY 75 had large outlays because of the construction of buildings and facilities.

[72] Appropriations for this program began in FY 70. This program is part of the Federal-Aid Highway Act of 1970, Public Law 91–605.

[73] The Federal Aviation Administration was an independent agency, and was transferred to the U.S. Department of Transportation in FY 67.

[74] Appropriations began in FY 72. No funds have been appropriated since FY 82.

[75] First year of appropriations was FY 70.

[76] This agency was established on July 1, 1971. This agency brings together a number of volunteer programs. Some of these funds were formerly in the Office of Economic Opportunity.

[77] These programs included the Service Learning Programs, University Year for Action, Youth Challenge Program, and the National Student Volunteer Program in FY 1975. In FYs 80 to 84, programs included were the University Year for Action, Young Volunteers for Action, and National Service Learning Programs. In fiscal years 1985 and 1986, the program included was the Service Learning Programs, and in FYs 87 to 90, programs included were the Literacy Corps and the Student Community Services Program.

[78] The Federal Emergency Management Agency was created on March 25, 1979, representing a combination of about five existing agencies. The two largest were the Defense Civil Preparedness Agency in the U.S. Department of Defense and the Federal Preparedness Agency in the General Services Administration.

[79] First year of appropriations was FY 68.

[80] First appropriations for the "other training programs" were in the late 1960s. These programs include the Fall-Out Shelter Analysis, Blast Protection Design, and Multi-Protection Design Summer Institute.

[81] This program was transferred from the General Services Administration to the National Archives and Records Administration in April 1985.

[82] This program makes grants for the promotion of scholarly, cultural, and artistic exchanges between Japan and the United States. Appropriations began in FY 76.

[83] The National Archives and Records Administration became an independent agency in April 1985.

[84] This program was established by the act of July 20, 1970, Public Law 91–345.

[85] This program was established by Congress to conduct and support research and scholarships in the fields of peace, arms control, and conflict resolution. This program began operation in February 1986.

[86] Includes Federal obligations for research and development centers administered by colleges and universities. FYs 89, 90, and 91 are estimated.

[87] Total outlays for FYs 65 and 70 include the "Research and Training" program. FY 75 includes the "National Institute of Education" program. FYs 80 to 91 include outlays for the Office of Educational Research and Improvement.

[88] Less than $50,000.

—Data not available or not applicable.

NOTE.—Some data have been revised from previously published figures. To the extent possible, amounts reported represent outlays rather than obligations.

SOURCE: U.S. Department of Education, National Center for Education Statistics, compiled from data appearing in U.S. Office of Management and Budget, *Budget of the U.S. Government,* fiscal years 1967 to 1992; National Science Foundation, *Federal Funds for Research and Development, fiscal years 1965 to 1991;* and unpublished data obtained from various Federal agencies. (This table was prepared April 1991.)

Table 339.—Federal on-budget funds obligated for programs administered by the Department of Education: Fiscal years 1980 to 1991

[In thousands of dollars]

Program	1980	1982	1984	1985	1986	1988	1989	1990	1991 [1]
1	2	3	4	5	6	7	8	9	10
Total	$14,102,165	$15,069,598	17,072,698	$18,818,201	$18,940,681	$20,697,311	$24,473,634	$25,214,653	$29,301,023
Elementary and secondary education	4,239,022	3,802,234	4,294,269	4,732,864	4,447,153	5,682,997	5,997,160	7,169,693	8,110,886
Grants for the disadvantaged	3,204,664	3,063,651	3,501,383	3,745,855	3,557,026	4,357,970	4,600,444	5,383,960	6,226,814
School improvement programs	788,918	524,730	549,117	748,000	658,676	1,067,213	1,129,444	1,524,001	1,610,678
Bilingual education	169,540	136,292	173,051	171,605	167,534	191,470	196,309	188,152	198,014
Indian education	75,900	77,561	70,718	67,404	63,917	66,344	70,963	73,580	75,380
School assistance in federally affected areas	812,873	457,227	608,791	695,746	677,055	731,241	731,768	815,573	808,286
Maintenance and operations	690,000	438,498	555,300	665,000	636,405	685,498	708,396	717,354	740,708
Construction	110,873	15,951	28,491	23,037	21,267	35,640	18,400	22,929	43,725
Disaster assistance	12,000	2,778	25,000	7,709	19,383	10,103	4,972	75,290	23,853
Education for the handicapped	1,555,253	2,023,536	2,416,799	2,666,056	2,573,399	3,075,456	3,814,846	3,480,122	5,091,091
State grant programs	815,805	933,657	1,082,180	1,245,219	1,087,249	1,115,333	1,642,647	1,258,871	2,407,086
Early childhood education [2]	38,745	40,673	53,164	27,625	15,991	210,752	319,012	280,341	612,914
Special centers, projects, and research	55,075	35,057	54,871	53,430	54,629	78,600	102,141	72,966	94,343
Captioned films and media services	17,778	11,438	14,000	35,670	36,105	13,026	13,346	15,191	16,424
Personnel training	55,375	48,911	55,540	68,025	68,339	66,153	67,023	70,838	69,289
Handicapped rehabilitation service and research	572,475	953,800	1,157,044	1,236,087	1,311,086	1,591,592	1,670,677	1,781,915	1,891,035
Vocational education and adult programs	1,153,743	751,118	954,320	856,271	1,016,302	1,000,055	1,052,470	1,138,674	1,317,000
Basic programs [3]	744,653	530,669	689,324	725,624	862,979	823,299	859,239	858,716	869,634
Consumer and homemaking	63,169	29,363	36,792	33,138	30,311	32,752	32,816	34,517	33,352
Program improvement and supportive services	162,512	91,650	117,249	5,202	—	—	—	—	—
State planning and advisory councils	13,423	8,800	11,200	7,584	6,761	7,681	7,945	7,923	9,128
Adult education, grants to States	153,724	90,636	99,755	84,723	109,791	129,183	139,771	188,280	268,903
Other	16,262	—	—	—	6,460	7,140	12,699	49,238	135,983
Postsecondary student financial assistance	5,108,534	6,584,012	7,478,401	8,534,205	8,932,803	8,807,929	11,482,608	11,112,068	12,185,673
Educational opportunity grants [4]	2,534,378	2,546,167	3,565,209	3,558,440	4,460,266	4,620,133	5,379,725	4,919,264	6,154,696
Work-study	596,065	523,910	561,322	599,467	576,145	604,445	620,644	615,269	598,574
Direct student loans	322,749	193,686	191,962	219,850	212,696	216,963	202,904	157,415	173,589
Guaranteed student loans	1,597,877	3,297,776	3,130,939	4,130,920	3,658,502	3,297,305	5,203,843	5,341,039	5,164,932
Other student assistance programs	57,465	22,473	28,969	25,528	25,194	69,083	75,492	79,081	93,882
Direct aid to postsecondary institutions	277,068	284,467	311,221	329,714	294,681	341,063	398,318	341,634	433,300
Aid to minority and developing institutions	114,680	119,829	132,081	140,374	125,895	135,222	179,062	99,812	99,542
Special programs for the disadvantaged	147,389	150,238	164,740	174,940	168,786	205,841	219,256	241,822	333,758
Cooperative education	14,999	14,400	14,400	14,400	—	—	—	—	—
Higher education facilities	268,493	449,191	216,893	194,556	206,017	162,528	77,362	84,035	107,391
Construction loans and insurance	35,362	38,690	54,105	33,188	26,800	89,820	37,109	30,000	29,277
Interest subsidy grants	24,626	23,759	23,925	24,968	23,981	24,466	22,524	38,471	43,064
College housing loans	208,505	386,742	138,863	136,400	155,236	48,242	17,729	15,564	35,050
Other higher education programs	34,927	38,226	82,410	74,340	64,032	79,305	73,574	188,999	225,603
International education and foreign languages	19,977	23,923	30,800	32,050	—	—	—	86,337	92,224
Fund for Improvement of Postsecondary Education	12,000	11,503	11,710	12,710	62,835	65,813	67,236	99,450	120,009
Other	2,950	2,800	39,900	29,580	1,197	13,492	6,338	3,212	13,370
Public library services	101,218	80,074	107,895	116,027	117,998	135,731	141,884	132,583	155,682
Public library services	66,451	60,000	65,000	75,000	71,774	78,922	80,944	82,505	83,898
Interlibrary cooperation	—	11,520	15,000	18,000	17,226	18,395	18,826	19,551	19,908
Public library construction	—	—	21,015	16,027	17,514	23,577	27,289	14,837	32,002
Research libraries	5,992	5,760	6,000	6,000	5,742	5,744	5,675	6,593	6,831
Other	28,775	2,794	880	1,000	5,742	9,093	9,150	9,097	13,043
Payments to special institutions	273,860	251,570	249,610	253,622	255,297	271,658	284,056	292,736	311,301
American Printing House for the Blind	4,349	5,000	5,000	5,500	5,263	5,266	5,335	5,663	6,136
National Technical Institute for the Deaf	19,799	26,300	28,000	31,400	30,624	31,594	33,326	35,594	37,688
Gallaudet College	49,409	64,815	56,288	59,092	59,334	62,195	65,998	67,643	72,262
Howard University	200,303	155,455	160,322	157,630	160,076	172,603	179,397	183,836	195,215
Departmental accounts	277,174	347,943	352,089	364,800	355,944	409,348	419,588	458,536	554,810
Educational research and improvement	51,415	61,550	57,165	60,556	57,514	68,147	78,263	87,074	135,215
Departmental management account	223,857	283,906	293,351	300,885	298,397	341,171	341,286	370,844	419,579
Other	1,875	2,290	1,401	3,349	—	—	—	—	—
Trust funds	27	197	172	10	33	30	39	618	16

[1] Estimated.

[2] Includes preschool incentive grants.

[3] Includes programs of national significance and special programs for the disadvantaged.

[4] Includes Pell Grants, Supplemental Education Opportunity Grants, State Student Incentive Grants, and Income Contingent Loans.

—Data are not available or not applicable.

NOTE.—Because of rounding, details may not add to totals. Data presented in this tabulation are obligations which differ from outlay figures reported in other tables in this chapter. Some data have been revised from previously published figures.

SOURCE: U.S. Office of Management and Budget, *Budget of the United States Government,* fiscal years 1982 to 1992. (This table was prepared March 1991.)

Table 340.—Department of Education outlays, by level of education and type of recipient: [1]
Fiscal years 1980 to 1991

[In millions of dollars]

Year and area of education	Total	Local education agencies	State education agencies	College students	Institutions of higher education	Federal	Multiple types of recipients	Other [2]
1	2	3	4	5	6	7	8	9
1980 total	**$13,137.8**	**$5,313.7**	**$1,103.2**	**$2,137.4**	**$2,267.2**	**$249.8**	**$693.8**	**$1,372.7**
Elementary/secondary	6,629.1	5,309.4	662.2	34.2	22.0	62.5	513.4	25.5
Postsecondary education	5,682.2	—	99.5	2,103.2	2,166.5	—	—	1,313.0
Other programs	747.7	4.3	341.5	—	—	187.3	180.4	34.2
Education research and statistics	78.7	—	—	—	78.7	—	—	—
1982 total	**14,109.3**	**5,425.8**	**1,414.2**	**1,610.2**	**1,951.8**	**268.3**	**535.4**	**2,903.6**
Elementary/secondary	6,456.3	5,420.8	593.8	48.9	21.9	2.6	340.3	27.9
Postsecondary education	6,418.8	—	196.6	1,561.3	1,847.7	—	195.1	2,813.2
Other programs	1,152.0	5.0	623.8	—	—	265.7	195.1	62.5
Education research and statistics	82.2	—	—	—	82.2	—	—	—
1983 total	**14,585.8**	**5,091.9**	**1,392.0**	**2,357.8**	**2,442.0**	**250.6**	**569.0**	**2,482.5**
Elementary/secondary	5,986.6	5,086.7	465.2	49.3	23.3	2.6	330.8	28.8
Postsecondary education	7,213.3	—	167.9	2,308.5	2,359.1	—	—	2,377.8
Other programs	1,326.3	5.2	758.9	—	—	248.0	238.2	75.9
Education research and statistics	59.6	—	—	—	59.6	—	—	—
1984 total	**15,534.7**	**5,256.5**	**1,879.0**	**2,193.4**	**2,167.4**	**330.2**	**516.7**	**3,191.4**
Elementary/secondary	6,220.8	5,252.4	536.0	55.5	35.3	22.9	259.9	58.8
Postsecondary education	7,341.2	—	211.5	2,137.9	1,972.5	—	—	3,019.3
Other programs	1,813.1	4.1	1,131.5	—	—	307.3	256.8	113.3
Education research and statistics	159.6	—	—	—	159.6	—	—	—
1985 total	**16,701.1**	**6,225.0**	**1,502.9**	**2,434.7**	**2,362.3**	**287.3**	**503.9**	**3,385.0**
Elementary/secondary	7,296.7	6,220.8	636.0	58.0	25.2	2.4	322.4	31.9
Postsecondary education	8,202.5	—	228.3	2,376.7	2,308.3	—	—	3,289.2
Other programs	1,173.1	4.2	638.6	—	—	284.9	181.5	63.9
Education research and statistics	28.8	—	—	—	28.8	—	—	—
1986 total	**17,740.1**	**6,435.1**	**1,823.3**	**2,685.9**	**2,637.2**	**265.4**	**625.8**	**3,267.5**
Elementary/secondary	7,552.0	6,432.1	558.5	68.3	45.2	2.2	372.0	73.8
Postsecondary education	8,444.9	—	215.6	2,617.6	2,523.0	—	—	3,088.7
Other programs	1,674.2	3.0	1,049.2	—	—	263.2	253.8	105.0
Education research and statistics	69.0	—	—	—	69.0	—	—	—
1987 total	**16,879.8**	**6,341.0**	**1,849.0**	**2,794.5**	**2,271.9**	**309.4**	**768.3**	**2,545.6**
Elementary/secondary	7,554.5	6,335.0	555.0	65.8	40.6	24.1	470.6	63.3
Postsecondary education	7,438.7	—	169.7	2,728.7	2,170.4	—	—	2,369.8
Other programs	1,825.8	6.0	1,124.3	—	—	285.3	297.7	112.6
Education research and statistics	60.9	—	—	—	60.9	—	—	—
1988 total	**18,326.9**	**6,614.8**	**2,234.6**	**3,103.4**	**2,519.5**	**319.4**	**838.8**	**2,696.3**
Elementary/secondary	8,098.4	6,606.3	717.9	66.2	39.5	23.8	616.7	28.0
Postsecondary education	8,247.1	—	184.60	3,037.2	2,437.6	—	—	2,587.7
Other programs	1,939.0	8.5	1,332.1	—	—	295.6	222.1	80.6
Education research and statistics	42.4	—	—	—	42.4	—	—	—
1989 total	**21,671.2**	**7,533.5**	**2,209.1**	**3,482.2**	**3,538.3**	**318.6**	**746.7**	**3,842.9**
Elementary/secondary	8,869.3	7,526.9	618.1	67.0	64.5	17.3	511.2	64.4
Postsecondary education	10,640.0	—	195.0	3,415.2	3,383.5	—	—	3,646.3
Other programs	2,071.6	6.6	1,396.0	—	—	301.3	235.5	132.2
Education research and statistics	90.3	—	—	—	90.3	—	—	—
1990 total	**23,198.6**	**8,000.7**	**2,490.3**	**3,859.6**	**3,649.8**	**441.4**	**912.2**	**3,844.5**
Elementary/secondary	9,681.3	7,995.0	700.3	80.5	85.4	113.1	650.7	56.3
Postsecondary education	11,176.0	—	261.6	3,779.1	3,475.0	—	—	3,660.4
Other programs	2,251.8	5.7	1,528.5	—	—	328.3	261.5	127.8
Education research and statistics	89.5	—	—	—	89.5	—	—	—
1991 total	**24,912.4**	**9,245.2**	**2,779.3**	**3,848.0**	**3,837.3**	**407.9**	**1,055.3**	**3,739.5**
Elementary/secondary	11,192.2	9,236.8	888.9	94.4	110.0	42.4	756.9	62.9
Postsecondary education	11,168.5	—	257.8	3,753.6	3,625.8	—	—	3,531.3
Other programs	2,450.2	8.4	1,632.6	—	—	365.5	298.4	145.3
Education research and statistics	101.5	—	—	—	101.5	—	—	—

[1] Outlays by type of recipient are estimated based on obligation data.
[2] Other recipients include Indian tribes, private nonprofit agencies, and banks.
—Data are not available or not applicable.

NOTE.—Some data have been revised from previously published figures. Because of rounding, details may not add to totals.

SOURCE: U.S. Department of Education, National Center for Education Statistics, unpublished data. (This table was prepared March 1991.)

Table 341.—Department of Education obligations for major programs, by State or other area: Fiscal year 1990

[In thousands]

State or other area	Total	Grants for the disad-vantaged [1]	Block grant to States for school improve-ment [2]	School as-sistance in federally affected areas [3]	Vocational and adult education [4]	Education for the handi-capped [5]	Bilingual educa-tion [6]	Indian educa-tion	Higher and con-tinuing educa-tion [7]	Student fi-nancial as-sistance [8]	Public library program	Rehabilita-tion services [9]
1	2	3	4	5	6	7	8	9	10	11	12	13
Total	$19,514,258	$5,321,387	$1,134,955	$680,000	$1,086,560	$1,524,819	$172,607	$66,255	$881,087	$6,952,994	$116,629	$1,576,967
Alabama	369,819	107,570	18,431	4,993	21,118	42,363	237	1,088	30,900	105,456	1,677	35,988
Alaska	130,252	17,923	5,121	73,418	5,000	5,187	1,087	6,354	1,922	8,180	424	5,636
Arizona	322,061	61,618	13,923	62,320	14,594	21,856	7,138	8,114	8,186	101,849	1,866	20,596
Arkansas	201,612	64,343	10,645	2,173	12,245	17,953	0	76	8,313	63,476	1,079	21,310
California	1,679,927	570,477	172,307	63,384	94,599	9,737	58,339	4,750	55,304	509,694	11,765	129,572
Colorado	226,687	49,036	12,744	7,561	12,589	18,145	1,703	655	9,317	95,220	1,396	18,321
Connecticut	186,785	56,853	11,645	7,383	19,655	25,229	822	27	5,857	44,529	1,685	13,099
Delaware	54,212	16,372	5,128	41	5,209	5,079	75	0	3,119	13,059	471	5,660
District of Columbia	262,867	24,987	5,106	1,345	5,276	1,693	1,732	27	193,663	19,085	456	9,497
Florida	780,793	235,657	42,591	13,696	45,230	88,567	3,814	248	17,268	259,583	5,434	68,706
Georgia	367,540	136,489	28,134	6,526	29,859	247	295	0	26,172	94,013	2,496	43,309
Hawaii	77,835	14,367	8,126	21,219	5,388	4,548	1,214	0	5,548	10,626	625	6,174
Idaho	86,334	17,923	5,217	4,815	5,327	11,641	605	190	2,547	29,231	745	8,093
Illinois	872,693	255,490	47,044	10,157	45,185	156,397	6,004	118	26,437	258,966	5,153	61,742
Indiana	340,226	79,476	35,597	1,790	25,505	1,637	728	14	9,653	144,038	2,582	39,205
Iowa	244,549	41,538	11,131	287	12,387	45,495	932	125	12,454	99,451	1,624	19,124
Kansas	187,122	37,229	9,709	9,302	10,163	14,323	312	312	7,986	81,084	1,388	15,313
Kentucky	291,891	91,522	16,247	1,150	19,481	34,500	146	0	11,920	83,223	1,545	32,158
Louisiana	390,128	122,630	20,766	5,079	22,303	23,161	1,654	411	19,145	136,923	1,784	36,271
Maine	100,805	27,767	5,849	2,888	5,741	13,149	340	67	7,443	26,857	825	9,879
Maryland	268,728	83,932	17,446	9,909	16,786	36,757	1,198	160	21,478	55,535	2,368	23,159
Massachusetts	439,032	128,291	20,855	5,249	22,000	55,759	4,573	323	21,253	146,071	2,716	31,942
Michigan	648,897	207,021	38,929	6,396	39,095	63,074	3,084	2,491	19,536	210,882	3,476	54,913
Minnesota	297,091	59,149	16,805	5,358	16,729	220	1,804	4,521	9,547	154,459	1,748	26,751
Mississippi	269,601	97,411	13,526	3,747	14,034	22,314	1,031	499	17,055	71,813	1,688	26,484
Missouri	341,619	84,695	20,128	5,374	21,964	36,646	488	2	9,275	124,934	2,424	35,689
Montana	107,141	14,563	5,161	21,363	5,252	12,474	2,362	3,103	4,516	31,170	612	6,566
Nebraska	171,828	23,868	6,422	8,006	7,058	12,586	331	467	4,073	97,634	999	10,382
Nevada	53,893	9,809	5,185	3,593	5,261	6,436	279	501	1,616	14,678	835	5,701
New Hampshire	53,670	13,284	5,192	2,534	5,349	7,439	75	0	2,124	10,347	778	6,548
New Jersey	476,364	167,682	29,162	11,814	26,334	72,084	2,081	81	14,041	115,733	3,455	33,897
New Mexico	178,279	39,379	7,059	36,041	7,588	12,870	7,321	5,913	4,684	44,140	911	12,375
New York	1,726,765	556,299	72,855	14,864	67,105	117,771	25,778	1,253	40,464	729,218	7,566	93,591
North Carolina	461,268	118,288	25,770	8,613	31,786	93,169	75	2,141	26,454	102,419	2,512	50,041
North Dakota	100,500	11,214	8,069	13,311	5,241	5,275	1,162	1,004	3,229	45,805	609	5,581
Ohio	714,236	176,473	43,594	4,384	47,020	74,270	792	47	17,031	271,513	4,865	74,248
Oklahoma	272,186	48,674	13,387	23,605	15,342	27,337	5,741	10,332	9,344	92,197	1,648	24,581
Oregon	190,386	54,297	10,530	3,333	11,554	18,032	2,332	1,035	6,731	63,046	1,456	18,040
Pennsylvania	920,002	256,376	45,407	3,484	49,091	80,166	1,046	198	25,371	373,045	6,039	79,779
Rhode Island	74,969	19,694	5,165	3,166	5,538	7,550	560	39	2,191	23,672	906	6,489
South Carolina	234,336	76,500	15,169	7,149	18,218	5,349	115	0	21,234	60,286	1,530	28,784
South Dakota	118,322	15,469	5,781	14,793	5,259	12,212	770	2,453	3,141	51,781	490	6,172
Tennessee	351,008	104,121	20,278	3,373	24,099	41,112	235	4	19,773	97,202	2,120	38,691
Texas	1,080,480	363,173	75,213	26,430	76,232	6,797	13,395	108	35,406	370,825	6,138	106,765
Utah	157,409	19,052	10,243	9,020	8,306	18,581	1,193	768	5,963	69,802	1,098	13,383
Vermont	50,790	13,871	5,114	11	5,135	4,768	75	94	2,454	13,155	441	5,673
Virginia	356,201	99,357	24,969	35,942	24,117	1,817	790	15	19,287	112,181	2,346	35,379
Washington	273,522	67,245	17,631	26,359	17,672	198	3,129	3,844	15,317	94,058	2,215	25,855
West Virginia	133,336	45,129	9,227	70	9,901	118	70	0	5,025	45,809	897	17,089
Wisconsin	342,121	72,814	19,372	6,083	20,583	38,121	491	1,629	11,355	136,563	2,362	32,747
Wyoming	55,232	6,937	5,114	7,316	5,066	7,975	667	655	1,601	14,093	469	5,337
Indian tribe setaside	86,034	27,345	1,365	0	12,971	38,113	0	0	0	0	2,419	3,821
Undistributed	727,683	11,680	0	46,506	0	0	0	0	0	669,480	0	18
Outlying areas												
American Samoa	8,961	3,013	1,059	0	398	3,248	280	0	241	113	84	526
Guam	17,758	2,994	2,814	1,709	795	4,684	75	0	1,723	1,279	92	1,593
Northern Marianas	6,093	2,212	507	0	384	1,719	97	0	463	299	78	334
Puerto Rico	546,958	182,319	21,677	800	19,615	27,363	1,128	0	13,094	252,741	1,122	27,100
Trust Territory of the Pacific	4,102	1,534	408	0	99	685	588	0	664	0	12	112
Virgin Islands	23,321	6,957	2,908	773	725	8,821	220	0	1,176	475	87	1,179

[1] Chapter 1, Education Consolidation and Improvement Act of 1981.

[2] Includes Chapter 2, Education Consolidation and Improvement Act of 1981, Science and Mathematics Education, Drug-Free Schools and Communities, and Education of Homeless Children and Youth.

[3] Includes Maintenance and Operations.

[4] Includes Vocational Education—Basic State Grants, Community Based Organizations, Consumer and Homemaker Education, State Councils, and Adult Education-State Administered Program.

[5] Includes State Grants, Preschool Incentive Grants to States, and Grants for Infants and Families.

[6] Also includes Emergency Immigrant Education Program and Transition Program for Refugee Children.

[7] Includes Institutional Aid to Strengthen Higher Education Institutions serving significant numbers of low-income students, Other Special Programs for the Disadvantaged, Cooperative Education, Fund for the Improvement of Postsecondary Education, Fellowships and Scholarships, and annual interest subsidy grants for facilities construction.

[8] Includes Basic Educational Opportunity Grants (Pell Grants), State Student Incentive Grants, and National Guaranteed Student Loan interest subsidies.

[9] Includes Rehabilitation Services Basic State Grants, Client Assistance for Handicapped Individuals, Independent Living, and Supported Employment Services.

NOTE.—Data reflect revisions to figures in the Budget of the United States Government, Fiscal Year 1992. To the extent possible, data represent obligations rather than outlays. Because of the exclusion of certain programs, totals in this table are lower than those reported in other tables. Because of rounding, details may not add to totals.

SOURCE: U.S. Department of Education, National Center for Education Statistics, based on unpublished tabulations from the Office of Management and Budget; and U.S. Department of Commerce, Bureau of the Census, Federal Expenditures by State for Fiscal Year 1990. (This table was prepared February 1991.)

Table 342.—Department of Education obligations for major programs, by State or other area: Fiscal year 1989 [1]

[In thousands]

State or other area	Total	Grants for the disad-vantaged [2]	Block grant to States for school improve-ment [3]	School as-sistance in federally affected areas [4]	Vocational and adult education [5]	Education for the handi-capped [6]	Bilingual educa-tion [7]	Indian educa-tion	Higher and con-tinuing educa-tion [8]	Student fi-nancial as-sistance [9]	Public library program	Rehabilita-tion services [10]
1	2	3	4	5	6	7	8	9	10	11	12	13
Total	$19,466,545	$4,525,724	$806,278	$723,216	$1,018,453	$1,961,609	$181,850	$80,118	$818,603	$7,729,590	$127,050	$1,494,055
Alabama	353,632	89,529	15,246	5,981	20,153	44,274	15	1,005	25,661	115,179	2,306	34,284
Alaska	126,179	16,355	4,402	73,787	4,771	5,352	1,043	6,859	1,332	6,492	421	5,365
Arizona	323,473	53,211	11,469	66,015	13,529	21,529	7,136	8,014	6,627	114,835	1,410	19,698
Arkansas	199,178	54,295	8,891	2,361	11,667	18,960	29	78	10,945	70,163	1,589	20,201
California	1,822,907	496,138	30,400	64,996	87,171	340,974	60,436	5,653	50,655	554,133	11,756	120,594
Colorado	227,705	42,155	10,953	8,110	12,113	22,026	2,081	786	8,663	101,898	2,163	16,758
Connecticut	176,039	49,056	9,986	7,169	1,896	23,107	869	22	7,117	62,099	1,670	13,047
Delaware	70,593	15,135	4,402	93	5,001	3,909	130	0	2,702	33,394	463	5,364
District of Columbia	258,059	22,190	4,402	1,870	5,059	5	1,266	233	188,539	24,151	1,176	9,169
Florida	748,142	198,303	35,183	14,486	42,391	81,818	6,420	272	17,475	281,939	5,358	64,495
Georgia	363,186	120,189	23,281	7,611	28,167	38,814	441	0	24,377	75,913	2,430	41,963
Hawaii	75,573	12,714	1,421	21,165	5,104	9,036	1,293	0	4,841	13,350	960	5,689
Idaho	90,514	15,788	4,402	4,658	5,102	12,516	533	427	2,372	36,385	910	7,422
Illinois	705,267	216,829	40,151	11,400	43,029	3,412	5,691	121	21,185	300,080	4,992	58,378
Indiana	341,241	68,937	6,544	1,932	24,530	35,464	795	14	9,941	152,811	2,822	37,452
Iowa	196,401	35,439	9,727	346	11,896	92	783	109	8,770	109,635	1,639	17,966
Kansas	253,333	32,284	8,312	10,652	9,357	17,140	328	556	9,544	149,324	1,321	14,516
Kentucky	297,871	76,752	13,689	1,599	18,653	35,995	206	0	12,014	106,690	1,878	30,396
Louisiana	414,371	103,256	17,401	7,848	21,686	48,644	1,847	511	16,433	161,833	2,350	32,563
Maine	103,628	23,547	3,767	3,080	5,544	23,227	289	60	5,021	28,565	1,011	9,517
Maryland	273,529	70,802	14,557	11,386	16,304	35,131	1,365	150	13,491	85,895	2,107	22,341
Massachusetts	410,218	110,928	17,776	5,709	21,261	50,114	4,532	628	19,423	145,504	2,756	31,587
Michigan	689,170	174,471	33,162	8,262	38,041	110,693	3,789	2,039	18,364	242,965	4,132	53,251
Minnesota	315,919	51,706	14,223	6,441	16,300	36,485	2,338	7,308	8,864	144,505	2,184	25,567
Mississippi	264,764	81,248	11,038	5,341	13,486	21,852	949	1,590	16,868	86,088	1,165	25,139
Missouri	379,868	69,991	17,012	5,531	20,993	68,140	709	3	8,050	152,392	3,163	33,885
Montana	93,682	13,754	4,402	21,456	5,038	366	2,022	4,559	6,118	29,024	674	6,270
Nebraska	184,315	20,990	5,484	8,525	6,633	12,184	409	510	4,135	114,887	891	9,668
Nevada	54,091	8,992	4,402	3,904	5,046	5,999	675	863	1,681	16,427	686	5,416
New Hampshire	53,479	10,842	4,402	2,307	5,121	6,168	89	0	3,949	13,360	776	6,465
New Jersey	478,216	142,058	24,533	12,056	25,023	71,456	2,528	72	11,325	151,649	3,506	34,010
New Mexico	170,641	33,801	5,800	36,758	7,225	11,706	7,321	6,509	3,966	44,864	1,017	11,675
New York	1,730,475	470,199	59,790	17,772	63,981	85,636	26,072	1,057	40,867	866,636	9,029	89,436
North Carolina	365,363	100,357	21,742	9,140	30,539	1,910	107	2,075	25,441	123,244	2,986	47,820
North Dakota	68,516	10,331	1,471	6,297	5,028	5,219	1,528	2,408	2,741	27,514	629	5,349
Ohio	674,810	147,022	37,386	5,156	44,846	70,341	1,105	40	17,614	276,304	4,818	70,179
Oklahoma	263,836	41,390	11,477	23,779	14,662	23,855	5,408	11,148	9,303	98,850	1,702	22,262
Oregon	195,709	45,396	9,131	3,465	10,918	29,171	1,728	946	7,184	69,593	1,464	16,713
Pennsylvania	910,115	218,266	38,693	4,383	47,584	79,704	1,376	390	21,670	416,605	5,333	76,112
Rhode Island	76,138	16,565	4,402	2,910	5,276	7,280	1,180	36	2,160	29,063	915	6,350
South Carolina	256,136	64,867	12,626	7,422	17,295	37,291	62	0	13,944	73,187	1,889	27,552
South Dakota	120,016	13,107	3,767	14,433	5,044	364	801	2,799	2,734	70,407	712	5,848
Tennessee	367,848	86,820	17,011	4,049	23,170	72,280	422	3	17,718	106,559	2,719	37,098
Texas	1,145,533	317,269	64,046	28,776	70,575	121,808	13,237	99	30,264	394,929	7,268	97,260
Utah	145,914	16,415	7,035	9,362	7,821	15,561	891	1,001	5,651	68,735	957	12,487
Vermont	55,928	11,521	4,402	19	5,380	6,761	79	83	5,581	16,174	529	5,397
Virginia	375,346	82,515	16,373	37,278	23,144	47,851	1,388	15	15,676	114,055	3,273	33,778
Washington	315,945	61,581	15,011	28,125	16,727	33,680	3,947	5,318	12,831	112,487	2,213	24,023
West Virginia	149,479	39,429	5,905	352	9,528	16,766	75	0	4,633	54,917	1,417	16,458
Wisconsin	398,180	63,997	16,499	6,214	19,875	59,664	732	2,921	14,389	181,141	2,564	30,185
Wyoming	47,721	6,725	4,402	7,212	4,838	530	536	738	1,297	15,518	542	5,384
Indian tribe setaside	63,153	25,217	3,499	0	13,493	18,495	0	0	0	0	2,449	0
Undistributed	686,276	0	7,000	61,910	0	0	0	91	0	617,275	0	0
Outlying areas												
American Samoa	3,254	402	1,085	0	373	106	210	0	279	220	85	495
Guam	14,844	160	2,490	0	1,265	4,896	261	0	2,722	1,394	232	1,424
Northern Marianas	2,726	180	672	0	362	209	206	0	584	117	78	318
Puerto Rico	504,990	154,144	17,007	1,550	18,669	1,307	1,458	0	11,614	267,279	1,415	30,547
Trust Territory ofthe Pacific	2,841	0	819	0	92	712	490	0	540	1	12	174
Virgin Islands	10,263	167	1,711	777	677	3,627	194	0	710	958	142	1,300

[1] Revised from previously published data.

[2] Chapter 1, Education Consolidation and Improvement Act of 1981.

[3] Includes Chapter 2, Education Consolidation and Improvement Act of 1981, Science and Mathematics Education, Drug-Free Schools and Communities, and Education of Homeless Children and Youth.

[4] Includes Maintenance and Operations.

[5] Includes Vocational Education—Basic State Grants, Community Based Organizations, Consumer and Homemaker Education, State Councils, and Adult Education-State Administered Program.

[6] Includes State Grants, Preschool Incentive Grants to States, and Grants for Infants and Families.

[7] Also includes Emergency Immigrant Education Program and Transition Program for Refugee Children.

[8] Includes Institutional Aid to Strengthen Higher Education Institutions serving significant numbers of low-income students, Other Special Programs for the Disadvantaged,

Cooperative Education, Fund for the Improvement of Postsecondary Education, Fellowships and Scholarships, and annual interest subsidy grants for facilities construction.

[9] Includes Basic Educational Opportunity Grants (Pell Grants), State Student Incentive Grants, and National Guaranteed Student Loan interest subsidies.

[10] Includes Rehabilitation Services Basic State Grants, Client Assistance for Handicapped Individuals, Independent Living, and Supported Employment Services.

NOTE.—Data reflect revisions to figures in the Budget of the United States Government, Fiscal Year 1991. To the extent possible, data represent obligations rather than outlays. Because of the exclusion of certain programs, totals in this table are lower than those reported in other tables. Because of rounding, details may not add to totals.

SOURCE: U.S. Department of Education, National Center for Education Statistics, based on unpublished tabulations from the Office of Management and Budget; and U.S. Department of Commerce, Bureau of the Census, Federal Expenditures by State for Fiscal Year 1989. (This table was prepared February 1991.)

Table 343.—Department of Education obligations for major programs, by State or other area: Fiscal year 1988 [1]

[In thousands]

State or other area	Total	Grants for the disadvantaged [1]	Block grant to States for school improvement [2]	School assistance in federally affected areas [3]	Vocational and adult education [4]	Education for the handicapped [5]	Bilingual education [6]	Indian education	Higher and continuing education [7]	Student financial assistance [8]	Public library program	Rehabilitation services [9]
1	2	3	4	5	6	7	8	9	10	11	12	13
Total	$17,262,360	$4,325,473	$785,981	$670,180	$973,793	$1,302,684	$133,353	$60,090	$547,601	$6,921,930	$120,894	$1,420,381
Alabama	298,216	80,577	13,427	5,431	19,106	47,057	94	972	26,125	70,849	2,093	32,484
Alaska	126,665	14,510	3,903	79,385	4,101	3,547	1,331	6,814	4,107	3,293	554	5,121
Arizona	269,107	45,388	9,959	52,710	12,690	20,757	5,605	5,101	7,403	89,613	1,658	18,223
Arkansas	168,622	57,336	7,781	2,174	11,087	17,213	144	75	7,506	44,898	1,369	19,039
California	1,281,811	467,828	78,250	61,841	81,920	829	36,454	3,862	33,977	394,445	11,193	111,213
Colorado	189,916	38,971	9,779	7,851	11,362	16,803	2,495	522	6,797	77,779	1,531	16,026
Connecticut	183,283	47,713	9,123	6,912	10,413	23,159	408	19	4,225	67,143	1,645	12,523
Delaware	67,397	14,509	3,903	65	4,905	4,511	50	0	1,811	32,064	452	5,127
District of Columbia	258,300	20,498	3,903	1,263	5,011	1,785	880	110	172,788	42,691	454	8,917
Florida	657,131	193,405	29,677	11,111	39,388	64,686	3,453	94	12,108	236,994	5,714	60,501
Georgia	333,939	107,568	20,150	7,067	26,353	37,313	193	0	23,467	69,712	2,570	39,547
Hawaii	65,215	13,534	3,903	20,246	5,059	339	1,104	0	2,736	11,942	940	5,412
Idaho	71,316	14,710	3,903	4,613	5,030	7,219	564	179	1,792	25,576	596	7,134
Illinois	737,366	203,724	36,083	11,862	41,903	77,999	3,770	115	18,095	282,141	5,998	55,676
Indiana	351,044	65,025	17,961	1,897	23,840	68,977	876	12	7,062	126,971	2,406	36,016
Iowa	207,952	33,092	9,091	219	11,883	21,780	246	240	8,029	104,285	1,557	17,530
Kansas	225,406	31,997	7,437	10,711	9,081	30,123	50	621	7,653	112,658	1,348	13,727
Kentucky	259,791	72,631	12,353	1,317	17,894	25,339	195	0	10,755	87,924	2,236	29,147
Louisiana	341,102	101,364	15,491	8,302	21,406	7,349	1,785	410	14,046	136,249	2,170	32,530
Maine	82,235	22,157	3,903	3,196	5,564	9,902	641	55	3,687	23,356	639	9,135
Maryland	281,215	72,001	13,022	8,206	16,096	64,336	642	145	13,985	69,781	1,744	21,258
Massachusetts	366,843	107,587	16,107	11,432	21,010	19,586	2,801	335	15,139	139,650	2,758	30,439
Michigan	522,186	168,575	30,059	6,800	37,581	2,453	4,225	2,094	17,930	198,633	4,082	49,753
Minnesota	298,148	48,909	12,956	5,270	16,115	28,519	1,731	3,901	8,478	145,141	2,656	24,471
Mississippi	246,385	75,073	9,604	3,653	12,910	28,306	872	835	12,440	77,392	1,370	23,931
Missouri	280,598	64,905	15,458	6,314	20,728	3,036	479	2	5,610	129,911	2,136	32,018
Montana	92,457	12,909	3,903	22,940	4,977	5,579	1,560	3,325	3,602	27,022	682	5,957
Nebraska	141,235	19,717	5,042	8,990	6,444	11,320	364	374	2,470	75,683	1,072	9,759
Nevada	49,833	8,840	3,903	3,047	4,971	5,968	688	487	1,289	14,720	725	5,194
New Hampshire	48,571	10,020	3,903	2,575	5,045	6,014	113	0	2,153	11,844	751	6,153
New Jersey	437,633	131,269	22,062	12,328	24,351	57,329	2,028	70	11,702	140,472	3,453	32,569
New Mexico	149,778	30,206	5,028	37,834	6,945	11,388	6,328	4,338	3,087	32,867	931	10,825
New York	1,529,260	440,869	55,817	14,546	63,120	1,486	22,069	1,166	37,339	800,693	6,314	85,840
North Carolina	395,008	96,705	19,614	9,006	29,005	71,341	124	1,843	23,257	95,639	2,919	45,554
North Dakota	77,013	9,627	3,903	9,998	4,952	4,710	1,352	1,319	2,530	32,915	611	5,097
Ohio	656,544	145,829	34,436	4,852	43,809	69,529	1,088	43	20,251	266,563	4,763	65,382
Oklahoma	238,722	42,431	10,335	22,828	13,919	25,540	3,788	10,213	7,757	78,661	1,720	21,530
Oregon	157,392	44,594	8,174	3,021	10,520	62	1,284	847	5,156	65,985	1,446	16,303
Pennsylvania	835,569	213,156	34,674	3,940	46,983	74,880	1,338	125	23,242	359,095	5,229	72,907
Rhode Island	70,637	15,630	3,903	2,811	5,173	7,885	714	36	5,912	21,676	735	6,162
South Carolina	220,011	62,059	11,148	5,809	16,299	25,606	0	0	12,561	58,210	2,060	26,260
South Dakota	108,011	11,448	3,903	14,790	4,978	5,776	962	1,728	1,733	56,557	486	5,650
Tennessee	274,414	83,517	15,183	3,579	22,034	4,030	236	3	13,950	94,472	2,142	35,268
Texas	1,029,020	310,755	55,295	26,784	65,074	116,773	10,529	84	27,434	315,346	8,310	92,636
Utah	131,605	14,886	6,929	8,937	7,366	15,973	884	864	6,896	56,070	1,017	11,783
Vermont	44,228	11,365	3,903	11	4,414	805	50	142	3,548	14,228	587	5,175
Virginia	332,177	78,250	16,928	34,221	22,367	38,627	481	15	11,795	94,707	2,684	32,103
Washington	275,722	60,700	13,365	26,849	15,682	28,990	2,094	4,144	9,387	89,550	2,192	22,770
West Virginia	140,235	37,118	6,404	97	9,215	16,764	0	0	3,512	50,154	1,059	15,912
Wisconsin	286,091	61,524	15,078	5,557	19,642	1,308	435	1,758	8,261	139,926	2,129	30,472
Wyoming	49,705	6,422	3,903	7,231	4,760	6,856	410	644	998	12,819	550	5,112
Indian tribe setaside	46,769	27,247	598	0	0	16,519	0	0	0	0	2,405	0
Undistributed	916,307	0	0	35,918	0	0	50	14	0	880,325	0	0
Outlying areas												
American Samoa	7,062	3,491	764	0	390	1,439	182	0	149	94	84	469
Guam	15,440	3,901	2,031	0	345	4,202	568	0	1,719	1,233	91	1,350
Northern Marianas	5,031	1,737	360	0	360	714	569	0	784	129	77	301
Puerto Rico	467,051	130,201	14,545	1,029	17,408	30,564	1,068	0	10,937	232,544	1,697	27,059
Trust Territory of the Pacific	13,763	8,976	1,567	0	97	1,580	752	0	93	0	13	686
Virgin Islands	13,440	6,490	2,197	804	714	207	156	0	896	643	87	1,246

[1] Data revised from previously published figures.

[2] Chapter 1, Education Consolidation and Improvement Act of 1981.

[3] Includes Chapter 2, Education Consolidation and Improvement Act of 1981, Science and Mathematics Education, Drug-Free Schools and Communities, and Education of Homeless Children and Youth.

[4] Includes Maintenance and Operations.

[5] Includes Vocational Education—Basic State Grants, Community Based Organizations, Consumer and Homemaker Education, State Councils, Adult Education-State Administered Program, and Adult Education for the Homeless.

[6] Includes State Grants, Preschool Incentive Grants to States, and Grants for Infants and Families.

[7] Includes Institutional Aid to Strengthen Higher Education Institutions serving significant numbers of low-income students, Other Special Programs for the Disadvantaged, Cooperative Education, Fund for the Improvement of Postsecondary Education, Fellowships and Scholarships, and annual interest subsidy grants for facilities construction.

[8] Includes Basic Educational Opportunity Grants (Pell Grants), State Student Incentive Grants, and National Guaranteed Student Loan interest subsidies.

[9] Includes Rehabilitation Services Basic State Grants, Client Assistance for Handicapped Individuals, Independent Living, and Supported Employment Services.

NOTE.—To the extent possible, data represent obligations rather than outlays. Because of the exclusion of certain programs, totals in this table are lower than those reported in other tables. Because of rounding, details may not add to totals.

SOURCE: U.S. Department of Education, National Center for Education Statistics, based on unpublished tabulations from the Office of Management and Budget; and U.S. Department of Commerce, Bureau of the Census, *Federal Expenditures by State for Fiscal Year 1988.* (This table was prepared March 1991.)

Table 344.—Appropriations for Chapter 1 and Chapter 2, Education Consolidation and Improvement Act of 1981, by State or other area: 1989–90 and 1990–91

[In thousands]

State or other area	Chapter 1 total, school year 1989–90 [2]	Chapter 1, school year 1990–91 [1]			State schools		Migrant children	State administration	Other [3]	Chapter 2	
		Total	Concentration grants	Local education agencies, basic grant	Handicapped children	Neglected and delinquent children				Fiscal year 1989	Fiscal year 1990
1	2	3	4	5	6	7	8	9	10	11	12
Total	$4,543,570	$5,318,284	$395,112	$4,373,146	$146,389	$32,791	$282,444	$50,176	$38,226	$462,977	$455,717
Alabama	89,528	107,565	11,354	92,295	358	354	1,915	943	346	7,969	7,805
Alaska	16,354	17,920	458	7,413	1,894	158	7,515	375	106	2,296	2,262
Arizona	53,210	61,618	5,389	47,227	733	406	7,041	540	280	6,127	6,233
Arkansas	54,294	64,340	6,034	51,609	1,431	244	4,236	564	222	4,605	4,536
California	494,559	570,437	47,290	415,885	1,970	3,010	93,156	5,002	4,125	48,473	48,717
Colorado	42,154	49,032	2,632	40,319	2,814	268	2,370	430	200	5,865	5,766
Connecticut	49,431	56,847	3,151	47,303	2,866	457	2,010	499	562	5,264	5,118
Delaware	15,134	16,371	1,001	12,389	1,755	94	586	375	172	2,296	2,262
District of Columbia	22,189	24,986	2,447	19,575	1,967	367	87	375	169	2,296	2,262
Florida	198,299	235,645	20,047	184,154	4,007	900	23,534	2,066	936	18,342	18,545
Georgia	120,186	136,479	12,461	118,031	1,226	677	2,435	1,197	452	12,205	12,198
Hawaii	12,714	14,533	648	12,792	549	52	0	375	118	2,296	2,262
Idaho	15,788	17,922	648	13,136	190	87	3,373	375	113	2,296	2,262
Illinois	216,825	255,476	18,456	205,643	24,728	949	1,949	2,240	1,511	21,076	20,432
Indiana	68,938	79,467	2,267	69,484	4,563	632	1,140	697	684	10,470	10,226
Iowa	35,438	41,533	1,075	38,394	745	313	219	375	412	5,196	4,975
Kansas	32,352	37,222	1,229	29,477	1,380	706	3,783	375	271	4,440	4,403
Kentucky	76,775	91,515	8,529	77,422	1,438	523	2,176	803	624	7,155	6,947
Louisiana	103,254	122,622	11,789	103,244	1,685	544	3,178	1,075	1,108	9,016	8,815
Maine	23,587	27,764	1,367	21,530	636	239	3,435	375	183	2,296	2,262
Maryland	70,798	82,835	5,315	73,743	1,114	1,121	376	726	439	7,678	7,624
Massachusetts	110,926	128,282	8,397	101,199	11,025	713	4,591	1,125	1,232	9,181	8,901
Michigan	174,970	207,005	13,457	171,159	7,685	1,401	10,500	1,815	987	17,402	16,935
Minnesota	51,705	59,146	2,801	52,433	210	256	2,058	519	868	7,639	7,576
Mississippi	81,247	97,407	9,985	83,481	357	323	1,914	854	492	5,623	5,489
Missouri	69,334	83,951	6,239	73,821	1,248	437	726	736	745	9,113	8,987
Montana	13,477	14,561	585	12,636	409	138	291	375	127	2,296	2,262
Nebraska	20,687	23,866	1,200	21,309	135	200	340	375	306	2,928	2,878
Nevada	8,992	9,806	428	7,791	265	210	631	375	106	2,296	2,262
New Hampshire	10,759	13,283	340	11,165	986	127	123	375	166	2,296	2,262
New Jersey	141,789	167,664	12,709	144,240	3,894	1,772	1,544	1,470	2,034	12,777	12,417
New Mexico	33,800	39,376	4,109	32,946	114	266	1,306	375	260	3,025	3,002
New York	470,188	556,258	46,821	470,005	18,011	3,448	6,349	4,878	6,746	30,179	29,371
North Carolina	100,353	118,271	8,960	103,086	1,052	1,031	2,782	1,037	324	11,527	11,341
North Dakota	10,330	11,208	603	9,188	320	38	526	375	158	2,296	2,262
Ohio	147,017	176,374	9,682	156,034	4,262	2,293	1,343	1,547	1,213	20,000	19,546
Oklahoma	41,389	48,665	3,551	43,044	337	171	977	427	157	6,156	6,042
Oregon	45,937	54,219	648	37,664	6,219	658	8,348	475	206	4,809	4,727
Pennsylvania	216,523	256,065	13,705	218,179	14,323	1,019	3,028	2,246	3,566	20,048	19,612
Rhode Island	16,565	19,684	1,470	16,622	624	245	158	375	191	2,296	2,262
South Carolina	64,864	76,486	7,003	67,308	283	759	252	671	210	6,641	6,557
South Dakota	13,106	15,465	1,194	13,378	175	81	61	375	201	2,296	2,262
Tennessee	86,817	104,102	10,554	90,925	524	707	185	913	293	8,948	8,758
Texas	317,269	363,056	29,038	278,436	6,263	1,340	43,297	3,184	1,499	33,756	33,335
Utah	16,414	18,906	648	15,740	1,023	166	850	375	103	4,314	4,317
Vermont	11,521	13,842	510	10,230	1,709	119	763	375	136	2,296	2,262
Virginia	82,731	100,359	7,601	89,962	678	519	415	880	305	10,063	9,911
Washington	61,581	69,258	2,453	50,589	2,060	1,063	12,181	607	304	8,017	8,034
West Virginia	39,429	45,113	3,798	39,240	1,279	221	42	396	139	3,616	3,469
Wisconsin	63,995	72,774	3,123	64,953	2,014	641	813	638	590	8,851	8,710
Wyoming	6,735	6,922	340	5,487	225	159	239	375	97	2,296	2,262
Other activities											
Bureau of Indian Affairs	25,217	27,345	0	27,345	0	0	0	0	0	0	0
Migrant coordination activities	7,780	8,415	0	0	0	0	8,415	0	0	0	0
Outlying areas											
American Samoa	1,962	3,014	0	2,926	23	0	0	50	15	448	449
Guam	2,201	2,988	0	2,765	158	0	0	50	15	1,266	1,270
Northern Marianas	1,072	2,210	0	2,103	26	0	16	50	15	225	225
Puerto Rico	154,570	182,317	19,568	156,532	225	168	2,866	1,599	1,359	8,535	8,390
Trust Territory of the Pacific	4,502	1,534	0	1,335	134	0	0	50	15	581	182
Virgin Islands	4,008	6,957	0	6,826	66	0	0	50	15	1,286	1,290

[1] Data are based on fiscal year 1990 budget authorizations. Excludes $11,853,000 for evaluation and studies; $4,445,000 for rural technical assistance (Rural Tacs); and $24,201,000 for Even Start.

[2] Data are based on fiscal year 1989 budget appropriations. Excludes $7,904,000 for evaluation and studies; $3,952,000 for rural technical assistance (Rural Tacs); and $14,820,000 for Even Start.

[3] Includes capital expenses and State program improvement grants.

NOTE.—Because of rounding, details may not add to totals.

SOURCE: U.S. Department of Education, Office of Planning, Budget, and Evaluation, special tabulations. (This table was prepared March 1991.)

Table 345.—Federal obligations to colleges and universities, by agency and State: Fiscal year 1988 [1]

[In thousands]

State or other area	Total	Department of Agriculture	Department of Defense	Department of Education	Department of Energy	Environmental Protection Agency	Department of Health and Human Services	National Aeronautics and Space Administration	National Science Foundation	Other [2]
1	2	3	4	5	6	7	8	9	10	11
United States	$17,541,962	$729,910	$1,753,034	$4,659,289	$2,992,082	$66,076	$4,755,474	$1,208,590	$1,151,552	$225,955
Alabama	249,118	19,413	11,454	101,365	12,214	8	82,737	13,670	5,516	2,741
Alaska	23,955	2,811	716	5,589	953	0	919	2,755	7,417	2,795
Arizona	186,707	10,830	9,909	48,647	13,567	1,085	41,697	13,802	40,963	6,207
Arkansas	84,001	14,361	515	57,996	783	365	8,292	184	1,300	205
California	3,420,059	25,851	151,039	319,997	1,107,699	5,327	690,683	925,720	180,557	13,186
Colorado	230,633	8,429	13,437	66,352	6,221	1,039	77,111	13,683	22,905	21,456
Connecticut	231,478	3,906	10,948	33,280	9,663	875	150,321	1,009	15,686	5,790
Delaware	27,618	3,686	3,634	9,756	660	48	3,422	720	4,331	1,361
District of Columbia	307,405	1,926	14,078	221,571	1,273	683	55,289	5,293	4,780	2,512
Florida	358,838	15,958	46,213	143,515	19,749	2,278	99,503	5,829	20,462	5,331
Georgia	299,505	21,237	66,004	87,026	12,348	2,213	88,190	4,536	13,589	4,362
Hawaii	58,779	5,097	2,140	12,547	1,801	37	12,316	6,492	10,026	8,323
Idaho	39,011	6,744	369	25,341	857	410	1,314	640	775	2,561
Illinois	958,145	20,801	30,961	202,744	438,356	2,773	176,584	9,054	72,085	4,787
Indiana	219,804	16,306	11,917	88,778	11,786	964	58,799	3,017	26,340	1,897
Iowa	217,027	24,122	3,742	80,538	21,882	1,424	69,431	7,749	7,143	996
Kansas	113,502	14,117	1,590	68,065	1,888	412	19,763	1,601	5,210	856
Kentucky	124,882	20,032	1,140	75,340	1,946	135	21,977	620	2,955	737
Louisiana	199,174	14,683	5,712	105,420	14,608	862	48,414	1,686	4,910	2,879
Maine	38,712	4,858	232	27,812	0	870	2,172	140	2,258	370
Maryland	761,456	9,955	416,344	71,903	8,797	1,271	206,925	14,454	25,820	5,987
Massachusetts	1,110,075	19,139	456,151	130,284	76,787	1,461	288,271	21,421	106,038	10,523
Michigan	433,177	20,831	16,942	167,423	11,861	1,816	156,006	9,904	43,200	5,194
Minnesota	248,301	16,878	5,416	105,999	4,990	964	93,415	1,865	18,002	772
Mississippi	146,500	23,614	12,342	90,770	4,267	181	9,989	1,041	1,292	3,004
Missouri	254,409	19,494	2,378	89,396	2,332	322	123,242	2,352	11,342	3,551
Montana	34,262	5,493	249	19,210	273	452	2,818	307	2,239	3,221
Nebraska	74,875	10,612	795	39,998	578	0	14,886	535	4,091	3,380
Nevada	20,986	2,455	90	4,930	615	3,185	3,598	98	2,272	3,743
New Hampshire	57,324	3,312	2,400	16,613	1,041	487	21,348	5,430	4,332	2,361
New Jersey	306,764	7,526	13,224	78,227	115,452	956	56,155	3,335	26,167	5,722
New Mexico	710,830	5,501	23,018	39,431	602,095	211	13,824	20,243	5,624	883
New York	1,587,867	21,432	68,705	449,485	281,268	7,265	575,836	14,184	152,761	16,931
North Carolina	412,890	28,272	15,117	119,052	6,196	5,385	210,898	3,878	19,564	4,528
North Dakota	54,401	18,093	352	26,974	1,196	71	4,107	90	659	2,859
Ohio	412,776	18,318	32,463	169,139	5,196	2,336	136,238	17,571	19,902	11,613
Oklahoma	127,973	14,536	1,685	76,889	10,948	991	13,827	3,203	4,349	1,545
Oregon	181,597	20,543	15,566	72,946	4,161	2,137	42,208	1,341	16,181	6,514
Pennsylvania	741,860	36,967	122,733	218,955	22,899	3,157	268,508	9,742	53,661	5,238
Rhode Island	77,967	2,622	10,174	26,155	3,204	1,216	16,036	1,903	13,884	2,773
South Carolina	126,927	14,652	4,081	68,554	9,698	288	23,090	680	5,351	533
South Dakota	35,883	5,971	520	23,097	265	110	1,441	389	860	3,230
Tennessee	254,186	19,550	8,264	89,984	30,860	565	92,435	4,055	7,427	1,046
Texas	720,480	38,564	66,942	249,480	21,498	3,050	270,509	22,084	41,355	6,998
Utah	163,120	4,849	24,469	68,090	4,888	682	44,920	1,744	11,334	2,144
Vermont	62,477	13,118	355	23,000	242	167	23,486	113	1,859	137
Virginia	276,943	18,515	10,634	81,908	50,391	1,631	76,603	13,172	13,922	10,167
Washington	333,978	25,845	24,127	94,380	7,930	1,172	140,199	5,103	28,947	6,275
West Virginia	98,065	7,964	1,028	38,410	7,136	1,114	10,751	211	29,693	1,758
Wisconsin	303,706	16,739	9,333	116,785	15,923	1,432	103,776	9,716	26,840	3,162
Wyoming	21,554	3,382	1,387	10,143	841	193	1,195	226	3,376	811
Outlying areas	251,323	16,892	315	215,235	400	106	15,112	96	2,117	1,050
American Samoa	768	665	0	103	0	0	0	0	0	0
Guam	4,203	1,664	0	2,117	0	0	307	0	10	105
Puerto Rico	240,524	11,508	315	210,671	400	106	14,561	96	2,027	840
Trust Territory of the Pacific	2,735	1,386	0	1,349	0	0	0	0	0	0
Virgin Islands	3,093	1,669	0	995	0	0	244	0	80	105

[1] Dollars reflect actual obligations during the fiscal year regardless of when the funds were actually spent by a recipient institution. Data include obligations to federally funded research and development centers administered by colleges and universities.

[2] Includes Department of Commerce, Department of Housing and Urban Development, Department of the Interior, Agency for International Development, Department of Labor, Department of Transportation, and Nuclear Regulatory Commission.

NOTE.—Totals exclude loans to individuals, such as the Federal Guaranteed Student Loan program sponsored by the Department of Education, and Federal training and development activities, as well as funds allocated to State agencies, even though the final recipient of such funds is known to be an academic institution. Tuition support programs such as Pell Grants are included in these figures.

SOURCE: National Science Foundation, *Federal Support to Universities, Colleges, and Selected Nonprofit Institutions, Fiscal Year 1988.* (This table was prepared January 1990.)

Table 346.—Summary of Federal funds for research, development, and R & D plant: Fiscal years 1983 to 1991

Item	Actual							Estimated		
	1983	1984	1985	1986	1987	1988	1989	1990	1991	Percent-age change, 1990 to 1991
1	2	3	4	5	6	7	8	9	10	11
Total outlays for research, development, and R & D plant	**$37,959.4**	**$41,330.1**	**$45,860.3**	**$52,090.3**	**$53,214.2**	**$56,556.6**	**$61,476.4**	**$63,352.5**	**$66,689.9**	5.3
Research and development	36,659.4	39,691.0	44,171.4	50,609.1	51,611.7	54,739.4	59,450.4	60,793.4	64,024.0	5.3
R & D plant	1,299.9	1,639.2	1,688.9	1,481.2	1,602.4	1,817.2	2,026.1	2,559.1	2,665.8	4.2
Total obligations for research, development, and R & D plant	40,009.6	44,012.2	50,180.4	52,951.2	57,101.4	58,992.2	63,570.9	65,286.7	68,868.1	5.5
Research and development obligations	38,711.5	42,224.9	48,359.6	51,412.4	55,255.4	56,935.1	61,405.8	62,320.1	66,107.3	6.1
Performers:										
Federal intramural [1]	10,581.9	11,572.3	12,945.4	13,534.9	13,413.1	14,280.9	13,184.5	16,094.1	16,396.3	1.9
Industrial firms	17,147.8	18,753.2	21,968.7	24,508.6	26,752.0	26,719.2	30,484.4	28,853.9	31,511.5	9.2
FFRDCS [2] administered by industrial firms	1,501.2	1,608.4	1,790.8	1,697.0	1,860.0	1,911.3	1,960.0	2,053.6	2,062.3	0.4
Universities and colleges	4,966.4	5,565.1	6,375.5	6,579.3	7,353.6	7,827.7	8,672.0	8,747.9	9,190.8	5.1
FFRDCS [2] administered by universities and colleges	2,265.8	2,324.9	2,534.9	2,439.8	3,209.5	3,473.9	3,497.1	3,410.3	3,653.8	7.1
Other nonprofit institutions	1,241.6	1,497.3	1,699.2	1,675.5	1,710.8	1,682.6	1,999.1	2,183.6	2,301.7	5.4
FFRDCS [2] administered by nonprofit institutions	581.3	597.1	689.2	552.6	510.6	505.6	522.0	444.7	482.2	8.4
State and local governments	186.0	130.9	129.4	128.4	148.3	142.1	167.4	174.6	184.1	5.5
Foreign	239.5	175.8	244.5	296.3	297.6	391.8	919.4	357.5	324.7	−9.2
Research	14,253.5	14,978.8	16,133.4	16,502.2	17,942.7	18,650.0	20,765.4	21,682.8	23,219.8	7.1
Performers:										
Federal intramural [1]	4,710.3	4,764.7	5,056.1	5,160.4	5,437.7	5,338.4	5,981.5	6,337.8	6,866.6	8.3
Industrial firms	2,152.6	2,185.9	2,159.1	2,379.3	2,448.6	2,642.5	2,875.1	3,162.0	3,427.3	8.4
FFRDCS [2] administered by industrial firms	522.7	496.5	485.9	482.1	433.5	455.2	519.8	519.2	505.1	−2.7
Universities and colleges	4,468.0	5,029.7	5,726.3	5,883.5	6,640.3	7,022.9	7,793.2	7,872.8	8,356.1	6.1
FFRDCS [2] administered by universities and colleges	1,211.6	1,287.5	1,336.5	1,192.9	1,470.9	1,564.8	1,703.4	1,732.9	1,863.2	7.5
Other nonprofit institutions	836.9	922.6	1,045.1	1,061.6	1,207.3	1,299.8	1,519.7	1,685.1	1,796.9	6.6
FFRDCS [2] administered by nonprofit institutions	85.2	87.3	97.0	89.2	89.8	82.9	109.5	121.7	137.3	12.9
State and local governments	136.7	88.2	89.5	91.0	90.2	103.1	121.2	127.0	125.3	−1.4
Foreign	129.6	116.5	137.9	162.4	124.3	140.4	142.1	124.2	141.9	14.2
Fields of science:										
Life sciences	5,177.0	5,636.0	6,362.5	6,464.3	7,343.8	7,724.5	8,495.1	8,913.6	9,407.0	5.5
Psychology	240.9	266.7	327.1	334.0	369.5	389.8	421.7	447.9	509.8	13.8
Physical sciences	2,891.4	2,969.0	3,046.0	3,069.1	3,252.7	3,317.3	3,705.2	3,895.0	4,191.5	7.6
Environmental sciences	1,251.2	1,275.9	1,403.7	1,481.7	1,511.6	1,607.0	1,773.3	2,103.9	2,344.8	11.4
Mathematics and computer sciences	419.4	440.3	574.9	615.4	640.6	642.9	735.5	720.9	792.2	9.9
Engineering	3,517.0	3,624.1	3,617.6	3,739.0	3,906.2	3,956.3	4,442.0	4,361.2	4,684.0	7.4
Social sciences	435.3	436.3	460.0	415.5	480.1	485.8	551.1	620.9	646.0	4.0
Other sciences	320.4	330.5	341.6	383.3	438.3	526.5	641.6	619.5	644.6	4.0
Basic research	6,260.1	7,067.4	7,818.7	8,153.1	8,944.1	9,473.6	10,602.0	11,347.6	12,254.6	8.0
Performers:										
Federal intramural [1]	1,689.8	1,861.1	1,923.4	2,018.9	2,046.2	2,050.3	2,370.7	2,573.0	2,782.3	8.1
Industrial firms	305.7	394.1	408.4	544.6	466.9	596.9	773.2	958.8	1,042.9	8.8
FFRDCS [2] administered by industrial firms	83.0	91.1	122.6	117.6	119.9	133.0	166.7	176.5	193.9	9.8
Universities and colleges	3,112.3	3,530.8	4,038.7	4,132.1	4,665.8	4,868.3	5,221.4	5,376.7	5,720.8	6.4
FFRDCS [2] administered by universities and colleges	591.2	652.7	695.9	691.1	906.6	989.8	1,098.1	1,146.2	1,266.9	10.5
Other nonprofit institutions	409.6	473.6	555.8	572.0	657.7	728.6	838.9	962.9	1,077.2	11.9
FFRDCS [2] administered by nonprofit institutions	8.0	8.2	12.4	13.1	13.3	17.7	42.2	55.4	67.6	22.1
State and local governments	32.1	28.1	30.5	31.0	37.5	42.7	43.6	48.5	51.4	5.9
Foreign	28.5	27.7	30.9	32.7	30.2	46.3	47.4	49.6	51.6	4.1
Fields of science:										
Life sciences	2,891.3	3,287.6	3,786.6	3,858.8	4,363.6	4,501.8	4,915.7	5,203.2	5,589.4	7.4
Psychology	92.9	107.9	132.8	133.0	147.2	177.8	187.1	202.2	221.4	9.5
Physical sciences	1,587.2	1,728.0	1,815.2	1,914.4	2,096.0	2,199.6	2,506.5	2,696.5	2,966.3	10.0
Environmental sciences	580.1	656.7	699.7	749.1	781.0	872.7	1,016.9	1,184.2	1,328.2	12.2
Mathematics and computer sciences	208.1	240.8	260.0	293.4	306.4	313.2	349.8	356.0	378.7	6.4
Engineering	689.5	845.0	884.2	968.5	989.5	1,006.2	1,183.7	1,198.7	1,253.3	4.6
Social sciences	137.7	132.6	140.7	113.5	129.5	146.8	154.6	188.2	189.0	0.5
Other sciences	73.3	68.8	99.4	122.5	130.9	255.5	291.7	318.5	328.1	3.0
Applied research	7,993.4	7,911.4	8,314.7	8,349.1	8,998.6	9,176.4	10,163.3	10,335.2	10,965.2	6.1
Performers:										
Federal intramural [1]	3,020.4	2,903.6	3,132.7	3,141.5	3,391.5	3,288.1	3,610.8	3,764.7	4,084.3	8.5
Industrial firms	1,846.9	1,791.8	1,750.7	1,834.7	1,981.7	2,045.6	2,101.8	2,203.1	2,384.4	8.2
FFRDCS [2] administered by industrial firms	439.7	405.4	363.3	364.5	313.6	322.2	353.2	342.8	311.2	−9.2
Universities and colleges	1,355.6	1,498.9	1,687.6	1,751.4	1,974.5	2,154.6	2,571.8	2,496.1	2,635.3	5.6
FFRDCS [2] administered by universities and colleges	620.5	634.8	640.6	501.8	564.3	575.0	605.4	586.8	596.3	1.6
Other nonprofit institutions	427.3	449.1	489.3	489.6	549.7	571.2	680.8	722.3	719.8	−0.3
FFRDCS [2] administered by nonprofit institutions	77.1	79.1	84.6	76.1	76.5	65.2	67.3	66.3	69.7	5.1
State and local governments	104.7	60.0	58.9	60.0	52.7	60.4	77.6	78.5	73.9	−5.8
Foreign	101.1	88.8	107.0	129.7	94.1	94.1	94.6	74.6	90.3	21.0
Fields of science:										
Life sciences	2,286.6	2,348.3	2,575.9	2,605.5	2,980.2	3,222.7	3,579.4	3,710.4	3,817.6	2.9
Psychology	147.9	158.8	194.3	201.0	222.4	212.0	234.5	245.7	288.4	17.4
Physical sciences	1,304.3	1,241.0	1,230.8	1,154.6	1,156.6	1,117.7	1,198.8	1,198.4	1,225.2	2.2
Environmental sciences	671.2	619.2	704.0	732.6	730.6	734.3	756.3	919.7	1,016.6	10.5
Mathematics and computer sciences	211.3	199.5	314.9	322.0	334.3	329.6	389.7	365.0	413.5	13.3
Engineering	2,827.5	2,779.1	2,733.4	2,770.5	2,916.7	2,950.0	3,258.3	3,162.4	3,430.6	8.5

Table 346.—Summary of Federal funds for research, development, and R & D plant:—Continued
Fiscal years 1983 to 1991

Item	Actual							Estimated		
	1983	1984	1985	1986	1987	1988	1989	1990	1991	Percentage change, 1990 to 1991
1	2	3	4	5	6	7	8	9	10	11
Social sciences	297.6	303.8	319.3	302.1	350.5	339.0	396.4	432.7	456.9	5.6
Other sciences	247.1	261.7	242.2	260.9	307.4	271.0	350.0	300.9	316.4	5.2
Development	24,458.0	27,246.1	32,226.1	34,910.2	37,312.7	38,285.1	40,640.4	40,637.3	42,887.6	5.5
Performers:										
Federal intramural [1]	5,871.7	6,807.6	7,889.3	8,374.6	7,975.4	8,942.5	7,203.0	9,756.3	9,529.7	−2.3
Industrial firms	14,995.2	16,567.3	19,809.5	22,129.3	24,303.4	24,076.7	27,609.3	25,692.0	28,084.1	9.3
FFRDCS [2] administered by industrial firms	978.5	1,112.0	1,304.9	1,215.0	1,426.4	1,456.1	1,440.2	1,534.3	1,557.2	1.5
Universities and colleges	498.5	535.4	631.2	695.8	713.2	804.8	878.8	875.0	834.8	−4.6
FFRDCS [2] administered by universities and colleges	1,054.2	1,037.4	1,198.3	1,246.9	1,738.6	1,909.1	1,793.6	1,677.4	1,790.6	6.7
Other nonprofit institutions	404.7	574.6	654.1	613.9	503.4	382.8	479.5	498.5	504.8	1.3
FFRDCS [2] administered by nonprofit institutions	496.1	509.8	592.2	463.4	420.8	422.7	412.4	323.0	344.8	6.7
State and local governments	49.3	42.8	39.9	37.4	58.0	39.0	46.3	47.5	58.8	23.6
Foreign	109.9	59.2	106.7	133.9	173.4	251.4	777.3	233.2	182.8	−21.6
R & D plant obligations	1,298.1	1,787.3	1,820.8	1,538.8	1,846.0	2,057.1	2,165.1	2,966.6	2,760.8	−6.9
Performers supported:										
Federal intramural [1]	393.9	632.8	630.2	317.1	301.6	319.6	329.5	448.4	383.3	−14.5
Industrial firms	260.8	451.7	298.5	409.7	668.7	719.5	900.4	1,250.3	1,034.4	−17.3
FFRDCS [2] administered by industrial firms	166.4	196.6	187.8	215.9	212.9	204.3	212.3	235.5	243.6	3.4
Universities and colleges	32.1	78.3	136.2	132.7	230.5	245.8	204.9	167.0	132.7	−20.6
FFRDCS [2] administered by universities and colleges	353.0	363.2	454.2	420.9	400.5	535.3	489.9	711.4	745.8	4.8
Other nonprofit institutions	82.1	55.6	69.4	11.8	20.6	23.7	14.2	141.0	203.9	44.6
FFRDCS [2] administered by nonprofit institutions	7.9	4.2	9.1	9.6	5.4	6.2	8.4	11.4	17.2	51.6
State and local governments	0.0	0.0	0.1	0.0	0.0	0.3	1.4	0.0	0.0	0.0
Foreign	1.8	4.9	35.5	21.0	5.8	2.4	4.2	1.6	0.0	−100.0

[1] Costs associated with the administration of intramural and extramural programs are covered as well as actual intramural performance.

[2] Federally funded research and development centers.

NOTE.—Some data revised from previously published figures. Because of rounding, details may not add to totals.

SOURCE: National Science Foundation, *Federal Funds for Research and Development,* various years. (This table was prepared February 1991.)

Table 347.—Federal obligations to colleges and universities for research and development, by field: United States and outlying areas, 1976–77 to 1987–88

Field of science or engineering	1976–77	1977–78	1979–80	1980–81	1983–84	1984–85	1985–86	1986–87	1987–88
1	2	3	4	5	6	7	8	9	10
Total, all fields	$2,803,017	$3,385,770	$4,160,543	$4,410,931	$5,448,821	$6,246,181	$6,456,743	$7,239,490	$7,717,052
Engineering, total	265,840	503,686	612,456	792,223	847,674	944,413	998,312	988,461	1,128,709
Aeronautical	13,053	20,840	28,044	31,056	40,678	39,903	42,257	40,019	47,746
Astronautical	1,674	849	4,634	4,875	12,405	14,765	24,147	23,474	32,516
Chemical	31,065	41,624	22,210	27,667	50,677	68,602	50,379	52,273	67,647
Civil	25,018	37,227	48,130	58,300	55,843	45,368	35,402	30,166	30,947
Electrical	45,449	76,337	86,916	115,011	161,336	231,457	212,175	197,133	251,336
Mechanical	22,109	25,156	42,593	37,954	45,952	53,214	56,416	60,392	60,506
Metallurgy and materials	35,577	40,681	63,057	52,815	75,341	80,416	101,457	98,033	120,983
Other engineering	91,895	260,972	316,872	464,545	405,442	410,688	476,079	486,971	517,028
All sciences, total	2,537,177	2,882,084	3,548,087	3,618,708	4,601,147	5,301,768	5,458,431	6,251,029	6,588,343
Physical sciences, total	401,211	445,482	507,884	500,657	715,948	789,184	770,254	824,643	859,503
Astronomy	32,427	37,864	52,736	54,835	78,124	78,654	78,435	84,587	89,756
Chemistry	123,744	139,507	170,048	165,189	230,689	256,156	255,593	271,146	281,433
Physics	198,591	231,405	249,661	250,342	359,757	397,061	379,289	406,264	425,919
Other physical sciences	46,449	36,706	35,439	30,291	47,378	57,313	56,937	62,646	62,395
Mathematical sciences	48,872	42,781	53,987	53,668	76,436	94,680	96,405	116,039	119,217
Computer sciences	26,671	34,856	37,585	37,493	58,667	78,634	82,691	80,672	84,304
Environmental sciences, total	302,645	304,116	379,453	330,079	398,538	453,789	468,882	496,444	473,849
Atmospheric sciences	88,304	85,496	86,486	95,112	114,183	135,562	124,657	151,294	131,778
Geological sciences	107,031	116,077	109,523	101,207	100,901	116,850	118,401	118,662	131,744
Oceanography	55,908	57,279	92,079	91,863	136,426	138,732	121,855	150,225	129,473
Other environmental sciences	51,402	45,264	91,365	41,897	47,028	62,645	103,969	76,263	80,854
Life sciences, total	1,488,155	1,719,103	2,137,751	2,290,587	2,932,582	3,362,712	3,463,114	4,035,516	4,348,171
Biological sciences	—	—	1,085,602	1,192,756	1,548,809	1,775,397	1,849,516	2,180,542	2,343,429
Environmental biology	—	—	13,137	14,636	80,595	79,601	86,088	87,628	97,126
Agricultural sciences	231,926	—	111,739	134,660	158,369	168,927	143,249	149,484	155,939
Medical sciences	779,667	711,002	885,898	904,963	1,120,032	1,294,571	1,325,157	1,546,711	1,691,610
Other life sciences	32,398	30,934	41,375	43,572	24,777	44,216	59,104	71,151	60,067
Psychological sciences, total	57,235	71,891	86,459	87,734	109,787	132,746	138,338	176,524	186,924
Biological aspects	19,715	22,816	28,269	26,273	33,515	39,700	39,049	46,194	53,287
Social aspects	21,318	27,457	31,129	28,846	30,261	36,205	38,589	51,557	52,113
Other psychological sciences	16,202	21,618	27,061	32,615	46,011	56,841	60,700	78,773	81,524
Social sciences, total	134,020	184,729	203,948	197,695	162,492	175,909	172,148	168,916	183,563
Anthropology	5,882	7,432	7,757	5,543	5,529	6,053	6,455	6,998	5,972
Economics	21,581	52,748	51,414	56,704	37,675	45,292	43,764	51,274	48,039
History	1,017	1,426	1,688	1,069	1,038	1,494	1,508	1,634	1,527
Linguistics	2,300	2,261	2,997	2,745	2,967	3,196	2,481	2,843	3,248
Political science	3,837	4,861	5,890	5,122	7,965	6,216	5,003	5,492	5,926
Sociology	27,457	39,951	34,903	38,136	33,232	34,887	34,580	41,797	55,201
Other social sciences	71,946	76,050	99,299	88,376	74,086	78,771	78,357	58,878	63,650
Other sciences	78,368	79,126	141,020	120,795	146,697	214,114	266,599	352,275	332,812

—Data not available.

NOTE.—Some data revised from previously published figures.

SOURCE: National Science Foundation, Science Resources Studies Division, unpublished data. (This table was prepared January 1990.)

Table 348.—Department of Agriculture obligations for child nutrition programs, by State or other area: Fiscal years 1989 and 1990

[In thousands]

State or other area	Total, fiscal year 1989	Fiscal year 1990								
		Total	Special milk [1]	School lunch [2]	School Breakfast	State administrative expenses	Commodities and cash in lieu of commodities [3]	Child and adult care	Summer food service	Nutrition education and training
1	2	3	4	5	6	7	8	9	10	11
Total	$5,358,096	$5,566,129	$22,043	$3,229,951	$591,536	$60,969	$678,740	$814,440	$163,450	$5,000
Alabama	125,810	127,348	36	77,017	14,064	1,363	15,782	14,660	4,354	73
Alaska	13,237	13,955	9	7,915	1,035	310	1,102	3,530	4	50
Arizona	74,413	78,376	174	47,129	10,219	870	5,978	12,404	1,546	56
Arkansas	65,129	68,024	40	40,972	9,060	970	8,617	7,527	787	50
California	598,899	640,913	960	392,630	82,174	6,156	51,812	94,192	12,522	466
Colorado	70,201	60,954	139	31,287	3,188	1,016	6,985	17,298	986	55
Connecticut	44,914	43,326	650	22,785	3,486	575	6,165	7,994	1,619	52
Delaware	12,700	13,736	37	5,666	1,142	298	1,561	3,848	1,134	50
District of Columbia	15,114	16,036	20	9,782	1,961	321	1,471	1,872	560	50
Florida	245,666	265,757	122	157,732	32,178	2,370	30,955	27,854	14,370	176
Georgia	174,718	178,800	249	106,012	21,078	1,829	24,037	20,323	5,159	112
Hawaii	24,171	24,623	8	14,274	2,477	353	4,129	2,996	336	50
Idaho	20,311	20,671	125	13,971	853	320	2,825	2,382	146	50
Illinois	209,924	214,191	2,644	131,287	14,971	2,262	25,724	28,591	8,508	204
Indiana	98,590	89,596	314	53,477	5,145	914	16,071	12,034	1,543	99
Iowa	54,818	54,141	243	31,094	2,697	651	9,649	8,858	899	50
Kansas	59,925	68,420	320	28,528	1,680	711	17,530	19,119	482	50
Kentucky	101,706	99,820	273	60,382	16,301	1,061	12,644	7,652	1,443	65
Louisiana	163,940	165,161	83	103,747	20,125	1,998	16,444	17,936	4,741	88
Maine	22,837	22,518	174	10,931	1,247	381	3,379	6,031	325	50
Maryland	68,809	73,254	379	39,371	6,637	886	9,912	14,082	1,914	73
Massachusetts	98,766	99,732	577	43,403	9,423	1,868	15,725	25,585	3,060	91
Michigan	144,269	145,538	1,377	82,632	6,292	1,628	18,440	30,711	4,288	168
Minnesota	92,087	101,871	901	41,416	3,561	1,287	12,831	40,621	1,179	75
Mississippi	130,603	128,678	14	75,345	17,482	1,410	12,451	17,326	4,597	52
Missouri	89,830	100,148	607	58,312	9,063	1,070	13,636	15,471	1,902	86
Montana	15,703	17,612	61	9,366	840	359	2,374	4,143	419	50
Nebraska	31,269	36,388	241	17,549	1,551	523	5,120	11,081	273	50
Nevada	12,107	13,404	68	7,749	1,707	283	1,774	1,721	52	50
New Hampshire	11,777	12,836	204	6,059	533	389	3,675	1,716	209	50
New Jersey	107,966	102,859	973	59,692	6,270	1,432	14,244	15,808	4,317	123
New Mexico	53,625	56,148	28	30,159	4,828	819	4,656	11,348	4,260	50
New York	399,670	410,097	1,574	231,363	44,770	2,769	46,208	49,399	33,718	296
North Carolina	155,555	154,372	133	90,386	22,835	1,560	19,379	16,496	3,475	108
North Dakota	17,617	18,237	71	8,167	606	377	2,236	6,453	277	50
Ohio	180,404	186,369	1,101	109,542	20,227	1,855	26,509	24,074	2,870	191
Oklahoma	74,802	78,927	133	46,301	10,132	903	10,358	10,189	855	56
Oregon	47,459	44,131	230	25,974	3,140	584	3,415	9,764	973	50
Pennsylvania	176,806	173,400	790	101,895	10,630	1,793	25,902	23,721	8,477	192
Rhode Island	12,950	13,686	101	7,463	897	419	1,640	2,190	927	50
South Carolina	95,958	99,085	25	60,149	12,859	989	12,268	7,895	4,838	62
South Dakota	21,511	21,744	60	11,758	1,832	425	4,264	2,661	694	50
Tennessee	111,930	115,115	33	67,981	17,716	1,186	16,061	10,111	1,944	84
Texas	482,637	507,604	104	304,092	81,754	4,665	51,739	57,866	7,065	319
Utah	37,378	44,867	57	24,467	1,083	550	6,767	11,147	746	50
Vermont	8,859	9,151	179	4,176	361	309	1,330	2,688	59	50
Virginia	98,981	101,339	248	58,525	10,681	761	17,214	11,818	1,995	98
Washington	79,359	80,918	323	42,800	5,153	1,032	9,492	21,228	814	76
West Virginia	47,439	49,393	34	28,281	9,541	598	5,932	4,358	599	50
Wisconsin	72,036	76,830	1,626	44,669	3,316	841	13,523	11,837	933	85
Wyoming	9,788	9,863	18	5,185	362	288	1,260	2,593	113	44
Department of Defense Dependents schools	2,512	6,593	0	2,510	0	0	4,083	0	0	0
Outlying areas										
American Samoa	4,351	4,925	0	2,898	1,440	164	373	0	0	50
Guam	3,580	3,059	0	1,885	681	200	283	10	0	0
Northern Marianas	2,535	2,538	0	1,626	554	163	146	0	0	50
Puerto Rico	128,859	137,859	0	104,516	20,219	1,362	8,613	37	3,043	70
Freely Associated States	3,639	229	0	0	0	0	225	0	0	4
Virgin Islands	5,440	4,246	3	2,815	39	233	486	364	257	50
Undistributed [4]	22,210	56,721	3,151	22,859	-2,562	264	11,335	20,831	843	0

[1] The Special Milk program total includes $1,660,485 in prior years unobligated balances restored.

[2] Special Meal Assistance program is combined with "School Lunch" program.

[3] Commodities are based on preliminary food orders for fiscal year 1990. Undistributed amount for Commodities and Cash in Lieu includes $7,506,282 for Study of Alternatives to Commodity Distribution.

[4] Undistributed amount reflects the difference between preliminary State earnings reports and Federal obligations as of September 30, 1990.

NOTE.—Data are based on obligations as reported September 30, 1990. Because of rounding, details may not add to totals.

SOURCE: U.S. Department of Agriculture, Food and Nutrition Service, Budget Division, unpublished data. (This table was prepared February 1991.)

Table 349.—Department of Health and Human Services allocations for Head Start and enrollment in Head Start, by State or other area: Fiscal years 1988, 1989, and 1990

State or other area	1988		1989		1990	
	Head Start allocations (in thousands)	Head Start enrollment [1]	Head Start allocations (in thousands)	Head Start enrollment [2]	Head Start allocations (in thousands)	Head Start enrollment [3]
1	2	3	4	5	6	7
Total	$1,176,224	448,464	$1,203,173	450,970	$1,517,240	540,934
Alabama	23,853	10,835	24,367	10,875	29,935	11,587
Alaska	2,446	800	2,462	800	2,840	800
Arizona	10,349	3,683	10,675	3,743	13,745	4,730
Arkansas	12,343	6,061	12,603	6,138	16,026	7,284
California	113,657	35,361	116,513	35,835	152,094	45,135
Colorado	10,752	4,456	10,936	4,730	13,674	5,625
Connecticut	11,021	4,220	11,243	4,199	13,609	4,726
Delaware	2,545	936	2,605	936	3,147	1,113
District of Columbia	6,687	2,285	6,761	2,285	7,747	2,493
Florida	32,874	13,031	33,763	13,234	45,381	16,975
Georgia	27,892	10,956	28,509	10,858	37,304	13,792
Hawaii	4,402	1,405	4,475	1,405	5,547	1,703
Idaho	3,332	1,166	3,450	1,154	4,452	1,369
Illinois	58,809	22,502	60,097	22,650	73,839	25,857
Indiana	16,536	7,036	16,917	7,108	21,890	8,689
Iowa	8,786	3,676	9,045	3,741	11,558	4,580
Kansas	7,405	3,390	7,548	3,394	9,778	3,938
Kentucky	22,708	10,188	23,030	10,148	27,793	11,292
Louisiana	24,898	10,465	25,557	10,654	34,383	13,686
Maine	4,888	2,385	4,998	2,388	6,239	2,724
Maryland	15,473	5,305	15,806	5,368	19,894	6,641
Massachusetts	25,383	8,147	25,854	8,217	30,731	9,257
Michigan	48,370	20,257	49,409	20,348	60,674	23,411
Minnesota	12,698	5,039	13,059	5,068	16,468	6,129
Mississippi	53,802	19,899	53,870	19,927	57,176	21,026
Missouri	20,297	8,777	20,753	8,883	26,207	10,726
Montana	2,955	1,177	3,058	1,201	3,874	1,535
Nebraska	4,782	2,044	4,894	2,044	6,254	2,535
Nevada	1,703	605	1,726	601	2,384	801
New Hampshire	2,213	748	2,234	748	2,746	865
New Jersey	34,365	9,645	35,018	9,625	41,481	10,765
New Mexico	6,996	3,658	7,154	3,603	9,408	4,381
New York	87,416	24,611	89,538	24,791	111,997	30,050
North Carolina	24,589	10,553	25,207	10,492	31,971	12,426
North Dakota	1,776	710	1,808	710	2,129	985
Ohio	48,356	22,117	49,468	22,352	62,438	26,250
Oklahoma	14,279	7,292	14,551	7,183	17,743	8,200
Oregon	9,353	2,952	9,640	2,974	12,223	3,436
Pennsylvania	49,439	17,062	50,465	17,130	61,536	20,061
Rhode Island	3,761	1,858	3,849	1,838	4,833	2,085
South Carolina	15,340	6,543	15,685	6,423	19,871	7,930
South Dakota	2,763	1,099	2,821	1,099	3,694	1,382
Tennessee	20,915	8,807	21,411	8,928	28,016	10,846
Texas	53,999	23,121	55,850	23,211	77,069	30,573
Utah	5,120	2,033	5,292	2,118	7,020	2,702
Vermont	2,422	871	2,444	871	2,821	973
Virginia	16,792	5,591	17,201	5,769	22,098	7,380
Washington	13,494	4,373	13,954	4,448	18,767	5,378
West Virginia	10,036	4,008	10,259	4,038	12,958	4,937
Wisconsin	17,651	7,205	18,074	7,241	22,931	8,612
Wyoming	1,590	698	1,624	699	1,876	826
American Indian programs	41,640	13,996	42,662	14,302	—	15,547
Migrant programs	44,345	19,042	45,419	19,103	111,096	23,529
Special projects	2,653	—	3,029	—	2,711	—
Outlying areas						
Puerto Rico	48,714	19,290	50,163	19,726	67,736	25,031
Pacific Territories	2,112	3,405	1,886	2,527	2,292	4,347
Virgin Islands	2,452	1,089	2,488	1,089	3,137	1,278

[1] The distribution of enrollment by age was: 10% were 5 years old and older; 62% were 4 years old; 25% were 3 years old; and 3% were under 3 years of age. Handicapped children accounted for more than 13% of all children in Head Start programs. The racial/ethnic composition was: American Indian, 4%; Hispanic, 22%; black, 38%; white, 33%; and Asian, 3%.

[2] The distribution of enrollment by age was: 8% were 5 years old and over; 64% were 4 year-olds; 25% were 3 year-olds; and 3% were under 3 years of age. Handicapped children accounted for almost 13.5 % of all children in Head Start programs. The racial/ethnic composition was: American Indian, 4%; Hispanic, 22%; black, 38%; white, 33%; and Asian 3%.

[3] The distribution of enrollment by age was: 7% were 5 years old and over; 63% were 4 year-olds; 27% were 3 year-olds; and 3% were under 3 years of age. Handicapped children accounted for 13.9 percent in Head Start programs. The racial/ethnic composition was: Native American, 4%; Hispanic, 22%; black, 38%; white, 33%; and Asian, 3%. —Not applicable.

NOTE.—Because of rounding, details may not add to totals.

SOURCE: U.S. Department of Health and Human Services, Office of Human Development Services. (This table was prepared April 1991.)

Table 350.—Public and private school students receiving publicly funded free or reduced price lunch, by selected school characteristics: School year 1987–88

School characteristics	All schools	Public				Private			
		Total	Elementary	Secondary	Combined	Total	Elementary	Secondary	Combined
1	2	3	4	5	6	7	8	9	10
Total	25.9	28.5	34.4	18.1	35.1	6.1	7.2	3.7	5.3
Community type:									
Rural/farming	30.5	31.6	35.8	22.5	35.5	10.8	12.6	(1)	(1)
Small city/town	23.2	25.0	29.8	16.7	27.9	4.5	5.5	(1)	(1)
Suburban	14.0	15.8	19.8	10.0	17.5	2.7	2.2	(1)	(1)
Urban	32.8	37.9	46.4	22.9	42.5	7.3	9.1	(1)	7.4
Other[2]	47.1	49.8	50.0	(1)	(1)	(1)	(1)	(1)	(1)
School size:									
Less than 150	21.9	38.2	37.3	35.4	45.5	8.2	7.9	(1)	8.5
150–299	24.1	32.4	34.4	23.0	37.6	7.5	7.9	(1)	(1)
300–499	27.1	30.0	31.0	23.2	34.5	4.2	4.2	(1)	(1)
500–749	29.9	31.5	34.4	21.5	33.3	5.6	7.2	(1)	(1)
750 or more	23.1	24.2	39.1	16.0	34.1	(1)	(1)	(1)	(1)
Minority students:									
Less than 5%	15.7	17.9	20.5	12.2	25.5	4.5	5.1	(1)	4.2
5 to 19%	15.4	17.2	21.5	10.3	26.6	3.5	3.5	(1)	(1)
20 to 49%	26.8	28.4	33.4	19.3	41.5	5.9	4.5	(1)	(1)
50% or more	49.9	52.5	61.7	34.0	55.6	16.0	19.7	(1)	(1)

[1] Too few sample cases (fewer than 30) for a reliable estimate.
[2] Includes military bases and Indian reservations.

SOURCE: U.S. Department of Education, National Center for Education Statistics, Schools and Staffing Survey, 1987–88. (This table was prepared April 1990.)

Table 351.—Public and private school students receiving publicly funded ECIA [1] Chapter I services, by selected school characteristics: School year 1987–88

School characteristics	All schools	Public				Private			
		Total	Elementary	Secondary	Combined	Total	Elementary	Secondary	Combined
1	2	3	4	5	6	7	8	9	10
Total	10.2	11.1	14.8	4.9	12.1	3.3	3.7	(2)	4.3
Community type									
Rural/farming	12.1	12.4	16.8	4.6	11.7	5.1	4.0	(2)	(2)
Small city/town	9.3	9.9	13.2	4.2	12.2	3.1	3.4	(2)	(2)
Suburban	5.9	6.6	8.9	3.3	(2)	1.6	2.7	(2)	(2)
Urban	12.4	14.1	18.5	6.7	13.7	3.9	4.3	(2)	5.6
Other[3]	20.9	22.1	21.2	(2)	(2)	(2)	(2)	(2)	(2)
School size									
Less than 150	10.2	17.7	17.5	13.2	24.5	3.8	1.9	(2)	7.6
150–299	10.7	13.2	15.0	5.9	13.6	5.4	5.7	(2)	(2)
300–499	11.2	12.3	13.9	4.0	11.3	2.5	3.0	(2)	(2)
500–749	11.6	12.4	14.4	5.7	11.9	(2)	(2)	(2)	(2)
750 or more	8.2	8.7	16.4	4.6	9.1	(2)	(2)	(2)	(2)
Minority students									
Less than 5%	6.4	7.3	9.9	2.6	9.0	1.8	2.5	(2)	(2)
5 to 19%	6.3	7.0	9.4	3.2	10.2	1.8	2.5	(2)	(2)
20 to 49%	9.0	9.4	12.5	3.9	14.2	5.0	3.1	(2)	(2)
50% or more	20.4	21.2	26.7	10.8	18.1	9.6	9.0	(2)	(2)

[1] Education Consolidation Improvement Act.
[2] Too few sample cases (fewer than 30) for a reliable estimate.
[3] Includes military bases and Indian reservations.

SOURCE: U.S. Department of Education, National Center for Education Statistics, Schools and Staffing Survey, 1987–88. (This table was prepared April 1990.)

CHAPTER 5
Outcomes of Education

This chapter consists primarily of tables comparing educational attainment and work force characteristics. The data show labor force participation and income levels of high school dropouts, high school graduates, and bachelor's degree recipients. Population characteristics are provided for many of the measures to help evaluate disparities among various demographic groups. The first set of tables contains data from the Bureau of the Census on educational attainment of the labor force and income of the labor force and data from the Bureau of Labor Statistics on employment and unemployment. These tables provide information on the educational attainment of the labor force, by occupation, sex, and race/ethnicity; money income, by level of education attained; and unemployment rates, by years of school completed, sex, and race/ethnicity.

The second group of tables was compiled from Bureau of Labor Statistics data on high school dropouts and graduates. These data show the labor force participation and college enrollment of high school students within the year after they leave school. The tabulations also provide comparative labor force participation and unemployment rates for graduates and dropouts. Additional information on college enrollment rates by race/ethnicity and sex have been included to help form a more complete picture of high school outcomes.

The third set of tables has been prepared from the National Center for Education Statistics survey, Recent College Graduates, and from a Bureau of the Census survey on earnings and education. These tables provide data on employment outcomes for high school and college graduates. A table provides a salary comparison by field of college degree for the entire population. Trends in salaries received by college graduates also are featured in this section.

Statistics on educational attainment of the entire population are in chapter 1. More detailed data on the number of degree recipients are contained in chapters 2 and 3. Chapter 2 contains trend data on the proportion of high school graduates going to college. Additional data on the income of persons by

educational attainment may be obtained from the Bureau of the Census in the *Current Population Reports,* Series P–60. The Bureau of Labor Statistics has a selection of publications dealing with the educational characteristics of the labor force. Further information on survey methodologies is in the "Guide to Sources" in the appendix and in the publications cited in the source notes.

Highlights

- The life goal most consistently rated "very important" by young men and women was "having a happy family life." Two of the other most highly rated goals in the 1986 survey were "being successful in work" and "finding steady work." (Table 352)

- Persons with lower levels of educational attainment were more likely to be unemployed than those who had higher levels of educational attainment. The March 1990 unemployment rate for those with 1 to 3 years of high school was 12.2 percent compared with 5.8 percent for those with 4 years of high school and 2.4 percent for those with 4 or more years of college.* Blacks, other minorities, and young people tended to have higher unemployment rates, even after allowing for level of educational attainment. (Table 355)

- Between 1979 and 1989, annual income generally rose more rapidly for men with higher levels of educational attainment than for those with lower levels. For example, the income of men who were year-round full-time workers with 4 years of college rose by 72 percent compared with 39 percent for men with 1 to 3 years of high school. Income for men who had completed 4 years of high school increased 47 percent. (Table 357)

---

*The unemployment rate for all persons with 8 years or less of school were lower than the rate for those who had completed 1 to 3 years of high school. The people with 8 years or less of schooling were generally older workers who tended to have low unemployment rates because of their greater experience in the work force.

- In general, women's incomes rose faster than men's incomes (86 percent compared with 63 percent) between 1979 and 1989. However, for full-time year-round workers, women's salaries remain significantly below those for men at all education levels. (Table 357)

- The problems of dropouts are highlighted by comparing the labor force and unemployment status of dropouts and high school graduates. Only 65 percent of 1988–89 dropouts were in the labor force (employed or looking for work) and, of those in the labor force, 28 percent were unemployed. Of the 1988–89 high school graduates who were not in college, 84 percent were in the labor force and 15 percent of those in the labor force were unemployed. (Tables 359 and 360)

- About 53 percent of the college graduates of the class of 1985–86 had jobs in professional, mana-

gerial, and technical areas in 1987. Thirty-one percent were employed in nonprofessional, nonmanagerial, and nontechnical areas, and 4 percent were unemployed. Many of the 11 percent who were not in the labor force were enrolled in graduate school. (Table 362)

- A large number of young adults participate in volunteer organizations. The most common organizations are sports groups (36 percent), church groups (32 percent), and social or hobby clubs (22 percent). (Table 367)

- A 1985 assessment of young adults found that the vast majority (about 96 percent) had basic literacy skills. On the other hand, only about one-fifth had high proficiency in several types of literacy skills. (Table 368)

Figure 23.--Unemployment rates for persons 16 years old and over, by years of school completed: 1990

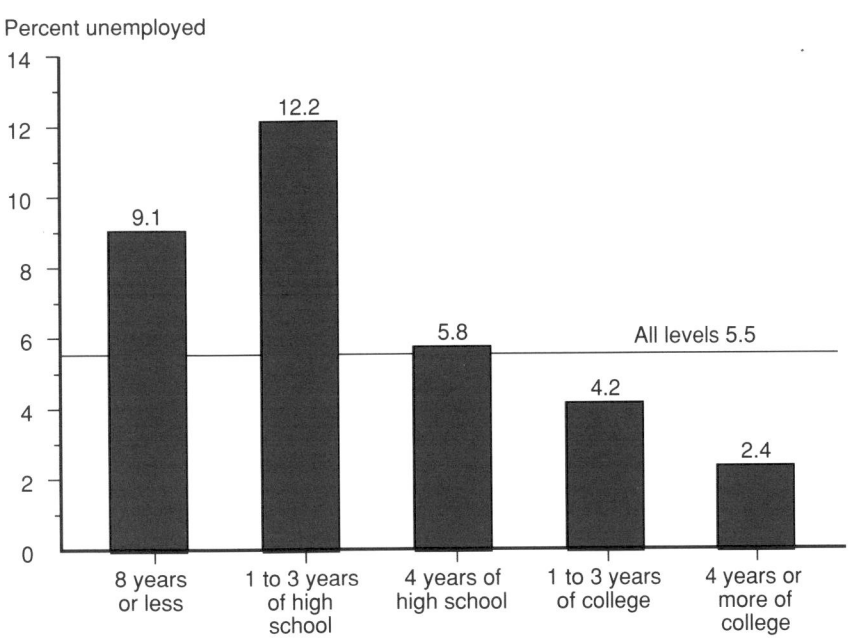

SOURCE: U.S. Department of Labor, Bureau of Labor Statistics, Office of Employment and Unemployment Statistics, unpublished data.

Figure 24.--Labor force status of 1988-89 high school dropouts and graduates: October 1989

SOURCE: U.S. Department of Labor, Bureau of Labor Statistics, "High School Graduates and Dropouts."

Figure 25.--Median annual income of full-time workers 25 years old and over, by years of school completed and sex: 1989

Income, in thousands

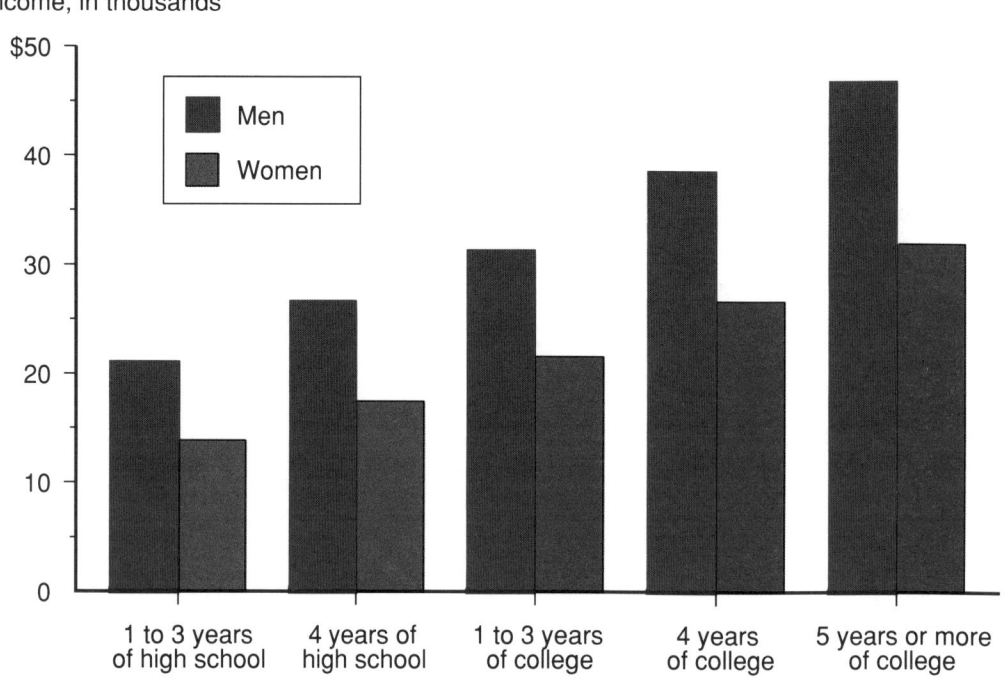

SOURCE: U.S. Department of Commerce, Bureau of the Census, *Money Income and Poverty Status of Families and Persons in the United States,* Series P–60, No. 161.

Figure 26.--Percentage of 1985-86 bachelor's degree recipients who have pursued additional higher education, by undergraduate major field of study: 1987

Undergraduate field of study

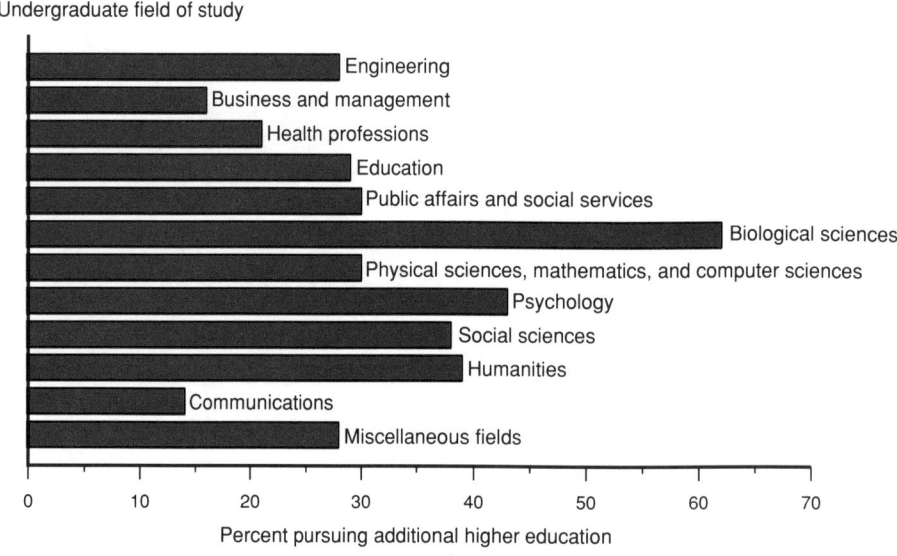

Percent pursuing additional higher education

SOURCE: U.S. Department of Education, National Center for Education Statistics, "Recent College Graduates" survey, 1987.

Table 352.—Percentage of 1972 and 1982 high school seniors who felt that certain life values were "very important," by sex: 1972 to 1986

Value	Percentage of 1972 seniors						Percentage of 1982 seniors					
	1972		1974		1976		1982		1984		1986	
	Male	Female	Male	Female	Male	Female	Male	Female	Male	Female	Male	Female
1	2	3	4	5	6	7	8	9	10	11	12	13
Being successful in work	86.5	83.0	81.2	74.9	80.3	69.7	88.2	85.5	88.7	84.2	84.0	77.2
Finding steady work	82.3	73.7	74.7	59.9	79.3	62.1	88.0	84.4	87.4	83.3	84.2	76.3
Having lots of money	26.0	9.8	17.8	9.1	17.7	9.4	41.3	24.1	35.8	20.9	27.8	16.9
Being a leader in the community	14.9	8.0	8.5	4.4	9.2	4.2	11.3	5.9	13.7	6.4	9.5	4.5
Correcting inequalities	22.5	31.1	16.6	18.2	16.2	17.1	11.8	11.7	13.3	13.9	10.7	10.9
Having children	—	—	—	—	—	—	37.0	47.0	42.7	56.3	41.4	56.2
Having a happy family life	78.6	85.7	83.1	86.7	84.2	86.4	81.6	86.3	86.1	90.2	86.8	87.8
Providing better opportunities for my children	66.6	66.2	59.5	61.6	59.8	58.8	71.0	68.7	72.1	69.9	68.4	67.4
Living closer to parents or relatives	6.8	8.2	8.3	12.4	7.7	11.9	15.0	15.7	15.6	20.1	12.9	19.8
Moving from area	14.3	14.6	8.3	7.4	6.7	6.4	14.4	12.8	10.5	9.1	9.0	7.4
Having strong friendships	81.2	78.7	76.5	74.7	76.1	72.1	80.4	79.1	80.1	79.7	76.5	75.0
Having leisure time	—	—	60.9	55.1	65.4	60.1	70.2	68.8	74.5	72.0	70.1	68.9

—Data not available.

NOTE.—Percentages are based on the total sample members who responded to the individual survey items in each survey period.

SOURCE: U.S. Department of Education, National Center for Education Statistics, National Longitudinal Study and High School and Beyond surveys. (This table was prepared June 1987.)

Table 353.—Labor force participation of persons 16 years old and over, by age, sex, race/ethnicity, and years of school completed: 1990

Age, sex, and race/ethnicity	Labor force participation rate [1]						Employment/population ratio [2]					
	Total	8 years or less [3]	High school		College		Total	8 years or less [3]	High school		College	
			1 to 3 years	4 years	1 to 3 years	4 years			1 to 3 years	4 years	1 to 3 years	4 years
1	2	3	4	5	6	7	8	9	10	11	12	13
Total, 16 years old and over	66.4	34.1	50.3	69.2	74.7	81.8	62.7	31.0	44.2	65.2	71.5	79.9
Men	76.1	46.6	61.4	80.7	82.0	87.8	71.9	42.6	54.0	75.9	78.5	85.8
Women	57.5	22.0	40.2	59.9	68.3	74.9	54.3	19.7	35.2	56.6	65.4	73.0
White [4]	66.8	35.3	51.3	68.8	74.3	81.6	63.6	32.2	45.9	65.4	71.6	79.8
Black [4]	63.4	27.5	46.4	72.9	78.5	85.9	56.2	24.2	36.6	64.3	72.2	83.0
Hispanic [5]	67.0	55.7	56.7	75.5	81.4	84.1	61.6	50.2	49.5	70.1	77.3	81.1
25 to 34 years old	83.7	65.6	71.7	83.6	85.9	90.1	79.1	58.8	62.5	78.4	82.3	87.9
Men	94.1	84.7	89.2	95.0	95.1	95.7	89.0	77.1	78.8	89.2	91.1	93.5
Women	73.7	43.8	53.1	72.4	78.0	84.5	69.5	38.0	45.2	67.8	74.7	82.2
White [4]	84.7	68.1	74.7	84.4	86.0	90.6	80.8	61.3	67.0	80.0	83.0	88.5
Black [4]	79.8	49.2	59.9	81.0	86.8	92.4	70.5	40.4	45.3	70.7	79.5	89.2
Hispanic [5]	77.9	71.0	71.6	80.4	86.4	85.8	72.1	64.2	64.1	74.4	82.5	83.2

[1] Percent of the civilian population who are employed or seeking employment.
[2] Number of persons employed as a percent of civilian population.
[3] Includes persons reporting no school years completed.
[4] Includes persons of Hispanic origin.

[5] Persons of Hispanic origin may be of any race.

SOURCE: U.S. Department of Labor, Bureau of Labor Statistics, Office of Employment and Unemployment Statistics, unpublished data. (This table was prepared April 1991.)

Table 354.—Occupation of employed persons 16 years old and over, by years of school completed and sex: 1990

Sex and occupation	Total employed, in thousands	Percentage distribution, by years of school completed								Median school years completed
		Total	Elementary school		High school		College			
			Less than 5 years	5 to 8 years	1 to 3 years	4 years	1 to 3 years	4 years	5 years or more	
1	2	3	4	5	6	7	8	9	10	11
All persons										
All occupational groups	99,032	100.0	1.0	4.2	7.9	39.1	20.8	15.5	11.5	12.4
Managerial and professional specialty	28,693	100.0	0.1	0.6	1.7	16.8	19.1	30.0	31.7	15.9
Executive, administrative, and managerial	13,934	100.0	0.2	1.0	2.7	26.3	23.4	28.7	17.7	15.0
Professional specialty occupations	14,759	100.0	0.0	0.3	0.7	7.8	15.1	31.3	44.8	16.3
Teachers, except college and university	3,718	100.0	0.0	0.1	0.4	5.8	7.5	36.7	49.5	16.5
Teachers, college and university	706	100.0	0.0	0.3	0.3	2.3	4.1	10.6	82.4	17.1
Technical, sales, and administrative support	29,713	100.0	0.2	1.2	4.4	44.4	28.2	16.1	5.6	12.5
Technicians and related support	3,373	100.0	0.1	0.4	1.8	28.2	35.5	22.5	11.5	14.1
Sales occupations	11,019	100.0	0.2	1.9	5.8	39.1	24.3	21.5	7.2	12.9
Administrative support, including clerical	15,321	100.0	0.1	0.9	3.9	51.8	29.4	10.8	3.1	12.4
Service occupations	11,684	100.0	2.3	8.9	14.6	48.4	18.2	5.7	1.9	12.0
Precision production, craft, and repair	11,988	100.0	1.1	6.3	13.2	52.7	20.1	5.1	1.6	12.1
Operators, fabricators, and laborers	14,232	100.0	2.8	10.1	17.1	53.2	12.8	3.2	0.9	11.9
Farming, forestry, and fishing	2,722	100.0	6.1	14.7	13.0	42.5	13.7	7.4	2.5	11.9
Men										
All occupational groups	54,571	100.0	1.3	5.0	8.5	36.8	19.7	15.8	12.9	12.5
Managerial and professional specialty	15,793	100.0	0.1	0.8	1.8	15.1	17.3	29.6	35.3	16.0
Executive, administrative, and managerial	8,489	100.0	0.2	1.3	2.9	22.2	21.3	31.4	20.7	15.6
Professional specialty occupations	7,304	100.0	0.1	0.3	0.6	6.8	12.6	27.4	52.3	16.6
Teachers, except college and university	995	100.0	0.0	0.2	0.3	5.1	7.1	29.8	57.2	16.7
Teachers, college and university	450	100.0	0.0	0.2	0.4	2.2	3.3	7.8	86.0	17.1
Technical, sales, and administrative support	10,777	100.0	0.3	1.5	3.9	33.2	28.5	23.4	9.1	13.7
Technicians and related support	1,703	100.0	0.1	0.5	1.8	26.3	34.6	23.3	13.4	14.3
Sales occupations	6,099	100.0	0.3	1.7	3.8	31.6	26.2	27.0	9.5	13.9
Administrative support, including clerical	2,975	100.0	0.4	1.8	5.4	40.4	29.7	16.3	6.0	12.7
Service occupations	4,414	100.0	2.9	9.2	11.0	43.5	22.4	8.0	3.0	12.1
Precision production, craft, and repair	10,959	100.0	1.0	6.3	13.1	52.5	20.4	5.1	1.6	12.1
Operators, fabricators, and laborers	10,359	100.0	2.5	9.7	16.3	53.0	14.0	3.6	0.9	11.9
Farming, forestry, and fishing	2,270	100.0	6.7	15.6	13.5	41.5	13.3	7.0	2.5	11.8
Women										
All occupational groups	44,458	100.0	0.7	3.2	7.3	41.9	22.1	15.1	9.7	12.4
Managerial and professional specialty	12,899	100.0	0.0	0.3	1.4	18.9	21.4	30.6	27.3	15.8
Executive, administrative, and managerial	5,445	100.0	0.1	0.5	2.4	32.7	26.7	24.5	13.2	14.1
Professional specialty occupations	7,455	100.0	0.0	0.2	0.8	8.8	17.6	35.1	37.6	16.1
Teachers, except college and university	2,723	100.0	0.0	0.1	0.5	6.0	7.6	39.1	46.7	16.4
Teachers, college and university	256	100.0	0.0	0.4	0.0	2.3	5.1	16.0	76.2	17.0
Technical, sales, and administrative support	18,936	100.0	0.1	1.0	4.6	50.8	28.0	11.9	3.5	12.4
Technicians and related support	1,671	100.0	0.1	0.2	2.0	30.0	36.5	21.7	9.5	14.0
Sales occupations	4,919	100.0	0.2	2.1	8.3	48.4	21.9	14.7	4.4	12.3
Administrative support, including clerical	12,346	100.0	0.1	0.6	3.5	54.6	29.3	9.5	2.4	12.3
Service occupations	7,270	100.0	1.9	8.7	16.9	51.4	15.7	4.3	1.2	11.9
Precision production, craft, and repair	1,028	100.0	1.4	6.2	14.2	54.6	16.6	5.4	1.6	12.0
Operators, fabricators, and laborers	3,873	100.0	3.4	11.2	19.4	53.6	9.6	2.1	0.7	11.8
Farming, forestry, and fishing	451	100.0	3.5	10.4	10.6	47.7	16.0	9.3	2.7	12.0

NOTE.—Because of rounding, details may not add to totals.

SOURCE: U.S. Department of Labor, Bureau of Labor Statistics, Office of Employment and Unemployment Statistics, Industry and Occupation tables, unpublished. (This table was prepared March 1991.)

Table 355.—Unemployment rate of persons 16 years old and over, by age, sex, race/ethnicity, and years of school completed: 1990

Sex, race/ethnicity, and years of school completed	Percent unemployed [1]							
	Total, 16 years and over	16 to 19 years	20 to 24 years	25 to 34 years	35 to 44 years	45 to 54 years	55 to 64 years	65 years and over
1	2	3	4	5	6	7	8	9
All persons								
All education levels	5.5	15.7	8.8	5.5	4.1	3.5	3.3	3.0
8 years or less	9.1	30.6	13.8	10.3	9.0	7.8	5.4	3.7
1 to 3 years of high school	12.2	18.0	19.3	12.7	8.6	6.2	4.3	4.0
4 years of high school	5.8	12.7	9.4	6.3	4.8	3.4	3.2	2.7
1 to 3 years of college	4.2	8.4	5.9	4.2	3.6	3.3	2.8	3.7
4 or more years of college	2.4	7.7	5.0	2.5	2.1	1.9	2.3	2.0
Men								
All education levels	5.6	16.5	9.2	5.4	4.0	3.7	3.7	3.0
8 years or less	8.4	28.0	11.2	9.0	8.4	7.0	5.8	3.3
1 to 3 years of high school	12.1	18.6	17.8	11.6	8.0	6.8	5.2	3.5
4 years of high school	6.0	13.2	9.5	6.2	5.0	3.7	3.7	2.9
1 to 3 years of college	4.2	8.9	6.3	4.2	3.6	3.1	3.1	4.7
4 or more years of college	2.3	4.5	5.1	2.3	1.9	2.0	2.6	1.8
Women								
All education levels	5.5	14.8	8.5	5.6	4.2	3.4	2.7	3.0
8 years or less	10.5	36.8	21.1	13.1	10.2	9.1	4.6	4.5
1 to 3 years of high school	12.4	17.4	22.2	14.8	9.4	5.5	3.1	4.6
4 years of high school	5.5	12.2	9.3	6.4	4.6	3.1	2.7	2.4
1 to 3 years of college	4.2	8.1	5.6	4.3	3.6	3.4	2.3	2.4
4 or more years of college	2.5	10.3	4.9	2.7	2.3	1.7	1.7	2.3
White [2]								
All education levels	4.8	13.6	7.2	4.6	3.6	3.3	3.2	2.8
8 years or less	8.7	28.2	12.2	10.1	8.6	7.2	5.2	3.2
1 to 3 years of high school	10.5	15.5	15.9	10.3	7.5	5.5	3.8	3.8
4 years of high school	4.9	11.0	7.4	5.2	4.1	3.2	3.1	2.6
1 to 3 years of college	3.7	7.2	5.0	3.5	3.1	3.1	2.8	3.4
4 or more years of college	2.2	8.4	4.4	2.3	2.0	1.9	2.2	1.9
Black [2]								
All education levels	11.4	31.7	20.1	11.7	7.9	5.4	4.5	5.2
8 years or less	12.2	47.3	51.1	17.9	12.3	9.1	6.3	6.1
1 to 3 years of high school	21.1	36.4	37.2	24.5	13.1	9.0	6.5	5.6
4 years of high school	11.9	25.3	20.8	12.7	8.9	5.0	3.6	3.2
1 to 3 years of college	7.9	18.8	12.2	8.5	6.6	3.6	2.0	9.8
4 or more years of college	3.4	—	10.5	3.6	3.1	1.2	2.6	3.4
Hispanic origin [3]								
All education levels	8.1	19.7	9.1	7.4	6.6	6.6	5.5	6.1
8 years or less	9.8	20.5	9.9	9.6	9.8	9.1	8.1	5.0
1 to 3 years of high school	12.6	22.2	12.1	10.6	8.7	9.8	4.1	6.3
4 years of high school	7.2	15.3	8.5	7.4	5.7	4.9	4.1	4.0
1 to 3 years of college	5.0	16.2	6.8	4.5	4.3	3.8	3.9	3.1
4 or more years of college	3.5	—	6.5	3.0	3.1	3.4	3.1	20.1

[1] The unemployment rate is the percent of individuals in the labor force who are not working and who made specific efforts to find employment sometime during the prior 4 weeks. The labor force includes both employed and unemployed persons.
[2] Includes persons of Hispanic origin.
[3] Persons of Hispanic origin may be of any race.

—Data not available.

SOURCE: U.S. Department of Labor, Bureau of Labor Statistics, Office of Employment and Unemployment Statistics, unpublished data. (This table was prepared April 1991.)

Table 356.—Employment status and hourly wages of 1972 high school graduates in Spring 1986, by race/ethnicity and socioeconomic status

Race/ethnicity, socioeconomic status, and level of education	Percent with specified level of education	Employment status				Average hourly wages of those employed	
		Continuous full-time	Intermittent full-time	Part-time	Not in labor force	Continous full-time	Intermittent full-time
1	2	3	4	5	6	7	8
Total, all persons	**100**	**39**	**34**	**6**	**20**	—	—
High school diploma	32	33	30	8	29	$7.01	$6.60
Some postsecondary education	30	42	33	6	19	7.17	7.18
1- or 2-year degree	12	40	37	9	14	7.59	7.65
Bachelor's degree	19	44	35	6	15	8.71	8.91
Advanced degree	7	40	46	5	9	10.80	10.70
Race/ethnicity							
White							
Total	100	40	34	7	19	—	—
High school diploma	32	34	31	8	28	7.11	6.76
Some postsecondary education	29	42	33	7	18	7.32	7.36
1- or 2-year degree	12	41	37	9	13	7.70	7.84
Bachelor's degree	20	45	35	6	14	8.76	9.03
Advanced degree	8	41	47	5	8	10.86	10.55
Black							
Total	100	38	35	7	20	—	—
High school diploma	31	36	35	10	18	5.89	5.38
Some postsecondary education	38	43	32	5	20	5.85	6.29
1- or 2-year degree	12	32	44	10	14	6.58	6.33
Bachelor's degree	16	36	34	4	26	7.97	7.30
Advanced degree	4	37	32	7	24	10.66	(1)
Hispanic							
Total	100	41	27	5	26	—	—
High school diploma	42	30	23	6	41	7.26	5.90
Some postsecondary education	35	52	28	4	15	7.28	6.24
1- or 2-year degree	12	46	34	4	16	6.87	7.93
Bachelor's degree	8	54	27	8	11	8.94	(1)
Advanced degree	4	27	47	9	17	(1)	(1)
Socioeconomic status quartile [2] (SES)							
Lower 25 percent	100	36	33	8	23	—	—
High school diploma	50	31	30	9	30	6.48	5.96
Some postsecondary education	27	43	32	7	18	6.67	6.25
1- or 2-year degree	11	37	38	9	15	6.71	7.03
Bachelor's degree	9	43	37	6	14	7.97	7.79
Advanced degree	3	37	40	8	16	9.74	10.24
Middle 50 percent	100	39	33	6	22	—	—
High school diploma	34	33	31	7	29	7.16	7.08
Some postsecondary education	31	41	32	6	21	7.21	7.45
1- or 2-year degree	13	41	37	9	13	7.53	7.79
Bachelor's degree	17	44	33	5	18	8.39	8.79
Advanced degree	5	43	44	3	11	10.46	9.89
Upper 25 percent	100	42	36	6	15	—	—
High school diploma	9	44	26	7	24	8.02	6.54
Some postsecondary education	31	32	33	6	17	7.54	7.45
1- or 2-year degree	10	39	35	9	17	8.62	7.96
Bachelor's degree	35	44	36	6	14	9.16	9.34
Advanced degree	15	38	48	6	7	11.19	11.29

[1] Too few respondents to produce reliable estimates.

[2] The SES index is a composite of five equally-weighted measures: father's education, mother's education, family income, father's occupation, and presence of certain items in the respondent's household.

—Data not available.

SOURCE: U.S. Department of Education, National Center for Education Statistics, "National Longitudinal Study, 1972," unpublished tabulations. (This table was prepared January 1989.)

Table 357.—Median annual income [1] of year-round full-time workers 25 years old and over, by years of school completed and sex: 1970 to 1989

Sex and year	Total	Elementary school			High school		College		
		Less than 8 years	8 years	8 years or less	1 to 3 years	4 years	1 to 3 years	4 years	5 years or more
1	2	3	4	5	6	7	8	9	10
Men									
1970	$9,521	$6,043	$7,535	—	$8,514	$9,567	$11,183	$13,264	$14,747
1971	10,038	6,310	7,838	—	8,945	9,996	11,701	13,730	15,300
1972	11,148	7,042	8,636	—	9,462	11,073	12,428	14,879	16,877
1973	12,088	7,521	9,406	—	10,401	12,017	13,090	15,503	17,726
1974	12,786	7,912	9,891	—	11,225	12,642	13,718	16,240	18,214
1975	13,821	8,647	10,600	—	11,511	13,542	14,989	17,477	19,658
1976	14,732	8,991	11,312	—	12,301	14,295	15,514	18,236	20,597
1977	15,726	9,419	12,083	—	13,120	15,434	16,235	19,603	21,941
1978	16,882	10,474	12,965	—	14,199	16,396	17,411	20,941	23,578
1979	18,711	10,993	14,454	—	15,198	18,100	19,367	22,406	25,860
1980	20,297	11,753	14,674	—	16,101	19,469	20,909	24,311	27,690
1981	21,689	12,866	16,084	—	16,938	20,598	22,565	26,394	30,434
1982	22,857	12,386	16,376	—	17,496	21,344	23,633	28,030	32,325
1983	23,891	14,093	16,438	—	17,685	21,823	24,613	29,892	34,643
1984	25,497	14,624	16,812	—	19,120	23,269	25,831	31,487	36,836
1985	26,365	14,766	18,645	—	18,881	23,853	26,960	32,822	39,335
1986	27,337	14,485	18,541	—	20,003	24,701	28,025	34,391	39,592
1987	28,232	—	—	16,691	20,863	25,490	29,820	35,527	41,973
1988	29,331	—	—	17,190	20,777	26,045	30,129	36,434	43,938
1989	30,465	—	—	17,555	21,065	26,609	31,308	38,565	46,842
Women									
1970	5,616	3,798	4,181	—	4,655	5,580	6,604	8,156	9,581
1971	5,872	3,946	4,400	—	4,889	5,808	6,815	8,451	10,581
1972	6,331	4,221	4,784	—	5,253	6,166	7,020	8,736	11,036
1973	6,791	4,369	5,135	—	5,513	6,623	7,593	9,057	11,340
1974	7,370	5,022	5,606	—	5,919	7,150	8,072	9,523	11,790
1975	8,117	5,109	5,691	—	6,355	7,777	9,126	10,349	13,138
1976	8,728	5,644	6,433	—	6,800	8,377	9,475	11,010	13,569
1977	9,257	6,074	6,564	—	7,387	8,894	10,157	11,605	14,338
1978	10,121	6,648	7,489	—	7,996	9,769	10,634	12,347	15,310
1979	11,071	7,414	7,788	—	8,555	10,513	11,854	13,441	16,693
1980	12,156	7,742	8,857	—	9,676	11,537	12,954	15,143	18,100
1981	13,259	8,419	9,723	—	10,043	12,332	14,343	16,322	20,148
1982	14,477	8,424	10,112	—	10,661	13,240	15,594	17,405	21,449
1983	15,292	9,385	10,337	—	11,131	13,787	16,536	18,452	22,877
1984	16,169	9,828	10,848	—	11,843	14,569	17,007	20,257	25,076
1985	17,124	9,736	11,377	—	11,836	15,481	17,989	21,389	25,928
1986	17,675	10,153	11,183	—	12,267	15,947	18,516	22,412	27,279
1987	18,608	—	—	11,018	12,939	16,549	19,946	23,399	30,060
1988	19,497	—	—	11,358	13,104	16,810	20,845	25,187	30,136
1989	20,570	—	—	12,188	13,923	17,528	21,631	26,709	32,050

[1] Data have not been adjusted for changes in the purchasing power of the dollar.
—Data not available or not applicable.

NOTE.—1987, 1988, and 1989 data were computed using a new processing procedure.

SOURCE: U.S. Department of Commerce, Bureau of the Census, *Current Population Reports*, Series P–60, Money *Income of Families and Persons in the United States*, various years; and *Money Income and Poverty Status of Families and Persons in the United States, 1988*, Series P-60, Nos. 161 and 166, and unpublished data. (This table was prepared January 1991.)

Table 358.—Total annual money earnings of persons 25 years old and over,[1] by years of school completed, sex, and age: 1989

Sex, income, and age	Total	8 years or less	High school			College					Mean school years completed
			Total	1 to 3	4	Total	1 to 3	4 or more			
								Total	4	5 or more	
1	2	3	4	5	6	7	8	9	10	11	12

Number, in thousands

Men

Total	74,421	8,561	34,426	8,000	26,426	31,435	13,270	18,164	10,042	8,122	12.6
With earnings	59,073	4,051	27,102	5,297	21,805	27,920	11,543	16,376	9,044	7,332	13.1

Percentage distribution of men with earnings

Total	100.0	100.0	100.0	100.0	100.0	100.0	100.0	100.0	100.0	100.0	13.1
$1 to $2,499 or loss	4.5	13.0	4.9	7.8	4.2	2.9	3.6	2.3	2.3	2.4	11.5
$2,500 to $4,999	3.1	7.8	3.8	6.2	3.2	1.8	2.5	1.4	1.4	1.4	11.5
$5,000 to $7,499	4.1	9.1	5.0	8.2	4.3	2.6	3.4	2.0	2.0	2.1	11.6
$7,500 to $9,999	3.8	9.4	4.6	6.6	4.1	2.3	3.0	1.8	2.0	1.5	11.5
$10,000 to $12,499	5.9	11.9	7.3	10.0	6.6	3.6	4.4	3.1	3.3	2.7	11.8
$12,500 to $14,999	4.1	6.8	5.1	6.5	4.8	2.7	3.9	1.9	2.1	1.7	11.9
$15,000 to $17,499	6.2	8.3	8.0	8.6	7.8	4.1	5.7	3.0	3.5	2.3	12.1
$17,500 to $19,999	5.2	6.4	6.3	6.6	6.2	4.0	5.4	3.0	3.7	2.1	12.4
$20,000 to $24,999	11.9	9.2	14.0	13.1	14.2	10.2	13.0	8.3	10.0	6.1	12.8
$25,000 to $29,999	10.3	7.4	11.3	9.3	11.8	9.7	11.5	8.5	9.3	7.5	13.0
$30,000 to $34,999	9.9	4.4	10.0	6.8	10.8	10.7	11.7	9.9	11.1	8.5	13.4
$35,000 to $49,999	17.6	5.1	14.1	8.0	15.6	22.8	21.1	24.1	23.9	24.3	14.1
$50,000 to $74,999	8.6	0.9	4.1	1.7	4.7	14.1	8.0	18.5	16.3	21.1	15.2
$75,000 and over	4.7	0.2	1.4	0.6	1.6	8.5	3.0	12.4	9.0	16.5	16.0

Median earnings

All ages, 25 and over	25,426	12,237	21,384	16,376	22,371	32,134	26,697	37,060	34,489	41,382	—
25 to 34 years	21,427	11,012	18,892	14,181	20,167	26,064	22,565	29,663	29,080	30,801	—
35 to 44 years	29,599	13,945	23,748	16,908	25,265	35,698	30,376	40,655	36,862	44,319	—
45 to 54 years	31,069	16,594	26,315	21,485	28,000	40,170	33,162	46,007	42,590	47,665	—
55 to 64 years	26,561	14,800	23,281	19,485	25,195	37,355	30,715	42,299	40,885	45,000	—
65 years and over	7,933	4,792	6,863	5,908	7,415	14,068	8,844	20,240	15,939	25,487	—

Number, in thousands

Women

Total	82,116	9,029	43,155	9,462	33,693	29,932	14,805	15,127	9,424	5,702	12.3
With earnings	49,256	2,076	24,860	3,911	20,949	22,320	10,535	11,785	7,122	4,664	13.1

Percentage distribution of women with earnings

Total	100.0	100.0	100.0	100.0	100.0	100.0	100.0	100.0	100.0	100.0	13.1
$1 to $2,499 or loss	11.2	23.8	12.9	18.5	11.8	8.2	9.7	6.8	7.1	6.3	12.2
$2,500 to $4,999	7.8	15.2	9.6	13.5	8.9	5.2	6.5	4.0	4.4	3.4	12.1
$5,000 to $7,499	9.2	15.9	11.0	14.0	10.5	6.5	7.9	5.3	5.7	4.8	12.3
$7,500 to $9,999	7.7	11.9	9.3	11.1	9.0	5.4	7.1	3.9	4.2	3.5	12.3
$10,000 to $12,499	10.1	10.6	12.8	13.2	12.7	7.0	8.5	5.7	6.4	4.5	12.5
$12,500 to $14,999	6.6	6.0	7.7	7.7	7.7	5.4	7.1	3.8	4.7	2.6	12.7
$15,000 to $17,499	8.9	7.2	10.0	7.4	10.5	7.9	10.0	6.0	6.8	4.6	12.8
$17,500 to $19,999	5.9	2.9	5.9	3.7	6.3	6.3	7.2	5.4	6.4	3.9	13.2
$20,000 to $24,999	11.6	3.6	10.1	6.1	10.8	14.1	14.0	14.3	15.6	12.2	13.7
$25,000 to $29,999	7.7	1.4	5.1	2.4	5.6	11.1	9.2	12.8	12.6	13.3	14.3
$30,000 to $34,999	5.0	0.4	2.7	0.9	3.0	8.0	5.6	10.1	9.3	11.3	14.7
$35,000 to $49,999	6.2	0.8	2.3	1.2	2.5	11.1	5.7	15.9	12.7	20.7	15.3
$50,000 to $74,999	1.6	0.1	0.5	0.2	0.6	2.8	1.2	4.3	3.2	6.0	15.6
$75,000 and over	0.6	0.1	0.2	0.1	0.2	1.0	0.4	1.6	0.9	2.8	15.7

Median earnings

All ages, 25 and over	**$14,037**	6,718	11,407	8,394	11,945	19,284	15,820	22,776	21,099	26,252	—
25 to 34 years	13,850	6,445	10,735	7,157	11,270	18,494	14,943	22,033	21,642	23,403	—
35 to 44 years	15,523	7,670	12,188	9,867	12,576	20,303	16,592	24,066	20,982	27,610	—
45 to 54 years	15,351	7,797	12,780	10,387	13,679	21,419	17,623	25,668	21,271	29,975	—
55 to 64 years	11,867	7,194	11,007	7,922	11,937	16,979	15,208	20,917	17,128	25,554	—
65 years and over	5,807	3,324	5,392	4,740	5,618	8,435	7,042	10,035	10,831	9,416	—

[1] Includes full-time and part-time workers.
—Not applicable.

NOTE.—Because of rounding, details may not add to totals.

SOURCE: U.S. Department of Commerce, Bureau of the Census, unpublished data. (This table was prepared February 1991.)

Table 359.—College enrollment and labor force status of 1988 and 1989 high school graduates 16 to 24 years old, by sex and race/ethnicity: October 1988 and October 1989

[Numbers in thousands]

Item	Civilian noninstitutional population			Civilian labor force [1]				
	Number	Percent	Percent of high school graduates	Number	Labor force participation rate	Employed	Unemployed	
							Number	Unemployment rate
1	2	3	4	5	6	7	8	9
1988 high school graduates [2]								
Total	2,673	100.0	100.0	1,677	62.7	1,450	227	13.5
Men	1,334	49.9	49.9	869	65.1	752	117	13.4
Women	1,339	50.1	50.1	808	60.3	698	110	13.7
White [3]	2,187	81.8	81.8	1,421	65.0	1,254	167	11.8
Black [3]	382	14.3	14.3	205	53.5	154	50	24.6
Hispanic origin [4]	179	6.7	6.7	103	57.8	77	27	25.9
Enrolled in college, October 1988	1,575	100.0	58.9	747	47.4	660	87	11.6
Men	761	48.3	28.5	362	47.6	328	35	9.5
Women	814	51.7	30.5	384	47.3	332	52	13.6
Full-time students	1,444	91.7	54.0	630	43.6	550	80	12.7
Part-time students	131	8.3	4.9	117	89.2	110	7	5.6
White [3]	1,328	84.3	49.7	668	50.3	598	70	10.5
Black [3]	172	10.9	6.4	49	28.5	37	12	([5])
Hispanic origin [4]	102	6.5	3.8	40	39.5	33	8	([5])
Not enrolled in college, October 1988	1,098	100.0	41.1	930	84.7	790	140	15.1
Men	572	52.1	21.4	506	88.5	424	82	16.2
Women	526	47.9	19.7	424	80.6	365	58	13.7
White [3]	859	78.2	32.1	754	87.7	656	97	12.9
Black [3]	211	19.2	7.9	156	73.9	117	38	24.5
Hispanic origin [4]	77	7.0	2.9	63	82.2	44	19	([5])
1989 high school graduates [6]								
Total	2,454	100.0	100.0	1,495	61.0	1,314	182	12.2
Men	1,208	49.2	49.2	763	63.1	680	83	10.9
Women	1,245	50.7	50.7	733	58.8	634	99	13.5
White [3]	2,051	83.6	83.6	1,306	63.7	1,165	141	10.8
Black [3]	337	13.7	13.7	162	48.0	122	40	24.8
Hispanic origin [4]	168	6.8	6.8	119	71.0	101	19	15.7
Enrolled in college, October 1989	1,463	100.0	59.6	659	45.1	600	59	8.9
Men	696	47.6	28.4	305	43.8	281	24	7.8
Women	767	52.4	31.3	354	46.2	319	35	9.9
Full-time students	1,353	92.5	55.1	557	41.2	503	54	9.7
Part-time students	110	7.5	4.5	102	93.0	97	5	4.8
White [3]	1,238	84.6	50.4	599	48.4	554	45	7.6
Black [3]	178	12.2	7.3	48	26.7	34	14	([5])
Hispanic origin [4]	93	6.4	3.8	63	68.3	63	—	([5])
Not enrolled in college, October 1989	991	100.0	40.4	836	84.4	713	123	14.7
Men	513	51.8	20.9	458	89.4	399	59	13.0
Women	478	48.2	19.5	378	79.1	314	64	16.9
White [3]	813	82.0	33.1	707	86.9	611	96	13.6
Black [3]	159	16.0	6.5	114	72.0	88	27	23.3
Hispanic origin [4]	75	7.6	3.1	56	74.3	37	19	([5])

[1] The labor force includes all employed persons plus those seeking employment. The labor force participation rate is the percentage of persons either employed or seeking employment.

[2] Includes persons who graduated from high school between January and October 1988.

[3] Includes persons of Hispanic origin.

[4] Persons of Hispanic origin may be of any race.

[5] Data not shown where base is less than 75,000.

[6] Includes persons who graduated from high school between January and October 1989.

—Data not available or not applicable.

NOTE.—Data are based upon sample surveys of the civilian noninstitutional population. Percents are only shown when base is 75,000 or greater. Even though the standard errors are large, smaller estimates are shown to permit users to combine categories in various ways. Because of rounding, details may not add to totals.

SOURCE: U.S. Department of Labor, Bureau of Labor Statistics, *Employment Status of School Age Youth, High School Graduates and Dropouts,* various years. (This table was prepared January 1991.)

Table 360.—Labor force status of 1979–80 to 1988–89 high school dropouts 16 to 24 years old, by sex and race/ethnicity: October 1980 to October 1989

[Numbers in thousands]

Year, sex, and race	Civilian noninstitutional population		Civilian labor force [1]				
	Number	Percent	Number	Labor force participation rate	Employed	Unemployed	
						Number	Unemployment rate
1	2	3	4	5	6	7	8
1979–80 high school drouputs [2] in October 1980	739	100.0	471	63.7	322	149	31.6
Men	422	57.1	305	72.3	212	93	30.5
Women	317	42.9	166	52.4	110	56	33.7
White [3]	580	78.5	392	67.6	286	106	27.0
Black [3]	146	19.8	73	50.0	33	40	([4])
Hispanic origin [5]	91	12.3	60	65.9	43	17	([4])
1984–85 high school dropouts [6] in October 1985	612	100.0	413	67.5	266	147	35.6
Men	321	52.5	261	81.3	163	98	37.5
Women	291	47.5	152	52.2	103	49	32.2
Single	220	35.9	117	53.2	78	39	33.3
Other marital status	72	11.8	36	([4])	26	10	([4])
White [3]	458	74.8	330	72.1	214	116	35.2
Black [3]	132	21.6	69	52.3	39	30	([4])
Hispanic origin [5]	106	17.3	73	68.9	40	33	([4])
1985–86 high school dropouts [7] in October 1986	562	100.0	359	63.9	259	100	27.9
Men	300	53.4	216	72.0	168	48	22.2
Women	262	46.6	143	54.6	91	52	36.4
Single	196	34.9	107	54.6	69	38	35.5
Other marital status	66	11.7	36	([4])	23	13	([4])
White [3]	449	79.9	289	64.4	213	76	26.3
Black [3]	90	16.0	50	55.6	29	21	([4])
Hispanic origin [5]	127	22.6	77	60.6	58	19	24.7
1986–87 high school dropouts [8] in October 1987	502	100.0	333	66.4	207	126	37.8
Men	274	54.6	202	73.7	125	77	38.1
Women	228	45.4	131	57.6	82	49	37.3
White [3]	373	74.3	257	68.9	172	85	33.0
Black [3]	115	22.9	69	60.1	30	39	([4])
Hispanic origin [5]	57	11.4	37	([4])	22	15	([4])
1987–88 high school dropouts [9] in October 1988	552	100.0	327	59.2	240	87	26.7
Men	307	55.6	229	74.4	164	65	28.5
Women	245	44.4	98	40.1	76	22	22.4
White [3]	436	79.0	283	64.8	213	70	24.7
Black [3]	107	19.4	42	39.4	25	18	([4])
Hispanic origin [5]	101	18.3	65	64.7	56	9	([4])
1988–89 high school dropouts [10] in October 1989	446	100.0	292	65.4	210	82	28.0
Men	243	54.5	181	74.6	127	54	29.6
Women	203	45.5	111	54.4	83	28	25.3
White [3]	324	72.6	228	70.6	176	52	22.9
Black [3]	112	25.1	59	52.2	31	27	([4])
Hispanic origin [5]	65	14.6	36	([4])	26	11	([4])

[1] The labor force includes all employed persons plus those seeking employment. The labor force participation rate is the percentage of persons either employed or seeking employment.

[2] Includes persons who dropped out of school between October 1979 and October 1980.

[3] Includes persons of Hispanic origin.

[4] Data not shown where base is less than 75,000.

[5] Persons of Hispanic origin may be of any race.

[6] Includes persons who dropped out of school between October 1984 and October 1985.

[7] Includes persons who dropped out of school between October 1985 and October 1986.

[8] Includes persons who dropped out of school between October 1986 and October 1987.

[9] Includes persons who dropped out of school between October 1987 and October 1988.

[10] Includes persons who dropped out of school between October 1988 and October 1989.

NOTE.—Data are based upon sample surveys of the civilian noninstitutional population. Includes dropouts from any grade, including a small number from elementary and middle schools. Percents are only shown when the base is 75,000 or greater. Even though the standard errors are large, smaller estimates are shown to permit users to combine categories in various ways. Because of rounding, details may not add to totals.

SOURCE: U.S. Department of Labor, Bureau of Labor Statistics, *Students, Graduates, and Dropouts, October 1980-82;* and *Employment Status of School Age Youth, High School Graduates and Dropouts,* various years; and "Nearly Half of College Freshman Also Hold a Job or Are Looking for One," June 1987; and "Sixty Percent of 1989 High School Graduates Enrolled in College," June 1990. (This table was prepared January 1991.)

Table 361.—Full-time employment status of bachelor's degree recipients 1 year after graduation, by field of study: 1976 to 1987

Field of study	Percent employed full-time				Percent employed full-time in a job closely related to field of study				Percent employed full-time in nonprofessional job [1]			
	1974–75 graduates in May 1976	1979–80 graduates in May 1981	1983–84 graduates in June 1985	1985–86 graduates in June 1987	1974–75 graduates in May 1976	1979–80 graduates in May 1981	1983–84 graduates in June 1985	1985–86 graduates in June 1987	1974–75 graduates in May 1976	1979–80 graduates in May 1981	1983–84 graduates in June 1985	1985–86 graduates in June 1987
1	2	3	4	5	6	7	8	9	10	11	12	13
Total	67	71	73	74	35	38	38	38	10	12	13	14
Professional/technical fields	77	80	82	81	51	51	47	47	9	10	13	11
Arts and sciences fields	56	56	56	62	18	17	15	25	12	14	15	15
Other	65	74	75	74	36	43	47	36	9	19	12	17
Newly qualified to teach	66	75	73	68	43	56	54	47	7	8	9	9
Not newly qualified to teach	67	71	73	74	33	36	36	37	12	13	13	14
Professional/technical fields	80	81	82	82	52	49	47	47	10	10	13	11
Engineering	79	84	84	83	57	55	53	46	4	2	3	5
Business and management	84	83	85	85	49	44	41	40	15	14	19	17
Health	75	77	75	76	71	66	70	65	2	4	2	3
Education [2]	66	67	63	73	22	29	24	57	12	18	16	9
Public affairs and services	—	77	74	72	—	46	31	37	—	10	15	20
Arts and sciences fields	57	56	56	63	17	16	15	25	13	15	15	15
Biological sciences	56	45	43	42	26	18	17	15	6	8	11	11
Physical sciences and mathematics ..	50	58	51	76	19	29	20	48	6	2	7	9
Psychology	61	56	57	66	22	17	12	22	18	17	16	19
Social sciences	59	61	61	61	12	10	13	12	15	21	14	17
Humanities	56	55	59	59	12	14	17	19	17	18	19	19
Other	68	75	77	75	36	43	42	36	10	20	14	21
Communications	—	71	76	77	—	31	31	33	—	24	16	18
Miscellaneous	66	76	77	74	35	46	46	38	11	19	13	23

[1] Includes those not working in technical, managerial, or administrative types of jobs who reported that they did not need a college degree to obtain their job.

[2] Includes those who have not finished all requirements for teaching certification or were previously qualified to teach.

—Data not available.

NOTE.—Data are from a sample survey of recent college graduates. Notes on methodology are included in the Guide to Sources. Data exclude bachelor's recipients from U.S. Service Schools. Deceased graduates and graduates living at foreign addresses at the time of the survey are not included. Data are not shown where sample size of base is less than 100 persons.

SOURCE: U.S. Department of Education, National Center for Education Statistics, "Recent College Graduates" surveys. (This table was prepared March 1989.)

Table 362.—Occupation of 1985–86 bachelor's degree recipients 1 year after graduation, by field of study and occupational area: 1987

[Percentage distribution]

Occupational area in June 1987	All fields of study	Professional/technical fields						Arts and sciences				Other fields	
		Business and management	Education	Engineering	Health professions	Public affairs/social services	Biological sciences	Mathematics, computer, and physical sciences	Social sciences	Humanities	Psychology	Communications	Miscellaneous[1]
1	2	3	4	5	6	7	8	9	10	11	12	13	14
Total	100	100	100	100	100	100	100	100	100	100	100	100	100
Professional, managerial and technical	53	52	75	71	79	49	28	59	32	39	40	47	37
Business	19	46	4	5	3	9	4	6	18	9	12	19	13
Educators	10	1	66	2	2	4	7	8	6	12	10	2	7
Engineers	6	1	(2)	57	(2)	(2)	(2)	6	(2)	(2)	(2)	1	1
Health professionals	5	(2)	1	(2)	65	1	2	(2)	(2)	7	5	(2)	3
Public affairs/social services	2	(2)	2	(2)	1	31	2	(2)	4	7	7	1	5
Biological scientists	(2)	(2)	(2)	(2)	(2)	(2)	4	(2)	(2)	(2)	(2)	(2)	1
Computer/physical scientist, mathematician	5	3	(2)	3	(2)	(2)	(2)	35	1	1	1	1	1
Communications	1	(2)	(2)	(2)	(2)	(2)	(2)	(2)	(2)	4	(2)	20	1
Writer	1	(2)	(2)	(2)	(2)	1	1	(2)	(2)	6	1	3	3
Technicians	3	1	1	4	7	3	10	4	3	1	4	1	5
Nonprofessional, nonmanagerial, and nontechnical	31	37	15	18	9	37	28	25	40	39	40	41	47
Unemployed	4	4	3	4	2	3	4	4	6	7	5	6	4
Not in labor force	11	6	6	7	10	10	39	10	21	15	15	5	12

[1] Includes agricultural and related studies, home economics, law, liberal/general studies, area studies, library science, recreation, and protective services.
[2] Less than 0.5 percent

SOURCE: U.S. Department of Education, National Center for Education Statistics, "Survey of 1985–86 Recent College Graduates." (This table was prepared March 1989.)

Table 363.—Percentage of 1985–86 bachelor's degree recipients who have pursued additional higher education, by type of degree sought or obtained, and undergraduate major field of study: 1987

Undergraduate major field of study	Total	No additional education	Courses not leading to degree or certificate	Associate or bachelor's degree	Post-baccalau-reate certificate	Master's degree	Doctor's degree	First-professional degree [1]	Other certificate
1	2	3	4	5	6	7	8	9	10
Total	100	72	3	1	1	15	1	4	2
Professional fields	100	79	2	1	([2])	14	([2])	2	1
Engineering	100	72	2	1	([2])	22	1	1	1
Business and management	100	84	2	1	([2])	9	([2])	2	1
Health professions	100	79	2	1	([2])	13	([2])	3	1
Education	100	71	3	1	1	19	([2])	([2])	3
Public affairs and social services	100	70	3	2	([2])	23	([2])	2	([2])
Arts and sciences fields	100	61	3	2	1	19	3	9	3
Biological sciences	100	38	5	3	1	13	6	28	5
Physical sciences, mathematics, and computer sciences	100	70	3	2	([2])	16	4	4	2
Psychology	100	57	2	1	1	29	4	3	2
Social sciences	100	62	2	1	1	16	2	12	3
Humanities	100	61	3	2	1	23	1	5	3
Other	100	77	4	2	1	10	([2])	3	4
Communications	100	86	3	1	1	6	([2])	2	1
Miscellaneous	100	72	4	2	1	12	1	4	5

[1] Includes chiropractic, dentistry, law, medicine, optometry, osteopathic medicine, pharmacy, podiatry, theological studies, and veterinary medicine.
[2] Less than 0.5 percent.

NOTE.—Data are from a sample survey of recent college graduates. Notes on methodology are included in the Guide to Sources. Data exclude bachelor's degree recipients from U.S. Service Schools. Deceased graduates and graduates living at foreign addresses at the time of the survey are not included. Because of rounding, details may not add to totals.

SOURCE: U.S. Department of Education, National Center for Education Statistics, "Recent College Graduates" survey. (This table was prepared March 1989.)

Table 364.—Percentage of 1985–86 bachelor's degree recipients who have applied for additional education and reasons for not applying, by major field of study: 1987

Undergraduate major field of study	Total	Applied for additional education	Did not apply for additional education, by reason				
			No plans to continue	Wanted to work	Wanted to take time off	Could not afford to continue	Other reasons
1	2	3	4	5	6	7	8
Total	100	36	16	34	6	5	3
Professional/technical fields	100	29	17	39	7	4	3
Engineering	100	37	13	40	4	4	2
Business and management	100	24	22	39	8	4	3
Health professions	100	29	15	39	8	6	3
Education	100	36	10	39	7	6	2
Public affairs and social services	100	43	14	34	4	5	([1])
Arts and sciences fields	100	47	13	27	5	4	3
Biological sciences	100	68	6	17	2	4	3
Physical sciences, mathematics, and computer sciences	100	37	16	35	5	4	2
Psychology	100	50	10	26	9	3	2
Social sciences	100	47	11	28	5	5	4
Humanities	100	49	15	23	5	4	3
Other	100	32	20	33	6	7	2
Communications	100	23	25	39	5	6	2
Miscellaneous	100	37	17	29	6	8	3

[1] Less than 0.5 percent.

NOTE.—Data are from a sample survey of recent college graduates. Notes on methodology are included in the Guide to Sources. Data exclude bachelor's degree recipients from U.S. Service Schools. Deceased graduates and graduates living at foreign addresses at the time of the survey are not included. Because of rounding, details may not add to totals.

SOURCE: U.S. Department of Education, National Center for Education Statistics, "Recent College Graduates" survey. (This table was prepared March 1989.)

Table 365.—Average annual salary of bachelor's degree recipients employed full-time 1 year after graduation, by field of study: 1976 to 1987

Field of study	Average salary[1] of 1974–75 degree recipients in February 1976		Average salary[1] of 1979–80 degree recipients in May 1981		Average salary[1] of 1983–84 degree recipients in June 1985		Average salary of 1985–86 degree recipients in June 1987	Percentage change in constant dollars, 1976 to 1981	Percentage change in constant dollars, 1981 to 1987
	Current dollars	Constant 1987 dollars	Current dollars	Constant 1987 dollars	Current dollars	Constant 1987 dollars	Current dollars		
1	2	3	4	5	6	7	8	9	10
Total	$7,600	$15,500	$15,200	$19,200	$17,700	$18,700	$20,300	25	6
Engineering	12,200	24,800	22,400	28,300	24,100	25,400	26,600	15	−6
Business and management	10,200	20,700	16,300	20,600	18,700	19,700	21,100	0	2
Health professions	8,600	17,500	17,300	21,900	20,800	21,900	22,600	25	3
Education[2]	6,300	12,800	11,500	14,500	13,800	14,600	15,800	14	9
Public affairs and social services	(3)	(3)	13,700	17,300	15,100	15,900	17,700	—	2
Biological sciences	6,500	13,200	14,500	18,300	15,100	15,900	16,400	40	−10
Physical sciences, mathematics, and computer sciences	7,000	14,200	16,300	20,600	17,500	18,500	22,500	45	9
Psychology	(3)	(3)	12,500	15,800	14,600	15,400	17,300	—	9
Social sciences	6,700	13,600	14,000	17,700	15,800	16,700	20,300	31	15
Humanities	5,800	11,800	12,600	15,900	14,000	14,800	16,200	36	2
Communications	(3)	(3)	(3)	(3)	16,200	17,100	(3)	—	—
Miscellaneous	6,800	13,800	15,100	19,100	18,600	19,600	17,600	39	−8

[1] Reported salaries of full-time workers under $2,600 in 1976, $4,200 in 1981, and $5,000 in 1985 were excluded from the tabulations.

[2] Most educators work 9- to 10-month contracts.

[3] Cell contains fewer than 75 respondents.

—Data not available.

NOTE.—Data exclude bachelor's recipients from U.S. Service Schools and graduates living at foreign addresses at the time of the survey. Constant dollar adjustments based on the Consumer Price Index.

SOURCE: U.S. Department of Education, National Center for Education Statistics, "Recent College Graduates" surveys. (This table was prepared February 1989.)

Table 366.—Income, earnings, and work activity of persons who held a bachelor's or advanced degree, by field of study: Spring 1984

Field of study	Mean monthly income[1]		Mean monthly earnings[2]		Number of months worked during previous 4 months		Standard errors for monthly income[3]	
	Bachelor's degrees	Advanced degrees	Bachelor's degrees	Advanced degrees	Bachelor's degrees	Advanced degrees	Bachelor's degrees	Advanced degrees
1	2	3	4	5	6	7	8	9
All degree recipients	$1,841	$2,711	$1,540	$2,341	3.08	3.35	$47	$80
Agriculture and forestry	1,945	(4)	1,559	(4)	3.25	(4)	203	(4)
Biology	1,559	(4)	1,201	(4)	2.73	(4)	218	(4)
Business and management	2,381	3,564	2,179	3,192	3.48	3.64	163	253
Economics	2,846	(4)	2,280	(4)	3.36	(4)	372	(4)
Education	1,290	2,062	1,012	1,695	2.76	3.23	51	140
Engineering	2,833	3,308	2,282	2,886	3.38	3.55	170	235
English and journalism	1,477	1,945	1,095	1,567	2.66	3.48	225	263
Home economics	1,065	(4)	525	(4)	2.12	(4)	208	(4)
Law	(4)	4,060	(4)	3,624	(4)	3.57	(4)	365
Liberal arts and humanities	1,400	1,720	1,072	1,466	2.87	3.17	92	192
Mathematics and statistics	2,116	(4)	1,809	(4)	3.20	(4)	270	(4)
Medicine and dentistry	(4)	4,234	(4)	3,797	(4)	3.53	(4)	385
Nursing, pharmacy, and health	1,424	1,804	1,196	1,610	2.99	2.98	92	310
Physical and earth sciences	2,529	2,913	2,068	2,431	3.08	3.21	391	406
Psychology	1,251	2,282	1,166	1,881	2.91	3.28	157	259
Religion and theology	(4)	1,584	(4)	1,211	(4)	3.36	(4)	139
Social sciences	1,610	2,124	1,371	1,745	3.00	3.20	157	234
Other	1,840	2,101	1,656	1,717	3.24	3.15	187	168

[1] Includes money wages and salary and net income from farm and nonfarm self-employment and all other income.

[2] Includes money wages or salary and net income from farm and nonfarm self-employment.

[3] See Guide to Sources for information on the use of standard errors.

[4] Data not shown where base is less than 200,000 persons.

NOTE.—Data are based on sample surveys of the civilian noninstitutional population.

SOURCE: U.S. Department of Commerce, Bureau of the Census, Current Population Reports, Series P-70, No. 11, "Educational Background and Economic Status: Spring 1984." (This table was prepared October 1987.)

Table 367.—Participation of young adults [1] in voluntary organizations, by selected characteristics: 1984 to 1986

Young adult characteristics	Percent participating in voluntary organizations											
	Sports teams or clubs	Church activities	Social or hobby clubs	Union trade, farm, or other professional associations	Literary, art discussion or study group	Community groups [2]	Youth organizations	PTA or other academic group	Political clubs	Organized volunteer work [3]	Service organizations [4]	Other voluntary group
1	2	3	4	5	6	7	8	9	10	11	12	13
Total	36.0	32.2	21.8	17.7	10.8	9.4	9.2	7.0	6.2	5.8	4.0	9.6
Sex												
Male	46.8	29.3	22.5	20.3	10.7	8.6	11.7	4.7	6.7	5.3	5.2	9.7
Female	25.8	34.9	21.1	15.3	11.0	10.2	6.9	9.1	5.8	6.2	2.9	9.4
Race/ethnicity												
White, non-Hispanic	36.5	30.6	22.3	18.2	10.2	8.5	8.7	6.4	5.9	5.5	3.9	9.7
Black, non-Hispanic	31.9	44.2	21.5	14.9	13.1	16.2	12.0	12.0	8.2	6.8	4.0	10.3
Hispanic	34.6	32.4	17.1	15.8	11.6	8.5	9.5	5.6	6.9	4.3	4.7	7.1
Asian	41.4	31.0	28.7	27.3	23.2	10.5	10.8	9.1	5.9	14.1	5.9	10.3
American Indian	41.1	30.0	27.9	19.7	8.9	13.0	11.6	6.5	9.6	4.2	7.2	7.8
Socioeconomic status												
Low	29.2	30.9	17.6	12.2	6.6	8.0	7.0	6.0	3.4	4.5	2.2	6.9
Low-middle	34.5	31.4	21.7	15.6	9.6	8.6	8.7	6.0	4.5	4.6	4.9	8.6
High-middle	39.9	35.4	23.5	21.8	11.6	9.4	10.6	7.2	7.8	6.9	4.7	10.6
High	43.1	33.9	26.4	22.4	16.0	12.2	10.7	10.0	9.9	7.4	4.1	13.0
High school curriculum												
General	35.8	30.9	21.3	14.5	8.8	8.4	9.3	5.0	5.2	4.5	3.8	9.0
Academic	40.7	35.8	25.0	24.2	15.7	11.8	10.3	11.5	9.1	8.2	4.7	12.6
Vocational	31.1	31.5	19.6	13.7	6.3	8.1	7.5	4.3	4.0	4.6	2.9	6.6
Level of participation in high school extracurricular activities [5]												
Never participated	18.4	14.6	17.1	14.1	5.6	4.6	3.4	2.4	1.5	2.3	2.1	4.6
Participated as a member	32.3	29.6	20.9	15.0	8.9	8.2	6.7	5.8	5.0	5.4	3.4	7.8
Participated as a leader	45.0	40.6	24.9	21.7	14.0	12.3	13.1	9.8	8.8	7.5	4.8	12.8

[1] Sample survey in 1986 based on people who were high school seniors in spring 1980. Respondents to the survey were asked about their voluntary participation in selected organizations over the previous 24-month period.

[2] Includes participation in community centers, neighborhood improvement, or social action associations or groups.

[3] E.g., hospital volunteer.

[4] Includes participation in organizations such as Rotary, Junior Chamber of Commerce, Veterans, etc.

[5] In 1980, the seniors were asked to indicate the level of participation in each of 15 different extracurricular activity areas (e.g., varsity sports, debate, band, subject-matter clubs, church activities, etc.). Responses to these earlier inquiries were used to classify overall level of participation in extracurricular activities.

NOTE.—Some adults participated in more than one organization.

SOURCE: U.S. Department of Education, National Center for Education Statistics, *High School and Beyond*. (This table was prepared October 1987.)

Table 368.—Literacy skills and reading scores of young adults,[1] by race/ethnicity and level of education: 1985

Young adult characteristic	Prose literacy scale,[2] percent with score of—				Document literacy,[3] percent with score of—				Quantitative literacy,[4] percent with score of—			
	200 or more	250 or more	300 or more	350 or more	200 or more	250 or more	300 or more	350 or more	200 or more	250 or more	300 or more	350 or more
1	2	3	4	5	6	7	8	9	10	11	12	13
Total	96.1	82.7	56.4	21.1	95.5	83.8	57.2	20.2	96.4	84.7	56.0	22.5
Race/ethnicity												
White, non-Hispanic	98.1	89.7	63.0	24.3	98.2	89.5	64.1	24.9	98.1	89.4	62.9	24.8
Black, non-Hispanic	86.3	57.2	21.3	3.5	84.4	56.5	20.1	2.2	87.8	58.0	21.4	3.3
Hispanic	93.5	73.6	40.9	13.5	92.0	69.8	35.9	9.4	92.8	72.5	35.2	9.2
Educational attainment												
Not high school graduate	85.4	57.9	24.1	3.4	83.4	53.6	18.8	1.5	86.1	57.7	20.6	3.5
High school graduate	99.6	81.6	45.1	10.5	96.5	81.8	46.2	9.0	96.9	80.5	45.2	10.1
Some postsecondary	98.8	92.0	67.0	26.8	99.0	92.1	68.0	27.2	99.3	92.7	66.8	27.0
College graduate	99.9	97.7	84.3	44.8	99.9	98.0	85.6	48.8	99.9	97.8	84.1	45.3

[1] Includes persons 21 to 25 years old. Excludes persons not living in households and those who were unable to speak English.

[2] Prose comprehension test measures the knowledge and skills needed to gain understanding and use information from texts such as editorials, news stories, and poems. A score of 200 indicates an ability to write a simple description of the type of job one would like to have. A score of 300 indicates an ability to locate information in a news article or an almanac. A score of 350 indicates an ability to synthesize the main argument from a lengthy newspaper editorial.

[3] Document literacy test measures the knowledge and skills required to locate and use information from documents such as indexes, tables, paycheck stubs, and order forms. A score of 200 indicates ability to match money-saving coupons to a shopping list of several items. A score of 300 indicates an ability to follow directions to travel from one location to another using a map. A score of 350 indicates an ability to use a bus schedule to select the appropriate bus for given departures and arrivals.

[4] Quantitative literacy test measures the knowledge and skills needed to apply the arithmetic operations of addition, subtraction, multiplication, and division, either alone or sequentially. A score of 200 indicates an ability to total two entries on a bank deposit slip. A score of 300 indicates an ability to enter deposits and checks and balance a checkbook. A score of 350 indicates an ability to determine the amount of a tip in a restaurant using a given percentage.

SOURCE: U.S. Department of Education, National Center for Education Statistics, *Young Adult Literacy and Schooling*. (This table was prepared May 1989.)

CHAPTER 6
International Education

This chapter offers a broad perspective on education among the nations of the world. It also provides an international context for examining the condition of education in the United States. Historically, the National Center for Education Statistics (NCES) has not been active in collecting international data. However, it has funded a number of research studies comparing mathematics and science performance among various nations. Included in these studies are the second International Assessment of Education Progress (IAEP) and the Third International Mathematics and Science Study (TIMSS). NCES has cooperated with international agencies in the compilation of statistics and the development of education indicators.

The data in this chapter were drawn from material prepared by the United Nations Educational, Scientific, and Cultural Organization (UNESCO), the Institute of International Education, the Organization for Economic Cooperation and Development (OECD), and the International Association for the Evaluation of Educational Achievement (IEA). The basic summary data on enrollments, teachers, enrollment ratios, and finances were synthesized from information appearing in the annual Statistical Yearbook published by UNESCO. Even though UNESCO tabulations are very carefully prepared, international data users should be cautioned about the many problems of definition and reporting involved in the collection of data about the educational systems in the world.

This chapter also contains data from recent international assessments of mathematics and science achievement. These assessments, most coordinated by the International Association for the Evaluation of Educational Achievement, provide comparative data for about 20 countries. Data from other mathematics and geography assessments also are included in this chapter. A different perspective is provided by data on the enrollment of foreign students in U.S. institutions of higher education. These data from the Institute of International Education provide information on the number of foreign students and their countries of origin.

Further information on survey methodologies is in the "Guide to Sources" in the appendix and in the publications cited in the source notes.

Highlights

- Enrollments at elementary and secondary levels have increased more rapidly in Africa than in other parts of the world. The smallest enrollment increases at these levels occurred in Northern America and Oceania with Europe actually decreasing. (Table 370)

- In 1987–88, about 939 million students were in schools around the world. Of these students, 590 million were in elementary-level programs, 291 million were in secondary programs, and 58 million were in postsecondary programs. (Table 370)

- Between 1979–80 and 1987–88, enrollments grew rapidly, particularly in the less-developed areas of the world. Elementary enrollment changes ranged from increases of 18 percent in Africa and 12 percent in Central and South America to modest increases of only 1 percent in Europe, 5 percent in Northern America and 6 percent in Asia. Oceania declined by 5 percent. Enrollment increases at the secondary level were more dramatic, especially in Africa (48 percent), Central and South America (33 percent) and Asia (24 percent). Secondary-level enrollment declined in Europe by 1 percent and Northern America by 4 percent. At the postsecondary level, Africa (52 percent) and Central and South America (43 percent) had the largest increases followed by Asia (35 percent). These increases are a result of large growth in the school attendance rates and sizeable rises in population. (Table 370)

- Preprimary enrollment rates are highest among 4-year-olds in Belgium, Spain, France and the Netherlands. Among 5-year-olds, enrollment rates also are high in Ireland, Austria, the U.S., and West Germany. (Table 369)

- Pupil/teacher ratios in elementary and secondary schools vary widely from country to country. Countries with relatively low ratios were Italy (10.1), Poland (14.0) and Australia (14.5) in 1988. Countries with relatively high ratios included Korea (31.1 in 1989), the Philippines (33.1) and Mexico (24.9) in 1988. (Table 371)

- A comparison of public expenditures on education as a percent of gross national product (GNP) reveals significant differences among nations. For example, in the U.S. the 1988 proportion of GNP for education was 5.8 percent. Other countries ranged from 2.1 percent for Mexico and 3.3 percent for Thailand to 7.3 percent for Norway and 7.9 percent for the U.S.S.R. (Table 383)

- U.S. students ranked below average in a 1981–82 international test of mathematical skills of eighth grade students. Few of the 19 other nations and Canadian provinces scored below the United States. U.S. students scored above the international average on statistics and about the international average on algebra and arithmetic, but they scored well below the international average on geometry and measurement. (Table 374)

- In an analysis of international mathematics testing for the most advanced 12th grade mathematics students, U.S. students ranked among the lowest scoring among the 13 participating nations. The best scores were made by Japanese students, who had the highest average scores on algebra, geometry, and calculus. Japanese schools were also among the most likely to cover material tested on the exam. American schools covered the smallest portion of such material, with the exception of schools in British Columbia. (Table 375)

- In the 1988 International Assessment of Educational Progress, the U.S. 13-year-olds scored among the lowest in mathematics and in the bottom third on science achievement among a group of countries and Canadian provinces. (Tables 372 and 376)

- In a series of science tests administered to a selected group of countries between 1983 and 1986, the U.S. 14-year-olds scored somewhat lower than their peers in 10 other countries, better than 1 other country, and about the same as 5 others. (Table 377)

- Ratios of bachelor's degrees conferred per thousand 22- and 23-year-olds ranged from 53 in Turkey and 72 in Austria to 241 in the U.S. and 263 in Canada. Over 50 percent of all bachelor's degrees were awarded to women in Canada, Finland, Greece, Norway, Spain, Sweden, and the U.S. (Table 380)

- In 1989–90 there were 387,000 foreign students studying at U.S. colleges and universities. This was 20,000 more than the year before, or a 5.6 percent increase, the largest since 1981–82 when the foreign student population rose 6 percent. Approximately 54 percent of the students were from Asian countries. (Table 384)

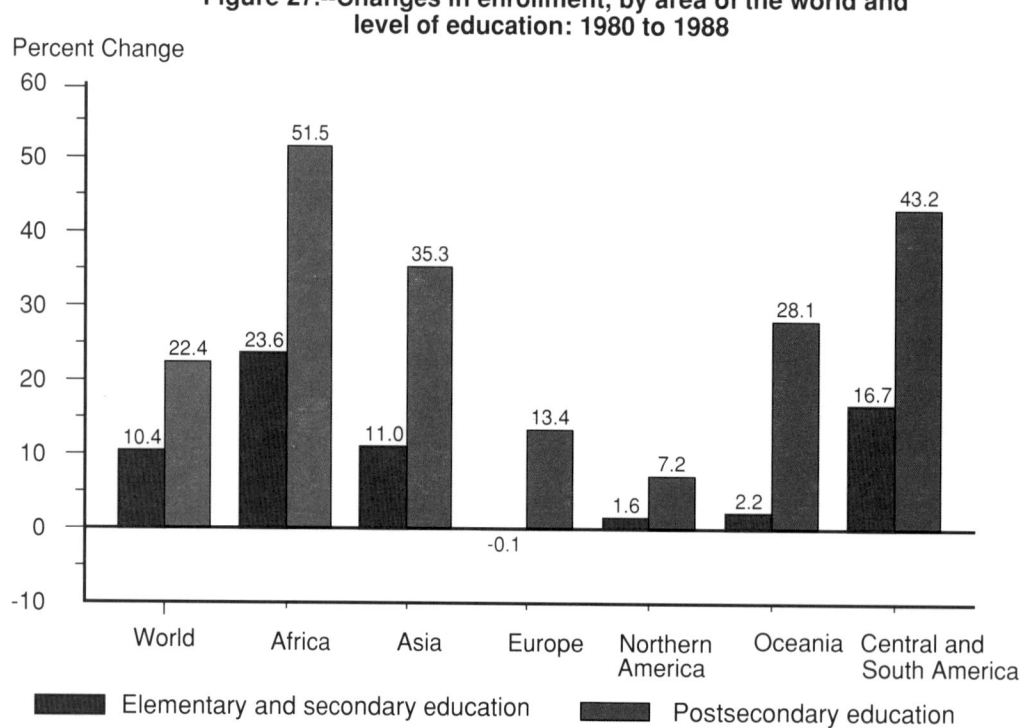

Figure 27.--Changes in enrollment, by area of the world and level of education: 1980 to 1988

Elementary and secondary education

Postsecondary education

SOURCE: United Nations Educational, Scientific, and Cultural Organization, Paris, *Statistical Yearbook, 1990.*

**Figure 28.--Public expenditures for education as a percentage
of gross national product: Selected countries, 1988**

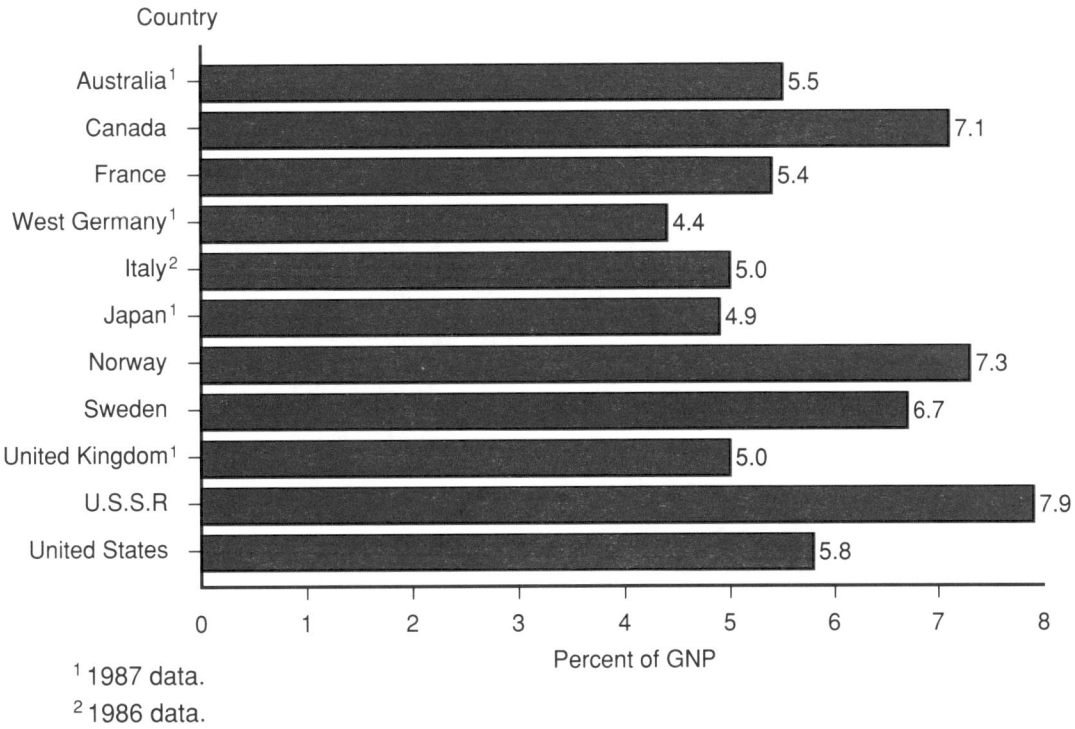

[1] 1987 data.
[2] 1986 data.

SOURCE: United Nations Educational, Scientific, and Cultural Organization, Paris, *Statistical Yearbook, 1990;* and U.S. Department of Commerce, Bureau of the Census, *Government Finances in 1987–1988.*

**Figure 29.--Distribution of elementary and secondary enrollment,
by major area of the world: 1988**

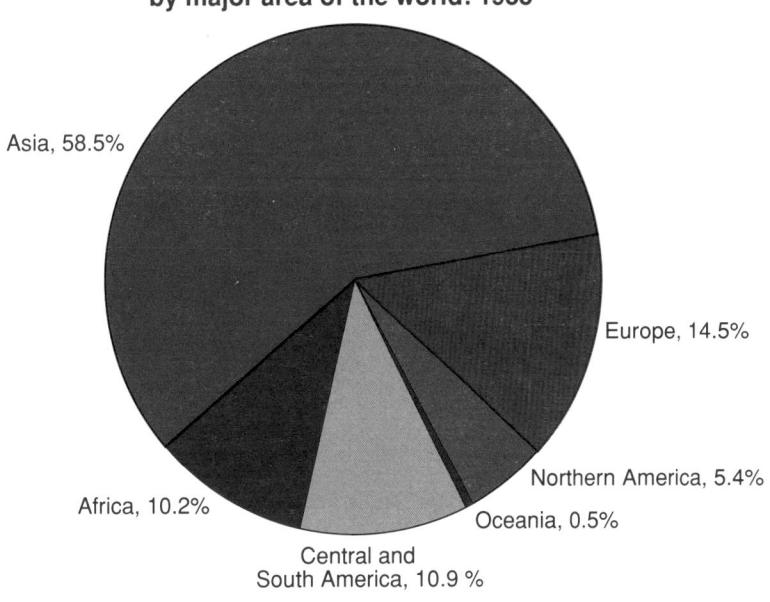

Total elementary and secondary enrollment = 881 million

SOURCE: United Nations Educational, Scientific, and Cultural Organization, Paris, *Statistical Yearbook, 1990.*

Figure 30.--Distribution of higher education enrollment, by major area of the world: 1988

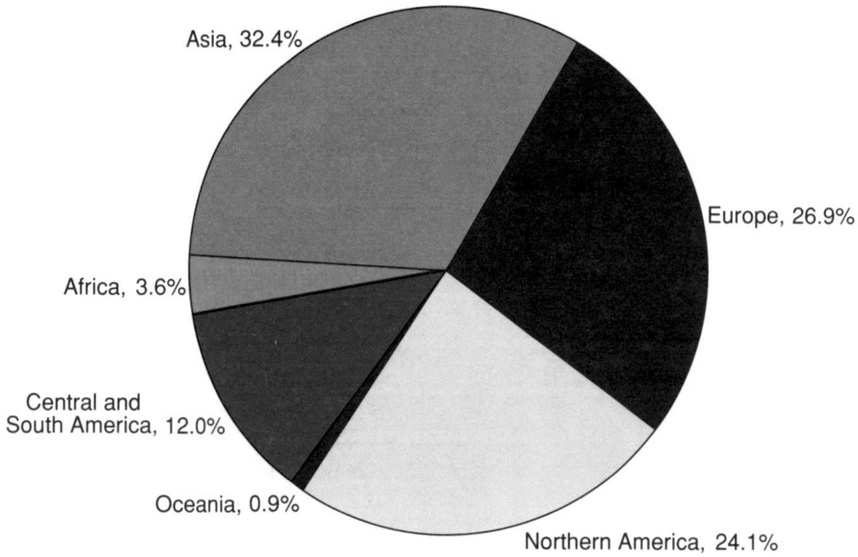

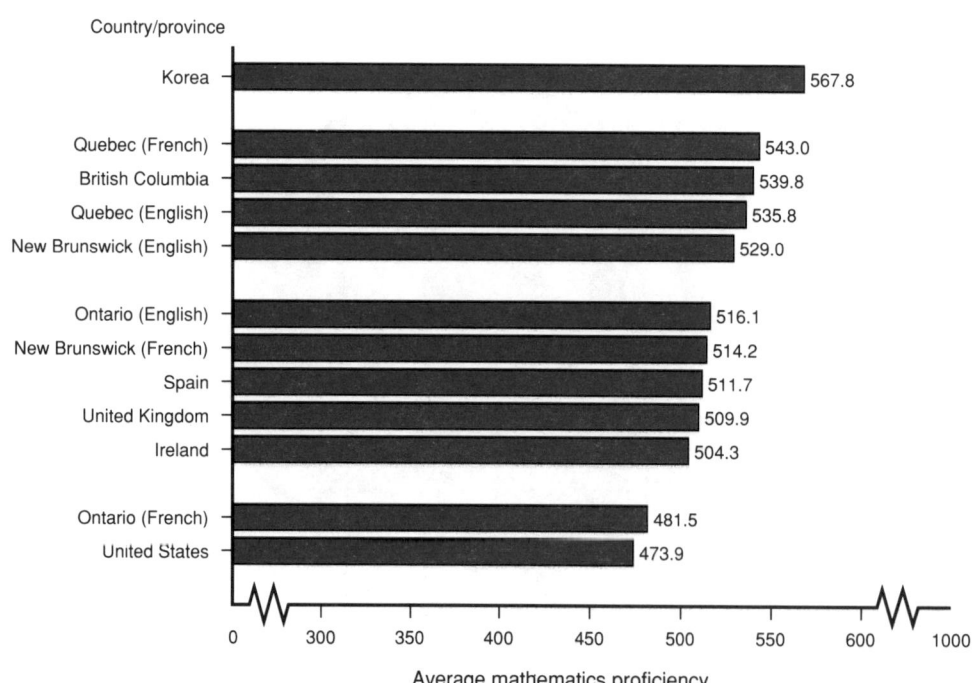

Asia, 32.4%

Europe, 26.9%

Africa, 3.6%

Central and
South America, 12.0%

Oceania, 0.9%

Northern America, 24.1%

Total higher education enrollment = 58 million

SOURCE: United Nations Educational, Scientific, and Cultural Organization, Paris, *Statistical Yearbook, 1990.*

Figure 31.--Mathematics proficiency at age 13, by country/province: 1988

Country/province

Country/province	Average mathematics proficiency
Korea	567.8
Quebec (French)	543.0
British Columbia	539.8
Quebec (English)	535.8
New Brunswick (English)	529.0
Ontario (English)	516.1
New Brunswick (French)	514.2
Spain	511.7
United Kingdom	509.9
Ireland	504.3
Ontario (French)	481.5
United States	473.9

Average mathematics proficiency

SOURCE: U.S. Department of Education, National Center for Education Statistics, International Assessment of Educational Progress, *A World of Differences,* by Educational Testing Services.

Figure 32.--Science proficiency at age 13, by country/province: 1988

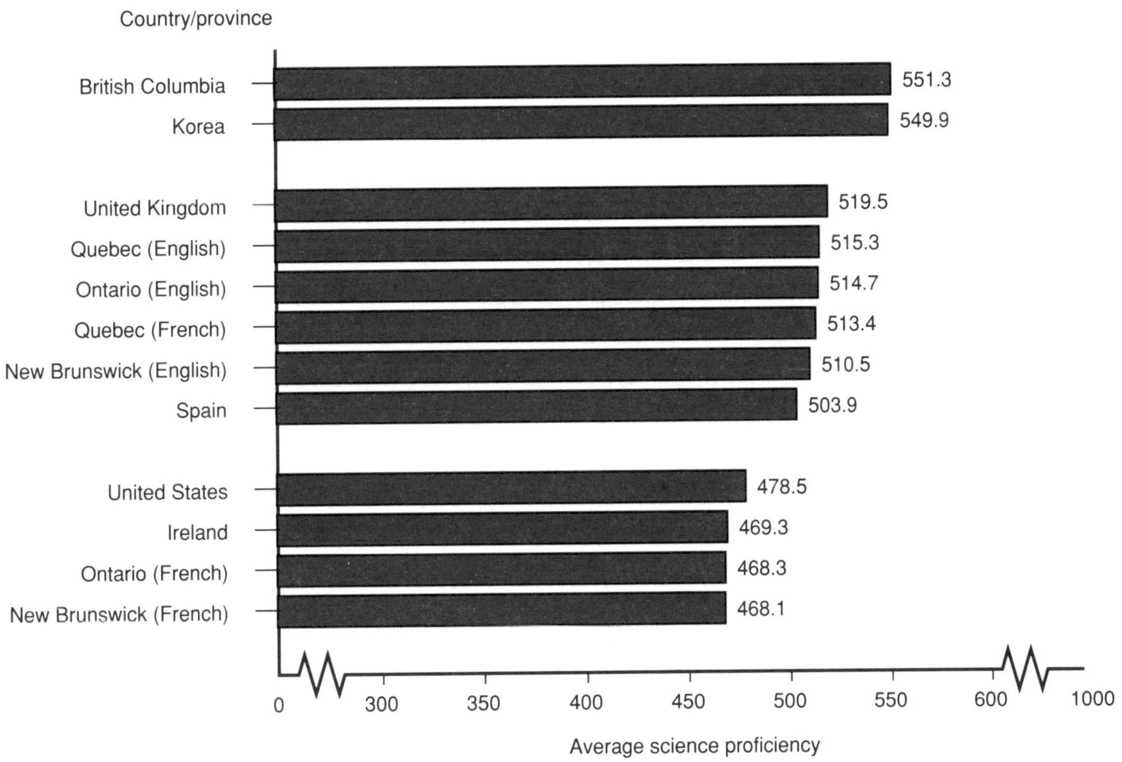

SOURCE: U.S. Department of Education, National Center for Education Statistics, International Assessment of Educational Progress, *A World of Differences,* by Educational Testing Service.

Table 369.—Preprimary enrollment and enrollment rates, by age: Selected countries, 1987–88

Country	Total enrollment	Enrollment rates in preprimary education				
		2 years old	3 years old	4 years old	5 years old	6 years old
1	2	3	4	5	6	7
Austria	192,571	1.0	28.5	63.4	92.3	24.1
Belgium	371,509	21.6	94.1	98.1	97.1	2.5
Canada	440,623	—	—	41.4	69.2	10.6
Denmark	51,988	—	—	—	—	96.8
Finland	99,442	20.2	16.0	19.6	24.3	48.0
France	2,518,602	35.7	96.3	100.0	99.8	1.6
Germany, West	1,660,284	9.1	32.3	71.6	86.5	79.5
Greece	155,527	—	9.1	43.2	57.0	1.1
Ireland	142,018	—	0.7	52.1	96.3	52.4
Italy	1,586,850	—	—	—	—	—
Japan	2,016,224	—	15.6	54.6	63.9	—
Netherlands	338,721	—	—	97.9	98.7	—
New Zealand	61,727	8.8	42.6	72.8	0.6	—
Norway	110,981	22.8	31.6	44.1	52.6	64.2
Portugal	104,438	—	—	—	—	—
Spain	1,054,241	4.5	17.8	90.6	100.0	—
Switzerland	132,879	0.6	5.4	18.7	67.1	78.1
United Kingdom	694,000	1.3	25.9	69.2	—	—
United States [1]	6,515,000	—	28.9	49.0	86.7	15.0
Yugoslavia	396,889	19.1	18.5	22.8	35.9	13.1

[1] 1986–87 data.
—Data not available.

SOURCE: Organization for Economic Cooperation and Development, *Education in OECD Countries 1987–88.* (This table was prepared February 1991.)

Table 370.—Estimated population, school enrollment, teachers, and public expenditures for education in major areas of the world: 1970, 1980, and 1988

Item	World total [1]	Major areas of the world					
		Africa [2]	Asia [3]	Europe [4]	Central and South America [5]	Northern America [5]	Oceania [6]
1	2	3	4	5	6	7	8
1970							
Population, all ages, [7] in thousands	3,672,000	363,000	2,077,000	702,000	284,000	227,000	19,000
Enrollment, all levels, [8] in thousands	617,811	34,226	324,137	135,746	56,323	63,192	4,188
First (primary) level	431,934	29,371	243,012	72,671	46,576	37,695	2,609
Second level [9]	157,781	4,454	74,239	53,269	8,107	16,357	1,355
Third level [10]	28,097	401	6,886	9,806	1,640	9,140	224
Teachers, all levels, [8] in thousands	25,937	967	11,478	7,959	2,314	3,037	182
First (primary) level	14,601	735	7,420	3,508	1,525	1,317	96
Second level [9]	9,211	202	3,490	3,713	629	1,104	72
Third level [10]	2,126	29	568	739	160	615	15
Public expenditures on education, in millions of U.S. dollars	$159,900	$2,406	$13,933	$64,098	$5,649	$71,830	$1,984
As a percent of gross national product	5.2	4.2	3.1	5.1	3.4	6.7	4.4
1980							
Population, all ages, [7] in thousands	4,428,000	481,000	2,561,000	750,000	361,000	252,000	23,000
Enrollment, all levels, [8] in thousands	845,865	74,295	478,481	141,421	87,262	59,594	4,811
First (primary) level	551,064	59,182	330,795	63,899	64,795	29,641	2,753
Second level [9]	247,399	13,718	133,776	63,782	17,595	16,885	1,642
Third level [10]	47,402	1,396	13,910	13,740	4,872	13,069	416
Teachers, all levels, [8] in thousands	36,913	2,153	18,630	8,820	3,734	3,304	272
First (primary) level	19,244	1,522	10,671	3,345	2,234	1,343	129
Second level [9]	14,288	548	6,937	4,375	1,113	1,204	112
Third level [10]	3,380	83	1,021	1,100	388	757	31
Public expenditures on education, in millions of U.S. dollars	$617,281	$18,054	$102,955	$251,343	$32,728	$201,780	$10,421
As a percent of gross national product	5.5	5.2	4.5	5.5	3.9	6.7	6.0
1988							
Population, all ages, [7] in thousands	5,076,000	611,000	2,958,000	781,000	429,000	272,000	26,000
Enrollment, all levels, [8] in thousands	939,301	92,213	534,471	143,141	103,153	61,300	5,023
First (primary) level	590,010	69,747	349,218	64,557	72,741	31,125	2,622
Second level [9]	291,252	20,350	166,436	62,997	23,434	16,166	1,868
Third level [10]	58,040	2,115	18,818	15,587	6,978	14,009	533
Teachers, all levels, [8] in thousands	43,742	3,127	22,112	9,928	4,858	3,403	313
First (primary) level	22,158	1,961	12,161	3,713	2,753	1,434	135
Second level [9]	17,383	1,035	8,500	4,971	1,542	1,194	141
Third level [10]	4,200	130	1,451	1,244	563	775	37
Public expenditures on education, in millions of U.S. dollars	$1,023,666	$21,740	$205,714	$375,519	$38,890	$365,714	$16,089
As a percent of gross national product	5.5	6.6	4.4	5.4	4.4	6.8	5.6

[1] Enrollment and teacher data exclude the Democratic People's Republic of Korea and South Africa. Expenditure data exclude Democratic Kampuchea, Democratic People's Republic of Korea, Lao People's Democratic Republic, Lebanon, Mongolia, Mozambique, South Africa, and Vietnam.

[2] Excludes South Africa.

[3] Excludes the U.S.S.R. and the Democratic People's Republic of Korea, but includes both the Asian and the European portions of Turkey.

[4] Includes the U.S.S.R.

[5] Northern America includes Bermuda, Canada, Greenland, St. Pierre, Miquelon, and the United States of America. Hawaii is included in North America, not Oceania. Central and South America includes the rest of America.

[6] Includes American Samoa, Australia, Guam, and New Zealand.

[7] Estimate of midyear population.

[8] Excludes preprimary, special, and adult education.

[9] General, teacher training, and other second-level education of a vocational and technical nature.

[10] Universities and other institutions of higher education.

NOTE.—Data have been revised from previously published figures. Because of rounding, details may not add to totals.

SOURCE: United Nations Educational, Scientific, and Cultural Organization, Paris, Statistical Yearbook, various years. (This table was prepared February 1991.)

Table 371.—Pupils per teacher in public and private elementary and secondary schools: Selected countries, 1970 to 1988

Country	All schools				Elementary schools				Secondary schools			
	1970	1980	1985	1988	1970	1980	1985	1988	1970	1980	1985	1988
1	2	3	4	5	6	7	8	9	10	11	12	13
Australia	—	16.0	13.9	14.5	28.0	[1]18.8	[1]15.9	[2]16.6	—	12.9	12.1	12.6
Brazil	—	23.5	22.3	22.4	23.6	25.6	23.9	23.9	13.2	14.2	14.6	14.6
Canada	20.9	[3]16.8	—	—	23.4	[3]15.8	[4]7.5	[4]7.3	16.9	[3]17.8	—	—
China	30.1	23.4	22.1	20.0	33.3	26.6	24.9	22.8	21.8	17.9	17.2	15.5
Egypt	33.2	—	26.2	[5]24.0	38.0	—	31.9	[5]29.9	25.0	24.0	20.4	[5]18.0
France	20.0	[6]21.4	[5,7]17.9	[7]15.6	26.0	[6]24.0	[5,7]20.5	[7]21.0	15.8	[6]19.6	[5,6]16.3	[6]13.0
Germany, Federal Republic of	19.4	16.3	[5]15.0	14.8	25.5	18.4	[5]17.3	17.5	12.3	14.4	[5]14.3	14.0
Indonesia	30.1	26.7	21.8	20.2	28.9	32.4	25.3	23.6	13.1	14.9	15.3	14.8
Iran, Islamic Republic of	32.8	—	—	24.1	32.4	[8]27.4	21.9	26.1	34.2	—	—	20.9
Italy	15.6	12.3	10.8	10.1	21.6	16.2	13.5	12.5	11.5	10.2	9.5	9.1
Japan	21.8	20.9	20.5	19.4	26.2	25.1	23.9	22.2	18.4	17.2	17.9	17.5
Korea	49.9	43.5	[9]35.4	[10]31.1	56.9	47.5	[9]37.9	[10]36.3	36.5	39.1	[9]33.2	[10]26.9
Mexico	34.8	30.2	26.1	24.9	45.9	39.1	33.6	31.3	14.5	17.7	17.2	17.3
Nigeria	32.3	35.7	—	—	34.1	37.2	44.1	40.4	21.2	28.8	—	—
Pakistan	[1]32.1	[1]27.9	[11]29.4	[1,9]29.3	[1]41.5	[1]36.5	[11]38.6	[1,9]39.3	[1]19.8	17.5	[12]18.2	[9]18.1
Philippines	29.4	31.3	31.2	33.1	28.6	30.4	30.9	33.0	33.1	34.1	32.3	33.4
Poland	17.5	16.6	16.5	14.0	23.0	19.7	20.7	15.6	10.2	12.0	10.6	10.8
Spain	28.5	23.9	22.6	[5]22.3	34.0	28.3	25.3	[5]24.7	21.5	20.9	21.0	[5]20.9
Sweden	13.6	—	—	—	20.0	[8]16.3	6.5	[13]6.2	10.1	—	—	—
Thailand	30.5	[7]31.1	[9]19.4	18.2	34.7	[7]24.7	[9]20.1	18.7	15.5	—	[9]17.6	16.8
United Kingdom	19.6	16.9	—	—	23.3	18.9	17.6	[5]20.3	15.9	15.3	—	—
United States	22.4	18.6	17.6	17.0	24.6	20.1	19.2	17.9	19.6	16.6	15.5	15.8
U.S.S.R.	—	—	—	—	[13]10.9	[13]9.1	9.4	[13]8.5	—	—	—	—
Yugoslavia	24.3	20.2	19.6	18.8	27.1	24.1	23.6	22.7	22.4	18.5	17.7	17.1

[1] Data include education preceding the first level.
[2] Teaching data include pre-primary classes and are in full-time equivalents.
[3] 1983 data, and teaching data include education preceding the first level.
[4] Data on teaching staff include all levels of education.
[5] 1987 data.
[6] Data on teachers refer to public education only.
[7] Data on teaching staff refer to public education only and include education preceding the first level.
[8] 1981 data.
[9] 1986 data.
[10] 1989 data.
[11] Data are for 1984 and they include education preceding the first level.
[12] 1984 data.
[13] Teaching data include general education at the second level.
—Data not available.

NOTE.—Coverage and grade groupings may vary somewhat from country to country and year to year. Some data have been revised from previous figures.

SOURCE: United Nations Educational, Scientific, and Cultural Organization, Paris, *Statistical Yearbook*, various years; and U.S. Department of Education, National Center for Education Statistics, Common Core of Data surveys and surveys of private schools. (This table was prepared February 1991.)

Table 372.—International Assessment of Educational Progress in mathematics for age 13, by content area: 1988

Country or province	Mathematics proficiency score			Percent correct on mathematics test, by content area					
	Mean [1]	Percent with score of 400 or more [2]	Percent with score of 500 or more [3]	Numbers and operations	Relations and functions	Geometry	Measurement	Data organization	Logic and problem solving
1	2	3	4	5	6	7	8	9	10
British Columbia	539.8	94.9	69.5	76.6	70.5	59.4	63.4	64.7	77.3
Ireland	504.3	86.3	54.7	67.9	69.0	56.4	55.3	48.1	72.3
Korea	567.8	95.3	78.1	79.2	80.0	72.3	71.2	74.7	73.9
New Brunswick (English)	529.0	95.5	65.4	73.2	71.1	58.0	64.9	60.3	73.8
New Brunswick (French)	514.2	94.6	58.3	72.9	69.2	52.6	59.3	52.4	66.5
Ontario (English)	516.1	91.8	58.3	70.1	67.7	56.1	58.4	59.7	73.5
Ontario (French)	481.5	84.8	40.5	62.7	68.2	47.4	52.1	50.2	59.7
Quebec (English)	535.8	96.7	67.3	75.9	72.3	59.4	62.8	62.3	74.1
Quebec (French)	543.0	97.2	72.7	77.9	75.6	60.9	65.1	62.1	73.9
Spain	511.7	90.7	57.0	68.6	70.6	62.7	59.4	56.5	72.3
United Kingdom	509.9	86.7	55.5	61.5	73.8	63.0	58.0	62.3	78.1
United States	473.9	77.7	40.3	61.4	59.9	49.1	43.9	54.7	63.0

[1] The scale for the scores ranges from 0 to 1,000, with a mean of 500 and a standard deviation of 100.
[2] Students at this level have the ability to select appropriate basic operations (addition, subtraction, multiplication, and division) to solve simple one-step problems. They can locate numbers on a number line and understand the most basic concepts of logic, percent, estimation, and geometry.
[3] Students at this level demonstrate an understanding of the concept of order and place value; the meaning of remainder in division; the properties of odd and even numbers and zero; elementary concepts of ratio and proportion; use of negative and decimal numbers; simple conversions involving fractions, decimals, and percents; and computation of averages. Students can use skills to solve problems requiring two or more steps.

SOURCE: U.S. Department of Education, National Center for Education Statistics, International Assessment of Educational Progress, *A World of Differences*, by Educational Testing Service. (This table was prepared May 1989.)

Table 373.—Selected statistics for countries[1] with populations over 10 million, by continent: 1970 to 1988

Country	Population, in millions			Persons per square kilometer in 1988	First level[2] Enrollment, in thousands			First level Enrollment ratio[5]		Second Level[3] Enrollment, in thousands			Second level Enrollment ratio[5]		Third Level[4] Enrollment, in thousands			Third level Enrollment ratio[5]		Age for compulsory attendance[6]
	1970	1980	1988	1988	1970	1980	1988	1970	1988	1970	1980	1988	1970	1988	1970	1980	1988	1970	1988	
1	2	3	4	5	6	7	8	9	10	11	12	13	14	15	16	17	18	19	20	21
World total[7]	3,672	4,428	5,076	37	431,934	551,064	590,010	[8]89	[9]100	157,781	247,399	291,252	[8]36	[9]53	28,097	47,401	58,040	[8]8.5	[9]13.5	—
Africa																				
Algeria[10]	13.8	18.7	23.8	10	[11]1,887	3,119	3,911	76	96	242	1,028	[12]1,999	11	62	20	[13]79	181	1.9	9.1	6-15
Cameroon	6.8	8.5	10.7	22	923	1,379	[14]1,875	91	[14]111	76	234	[14]417	8	[14]27	3	12	[15]18	0.5	[12]2.7	[16]6-12
Cote D'Ivoire	5.5	8.3	11.6	36	503	1,025	[17]1,215	63	[17]70	70	222	[15]267	9	[17]19	4	[15]20	[15]20	0.9	[15]2.4	7-13
Egypt	33.1	42.1	51.9	52	3,795	4,663	[17]7,035	72	[17]90	1,448	2,929	[14]4,131	35	[14]69	233	716	[14]875	8.6	[14]19.8	6-15
Ethiopia	30.6	38.8	47.9	39	655	2,131	2,856	16	36	135	[17]666	882	4	15	5	14	31	0.2	0.9	7-13
Ghana	8.6	10.7	14.1	59	1,420	[18]1,378	1,706	64	73	99	693	793	14	39	5	[19]16	[14]27	0.8	[12]1.5	6-16
Kenya[10]	11.3	16.7	23.9	41	1,428	3,927	5,124	58	93	136	428	563	9	23	8	13	37	0.8	[14]1.5	
Madagascar	6.7	8.8	11.2	19	938	1,724	1,534	58	97	113	234	345	9	19	6	23	37	0.8	3.7	6-13
Morocco	15.3	20.1	23.9	54	1,175	2,172	2,111	52	67	299	797	1,366	13	36	16	112	[14]212	1.5	[14]9.8	7-14
Mozambique	8.9	12.1	14.9	19	497	1,387	1,288	47	[14]68	43	[20]121	[14]117	5	[14]5	2	1	[14]2	0.3	[14]0.2	7-14
Nigeria[10]	57.2	80.6	105.0	114	3,516	13,760	12,225	37	[20]66	357	2,346	[20]3,561	4	23	16	150	[20]208	0.5	[15]2.9	6-12
South Africa	22.5	28.3	33.8	28																
Sudan[10]	13.9	18.7	23.8	9	826	1,464	[12]1,767	38	[12]49	133	384	[17]557	7	[12]20	14	29	[14]35	1.2	[14]1.8	—
Uganda	9.8	13.1	17.2	73	720	1,292	2,632	38	77	[21]48	[21]87	260	4	13	4	6	[14]13	0.5	[14]0.9	7-14
United Republic of Tanzania	13.3	18.6	24.0	25	856	3,368	[14]3,160	34	[14]66	45	79	[14]114	3	[14]4	2	[19]3	[14]6	0.2	[14]0.3	7-14
Zaire[10]	21.6	26.4	33.5	14	3,088	4,196	[14]4,282	88	[14]76	248	1,207	[12]983	9	[12]23	12	28	[17]41	0.7	[17]1.5	6-12
Asia																				
Afghanistan[10]	13.6	16.0	15.5	24	541	1,116	750	28	25	116	137	—	7	[23]8	8	[22]23	[14]17	0.7	1.3	7-15
Bangladesh	68.1	88.7	104.5	726	5,284	8,240	[23]11,285	54	[23]70	791	2,659	3,340	21	[23]17	118	240	430	2.3	4.5	6-10
Burma	27.0	33.6	[14]39.1	[14]58	3,178	4,773	[20]4,696	83	[20]95	846	1,066	[20]1,234	21	[20]24	46	[19]165		2.2	[19]5.1	5-10
China[10]	830.7	996.1	1,104.0	115	105,280	146,270	125,357	89	134	26,483	56,778	52,461	24	44	[24]48	[24]1,161	[24]2,066	0.1	1.7	7-16
India	[25]539.1	[25]675.0	[25]796.6	[25]242	57,045	73,873	95,740	73	99	20,114	30,532	—	26	41	2,904	[25]5,346	[17]4,471	6.2	[16]6.4	[26]6-14
Indonesia	117.9	146.4	175.0	92	14,870	25,537	30,131	80	119	2,460	5,722	11,693	16	48	248	[19]566	[15]980	2.6	[15]6.5	7-13
Iran, Islamic Republic of[10]	28.7	39.3	52.5	32	3,416	4,799	8,262	72	116	1,057	[12]2,836	4,297	27	53	75	151	316	3.1	6.6	6-10
Iraq	9.4	13.2	17.3	39	1,099	2,616	3,023	69	96	314	1,033	1,167	24	47	42	107	209	5.2	13.8	6-12
Japan	103.4	116.8	122.6	325	9,558	11,827	9,872	99	102	8,667	9,558	11,310	86	95	1,819	[27]2,412	[27]2,588	17.0	30.1	6-15
Korea, North (DPR)	13.9	18.0	21.9	182			[14]1,543		[23]108					[14]100			390			5-15
Korea, South (Republic of)	32.2	38.1	42.0	424	5,749	5,658	[23]4,894	103	102	1,907	4,286	[23]4,546	42	[23]86	201	648	1,573	7.9	[23]37.7	6-12
Malaysia	10.4	13.7	16.9	51	1,684	2,009	2,338	87	102	609	1,084	1,433	34	57	[24]24	58	[28]108	1.6	6.7	6-14
Nepal[10]	11.5	14.0	18.0	128	390	1,068	2,109	26	86	116	512	613	10	30	24	[29]38	[14]83		[14]5.0	6-11
Pakistan	[30]60.6	[30]82.6	[30]105.4	[30]132	3,993	[35]5,474	[37]7,609	40	[14]40	1,463	2,166	[14]3,191	13	[14]19	115	[22]157	[33]316	2.3	[14]5.0	
Philippines	36.9	48.3	58.9	196	6,969	[19]8,518	9,973	108	110	1,719	2,929	3,737	46	71	652	1,276	1,580	19.8	[14]28.2	7-13
Saudi Arabia	5.8	9.4	14.0	7	423	927	[12]1,460	45	[12]71	89	349	[12]654	12	[12]44	8	62	[12]131	1.7	1.7	
Sri Lanka[10]	12.5	14.8	16.6	253	1,671	2,081	[14]2,037	99	[14]107	941		—	47	[14]71	12	[24]43	[12]62	1.2	[12]13.4	5-15
Syrian Arab Republic	6.3	8.7	11.3	61	925	1,556	[34]2,304	78	110	328	604	[35]934	38	57	43	140	[14]43	9.2	[12]12.0	6-11
Thailand[10]	36.4	46.7	54.5	106	5,635	7,393	[14]6,518	83	87	695	1,920	2,071	17	28	55	[36]361	[12]183	1.7	[12]17.8	7-15
Turkey	35.3	44.4	52.4	67	5,012	5,656	[14]6,880	110	117	1,309	2,218	[14]3,288	27	[14]46	170	246	[14]884	6.0	[14]15.9	6-14
Vietnam[10]	42.7	53.7	64.2	194		7,887	[17]8,126		[17]102			—		[17]42	[37]80	[27]115	595	2.3	11.3	6-11
Europe																				
Czechoslovakia[10]	14.3	15.3	15.6	122	1,966	1,904	2,013	98	94	[37]657	781	812	[37]72	85	131	197	185	10.4	17.5	6-16
France	50.8	53.9	55.9	101	4,940	4,610	4,176	117	114	4,281	5,014	5,390	74	94	801	[38]1,077	[38]1,477	19.5	34.5	6-16
Germany, East (Dem. Republic)	[39]16.7	16.9	[39]16.7	[39]154	2,534	852	956	93	105	486	1,896	1,418	92	78	303	401	[40]439	32.8	33.1	6-16
Germany, West (Fed. Republic)	[39]60.7	[39]61.6	[39]61.2	[39]246	6,345	2,784	2,387		105	2,705	6,561	6,219		99	504	1,223	1,687	13.4	31.8	6-18
Hungary	10.3	10.7	10.6	114	1,116	1,162	1,243	97	96	465	357	446	63	71	81	101	[40]99	10.1	14.8	6-16
Italy	53.8	56.4	57.4	191	4,857	4,423	3,238	110	95	3,824	5,308	5,285	61	76	687	1,118	1,296	16.7	26.3	6-13
Netherlands[10]	13.0	14.1	14.8	361	1,462	1,333	1,429	102	117	1,006	1,391	[14]1,342	75	[14]104	231	360	[14]1,413	19.5	32.4	5-16
Poland	32.5	35.6	37.9	121	5,257	4,167	5,087	101	100	1,734	1,674	[17]580	62	81	398	[40]493	[40]493	14.0	19.6	7-14
Portugal[10]	8.9	9.8	10.3	113	992	1,240	[12]1,234	98	[12]126	446	398	[40]1,529	57	[12]59	50	92	210	8.0	17.5	6-14
Romania	20.3	22.2	23.1	97	2,879	3,237	3,027	112	[14]97	660	871	[14]1,479	44	[14]79	152	[40]193	[41]157	10.1	[14]9.8	6-16
Spain	33.8	37.5	39.1	77	3,930	3,610	[14]3,247	123	[14]111	1,950	3,977	[40]4,798	56	[14]105	225	698	[14]1,010	8.9	[14]31.5	6-15
United Kingdom	55.6	56.3	57.1	234	5,806	4,911	[14]4,370	104	[14]107	4,149	5,342	[14]4,508	73	[14]83	601	827	[14]1,086	14.1	[14]22.8	5-16
Yugoslavia	20.4	22.3	23.6	92	1,579	1,432	1,422	106	94	1,982	2,426	2,362	63	80	261	412	341	15.9	18.3	7-15
North America																				
Canada	21.3	24.0	26.0	3	3,736	2,185	2,319	101	105		2,323	2,249	[42]65	105	642	888	1,309	34.6	62.2	6-16
Cuba[10]	8.6	9.7	10.4	94	1,530	1,469	899	121	104	235	1,146	1,127	22	91	26	152	251	3.7	21.6	6-11

Table 373.—Selected statistics for countries[1] with populations over 10 million, by continent: 1970 to 1988—Continued

Country	Population, in millions			Persons per square kilometer in 1988	First level[2]					Second Level[3]					Third Level[4]					Age for compulsory attendance[6]
					Enrollment, in thousands			Enrollment ratio[5]		Enrollment, in thousands			Enrollment ratio[5]		Enrollment, in thousands			Enrollment ratio[5]		
	1970	1980	1988	1988	1970	1980	1988	1970	1988	1970	1980	1988	1970	1988	1970	1980	1988	1970	1988	
1	2	3	4	5	6	7	8	9	10	11	12	13	14	15	16	17	18	19	20	21
Mexico	51.2	69.4	82.7	42	9,248	14,666	14,656	104	117	1,584	4,742	6,866	22	53	248	930	1,310	5.9	15.2	6-14
United States[43]	205.1	227.8	246.3	26	36,629	31,669	32,539	99	104	14,643	14,581	12,893	94	92	8,581	12,097	13,055	49.4	68.1	6-16
South America																				
Argentina	24.0	28.2	32.0	12	3,386	3,917	4,999	105	111	977	[19]1,366	[14]1,862	44	[14]74	275	491	[14]958	14.0	[14]40.8	6-14
Brazil[10]	95.9	121.3	144.4	17	17,066	22,598	26,821	[44]82	104	4,086	2,819	3,340	[44]17	38	430	1,409	1,504	5.1	10.9	7-14
Chile	9.5	11.1	12.8	17	2,040	2,185	1,988	107	[23]100	302	538	[23]742	39	[23]75	78	145	[14]224	9.4	[14]17.8	6-13
Colombia	20.5	25.9	30.2	27	3,286	4,168	[12]4,003	108	[12]114	750	1,733	[12]2,136	25	[12]56	86	[45]272	[14]435	4.8	[14]13.9	6-14
Peru	13.2	17.3	21.3	17	2,341	3,161	[17]3,712	107	[17]122	546	1,203	—	31	[17]65	126	306	[12]473	11.4	[14]25.5	6-12
Venezuela	10.6	15.0	18.8	21	1,770	2,530	[14]2,926	94	[14]106	425	850	[14]1,076	33	[14]54	101	307	500	10.9	[14]26.5	5-14
Oceania																				
Australia	12.5	14.7	16.5	2	1,812	1,718	1,529	115	106	1,137	1,100	1,297	82	99	180	324	421	16.6	[14]28.8	6-16
U.S.S.R																				
U.S.S.R.[46]	242.8	265.5	283.7	13	25,798	21,714	24,711	104	105	20,764	20,275	21,424	85	98	4,581	[40]5,235	[40]5,098	25.4	23.6	7-17
Byelorussian S.S.R.	9.0	9.6	[14]10.1	[14]49	750	949	852	104	—	818	760	720	85	—	140	[40]177	[40]182	25.4	—	7-17
Ukrainian S.S.R.	47.3	50.0	[14]51.3	[14]85	6,668	3,595	[14]3,946	104	—	1,628	3,406	[14]3,467	85	—	807	[40]880	[40]867	25.4	—	7-17

1 Selection based on total poption for midyear 1988.

2 First-level enrollment genery consists of elementary grades.

3 Second-level enrollment includes general education, teacher training (at the second level), and technical and vocational education. This level generally corresponds to secondary education the United States.

4 Third-level enrollment includes college and university enrollment, and technical and vocational education beyond the high school level. There is considerable variation in reporting from country to country.

5 Data are the total enrollment all ages in the school level divided by the population of the specific age groups which correspond to the school level. Adjustments have been made for varying lengths of first- and second-level programs. All third-level ratios are based on the 20- to 24-year-old population. Because some countries have many students from outside the normal age range, first-level ratios may exceed 100.

6 In many countries and territories, a child may be exempt from school attendence if there is no suitable school within a reasonable distance of his/her home.

7 Enrollment totals and enrollment ratios exclude North Korea. Enrollment ratios exclude China.

8 All enrollment ratio data for gross enrollment.

9 World gross enrollment ratio estimated for 1990.

10 Classification of first and/or second levels have been revised. Data by level may not be comparable over time.

11 Provisional or estimated data.

12 Data for 1986.

13 Data refer only to institutions under the Ministry of Education.

14 Data for 1987.

15 Data for 1984.

16 Eastern Cameroon.

17 Data for 1985.

18 Includes public schools only.

19 Data for 1981.

20 Data for 1983.

21 Includes government maintained and aided schools only.

22 Data for 1979.

23 Data for 1989.

24 Includes full-time students only.

25 Including data from the Indian-held part of Jammu and Kashmir.

26 Data pertain to the majority states.

27 Including correspondence courses.

28 Not including polytechnics.

29 Data refer to public universities only.

30 Excluding data for Jammu and Kashmir. Also excluded are Junagardh, Manavadar, Gilgit and Baltistan.

31 Data include education preceding the first level.

32 Data are for 1987 and exclude education preceding the first level.

33 1987 data for universities only.

34 Including UNRWA schools with 36,741 pupils.

35 Inlucing UNRWA schools with 16,306 pupils.

36 Excludes Open University with an enrollment of 243,825.

37 Data for 1975.

38 The total number of students (all institutions) is overestimated due to inclusion of enrollment of non-university institutions.

39 Includes relevant data for Berlin.

40 Includes evening and correspondence courses.

41 1987 data including eveningd correspondence courses.

42 Data are for 14- to 19-years.

43 Enrollment data and ratios based on data reported by the National Center for Education Statistics and the U.S. Department of Commerce, Bureau of the Census.

44 Data for 1971.

45 Data include students at the Open University.

46 Includes Byelorussian S.S.R and Ukrainian S.S.R.

—Data not available.

SOURCE: United Nations Educational, Scientific, and Cultural Organization (UNESCO), *Statistical Yearbook*, various years; U.S. Department of Commerce, Bureau of the Census, *Current Population Reports*, Series P–20; and U.S. Department of Education, National Center for Education Statistics, Common Core of Data and "Fall Enrollment in Institutions of Higher Education" surveys, and Integrated Postsecondary Education Data System (IPEDS), "Fall Enrollment" survey. (This table was prepared February 1991.)

Table 374.—Average percentage of items answered correctly on an international mathematics test of 8th grade students: Selected countries, 1981–82

Country or province	Mean percent correct, all items [1]	Arithmetic	Algebra	Geometry	Measurement	Statistics
1	2	3	4	5	6	7
Average	**47.4**	**50.5**	**43.1**	**41.4**	**50.8**	**54.7**
Belgium						
Flemish	53.2	58.0	52.9	42.5	58.2	58.2
French	51.4	57.0	49.1	42.8	56.8	52.0
Canada						
British Columbia	51.6	58.0	47.9	42.3	51.9	61.3
Ontario	49.0	54.5	42.0	43.2	50.8	57.0
England and Wales	47.2	48.2	40.1	44.8	48.6	60.2
Finland	46.8	45.5	43.6	43.2	51.3	57.6
France	52.5	57.7	55.0	38.0	59.5	57.4
Hong Kong [2]	49.4	55.1	43.2	42.5	52.6	55.9
Hungary	56.0	56.8	50.4	53.4	62.1	60.4
Israel	45.0	49.9	44.0	35.9	46.4	51.9
Japan [2]	62.1	60.3	60.3	57.6	68.6	70.9
Luxembourg	37.5	45.4	31.2	25.3	50.1	37.3
Netherlands	57.1	59.3	51.3	52.0	61.9	65.9
New Zealand	45.5	45.6	39.4	44.8	45.1	57.3
Nigeria	33.6	40.8	32.4	26.2	30.7	37.0
Scotland	48.4	50.2	42.9	45.5	48.4	59.3
Swaziland	31.5	32.3	25.1	31.1	35.2	36.0
Sweden	41.8	40.6	32.3	39.4	48.7	56.3
Thailand	42.2	43.1	37.7	39.3	48.3	45.3
United States	45.3	51.4	42.1	37.8	40.8	57.7

[1] Weighted average determined by the number of items in each test component.
[2] Students in Japan and Hong Kong were attending the seventh grade.

SOURCE: U.S. Department of Education, National Center for Education Statistics, contractor report, *Perceptions of the Intended and Implemented Curriculums,* by Ian Livingston. This table was based on the "Second International Mathematics Study" conducted by the International Association for the Evaluation of Educational Achievement. (This table was prepared October 1986.)

Table 375.—International mathematics test scores and percentage of age group taking tests in the 12th grade: [1] Selected countries, 1981–82

Country or province	Average age of students	Percent of age group taking test	Percent of analysis items students had been taught	Achievement scores for top 5 percent of age group			
				Average score [2]	Algebra	Geometry	Analysis (calculus)
1	2	3	4	5	6	7	8
Average	**17**	**16**	**76**	**57.1**	**57.6**	**57.2**	**56.4**
Belgium							
Flemish	17	10	88	56.3	57.5	55.9	55.5
French	17	10	—	54.2	55.3	53.6	53.7
Canada							
British Columbia	17	30	32	57.3	60.9	59.2	51.8
Ontario	18	19	83	59.4	59.6	59.3	59.4
England and Wales	17	6	85	55.5	54.9	55.5	56.1
Finland	18	15	87	60.5	60.7	59.8	61.0
Hungary	17	50	67	59.9	60.9	61.1	57.7
Israel	17	6	78	50.0	51.5	47.7	50.9
Japan	17	12	92	65.0	63.7	64.9	66.5
New Zealand	17	11	93	57.2	56.8	57.0	57.7
Scotland	16	18	—	55.7	56.2	58.0	52.9
Sweden	18	12	86	58.9	58.5	59.0	59.2
Thailand	—	—	63	—	—	—	—
United States	17	13	54	52.2	52.8	53.0	50.9

[1] For all countries, this table includes students attending precollege mathematics classes at the highest level of secondary school. In some countries, the students had been in school longer than 12 years.
[2] Average of scores on algebra, geometry, and analysis tests with 98 items. This score is based on a standardized distribution of data from all 15 participating countries, then adjusted to a mean of 50 and a standard deviation of 10.

—Data not available.

SOURCE: U.S. Department of Education, National Center for Education Statistics, unpublished contractor report based on the "Second International Mathematics Study" conducted by the International Association for the Evaluation of Educational Achievement. (This table was prepared October 1986.)

Table 376.—International Assessment of Educational Progress in science for age 13, by content area: 1988

Country or province	Science proficiency score			Percent correct on science test, by content area				
	Mean [1]	Percent with score of 400 or more [2]	Percent with score of 500 or more [3]	Life sciences	Physics	Chemistry	Earth and space sciences	Nature of science
1	2	3	4	5	6	7	8	9
British Columbia	551.3	95.2	71.9	72.6	63.7	64.4	73.0	69.8
Ireland	469.3	75.6	37.2	60.0	53.0	46.7	61.0	54.5
Korea	549.9	93.1	72.7	72.7	67.6	65.9	71.3	65.8
New Brunswick (English)	510.5	90.4	55.4	66.0	59.3	53.8	68.2	63.0
New Brunswick (French)	468.1	77.9	35.3	58.5	56.0	48.8	55.2	57.3
Ontario (English)	514.7	90.8	55.9	67.4	59.8	52.8	68.0	63.9
Ontario (French)	468.3	78.8	34.8	60.1	55.1	46.9	57.4	56.6
Quebec (English)	515.3	91.8	57.4	68.9	58.3	51.4	66.3	64.4
Quebec (French)	513.4	91.5	56.3	70.8	59.6	54.0	60.7	64.0
Spain	503.9	88.0	53.5	69.0	60.2	51.6	65.6	59.5
United Kingdom	519.5	89.0	59.0	68.4	62.2	52.4	68.8	64.2
United States	478.5	78.3	41.8	64.0	52.9	47.7	61.4	56.0

[1] The scale for the scores ranges from 0 to 1,000, with a mean of 500 and a standard deviation of 100.

[2] Students at this level exhibit a growing knowledge in life sciences and can apply some basic principles from the physical sciences, including force. They also display a beginning understanding of some of the basic methods of reasoning used in science, including classification and interpretation of statements.

[3] Students at this level have a grasp of experimental procedures used in science, such as designing experiments, controlling variables, and using equipment. They can identify the best conclusions drawn from data on a graph and the best explanation for observed phenomena. Students understand some concepts in a variety of science content areas, including the life sciences, physical sciences, and earth and space sciences.

SOURCE: U.S. Department of Education, National Center for Education Statistics, International Assessment of Educational Progress, *A World of Differences*, by Educational Testing Service. (This table was prepared January 1989.)

Table 377.—Science test scores for 10- and 14-year-olds, percentage of age groups in school, and mean ages of students tested in selected countries: 1983 to 1986 [1]

Country	10-year-olds					14-year-olds				
	Grade tested	Average test scores	Percent of age group in school	Mean age, in years and months	Standard deviation of age, in months	Grade tested	Average test scores	Percent of age group in school	Mean age, in years and months	Standard deviation of age, in months
1	2	3	4	5	6	7	8	9	10	11
Australia	4, 5, 6	12.9	99	10:6	3.3	8, 9, 10	17.8	98	14:5	3.3
Canada (English)	5	13.7	99	11:1	7.1	9	18.6	99	15:0	6.1
England	5	11.7	99	10:3	3.6	9	16.7	98	14:2	3.6
Finland	4	15.3	99	10:10	4.1	8	18.5	99	14:10	4.1
Hong Kong	4	11.2	99	10:5	9.8	8	16.4	99	14:7	10.9
Hungary	4	14.4	99	10:3	5.2	8	21.7	98	14:3	4.7
Italy	5	13.4	99	10:9	5.2	8, 9	16.7	99	14:7	5.4
Japan	5	15.4	99	10:7	3.5	9	20.2	99	14:7	3.5
Korea (South)	5	15.4	99	11:2	7.4	9	18.1	99	15:0	7.2
Netherlands	—	—	—	—	—	9	19.8	99	15:6	12.5
Norway	4	12.7	99	10:11	4.0	9	17.9	99	15:10	4.0
Philippines	5	9.5	97	11:1	11.3	9	11.5	60	16:1	18.9
Poland	4	11.9	99	10:11	5.4	8	18.1	91	15:0	5.8
Singapore	5	11.2	99	10:10	5.7	9	16.5	91	15:3	9.0
Sweden	4	14.7	99	10:10	4.1	8	18.4	99	14:9	3.8
Thailand	—	—	—	—	—	9	16.5	32	15:4	8.9
United States	5	13.2	99	11:3	6.9	9	16.5	99	15:4	9.1

[1] Tests were conducted between 1983 and 1986.

—Data not available.

SOURCE: International Association for the Evaluation of Educational Achievement, *Science Achievement in Seventeen Countries, A Preliminary Report.* Copyright © 1988 by Pergamon Press. (This table was prepared January 1989.)

Table 378.—Science test scores for 12th graders enrolled and not enrolled in science classes, by subject: Selected countries, 1983 to 1986 [1]

Country	Grade tested	Average age, years: months	Percent enrolled in school	Biology students		Chemistry students		Physics students		Non-science students [2]
				Biology test, percent correct	As a percent of total enrollment	Chemistry test, percent correct	As a percent of total enrollment	Physics test, percent correct	As a percent of total enrollment	As a percent of total enrollment
1	2	3	4	5	6	7	8	9	10	11
Australia	12	17:3	39	48.2	18	46.6	12	48.5	11	10
Canada	12, 13	18:3	71	45.9	28	36.9	25	39.6	19	—
England	13	18:0	20	63.4	4	69.5	5	58.3	6	10
Finland	12	18:7	[3]45	51.9	45	33.3	14	37.9	14	—
Hong Kong (6) [4]	12	18:4	20	50.8	7	64.4	14	59.3	14	—
Hong Kong (7) [5]	13	19:2	—	55.8	4	77.0	8	69.9	8	—
Hungary	12	18:0	[6]18	59.7	3	47.7	1	56.5	4	9
Italy	12	19:0	52	42.3	14	38.0	2	28.0	19	25
Japan	12	18:2	63	46.2	12	51.9	16	56.1	11	35
Norway	12	18:11	40	54.8	10	41.9	15	52.8	24	—
Poland	12	18:7	28	56.9	9	44.6	9	51.5	9	—
Singapore	13	18:1	17	66.8	3	66.1	5	54.9	7	8
Sweden	12, 13	19:0	[7]15	48.5	15	40.0	15	44.8	15	—
United States [8]	12	17:7	90	37.9	6	37.7	1	45.5	1	[9]66

[1] Tests were conducted between 1983 and 1986.

[2] Data for students not enrolled in science classes.

[3] 63 percent of age group were in full-time schooling, but the 18 percent in vocational programs were not sampled.

[4] Form 6 represents grade 12.

[5] Form 7 represents grade 13.

[6] 40 percent of age group were in full-time schooling, but the 22 percent in vocational programs were not sampled.

[7] An additional 15 percent were enrolled in non-science academic programs and were not sampled.

[8] United States test scores are included in this table even though they are not directly comparable with scores from other countries. U.S. students were tested for 25 items in biology and chemistry and 26 items in physics. Other countries were tested with 30 items in each subject.

[9] Includes students in first-year physics courses.

—Data not available.

NOTE.—The primary sampling units in Hong Kong were classes rather than schools.

SOURCE: International Association for the Evaluation of Educational Achievement, *Science Achievement in Seventeen Countries, A Preliminary Report.* Copyright © 1988 by Pergamon Press. (This table was prepared January 1989.)

Table 379.—Mean number of areas [1] correctly identified in a test of geography knowledge, by country and age: 1988

Country	Age				
	18 to 24	25 to 34	35 to 44	45 to 54	55 and over
1	2	3	4	5	6
Canada	9.3	9.2	10.5	8.3	8.7
France	9.2	9.6	10.1	9.0	8.8
Germany, West	11.2	11.2	11.0	11.8	10.9
Italy	9.3	9.3	8.4	7.8	5.5
Japan	9.5	10.8	10.5	9.7	7.9
Mexico	8.2	6.9	7.6	6.4	5.7
Sweden	11.9	12.3	12.5	11.5	10.3
United Kingdom	9.0	8.4	9.2	8.9	7.8
United States	6.9	8.8	9.6	8.8	8.4

[1] Individuals were asked to identify 16 countries or bodies of water on a world map: Canada, Central America, Egypt, France, Italy, Japan, Mexico, Pacific Ocean, Persian Gulf, South Africa, Sweden, United Kingdom, U.S.A., U.S.S.R., West Germany, and Vietnam.

SOURCE: The Gallup Organization, Inc., *Geography: An International Gallup Survey, 1988.* (This table was prepared March 1989.)

Table 380.—Higher education degrees conferred, by sex and as a ratio of age group: Selected countries, 1987

Country	Higher education degrees			Percentage female graduates			Graduates as a ratio of age group (Number per thousand)					
	Associate	Bachelor's	Graduate[1]	Associate	Bachelor's	Graduate[1]	Associate		Bachelor's		Graduate[1]	
							Age	Ratio	Age	Ratio	Age	Ratio
1	2	3	4	5	6	7	8	9	10	11	12	13
Australia[2]	27,375	47,031	4,144	59.2	49.6	32.3	19	104	21	182	23	15
Austria	3,701	9,608	742	66.3	39.7	21.8	20–21	29	22–23	72	24–25	6
Belgium[3]	28,020	23,519	—	58.9	40.1	—	20–21	184	22–23	146	—	—
Canada	59,057	120,062	20,033	56.7	54.0	43.8	20–21	146	22–23	263	24–25	43
Denmark[3]	8,302	10,729	—	63.4	41.6	—	21–22	95	23–24	129	—	—
Finland	12,640	9,434	842	52.7	56.2	26.8	21–22	172	23–24	124	25–26	11
France	128,730	137,690	50,944	54.3	49.0	40.6	20–21	152	22–23	159	24–25	60
Germany, West	85,047	138,805	16,035	63.3	38.0	26.3	21–22	81	23–24	128	25–26	15
Greece	7,732	16,303	591	56.2	51.1	32.5	19–20	53	21–22	117	23–24	4
Ireland[4]	4,641	9,616	1,073	—	—	—	19–20	75	21–22	170	23–24	20
Italy	5,393	74,085	15,943	58.3	47.6	32.9	21–22	6	23–24	76	24–25	17
Japan	175,970	385,092	25,037	87.5	26.0	12.1	20–21	107	22–23	223	24–25	16
Netherlands[3]	38,308	20,545	—	50.0	34.6	—	20–21	155	22–23	80	—	—
New Zealand[5]	2,571	6,561	2,666	57.1	46.7	35.9	20–21	47	22–23	124	24–25	49
Norway[6]	21,283	14,620	4,650	55.3	65.0	32.4	21–22	317	23–24	224	25–26	74
Spain	42,590	63,947	3,474	63.5	52.5	25.9	20–21	64	22–23	96	24–25	5
Sweden	24,688	14,566	1,200	53.0	53.3	21.8	—	—	—	—	—	—
Turkey	17,685	52,878	5,264	35.4	34.4	34.8	20–21	17	22–23	53	24–25	6
United Kingdom	125,349	143,110	46,592	53.9	44.7	35.2	20–21	134	22–23	148	24–25	49
United States[4]	466,279	968,203	395,518	53.9	51.7	45.9	20–21	127	22–23	241	24–25	97
Yugoslavia	21,155	27,364	2,982	51.5	48.2	30.2	21–22	57	23–24	75	25–26	8

[1] Includes master's, doctor's, and professional degrees.
[2] Excluding Technical and Further Education (TAFE).
[3] Data on graduate degrees included in data on bachelor's degrees.
[4] Data are for 1986.
[5] Universities and teacher training colleges only.

[6] Data are high due to the frequency with which Norwegian students gain several qualifications during the same year.
—Data not available.

SOURCE: Organization for Economic Cooperation and Development, *Education in OECD Countries 1987–88*. (This table was prepared February 1991.)

Table 381.—Enrollment and current fund expenditures: Selected countries, 1979–80 and 1987–88

Country	1979–80				1987–88			
	Elementary and secondary enrollment	Elementary and secondary expenditures in thousands of U.S. dollars[1]	Expenditure per student[1]	Purchasing power parity rate[2]	Elementary and secondary enrollment	Elementary and secondary expenditures in thousands of U.S. dollars[1]	Expenditure per student[1]	Purchasing power parity rate[2]
1	2	3	4	5	6	7	8	9
United States[3]	43,403,406	$86,984,142	$2,004	1.00	41,491,000	$149,492,073	$3,603	1.00
Australia	2,818,820	4,321,251	1,533	1.07	[4]2,809,912	[4]5,976,683	[4]2,127	[4]1.35
Austria	1,140,099	1,987,193	1,743	16.80	966,865	3,119,106	3,226	16.50
Belgium	1,677,641	3,457,618	2,061	43.30	[5]1,534,365	[5]4,399,024	[5]2,867	[5]44.20
Canada	4,508,147	11,414,628	2,532	1.17	4,568,605	19,220,121	4,207	1.25
Denmark	933,579	1,841,018	1,972	8.69	[4]865,891	[4]3,125,867	[4]3,610	[4]10.21
Finland	817,512	1,365,242	1,670	5.08	790,748	2,581,001	3,264	6.45
France	9,624,027	13,646,870	1,418	6.00	9,566,880	22,893,544	2,393	7.45
Germany, West	9,345,164	15,494,282	1,658	2.72	[4]8,791,070	[4]20,218,963	[4]2,300	[4]2.47
Ireland	720,599	608,186	844	0.55	[6]763,831	[6]955,553	[6]1,251	[6]0.75
Italy[7]	9,730,877	10,558,002	1,085	784.00	8,880,518	16,961,789	1,910	1366.00
Japan	21,384,136	26,174,182	1,224	262.00	[4]21,566,159	[4]45,202,669	[4]2,096	[4]214.00
Netherlands	2,724,827	4,430,569	1,626	2.76	[4]2,773,671	[4]6,265,723	[4]2,259	[4]2.41
New Zealand	733,689	747,629	1,019	1.02	[4]661,300	[4]1,104,371	[4]1,670	[4]1.68
Norway	750,962	1,598,047	2,128	7.43	678,322	2,962,910	4,368	8.65
Portugal	1,638,627	1,124,098	686	31.60	[8]1,815,482	[8]1,778,962	[8]980	[8]84.10
Spain[9]	7,586,370	2,162,115	285	48.90	8,097,678	6,923,515	855	103.20
Sweden	1,273,512	3,414,286	2,681	6.97	1,189,433	5,108,615	4,295	8.94
Switzerland	910,532	2,417,462	2,655	2.42	[4]763,628	[4]3,447,780	[4]4,515	[4]2.44
Turkey	7,874,403	1,685,122	214	39.00	[5]10,168,613	[5]6,497,744	[5]639	[5]196.90
United Kingdom	10,252,573	15,450,628	1,507	0.52	[4]8,878,000	[4]23,855,186	[4]2,687	[4]0.60

[1] Conversion to U.S. dollars based on purchasing power parity exchange rate.
[2] Rate used to convert foreign currency to U.S. dollars.
[3] Per pupil expenditure for the United States was based on enrollment of public and private students and public current expenditures. If only public enrollment and public current expenditures had been used, the per pupil expenditures would be: 1979–80=$2,089, 1987–88=$3,927.
[4] Data are for 1986–87.
[5] Data for enrollment are for 1986–87, data for expenditures and distribution figures are for 1987–88.
[6] Data are for 1985–86.
[7] Data for enrollment are for 1979–80 and 1985–86; and data for expenditures and distribution figures are for 1978–79 and 1985–86.

[8] Data for enrollment are for 1984–85, data for expenditures and distribution figures are for 1986–87.
[9] Data for enrollment are for 1979–80 and 1985–86; and data for expenditures are for 1975–76 and 1985–86, with 1979–80 and 1985–86 figures based on distribution figures from 1975–76 and 1978–79.

NOTE.—Elementary and secondary expenditures for all countries exclude "Other" and "Not Distributed" expenditures. Data have been revised from previous figures.

SOURCE: United Nations Educational, Scientific and Cultural Organization, *Statistical Yearbook, 1989, 1990*; and U.S. Department of Education, National Center for Education Statistics, Common Core of Data survey. (This table was prepared February 1991.)

Table 382.—Public expenditures for education as a percentage of government expenditures for all purposes: Selected countries, 1960 to 1988

Country	1960	1970	1975	1979	1980	1981	1982	1983	1984	1985	1986	1987	1988
1	2	3	4	5	6	7	8	9	10	11	12	13	14
Australia	—	13.3	14.8	15.0	14.8	14.5	14.0	13.6	13.2	12.8	12.6	12.5	—
Canada	[1]14.3	24.1	17.8	18.3	17.3	17.0	—	—	15.2	12.7	15.5	15.4	15.6
Chile	12.6	22.0	12.0	—	11.9	—	—	—	—	15.3	—	—	—
France	—	—	—	[2]17.8	—	—	—	18.0	—	—	—	—	—
Germany, Federal Republic of	—	9.2	10.7	10.0	10.1	—	—	9.5	9.2	9.2	9.2	9.0	—
Hungary	8.4	6.9	4.2	4.2	5.2	5.5	5.8	6.6	6.4	6.4	6.4	6.3	6.4
Italy	—	11.9	9.4	11.1	—	—	—	9.6	8.5	8.3	8.3	—	—
Japan	—	20.4	22.4	20.1	19.6	19.4	19.1	18.7	18.1	17.9	17.7	16.9	—
Mexico	—	8.5	11.9	—	[2]16.7	[2]17.2	[2]17.2	[2]6.4	—	[2]25.3	—	—	—
Netherlands	—	—	23.7	24.1	23.1	19.6	18.8	18.1	16.8	16.4	—	—	—
Nigeria	—	—	[3]16.5	16.2	—	24.7	[2]9.6	[2]9.3	[2]11.6	[2]8.7	[2]12.0	—	—
Norway	—	15.5	14.7	—	13.8	13.5	13.5	12.9	12.8	13.6	13.6	13.8	13.5
Sweden	—	—	13.4	13.6	14.1	13.9	13.0	12.5	12.2	12.6	12.6	12.8	12.3
Thailand	—	17.3	21.0	18.8	20.6	20.0	20.1	21.1	—	18.5	19.4	17.9	16.6
United Kingdom	—	14.1	14.3	13.6	13.9	12.2	11.9	11.5	11.3	—	—	—	—
United States	15.1	20.3	18.1	20.5	19.9	19.1	18.1	17.7	17.7	17.3	17.5	17.5	17.6
U.S.S.R.	11.7	12.8	12.9	11.6	11.2	10.9	10.3	10.2	10.2	—	—	—	—
Yugoslavia	—	23.3	24.4	28.4	32.5	—	—	—	—	—	—	—	—

[1]—Data for 1961.
[2] Expenditures by the Federal Government only.
[3] Data for 1976.
—Data not available.

NOTE.—Some data have been revised from previously published figures.

SOURCES: United Nations Educational, Scientific, and Cultural Organization, Paris, *Statistical Yearbook*, various years; and U.S. Department of Commerce, Bureau of the Census, *Governmental Finances*, various years. (This table was prepared February 1991.)

Table 383.—Public expenditures for education as a percent of gross national product: Selected countries, 1960 to 1988

Country	1960	1970	1975	1979	1980	1981	1982	1983	1984	1985	1986	1987	1988
1	2	3	4	5	6	7	8	9	10	11	12	13	14
Australia	2.9	4.2	6.5	5.9	5.9	5.9	5.9	6.3	6.0	5.9	5.7	5.5	—
Canada	[1]4.6	8.9	7.6	7.7	7.3	7.8	8.3	7.7	7.2	7.0	7.5	[1]7.3	7.1
Chile	[2]2.7	5.1	4.1	3.8	4.6	5.4	5.7	4.9	4.8	4.4	—	3.6	—
France	[3]2.4	4.9	5.2	—	5.0	5.6	5.8	5.8	5.8	5.8	5.6	5.5	5.4
Germany, Federal Republic of	—	3.5	5.1	4.6	4.7	4.7	4.6	4.8	4.6	4.5	4.4	4.4	—
Hungary	[4]4.4	[4]4.4	4.1	4.1	4.7	5.1	5.0	5.8	5.4	5.4	5.7	[1]5.5	5.4
Italy	[5]3.6	4.0	4.1	4.4	—	—	—	4.8	5.1	5.0	5.0	—	[3]—
Japan	4.1	3.9	5.5	5.8	5.8	5.9	5.6	5.6	5.2	5.1	5.0	4.9	—
Mexico	[1][2]1.3	2.4	3.6	4.0	[2]3.0	[2]4.2	[2]4.3	[2]2.8	[2]2.5	[2]3.9	[2]3.8	3.6	2.1
Netherlands	[6]4.9	7.3	8.2	8.1	7.9	7.8	7.6	7.4	6.8	6.8	6.9	7.3	—
Nigeria	[3][5]2.2	—	[7]4.3	3.9	—	5.5	[2]2.1	[2]1.6	[2]1.2	[2]1.0	[2]1.5	—	—
Norway	4.2	6.0	7.1	—	7.2	6.9	7.0	7.0	6.7	6.5	6.8	[1]7.1	[1]7.3
Sweden	[3]4.6	7.7	7.3	9.1	9.0	9.2	9.0	8.4	8.0	7.7	7.5	[1]7.3	6.7
Thailand	[5][8]2.5	3.5	3.5	3.2	3.4	3.7	3.9	3.9	—	3.9	3.8	3.6	3.3
United Kingdom	[1]4.3	5.3	6.6	5.4	5.6	5.5	5.4	5.2	5.1	4.9	5.0	[1]5.0	—
United States	4.0	5.9	6.6	5.7	5.8	5.4	5.6	5.6	5.5	5.5	5.7	5.8	5.8
U.S.S.R. [4]	5.9	6.8	7.6	7.3	7.3	6.9	6.7	6.8	6.8	7.0	7.2	[1]7.5	[1]7.9
Yugoslavia	[9]2.5	4.9	5.4	5.4	4.7	4.5	4.4	3.7	3.5	3.4	3.8	[1]4.2	4.3

[1] Data for 1961.
[2] Expenditures by the Ministry of Education only.
[3] As percentage of gross domestic product at market prices.
[4] Data are as a percentage of net material product.
[5] Data for 1959.
[6] Includes private expenditures relating to private education.
[7] Data for 1976.
[8] Central or federal government only; not including foreign aid.

[9] As a percent of gross material product.
—Data not available.

NOTE.—Some data have been revised from previously published figures.

SOURCE: United Nations Educational, Scientific, and Cultural Organization, Paris, *Statistical Yearbook;* and U.S. Department of Commerce, Bureau of the Census, *Governmental Finances*, various years. (This table was prepared February 1991.)

Table 384.—Foreign students enrolled in institutions of higher education in the United States and outlying areas, by continent, region, and selected countries of origin: 1980–81 to 1989–90

Continent, region, and country	1980–81		1984–85		1985–86		1986–87		1987–88		1988–89		1989–90	
	Number	Percent	Number	Percent	Number	Percent	Number	Percent	Number	Percent	Number	Percent	Number	Percent
1	2	3	4	5	6	7	8	9	10	11	12	13	14	15
Total	311,880	100.0	342,110	100.0	343,780	100.0	349,610	100.0	356,190	100.0	366,650	100.0	386,850	100.0
Africa	38,180	12.2	39,520	11.6	34,190	9.9	31,580	9.0	28,450	8.0	26,730	7.3	24,570	6.4
Eastern Africa	6,260	2.0	7,080	2.1	6,730	2.0	6,600	1.9	6,700	1.9	7,040	1.9	7,330	1.9
Central Africa	1,130	0.4	1,350	0.4	1,540	0.4	1,770	0.5	1,880	0.5	1,890	0.5	1,800	0.5
North Africa	7,310	2.3	6,490	1.9	5,980	1.7	5,470	1.6	5,360	1.5	5,030	1.4	4,740	1.2
Southern Africa	1,480	0.5	2,160	0.6	2,360	0.7	2,530	0.7	2,770	0.8	2,830	0.8	2,750	0.7
West Africa	22,000	7.1	22,440	6.6	17,580	5.1	15,210	4.4	11,740	3.3	9,940	2.7	7,950	2.1
Nigeria	17,350	5.6	18,370	5.4	13,710	4.0	11,700	3.3	8,340	2.3	6,150	1.7	4,480	1.2
Europe	25,330	8.1	33,350	9.7	34,310	10.0	36,140	10.3	38,820	10.9	42,770	11.7	46,040	11.9
Eastern Europe	1,670	0.5	1,690	0.5	1,770	0.5	1,880	0.5	2,000	0.6	2,460	0.7	3,360	0.9
Western Europe	23,660	7.6	31,660	9.3	32,540	9.5	34,260	9.8	36,820	10.3	40,310	11.0	42,680	11.0
Germany, Federal Republic of	3,310	1.1	4,190	1.2	4,730	1.4	5,090	1.5	5,730	1.6	6,340	1.7	6,750	1.7
Greece	3,750	1.2	4,870	1.4	4,440	1.3	4,240	1.2	4,140	1.2	4,360	1.2	4,430	1.1
United Kingdom	4,440	1.4	6,030	1.8	5,940	1.7	6,240	1.8	6,600	1.9	6,800	1.9	7,100	1.8
Latin America	49,810	16.0	48,560	14.2	45,480	13.2	43,480	12.4	44,550	12.5	45,030	12.3	48,090	12.4
Caribbean	10,650	3.4	11,010	3.2	11,100	3.2	11,250	3.2	11,580	3.3	11,960	3.3	12,580	3.3
Central America	12,970	4.2	12,550	3.7	12,740	3.7	13,070	3.7	14,550	4.1	14,850	4.1	16,540	4.3
Mexico	6,730	2.2	5,750	1.7	5,460	1.6	5,330	1.5	6,170	1.7	5,780	1.6	6,540	1.7
South America	26,190	8.4	25,000	7.3	21,640	6.3	19,160	5.5	18,420	5.2	18,220	5.0	18,970	4.9
Venezuela	11,750	3.8	10,290	3.0	7,040	2.0	4,870	1.4	3,790	1.1	3,040	0.8	2,740	0.7
Middle East	84,710	27.2	56,580	16.5	52,720	15.3	47,000	13.4	43,630	12.2	40,200	11.0	37,330	9.6
Iran	47,550	15.2	16,640	4.9	14,210	4.1	12,230	3.5	10,420	2.9	8,950	2.4	7,440	1.9
Jordan	6,140	2.0	6,750	2.0	6,590	1.9	5,650	1.6	5,140	1.4	4,940	1.3	5,250	1.4
Lebanon	6,770	2.2	6,940	2.0	7,090	2.1	6,450	1.8	5,820	1.6	5,130	1.4	4,450	1.2
Saudi Arabia	10,440	3.3	7,760	2.3	6,900	2.0	5,840	1.7	5,490	1.5	4,970	1.4	4,110	1.1
North America [1]	14,790	4.7	15,960	4.7	16,030	4.7	16,300	4.7	16,360	4.6	16,730	4.6	18,590	4.8
Canada	14,320	4.6	15,370	4.5	15,410	4.5	15,700	4.5	15,690	4.4	16,030	4.4	17,870	4.6
Oceania	4,180	1.3	4,190	1.2	4,030	1.2	4,230	1.2	3,620	1.0	3,610	1.0	4,010	1.0
South and East Asia	94,640	30.3	143,680	42.0	156,830	45.6	170,700	48.8	180,540	50.7	191,430	52.2	208,110	53.8
East Asia	51,650	16.6	72,630	21.2	80,720	23.5	91,890	26.3	101,210	28.4	113,140	30.9	127,320	32.9
China	2,770	0.9	10,100	3.0	13,980	4.1	20,030	5.7	25,170	7.1	29,040	7.9	33,390	8.6
Hong Kong	9,660	3.1	10,130	3.0	10,710	3.1	11,010	3.1	10,650	3.0	10,560	2.9	11,230	2.9
Japan	13,500	4.3	13,160	3.8	13,360	3.9	15,070	4.3	18,050	5.1	24,000	6.5	29,840	7.7
Korea, Republic of	6,150	2.0	16,430	4.8	18,660	5.4	19,940	5.7	20,520	5.8	20,610	5.6	21,710	5.6
Taiwan	19,460	6.2	22,590	6.6	23,770	6.9	25,660	7.3	26,660	7.5	28,760	7.8	30,960	8.0
South Central Asia	14,540	4.7	23,340	6.8	25,800	7.5	28,700	8.2	32,410	9.1	35,500	9.7	38,840	10.0
India	9,250	3.0	14,610	4.3	16,070	4.7	18,350	5.2	21,010	5.9	23,350	6.4	26,240	6.8
Pakistan	2,990	1.0	4,750	1.4	5,440	1.6	5,950	1.7	6,570	1.8	7,050	1.9	7,070	1.8
South East Asia	28,450	9.1	47,710	13.9	50,310	14.6	50,110	14.3	46,920	13.2	42,790	11.7	41,950	10.8
Indonesia	3,250	1.0	7,190	2.1	8,210	2.4	9,240	2.6	9,010	2.5	8,720	2.4	9,390	2.4
Malaysia	6,010	1.9	21,720	6.3	23,020	6.7	21,640	6.2	19,480	5.5	16,170	4.4	14,110	3.6
Thailand	6,550	2.1	7,220	2.1	6,940	2.0	6,480	1.9	6,430	1.8	6,560	1.8	6,630	1.7
Stateless [3]	240	0.1	270	0.1	190	0.1	180	0.1	220	0.1	150	(2)	110	(2)

[1] Excludes Mexico and Central America, which are included with Latin America.

[2] Less than .05 percent.

[3] Home country unknown or undeclared.

—Data not available.

NOTE.—Data are for "nonimmigrants," i.e., students who have not migrated to this country. The distribution by continent and region includes estimates for students whose country of origin is unknown. Because of rounding, details may not add to totals.

SOURCE: Institute of International Education, Open Doors, various years, and unpublished data. (Latest edition copyright © 1990 by the Institute of International Education. All rights reserved.) (This table was prepared March 1991.)

CHAPTER 7
Learning Resources and Technology

This chapter contains statistics on libraries and on the use of information technologies. These data show the extent of America's access to information technologies outside of formal classroom activities. The data also provide a capsule description of the magnitude and availability of library resources. Access to information has been widely cited as the key to success in a growing number of endeavors. Thus, how information is made available and to whom become matters of concern.

The tables in this chapter are based on periodic surveys conducted by the National Center for Education Statistics (NCES).

The first section of the chapter has tables dealing with public libraries, public and private school libraries, and college and university libraries. They contain data on collections, population served, staff, and expenditures. Two tables provide institutional-level information for the largest public libraries and the largest college libraries in the country.

The second half of the chapter provides information on the availability and use of technology. For example, the proportion of schools with microcomputers was tabulated for a period of years to permit trend comparisons. Also included are new data on the use of computers by adults and school children, with comparisons between various demographic groups.

Related data may be found in various sections of this report. For example, statistics on the number of degrees conferred in computer and information sciences and library sciences are in chapter 3. Further information on survey methodologies are in the "Guide to Sources" and in the publications cited in the source notes.

Highlights

- In fall 1985, almost 94 percent of all public schools and 75 percent of all private schools had libraries or media centers. (Tables 385 and 388)

- During the 1984–85 school year, public school libraries held an average of 7,668 book titles, 34 periodical subscriptions, 353 audio materials, and 540 films and filmstrips. (Table 387)

- Total expenditures for college libraries rose by 154 percent between 1974–75 and 1987–88. However, the proportion of college budgets spent on libraries

fell from 3.9 percent to 2.9 percent during the same period. (Table 389)

- The number of public schools using microcomputers has risen rapidly in recent years. Between fall 1981 and fall 1986, the proportion of public schools with computers rose from 18 percent to 96 percent. (Table 393)

- About 36 percent of all American workers used computers on their jobs in October 1989. The percentages ranged from 7 percent for workers who did not complete high school to 58 percent for those with 4 or more years of college. Women who have not completed college were more likely to use computers than men who have not completed college. For men and women who have completed 4 years of college, the percentages using computers were about the same. Computer users with higher levels of education were more likely to use their computers for more diverse applications than those with lower levels of education. (Table 394)

- The total computer usage rate of students at school increased from 27.3 percent in October 1984 to 42.7 percent in October 1989. The rate at the pre-kindergarten and kindergarten level increased more than twofold. The rate at the first-through eighth-grade level increased by about two-thirds. (Table 395)

- More than half (52 percent) of all elementary school children used computers at school in October 1989. The computer usage rate was 39 percent for students in high school and college. Sizeable percentages of students used computers at home, though fewer actually used them for schoolwork. About 18 percent of elementary school children used computers at home and about 6 percent used them for schoolwork. Students at the high school and undergraduate level were about twice as likely as the elementary school children to use home computers for schoolwork. In general, students in higher income families were more likely to use computers at home and use them for schoolwork than were students from lower income families. (Table 395)

Figure 33.--Books held by public school libraries, by size of school and level of education: Fall 1985

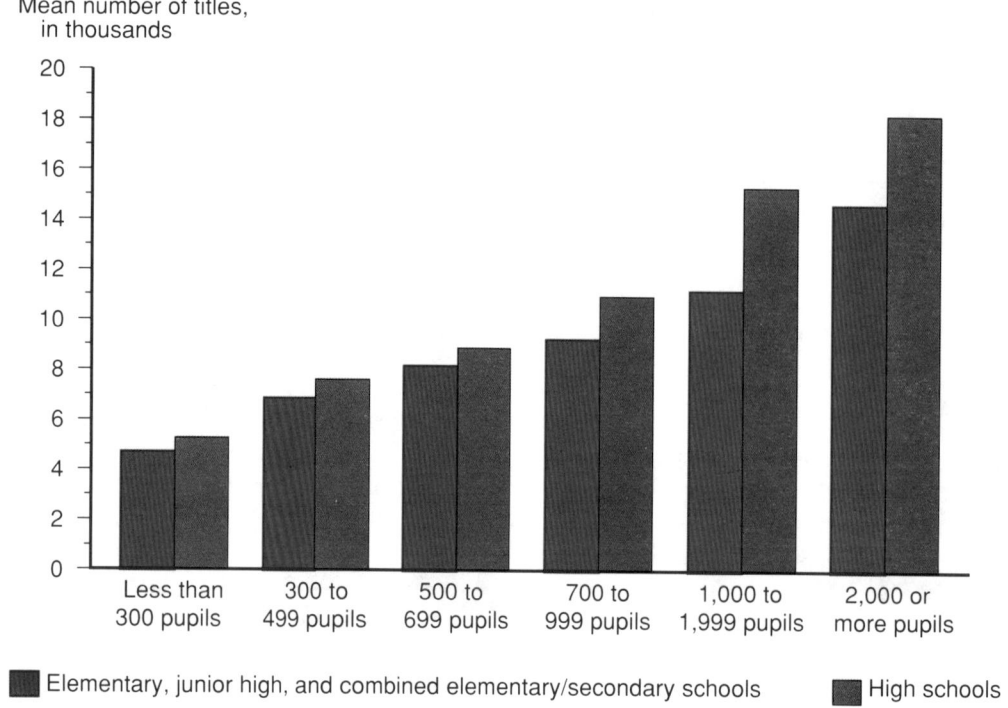

Mean number of titles, in thousands

SOURCE: U.S. Department of Education, National Center for Education Statistics, "National Survey of Public and Private School Libraries and Media Centers, 1985."

Figure 34.--Public schools with microcomputers, by level of school: 1982 to 1986

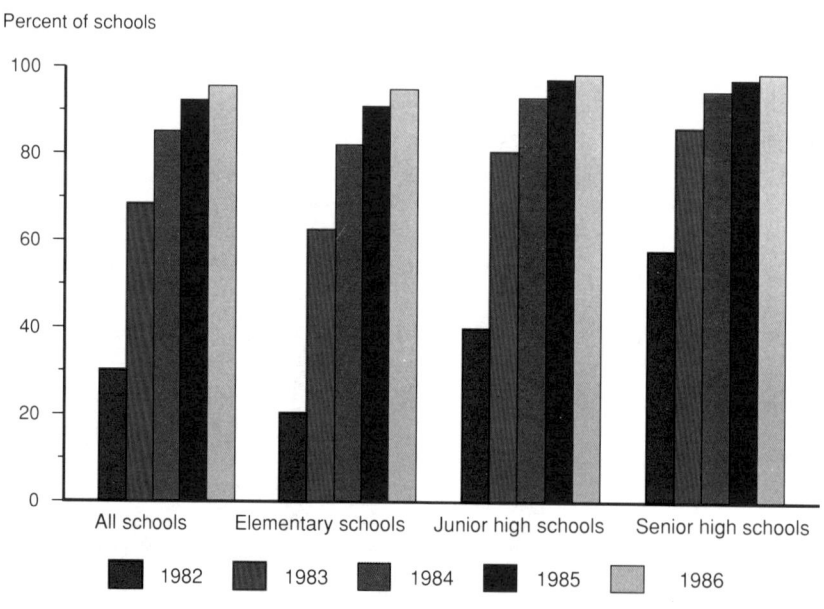

Percent of schools

SOURCE: Market Data Retrieval, Inc., *Microcomputers in Schools, 1983–84, 1985.*

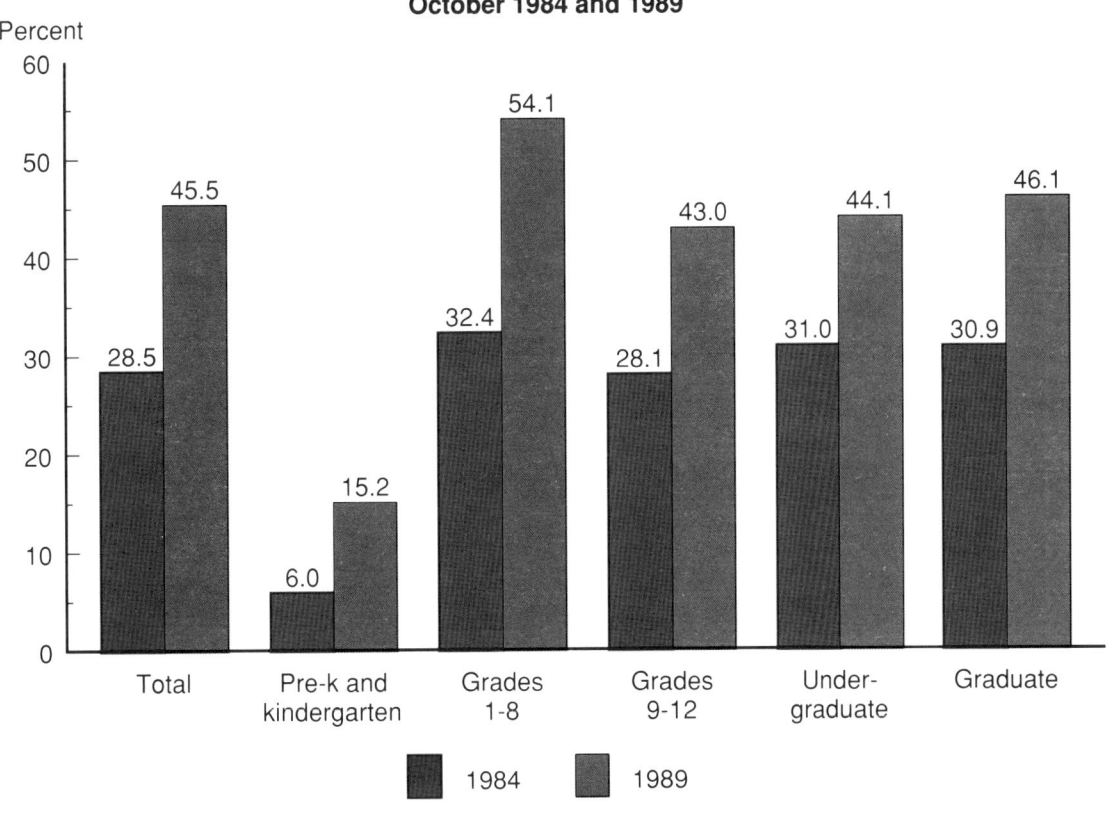

Figure 35.--Student use of computers, by level of instruction: October 1984 and 1989

■ 1984   □ 1989

SOURCE: U.S. Department of Commerce, Bureau of the Census, Current Population Survey, October 1984 and 1989, unpublished data.

Table 385.—Selected statistics on public school libraries/media centers, by level and size of school: Fall 1985

School level and size	Number of library/ media centers	Percent of schools with library/ media centers	Library/media center staff					Mean circulation per week	
			Total staff	Mean number of staff per school	Certified library staff	Other professional staff	Other staff	Per school	Per pupil
1	2	3	4	5	6	7	8	9	10
All schools	**73,352**	**93.5**	**96,324**	**1.3**	**54,215**	**5,252**	**36,857**	**523**	**1.2**
Fewer than 300 pupils	19,070	82.4	15,806	0.8	9,560	1,046	5,200	261	1.4
300 to 499 pupils	23,744	97.5	27,297	1.1	15,552	1,886	9,859	525	1.3
500 to 699 pupils	14,916	98.5	19,997	1.3	11,296	1,214	7,487	679	1.2
700 to 999 pupils	8,721	98.2	13,961	1.6	7,819	613	5,530	672	0.8
1,000 to 1,999 pupils	5,834	99.3	15,188	2.6	7,936	433	6,819	678	0.5
2,000 or more pupils	1,068	100.0	4,075	3.8	2,053	60	1,962	879	0.3
Elementary, junior high, and combined schools ..	61,013	92.6	70,918	1.2	39,682	4,394	26,842	550	1.3
Fewer than 300 pupils	16,567	81.1	13,232	0.8	7,693	804	4,734	284	1.5
300 to 499 pupils	21,883	97.5	24,696	1.1	13,808	1,775	9,113	547	1.4
500 to 699 pupils	13,428	98.4	17,703	1.3	9,828	1,132	6,742	720	1.2
700 to 999 pupils	6,918	97.7	10,660	1.5	5,904	515	4,241	758	0.9
1,000 to 1,999 pupils	2,169	98.2	4,506	2.1	2,369	169	1,968	878	0.8
2,000 or more pupils	49	100.0	121	2.5	78	0	43	1,215	0.5
High schools [1]	12,339	98.0	25,406	2.1	14,534	858	10,015	388	0.5
Fewer than 300 pupils	2,503	91.7	2,574	1.0	1,867	242	465	109	0.6
300 to 499 pupils	1,861	98.5	2,601	1.4	1,743	112	746	276	0.7
500 to 699 pupils	1,488	100.0	2,294	1.5	1,468	82	744	308	0.5
700 to 999 pupils	1,803	100.0	3,301	1.8	1,914	98	1,289	340	0.4
1,000 to 1,999 pupils	3,665	100.0	10,682	2.9	5,566	264	4,851	560	0.4
2,000 or more pupils	1,019	100.0	3,955	3.9	1,975	60	1,919	863	0.3

[1] Excludes vocational/technical centers and intermediate schools. Intermediate schools are included under elementary and combined schools.

NOTE.—Data are derived from a sample survey and are subject to sampling error. Because of rounding, details may not add to totals.

SOURCE: U.S. Department of Education, National Center for Education Statistics, "National Survey of Public and Private School Libraries and Media Centers, 1985." (This table was prepared September 1986.)

Table 386.—General statistics of public school libraries/media centers, by level of school: 1973–74 to fall 1985

Item	1973–74			1977–78			1984–85 and fall 1985 [1]		
	Total	Elementary and combined schools	Secondary schools	Total	Elementary and combined schools	Secondary schools	Total	Elementary, junior high, and combined schools	High schools
1	2	3	4	5	6	7	8	9	10
Number of public school libraries/media centers	74,625	52,310	22,315	70,854	52,087	18,767	73,352	61,013	12,339
Number of pupils served fall membership, in thousands	43,929	25,830	18,099	40,606	24,098	16,509	39,135	27,965	11,169
Collections, in thousands									
Volumes of books held at end of year	506,965	308,232	198,733	531,470	343,070	188,400	620,974	468,395	152,579
Volumes of books added during year	37,487	22,206	15,281	28,999	18,410	10,589	23,082	17,290	5,792
Periodical subscriptions held at end of year	2,892	1,319	1,573	4,026	2,347	1,679	2,487	1,586	901
Audiovisual materials held at end of year	68,024	43,719	24,305	75,938	26,734	49,204	—	—	—
Collections per pupil in membership									
Book volumes per pupil	11.5	11.9	11.0	13.1	14.2	11.4	15.9	16.7	13.7
Book volumes added per pupil	0.9	0.9	0.8	0.7	0.8	0.6	0.6	0.6	0.5
Staff, in full-time-equivalents									
Certified staff [2]	62,659	35,045	27,614	68,058	44,764	23,294	54,215	39,682	14,534
Men	7,378	2,749	4,629	—	—	—	—	—	—
Women	55,281	32,296	22,985	—	—	—	—	—	—
Less than a bachelor's degree	3,686	2,109	1,577	1,520	1,216	304	—	—	—
Bachelor's or higher degree	58,974	32,937	26,037	66,538	43,548	22,990	—	—	—
Noncertified staff (e.g., technical, secretarial, clerical, etc.)	38,807	21,482	17,325	—	—	—	42,109	31,236	10,873
Operating expenditures, in thousands									
Total operating expenditures	$1,182,280	$636,390	$545,890	$1,385,608	$834,744	$550,864	—	—	—
Salaries and wages	818,320	441,660	376,660	1,000,550	611,247	389,303	—	—	—
Books	162,960	86,860	76,100	172,473	106,199	66,274	$205,234	$143,564	$61,670
Periodicals	24,870	10,560	14,310	30,012	14,054	15,958	48,036	27,578	20,458
Equipment	66,450	38,440	28,010	69,587	40,486	29,101	—	—	—
Other operating expenditures [3]	109,680	58,870	50,810	112,987	62,758	50,229	—	—	—
Expenditures per student in membership									
Total operating expenditures	26.91	24.64	30.16	34.12	34.64	33.37	—	—	—
Salaries and wages	18.63	17.10	20.81	24.64	25.37	23.58	—	—	—
Books	3.71	3.36	4.20	4.25	4.41	4.01	6.24	6.00	7.40

[1] Data on numbers of library/media centers, membership, and staff are for fall 1985. Data on collections and expenditures are for 1984–85. Definitions of types of schools differ from tabulations for earlier years.

[2] Includes staff holding State certification as librarians, media specialists, or classroom teachers.

[3] Includes audiovisual materials.

—Data not available.

NOTE.—Data are derived from a sample survey and are subject to sampling error. Because of rounding, details may not add to totals.

SOURCE: U.S. Department of Education, National Center for Education Statistics, *Statistics of Public School Libraries/Media Centers,* fall 1974 and fall 1978; "National Survey of Public and Private School Libraries and Media Centers, 1985". (This table was prepared September 1986.)

Table 387.—Holdings and expenditures of public school libraries/media centers, by level and size of school: 1984–85

School level and size	Mean number of titles held per library/media center				Mean annual expenditure per pupil [1] by object					
	Book titles	Periodical subscriptions	Films and filmstrips	Audio materials	Total [2]	Books	Periodical subscriptions	Audio-visual materials	Computer hardware [3]	Computer software [3]
1	2	3	4	5	6	7	8	9	10	11
All schools	**7,668**	**34**	**540**	**353**	**$17.58**	**$6.24**	**$1.49**	**$1.80**	**$3.41**	**$0.84**
Fewer than 300 pupils	4,793	23	300	175	27.54	9.18	2.52	2.54	5.96	1.48
300 to 499 pupils	6,927	27	499	311	15.37	5.58	1.18	1.65	3.04	0.80
500 to 699 pupils	8,250	32	640	396	13.89	5.25	1.01	1.46	2.41	0.54
700 to 999 pupils	9,602	46	705	444	12.64	4.67	1.14	1.52	1.94	0.48
1,000 to 1,999 pupils	13,802	73	928	765	12.05	4.47	1.23	1.41	1.71	0.35
2,000 or more pupils	18,082	115	912	846	11.13	4.53	1.14	1.15	0.94	0.13
Elementary, junior high, and combined schools	7,003	26	523	337	16.79	6.00	1.22	1.69	3.44	0.89
Fewer than 300 pupils	4,720	19	313	184	25.18	8.63	2.00	2.12	5.57	1.53
300 to 499 pupils	6,867	24	509	313	14.65	5.29	1.00	1.62	3.08	0.80
500 to 699 pupils	8,178	28	637	396	13.35	5.07	0.86	1.44	2.36	0.55
700 to 999 pupils	9,242	38	742	461	12.16	4.44	0.90	1.45	2.09	0.48
1,000 to 1,999 pupils	11,214	45	888	991	10.65	3.81	0.70	1.44	1.88	0.36
2,000 or more pupils	14,644	73	253	422	8.84	5.13	0.53	1.22	0.00	0.02
High schools [4]	10,960	73	625	429	21.46	7.40	2.84	2.36	3.24	0.59
Fewer than 300 pupils	5,275	45	216	113	43.13	12.76	5.94	5.37	8.55	1.16
300 to 499 pupils	7,624	57	384	288	23.77	9.01	3.31	2.00	2.62	0.79
500 to 699 pupils	8,901	68	665	398	18.70	6.87	2.35	1.65	2.87	0.45
700 to 999 pupils	10,987	76	563	380	14.48	5.56	2.05	1.77	1.36	0.48
1,000 to 1,999 pupils	15,334	90	952	631	12.88	4.86	1.55	1.39	1.62	0.34
2,000 or more pupils	18,247	117	943	866	11.24	4.50	1.17	1.15	0.98	0.14

[1] Excludes salaries and wages.

[2] Includes expenditures not shown separately.

[3] Includes expenditures for computer installations that are administered by library/media centers.

[4] Excludes vocational/technical centers and intermediate schools. Intermediate schools are included under elementary and combined schools.

NOTE.—Data are derived from a sample survey and are subject to sampling error. Because of rounding, details may not add to totals.

SOURCE: U.S. Department of Education, National Center for Education Statistics, "National Survey of Public and Private School Libraries and Media Centers, 1985." (This table was prepared September 1986.)

Table 388.—Selected statistics on private school libraries/media centers, by level and size of school: 1984–85

Selected characteristics	All private schools	Level of school				Number of pupils in school				
		Elementary	Secondary	Combined	Other [1]	Less than 50	50 to 149	150 to 299	300 to 599	600 or more
1	2	3	4	5	6	7	8	9	10	11
Number of schools, fall 1985	25,615	15,117	2,479	4,975	3,044	4,649	8,143	6,405	4,670	1,748
Number of schools with library/media centers	19,186	11,747	2,364	3,566	1,509	2,356	5,581	5,280	4,225	1,745
Percent of schools with library/media centers	75	78	95	72	50	51	69	82	90	100
Percent of pupils in schools with library/media centers	88	87	99	83	66	53	70	83	91	100
Library/media FTE staff, total, fall 1985	16,627	7,853	4,120	3,033	1,622	705	2,996	4,355	4,946	3,625
Certified library staff	5,390	1,900	1,940	1,267	284	47	735	1,299	1,855	1,454
Other professional staff	3,534	1,778	651	577	528	114	625	1,039	1,073	683
Other staff	7,704	4,175	1,530	1,189	810	545	1,636	2,016	2,018	1,488
Library/media staff, mean FTE per school	0.87	0.67	1.74	0.85	1.07	0.30	0.54	0.82	1.17	2.08
Certified library staff	0.28	0.16	0.82	0.36	0.19	0.02	0.13	0.25	0.44	0.83
Mean number of titles held per library/media center, 1984–85.										
Book titles, all centers	5,154	4,001	10,583	6,013	3,589	2,242	2,857	4,450	7,603	12,628
Catholic	6,117	4,834	11,641	—	—	—	2,884	4,490	6,485	12,562
Other religious orientation	3,366	2,290	7,444	4,182	1,678	1,733	2,226	3,854	7,657	—
Not religiously affiliated	6,413	4,326	10,452	11,783	3,589	2,921	4,105	6,127	14,788	—
Periodical subscriptions	19	10	61	22	18	5	9	16	28	62
Films and filmstrips	253	259	492	124	139	42	78	191	512	660
Audio materials	225	183	600	121	206	50	111	152	313	832
Mean circulation per week, 1984–85										
Per school	200	230	154	171	106	40	96	199	329	441
Per pupil	0.9	1.0	0.4	0.9	1.0	1.3	0.9	0.9	0.8	0.5
Mean annual expenditure [2] per pupil, 1984–85										
Total [3]	$21.56	$15.52	$22.35	$34.26	$37.29	$59.75	$20.48	$14.26	$13.92	$13.99
Books	9.64	6.03	10.51	16.59	19.88	27.68	9.92	5.66	5.86	5.56
Periodical subscriptions	1.42	0.73	3.36	1.35	3.94	1.52	1.80	1.01	1.35	1.47
Audiovisual materials	1.84	1.11	1.92	4.31	1.57	5.50	1.43	1.15	1.29	1.66
Computer hardware [4]	3.08	3.35	1.97	2.89	3.16	7.83	2.69	2.68	2.08	1.50
Computer software	0.93	1.13	0.44	0.42	1.29	1.35	1.00	1.04	0.66	0.42
Mean annual expenditure [2] per pupil, by control										
Total [3]	21.56	15.52	22.35	34.26	37.29	59.75	20.48	14.26	13.92	13.99
Catholic	13.39	12.29	16.97	—	—	—	15.88	13.73	11.36	12.32
Other religious orientation	25.80	20.04	26.07	34.76	9.81	59.61	14.95	13.23	17.17	—
Not religiously affiliated	36.54	25.25	44.47	34.30	42.27	62.65	36.73	21.01	25.66	—

[1] Includes special education and alternative schools.
[2] Excludes salaries and wages.
[3] Includes items not shown separately.
[4] This figure often includes the total school budget for computer hardware.
— Data not shown because of small sample size.

NOTE.—Data are derived from a sample survey and are subject to sampling error. Because of rounding, details may not add to totals.

SOURCE: U.S. Department of Education, National Center for Education Statistics, *Statistics of Public and Private School Library Media Centers, 1985–86 (with historical comparisons from 1958 to 1985).* (This table was prepared February 1988.)

Table 389.—General statistics of college and university libraries: United States and outlying areas, 1974–75 to 1987–88

Item	1974–75	1975–76	1976–77	1978–79	1981–82[1]	1984–85[1]	1987–88[1]
1	2	3	4	5	6	7	8
Number of libraries	2,972	2,987	3,058	3,122	3,104	3,322	3,438
Total enrollment[2]	10,322	11,291	11,121	11,392	12,372	12,242	12,767
Collections, thousands of units							
Number of volumes at end of year	447,059	468,033	481,442	519,895	567,826	631,727	718,504
Number of volumes added during year	23,242	22,977	22,367	21,608	19,507	20,658	21,907
Number of serial subscriptions[3]	4,434	4,618	4,670	4,775	4,890	6,317	6,416
Library staff, in full-time equivalents							
Total staff in regular positions[3]	56,836	56,852	57,087	58,416	58,476	58,476	67,251
Librarians and professional staff	23,530	23,104	23,308	23,676	23,816	21,822	25,115
Other paid staff	33,306	33,748	33,779	34,740	34,660	38,026	40,733
Contributed services	—	—	—	—	—	—	1,403
Student assistants	—	—	—	—	—	—	33,821
Hours of student and other assistance, in thousands	34,687	36,725	39,950	39,552	40,068	28,360	—
Library operating expenditures (excluding capital outlay)							
Operating expenditures, total, in thousands	$1,091,784	$1,180,128	$1,259,637	$1,502,158	$1,943,769	$2,404,524	$2,770,075
Salaries[4]	592,568	649,374	698,090	824,438	1,081,894	1,156,138	1,451,551
Hourly wages	61,474	66,175	68,683	79,535	100,847	—	—
Fringe benefits	—	—	—	—	—	231,209	—
Preservation	22,206	22,375	22,521	25,274	30,351	32,939	34,144
Collection	327,904	357,544	373,699	450,180	561,199	750,282	891,281
Other library operating expenditures	87,632	84,660	96,643	122,731	169,478	233,957	393,099
Operating expenditures, total, in percents	100.0	100.0	100.0	100.0	100.0	100.0	100.0
Salaries[4]	54.3	55.0	55.4	54.9	55.7	48.1	52.4
Hourly wages	5.6	5.6	5.5	5.3	5.2	—	—
Fringe benefits	—	—	—	—	—	9.6	—
Preservation	2.0	1.9	1.8	1.7	1.6	1.4	1.2
Collection	30.0	30.3	29.7	30.0	28.9	31.2	32.2
Other library operating expenditures	8.0	7.2	7.7	8.2	8.7	9.7	14.2
Library operating expenditures as percent of total institutional expenditures for education and general purposes	3.9	3.8	3.8	3.7	3.5	3.4	[5]2.9

[1] Data are for the 50 States and the District of Columbia only.
[2] Fall enrollment for the academic year specified.
[3] Data are for end of year.
[4] Includes expenditures for fringe benefits (except for 1984–85 and 1987–88) and salary equivalents of contributed services staff.
[5] Data are for 1986–87.
—Data not available.

NOTE.—Because of rounding, details may not add to totals.

SOURCE: U.S. Department of Education, National Center for Education Statistics, *Library Statistics of Colleges and Universities,* various years. (This table was prepared January 1991.)

Table 390.—Selected statistics on the collections, staff, and operating expenditures of 50 large college and university libraries: 1985

Institution	Rank order, by number of volumes	Number of volumes at end of year, in thousands	Full-time-equivalent staff [1]		Operating expenditures, in thousands [2]				
			Total	Profes-sional	Total	Salaries and wages [3]	Books and other materi-als [4]	Binding and rebinding	Other
1	2	3	4	5	6	7	8	9	10
Harvard University (Mass.)	1	10,930	1,001	310	$30,452	$17,905	$6,872	$621	$5,054
Yale University (Conn.)	2	8,192	595	176	18,982	11,242	4,916	279	2,544
University of Illinois—Urbana Campus	3	6,808	551	122	15,500	8,932	4,724	228	1,616
University of California—Berkeley	4	6,611	721	170	26,024	17,603	5,115	520	2,786
University of Michigan, Ann Arbor	5	5,802	544	143	14,795	10,072	3,335	275	1,112
Columbia University, Main Division (N.Y.)	6	5,461	559	128	18,340	11,316	4,260	393	2,370
University of California—Los Angeles	7	5,453	692	190	27,586	16,805	5,850	614	4,317
University of Texas at Austin	8	5,402	593	131	19,441	11,261	6,539	182	1,458
Stanford University (Calif.)	9	5,318	590	155	25,202	16,377	5,755	351	2,720
University of North Carolina at Chapel Hill	10	4,851	370	109	12,639	6,475	4,228	246	1,690
University of Chicago (Ill.)	11	4,661	334	77	12,433	6,942	2,980	247	2,265
University of Wisconsin—Madison	12	4,495	519	132	17,179	9,936	4,141	218	2,885
University of Washington	13	4,416	483	125	14,833	8,445	4,313	373	1,702
Indiana University at Bloomington	14	4,366	495	109	12,092	7,399	3,516	210	967
University of Minnesota, Minneapolis–St. Paul	15	4,229	412	109	15,138	9,255	3,570	382	1,932
Cornell University (N.Y.)	16	4,065	448	91	12,475	7,142	4,146	249	939
Ohio State University, Main Campus	17	3,983	467	109	15,078	8,248	4,387	212	2,232
Rutgers University, New Brunswick (N.J.)	18	3,807	357	78	10,557	6,091	2,582	287	1,596
Princeton University (N.J.)	19	3,752	388	98	12,603	7,725	3,557	252	1,069
Duke University (N.C.)	20	3,459	302	97	9,895	5,621	3,103	190	981
University of Florida	21	3,409	430	98	9,511	5,061	3,022	117	1,310
University of Pennsylvania	22	3,282	319	101	11,942	7,332	2,512	280	1,818
Northwestern University (Ill.)	23	3,125	348	104	10,352	5,951	3,169	218	1,014
Michigan State University	24	3,063	318	75	10,024	5,916	2,681	186	1,241
University of Arizona	25	2,966	362	91	13,862	6,075	4,425	301	3,062
New York University	26	2,879	372	76	12,301	7,736	3,258	206	1,101
University of Virginia, Main Campus	27	2,770	348	90	10,711	4,915	4,333	214	1,248
University of Iowa	28	2,662	251	79	8,799	4,475	3,407	235	682
University of Pittsburgh, Main Campus (Penn.)	29	2,584	328	86	9,802	6,056	2,555	169	1,021
University of Utah	30	2,530	283	59	8,048	4,580	2,392	142	934
University of Rochester (N.Y.)	31	2,473	204	54	7,268	3,592	2,193	104	1,379
University of Southern California	32	2,436	342	97	10,402	5,577	2,962	139	1,724
University of Georgia	33	2,416	301	76	8,296	3,905	3,447	239	704
University of Kansas, Main Campus	34	2,374	250	64	8,244	4,214	2,837	159	1,034
Johns Hopkins University (Md.)	35	2,296	241	56	7,786	4,371	2,104	60	1,251
Southern Illinois University, Carbondale	36	2,263	269	64	6,944	3,608	2,306	139	891
University of Missouri, Columbia	37	2,255	211	50	5,707	2,683	2,146	142	736
University of California, Santa Barbara	38	2,252	238	57	9,579	5,799	2,673	216	892
Arizona State University	39	2,188	311	73	9,442	4,252	3,809	175	1,205
Syracuse University, Main Campus (N.Y.)	40	2,186	243	55	7,973	4,237	2,446	103	1,186
Louisiana State University and A & M College	41	2,158	273	68	8,289	3,410	3,142	178	1,559
University of Hawaii at Manoa	42	2,119	234	68	8,210	4,934	2,289	184	803
Wayne State University (Mich.)	43	2,084	210	55	8,253	3,460	2,445	99	2,249
State University of New York at Buffalo, Main Campus	44	2,066	230	61	7,802	4,400	2,097	100	1,205
University of Colorado at Boulder	45	2,052	193	45	6,233	3,377	2,224	122	510
University of Massachusetts at Amherst	46	2,033	219	45	6,653	4,199	1,813	67	575
Washington University (Missouri)	47	2,030	229	66	7,828	3,434	2,518	133	1,743
University of California at Davis	48	1,995	295	66	12,898	7,695	3,703	345	1,155
Massachusetts Institute of Technology	49	1,994	275	86	9,729	6,318	1,811	125	1,475
Brown University (R.I.)	50	1,966	220	59	6,714	3,475	2,105	139	995

[1] Data are for fall 1985.
[2] Data are for 1984–85.
[3] Includes salary equivalents of contributed services staff, fringe benefits of total staff, and wages of student assistants charged to the library budget.
[4] Includes operating expenses for book stock, periodicals, microforms, audiovisual materials, and other library materials.

SOURCE: U.S. Department of Education, National Center for Education Statistics, "Library Statistics of Colleges and Universities, Fall 1985" survey. (This table was prepared October 1986.)

Table 391.—General statistics of public libraries, by population of area served: Fiscal year 1982

Item	Population of area served						
	Total	Under 10,000	10,000 to 49,999	50,000 to 99,999	100,000 to 249,999	250,000 to 499,999	500,000 and over
1	2	3	4	5	6	7	8
Number of public service outlets	70,573	9,422	24,134	14,132	12,225	5,390	5,271
Central libraries	8,597	5,495	2,224	483	257	76	63
Branch libraries	6,943	350	1,389	1,271	1,361	924	1,649
Bookmobiles and mobile unit stops	49,981	3,036	19,227	11,461	9,034	4,029	3,195
Other outlets	5,051	542	1,295	918	1,573	361	363
Collections, in thousands							
Volumes of books held at end of year	494,149	80,600	127,069	63,984	65,874	48,274	108,347
Volumes of books added during year	30,204	4,652	7,847	3,761	3,856	3,419	6,669
Direct circulation of all materials	1,113,246	130,361	288,822	158,841	163,785	121,380	250,057
Staff, in full-time-equivalents							
Librarians	37,570	6,902	9,861	4,782	4,708	3,631	7,685
Technical, clerical, and other staff	49,283	3,114	11,945	7,760	7,589	5,849	13,027
Plant operation and maintenance staff	5,324	724	1,253	541	636	478	1,694
Finances, in millions							
Library receipts	$2,271	$178	$512	$308	$343	$264	$666
Library expenditures	2,210	165	499	305	333	264	643

NOTE.—Because of rounding, details may not add to totals.

SOURCE: U.S. Department of Education, National Center for Education Statistics, "Public Libraries, 1982" survey.

Table 392.—Public libraries, books and serial volumes, annual attendance, and reference transactions, by State: 1989 [1]

State	Number of libraries	Number of books and serial volumes	Number of books and serial volumes per capita	Annual attendance in libraries per capita [2]	Annual reference transactions in libraries per capita [3]	State	Number of libraries	Number of books and serial volumes	Number of books and serial volumes per capita	Annual attendance in libraries per capita [2]	Annual reference transactions in libraries per capita [3]
1	2	3	4	5	6	1	2	3	4	5	6
United States	8,968	600,318,617	2.53	2.63	0.92						
Alabama	200	6,388,341	1.76	—	0.35	Missouri	142	14,715,308	3.33	3.67	0.67
Alaska	88	1,548,050	2.88	1.97	0.20	Montana	81	2,373,635	2.69	0.05	0.01
Arizona	83	6,291,452	1.82	3.45	0.73	Nebraska	261	4,849,020	3.61	3.96	0.55
Arkansas	38	4,244,872	1.87	—	0.21	Nevada	26	1,992,488	1.49	—	0.63
California	169	54,275,436	1.89	0.09	1.30	New Hampshire	229	4,272,840	3.97	4.24	0.52
Colorado	134	8,502,516	2.56	3.02	0.98	New Jersey	313	26,696,923	3.49	3.27	0.68
Connecticut	192	11,674,642	3.76	6.70	0.86	New Mexico	70	2,953,125	2.47	4.74	0.50
Delaware	29	1,105,177	1.65	2.22	0.49	New York	759	62,780,293	3.58	2.87	1.01
District of Columbia ...	1	1,620,073	2.58	3.47	1.23	North Carolina	100	11,942,928	1.82	2.37	0.51
Florida	115	20,943,640	1.64	2.38	1.02	North Dakota	93	1,146,172	3.06	3.04	0.59
Georgia	53	11,952,949	1.85	—	—	Ohio	250	35,247,494	3.25	5.07	1.36
Hawaii	1	2,320,850	2.29	3.30	1.17	Oklahoma	106	5,472,709	2.02	2.74	0.75
Idaho	111	2,563,364	2.98	3.67	0.53	Oregon	123	5,793,198	2.27	4.08	0.65
Illinois	597	30,478,879	3.03	—	1.09	Pennsylvania	441	23,761,036	2.06	2.41	0.59
Indiana	238	17,047,104	3.27	3.57	1.07	Rhode Island	51	3,447,974	3.67	4.48	0.01
Iowa	494	10,446,934	3.59	4.20	0.64	South Carolina	40	5,067,967	1.62	1.91	0.64
Kansas	317	7,962,499	4.07	0.09	0.37	South Dakota	110	2,057,972	4.11	3.22	0.82
Kentucky	115	6,674,015	1.84	—	0.01	Tennessee	178	7,604,208	1.55	—	—
Louisiana	64	8,607,785	2.05	1.00	0.21	Texas	468	31,253,070	2.12	2.32	0.91
Maine	238	4,830,102	4.78	3.66	0.64	Utah	69	4,118,309	2.43	5.47	0.68
Maryland	24	10,303,959	2.29	—	—	Vermont	200	2,233,578	4.50	3.43	0.41
Massachusetts	348	26,941,840	4.59	—	—	Virginia	88	13,188,444	2.25	0.33	1.09
Michigan	379	23,445,891	2.53	3.35	1.88	Washington	70	10,557,563	2.52	4.00	0.78
Minnesota	133	11,213,914	2.65	3.74	1.25	West Virginia	98	4,144,930	2.15	2.35	0.48
Mississippi	46	4,853,453	1.84	1.65	0.37	Wisconsin	372	14,642,990	3.03	4.34	1.28
						Wyoming	23	1,766,760	3.82	4.73	0.82

[1] The time period covered was generally calendar or fiscal 1989, although for some states, the latest data available covered calendar year 1988.

[2] Attendance is the total number of persons entering the library including persons attending activities, meetings, and those persons requiring no staff services.

[3] A reference transaction is an information contact which involves the knowledge, use, recommendation, interpretation or instructions in the use of one or more information sources by a member of the library staff.

—Data not available.

SOURCE: U.S. Department of Education, National Center for Education Statistics, Federal-State Cooperative System for Public Data, July 1990. (This table was prepared June 1991.)

Table 393.—Microcomputer use by elementary and secondary schools, by level, control, and size of school: 1981 to 1986

Control and size	Percent of schools using microcomputers			
	All schools	Elementary schools	Junior high schools	Senior high schools
1	2	3	4	5
Public schools				
Fall 1981	18.2	11.1	25.6	42.7
Fall 1982	30.0	20.2	39.8	57.8
Fall 1983	68.4	62.4	80.5	86.1
Fall 1984	85.1	82.2	93.1	94.6
Fall 1985	92.2	91.0	97.3	97.4
Fall 1986	95.6	94.9	98.5	98.7
Enrollment size, fall 1985				
Under 200	81.5	82.0	93.3	92.5
200 to 299	92.7	92.1	97.1	96.6
300 to 499	94.1	93.4	97.3	97.4
500 to 999	95.2	93.2	97.9	98.6
1,000 and over	97.9	94.7	96.8	98.9
Private schools 1982–83 [1]				
Catholic	22.8	16.3	27.8	57.8
Other private	24.6	21.1	43.4	54.8
1983–84 [1]				
Catholic	63.4	—	—	—
Other private	46.4	—	—	—
1984–85 [1]				
Catholic	82.9	81.5	87.7	92.8
Other private	61.9	—	—	—
1985–86 [1]				
Catholic	91.4	—	—	—
Other private	67.3	—	—	—

[1] Private schools were surveyed in the middle of the school year.
—Data not available.

NOTE.—Some data have been revised from previously published figures.

SOURCE: Market Data Retrieval, Inc., *Microcomputers in Schools, 1984, 1985, 1987;* and unpublished tabulations. (This table was prepared May 1989.)

Table 394.—Percentage of workers using computers on the job, by sex, educational attainment, and selected computer activities: October 1989

Highest educational attainment and sex	Percent using computers at work	Distribution of on-the-job computer users, by selected computer activities [1]				
		Word processing	Bookkeeping	Inventory control	Communications	Databases
1	2	3	4	5	6	7
Total	**36.01**	**41.41**	**26.78**	**25.92**	**26.37**	**27.78**
Not high school graduate	7.31	18.36	20.14	39.20	13.85	13.14
High school graduate	27.93	32.02	27.56	29.83	20.83	19.45
Some college	44.44	39.85	28.81	28.34	27.06	27.62
4 years of college	57.60	46.34	27.08	23.42	30.10	33.42
More than 4 years of college	58.03	56.64	22.76	16.49	31.49	36.82
Male	30.98	37.53	24.24	31.32	28.33	30.16
Not high school graduate	5.64	12.23	12.03	44.13	11.38	10.11
High school graduate	18.94	19.39	20.56	42.50	19.18	16.83
Some college	36.81	30.87	24.17	35.62	27.85	28.73
4 years of college	58.17	45.22	28.76	27.95	32.56	36.08
More than 4 years of college	59.43	56.37	24.11	18.28	34.51	39.77
Female	42.09	44.95	29.10	20.99	24.58	25.60
Not high school graduate	9.87	23.88	27.43	34.76	16.06	15.86
High school graduate	37.79	39.02	31.43	22.71	21.74	20.90
Some college	52.36	47.91	32.34	22.80	26.46	26.77
4 years of college	56.84	57.09	24.71	17.07	26.65	29.69
More than 4 years of college	55.94	57.05	20.55	13.56	26.54	31.98

[1] Individuals may be counted in more than one job category.

NOTE.—Data are based on a sample survey of households and are subject to sampling and nonsampling error. Data have been revised from previously published figures.

SOURCE: U.S. Department of Commerce, Bureau of the Census, *Current Population Survey, October, 1989.* (This table was prepared March 1991.)

Table 395.—Student use of computers, by level of instruction and selected characteristics: October 1984 and October 1989

Student and school characteristics	October 1984						October 1989 [1]					
	Total	Prekinder-garten and kinder-garten	Grades 1 through 8	Grades 9 through 12	1st through 4th year of college	5th or later year of college	Total	Prekinder-garten and kinder-garten	Grades 1 through 8	Grades 9 through 12	1st through 4th year of college	5th or later year of college
1	2	3	4	5	6	7	8	9	10	11	12	13
Percent of students using computers at school												
Total	**27.3**	**5.8**	**31.5**	**26.3**	**29.2**	**29.3**	**42.7**	**14.7**	**52.3**	**39.2**	**39.2**	**40.7**
Sex												
Male	29.0	6.2	32.1	28.0	34.4	33.2	43.5	13.9	52.9	38.7	42.1	47.0
Female	25.5	5.4	30.9	24.4	24.3	25.1	41.9	15.6	51.7	39.8	36.8	34.9
Race/ethnicity												
White, non-Hispanic	30.0	6.4	36.5	28.5	29.3	29.4	45.7	17.0	58.4	40.6	40.0	39.6
Black, non-Hispanic	16.8	2.5	16.1	18.0	27.2	22.4	32.6	7.4	35.7	36.0	35.1	35.2
Hispanic	18.6	3.9	18.7	18.4	29.7	22.5	34.9	10.1	40.2	33.6	32.4	37.8
Other	28.6	10.5	28.6	29.6	31.0	45.8	42.7	8.5	47.0	41.4	43.9	58.0
Household income.												
Less than $5,000	18.7	1.9	18.1	17.6	28.5	30.2	36.7	8.5	40.4	35.6	40.1	53.5
$5,000–9,999	21.0	2.2	21.3	20.0	30.2	33.9	36.1	9.2	40.3	32.7	40.5	60.2
$10,000–14,999	22.4	5.0	24.9	24.0	24.5	26.0	38.4	14.6	44.4	39.1	30.8	55.2
$15,000–19,999	25.9	4.9	30.0	24.9	27.4	28.6	41.5	11.9	50.9	34.8	39.6	44.0
$20,000–24,999	26.7	6.0	31.9	25.4	25.4	29.0	42.4	14.6	51.8	40.1	32.5	44.4
$25,000–29,999	30.5	6.7	37.2	28.7	29.8	26.7	46.1	16.1	56.4	43.8	40.4	42.1
$30,000–34,999	30.5	6.1	37.8	28.4	28.2	33.2	44.2	17.4	56.8	37.8	37.1	33.3
$35,000–39,999	32.3	9.6	39.9	31.5	28.1	28.5	45.2	16.1	58.3	41.5	34.5	45.3
$40,000–49,999	32.8	10.8	40.6	30.3	31.1	30.4	44.7	15.4	59.7	36.7	38.1	35.4
$50,000–74,999	35.5	9.1	45.9	32.7	35.1	26.8	47.0	16.2	61.2	44.6	43.4	31.8
More than $74,999	36.0	8.2	51.6	31.3	34.1	26.5	51.2	21.2	67.0	45.8	49.6	31.0
Control of school												
Public	27.4	5.9	30.8	26.1	28.9	28.7	43.3	16.4	51.9	39.0	37.5	41.3
Private	26.5	5.8	37.7	28.6	30.2	30.4	38.9	11.8	56.6	42.6	46.3	39.7
Percent of students using computers at home												
Total	**11.5**	**7.6**	**12.6**	**12.9**	**9.0**	**12.2**	**18.8**	**10.2**	**17.8**	**20.7**	**21.3**	**33.4**
Sex												
Male	14.0	7.2	14.7	16.7	12.1	14.2	20.7	11.0	18.7	23.9	25.4	36.0
Female	9.0	8.0	10.4	8.8	6.2	10.1	17.0	9.3	16.9	17.4	18.0	31.1
Race/ethnicity												
White, non-Hispanic	13.7	9.1	15.4	15.5	9.9	13.7	22.7	12.2	22.3	25.3	23.6	35.6
Black, non-Hispanic	4.9	3.6	5.2	5.0	4.9	3.3	7.3	3.7	6.8	8.5	9.1	18.6
Hispanic	3.6	2.5	3.7	3.1	3.7	6.4	7.5	3.4	6.6	8.2	11.5	27.1
Other	9.0	3.8	9.2	9.5	9.4	11.8	18.8	9.9	16.6	21.6	23.7	24.7
Household income												
Less than $5,000	2.9	1.0	2.1	3.5	5.4	4.3	8.4	4.5	4.1	6.6	17.7	29.4
$5,000–9,999	3.2	2.3	3.2	3.4	2.9	5.1	5.4	1.0	2.7	4.4	14.2	28.4
$10,000–14,999	5.0	2.7	4.9	5.4	5.3	8.8	7.2	1.9	6.2	6.5	11.8	26.5
$15,000–19,999	7.5	4.6	8.3	8.0	5.4	8.7	11.3	3.2	9.2	13.6	15.8	33.6
$20,000–24,999	9.9	9.4	10.3	11.0	7.2	10.3	12.9	6.8	11.6	13.6	16.9	32.2
$25,000–29,999	12.8	8.3	15.1	13.1	9.6	9.2	17.0	11.9	16.5	17.1	19.2	29.6
$30,000–34,999	15.8	8.8	19.6	15.0	10.9	14.9	17.7	8.0	17.6	20.2	19.4	30.7
$35,000–39,999	19.4	13.2	23.6	20.4	11.4	18.6	21.4	8.7	22.2	25.1	22.1	26.5
$40,000–49,999	20.4	12.4	24.9	21.0	13.9	23.8	25.7	14.8	27.5	27.7	21.7	40.7
$50,000–74,999	24.2	18.5	32.0	27.1	13.8	21.1	31.6	20.6	33.8	34.3	27.6	41.1
More than $74,999	22.1	21.2	26.9	27.8	12.5	18.9	43.8	25.2	50.9	53.4	33.9	41.4
Control of school												
Public	11.2	6.3	11.9	12.4	8.9	12.5	17.9	8.3	16.8	19.7	20.7	32.2
Private	13.8	9.8	18.8	18.5	9.6	11.7	24.4	13.4	27.7	35.9	23.8	35.9
Percent of students using computers at home for school work												
Total	**4.6**	**0.9**	**4.0**	**6.6**	**4.9**	**7.7**	**8.9**	**0.6**	**6.3**	**12.2**	**13.7**	**23.9**
Sex												
Male	5.9	0.8	4.8	8.9	7.1	9.2	9.5	0.6	6.3	13.6	16.0	25.9
Female	3.3	1.0	3.2	4.1	2.8	6.1	8.3	0.6	6.2	10.8	11.7	22.0
Race												
White, non-Hispanic	5.4	1.0	4.8	7.7	5.4	8.7	10.7	0.6	7.7	15.2	15.1	25.5
Black, non-Hispanic	2.3	1.1	2.0	3.2	2.4	2.7	3.4	0.9	2.7	4.0	6.2	12.6
Hispanic	1.4	—	1.3	1.9	1.0	4.2	3.6	—	2.8	4.4	6.4	24.8
Other	3.8	—	3.0	5.3	5.7	4.8	9.1	—	5.8	13.4	15.5	14.8
Household income												
Less than $5,000	1.0	—	0.2	1.0	3.7	2.9	5.0	—	1.5	4.1	12.6	23.8
$5,000–9,999	1.5	0.4	1.5	1.2	1.6	5.1	3.2	—	0.6	2.6	10.3	26.5
$10,000–14,999	1.9	0.3	1.6	2.8	2.7	3.7	3.5	0.7	1.8	3.6	8.1	19.3
$15,000–19,999	3.0	1.3	2.6	4.6	2.7	4.9	4.5	—	2.1	5.2	9.3	30.2
$20,000–24,999	3.1	0.6	1.8	5.4	3.7	7.7	5.7	0.3	3.8	7.6	10.5	23.8
$25,000–29,999	5.1	1.8	5.8	5.9	4.0	5.1	6.4	0.3	4.1	8.2	12.3	19.7
$30,000–34,999	4.9	1.1	4.9	6.2	5.3	6.6	8.0	0.1	5.7	12.0	12.8	19.8
$35,000–39,999	7.1	1.3	8.2	8.1	5.0	14.0	10.5	1.2	7.9	15.0	15.9	18.7
$40,000–49,999	9.2	0.9	8.9	12.1	7.8	15.1	11.9	0.7	9.7	17.1	14.3	29.4
$50,000–74,999	11.5	1.8	10.8	16.9	9.2	14.0	15.2	0.8	12.7	21.2	17.5	28.5
More than $74,999	9.8	2.8	8.4	15.7	8.1	12.2	22.0	2.4	21.9	34.2	21.2	22.2
Control of school												
Public	4.5	1.0	3.8	6.3	4.7	7.6	8.5	0.6	5.9	11.5	13.1	22.2
Private	5.4	0.7	6.0	10.0	5.8	7.8	11.4	0.5	9.4	23.6	15.8	27.1

[1] Data have been revised from previously published figures.
—Data not available.

NOTE.—Data are based on a sample survey of households and are subject to sampling and nonsampling error.

SOURCE: U.S. Department of Commerce, Bureau of the Census, *Current Population Survey, October, 1984 and 1989*, unpublished data. (This Table was prepared February 1991.)

Guide To Tabular Presentation

This section is intended to assist the reader in following the basic structure of the *Digest* tables and to provide a legend for some of the common symbols and indexes used throughout the book. Unless otherwise noted, all data are for the 50 States and the District of Columbia.

Table Components

Title Describes the table content concisely.

Unit indicator Informs the reader of the measurement unit in the table—"In thousands," "In millions of dollars," etc. Noted below the title unless several units are used, in which case the unit indicators are generally given in the spanner or individual column heads.

Spanner Describes a group of two or more columns.

Column head Describes specific column.

Stub Describes a row or a group of rows. Each stub is followed by a number of dots (leaders) or by a semicolon if no data appears in the data fields.

Field The area of the table which contains the data elements.

Rules in the field

Single horizontal rules indicate
— that the data below the line add to the figure immediately above the line, or
— in the case of derived figures (e.g., percents, medians) that the datum above the line represents a cumulative figure.

Double horizontal rules demarcate groups of related rows.

Single vertical rules delineate columns.

Double vertical rules divide the table into sections with unique stubs.

Example of Table Structure

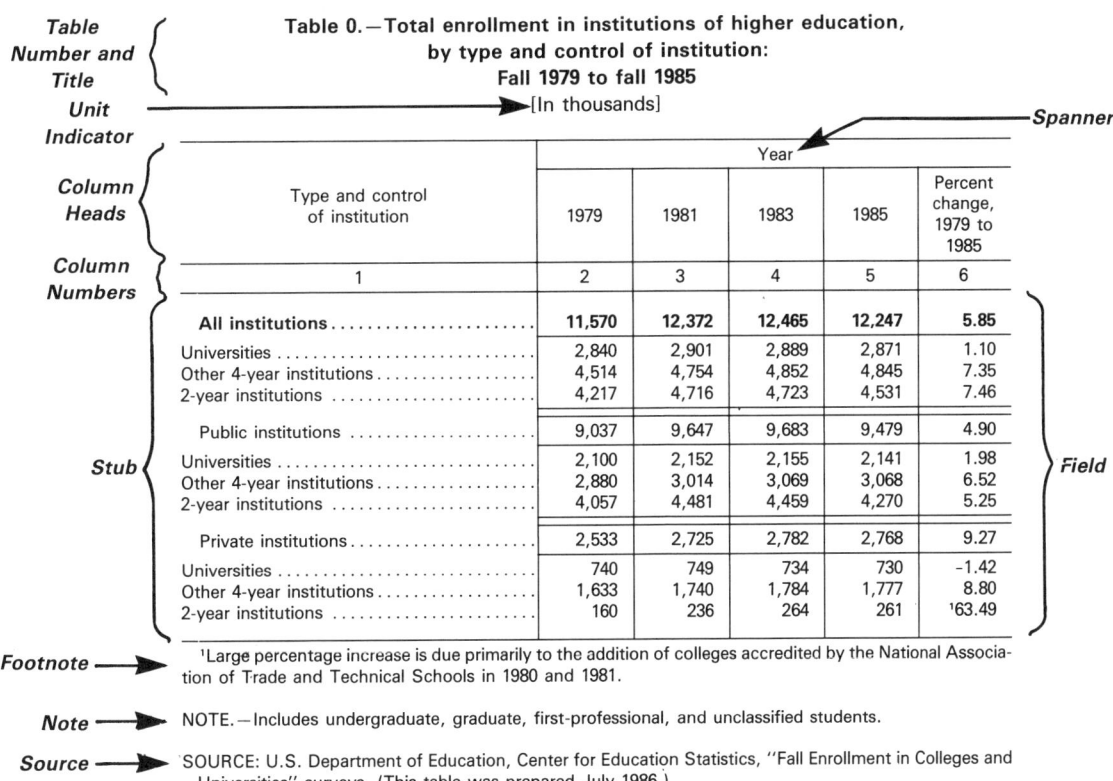

Table 0.—Total enrollment in institutions of higher education, by type and control of institution: Fall 1979 to fall 1985

[In thousands]

Type and control of institution	Year				
	1979	1981	1983	1985	Percent change, 1979 to 1985
1	2	3	4	5	6
All institutions	**11,570**	**12,372**	**12,465**	**12,247**	**5.85**
Universities	2,840	2,901	2,889	2,871	1.10
Other 4-year institutions	4,514	4,754	4,852	4,845	7.35
2-year institutions	4,217	4,716	4,723	4,531	7.46
Public institutions	9,037	9,647	9,683	9,479	4.90
Universities	2,100	2,152	2,155	2,141	1.98
Other 4-year institutions	2,880	3,014	3,069	3,068	6.52
2-year institutions	4,057	4,481	4,459	4,270	5.25
Private institutions	2,533	2,725	2,782	2,768	9.27
Universities	740	749	734	730	-1.42
Other 4-year institutions	1,633	1,740	1,784	1,777	8.80
2-year institutions	160	236	264	261	[1]63.49

[1]Large percentage increase is due primarily to the addition of colleges accredited by the National Association of Trade and Technical Schools in 1980 and 1981.

NOTE.—Includes undergraduate, graduate, first-professional, and unclassified students.

SOURCE: U.S. Department of Education, Center for Education Statistics, "Fall Enrollment in Colleges and Universities" surveys. (This table was prepared July 1986.)

Footnote Describes a unique circumstance relating to a specific item within the table. Usually listed below the bottom rule of the table.

Note Furnishes general information that relates to the entire table.

Source The document or reference from which the data are drawn. This note may also include the organizational unit responsible for preparing the data.

Descriptive Terms

Average A number that is used to represent the "typical value" of a group of numbers. It is regarded as a measure of "location" or "central tendency" of a group of numbers.

> ***Arithmetic mean*** is the most commonly used average. It is derived by summing the individual item values of a particular group and dividing that sum by the number of items. This value is often referred to simply as the "mean" or "average."
>
> ***Median*** is the measure of central tendency that occupies the middle position in a rank order of values. It generally has the same number of items above it as below it. If there is an even number of items in the group, the median is the average of the middle two items.
>
> ***Per capita,*** or per person, figure represents an average computed for every person in a specified group, or population. It is derived by dividing the total for an item (such as income or expenditures) by the number of persons in the specified population.

Index number A value that provides a means of measuring, summarizing, and communicating the nature of changes that occur from time to time or from place to place. An index is used to express changes in prices over periods of time but may also be used to express differences between related subjects at a single point in time.

The *Digest* most often uses the Consumer Price Index to compare purchasing power over time.

To compute a price index, a base year or period is selected. The base year price is then designated as the base or reference price to which the prices for other years or periods are related.

A method of expressing the price relationship is:

Index number =

$$\frac{\text{Price of a set of one or more items for related year}}{\text{Price of the same set of items for base year}} \times 100$$

When 100 is subtracted from the index number, the result equals the percent change in price from the base year.

Current and constant dollars are used in a number of tables to express finance data. Unless otherwise noted, all figures are in current dollars, not adjusted for inflation. Constant dollars provide a measure of the impact of inflation on the current dollars.

> ***Current dollar*** figures reflect actual prices or costs prevailing during the specified year(s).
>
> ***Constant dollar*** figures attempt to remove the effects of price changes (inflation) from statistical series reported in dollar terms.

The constant dollar value for an item is derived by dividing the base year price index (for example, the Consumer Price Index for 1986) by the price index for the year of data to be adjusted and multiplying by the item to be adjusted. The result is an adjusted dollar value as it would presumably exist if prices were the same as the base year—in other words, as if the dollar had constant purchasing power. Any changes in the constant dollar amounts would reflect only changes in the real values.

NOTE: Tables may not include data for all years implied in table titles.

Guide to Sources
Sources and Comparability of Data

The information presented in this report was obtained from many sources, including Federal and State agencies, private research organizations, and professional associations. The data were collected using many research methods, including surveys of a universe (such as all colleges) or of a sample, compilations of administrative records, and statistical projections. *Digest* users should take particular care when comparing data from different sources. Differences in procedures, timing, phrasing of questions, interviewer training, and so forth mean that the results from the different sources may not be strictly comparable. Following the general discussion of data accuracy below, descriptions of the information sources and data collection methods are presented, grouped by sponsoring organization. More extensive documentation of a particular survey's procedures does not imply more problems with the data, only that more information is available.

Accuracy of Data

The accuracy of any statistic is determined by the joint effects of "sampling" and "nonsampling" errors. Estimates based on a sample will differ somewhat from the figures that would have been obtained if a complete census had been taken using the same survey instruments, instructions, and procedures. In addition to such sampling errors, all surveys, both universe and sample, are subject to design, reporting, and processing errors and errors due to nonresponse. To the extent possible, these nonsampling errors are kept to a minimum by methods built into the survey procedures. In general, however, the effects of nonsampling errors are more difficult to gauge than those produced by sampling variability.

Sampling Errors

The samples used in surveys are selected from a large number of possible samples of the same size that could have been selected using the same sample design. Estimates derived from the different samples would differ from each other. The difference between a sample estimate and the average of all possible samples is called the sampling deviation. The standard or sampling error of a survey estimate is a measure of the variation among the estimates from all possible samples and, thus, is a measure of the precision with which an estimate from a particular sample approximates the average result of all possible samples.

The sample estimate and an estimate of its standard error permit us to construct interval estimates with prescribed confidence that the interval includes the average result of all possible samples. If all possible samples were selected under essentially the same conditions and an estimate and its estimated standard error were calculated from each sample, then: 1) approximately 2/3 of the intervals from one standard error below the estimate to one standard error above the estimate would include the average value of all possible samples; and 2) approximately 19/20 of the intervals from two standard errors below the estimate to two standard errors above the estimate would include the average value of all possible samples. We call an interval from two standard errors below the estimate to two standard errors above the estimate a 95 percent confidence interval.

To illustrate this concept, consider the table of standard errors and 95 percent confidence intervals for estimates from the "1985 Survey of Public and Private School Libraries and Media Centers" sample (table A1, below). For the estimate that 93.5 percent of all schools have library programs, the table shows that the standard error is 0.54 percent. Therefore, we can create a 95 percent confidence interval which is approximately 92.4 to 94.6 (93.5 percent ± 2 times 0.54 percent).

Analysis of standard errors can help assess how valid a comparison between two estimates might be. The standard error of a difference between two independent sample estimates is equal to the square root of the sum of the squared standard errors of the estimates. The standard error (se) of the difference between independent sample estimates "a" and "b" is:

$$se_{a,b} = \sqrt{se_a^2 + se_b^2}$$

It should be noted that most of the standard error estimates presented in subsequent sections and in the original documents are approximations. That is, to derive estimates of standard errors that would be applicable to a wide variety of items and could be prepared at a moderate cost, a number of approximations were required. As a result, the standard error estimates provide a general order of magnitude rather than the exact standard error for any specific item. The preceding discussion on sampling variability was directed toward a situation concerning one or two estimates. Determining the accuracy of statistical projections is more difficult. In general, the further away the projection date is from the date of the actual data being used for the projection, the greater the probable error in the projections. If, for instance, annual data from 1970 to 1988 are being used to project enrollment in institutions of higher education, the further beyond 1989 one projects, the more variability in the projection. One will be less sure of the 1995 enrollment projection than of the 1990 projection. A detailed discussion of the projections methodology is contained in *Projections of Education Statistics to 2000* (National Center for Education Statistics, 1989).

Nonsampling Errors

Universe and sample surveys are subject to nonsampling errors. Nonsampling errors may arise when respondents or interviewers interpret questions differently, when respondents must estimate values, or when coders, keyers, and other processors handle answers differently, when persons who should be included in the universe are not, or when persons fail to respond (completely or partially). Nonsampling errors usually, but not always, result in an understatement of total survey error and thus an overstatement of the precision of survey estimates. Since estimating the magnitude of nonsampling errors often would require special experiments or access to independent data, these magnitudes are seldom available.

To compensate for nonresponse, adjustments of the sample estimates are often made. An adjustment made for either type of nonresponse, total or partial, is often referred to as an imputation—substitution of the "average" questionnaire response for the nonresponse. Imputations are usually made separately within various groups of sample members which have similar survey characteristics. Imputation for item nonresponse is usually made by substituting for a missing item the response to that item of a respondent having characteristics that are similar to those of the nonrespondent.

Although the magnitude of nonsampling error in the data collected in this *Digest* is frequently unknown, idiosyncrasies that have been identified are noted on the appropriate tables.

Federal Agency Sources

National Center for Education Statistics (NCES)

Common Core of Data

NCES uses the Common Core of Data (CCD) survey to acquire and maintain statistical data on the 50 States, the District of Columbia, and the outlying areas from the universe of State-level education agencies. Information about staff and students is collected annually at the school, LEA (local education agency or school district), and State levels. Information about revenues and expenditures is also collected at the State level.

Data are collected for a particular school year (July 1 through June 30) via survey instruments sent to the States by October 15 of the subsequent school year. States have 2 years in which to modify the data originally submitted.

Since the CCD is a universe survey, the CCD information presented in this edition of the *Digest* is not subject to sampling errors. However, nonsampling errors could come from two sources—nonreturn and inaccurate reporting. Almost all of the States submit the six CCD survey instruments each year, but submissions are sometimes incomplete or too late for publication.

Understandably, when 57 education agencies compile and submit data for over 85,000 public schools and approximately 15,000 local school districts, misreporting can occur. Typically, this results from varying interpretation of NCES definitions and differing recordkeeping systems. NCES attempts to minimize these errors by working closely with the Council of Chief State School Officers (CCSSO) and its Committee on Evaluation and Information Systems (CEIS).

The State education agencies report data to NCES from data collected and edited in their regular reporting cycles. NCES encourages the agencies to incorporate into their own survey systems the NCES items they do not already collect so that those items will also be available for the subsequent CCD survey. Over time, this has meant fewer missing data cells in each State's response, reducing the need to impute data.

NCES subjects data from the education agencies to a comprehensive edit. Where data are determined to be inconsistent, missing, or out of range, NCES contacts the education agencies for verification. NCES-prepared State summary forms are returned to the State education agencies for verification. States are also given an opportunity to revise their State-level aggregates from the previous survey cycle. Questions concerning the Common Core of Data can be directed to:

John Sietsema
Elementary and Secondary Education Statistics
  Division
National Center for Education Statistics
555 New Jersey Avenue NW
Washington, DC 20208–5651

Federal Funds for Education

NCES prepares an annual compilation of Federal funds for education. Data for U.S. Department of Education program totals came from the *Budget of the U.S. Government*. Budget offices of other Federal agencies provided information for all other Federal program support except for research funds, which are obligations reported by the National Science Foundation in *Federal Funds for Research and Development*, fiscal years 1965 to 1990. Some data are estimated, based on reports from the Federal agencies contacted and the *Budget of the U.S. Government, Fiscal Year 1992.*

Except for money spent on research, outlays were used to report program funds to the extent possible. Some tables are obligations as noted in the title of the table. Some Federal program funds not commonly recognized as education assistance are also included in the totals reported. For example, portions of Federal funds paid to some States and counties as shared revenues resulting from the sale of timber and minerals from public lands have been estimated as funds used for education purposes. Parts of the funds received by States (in 1980) and localities (throughout the period) under the General Revenue Sharing Program are also included, as are portions of Federal funds received by the District of Columbia. The share of these funds allocated to education was assumed equal to the share of general funds expended for elementary and secondary education by States and localities in the same year as reported by the U.S. Bureau of the Census in its annual publication, *Governmental Finances.*

All State intergovernmental expenditures for education were assumed earmarked for elementary/secondary education. Contributions of parent governments of dependent school systems to their public schools amounted to approximately 9 percent of local government revenues and local government revenue sharing in each year. Therefore, 9 percent of local government revenue-sharing funds were assumed allocated each fiscal year to elementary and secondary education. Parent government contributions to public school systems were obtained from the U.S. Bureau of the Census, *Finances of Public School Systems.* The amount of State revenue-sharing funds allocated for postsecondary education in 1980 was assumed to

be 13 percent, the proportion of direct State expenditures for institutions of higher education reported in *Governmental Finances* for that year.

The share of Federal funds for the District of Columbia assigned to education was assumed equal to the share of the city's general fund expenditures for each level of education.

For the job training programs conducted by the Department of Labor, only estimated sums spent on classroom training have been reported as educational program support.

During the 1970s, the Office of Management and Budget (OMB) prepared annual reports on Federal education program support. These were published in *Budget of the U.S. Government [Special Analyses].* The information presented in this report is not, however, a continuation of the OMB series. A number of differences in the two series should be noted. OMB required all Federal agencies to report outlays for education-related programs using a standardized form, thereby assuring agency compliance in reporting. The scope of education programs reported here differs from OMB. Off-budget items such as the annual volume of guaranteed student loans were not included in OMB's reports. Finally, while some mention is made of an annual estimate of Federal tax expenditures, OMB did not include them in its annual analysis of Federal education support. Estimated Federal tax expenditures for education are the difference between current Federal tax receipts and what these receipts would be without existing education deductions to income allowed by Federal tax provisions.

Recipients' data are estimated based on *Estimating Federal Funds for Education: A New Approach Applied to Fiscal Year 1980,* U.S. Department of Education, "Federal Support for Education, Fiscal Years 1980 to 1984," and *Catalog of Federal Domestic Assistance.* The recipients' data are estimated and tend to undercount institutions of higher education (IHEs), students, and local education agencies (LEAs). This is because some of the Federal programs have more than one recipient receiving funds. In these cases the recipients were put into a "mixed recipients" category, because there was no way to disaggregate the amount each recipient received.

High School and Beyond

High School and Beyond (HSB) is a national longitudinal survey of 1980 high school sophomores and seniors. The base-year survey was a probability sample of 1,015 high schools with a target number of 36 sophomores and 36 seniors in each of the schools. A total of 58,270 students participated in the base-year survey. Substitutions were made for noncooperating schools—but not for students—in those strata where it was possible. Overall, 1,122 schools were selected in the original sample and 811 of these schools participated in the survey. An additional 204 schools were drawn in a replacement sample. Student refusals and student absences resulted in an 82 percent completion rate for the survey.

Several small groups in the population were oversampled to allow for special study of certain types of schools and students. Students completed questionnaires and took a battery of cognitive tests. In addition, a sample of parents of sophomores and seniors (about 3,600 for each cohort) was surveyed.

HSB first followup activities took place in the spring of 1982. The sample design of the first followup survey called for the selection of approximately 30,000 persons who were sophomores in 1980. The completion rate for sophomores eligible for on-campus survey administration was about 96 percent. About 89 percent of the students who left school between the base year and first followup surveys (dropouts, transfer students, and early graduates) completed the first followup sophomore questionnaire.

As part of the first followup survey of High School and Beyond, transcripts were requested in fall 1982 for an 18,152-member subsample of the sophomore cohort. Of the 15,941 transcripts actually obtained, 1,969 were excluded because the students had dropped out of school before graduation, 799 were excluded because they were incomplete, and 1,057 were excluded because the student graduated before 1982 or the transcript indicated neither a dropout status nor graduation. Thus 12,116 transcripts were utilized for the overall curriculum analysis presented in this publication. All courses in each transcript were assigned a six-digit code based on *A Classification of Secondary School Courses* (developed by Evaluation Technologies, Inc. under contract with NCES). Credits earned in each course were expressed in Carnegie units. (The Carnegie unit is a standard of measurement that represents one credit for the completion of a 1-year course. To receive credit for a course, the student must have received a passing grade— "pass," "D," or higher.) Students who transferred from public to private schools or from private to public schools between their sophomore and senior years were eliminated from public/private analyses.

In designing the senior cohort first followup survey, one of the goals was to reduce the size of the retained sample, while still keeping sufficient numbers of minorities to allow important policy analyses. A total of 11,227 (94 percent) of the 11,995 persons subsampled completed the questionnaire. Information was obtained about the respondents' school and employment experiences, family status, and attitudes and plans.

The sample for the second followup, which took place in spring 1984, consisted of about 12,000 members of the senior cohort and about 15,000 members of the sophomore cohort. The completion rate for the senior cohort was 91 percent, and the completion rate for the sophomore cohort was 92 percent.

HSB third followup data collection activities were performed in spring of 1986. Both the sophomore and senior cohort samples for this round of data collection were the same as those used for the second followup survey. The completion rates for the sophomore and senior cohort samples were 91 percent and 88 percent, respectively.

Table A2 contains the maximum number of cases that are available for the tabulations of the specific classification variables used throughout this publication.

The standard error (se) of an individual percentage (p) based on HSB data can be approximated by the formula

$$se_p = DEFT \sqrt{p(100-p)/n}$$

where n is the sample size and DEFT, the square root of the design effect, is a factor used to adjust for the particular sample design used in HSB. Table A3 provides the DEFT factors for different HSB samples and subsamples.

In evaluating a difference between two independent percentages, the standard error of the difference may be conservatively approximated by taking the square root of the sum of the squared standard errors of the two percentages. For example, in the 1986 followup of 1980 sophomores, 84.0 percent of the men and 77.2 percent of the women felt that being successful in work was "very important," a difference of 6.8 percentage points. Using the formula and the sample sizes from table A2 and the DEFT factors from table A3, the standard errors of the two percentages being compared are calculated to be:

$$1.43 \sqrt{(84.0)(16.0)/5,391} = .714$$

$$1.43 \sqrt{(77.2)(22.8)/5,857} = .784$$

The standard error of the difference is therefore

$$\sqrt{.714^2 + .784^2} = \sqrt{.510 + .615} = 1.06$$

The sampling error (95 chances in 100) of the difference is approximately double the standard error, or approximately 2.1 percentage points, and the 95 percent confidence interval for the difference is 6.8 ± 2.1, or 4.7 to 8.9 percentage points.

The standard error estimation procedure outlined above does not compensate for survey item nonresponse, which is a source of nonsampling error. (Table A2 reflects the maximum number of responses that could be tabulated by demographic characteristic.) For example, of the 10,925 respondents in the 1984 followup survey of 1980 high school graduates, 372, or 3.4 percent, did not respond to the particular question on whether they had ever used a pocket calculator. Item nonresponse varied considerably. A very low nonresponse rate of 0.1 percent was obtained for a question asking whether the respondent had attended a postsecondary institution. A much higher item nonresponse rate of 12.2 percent was obtained for a question asking if the respondent had used a micro or minicomputer in high school. Typical item nonresponse rates ranged from 3 to 4 percent.

The Hispanic analyses presented in this report relied on students' self-identification as members of one of four Hispanic subgroups: Mexican, Mexican-American, Chicano; Cuban, Cubano; Puerto-Rican, Puertorriqueno, or Boricua; or other Latin American, Latino, Hispanic, or Spanish descent.

An NCES series of technical reports and data file users manuals provides additional information on the survey methodology.

Further information on the High School and Beyond survey may be obtained from:

Paula Knepper
Postsecondary Education Statistics Division
National Center for Education Statistics
555 New Jersey Avenue NW
Washington, DC 20208–5652

1987 High School Transcript Study

Transcripts of 1987 high school graduates were compared with transcripts of 1982 graduates to describe changes in course taking across this 5-year period. The analyses were based on approximately 22,700 transcripts of 1987 graduates selected for the National Assessment of Educational Progress (NAEP), and 12,000 transcripts of 1982 graduates who participated in the High School and Beyond study (see corresponding source note above in this appendix).

The sample of schools for the 1987 High School Transcript Study consisted of a nationally representative sample of 471 eligible secondary schools selected for the 1986 NAEP for grade 11 students; 433 of the schools participated. Only those students who graduated from high school were selected from both studies. Handicapped students (those students receiving special education) were not included.

Further information can be obtained from:

Andrew Kolstad
Education Assessment Division
National Center for Education Statistics
555 New Jersey Avenue NW
Washington, DC 20208–5653

Integrated Postsecondary Education Data System

The Integrated Postsecondary Education Data System (IPEDS) surveys all postsecondary institutions, including universities and colleges, as well as institutions offering technical and vocational education beyond the high school level. This survey, which began in 1986, replaces and supplements the Higher Education General Information Survey (HEGIS).

The IPEDS consists of several integrated components that obtain information on who provides postsecondary education (institutions), who participates in it and completes it (students), what programs are offered and what programs are completed, and both the human and financial resources involved in the provision of institutionally based postsecondary education. Specifically, these components include: institutional characteristics, including institutional activity; fall enrollment, including age and residence; fall enrollment in occupationally specific programs; completions; finance; staff; salaries of full-time instructional faculty; and academic libraries.

The higher education portion of this survey is a census of accredited 2- and 4-year colleges. However, data from the technical and vocational institutions are collected through a sample survey. Thus, some portions of the data will be subject to sampling and nonsampling errors, while some portions will be subject only to nonsampling errors. The tabulations on institutional characteristics developed for this edition of the Digest are based on lists of all institutions and are not subject to sampling errors.

Prior to the establishment of IPEDS in 1986, the Higher Education General Information Survey (HEGIS) acquired and maintained statistical data on the characteristics and operations of institutions of higher education. Implemented in 1966, HEGIS was an annual universe survey of institutions listed in the latest NCES Education Directory, Colleges and Universities.

The trend tables presented in this report draw on HEGIS surveys which solicited information concerning institutional characteristics, faculty salaries, finances, enrollment, and degrees. Since these surveys were distributed to all higher education institutions, the data presented were not subject to sampling error. However, they were subject to nonsampling error, the sources of which varied with the survey instrument. Each survey is, therefore, discussed separately. Information concerning the nonsampling error of the enrollment and degrees surveys draws extensively on the "HEGIS Post-Survey Validation Study" conducted in 1979.

Further information on IPEDS may be obtained from:

William Freund
Postsecondary Education Statistics Division
National Center for Education Statistics
555 New Jersey Avenue NW
Washington, DC 20208–5652

Institutional Characteristics

This survey provided the basis for the universe of institutions presented in the *Education Directory, Colleges and Universities,* and it was used in all other IPEDS data collection activities. The universe comprised institutions that met certain accreditation criteria and offered at least a 1-year program of college-level studies leading toward a degree. All of these institutions were certified as eligible by the U.S. Department of Education's Division of Eligibility and Agency Evaluation. Each fall, institutions listed in the previous year's Directory were asked to update a computer printout of their information.

Fall Enrollment

This survey has been part of the IPEDS or HEGIS series since 1966. The enrollment survey response rate was relatively high; the 1989 response rate was 86.1 percent. Major sources of nonsampling error for this survey were classification problems, the unavailability of needed data, interpretation of definitions, the survey due date, and operational errors. Of these, the classification of students appears to have been the main source of error. Institutions had problems in correctly classifying first-time freshmen, other first-time students, and unclassified students for both full-time and part-time categories. These problems occurred most often at 2-year institutions (private and public) and private 4-year institutions. In the 1977–78 HEGIS validation studies, the classification problem led to an estimated overcount of 11,000 full-time students and an undercount of 19,000 part-time students. Although the ratio of error to the grand total was quite small (less than 1 percent), the percentage of errors was as high as 5 percent for detailed student levels and even higher at certain aggregation levels.

Beginning with fall 1986, the survey system was redesigned with the introduction of the Integrated Postsecondary Education Data System (IPEDS) (see above). The new survey system comprises all postsecondary institutions, but also maintains comparability with earlier surveys by allowing HEGIS institutions to be tabulated separately. The new system also provides for preliminary and revised data releases. This allows the Center flexibility to release early data sets while still maintaining a more accurate final data base.

Salaries, Tenure, and Fringe Benefits of Full-Time Instructional Faculty

This survey has been conducted for most years from 1966-67 to 1985–86, and in 1987–88 and 1989–90. Although the survey form was changed a number of times during those years, only comparable data are presented in this report. The data were collected from the individual colleges and universities.

This survey differed from other HEGIS surveys in that imputations were not made for nonrespondents. Thus, there is some possibility that the salary averages presented in this report may differ from the results of a complete enumeration of all colleges and universities. Beginning with the surveys for 1987–88, the IPEDS data tabulation procedures included imputations for survey nonrespondents. The response rate for the 1989–90 survey was 80.5 percent. The response rate for public colleges was substantially higher than the response rate for private colleges. Thus it is probable that the public colleges' salary data are more accurate than the data for private colleges. Other sources of nonsampling error included computational errors and misclassification in reporting and processing. NCES checked individual colleges' data for internal and longitudinal consistency and contacted the colleges to check inconsistent data.

Completions

This survey was part of the HEGIS series throughout its existence. However, the degree classification taxonomy was revised in 1970–71 and 1982–83. Collection of degree data has been maintained through the IPEDS system.

Though information from survey years 1970–71 through 1981–82 is directly comparable, care must be taken if information before or after that period is included in any comparison. Degrees-conferred trend tables arranged by the 1982–83 classification were added to the *Digest* to provide consistent data from 1970–71 to 1988–89. Data in this edition on associate and other formal awards below the baccalaureate, by field of study, are not comparable with figures for earlier years. The nonresponse rate did not appear to be a significant source of nonsampling error for this survey. The return rate over the years was extremely high, with the response rate for the 1988–89 survey at 76.3 percent. Because of the high return rate, nonsampling error caused by imputation was also minimal.

The major sources of nonsampling error for this survey were differences between the NCES program taxonomy and taxonomies used by the colleges, classification of double majors and double degrees, operational problems, and survey timing. In the 1979 HEGIS validation study, these sources of nonsampling were found to contribute to an error rate of 0.3 percent overreporting of bachelor's degrees and 1.3 percent overreporting of master's degrees. The differences, however, varied greatly among fields. Over 50 percent of the fields selected for the validation study had no errors identified. Categories of fields that had large differences were business and management, education, engineering, letters, and psychology. It was also shown that differences in proportion to the published figures were less than 1 percent for most of the selected fields that had some errors. Exceptions to these were: master's and Ph.D. programs in labor and industrial relations (20 percent and 8 percent); bachelor's and master's programs in art education (3 percent and 4 percent); bachelor's and Ph.D. programs in business and commerce, and in distributive education (5 percent and 9 percent); master's programs in philosophy (8 percent); and Ph.D. programs in psychology (11 percent).

Financial Statistics

This survey was part of the HEGIS series and has been continued under the IPEDS system. Changes were made in the financial survey instruments in fiscal years (FY) 1976, 1982, and 1987. The FY 76 survey instrument contained numerous revisions to earlier survey forms and made direct comparisons of line items very difficult. Beginning in FY 82, Pell Grant data were collected in Federal restricted grants and contracts revenues and restricted scholarships and fellowships expenditures. The introduction of the Integrated Postsecondary Education Data System (IPEDS) in the FY 87 survey included several important changes to the survey instrument and data processing procedures. While these changes were significant, considerable effort has been made to present only comparable information on trends in this report and to note inconsistencies. Finance tables for this publication have been adjusted by subtracting the largely duplicative Pell Grant amounts from the later data to maintain comparability with pre-FY 82 data.

Possible sources of nonsampling error in the financial statistics include nonresponse, imputation, and misclassification. The response rate has been about 85 to 90 percent for most of the years reported. The response rate for the FY 1989 survey was 83.5 percent.

Two general methods of imputation were used in HEGIS. If the prior year's data were available for a nonresponding institution, these data were inflated using the Higher Education Price Index and adjusted according to changes in enrollments. If no previous year's data were available, current data were used from peer institutions selected for location (State or region), control, level, and enrollment size of institution. In most cases estimates for nonreporting institutions in IPEDS were made using data from peer institutions.

Beginning with FY 87, the new survey system (IPEDS, see above) comprises all postsecondary institutions, but also maintains comparability with earlier surveys by allowing 2- and 4-year HEGIS institutions to be tabulated separately. The finance data tabulated for this publication reflect totals for the HEGIS or higher education institutions only. In order to maintain comparability with the historical time series of HEGIS institutions, data were combined from two of the three different survey forms that make up the IPEDS survey system. The vast majority of the data were tabulated from Form 1, which was used to collect information from public and private nonprofit 2- and 4-year colleges. Form 2, a condensed form, was used to gather data for the 2-year proprietary institutions. Because of the differences in the data requested on the two forms, several assumptions were made about the Form 2 reports so that their figures could be included in the institutions of higher education totals.

In the section on revenue, the Form 2 institutions were not asked to separate appropriations from grants and contracts, nor State from local sources of funding. For the Form 2 institutions, all the Federal revenues were assumed to be Federal grants and contracts and all of the State and local revenues were assumed to be restricted State grants and contracts. All other Form 2 sources of revenue, except for tuition and fees and sales and services of educational activities, were included under "other." Similar adjustments were made to the expenditures accounts. The Form 2 institutions reported instruction and scholarship and fellowship expenditures only. All other educational and general expenditures were allocated to academic support.

To reduce reporting error, NCES used national standards for reporting finance statistics. These standards are contained in *Colleges and University Business Administration: Administrative Services (1974 Edition),* published by the National Association of College and University Business Officers; *Audits of Colleges and Universities* (as amended August 31, 1974), by the American Institute of Certified Public Accountants; and *HEGIS Financial Reporting Guide (1980),* by NCES. Wherever possible, definitions and formats in the survey form are consistent with those in these three accounting texts.

Questions concerning the surveys used as data sources for this report or other questions concerning HEGIS can be directed to:

Postsecondary Education Statistics Division
National Center for Education Statistics
555 New Jersey Avenue NW
Washington, DC 20208–5652

National Assessment of Educational Progress

The National Assessment of Educational Progress (NAEP) is a cross-sectional study designed and initially implemented in 1969. NAEP has gathered information about selected levels of educational achievement across the country. NAEP has surveyed the educational attainments of 9-, 13-, and 17-year-olds and young adults (ages 25-35) in 10 learning areas. Different learning areas have been assessed periodically, and all areas have been reassessed in order to measure possible changes in educational achievement.

The assessment data presented in this publication was designed and conducted by the Education Commission of the States (1969–1983) and by the Educational Testing Service (1983 to present). Three-stage probability samples have been used. The primary sampling units have been stratified by region and, within region, by State, size of community, and, for the two smaller sizes of community strata, by socioeconomic level. The first stage of sampling entails defining and selecting primary sampling units (PSU's). For each age/grade level (3,7, and 11), the second stage entails enumerating, stratifying, and randomly selecting schools, both public and private, within each PSU selected at the first stage. The third stage involves randomly selecting students within a school for participation in NAEP. Assessment exercises have been administered either to individuals or to small groups of students by specially trained personnel.

After NAEP data are scored, they are weighted in accordance with the population structure and adjusted for nonresponse. Analyses include computing the percentage of students giving various responses and using Item Response Theory (IRT) technology to estimate levels of achievement for the nation and various subpopulations. IRT technology enables the assessment of a sample of students in a learning area or subarea on a single scale even if different students have been administered different exercises. The underlying principle is that when a number of items require similar skills, the regularities observed across patterns of response can often be used to characterize both respondents and tasks in terms of a relatively small number of variables. When aggregated through appropriate mathematical formulas, these variables capture the dominant features of the data.

Sample sizes for the reading proficiency portion of the 1987–88 NAEP study were 3,782 for the 9-year-olds, 4,005 for the 13-year-olds, and 3,652 for the 17-year-olds. Response rates were 92 percent, 88 percent, and 77 percent, respectively. Response rates for earlier years (1970–71, 1974–75, and 1979–80) were generally lower. For example, the lowest response rate for the 9-year-olds was 88 percent in 1974–75, and the lowest response rate over all was 70 percent for the 17-year-olds in 1974–75. Data on standard errors are provided in table A4.

The 1987–88 U.S. history assessment data in this report are based on a nationally representative sample of 3,950 4th graders, 6,462 8th graders, and 5,507 12th graders. The response rates were: 93 percent for 4th graders, 88 percent for 8th graders, and 78 percent for 12th graders. Data on standard errors are provided in table A5.

The 1987–88 U.S. civics assessment trend data in this report are based on a nationally representative sample of 1,938 13-year-olds and 1,786 17-year-olds. The response rates were 90 percent for the 8th graders and 79 percent for the 17-year-olds in 1987–88. Sample sizes for the earlier years were much larger with 19,952 13-year-olds and 17,866 17-year-olds in 1976 and 7,268 13-year-olds and 6,751 17-year-olds in 1982. The 1987–88 analyses for 4th, 8th, and 12th graders were based on a somewhat different 1987–88 sample. The sample sizes were 1,974 4th graders, 4,487 8th graders, and 4,275 12th graders. The response rates were: 93 percent for 4th graders, 88 percent for 8th graders, and 78 percent for 12th graders. Data on standard errors are provided in table A5.

The 1983–84 NAEP writing assessment used a stratified, three-stage sampling design. The first stage was counties (or aggregates of counties). The second stage was schools, and the third stage involved selecting students within the schools at random. The 1983–84 assessment included 24,437 students at age 9; 26,228 students at age 13; and 28,992 students at age 17. Student response rates for the 1987–88 writing assessment were 92 percent for the 9-year-olds, 88 percent for the 13-year-olds, and 77 percent for the 17-year-olds. Sample sizes varied depending on the test items and the scoring method used. Table A5 contains standard errors for selected estimates.

The 1985–86 NAEP mathematics and science assessments were administered to 6,932 students age 9; 6,200 students age 13; and 3,868 students still in school at age 17. The response rates were: 93 percent for the 9-year-olds, 89 percent for the 13-year-olds, and 79 percent for the 17-year-olds. Table A6 contains standard errors for selected estimates.

The 1987–88 geography assessment was administered to 3,030 high school students. The response rate for the assessment was 77 percent. The National Geographic Society provided support for conducting the assessment.

The literacy assessment data used in this report are based on a nationally representative household sample of 21- to 25-year-olds. Blacks and Hispanics were oversampled to allow samples of sufficient size for reliable results. A total of 38,400 households were screened to locate 4,494 potential respondents. (No more than one person was surveyed from any one household.) Of the potential respondents, 3,618 young adults participated, resulting in a response rate of 80 percent.

Information from NAEP is subject to both nonsampling and sampling error. Two possible sources of nonsampling error are nonparticipation and instrumentation. Certain populations have been oversampled to assure samples of sufficient size for analysis. Instrumentation nonsampling error could result from failure of the test instruments to measure what is being taught and, in turn, what is being learned by the students.

For further information on NAEP, contact:

Gary Phillips
Education Assessment Division
National Center for Education Statistics
555 New Jersey Avenue NW
Washington, DC 20208–5653

National Education Longitudinal Study of 1988

The National Education Longitudinal Study of 1988 (NELS:88) is the third major longitudinal study sponsored by the National Center for Education Statistics. The two studies that preceded NELS:88, the National Longitudinal Study of the High School Class of 1972 (NLS-72) and High School and Beyond (HS&B), surveyed high school seniors (and sophomores in HS&B) through high school, postsecondary education, and work and family formation experiences. Unlike its predecessors, NELS:88 begins with a cohort of eighth grade students. In 1988, some 26,000 eighth graders, their parents, their teachers, and their school principals were surveyed. The first followup will revisit the same sample of students in 1990, when they are in the 10th grade.

NELS:88 is designed to provide trend data about critical transitions experienced by young people as they develop, attend school, and embark on their careers. It will complement and strengthen State and local efforts by furnishing new information on how school policies, teacher practices, and family involvement affect student educational outcomes (i.e., academic achievement, persistence in school, and participation in postsecondary education). For the base year, NELS:88 is a multifaceted study questionnaire and four cognitive tests, a parent questionnaire, a teacher questionnaire, and a school questionnaire.

Designed to ensure that private schools, rural schools, and schools with high minority membership were adequately represented, sampling was first conducted at the school level and then at the student level within schools. Additionally, oversamples of students with Hispanic and Asian or Pacific Island heritage were drawn. The data represented in this edition of the Digest are drawn from a nationally representative sample of 1,000 schools (800 public schools; and 200 private schools, including parochial institutions). Within this school sample, 26,000 eighth-grade students were selected at random. Followups to this survey are to be conducted every 2 years, the first occurring in 1990.

Further information about the NELS:88 survey can be obtained from:

Jeffrey Owings
Elementary and Secondary Education Statistics
  Division
National Center for Education Statistics
555 New Jersey Avenue NW
Washington, DC 20208–5651

National Longitudinal Study

The National Longitudinal Study (NLS) of the High School Class of 1972 began with the collection of base-year survey data from a sample of about 19,000 high school seniors in spring of 1972. Five more followup surveys of these students were conducted in 1973, 1974, 1976, 1979, and 1986. The NLS was designed to provide the education community with information on the transitions of young adults from high school through postsecondary education and the workplace.

The sample design for the NLS is a stratified, two-stage probability sample of students from all schools, public and private, in the 50 States and the District of Columbia with a 12th-grade enrollment during the 1971–72 school year. During the first stage of sampling, about 1,070 schools were selected for participation in the base-year survey. As many as 18 students were selected at random from each of the sample schools. Both the size of the school and student samples were increased during the first followup survey. Beginning with the first followup and continuing through the fourth followup, about 1,300 schools participated in the survey and slightly under 23,500 students were sampled. The response rates for each of the different rounds of data collection have been 80 percent or higher.

Sample retention rates across the survey years have been quite high. For example, of the individuals responding to the base-year questionnaire, the percentages who responded to the first, second, third, and fourth followup questionnaires were about 94, 93, 89, and 83 percent, respectively.

Approximate standard errors for the percentage estimates based on NLS data reported in this publication may be estimated by the formula

$$se_p = DEFT \sqrt{p(100-p)/n}$$

where p is the estimated percentage and n is the sample size. DEFT is the root design effect factor used to adjust for the sample design used in NLS. For the first, second, and third followup surveys, the root design effect adjustment factors are 1.18, 1.16, and 1.20. Standard errors for the fourth followup survey data are adjusted by a generalized design effect factor of 1.20. Table A7 lists the approximate respondent counts for the classification variables used in this year's *Digest*. Table A8 gives examples of the approximate standard errors of percentage estimates based on the fourth followup survey for different sample sizes.

Further information may be obtained from:

Carl Schmitt
Postsecondary Education Statistics Division
National Center for Education Statistics
555 New Jersey Avenue NW
Washington, DC 20208–5652

National Postsecondary Student Aid Study

The National Postsecondary Student Aid Study (NPSAS) is the most comprehensive nationwide study of how students and their families pay for postsecondary education. It includes national representative samples of undergraduates, graduates, and first-professional students; students attending less than 2-year institutions, 2- to 3-year schools, 4-year colleges, and major universities. Participants included students who do not receive aid and their parents as well as the students and parents who do receive financial aid. Study results are used to help determine future Federal policy regarding student financial aid. The study is conducted every three years.

The first NPSAS was conducted during the 1986–87 school year. Data were gathered from about 1,130 colleges, universities, and other postsecondary institutions; 55,000 students; and 16,000 parents. These data provided information on the cost of postsecondary education, the distribution of financial aid, and the characteristics of both aided and nonaided students and their families.

As a part of the 1989–90 NPSAS, information on nearly 70,000 undergraduates and graduate students enrolled during the school year was collected at more than 1,130 postsecondary institutions. The sample included students enrolled at any time between July 1, 1989 and June 30, 1990. About 51,000 students and a subsample of about 16,000 of their parents were interviewed by telephone.

This *Digest* contains preliminary information from the 1989–90 NPSAS based on institutional records of 25,000 aided undergraduates, in addition to data from the 1986–87 survey.

Further information may be obtained from:

Andrew Malizio
Postsecondary Education Statistics Division
National Center for Educational Statistics
555 New Jersey Avenue NW
Washington, DC 20208–5652

National Survey of Postsecondary Faculty

The National Survey of Postsecondary Faculty (NSOPF), a survey of instructional faculty in postsecondary institutions, was conducted for the first time in the 1987–88 academic year by NCES. The study consisted of three major components: the Institutional Survey, a stratified random sample of 480 institution-level respondents; the Faculty Survey, a stratified random sample of 11,013 eligible faculty members within the participating institutions; and the Department Chair Survey, a stratified random sample of 3,029 eligible department chairpersons (or their equivalent) within the participating 2- and 4-year institutions.

Institutions were selected from nonproprietary U.S. postsecondary institutions that grant a 2-year (A.A.) or higher degree, and have been accredited by organizations recognized by the U. S. Department of Education. Included in this group are religious, medical, and other specialized institutions, as well as 2- and 4-year non-specialized institutions. This universe consisted of 3,159 institutions, from the 1987 Integrated Postsecondary Education Data System (IPEDS).

Information was gathered on the following: backgrounds, responsibilities, workloads, salaries, benefits, and attitudes of both full- and part-time faculty. Additional information was collected on faculty composition, turnover and recruitment, and retention and tenure policies from institutional and department-level respondents. The survey, to be renamed the National Study of Postsecondary Faculty, will be repeated in the 1992-93 academic year so that changes over time in institutional policies, and faculty characteristics, behaviors, and attitudes can be assessed.

For more information contact:

Linda J. Zimbler
Postsecondary Education Statistics Division
National Center for Education Statistics
555 New Jersey Avenue, NW
Washington, DC 20208–5652

Survey on Principal's Perceptions of Academic Reform

This sample survey used the NCES Fast Response Survey System (FRSS), which is designed to gather timely information for policymakers. In October 1987, questionnaires were mailed to a national probability sample of 930 public high schools from a universe of approximately 14,500. A public high school was defined as any regular public school with a principal, enrollment in grade 12, and no pupils below grade 7. Questionnaires were completed by the high school principal. Data collection was completed in December with a response rate of 98 percent. The sampling frame used for the survey was the 1985–86 Common Core of Data Universe of Public School Systems. States were classified by patterns of academic reforms, each of which might be present or absent, giving 64 patterns. Six possible reforms were examined. Twenty-seven patterns occurred and each of the 27 was used as a stratum. The survey data were weighted using the universe of the probability of selection as the weights, and were adjusted for nonresponse. Since the estimates were obtained from a sample of districts, they are subject to sampling variability. Estimates of standard errors for the estimates were computed using a replication technique known as jackknife replication. This survey is also subject to nonsampling error which can occur from a variety of sources such as differences in the respondents' interpretation of the meaning of the questions, differences related to the particular time the survey was conducted, or errors in data preparation. Considerable effort was made to eliminate these biases. Thus, it appears unlikely that nonsampling errors severely biased the data from this survey.

For more information about this survey, contact:

Elementary and Secondary Education Statistics
  Division
National Center for Education Statistics
555 New Jersey Avenue NW
Washington, DC 20208–5651

1985–86 Private School Survey

The 1985–86 Private School Survey was based on the sampling system developed for the 1983 Private School Survey. The "1983 Private School Survey" was carried out in two parts, one based on a "list" frame and one based on an "area" frame. The area frame was used under the assumption that the lists available to NCES were not comprehensive and that list-building techniques applied to a sample of census areas would reveal some additional private schools. NCES started with the most complete list available, comprising some 21,000 schools, and updated it in 1983, based on review of new directories and other published sources. This effort resulted in a list of just under 27,000 schools. This frame was then stratified into 12 strata based on various combinations of religious affiliation and school level. A systematic sample of 1,320 schools was selected with probabilities equal to the square root of the enrollment of the school divided by the sum of the square roots of enrollment for all of the schools in the stratum. Inflating this sample provided an estimated universe, which was subsequently reduced by removing the estimated numbers of duplicates, nonrespondents, coding errors, and ineligibles. The final estimated list universe of schools was 21,710. The response rate for the list sample was 91 percent (1,074 of 1,176 schools), and the response rate for the area sample was 81 percent (733 of 901 schools).

For the area sample, the basic frame was a list of all counties reported from the 1980 census, adjusted so that independent cities were treated as counties and smaller counties were combined with other contiguous counties. This produced a list of 2,497 sampling units. These sampling units were stratified according to census region, in or out of a Standard Metropolitan Statistical Area (SMSA), and above or below the median private school enrollment for that region and SMSA status, yielding 16 strata. The final sample was a systematic one comprising 75 sampling units, 8 of which were drawn with certainty based upon populations exceeding 1.7 million in the 1980 census. The remaining units were selected with probabilities proportionate to the square root of the population of the unit within the stratum.

For each of the sampling units in the area design, schools not overlapping with the list-frame schools were sought by reviewing directories of various types (e.g., private school organizations, telephone) and by telephoning officials, churches, chambers of commerce, and selected vendors, such as milk companies. This search produced 901 schools which met NCES criteria for functioning private schools. When weighted, these data inflated to approximately 6,000 schools nationally. Since the area frame was designed not to overlap with the list frame, results for the area sample were combined with those for the list sample.

A followup survey was conducted in 1985. The schools within the sampling areas were drawn from the lists of schools created in the same sample areas from the "1983 Private School Survey." Since the lists were not updated, schools established after 1983 were not generally eligible for sampling. The estimates for the 1985–86 study are valid for schools that were in existence in 1983. Some of the estimates contain extrapolations for newly established schools, based on assumptions made from the 1983 survey data.

During the fall of 1985, the principal of each sampled school was contacted to obtain the school's participation in the study and to sample up to 10 teachers at the school. During January 1986, questionnaires were mailed to schools and teachers. Follow-up for questionnaire and item nonresponse was conducted during the spring of 1986. Imputations were made for item nonresponse. Of the 1,387 eligible schools, 1,174 responded (85 percent). A total of 5,295 teacher questionnaires were completed, for a teacher response rate of 76 percent.

Additional information is available from:

Marilyn McMillen
Elementary and Secondary Education Statistics
  Division
National Center for Education Statistics
555 New Jersey Avenue NW
Washington, DC 20208–5651

Projections of Education Statistics

Since 1964, NCES has published projections of key statistics for elementary and secondary schools and institutions of higher education. These projections include statistics such as enrollments, instructional staff, graduates, and earned degrees. The Projections reports include several alternative projection series and a methodology section describing the techniques and assumptions used to prepare them. Data in this edition of the *Digest* reflect the intermediate projection series only.

Differences between the reported and projected values are, of course, almost inevitable. An evaluation of past projections revealed that, at the elementary and secondary level, projections of enrollments have been quite accurate: mean absolute percentage differences for enrollment were less than 1 percent for projections from 1 to 5 years in the future, while those for teachers were less than 4 percent. At the higher education level, projections of enrollment have been fairly accurate: mean absolute percentage differences were 5 percent or less for projections from 1 to 5 years into the future.

Since projections of time series are subject to errors both by the nature of statistics and the properties of projection methodologies, users are cautioned not to place too much confidence in the numerical values of the projections. Important, but unforeseeable, economic and social changes may lead to differences, particularly at the higher education level. Rather, projections are to be considered as indicators of broad trends.

For further information about projection methodology and accuracy, contact:

Debra E. Gerald
Statistical Standards and Methodology Division
National Center for Education Statistics
555 New Jersey Avenue NW
Washington, DC 20208–5654

1985 Survey of Public and Private School Libraries and Media Centers

Statistics of public school libraries have been collected periodically since 1958. Prior to 1985, the last survey was conducted in 1978. The 1978 survey form was substantially revised for the 1985 data collection, based on consultations with various associations and individuals, including the American Library Association and the American Association of School Librarians. This sample survey was conducted under contract to NCES. The survey forms were mailed to a nationally representative sample of 4,500 public schools in the fall of 1985 and to a sample of 1,700 private schools in January of 1986. Data collection continued throughout the 1985–86 school year until a response rate of 92 percent for public schools and 85 percent for private schools was attained.

Estimates in the library survey tables are based on samples and are subject to sampling variability. Caution should be exercised in interpreting figures based on a relatively small number of cases. Although the standard errors are quite low for most of the national statistics, they can be substantial when comparing data from State to State. In a number of States, budgets restricted sample sizes to 75. Table A1 gives standard errors for several representative statistics. For example, the national estimate of per-pupil expenditures for books is $6.24, and the standard error is $.15. Thus, the chances are 95 out of 100 that the result from a complete census would differ from the estimate by less than $.30 (1.96 times the standard error). The 95 percent confidence interval is thus $5.94 to $6.54.

Additional information on these school library studies is available from:

Postsecondary Education Statistics Division
National Center for Education Statistics
555 New Jersey Avenue NW
Washington, DC 20208–5652

Survey of Recent College Graduates

NCES has conducted periodic surveys of persons, about 1 year after graduation, to collect information on college outcomes. The "Recent College Graduates" surveys have concentrated on those graduates entering the teaching profession. To obtain accurate results on this subgroup, graduates who are newly qualified to teach have been oversampled in each of the surveys. The survey involves a two-stage sampling procedure. First, a sample of institutions awarding bachelor's and master's degrees is selected and stratified by percentage of education graduates, control, and type of institution. Second, for each of the selected institutions, a sample of degree recipients is chosen. The response rates on the Recent College Graduates survey have tended to be low because of the great difficulty in tracing the students after graduation. Much more of the nonresponse can be attributed to invalid mailing addresses than to refusals to participate. Despite their shortcomings, the data are presented in this report because they provide valuable information not available elsewhere about college outcomes. Users should be cautious about drawing conclusions based on data from small samples. It is also likely that the data are somewhat biased since the more mobile students, such as graduate students, are the most difficult to track for the survey.

The 1976 survey of 1974–75 college graduates was the first and smallest of the series. The sample consisted of 209 schools, of which 200 (96 percent) responded. Of the 5,506 graduates in the sample, 4,350 responded, for a response rate of 79 percent.

The 1981 survey was somewhat larger, with a coverage of 301 institutions and 15,852 graduates. Responses were obtained from 286 institutions, for an institutional response rate of 95 percent, and from 9,312 graduates (716 others were determined to be out of scope), for a response rate of 62 percent.

The 1985 survey requested data from 18,738 graduates from 404 colleges. Responses were obtained from 13,200 students, for a response rate of 74 percent (885 were out of scope). The response rate for the colleges was 98 percent. The 1987 survey form was sent to 21,957 graduates. Responses were received from 16,878, for a response rate of 79.7 percent. Table A9 contains sample sizes for number of graduates, by field, for the 1976, 1981, 1985, and 1987 surveys.

Further information on this survey may be obtained from:

Postsecondary Education Statistics Division
National Center for Education Statistics
555 New Jersey Avenue NW
Washington, DC 20208–5652

Survey of School Discipline Policies and Practices

This sample survey used the NCES Fast Response Survey System (FRSS), which is designed to gather timely information for policymakers. In February 1985, questionnaires were mailed to a stratified national probability sample of 900 public junior and senior high schools, representing approximately 30,000 schools. About 60 schools were determined to be out of the scope for the survey since they did not have regular secondary school programs. The final sample represents an estimated 26,365 schools. The sample was allocated proportionately to the number of schools in each of four strata—junior high, senior high, combined, and other (including ungraded, vocational education, special education, and alternative schools). The survey form was completed by the school administrator (often the principal) most familiar with discipline policies of the school. The response rate for the survey was 93 percent. Responses were adjusted for nonresponse and weighted to national totals. Standard errors for selected items are shown in table A10 as a general guide to the precision of the numbers.

For more information about this survey contact:

Elementary and Secondary Education Statistics Division
National Center for Education Statistics
555 New Jersey Avenue NW
Washington, DC 20208–5651

Second International Mathematics Study

The "Second International Mathematics Study" was organized as a cooperative undertaking of research institutes in about 24 countries represented in the International Association for Evaluation of Educational Achievement (IEA). Sample surveys of two population groups were conducted during the 1981–82 school year in 20 countries. Data were collected from school administrators, teachers, and students.

"Population A" included all students in the grade in which the majority of students had attained the age of 13.0 to 13.1 years by the middle of the school year. In all countries, school enrollment is nearly universal at that age, which represents the final year of elementary school for most countries. For the United States, Population A was the eighth grade. For Japan and Hong Kong, the seventh grade was chosen for study because the cognitive mathematics tests were more appropriate for that grade level.

"Population B" was defined as all students who were in the terminal grade of secondary education and who were studying mathematics as a substantial part of their academic program, taking at least 5 hours of mathematics classes each week. In the United States, classes of precalculus and calculus were chosen. These classes represented about 12 percent of the total age group. In other countries, Population B represented between 6 and 50 percent of the age group.

About 20 countries' education systems participated in the Population A survey and 15 systems participated in the Population B survey. The 35 samples ranged in size from 1,000 to 8,800 students.

Because of the variations in student curriculum, survey design, and other factors from country to country, the results of this survey should be used with care. Further information on the sampling methodology and response rates is available from:

Data Development Division
National Center for Education Statistics
555 New Jersey Avenue NW
Washington, DC 20208–5650

Schools and Staffing Survey

The "Schools and Staffing Survey" (SASS) data were collected through a sample survey of school districts, schools, school administrators, and teachers. The surveys of schools and school principals were based on the 9,317 public and 3,513 private schools in the school samples. In addition, 56,242 public school teachers and 11,529 private school teachers participated in the teacher survey.

The public school sample was selected from the Quality Education Data (QED) file of public schools. All public schools in the file were stratified by State and by three grade levels (elementary, secondary, and combined). Within each stratum, the schools were sorted by urbanicity, zip code, highest grade in the school, and the enrollment. For each stratum within each State, sample schools were selected by systematic sampling with probability proportional to the square root of the number of teachers within a school.

The private school sample was selected primarily from the QED file of private schools. To improve coverage, two additional steps were taken. The first step was to update the QED file with current lists of schools from 17 private school associations. All private schools in the file were stratified by State and then by three grade levels (elementary, secondary, and combined) and 13 affiliation groups. Within each stratum, the schools were sorted by urbanicity, zip code, highest grade in the school, and the enrollment. For each stratum within each State, sample schools were selected by systematic sampling with probability proportional to the square root of the number of teachers within a school. The second step was to include an area-frame sample, contained in 75 Primary Sampling Units (PSUs), each PSU consisting of a county or group of counties. Within each PSU, an attempt was made to find all eligible private schools. A telephone search was made, using such sources as yellow pages, religious institutions, local education agencies, chamber of commerce, local government offices, commercial milk companies, and real estate offices. The PSUs were stratified by Census geographic region, Standard Metropolitan Statistical Area status, and private school enrollment. These PSUs were selected from the universe of 2,497 PSUs with probability proportional to the square root of the PSU population. All schools not on the QED file or the lists from the private school associations were eligible to be selected for the area-frame sample. Schools in the area frame that could be contacted were sampled with probability proportional to the square root of the number of teachers. A systematic equal probability sample was then drawn from the schools in the area frame that could not be contacted.

The School Administrator Questionnaire was mailed to the administrator of each sampled school in February 1988. Weighted response rates for the School Administrator Questionnaire were 94.4 percent for public school administrators and 79.3 percent for private school administrators. There was no explicit imputation for item nonresponse and for a small number of schools which were found to be missing from the QED lists of public schools. The national estimate for public school principals is underestimated because of missing schools.

The weighted response rate for the Private School Questionnaire was 78.6 percent for private schools. The data were weighted to reflect the universe of private schools, and the weights were adjusted for nonresponse. A private school was excluded from the sample if it did not have any students in any of the grades from 1 to 12, if it operated in a private home that was used as a family residence, or if it was undetermined whether it operated in a private home and its enrollment was less than 10 or it had only one teacher.

For more information about this survey, contact:

Charles Hammer or Marilyn M. McMillen
Elementary and Secondary Education Statistics
  Division
National Center for Education Statistics
555 New Jersey Avenue NW
Washington, DC 20208–5651

Second International Science Study

The "Second International Science Study" was organized by the International Association for the Evaluation of Educational Achievement (IEA). Sample surveys were conducted in 19 countries in 1970 and, in the mid-1980s, the same was done in 24 countries.

"Population 1" is defined as either 10-year-olds or all children in grades where most 10-year-olds were to be found in the system. This population was given a core test of 24 items.

"Population 2" is constituted in the same manner as Population 1, but the test population consists of 14-year-olds. This population was given a core test of 30 items.

"Population 3" includes science students in the terminal grade. This is grade 12 except for Ontario, Canada (English), England, Hong Kong, Singapore, and the technology track in Sweden, where it is grade 13. Population 3 consists of two groups: a) the group studying biology, chemistry, or physics (these three subgroups are known as populations 3B, 3C, and 3P, respectively); and b) those students not studying science (population 3N) in the terminal grade.

Further information on the sampling methodology and response rates is available from:

Data Development Division
National Center for Education Statistics
555 New Jersey Ave NW
Washington, DC 20208–5650

State Survey on Substance Abuse Education

This survey used the NCES Fast Response Survey System (FRSS), which is designed to gather timely information for policymakers. In May of 1987, questionnaires were mailed to each State's coordinator of alcohol and drug abuse education, who was asked to have it completed by the person most knowledgeable about the State's substance abuse prevention activities. Surveys were mailed to the 50 States and the District of Columbia. Data collection was completed in June with a response rate of 100 percent. Because this survey was a census and had a 100 percent response rate, sampling error is not a factor. However, nonsampling error can occur for a variety of reasons, such as differences in the respondents' interpretation of the meaning of the questions, differences related to the particular time the survey was conducted, or errors in data preparation. Considerable effort was made to eliminate these biases. Thus, it appears unlikely that nonsampling errors severely biased the data from this survey.

For more information about this survey, contact:

Elementary and Secondary Education Statistics
    Division
National Center for Education Statistics
555 New Jersey Avenue NW
Washington, DC 20208–5651

District Survey on Substance Abuse Education

This sample survey, compiled by NCES, used the NCES Fast Response Survey System (FRSS), which is designed to gather timely information for policymakers. In May of 1987, questionnaires were mailed to a national probability sample of 700 public school districts from a universe of approximately 15,300. Questionnaires were mailed to the school district su-

perintendents who were asked to have it completed by the person most knowledgeable about the district's substance abuse prevention activities. Data collection was completed in June with a response rate of 98 percent. The sampling frame used for the survey was the 1983–84 Common Core of Data, "Universe of Public School Systems." The sample was stratified by enrollment size and metropolitan status. Districts within a stratum were sampled with equal probability. The survey data were weighted to reflect these sampling rates and were adjusted for nonresponse. Since the estimates were obtained from a sample of districts, they are subject to sampling variability. Estimates of standard errors for the estimates were computed using a balanced half-sampling technique known as balanced repeated replications. This survey is also subject to nonsampling error which can occur for a variety of reasons, such as differences in the respondents' interpretation of the meaning of the questions, differences related to the particular time the survey was conducted, or errors in data preparation. Considerable effort was made to eliminate these biases. Thus, it appears unlikely that nonsampling errors severely biased the data from this survey.

For more information about this survey, contact:

Elementary and Secondary Education Statistics
    Division
National Center for Education Statistics
555 New Jersey Avenue NW
Washington, DC 20208–5651

Other Governmental Agencies

Office for Civil Rights

Civil Rights Survey of Elementary and Secondary Schools

The Office for Civil Rights (OCR), U.S. Department of Education, conducts biennial surveys of public school districts and of schools within those districts. Data are obtained on the characteristics of pupils enrolled in public schools throughout the Nation. Such information is required under Title VI of the Civil Rights Act of 1964, Title IX of the Education Amendments of 1972, and Section 504 of the Rehabilitation Act of 1973 to enable OCR to carry out its compliance responsibilities. The 1986 survey included the 100 largest public school districts, those of special interest (i.e., court order, compliance review), and a stratified random sample of approximately 3,700 districts representing approximately 37,000 schools. The sample was stratified by State, district size, and estimated number of minority students.

Further information is available from:

Lawrence Bussey
Chief, Surveys Branch
Office for Civil Rights
U.S. Department of Education
330 C Street SW
Washington, DC 20202

Office of Special Education and Rehabilitative Services

Annual Report to Congress on the Implementation of the Education of the Handicapped Act

The Education of the Handicapped Act (EHA) requires the Secretary of Education to transmit to Congress annually a report describing the progress in serving the Nation's handicapped children. The annual report contains information on children served by the public schools under the provisions of Part B of the EHA and for children served in State-operated programs (SOP) for the handicapped under Chapter I of the Education Consolidation and Improvement Act (ECIA). Statistics on children receiving special education and related services in various settings and school personnel providing such services are reported in an annual submission of data to the Office of Special Education and Rehabilitative Services (OSERS) by the 50 States, the District of Columbia, and the outlying areas. The child count information is based on the number of handicapped children receiving special education and related services on December 1st of each year for EHA and October 1st for Chapter I of ECIA/SOP.

Since each participant in programs for the handicapped is reported to OSERS, the data are not subject to sampling error. However, nonsampling error can occur from a variety of sources. Some States follow a noncategorical approach to the delivery of special education services, but produce counts by handicapping condition because EHA-B requires it. In those States that do categorize their handicapped students, definitions and labeling practices vary.

Further information on the Annual Report to Congress may be obtained from:

Office of Special Education and Rehabilitative
  Services
Office of Special Education Programs
Room 3523, Switzer Building
330 C Street SW
Washington, DC 20202

National Longitudinal Transition Study of Special Education Students

As part of the 1983 amendments to the Education of All Handicapped Children Act (EHA), Congress requested that the U.S. Department of Education conduct a national longitudinal study of the transition of secondary special education students to determine how they fare in terms of education, employment, and independent living. A 5-year study was mandated, which was to include youth from ages 13 to 21 who were in special education at the time they were selected and who represented all 11 Federal disability categories. Data are drawn from extensive telephone interviews with parents, from school records, and from a survey of educators in secondary schools attended by youth in the study.

The study is being conducted by SRI International and began in April 1987. The National Transition Study involves a nationally representative sample of more than 8,000 secondary-age youth with disabilities. A sample of 450 school districts was randomly selected from the universe of approximately 14,000 school districts serving secondary special education students. An additional replacement sample of 176 additional districts was selected due to a low rate of agreement to participate from the initial group of districts. Participation in the study was invited from the approximately 80 special schools serving secondary-age deaf, blind, and deaf-blind students. A total of approximately 300 school districts and 25 special schools agreed to have youth selected for the study.

For further information about this study, contact:

Office of Special Education and Rehabilitative
  Services
Office of Special Education Programs
330 C Street SW
Washington, DC 20202

Bureau of the Census

Current Population Survey

Current estimates of school enrollment, as well as social and economic characteristics of students, are based on data collected in the Census Bureau's monthly household survey of about 60,000 households. The monthly Current Population Survey (CPS) sample consists of 729 areas comprising 1,973 counties, independent cities, and minor civil divisions throughout the 50 States and the District of Columbia. The sample was initially selected from the 1980 census files and is periodically updated to reflect new housing construction.

The monthly CPS deals primarily with labor force data for the civilian noninstitutional population (i.e., excluding military personnel and their families living on post and inmates of institutions). In addition, in October of each year, supplemental questions are asked about highest grade completed, level and grade of current enrollment, attendance status, number and type of courses, degree or certificate objective, and type of organization offering instruction for each member of the household. In March of each year, supplemental questions on income are asked. The responses to these questions are combined with answers to two questions on educational attainment: highest grade of school ever attended, and whether that grade was completed.

The estimation procedure employed for the monthly CPS data involves inflating weighted sample results to independent estimates of characteristics of the civilian noninstitutional population in the United States by age, sex, and race. These independent estimates are based on statistics from decennial censuses; statistics on births, deaths, immigration, and emigration; and statistics on the population in the armed services. Generalized standard error tables are provided in the *Current Population Reports.* The data are subject to both nonsampling and sampling errors.

Further information is available in the *Current Population Reports,* Series P–20, or by contacting:

Education and Social Stratification Branch
Population Division
Bureau of the Census
U.S. Department of Commerce
Washington, DC 20233

School Enrollment

Each October, the Current Population Survey (CPS) includes supplemental questions on the enrollment status of the population 3 years old and over. The main sources of nonsampling variability in the responses to the supplement are those inherent in the survey instrument. The question of current enrollment may not be answered accurately for various reasons. Some respondents may not know current grade information for every student in the household, a problem especially prevalent for households with members in college or in nursery school. Confusion over college credits or hours taken by a student may make it difficult to determine the year in which the student is enrolled. Problems may occur with the definition of nursery school (a group or class organized to provide educational experiences for children), where respondents' interpretations of "educational experiences" vary.

Examples of sampling variability in the estimates of school enrollment rates are given in table A11. Questions concerning the CPS "School Enrollment" survey may be directed to:

Education and Social Stratification Branch
Bureau of the Census
U.S. Department of Commerce
Washington, DC 20233

Educational Attainment

Data on years of school completed are derived from two questions on the Current Population Survey (CPS) instrument. Formal reports documenting educational attainment are produced by the Bureau of the Census using March CPS results. The latest report is *Educational Attainment in the United States, March 1987 and 1986,* Series P–20, No. 415, which is available from the Government Printing Office.

In addition to the general constraints of the CPS, some data indicate that the respondents have a tendency to overestimate the educational level of members of their household. Some inaccuracy is due to a lack of the respondent's knowledge of the exact educational attainment of each household member and the hesitancy to acknowledge anything less than a high school education. Another cause of nonsampling variability is the change in the numbers in the armed services over the years. In 1970, 25 percent of all males 20 and 21 years old were in the armed services. By 1974, this had decreased to less than 10 percent. The exclusion of members of the armed services appears to increase the proportion of the CPS population with some college and decrease the proportion of those who finished high school but went no further. After 1974, there was more stability in the proportion of young men in the military.

Beginning with the data for March 1980, tabulations have been controlled to the 1980 census. Examples of the sampling variability in the estimates of educational attainment are given in table A12. The figures shown in the table hold for total or white population estimates only. The variability in estimates for subgroups (region, household relationships, etc.) can be estimated using the tables presented in *Current Population Reports.*

Questions concerning "Educational Attainment in the United States" may be directed to:

Education and Social Stratification Branch
Bureau of the Census
U.S. Department of Commerce
Washington, DC 20233

Participation in Adult Education Survey

In May of 1969, 1972, 1975, 1978, 1981, and 1984, the Current Population Survey (CPS) included a supplemental inquiry on "Participation in Adult Education" (PAE). In addition to the questions on the CPS, interviewers asked if anyone in the household 17 years of age or older had participated in adult education in the 12-month period prior to the survey date. A survey form was filled out by the interviewer or left with a proxy member of the household for participants who were not at home at the time of the interview. In 1981, the supplement form was no longer left with the proxy but completed by the interviewer.

The PAE response rate of 94 percent in 1981 must be viewed in conjunction with the 96 percent response rate of the CPS. The overall response rate for the PAE survey in 1981 is then 90 percent. Examples of the sampling variability in the estimates from the PAE survey are given in tables A13 and A14.

The figures shown in the tables hold for total or white population estimates only. The variability in estimates for subgroups (employment status, income, education, etc.) can be estimated using the tables presented in *Current Population Reports.*

Further information concerning the PAE survey may be obtained from:

Postsecondary Education Statistics Division
National Center for Education Statistics
555 New Jersey Avenue NW
Washington, DC 20208–5652

Governmental Finances

The Census Bureau conducts an Annual Survey of Government Finances as authorized by law under Title 13, United States Code, Section 182. This survey covers the entire range of government finance activities: revenue, expenditure, debt, and assets. Revenues and expenditures comprise actual receipts and payments of a government and its agencies, including government-operated enterprises, utilities, and public trust funds. The expenditure reporting categories comprise all amounts of money paid out by a government and its agencies with the exception of amounts for debt retirement and for loan, investment, agency, and private trust transactions.

Most of the Federal Government statistics for 1988 are based on figures for 1986 that appear in *The Budget of the United States Government for the Fiscal Year 1990.* Since the classification used by the Census Bureau for reporting State and local government finance statistics differs in a number of important respects from the classification used in the United States budget, it was necessary to adjust the Federal data. For this report, Federal budget expenditures include interest accrued, but not paid, during the fiscal year; Census data on interest are on a disbursement basis.

The State government finances for 1988 are based primarily on the annual Census Bureau survey of State finances for fiscal year 1988. Census staff compiled figures from official records and reports of the various States for most of the State financial data.

The sample of local governments is drawn from the 1982 Census of Governments and consists of certain local governments taken with certainty plus a sample below the certainty level.

The statistics in this Census report, *Governmental Finances,* that are based wholly or partly on data from the sample are subject to sampling error. State government finance data are not subject to sampling error. Estimates of major United States totals for local governments are subject to a computed sampling variability of less than one-half of l percent. The estimates are also subject to the inaccuracies in classification, response, and processing which would occur if a complete census had been conducted under the same conditions as the sample.

Further information can be obtained from:

Governments Division
Bureau of the Census
U.S. Department of Commerce
Washington, DC 20233

National Center for Health Statistics

Monthly Vital Statistics Report

Data in this report are based on the birth certificates in all States and the District of Columbia. The data are provided to the National Center for Health Statistics through the Vital Statistics Cooperative Program. In 1983 and 1984, the program included 46 States, accounting for 83 to 84 percent of all births in the United States. Data for Arizona, California, the District of Columbia, and Georgia were based on a 50 percent sample of birth certificates filed as far back as 1982.

Birth and fertility rates are based on population estimates by the Census Bureau. Birth and fertility rates for 1985 are based on the 1980 Census count.

Further information may be obtained from:

U.S. Department of Health and Human Service
Public Health Services
National Center for Health Statistics
3700 East-West Highway
Hyattsville, MD 20782

National Institute on Drug Abuse

The National Institute on Drug Abuse of the U.S. Department of Health and Human Services is the primary supporter of the long-term study entitled "Monitoring the Future: A Continuing Study of the Lifestyles and Values of Youth," conducted at the University of Michigan, Institute for Social Research. One component of the study deals with student drug abuse. Results of a national sample survey have been published annually since 1975. Approximately 125 to 135 schools have participated each year. With the exception of 1975 when about 9,400 students participated in the survey, more than 15,000 students have participated in the survey annually. For the class of 1988, about 16,300 students responded to the survey. Over the years, the response rate has varied from 77 to 84 percent. Table A15 provides examples of the survey's sampling error.

The data in this survey represent only high school seniors. Understandably, there will be some reluctance to admit illegal activities. Also, students who were out of school on the day of the survey were nonrespondents. The survey did not include high school dropouts. The inclusion of these two groups would tend to increase the proportion of individuals who had used drugs. A 1983 study found that the inclusion of the absentees could increase some of the drug usage estimates by as much as 2.7 percent. (Details on that study and its methodology were published in *Drug Use Among American High School Students, College Students, and Other Young Adults,* by Lloyd D. Johnston, Patrick M. O'Malley, and Jerald G. Bachman, available from the National Clearinghouse on Drug Abuse Information, 5600 Fishers Lane, Rockville, MD 20857.)

Further information on this survey may be obtained from:

National Institute on Drug Abuse
Division of Epidemiology and Statistical Analysis
5600 Fishers Lane
Rockville, MD 20857

National Science Foundation

Survey of Earned Doctorates Awarded in the United States

The Survey of Earned Doctorates Awarded in the United States has collected basic statistics from the universe of doctoral recipients in the United States each year since the 1920s. It has been supported by five Federal agencies: the National Science Foundation, in conjunction with the U.S. Department of Education; the National Endowment for the Humanities; the U. S. Department of Agriculture; and the National Institute of Health.

A survey form is distributed, with the assistance of graduate deans, to each person completing the requirements for a doctorate. Of the approximately 31,000 persons eligible for the survey, approximately 95 percent respond. The questionnaire obtains information on sex, race/ethnicity, marital status, citizenship, handicaps, dependents, specialty field of doctorate, educational institutions attended, time spent in completion of doctorate, financial support, educational debt, postgraduation plans, and educational attainment of parents. The data are collected, edited, and published by the National Academy of Sciences.

For further information contact:

Susan Hill
National Science Foundation
1800 G Street NW
Washington, DC 20550

Federal Obligations to Colleges and Universities and Selected Nonprofit Institutions

Each year, the National Science Foundation collects data on obligations to colleges and universities from Federal agencies. Obligations differ from expenditures in that funds obligated during one fiscal year may be spent by the recipient in later years. The fiscal year 1987 data were submitted by 15 Federal agencies. Obligation amounts include direct Federal support, so that amounts subcontracted to other institutions are included. Those funds received through subcontracts are excluded. Also excluded from the data are certain types of financial assistance, such as the Department of Education's Guaranteed Student Loan Program and obligations to the U.S. service academies. For purposes of tabulations in this publication, university administered federally funded research and development centers (FFRDCs) have been included in appropriate State totals.

The universe of academic institutions for this survey is based on the Integrated Postsecondary Education Data Survey conducted by the National Center for Education Statistics (see above). Institutions without Federal support were excluded and some systems were combined into single reporting units.

Further information on this survey may be obtained from *Federal Support to Universities, Colleges, and Selected Nonprofit Institutions,* published by the National Science Foundation, or by contacting:

Universities and Nonprofit Institutions Study Group
Division of Science Resources Studies
National Science Foundation, Room L–602
Washington, DC 20550

Survey of Scientific and Engineering Expenditures at Universities and Colleges

The universe for this survey included 563 institutions in the United States and outlying areas that had a master's or doctor's degree program in the sciences or engineering. In addition, schools that had $50,000 or more in separately budgeted research and development expenditures and the 19 federally funded research and development centers were included. Altogether, these institutions represented approximately 99 percent of all college and university research and development.

The survey instrument has remained essentially unchanged in recent years to facilitate consistent responses. The field of study details match the standard field codes in the *Classification of Instructional Programs,* published by NCES. The response rate for the 1982 survey was 81 percent. The remaining institutions were imputed. The imputation amounted to only 6 percent of the total expenditures reported, since the nonrespondents tended to be smaller institutions. The survey process included a verification procedure in which trend data for the past two reports and the current survey were sent to each institution. The institutions were given an opportunity to amend the current and past figures. These revisions have been incorporated in the National Science Foundation database.

Further information on this survey may be obtained from Academic Science/Engineering, R&D Funds, published by the National Science Foundation, or by contacting:

Universities and Nonprofit Institutions Study Group
Division of Science Resources Studies
National Science Foundation, Room L–602
Washington, DC 20550

Other Organization Sources

American Association of Colleges for Teacher Education

The Committee on Research and Information of the American Association of Colleges for Teacher Education (AACTE) initiated the Research About Teacher Education (RATE) Project in 1985. The project is devoted to collecting information about institutions of higher education that engage in teacher education. The data in the report, *Teaching Teachers: Facts and Figures,* were culled from analyses of three survey instruments—institutional, faculty, and student. Archival data from institutions covered the 1985 calendar year. Self-reported perceptual and factual data from faculty and students were collected in spring 1986. The institutions were selected from a stratified random sample of the 713 member institutions of AACTE in 1985. The institutions were stratified according to the highest degree offered within the school, college, or department of education. Thirty institutions were randomly selected from each stratum for a total of 90 institutions. Of these, 76 institutions provided complete data, representing 84 percent of the sample.

To provide a more complete picture, surveys were administered to 360 education faculty and 900 students. These groups were drawn from secondary education methods courses. The current report contains data from 215 faculty and 876 students.

For those interested in more technical information from the RATE Project, supporting documentation for this report is available from:

American Association of Colleges for Teacher Education
One Dupont Circle
Suite 610
Washington, DC 20036–2412

American College Testing Program

The American College Testing (ACT) Assessment is designed to measure educational development in the areas of English, mathematics, social studies, and natural sciences. The ACT Assessment is taken by college-bound high school students and the test results are used to predict how well students might perform in college.

Prior to the 1984–85 school year, national norms were based on a 10 percent sample of the students taking the test. Since then, national norms are based on the test scores of all students taking the test. Moreover, beginning with 1984–85, these norms have been based on the most recent ACT scores available from students scheduled to graduate in the spring of the year. Duplicate test records are no longer used to produce national figures.

Separate ACT standard scores are computed for English, mathematics, social studies, and natural science. ACT standard scores are reported for each subject area on a scale from 1 to 36. The four ACT standard scores have a mean (average) of about 19 and a standard deviation of about 6 for college-bound students nationally. A composite score is obtained by taking the simple average of the four standard scores and is an indication of student's overall academic development across these subject areas.

It should be noted that college-bound students who take the ACT Assessment are not representative in some respects of college-bound students nationally. First, students who live in the Midwest, Rocky Mountains and Plains, and the South are overrepresented among ACT-tested students as compared with college-bound students nationally. Second, ACT-tested students tend to enroll in public colleges and universities more frequently than do college-bound students nationally.

For further information, contact:

American College Testing Program
2201 North Dodge Street
P.O. Box 168
Iowa City, IA 52243

American Federation of Teachers

The American Federation of Teachers (AFT) reports national and State average salaries and earnings for teachers, other school employees, government workers, and professional employees over the past 25 years. The AFT's survey of State departments of education obtains information on minimum salaries, experienced teachers reentering the classroom, and teacher age and experience. Most data from the survey are reported as received, although some data are confirmed by telephone. These data are available in the AFT's annual report *Salary and Analysis of Salary Trends*. While serving as the primary vehicle for reporting the results of the AFT's annual survey of State departments of education, several other data sources are also used in this report.

Further information on this survey can be obtained from:

American Federation of Teachers
555 New Jersey Avenue NW
Washington, DC 20001

Carnegie Foundation for the Advancement of Teaching

The Carnegie Foundation for the Advancement of Teaching (CFAT) conducted the National Survey of Public School Teachers in the spring of 1987. The survey was mailed to 40,000 public elementary and secondary school teachers in all 50 States. Questionnaires were returned by 21,698 teachers, representing a response rate of 54.3 percent. Elementary teachers compose 29.6 percent (11,827) of the sample and secondary teachers compose 29.1 percent (11,651). Some of the teachers taught at both levels.

A stratified random sample design was used. The total survey size is composed of simple random samples from each State. Each survey response was weighted based on the level and State of the responding teacher. The maximum sampling error for this survey is less than plus or minus l percent for the total sample. In general, more than 95 percent of the teachers who returned the questionnaire answered each question.

Results from this survey may be found in *Teacher Involvement in Decisionmaking: A State-By-State Profile and The Condition of Teaching: A State-By-State Analysis, 1988*. For additional information on the data obtained from this survey, contact:

Robert Hochstein
Carnegie Foundation for the Advancement of
   Teaching
1775 Massachusetts Avenue NW
Washington, DC 20036

College Entrance Examination Board

The Admissions Testing Program of the College Board comprises a number of college admissions tests, including the Preliminary Scholastic Aptitude Test (PSAT) and the Scholastic Aptitude Test (SAT). High school students participate in the testing program as sophomores, juniors, or seniors—some more than once during these 3 years. If they have taken the tests more than once, only the most recent scores are tabulated. The PSAT and SAT report subscores in the areas of mathematics and verbal ability.

The SAT results are not representative of high school students or college-bound students nationally since the sample is self-selected. Generally, tests are taken by students who need the results to attend a particular college or university. The State totals are greatly affected by the requirements of its State colleges. Public colleges in a number of States require ACT scores rather than SAT scores. Thus, the proportion of students taking the SAT in these States is very low and is inappropriate for any comparison. In recent years, about 1 million high school students have taken the examination annually.

Further information on the SAT can be obtained from:

College Entrance Examination Board
Educational Testing Service
Princeton, NJ 08541

Council for Aid to Education

The Council for Aid to Education, Inc., (CFAE) is a not-for-profit corporation funded by contributions from business. CFAE sponsors public service campaigns and provides consulting and research services on voluntary support for education institutions. Each year, CFAE conducts a survey of colleges and universities and private elementary and secondary schools to obtain information on the amounts, sources, and purposes of private gifts, grants, and bequests received during the academic year. In the 1986–87 study, survey forms were sent to approximately 2,800 colleges and universities and 1,174 responded, which was 1.7 percent below the 1985–86 level. The response rates were much higher for the 4-year colleges than for the 2-year colleges. For example, 90 percent of the doctoral-level institutions and 63 percent of the comprehensive and general baccalaureate colleges participated in the survey. CFAE estimates that about 85 percent of all voluntary support is reported in the survey because of the high participation of institutions receiving large amounts of funding. Survey forms are reviewed by CFAE for internal consistency before preparing a computerized database. Institutional reports of voluntary support data from the CFAE "Survey of Voluntary Support of Education" are more comprehensive and detailed than the related data in the "Financial Statistics of Institutions of Higher Education" survey conducted by NCES. The results from the "Survey of

Voluntary Support of Education" are published in the annual Voluntary Support of Education, which may be purchased from CFAE.

Further information is available from:

Director of Research
Council for Aid to Education, Inc.
680 Fifth Avenue
New York, NY 10019

Council of Chief State School Officers

The Council of Chief State School Officers (CCSSO) is a nonprofit organization of the 57 public officials who head departments of public education in every State, the outlying areas, the District of Columbia, and the Department of Defense Dependents Schools. In 1985, the CCSSO founded the State Education Assessment Center to provide a locus of leadership by the States to improve the monitoring and assessment of education. *State Education Indicators, 1988* is the principal report of the Assessment Center's program of indicators on education. Most of the data is obtained from a member questionnaire; the remainder of the data is obtained from Federal Government agencies.

For additional information on this report, contact:

Ramsay Selden
State Education Assessment Center
Council of Chief State School Officers
379 Hall of States
400 North Capitol Street NW
Washington, DC 20001

Council of State Directors of Programs for the Gifted

The Council of State Directors of Programs for the Gifted is composed of the director or individual in the leadership position for gifted education in each of the 50 States, the District of Columbia, and the outlying areas. The Council has conducted many surveys in the past and most recently conducted two comprehensive State surveys in order to produce a profile of gifted education throughout the Nation. These data are reported in the 1985 and 1987 "State of the States Gifted and Talented Education" reports. This edition of the *Digest* uses data from the 1986–87 school year. Responses for the 1986–87 survey were received from all 50 States, Puerto Rico, and Guam. The Council is in the process of deciding whether future surveys will be conducted annually or biennially.

Further information is available from:

Nancy Lukenbill, President
Council of State Directors of Programs for the Gifted
Office of Public Instruction
Room 106, State Capitol
Helena, MT 59620

Education Commission of the States

The Education Commission of the States (ECS) Clearinghouse collects information on laws and standards in the field of education and reports them periodically in "Clearinghouse Notes." The Commission collects information about administrators, principals, and teachers. It also examines policy areas, such as assessment and testing, collective bargaining, early childhood issues, quality education, and school schedules. The information is collected by reading State newsletters, tracking State legislation, and surveying State education agencies. Data are verified by the individual States when necessary. Even though ECS monitors State activity on a continuous basis, it updates the reports only when there is significant change in State activity.

Further information is available from:

Melody Bush or Chris Pipho
Education Commission of the States
1860 Lincoln Street, Suite 300
Denver, CO 80295

Gallup Poll

Each year the Gallup Poll conducts the "Public Attitudes Toward the Public Schools" survey, funded by Phi Delta Kappa. The survey includes interviews with over 1,600 adults representing the civilian noninstitutional population 18 years old and over.

The sample used in the 22nd annual survey was made up of a total of 1,594 respondents and is described as a modified probability sample of the Nation. Personal, in-home interviewing was conducted in representative communities of the Nation.

The survey is a sample survey and is subject to sampling error. The size of error depends largely on the number of respondents providing data. Table A16 shows the approximate sampling errors associated with different percentages and sample sizes for the survey. Table A17 also provides approximate sampling errors for comparisons of two sample percentages.

For example, an estimated percentage of about 10 percent based on the responses of 1,000 sample members has an approximate sampling error of 2 percent at the 95 percent confidence level. The sampling error for the difference in two percentages (50 percent versus 41 percent) based on two samples of 750 members and 400 members, respectively, is about 8 percent at the 95 percent confidence level. Table A17 contains approximate sampling errors for the difference in two percentages.

Further information on this survey can be obtained from:

Gallup Poll
Phi Delta Kappa
P.O. Box 789
Bloomington, IN 47402–0789

Independent Sector

In 1988, Independent Sector commissioned the Gallup Poll to conduct a national survey on the giving and volunteering behavior of Americans. This survey is the beginning of a series of surveys that will be conducted every 2 years. The information was obtained from in-home personal interviews conducted from March 8 to March 22, 1988, with a representative national sample of 2,775 adult Americans 18 or more years old. The sampling procedure did not include those with incomes above $200,000 because they constitute such a small percentage of the population.

The results from this survey are published in *Giving and Volunteering in the United States* and may be purchased from:

Independent Sector
1828 L Street NW
Washington, DC 20036

Institute of International Education

Each year the Institute of International Education (IIE) conducts a survey of the number of foreign students studying in American colleges and universities and reports these data in *Open Doors,* an annual publication. All of the regionally accredited institutions in the *Education Directory, Colleges and Universities,* published by NCES, are surveyed by IIE. The data presented in the *Digest* are drawn from the IIE survey, which requests the total enrollment of foreign students in an institution and information on student characteristics, such as country of origin. For the 1989–90 survey, 2,546 out of 2,840 (90 percent) institutions surveyed reported data for the survey.

Additional information can be obtained from the publication *Open Doors* or by contacting:

Alfred Julian
Institute of International Education
809 United Nations Plaza
New York, NY 10017

Market Data Retrieval

Market Data Retrieval (MDR) is a market research company that compiles mailing lists of schools and school districts. MDR also conducts special analyses of school characteristics. In recent years, MDR has conducted surveys of computer use in public and private schools.

During its annual summer survey of public school districts, MDR included questions on computer use in public schools. All school districts were asked about the number of their schools using computers. In the fall, an additional mail survey was conducted to gather more information on the number and type of computers being used. Data on computer utilization were reported for 86 percent of public schools. These data were used to generate State-by-State estimates which were aggregated to construct a national total.

Private school data were compiled through mail and telephone surveys during the middle of the 1982–83 and 1983–84 school years. The 1983–84 response rate for Catholic schools was 96 percent, and the rate for other private schools was 89 percent.

Further information on these surveys may be obtained from:

Market Data Retrieval
16 Progress Drive
Shelton, CT 06484

Metropolitan Life Insurance Company

Louis Harris and Associates conducted the 1989 Metropolitan Life Survey of the American Teacher for the Metropolitan Life Insurance Company. During May and June 1989, 2,000 telephone interviews were conducted with current public school teachers in kindergarten through grade 12. The survey included all states of the U.S. and the District of Columbia.

A list of 1.2 million teachers was compiled by Market Data Retrieval of Westport, Connecticut, from which Louis Harris and Associates drew a random sample of current teachers. NCES statistics on public school teachers were used to compute sample sizes for complete interviews for each state.

Thirty open-ended in-depth interviews with teachers around the country were used to develop the final questionnaire. School contacts numbered 6,642, of which 2,000 became interviews. The rate of completion for the teacher interviews was 83 percent. The sampled data were adjusted by race and regional data provided by the respondents to accurately reflect their actual proportions in the population.

For more information contact:

Metropolitan Life Survey of the American Teacher
Metropolitan Life Insurance Company
One Madison Avenue
New York, NY 10010

National Association of Secondary School Principals

The National Association of Secondary School Principals (NASSP) survey is the third in a series of national studies of high school principals dating back to 1965. The major purpose of this study is to analyze and describe high school leaders and their schools.

A sample of 1,028 secondary schools was drawn randomly from NASSP's national database of all American schools with grade 12. Survey forms were mailed in early 1987. A preliminary analysis of the returns indicated a disproportionate response rate, primarily from smaller schools in the Midwest. A second set of surveys was mailed in late March of 1987 and targeted by zip codes to redress the imbalance in preliminary returns. In all, 1,544 survey forms were sent and 716 were returned by principals. The response rate for principals was 46 percent.

Further information on this survey may be obtained from *High School Leaders and Their Schools* or by contacting:

National Association of Secondary School Principals
1904 Association Drive
Reston, VA 22091

National Association of State Scholarship and Grant Programs

The National Association of State Scholarship and Grant Programs (NASSGP) is an association of States with general programs of scholarship or grant assistance for undergraduate study. Executive officers responsible for grant program administration represent each State in the Association. The publication of the *19th Annual Survey Report: 1987–88 Academic Year* represents the eighth year that the Pennsylvania Higher Education Assistance Agency has produced the NASSGP annual report. Data are reported for all 50 States, the District of Columbia, and Puerto Rico.

For more information on this survey, contact:

Jerry S. Davis
Research and Statistics
Pennsylvania Higher Education Assistance Agency
Towne House
660 Boas Street
Harrisburg, PA 17102

National Education Association

The National Education Association (NEA) reports enrollment, expenditure, revenue, graduate, teacher, and instructional staff salary data in its annual publication, *Estimates of School Statistics*. Each year NEA prepares regression-based estimates of financial and other education statistics and submits them to the States for verification. Generally about 30 States adjust these estimates based on their own data. These preliminary data are published by NEA along with revised data from previous years. States are asked to revise previously submitted data as final figures become available. The most recent publication contains all changes reported to the NEA.

Further information on NEA surveys can be obtained from:

National Education Association—Research
1201 16th Street NW
Washington, DC 20036

Status of the American Public School Teacher

The "Status of the American Public School Teacher" survey is conducted every 5 years by the National Education Association (NEA). The survey was designed by the NEA Research Division and initially administered in 1956. The intent of the survey is to solicit information covering various aspects of public school teachers' professional, family, and civic lives.

Participants for the survey are selected using a two-stage sample design, with the first-stage stratum determined by the number of students enrolled in the districts. Selection probabilities are determined so that the resulting sample is self-weighting. In 1985–86, a sample of 1,998 was selected from the approximately 2,207,000 public school teachers. The sample was adjusted to 1,784 to reflect the 214 responses that were unusable because the respondent could not be located or the respondent was not a teacher. After followup procedures, 1,291 usable replies were obtained, yielding a response rate of 72 percent.

Possible sources of nonsampling errors are nonresponses, misinterpretation, and—when comparing data over years—changes in the sampling method and instrument. Misinterpretation of the survey items should be minimal, as the sample responding is not from the general population but one knowledgeable about the area of concern. Since the sampling procedure changed after 1956, and some wording of items has changed over the different administrations, care is taken to present only comparable data.

Since sampling is used, sampling variability is inherent in the data. An approximation to the maximum standard error for estimating the population percentages is 1.4 percent. To estimate the 90 percent confidence interval for population percentages, the maximum standard error of 1.4 percent is multiplied by 1.65 (1.4 x 1.65). The resulting percentage (2.3) is added and subtracted from the population estimate to establish upper and lower bounds for the confidence interval. For example, if a sample percentage is 60 percent, there is a 90 percent chance that the population percentage lies between 57.7 percent and 62.3 percent (60 percent ± 2.3 percent). If comparisons of two percentages are to be made, table A20 gives maximum differences for significance at the 90 percent confidence level.

Questions concerning the "Status of the American Public School Teacher" survey may be directed to:

National Education Association—Research
1201 16th Street NW
Washington, DC 20036

United Nations Educational, Scientific, and Cultural Organization

The United Nations Educational, Scientific, and Cultural Organization (UNESCO) conducts annual surveys of education statistics of its member countries. Besides official surveys, data are supplemented by information obtained by UNESCO through other publications and sources. Each year more than 200 countries reply to the UNESCO surveys. In some cases, estimates are made by UNESCO for particular items such as world and continent totals. While great efforts are made to make them as comparable as possible, the data still reflect the vast differences among the countries of the world in the structure of education. While there is some agreement about the reporting of first- and second-level data, the third level (postsecondary education) presents numerous substantial problems. Some countries report only university enrollment while other countries report all postsecondary, including vocational and technical schools and correspondence programs. A very high proportion of some countries' third-level students attend institutions in other countries. While definition

problems are many in this sort of study, other survey problems should not be overlooked. The member countries that provide data to UNESCO are responsible for their validity. Thus, data for particular countries are subject to nonsampling error and perhaps sampling error as well. Some countries may furnish only rough estimates, while data from other countries may be very accurate. Other difficulties are caused by the varying periodicity of data collection among the countries of the world. In spite of such problems, many researchers use UNESCO data because they are the best available. Users should examine footnotes carefully to recognize some of the data limitations.

More complete information may be obtained from the *Statistical Yearbook* published by UNESCO or from:

Office of Statistics
UNESCO
7, Place de Fontenoy
75700 Paris
France

Organization for Economic Cooperation and Development

The Organization for Economic Cooperation and Development (OECD) publishes analyses of national policies in education, training, and economics in 23 countries. The countries surveyed are: Australia, Austria, Belgium, Canada, Denmark, Finland, France, Germany (West), Ireland, Italy, Japan, Luxembourg, Netherlands, New Zealand, Norway, Portugal, Spain, Sweden, Switzerland, Turkey, United Kingdom, United States, and Yugoslavia. Two OECD publications, *A Compendium of Statistical Information* and *National Accounts,* were used to develop tables for the *Digest* chapter on international education.

Since only developed nations, mostly European, are included in these studies the range of analysis is limited. However, OECD data allow for some detailed international comparison of financial resources or other education variables to be made for this selected group of countries.

More complete information may be obtained from:

OECD
2, rue Andre-Pascal
75775 PARIS CEDEX 16, France

Table A1.—Selected standard errors for selected items in the 1985 Survey of Public and Private School Libraries and Media Centers

Items for public school libraries	Estimate	Standard error	95% confidence interval	
			Lower	Upper
Percent of schools having library/media centers				
All schools	93.5	0.54	92.4	94.6
Secondary schools	98.0	0.97	96.1	99.9
Schools with 500 to 699 pupils	98.5	0.39	97.7	99.3
Average expenditure per pupil for books				
All schools	$6.24	0.1524	$5.94	$6.54
Secondary schools	7.40	0.3253	6.77	8.04
Schools with 700 to 999 pupils	4.67	0.1743	4.33	5.01
Average book volumes held per pupil				
All schools	20.3	0.3784	19.5	21.0
Elementary and combined schools	20.6	0.4275	19.8	21.5
Schools with over 2,000 pupils	9.5	0.3782	8.7	10.2

Table A2.—Respondent counts for selected High School and Beyond surveys

Classification variable and subgroup	Followup survey of 1980 sophomores in 1982	Followup survey of 1980 seniors in 1982	Followup survey of 1980 sophomores in 1984	Followup survey of 1980 seniors in 1984	Followup survey of 1980 sophomores in 1986	Followup survey of 1980 seniors in 1986
Total respondents (unweighted)	25,830	11,227	11,463	10,925	11,248	10,536
Sex						
Male	12,717	5,213	5,514	5,058	5,391	4,832
Female	13,113	6,014	5,949	5,867	5,857	5,704
Race/ethnicity						
White, non-Hispanic	17,295	5,180	7,285	5,057	7,194	5,246
Black, non-Hispanic	3,338	2,724	1,651	2,625	1,585	2,726
Hispanic	4,439	2,749	1,795	2,654	1,745	1,950
Asian or Pacific Islander	413	367	425	355	413	356
American Indian or Alaskan. Native	248	191	253	185	246	200
Other or unclassified	97	16	54	49	65	58
Socioeconomic status composite (SES) [1]						
Low	6,752	3,940	2,831	3,857	2,751	3,668
Low-middle	6,234	2,390	2,624	2,314	2,559	2,289
High-middle	6,134	2,168	2,849	2,107	2,817	1,995
High	6,341	1,988	3,086	1,936	3,044	1,900
Unclassified	369	741	73	711	77	684
Father's highest level of education						
Less than high school	5,179	—	—	—	—	—
High school graduate [2]	11,961	—	—	—	—	—
College graduate [3]	5,169	—	—	—	—	—
Don't know/missing	3,521	—	—	—	—	—
High school program (self-reported)						
Academic	10,152	4,145	6,547	4,007	—	3,899
General	8,789	3,829	3,468	3,764	—	3,602
Vocational	6,664	2,660	3,611	2,581	—	2,481
Unclassified	225	593	56	573	—	554
High school type						
Public	—	9,969	8,647	9,727	—	9,385
Catholic	—	964	2,479	911	—	876
Other private	—	294	337	287	—	275
Postsecondary education status [4]						
Full-time	—	—	4,466	—	—	—
Part-time	—	—	3,275	—	—	—
Never enrolled	—	—	3,678	—	—	—
Missing/unclassified	—	—	44	—	—	—
October 1980 postsecondary education attendance status						
Part-time 2-year public institution	—	—	—	—	—	352
Part-time 4-year public institution	—	—	—	—	—	152
Full-time 2-year public institution	—	—	—	—	—	1,312
Full-time 4-year public institution	—	—	—	—	—	1,986
Full-time 4-year private institution	—	—	—	—	—	1,015
Not a student	—	—	—	—	—	4,523
Other and missing	—	—	—	—	—	1,196
Postsecondary education plans						
No plans	—	—	—	—	—	1,623
Attend vocational/technical school	—	—	—	—	—	1,835
Attend college less than four years	—	—	—	—	—	1,528
Earn bachelor's degree	—	—	—	—	—	2,631
Earn advanced degree	—	—	—	—	—	2,265
Missing	—	—	—	—	—	654
Participation in high school extracurricular activities [5]						
Never participated	—	—	—	—	—	1,024
Participated as a member	—	—	—	—	—	4,104
Participated as a leader	—	—	—	—	—	4,457

[1] The SES index is a composite of five equally-weighted measures: father's education, mother's education, family income, father's occupation, and presence of certain items in the respondent's household.

[2] Includes attendance at a vocational, trade, or business school, or 2-year college; or attendance at a 4-year college resulting in less than a bachelor's degree.

[3] Includes those with a bachelor's or higher level degree.

[4] Postsecondary education status was determined by students' enrollment in academic or vocational study during the four semesters—fall 1982, spring 1983, fall 1983, and spring 1984—following their scheduled high school graduation. Students who enrolled in full-time study in each of the four semesters were classified as full-time. Students who were enrolled in part-time study in any of the four semesters and those who were enrolled in full-time study in fewer than four semesters were classified as part-time. Students who had neither enrolled on a full-time nor part-time basis in each of the four semesters were classified as never enrolled.

[5] Responses to questions concerning participation in each of 15 different extracurricular activity areas (i.e., varsity sports, debate, band, subject-matter clubs, etc.) were used to classify students' overall level of participation in extracurricular activities. The difference between the sum of the three category respondent counts and the total sample size is due to missing data.

—Data not applicable.

NOTE.—Data from students who dropped out of school between the 10th and 12th grades were not used in analyses of sophomore samples.

Table A3.—Design effects (DEFF) and root design effects (DEFT) for selected High School and Beyond surveys and subsamples

Subsample characteristic	Followup survey of 1980 sophomores in 1984		Followup survey of 1980 seniors in 1984		Followup survey of 1980 sophomores in 1986		Followup survey of 1980 seniors in 1986	
Total sample	**2.40**	**(1.54)**	**2.87**	**(1.69)**	**2.19**	**(1.47)**	**2.28**	**(1.50)**
Sex								
Male			—		2.07	(1.43)	2.13	(1.45)
Female			—		2.06	(1.43)	2.26	(1.50)
Race/ethnicity								
White and other	2.06	(1.42)	2.09	(1.44)	1.92	(1.38)	1.70	(1.30)
Black	2.22	(1.47)	2.26	(1.50)	2.19	(1.47)	2.40	(1.54)
Hispanic	3.15	(1.73)	3.72	(1.92)	3.11	(1.76)	4.06	(2.01)
Socioeconomic status composite (SES)								
Low	1.91	(1.37)	2.28	(1.50)	1.83	(1.35)	2.31	(1.51)
Middle	1.95	(1.39)	1.81	(1.34)	2.06	(1.42)	2.02	(1.42)
High	2.05	(1.42)	1.93	(1.38)	1.92	(1.38)	1.71	(1.30)

—Not available.

NOTE.—The average design effect for the 1980 sophomore cohort first followup (1982) survey is 3.59(1.89) and the average design effect for the 1980 senior first followup (1982) survey is 2.64(1.62).

Table A4.—Standard errors for the NAEP reading proficiency study: 1970–71 to 1987–88

Item	Standard error for estimate (mean) [1]		Standard error for percent of students reading at or above a basic level					Standard error for percent of students reading at or above intermediate level				
	1983–84	1987–88	1970–71	1974–75	1979–80	1983–84	1987–88	1970–71	1974–75	1979–80	1983–84	1987–88
9-year-olds												
Total	1.0	1.2	0.9	0.8	0.9	1.0	1.2	0.5	0.5	0.8	0.6	0.9
White	0.8	1.5	0.9	0.8	0.7	0.8	1.6	0.6	0.5	0.8	0.7	1.2
Black	1.2	2.6	1.4	1.1	1.6	1.2	2.4	0.3	0.2	0.5	0.5	0.8
Hispanic	1.6	3.9	—	2.7	2.6	1.6	3.2	—	0.5	1.0	0.4	1.9
13-year-olds												
Total	0.7	0.9	0.4	0.4	0.4	0.3	0.5	1.1	1.0	1.0	0.7	1.1
White	0.6	1.0	0.3	0.2	0.2	0.2	0.5	0.9	0.8	0.7	0.6	1.4
Black	1.2	2.3	1.4	1.2	1.5	0.9	1.8	1.0	1.4	1.4	1.2	2.1
Hispanic	1.6	3.5	—	2.2	1.8	1.1	2.2	—	3.8	2.1	1.8	3.4
17-year-olds												
Total	0.9	1.1	0.3	0.3	0.4	0.1	0.2	0.9	0.7	1.0	0.7	0.7
White	0.7	1.3	0.2	0.1	0.1	0.1	0.1	0.7	0.5	0.7	0.4	0.8
Black	1.2	2.6	1.2	1.6	2.1	0.4	0.8	1.4	1.6	2.2	1.1	1.9
Hispanic	1.9	4.0	—	2.3	1.5	0.5	1.5	—	4.0	2.5	1.5	4.0

[1] Item response theory used as a basis to estimate performance at the three levels on a common scale from 0 to 500.

—Data not available.

Table A5.—Standard errors for the NAEP writing, history, and civics proficiency studies: 1976 to 1988

Item	Standard error for estimated (mean) [1] writing performance						Standard error for estimated (mean) [1] history performance, 1988			Standard error for estimated percent correct in civics					
	4th grade		8th grade		11th grade		4th grade	8th grade	12th grade	13-year-olds			17-year-olds		
	1984	1988	1984	1988	1984	1988				1976	1982	1988	1976	1982	1988
Total	**1.7**	**1.3**	**1.4**	**0.8**	**2.1**	**1.2**	**0.9**	**0.7**	**1.0**	**0.2**	**0.4**	**0.4**	**0.3**	**0.5**	**0.5**
Male	2.7	1.9	2.4	1.4	3.0	1.6	1.2	1.0	1.3	0.2	0.4	0.6	0.3	0.6	0.7
Female	1.9	1.6	1.5	1.1	2.4	1.4	1.0	0.8	1.1	0.3	0.4	0.4	0.3	0.5	0.6
White	1.9	1.6	1.5	1.0	2.1	1.3	1.0	0.8	1.2	0.2	0.3	0.5	0.3	0.4	0.6
Black	4.0	3.1	4.1	2.3	4.1	2.6	1.9	1.5	1.7	0.3	0.4	0.6	0.5	0.5	1.0
Hispanic	4.5	3.6	6.9	3.2	4.6	3.2	1.7	1.9	1.8	0.6	0.5	1.8	0.8	1.2	1.7

[1] Item response theory used as a basis to estimate performance at the three levels on a common scale from 0 to 400.

Table A6.—Standard errors for the NAEP mathematics and science proficiency studies: 1976–77 to 1985–86

Item	Basic operations mathematics proficiency			Moderately complex mathematics proficiency			Understand scientific principles			Apply basic scientific information		
	1977–78	1981–82	1985–86	1977–78	1981–82	1985–86	1976–77	1981–82	1985–86	1976–77	1981–82	1985–86
9-year-olds												
Total	0.6	0.8	0.9	0.1	0.1	0.2	1.1	1.6	1.0	0.7	1.7	1.0
White	0.7	0.9	1.0	0.1	0.1	0.2	0.7	1.6	0.9	0.6	2.0	1.1
Black	0.5	0.5	0.7	0.0	0.0	0.0	1.5	2.6	1.9	0.5	1.0	0.9
Hispanic	1.3	1.1	2.5	0.4	0.0	0.0	3.1	5.0	3.3	1.6	2.3	1.9
13-year-olds												
Total	1.2	1.2	1.5	0.7	0.9	1.0	0.7	0.7	0.9	1.1	1.4	1.4
White	0.8	0.9	1.6	0.7	0.9	1.1	0.4	0.4	0.7	0.9	1.3	1.5
Black	1.8	1.7	3.6	0.4	0.9	1.4	2.1	1.6	2.0	1.6	1.4	2.7
Hispanic	2.5	2.1	4.9	0.6	1.0	1.0	2.7	2.6	3.1	1.6	5.0	3.7
17-year-olds												
Total	0.5	0.5	0.4	1.1	1.2	1.2	0.2	0.4	0.4	0.7	1.0	1.2
White	0.3	0.3	0.2	1.1	1.3	1.4	0.1	0.2	0.3	0.4	0.8	1.4
Black	1.4	1.3	1.7	1.3	1.5	2.6	0.9	1.4	1.7	1.4	1.6	2.7
Hispanic	2.2	1.0	2.1	2.4	2.2	3.9	1.5	1.8	1.7	1.6	1.8	5.0

Standard error for percent of students at or above—

Table A7.—Respondent counts for selected National Longitudinal Study surveys

Classification variable and subgroup	Base year survey of 1972 seniors	Followup survey of 1972 seniors in 1974–75	Followup survey of 1972 seniors in 1976–77	Followup survey of 1972 seniors in 1979–80
Total respondents (unweighted)	**16,409**	**19,328**	**19,422**	**17,519**
Sex				
Male	7,081	9,350	9,394	8,385
Female	7,290	9,962	9,898	9,036
Race/ethnicity				
White, non-Hispanic	14,371	—	—	15,914
	12,333			13,812
Black, non-Hispanic	2,038	—	—	2,102
Hispanic	—	—	—	665
Asian	—	—	—	210
Socioeconomic status composite (SES) [1]				
Low	—	—	—	4,786
Middle	—	—	—	8,322
High	—	—	—	4,171
Father's highest level of education				
Less than high school	3,811	—	—	—
High school graduate [2]	6,223	—	—	—
College graduate [3]	2,404	—	—	—
High school program (self-reported)				
Academic	4,471	—	—	—
General	6,336	—	—	—
Vocational	3,564	—	—	—

[1] The SES index is a composite of five equally-weighted measures: father's education, mother's education, family income, father's occupation, and presence of certain items in the respondent's household.

[2] Includes attendance at a vocational, trade, or business school, or 2-year college; or attendance at a 4-year college resulting in less than a bachelor's degree.

[3] Includes those with a bachelor's or higher-level degree.

—Data not applicable.

NOTE.—Sample sizes for categories of classification variables may not sum to the total number of respondents because of missing or excluded data. Because of item nonresponse, the actual number of respondents answering each question in a series of related questions will vary.

**Table A8.—Approximate standard errors for percentages estimated from
National Longitudinal Study survey: 1979**

Size of sample	Estimated percentages				
	10 or 90	20 or 80	30 or 70	40 or 60	50
250	2.28	3.04	3.48	3.72	3.79
500	1.61	2.15	2.46	2.63	2.68
1,000	1.14	1.52	1.74	1.86	1.90
2,000	0.81	1.07	1.23	1.31	1.34
3,000	0.66	0.88	1.00	1.07	1.10
4,000	0.57	0.76	0.87	0.93	0.95
5,000	0.51	0.68	0.78	0.83	0.85
6,000	0.46	0.62	0.71	0.76	0.77
8,000	0.40	0.54	0.61	0.66	0.67
10,000	0.36	0.48	0.55	0.59	0.60
12,000	0.33	0.44	0.50	0.54	0.55
16,000	0.28	0.38	0.43	0.46	0.47
20,000	0.25	0.34	0.39	0.42	0.42

**Table A9.—Respondent counts of full-time workers from the Recent College Graduate survey:
1976 to 1987**

Field of study	Number employed full time			
	1974–75 graduates in May 1976	1979–80 graduates in May 1981	1983–84 graduates in June 1985	1985–86 graduates in June 1987
Total respondents (unweighted)	**2,464**	**5,521**	**6,799**	**15,024**
Professions	1,840	4,260	2,743	8,987
Arts and sciences	514	811	1,373	4,869
Other	110	450	2,683	1,168
Newly qualified to teach	1,337	2,469	1,215	2,546
Not newly qualified to teach	1,127	3,052	5,584	12,478
Professions	601	1,841	2,743	7,043
Engineering	80	270	601	915
Business and management	290	749	1,522	2,407
Health	72	252	379	3,106
Education [1]	141	464	100	521
Public affairs and services	18	106	141	94
Arts and sciences	433	770	1,373	4,369
Biological sciences	83	116	136	380
Physical sciences and mathematics	40	103	136	1,782
Psychology	64	105	188	366
Social sciences	107	252	432	780
Humanities	139	194	481	1,061
Other	93	441	1,468	1,066
Communications	7	73	240	392
Miscellaneous	86	368	1,228	674

[1] Includes those who had not finished all requirements for teaching certification or were previously qualified to teach.

Table A10.—Standard errors for selected items in the 1985 Survey of School Discipline Policies and Practices

Items for secondary schools	Estimate	Standard error	95% confidence interval	
			Lower	Upper
Percent of secondary schools indicating that compared with 5 years ago, disruptive classroom behavior is				
Less now, all schools	65.9	1.6	62.8	69.0
Less now, junior high schools	59.1	2.5	54.2	64.0
Less now, senior high schools	72.7	2.2	68.4	77.0
More now, all schools	12.0	1.3	9.5	14.5
Percent of schools with one or more occurrences of the following infractions [1]				
Student caught selling illegal drugs at school, all schools	34.9	1.9	31.2	38.6
Student caught selling illegal drugs at school, junior high schools .	30.5	2.9	24.8	36.2
Student caught selling illegal drugs at school, senior high schools	39.4	2.3	34.9	43.9
Thefts of personal items, [2] all schools	82.3	1.7	79.0	85.6
Thefts of personal items, [2] small schools (less than 400 students).	71.3	4.3	62.9	79.7
Thefts of personal items, [2] large schools (1,000 or more students).	93.2	1.6	90.1	96.3
Percent of schools with one or more occurrences of the following disciplinary actions [1]				
Suspension for disciplinary reasons, all schools	95.7	0.8	94.1	97.3
Suspension for disciplinary reasons, small schools (less than 400 students).	89.3	2.7	84.0	94.6
Suspension for disciplinary reasons, large schools (1,000 or more students).	99.3	0.5	98.3	100.3
Expulsions, all schools	36.8	1.8	33.3	40.3
Expulsions, urban schools	44.9	4.9	35.3	54.5
Expulsions, rural schools	35.4	2.6	30.3	40.5
Average number of occurrences per 100 students of the following disciplinary actions: [1]				
Suspension for disciplinary reasons, all schools	10.0	0.50	9.0	11.0
Suspension for disciplinary reasons, small schools (less than 400 students).	7.1	1.10	4.9	9.3
Suspension for disciplinary reasons, large schools (1,000 or more students).	13.7	1.00	11.7	15.7
Expulsions, all schools	0.3	0.04	0.2	0.4
Expulsions, urban schools	0.6	0.20	0.2	1.0
Expulsions, rural schools	0.2	0.03	0.1	0.3

[1] Data are for the 1983–84 school year.
[2] Includes only reported thefts of personal items valued at $10.00 or more.

Table A11.—Standard errors for selected items on full-time faculty in the National Survey of Postsecondary Faculty: 1988

Selected characteristics	Number of respondents	Percent total	Sex		Race/ethnicity				
			Male	Female	American Indian	Asian	Black	Hispanic	White
All institutions [1]	6,265	100	72.72	27.28	0.84	4.36	3.26	2.05	89.49
Standard error	—	—	0.86	0.86	0.15	0.42	0.58	0.24	0.87
Type and control.									
Public research	1,283	100	79.30	20.70	0.72	4.98	1.69	2.18	90.42
Standard error	—	—	1.65	1.65	0.35	0.78	0.46	0.34	1.00
Private research	429	100	80.53	19.47	0.00	3.74	6.14	4.70	85.42
Standard error	—	—	2.75	2.75	0.00	1.08	4.22	1.66	4.72
Public doctoral [2]	770	100	76.25	23.75	1.06	5.25	1.86	0.71	91.12
Standard error	—	—	2.34	2.34	0.49	1.31	0.77	0.24	1.41
Private doctoral [3]	216	100	73.44	26.56	0.36	10.40	1.81	1.45	85.98
Standard error	—	—	8.35	8.35	0.40	5.68	1.99	0.95	6.66
Public comprehensive	1,276	100	71.10	28.90	0.77	5.82	3.51	1.88	88.03
Standard error	—	—	1.70	1.70	0.31	1.16	1.16	0.51	1.80
Private comprehensive	653	100	72.48	27.52	1.19	4.40	1.79	1.40	91.22
Standard error	—	—	3.21	3.21	0.65	1.07	0.87	0.62	1.78
Liberal arts	555	100	70.93	29.07	1.19	2.68	8.30	0.95	86.88
Standard error	—	—	4.04	4.04	0.53	1.23	3.22	0.50	4.06
Public 2–year [4]	849	100	62.13	37.87	1.27	1.94	3.06	2.75	90.97
Standard error	—	—	2.16	2.16	0.35	0.73	0.73	0.71	1.67
Other [5]	162	100	78.74	21.26	0.00	0.98	2.94	0.99	95.10
Standard error	—	—	3.96	3.96	0.00	0.27	1.97	0.83	2.05

[1] All accredited, nonproprietary U.S. postsecondary institutions that grant a two–year (A.A.) or higher degree and whose accreditations at the higher education level is recognized by the U. S. Department of Education.
[2] Includes publicly controlled institutions classified by the Carnegie Foundation as specialized medical schools.
[3] Includes privately controlled institutions classified by the Carnegie Foundation as specialized medical schools.
[4] Respondents from private two-year colleges are included only in "all institutions" because there are too few cases for a reliable estimate.
[5] Religious and other specialized institutions, except medical, that offer degrees ranging from bachelors to doctorates.
—Data not available or not applicable.

Table A12.—Undergraduates responding to the National Postsecondary Student Aid Study and coefficients of variation, by source of aid and selected characteristics: 1987

Selected characteristics	Number of respondents						Coefficient of variation [1]					
	Total under-graduates	Source of aid [2]					Total under-graduates	Source of aid				
		Any aid [3]	Federal	State	Institutional	Other		Any aid	Federal	State	Institutional	Other
Total undergraduates	**34,882**	**20,374**	**15,969**	**6,653**	**7,554**	**2,744**	**0.19**	**0.21**	**0.25**	**0.52**	**0.53**	**0.47**
Sex												
Male	15,583	8,911	6,948	2,796	3,409	1,175	0.25	0.27	0.32	0.67	0.60	0.76
Female	19,298	11,462	9,020	3,856	4,144	1,569	0.26	0.24	0.27	0.57	0.63	0.67
Race/ethnicity												
American Indian	246	159	146	43	42	26	2.36	1.75	1.96	2.82	3.31	5.43
Asian American	1,572	843	668	341	331	126	0.98	0.90	1.07	1.54	1.71	2.15
Black, non-Hispanic	3,395	2,624	2,348	793	631	208	1.04	0.53	0.59	1.17	1.22	1.85
Hispanic	2,024	1,302	1,118	449	337	129	1.10	0.63	0.78	1.27	1.70	2.02
White, non-Hispanic	27,503	15,357	11,621	4,997	6,189	2,242	0.23	0.26	0.33	0.66	0.56	0.50
Age												
23 or younger	23,505	14,455	11,379	5,214	6,357	1,735	0.23	0.23	0.25	0.48	0.53	0.64
24–29	5,151	2,909	2,382	672	621	390	0.41	0.40	0.51	1.18	1.20	1.10
30 or older	6,218	3,006	2,206	767	576	619	0.47	0.45	0.56	1.14	1.06	1.04
Marital status												
Married	6,712	3,246	2,391	687	718	631	0.42	0.47	0.61	1.40	1.31	1.09
Not married [4]	28,133	17,115	13,571	5,966	6,835	2,111	0.18	0.21	0.24	0.48	0.53	0.53
Attendance status												
Full-time	25,550	16,988	13,802	6,016	6,764	1,918	0.20	0.18	0.23	0.43	0.49	0.57
Part-time	8,112	2,727	1,637	477	590	746	0.54	0.59	0.74	1.74	1.30	0.84
Dependency status												
Dependent	23,694	13,645	10,409	4,861	6,148	1,773	0.21	0.24	0.26	0.52	0.54	0.61
Independent	11,047	6,697	5,545	1,789	1,395	965	0.40	0.29	0.37	0.89	0.92	0.96
Housing status												
School-owned	10,045	6,913	5,302	2,587	4,102	1,054	0.54	0.25	0.33	0.54	0.52	0.85
Off campus, not with parents	15,538	8,441	6,727	2,273	2,113	1,245	0.32	0.24	0.32	0.77	0.68	0.80
With parents	9,282	5,011	3,932	1,792	1,339	443	0.47	0.42	0.40	0.76	1.01	1.19

[1] Coefficients of variation in percents.
[2] Numbers added across the various sources total more than the number of students receiving any aid because some students received aid from multiple sources.
[3] Includes students who said they were awarded aid but did not specify the source of aid.
[4] Includes students who were single, separated, divorced, or widowed.

Table A13.—Estimated enrollment rates and standard errors in the October Current Population Survey

Base of percentage, in thousands	Estimated percentage				
	2 or 98	5 or 95	10 or 90	25 or 75	50
	Total or white persons				
100	2.1	3.3	4.6	6.6	7.6
250	1.3	2.1	2.9	4.2	4.8
500	1.0	1.5	2.0	2.9	3.4
1,000	0.7	1.0	1.4	2.1	2.4
2,500	0.4	0.7	0.9	1.3	1.5
5,000	0.3	0.5	0.6	0.9	1.1
10,000	0.2	0.3	0.5	0.7	0.8
25,000	0.13	0.2	0.3	0.4	0.5
50,000	0.09	0.15	0.2	0.3	0.3
100,000	0.07	0.10	0.05	0.2	0.2
150,000	0.05	0.12	0.12	0.2	0.2
	Black or Hispanic persons				
75	2.6	4.1	5.6	8.1	9.3
100	2.3	3.5	4.8	7.0	8.1
250	1.4	2.2	3.1	4.4	5.1
500	1.0	1.6	2.2	3.1	3.6
1,000	0.7	1.1	1.5	2.2	2.5
2,500	0.5	0.7	1.0	1.4	1.6
5,000	0.3	0.5	0.7	1.0	1.1
10,000	0.2	0.4	0.5	0.7	0.8
15,000	0.2	0.3	0.4	0.6	0.7
20,000	0.2	0.2	0.3	0.5	0.6

Table A14.—Estimated educational attainment rates and standard errors in the March Current Population Survey

Estimate	Base of percentage, in thousands	Standard error	90 percent confidence interval
2 or 98 [1]	100	2.00	0 to 5.2
	100,000	0.06	1.9 to 2.1
10 or 90	100	4.3	3.1 to 16.9
	100,000	0.14	9.8 to 10.2
50	100	7.20	38.5 to 61.5
	100,000	0.20	49.7 to 50.3

[1] The confidence interval for the larger values can be found by taking the complement of that shown, e.g. for 98 it would be 94.8 to 100.

Table A15.—Estimated standard errors for selected estimates of persons from the "Participation in Adult Education" CPS supplement

Estimate	Standard Error	90 percent confidence interval
10	4.5	2.8 to 17.2
50	10.2	33.7 to 66.3
500	30.0	452 to 548
50,000	253.0	49,595 to 50,405

Table A16.—Estimated participation rates and standard errors in the "Participation in Adult Education" CPS supplement

Estimate	Base of Percentage in thousands	Standard error	90 percent estimate confidence interval
1 or 99 [1]	50	2.4	0 to 4.8
	5,000	0.2	0.68 to 1.3
10 or 90	50	7.1	0 to 21.4
	5,000	0.7	8.9 to 11.1
50	50	11.8	31.1 to 68.9
	5,000	1.2	48.1 to 51.9

[1] The confidence interval for the larger values can be found by taking the complement of that shown, e.g., for 99 it would be 95.2 to 100.

Table A17.—Percent of seniors who had ever used selected drugs and 95 percent confidence limits: 1986 [1]

Drug	Lower limit	Observed estimate	Upper limit
Alcohol	89.7	91.3	92.7
Marijuana/hashish	48.7	50.9	53.1
LSD	6.3	7.2	8.2
PCP	3.8	4.8	6.0
Cocaine	15.5	16.9	18.4
Heroin	0.8	1.1	1.4

[1] Approximate sample size = 15,200.

Table A18.—Sampling errors (95 percent confidence level) for percentages estimated from the Gallup Poll, 1987

Percent	Size of sample						
	1,500	1,000	750	600	400	200	100

Recommended allowance for sampling error of a percentage

Percent	1,500	1,000	750	600	400	200	100
Percentages near 10 or 90	2	2	3	3	4	5	8
Percentages near 20 or 80	3	3	4	4	5	7	10
Percentages near 30 or 70	3	4	4	5	6	8	12
Percentages near 40 or 60	3	4	5	5	6	9	12
Percentages near 50	3	4	5	5	6	9	13

Table A19.—Sampling errors (95 percent confidence level) for the difference in two percentages estimated from the Gallup Poll: 1987

Size of sample	Size of sample					
	1,000	750	600	400	200	100

Recommended allowance for sampling error of a difference in percentages (percentages near 80 or 20)

Size of sample	1,000	750	600	400	200	100
1,500	4					
1,000	4	5				
750	5	5	5			
600	5	5	6	6		
400	6	6	6	7	7	
200	8	8	8	8	9	10

Recommended allowance for sampling error of a difference in percentages (percentages near 50)

Size of sample	1,000	750	600	400	200	100
1,500	5					
1,000	5	6				
750	6	6	7			
600	6	7	7	7		
400	7	8	8	8	9	
200	10	10	10	10	11	13

Table A20.—Approximate sampling errors (95 percent confidence level) for percentages estimated from Metropolitan Life Survey of the American Teacher, 1987

Percentage	Size of sample					
	2000	1500	1000	500	200	100
	Recommended allowance for sampling error of a percentage					
Percentages near 10 or 90	1	2	2	3	4	6
Percentages near 20 or 80	2	2	2	4	6	8
Percentages near 30 or 70	2	2	3	4	6	9
Percentages near 40 or 60	2	3	3	4	7	10
Percentages near 50	2	3	3	4	7	10

Table A21.—Approximate sampling errors (95 percent confidence level) for the differences in two percentages estimated from the Metropolitan Life Survey of the American Teacher, 1987

Sample sizes of two groups being compared	Recommended allowance for sampling error of a difference in percentages				
	Percentage result at 10% or 90%	Percentage result at 20% or 80%	Percentage result at 30% or 70%	Percentage result at 40% or 60%	Percentage result at 50%
2,000 vs. 1,000	2	3	4	4	4
1,000 vs. 1,000	3	4	4	4	4
1,000 vs. 200	5	6	7	7	8
1,000 vs. 100	6	8	9	10	10
200 vs. 100	7	10	11	12	12

Table A22.—Maximum differences required for significance (90 percent confidence level) between sample subgroups of the Status of the American Public School Teacher survey

Size of one subgroup	Size of other subgroup						
	100	200	300	400	500	600	700
100	11.6	10.1	9.5	9.2	9.0	8.9	8.8
200	10.1	8.2	7.5	7.1	6.9	6.7	6.6
300	9.5	7.5	6.7	6.3	6.0	5.8	5.7
400	9.2	7.1	6.3	5.8	5.5	5.3	5.2
500	9.0	6.9	6.0	5.5	5.2	5.0	4.8
600	8.9	6.7	5.8	5.3	5.0	4.7	4.6
700	8.8	6.6	5.7	5.2	4.8	4.6	4.4

Definitions

Academic support This category of college expenditures includes expenditures for support services that are an integral part of the institution's primary missions of instruction, research, or public service. Includes expenditures for libraries, galleries, audio/visual services, academic computing support, ancillary support, academic administration, personnel development, and course and curriculum development.

Achievement test An examination that measures the extent to which a person has acquired certain information or mastered certain skills, usually as a result of specific instruction.

Agriculture Courses designed to improve competencies in agricultural occupations. Included is the study of agricultural production, supplies, mechanization and products, agricultural science, forestry, and related services.

American College Testing Program (ACT) The ACT assessment program measures educational development and readiness to pursue college-level coursework in English, mathematics, natural science, and social studies. Student performance on the tests does not reflect innate ability and is influenced by a student's educational preparedness.

Appropriation (institutional revenues) An amount (other than a grant or contract) received from or made available to an institution through an act of a legislative body.

Appropriations (Federal funds) Budget authority provided through the congressional appropriation process that permits Federal agencies to incur obligations and to make payments.

Associate degree A degree granted for the successful completion of a sub-baccalaureate program of studies, usually requiring at least 2 years (or equivalent) of full-time college-level study. This includes degrees granted in a cooperative or work-study program.

Auxiliary enterprises This category includes those essentially self-supporting operations which exist to furnish a service to students, faculty, or staff, and which charge a fee that is directly related to, although not necessarily equal to, the cost of the serv-ice. Examples are residence halls, food services, college stores, and intercollegiate athletics.

Average daily attendance (ADA) The aggregate attendance of a school during a reporting period (normally a school year) divided by the number of days school is in session during this period. Only days on which the pupils are under the guidance and direction of teachers should be considered days in session.

Average daily membership (ADM) The aggregate membership of a school during a reporting period (normally a school year) divided by the number of days school is in session during this period. Only days on which the pupils are under the guidance and direction of teachers should be considered as days in session. The average daily membership for groups of schools having varying lengths of terms is the average of the average daily memberships obtained for the individual schools.

Bachelor's degree A degree granted for the successful completion of a baccalaureate program of studies, usually requiring at least 4 years (or equivalent) of full-time college-level study. This includes degrees granted in a cooperative or work-study program.

Budget authority (BA) Authority provided by law to enter into obligations that will result in immediate or future outlays. It may be classified by the period of availability (1-year, multiple-year, no-year), by the timing of congressional action (current or permanent), or by the manner of determining the amount available (definite or indefinite).

Business Program of instruction that prepares individuals for a variety of activities in planning, organizing, directing, and controlling business office systems and procedures.

Carnegie unit A standard of measurement that represents one credit for the completion of a 1-year course.

Catholic school A private school over which a Roman Catholic church group exercises some control or provides some form of subsidy. Catholic schools for the most part include those operated or supported by: a parish, a group of parishes, a diocese, or a Catholic religious order.

Central cities The largest cities, with 50,000 or more inhabitants, in a Metropolitan Statistical Area (MSA). A smaller city within a MSA may also qualify if it has at least 25,000 inhabitants or has a population of one-third or more of that of the largest city and a minimum population of 25,000. An exception occurs where two cities have contiguous boundaries and constitute, for economic and social purposes, a single community of at least 50,000, the smaller of which must have a population of at least 15,000.

Class size The membership of a class at a given date.

Classroom teacher A staff member assigned the professional activities of instructing pupils in self-contained classes or courses, or in classroom situations. Usually expressed in full-time equivalents.

Cohort A group of individuals that have a statistical factor in common, for example, year of birth.

College A postsecondary school which offers general or liberal arts education, usually leading to an associate, bachelor's, master's, doctor's, or first-professional degree. Junior colleges and community colleges are included under this terminology.

Combined elementary and secondary school A school which encompasses instruction at both the elementary and the secondary levels. Examples of combined elementary and secondary school grade spans would be 1 through 12 or 5 through 12.

Computer science A group of instructional programs that describes computer and information sciences, including computer programming, data processing, and information systems.

Constant dollars Dollar amounts that have been adjusted by means of price and cost indexes to eliminate inflationary factors and allow direct comparison across years.

Consumer, personal, and miscellaneous services A group of instructional programs that describes the fundamental skills a person is normally thought to need in order to function productively in society. Some examples are child development, consumer education, and family relations.

Consumer Price Index (CPI) This price index measures the average change in the cost of a fixed market basket of goods and services purchased by consumers.

Consumption That portion of income which is spent on the purchase of goods and services rather than being saved.

Credit The unit of value, awarded for the successful completion of certain courses, intended to indicate the quantity of course instruction in relation to the total requirements for a diploma, certificate, or degree. Credits are frequently expressed in terms such as "Carnegie units," "semester credit hours," and "quarter credit hours."

Current dollars Dollar amounts that have not been adjusted to compensate for inflation.

Current expenditures (elementary/secondary) The expenditures for operating local public schools, excluding capital outlay and interest on school debt. These expenditures include such items as salaries for school personnel, fixed charges, student transportation, school books and materials, and energy costs. Beginning in 1980–81, expenditures for State administration are excluded.

Current expenditures per pupil in average daily attendance Current expenditures for the regular school term divided by the average daily attendance of full-time pupils (or full-time equivalency of pupils) during the term. See also *Current expenditures* and *Average daily attendance*.

Current-fund expenditures (higher education) Money spent to meet current operating costs, including salaries, wages, utilities, student services, public services, research libraries, scholarships and fellowships, auxiliary enterprises, hospitals, and independent operations. Excludes loans, capital expenditures, and investments.

Current-fund revenues (higher education) Money received during the current fiscal year from revenue which can be used to pay obligations currently due, and surpluses reappropriated for the current fiscal year.

Current Population Survey See Guide to Sources.

Disposable personal income Current income received by persons less their contributions for social insurance, personal tax, and nontax payments. It is the income available to persons for spending and saving. Nontax payments include passport fees, fines and penalties, donations, and tuitions and fees paid to schools and hospitals operated mainly by the government. See also *Personal income*.

Doctor's degree An earned degree carrying the title of Doctor. The Doctor of Philosophy degree (Ph.D.) is the highest academic degree and requires mastery within a field of knowledge and demonstrated ability to perform scholarly research. Other doctorates are awarded for fulfilling specialized requirements in professional fields, such as education

(Ed.D.), musical arts (D.M.A.), business administration (D.B.A.), and engineering (D.Eng. or D.E.S.). Many doctor's degrees in academic and professional fields require an earned master's degree as a prerequisite. First-professional degrees, such as M.D. and D.D.S., are not included under this heading.

Educational attainment The highest grade of regular school attended and completed.

Educational and general expenditures The sum of current funds expenditures on instruction, research, public service, academic support, student services, institutional support, operation and maintenance of plant, and awards from restricted and unrestricted funds.

Elementary education/programs Learning experiences concerned with the knowledge, skills, appreciations, attitudes, and behavioral characteristics which are considered to be needed by all pupils in terms of their awareness of life within our culture and the world of work, and which normally may be achieved during the elementary school years (usually kindergarten through grade 8 or kindergarten through grade 6), as defined by applicable State laws and regulations.

Elementary school A school classified as elementary by State and local practice and composed of any span of grades not above grade 8. A preschool or kindergarten school is included under this heading only if it is an integral part of an elementary school or a regularly established school system.

Elementary/secondary school As reported in this publication, includes only regular school, i.e., schools that are part of State and local school systems, and also most not-for-profit private elementary/secondary schools, both religiously affiliated and nonsectarian. Schools not reported include subcollegiate departments of institutions of higher education, residential schools for exceptional children, Federal schools for American Indians, and Federal schools on military posts and other Federal installations.

Employment Includes civilian, noninstitutional persons who (1) worked during any part of the survey week as paid employees; worked in their own business, profession, or farm; or worked 15 hours or more as unpaid workers in a family-owned enterprise; or (2) were not working but had jobs or businesses from which they were temporarily absent due to illness, bad weather, vacation, labor-management dispute, or personal reasons—whether or not they were seeking another job.

Endowment A trust fund set aside to provide a perpetual source of revenue from the proceeds of the endowment investments. Endowment funds are often created by donations from benefactors of an institution, who may designate the use of the endowment revenue. Normally, institutions or their representatives manage the investments, but they are not permitted to spend the endowment fund itself, only the proceeds from the investments. Typical uses of endowments would be an endowed chair for a particular department or for a scholarship fund. Endowment totals tabulated in this book also include funds functioning as endowments, such as funds left over from the previous year and placed with the endowment investments by the institution. These funds may be withdrawn by the institution and spent as current funds at any time. Endowments are evaluated by two different measures, book value and market value. Book value is the purchase price of the endowment investment. Market value is the current worth of the endowment investment. Thus, the book value of a stock held in an endowment fund would be the purchase price of the stock. The market value of the stock would be its selling price as of a given day.

English A group of instructional programs that describes the English language arts, including composition, creative writing, and the study of literature.

Enrollment The total number of students registered in a given school unit at a given time, generally in the fall of a year.

Expenditures Charges incurred, whether paid or unpaid, which are presumed to benefit the current fiscal year. For elementary/secondary schools, these include all charges for current outlays plus capital outlays and interest on school debt. For institutions of higher education, these include current outlays plus capital outlays. For government, these include charges net of recoveries and other correcting transactions other than for retirement of debt, investment in securities, extension of credit, or as agency transaction. Government expenditures include only external transactions, such as the provision of perquisites or other payments in kind. Aggregates for groups of governments exclude intergovernmental transactions among the government.

Expenditures per pupil Charges incurred for a particular period of time divided by a student unit of measure, such as average daily attendance or average daily membership.

Extracurricular activities Activities that are not part of the required curriculum and that take place outside of the regular course of study. As used here, they include both school-sponsored (e.g., varsity athletics, drama and debate clubs) and community-sponsored (e.g., hobby clubs and youth organizations like the Junior Chamber of Commerce or Boy Scouts) activities.

Family A group of two persons or more (one of whom is the householder) related by birth, marriage, or adoption and residing together. All such persons (including related subfamily members) are considered as members of one family.

Federal funds Amounts collected and used by the Federal Government for the general purposes of the Government. There are four types of Federal fund accounts: the general fund, special funds, public enterprise funds, and intragovernmental funds. The major Federal fund is the general fund, which is derived from general taxes and borrowing. Federal funds also include certain earmarked collections, such as those generated by and used to finance a continuing cycle of business-type operations.

First-professional degree A degree that signifies both completion of the academic requirements for beginning practice in a given profession and a level of professional skill beyond that normally required for a bachelor's degree. This degree usually is based on a program requiring at least 2 academic years of work prior to entrance and a total of at least 6 academic years of work to complete the degree program, including both prior-required college work and the professional program itself. By NCES definition, first-professional degrees are awarded in the fields of dentistry (D.D.S or D.M.D.), medicine (M.D.), optometry (O.D.), osteopathic medicine (D.O.), pharmacy (D.Phar.), podiatric medicine (D.P.M.), veterinary medicine (D.V.M.), chiropractic (D.C. or D.C.M.), law (J.D.), and theological professions (M.Div. or M.H.L.).

First-professional enrollment The number of students enrolled in a professional school or program which requires at least 2 years of academic college work for entrance and a total of at least 6 years for a degree. By NCES definition, first-professional enrollment includes only students in certain programs. See *First-professional degree* for a list of programs.

Fiscal year The yearly accounting period for the Federal Government, which begins on October 1 and ends on the following September 30. The fiscal year is designated by the calendar year in which it ends; e.g., fiscal year 1988 begins on October 1, 1987, and ends on September 30, 1988. (Prior to fiscal year 1976, the fiscal year began on July 1 and ended on the following June 30.)

Foreign languages A group of instructional programs that describes the structure and use of language that is common or indigenous to people of the same community or nation, the same geographical area, or the same cultural traditions. Programs cover such features as sound, literature, syntax, phonology, semantics, sentences, prose, and verse, as well as the development of skills and attitudes used in communicating and evaluating thoughts and feelings through oral and written language.

Full-time enrollment The number of students enrolled in higher education courses with total credit load equal to at least 75 percent of the normal full-time course load.

Full-time-equivalent (FTE) enrollment For institutions of higher education, enrollment of full-time students, plus the full-time equivalent of part-time students as reported by institutions. In the absence of an equivalent reported by an institution, the FTE enrollment is estimated by adding one-third of part-time enrollment to full-time enrollment.

Full-time instructional faculty Those members of the instruction/research staff who are employed full time as defined by the institution, including faculty with released time for research and faculty on sabbatical leave. Full-time counts exclude faculty who are employed to teach less than two semesters, three quarters, two trimesters, or two 4-month sessions; replacements for faculty on sabbatical leave or those on leave without pay; faculty for preclinical and clinical medicine; faculty who are donating their services; faculty who are members of military organizations and paid on a different pay scale from civilian employees; academic officers, whose primary duties are administrative; and graduate students who assist in the instruction of courses.

Full-time worker In educational institutions, an employee whose position requires being on the job on school days throughout the school year at least the number of hours the schools are in session. For higher education, a member of an educational institution's staff who is employed full time.

GED recipient A person who has obtained certification of high school equivalency by meeting State requirements and passing an approved exam, which is intended to provide an appraisal of the person's achievement or performance in the broad subject matter areas usually required for high school graduation.

General Educational Development (GED) program Academic instruction to prepare persons to take the high school equivalency examination. See *GED recipient*.

General program A program of studies designed to prepare students for the common activities of a citizen, family member, and worker. A general program of studies may include instruction in both academic and vocational areas.

Geographic region   1) One of four regions used by the Bureau of Economic Analysis of the U.S. Department of Commerce, the National Assessment of Educational Progress, and the National Education Association, as follows: (The National Education Association designated the Central region as Middle region in its classification.)

Northeast	Southeast
Connecticut	Alabama
Delaware	Arkansas
District of Columbia	Florida
Maine	Georgia
Maryland	Kentucky
Massachusetts	Louisiana
New Hampshire	Mississippi
New Jersey	North Carolina
New York	South Carolina
Pennsylvania	Tennessee
Rhode Island	Virginia
Vermont	West Virginia

Central (Middle)	West
Illinois	Alaska
Indiana	Arizona
Iowa	California
Kansas	Colorado
Michigan	Hawaii
Minnesota	Idaho
Missouri	Montana
Nebraska	Nevada
North Dakota	New Mexico
Ohio	Oklahoma
South Dakota	Oregon
Wisconsin	Texas
	Utah
	Washington
	Wyoming

2) One of the regions or divisions used by the U.S. Bureau of the Census in Current Population Survey tabulations, as follows:

Northeast	Midwest
(New England)	*(East North Central)*
Maine	Ohio
New Hampshire	Indiana
Vermont	Illinois
Massachusetts	Michigan
Rhode Island	Wisconsin
Connecticut	

(Middle Atlantic)	*(West North Central)*
New York	Minnesota
New Jersey	Iowa
Pennsylvania	Missouri
	North Dakota
	South Dakota
	Nebraska
	Kansas

South	West
(South Atlantic)	*(Mountain)*
Delaware	Montana
Maryland	Idaho
District of Columbia	Wyoming
Virginia	Colorado
West Virginia	New Mexico
North Carolina	Arizona
South Carolina	Utah
Georgia	Nevada
Florida	

(East South Central)	*(Pacific)*
Kentucky	Washington
Tennessee	Oregon
Alabama	California
Mississippi	Alaska
	Hawaii

(West South Central)
Arkansas
Louisiana
Oklahoma
Texas

Government appropriation   An amount (other than a grant or contract) received from or made available to an institution through an act of a legislative body.

Government grant or contract   Revenues from a government agency for a specific research project or other program.

Graduate   An individual who has received formal recognition for the successful completion of a prescribed program of studies.

Graduate enrollment   The number of students who hold the bachelor's or first-professional degree, or the equivalent, and who are working towards a master's or doctor's degree. First-professional students are counted separately. These enrollment data measure those students who are registered at a particular time during the fall. At some institutions, graduate enrollment also includes students who are in postbaccalaureate classes but not in degree programs. In specified tables, graduate enrollment includes all students in regular graduate programs and all students in postbaccalaureate classes but not in degree programs (unclassified postbaccalaureate students).

Graduate Record Examination (GRE) Multiple-choice examinations administered by the Educational Testing Service and taken by applicants who are intending to attend certain graduate schools. Two generalized tests are offered, plus specialized tests in a variety of subject areas. Ordinarily, a student will take only the specialized test that applies to the intended field of study.

Graduation Formal recognition given an individual for the successful completion of a prescribed program of studies.

Gross national product (GNP) The total national output of goods and services valued at market prices. GNP can be viewed in terms of expenditure categories which include purchases of goods and services by consumers and government, gross private domestic investment, and net exports of goods and services. The goods and services included are largely those bought for final use (excluding illegal transactions) in the market economy. A number of inclusions, however, represent imputed values, the most important of which is rental value of owner-occupied housing. GNP, in this broad context, measures the output attributable to the factors of production—labor and property—supplied by U.S. residents.

Handicapped Those children evaluated as having any of the following impairments, who because of these impairments need special education and related services. (These definitions apply specifically to data from the Office of Special Education and Rehabilitative Services presented in this publication.)

Deaf Having a hearing impairment which is so severe that the student is impaired in processing linguistic information through hearing (with or without amplification) and which adversely affects educational performance.

Deaf-blind Having concomitant hearing and visual impairments which cause such severe communication and other developmental and educational problems that the student cannot be accommodated in special education programs solely for deaf or blind students.

Hard of hearing Having a hearing impairment, whether permanent or fluctuating, which adversely affects the student's educational performance, but which is not included under the definition of "deaf" in this section.

Mentally retarded Having significantly subaverage general intellectual functioning, existing concurrently with defects in adaptive behavior and manifested during the developmental period, which adversely affects the child's educational performance.

Multihandicapped Having concomitant impairments (such as mentally retarded-blind, mentally retarded-orthopedically impaired, etc.), the combination of which causes such severe educational problems that the student cannot be accommodated in special education programs solely for one of the impairments. Term does not include deaf-blind students but does include those students who are severely or profoundly mentally retarded.

Orthopedically impaired Having a severe orthopedic impairment which adversely affects a student's educational performance. The term includes impairment resulting from congenital anomaly, disease, or other causes.

Other health impaired Having limited strength, vitality, or alertness—due to chronic or acute health problems such as a heart condition, tuberculosis, rheumatic fever, nephritis, asthma, sickle cell anemia, hemophilia, epilepsy, lead poisoning, leukemia, or diabetes—which adversely affects the student's educational performance.

Seriously emotionally disturbed Exhibiting one or more of the following characteristics over a long period of time, to a marked degree, and adversely affecting educational performance: an inability to learn which cannot be explained by intellectual, sensory, or health factor; an inability to build or maintain satisfactory interpersonal relationships with peers and teachers; inappropriate types of behavior or feelings under normal circumstances; a general pervasive mood of unhappiness or depression; or a tendency to develop physical symptoms or fears associated with personal or school problems. This term does not include children who are socially maladjusted, unless they also display one or more of the listed characteristics.

Specific learning disabled Having a disorder in one or more of the basic psychological processes involved in understanding or in using spoken or written language, which may manifest itself in an imperfect ability to listen, think, speak, read, write, spell, or do mathematical calculations. The term includes such conditions as perceptual handicaps, brain injury, minimal brain dysfunction, dyslexia, and developmental aphasia. The term does not include children who have learning problems which are primarily the result of visual, hearing, or environmental, cultural, or economic disadvantage.

Speech impaired Having a communication disorder, such as stuttering, impaired articulation, language impairment, or voice impairment, which adversely affects the student's educational performance.

Visually handicapped Having a visual impairment which, even with correction, adversely affects the student's educational performance. The term includes partially seeing and blind children.

High school A secondary school offering the final years of high school work necessary for graduation, usually including grades 10, 11, 12 (in a 6-3-3 plan) or grades 9, 10, 11, and 12 (in a 6-2-4 plan).

High school program A program of studies designed to prepare students for their postsecondary education and occupation. Three types of programs are usually distinguished—academic, vocational, and general. An academic program is designed to prepare students for continued study at a college or university. A vocational program is designed to prepare students for employment in one or more semiskilled, skilled, or technical occupations. A general program is designed to provide students with the understanding and competence to function effectively in a free society and usually represents a mixture of academic and vocational components.

Higher education Study beyond secondary school at an institution that offers programs terminating in an associate, baccalaureate, or higher degree.

Higher education institutions (alternative classification)

Comprehensive Characterized by diverse post-baccalaureate programs (including first-professional) but not engaged in significant doctoral-level education.

Doctoral-granting Characterized by a significant level and breadth of activity in commitment to doctoral-level education as measured by the number of doctorate recipients and the diversity in doctoral-level program offerings.

General baccalaureate Characterized by primary emphasis on general undergraduate, baccalaureate-level education. Not significantly engaged in postbaccalaureate education.

Specialized Baccalaureate or postbaccalaureate institution emphasizing one area (plus closely related specialties), such as business or engineering. The programmatic emphasis is measured by the percentage of degrees granted in the program area.

New These institutions, though not necessarily newly organized, are new additions to the Integrated Postsecondary Education Data System (IPEDS) universe. When degree and award data become available, they will be reclassified.

Non-degree-granting Offering undergraduate or graduate study but not conferring degrees or awards. In this volume, these institutions are included under *Specialized*.

2-year Conferring at least 75 percent of its degrees and awards for work below the bachelor's level.

Higher education institutions (traditional classification)

4-year institution An institution legally authorized to offer and offering at least a 4-year program of college-level studies wholly or principally creditable toward a baccalaureate degree. In some tables, a further division between universities and other 4-year institutions is made. A "university" is a postsecondary institution which typically comprises one or more graduate professional schools (also see *University*). For purposes of trend comparisons in this volume, the selection of universities has been held constant for all tabulations after 1982. "Other 4-year institutions" would include the rest of the nonuniversity 4-year institutions.

2-year institution An institution legally authorized to offer and offering at least a 2-year program of college-level studies which terminates in an associate degree or is principally creditable toward a baccalaureate degree.

Higher Education Price Index A price index which measures average changes in the prices of goods and services purchased by colleges and universities through current-fund education and general expenditures (excluding expenditures for sponsored research and auxiliary enterprises).

Household All the persons who occupy a housing unit. A house, apartment, or other group of rooms, or a single room, is regarded as a housing unit when it is occupied or intended for occupancy as separate living quarters, that is, when the occupants do not live and eat with any other persons in the structure, and there is direct access from the outside or through a common hall.

Imaginative writing This type of writing can take a variety of forms, such as stories, poems, plays, or lyrics. It represents a special approach to sharing experiences and understanding the world and ourselves. In this form of writing, special attention is given to rhythm and tone; the use of anecdote; the presence of metaphor and simile; shifts in plots; and the unexpected use of words, phrases, or punctuation.

Income tax Taxes levied on net income, that is, on gross income less certain deductions permitted by law. These taxes can be levied on individuals or on corporations or unincorporated businesses where the income is taxed distinctly from individual income.

Independent operations A group of self-supporting activities under control of a college or university. For purposes of financial surveys conducted by the National Center for Education Statistics, this category is composed principally of Federally Funded Research and Development Centers (FFRDC).

Informative writing This type of writing is used to share information and to convey messages, directions, and ideas. It often involves reporting or retelling events or experiences that have already occurred.

Institutional support The category of higher education expenditures that includes day-to-day operational support for colleges, excluding expenditures for physical plant operations. Examples of institutional support include general administrative services, executive direction and planning, legal and fiscal operations, and community relations.

Instruction That category including expenditures of the colleges, schools, departments, and other instructional divisions of higher education institutions and expenditures for departmental research and public service which are not separately budgeted. Includes expenditures for both credit and noncredit activities. Excludes expenditures for academic administration where the primary function is administration (e.g., academic deans).

Instructional staff Full-time-equivalent number of positions, not the number of different individuals occupying the positions during the school year. In local schools, includes all public elementary and secondary (junior and senior high) day-school positions that are in the nature of teaching or in the improvement of the teaching-learning situation. Includes consultants or supervisors of instruction, principals, teachers, guidance personnel, librarians, psychological personnel, and other instructional staff. Excludes administrative staff, attendance personnel, clerical personnel, and junior college staff.

Junior high school A separately organized and administered secondary school intermediate between the elementary and senior high schools, usually including grades 7, 8, and 9 (in a 6-3-3 plan) or grades 7 and 8 (in a 6-2-4 plan).

Labor force Persons employed as civilians, unemployed (but looking for work), or in the armed services during the survey week. The "civilian labor force" comprises all civilians classified as employed or unemployed.

Local education agency See *School district*.

Mandatory transfer A transfer of current funds that must be made in order to fulfill a binding legal obligation of the institution. Included under mandatory transfers are debt service provisions relating to academic and administrative buildings, including (1) amounts set aside for debt retirement and interest and (2) required provisions for renewal and replacement of buildings to the extent these are not financed from other funds.

Master's degree A degree awarded for successful completion of a program generally requiring 1 or 2 years of full-time college-level study beyond the bachelor's degree. One type of master's degree, including the Master of Arts degree, or M.A., and the Master of Science degree, or M.S., is awarded in the liberal arts and sciences for advanced scholarship in a subject field or discipline and demonstrated ability to perform scholarly research. A second type of master's degree is awarded for the completion of a professionally oriented program, for example, an M.Ed. in education, an M.B.A. in business administration, an M.F.A. in fine arts, an M.M. in music, an M.S.W. in social work, and an M.P.A. in public administration. A third type of master's degree is awarded in professional fields for study beyond the first-professional degree, for example, the Master of Laws (LL.M.) and Master of Science in various medical specializations.

Mathematics A group of instructional programs that describes the science of logical symbolic language and its application.

Mean test score The score obtained by dividing the sum of the scores of all individuals in a group by the number of individuals in that group.

Metropolitan population The population residing in Metropolitan Statistical Areas (MSAs). See *Metropolitan Statistical Area*.

Metropolitan Statistical Area (MSA) A large population nucleus and the nearby communities which have a high degree of economic and social integration with that nucleus. Each MSA consists of one or more entire counties (or county equivalents) that meet specified standards pertaining to population, commuting ties, and metropolitan character. In New England, towns and cities, rather than counties, are the basic units. MSAs are designated by the Office of Management and Budget. An MSA includes a city and, generally, its entire urban area and the remainder of the county or counties in which the urban area is located. An MSA also includes such additional outlying counties which meet specified criteria relating to metropolitan character and level of commuting of workers into the central city or counties. Specified criteria governing the definition of MSAs recognized before 1980 are published in *Standard Metropolitan Statistical Areas: 1975*, issued by the Office of Management and Budget. New MSAs were designated when 1980 counts showed that they met one or both of the following criteria:

1. Included a city with a population of at least 50,000 within their corporate limits, or

2. Included a Census Bureau-defined urbanized area (which must have a population of at least 50,000) and a total MSA population of at least 100,000 (or, in New England, 75,000).

Migration Geographic mobility involving a change of usual residence between clearly defined geographic units, that is, between counties, States, or regions.

Minimum-competency testing Measuring the acquisition of competence or skills to or beyond a certain specified standard.

National Assessment of Educational Progress (NAEP) See Guide to Sources.

Newly qualified teacher Persons who (1) first became eligible for a teaching license during the period of the study referenced or who were teaching at the time of survey but were not certified or eligible for a teaching license and (2) had never held full-time, regular teaching positions (as opposed to substitute) prior to completing the requirements for the degree which brought them into the survey.

Nonmetropolitan residence group The population residing outside Metropolitan Statistical Areas. See *Metropolitan Statistical Area*.

Nonresident alien A person who is not a citizen of the United States and who is in this country on a temporary basis and does not have the right to remain indefinitely.

Nonsupervisory instructional staff Persons such as curriculum specialists, counselors, librarians, remedial specialists, and others possessing education certification but not responsible for day-to-day teaching of the same group of pupils.

Obligations Amounts of orders placed, contracts awarded, services received, or similar legally binding commitments made by Federal agencies during a given period that will require outlays during the same or some future period.

Occupational home economics Courses of instruction emphasizing the acquisition of competencies needed for getting and holding a job or preparing for advancement in an occupational area using home economics knowledge and skills.

Off-Budget Federal entities Organizational entities, federally owned in whole or in part, whose transactions belong in the budget under current budget accounting concepts but that have been excluded from the budget totals under provisions of law.

Outlays The value of checks issued, interest accrued on the public debt, or other payments made, net of refunds and reimbursements.

Part-time enrollment The number of students enrolled in higher education courses with a total credit load less than 75 percent of the normal full-time credit load.

Personal income Current income received by persons from all sources minus their personal contributions for social insurance. Classified as "persons" are individuals (including owners of unincorporated firms), nonprofit institutions serving individuals, private trust funds, and private noninsured welfare funds. Personal income includes transfers (payments not resulting from current production) from government and business such as social security benefits, military pensions, etc., but excludes transfers among persons.

Persuasive writing This type of writing attempts to bring about some action or change. Its primary purpose is to influence others. It is concerned with the positions, beliefs, and attitudes of the readers.

Physical plant assets Includes the values of land, buildings, and equipment owned, rented, or utilized by colleges. Does not include those plant values which are a part of endowment or other capital fund investments in real estate. Excludes construction in progress.

Postbaccalaureate enrollment The number of graduate and first-professional students working towards advanced degrees and of students enrolled in graduate-level classes but not enrolled in degree programs. See also *Graduate enrollment* and *First-professional enrollment*.

Postsecondary education The provision of formal instructional programs with a curriculum designed primarily for students who have completed the requirements for a high school diploma or equivalent. This includes programs of an academic, vocational, and continuing professional education purpose, and excludes avocational and adult basic education programs.

Private school or institution A school or institution which is controlled by an individual or agency other than a State, a subdivision of a State, or the Federal Government, which is usually supported primarily by other than public funds, and the operation of whose program rests with other than publicly elected or appointed officials.

Property tax The sum of money collected from a tax levied against the value of property.

Proprietary institution An educational institution that is under private control but whose profits derive from revenues subject to taxation.

Public school or institution A school or institution controlled and operated by publicly elected or appointed officials and deriving its primary support from public funds.

Pupil/teacher ratio The enrollment of pupils at a given period of time, divided by the full-time-equivalent number of classroom teachers serving these pupils during the same period.

Racial/ethnic group Classification indicating general racial or ethnic heritage based on self-identification, as in data collected by the Bureau of the Census, or on observer identification, as in data collected by the Office for Civil Rights. These categories are in accordance with the Office of Management and Budget standard classification scheme presented below:

> **American Indian or Alaskan Native** A person having origins in any of the original peoples of North America and maintaining cultural identification through tribal affiliation or community recognition.

> **Asian or Pacific Islander** A person having origins in any of the original peoples of the Far East, Southeast Asia, the Indian subcontinent, or the Pacific Islands. This area includes, for example, China, India, Japan, Korea, the Philippine Islands, and Samoa.

> **Black** A person having origins in any of the black racial groups in Africa. Normally excludes persons of Hispanic origin except for tabulations produced by the Bureau of the Census, which are noted accordingly in this volume.

> **Hispanic** A person of Mexican, Puerto Rican, Cuban, Central or South American, or other Spanish culture or origin, regardless of race.

> **White** A person having origins in any of the original peoples of Europe, North Africa, or the Middle East. Normally excludes persons of Hispanic origin except for tabulations produced by the Bureau of the Census, which are noted accordingly in this volume.

Remedial education Instruction for a student lacking those reading, writing, or math skills necessary to perform college-level work at the level required by the attended institution.

Resident population Includes civilian population and armed forces personnel residing within the United States. Excludes armed forces personnel residing overseas.

Revenues All funds received from external sources, net of refunds, and correcting transactions. Noncash transactions such as receipt of services, commodities, or other receipts "in kind" are excluded as are funds received from the issuance of debt, liquidation of investments, and nonroutine sale of property.

Salary The total amount regularly paid or stipulated to be paid to an individual, before deductions, for personal services rendered while on the payroll of a business or organization.

Sales tax Tax imposed upon the sale and consumption of goods and services. It can be imposed either as a general tax on the retail price of all goods and services sold or as a tax on the sale of selected goods and services.

Scholarships and fellowships This category of college expenditures applies only to money given in the form of outright grants and trainee stipends to individuals enrolled in formal coursework, either for credit or not. Aid to students in the form of tuition or fee remissions is included. College Work-Study funds are excluded and are reported under the program in which the student is working. In the tabulations in this volume, Pell Grants are not included in this expenditure category.

Scholastic Aptitude Test (SAT) An examination administered by the Educational Testing Service and used to predict the facility with which an individual will progress in learning college-level academic subjects.

School A division of the school system consisting of students in one or more grades or other identifiable groups and organized to give instruction of a defined type. One school may share a building with another school or one school may be housed in several buildings.

School climate The social system and culture of the school, including the organizational structure of the school and values and expectations within it.

School district An education agency at the local level that exists primarily to operate public schools or to contract for public school services. Synonyms are "local basic administrative unit" and "local education agency."

Science The body of related courses concerned with knowledge of the physical and biological world and with the processes of discovering and validating this knowledge.

Secondary instructional level The general level of instruction provided for pupils in secondary schools (generally covering grades 7 through 12 or 9 through 12) and any instruction of a comparable nature and difficulty provided for adults and youth beyond the age of compulsory school attendance.

Secondary school A school comprising any span of grades beginning with the next grade following an elementary or middle-school (usually 7, 8, or 9) and ending with or below grade 12. Both junior high schools and senior high schools are included.

Senior high school A secondary school offering the final years of high school work necessary for graduation and invariably preceded by a junior high school.

Social studies A group of instructional programs that describes the substantive portions of behavior, past and present activities, interactions, and organizations of people associated together for religious, benevolent, cultural, scientific, political, patriotic, or other purposes.

Socioeconomic status (SES) For the High School and Beyond study and the National Longitudinal Study of the High School Class of 1972, the SES index is a composite of five equally weighted, standardized components: father's education, mother's education, family income, father's occupation, and household items. The terms high, middle, and low SES refer to the upper, middle two, and lower quartiles of the weighted SES composite index distribution.

Special education Direct instructional activities or special learning experiences designed primarily for students identified as having exceptionalities in one or more aspects of the cognitive process or as being underachievers in relation to general level or model of their overall abilities. Such services usually are directed at students with the following conditions: (1) physically handicapped; (2) emotionally handicapped; (3) culturally different, including compensatory education; (4) mentally retarded; and (5) students with learning disabilities. Programs for the mentally gifted

and talented are also included in some special education programs. See also *Handicapped*.

Standardized test A test composed of a systematic sampling of behavior, administered and scored according to specific instructions, capable of being interpreted in terms of adequate norms, and for which there is data on reliability and validity.

Standardized test performance The weighted distributions of composite scores from standardized tests used to group students according to performance.

Standard Metropolitan Statistical Area (SMSA) See *Metropolitan Statistical Area (MSA)*.

Student An individual for whom instruction is provided in an educational program under the jurisdiction of a school, school system, or other education institution. No distinction is made between the terms "student" and "pupil," though "student" may refer to one receiving instruction at any level while "pupil" refers only to one attending school at the elementary or secondary level. The term "student" is used to include individuals at all instructional levels. A student may receive instruction in a school facility or in another location, such as at home or in a hospital. Instruction may be provided by direct student-teacher interaction or by some other approved medium such as television, radio, telephone, and correspondence.

Subject-matter club Organizations that are formed around a shared interest in a particular area of study and whose primary activities promote that interest. Examples of such organizations are math, science, business, and history clubs.

Supervisory staff Principals, assistant principals, and supervisors of instruction. Does not include superintendents or assistant superintendents.

Tax base The collective value of objects, assets, and income components against which a tax is levied.

Tax expenditures Losses of tax revenue attributable to provisions of the Federal income tax laws that allow a special exclusion, exemption, or deduction from gross income or provide a special credit, preferential rate of tax, or a deferral of tax liability affecting individual or corporate income tax liabilities.

Teacher shortage The number of teaching positions vacant, abolished, or withdrawn because a candidate was sought and not found, courses were eliminated because of budget cuts or administrative decisions not to offer courses in a given field, a teacher was laid off, or a position was filled by a temporary substitute.

Technical education A program of vocational instruction that ordinarily includes the study of the sciences and mathematics underlying a technology, as well as the methods, skills, and materials commonly used and the services performed in the technology. Technical education prepares individuals for positions—such as draftsman or lab technician—in the occupational area between the skilled craftsman and the professional person.

Total expenditure per pupil in average daily attendance Includes all expenditures allocable to per pupil costs divided by average daily attendance. These allocable expenditures include current expenditures for regular school programs, interest on school debt, and capital outlay. Beginning in 1980–81, expenditures for State administration are excluded and expenditures for other programs (summer schools, community colleges, and private schools) are included.

Trade and industrial occupations The branch of vocational education which is concerned with preparing persons for initial employment or with updating or retraining workers in a wide range of trade and industrial occupations. Such occupations are skilled or semiskilled and are concerned with layout designing, producing, processing, assembling, testing, maintaining, servicing, or repairing any product or commodity.

Transcript An official list of all courses taken by a student at a school or college showing the final grade received for each course, with definitions of the various grades given at the institution.

Trust funds Amounts collected and used by the Federal Government for carrying out specific purposes and programs according to terms of a trust agreement or statute, such as the social security and unemployment trust funds. Trust fund receipts that are not anticipated to be used in the immediate future are generally invested in interest-bearing Government securities and earn interest for the trust fund.

Tuition and fees A payment or charge for instruction or compensation for services, privileges, or the use of equipment, books, or other goods.

Unclassified students Students who are not candidates for a degree or other formal award, although they are taking higher education courses for credit in regular classes with other students.

Undergraduate students Students registered at an institution of higher education who are working in a program leading to a baccalaureate degree or other formal award below the baccalaureate, such as an associate degree.

Unemployed Civilians who had no employment but were available for work and (1) had engaged in any specific jobseeking activity within the past 4 weeks, (2) were waiting to be called back to a job from which they had been laid off, or (3) were waiting to report to a new wage or salary job within 30 days.

U.S. Service Schools These institutions of higher education are controlled by the U.S. Department of Defense and the U.S. Department of Transportation. The 10 institutions counted in the NCES surveys of higher education institutions include: the Air Force Institute of Technology, Community College of the Air Force, Naval Postgraduate School, Uniformed Services University of the Health Sciences, U.S. Air Force Academy, U.S. Army Command and General Staff College, U.S. Coast Guard Academy, U.S. Merchant Marine Academy, U.S. Military Academy, and the U.S. Naval Academy.

University An institution of higher education consisting of a liberal arts college, a diverse graduate program, and usually two or more professional schools or faculties and empowered to confer degrees in various fields of study. For purposes of maintaining trend data in this publication, the selection of university institutions has not been revised since 1982.

Visual and performing arts A group of instructional programs that generally describes the historic development, aesthetic qualities, and creative processes of two or more of the visual and performing arts.

Vocational education Organized educational programs, services, and activities which are directly related to the preparation of individuals for paid or unpaid employment, or for additional preparation for a career, requiring other than a baccalaureate or advanced degree.

Vocational home economics Vocational courses of instruction emphasizing the acquisition of competencies needed for getting and holding a job or preparing for advancement in an occupational area using home economics knowledge or skills.

Index of Table Numbers

ISBN 0-16-035996-1

9 780160 359965

90000